The Criminal Law: Explanations and C

Brian Ashton B.Sc, Cert Ed.
Formerly Superintendent, West Midlands Police.
Author of the long-running Promotion Exam Questions
and Answers articles in Police Review

Alan Slater LLB (Hons), LLM
Detective Inspector, West Midlands Police.

© Police Review 1998

1st edition 1998

ISBN 0 7106 1932 4

Police Review Publishing Co
Celcon House
289–293, High Holborn
London WC1V 7HU

Designed and typeset by Mark Annison, HT Graphic Design, London.
Proof read and indexed by Mandy Preece, Bitterne Village, Southampton.
Printed and bound in Great Britain by The Cromwell Press Ltd, Trowbridge, Wiltshire.

Preface

The book is intended as an easily understood source of information for law students, police officers and anyone else who requires explanation of aspects of criminal law. It is not a comprehensive reference book, but should serve to answer many queries without the need for access to one of the more authorative references. The actual wording of sections and regulations, together with the everyday language of the explanations, should meet the needs of the novice and the more learned alike. A brief mention of the effects of particular cases is included in the text, and this may suffice for some readers. For the more enquiring minds, lengthier accounts of certain **keynote cases** appear at the end of chapters. Chapter 1 – Learning the Law – offers guidance on the use of law reports, for those who wish to study a case decision in more depth.

Brian Ashton
Alan Slater   February 1998

Contents

PART XI   TRAFFIC

Note: Where a "(K)" is shown, this denotes that the case is a Keynote case.

case name	year	reference 1	reference 2	reference 3	chapter	paragraph
DPP v Morgan	1976	AC 182			7	2.1
DPP v Morgan	1975	2 All ER 347	2 WLR 913		6	10.3
DPP v Newbury, DPP v Jones	1977	62 Cr App R 291	AC 500	Crim LR 359	9	4.2.1
DPP v Orum	1988	3 All ER 449			16	8.1.1
DPP v Pidhajeckyj	1991	155 JP 318	Crim LR 471		60	1.3
DPP v Smith	1960	3 All ER 161	44 Cr App R 261	Crim LR 728	5 8	8.1 3.1.1, 4.1.1
DPP v Taylor and Little	1992	1 All ER 299	QB 645	95 Cr App R 28	8	1.4
DPP v Warren (K)	1992	4 All ER 865	TLR 6.11.92		51	4.1.1, 4.2.2
DPP v Whyte	1972	2 All ER 446	AC 849	3 WLR 897	24	2.4
DPP v Wilson	1991	Crim LR 441	RTR 284		51	3.1.1
Duport Steels v Sirs	1980	1 All ER 529	1 WLR 157		1	3.3
Eden v Mitchell	1975	RTR 425			52	1.3.4
Edwards v Toombs	1983	Crim LR 43	LS Gaz R 93		13	10.1
Elliot v DPP	1989	TLR 19.1.89			12	12.3.2
Elliott v Gray	1960	1 QB 367			52	1.3.4
Elsey v Smith	1983	IRLR 292			20	3.1.2
Evans v Hughes (K)	1972	56 Cr App R 813	3 All ER412	Crim LR 558	17 47	3.1.1 1.1.2, 2.1.1

case name	year	reference 1	reference 2	reference 3	chapter	paragraph
Moses v Winder	1981	RTR 37			50	6.1
Myers v DPP	1965	AC 1009			7	5.1
Nagy v Weston	1965	1 All ER 78	1 WLR 280		20 / 47	4.2 / 2.1.1
Nakhla v R	1975	2 All ER 138			42	2.5.4
Neal v Gribble	1978	68 Cr App R 9	Crim LR 500		13	5.2
Newman v Overington, Harris and Ash Ltd	1928	93 JP 46	27 LGR 85		6	3.3
News Group Newspapers v SOGAT 82 (No.2)	1987	ICR 181			20	2.1.3, 4.5
News of the World v Friend	1973	1 All ER 442	Crim LR 237		42	4.10.2
Nichol v Carton	1985	81 Cr App R 339	Crim LR 233	149 JP 424	29	1.2.3
Nichol v Leach and another	1972	Crim LR 571			50	1.2
Noor Mohamed v R (K)	1949	AC 182	1 All ER 365	93 SJ 180	1 / 7	5.6 / 5.16
Norton v Knowles	1967	3 All ER 1061	(1969) 1 QB 572		39	2.2.2
O'Moran v DPP	1975	1 All ER 473	QB 864		16 / 18	12.2.2 / 2.5.2
Parkin v Norman	1982	2 All ER 583	(1983) QB 92	(1983) Crim LR 528	16	6.1.1
Paul v DPP	1990	90 Cr App R 173	(1989) Crim LR 660		12	4.1.1

case name	year	reference 1	reference 2	reference 3	chapter	paragraph
Pawley v Wharldall	1966	2 All ER 757	1 QB 373	3 WLR 496	50	4.1.1
Piddington v Bates (K)	1960	3 All ER 660			8	7.1.1
					20	4.4, 5.2
Pilgrim v Rice-Smith	1977	All ER 658	1 WLR 671		13	1.7
Pointon v Hill, Boot v Hill	1884	12 QBD 306			49	4.1.1
Police v Mudd	1968	Crim LR 269			4	4.12
Price v Civil Service Commission and Others	1978	1 All ER 1228			36	2.1.4
Quelch v Phipps	1955	2 All ER 302			53	1.4
R v Adomako (K)	1994	3 All ER 79	99 Cr App R 362	(1995) 1 AC 171	9	4.2.2
R v Ahluwalia (K)	1992	4 All ER 889	96 Cr App R 13		9	4.1.1
R v Allen	1985	2 All ER 641			13	9.5
R v Allen	1872	36 JP 820	LR 1 CCR 367	20 WR 756	23	3
R v Andrews	1987	1 All ER 513	2 WLR 413	151 JP 548	7	4.19
R v Andrews Weatherfoil Ltd	1972	1 All ER 65	1 WLR 118	136 JP 128	27	1.2
R v Ansell	1974	3 All ER 568	(1975) QB 215	Crim LR 616	12	6.1.1
R v Arnold	1996	TLR 3.10.96			24	2.1.5
R v Ashton-Rickardt	1977	65 Cr App R 67	(1978) 1 All ER 173	Crim LR 424	26	12.2.2
R v B (Evidence of Propensity)	1997	TLR 19.2.97			7	5.17

case name	year	reference 1	reference 2	reference 3	chapter	paragraph
R v Preece and Howells (K)	1976	66 Cr App R 28			10	16.1.1
R v Proctor	1923	17 Cr App R 124			13	11.1
R v Rasool	1997	TLR 17.2.97			25	2.8
R v Ratten	1972	AC 378			7	4.18
R v Reakes (K)	1974	Crim LR 615		Crim LR 553	10	15.3.1
R v Reid	1972	2 All ER 1350	56 Cr App R 703		11	2.1.1
R v Roberts	1964	2 All ER 541	(1965) 1 QB 85		50	1.3
R v Robins	1884	1 Car and Kir 456			11	4.1.2
R v Robinson (K)	1977	Crim LR 173			13	1.19
R v Rogers	1993	Crim LR 386			7	6.4
R v Rolfe (K)	1952	36 Cr App R 4			10	17.1.1
R v Rowton	1865	Le & Ce 520	(1861-73) All ER R 54	5 New Rep 428	7	5.15
R v Samuel	1988	2 All ER 135	QB 615	2 WLR920	1 4 7	5.3 4.12 4.7, 10.13
R v Sang	1980	AC 402	(1979) 2 All ER 46	(1979) 2 WLR 439	7	4.9
R v Satnam, R v Kewal (K)	1984	78 Cr App R 149	(1985) Crim LR 236		10	1.1.1

statute	year	section	chapter	paragraph
Child Abduction Act	1984	1	11	3.1
		2	11	3.2
Children Act	1989	2	34	2.5
		20	34	8.2
		21	34	8.2
		31	34	2.6, 8.3
		38A	34	10
		44	34	8.4
		44A	34	10
		46	34	8.5
		48	34	8.4.4, 8.4.5
		49	34	8.6
		50	34	8.6.3
		51	34	2.3
		95	34	8.7
		102	34	8.8
Children and Young Persons (Harmful Publications) Act	1955	1	24	1.2
		2	24	2.1
Children and Young Persons (Protection from Tobacco) Act	1991	3	34	4.5.4
Children and Young Persons Act	1933	1	34	3
		3	12	12.7.2
			34	4.1
		4	34	4.2
		5	34	4.4
		7	34	4.5, 4.5.7, 4.6
		10	34	4.7
		11	34	4.3
		12	34	7
			41	7
		18	34	6.1
		21	34	6.1
		25	34	6.2.4
		28	34	6.1.4, 6.2.3
		50	7	3.1
		99	34	2.1.4
Children and Young Persons Act	1963	23	34	6.2.2
		24	34	6.2.2
		37	34	6.2.1
		38	34	6.2.1
Children and Young Persons Act	1969	32	34	9
Cinemas Act	1985	1	41	6.1

statute	year	section	chapter	paragraph
Abandonment of Animals Act	1960	1	43	1.2.7
Air Force Act 1955 / Army Act	1955	70	33	4.1
		186	33	2
		187	33	2.2
		188	33	2.2.2
		190A	33	3.1
		190B	33	3.2
		191	33	5.1
		192	33	5.2
		197	33	5.3
Alcoholic Liquors Duties Act	1979	65	40	1.1
Animal Health Act	1981	15	43	4.2, 4.4.1
		60	43	4.3.1
		61	43	4.4.2
		62	43	4.4.3
		65	43	4.3.4
		66	43	4.3.4
Animals Act	1971	9	43	5.7.8
Army Act 1955 – see Air Force Act	1955			
Aviation Act	1992	27	4	5.1
Aviation and Maritime Security Act	1990	12	14	7.1
Badgers Act	1973		44	4.4.1
Bail Act	1976	3A	2	7.7, 7.8
		6	2	7.11, 7.12
		7	2	7.7, 7.11
		9	2	7.17
Betting, Gaming and Lotteries Act	1963	1	42	2.3.1
		2	42	2.2.4
		3	42	2.2.5
		8	42	2.5
		9	42	2.2.6
		10	42	2.4
		22	42	2.6
		51	42	2.7
		55	42	2.2
		Sch. 1	42	2.2.3
British Transport Commission Act	1949	56	14	7.6
Caravan Sites Act	1968		39	2.5
Charities Act	1992	74	49	5.3,5.4

statute	year	section	chapter	paragraph
Cinemas Act	1985	2	41	6.1.3
		4	41	6.2.1
		5–8	41	6.1.4
		10	41	6.1.6
		13	41	6.3
Civil Evidence Act	1965	5	7	5.4
Cockfighting Act	1952		43	1.2.6
Computer Misuse Act	1990	1	37	6.2.1
		2	37	6.2.2
		3	37	6.2.3
		8	6	6.1
		14	37	6.5
Confiscation of Alcohol (Young Persons) Act	1997	1	40	6.5
Coroners Act	1988	10	2	1.21
Crime (Sentences) Act	1997	2	2	11.1
		3	2	11.2
		4	2	11.3
		52	10	19.1.2
Criminal Attempts Act	1981	1	6	6.1
		2-4	6	6.5
		9	48	3.1
Criminal Damage Act	1971	1	2	2.4
			14	1.1
		2	14	2.1
		3	14	3.1
		5	14	4.1, 5.1
		10	14	6.1
Criminal Evidence Act	1898	1	3	1.1
			7	5.14
Criminal Justice Act	1961	22	29	1.2.2
Criminal Justice Act	1967	9	2	6.12
			7	4.5
		91	40	7.5.3
Criminal Justice Act	1988	23	7	5.1
			35	6.3
		24	7	5.1
		32	3	4.1
		39	8	1

statute	year	section	chapter	paragraph
Criminal Justice Act	1988	134	8	10
		139	47	3
		139A	47	4
		139B	47	4.4
		141	47	6.2
		141A	47	5
		142	47	6.3
		160	24	2.16
Criminal Justice Act	1991	1	2	9.2
		52	3	1.2
		55	3	4.1
		78	8	8.2
		80–92	29	2.1
		90	8	8.1
Criminal Justice and Public Order Act	1994	25	2	7.1, 7.2, 7.4
		27	2	7.5
		36–37	7	10.7
		51	3	5.1
		56	7	9.10
		57	7	9.8
		60	4	6.1
			16	10
		61	17	7
		62	17	7.2
		63	17	8
		64	17	8.4
		65	17	9
		66	17	8.3.1
		68	17	10
		69	17	11
		75	17	6
		76	17	6
		137	4	3.9
		166	19	5
		167	49	6.1
Criminal Justice (International Co-operation) Act	1990		26	15
Criminal Law Act	1967	3	6	10.1
		4	29	4.2
		5	29	4.4
Criminal Law Act	1977	1	6	5.2
		6	17	1
		7	17	2

statute	year	section	chapter	paragraph
Criminal Law Act	1977	8	17	3
			47	1.1.1
		9	17	4
		10	17	5
		38	4	2.5
		51	25	2.4
		54	10	14
		56	2	1.22
Criminal Procedure and Investigations Act	1996	1	7	12.9
		3	7	12.6
		5	3	2.1
			7	12.9
		6	7	12.9
		9	7	12.8, 12.23
		23	7	12.13
Crossbows Act	1987	1	22	7.2.1
		2	22	7.2.2
		3	22	7.2.3
		4	22	7.4
Dangerous Dogs Act	1991	1	43	5.4.1
		3	43	5.6.1
		4	43	5.4.10, 5.4.12
		4A	43	5.4.12
		5	43	5.4.6, 5.4.7, 5.6.8
Dangerous Wild Animals Act	1976		43	7
Data Protection Act	1984	1	37	1.5
		5–6	37	3
		21	37	4
		22–24	37	4.2
		27	37	5.2
		28	37	5.1
		33	37	5.3
		Sch. 1	37	2
Deer Act	1991	1	44	6.2
		2	44	6.4
		3	44	6.3.1
		4	44	6.5
			55	6.5
		6	44	6.3.2
			58	6.3.2
		10	44	6.6
		12	44	6.7

statute	year	section	chapter	paragraph
Firearms Act	1968	9	21	8.2.2
		10	21	8.2.3
		11	21	8.1.3, 8.2.4–8.2.9
		12	21	8.2.13
		13	21	8.2.14
		15	21	8.2.16, 8.3.2
		16	22	4.2
		16A	22	4.3
		17	22	4.4, 4.5
		18	22	4.6
		19	22	3.1
		20	22	3.2
		21	22	4.7
		22–24	22	2
		25	21	10.9
		27	21	3.2
		28	21	4.2.1
		30A	21	6.1
		30B	21	6.1.2
		30C	21	6.1.3
		33	21	9.2.2
		34	21	9.3
		38	21	9.4
		39	21	9.5
		40	21	9.6
		42	21	10.3
		44	21	1.3
		46	21	8.3.3
			22	5.3
		47	22	5.1, 5.1.3
		48	21	8.3.1
			22	5.2
		51	22	6
		52	22	5.4
		54	21	8.1.4
		57	21	2.1
			22	3.1.2
		58	21	2.8, 8.2.15
Firearms (Amendment) Act	1988	5	21	4.2.1
		12	21	6.3
		15	21	8.2.10
		16	21	8.2.8
		17	21	8.2.11
		18	21	8.2.12
		19	21	8.1.5

statute	year	section	chapter	paragraph
Firearms (Amendment) Act	1997	2	21	5.2
		7	21	2.8
		32–33	21	10.4
		34	21	10.5
		35	21	10.6
		39	21	7.5
		48	21	2.7
Football (Offences) Act	1991	2	19	3.2.1
		3	19	3.2.2
		4	19	3.2.3
Football Spectators Act	1989	15	19	4.4
		16	19	4.5
Forgery and Counterfeiting Act	1981	1	28	2.1
		2	28	3.1
		3	28	4.1
		4	28	5.1
		5	28	6.1
		6	28	7.1
		7	28	7.2
		8–10	28	8.1
		14	28	9.1
		15	28	10.1
		16	28	11.1
		17	28	12.1
		18	28	13.1
		19	28	14.1
		20–21	28	15.1
		22	28	16.1
		24	28	17.1
		27	28	18.1
		28	28	18.2
Game Act	1831	30	44	5.2.1
		31, 31A	44	5.2.3
		32	44	5.2.1
		35	44	5.2.2
Game Laws (Amendment) Act	1960	2	44	5.2.4
		4	44	5.2.4
		4A	44	5.2.6
Gaming Act	1968	2	42	3.2.2
		3–4	42	3.2.5
		5	42	3.2.7
		6	42	3.2.8

statute	year	section	chapter	paragraph
Gaming Act	1968	8	42	3.2.12
		12	42	3.4
		13	42	3.6.1
		14–15	42	3.6.2
		17	42	3.4.5
		19	42	3.3.4
		20	42	3.4.6
		23	42	3.7
		26	42	3.8.1
		27–28	42	3.8.9
		31	42	3.8.3
		32	42	3.8.5
		33	42	3.8.8
		34	42	3.8.5
		36	42	3.8.9
		38	42	3.8.10
		41	42	3.2.13
		43	42	3.9
		52	42	1.2.2–1.2.3
		Sch. 1	42	3.3.2
		Sch. 2	42	3.3.3
		Sch. 3	42	3.5
Goods Vehicles (Licensing of Operators) Act	1995	38	28	19.2
Greater London Council (General Powers) Act	1986	12	41	9.2.2
Guard Dogs Act	1975		43	5.8
Health and Safety at Work Act	1974	15	60	8.2
Highways Act	1980	137	46	2.1
		139–140A	46	5
		155	43	8
		161	22	3.4
		161A	46	4
		162	46	3
Homicide Act	1957		9	4.1.2, 4.1.4
		3	6	7.2
House to House Collections Act	1939	5	49	5.3
		6	49	5.4
Housing Act	1996	152	45	3.2
		153	45	3.3
		155	45	3.4

statute	year	section	chapter	paragraph
Licensing Act	1964	10	40	1.3.3
		39	40	4.1.6
		41	40	3.1.2
		44	40	3.1.3
		45	40	3.1.4
		48	40	3.1.5
		49	40	3.1.7
		54	40	10.2
		59	40	4.1.7
		60	40	4.1
		63	40	4.2
		65	40	1.1
		67A	40	7.9
		68	40	5.2
		70	40	5.3
		73	40	5.7.2
		74	40	5.5, 5.6
		76–78	40	5.4
		81	40	5.7.3
		81A	40	5.7.4
		84	40	11
		85	40	11.5
		86	40	4.1.4
		86A	40	4.3.2
		87	40	4.3
		87A	40	4.4
		89	40	5.8
		94	40	8
		148	40	1.2.8
		160	40	1.5.1, 1.5.2
		161	40	1.2.6, 8.5.2
		163	40	1.6
		164	40	1.5.7
		166	40	1.5.4
		168	40	6.2
		168A	40	6.3
		169	40	6.4
		170	40	6.4.4
		171	40	2.3
		171A	40	6.4.5
		172	40	7.2
		173	40	7.2
		174	40	7.3
		175	40	7.6
		176	12	12.7, 13.2

statute	year	section	chapter	paragraph
Licensing Act	1964	178	40	7.7
		181A	40	6.4.5
		182	41	2.2.2
		186	40	9
		187	40	10.3
		199	40	1.2.9
		200	40	2.2
		201	40	2.1, 2.3
		Sch. 7	40	3.1.5
Licensing (Occasional Permissions) Act	1983		40	1.3.2
Litter Act	1983	5	45	1.2.1
Local Government (Miscellaneous Provisions) Act	1982		41	2
		40	45	4.1
		46	59	4.1.1
		47	59	3.1.2
		48	59	4.1.2
		50	59	5.2, 6.1.2
		51	59	4.1.3
		53	59	6.1.1
		56	59	4.2
		59	59	3.1.3
		60	59	6.2.1
		61	59	6.2.2
		62	59	6.2.3
		64	59	3.2.2
		68	59	5.1
		73	59	5.3
		88	59	2.2
		Sch. 1	41	2.5–2.7
		Sch. 3	41	9
London Government Act	1963		41	3.1
		Sch. 12	41	3.3–3.5
London Local Authorities Act	1990	4	41	8.3.1
		6	41	8.3.2
		8	41	8.3.3
		15	41	8.3.5
		17	41	8.3.6
Lotteries and Amusements Act	1976	1	42	4.2
		2	42	4.2
		3	42	4.3
		4	42	4.4

statute	year	section	chapter	paragraph
Lotteries and Amusements Act	1976	5	42	4.5
		6	42	4.6
		9A	42	4.7.3
		14	42	4.10
		15–16	42	4.8
		19	42	4.9
Magistrates' Courts Act	1980	55	4	2.6
		76	4	2.6
		93	4	2.6
		97	4	2.2, 2.6
		144	2	3.2
Malicious Communications Act	1988	1	25	1.7
Malicious Damage Act	1861	35	14	7.5
		36	14	7.5
		47	14	7.3
		48	14	7.4
Mental Health Act	1959	128	10	8
Mental Health Act	1983	18	38	4.2, 4.3
		35–36	38	4.4
		38	38	4.4
		40	38	3.2
		127	38	7
		128	38	5
		135	38	6
		136	38	2
		137	38	3
		138	38	4.5
		145	38	1.2
Metropolitan Public Carriage Act	1869		59	1.1
Misuse of Drugs Act	1971	3	26	2
		4	26	3, 5
		5	26	6, 7
		6	26	4
		8	26	8
		9	26	9.1
		9A	26	10
		20	26	11
		23	26	13, 13.2, 13.3
		28	26	12
National Lottery etc. Act	1993	16	42	4.2.5
Naval Discipline Act	1957	42	33	4.1

statute	year	section	chapter	paragraph
Naval Discipline Act	1957	96	33	5.1
		97	33	5.2
		103	33	3.1
		104	33	3.2
		105	33	2.1
		108	33	2.2.2
		109	33	2.2.1
Night Poaching Act	1828	1–2	44	5.3
		9	44	5.3
Noise Act	1996	2–4	45	2.5.1–2.5.4
		10	45	2.5.8
Obscene Publications Act	1959	1	24	2.3
		4	24	2.6
		29	24	2.5
Offences Against the Person Act	1861	4	9	2
		16	9	3
		18	8	4
		20	8	5
		21	8	9.1
		22	8	9.2
		23	8	9.3
		24	8	9.4
		27	8	3.3
		28	15	2.2
		29	8	9.6
			15	2.3
		30	15	2.4
		32–33	14	7.7
		35	8	9.7
		36	8	8.3
		38	8	6
		47	8	3
		57	23	1
		58–59	9	7
		60	9	8
Pedlars Act	1871	2–5	49	2.1
		19	49	2.5
Perjury Act	1911	1	29	3.1, 3.3
		6	29	3.4
		7	29	3.4
		13	29	3.5
Pet Animals Act	1951	1	43	6.1

statute	year	section	chapter	paragraph
Pet Animals Act	1951	2,3	43	6.2
		4	43	6.1
Poaching Prevention Act	1862	2	44	5.4.2, 5.4.3
Police Act	1996	30	32	10
		68	32	2.2
		69	32	2.2
		70	32	2.3
		72	32	2.4
		84	32	5.1
		85	32	6.1
		86	32	2.8
		88	32	7.1
		89	8	7
			32	11.1
		90	32	11.2–11.4
		91	32	11.5
		Sch. 6	32	6.2
Police Act	1997	112	37	7.2
		113, 114	37	7.3
		115, 116	37	7.4
		119	37	7.6
		123	37	7.7.1
		124	37	7.7.2
Police and Criminal Evidence Act	1984	6	4	5.1
		10	2	5.1
		15	4	2.8
		16	4	2.8
		17	4	2.10
		18	4	2.11
		22	7	12.18
		24	4	3.3
		25	4	3.5
		27	4	3.7
			7	7.4
		28	4	3.10
		30	4	4.4, 4.7
		32	4	2.13
			19	5.2.2
		38	2	7.2
		40	4	4.9
		41	4	4.12, 4.17
		42	4	4.7, 4.12
		43	4	4.7, 4.12

statute	year	section	chapter	paragraph
Police and Criminal Evidence Act	1984	46	2	7.14
			4	4.20
		54	4	7.1
		55	4	7.3
		56	4	7.6
		57	4	7.9
		·58	4	7.10
		61	7	7.1
		63	7	9.7
		63A	7	9.10
		64	7	9.8
		69	7	5.4
		76	4	7.23
			7	4.6, 10.12
		77	4	7.26
		78	4	7.2.3–7.2.4
			7	4.6
		80	3	1.3, 1.4
		82	7	4.8
		104	32	4.1
Post Office Act	1953	11	25	1.5
		65	16	14.1
Prevention of Terrorism (Temporary Provisions) Act	1989	2	18	2.3
		3	18	2.5
		5–8	18	5
		9	18	3
		10	18	2.4
		11	18	4
		12	18	2.4.4
		13A	5	5.4
			18	8.5
		13B	18	8.6
		14	4	4.2
			18	8, 9.4
		15	18	8.2–8.4
		16A	18	6
		16B	18	6.2
		16C	18	8.7
		16D	18	8.8
		17	18	7.3
		18	18	7
		18A	18	7.2
		Sch. 7	18	8.4.2–8.4.4
Prevention of Corruption Act	1906	1	27	5.1

statute	year	section	chapter	paragraph
Prevention of Corruption Act	1916	2	27	5.2
Prevention of Crime Act	1953	1	47	1.1.1,2.1
Prison Act	1952	39	29	1.2.1
		40	29	1.4
		49	29	1.3
Private Places of Entertainment (Licensing) Act	1967		41	2.1
Prosecution of Offences Act	1985	3	7	12.14
Protection from Eviction Act	1977	1	39	2.2–2.3
Protection from Harassment Act	1997	1,2	39	1.1
		3	39	1.2
		4	39	1.3
		5	39	1.4
		12	39	1.5
Protection of Animals Act	1911	1	43	1.2
		5	43	1.3.4
		5A, 5B	43	1.2.4
		11	43	2
		12	43	1.3
		15	43	1.1
Protection of Badgers Act	1992	1	44	4.2
		2	44	4.2.3
		3	44	4.2.5
		4	44	4.2.8
		5	44	4.2.11
		6	44	4.2.12
		7	44	4.2.4
		8	44	4.2.6
		9	44	4.2.9
		10	44	4.3
		11	44	4.4
		12	44	4.5
		13	44	4.6
Protection of Children Act	1978	1	24	2.12
Public Bodies Corrupt Practices Act	1889	1	27	1.1
		2	27	2.1
		7	27	4.1
Public Meeting Act	1908	1	16	13
Public Order Act	1936	1	16	12.2

statute	year	section	chapter	paragraph
Public Order Act	1936	2	16	12.3
		7	16	12.2.3
Public Order Act	1986	1	16	2
		2	16	3
		3	16	4
		4	16	6
		4A	16	7
		5	16	8
		6	16	2.4
		11	16	11.1
		12	16	11.2
		13	16	11.3
		14	16	11.4
		14A, 14B	17	12
		14C	17	12
		18	16	9.2
		19	16	9.3
		20	16	9.6
		21	16	9.5
		23	16	9.4
		30	19	4.2
		31	19	4.2.2
		38	14	8
Race Relations Act	1976	1	36	3.1
		2	36	4.1
		4	36	4.2
		5	36	3.2
		16	36	7.4.1
		30	36	6.2
		31	36	6.4
		32	36	7
		33	36	6.1
		35–38	36	8
Refuse Disposal (Amenity) Act	1978	2	45	1.3.1
		3	45	1.3.4
			60	5.2
Rehabilitation of Offenders Act	1974		37	7.5
		4	2	10.1
Representation of the People Act	1983	60	31	2.1
		61	31	2.2
		97	16	13.4
			31	3.1
		Sch. 1	31	3.2.1–3.3.2

statute	year	section	chapter	paragraph
Restriction of Offensive Weapons Act	1959	1	47	6.1
Road Traffic Act	1988	1	9	4.2.3
			50	3
		2	50	2
		3	50	4
		3A	51	8.1
		4	51	1.1, 7.1, 9.1
		5	51	2.1, 7.1
		6	51	3.1, 9.2
		7	51	4.1
		8	51	4.2
		9	51	5.1
		10	51	6.1
		14,15	52	11.3
		16	58	1.2
		17	58	1.3
		22	60	2.1
		22A	60	2.2
		23	58	2
		24	58	3.2
		25	48	3.1.1
			60	3.1
		26	60	3.2
		27	43	5.3.4
		28–30	58	3.1
		34	60	4.1
		35	57	3.1
		36	57	2.1.1
		37	57	3.3
		40A	52	1.3.2, 9.1
		41A	52	1.3
		41B	52	1.3.1
		42	52	1.3.1
			56	2.7
		63	52	1.3.1
		67	60	7.2
		75–76	52	9.3
		81	58	4.3
		87	54	1.1
		91	56	2.17
		96	54	3.1
		97	54	2.1
		99, 100	60	5.1.2–5.1.3
		101	54	4.2
		102	54	4.3

statute	year	section	chapter	paragraph
Road Traffic Act	1988	103	54	4.4–4.5
		163	57	3.2
			60	3.1
		164	60	6.1
		165	60	6.2
		169	57	3.4
		170	53	1.1
		172	60	6.3
		173	60	6.4
		174	60	6.5
		175	60	6.6
		176	60	6.7
		192	50	1.2–1.4
Road Traffic Offenders Act	1988	1	60	1.1
		2	60	1.2
		15	51	10.1, 10.2
		16	51	10.3
		28–49	54	4
		34	54	4.1.5
		54	55	2.1
		62	55	2.2
		75	55	3.1
		91	57	2.1.1
		Sch. 1	60	1.4
Road Traffic Regulation Act	1984	14	57	6.1
		17	57	6.1
		25	57	5.2
		28	57	4
		64	57	1.2
		67	57	1.4
		81	57	6.1
		84	57	6.1
		86	57	6.1
		87	57	6.3
		88	57	6.1
		89	57	6.2
Safety of Sports Grounds Act	1975	2	41	10.3
		10	41	10.4
		11	41	10.2
Salmon Act	1986	32	44	7.6
Salmon and Freshwater Fisheries Act	1975	25–28	44	7.2
		31–36	44	7.3
Scrap Metal Dealers Act	1964	1 – 6	49	3

statute	year	section	chapter	paragraph
Sex Discrimination Act	1975	1	36	2.1.1
		2	36	2.1.2
		3	36	2.1.3
		4	36	4.1
		6	36	4.2
		7	36	2.2
		17	36	7.4.1
		39	36	6.2
		40	36	6.3
		41	36	7
		42	36	6.1
		47–49	36	8
Sex Offenders Act	1997	1	10	22.1
		2	10	22.2
		3	10	22.4
		7	10	20.2
		Sch. 1	10	22.3
Sexual Offences Act	1956	1	10	1
		2	10	2
		3	10	3
		4	10	4
		5	10	5
		6	10	6
		7	10	7
		9	10	10
		10	10	12
		11	10	13
		12	10	15
		13	10	16
		14	10	17
		15	10	18
		16	10	15.2
		17	11	4.4
		19	11	4.2
		20	11	4
		21	11	4.3
		22	12	8
		23	10	11
		24	12	12.6
		25–27	10	9
		28	12	9
		29	12	10
		30	12	6
		31	12	7

statute	year	section	chapter	paragraph
Sexual Offences Act	1956	32	12	5
		33	12	12.3
		34	12	12.4
		35	12	12.5
		36	12	13
		42	12	6.2
		43	11	5
		12	12.6.3	
Sexual Offences Act	1967	1	10	15.3
		4	10	15.6
		5	12	11
		6	12	12.2
Sexual Offences Act	1985	1,2	12	4
Sexual Offences (Amendment) Act	1976		10	21
Sexual Offences (Amendment) Act	1992		10	21
Sexual Offences (Conspiracy and Incitement) Act	1996	10	20.1	
Sporting Events (Control of Alcohol, etc.) Act	1985	1, 1A	19	2
		2	19	2.2
		2A	19	2.3
		3	19	2.4, 2.4.4
		6	19	2.4.4
		7	19	2.1.5, 2.2.3, 2.5
Street Offences Act	1959	1	12	2
Suicide Act	1961	2	9	9
Telecommunications Act	1984	42	25	2.3
		43	25	2.1
Telegraph Act	1863	45	25	1.1
Telegraph Act	1868	20	25	1.3
Theatres Act	1968	2	41	4.2
		6	41	4.2.5
		7	41	4.2.6
		9	41	4.2.8
		10	41	4.3.1
		12	41	4.1
		13	41	4.1.3
		15	41	4.3.3–4.3.5
Theft Act	1968	1–6	13	1.1
		8	13	2.1

statute	year	section	chapter	paragraph
Theft Act	1968	9	13	3.1
		10	13	3.4
			47	1.1.1
		11	13	4.1
		12	13	5.1
		12A	13	5.2
		13	13	6.1
		14	13	7.1
		15	13	8.11
		15A	13	8.12
		16	13	8.13
		17	13	10.1
		18	13	12.1
		19	13	13.1
		20	13	9.1, 14.1
		21	13	15.1
		22	13	16.1
		23	13	20.1
		24	13	19.1
		25	48	1.1
		27	13	17.1, 18.1
		34	13	9.2
		Sch. 1	44	7.5
Theft Act	1978	1–4	13	9.3–9.6
Town Police Clauses Act	1847	37	59	3.1
		38	59	2.1
		45	59	3.2.1
		46–50	59	3.1.3
		47	59	3.2.1
		52,53	59	3.2.1
		58	59	3.2.1
Trade Marks Act	1994	97	28	20.1–20.3
Trade Union and Labour Relations (Consolidation) Act	1992	220	20	2
		241	20	3
Transport Act	1985	10–16	59	2.3
Treasure Act	1996	2	1	20
Vagrancy Act	1824	3	49	4.1
		4	48	2.1
			49	4.2
		6	48	2.2
		49	4.3	

statutory instrument	year	regulation	chapter	paragraph
Road Vehicles (Construction and Use) Regulations	1986	18	52	2.1
		26	52	3.1
		27	52	3.2
		29	52	4.1
		30	52	5.1
		34	52	5.2
		35	52	6.1
		36	52	6.2
		37	52	8.4
		39	52	7.1
		46, 47	52	11.1
		54	52	8.1
		74	56	1.7
		76	60	7.1
		97	52	8.2
		98	52	8.3
		99	52	8.4.4
		100	52	9.2
		101	52	10.1
		102	52	10.2
		103	46	2.2
		104	52	10.4
		105	52	10.5
		106	52	10.6
		107	52	10.7
		109	52	10.8
Road Vehicles Lighting Regulations	1989	23	56	1.2
		24	56	2.1
		25	56	2.5
		27	56	2.6
Traffic Signs Regulations and General Directions	1994	10	57	2.1.3
		16	57	2.2
		26	57	2.3
Traffic Signs (Temporary Obstructions) Regulations	1985	8–11	57	1.5.1–1.5.4
Zebra, Pelican and Puffin Pedestrian Crossing Regulations	1997	18–26	57	5.1–5.2.11

Chapter 1: Learning the Law

INTRODUCTION

1.1 English law is not written with a view to its being readily understood by a lay person; indeed it is not wholly written in English, Latin and French phrases are frequently encountered. The aim in this chapter is to remove some of the mystique surrounding this country's legal system and to explain:
- how an act of Parliament is constructed, and the purposes of its several parts
- what the result of an appeal case really means
- how judges and lawyers may interpret acts of Parliament and case decisions
- how to distinguish the crucial elements from the additional comments in a court's judgement.

1.2 This book is aimed at students of law, at police officers and at anyone else who may have the need or inclination to study the criminal law. Case decisions are referred to throughout the text, and some which illustrate clearly a particular aspect of law are described in more detail in 'Keynote Cases' at the end of a chapter. A list of law reports, where the text of case decisions may be found, is provided towards the end of the chapter, for the reader who seeks more detail than is provided in these pages. A glossary of Latin terms, such as 'ratio decedendi' and 'obiter dictum' is included at the end of this chapter.

1.3 The law is a living thing, changing from day to day to cater for changes in society and circumstances, which even the most able of minds cannot predict. It is hoped that the introduction to case law which the book provides will encourage the reader to follow the law reports to found in newspapers such as The Times and The Independent, to keep up with these changes as they take place

ACTS OF PARLIAMENT

2.1 The laws of the United Kingdom arise from numerous sources, the first and probably the most important, is Acts of Parliament. The government in power generally decides what matters it wishes to make subject of legislation. Most governments will have lists of subjects from their election manifestos. Most of these will not, however, affect the criminal law.

2.2 When you need to research the law it is often necessary to read Acts of Parliament. This is what you can expect the first page of an Act of Parliament to look like *(see fig 1)*. Note that the numbers in parentheses which appear in Figure 1 do not appear in an actual act. They are to aid explanation, and relate to the matters listed below.

1) Short title, in this case a very precise phrase naming the Act.

2) Official citation. Chapter 24 is the twenty-fourth piece of law passed during this session of parliament in 1978. Originally an Act was the total legislation passed during the session in Parliament, each part or subject being a chapter, these being numbered in the order they were made. More recently, the word Act has been used for each chapter. Acts are cited, for example, as 'Theft Act 1968' using the short title, or 1968 chapter 74. Prior to 1963, Acts were not cited by their calendar year but by the regnal year, or years of the

Figure 1

(1) Coffee Shops Trust (Scotland) Act 1978

(2) 1978 Chapter 24

(3) An Act to extend the Coffee Shops Trust Act 1977 to Scotland

(4) [30th June 1978]

(5) Be it enacted by the Queen's most Excellent Majesty, by and with the advice and consent of the lords Spiritual and Temporal, and Commons, in this Present Parliament assembled, and by the authority of the same, as follows:

(6) Extension of Coffee Shops Trust Act 1976 to Scotland 1976 c27

(7)

1–(1) The Coffee Shops Trust Act 1977 shall be amended as follows, and as so amended shall extend to Scotland and come into force there on the passing of this Act.

(2) In section 2 (objects of the trust and powers of trustees), after subsection (2) there shall be added –

"(3) Subsection (2) above shall have effect in relation to Scotland with the substitution for paragraph (d) of the following paragraph –

"(d) from time to time to sell, let, surrender or otherwise dispose of, or apply as security for borrowing, any heritable or moveable property vested in or acquired by the trustees;".".

(3) In section 6(4) (extent), the words "Scotland or" are hereby repealed.

(8) Short title and extent

2–(1) This Act may be cited as the Coffee Shops Trust (Scotland) Act 1978.

(2) This Act does not extend to Northern Ireland.

monarch's reign. Acts were numbered consecutively throughout the parliamentary session which normally runs from November to the following October, and then cited accordingly, e.g., 2 & 3 Vict. c.5, so the reference given is to the fifth act to be passed in the parliamentary session covering the second and third years of Queen Victoria's reign.

3) The long title. This describes in more detail the purpose of the Act.

4) The date of Royal assent. The date upon which the legislation became an Act, this is not necessarily the date that the Act came (or comes) into force.

5) The enacting formula. This is an explanation of whose authority was invoked to bring into effect the Act and is a historical phrase.

6) This left edge or margin of the Act may contain notes used to show how the authors of the legislation used prior legislation as a guide. In this case the purpose of this Act is to extend the powers of trustees of coffee shops in Scotland in a similar manner to those in the rest of England and Wales. A useful reference to the legislation in chapter 27 of the 1976 session of Parliament is provided.

7) Text of the Act. This is divided into sections, sub-sections and paragraphs.

8) Short title, commencement and extent. This part sets out the date the Act will come into force if it is not at the date of Royal assent. The subsequent date or grant to the Minister giving power to bring all or part of the Act into force by use of statutory instrument.

2.3 The naming and numbering of an act of Parliament is a fairly straightforward matter. Take for example the Theft Act 1968. The name gives some indication of the subject matter, in this case the Act defines offences of theft, burglary and deception, connected with the dishonest obtaining of property. The name includes the year in which it became law, which serves to distinguish it from other Acts of the same name, e.g. the Theft Act 1978. Some Acts are of a more general nature. For example, the Criminal Law Act 1977 deals with a range of matters, from bomb hoaxes to the use of force to regain possession of premises. Even so, the title does indicate that the Act is unlikely to deal with such matters as social security benefits or income tax.

Numbering of Sections in an Act of Parliament

2.4 In order to sub-divide an Act of Parliament into an understandable form, the document known simply as an Act is split into sections. Sections are usually paragraphs dealing with a subject or part of a subject. Each section is individually numbered in rising order. Some more complex sections are again sub-divided into sub-sections. To make the numbering easier to follow these are usually numbered but the numbers are put into brackets, e.g. Section 1(1). Some really complex matters are again split up by using letters in brackets, e.g. Section 1(2)(a). This greatly assists when researching the law or dealing with offences. In the Theft Act 1968, the definition of 'theft' is contained in Section 1, while the various terms used in that definition are explained in detail in Sections 2–6. This type of arrangement is not unusual. There are many Acts of Parliament having hundreds of Sections, the majority of which explain the workings of a few sections that define offences. Most Acts also have Schedules attached to the back. Schedules generally include lists of other Acts affected by the new legislation passed in the Act, or list people affected and Acts and Sections that have been repealed or amended. A great deal of some Acts relates to administrative tasks relating to the subject matter. Some will come into effect in stages and dates will be set for the activation of various parts and sections.

Codified Statutes

2.5 In the English legal system a codifying Act is simply a tidying up Act. It is a piece of legislation that brings together all the existing law. A good example of this is the 1968 Theft Act. It brought together all of the existing law on theft at the time and incorporated it.

2.6 By contrast, the Police and Criminal Evidence Act 1984 has 'Codes of Practice' contained in it, which may from time to time be changed. The intention when the Act was being prepared was that these codes could be easily changed to cater for changes in society, to be responsive to the needs of the time. The Act itself contains all of the relevant legislation concerning the collection and organisation of criminal evidence from police enquires. All of the previously relevant legislation on that topic is repealed by the Act.

2.7 In Europe, where legal systems are different, codification means something else. In France, for example, the criminal law is contained in the 'Code Napoleon' which sets out broad descriptions of offences. Judges and magistrates then interpret the law and apply it to particular cases.

Delegated or Sub-Ordinate Legislation

2.8 The power to make rules and pass laws can be delegated by Parliament to a person or body. Local authorities can, for example, make bye-laws to cover local problems in particular boroughs. An Act of Parliament may set up a structure for the appropriate Minister of State to make regulations and rules relating to specific topics. Road Traffic Acts are a good example of Acts that have powers extended to the Minister of State. These allow very complex matters (such as the design and placement of instruments, lights, and many other features of vehicles) to be regulated by the passing of statutory instruments. The amount of delegated legislation issued far exceeds the number of Acts of Parliament.

2.9 The development of the welfare state since the Second World War has been controlled mainly by regulations made by ministers under authority of Acts of Parliament. Many of the major institutions of state are controlled in this way. It is often the case, however, that the regulations are drawn up by civil servants; the minister's role is limited to directing that the work should be done and to an overview of the content.

2.10 Control over delegated legislation because of its sheer volume is difficult. In the case of statutory instruments, the proposed new regulations are placed before Parliament with a set period for consideration given, i.e. 40 days. If there is no objection, the regulations will become law. This is called a 'negative resolution'. An alternative method is for the minister to propose the regulations before the House of Commons and for them to be agreed by resolution. This is called a 'positive resolution'.

2.11 Such regulations are subject of scrutiny by the courts. Where a delegatee of a power exceeds or is considered to have exceeded the authority given to him, the exercise of that authority can be the subject of consideration by the courts. The courts may rule that the minister has acted unlawfully or 'ultra vires' (beyond or outside the power). In all cases where persons have a grievance at the way legislation, delegated and otherwise, has been interpreted they can seek judicial review by the courts of the operation of the law.

2.12 An example of the courts' exercising control over what may be mis-placed use of powers by ministers, is afforded by the case of *R v Secretary of State for the Home Department, ex parte Naughton* (1996) (keynote case). The case concerned the authority delegated to the Home Secretary to rule on the computation of reductions and remissions in prison sentences.

2.13 In order that the rules passed under statutory instruments should be more widely known, the Statutory Instruments Act 1946 was passed, providing that statutory instruments should be numbered, printed, published and sold. Unfortunately most statutory instruments are very difficult to read and understand and they frequently quote other complicated sources of information and legislation.

Bye-laws

2.14 Local authorities are empowered to pass bye-laws. This allows a local authority power to make rules which will directly resolve local problems that are often peculiar to an area or region. Local bye-laws will include such things as the rule for good conduct in local parks. It is often worth looking at the local bye-laws to see what offences are set out, as a person may be required to provide personal details for the purpose of being summoned for a minor breach of the bye-laws. Failure to provide such details, however, may render a person liable to arrest under Section 25 of the Police and Criminal Evidence Act 1984, under the general powers of arrest provisions.

European Law

2.15 The United Kingdom joined the European Community on the 1st of January 1973. In so doing, it gave powers to the European Community legislature to pass laws that are binding in the UK. The European Communities Act 1972 provides that '…all rights, powers, liabilities, obligations, restrictions, remedies and procedures under the European treaties are to be given effect immediately in English law.' Such rights are to be referred to as 'enforceable Community rights'. English judges must give authority to Community law. It is apparent, even to the casual reader of most newspapers, that the effects of European law are slowly becoming more and more important.

2.16 An example of this legislation is that of the common agricultural policy. Agreed rules for farming are arrived at by the Community. These then become law within the individual member states. Breach of the rules, or questions arising from the interpretation of the rules, are decided by the European Court of Justice in Luxembourg, rather than the national courts of the member states.

2.17 The European Court has developed a number of principles that the member state authorities must follow in pursuit of common policy between states. A good example of the way in which the European Court may become involved with national laws is in the case of Mr Bosnan, the French footballer, who claimed that his freedom of employment was unfairly impeded by contractual restraints of the football transfer system. The European Court gave a reasoned judgment of over one hundred pages. The judgment, however, gave not only the results of its findings but also some guidelines of how it thought the system of transfers should be operated.

2.18 By contrast, an English court would expect that its rulings would become a precedent to be accepted and followed. Comment about what should occur would only be by way of opinion which would not form part of the ruling. Such statements are said to be 'obiter dictum' or outside the ruling of the case. Obiter dictum is a Latin phrase which means that the comment, although falling within the case, refers to a point which is not at issue and is given only by way of an example as to how the decision may have been made under the example situation. A judge may give an example result which would have happened if circumstances alluded to had prevailed. At this time, however, there are few rulings of the European Court that will directly affect the criminal law.

INTERPRETATION OF THE LAW

3.1 Acts of Parliament are written in a standard format and can be very complex. Most criminal law legislation is by its very nature complex. Lawyers and judges often disagree with how such statutes are interpreted. Even simple phrases can be read to give different meanings.

3.2 Over the years, judges and lawyers have formulated rules to allow interpretation of legislation. Provided a good enough reason is given, almost any interpretation is possible to enable the judge to attain a desired result. In the adversarial courts of the United Kingdom, it is the lawyers who argue the interpretation they would most like the judge to accept as being correct according to their case and desired result. Principally there are three rules, the literal rule, the golden rule and the mischief rule.

The Literal Rule

3.3 It is within the power of Parliament to make the law. Judges should interpret the words of Parliament as they are set out in statutes, nothing added or taken away. In essence that is the literal rule. Lord Diplock expressed this point when he said, 'At a time when more and more cases involve the application of legislation which gives effect to policies which are the subject of bitter public and parliamentary controversy, it cannot be too strongly emphasised that the British constitution, though largely unwritten, is firmly based upon the separation of powers; Parliament makes the laws, the judiciary interpret them' (*Duport Steels Ltd v Sirs* (1980)). This view clearly shows that if the statute is clear and unambiguous, the court should interpret the words as they are written. This is so even if it is obvious to the court that Parliament would have used other words if it had foreseen the situation before the court.

3.4 Generally statutes are written with a specific intention. If they do not fulfil that aim, it is clearly within the power of Parliament to review and amend the law. This was the case with the problems relating to the interpretation of obtaining of services by deception under the 1968 Theft Act. The matters became so complex that further legislation (Theft Act 1978) was passed to clarify and deal with the conflicts in this difficult area of law.

The Golden Rule

3.5 This rule departs from the literal rule and arises from circumstances where the statute would, if read literally, lead to an absurd situation. The rule appears to apply only in circumstances where the court may achieve a less absurd, more sensible meaning of a word or phrase, by linguistic interpretation. It does not necessarily matter, that the more natural use of the word or phrase brings about the absurd meaning. Lord Reid (*Coutts & Co v I.R.C.* (1953)) said, 'Where a statutory provision on one interpretation brings about a startling and inequitable result, this may lead the court to seek another possible interpretation which will do better justice'.

3.6 An example would be to suggest that a literal interpretation of Section 57 of the Offences Against the Person Act 1861, which creates the offence of bigamy, would not allow anyone to commit the offence. The Section states in clear English that any person who, being married, shall marry any other person, commits an offence of bigamy. The legal definition of marriage states that both parties to a marriage must be single. It would therefore be impossible to commit the offence because anyone who was married could not marry again. The courts seeing this as absurd have interpreted the words 'shall marry' as being where the parties go through a ceremony of marriage as if they were able and entitled to enter into such a contract.

3.7 It is probably true to suggest that the 'golden rule' has developed to prevent potential injustice being caused by the court interpreting statutes using the literal rule.

3.8 It is suggested by learned writers that another use of the golden rule is where judges imply words into the interpretation of statutes. An example of this concerns the Factories Act 1861 which has a provision stating that dangerous parts of machines must be fenced while they are 'in motion'. Failure to ensure the safety of employees by allowing unguarded machines to be used renders the employer liable for breach of the Act. A worker who was attempting to adjust a machine had to remove the frame to allow access. He turned the machine manually whilst effecting adjustments. Unfortunately, his finger became caught in the machine and he suffered injury. The question for the court was were the employers liable for breach of the Act. On a strict interpretation the machine was in motion, albeit not propelled other than by the worker's own hand. The employers should on a strict literal interpretation have been liable. The case came before the House of Lords on appeal. The decision of their Lordships was that 'in motion' for the purposes of this incident meant 'mechanical propulsion' (*Richards Thomas & Baldwins Ltd v Cummings* (1955)).

The Mischief Rule

3.9 This rule of interpretation is aimed at looking behind the statute at the reason why it was passed. What is it that the Act was meant to do, why was it needed? For this type of interpretation, the judge may look at the words used in their common parlance and look at the words around them and the context in which they are used. The term used by lawyers is the Latin 'noscitur a socis' which may be interpreted as 'within its society' or 'in context.' A judge, applying this principle, may look not only at the Section of an Act which she is seeking to interpret, but at the statute as a whole, or indeed, at other statutes dealing with the same topic. Particular words or phrases may, however, have different meanings even within the same Section.

3.10 The case of *National Real Estate v Hassan* (1939) illustrates the use of the mischief rule. In the early 1930's speculators bought up dilapidated houses which were already rented out to tenants. Many of the tenancies were subject to a 'covenant to repair'. i.e. the tenant was responsible for keeping the property in good repair. Once a speculator had completed a purchase of such a property, the tenants were threatened with legal action if they failed to carry out repairs. A law was enacted to prevent speculators abusing the law in order to make profits out of tenants. In National Real Estate v Hassan, the court had to decide 'did the Act apply to speculators who had begun their actions prior to the passing of the Act, or did it apply to court actions commenced after the commencement date of the Act?' Applying the mischief rule, the court effectively back-dated the Act. It is very unusual in this country for a new law to apply retrospectively, but in this case, the hardship being caused at the time warranted such a decision.

THE COMMON LAW

4.1 The phrase 'common law' has for some reason come to mean many things to many people. Generally it is viewed as the results of decisions made by judges when they interpret the law to resolve disputes in court. The 'common law' has developed within our society to reflect the needs not catered for by written law.

4.2 When the Normans invaded Britain, there was no true central government or legal system as we now know it. William the Conqueror began a policy of centralisation that led to one body for government and one for the law. This was achieved not by imposing laws upon the country but by settling disputes according to local tradition and custom. Disputes were settled by travelling justices who held commissions under the Crown. From the times of Henry II these travelling justices were sent out at regular intervals.

4.3 These local travelling justices gradually increased their powers, generally there were three types of justices. First, those who tried persons found in gaols – at that time it was not a punishment to be kept imprisoned – were commissioned as Justices of Goal Delivery. Secondly, those who could try anyone for crime caught since the last visit, were commissioned as Justices of Oyer and Terminer. Finally, there were those who had power to try civil cases, these were commisioned as Justices of Assize. At this time most civil disputes were generally tried at Westminster (this court was called Nisi Pruis) but for convenience to the parties, trials were allowed in the local courts. Civil disputes were listed for hearing at the Westminster Court 'unless before' so they could be heard earlier at the local court if that occurred first. The modern version of these courts are the Assizes which remained in operation until 1974.

4.4 The early commissioners were clerics, as these were the only people who could read and write. The legal profession slowly evolved and lawyers were commissioned. At first the local justices administered local customs, accepting advice on custom and help from juries taken from the local population. Judges would hold discussions between themselves about cases they had dealt with and prevailing customs, thus discovering good and bad custom. They frequently refused to apply bad custom. The system developed into a more and more consistent approach and in this way judges developed the common law.

4.5 As the 'Curia Regis', or Kings Court developed, specialisation occurred with its divisions. The Court of Exchequer, whose judges were known as Barons, emerged at about 1200. Initially, its sole purpose was to deal with revenue disputes but as the judges were paid on a commission basis various legal devices were used to widen the actions coming within the court's jurisdiction. At around 1272, 'The Court of Common Pleas' or 'Common Bench', developed from the Curia Regis, this courts' first chief justice was appointed. He was assisted by other judges (lesser or younger) called puisne. The Court of Common Pleas was set up because the Magna Carta of 1215 had stated that there should be a court in a fixed place to carry out the work of the travelling justices. The court was based in Westminster. This court was to deal with trespass and debt, trespass included what is now known as theft in all its forms. The third court of common law was the King's Bench, so called as it originally followed the King around the country dealing with similar problems to that of the Court of Common Pleas. The proximity of this court to the King, however, gave it greater importance. This court specifically dealt with criminal matters, and by virtue of its position, exercised control over the other courts by prerogative writ (powers derived from the monarch). These courts remained in this form until the Judicature Acts of 1875.

4.6 The cumulative effect of the body of decisions made by Judges and Justices over the centuries has brought about what we now know as common law. Built into this system of decisions are those made by the courts on the grounds of equity. Equity (fairness) is not based so much on the literal interpretation of facts but rather on morals and maxims. One example would be the maxim 'he who comes to equity must do so with clean hands'. This meant that if, for example, two neighbours were involved in a dispute, one took action to stop the other taking a short cut accross his property, if the one seeking the remedy of injunction had for example used tricks or some other unfair method to deter the trespasser, at equity there could be no help. Also, the common law courts could only give damages to someone who had been wronged. It would be possible for the courts to give damages against a trespasser, but they could not stop the trespasser from doing the same again. A person who wished for some other remedy would have to petition the King. Such matters were delegated to the King's Chief Minister, the Chancellor. The Chancellor's Court, or Chancery Court, developed rules of fairness rather than legality. These maxims had the authority of law but were discretionary. The court did not have to grant the remedy sought if it thought this was unfair.

4.7 The common law position with regard to mortgages was that if a person mortgaged his land to another for the loan of money, the money would be due for repayment by a set date. If this loan was not repaid on time or as specified, the ownership of the land then went to the money lender. The borrower remained liable to repay the loan. Even when the loan was repaid, the borrower could not recover his land. The courts of equity developed a maxim 'once a mortgage always a mortgage' which allowed the borrower of money using land as security to have his land back when the loan was repaid. There would, of course, in fairness be increased interest for the overdue period.

4.8 In 1875 the whole structure of the court and how it dealt with the law was reviewed. The Judicature Act 1875 set out the system of courts that continued until 1975. The current structure and order is discussed in full in chapter two.

CASE LAW INTERPRETATION AND LEGAL PRECEDENT

5.1 One of the rare forms of art is the ability to distinguish between the way one court's judgment affects another court's decisions. All cases have grounds for the decision or give a legal reason why a judge decides in favour of one party or another. This reason is the ratio decidendi (often shortened to 'ratio') a Latin phrase meaning the decision or central point of the case. The importance of the ratio is that the decision may include interpretation of a statute which will affect other cases coming before other courts. A decision made by a higher court will bind all other lower courts to use the same type of interpretation of the law under similar circumstances. Thus the magistrates' court must follow precedent set out by the Crown Court, the Crown Court is bound by the precedents of the Court of Appeal, the Court of Appeal is bound by the House of Lords, and to some extent the House of Lords is bound in precedent by the European Court of Justice in Luxembourg.

Legal Precedent

5.2 If, during the trial of a person for an offence, a question arises as to how a particular piece of legislation or phrase should be applied or interpreted, the court will look to see whether the question has been considered before. In this way judges use earlier judgments made by other more senior courts as guidance in their decision making. We can use an example to illustrate this. In 1984 the Police and Criminal Evidence Act legislated for the first time on the exclusion of evidence in criminal cases. The law relating to how evidence is accepted by the courts is very important. Section 76 of the Police and Criminal Evidence Act 1984 deals with confessions that must be excluded if obtained by oppression. But what is 'oppression'. This question arises in numerous trials. In the case of *R v Miller* (1976) it was held that lengthy interviews with a schizophrenic, taking place over two days, resulting in a confession by Miller to the killing his girlfriend, was not so oppressive as to exclude the confession from evidence.

5.3 On the same question of exclusion of confession evidence for oppression in *R v Fulling* (1987) the Court of Appeal decided that it was not oppressive for the police to tell the defendant that her lover was having an affair with another woman, which she claimed had so affected her that she had made a full confession. The court held that the word oppression should be given its normal meaning as stated in the *Oxford English Dictionary*: 'the exercise of authority in a burdensome, harsh or wrongful manner, unjust or cruel treatment of subjects, inferiors etc, the imposition of unreasonable or unjust burdens.' It is possible to see from these two examples, covering the very narrow subject of how to interpret the word 'oppressive', just how different the views of the courts may be, given the differing circumstances and backgrounds to cases coming before them. In *R v Samuel* (1988) the court stated that denial of access to a solicitor might be oppressive.

Distinguishing Cases on their Facts

5.4 As a general rule, all courts are bound to follow the precedent of legal decisions, including the interpretation of statutes and case law of the higher courts. This rule applies unless such earlier decisions can be distinguished from the facts of the matter being decided by the court.

5.5 Two cases, distinguished one from another, relate to the admission of similar fact evidence in cases of murder. In *R v Smith* (1915) (keynote case) Smith was charged with the murder of a woman with whom he had gone through a ceremony of marriage. Evidence was presented that Smith had been married on two previous occasions and each of the women had been found dead in very similar circumstances. The decision of the court was that for similar fact evidence to be admissible the evidence must be of striking similarity.

5.6 In *Noor Mohammed v R* (1949) a similar question arose and the court stated that the evidence was not so strikingly similar as to allow its introduction. In this case, the defendant was charged with murder: it was alleged that he had killed the woman he lived with by giving her cyanide. There was weak evidence that the defendant's first wife had died having taken an overdose of cyanide, which the defendant had supposedly administered to her on the pretext that it cured toothache. This was initially admitted into evidence. The defendant, as a goldsmith, was legitimately in possession of the cyanide. Reviewing the evidence, the court made the following points: the defendant's second wife may have committed suicide, there was some evidence to suggest that this had occurred; the evidence relating to the first wife was poor and there was no evidence to show its relevance as being 'strikingly similar'. The case was dismissed.

5.7 The above examples show how cases can be distinguished from each other on their facts although the substance of the decision relates to the same point of law, in this case the admissibility of similar fact evidence.

5.8 All criminal cases begin at the magistrates' courts and most cases will be dealt with by the magistrates. Other cases, often the more serious, will be committed for trial at the Crown Court. The magistrates' courts' decisions do not form precedent for other courts. The rights of appeal from the various courts are dealt with in chapter two. Civil cases will be started by the issue of a writ of action in either the county court or the High Court.

5.9 A major problem that most law students will have is learning where to find case reports. Problems will occur if a case citation is not understood, here we give the example of a criminal case reference:

R v Smith [1949] 2 QB 423.

If we break this down, the:
- 'R' stands for Regina or Queen or complainant
- 'v' is versus,
- 'Smith' is the name of the defendant or respondent,
- '[1949]' is the year,
- '2 QB' is the second volume of the Queen's Bench Division reports (the report may be cited under any of the case report systems, see case reports in keynote case section),
- '423' is the page number in the second volume of the report.

Note: [ ] type brackets indicate that without the year being given, the case report will be difficult to trace. The other sort, ( ), are used where other references are included, such as a volume number, so that the case report may be found without having to rely on the year.

5.10 Law reports have since 1881 been consistently recorded with standard abbreviations for the divisions of the courts. A more comprehensive list is given at the end of this chapter, but some examples are given below.

1881 - 1890		1891 to Present	
Appeal Cases	(...App. Cas.)	Appeal Cases	([year]) A.C.
Chancery Division	(...Ch.D)	Chancery Division	([year]) Ch.
Queen's Bench Division or King's Bench Division	(...Q.B.D.) (...K.B)	Queen's Bench Division or King's Bench Division	([year] QB) ([year] KB)
Probate Division	(...P.D.)	Probate Division since 1972 Family Division	([year]) P.) ([year] Fam.)

THE CLASSIFICATION OF OFFENCES

6.1 The classification of offences is set out in law (part VI Criminal Law Act 1977). There are basically two classes, summary and indictable. A third class is created by offences which can fall into either class subject to the circumstances relating to the commission of the offence involved. This third class of offence is called for simplification 'either-way', the phrase denoting that the offence can be tried either on indictment or summarily.

Indictable Offence

6.2 Means an offence, which if committed by an adult, is triable on indictment, whether it is exclusively so or triable either-way. Some offences can only be tried on indictment, these include murder, treason, manslaughter and other very serious offences. Such offences are always tried at the Crown Court with a judge and jury.

Summary Offence

6.3 Means an offence, which if committed by an adult, is triable summarily. A summary trial will always take place in the magistrates' court.

Either-way Offence

6.4 Means an offence, which if committed by an adult, is triable either on indictment or summarily.

Summons

6.5 Is a written order issued and signed by a Justice of the Peace, or Justices' Clerk on behalf of the Justice. The summons is directed to the named person in the information requiring him to appear before a named magistrates' court for the area specified in the summons to answer specified charges set out in the summons. Summonses are issued as a result of information or complaint made to the Magistrates. Complaints can be either verbal or written and are concerned with matters which are generally not subject to the criminal law. Examples include nuisance by way of breach of the peace, or threats to breach the peace resulting in a binding over of the named person to keep the peace, or a recognisance of the peace. Generally, summonses are delivered by post. Magistrates may also require the attendance of a witness by way of summons if it is unlikely that the person will attend the court voluntarily. Such summonses will not be effective unless service can be proven so they cannot be delivered or served by post.

Keynote Cases

7.1 *Regina v Sec of State Home Department ex parte Naughton* (1996) Times Sept 17th QBD

Problem

How do we know when a minister or someone who has legal authority to take an action has abused their powers? What can be done to question those powers and the exercise of the powers? In this case, the question was about how to calculate the time owed to prisoners for periods in custody on remand.

Circumstances

This case was brought by way of review of the decision taken not to release a prisoner. A problem had occurred when interpreting Section 67 of the Criminal Justice Act 1967, as amended by Section 47 of the Police and Criminal Evidence Act 1984. The application for review in this matter was brought in the name of a prisoner named Naughton. Naughton had been arrested on September 26th 1994 for possession of cannabis, he was remanded in custody by the Magistrates initially. He was eventually bailed to Crown Court, some 106 days later, on January 9th 1995. During the period on remand prior to January 1995 he was sentenced to a short detention for burglary, this amounted to 25 days. On March 26th 1995 he was again arrested, this time for burglary, and remanded in custody be the Magistrates. On the 17th of November 1995 at Sheffield Crown Court, Naughton was sentenced to 18 months' imprisonment for each offence to run consecutively, a total of 36 months imprisonment. There was no dispute about the computation of days served on remand, they amounted to 239, plus 81 credited for remission. Naughton claimed he was due this period of remission from each sentence. Naughton relied on four cases relating to concurrent sentences, contending that the court should adopt an approach which allowed for the fact that the 1967 legislation was ambiguous, and that ambiguity should be in his favour. The Home Office claimed that it was wrong to allow the time served on remand against each sentence passed in a consecutive sentence as this would produce absurd results. Lord Justice Brown, accepting the argument of the Home Office, said there could be no possible justification or logic for remand prisoners being advantaged as the applicant contended. Such a situation was almost too absurd to contemplate.

Decision
When calculating time to be deducted from a sentence by the time the prisoner is held on remand, the calculation should be on the sentence as a whole.

Comment
The method of calculating the length of sentences, by reducing the time a prisoner has spent in custody between being arrested and being sentenced, would produce absurd results if Naughton's arguments had been accepted. His argument was that the 239 days should, in effect, be deducted twice, once from each of the two sentences. In his circumstances, this would still leave him with a proportion of the sentences to serve, but it is not difficult to come up with absurd examples. e.g. A and B are arrested for burglaries; A abides by condition of bail and serves no period in custody prior to sentence, while B breaks bail conditions and is in custody for three months prior to sentence. They each receive two 6 month sentences, to be served consecutively. B would walk out of prison almost immediately (given that with remission, some sentences are in effect, halved), while A would go on to serve 6 months in prison.

7.2 *R v Smith* (1915) 11 Cr App R 229

Problem
In what circumstances will evidence of similar facts be admissible in evidence?

Circumstances
Smith, the defendant, was charged with murder. He had gone through a marriage ceremony with a woman who had later died. At the trial, the prosecution brought evidence that Smith had been married twice before: on each occasion the woman had been found dead drowned in her bath; the woman had been insured to the benefit of Smith; Smith had called a medical practitioner to the bodies informing them that the deceased woman had suffered from epileptic fits; and the bathroom door had not been capable of being locked. The amazing similarities between the deaths of all three woman meant that the relevance to the prior deaths ruled out the possibility of natural causes being the reason for death. The courts accepted the evidence, which would not otherwise have been allowed, under the rule for admissibility of similar facts.

Decision
Similar evidence will only be admissible if it can be shown that it is strikingly similar.

Comment
The purpose of similar evidence and the rule allowing its admission into evidence, is to prevent the defendant from claiming accident or coincidence as a defence. It would normally not be considered unless the case was of a serious nature, but its main thrust is to prevent a defendant using the same defence on numerous occasions.

Glossary of Some Common Legal Terms

Term	Meaning
Aliter or secus	otherwise
CA	Court of Appeal
contra	a contradiction
CPS	Crown Prosecution Service
DPP	Director of Public Prosecutions
ibid (short for ibidem)	in the same place
ie, ibid	as applied to the reported case
infra vires	inside the power (within the power)
loc cit	the page previously cited
obiter dictum	a statement outside the main decision, an aside
op cit	the book previously cited
passim	everywhere in the book
per curiam	statement by the whole court
per incuriam	judge's remark made by mistake
per semble	it seems that
prima facie	on the face of it
ratio/ratio decidendi	the legal point decided
SC	the same case
ultra vires	outside the power

Law Reports for Criminal Cases

Abbreviation	Report Name	Years	Courts reported
Acton	Action (Prize Causes)	1809 – 1811	Privy Council
AC	Appeal Cases	1891 – present	
Ad &El or A&E	Adolphus and Ellis	1834 – 1840	King's or Queen's Bench
Aleyn	Aleyn	1646 – 1649	King's Bench
All ER	All England Reports	1936 – present	All superior courts
All ER Rep	All England Reprint	1558 – 1935	All Courts
Barnard KB	Barnardiston (KB)	1726 – 1734	King's Bench
Barn & Ad. or B & A.	Barnewell and Adolphus	1830 – 1834	King's Bench
Benl	Benloe	1530 – 1627	King's Bench
Bro P.C.	Browns Reports of cases in Parliament	1702 – 1800	House of Lords
Cab & El	Cababe & Ellis	1882 – 1885	Queen's Bench
Colles	Colles	1697 – 1713	House of Lords
Cox's C.C.	Cox (Criminal Law)	1843 – 1945	Criminal Courts
Cr App R	Criminal Appeal Reports	1908 – present	
Crim LR	Criminal Law Review	1954 – present	
Den C.C.	Dennison	1844 – 1852	Criminal Courts
East	East	1800 – 1812	King's Bench
Ell & Bl or E & B	Ellis and Blackburn	1851 – 1858	Queen's Bench
Fost. CL	Foster (Crown Law)	1708 – 1760	Criminal Courts
J.P.	Justice of the Peace	1837 – present	magistrates' courts
Law Rep or L.R	Law Reports	1865 – present	All the courts
Mod	Modern reports (Leaches)	1669 – 1755	All the courts
Mood. C. C.	Moody	1824 – 1844	Criminal Courts
RTR	Road Traffic Reports	1970 – present	
SCT	Scots Law Times	1893 – present	
T.L.R.	Times Law Reports	1884 – 1952	All the courts
Traff. Cas	Traffic cases	1951 – present	All the courts
W.L.R.	Weekly Law Reports	1953 – present	All the courts

Note: There are many more law reports which have been compiled over the past three centuries, all recording different courts at different times. For practical purposes it is thought that most students of criminal law will survive having the ability to look up the above abbreviations if required.

Chapter 2: Courts and the Legal Process

TYPES OF CRIMINAL LAW COURT

Criminal Law Courts	Functions
Magistrates' court	Summary Trials
Crown Court	Trial on indictment, appeals on fact and law from magistrates' courts
High Court (Queen's Bench Division)	Appeals from Magistrates on law only (case stated)
Court of Appeal	Appeals from Crown Court on fact or law
House of Lords	Appeals on points of law from the Court of Appeal
Privy Council	Highest Court of Appeal for some Commonwealth Countries
Coroners' Court	Decisions about cause of death, and ownership of treasure trove

Magistrates' Court

1.1 This is the court where the majority of police investigations will become prosecutions. It is the 'court of first instance' for all criminal matters. The court comprises of two or more, but not more than seven, lay magistrates (Magistrates are drawn from the general public and are trained to make decisions about matters brought before them). These magistrates also have the title Justices of the Peace. Occasionally there may be a single stipendiary magistrate sitting in the court. This person is legally qualified and paid to sit as a magistrate. He or she will have all the powers of a bench of lay magistrates. The magistrates' court will also have a clerk. The clerk is very important. It is the function of the clerk to advise the lay magistrates about the law. The clerk cannot advise about the finding of guilt, but can and should advise about the admissibility of evidence.

1.2 The magistrates' court normally deals with all summary cases arising within its jurisdictional area. There is a facility for magistrates to transfer authority to deal with cases in another area, subject to agreement between the relevant clerks, if necessary or expedient. Such transfers are possible to allow a defendant's cases all to be dealt with by one court. If, for instance, a youth steals a car then drives around the country committing minor thefts, when he is arrested all of the matters can be dealt with by one court.

1.3 The court will also act as an examining court for matters that are to be dealt with on indictment. Here the court examines the evidence by way of committal proceedings. One method is to hold a court that actually hears the evidence to be given later at the Crown Court. This is often referred to as an old-style committal: each witness is questioned by the prosecution and defence representatives about their knowledge of the incident, and or their version of events. The examining magistrates have to be satisfied that there is sufficient evidence to form a 'prima facie' case (*prima facie* is a Latin phrase meaning 'on the face of it' used to show that there is a case to answer). The alternative method for committals is by the submission of written statements, this is known as a paper committal. The prosecution formally hand to the defence copies of the statements it intends to use to prove the allegations formed in the indictments(s) to be heard later at Crown Court. After committal proceedings, the defence will normally tell the court which of the prosecution witnesses it requires to attend Crown Court to give evidence. Some witnesses will be given summonses to attend the trial, others will be conditionally warned to attend. This means that some witnesses will have to attend, others may have to attend if later warned. At this stage, the defence will have some idea on what grounds they intend to defend an allegation and which witnesses they will need to question to adduce evidence favourable to their defence. Many facts will be accepted by the defence as being true, often without dispute.

1.4 There are some cases that fall between indictable and summary, these are called either-way offences. The magistrates will ask the defendant(s) where they wish the matter to be dealt with, either on indictment in the Crown Court or summarily before the Magistrates. Section 47 of the Offences Against the Person Act 1861 can be dealt with either on indictment or summarily. This offence is subject to a maximum penalty on first conviction of five years' on indictment, but only twelve months if convicted summarily. The problem for a defendant is, however, that if the magistrates find that their ability to sentence the offender is insufficient they can commit the matter to Crown Court for sentence. This is not normally necessary as the prosecution and defence usually agree the 'mode of trial' based upon the probability of the type of sentence the defendant may be subject to under the prevailing circumstances. The practical experience shown by prosecutors making these decisions is normally correct.

1.5 A trial in the magistrates' courts occurs when a defendant pleads not guilty to the charge or summons read out by the clerk. The prosecution will call the witnesses it requires to prove the case. The defence will also call its own witnesses. Both prosecution and defence question the witnesses in an attempt to adduce the evidence required to prove or disprove the case. This is called 'examination in chief'. The progress of a case is dealt with later in this chapter.

The Youth Court

1.6 A youth court is a magistrates' court specially set aside for dealing with young people aged under 18 years (juveniles). The magistrates are specially selected and trained. The youth court should normally be held in a different room or building to the normal magistrates' court. If this is not possible, there must be at least one hour between the youth court sitting and the magistrates' court rising. The court consists of no more than three magistrates, there must be at least one male and one female magistrate. In exceptional circumstances the court may sit without a representation of both sexes. There is no right of access for the general public to the youth court.

1.7 The youth court must deal with all cases involving a defendant under 18 years of age summarily unless the offence, if committed by an adult, would have been indictable or triable as an either-way offence and:
  - the charge is one of homicide
  - the charged offence is so grave that under statutory powers the juvenile if found guilty would be sentenced to be detained for a long period; or
  - the defendant is charged jointly with an adult (a person over 18), and the court deems it in the interests of justice to commit them both for trial.

1.8 Subject to certain exceptions, no juvenile (under 18) charged with offences will appear before a magistrates' court, other than a youth court except where:

- the juvenile is charged jointly with an adult
- an adult is charged with aiding, abetting, counselling, procuring, allowing or permitting an offence with which a juvenile is charged
- where the fact that the defendant is a juvenile is discovered by the court
- where the juvenile is charged with aiding or abetting an adult, and
- the charge against the juvenile is from circumstances which are the same as, or connected with, those giving rise to an offence by an adult (e.g. the juvenile steals a car and the adult disposes of it).

1.9 The importance of the specialist role performed by the youth court is acknowledged under the Magistrates' Court Act 1980. Any court finding a juvenile guilty of any offence other than homicide must refer the case to the youth court for sentence.

1.10 Adult courts have discretion and power (if the juvenile is jointly charged with an adult, if the adult pleads guilty, is discharged or is committed for trial) to remit the juvenile for hearing by the youth court. In other words, if the adult defendant with whom the juvenile would have stood trial has the case disposed of by way of plea or committal, the adult court can send the juvenile's case to youth court for hearing and disposal.

1.11 Provisions for summary matters to be dealt with by post only apply to juveniles over 16 when the summons is issued. Where a juvenile is charged with an offence and his or her appearance before the court to decide mode of trial does not occur until after he or she becomes 18 that person is treated as an adult.

Crown Court

1.12 All matters that are subject of indictment are brought before the Crown Court. These are the really serious cases where the defendant is likely to be sent to prison upon first conviction. The Crown Court has a judge who sits and decides on all points of law and makes decisions about the admissibility of evidence. The judge may be a circuit judge, who is addressed as 'Your Honour', or a Recorder who is addressed as 'Sir', or a High Court judge who is addressed as 'My Lord'. The judge will wear a white wig with a short tail. Which level of judge is running the court will dictate whether he or she wears a red or purple gown. The judge sits in the highest chair on the floor of the court usually behind a high bench.

1.13 The Crown Court is organised into three tiers. In each tier the judge sits to hear a trial with a jury of 12. The most serious cases are heard by the first tier of the court that has a High Court judge sitting. The second tier usually has a circuit judge. The third tier deals with the less serious indictable offences and is usually presided over by a Recorder. New circuit judges can be appointed from barristers of ten years' standing. Recorders originally had to have five years' experience to become a circuit judge. This was shortened in 1977 (Administration of Justice Act 1977) to three years. A Recorder is appointed from the ranks of barristers and solicitors who have more than ten years' standing. The route via Recorder is currently the only method for a solicitor to become a judge. There is a clerk to the Crown Court. His duty is to ensure the efficient and smooth running of the court. The clerk is guided and advised by the judge.

1.14 The right of trial by jury is exercised at Crown Court. The jury in a trial decides upon the facts whether a person is guilty or not. The judge guides the jury by directing them on points of law, advising them about the relevance of certain evidence and the dangers of identification evidence by eye witnesses.

1.15 Only barristers are allowed to address the judge whilst actually in court. Barristers will be seen to wear wigs similar to the judge and scholars black gowns. Witnesses must answer the barrister's questions addressing their replies to the judge. Outside the court barristers are not supposed to talk directly with witnesses or defendants but to take instructions from solicitors who act as 'go betweens'. Barristers can, however, talk to directly to professionally-qualified witnesses such as doctors, pathologists or people qualified to give legal opinion.

1.16 The Crown Court was set-up in 1971 by the Crown Courts Act. The Crown Court may sit in any part of England or Wales. Jurisdiction of all criminal matters above magistrates' courts lies with the Crown Court. This is exercised in six regional areas or circuits: Northern; Midland and Oxford; South Eastern; Wales and Chester; Western; and North-Eastern.

1.17 Appeals from the magistrates' courts are also held in the Crown Court. Appeals to the Crown Court are heard by a panel consisting of a professional judge and up to four lay magistrates. The Court acting as an appeal venue may if the appeal is on sentence, vary, increase, decrease any sentence, or, if the appeal is against conviction it may confirm or acquit. There is a further appeal on a point of law from the magistrates' court to the High Court, this is known as 'Case Stated'.

1.18 An example of how the trial progresses is included later in the chapter.

The Coroners' Court

1.19 Coroners jurisdictional areas tend to follow the boundaries of local authorities. The duty of the Coroners' Court is to hold inquests, to identify the person who has died and to decide the reason why they died, whether the death was lawful, and to give a reason for death. Coroners are allowed to give a variety of reasons for death: suicide, unlawful killing, misadventure and accident are among the options. Coroners become involved in deciding the cause of death only when a doctor is unwilling to issue a death certificate stating the cause of death, or where such deaths are sudden, unexpected or unnatural. All deaths in custody, including those at police stations, prisons or mental hospitals are subject of coroners' court enquires.

1.20 Another function of the Coroner is to decide who has the legitimate claim to property found hidden (treasure trove). The rules for dealing with 'treasure' were changed under the Treasure Act 1996, which came into effect on the 24th of September 1997. Treasure is now defined under Section 1 of that Act:

Section 1(1)(a) Objects other than coins

Any object other than a coin, provided at least 10 per cent by weight of metal is precious metal (gold or silver) and that it is at least three hundred years old when found. This means that object plated with gold or silver will not normally be treasure (unless found with other objects which are treasure).

Section 1(1)(a) and Section 3(2) Coins

All coins that contain at least 10 per cent of gold or silver by weight of metal and that come from the same find; provided that the find consists of at least two coins with gold, or

silver content of at least 10 per cent. The coins must be at least three hundred years old at the time of discovery. In the case of a find consisting of coins that contain less than 10 per cent of gold or silver, there must be at least ten such coins, of at least three hundred years of age'.

The purpose of the Treasure Act is to provide general guidelines under which there can be certainty of ownership for persons finding property, where no owner is apparent. In general terms, any find of property thought to be over three hundred years old, must be reported to the coroner for the area within 14 days. (Failure to report a find, brings criminal liability to the finder, subject of a maximum fine – currently up to £5,000.) The Coroner will then direct the finder to an appropriate museum, for the find to be evaluated and a report prepared. The Coroner will then hold an inquest to determine the true status of the find and its rightful ownership. In general terms, if an item is declared to be treasure, the British Museum or National Museum and Galleries of Wales, are contacted to see if they wish to acquire it. If this is so, an agreed valuation is made for the find and this is paid to the finder. If no museum wishes to acquire the find, the Secretary of State may disclaim it. The owner of the land is notified that, unless there is an objection, the Coroner intends to return the find to the finder. If the Coroner receives an objection, he will retain the property until the dispute between the finder and the landowner is settled.

1.21 The rules of evidence adhered to strictly in all other courts are not quite so strictly enforced at coroners' court. The inquest is carried out in a more inquisitorial manner. The coroner will frequently ask all of the questions to clarify points raised. There is as such no prosecution or defence. Relatives or representatives acting for relatives of the deceased, or any interested party, may ask pertinent questions of anyone called to give evidence as to the cause of death. There are offences committed by jurors and witnesses who fail to answer summons or questions:

1: Where a person duly summoned as a juror at an inquest:
   – does not, after being openly called three times, appear to the summons; or,
   – appears to the summons but refuses without reasonable excuse to serve as a juror;
   the coroner may impose on that person a fine not exceeding £1,000.

2: Where a person duly summoned to give evidence at an inquest:
   – does not after being openly called three times, appear to the summons, or;
   – appears to the summons but refuses without lawful excuse to answer a question
     put to him;
   the coroner may impose on that person a fine not exceeding £1,000.

Section 10 Coroners Act 1988
as amended by Section 10 of the Criminal Justice Act 1991.

Explanation
These powers conferred on the coroner are in addition to other powers under other enactments regarding the attendance of witnesses and jurors. The purpose is to enable a coroner to make a full enquiry into the cause of death.

1.22 Coroners have juries to assist them to decide the cause of death where the death is unnatural or occurred in custody. Coroners have held office under the Crown since about the twelfth century. A Coroner must have at least five years' standing as a barrister, solicitor or doctor. They are usually appointed by the local authority for the area they serve. Since the passing of Section 56 of the Criminal Law Act 1977 the jury in a coroners' case must not name the person they blame for the cause of death. In cases involving murder it was historically the purpose of the jury to name where possible the person responsible.

1.23 Most police areas now have civilian employee coroners' officers who regularly make and complete enquires into the cause of death, where such deaths are unnatural or unexpected. Police officers, however, usually make the first enquires. In the case of murder or death whilst travelling in a vehicle police officers usually complete the inquiry and the coroner calls the police officers to produce the evidence discovered. Where death occurs at work, factory inspectors and the Health and Safety Executive may also become involved in the enquires, they then become 'interested parties' for the purpose of questioning witnesses at the inquest. Where incidents involve aircraft, the specialist investigators of the Civil Aviation Authority will become involved.

The Privy Council

1.24 The countries of the Commonwealth use the Privy Council as the highest appeal court for their criminal cases. The Judicial Committee of the Privy Council as a Court is composed of the senior members of the Law Lords from the House of Lords. Cases decided by the Privy Council have persuasive effect on English law. They do not normally become precedent unless the decision is used to provide support for other decisions brought through the normal criminal appeal system.

Civil Court

1.25 Within the United Kingdom the structure of the civil courts is very complex. This is because of the diversity of cases likely to be considered. Matters as different as shipping, contract disputes and domestic violence all come before different branches of the civil court for resolution. For the purpose of this book we are confined to brief discussion of the role of the family courts.

1.26 The Family Division of the High Court is the most likely of the civil courts to affect police officers. Injunctions giving powers of arrest and or restraining freedom to approach, molest and control are issued by this court. Domestic disputes can also be settled by the magistrates' court acting as a domestic court. When the magistrates' court acts as a domestic court, appeals on its decisions will be to the Family Division of the High Court. The civil courts have a hierarchy, a structured order which sets out which court has precedence over other courts within the structure. The most important court is the House of Lords. The Appeal Court is next, this has four divisions: Chancery; Criminal; Civil; Family. Then there are the main courts: High Court and County Courts.

PROGRESS OF A CASE

2.1 What has gone before is a very brief outline of the functions of the various courts in trying criminal cases. There are alternative stages through which a case may progress, dependent on whether the defendant pleads guilty and whether, in the case of an either-way offence, the matter is tried at magistrates court or at Crown Court.

Progress of Trial

2.2 The progress of a criminal matter to trial – *see flow diagram on opposite page.*

Options and Benefits of Trial by Jury

2.3 Jury trials tend to be less predictable than trial before magistrates. Most jurors will have sat

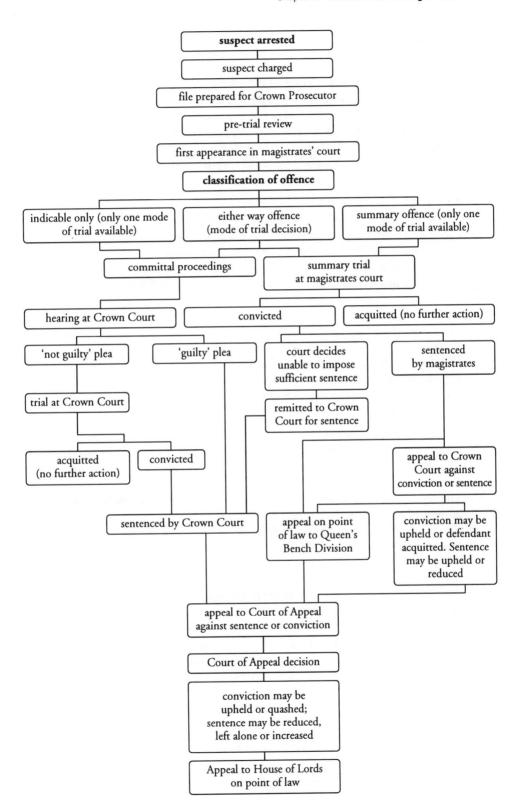

only once, or possibly twice in their lives as part of a jury. They have no prior knowledge of decision making in the criminal courts. Equally most jurors bring the layman's point of view and decision making to the courts. A defendant has the choice of electing for trial by jury at Crown Court or by the magistrates provided the offence is either-way. The defendant must be warned, however, that if the magistrates find the defendant guilty and they feel that under the circumstances they do not have sufficient power to sentence, they may commit the defendant to Crown Court for sentence. This can be very important for a defendant who is on trial for such offences as burglary. The powers to sentence at magistrates' court is limited to 12 months' imprisonment, this is greatly increased at Crown Court to five years' imprisonment.

Mode of Trial

2.4 To assist the magistrates when dealing with considerations as to where an either-way offence should be tried, the Law Lords have issued a practice statement (Practice Note (Mode of Trial; Guidelines) (1990)). The objective of the practice statement was not to impinge upon the magistrates' duty to consider each case individually, and on its own facts, but to provide guidance which will apply to all defendants over 17 years of age. When magistrates have to make a decision on the mode of trial for an either-way offence, they may take into account a number of factors, including:

— The nature of the case.
— Any circumstances which make the offence a serious one.
— Whether their sentencing powers are likely to be sufficient.
— Representations made by prosecution or defence.
— Any attendant circumstances which would make one mode of trial more suitable than the other.

The following observations have been made by the Law Lords, to guide magistrates:
— The court should never make its decision on the grounds of convenience or expedition.
  — The court should assume for the purpose of making its decision that the prosecution's version of the facts is correct.
  — The defendant's personal circumstances and mitigating factors are irrelevant for the purpose of making the mode of trial decision.
  — The fact that the charges are alleged to be specimen ones, or that the defendant will be asking for other offences to be taken into consideration, are relevant.
  — Where the case concerns complex questions of fact or difficult questions of law, the court should consider committal for trial.
  — If one defendant elects trial the court must proceed with all defendants as if an examining court for committal.
  — A youth (under 18) if charged jointly with an adult (over 18) should only be committed for trial at Crown Court if it is in the interests of justice.
  — In general, either-way offences should be tried summarily unless the circumstances reveal features set out in the practice statement listings:

Burglary
Dwelling
1 Entry during daytime, occupier present.
2 Entry at night where normally the occupier would be present, whether or not occupier actually present.
3 The offence is alleged to be one of a series.

4 Soiling, ransacking, damage or vandalism occurs.
5 The offence has professional hallmarks.
6 Unrecovered property of high value (high value means, a figure equal to at least twice the maximum compensation value the magistrates can award (currently £5,000)).

Non-dwelling
1 Entry to doctors surgery or pharmacy.
2 Fear is caused, or violence offered to anyone lawfully on the premises.
3 The offence has professional hallmarks.
4 Vandalism on a substantial scale.
5 Unrecovered property of a high value.

Theft and Fraud
1 Breach of trust by a person in substantial authority, or person in whom a high degree of trust is placed.
2 Theft or fraud committed or disguised in a sophisticated manner.
3 Theft or fraud committed by an organised gang.
4 Theft or fraud where committed on a vulnerable victim.
5 Unrecovered property of a high value.

Handling Stolen Property
1 Dishonest handling of stolen property by receiver who has commissioned the theft.
2 The offence has professional hallmarks.
3 Involves property of high value.

Social Security Fraud
1 Organised fraud on a large scale.
2 Substantial fraud carried out over a long period of time.

Violence (Sections 20 and 47 Offences Against the Person Act 1861)
1 The use of any form of weapon likely to cause serious injury.
2 More than minor injuries caused by kicking the head, headbutting or similar forms of assault.
3 Serious violence is caused to a person who has to work in contact with the public (e.g., police officers, bus or taxi drivers, publicans, shopkeepers).
4 Violence towards vulnerable people (elderly or infirm).

Public Order Offences
1 Organised violence or use of weapons.
2 Significant injury or substantial damage.
3 The offence has clear racial motivation.
4 Attack upon police officers, ambulance crew, fire fighters or similar.

Violence Towards or Neglect of Children
1 Substantial injury.
2 Repeated violence or serious neglect, even if the injury is minor.
3 Sadistic violence (e.g., deliberate burning or scalding).

Indecent Assault

1 Substantial difference of ages between offender and victim, and the assault is more than trivial.
2 Violence or threats of violence.
3 Occurs during a trust relationship between offender and victim.
4 Several similar offences, and the assaults are more than trivial.
5 The victim is particularly vulnerable.
6 Serious nature of the assault.

Unlawful Sexual Intercourse

1 Wide disparity of age.
2 Breach of position of trust.
3 The victim is particularly vulnerable.

Drugs

Class A

1 Supply, possession with intent to supply; should be committed for trial.
2 Possession: should be committed for trial unless the amount is consistent with only personal use.

Class B

1 Supply, possession with intent to supply; should be committed for trial unless there is only small scale supply without payment.
2 Possession should be committed for trial where the quantity involved is substantial.

Dangerous Driving

1 Alcohol or drugs contributed to the danger.
2 Grossly excessive speed.
3 Racing.
4 Prolonged course of dangerous driving.
5 Other related offences.

Criminal Damage

1 Deliberate fire-raising.
2 Committed by a group.
3 Damage of a high value.
4 The offence has a clear racial motivation.

In general, all cases should be tried summarily unless the court considers that one or more of the listed factors is present in the case coming before them, and, that its sentencing powers are insufficient. Criminal damage under Section 1 of the Criminal Damage Act 1971 which is not arson, and, where less than £5,000 worth of damage has occurred, must be tried summarily.

RULES FOR DISCLOSURE OF EVIDENCE IN CRIMINAL CASES

3.1 A broad rule is that the prosecution must always allow the defence access to the evidence upon which it intends to base its prosecution. This follows the general rule that a man must know the evidence against him to be able to defend himself.

3.2 Magistrates' courts have authority to force (Section 144 Magistrates' Courts Act 1980, as extended by Section 48 Criminal Law Act 1977 and Magistrates' Courts (Advance Information) Rules 1985) the prosecution to disclose to the accused or representative of the accused all or any prescribed class of the facts and matters which the prosecution proposes to adduce as evidence. If the magistrates are satisfied that this has not been complied with, they must adjourn the proceedings pending compliance, unless the conduct of the case for the accused will not be substantially prejudiced.

3.3 The only grounds for refusal to disclose particular facts or matters are those of privilege or that the prosecutor believes that to do so might lead to attempts to intimidate the witness, or otherwise to cause the course of justice to be interfered with. Privilege is dealt with below. If the prosecutor does refuse access to any evidence he must give the person requesting the advance disclosure a written notice to the effect that certain advance information is being withheld (Rule 5 Magistrates' Courts (Advance Information) Rules 1985). See also later in Chapter 7 (evidence), disclosure and the Criminal Procedure and Investigations Act 1996.

DISCOVERY IN CIVIL CASES

4.1 A person taking a civil action is entitled to ask the court for access to any information or material considered likely to assist in founding the action provided an action has been started. This is called discovery. Discovery is restricted by the Limitation Act 1980 and what is called 'privilege'. Certain classes of documents and communications are subject of restrictions because of their very nature, an example being solicitor-client communication.

PRIVILEGE IN CRIMINAL CASES

5.1 An item of potential evidence will not be available to be submitted as evidence in court proceedings if it is subject to privilege. Privileged material will include communications between a priest and a parishioner at confession, or between a solicitor and her client about a case. This type of material is catered for in Section 10 of the Police and Criminal Evidence Act 1984. Material subject of legal privilege may not be searched for by police when premises are being searched.

Section 10 Police and Criminal Evidence Act 1984

1: Subject to subsection (2) below, in this Act 'items subject to legal privilege' means:
   - communications between a professional legal advisor and his client, or any
     person representing his client made in connection with the giving of legal advice
     to the client
   - communications between a professional legal adviser and his client, or any person representing
     the client, or between such client and an adviser, or his client and any such representative and
     any other person made in connection with or contemplation of legal proceedings; and
   - items enclosed with or referred to in such communications and made:
     i) in connection with the giving of legal advice; or
     ii) in connection with or in contemplation of legal proceedings and for the purpose of
        such proceedings, when they are in possession of someone who is entitled to be
        in possession of them.

2: Items held with the intention of furthering a criminal purpose are not items subject to legal privilege.

5.2 The subject of privilege is quite complex, the courts have interpreted the law in a practical manner. In *R v Inner London Sessions Crown Court, ex p Baines & Baines* the police were seeking information about the purchase of various properties following a £26 million Brinks Mat Security Company robbery at Heathrow Airport. A judge granted officers a production order against a firm of solicitors requiring them to make available for inspection 'all client account records including ledgers, day books, cash books, account books and other records used in the ordinary course of business of the firm' in whatever form, in connection with the purchase of a named property. This decision was quashed by the Divisional Court on the grounds of failure to comply with legal formalities. The court considered briefly what would be covered as being legal advice and it held that an item was covered if it was a communication made in the course of giving advice. Records of conveyancing transactions were not privileged since they were not within the giving of advice. However, correspondence between a client and his solicitor seeking or giving advice would be privileged. Correspondence regarding financial transactions might therefore be privileged because it could contain advice.

5.3 A legal aid application which could possibly reveal an offence of attempting to pervert the course of justice was subject of legal privilege, even though the application may have been made in furtherance of a criminal purpose. The Law Society who held the form did not do so in the furtherance of any criminal activity and so could not be made to deliver up the form (*R v Snaresbrook Crown Court ex p DPP* (1988)). In this case the Law Society had claimed legal privilege. On this basis the holder of privileged documents could claim legal privilege provided that that person or institution did not hold the documents 'in furtherance of a criminal purpose'. It would be quite natural to accept that documents in possession of solicitors or barristers would not normally be held in furtherance of criminal purposes. This would then mean that all documents held by solicitors would be capable of being subject to legal privilege.

5.4 This position changed with the case *R v Central Criminal Court, ex p Francis and Francis* (1989). Police officers suspected that an innocent person had been given monies (the proceeds of drug sales), and that records of the transactions were held with solicitors. Sections 27 to 32 of the Drug Trafficking Act 1986 set out the procedure to obtain excluded material. This is very similar to the provisions of the Police and Criminal Evidence Act 1984, and uses the same definition of 'legal privilege'. The police sought a court order for disclosure of documents by the solicitors relating to transactions with regard to property.

5.5 A production order was obtained giving the police access to all the solicitors' files relating to the property transaction. The Divisional Court refused the solicitors judicial review on the grant of the order stating that the documents were held with the intention of the furtherance of a criminal purpose within Section 10(2) Police and Criminal Evidence Act 1984. The criminal intention was not that of the solicitor or his client but of the third party who had given the client the monies which were the subject of the transaction. This decision was upheld on appeal at the House of Lords. Lord Brandon expressed the view supported by the majority of the Law Lords that since crooked solicitors were rare, a contrary view would not advance the purpose of the legislation and would protect the perpetrators of serious crime. By contrast, the broader construction of the Section, 'would materially assist in achieving the purpose of Part II of the Act and would prevent the principle of legal privilege being used to protect the perpetrators of serious crimes'. It is sufficient that the criminal purpose is just to salt away the proceeds of crime (per Lord Goff). The question as to at which stage the criminal purpose arises was also considered. Lord Goff commented that the critical moment was when the communication was made; did the client or some third party have a criminal purpose at the moment the communication came into the solicitor's possession. That is the point in time when Section 10(2) negates legal privilege. Commentary by learned writers about this case considers that legal privilege is lost where a third party uses a client as an intermediary or innocent tool. This could cause problems for solicitors claiming privilege for their clients where they have to prove the nature of that client's relationship with a third party.

SUMMARY TRIALS

6.1 All summary trials are conducted before the magistrates' court. There are two methods of starting proceedings:
- The arrest and charging of a suspect to attend court on bail or in custody
- The reporting of a suspected offender for issue of summons to attend court.

6.2 Persons who appear before the court will have the charge or summons read to them by the magistrates' clerk. The clerk will ask if they understand the charge and if they plead guilty or not guilty. The court must be satisfied that if an accused pleads guilty that it is a clear, unequivocal plea. A court may convict without hearing the evidence but in practice the prosecutor will give an outline of the evidence. The accused or his legal representative is at liberty to dispute the facts and may also put forward any mitigation for the offence. This is prior to the passing of sentence.

6.3 In the event of a not guilty plea the magistrates will hear any evidence called by the prosecution and defence. The conduct of such a trial is subject to strict rules. Again the trial will start by the clerk reading out to the accused a charge or summons alleging an offence. The accused having pleaded not guilty, the clerk will order that all witnesses in the matter leave the court.

6.4 Opening the case, the prosecutor will outline the facts. The prosecutor will then call such witnesses as are necessary to prove the case. Each witness will be called into court and will give evidence of matters within their knowledge. Initially the prosecutor will ask each witness pertinent questions in an attempt to adduce evidence to prove the facts alleged. Then the defendant or his legal representative will ask questions in cross-examination to prove a defence or an excuse to the allegations made. Witnesses are not normally allowed to give evidence of opinion unless they are an expert in a particular field, e.g., a doctor giving evidence of how a particular injury may or may not have been caused, or a police officer may give evidence of drunkenness.

6.5 At the conclusion of the case for the prosecution, the defence will call any witnesses they have to rebut evidence given by the prosecution. At this time the defence will ask questions first to adduce evidence in their favour then the prosecutor will have an opportunity to cross-examine defence witnesses to adduce evidence favourable to the prosecution.

6.6 This type of trial is called adversarial. Prior to the start of the trial, the prosecution will have considered what are the matters or issues in dispute and will attempt by questioning the witnesses to prove those points. The prosecutor may not ask leading questions: these are questions which would normally be answered either 'yes' or 'no'. An example of a leading question would be, 'did you see the defendant standing on the pavement outside the restaurant hitting the injured person with the hammer'. The questions should have been, 'Where was the defendant standing?', 'What was he doing?'.

6.7 At the conclusion of the evidence given by the witnesses, the prosecution will be given an opportunity to make a closing speech. This should draw together the evidence given by the witnesses and additionally commenting upon statements admitted into evidence without the makers being called. The last to speak is the defendant or his legal representative. They will have an opportunity to review the evidence given, often giving differing views of the evidence or different emphasis so as to discredit prosecution witnesses, or prove a defence or excuse for the commission of the offence.

6.8 At this stage the magistrates will normally retire to consider their verdict The magistrates may seek the advice of the clerk of the court if they wish on points of law but not on the facts.

6.9 If the magistrates return a not guilty verdict the defendant is released from court immediately, no further action is taken. If, however, the magistrates find the defendant guilty, the prosecutor may then reveal any relevant convictions and give a brief outline of the defendant's character in order to allow the court to pass a suitable sentence. A speech or plea in mitigation is then allowed to the defence. The accused may also ask the court to take into consideration any other matters, which he also admits to having committed. The magistrates will then consider what has been said, and then pass sentence.

6.10 Where a matter is subject to the issue of summons to attend the court, some offences allow the accused to plead guilty by post giving such mitigating statement as they wish the court to consider. Under such circumstances there is no need to attend court. A written statement of sentence is issued by the court. This procedure is set out in the Magistrates' Courts Act 1980. Certain conditions must be fulfilled before this procedure can take place:
- The proceedings must be by way of summons
- The maximum sentence must not exceed three months' imprisonment
- The prosecutor must notify the court that the accused was served with a notice of the facts which will be presented to the court, together with the summons and a notice outlining the prescribed procedure, and the fact that the accused does not wish to attend court, and
- The accused or his solicitor must have notified the clerk to the court that the accused wishes to plead guilty.

Additionally, the prosecutor must serve on the accused, not less than seven days prior to the hearing date, a copy of any previous convictions that it is intended to bring to the attention of the court.

Trial on Indictment at Crown Court

6.11 An indictment is a written accusation that one or more persons have committed a certain crime. The accusation is written down in a set format. At the start of proceedings in the Crown Court, an accused person will have an indictment read out and will then be given an opportunity to state whether they plead guilty or not guilty to the matter. The indictment is prepared by the magistrates' court committing the case for trial at Crown Court. Part of the purpose of the committal proceedings is to ensure that there is sufficient evidence to warrant prosecution.

6.12 The trial will follow the same basic pattern as that of a summary trial. The prosecution will outline its case and then call its witnesses to give evidence. Witnesses whose evidence is agreed as acceptable by the defence may have their statements read out to the court. To be admissible these statements must conform to the format set out in Section 9 Criminal Justice Act 1967 and such statements are known as Criminal Justice Act (CJA) statements. The defence will have an opportunity to cross examine all of the prosecution witnesses. Once the case for the prosecution is complete, the defence has an opportunity to address the judge. At this stage the counsel for the defence may make a submission of 'no case to answer', alleging that the prosecution have not proven their case. If the judge rules that there is no case to answer the matter ends there and then, the defendant is released immediately. This may occur when a prosecution witness fails to attend court and the judge refuses a prosecution application for an adjournment.

6.13 The defence then have an opportunity to bring to court any witnesses they wish to refute the evidence given by the prosecution witnesses. Each witness will give evidence firstly being questioned by the defence barrister then being cross examined by the prosecution. At the conclusion of the defence case, closing speeches are made which bring together the basis of each side's argument, effectively as a précis of the points proving or disproving the accused person's guilt.

BAIL

7.1 Bail is defined as 'a recognisance entered into, with or without surety, to attend at a court or police station named therein, at a time and date specified therein'. Bail may be conditional or unconditional. Bail may be granted by a custody officer at a police station or by the magistrates' court, or during proceedings by the Crown Court. If a defendant appears before magistrates court to be remanded and the magistrates refuse an application for bail, an appeal against this decision may be made to a Crown Court judge. This appeal will normally be heard by a 'judge in chambers', i.e., it does not come before the judge in open court, but is heard by her in private, in a room.

7.2 Subject to Section 25 of the Criminal Justice and Public Order Act 1994 bail must be granted to every person arrested and charged with an offence (Section 38 Police and Criminal Evidence Act 1984), unless one or more of the conditions of Section 38(1) (Police and Criminal Evidence Act 1984, as amended by Section 28 of the Criminal Justice and Public Order Act 1984) apply:

1: If the person arrested is not a juvenile, and:
   - his name and address cannot be ascertained, or, the custody officer has reasonable grounds for doubting that the name or address furnished by him as his name or address are his real name or address, or
   - the custody officer has reasonable grounds for believing that the arrested person will fail to appear at court to answer bail, or
   - in the case of a person arrested for an imprisonable offence, the custody officer has reasonable grounds for believing that the detention of the arrested person is necessary to prevent him from committing a further offence, or
   - in the case of a person arrested for an offence which is not imprisonable, the custody officer has reasonable grounds for believing that the detention of the person is necessary to prevent him from causing physical injury to any other person or from causing loss or damage to property, or

- the custody officer has reasonable grounds for believing that the detention of the person arrested is necessary to prevent him from interfering with the administration of justice or with the investigation of offences or of a particular offence, or
- the custody officer has reasonable grounds for believing that the detention of the person arrested is necessary for his own protection.

2: If the person arrested is a juvenile:
- any of the requirements of paragraph (1) above is satisfied, or
- the custody officer has reasonable grounds for believing that the arrested juvenile ought to be detained in his own interest.

7.3 Put simply, when reaching a decision, whether to grant bail, the custody officer has to consider:
- the nature and seriousness of the offence (which may have a bearing on the accused's own safety, or whether he is likely to commit further offences)
- the likely sentence, his previous convictions, his previous history as far as bail is concerned (all factors which may relate to whether he will answer to bail)
- any other matters relating to the particular offence or particular accused.

7.4 The general rule that bail must be granted was altered by Section 25 of the Criminal Justice and Public Order Act 1994. Bail must not be granted if the person arrested has been charged with murder, attempted murder, manslaughter, rape or attempted rape and has been:
- convicted of murder, attempted murder, rape, or attempted rape, whether or not sentenced or an appeal against conviction or sentence is pending, or
- convicted of manslaughter or culpable homicide (in Scotland) and sentenced to imprisonment or long-term detention as a child or young person, for the offence, whether or not an appeal against conviction or sentence is pending.

7.5 In order to allow custody officers the ability to bail persons who would otherwise have to be detained, Section 27 of the Criminal Justice and Public Order Act 1994 sets out circumstances under which conditions may be imposed on a suspect being considered for bail. The custody officer must justify the imposition of any conditions in writing on the custody record. Conditions which may be imposed are:
- to provide sureties to secure surrender to custody
- to give a security if it appears the person is unlikely to remain in the United Kingdom
- to comply with any other requirement *(see below)*
- if under 17, a parent or guardian may be bound in the sum of no more than £50.

Conditions may be imposed only if it appears necessary to do so in order to prevent the person from:
- failing to surrender to his bail
- committing offences whilst on bail
- interfering with witnesses.

Requirements which may be imposed include:
- as to place of residence, i.e. to live and sleep at a specified address
- to notify any change of address
- curfew, not to be away from the place of residence between specified hours
- not to enter a specified area or building, or go within a specified distance of a named address
- not to contact a specified person, directly or otherwise

- to surrender a passport
- to report to a local police station at a specified time, or, during a specified event (football match etc).

7.6 The refusal to sign acknowledgement of bail conditions is not in itself sufficient grounds for the custody officer to refuse bail. It may, however, indicate that conditions of Section 38(1) (Police and Criminal Evidence Act 1984) are satisfied and that detention after charge may be justified. The refusal to accept conditional bail means that the very purpose of the conditions is likely to be defeated.

7.7 The decision to alter bail conditions imposed and accepted may be reviewed and varied by another custody officer or by the court. This is a very important power granted under Section 3A Bail Act 1976 (as amended by Section 27 Criminal Justice and Public Order Act 1994) as suspected or anticipated breaches may result in the arrest of the person for bail breach under Section 7(3) Bail Act 1976.

7.8 A person bailed after charge to appear before a court may request the custody officer at the police station where the bail was granted to vary the conditions of such bail. There is no limit on how many applications for variance of bail set by a custody officer may be made. Each request for variation must be recorded and dealt with separately. Applications for variation will entail a repeat of the initial decision process in accordance with Section 38 (Police and Criminal Evidence Act 1984), and Section 3A Bail Act 1976, as amended by Section 27 Criminal Justice and Public Order Act 1994). The custody officer making such a decision cannot alter the date of appearance or refuse bail. Consideration may have to be given to arresting a person if he refuses to accept a decision not to vary the bail as requested and threaten to commit offences in relation to breach of the bail set.

7.9 The magistrates' court may hear applications to vary conditional bail, an application must:
- be made in writing
- contain a statement of grounds upon which it is made
- specify the offence for which bail was granted
- specify which condition or conditions are to be reviewed
- specify the name and address of any surety(ies).

The magistrates' clerk will set a time and date for hearing the application. He will then inform the applicant and any surety(ies). A copy of the application will also be forwarded to the police. The time set for hearing the application must be less than 72 hours after receipt of the application, excepting any Sunday or bank holiday. The court will accept written or oral argument for alteration of conditions. If heard in the absence of the applicant, a written notification of the court's decision must be sent to the applicant's last known or usual place of abode.

7.10 Once an application has been made by the defendant to the court, police may not thereafter, vary any of the conditions. When reaching bail decisions, the courts should take account of the same considerations as do custody officers.

Bail Breach
7.11 The general principle is that a person granted bail in criminal proceedings is under a duty to surrender to custody at the appointed time and place. That duty is enforceable under Section 6 of the Bail Act 1976. If the bail is subject to appearance at court the court may also issue a warrant for the arrest of the person in breach of bail (Section 7 Bail Act 1976).

7.12 When a person released on bail in criminal proceedings fails without reasonable cause to surrender to custody he is guilty of an offence (Section 6(1) Bail Act 1976). Where a person has been released on bail in criminal proceedings, and having reasonable cause for the failure to surrender, fails to attend at the appointed time and place as soon as reasonably practicable after that time, he shall be guilty of an offence (Section 6(2) Bail Act 1976). The fact that a defendant mistakenly attended on the wrong date is not a reasonable cause (*Laidlaw v Atkinson* (1986)). If a defendant is the subject of court bail, it is for the court to decide if it wishes to take action for breach of bail. The court may be invited by the prosecutor to consider action. If the matter is pursued, however, the prosecutor must conduct the proceedings against the defendant. If the magistrates indicate that they are not going to institute any action for bail breach they cannot at a later time take action (*France v Dewsbury Magistrates' Court* (1987)). It is for the accused to prove that he had reasonable cause for the failure to attend. Bail breach offences are summary offences; if committed at Crown Court the sentence is as if the offender has committed contempt of court.

7.13 A person who has been released on bail in criminal proceedings is under a duty to surrender to the court, and if he fails to surrender, the court may issue a warrant for his arrest. If a person absents himself from court during a hearing, the court may issue a warrant for his arrest. A person having been bailed to appear at court in criminal proceedings may be arrested if:
- a constable has reasonable grounds for considering that the person is not likely to surrender to custody, or
- a constable has reasonable grounds for believing that the person is likely to break any conditions of his bail, or has broken any of the conditions of the bail, or
- where a person has been released on surety, a constable is notified in writing that the surety wishes to be relieved of the obligation of a surety.

7.14 Where a person is bailed to reappear at a police station under the provisions of Section 47(3) of the Police and Criminal Evidence Act 1984, and that person fails to surrender to bail, he may be arrested without warrant and charged with the bail breach offences (Section 46 Police and Criminal Evidence Act 1984, as amended by Section 29(2) Criminal Justice and Public Order Act 1994).

7.15 A person who in accordance with the requirements of conditional bail sends another person to sign the bail record at a police station, or attend court for him, may be guilty of the offence under the Forgery Act 1861:
- Whosoever, without lawful authority or excuse
  (the burden of proof lies with the accused)
- shall in the name of any other person acknowledge
- any recognisance or bail (*R v McKenzie* (1971))
- or any cognovit actionem
- or judgment
- or any deed
- or other instrument
- before any court judge, or any other person authorised in that behalf
- shall be guilty of an offence (Section 34 Forgery Act 1861, as amended by the Statute Law Revision Act 1892, the Statute Revision (No 2) Act 1893, and Section 1 Criminal Law Act 1967).

The maximum penalty for breach of this Section is seven years' imprisonment.

Explanation

7.16 This is not a frequently used offence. The facts revealing such an offence would potentially lead to a serious interference with the administration of justice. This could be classified as a serious arrestable offence under the Police and Criminal Evidence Act 1984. The Section does not specify any requirement to obtain anything or act for any particular purpose. The mere fact that a person acknowledged the legal requirement of bail, judgment, or cognovit actionem, deed or other instrument, before any authorised person of another person not himself is sufficient for the offence to be complete. Thus a person attending at a police station to comply with bail conditions on behalf of another could be guilty of this offence.

7.17 Where an accused person who, is bailed subject to the provision of sureties and agrees to indemnify the surety(ies) against any liability that surety(ies) may incur should the accused person fail to attend on bail, both the accused and the surety(ies) commit an offence (Section 9 Bail Act 1976, as amended by Section 28 Criminal Law Act 1977). No proceedings may be taken however without the consent of the Director of Public Prosecutions. Indemnifying surety(ies) is an either-way offence, the maximum penalty at magistrates' court is three months' imprisonment and or a fine, at Crown Court twelve months' imprisonment and/or a fine.

REMANDS

8.1 When a person has been released on bail in criminal proceedings, he may be liable for one of two offences, should he fail to answer bail:
- fail (without reasonable cause) to surrender to custody
- having reasonable cause, has failed to surrender to custody (and thereafter fails to surrender at the appointed place, as soon after the appointed time as is reasonably practicable).

Explanation

Without reasonable cause: If a person is bailed to attend magistrates court at 10.00am on a particular day, but is too ill to attend, he may be able to show that he had a good reason for failing to turn up, so not be liable for an offence. Other excuses such as 'My Mum forgot to wake me' may prove less convincing.

As soon after as practicable: A person may have a reasonable excuse for being late, but will then be liable if she fails to answer bail as soon after the required time as was practicable. For example, Mary sets off to get to court for 10.00am, to surrender to her bail . Her car breaks down, which makes her late, there being no suitable public transport. She arrives in town at 11.00am, but instead of going straight to court, decides to go shopping instead. She eventually wanders into the court building at 1.00pm. just as the court is about to rise for the day. She became liable for the second offence as soon as she failed to surrender at the earliest opportunity, i.e., at 11.00am.

8.2 If the person on remand is a juvenile, and is remanded into the care of the local authority, a constable may arrest without warrant a child or young person so remanded or committed to the local authority, whom the officer reasonably suspects has broken any of the conditions of that committal or remand. Such breaches will be treated as if breaching bail from a court. It is at the court's discretion to take further action for any breach. If the court takes action the prosecutor will conduct the case and bring such evidence as is available. After arrest the child or young person is to be brought before the next available court for it to reconsider the remand decision.

8.3 A juvenile who has been arrested may be detained in custody at a police station after being charged if:
- the conditions for refusing to release an adult with or without bail are met; and
- either it is impracticable to transfer her to local authority accommodation; or
- she has attained the age of 12 years, no secure accommodation is available and keeping her in other local authority accommodation will not be adequate to protect the public from serious harm from her.

SENTENCING

9.1 The courts are bound by the set scales of punishment which are laid down by Parliament when Acts are passed. Breach of bail, for example, is subject of a maximum sentence of three months' imprisonment and/or a fine not exceeding scale level five upon summary conviction. Where the offence is dealt with at Crown Court, the punishment is as for contempt of court and a maximum sentence of twelve months' imprisonment and/or a fine. Courts can only impose a sentence upon either finding of guilt or guilty plea. Under certain conditions, however, an offender may agree to accept a recognisance to keep, or be bound over to keep the peace. As such this is not a sentence, it is an agreement to keep the peace subject to a potential penalty for failure to do so. Hence the phrase, bound over in the sum of £50. If the person bound over fails to behave he or she may have to forfeit £50 to the court.

9.2 A court may only pass a custodial sentence where the offence is one for which there is a liability to a custodial sentence and the court is of the opinion that:
- the offence, or combination of the offence and any other offence associated with it, was so serious that only such a sentence can be justified for the offence, or
- where the offence is a violent or sexual offence, that only such a sentence would be adequate to protect the public from serious harm from the offender (Section 1 Criminal Justice Act 1991).

9.3 Records of convictions, may be read to the court after a finding of guilt or guilty plea. The purpose of this is to allow the court to have regard to the offender's prior conduct when setting a sentence. Quite obviously a person who is frequently arrested and convicted of a certain type of offence must aggravate the seriousness of the matter so as to deserve a harsher sentence. A first time offender for a simple theft from a shop would normally be liable to a fine. A repeat offender or career criminal would possibly warrant imprisonment. The punishment should fit the crime and the circumstances of its commission.

9.4 Where a defendant has been sentenced to a longer sentence than was legally allowed, it is a matter for a court to alter the sentence rather than the institution where the offender is detained. In *R v Clue* (1995) a young offender was sentenced under the provisions of the Criminal Justice and Public Order Act 1994 which increased the maximum sentence from 12 months to 24 months' imprisonment. One of the offences for which he was sentenced had been committed before the provisions, allowing for the increased sentence had come into force. The head of prison services at the young offenders institution wrote to the Lord Chancellor's Department suggesting that the sentence should be reduced taking account of the error made. The Court of Appeal took the view that the sentence had been passed in a public court and although in error should be corrected in a public court. Apart from Her Majesty's use of prerogative power, no other method of alteration of the sentence was appropriate.

REHABILITATION OF OFFENDERS

10.1 Subject to certain exceptions, the convictions of a person become spent in accordance with the Rehabilitation of Offenders Act 1974 (Section 4, as amended by the (Exceptions) Order 1975). The intention of this piece of legislation is to allow people who have made one minor mistake in their lives to effectively have their prior convictions recorded, but treated as spent. Records of such convictions may not be brought to the attention of the courts after a period of rehabilitation has elapsed. Certain types of offences are not subject of rehabilitation, i.e., murder, manslaughter, treason etc.

10.2 Whereas in some occupations, it is quite acceptable for a person to be so employed, having a spent conviction, in other occupations, and to be the holder of certain licences, however, a completely 'spotless' record may be required. For this reason, certain professions are exempt from the rehabilitation provisions. An applicant for any of these, or for certain licences, may be required to reveal details of previous convictions even though these may otherwise be considered 'spent'. Such professions and/or licence holdings include:
- medical practitioners, dentists and nurses
- barristers, judicial appointments, magistrates' clerks
- police constables, prison officers
- holder of firearms dealer certificate, etc
  (Rehabilitation of Offenders Act 1974 (Exceptions) Order 1975).

CRIME (SENTENCES) ACT 1997

11.1 The purpose of this particular piece of legislation is to try to ensure that prolific offenders are given mandatory minimum sentences. The efforts of the Home Secretary have been somewhat blunted by exception clauses which allow judges to retain the discretion to give lesser or greater sentences dependent on the circumstances prevailing when the offence took place and in relation to a particular offender.

Section 2 Crime (Sentences) Act 1997

Mandatory life sentences for serious second offence:

1: This Section applies where:
   - a person is convicted of a serious offence committed after the commencement of this Section; and
   - at the time when that offence was committed, he was 18 or over and had been convicted in any part of the United Kingdom of another serious offence.

2: The court shall impose a life sentence, that is to say:
   - where the person is 21 or over, a sentence of imprisonment for life
   - where he is under 21, a sentence of custody for life under Section 8(2) of the Criminal Justice Act 1982, unless the court is of the opinion that there are exceptional circumstances relating to either of the offences or to the offender which justify not doing so.

3: Where the court does not impose a life sentence, it shall state in open court that it is of that opinion and what the exceptional circumstances are.

4: An offence the sentence for which is imposed under subsection (2) above shall not be regarded as an offence the sentence for which is fixed by law.

5: An offence committed in England and Wales is a serious offence for the purposes of this Section if it is any of the following, namely:
   - an attempt to commit murder, a conspiracy to commit murder, or an incitement to murder
   - an offence under Section 4 of the Offences Against the Person Act 1861 (soliciting murder)
   - manslaughter
   - an offence under Section 18 of the Offences Against the Person Act 1861 (wounding, or causing grievous bodily harm, with intent)
   - rape or attempt to commit rape
   - an offence under Section 5 of the Sexual Offences Act 1956 (intercourse with a girl under 13)
   - an offence under Section 16 (possession of a firearm with intent to injure), Section 17 (use a firearm to resist arrest) or Section 18 (carrying a firearm with criminal intent) of the Firearms Act 1968; or
   - robbery where, at some time during the commission of the offence, the offender had in his possession a firearm or imitation firearm within the meaning of the Firearms Act 1968.

Explanation

When a person is convicted for the second time of one of the specified 'serious' offences, the court should normally impose a life sentence. Only in exceptional circumstances may the judge do otherwise, and in such a case, must give his reasons in open court for coming to the conclusion that the circumstances are exceptional. In this context 'exceptional' may relate either to the offender himself, or to the circumstances of the offence. The previous conviction may have been in any part of the United Kingdom, not necessarily in England or Wales. Because of differences in the legal systems in Scotland and in Northern Ireland, the lists of relevant offences for those countries differs from that set out above. The offender must have been at least 18 years of age when the second offence was committed.

Drug offences: Section 3 of the Act provides that upon a person over 18 receiving a second conviction for an offence of trafficking in a Class A drug, the court shall impose a sentence of not less than seven years imprisonment. The court may disregard this provision if it considers that there are specific circumstances relating either to the offence or to the offender, which would make such a sentence unjust. These circumstances must be stated in open court.

Domestic burglary: Section 4 makes provision for mandatory minimum sentences of three years imprisonment for persons convicted on a second occasion of a burglary of domestic premises. This provision has not yet been brought into force.

Chapter 3: Witnesses

COMPETENCE AND COMPELLABILITY

Competence

1.1 The question as to whether a person is able to give evidence before a court relates to his competence, that is his ability to give credible evidence relevant to the issue under consideration. This matter is subject of the Criminal Evidence Act 1898 (as amended by the Civil Evidence Act 1979 and the Police and Criminal Evidence Act 1984). This states that a defendant cannot be called as a witness unless he wishes to give evidence (Section 1(a) Criminal Evidence Act 1898). A co-defendant who has already pleaded guilty is competent and compellable by the defence (*R v Boal* (1964)). In this case a defendant having pleaded guilty was held not to have been before the jury as a person 'so charged' within the meaning of Section 1(a). In *R v Turner* (1975) it was stated that an accomplice having a hope of immunity was still a competent witness. This is however a matter of degree and the judge will always retain discretion to refuse to allow evidence dependent on how prejudicial it is and the circumstances which bring it before the court.

1.2 The question of the competence of child evidence under oath was considered in *R v Hayes* (1977). The test as to whether a child is competent to give evidence is not that he is aware of the divine sanction, but that 'the child had sufficient appreciation of the solemnity of the occasion, and the added responsibility to tell the truth, which is involved in taking the oath, over and above the normal duty to tell the truth in normal social conduct'. In *R v Campbell* (1983) the *Hayes* test was applied and approved, the court stating that 'the child should realise the seriousness of the occasion and that more was involved than the ordinary duty in everyday life to tell the truth'. The ability of the court to accept the 'unsworn' (Section 52 Criminal Justice Act 1991) evidence of a child under 14 to some extent removes necessity to enquire into the question of whether a child under 14 years old understands the oath. The effect of Section 52 of the Criminal Justice Act 1991 is that the evidence of those under 14 will not be given on oath, whereas evidence of those 14 and above will be sworn.

1.3 The competence or otherwise of a person to give evidence against his spouse is the subject of provisions in Section 80 Police and Criminal Evidence Act 1984. In any criminal proceedings the wife or husband of the accused is competent to give evidence for the prosecution and on behalf of the accused and any person jointly charged with the accused. This is true unless the husband and wife are jointly charged. However, even if they are jointly charged initially, if the husband or wife become no longer liable to be found guilty because he or she has pleaded guilty, or for any other reason then they will again become competent witnesses.

Compellability

1.4 If a witness is competent to be called as a witness he will usually be compellable. The subject is complicated in the cases of spouses: a husband and wife will only be compellable if Section 80(3) applies.

Section 80 Police and Criminal Evidence Act 1984

(3) In any proceedings the wife or husband of the accused shall, subject of subsection 4 (being jointly charged) be compellable to give evidence for the prosecution or on behalf of any person jointly charged with the accused if and only if:

a) the offence charged involves an assault on, or injury, or threat of injury to, the wife or husband of the accused, or a person who was at the material time under the age of sixteen; or

b) the offence charged is a sexual offence alleged to have been committed in respect of a person who was at the material time under that age; or

c) the offence charged consists of attempting or conspiring to commit, or of aiding or abetting, counselling, procuring or inciting the commission of, an offence falling within either (a) or (b) above.

Explanation

To make the spouse compellable to give evidence, the offence must involve an assault, injury or threat of injury to the other spouse, or a person who at that time is under sixteen years old, or involve sexual offences upon a person under sixteen, or aid, abet, counsel, incite or procure such offences. From the practical standpoint these provisions are not that frequently invoked. Evidentially a spouse under such circumstances may either be a willing witness, or is likely to be very hostile to giving evidence.

ALIBI NOTIFICATION

2.1 The rules regarding the notification by the defendant involved in criminal proceeding to adduce evidence of alibi are set out in statute. The basic principle is that an alibi must be served as part of the defence statement under Section 5 of the Criminal Procedure and Investigations Act 1996. This will form part of a compulsory statement of defence disclosure.

Section 5 Criminal Procedure and Investigations Act 1996

(7) If the defence statement discloses an alibi the accused must give particulars of the alibi in the statement, including:

a) the name and address of any witness the accused believes is able to give evidence in support of the alibi, if the name and address are known to the accused when the statement is given

b) any information in the accused's possession which might be of material assistance in finding any such witness, if his name or address is not known to the accused when the statement is given.

(8) For the purposes of this Section evidence in support of an alibi is evidence tending to show that by reason of the presence of the accused at a particular place or in a particular area at a particular time he was not, or was unlikely to have been, at the place where the offence is alleged to have been committed at the time of its commission.

Explanation

Subsection 7(8) indicates that the alibi is linked to a location. The alibi notice must now be part of any defence statement served on the prosecution as part of the disclosure system.

2.2 The question then arises 'what is evidence of alibi?' and what is evidence in chief for the defendant? In *R v Hassan* (1970) the defendant was charged with living on the immoral earnings of a prostitute. Part of the evidence was that upon entering a prostitute's address officers saw the defendant exiting via a window. The defendant wished to call evidence that he was elsewhere. The judge ruled that notice of alibi should have been given and refused to hear the evidence. On appeal, the court stated that this is wrong, the defence were adducing evidence which was not anchored to a particular location. It was thus not evidence of alibi, the evidence was therefore not subject of the requirement to give a notice of alibi. Lord Edmund Davies in considering this case and the applicability of evidence of alibi to continuing offences said he could see difficulties, but the mere fact an offence was continuing did not rule out the need to use alibi notice.

2.3 Although the 1996 legislation places a responsibility on the defence to give advance notice of alibi evidence, on pain of having such evidence excluded, situations will arise where the requisite notice is not given, e.g., the defence representative is brought in at a late stage in proceedings, or there has been an omission on the defence solicitor's part. It remains to be seen whether a court will accept that a defendant should lose his liberty because of his legal adviser's neglect, or whether alibi evidence will be admitted in circumstances where the requirements for advance notice have not been complied with.

2.4 It appears that the facts at issue and the effect of the notice or rather its content will be the deciding factor. In *R v Sullivan* (1970) an unrepresented defendant was committed for trial, no notice of alibi was given. A month later the defendant was granted legal aid and his solicitors served a notice of alibi. The notice was partially defective, the defect being remedied by letter within a couple of days. The prosecution obtained an adjournment to check the facts. At the subsequent trial, the prosecution objected to the alibi notice and the court ruled that the alibi would be inadmissible. On appeal, it was stated that the court had been wrong to exclude the evidence of alibi, the mere fact that the notice was not served within the then required seven days did not by itself justify excluding the evidence. In this case, however, it also appeared that the information given in the notice was itself highly suspect, in that of the three witnesses named, one failed to keep an appointment with the police, another had provided an address which could not be traced, and the third supplied an address which was fictitious. If these facts had been brought to the original court it would be reasonable to expect that court would have excluded the evidence.

HOSTILE WITNESSES

3.1 A hostile witness is one who gives evidence which is adverse or contradicts that given earlier by way of statement. The prosecution or defence cannot when they have called a witness contradict their own witness or give evidence of the witness's bad character (Sections 3 and 4 Criminal Procedure Act 1865). However, if the judge gives authority they may treat the witness as 'hostile' and may contradict him by way of other evidence. By leave of the judge the witness may be confronted with prior inconsistent statements made by him. The witness must first be asked if he or she made the statement. If the witness does not openly admit making the prior statement, evidence may have to be called to prove the statement. A witness being declared hostile to the side calling him is a rare occurrence, it is only at the discretion of the judge that a witness may be declared 'hostile' and proof must be given of any prior and inconsistent statements. It must be remembered that such witnesses may be motivated by malice or other factors, including the fact that they are now giving evidence under oath.

VIDEO LINKS

4.1 With the leave of the court, child witnesses below the age of 14, are allowed to give evidence via live television link to the court (Section 32 Criminal Justice Act 1988). This applies to cases involving sexual offences, child cruelty and violence or threatened violence. The scope for use of video links to courts was extended to those under 17 years old in Youth Courts (Section 55 Criminal Justice Act 1991). The evidence of a child may also be obtained using video recording, but this will be subject to the discretion of the judge to exclude it if the witness is not available for cross examination, or any of the rules regarding the making of such recording is breached. Further, the judge may exclude the evidence if it is considered to be not in the interests of justice to admit it.

INTERFERENCE WITH WITNESSES OR JURORS, OR POTENTIAL WITNESSES OR JURORS

5.1 The possibility of justice being perverted by what is known as 'witness interference' and 'jury knobbling' was considered to require some form of legislation to prevent the practice and provide a sanction. This was catered for in the Criminal Justice and Public Order Act 1994 under Section 51. Not only does this legislation cover the period of any forthcoming investigation and proceedings but also up to twelve months after the conclusion of a court action.

Section 51 Criminal Justice and Public Order Act 1994

(1) A person who does to another person:
   a) an act which intimidates, and is intended to intimidate, that other person
   b) knowing or believing that the other person is assisting in the investigation of an offence, or is a witness, or potential witness, or a juror, or potential juror in proceedings for an offence; and
   c) intending thereby to cause an investigation or the course of justice to be obstructed, perverted or interfered with;
   commits an offence.

(2) A person who does, or threatens to do, to another person:
   a) an act which harms, or would harm, and is intended to harm, that other person
   b) knowing or believing that the other person, or some other person, has assisted in an investigation into an offence, or has given evidence, or particular evidence in proceedings for an offence, or has acted as a juror, or concurred in a particular verdict in proceedings for an offence; and
   c) does or threatens to do the act because of what (within paragraph (b)) he knows or believes;
   commits an offence.

(3) A person does an act 'to' another person with the intention of intimidating, or harming, that other person not only where the act is done in the presence of the other and

directed at him directly but also where the act is done to a third person and is intended, in the circumstances, to intimidate or harm the person at whom the act is directed.

Explanation

This Section covers not only actual witnesses, but also potential witnesses and jurors. Thus if everyone on a panel list for jury service was sent a threat the offence is complete. There is no need to prove that the person making the threat is in a physical position to carry out the threat.

5.2 The harm that is done or threatened may be financial as well as physical, whether to the person or the person's property, and similarly as respects an intimidatory act which consists of threats (Section 51(4) Criminal Justice and Public Order Act 1994). The intention required by Section 51(1)(c) and the motive required by Section 51(2)(c) need not be the only or the predominating intention or motive with which the act is done or, in the case of Section 51(2), threatened (Section 51(5)). This means that the accused may have had another reason as well as witness or juror intimidation for his actions.

5.3 There is a rebuttable presumption of intention to intimidate with the intent to obstruct, interfere or pervert justice written into Section 51(7) as far as it relates to the offence under Section 51(1). A similar rebuttable presumption relating to the intention for the Section 51(2) offence is contained in Section 51(8). This presumption make the two offences which are contrary to this Section easier to prove for the prosecution, and places the burden on the defence to disprove the intention for the actions taken.

5.4 The Section does not remove or replace any of the common law offences relating to attempts to pervert justice by witness interference (Section 51(11)), it is intended to provide a legislative alternative.

5.5 The two offences set out in Section 51 are arrestable and either-way offences. When dealt with by trial on indictment first conviction carries a potential imprisonment of five years, summary conviction carries a potential six months' imprisonment and/or a fine.

Chapter 4: Methods of Securing Evidence

SUMMONS

1.1 A summons to attend is a written order issued and signed by a justice of the peace or a justice's clerk on behalf of the justice, for a person named therein to attend a court at a time and date stated therein to answer an allegation set out therein, or to give evidence in relation to a matter stated therein. Failure to attend may lead to a warrant for the arrest of a person to force his attendance. Magistrates' courts use summonses to start proceedings and to ensure the attendance of the parties to those matters. A summons may be issued as the result of a complaint, which is a written allegation that a person has committed a breach of the law which is not a criminal offence. An example of a complaint is where a person is threatening to commit a breach of the peace; the justices may issue a summons requiring the attendance of the person and if satisfied may require the person to be bound over to keep the peace. A summons may be issued by the court and delivered by post.

1.2 The courts may order a person or persons to deliver up to them any document or other thing for examination in relation to any proceedings being heard by them. This can also be done by summons but in such cases the summons must be delivered in person.

A summons may be effectively served by (Magistrates' Courts Rules 1981):
- delivering it to the person to whom it is directed; or
- by leaving it with someone at his last known or usual place of abode; or,
- by sending it by post in a letter addressed to him at his last known or usual place of abode.

Service of a summons on a corporation may be affected by delivering it at, or sending it by post to:
- the registered office of the corporation, if in the United Kingdom, or,
- any place in the United Kingdom where the corporation trades, or conducts its business, if there is no registered office in the United Kingdom.

In the case of sending by post this must be recorded delivery or registered post to be lawful and accepted as good service. Proof of service is by way of certificate signed by the person who effected service.

WARRANTS

2.1 A warrant is a written order signed by a magistrate or judge directing a person named therein to take a course of action stated therein (clerks to the justices cannot sign warrants). Warrants may be issued by the courts to force action to be taken. A warrant remains in force until it is either withdrawn or executed. A warrant may be issued when evidence has been given on oath to the effect that a person has, or is suspected of having committed an offence. An arrest warrant must not be issued unless a summons has proven ineffective, or the offence committed is triable on indictment, or imprisonable, or the accused's address is not sufficiently established for a summons to be served on him. When a warrant has been executed it must be endorsed accordingly. In the case of commitment warrants this should include a receipt for the defaulter from the prison authorities, or custody officer.

Witness Warrant

2.2 A warrant may be issued to force attendance of a witness who would otherwise be unlikely to voluntarily attend court (Section 97 Magistrates' Courts Act 1980). Such a warrant will only be issued where a summons would be ineffective.

Distress Warrants

2.3 Distress warrants can be issued by the courts to levy unpaid sums from fines and compensation orders made by the court. Such warrants are usually executed by a bailiff and are more frequently issued by judges at civil courts than by magistrates. The warrant requires that goods to the value of the outstanding balance be seized; initially this is done by labelling the goods and identifying them. Tools of trade, clothing, bedding and the property of public utilities cannot be seized. Before a distress warrant can be issued the court must consider evidence whether there is likely to be assets to the value of the default *(R v Birmingham Justices (Ex P Beneath) [1983])*.

Commitment Warrant

2.4 Before a person is accepted into a prison, the prison authorities must receive a warrant of commitment. Persons taking someone to prison from a court (usually prisoner custody officers) must ensure that the court has provided a warrant, otherwise they run the risk of being turned away with the prisoner. The warrant gives the governor (or director, in the case of a contracted-out prison) lawful authority to detain the prisoner in accordance with the instructions contained in the warrant. In the case of a person remanded in custody, the warrant may instruct the governor to keep him for 7 days, and then to bring him back to the magistrates' court. If the prisoner has been sentenced, the warrant will be the official record of the length of that sentence, providing the starting point for calculation of his release date.

Execution of Warrants

2.5 Warrants for arrest, distress, and commitment issued by the magistrates' courts in England and Wales may be executed anywhere in England and Wales by a constable. A constable may also execute a warrant issued in one of the other parts of the United Kingdom (England and Wales, Scotland, Northern Ireland (Section 38 Criminal Law Act 1977)).

2.6 Certain warrants may be executed by a constable who does not have possession of them at the time they are executed. They are:
- warrants to arrest for an offence
- warrants issued for detention of deserters (Army Act 1955, Air Force Act 1955, Naval Discipline Act 1957, Reserve Forces Act 1980)
- warrants of commitment for lack of sufficiency for distress
- warrants for; non-appearance, commitment, witness arrest (Magistrates' Courts Act 1980, Section 55, 76, 93, and 97)
- warrants for family protection (Family Law Act 1996, Section 47).

Entry to Execute Warrants

2.7 Police officers may enter and search premises which includes any vehicle, vessel, aircraft or tent, for the purpose of executing a warrant to arrest arising out of or in connection with criminal proceedings (Section 17 Police and Criminal Evidence Act 1984) or for commitment to prison (Section 76, Magistrates' Courts Act 1980). This power is only excercisable where the constable has reasonable grounds for believing that the person he is seeking is in the premises. If the premises consist of two or more separate dwelling the entry and search is restricted to the dwelling in which the constable has reasonable grounds to believe the wanted person is. The search is only allowed to the extent necessary to discover the person.

Search Warrants

2.8 The safeguards for the issue of search warrant are contained in Sections 15 and 16 of the Police and Criminal Evidence Act.

Section 15 Police and Criminal Evidence Act 1984

(1) This Section and Section 16 below have effect in relation to the issue to constables under any enactment , including an enactment contained in an Act passed after this Act, of warrants to enter and search premises, and an entry on or search of premises under warrant to enter and search premises, and an entry on or search of premises under warrant is unlawful unless it complies with this Section and Section 16 below.

(2) Where a constable applies for any such warrant, it shall be his duty:
  a) to state:
    i) the grounds on which he makes the application; and
    ii) the enactment under which the warrant would be issued.
  b) to specify the premises to which it is desired to enter and search; and
  c) to identify, so far as practical, the articles or persons to be sought.

(3) An application for such a warrant shall be made ex parte and supported by an information in writing.

(4) The constable shall answer on oath any questions that the justice of the peace or judge hearing the application asks him.

(5) A warrant shall authorise entry on one occasion only.

(6) A warrant:
  a) shall specify:
    i) the name of the person who applies for it
    ii) the date on which it is issued
    iii) the enactment under which it is issued; and
    iv) the premises to be searched; and
  b) shall identify, so far as practical, the articles or persons to be sought.

(7) Two copies shall be made of the warrant.

(8) The copies shall be clearly marked as copies.

Explanation

This Section details what information is required to obtain a warrant, how it is to be obtained by giving evidence on oath. An important note is made at subsection (5) that entry is only to be made once.

Section 16 Police and Criminal Evidence Act 1984

(1) A warrant issued to enter and search premises may be executed by any constable.

(2) Such a warrant may authorise persons to accompany any constable who is executing it.

(3) Entry and search under a warrant must be within one month from the date of issue.

(4) Entry and search under a warrant must be at a reasonable hour unless it appears to the constable executing it that the purpose of a search may be frustrated on entry at a reasonable hour.

(5) Where the occupier of premises which are to be entered and searched is present at the time when the constable seeks to execute a warrant to enter and search them, the constable:
   a) shall identify himself to the occupier and, if not in uniform produce to him documentary evidence that he is a constable
   b) shall produce the warrant to him; and
   c) shall supply him with a copy of it.

(6) Where:
   a) the occupier of such premises is not present at the time when a constable seeks to execute such a warrant; but
   b) some other person who appears to the constable to be in charge of the premises is present;

subsection (5) above shall have effect as if any reference to the occupier were a reference to that other person.

(7) If there is no person present who appears to the constable to be in charge of the premises, he shall leave a copy of the warrant in a prominent place on the premises.

(8) A search under a warrant may only be a search to the extent required for the purpose for which it was issued.

(9) A constable executing a warrant shall make an endorsement on it stating:
   a) whether any articles or persons sought were found; and
   b) whether any articles were seized, other than articles which were sought.

(10) A warrant which:
   a) has been executed; or
   b) has not be executed within the time authorised for its execution, shall be returned:
      i)   if it was issued by a justice of the peace, to the clerk to the justices for the petty sessions area for which he acts; and
      ii) if it was issued by a judge, to the appropriate officer of the court from which he issued it.

(11) A warrant which is returned under subsection (10) above shall be retained for 12 months from its return:
   a) by the clerk to the justices, if it was returned under paragraph (i) of that subsection; and
   b) by the appropriate officer, if it was returned under paragraph (ii).

(12) If during the period for which a warrant is to be retained the occupier of the premises to which it relates asks to inspect it, he shall be allowed to o so.

2.9 In *R v South Western Magistrates and another Ex P Cofie* (1996) the magistrates had issued a warrant to search an address. The occupier Mrs Cofie had sought judicial review stating that the issue of the warrant was illegal. The grounds for this claim were that the application and warrant were not specific as to the exact location the constables wished to search. The premises involved were used by numerous persons and had been sub-divided for multiple occupiers as separate dwellings. The court on appeal stated that where the premises were multi-occupied, the constable must state which part of the premises he wishes to search in the initial application. Where a warrant is issued to search for a person, officers could not conduct a search of small drawers and other impossible places for a person to hide.

Entry and Search of Premises to Arrest or Find Evidence

2.10 Sections 17, 18 and 32 of the Police and Criminal Evidence Act 1984 give police wide powers to search persons and premises in connection with an arrest for a criminal offence. There is a power to enter and search any premises to arrest someone for an arrestable offence (and in connection with other specified matters); there is power to search premises where an arrested person was at the time of or immediately prior to his arrest. There is also power to search premises occupied or controlled by a person who has been arrested for an arrestable offence.

Police and Criminal Evidence Act 1984 Section 17

(1) Subject to the following provisions of this Section, and without prejudice to any other enactment, a constable may enter and search any premises for the following purposes:
   a) of executing:
      i) a warrant of arrest issued in connection with and arising out of criminal proceedings; or
      ii) a warrant of commitment issued under Section 76 of the Magistrates' Courts Act 1980;
   b) of arresting a person for an arrestable offence;
   c) of arresting a person for an offence under:
      i) Section 1 (prohibition of uniforms in connection with political object) of the Public Order Act 1936.
      ii) any enactment contained in Section 6 to 8 or 10 of the Criminal Law Act 1977 (offences of entering and remaining on property)
      iii) Section 4 of the Public Order Act 1986 (fear or provocation of violence)
   d) of recapturing a person unlawfully at large and whom he is pursuing; or
   e) of saving life or limb or preventing serious damage to property.

(2) Except for the purposes specified in paragraph (e) of subsection (1) above, the powers of entry and search conferred by this Section:
   a) are only excercisable if the constable has reasonable grounds for believing that the person whom he is seeking is on the premises; and
   b) are limited, in relation to premises consisting of two or more separate dwellings, to powers to enter and search:
      i) any parts of the premises which the occupiers of any dwelling comprised in the premises use in common with the occupiers of any other such dwellings; and
      ii) any such dwelling in which the constable has reasonable grounds for believing that the person whom he is seeking may be.

(3) The powers of entry and search conferred by this Section are only excercisable for the purposes specified in subsection (1) (c) (ii) above by a constable in uniform.

(4) The power to search conferred by this Section is only a power to search to the extent that is reasonably required for the purpose for which the power of entry is exercised.

(5) Subject to subsection (6) below, all the rules of common law under which a constable has power to enter premises without a warrant are hereby abolished.

(6) Nothing in subsection (5) above affects any power of entry to deal with or prevent a breach of the peace.

Explanation

Section 17 is designed to allow officers to enter to effect an arrest for an arrestable offence, and for the three specified offences, political objects under Section 1 of the 1936 Public Order Act, adverse entry of premises under the 1977 Criminal Law Act, and Section 4 of the Public Order Act 1986 i.e., provocation of violence. The common law powers of entry are specifically revoked with the exception of preventing and dealing with breaches of the peace. The search for wanted persons is limited by reasonableness. Following *R v South Western Magistrates and Another Ex P Cofie* the officers would have to justify searching where a person could not possibly hide, or in areas which belonged to another tenant in a multi-occupational set of dwellings.

Entry and Search after Arrest

2.11 Police officers may use the powers contained in Section 18 of the Police and Criminal Evidence Act 1984, to search for other property suspected of being proceeds of crime which has been stored by a suspect who has been arrested.

Police and Criminal Evidence Act 1984 Section 18

(1) Subject to the following provisions of this Section, a constable may enter and search, any premises occupied or controlled by a person who is under arrest for an arrestable offence, if he has reasonable grounds for suspecting that there is on the premises evidence other than items subject to legal privilege, that relates:
   a) to that offence; or
   b) to some other arrestable offence which is connected with or similar to that offence.

(2) A constable may seize and retain anything for which he may search under subsection (1) above.

(3) The power to search conferred by subsection (1) above is only a power to search to the extent that is reasonably required for the purposes of discovering such evidence.

(4) Subject to subsection (5) below, the powers conferred by this Section may not be exercised unless an officer of the rank of inspector or above has authorised them in writing.

(5) A constable may conduct a search under subsection (1) above:
   a) before taking a person to a police station; and
   b) without obtaining an authorisation under subsection (4) above, if the presence of the person at a place other than a police station is necessary for the effective investigation of the offence.

(6) If a constable conducts a search by virtue of subsection (5) above, he shall inform an officer of the rank of inspector or above that he has made the search as soon as practical after he has made it.

(7) An officer who:
   a) authorises a search; or
   b) is informed of search under subsection (6) above, shall make a record in writing:
      i) of the grounds for the search; and
      ii) of the nature of the evidence that was sought.

(8) If the person who was in occupation or control of the premises at the time of the search is in police detention at the time the record is made, the officer shall make the record as part of his custody record.

Explanation

A search of premises may only be justified to look for items from similar offences. If property is found from other offences this will not however preclude it from being used as evidence provided the search was based on good reasons. An example may be that a person caught committing burglaries had used a 'modus operandi' which was unusual. The investigating officers were searching for goods from other similar offences in the area committed using the peculiar 'modus operandi'. If the officers discover quantities of drugs these would provide evidence of other offences not those for which the suspect was already detained. This does not mean that the suspect could not be arrested or questioned about the drugs even though the search was for the proceeds of burglaries. It means however that the officer authorising the search would have to be able to justify the reason for the search, e.g., 'to look for property from other similar burglaries in and around the area using a similar modus operandi to that which the suspect was found using when arrested'.

2.12 A speculative search cannot be lawfully carried out without good and reasonable grounds to expect the discovery of evidence. Evidence discovered in an unauthorised manner could be subject of exclusion under Section 78 of the Police and Criminal Evidence Act 1984. Such exclusion is a matter for the court to excercise its discretion.

Search Upon Arrest

2.13 Where a person is arrested at a place other than a police station the person may be searched, as may the premises in which he is arrested, or in which he was immediately prior to his arrest.

Section 32 Police and Criminal Evidence Act 1984

(1) A constable may search an arrested person, in any case where the person to be searched has been arrested at a place other than a police station, if the constable has reasonable grounds for believing that the person may present a danger to himself or others.

(2) Subject to subsections (3) and (5) below, a constable shall also have power in any such case:
   a) to search the arrested person for anything:
      i)   which he might use to assist him to escape from lawful custody; or
      ii) which might be evidence relating to an offence; and
   b) to enter and search any premises in which he was when arrested or immediately before he was arrested for evidence relating to the offence for which he was arrested.

Explanation

2.14 The power to search under Section 32 is subject to provisos that it can only be to such an extent to discover any article or thing which is evidence or may be used to aid escape (Section

32 (3)). The officer may not require a person to remove clothing in a street or public place other than coat, jacket or gloves (Section 32(4)). The constable may not search unless there are reasonable grounds for believing that there is evidence or articles to be found (Section 32(6), and the same provisions apply to the search of multi-occupied buildings as for Section 18 being only those areas which the suspect had access to immediately prior to his arrest and common areas within the building.

The arrest of a person for a breach of the peace where no weapon was used would therefore not justify the search of premises, but may justify search of the person for articles which may be used to aid escape or which may pose a danger to others.

Power to Seize Property

2.15 A constable lawfully on premises may seize property except property subject of privilege if he has reasonable grounds for believing that the property has been:
- obtained in consequence of the commission of an offence, and that it is necessary to seize it to prevent it being concealed, lost, damaged, altered or destroyed; or
- that it is evidence relating to an offence which he is investigating, or any other offence, and that in order to prevent it being concealed, lost, altered or destroyed it must be seized.

2.16 A constable may require information except that to which privilege applies contained in a computer and which is accessible from the premises, to be produced in a form which is visible and legible if he has reasonable grounds for believing that:
- it is evidence in relation to an offence which he is investigating, or any other offences or, that it is necessary to do so in order to prevent it being concealed, lost tampered with or destroyed.

ARREST AND POLICE DETENTION

3.1 Arrest and detention in police custody is covered extensively by the Police and Criminal Evidence Act 1984. The codes of practice issued with the Act have been updated on several occasions.

Arrest

3.2 Arrest is defined as the taking or restraining of a person's liberty. The purpose of powers of arrest is to allow police officers to detain a person to secure evidence of matters under investigation. Not all offences give rise to a power to arrest. There are however instances where the attendant circumstances will authorise a constable to arrest (Section 25 Police and Criminal Evidence Act 1984).

3.3 Powers of arrest are provided in Section 24 of the Police and Criminal Evidence Act 1984, which defines the circumstances under which offences become arrestable in themselves.

Section 24 Police and Criminal Evidence Act 1984

(1) The powers of summary arrest conferred by the following subsection shall apply;
   a) to offences for which the sentence is fixed by law; or

b) to offences for which a person of 21 years of age or over (not previously convicted) may be sentenced to imprisonment for a term of five years (or might be so sentenced but for the restrictions imposed by Section 33 of the Magistrates' Courts Act 1980); and

c) offences to which subsection (2) applies.

Explanation

Sentence fixed by law: There are few offences left where the judge has no discretion, being required to impose a fixed sentence. The only everyday example is murder, for which a penalty of life imprisonment must be imposed. Thus, murder is an arrestable offence.

Five years or more: To come within this group, the offence must be one for which an adult may be sentenced to five years or more on first conviction. There may be restrictions placed upon the maximum length of sentence to be imposed on a person under 21, for example, but this does not mean that the offence ceases to be an arrestable one when committed by a person under that age. If there was an offence for which the maximum punishment was three years imprisonment for a person never convicted of such an offence before, and seven years for someone who had a previous conviction, this would not amount to an arrestable offence.

Other offences: There are a fair number of offences which, although carrying a maximum sentence of less than five years' imprisonment, are nevertheless arrestable offences. These include offences:

a) covered by Section 1 of the Customs and Excise Management Act 1979

b) offences under the Official Secrets Act 1920 that would otherwise not be arrestable by virtue of the sentence

bb) offences under the Official Secrets Act 1989 with the exception of Section 8(1), 8(4) or 8(5)

c) Sections 22 (causing prostitution) and 23 (procuration of girl under 21) of the Sexual Offences Act 1956

d) offences under Section 12(1)(Unauthorised taking of a motor vehicle) and Section 25(1) (going equipped) Theft Act 1968

e) offences under the Football (Offences) Act 1991

f) publication of obscene matter (Section 2 of the Obscene Publications Act 1959)

g) indecent photographs and pseudo photographs of children (Section 1 of the Protection of Children Act 1978)

h) sale of tickets by unauthorised persons (Section 166 of the Criminal Justice and Public Order Act 1994)

i) publication of materials likely to stir up racial hatred (Section 19 of the Public Order Act 1986)

j) touting for car hire services (Criminal Justice and Public Order Act 1994)

k) carrying an offensive weapon in a public place without lawful authority or reasonable excuse (Section 1 of the Prevention of Crime Act 1953)

l) carrying a bladed or pointed article in public without good reason or lawful authority (Section 139 of the Criminal Justice Act 1988)

m) having an article with a blade or point, or offensive weapon on school premises (Section 139A(1) or (2) Criminal Justice Act 1988)

n) harassment (Section 2 Protection of Harassment Act 1997)

Powers of arrest are also conferred under Section 24(3) for:

a) conspiring to commit an arrestable offence

b) attempting to commit any arrestable offence other than under Section 12(1) Theft Act 1968

c) inciting, aiding, abetting, counselling or procuring the commission of any such offence.

Powers of Arrest Without Warrant for Arrestable Offences

3.4 Section 24(4) and (5) of the Police and Criminal Evidence Act 1984 provide that:

24(4) 'any person' may arrest without warrant:
  a) anyone who is in the act of committing an arrestable offence;
  b) anyone whom he has reasonable grounds for suspecting to be committing an arrestable offence;

24(5) Where an arrestable offence has been committed, any person may arrest without warrant:
  a) anyone who is guilty of the offence;
  b) anyone whom he has reasonable grounds for suspecting to be guilty of it.

In addition police officers have the powers conferred by subsections (6) and (7):

24(6) Where a constable has reasonable grounds for suspecting that an arrestable offence has been committed, he may arrest without warrant anyone whom he has reasonable grounds for suspecting to be guilty of the offence.

24(7) A constable may arrest without warrant:
  a) anyone who is about to commit an arrestable offence;
  b) anyone whom he has reasonable grounds for suspecting to be about to commit an arrestable offence.

General Arrest Conditions

3.5 There are circumstances where it is not possible to deal with minor offences without arresting the offender. Section 25 of the Police and Criminal Evidence Act 1984 caters for these circumstances by providing a power of arrest subject to conditions which relate to the offender rather than to the offence.

Section 25 Police and Criminal Evidence Act 1984

(1) Where a constable has reasonable grounds for suspecting that any offence which is not an arrestable offence has been committed or attempted, he may arrest the relevant person if it appears to him that service of a summons is impracticable or inappropriate because any of the general arrest conditions is satisfied.

(2) In this Section, 'the relevant person' means any person whom the constable has reasonable grounds to suspect of having committed or having attempted to commit the offence or of being in the course of committing or attempting to commit it.

(3) The general arrest conditions are:
  a) the name of the relevant person is unknown to, and cannot be readily ascertained by, the constable
  b) that the constable has reasonable grounds for doubting whether a name furnished by the relevant person as his name is his real name

  c) that:
     i)   the relevant person has failed to furnish a satisfactory address for service; or
     ii) the constable has reasonable grounds for doubting whether an address
          furnished by the relevant person is a satisfactory address for service
  d) that the constable has reasonable grounds for believing that the arrest is necessary
      to prevent the relevant person:
     i)   causing harm to himself or any other person
     ii)   suffering physical injury
     iii) causing loss or damage to property
     iv)   committing an offence against public decency; or
     v)   causing an unlawful obstruction of the highway.
  e) that the constable has reasonable grounds for believing that the arrest is necessary
      to protect a child or other vulnerable person from the relevant person.

(4) For the purpose of Section 25(3) above an address is a satisfactory address for service
    of a summons if it appears to the constable:
  a) that the relevant person will be at it for a sufficiently long period for it to be
      possible for him to serve a summons; or
  b) that some other person specified by the relevant person will accept service of the
      summons for the relevant person at it.

3.11 The decision in the case of *Christie v Leachinsky* (1947) provides guidelines as to the manner
of informing a person of the fact that he is under arrest. The suspect should understand, firstly
that he is under arrest, and secondly, the reasons for his arrest. There is no requirement that he
should be informed of the power of arrest, or be given details of the relevant statute. An
explanation in plain, simple language will suffice.

Powers to Arrest for Fingerprinting
3.7 Section 27 of the Police and Criminal Evidence Act 1984 gives police officers powers to
arrest a person to take fingerprints.

Section 27 Police and Criminal Evidence Act 1984

(1) If a person:
  a) has been convicted of a recordable offence;
  b) has not at any time been in police detention for the offence; and
  c) has not had his fingerprints taken:
     i)   in the course of the investigation of the offence by the police; or
     ii) since the conviction;

any constable may at any time not later than one month after the date of the conviction
require him to attend a police station in order that his fingerprints may be taken.

(2) A requirement under subsection (1) above:
  a) shall give the person a period of at least seven days within which he must attend; and
  b) may direct him so to attend at a specified time of day or between specified
      times of day.

(3) Any constable may arrest without warrant a person who has failed to comply with
    a requirement of subsection (1) above.

(There are similar powers relating to the taking of samples – *See chapter 7, paragraph 9.10.*)

Common Law Powers of Arrest

3.8 At common law police officers and others have powers of arrest without warrant. These powers were not affected by the 1984 Police and Criminal Evidence Act. The common law powers are:

- where a breach of the peace is committed by the person arrested in the presence of the person making the arrest; or
- where there is an imminent threat of a breach of the peace by the person arrested, although no breach of the peace has occurred at the time; or
- where a breach of the peace has been committed by the person arrested and there is a threat of a renewal of the breach of the peace.

These common law powers are not restricted by the location, whether public or private. Even if no other member of the public is present, a fight between two men in a private dwelling is still a breach of the peace. Even if the fight has ended the mere threat of renewal is sufficient to justify arrest. Once a constable reasonably foresees a breach of the peace he is entitled to enter and remain in the premises where until that time he may have been regarded as a trespasser (*Robson v Hallett* [1967]).

Cross Border Arrests

3.9 Any constable of a police force in England, Wales, Scotland, or Northern Ireland, who has reasonable grounds for suspecting that an offence has been committed in or attempted in his country, and that the suspected person is in another of the countries (England, Wales, Scotland or Northern Ireland) may arrest that person without warrant on condition that the suspected offence is an arrestable offence in that country (Section 137 Criminal Justice and Public Order Act 1994).

Information Required to be Given Upon Arrest

3.10 The prescribed information to be given to a suspect is set out in Section 28 of the Police and Criminal Evidence Act as:

(1) Subject to subsection (5) below, when a person is arrested without being informed that he is under arrest, the arrest is not lawful unless the person arrested is informed that he is under arrest as soon as is practicable after his arrest.

(2) Where a person is arrested by a constable subsection (1) above applies regardless of whether the reason for the arrest is obvious.

(3) Subject to subsection (5) below, no arrest is lawful unless the person arrested is informed of the ground of the arrest at the time, or as soon as is practicable after, the arrest.

(4) Where the person is arrested by a constable, subsection (3) applies regardless of whether the ground for arrest is obvious.

(5) nothing in this Section is to be taken to require a person to be informed:
  a) that he is under arrest; or
  b) of the ground for the arrest,

if it was not reasonably practicable for him to be so informed by reason of his having escaped from arrest before the information could be given.

3.11 The decision in the case of Christie v. Leachinsky (1947) provides guidelines as to the manner of informing a person of the fact that he is under arrest. The suspect should understand, firstly that he is under arrest, and secondly, the reasons for his arrest. There is no requirement that he should be informed of the power of arrest, or be given details of the relevant statute. An explanation in plain, simple language will suffice.

The Caution

3.12 When a person is arrested or informed he may be reported for an offence he must be cautioned if the reply made is to be admissible in evidence. The caution must be in the following terms:

'You do not have to say anything,
but it may harm your defence,
if you do not mention when questioned,
something which you later rely on in court,
anything you do say may be given in evidence'.

Provided the meaning of the caution is clear the exact wording need not be given but it is advisable that police officers should learn the caution verbatim, to avoid problems when giving evidence in court.

3.13 A caution must be given as soon as there are reasonable grounds to suspect a person of an offence, before questions or further questions are put to him regarding his suspected involvement in the offence. Failure to do may lead to the answers to such questions being excluded from evidence in subsequent court proceedings. A person must always be cautioned before he is reported for an offence or charged with it. Notes should be made of the replies of a person when being told he is being reported for an offence, charged, or when questioned about an offence. The person cautioned should be given an opportunity to read any notes or records made and verify the accuracy by signing the notes if at all possible. A person who is violent or is incapable of understanding should be given an opportunity to review the evidence contained in the notes when calm or capable of understanding them.

POLICE DETENTION, TREATMENT AND CONDITIONS

4.1 Provisions of the Police and Criminal Evidence Act 1984 and Code C of the Codes of Practice lay down requirements in relation to the detention, welfare and treatment of persons in police custody. There are requirements common to all detained persons, with additional ones for those categories considered at special risk, such as juveniles, the mentally impaired and those unable to speak good English.

4.2 Any person arrested in England or Wales is subject of time limits to detention in police custody. Police detention is defined as 'he has been taken to a police station after being arrested for an offence, or after being arrested under Section 14 of the Prevention of Terrorism (Temporary Provisions) Act 1989, or under paragraph 6 of Schedule 5 to that Act by an examining officer who is a constable; or, he is arrested at a police station after attending there voluntarily at the station or accompanying a constable to it; and, is detained there; or, is detained elsewhere in the charge of a constable' (Section 118(2) (a) and (b) Police and Criminal Evidence Act 1984).

4.3 A person detained at court after being charged with an offence is no longer considered to be 'in police custody' for the purposes of PACE and Code C of the Codes of Practice.

However, the requirements will apply where a person is detained other than for an offence, e.g. where he has been brought to a police station in its capacity as a place of safety, under provisions of the Mental Health Act 1983. However, the requirement for regular reviews of a person's detention shall apply only in the case of a person arrested for an offence.

In other cases where a person is detained at a police station, e.g. persons held there who should be in prison, during a period of prison overcrowding, none of the provisions of Code C will apply, but the provisions relating to treatment – quality and frequency of meals, clean bedding, etc – should be regarded as the minimum standards required in these cases (Code C, Sections 1.10 – 1.12).

4.4 A person having been arrested should be taken to a designated police station 'as soon as is practicable' (Section 30 PACE 1984). A designated police station is one whose custody facilities are approved for the detention of persons under the Police and Criminal Evidence Act 1984. The reason the phrase 'as soon as practicable' is included in the Section is to allow for situations where it is reasonable to continue investigations, for example where a person is arrested and it is necessary to search a route taken by him to recover property which otherwise might be lost. In such cases any questions put to the suspect must be confined to those investigations. In exceptional circumstances an arrested person may be taken to any police station, these are:

– the constable is working in an area where no designated station exists, or
– he is a constable belonging to a police force maintained by an authority other than a police authority eg, British Transport Police.

4.5 Additionally a constable may take an arrested person to any police station if:

– the constable has arrested the person without the assistance of another constable, and no other constable is available to assist him, or
– the constable has taken the person into custody from a person, not a constable, without the assistance of any other constable, and no other constable is available to assist him, and
– it appears to the constable that he will be unable to take the arrested person to a designated police station without the arrested person injuring himself, the constable, or some other person.

4.6 This provision allows police in rural areas to take into custody persons under circumstances where it is impractical to transfer an arrested person with safety to a designated station. Under this provision if the first station the arrested person is taken to is not a designated station, the arrested person must be transferred to a designated station within six hours unless he is released from custody.

4.7 A person arrested and taken into custody at a designated police station may only be detained subject to time limits (Section 40 PACE 1984), or relevant detention periods. A person so detained must not be kept in custody for more than twenty-four (24) hours, without charge (Section 41 PACE 1984). Detention beyond that period may be authorised in certain circumstances by an officer of the rank of superintendent or above (Section 42 PACE 1984), or by a magistrates' court (Section 42 and 43 PACE 1984). At the end of each relevant period the purpose of the detention and the current state of the investigation must be reviewed and a decision to authorise further detention or not must be made. Further detention may be authorised:

– Where a detained person is unfit through drink or drugs to be charged or released without charge, with or without bail, the review officer must consider whether the arrested person is in a fit state to be charged or released; if he is fit one of these options must be taken. If he remains unfit further detention may be authorised, but consideration should be given to whether there is sufficient evidence to charge with an offence.

— Where there is at the time insufficient evidence upon which to charge, and the custody officer has authorised detention on the basis that there are reasonable grounds to believe that his detention without charge is necessary to secure or preserve evidence relating to an offence for which he is under arrest or to obtain such evidence, the review officer may authorise further detention on the same basis.

4.8 After charge the review officer must release the person, with or without bail unless:
— his name and address cannot be ascertained, or there are reasonable grounds to doubt the name and address given; or
— there are reasonable grounds to believe that detention is necessary for his own protection, or to prevent him causing physical injury to any person or loss of or damage to property; or
— there are reasonable grounds to believe that the person will fail to answer bail, or that his detention is necessary to prevent him interfering with the administration of justice or with police investigations; or
— in the case of a juvenile, detention is necessary in his own interests.

4.9 The reviews of detention after charge are completed by the custody officer. Prior to charge the review is carried out by an officer not below the rank of inspector who is not directly involved in the investigation. Section 40 of the Police and Criminal Evidence Act 1984 details the time periods for reviews to be conducted as being:
— the first review must be not less than six hours after detention was authorised
— the second review must not be later than nine hours after the first review
— subsequent reviews must be at intervals not greater than nine hours.

4.10 The review of a person's custody must be recorded on the custody record by the reviewing officer. This should be done in the presence of the detained person unless he is incapable of understanding, or violent or likely to become violent. The detained person (unless he is asleep) or any solicitor representing him must be able to make any representations about the review. If any comments or representations are made they should be recorded on the custody record. Before conducting a review the review officer should remind the detained person of his right to free legal advice. If the detained person is likely to be asleep when the review is due, the reviewing officer should bring forward the review to allow any representations to be made without having to wake up the detained person. There is discretion for the review officer to have representations from a person other than the detained person and his solicitor, such persons who would have an interest in the detained person's welfare. If the detained person is unfit, by reason of behaviour or condition, the review officer may refuse to hear oral representations for the person. If a review is delayed the reasons for the delay must be recorded on the person's custody record.

4.11 A review may be postponed:
a) if, having regard to all the circumstances prevailing at the latest time for the review in question, it is not practicable to carry out the review at that time
b) without prejudice to the generality of (a) above
    i) if at that time the person in detention is being questioned by a police officer and the review officer is satisfied that an interruption of the questioning for the

purpose of carrying out the review would prejudice the investigation in connection with which he is being questioned; or

ii) if at that time no review officer is readily available.

The reason for any postponement must be recorded on the person's custody record. Such a postponement does not affect the later reviews if any are required.

Authority for Continued or Further Detention
Police and Criminal Evidence Act 1984, Sections 41–43

4.12 The normal maximum period for which a person may be kept in police detention without being charged is 24 hours. However, detention without charge may be continued upon the authority of a superintendent or above, then further extended under the authority of a warrant granted by magistrates. (The phrases 'continued detention' and 'extended detention' are used in the Act, to distinguish the two phases of further detention.)

A police officer of the rank of superintendent or above who is responsible for the police station at which the person is detained may authorise the person to kept in police detention for a period of up to 36 hours from the relevant time, if she has reasonable grounds for believing:

a) that detention of that person without charge is necessary to secure or preserve evidence relating to an offence for which he is under arrest, or to obtain such evidence by questioning him; and

b) an offence for which he is under arrest is a serious arrestable offence; and

c) the investigation is being conducted diligently and expeditiously.

Explanation
Superintendent, etc: The officer who gives the authorisation must be of the rank of superintendent or above, but not just any superintendent. If officers from the Drug Squad, for example, arrest a person for serious drug trafficking offences and take him to a designated police station, it will an officer responsible for that station, not the superintendent from the Drug Squad, who may authorise continued detention.

Grounds for continuance: The matters at (a) which must be satisfied are the same grounds upon which a custody officer may authorise the initial detention of a person who has been arrested for an offence. In effect, this provision is saying that the original reasons for detaining the person still exist, i.e. the search for evidence is continuing.

The offence, or at least one of the offences for which the person is detained is a serious arrestable offence. The last point on which the authorising officer must be satisfied is that time has not been wasted during the investigation. It is no good the officers in the case going off to play golf for half a day, then seeking continued detention because enquiries are not complete.

Up to 36 hours: Continued detention may be for a period of up to 12 hours in addition to the original 24 hours. If detention is authorised for 28 hours, i.e. an extra four hours, in the expectation that the detained person will be charged within that period, but enquiries take longer than anticipated, an additional authorisation may be given, up to a total of 36 hours, so long as the grounds for continuing the detention are still satisfied. This provision does not authorise a delay in charging a person once there is sufficient evidence do so (*R v Samuel* (1988)).

When to decide: A decision to continue detention must be made after the second review of detention, but before the 24 hour period has expired. The second review should normally take place no later than 15 hours after detention is authorised. To decide at an earlier stage to continue detention beyond 24 hours may indicate that proper consideration is not being given, it being far too early to decide that further detention will be necessary. It is no good waiting until the 24 hours is up, because any time over the 24 hours before authorisation is given, will amount to unlawful detention.

Representations: Before reaching a decision to continue detention, the officer concerned must give the detained person, his solicitor and any appropriate adult an opportunity to make representations about the matter. The opportunity for representations is mandatory, and failure to allow same may result in the courts refusing an application for further detention (*Police v Mudd* (1968)).

Additionally, the officer has a discretion to allow any other person with an interest in the detained person's welfare to make representations.

Tell the detained person: The officer who authorises continued detention must inform the person concerned of the grounds for his continued detention. She must also record those grounds on the custody record.

Magistrates' Warrants of Extended Detention

4.13 Police may apply to a magistrates' court for a warrant of extended detention without charge beyond 36 hours. Evidence must be given on oath, a copy of the application being given to the detained person beforehand. The hearing shall be in the presence of the detained person. The court may issue a warrant on being satisfied that the same grounds exist, as apply to an authorisation of a superintendent or above for continued detention *(see preceding paragraph)*. Magistrates may hear an application up to six hours after the expiry of the initial 36 hour period of detention, in exceptional circumstances. However, if the court believes that the application could have been made within the 36 hour period, it may dismiss the application. The time which counts in this regard is the time of the hearing, not the time at which the police first contacted the magistrates' clerk to make the arrangements (*Sedgefield Justices, ex parte Milne v R* (1987)).

4.14 The magistrates may grant an extension for up to thirty-six additional hours, or any lesser period they feel suitable (Section 43 sub Sections (10)(11) and (12)). They may dismiss the application and release immediately the detainee. An information for the purpose of Section 43 must be on oath and in writing, it must state the nature of the offence, generally outline the evidence of arrest, what enquires have been completed and those still to be made, and outline the reason for the request for further detention. Where the application is refused the person must be released, on bail or unconditionally, unless time remains of the superintendent's authorisation. The fact that a court refuses to extend authority to detain over thirty six hours does not negate the authority of the superintendent up to that time.

4.15 When the detainee is to appear before the court he should be informed of the right to free legal advice. A solicitor acting for the detainee must be given appropriate time to prepare for the application under Section 43, to consult his client, to examine the custody record and make such enquires as are required.

4.16 The police can apply to the magistrates for one or more warrants of extended detention subject of a total limit of ninety-six hours (Section 44). The conditions relating to the application remain the same as under Section 43 – evidence given under oath, copies of the information supplied to the detainee prior to the hearing, the right to free legal advice.

The Calculation of Relevant Periods of Detention

4.17 Because an arrested person should not normally be detained without charge for more than twenty-four hours, the need to ensure compliance requires explanation of how that period will be calculated. Section 41 of the Police and Criminal Evidence Act 1984 clarifies the subject.

Section 41 Police and Criminal Evidence Act 1984

(1) Subject to the following provisions of this Section and of Section 42 and 43 (PACE), a person shall not be kept in police detention for more than 24 hours without being charged.

(2) The time from which the period of detention of a person is to be calculated (in the PACE Act 1984 referred to as the 'relevant time'):
   a) in the case of a person to whom the Section applies, shall be:
      i)   the time at which a person arrives at the relevant police station, or
      ii) the time 24 hours after the time of the persons arrest, whichever is the earlier
   b) in the case of a person arrested outside England and Wales, shall be:
      i)   the time at which that person arrives at the first police station to which he is taken in the police area in England or Wales in which the offence for which he is arrested is being investigated; or
      ii) the time 24 hours after the time of that person's entry into England or Wales, whichever is the earlier.
   c) in the case of a person who:
      i)   attends voluntarily at a police station; or
      ii) accompanies a constable to a police station without being arrested, and is arrested at the station, the time of arrest;
   d) in any other case, except when subsection (5) below applies, shall be the time at which the arrested person arrives at the first police station to which he is taken after his arrest.

(3) Subsection 2(a) above applies to a person if:
   a) his arrest is sought in one police area in England and Wales
   b) he is arrested in another police area; and
   c) he is not questioned in the area in which he is arrested in order to obtain evidence in relation to an offence for which he is arrested.

And in sub-paragraph (i) of that paragraph 'the relevant police station' means the first police station to which he is taken in the police area in which his arrest is sought.

(4) Subsection (2) above shall have the effect in relation to a person arrested under Section 31 above as if every reference in it to his arrest or his being arrested were a reference to his arrest or his being arrested for the offence for which he was originally arrested.

(5) If:
   a) a person is in police detention in a police area in England and Wales (the first area); and
   b) his arrest for an offence is sought in some other police area in England and Wales (the second area); and
   c) he is taken to the second area for the purpose of investigating that offence, without being questioned about it in the first area in order to obtain evidence about it, the relevant time shall be:
      i)   the time 24 hours after he leaves the place where he is detained in the first area; or

ii) the time at which he arrives at the first police station to which he is taken in the second area;

whichever is the earlier.

(6) When a person who is in police detention is removed to hospital because he is in need of medical treatment, any time during which he is being questioned in hospital or on the way there or back by a police officer for the purpose of obtaining evidence relating to the offence shall be included in any period which falls to be calculated for the purposes of this part of the Act, but any other time while he is in hospital, or on his way there or back shall not be so included.

(7) Subject to subsection (8) below, a person who at the expiry of 24 hours after the relevant time is in police detention and has not been charged shall be released at that time, either on bail or without bail.

(8) Subsection (7) above does not apply to a person whose detention for more than 24 hours after the relevant time has been authorised or is otherwise permitted in accordance with Section 42 or 43 of the Act.

(9) A person released under subsection (7) above shall not be re-arrested without a warrant for the offence for which he was previously arrested unless new evidence justifying a further arrest has come to light since his release.

4.18 Although the legislation at first appears difficult to grasp, in its simplest form the rules regarding the starting of the detention clock mean that it starts:

1: at the time of arrest, if that arrest occurs at a police station.

2: at the time of arrival of the prisoner at the first police station in the area where the offence occurred, if the arrest was made in a different area.

3: not more than 24 hours after the arrest, (in the unlikely event of it taking longer than that to get the prisoner to a police station).

4: if the person is arrested outside England or Wales, on arrival at the first police station in the area of the offence, or 24 hours after the arrival of the prisoner in England or Wales, whichever is the earlier.

5: If a person is arrested in one force area and is wanted for an offence in another force area, (and is not questioned about the offence in the first force) 24 hours after leaving the force where first arrested, or upon arrival at the first police station in the second force area, which ever is the earlier.

4.19 Where the suspect is wanted in two force areas for different offences there will be effectively two relevant times. This does not however mean that where a person is arrested in one force that the same force can re-start the clock by arresting him for another offence at the end of the relevant period. Section 41 contains a safeguard to prevent the second arrest from restarting the clock, the relevant time for the second and subsequent arrests, if any, starts from the relevant time of the initial detention.

Detention After Charge

4.20 Section 46 details when a person must be brought before a court after he has been charged with an offence and kept in police detention, or in the case of a juvenile detained by the local authority. The broad principle is that the person should be brought before the magistrates 'as soon as practicable' (Section 46(2) PACE 1984), and in any event not later than the first sitting after he is charged with the offence. If there is no sitting of the court for the day when the detainee is charged, or the next day, the custody officer must inform the clerk of the court so that he may arrange a special sitting. If the person charged is to be brought before a magistrate in another area he must be taken to that area as soon as possible and brought before the next available court. Sundays, Good Friday and Christmas Day do not count as days for the calculation of the period before bringing a detainee before court. A person detained in hospital need not be brought to court until he is well enough (Section 46(9) PACE 1984).

4.21 There is a provision whereby magistrates may remand a person into police custody for a period of up to three days, to allow questioning. This provision is used, for example, when a person has been charged with an offence and has indicated that he has committed a number of other offences. During the three day period, he may be asked questions about these other offences (in police parlance this period may be referred to as a 'three day lie down').

(8) Where a person is committed to detention at a police station under subsection (7):
  a) he shall not be kept in such detention unless there is a need for him to be so detained for the purposes of enquires into other offences;
  b) if kept in such detention, he shall be brought back before the magistrate's court which committed him as soon as that need ceases
  c) he shall be treated as a person in police detention to whom the duties under Section 39 of the Police and Criminal Evidence Act 1984 (responsibilities in relation to persons detained) relate
  d) his detention shall be subject to periodic review at the times set out in Section 40 of that Act (review of police detention).

4.22 Police forces are required to keep statistical information relating to the detention of persons. This information must also be published in the annual report of the chief officer for each policing area. The information is:
  a) the numbers of persons kept in custody for more than twenty four hours who are later released without charge
  b) the number of applications for warrants of further detention, and the result of those applications; and
  c) in relation to each warrant of further detention:
      i)   the period of detention authorised by it
      ii) the period the person spent in police detention on its authority; and
      iii) where he was charged or released without charge.

The purpose of this requirement is to ensure that some figures relating the effectiveness of the use of further detention, or its abuse, would be available. The Home Office has issued research figures (Detention at the Police Station under the Police and Criminal Evidence Act 1984 (by David Brown) (Home Office Research Study No. 104)) that show most detainees are only in custody under investigation at a police station for less than six hours.

POWERS TO STOP AND SEARCH

5.1 Apart from the special provisions relating to constables employed by the railway, docks and harbour boards (Section 6 Police and Criminal Evidence Act 1984 (special provisions for statutory undertakings)), and under the Aviation Act 1982 (Section 27(2) Aviation Act 1982) police officers are required to have a reasonable suspicion that a vehicle is carrying stolen or prohibited goods before they can excercise stop and search powers under the Police and Criminal Evidence Act 1984.

5.2 Code 'A' of the Police and Criminal Evidence Act 1984 covering stop and search applies to searches conducted under:

a) The Police and Criminal Evidence Act 1984, where the constable is required to have reasonable grounds for suspicion that articles unlawfully obtained or possessed are being carried; and

b) authorised under Section 60 of the Public Order and Criminal Justice Act 1994 based upon a reasonable belief that incidents involving serious violence may take place within a locality; and

c) authorised under Section 13A of the Prevention of Terrorism (Temporary Provisions) Act 1989 as amended by the Criminal Justice and Public Order Act 1994; and

d) exercised under paragraph 4(2) of Schedule 5 to the Prevention of Terrorism (Temporary Provisions) Act 1989.

5.3 Code A of the Codes of Practice requires that there must be some objective basis for 'reasonable suspicion', that it can never be supported on personal factors alone, unless there is supporting intelligence or information. For example, such factors as a person's age, colour or manner of dress cannot be used singly or in combination as a sole basis on which to search a person. However, if for example, there is reliable information that members of a gang regularly carry offensive weapons, and that membership of that gang is signified by a particular item of clothing, tattoo or other distinguishing characteristic, a search may be justified on the basis of that item of clothing or other factor.

5.4 Authorisation under Section 13A of the Prevention of Terrorism Act (Temporary Provisions) Act 1989 to stop and search may be given where it appears expedient to do so in order to prevent acts of terrorism. It must be given by an assistant chief constable (or equivalent) in writing, specifying where the powers may be exercised, the period over which they will remain in effect (which should not exceed twenty eight days). These powers may be extended by periods of up to twenty-eight days.

5.5 Section 60 of the Criminal Justice and Public Order Act 1994 is covered later in the chapter.

5.6 In the case of a search requiring reasonable suspicion, the person may be detained in order to carry out the search, but he may not be detained in order to obtain grounds for a search. Before carrying out a search the officer may question the person about his behaviour, or presence under those circumstances which give rise to suspicion; there may be a satisfactory explanation which will negate the need to search. If the answers given during questioning negate the grounds for reasonable suspicion there is no longer a power to stop or search.

5.7 Before a search of a person or vehicle is conducted the officer must take reasonable steps to inform the driver, or person of:

i) his name (except in terrorism cases, in which case he must provide his warrant or other roll number) and the name of the police station to which he is attached

ii) the object of the search; and

iii) the grounds for undertaking it.

If not in uniform the officer must show his warrant card, in terrorism cases he need not reveal his name. Searches under Section 13A of the Prevention of Terrorism (Temporary Provisions) Act 1989 and Section 60 Criminal Justice and Public Order Act 1994 may only lawfully be carried out by officers in uniform.

Records Required

5.8 Unless it is impractical to make a record of a search, the officer must make a record and inform the owner or person in charge of the vehicle searched, or person searched that he is entitled to a copy of the search record. If the person wishes a copy and is not given one on the spot he must be told which police station to apply to. If the person appears not to understand, or there is any doubt about his ability to understand English, the officer must take reasonable steps to explain the reasons for the search, the grounds, and the details required to be given to the person.

5.9 Every reasonable effort must be made to reduce embarrassment to the person being searched, his co-operation should be sought in every case. A forcible search may only be made if the person resists, or is unwilling to co-operate. This should be as a last resort only. The search must be conducted at or nearby the place where the person or vehicle was first detained.

5.10 The extent of any search should only be to discover the articles sought, the thoroughness and extent will depend upon what is expected to be found. If the suspicion extends to an article slipped into one pocket, and the opportunity to move it to another pocket has not arisen then the search should be confined to that pocket. If the search is for a small article such as drugs a more extensive search may be required. Searches not requiring reasonable suspicion may be to the extent required to find what is being searched for. Searches in public must be restricted to superficial examination of outer clothing. There is no power to require a person to remove any clothing in public other than an outer coat, jacket or gloves. Where the removal of other clothing is justified, this should be carried on out of public view, e.g., in a nearby police van or at a station if nearby. Any search involving more than the removal of outer clothing must be carried out by an officer of the same sex as the person detained.

5.11 A record of search must be made and the following details are required even if the person does not wish to identify himself or give his date of birth:

1: The name of the person searched, or if he withholds it a description of him.
2: A note of the person's ethnic origin.
3: When a vehicle is searched a description of it including the registration number.
4: The object of the search.
5: The grounds for making it.
6: The date and time it was made.
7: The place where it was made.
8: Its results.
9: A note of any injury or damage to property resulting from it.
10: The identity of the officer making it (except in terrorism cases where warrant or roll number and station of operation will suffice).

A record is required for each person and each vehicle searched. If a person and his vehicle are searched and the object of the search and grounds are the same only one record is required. The record must be briefly informative, giving the reason for the reasonable suspicion, whether by reference to his behaviour or other circumstances, or by stating the authority for the search if carried out under a provision not requiring reasonable suspicion.

5.12 Where a search is carried out of an unattended motor vehicle, or anything in or on it, the officer conducting the search must leave a notice on or in it recording the fact that it has been searched. Where the vehicle has not been opened but something on the vehicle has been searched the notice may be left on the vehicle. The notice must include the name of the police station the police officer conducting the search is from, where a copy of the search record can be obtained and the details of where any claim for compensation should be directed.

5.13 If a search is conducted by more than one officer the names of all the officers involved must be recorded on the record. If a vehicle has no registration number the search record should reflect this. For the purposes of (Code 'A') a written statement means a record that the person or vehicle was stopped and of the facts required to be kept.

SPECIAL POWERS FOR POLICE

6.1 As a result of various instances of civil disorder involving offensive weapons, and the continued potential for the use of such weapons, the Criminal Justice And Public Order Act 1994 gave additional powers to police to designate areas for the purpose of searching for such weapons (Section 60 Criminal Justice and Public Order Act 1994). A police officer of or above the rank of inspector may authorise police officers in uniform to:

a) stop any pedestrian and search him or anything carried by him for offensive weapons or dangerous instruments

b) stop any vehicle and search the vehicle, its driver and any passenger, for offensive weapon or dangerous instrument.

The authorisation may be given where the inspector (or officer of higher rank):

i) reasonably believes that incidents involving serious violence may take place in any locality in the officer's area, and

ii) it is expedient to do so to prevent their occurrence.

6.2 These provisions are detailed in chapter 16, paragraph 10.

THE QUESTIONING AND TREATMENT OF DETAINED PERSONS

7.1 The treatment and questioning of persons by police officers is regulated the Police and Criminal Evidence Act 1984. Section 53 of that Act abolished all common law and statutory powers to search persons at police station, including intimate searches. The only exceptions to this are powers in prevention of terrorism legislation. The powers to search arrested persons are contained in Sections 54 and 55 of the Act.

Section 54 Police and Criminal Evidence Act 1984

(1) The custody officer at a police station shall ascertain and record or cause to be recorded everything which a person has with him when he is:

a) brought to the station having been arrested elsewhere or after being committed to custody by an order or sentence of the court; or

b) arrested at the station and detained there under Section 47(5) (person attending on bail subject of Section 47(3) when there is need to preserve and secure evidence possibly by questioning).

(2) In the case of an arrested person the record shall be made as part of his custody record.

(3) Subject to (4) below, a custody officer may seize and retain any such thing or cause any such thing to be seized and retained.

(4) Clothes and personal effects may only be seized if the custody officer:
  a) believes that the person from whom they are seized may use them:
    i)   to cause physical injury to himself or any other person
    ii) to damage property
    iii) to interfere with evidence; or
    iv) to assist him to escape; or
  b) has reasonable grounds for believing that they may be evidence relating to an offence.

(5) Where anything is seized, the person from whom it is seized shall be told the reason for the seizure unless he is:
  a) violent or likely to become violent; or
  b) incapable of understanding what is said to him.

(6) Subject to subsection (7) below, a person may be searched if the custody officer considers it necessary to enable him to carry out his duty under subsection (1) above and to the extent that the custody officer thinks necessary for that purpose.

(6A)   A person who is in custody at a police station or who is in police detention otherwise than at a police station may at any time be searched in order to ascertain whether he has with him anything which he could use for any of the purposes specified in subsection (4)(a) above.

(6B)   Subject to subsection (C) below, a constable may seize and retain or cause to be seized or retained, anything found in such a search.

(6C)   A constable may only seize clothes and personal effects in the circumstances specified in (4) above.

Explanation

7.2 A search under Section 54 must be carried out by a constable, who shall be of the same sex as the person being searched. Although a search must be carried out at an early stage, in order that the custody officer may fulfil the requirement to make a record of the arrested person's property, the Section allows for a detained person to be searched at any time. There may be reason to believe, for example, that something has been missed on an earlier search, or that the person has acquired an article since coming into the police station. There is no limit on the timing or number of searches.

A strip search, one which involves the removal of items of clothing other than outer clothing, may be authorised by the custody officer, and shall be carried out in accordance with the provisions of Annex A to Code C.

Where it is clear that a person will be detained for only a short period, and is not to be placed in a cell, the custody officer may decide not to search him (Codes of Practice, Code C, Notes for Guidance, note 4A).

Intimate Searches

7.3 An intimate search is a search which consists of a physical examination of a person's body orifices, other than the mouth. Such a search is subject to the provisions of Section 55 of PACE, and to Annex A to Code C of the Codes of Practice.

Section 55 Police and Criminal Evidence Act 1984

(1) Subject to the following provisions of this Section if an officer of the rank of at least superintendent has reasonable grounds for believing:

   a) that a person who has been arrested and is in police detention, may have concealed on him any thing which:

     i) he could use to cause physical injury to himself or others; and

     ii) he might so use while he is in police detention or in custody of a court; or

   b) that such a person:

     i) may have a Class A drug concealed on him; and

     ii) was in possession of it with the appropriate criminal intent, before his arrest,

   he may authorise an intimate search of that person.

7.4 An intimate search for anything cannot be authorised unless the authorising officer has reasonable grounds for believing that without an intimate search it would not be found (subsection (2)). The authorisation for such a search may be given orally but must be put in writing as soon as practicable. This would normally be an endorsement of the custody record relating to the person. An intimate search which is authorised only for the purpose of finding drugs must be done by a 'suitably qualified person' (registered medical practitioner, or registered nurse). In any other case, the search should be by a qualified person, except where an officer of at least the rank of superintendent considers that this is not practicable. In such cases the search must be carried out by a constable (subsections (4), (5) and (6)) who must be of the same sex as the arrested person. Intimate searches can only be done at a police station, a hospital, a registered medical practitioner's premises or some other place used for medical purposes. Intimate searches which are drug only searches may not be conducted at a police station (subsection (9)). The custody record must be endorsed with details of the parts of the body searched, and why they were searched. The custody officer may seize and retain anything found or authorise it to be seized and retained if he believes it will be used to cause physical injury, to the suspect, or any other person, to damage property, interfere with evidence, or assist in escape, or he has reasonable grounds for believing it to be evidence relating to an offence. The detained person must be informed of the retention of such an item unless he is violent or likely to become violent or is incapable of understanding what is said to him.

7.5 The number of intimate searches conducted in an area and details of all such intimate searches must be recorded in the annual report of the Chief Officer for an area. This must include details of searches conducted other than by a qualified person.

The Right to Have Someone Informed when Arrested
Police and Criminal Evidence Act 1884, Section 56

7.6 When a person has been arrested and is being held in custody at a police station or other premises, she shall be entitled, if she so requests, to have someone informed – a friend, relative, or other person who is known to her or who is likely to take an interest in her welfare – that she has been arrested and is being detained there. This must be done as soon as is practicable, unless delay is permitted in the terms of the following provisions. Delay is permitted only:

- in the case of a person who is in police detention for a serious arrestable offence; and
- if an officer of the rank of at least superintendent authorises it.

Delay may be authorised when the officer concerned has reasonable grounds for believing that telling the named person of the arrest:
- will lead to interference with or harm to evidence connected with a serious arrestable offence or interference with or physical injury to other persons; or
- will lead to the alerting of other persons suspected of having committed a serious arrestable offence but not yet arrested for it; or
- will hinder the recovery of property obtained as the result of a serious arrestable offence;
- (where the serious arrestable offence in question is a drug trafficking offence, and there is reason to believe that the detained person has benefitted from drug trafficking) will lead to the recovery of the value of that person's proceeds of drug trafficking being hindered;
- (where the offence is one in respect of which confiscation orders may be made, and there is reason to believe that the detained person has benefitted from the offence) will lead to the recovery of the value of the property or pecuniary advantage obtained by that person from or in connection with the offence, being hindered.

7.7 Matters relating to a delay in notification.

The following provisions apply to a delay in notification of a named person:
- delay in notification may not last for more than 36 hours
- authorisation may be given orally or in writing, but if given orally, must be confirmed in writing as soon as is practicable
- the detained person must be told the reason for the delay, as soon as is practicable
- the reason shall be noted on her custody record, as soon as is practicable
- once the reason for the delay ceases to subsist, there may be no further delay permitted.

Explanation

In custody: This term includes 'detained' under prevention of terrorism legislation.

At a police station or other premises: A person may be arrested and taken to hospital for treatment; he will then be in 'other premises', and the entitlement will still apply. When a detained person is moved from one police station to another, or to other premises, the right will be exercisable on each occasion.

Known... or likely to take an interest: The detained person is not permitted to select just anyone to be informed that he has been arrested, otherwise the prime minister, members of the Royal Family, and other well known people would be inundated with calls from police stations. The right to have a person informed is limited to friends, relatives or other persons known to the detained person. In addition, someone who does not necessarily know him, but who for whatever reason, is likely to take an interest in his welfare, may be nominated.

Grounds for delay: The person must be detained for a serious arrestable offence, as defined in Section 116 of the Police and Criminal Evidence Act 1984. Note that the various grounds relate to 'a serious arrestable offence' not necessarily the same offence as that for which the person is detained. So, for example, if Peter is detained for a serious crime and it is believed that Paul has committed a related serious arrestable offence, a belief that notifying someone known to Peter and to Paul will lead to Paul disposing of the proceeds of his crime, or disposing of evidence relating to it, will be a valid ground for delay.

Drug trafficking/confiscation order offence: The ground relating to specifically to drug trafficking offences is an additional ground. The drug trafficking offence must be a serious arrestable offence before delay may be authorised, and any of the grounds for delay applicable to all serious arrestable offences, may apply. Likewise, where the offence is one in respect of which a confiscation order may be made, the specific ground applicable to these offences, together with the grounds relating to serious arrestable offences generally, may give ground for delay.

Limit on delay: Delay may be for not more than 36 hours. Since police may not hold a person beyond 36 hours without obtaining a warrant to do so from magistrates, this limit is of limited practical significance.

7.8 Where the intimation of arrest is delayed or denied the reasons must be recorded on the person's custody record, and the detained person informed. Delay in notification must be reviewed when the suspect is moved from one police station or premises to another. These provisions apply equally to persons who have been arrested under the provisions of prevention of terrorism legislation, and arrest includes detention under such provisions.

Additional Rights of Children and Young Persons
Section 57 Police and Criminal Evidence Act 1984

7.9 The rights of an arrested suspect to have someone informed of the arrest require that with children or young persons specific information must be given to those responsible for the detained person. Where a child or young person is in police detention, the police must make such enquires as are practical to ascertain the identity of the person responsible for the detained person's welfare. The responsible person must be informed as soon as practicable, unless such intimation is impractical in itself, of the detention, the reason for such detention, and where the detention is taking place. The responsible person is the parent, guardian, or any other person who has for the time being assumed responsibility for that child or young person.

Access to Legal Advice
7.10 The general rule is that every person arrested has the right to legal advice. This provision is qualified by the right of the police to delay access to legal advice.

Section 58 Police and Criminal Evidence Act 1984

(1) A person arrested and held in custody in a police station or other premises shall be entitled, if he requests, to consult a solicitor privately at any time.

(2) Subject to subsection (3) below, a request under subsection (1) above and the time at which it was made shall be recorded in the person's custody record.

(3) Such a request need not be recorded in the custody record of a person who makes it at a time while he is in court after being charged with an offence.

(4) If a person makes such a request, he must be permitted to consult with a solicitor as soon as is practicable except where the delay is permitted by this Section.

(5) In any case he must be permitted to consult with a solicitor within 36 hours from the relevant time as defined under Section 41(2).

(6) Delay in compliance with a request is only permitted:
   a) in the case of a person in police detention for a serious arrestable offence; and

b) if an officer of at least the rank of superintendent authorises it.

(7) An officer may give an authorisation under subsection (6) above orally or in writing, but if he gives it orally, he shall confirm it in writing as soon as practicable.

(8) Subject to subsection (8A) below, an officer may only authorise delay where he has reasonable grounds for believing that the excercise of the right conferred by subsection (1) above at the time when the person in police detention desires to exercise it:
  a) will lead to interference with or harm to evidence connected with a serious arrestable offence or interference with or physical injury to other persons; or
  b) will lead to the alerting of other persons suspected of having committed such an offence but not yet arrested for it; or
  c) will hinder the recovery of any property obtained as a result of such an offence.

(8A) An officer may also authorise delay where the serious arrestable offence is a drug trafficking offence or an offence to which Part VI of the Criminal Justice Act 1988 applies and the officer has reasonable grounds for believing:
  a) where the offence is a drug trafficking offence, that the detained person has benefited from drug trafficking and that the recovery of the value of that persons proceeds of drug trafficking will be hindered by the exercise of the right conferred in subsection (1) above; and
  b) where the offence is one to which Part VI of the Criminal Justice Act 1988 applies, that the detained person has benefited from the offence and the recovery of the value of the property obtained by that person from or in connection with the offence or, of the pecuniary advantage derived by him from or in connection with it will be hindered by the excercise of the right conferred by subsection (1) above.

(9) If delay is authorised:
  a) the detained person shall be told the reasons for it; and
  b) the reasons shall be noted on the custody record.

(10) The duties imposed under subsection (9) above shall be performed as soon as practicable.

(11) There may be no further delay in permitting the excercise of the right conferred by subsection (1) above once the reason for authorising delay ceases to subsist.

7.11 Section 58 also covers the application of denying of access to legal advice to persons detained for terrorism offences under the prevention of terrorism legislation. For this purpose the authority must be from an officer of at least the rank of commander or assistant chief constable. Subsection (8) of Section 58 is extended to add the provisions:
  d) will lead to interference with the gathering of information about the commission, preparation, or instigation of acts of terrorism; or
  e) by alerting any person, will make it more difficult:
    i) to prevent an act of terrorism; or
    ii) to secure the apprehension, prosecution or conviction of any person in connection with the commission, preparation or instigation of an act of terrorism.

Interviews with Detained Persons

7.12 Interviews with persons who are detained, in relation to offences of which they are suspected, are governed by Code C of the Codes of Practice.

7.13 If a police officer wishes to interview a person in custody, or conduct any enquires which require that person to be present, the custody officer will be responsible for deciding whether to hand the detained person over for such an interview. During the time that the person is in custody at a designated police station it is the custody officer who authorises the normal movements of the detained person, and he will hand custody to the interviewing/investigating officers for the duration of their enquires. Upon completion of the interview/investigation the custody officer will take back custody. The investigating officers have a duty to state if the Codes of Practice have been complied with or not, and any reason for the breach of the codes.

7.14 In any twenty-four hour period the detainee must be given a rest period of at least eight hours, which must not be interrupted by questioning, travel or any disruption by the investigating officers. The rest period must not be delayed or interrupted, except at the request of the person, his appropriate adult or legal representative, unless there are reasonable grounds for believing that not to do so would:

    i)   involve a risk of harm to people, or serious loss of, or damage to property; or

    ii) delay unnecessarily the person's release from custody; or

    iii) otherwise prejudice the outcome of the investigation.

If a person voluntarily attends the police station and is later arrested, the period is calculated from the time of arrest.

7.15 Detained people may not be given intoxicating liquor unless under medical supervision, and people who are unfit through drink or drugs to the extent that they will not fully comprehend the significance of the questions being put to them must not be questioned. If there is any doubt the advice of a police surgeon should be sought.

7.16 The rooms used for interviews should be well lit, ventilated and adequately heated. People being questioned must not be required to stand. Breaks from interviews should be taken at recognised meal times. Short breaks should be taken at intervals of approximately two hours for refreshments, subject to the same provisions set out at **7.14** (i) (ii) (iii) *(above)*.

7.17 Before the commencement of any interview, each officer present must identify himself by name, rank and number to the person being interviewed. The only exception to this is where a person is being interviewed in connection with terrorism, in which case the officer should identify himself by warrant number and rank, rather than by name.

The Right to Legal Advice

7.18 All persons in detention have the right to free and independent legal advice. Upon arrival at a designated police station under arrest the custody officer must inform the detained person of his rights, and that these are continuing rights throughout the period of detention. The rights are:

(1) The right to have someone informed of his arrest.

(2) The right to consult privately with a solicitor and that the fact the legal advice is free of charge.

(3) The right to consult a copy of the codes of detention.

In addition the custody officer must serve a written notice on the detainee explaining these three rights and the right to a copy of the custody record.

7.19 A poster explaining the right to free legal advice must be prominently displayed in every charging area of a police station. Police officers should not do anything which dissuades a person from seeking legal advice. Unless otherwise authorised (Annex B Code C) the custody officer must act without delay to secure the provision of legal advice for a detainee. If a person declines the legal advice he must be informed that he can communicate with a legal advisor by phone. If the person continues to waive his right to free legal advice the custody officer must ask the reasons for this and record the reason on the custody record. Once a person makes it clear he neither wishes to speak to a solicitor in person nor via telephone he need not be reminded of this right. The right remains should he change his mind.

7.20 A person who has requested legal advice must not be interviewed, or any interview being conducted cannot continue unless:
  a) annex B to Code C of the Codes of Practice applies; or,
  b) an officer of the rank of superintendent or above has reasonable grounds for
      believing that:
      i)   delay will cause an immediate risk of harm to persons or serious loss of, or
           damage to, property; or
      ii) where a solicitor, including a duty solicitor, has been contacted and has agreed
           to attend, awaiting his arrival would cause unreasonable delay to the process of
           the investigation; or
  c) the solicitor nominated by the person, or selected by him from a list:
      i)   cannot be contacted; or
      ii) has previously indicated that he does not wish to be contacted; or
      iii) having been contacted, declines to attend
      and the person has been advised of the duty solicitor scheme but has declined to ask
      for the duty solicitor, or the duty solicitor is unavailable.

      If (c) then applies an officer of the rank of inspector or above has given agreement
      for the interview to proceed. This must be recorded on the custody record. In taking
      such a decision the inspector must consider that the detainee must have been given at
      least two alternative solicitors before authorising any interview to continue *(see note
      6B Code C Codes of Practice).*

  d) the person who wanted legal advice changes his mind.

In these circumstances, the reasons for changing his mind must be recorded on the custody record and an officer of the rank of inspector or above must authorise the continuation of the interview. This authorisation may be given by telephone. Confirmation of this change of mind must be given including the authorising officer's name at the beginning of any interview or at the point of re-commencement of interview.

7.21 Where a person has been given access to free legal advice, and the solicitor is present he shall be entitled to be present at any interview. A solicitor may only be required to leave an interview if an investigating officer is unable to properly put questions to the suspect. If the investigating officer considers that a solicitor is acting in such a way he should stop the interview, he must then inform an officer not below the rank of superintendent of the circumstances leading up to the stopping of the interview with the suspect. If a superintendent is not readily available, an officer not below the rank of inspector who is not connected with the investigation may deal with the matter. After speaking with the solicitor this officer will decide whether the interview can continue with that solicitor present. If he decides it should not, the suspect should be given opportunity to consult with another solicitor before the interview continues, and that solicitor then has the right to be present during any interview with the suspect.

7.22 The removal of a solicitor from an interview is a very serious step and the officer authorising this must consider whether the matter should be reported to the Law Society. Where the solicitor concerned is the duty solicitor the report must also be sent to the Legal Aid Board. This said, it is important that the position of the solicitor is understood. He is present to protect and advance the legal rights of his client. On occasions this may require the solicitor to give advice which has the effect of his client avoiding giving evidence which strengthens the prosecution case. The solicitor may intervene to seek clarification or to challenge an improper question to his client or the manner in which a question is put, or to advise his client not to reply to particular questions, or if he wishes to give his client further legal advice. A solicitor can only be removed from an interview if his approach or conduct obstructs proper questions being put to the suspect or his response being recorded. Examples of unacceptable conduct include answering questions on a suspect's behalf or providing written replies for the suspect to quote. Any decision to exclude the solicitor from an interview will need to be explained and justified to the court which may eventually try the matter. For the purposes of the Police and Criminal Evidence Act 1984 the term solicitor means a solicitor who holds a current practising certificate, a trainee solicitor, a duty solicitor's representative or an accredited representative included on the register of representatives maintained by the Legal Aid Board. If a solicitor wishes to send a non-accredited or probationary representative to provide advice on his behalf, then that person shall be admitted to the police station for this purpose unless an officer of the rank of inspector or above considers that such a visit will hinder the investigation of crime and directs otherwise. Hindering the investigation of crime does not include giving proper legal advice to a detained person. If an inspector refuses access to a non-accredited or probationary representative or a decision is taken that the person should not remain in the interview, the inspector must forthwith inform the solicitor on whose behalf the representation was being made, and give him an opportunity to make alternative arrangements for his client. The detained person must also be informed and his custody record endorsed with the relevant facts.

Exclusion of Evidence Obtained During Interview

7.23 Under the provisions of the Police and Criminal Evidence Act 1984, the gathering of prosecution evidence from whatever source, is subject to strict rules. If these rules are broken, related evidence may be excluded by the court. Confessions obtained by interview with a suspect are subject to the conditions contained in Sections 76, 78 and 82(3) of the Act. (This topic is dealt with in greater detail in Chapter 7.)

7.24 A court has no discretion under the provisions of Section 76 – if a confession is obtained by oppression, or in circumstances likely to render it unreliable, it must be excluded from evidence. Section 76(2) puts the onus on the prosecution, to prove that a confession was obtained without oppression, and without anything being said or done which may be likely to render it unreliable. Questioning, by its very nature, duration or other attendant circumstances, or the very fact of being in custody, are all factors which may affect the reliability of a confession (*R v Prager* (1972)). The term 'oppression' is to be given its ordinary, dictionary meaning, 'The exercise of authority in a burdensome, harsh or wrongful manner; unjust or cruel treatment of inferiors, etc; the imposition of unreasonable or unjust burdens.' (*R v Fulling* (1987)). To mislead a suspect, or lie to him, may regarded as oppressive. (*R v Heron*

(1993)) In this case, Heron was charged with the murder of a seven year old girl, in circumstances which were highly emotive. During interviews, police officers repeatedly misrepresented facts about identifications, by stating that there were witnesses who had seen the defendant with the victim at crucial times.

To ask the same question a number of times, effectively refusing to accept a denial, will be considered oppressive. (*R v Paris, Abdullai and Miller* (1993)). Miller's admission, in particular, was excluded from evidence because he had confessed only after making more than 300 denials.

7.25 A question which arises is 'Should evidence be heard by the court before the defence raises objection to it?' In Crown Court, there is not too much of a problem because representations as to admissibility may be heard by the judge in the absence of the jury. In magistrates' court, the magistrates have to hear the evidence before they are able to decide whether to exclude it or not. If they decide that the evidence should be excluded, they then have to eliminate its prejudicial effect from their minds.

Confessions Made by Mentally Handicapped Persons

7.26 There is a need for caution when dealing with those who suffer from a mental handicap, who may be readily open to suggestion. This need was recognised in:

Section 77 The Police and Criminal Evidence Act 1984

(1) Without prejudice to the general duty of the court at a trial on indictment to direct a jury on any matter on which it appears to the court appropriate to do so, where at such a trial:
   a) the case against the accused depends wholly or substantially on a confession by him; and
   b) the court is satisfied:
      i) that he is mentally handicapped; and
      ii) the confession was not made in the presence of an independent person, the court shall warn the jury that there is special need for caution before convicting the accused in reliance on the confession, and shall explain that the need arises because of the circumstances mentioned in paragraph (a) and (b) above.

(2) In any case where at the summary trial of a person for an offence it appears to the court that a warning under subsection (1) above would be required if the trial were on indictment, the court shall treat the case as one in which there is a special need for caution before convicting the accused on his confession.

(3) In this Section:
   'independent person' does not include police officer or a person employed for, or engaged on police purposes
   'mentally handicapped' in relation to a person means that he is in a state of arrested or incomplete development of mind which includes significant impairment of intelligence and social functioning;

Interpreters

7.27 A person must not be interviewed in the absence of a person capable of acting as an interpreter if:
   a) he has difficulty in understanding English

b) the interviewing officer cannot speak the person's own language; and
c) the person wishes an interpreter to be present.

7.28 The interviewing officer must ensure that the interpreter makes a note of the interview at the time in the language of the person being interviewed for use in the event of his being called to give evidence, and certifies its accuracy. He must allow sufficient time for the interpreter to make a note of each question and answer after each has been put or interpreted. The person shall be given an opportunity to read the interview or have it read to him and sign it as correct or to indicate the respects in which he considers it inaccurate. If the interview is tape recorded the normal tape arrangements apply. In the case of a person making a statement in a language other than English:

a) the interpreter shall take down the statement in the language in which it is made
b) the person making the statement shall be invited to sign it; and
c) an official English translation shall be made in due course.

7.29 If the person appears to be deaf, or there is doubt about his hearing or speaking ability, he must not be interviewed in the absence of an interpreter unless he agrees in writing to be interviewed without one. An interpreter must also be called if the person being interviewed is a juvenile and it appears that the appropriate adult is deaf or there is doubt about his hearing or speaking ability, unless he agrees in writing that the interview can continue without one. The interviewing officer in such cases must ensure that the interpreter is given an opportunity to read the record of the interview and certify its accuracy in the event of being called to give evidence. A police officer must not be used to interpret for a person who cannot communicate with his solicitor, whether because of language, hearing or speech difficulties. A police officer may otherwise only interpret where the detained person and, if applicable, his appropriate adult consent in writing. If the interview is by way of tape this consent to have a police officer interpret may be also recorded on tape. In all cases where a person is detained the fact that an interpreter is available free of charge must be made clear to the detainee. If the matter does go to trial the interpreter used to facilitate the interview cannot be used in court other than as a witness for the prosecution to produce original notes from the interview and translations made of those notes. A second interpreter must be arranged to assist the court.

Chapter 5: Elements of Offences

1.1 A person is walking along a pavement in winter when he slips on a patch of ice and begins to fall. As he flails his arms in an effort to regain balance, the man's hand catches another person in the face, causing injury. Common sense tells us that the falling man has not committed a criminal assault, even though his actions have caused injury to another person. Assault, in common with most crimes, requires a mental element – the Latin term is Mens Rea – quite apart from any physical action.

1.2 There are very few offences for which mere thoughts could be said to constitute guilt, although some offences especially conspiracies require very little evidence of physical action. Generally for a person to be guilty of committing an offence, both the state of mind and the physical action will be required. The Latin phrase for this is 'actus non facit reus, nisi sit mens rea', (an act does not make a person legally guilty unless the mind is legally blameworthy).

1.3 We will consider the various states of mind required to make a person culpable, also the acts which must be carried out to complete offences. The mental element or 'mens rea' and the physical acts associated with committing crime or 'actus reus', will both normally be required if an offence is to be complete. However a small number of minor offences do not require guilty knowledge, such offences are called absolute offences. Absolute offences have strict liability for the consequences of actions undertaken.

MENS REA

2.1 When considering whether a person accused of an offence is guilty of it, the court must have regard to his 'mens rea', or 'guilty mind'. In some cases, the court has to be satisfied that the accused intended to carry out the criminal acts. In other cases, it may suffice if the prosecution prove that the accused acted recklessly without proper regard to the consequences of what he was doing. A court or jury shall not be bound to infer that an accused intended or foresaw the result of his actions just because this result was a likely outcome. Instead the court shall decide whether he did actually foresee or intend that result by taking account of the available evidence. For some offences to be complete, it is necessary to prove that the accused had knowledge of certain facts, before he may properly be declared guilty. For example, a motor vehicle owner will not be guilty of permitting another person to use the motor vehicle on a road with a defective tyre, unless he knew that the tyre was defective. The driver however, will be guilty of using the vehicle with a defective tyre, whether or not he was aware of the defect.

2.2 The mental element or mens rea required to constitute an offence of parking in the controlled area of a Pelican crossing will be considerably different from that which goes to make for an offence of assault with intent to injure. Generally when considering statutory offences the statute will detail the type of culpability required to prove guilt. Typically this 'state of mind' falls into three categories – intention, recklessness and knowledge. There are other phrases such as due care, and negligence; these are however covered by the main categories and to some extent are divisions within them. It is an over simplification to suggest that an accused's state of mind will fall distinctly into one or more of these categories. Some offences such as malicious wounding will require recklessness proven almost to the point of intention to satisfy the requirement of 'proof beyond reasonable doubt' for a finding of guilt. Criminal damage by contrast may require nothing more than that the accused just did not stop to think about what he or she was doing to establish the recklessness sufficient for a finding of guilt. There is no general requirement to show an evil mind or blatant knowledge of the wrongfulness of the act. Ignorance of the law or ignorance that society in general would view a person's conduct as unlawful is no defence.

Intention

3.1 The dictionary shows the ordinary meaning of this word to be 'done on purpose'. In law the same meaning is followed, a person may be regarded as having intended the natural consequences of his or her actions. In some offences the consequence of an act must occur before there can be any liability. For others such as attempts under the Criminal Attempts Act 1981, the act need not be complete for liability to occur. In the latter case the need to prove the intent to commit the offence is greater as you cannot infer from the result that it was intended. With an incomplete offence, such as an attempt, it may be that the accused's admission is the only available evidence of his intent. To prove the offence of murder, the prosecution have to show that the accused acted with intent unlawfully to kill or cause grievous bodily harm. Any lesser intent, and the offence is not made out. For theft, a person must intend permanently to deprive. A defence, that the accused intended only to 'borrow' the goods subject of the charge may well succeed. Proving a specific intention is often very difficult.

3.2 Intention is tested according to the results occurring and the accused's own stated desired result. There is some dispute as to whether an intention to kill as mens rea for murder is required or whether the fact that, although the accused did not intend to kill, a realisation that this was the highly probable outcome would be sufficient. In *Hyam v DPP* [1975] *(see keynote case)* the House of Lords did not decide what intention was but stated that a person has the mens rea for murder if, when he does an act which kills, he knows that it is highly probable that this act will cause death or grievous bodily harm. This case should be read in conjunction with *R v Hancock and Shankland* [1986] *(see keynote case)* which discusses intention to murder, and *R v Moloney* [1985] *(see keynote case)*.

Recklessness

4.1 Recklessness describes the state of mind of the accused at the time he carried out a particular action. For the accused to be culpable, the recklessness may relate to his decision, whether to act or not, or to the manner or circumstanes in which he carried out his action. When recklessness is sufficient to establish the mens rea of an offence, there is no requirement that the prosecution should prove that the accused intended a particular consequence of his action; instead, it may be shown that he realised that such a consequence was likely, but continued in his course of conduct, regardless of that risk.. This is called subjective recklessness and requires the conscious taking of an unjustified risk. The courts have also recognised another type of recklessness, this is often called Caldwell type recklessness. This arises where there was a risk which would be obvious to an ordinary person and the accused either:
- recognised that risk, but nevertheless went on to take it; or
- gave no thought to the possible consequences of his actions (*R v Caldwell* (1981)).

This is partly an objective and partly subjective test. The objective part is whether an ordinary person (the man on the Clapham omnibus) looking at the circumstances, would see an obvious risk. The subjective part is whether the accused foresee the risk, or turn a blind eye?

4.2 Subjective recklessness, that is, recklessness viewed from the accused's position, is required (as an alternative to actual intent) for offences such as rape, malicious wounding and common assault. The Caldwell type of recklessness, where the accused's actions are viewed in comparison to the standards of others, will suffice for offences such as criminal damage. However, to be guilty of malicious wounding or causing grievous bodily harm, the phrase 'maliciously', if not quite intent, is held to require a conscious decision on the part of the accused to do something regardless of the outcome, i.e. in a reckless manner. This type of recklessness is closer to actual intention.

Knowledge
5.1 Many offences either expressly or impliedly require knowledge of the facts by which an act, circumstance or omission, is criminal. It is sufficient that the accused knew the relevant facts, or was wilfully blind to them. A man driving someone else's car who failed to check that he was insured could be said to have knowledge, or was blind to the consequences of his action in circumstances that would make him liable.

Strict Liability or Absolute Offences
6.1 An offence of strict liability, otherwise known as an 'absolute offence' is one which requires no proof of mens rea, or guilty knowledge, on the part of the accused. Such offences are usually associated with participation in a potentially risky enterprise, where high standards are required in the interests of public safety. For example, if a lorry being driven on a road is found to have defective brakes, the owner of a lorry will be liable for using the vehicle with defective brakes, even if he had no knowledge that the brakes were faulty. A baker will be criminally liable if a dead mouse is found in one of her loaves, without the need to prove intent or recklessness on her part. It is not enough for the haulage contractor or the baker to say, 'I did not know'. It is their responsibility to ensure that safe standards are maintained in the conduct of their business.

ACTUS REUS

7.1 Lawyers sometimes find difficulty in separating the mental culpability of offenders and the nature of the act required to complete a crime. Some acts done in innocence can be sufficient to form part of crime. It would also be wrong to suggest that in every case an act is necessary. In some circumstances the failure to do something may render a person under a legal obligation to act liable to the sanction of the law. A good example of this is failure to provide specimens for drink driving procedures.

7.2 The existence of a state of affairs can also complete the offence, such as being found drunk in a public place. As being drunk when not in a public place is not an offence, the mere fact that a drunk wanders into a public place creates the offence. Other factors can also form part of the actus reus of an offence, such as time, place or consequence of actions. To be found guilty of murder someone must have died in consequence of action's taken by an accused. The definitions of offences set out the additional factors which form the actus reus.

7.3 It is an over simplification to state that everything contained in the definition of an offence other than that forming the 'mens rea' is actus reus. At times the mens rea and actus reus appear to be contained in the same part of a definition, an example being, appropriation for theft. Appropriation can be achieved by either a change of mind or a state of affairs. Lifting goods from a shop shelf can be the appropriation by physical act; merely making one's mind up to take the goods can provide the mental element within the same outward act. An example of this confusion can be that the person has removed goods from the shelf, put them into a shopping trolley and then whilst going about the store decides to steal the goods. In this way the appropriation contains both a physical act and a state of mind. The question for the courts is which is the appropriation. Practically, store detectives find it easier to wait until the person has left the store having failed to pay for goods, to ensure that the offence has physically shown itself to be complete. There are some interesting arguments about appropriation in the chapter covering theft.

Keynote Cases

8.1 Case One: Intention
Hyam v DPP [1974] 2 All ER 41

Problem

How can we decide what someone intended? How can we categorise what they intended?

Circumstances

Hyam was convicted of murder. She had poured petrol through the letter box of a house in Coventry belonging to a Mrs Booth. In the resultant fire the two daughters of Mrs Booth died, she and her son escaped via a window. Hyam stated that her intention was merely to frighten Mrs Booth, and that she did not intend to cause death or grievous bodily harm The problem for the court on appeal however was that Hyam's stated intention was not to kill. The court took the view that where death was a highly probable consequence of an act then sufficient mens rea for murder had been shown. This contradicts the early cases including *DPP v Smith* [1960] where there has to be clear intention to kill or cause grievous bodily harm to someone to convict of murder.

Decision

Where the result of a premeditated action is such that there is a high degree of probability of that result, then where death occurred there is sufficient mens rea for murder.

Comment

An act that is highly dangerous carried out regardless of the danger to third parties could then prove to hold sufficient mens rea for murder.

8.2 Case Two: Intention
R v Moloney [1985] 1 All ER 1025

Problem

Does drink have any relevance to intention? How can we judge what was intended?

Circumstances

Moloney and his stepfather had been drinking very heavily at a ruby wedding party. The rest of the party went to bed at about 1am. Moloney and his stepfather continued drinking until late into the night in an apparently friendly manner until about 4am when Moloney rang the police to say, 'I've just murdered my Father'. He stated that they had disagreed about who was the faster at loading and firing a shotgun. At the stepfather's request he had got down two shotguns, Moloney had loaded first and when the stepfather said 'I didn't think you'd got the guts but if you have, pull the trigger'. Moloney had stated, 'I didn't aim but just pulled the trigger and he was dead'. Plainly there was no intention to cause grievous bodily harm or death to the step father. The question was did Moloney have sufficient intent to kill. Moloney was convicted at first instance and appealed, the appeal was dismissed and at appeal to the House of Lords, Lord Bridge said:

> 'In law a man intends the consequences of his voluntary act,
>   a) when he desires it to happen, whether or not he foresees that it probably will happen, or
>   b) when he foresees that it will probably happen, whether he desires it or not.'

Decision
Intention is doing what you set out to do, even if you think it unlikely to happen, or knowing that it will probably happen whether you want it to or not.

Comment
Intention is the result of a voluntary act, when done because you wanted to, or when you realise what will probably happen as a result of that voluntary act, whether or not you want that result. When you hit a nail with a hammer it may be said that your intention is to knock the nail into a piece of wood. If you are aware that the nails are quite weak and that the wood is very hard, you may foresee that it is likely the nails will bend, rather than being driven into the wood. If you continue to hammer the nail and it bends, you may be seen as having the intention to cause it to bend, in order to fulfil your primary intention (to knock it into the wood).

8.3 Case Three: Intention and Recklessness
R v Hancock and Shankland [1986] 1 All ER 641

Problem
What is the difference between intent and recklessness?

Circumstances
Both defendants were miners on strike during the bitter and protracted dispute of the 1980's. The accused objected to a miner going to work whilst they were on strike. They waited on the route taken, on a bridge, and as the taxi taking the miner to work passed underneath, pushed a concrete block off the bridge onto the taxi. The block passed through the windscreen killing the driver. Both men were prepared to plead guilty to manslaughter but the Crown wished to pursue the charge of murder. The defence was that they intended to block the road not to kill or do grievous bodily harm. At Crown Court both were convicted, they appealed to the Court of Appeal and the conviction was quashed. The Crown then appealed to the House of Lords. The appeal was dismissed Lord Bridge clarifying his earlier speech from Moloney saying: 'But looking on their facts at the decided cases where a crime of specific intent was under consideration, including (Hyam v DPP) itself, they suggest to me that the probability of the consequences to have been foreseen must be little short of over-whelming before it will suffice

to establish the necessary intent'. This seems to clarify that intention requires a very high degree of proof, such as to make the finding of guilt a matter more of evidence on the facts than pre-determined application of a definition. Lord Bridge further clarified the point saying: 'foresight of consequences, as an element of bearing on the issue of the intention in murder, or indeed in any other crime of specific intent, belongs, not to the substantive law, but to the law of evidence'.

Decision
Intention must be viewed in the light of the known circumstances, according to the evidence of the particular case.

Comment
The courts appear to be giving a broader brush approach by stating the policy which should dictate in future cases what intention should be viewed as. In all cases where the courts are looking at intention they are viewing it on the basis only of the available evidence, they cannot know what the accused thought at the time of the offence unless he makes admissions.

8.4 Case Four: Recklessness and Self Induced Intoxication
R v Caldwell [1981] 1 All ER 961

Problem
Does self induced intoxication affect recklessness?

Circumstances
Caldwell had been doing work for the proprietor of a residential hotel. He considered that he had a grievance against the proprietor. One night Caldwell got very drunk and decided to revenge himself on the proprietor by setting fire to the hotel. At that time there were several guests in residence. Caldwell broke a window and succeeded in starting a fire. This was discovered and quickly put out before serious harm could occur. Caldwell was indicted for causing fire with intent to endanger life or being reckless as to whether life would be endangered. He pleaded not guilty to the offence on the grounds that he was so drunk he could not form the specific intent required. The second count on the indictment was that of criminal damage under Section 1(1) of the Criminal Damage Act of 1981, requiring proof of recklessness, for guilt to which Caldwell pleaded guilty. At Crown Court the recorder directed the jury that self induced intoxication was no defence, Caldwell was convicted on both counts and sentenced to three years. Caldwell appealed on the basis that the direction on drunkenness was wrong. The appeal was upheld on count one but the court left the sentence for count two as three years, as it was considered an appropriate sentence. The prosecutor appealed to the House of Lords to clarify the position on self-induced drunkenness and recklessness as it relates to endangering lives. Five Law Lords sat and considered the case, Lord Diplock's speech was supported by Lord Roskill and Lord Keith in which he said, 'reckless is; when he does that act he has either not given any thought to the possibility of there being such a risk or has recognised the risk and none the less gone on to do it'.

On the point raised regarding self-induced intoxication it was said 'when recklessness establishes an element of the offence, if the actor, due to self induced intoxication, is unaware of a risk of which he would have been aware had he been sober such unawareness is immaterial'.

Decision

Recklessness is where a person does an act, and he either has not given any thought to the possibility of there being a risk, or has recognised that there is a risk and carries on regardless. Self induced intoxication is no defence to an offence for which recklessness suffices as the mens rea.

Comment

In this case the courts have taken a policy decision, self induced intoxication is no defence when recklessness suffices as the 'mens rea' for a crime. Caldwell was unaware of the risk of endangering lives, due to his state of self induced intoxication. However, for recklessness this made no difference, he was still guilty.

Chapter 6: Principles of Criminal Liability

PARTIES TO OFFENCES

Principal

1.1 The principal offender is the person with the necessary mens rea who is responsible for carrying out a criminal activity. He or she will be the person who commits the crime, e.g., a person who uses someone who is below the age of criminal responsibility to commit crime for him. In this example the person who actually commits the act completing the crime does not have the mens rea, it is the person who causes the acts to be committed who is to be treated as the principal or main offender.

Accomplices

2.1 A person who aids, abets, counsels or procures the commission by another of an offence has the same criminal liability as that person. This applies to both summary and indictable offences. It is important to note that you cannot aid, abet, counsel or procure without there being a principal offender (*R v Loukes* [1991]). Loukes was a passenger in a car, the driver of the motor vehicle had been acquitted of dangerous driving, Loukes was charged with aiding and abetting him. As the driver was not convicted of dangerous driving, no-one could be convicted of aiding and abetting him in causing death by dangerous driving, so Loukes was not liable.

Aid, Abet, Counsel or Procure

3.1 Aiding means actively helping the principal offender in the commission of crime. An abettor is one who is present assisting or actively encouraging the principal offender to commit an offence (*R v Clarkson* [1971]). A person who provides transport for the offender to facilitate a crime is an aider, provided knowledge can be shown of the purpose of the provision of the transport. An abettor is one who gives support and encouragement possibly to overcome nervousness. Phrases such as 'go on you can do it if you want', 'it's yours for the taking' etc, would be sufficient to prove that the requisite knowledge or 'mens rea' for abetting the crime is present. To show that a person abets or aids another it must be shown that he knew what the other intended to do.

3.2 Counselling principals to crime is usually confined to advice and encouragement prior to the commission of the offence. To make out the offence of counselling it must be proven that the offence was committed by the person counselled and that the person counselled was acting within the scope of his authority and not accidentally (*R v Clarkson* [1971]). A person who procures a crime however is one who desires the commission but takes no direct part. A procurer sets out to bring about a crime and ensures that it is committed.

3.3 The words aids, abets, counsels or procures do not signify different offences (*Gough v Rees* (1929)), although an aider or abettor cannot be convicted unless he was present when the offence was committed (*Newman v Overington, Harris and Ash Ltd* (1928)). For evidential purposes it is better to use the complete phrase when framing an allegation; 'that you did aid, abet, counsel or procure' in order to secure conviction even when the defendant was not physically present at the crime scene. Evidentially it will be necessary to prove that the defendant who aids, abets, counsels or procures knew that the acts which constitute an offence were being committed by the principal, and that the person gave assistance, or encouragement to the principal or perpetrator of that offence.

Incitement

4.1 A person who incites another to commit crime is guilty of an offence at common law even though the offence is not committed. If the offence is actually committed the inciter may become liable as accessory. The actual involvement must then be considered to discover the depth of involvement and criminal liability. A person has been convicted of attempting to incite by sending a letter that did not arrive (*R v Banks* (1873)). It is a requirement however, that the person being incited must be capable of committing the crime (*R v Whitehouse* [1977]).

Conspiracy

5.1 The offence of conspiracy at common law has almost been abolished, the only remaining common law offences being conspiracy to defraud, conspiracy to corrupt public morals or outrage public decency.

5.2 All other conspiracies are covered by:

Section 1 Criminal Law Act 1977

(1) If a person agrees with any other person or persons that a course of conduct shall be pursued which, if the agreement is carried out in accordance with their intentions, either:
   a) will necessarily amount to or involve the commission of any offence or offences by one or more parties to the agreement, or
   b) would do so but for the existence of facts which render the commission of the offence or any other offence impossible;

   he is guilty of conspiracy to commit the offence in question.

Explanation

If parties agree on a course of action, and if that action is completed it will amount to a crime, they are guilty of conspiracy.

5.3 A person will not be guilty of conspiracy who is to be the intended victim of that offence (Section 2(1) Criminal Law Act 1977). Nor can a person conspire with a person under the age of criminal responsibility or a spouse. The defence afforded to a spouse will not apply however if there is a group or co-conspirators and the spouse is aware of the existence of others with whom the agreement has been made to commit crime. Effectively, the person will have conspired with others not including the spouse (*R v Chrastny* [1992]). Generally the authority of the Director of Public Prosecutions is required to proceed with an offence of conspiracy. The punishment is dependent upon which offence the conspiracy involves.

Attempts

6.1 Attempting to commit an offence is in itself an offence by virtue of:

Section 1 Criminal Attempts Act 1981

(1) If with intent to commit an offence to which this Section applies, a person does an act

which is more than merely preparatory to the commission of the offence, he is guilty of attempting to commit the offence.

(1A) Subject to Section 8 of the Computer Misuse Act 1990 (relevance of external law), if this subsection applies to an act, what the person doing it had in view shall be treated as an offence to which this Section applies.

(1B) Subsection 1A above applies to an act if:
   a) it is done in England and Wales; and
   b) it would fall within subsection (1) above as more than merely preparatory to the commission of an offence under subsection 3 of the Computer Misuse Act 1990 but for the fact that the offence, if completed, would not be an offence triable in England and Wales.

(2) A person may be guilty of attempting to commit an offence to which this Section applies even though the facts are such that the commission of the offence is impossible.

(3) In any case where:
   a) apart from this subsection a persons intention would not be regarded as having amounted to the intention to commit the offence; but,
   b) if the facts of the case had been as he believed them to be, his intention would be so regarded,

then for the purposes of subsection (1) he shall be regarded as having the intent to commit that offence.

Explanation
6.2 Intention to commit: For a person to be guilty of an attempt, he must first intend to commit an indictable offence. Where an offence may be committed by acting recklessly, rather than intentionally, e.g. criminal damage, a person will not be guilty of an attempt, because he is shown to have acted recklessly in a manner which almost caused damage (*R v Millard and Vernon* (1987)). Intention may be something which the court can infer from foresight of consequences, but foresight should not itself be equated with intent (*R v Pearman* (1985)).

Attempts are limited to indictable offences, a person may not be convicted of an attempt to commit an offence which is triable only summarily.

More than merely preparatory: To amount to an attempt, the accused's action must be more than merely preparatory; the action must have an immediate connection, not merely a remote connection, with the commission of the intended crime. If Bill Sykes buys a hacksaw from a hardware shop, intending to use it to cut through the padlock on the gate of a building he plans to break into, the buying of the hacksaw blade is an act of preparation for the burglary; he is not guilty of attempted burglary at this stage. If, however, he is caught inside the fence surrounding a building, having cut through the padlock on the gate, he may at that stage have done enough to be guilty of attempted burglary. It will be a matter of fact for the court to determine in any particular case, whether an action has progressed beyond mere preparation. (In the Sykes example quoted here, there are other offences which may be more readily proved, such as 'going equipped' and 'found on enclosed premises. These offences are referred to collectively as 'preventive measures' and are dealt with in Chapter 48.)

Where a man concealed his motor vehicle then falsely reported it stolen, he was held to be not guilty of attempting to obtain property by deception when he wrote to his insurance company, to ask whether he could make a claim in respect of the 'stolen' van. Writing the letter was merely an act of preparation; further action, such as submitting a completed claim form, may have amounted to the attempt (*Comer v Bloomfield* (1970)).

6.3 Computer misuse: The Computer Misuse Act 1990 creates offences related to 'computer hacking', where a person seeks to gain unauthorised access to a computer system, or to interfere with its operation. (These provisions are dealt with in Chapter 37.) The effect of subsections 1A and 1B is to render a person liable for an attempt to commit an offence of computer misuse, for something done in this country even if the full offence, had it been completed, would not have been triable here. This provision takes cognisance of the world-wide nature of modern communications and computer systems.

6.4 Attempting the impossible: Subsections 2 and 3 provide that a person may be guilty of attempting to commit a crime, even though the facts are such that either, it would be impossible to commit the crime, or his intention did not actually amount to the intention to commit the full offence.

Prior to the coming into force of this legislation, the common law rule was that a person would not be liable, for attempting to commit the impossible. There are examples, post 1981, where the courts sought to reconcile the old common law rule with the new legislation. In *Anderton v Ryan* (1985), for example, a woman who bought an item very cheaply, believing it to be stolen, was held not to be guilty of an attempt to handle stolen goods, because the item was not in fact stolen! However, this ruling was not followed in *R v Shivpuri* (1987), where the defendant was convicted of attempting to commit offences of dealing in a controlled drug. He thought he was dealing in a controlled drug, but the substance in question was harmless vegetable matter.

6.5 Arrest, punishment, etc:
Sections 2–4 Criminal Attempts Act 1981
Other Acts: In any other legislation, where an attempt to commit an offence is itself an offence, the provisions relating to actions more than merely preparatory, attempting the impossible, etc, will apply to the interpretation of the term 'attempt'.

Procedural provisions: Provisions which apply to an offence will apply likewise to any attempt to commit the offence. Such provisions include:
- restrictions on proceedings, e.g. if a prosecution for an offence requires the consent of the Attorney General, the same applies to a prosecution for an attempt to commit it
- powers to arrest, to search, to seize property
- provisions for the forfeiture of property
- provisions relating to corroboration of evidence, etc.

Punishment: Generally, the maximum punishment for an attempt is the same as the maximum which may be imposed for the full offence. In the case of an offence triable either way, this applies to the maximum if tried on indictment, and to the maximum if the offence is tried summarily.

One exception is an offence for which the sentence is fixed by law. In the case of murder, the sentence is fixed as life imprisonment. For attempted murder, the maximum sentence shall be life imprisonment. The significant difference is that upon a conviction for murder, the judge has no option, she must impose a sentence of life imprisonment. If the defendant is convicted of attempted murder, the judge may impose a sentence she considers appropriate, to a maximum of life imprisonment.

DEFENCES TO CRIMINAL ACTS

Provocation

7.1 This defence is usually confined to reducing liability for murder to that of manslaughter although it does have a role to play in the mitigation of offences of assault (*R v Cunningham* [1959]). Generally as a mitigating factor in assault similar questions will be raised to those considered when the defence is used for murder.

7.2 A defendant charged with murder has a specific defence of provocation, this is a statutory defence under the Homicide Act of 1957.

Section 3 Homicide Act 1957

- Where on a charge of murder there is evidence
- on which the jury can find that the person charged was provoked
- whether by things said or done
- or by both together
- to lose his self control.

the question whether the provocation was enough to make a reasonable man do as he did shall be a matter for the jury, and in determining the question the jury shall take into account everything done and said according to the effect that, in their opinion, it would have on a reasonable man.

7.3 Section 3 provides a two-stage test:
- whether the defendant lost his self-control;
- if so, would the provocation have been sufficient for a reasonable man to lose control in the same circumstances?

The judge must direct the jury, as a question of law, as to whether there is any evidence which requires consideration, of possible provocation. If the judge so directs, it will then be questions of fact for the jury to decide on each of the two stages.

7.4 If provocation is to amount to a defence to murder, the provocation must be such as to overcome the self-control of someone, given his nature or characteristics. It is not enough to establish the defence, to prove that the defendant loss of self-control arose in circumstances where he was drunk and depressed, these being temporary states (see *R v Newell* (1980), keynote case).

7.5 Consideration of the defendant's characteristics was a feature in *DPP v Camplin* (1978) (keynote case) where the defendant was a 15-year old boy. The proper course was to consider the reaction of another 'reasonable' 15 year old, not that of a reasonable adult.

Duress

8.1 Once raised by a defendant duress must be rebutted by the prosecution otherwise the defendant must be acquitted. It is a question of fact that must be decided by a jury on the basis of the evidence before it only. Duress is the compulsion by fear or threats to do an illegal act. Generally the threats must be of bodily harm or violence.

8.2 The perception of fear for personal safety is the main ground for this defence. In *R v Graham* [1982] it was decided that voluntary consumption of drugs and intoxicants which would lower the defendant's susceptibility to these threats could not be a factor.

8.3 What then is the case where a person joins a secret organisation such as the triads, Mafia or IRA and acts under duress of the organisation? This question arose in *R v Fitzpatrick* [1977] when the defendant taking part in an armed robbery shot and killed an innocent person. Fitzpatrick claimed to be acting under duress and was convicted of murder. On appeal it was held that having voluntarily joining such an illegal organisation he could not claim duress from it.

Automatism and Insanity

9.1 Insanity is a defence to a criminal charge if:

> 'Through defect of reason due to disease of the mind, the defendant either did not know the nature and quality of his act or, if he did, then he did not know he was doing wrong.' (McNaughten's Case (1843).)

The directions given by this case have become known as the McNaughten Rules and are used to guide consideration by the courts on pleas relating to sanity. The burden of proof is with the defence unless the prosecution alleges insanity.

The rules comprise of three elements:

a) The accused must have been suffering from a disease of the mind, an impairment of the mental faculties of reason, memory and understanding, due to a disease. This disease may be organic or functional and permanent or transient. Not due to some external factor such as a blow on the head.

b) The accused must have been suffering from a 'defect of reason' due to the disease of the mind. This is a deprivation of the power to reason as opposed to momentary confusion or absent mindedness.

c) As a result the accused must not have known the physical nature and quality of his act, or, if he did know this, not to have known he was doing 'a legal wrong'. It is not enough to show that due to a defect of reason caused by disease the accused acted under an irresistible impulse.

9.2 If a plea of insanity is successful, the defendant will be 'not guilty' of the offence charged, but may nevertheless be detained in a secure mental institution until the Home Secretary is satisfied that this is no longer necessary for the protection of the public.

9.3 Where it is an element of an offence, that the accused has committed a voluntary act, the defence of automatism may be brought, proving that the accused's act was involuntary, not carried out of his own free will. The defence must raise sufficient evidence to support the plea. The key word is 'involuntary', the circumstances must be such that the defendant could not stop the action which he took. A simple example is that of the man who, stung by a bee while driving his car, momentarily lost control as his body reacted involuntarily to the effects of the bee sting. The defence of automatism would then be open, as a defence to a charge of dangerous driving, for example. The question must be whether the defendant's actions constituted an automatic or involuntary response (*Broome v Perkins* (1987)).

An epileptic fit is considered in law to be akin to insanity and is dealt with under the McNaughten Rules.

Reasonable Force

10.1 This is a specific defence to assault, e.g., arising from force used to effect the lawful arrest of a person.

Section 3 Criminal Law Act 1967

(1) A person may use such force as is reasonable in the circumstances in the prevention of crime, or in effecting or assisting in the lawful arrest of offenders or suspected offenders or person unlawfully at large.

(2) Subsection (1) above shall replace the rules of the common law on the question when force used for the purpose mentioned in the subsection is justified by that purpose.

Explanation

10.2 Reasonable force can be used to prevent a crime, arrest an offender or person unlawfully at large. There have been many essays and even books written on this particular topic. It is a matter for a court to decide based upon the evidence before it what is reasonable and under what circumstances. Suffice it to say that it would appear to be lawful to kill a person threatening to kill, provided that person had at hand the means and ability to carry out the threat.

10.3 What then of the person who thinks he sees an offence taking place but is mistaken. If he uses force can he rely on this defence? These circumstances arose for a decision by the court in *R v Gladstone* (1983). A street robbery took place in which a youth took property from a woman. A man who witnessed the crime gave pursuit and caught the youth. He then attempted to detain him and a struggle ensued, in which the witness punched the youth. Gladstone then, in turn, saw this struggle taking place, but, knowing nothing of the robbery, assumed that he was witnessing a youth being attacked by a man. Gladstone then assaulted the man (the robbery witness) to protect the youth (the robber) The robbery witness had claimed (falsely) that he was a police officer, but was unable to produce identification. Gladstone was convicted of assaulting the robbery witness, but the conviction was quashed on appeal. The grounds for finding in Gladstone's favour were:
  i) where the defendant claims to have been acting reasonably to prevent a crime being committed, it is for the prosecution to prove that the defendant acted unreasonably;
  ii) the court must decide as a question of fact, whether the defendant's claim, to have a reasonable belief that he was acting to prevent an offence being committed, was genuine.

10.4 It is the defendant's belief, based on what knowledge of the facts he has, which must be considered. Whether the use of force is reasonable within the provisions of Section 3, will be a matter for the court to decide, taking account of the prevailing circumstances, as they were known to the defendant.

Intoxication

11.1 Intoxication in law must be considered as arising from any form of external stimulus or depressant, whether drugs, alcohol or other stimulant, to whatever degree affecting the defendant. There are only two instances where self induced intoxication may provide a defence to crime. Firstly where the intoxicant is taken under medical advice. Secondly where a non-dangerous drug, sedative or similar is taken without knowledge of potential side effects. It is a matter of public policy that self induced intoxication is not a defence to crime *(see keynote cases on duress and provocation).*

Keynote Cases

12.1 Case One: Provocation
R v Newell (1980) 71 Cr App R 331 CA

Problem

What is provocation, does it depend on the person or the circumstances?

Circumstances

A young man who was also a chronic alcoholic became very depressed when his girlfriend left him, he had been very attached to her. It is probable he was also dependent upon her for support. At a later date he was drinking with a friend, both men becoming very drunk. The friend, thinking he was cheering up Newell, made some derogatory remarks about the estranged girlfriend. Newell attacked his friend and killed him. The question for the court was whether the circumstances warranted the claimed defence of provocation. The prosecution proved that Newell had struck his friend Mike over the head twenty-two times with an ashtray weighing almost two pounds. Mike died as a result of the blows. The judge during his summing up made the following observation, 'would a sober man in relation to that drunken observation, batter his friend over the head with a nearly two pound weight ashtray'. On appeal it was submitted that the judge should have said, 'Do you consider that the accused, being emotionally depressed and upset, as he was, and in the physical condition of a chronic alcoholic, was reasonably provoked by the words used and reacted in a way in which he might reasonably be expected to have acted, on the basis that he had had a very large amount to drink and a suicidal overdose of drugs four days previously, and that he was in a state of toxic confusion'. The question being put to the court is, do we impose a reasonable man test for provocation or must we accept the very subjective test of the individual's personal situation and attributes. The Court of Appeal led by Lord Lane stated that 'it is not enough to constitute a characteristic that the offender should merely in some general way be mentally deficient or weak minded. To allow this to be said would have we have indicated earlier, deny any real operation to the reference made in the Section to the ordinary man, and it would, moreover, go far towards the admission of a defence of diminished responsibility... there must be something more, such as provocative words or acts directed to a particular phobia from which the offender suffers, beyond that, we do not think it is advisable that we should attempt to go'. The appellant's drunkenness, or lack of sobriety, his having taken an overdose of drugs and written a suicide note a few days previously, his grief at the defection of his girlfriend, and so on, are none of them matters which can be described properly as characteristics. They are all transitory in nature. The appeal was dismissed.

Decision

For provocation to be a defence to murder the provocation must be more than merely derogatory, they must be acts or provocation directed towards a particular phobia rather than some transient factor in a person's life.

Comment

The self induced drunkenness may have affected the resilience of Newell to comments no doubt made with the best intentions by his friend Mike. However, the state was transitory and not intrinsic to Newell. As such the court would not accept this as being grounds for a defence of provocation.

12.2 **Case Two: Provocation**
DPP v Camplin **[1978] QB 254, [1978] 1 All ER 1236**

Problem
How do we judge what should be accepted as provocation?

Circumstances
A fifteen year old boy was charged with the murder of a middle aged Pakistani man. The facts briefly were that the man and boy were alone in a flat. The man had taken advantage of the situation and buggered the boy and then as the boy cried with pain and despair the man had laughed and made fun of him. The boy took up a chapati pan, a heavy kitchen utensil similar to a rimless frying pan, and struck his assailant splitting his skull and killing him. The boy put up the defence of provocation. Counsel for defence asked the jury to consider the provocation on the basis of the age of the offender, to compare what a reasonable fifteen-year-old's response would have been. The judge however directed the jury that the test was what would a reasonable man have done. Convicted, Camplin appealed on the basis of the judge's direction to the jury. The Court of Criminal Appeal substituted a conviction for manslaughter and stated that the judge should have summed up... 'whether the provocation was enough to have made a reasonable person of the same age as the appellant in the same circumstances do as he did'.

Decision
In considering whether the defence of provocation lies, the 'reasonable person' whom the jury must consider is a person with the same intrinsic characteristics as the accused.

Comment
This decision is compatible with that in R v Newell (above). In considering whether a reasonable person would have acted as the defendant did in the same circumstances, the court shall take account of his intrinsic characteristics, but shall discount features of a temporary nature, such as a mood of depression, or drunkenness. The court should not, however, discount features such as the age of the defendant.

12.3 **Case Three: Duress**
R v Graham **[1982] 1 All ER 801 CA**

Problem
Is duress subjective to the person claiming to be acting under it?

Circumstances
Graham was a practising, homosexual living in a 'bizarre menage a trois' with his wife and another homosexual, King. Graham was suffering from an anxiety state for which he was taking valium. According to medical evidence this would make him more susceptible to bullying. King was known to Graham as a violent man; he was aware of various violent acts committed by King. On the 27th of June 1980, Mrs Graham went to visit her mother in law. Graham and King remained at home drinking heavily. Graham was also at this time taking the prescribed valium. King suggested getting rid of Mrs Graham. Graham induced the return of his wife by pretending he had cut his wrists. Upon her return, Graham lay face down on the floor pretending to be seriously hurt. As Mrs Graham knelt down to minister to him King approached her from behind and put a flex cord around her neck. King urged Graham to pull

the cord which he did. King is also said to have said 'What's it like knowing you are going to die! The plug came off Graham's end of the flex and it was considered that Graham's efforts may not even have caused the death. The question for the court was did these circumstances reveal the defence of duress? If the jury decided that Graham was acting under duress for fear of his own life he would be entitled to be set free and acquitted. Graham was convicted and appealed.

The Court of Appeal dismissed Grahams appeal stating that the court's approach to this matter should have been:

a) was the defendant, or may he have been, impelled to act as be did because, as a result of what he reasonably believed King had said or done, he had good cause to fear that if he did not so act King would kill him or cause him serious physical injury, and

b) if so, have the prosecution made the jury sure that a sober person of reasonable firmness, sharing the characteristics of the defendant, would not have responded to whatever he reasonably believed King said or did by taking part in the killing!

The fact that this defendant's will was eroded by the voluntary consumption of alcohol and drugs or both is not relevant to this test. The appeal court went further by doubting that the prosecution should have conceded that the question of duress arose on the facts outlined. The words and deeds of King were far short of those needed to raise a threat of the required gravity. The appeal was dismissed.

Decision

Drugs and alcohol voluntarily taken will not assist a person claiming to act under duress. The threats needed to warrant such a course of action, i.e. murder, are such that one must reasonably fear for one's own life.

Comment

Again the court ruled that self induced intoxication is not to be a factor in defences. The comment that the prosecution should have argued against rather than conceding to the duress consideration put forward by the defence, says a great deal about the Court of Appeal's views on defences. Public policy dictates that such defences should not be too readily conceded.

12.4 Case Four: Duress
R v Fitpatrick [1977] NI 20 Court of Criminal Appeal Northern Ireland

Problem

Is there a public policy upon which duress cannot stand?

Circumstances

Fitzpatrick had voluntarily joined the IRA. After a year of being a member he decided he wanted to leave. Fitzpatrick was induced, he claims, by threats not to leave but also to take part in an armed robbery. He stated that threats were made against himself and his mother. Fitzpatrick took part in an armed robbery and during the robbery shot and killed an innocent person. Fitzpatrick was convicted of murder, robbery and belonging to a proscribed organisation. The only defence raised was one of duress. The trial judge cited Stephen's History of the Criminal Law of England (volume 2 page 108):

'If a man chooses to expose, and still more, if he chooses to submit himself to illegal compulsion, it may not operate even in mitigation of punishment. It would surely be monstrous to mitigate the punishment of a murderer on the ground that he was a member of a secret society by which he would have been assassinated if he had not committed murder.'

Fitzpatrick appealed on the grounds that the judge had wrongly directed that duress was not available to a person who voluntarily joined a terrorist organisation. During the appeal there was extensive consideration of the effect of duress within organised gangs of criminals, especially that the more ruthless the organisation the better the defence would operate if it were allowed. The appeal was rejected by the court which said:

'If a person voluntarily exposes and submits himself, as the appellant did, to illegal compulsion, he cannot rely on the duress to which he has voluntarily exposed himself as an excuse either in respect of the crimes he commits against his will, or in respect of his continued but unwilling association with those capable of exercising upon him in duress which he calls in aid'.

Decision
If you belong to an illegal organisation or secret society which you joined freely and at your own volition you cannot claim that it or members of it made you do illegal acts under duress.

Comment
Again the freedom of choice to chose right from wrong is a strong influence in public policy decisions as they relate to defences. Note the comment that if duress was allowed to be claimed under these circumstances would mean that the more ruthless the organisation the stronger the defence of duress would be. Clearly this cannot be right and accordingly duress in such circumstances should not succeed as a defence.

Chapter 7: Evidence

1.1 The term evidence denotes 'the means by which any point or fact in issue may be proved or disproved in a manner complying with the legal rules governing the subject'. It is essential that the word evidence in not confused with information. A criminal investigation will include the collection of various pieces of information, some documentary, some real artefacts, and some will be verbal. What of this is admissible as evidence can be decided by applying the rules.

THE STANDARD OF PROOF

1.2 It is important to understand the difference between civil and criminal cases and the differing standards of proof. At civil law the standard of proof required to prove a matter is 'on the balance of probability'. This means that once evidence has been adduced to show that a set of circumstances is more likely to prevail than not, then the standard has been met. In criminal law however an entirely different and higher standard is required. It was stated in *Woolmington v DPP* [1935] that there is a golden thread which passes through the criminal law, 'in criminal cases it is always for the prosecution to prove the actus revs and men rea beyond reasonable doubt'. In *R v Mancini* [1942] it was said that the judge must direct the jury so that they are 'certain so as to be sure of guilt', but also that there is no magical formula for what must be said. There is no set prescriptive wording that must be used by the judge when directing a jury on the standard of proof in criminal matters. It must be made clear to the jury however that they must be sure that they are convinced of the guilt of a person before they can properly return a verdict of guilty.

1.3 If a defendant in a criminal matter raises an alibi or defence to an allegation it is required that sufficient evidence is brought out by the defendant to put the onus on the prosecution to disprove it. However, the standard of proof required for the defence to raise such a defence or alibi is not as onerous as that placed upon the prosecution. The defence in such circumstances must provide sufficient evidence to 'pass the judge', satisfy the judge that there is a defence or alibi for the prosecution to negate before it can successfully convict a defendant. The phrase 'pass the judge' arises from the case of *R v Lobell* [1957] where self defence became an issue in a trial for murder. It is for the prosecution to negate self defence if this is raised as an issue.

1.4 There are three circumstances where the evidence raised by the defence must be on the balance of probability. They are, where the defendant relies upon a statutory exemption from liability or proviso, where the defence of insanity is raised and, where a specific statutory exemption from liability is raised. An example of the latter relates to possession of an offensive weapon 'without lawful authority or reasonable excuse, proof whereof shall lie on the accused' (Section 1 Prevention of Crime Act 1953).

THE BURDEN OF PROOF

2.1 In criminal cases it is for the prosecution to prove beyond all reasonable doubt that a person is guilty of an offence, otherwise the court must acquit the defendant. That is the normal rule giving the onus or rather burden of proof and standard of proof in criminal matters. It is however possible for the burden of proof to shift from prosecution to defence and vice versa. This may seem odd but if a defendant provides an excuse or defence to a crime he or she must provide sufficient proof of that alibi or defence to allow it to be accepted by the court so as to need evidence in rebuttal. In the case of *DPP v Morgan* [1976] where an allegation of rape was made by the prosecutor, the defence of consent was raised. The court held that once the defence was raised it was for the prosecution to prove the absence of consent. Where a case involved an allegation of the misuse of drugs, as in *R v Oliver* [1944], it is for the defendant under such circumstances to prove that the drugs were being used legitimately under medical supervision. In *R v Turner* [1910] it was stated that 'if a negative averment is made by one side which is peculiar in the knowledge of the other, the party with whom the knowledge lies and upon whom the positive averment is must prove, not he in the negative'. That is quite a difficult concept to grasp. It would be better explained that where an exception or proviso occurs in an offence it is for those who rely on that proviso to show that it operates in their favour. This is now simplified by legislation under Section 101 of the Magistrates' Courts Act 1980. The standard of proof required by a defendant under such circumstances is only on the balance of probability.

PRESUMPTIONS

3.1 The purpose of presumptions is to attempt to simplify the process of proving facts by evidence. Presumptions tend to be about matters of which the probability of them being correct is almost certain within the common sense approach of most people, until evidence is brought to question them. An example is that it is presumed in law the earth revolves on its axis once in every twenty four hours and that as such there are twenty four hours in the day. This example is a presumption of fact and unless evidence is brought to contradict the presumption the court will accept the fact without proof. An example of a presumption in law is that a person under the age of 10 years is incapable of committing any criminal offence. This is set down in statute (Section 50 Children and Young Persons Act 1933). Everyone is presumed to know the law, so a defence plea that the accused was ignorant of a particular provision will be no excuse. Common sense dictates that without presumptions the onus to prove facts placed upon a prosecutor would be too great to finalise a prosecution. In every case at the outset there would be a need to prove the sanity of a defendant. Thus there is an automatic presumption that the defendant is sane unless evidence is brought to prove otherwise. Society itself has moulded some presumptions from moral conscience; the presumption of legitimacy at the birth of a child born during the period its mother was married is an example of this. It is undesirable for parents to have to prove the paternity of children.

3.2 Presumptions fall into two categories, presumptions of fact and presumptions at law. In either category the presumption may be absolute or rebuttable. For a rebuttable presumption, is one which evidence can be brought to rebut or deny the presumption. In English law there is a rebuttable presumption of innocence, a person is innocent until proven guilty. There are many examples of matters which are accepted by the courts as being correct without evidence being called to prove them, which if evidence was brought to rebut the situation would require proof. Absolute presumptions are matters which are accepted as being the state of things and no amount of evidence to the contrary will change the courts' view. That a child under 10 is incapable of committing a crime is one such example. There may well be evidence, in a particular case, that a 9-year-old child acted in a manner which showed malice or guilty knowledge, but such evidence will not be admitted to seek to disprove the presumption. There is a presumption that in the absence of other evidence the natural consequence of action proves an event. In

Latin this is known as 'res ipsa loquitor'. If a car runs off the road and collides with a tree and there are no other cars or other external factors causing the accident it must be presumed that the driver was at fault. Evidence to the contrary can rebut this proposition but until it does 'the facts speak for themselves'.

JUDICIAL NOTICE

4.1 The court will not require proof of facts which are subject to judicial notice. It will take notice of notorious facts, these are facts which are common knowledge, e.g., schools exist to teach pupils, water runs downhill etc. Judicial notice will also cover facts ascertained after enquires properly made, facts within the general knowledge of the judge, or those provided by the Secretary of State, such as the extent of territorial waters. Judges will also take notice of statutes although they are not required normally to be proved in court. Seals and signatures on court documents are also subject of judicial notice and accepted without proof of making, unless challenged.

Relevant Facts

4.2 These are facts which are pertinent to a case. In any prosecution or defence of a case at court there is only need to provide evidence of relevant facts. It would be of little point in a case of assault, proving that the offender had a timeshare in Portugal, unless this fact was directly involved and pertinent to the case. In order to be admissible in evidence, facts must be relevant to the offence which it is sought to prove.

Facts at Issue

4.3 In most cases coming before the court there can be agreement, if only informally, that certain points of law and or fact are at issue. Any student of law attending court for the first time cannot fail to notice that many of the circumstances related to the court by the prosecution are accepted without question. The formality of reading much of the evidence to the court as undisputed leaves the court free to consider the points in dispute, or as they are known in legal parlance 'facts at issue'. Very few cases will require every fact to be proved in open court, some if not most will be accepted without dispute. Once the disputed facts are identified, the majority of the legal argument and evidence will be called to settle what is perhaps a small difference in opinion about certain facts or disputed events. In a case of theft, the accused may agree that the goods were taken but dispute dishonesty. The trial at court will quickly go over the attendant facts and be primarily concerned with the intentions and understanding of the accused as relates to the goods and the appropriation of them. If it were otherwise, simple cases of theft would take weeks to resolve before courts with many facts having to be proved, which might otherwise have been accepted.

The Best Evidence Rule

4.4 It is important that the evidence brought before a court is the best available. This rule was first propounded in the mid eighteenth century, 'there is but one general rule of evidence, the best that the nature of the case will allow'. Direct evidence by witnesses and production of artefacts used in crime provide the best evidence. For a witness to be able to stand in court and produce a knife taken from an offender who is known to the witness, is direct evidence of facts in the personal knowledge of the witness. It is not always possible to produce evidence in such a simple manner. The witness may have made a statement and now be out of the court's jurisdiction, or dead, or merely unable or unwilling to attend court. In this case the evidence adduced from the statement of the witness may be acceptable. However, the court should always be presented with the best possible evidence upon which to base its judgement. The best evidence rule applies to documentary evidence. The original of a letter or other paper exhibit is the 'primary' evidence, any copy made of that original is considered to be 'secondary' evidence. The original should be produced unless failure to do so can be explained. The court will usually accept failure to produce an original document if the original, for example, has been destroyed, production would be physically impossible for some reason, it is being withheld for reasons relating to the security of the state, etc. In *Kajaala v Noble* (1982) it was stated that the court is not confined to the best evidence, but may admit all relevant evidence. This decision appears to contradict that in *R v Stevenson, Hulse and Whitney* (1971) where a court refused to accept a copy of a tape recording because it was a copy, not the original. Perhaps the two decisions may be reconciled by considering the availability in each case of the primary evidence.

The Admissibility of Evidence

4.5 There are numerous rules of evidence which make evidence inadmissible in court proceedings. In criminal cases, interviews with suspects are covered by the Police and Criminal Evidence Act 1984. This Act gives the rules for acceptability of evidence obtained during interview but does not consider the manner and method for obtaining evidence from witnesses. The rules for obtaining evidence from witnesses have been settled for many years. A witness may, if called to do so, give verbal evidence of the incident as far as relates to direct evidence of things he has himself seen, heard or experienced. A witness to an incident may be interviewed by a police officer. Anything he says to the police officer is normally hearsay evidence unless the account is given in the presence and hearing of the suspect, and the suspect is allowed to challenge the accuracy of the statement made. Witnesses may make written statements which may be tendered in evidence without the requirement for verbal evidence to be given in court hearings, provided the statement is to be unchallenged and in the format laid down. Such statements are only acceptable in court if they are written down in a set format and comply with conditions laid out by law (Section 9(2) Criminal Justice Act 1967). The statement must be signed by the maker on each page, it must contain a declaration in the prescribed format, a copy of the statement must be served upon the other party in the matter not less than seven days prior to any hearing, and there must have been no written notification of objection to the statement. Even if the seven day notification and service of the statement on the other party have nor been complied with, provided the parties agree, the statement may still be admitted into evidence.

Rules for the Exclusion of Evidence in Criminal Cases

4.6 The Police and Criminal Evidence Act 1984 gives statutory guidance to the courts when considering the evidence before it as to what must be excluded (Section 76 Police and Criminal Evidence Act 1984), and how the court can exercise its discretion to exclude (Section 78 Police and Criminal Evidence Act 1984). Section 76 is concerned solely with confessions obtained during interviews and is covered later in this chapter. Section 78 deals with all evidence and gives a discretion to judges to exclude any evidence including confessions.

Section 78 Police and Criminal Evidence Act 1984

(1) In any proceedings the court may refuse to allow evidence on which the prosecution proposes to rely to be given if it appears to the court that, having regard to all the

circumstances including the circumstances in which the evidence was obtained, the admission of the evidence would have such an adverse effect on the fairness of the proceedings that the court ought not to admit it.

(2) Nothing in this Section shall prejudice any rule of law requiring the court to exclude evidence.

Explanation

The court may exclude any evidence it considers to have been unfairly obtained which it considers to prejudice the proceedings.

4.7 The purpose of the Section is to prevent police officers from being devious or from using trickery to obtain confessions. In *R v Mason* [1988] the Court of Appeal quashed a conviction for arson where the police officers deceived the suspect into thinking they had evidence they did not have. In *R v Samuel* [1988] in a conviction for robbery, there had been a wrongful denial of legal advice. At trial the judge had considered the denial of legal advice but decided wrongly that it was not a breach of the codes of practice.

4.8 In practice the admissibility of confession evidence can be challenged under Section 76, 78 or 82(3) of the Police and Criminal Evidence Act 1984. The courts have refused to lay down guidelines as to how Section 78 is applied. Unfairness to the defendant is not the sole criterior for use of the discretion to exclude evidence, the judge must consider the interests of the prosecution as well as the defence. If the trial judge has not exercised his discretion to exclude evidence or has misdirected himself then the appeal court can exercise the discretion to exclude. The majority of cases where evidence has been excluded seem to be where police officers have breached Codes of Practice. The burden of proof of impropriety to give grounds for exclusion of evidence under Section 78 is on the defence.

Section 82(3) Police and Criminal Evidence Act 1984

Nothing in this part of this Act shall prejudice any power of the court to exclude evidence (whether by preventing questions from being put or otherwise) at it's discretion.

Explanation

4.9 The retention of the court's common law powers is effected by this subsection. The general view is that this subsection allows the retention of the power to exclude evidence set out in *R v Sang* [1980], i.e., where the prejudicial effect of the evidence is greater than the probative value. The wide interpretation by the courts of Section 76 and 78 has meant that none of the currently cited cases have required the safety net of subsection 82(3).

Hearsay

4.10 There is a general rule that hearsay evidence is inadmissible in court proceedings. This rule is subject to many exceptions. The rule against hearsay is mainly based in the fact that statements made in the absence of the accused cannot be questioned or denied. Another reason is that such statements emanate from those not in court, not under oath nor in a position to be cross examined. Changes in the laws of disclosure for unused materials obtained during investigations will require police officers to record some hearsay statements in a permanent and retrievable form, especially where these statements are oral assertions of facts which may not be provable but which may affect the value of other evidence available. For example, during the course of observations on a group of youths suspected of burglary, the investigating officer is made aware of anonymous information that a particular youth is responsible and that youth is not one of those suspected. Clearly this is hearsay, but as it is relevant to the suspect under investigation it must be retained. The revelation of unused materials is dealt with later in this chapter.

4.11 Hearsay evidence is the 'assertion of evidence which cannot be proved by the maker'. This is probably the most complex area of the rules of criminal evidence. Verbal assertions made in the form of a statement will be hearsay if the maker cannot prove the truth of them. Documents are treated as hearsay unless they can be proved by the maker. Fortunately there are numerous rules which now allow for the admission into evidence of documents which strictly speaking cannot be proved by the maker. We will look at those rules which make documents admissible later in this chapter. In the case of *Subramaniam v Public Prosecutor* [1956]' *(see keynote case)* it was stated 'evidence of a statement made to a witness by a person who himself is not called to give evidence may or may not be hearsay'. If the statement is given in evidence to prove its content it will be hearsay; if the evidence is given merely to prove that a statement was made rather than its content, it will be admissible.

Admissible Hearsay

4.12 Statements made in the presence and hearing of the accused are accepted as being admissible by a witness who heard the maker of the statement. A good example of this rule is where a police officer gives evidence of the facts related by a shop assistant who has detained a suspect for theft. Here the officer can repeat in evidence what was said provided it was in the presence and hearing of the suspect and the suspect was given a right of reply. Obviously if the suspect could not hear or understand the facts related then the officer could not give the statement as evidence.

Dying Declarations

4.13 Statements made by a person who has been fatally injured and has no hope of survival, as to the cause of and circumstances relating to the injuries causing death, are admissible in evidence although they cannot be proved by the maker. It must be shown that at the time of making the statement the person had a settled expectation of death. The reason for this exception to the hearsay rule is that it is believed that a person about to die is likely to tell the truth about the circumstances relating to the death. In *R v Woodcock* (1989) *(see keynote case)* it was said 'the general principle on which this species of evidence is admitted is that they are declarations made in the extremity, when the party is at the point of death, and when every hope of this world is gone; when every motive of falsehood is silenced, and the mind is induced by the most powerful considerations to speak the truth; a situation so solemn, and so awful, is considered by the law as creating an obligation equal to that imposed by a positive oath administered in a court of justice'.

Contemporaneous Business Records

4.14 A statement made in the course of a person's duty, written or oral, may be admissible as an exception to the exclusion of hearsay evidence. A verbal statement made to the duty officer by a constable, that he was going to watch a particular prisoner, was admitted in evidence at the trial of that prisoner for the murder of the constable.

Declarations Against Self Interest

4.15 This covers all statements oral or written made by a deceased person of facts which the maker knew to be against his or her pecuniary or proprietary interest at the time the statement was made. The reason for allowing such statements into evidence is that the maker is unlikely to lie about something which is against his own personal interest. This rule arose more in contract and land law than through the criminal law. The effect of the rule is that an accused person cannot tender in evidence a third party's admission to murder as part of his defence.

Note that here, the term 'against' is the one used by lawyers in this context. In this sense, it means 'relating to', rather than 'contrary to', so 'against his own personal interest' actually means, 'in favour of his own personal interest.' Quite simple, really!

Entries in Public Documents

4.16 The statement must have been made by an authorised agent of the public in the course of official duty, and the facts recorded are of public interest, or are required to be recorded for the benefit of the public. This would allow a Registrar of Births and Deaths to produce official records. In effect this rule allows production of public documents and records which cannot be produced by the person who made them.

Res Gestae

4.17 This Latin phrase means 'transaction'. Its use in legal terminology indicates that the evidence arises from its part in 'the transaction' or event. The evidence must be seen to be part of the transaction. In *R v Bedingfield* (1879) the deceased staggered from one room to another, her throat cut across saying words to the effect 'Oh dear, aunt, see what Bedingfield has done to me!' this evidence was excluded from the court as it was not part of the event or transaction. The statement of the deceased was after the event.

4.18 The rules as to what is or is not evidence admissible as 'res gestae' are very complex, essentially they depend on a very high degree of relevance. *R v Ratten* [1972] confirmed the view that 'res gestae' is admissible hearsay to the truth of the assertion in the statement made.

4.19 The case of *R v Andrews* [1987] resolved many of the uncertainties of 'res gestae'. The deceased witness was stabbed by burglars. Being mortally wounded he staggered to neighbours and said words to the effect of 'Andrews did it'. Lord Ackner reviewed the case by asking five questions:
   i)   can concoction be ruled out
   ii) was the incident so dramatic as to overwhelm the victims thoughts
   iii) was the statement spontaneous
   iv) are there any special features such as malice
   v)   is the evidence accurate or doubtful.

These questions will govern the admissibility of hearsay statements as to whether they will be admitted as part of the 'res gestae'. This case supports the views of Lord Wilberforce in R v Ratten and has overturned the narrow view expressed by the court in Bedingfield. In any case where such evidence is potentially available it would be proper and necessary to seek the views of the Crown Prosecution Service as to the suitability and admissibility of evidence under this rule.

Early Complaint

4.20 A statement of early complaint may be admissible in a prosecution for a sexual offence. Evidence of 'early complaint' is, strictly speaking, not an example of hearsay evidence.

Although 'Mary told me that Kevin had just indecently assaulted her.' is evidence of what a witness has heard another person, not the defendant, say, its value is not support the truth of what was said, but as evidence of the fact that a complaint of assault was made at an early stage.

4.21 There is a change in attitude towards statements taken from witnesses which contain evidence falling into the category of hearsay. The Criminal Procedure and Investigations Act 1996 will change the way that the prosecution deals with certain aspects of evidence. Some statements made about the matter under investigation, even though hearsay, may prove to be evidentially beneficial to the suspect, or clarify points which at a later date may form part of a defence statement. Police officers should understand what is and what is not hearsay simply to be able to deal with those matters which must be disclosed to the defence and those which are not strictly evidential but which should be revealed to the prosecutor so that a fair and balanced decision can be made about whether or not to continue with any prosecution.

DOCUMENTARY EVIDENCE

5.1 Prior to 1965 all documentary evidence had to be proven by its maker as being an accurate record of notes made at the time. The law on the admissibility of such records was changed following the case of *Myers v DPP* [1965]. Myers was allegedly involved in changing vehicle details in order to pass them off as other vehicles, During the trial evidence was given of vehicle identification serial numbers from records kept by the car company during manufacture of the vehicles. It was impossible to say who had made the records, so no one could be identified to actually produce the records in court. The records were held to be hearsay and inadmissible. Without the records Myers was acquitted as the original identities of the cars could not be proved. The Criminal Evidence Act 1965 was passed to allow evidence of records made in the course of trade or profession to be admissible without proof of the maker, provided they were kept in the normal course of business. Although this dealt with records kept in trade or professional circumstances this did not cover public records. In *R v Patel* [1981] immigration records were ruled to be inadmissible under the Criminal Evidence Act 1965. This matter was corrected by the Criminal Justice Act 1988.

Section 23 Criminal Justice Act 1988

(1) Subject:
 a) to subsection 23(4)
 b) to paragraph 1a of Schedule 2 to the Criminal Justice Act 1968, (oral evidence given at the original trial must be given orally at any re-trial); and
 c) to Section 69 of the Police and Criminal Evidence Act 1984 (evidence of computer print-outs)
   A statement made by a person in a document shall be admissible in criminal proceedings as evidence of any fact of which direct oral evidence would be admissible if:
   i) the requirements of one of the paragraphs of subsection 23(2) are satisfied; or
   ii) the requirements of subsection 23(3) are satisfied.

(2) The requirements mentioned in subsection 2 3(1)(i) above are:
 a) that the person who made the statement is dead or by reason of his bodily or mental condition unfit to attend as a witness, or
 b) that:

i)   the person who made the statement is outside the United Kingdom, and

ii) it is not reasonably practicable to secure his attendance, or

iii) that all reasonable steps have been taken to find the person who made the statement, but that he cannot he found.

(3) The requirements mentioned in subsection (1)(ii) above are:

a) that the statement was made to a police officer or some other person charged with the duty of investigating offences or charging offenders, and

b) that person does not give oral evidence through fear or because he is kept out of the way.

Subsection 23(1) does not render admissible a confession made by an accused person that would not be admissible under Section 76 of the Police and Criminal Evidence Act l984.

Explanation

The purpose of this Section is to allow first hand hearsay evidence. Section 23 cannot affect the admissibility of confession. If the evidence is initially given orally it must also be given orally at any re-trial or appeal. The Section covers non-paper records and facts only are admissible. If the witness was not competent to give the evidence initially, his record of events will be inadmissible.

Section 24 Criminal Justice Act 1988

(1) A statement in a document shall be admissible in criminal proceedings as evidence of any fact of which direct oral evidence would be admissible. If the following conditions are satisfied:

i)   the document was created or received by a person in the course of a trade, business, profession or other occupation, or as the holder of a paid or unpaid office, and

ii) the information contained in the document was supplied by a person (whether or not the maker of the statement) who had, or may reasonably be supposed to have had, personal knowledge of the matter dealt with.

(2) Subsection(l) applies whether the information contained in the document was supplied directly or indirectly but, if it was supplied indirectly, only if each person through whom it was supplied received it:

a) in the course of trade, business, profession or other occupation, or

b) as the holder of a paid or unpaid office.

(3) Subsection (1) does not render admissible a confession made by an accused person that would not be admissible under Section 76 of the Police and Criminal Evidence Act 1984.

(4) A statement prepared for the purpose of:

a) pending or contemplated criminal proceedings, or

b) of a criminal investigation,

shall not be admissible by virtue of subsection (1) unless:

i)   the requirements of subsection (2) of Section 23 are satisfied, or

ii) the requirements of subsection (3) of Section 23 are satisfied, or

iii) the person who made the statement cannot reasonably be expected (having regard to the time elapsed since he made the statement and to all the circumstances) to have any recollection of the matters dealt with in the statement.

Explanation

This Section is subject of the conditions of Section 23 (person being unable to attend unfit etc). The Section is not limited to first hand hearsay, and also allows admission of documents the maker cannot remember making.

5.2 The admissibility of notes made during the 'course of trade or business' has been subject of review by the courts. In *R v Carrington* [1994] a note made in response to information about an offender's car was used to refresh a store supervisor's memory of events and details. The defence argued that such use was not permitted under Section 24(3) Criminal Justice Act 1988 as the witness could remember some of the evidence given to the police in an earlier statement, but not all of it. The Court of Appeal held that any record made must be viewed as each part being separate to the rest. The fact that the witness could remember the description of the suspect but not a vehicle registration number from memory did not matter. Section 24 refers to 'statements' in documents, meaning almost any sort of written, visual, audible or electronic record which can be stored in practically any medium. 'Statement' in policing terms has always been given a much narrower definition and this should not confuse or constrict the true meaning.

Constraints on Admissibility

5.3 Courts have discretion to exclude hearsay documentary evidence on the following grounds:
   i)   where the authenticity of the document is in question;
   ii)   where direct evidence could be given;
   iii) because of the risks involved, e.g. the defence cannot rebut the evidence and to
         admit it would be unfair to the defendant;
   iv)   when to admit the evidence would not be in the interests of justice, e.g. in that the
         result would be unfair to the defendant.
(Criminal Justice Act 1988, ss 25(2), 26)

Computer Recorded Evidence

5.4 The growth in use of computers has brought problems for courts as to how to deal with the evidence contained within them. A computer is defined as 'any device for storing and processing information' (Section 5 Civil Evidence Act 1965). This is a very broad definition and could be said to encompass anything from a small pocket calculator to a very large mainframe number cruncher.

Section 69 Police and Criminal Evidence Act 1984

(1) In any proceedings, a statement in a document produced by a computer shall not
    be admissible as evidence of any fact stated therein unless it is shown:
    a) that there are no reasonable grounds for believing that the statements are inaccurate
        because of improper use of the computer
    b) that at all material times the computer was operating properly, or if not, that any
        aspect in which it was not operating properly or was out of operation was not such
        as to affect the production of the documents or the accuracy of the contents; and
    c) the relevant conditions specified in the rules of court are satisfied

(2) Provisions may be made by rules of court requiring that in any proceedings where it is
    desired to give a statement in evidence by virtue of this Section, such information
    concerning the statement as may be required by the rules shall be provided in such
    form and at such time as may be so required.

Explanation

Court rules may govern production of computer records. All statements produced from computer print-outs must relate to fact and not opinion. The court will have to be satisfied that the computer was operating properly and was not being misused. Such evidence can be produced under certificate. A computer engineer or specialist must certify that at the time of the record being made by the computer it was functioning properly.

5.5 Problems will arise as to what is a computer print out, and when it may be admitted into evidence under certificate. In *R v Spiby* [1990] *(see keynote case)* it was held that a printout from an automatic telephone system, very similar to a receipt, would be real evidence as opposed to having to be produced into evidence under Section 69(1) of the Police and Criminal Evidence Act or Section 23 of the Criminal Justice Act 1988. The main reason for this was that the machine automatically issued the printout.

5.6 The operation of a computer which automatically prints its results has also been considered by the appeal courts, In *Sophocleous v Ringer* [1987] an analyst used the printout from a computer operated on gas chromatography to refer to during evidence. The results of the machine were printed automatically once the operator had fed in the initial information. The defence argued that Section 69 of the Police and Criminal Evidence Act 1984 applied to the evidence contained in the printout and certification was required. The appeal court took the view that as the scientist who operated the computer was present and gave evidence, it would only be reasonable to allow her to refer to the printout generated as a result of her input into the computer.

5.7 This would probably not be the case however if the machine had been operated by a lab technician with no real expertise or knowledge of the workings of the computer, or if the evidence concerned was given by a data inputter whose sole role was to input rather than to have an understanding of how the system actually functioned.

5.8 There is no need to prove however that a clock within a computer is telling the correct time, provided that this does not affect the computer's other functions. In *DPP v McKeown* and *DPP v Jones* (1997) it was held that although a breath test machine's internal computer clock was inaccurate this does not show that the machine's ability to analyse breath was impaired.

Corroboration

5.9 Corroboration is evidence which tends to support the truthfulness and accuracy of that already given. Corroborative evidence adds weight and credibility to evidence given earlier. Whether evidence amounts to corroboration of other evidence, is a matter of fact for the magistrates or jury to decide on.

5.10 There are very few instances of corroboration being required by law One is in a prosecution for perjury, it being a statutory requirement that a person cannot be convicted on the evidence of one witness alone. There must either be two witnesses, or substantial corroboration of one witness's evidence. A substantial number of similar requirements for corroboration, particularly in relation to sexual offences, have been abolished in recent years.

5.11 Although there may be very few occasions on which corroboration is required by law, corroborated evidence will continue to carry more weight than uncorroborated testimony, and there is little doubt that courts and the legal profession will continue to look for it in practice.

Evidence of Character

5.12 It is a fundamental principle of English law that a person is innocent until proved guilty. In order to prevent prejudice against the 'innocent' defendant, there are restrictions on revealing the accused's previous bad character before a verdict is reached. There are also rules relating to disclosure of the character of a witness in criminal proceedings.

5.13 Any known convictions of witnesses will be required to be made available to the defence in criminal proceedings. The character of a witness will always be relevant to proceedings as it relates to the witness's credibility. A witness may be asked about any relevant convictions but to do so may cause the defendant to lose his protection against being asked about his prior convictions or character.

5.14 The defendant's character is protected by a shield. No evidence can be mentioned in court about the accused's previous convictions without permission of the court. The circumstances as set out in Section 1 of the Criminal Evidence Act 1898 are:

Section 1 Criminal Evidence Act 1898

Every person charged with an offence is competent for the defence provided:
   a) he gives evidence at his own request
   c) if he gives evidence he may be asked questions in cross examination which would encriminate him
   f) he may not be asked questions about his character, prior charges or convictions unless:
      i) such are admissible to prove that charge, (e.g. disqualified driver, common prostitute)
      ii) he produces evidence of his own good character, or attacks that of the prosecutor,
      iii)he gives evidence against a co-accused
   g) he gives evidence from the witness box.

Explanation

These provisions dictate when the court has discretion to allow the prosecutor to reveal the prior bad character of the accused. The prosecution can never force a defendant to give evidence. It is for the prosecution to prove its case beyond all reasonable doubt without the defendant's evidence. Effectively this Section will shield the defendant's character from attack unless he or his representatives attack the character of the prosecution witnesses.

5.15 If the defendant does not give evidence he cannot lose the protection of the Section 1 shield (*R v Butterwasser* [1948]). At common law the defendant is allowed to call evidence of good prior character and the prosecution may rebut such evidence after it has been made an issue. Any evidence of character called for the defendant may only be of a general nature (*R v Rowton* (1865)).

Similar Fact Evidence

5.16 A court will accept in evidence which otherwise would not be admissible and relevant to the trial if that evidence relates to a tendency to think or act in a particular way. It may relate to the accused's conduct on other occasions, his character, or previous convictions for similar crimes. It is the provable propensity to act and or think in a similar manner which may allow for the admissibility of the evidence. It is no good just showing that an accused had a tendency towards wrongdoing generally. To be admissible the evidence of similar conduct must be 'strikingly similar'. In *Noor Mohammed v R* [1949] weak evidence that a goldsmith's first wife had died of a cyanide overdose was inadmissible as there was only weak and tenuous evidence to support this proposition *(see keynote case)*. The phrase 'strikingly similar' arises from the case of *R v Smith* (1915) *(see keynote case)*.

5.17 The fact that a defendant has a propensity towards a particular lifestyle or form of behaviour is generally not admissible, as being prejudicial without serving to prove his guilt. This was considered in *R v B (evidence of propensity)* (1997). B was interviewed about his possession of various articles, including magazines of a pornographic and homosexual nature, seeking to support the claim that he had a propensity to act in a particular way. The defence argued that this evidence should not have been admitted, and the court supported this argument. The evidence did not help to prove the defendant's guilt, but was prejudicial to him. This does not mean that a suspect may not be asked questions by the police about his propensity towards particular styles of behaviour. Such questions may yield valuable evidence. Such matters may not however, be included in evidence at court.

EYEWITNESS IDENTIFICATIONS

6.1 Evidence given by a witness as to what he or she saw is acceptable to a court. The credibility of any identification of an accused will depend upon many factors. The courts have long recognised that there is a possibility of witnesses being honestly mistaken in identifying an offender. A mistaken witness can be just as convincing as to the certainty of his identification as one who gives an accurate version of events. The problem for the courts has always been how to warn juries of the potential for mistakes. The case of *R v Turnbull (and others)* [1976] *(see keynote case)* set out matters which the jury should consider when evaluating the eyewitness testimony of identification. These matters are:
   i)   the length of time during which the witness had the person under observation
   ii) whether the observations were uninterrupted or impeded in any way,
        e.g., by passing traffic
   iii) the prevailing conditions of visibility
   iv) the distance between the witness and the person observed
   v)   has the witness seen the accused before?, if so, how often? if only occasionally, is there
        any special reason why she should remember the accused?
   vi) the length of time which elapsed between the original observations and identification
        of the accused to the police
   vii) was there any material discrepancy between the description given of the suspect by
        the witness when first seen by the police, and the accused's actual appearance?

6.2 There are several methods of testing the ability of witnesses to identify a suspect as an offender. These methods are set out in Code 'D' of the Codes of Practice to the Police and Criminal Evidence Act 1984:
   a) identification parade
   b) group identification
   c) video identification
   d) confrontation.

There is no set order of preference for these methods of identification, subject to the provisos:
   i)   that video identification may be used if the identification officer feels it to be the most
        satisfactory course, whether because of the suspect's refusal to take part in an

identification parade or group identification, or for other reasons;
(Codes of Practice, Code D, Section 2.10)

ii) that a confrontation may take place only if none of the other three methods is arranged, on the ground that it is not practicable to arrange any of them
(Codes of Practice, Code D, Section 2.12)

The first implies that video identification is a third option, after the parade and group methods have been considered. The second requires that confrontation is the last resort, of the four.

Dock identification should not be used. The methods for carrying out the above listed identification procedures are called the formal methods and are used where the suspect is known and available. Known and available means that the police are able to arrange for the suspect to take part in an arranged procedure.

6.3 The phrase 'known and available' used in Code D paragraph 2.1 of the revised codes of practice is the crucial factor as to whether formal or informal identification methods are required. The case or *R v Kitchen* [1994] *(see keynote case)* indicates that a suspect is known and available, when it is known that he could be arrested within a relatively short period. If a suspect is known and available, formal methods should be used, otherwise less strictly controlled methods may be used. We may call these alternative methods informal.

6.4 Informal identification is sometimes referred to as 'Street Identification'. This is not to be confused with the Code 'D' group identification. A street identification can take place to identify a suspect in certain limited circumstances. The rules for such are to be found in the Court of Appeal judgements of *R v Oscar* [1992], *R v Kelly* [1992] and *R v Rogers* [1993]. The court indicated that an instant confrontation would apply where the suspect is located within minutes of an offence and the witness is readily available. In the immediate aftermath of a crime a witness can be taken on a tour of the area by police officers to try to locate a suspect. This should be part of an uninterrupted chain of events forming the immediate post event investigation. The purpose of such an instant confrontation is to prevent a guilty person from evading detection and any unreasonable delay in releasing an innocent person. Once the suspect is at a police station, whether detained or not, instant confrontation should not be used. There is no need to warn the suspect. The witnesses should have their attention drawn to the particular individual. If at all possible in the presence of the suspect, the witness should be asked 'is the person present a person concerned with the incident?' If the witness answers in the affirmative and the suspect is identified, no other witnesses should be allowed to see the suspect. At this stage the suspect becomes 'known and available' for the purpose of formal identification methods.

6.5 Formal identification procedures must be carried out in accordance with Code D of the Codes of Practice (issued under the provisions of the Police and Criminal Evidence Act 1984). Whenever a suspect disputes an identification, or the officer in charge of an investigation considers that it would be useful, one of the three methods – identification parade, group identification or video film identification – shall be arranged. The suspect's consent is required for a parade or video identification. A group identification may take place with or without the suspect's consent.

6.6 Before any formal procedures take place the suspect and/or his legal adviser must be provided with the details of the first descriptions given of the suspect(s) by any witnesses, also details of any prepared photograph, photofit or similar circulation issued to assist in obtaining or tracing suspects to the matter under investigation. Formal identification procedures must be conducted by an officer not below the rank of Inspector who must not be connected with the investigation.

6.7 Prior to any formal identification procedure the suspect must be given a notice which states:

i) the purposes of the parade or group identification or video identification

ii) that he or she is entitled to free legal advice

iii) the procedure for holding it, including the right to have a solicitor or friend present

iv) where appropriate, the special arrangements for juveniles

v) that he or she does not have to take part in any parade, or co-operate in any group identification, or with the making of any video film and, if it is proposed to hold a group or video identification, his or her entitlement to a parade if this can be practicably arranged

vi) if he or she does not consent to taking part in a parade or co-operate in a group identification or with the making of a film, his refusal may be given in evidence in any subsequent trial and police may proceed covertly without his consent or make other arrangements to test whether a witness identifies him

vii)(a) that if he should significantly alter his appearance between the taking of any photograph at the time of his arrest or after charge and any attempt to hold an identification procedure, this may be given in evidence if the case comes to trial; and the identification officer may then consider other forms of identification

vii)(b) that a photograph may be taken of him when he attends for any identification procedure

viii) whether the witness had been shown photographs, photofit, identikit or similar pictures by the police during the investigation before the identity of the suspect became known

ix) that if he changes his appearance before a parade it may not be practicable to arrange a parade on the day in question or subsequently and, because of his change in appearance, the identification officer may then consider alternative methods of identification

x) that he or his solicitor will be provided with details of the descriptions of the suspect as first given by any witnesses who are to attend the parade, group identification, video identification or confrontation.

6.8 The identification officer should also read the notice to the suspect to ensure he understand what is to occur and his rights. The suspect should then be asked to indicate whether he is willing to take part in any of the formal identification procedures and sign a second copy of the form. If the identification officer considers that it is impracticable to hold a parade he must tell the suspect why and make a written record of his reasons on the appropriate forms. In practice, the suspect will have to be of a very striking appearance or have unusual physical deformities to justify such a decision.

6.9 An identification parade should comprise of no less than eight other persons of similar appearance to the suspect, in relation to age, height, general appearance and position in life. If there are two suspects of similar description, not less than twelve others should be used. In no circumstances should there be more than two suspects on one parade. Where the parade consists of police officers in uniform, numbers and identifying badges must be concealed.

6.10 Witnesses should not prior to the parade be able to:

i) communicate with each other about the case or overhear a witness who has already seen the parade

ii) see any member of the parade

iii) on that occasion see or be reminded of any photograph or description of the suspect or be given any other indication of his identity; or

iv) on that occasion see the suspect either before or after the parade.

Identification Parades

6.11 Immediately prior to the parade the identification officer must:

i)   remind the suspect of his rights and caution him

ii) exclude all unauthorised persons from the area where the parade is to be held

iii) allow the suspect an opportunity to object to anyone taking part in the line up

iv) allow the suspect or suspects to choose their own position in the line-up.

Once the parade has been formed the following rules apply:

i)   once the parade has been formed, everything thereafter in respect of it shall take place in the presence and hearing of the suspect (and of any appropriate adult, solicitor, interpreter or friend who may be present). However, if the parade involves use of a screen, everything said to or by any witness in the place where the parade is held, must be said in the hearing and presence of the suspect's solicitor, appropriate adult or friend, or it must be recorded on video. In other words, if there is no screen, the action must take place in the presence of the solicitor, friend, etc, who may be present. If no such person is present, so be it. Where the parade involves a screen, if no such person is present, the proceedings must be recorded on video.

ii) the officer conducting the witness to the parade does not discuss anything with the witness regarding the parade, its composition or whether any earlier witness has identified anyone

iii) if a witness wishes to hear anyone on the parade speak, move or adopt a particular posture, the identification officer should first ask the witness if she can identify any persons on the parade by appearance alone. If a request is made for members of the parade to speak, the witness should be reminded that persons on the parade have been selected on the basis of physical appearance only. Members of the parade may then be asked to comply with the witness's request, to move, speak or adopt a specified posture

iv) where video films, or other method of broadcasting descriptions or look alike images have been used, the identification officer must ask each witness after they have seen the parade if they have seen such materials. He must note their reply.

v)   at the conclusion of the parade the identification officer must ask the suspect if they are any comments he wishes to make about the conduct of the parade. The identification officer must note any reply.

Documentation:

i)   the identification officer is responsible for keeping records of all parades and action taken during parades. This including a record of all those present who are known to the police, and of those persons taking part

ii) a copy of any photograph or video film taken of the assembled parade must be supplied if requested to the suspect or his solicitor within a reasonable time. Any video film or photograph shall be destroyed or wiped clean at the conclusion of the proceedings unless the suspect is convicted or admits the offence and is cautioned for it

iii) if the identification officer asks any person present to leave the parade because he is interfering with the conduct of the parade, he must record the reasons

iv) if prison inmates make up the parade, the reasons and circumstances must be recorded.

Video Identification

6.12 Where a video identification is carried out, the following procedure must be followed:

i) the making, showing and arranging of the film must be the responsibility of identification officer, or officers who are not connected with the case

ii) the film must include the suspect and at least eight other people who so far as possible resemble the suspect in age, height, general appearance and position in life. Only one suspect should normally appear on one film unless there are two suspects of similar description, in which case at least twelve others must be used to compile the film

iii) the suspect and the others must all as far as possible be filmed in the same positions, or carrying out the same activity and under identical conditions

iv) provision must be made for each person filmed to be identified by a number

v) if police officers are filmed they should not have numerals or badges displayed. If prison inmates are filmed then all or none should be in prison uniform

vi) the suspect and or his solicitor must be given an opportunity to view the prepared film before it is shown to the witnesses. If he has any reasonable objections to the film or anyone contained in it, steps should be taken if practicable to remove the grounds for objection. If this is not practicable the identification officer must explain the reasons to the suspect and or his solicitor and record both the objection and the reason for failure to correct the objection on the forms provided.

vii) the suspect's solicitor, or if not represented the suspect, must be informed of the time and place that it is intended to conduct the video identification so that the representative or someone acting on his behalf may be present. The suspect himself may not be present when the film is shown to the witnesses. In the absence of a person representing the suspect, the viewing itself shall be recorded on video. No unauthorised persons may be present during the witness viewing

viii) only one witness may view the film at a time

ix) the identification officer is responsible for ensuring that the witnesses do not communicate with each other about the case or overhear a witness who has already seen the film.

x) the identification officer must take care not to draw the witnesse's attention to any one individual on the film.

xi) the witness will be asked to view the film at least twice before being asked if he can identify anyone in it as being involved in the incident he witnessed. If the witness identifies anyone by number, the identification officer will show that person again to confirm the identification by the witness

xii) where video film or photographs have been released through the media to identify a suspect, the witness must be asked by the investigating officer after the identification whether he has seen any such material relating to the offence, and record the reply.

xiii) it is the responsibility of the identification officer to ensure the security of all tapes made for viewing. No officer involved in the investigation of the offence can be permitted to view the tape prior to it being shown to the witnesses.

xiv) at the conclusion of the case, any video tapes must be destroyed unless the suspect is convicted or has admitted the offence and been cautioned for it

xv) the identification officer is responsible for recording the names and details of those participating in the tape and those viewing it. A full record of the viewing must be made on the forms provided.

Group Identifications

6.13 In a group identification, witnesses are given the opportunity to pick out a suspect when he is in a group of people. The composition of this type of identification is less formal than for an identification parade in which those involved stand in a line. A group identification may be held in a room in a police station, as a last resort, but may take place in a shopping centre, railway station foyer or other public place. In common with video identification, group identifications can take place with or without the consent of the suspect. The location selected for such identifications is a matter controlled by the identification officer. The factors to be considered involve the type of persons expected to be present, the numbers of such persons, and the likelihood that they will be similar in age, height and general position in life to the suspect. A group identification need not be held if the possible location would not be suitable because of the suspect's unusual appearance. Immediately after a group identification has taken place, with or without the suspect's consent, a video film or photograph must be taken of the location and of those present. Again as with all formal identification procedures the suspect and his legal advisors must be provided with the first descriptions given by any witnesses.

6.14 When a group identification takes place, with the suspect's consent, he must be served with a notice explaining the procedure. The witness, identification officer and suspect's solicitor or friend may be concealed from the group being viewed. The identification officer is responsible for ensuring that the witnesses are not able:

i) to communicate with each other about the case or overhear a witness who has already been given an opportunity to see the suspect in the group

ii) on that occasion to see the suspect; or

iii) on that occasion to see or be reminded of any photographs or description of the suspect or be given any indication of his identity further

iv) the witnesses should be brought to view the group one by one. They must be reminded that the person they came to identify may or may not be there, and that if they cannot make a positive identification they should say so.

Moving Group Identifications

6.15 Where a moving group is used, such as on an escalator, only one suspect may be put into the group at a time, although two may be put through consecutively. The identification officer must tell the witness to look at the group to see if he can identify someone. If the witness makes an intimation of identification the identification officer should try to get the witness to move closer to confirm the identification. If this is not possible the identification officer must ask the witness how sure he is that the person indicated is the relevant person. The identification officer must try to ensure sufficient time for identification has taken place.

Stationary Group Identifications

6.16 Where the group is stationary, for example in a queue, the identification officer should ask the witness to pass through at least twice to see if an identification can be made. The suspect may take up any position in the group he or she wishes. All instructions to the suspect must be done away from the hearing of the witnesses. The identification officer must attempt to get the witness to point out any person identified in a clear and unambiguous manner if at all possible.

6.17 In both cases, where the suspect unreasonably delays, or conceals himself in the group, the identification officer may treat this as a refusal to take part or co-operate in the group identification. If the witness identifies anyone who is not a suspect, the identification officer should try to obtain that persons name and address if at all possible and explain to him what has happened. When the group identification is completed the identification officer should ask the suspect if he has any comments to make about the conduct of the procedure. If the suspect is not already informed, the identification officer must tell him of any identifications made.

6.18 Where the suspect does not consent and the identification is made covertly, the rules for conduct of a group identification should be complied with where possible. Any number of suspects can be identified at the same time. The suspect will not have the right to legal advice at the time of identification.

6.19 Group identifications should not normally take place in a police station unless for reasons of security or safety. In such case they may take place in a room with or with a two way screen, or anywhere else in the police station the identification officer consider appropriate.

6.20 Where a photograph or film is taken of the area where a group identification takes place a copy must be made available to the defence within a reasonable time. If the film or photograph include the suspect, all copies must be destroyed unless the suspect is convicted or admits the offence and is cautioned. A full record of the conduct of the group identification must be made by the identification officer on the forms provided.

Confrontations

6.21 Confrontation of witness and suspect as part of the formal identification procedure should be carried out as a last resort only, normally on police premises. The witness must be told that the person he is about to see may or may not be the one involved in the incident, and that if he cannot make a positive identification he should say so. Before a confrontation takes place the suspect and or his solicitor must be provided with details of the first descriptions of the witness(s). The suspect or his solicitor must also be allowed to view any materials issued to trace a suspect unless it is impractical to do so and this would delay the investigation unreasonably. The suspect is confronted with the witness, who is asked, 'Is this the person'? Confrontations must take place in the presence of the suspect's legal advisor, interpreter if required and friend, unless this would cause unreasonable delay. Where video films or photographs have been released by the police to trace a suspect, the witness shall be asked by the investigating officer if has seen any such materials. The reply must be recorded.

Photographs

6.22 The showing of photographs to witnesses of crime, to identify a suspect when the suspect is unknown, is set out in Code D annex D. An officer of the rank of sergeant or above must be responsible for supervising and directing the showing of the photographs but the actual showing may be done by a constable or a civilian police employee. The photographs must be made up into an album, or if loose mounted in a frame, or if on optical disc in a sequence of not less than twelve.

6.23 The officer must confirm that the first description of the suspect as given by the witness has been recorded before any photographs are shown. If this cannot be done the showing must be postponed. Only one witness must view the photographs at a time. He or she must be given as much privacy as possible and should not be allowed to communicate with any other witness in the case. The witness should be shown at least twelve photographs at a time, all of which, as far as possible, shall be of a similar type. The witness must be informed that the person he saw may or may not be amongst those depicted in the group of photographs. He should not be guided through or in any way prompted to make a selection, but must be left to make any selection on his own.

6.24 If a witness identifies anyone, unless that person is eliminated from the enquiry, no other witness should be shown the photographs. They should instead be asked to attend a parade or group or video identification. Where the use of a photofit, identikit or similar picture has led to a suspect being available for identification procedures, that picture shall not be shown to any other potential witness. If the witness has been shown photographs, photfit or similar pictures which have made the suspect available for formal identification procedures, this must be brought to the attention of the suspect before any formal identification procedure takes place.

6.25 It is the responsibility of the investigating officer to ensure that the identification officer is aware of any prior identification procedures carried out. The photographs used in any attempt to identify a suspect must be kept available for the court. The photographs must be numbered and a separate photograph must be taken of the frame or part of the album from which the witness made the identification, as an aid to reconstituting it.

6.26 Whether or not an identification is made, the matter must be documented together with any comments made by the witnesses viewing the photographs.

IDENTIFICATION BY FINGERPRINTS

7.1 The process of taking fingerprints from suspects and the later destruction if required is covered by the Police and Criminal Evidence Act 1984, Section(s) 61 and 64. The fingerprints of a person 10 years old and above may not be taken without consent unless authorised by Section 61. Consent must always be given in writing and should normally be recorded on the custody record Consent for a juvenile, means, as it does in relation to other methods of identification covered by Code D:

  i)   in the case of a person aged under 14 years, the consent of his parent or guardian
  ii) in the case of a person aged 14 and under 17 years, the consent of that person, and
       of his parent or guardian

A person whose fingerprints are taken with or without consent must be informed beforehand that his prints may be subject of a speculative search against other fingerprints found during investigations into other crimes.

Section 61 Police and Criminal Evidence Act 1984

(3) The fingerprints of a person detained at a police station may be taken without the appropriate consent:
  a)   if an officer of at least the rank of superintendent authorises them to be taken; or
  b)   if:
    i)   he has been charged with a recordable offence or informed that he will be reported for such an offence; and
    ii) he has not had his fingerprints taken in the course of the investigation of the offence by the police.

(4) An officer may only give authorisation under subsection 3(a) above if he has reasonable grounds:
  a)   for suspecting involvement of the person whose fingerprints are to be taken in a criminal offence; and
  b)   for believing that his fingerprints will tend to confirm or disprove his involvement.

7.2 The authority under subsection 3(a) may be given orally but must be confirmed in writing. Any person convicted of a recordable offence may have their fingerprints taken for that offence without consent. If the person is later acquitted at court the fingerprints must be destroyed and the person charged or reported may be present to witness the destruction. The person may apply for a certificate to prove his fingerprints have been destroyed within three months. Reference to fingerprints includes palm prints.

7.3 Recordable offences are those offences for which the offence is punishable with imprisonment on first conviction; and certain non-imprisonable offences, e.g. Section 1 Street Offences Act 1959 (loitering for the purposes of prostitution), Section 43 of the Telecommunications Act 1984 (improper use of public telecommunication system) Section 25 Road Traffic Act 1988 (tampering with a motor vehicle), Section 1 of the Malicious Communications Act 1988 (sending letters with the intention to cause distress or anxiety). Reasonable force may be used when taking fingerprints either with or without consent (Code D Para 3.2 and Section 117 Police and Criminal Evidence Act 1984).

7.4 When a person is convicted of a recordable offence without having been detained at a police station at any stage of the proceedings, there is provision to require him to attend a police station to have his fingerprints taken.

Section 27 Police and Criminal Evidence Act 1984

(1) If a person:
    a) has been convicted of a recordable offence
    b) has not at any time been in police detention for the offence; and
    c) has not had his fingerprints taken:
        i) in the course of the investigation of the offence by the police; or
        ii) since his conviction;
any constable may at any time not later than one month after the date of the conviction require him to attend a police station in order that his fingerprints may be taken.

(2) A requirement under subsection (1) above:
    a) shall give the person a period of at least 7 days within which he must attend; and
    b) may direct him to so attend at a specified time of day or between specified times of day.

(3) Any constable may arrest without warrant a person who has failed to comply with the requirement under subsection (1) above.

Explanation
In the majority of cases, persons convicted of recordable offences will have been arrested at some stage and taken to a police station to be interviewed and charged. In any case where a person has been dealt with by summons instead of being arrested and charged, police may make a requirement of that person to attend a police station, at some time during the month following his conviction. Failure to comply may lead to arrest – not for an offence but in order that his fingerprints may then be taken.

PRISONER'S PHOTOGRAPHS

8.1 The photograph of a person arrested may be taken at a police station only with his written consent or if authorised by legislation. Under Code D the photograph of a person who has been arrested may be taken if:

    i) he is arrested at the same time as other people, or at a time when it is likely that other people will be arrested, and a photograph is necessary to establish who was arrested, at what time and what place; or

    ii) he has been charged with, or reported for a recordable offence and has not yet been released or brought to court; or

    iii) he is convicted of such an offence and his photograph is not already on record as a result of (i) or (ii). There is no power to arrest to take a photograph; this would take effect where a person is in custody as a result of another power, (e.g. where arrested for fingerprinting under Section 27 of the Police and Criminal Evidence Act 1984); or

    iv) an officer of at least the rank of superintendent authorises it, having reasonable grounds for suspecting involvement of the person in a criminal offence and where there is identification evidence in relation to that offence.

Note: There is no power to take photographs by force.

8.2 Where a person's photograph has been taken in accordance with these rules, the photograph, negative and any copies must be destroyed if:

    a) he is prosecuted for the offence and cleared, unless he has a previous conviction for a recordable offence; or

    b) he has been charged but not prosecuted (unless he admits the offence and is cautioned for it or he has a previous conviction for a recordable offence).

The opportunity to witness the destruction or a certificate confirming the destruction of the photographs must be given if requested, provided he applies to be present within five days of the destruction becoming a requirement. A record must be made of the reasons for taking a person's photograph under this Section without consent and also any destruction.

INTIMATE AND NON-INTIMATE SAMPLES

9.1 The ability of scientists to reconstruct crime scenes from debris left at the scene can be almost unbelievable. The certainty of expert evidence can convict in the absence of a confession. Recent changes in the law now allow the preparation of a national database of D.N.A samples taken from persons charged with recordable crimes. It is anticipated that this database of samples will assist in the prevention and detection of crimes. The taking of intimate and non-intimate samples from a suspect are subject of Code D Section 5.

9.2 Intimate samples may be taken from a person in police detention only:

    i) if an officer of the rank of superintendent or above has reasonable grounds to believe that such an impression or sample will tend to confirm or disprove the suspect's involvement in a recordable offence and gives authorisation for a sample to be taken; and

    ii) with the suspect's written consent.

9.3 Nothing in Code D prevents intimate samples being taken from a person, with his consent, for elimination purposes. This would allow, for example, all the men between certain ages in an area to be tested, following the commission of a very serious crime. In this regard however, attention is drawn to the need for care in obtaining the consent of a juvenile or person who suffers from mental disorder or mental handicap. Consent means:

    i) in the case of a juvenile, as set out in paragraph 7.1 above

ii) in the case of a person suffering from mental disorder or mental handicap, a consent which has been obtained in the presence of the appropriate adult

(Code D, Section 1.11)

9.4 The terms 'intimate' and 'non-intimate' as far as they relate to samples taken from persons suspected of crime are defined in Section 65 of the Police and Criminal Evidence Act 1984 (amended by the Criminal Justice and Public Order Act 1994 Section 58), and are:

i) 'intimate sample' means a dental impression or sample of blood, semen or any other tissue fluid, urine, or pubic hair, or swab taken from a person's body orifice other than the mouth.

ii) 'non-intimate sample' means:

a) sample of hair (other than pubic hair) which includes hair plucked from the root. (Where hair samples are taken for DNA analysis the suspect should be given a reasonable choice of where he or she wishes them taken from)

b) a sample taken from a nail or from under a nail

c) a swab taken from any part of a person's body including the mouth, but not any other body orifice

d) saliva

e) a footprint or similar impression of any part of the body other than a part of the hand.

9.5 The person must be told that any sample taken may be subject of a speculative search, also the authority by which the sample is being taken. Where a sample is being taken and clothing is required to be removed this should only be done in the absence of members of the opposite sex, with the exception of those medically qualified, or where the person subject of the sample is a juvenile or mentally disordered or mentally handicapped who requests the presence of an appropriate adult of the opposite sex who is readily available.

9.6 Where a person is required to provide an intimate sample the Code suggests an appropriate warning to be given to the person prior to the taking of any sample:

'You do not have to [provide this sample] [allow this swab or impression] to be taken, but I must warn you that if you refuse without good cause, your refusal may harm your case if it comes to trial'

Non-Intimate Samples

9.7 Non intimate samples may be taken from a detained person only with his written consent unless under conditions specified by Section 63 of the Police and Criminal Evidence Act 1984 as amended by Section 55 of the Criminal Justice Act 1994 apply (Code D para 5.5):

i) if an officer of the rank of superintendent or above has reasonable grounds to believe that the sample will tend to confirm or disprove the person's involvement in a recordable offence and gives authorisation for a sample to be taken; or

ii) where the person has been charged with a recordable offence or informed that he will be reported for such an offence; and he has not had a non-intimate sample taken from him in the course of the investigation or if he has had a sample taken from him, it has proved unsuitable, or insufficient for the same form of analysis.

9.8 The information obtained from the samples taken may be added to the National Database by virtue of Section 57 of the Criminal Justice and Public Order Act 1994 which amends Section 64 of the Police and Criminal Evidence Act 1984. Section 64 relates to the destruction of fingerprints and other samples and is amended as follows:

Samples which are required to be destroyed, need not be destroyed if they are taken for the purpose of the same investigation for which a person from whom one was taken has been convicted, but the information derived from the sample of any person entitled to its destruction shall not be used:
   a) in evidence against the person so entitled; or
   b) for the purposes of any investigation of an offence.

9.9 This means that where a sample has been taken from a person during an investigation and the person is convicted the sample may be retained and its information kept on database. Where samples have been taken from a number of persons during an investigation and one of them has been convicted, the samples taken from the others need not be destroyed. However, the information derived from the samples of the innocent persons must not be used in evidence against any of them, nor must it be used in the investigation of any offence.

Power to Take Samples

9.10 Section 56 of the Criminal Justice and Public Order Act 1994 introduced a new section into the Police and Criminal Evidence Act 1984, which makes provision for the taking of samples from convicted persons:

Section 63A Police and Criminal Evidence Act 1984

(4) Any constable may, within the allowed period, require a person who is neither in police detention nor held in custody by the police on the authority of the court to attend a police station in order to have a sample taken where:
   a) the person has been charged with a recordable offence, or informed that he will be reported for such an offence and, either he has not had a sample taken from him in the course of the investigation of the offence by the police , or he has had a sample so taken from him but either, it was not suitable for the same means of analysis or, though suitable, the sample proved insufficient; or
   b) the person has been convicted of a recordable offence and either he has not had a sample taken from him since the conviction or he has had a sample taken from him (before or after his conviction) but either, it was not suitable for the same means of analysis or, though suitable, the sample proved insufficient.

(5) The period allowed for requiring a person to attend a police station for the purpose specified in subsection (4) above is:
   a) in the case of a person falling within paragraph (a), one month beginning with the date of charge, or one month beginning with the date on which the appropriate officer is informed of the fact that the sample is not suitable for the same means of analysis, or has proved insufficient, as the case may be
   b) in the case of a person falling within paragraph (b), one month beginning with the date of the conviction, or one month beginning with the date on which the appropriate officer is informed of the fact that the sample is not suitable for the same person means of analysis or has proved insufficient, as the case may be.

(6) A requirement under subsection (4) above:
   a) shall give the person at least 7 days within which he must attend; and
   b) may direct him to attend at a specified time of day or between specified times of day.

(7) Any constable may arrest without warrant a person who has failed to comply with a requirement under subsection (4) above.

Explanation

The power of arrest is almost identical to that for the taking of fingerprints.

9.11 This power of arrest is summarised as being, one month from the date of conviction, charge or being reported for a recordable offence, or the constable being informed that the sample taken from that person is insufficient in quality or quantity for analysis. The person must then be given at least seven days to attend at a specified time or between specified times. Failure to comply renders a person liable to arrest.

INTERVIEWS AND CONFESSIONS

10.1 The rules governing the questioning of suspects are set out in Code C of the Codes of Practice. An interview is defined as 'the questioning of a person regarding his involvement in a criminal offence'. Such interviews are required to be carried out under caution.

10.2 A caution must be given to a person when there are grounds to suspect that he is involved in an offence. The caution must be given before any questions are asked if the person is already suspected of involvement, or further questions are asked once the answers to initial questions make the person a suspect. Otherwise, any reply given to questioning may be inadmissible in evidence at a later prosecution. A person need not be cautioned if the questions put to him are solely to establish his identity, or ownership of any vehicle, or to obtain information in accordance with statutory requirements, for example where a driver is required to give his name and address.

10.3 The caution is:
'You do not have to say anything, but it may harm your defence if you do not mention when questioned something which you later rely on in court. Anything you do say may be given in evidence.'

10.4 Minor deviations from the caution, provided the sense of the caution is preserved will not constitute a breach of the requirement to caution someone.

10.5 At a police station the interview should normally be conducted by way of contemporaneously recorded tape. At the commencement of the recording, the interviewing officer should introduce those present in the interview room, each in turn stating who they are and their role in the interview. The suspect must be reminded of his right to have free and independent legal advice throughout the interview and the fact that if he is not legally represented at that time he can at any time ask for free and independent legal advice. The officer conducting the interview must record on the tape the time, date and location of the interview, also he must inform the suspect that at the conclusion of the interview a notice will be given to him explaining how to obtain a copy of the taped interview. The suspect must be cautioned in the prescribed form and questions may then be put to him relating to the allegation being made. The suspect must be given an opportunity to answer any allegation made against him. If the suspect declines to be interviewed on tape, the interviewing officer must record the reasons why the suspect declines to be interviewed on tape during the normal introduction, after first attempting to get the suspect to detail his reasons on tape. Any such request from a suspect must be noted on the custody record. If the suspect elects of his own free will to discuss any other matter during a taped interview this should normally be done on tape after the conclusion of the formal interview for the offence under investigation. Any comments made whilst the tape is not running, during breaks, or whilst changing tapes if the interview is protracted, should be mentioned and covered as soon as practicable when the recording restarts. When a break is to be taken during the course of an interview, at which the suspect is to leave the interview room, the fact that the break is taken, the reason for it and the time, shall be recorded on the tape. The tapes shall then be removed from the machine and the procedure for conclusion of an interview shall be followed.

If, however, the break is to be a short one, with the suspect and a police officer remaining in the interview room, the fact that the break is taken, the reason for it and the time shall be recorded as before. The tape recorder may be turned off, but there will be no need to remove the tapes. The interview may then be resumed using the same tapes, with the time it recommences being recorded on the tape (Code E, Sections 4.9 and 4.10).

10.6 At the conclusion of the interview the suspect must be asked if there is anything he would like to add alter or correct. This is equally so where a written record of the interview is made rather than a taped interview. Any documents used or made during an interview should be clearly explained and identified on tape and signed by the persons present. Where possible, these documents should be treated as exhibits, and identified by their reference numbers. Where the interview has been recorded by audio tape or video, the tape or video should be sealed in accordance with Code E and signed by those present. The tape seal must contain the details of those present during an interview, the time started and concluded, the number of tapes used and the details of the suspect. If during the conduct of an interview, the suspect makes a complaint about his detention or any aspect of the policing of his case he should be told that the matter will be referred to the custody officer at the conclusion of the interview.

10.7 If a suspect has been arrested and there are certain matters which police officers wish to interview him about, he may be warned that his failure to answer questions can be brought to the attention of the court. Section 36 and 37 of the Criminal Justice and Public Order Act 1994 set out a 'special warning' which must be given to the suspect

10.8 The special warning is to be given when:
   a) a suspect is arrested by a constable and there is found on his person, or in or on his clothing or footwear, or otherwise in his possession, or in the place where he was arrested, any objects, marks or substances, or marks on such objects, and the person fails or refuses to account for the objects, marks or substances found; or
   b) an arrested person was found by a constable at the place at or about the time the offence for which he was arrested, is alleged to have been committed, and the person fails or refuses to account for his presence at that place.

10.9 For an inference to be drawn from the suspect's failure or refusal to answer a question or questions about one of the matters, or to answer in a satisfactory manner the investigating officer must first tell the suspect in ordinary language:
   a) what offence he is investigating
   b) what fact he is asking the suspect to account for
   c) that he believes this fact may be due to the suspect's taking part in the commission of the crime in question
   d) that a court may draw proper inference if he fails or refuses to account for the fact about which he is being questioned

e) that a record is being made of the interview and that it may be given in evidence if he is brought to trial.

10.10 The security of the tapes used in any interview is the responsibility of the officer in charge of the police station. Seals must not be broken on master tapes required for criminal proceedings, except in the presence of a member of the Crown Prosecution Service, the defendant and or his legal advisor. Where tapes have been sent for committal proceedings an application is required to the chief clerk to the Crown Court for release of the tapes for unsealing. A tape recording of an interview is primary evidence which can be played to the court rather than the reading of a transcript. It becomes an exhibit once produced for the court.

10.11 Following the arrest of a suspect, he must not be interviewed about the relevant offence except at a police station or other authorised place of detention unless the consequent delay would be likely:

i) to lead to interference with or harm to evidence connected with an offence, or interference with or physical harm to other people; or

ii) to lead to the alerting of other people suspected of having committed an offence but not yet arrested for it; or

iii) to hinder the recovery of property obtained in consequence of the commission of an offence.

The interview conducted on any of these grounds should cease as soon as the reasons for holding such an interview cease to exist.

10.12 Immediately prior to the start of any interview the officer in charge of the interview must remind the suspect of his right to free and independent legal advice, he should then put to the suspect any significant statement made prior to arrival at the police station. A statement will be any comment or silence which is relevant and which may be used in evidence. In particular, this must include any admissions of guilt or partial admissions, and any comments or silence which may give rise to inferences. Police officers must not try to elicit answers by force, fear or fraud. Oppression used during interviews of suspects will automatically cause any evidence obtained through the interview to be excluded. It does not matter if a suspect is telling the truth in a confession; if it is obtained by oppression, or because of things said or done which would render any admission unreliable, the courts must exclude it. Section 76 of the Police and Criminal Evidence Act 1984 is not a discretionary power. Courts must exclude confessions made in breach of the Section.

Section 76 Police and Criminal Evidence Act 1984

(1) In any proceedings a confession made by an accused person may be given in evidence against him so far as it is relevant to any matter in issue in the proceedings and is not excluded by the court in pursuance of this Section.

(2) If, in any proceedings where the prosecution proposes to give in evidence a confession made by an accused person, it is represented to the court that the confession was or may have been obtained:

a) by oppression of the person who made it; or

b) in consequence of anything said or done which was likely, in the circumstances existing at the time, to render unreliable any confession which might be made by him in consequence thereof, the court shall not allow the confession to be given in evidence against him except in so far as the prosecution proves to the court, beyond reasonable doubt that the confession (not-withstanding that it may be true) was not obtained as aforesaid.

(3) In any proceedings where the prosecution proposes to give in evidence a confession made by an accused person, the court may of its own motion require the prosecution, as a condition of allowing it to do so, to prove that the confession was not obtained as mentioned in subsection (2) above.

(4) The fact that a confession is wholly or partly excluded in pursuance of this Section shall not affect the admissibility in evidence:
   a) of any facts discovered as a result of the confession; or
   b) where the confession is relevant as showing that the accused speaks, writes or expresses himself in a particular way, of so much of a confession as is necessary to show that he does so.

(5) Evidence that a fact to which this subsection applies was discovered as a result of a statement made by an accused person shall not be admissible unless evidence of how it was discovered is given by him or on his behalf.

(6) Subsection (5) above applies:
   a) to any fact discovered as a result of a confession which is wholly excluded in pursuance of this Section; and
   b) to any fact discovered as a result of a confession which is partly so excluded, if that fact is discovered as a result of the excluded part of the confession.

Explanation

Section 76 only applies to evidence of confessions, and basically the court must exclude any confession obtained by oppression, or other inducements which make it unsafe.

10.13 Oppression can include, torture, inhuman or degrading treatment, and the use of threats of violence whether or not amounting to torture. The term oppression has been interpreted by the courts. In *R v Samuel* [1988] the court stated that the denial of access to a solicitor might be oppressive. In *R v Fulling* [1987] the court held that it was not oppressive for the police to tell the suspect that her lover had been having an affair with another woman. In this case the court held that the word oppression should take its meaning from the Oxford English Dictionary as 'the exercise of authority or power in a burdensome, harsh or wrongful manner; unjust or cruel treatment of subjects, inferiors, etc; the imposition of unreasonable or unjust burdens'. It was argued in this case that oppression could occur where there had been no impropriety by the police. Lord Lane however stated that he felt that it was difficult to envisage circumstances where oppression would not entail some form of impropriety by the police.

10.14 Unreliability as mentioned in Section 76(2)(b) is the second instance where evidence of confession must be excluded. This may be where other breaches of the Codes of Practice have occurred and a confession has arisen as a result. In the case of *R v Harvey* [1988] a confession to murder done in the presence of her lesbian lover was excluded. The defendant had a low IQ and she suffered from a psyhcopathic disorder which was aggravated by alcohol abuse. Both woman had blood on their clothes. The other woman had confessed, and upon hearing of the confession, the defendant made a full confession. The other woman then retracted her own confession. There was psychiatric evidence before the court that it was possible that the defendant had confessed having heard of her lover's confession, in a child like attempt to take the blame on herself. The judge said that the prosecution had not discharged the burden of proof regarding the reliability of the confession. The jury were directed to acquit. There are many other cases where the confession has been excluded for a variety of reasons.

10.15 Read literally, Section 76 requires the court to consider the validity of any evidence of confession before it can be put before the court. This is normally done on a 'voire dire' (trial within a trial, without the jury), in the absence of the jury as it is a point of law, rather than a question of fact. Confessions can of course also be challenged under Section 78 and 82(3) of the Police and Criminal Evidence Act (see paragraphs 4.6 – 4.9).

PROSECUTION POLICIES

The Crown Prosecution Code

11.1 The Crown Prosecution Service has a prosecution policy code which dictates the approach that individual prosecutors should adopt for all cases. The code is designed to bring consistency and fairness to all involved. The code sets out two tests for prosecution, 'the evidential test' and the 'public interest test'. If the case papers do not reveal sufficient evidence and information to give a realistic prospect of conviction then the case should go no further.

The 'Evidential Test'

11.2 i) Can the evidence be used in court:
- is it likely that the evidence will be excluded by a court?
- is the evidence admissible to the court under the rules governing evidence?
- is there enough evidence to give a realistic prospect of a conviction?

ii) Is the evidence reliable:
- is any confession unreliable due to the age of the suspect, mental illness, lack of understanding or other viable objection to it?
- is the witness's background such that his evidence will weaken the prosecution case? does the witness have any motive such as malice? or have a relevant recent conviction?
- is the identification of the accused as the offender likely to be questioned? if so how strong is the evidence of identification?

The Public Interest Test

11.3 The question as to whether or not a prosecution is to take place will depend on not only the prospect of a conviction, but also showing that justice must be seen to be done in a manner which is fair to all.

Lord Shawcross said in 1951:
   'It has never been the rule in this country, I hope it never will be, that suspected
   criminal offences must automatically be the subject of prosecution'.

There will obviously be factors which weigh either in favour or otherwise of prosecution or not dependent upon the circumstances. Those factors may be:
- a conviction is likely to result in a significant sentence
- a weapon was used or violence was threatened during the commission of the offence
- the offence was committed against a public servant, e.g. police, fire, nurse or similar
- the defendant was in a position of trust
- evidence shows that the defendant was a ringleader or organiser of the crime

- evidence of premeditation when committing the offence
- evidence of group action
- vulnerable victim was subject of the offence
- offence motivated by victimisation on the grounds of ethnic, political, sexual or religious beliefs
- marked difference between the mental ability of offender and victim, or any element of corrupting vulnerable victim
- relevant previous cautions or convictions of the offender
- offence committed against or contrary to any court order of prohibition
- offender is likely to continue committing similar offences, history of similar offending
- the offence although not serious in itself is prevalent in the area.

11.4 There will always be reasons not to prosecute. Some of the common public interest reasons are:
- probability of nominal or very small penalty
- the offence was committed by misunderstanding of the facts which mitigate the seriousness of the offence
- the loss or harm created by the offence is minimal and was as a result of a single incident which is more in the nature of a misjudgement or accident
- a long delay in bringing the prosecution between the date of the offence and the date of trial unless:
  - the offence is serious
  - delay caused by the defendant
  - the offence has only recently become known
  - the complexity of the offence has protracted the investigation
- any prosecution is likely to have a very detrimental effect on the victim's physical or mental health, always bearing in mind the seriousness of the offence
- elderly defendant suffering from poor mental or physical health unless the offence is serious and there is a real likelihood of repeated offending. The prosecutor will have to balance desirability of diverting an offender suffering significant mental or physical health problems with the need to safeguard the public
- the offender has made full and appropriate compensation, this should not be merely to avoid prosecution
- details may be made public which could harm sources of information, international relations or security.

11.5 The decision whether or not to proceed will be taken by weighing all the factors which dictate prosecution policy. It is clear that decisions will be very individual and what in one case seems reasonable may in another seem totally at odds with the decision arrived at. Not all factors are such that they will become common knowledge. The interests of the victim are always a very important consideration to the Crown Prosecutor. The age of the victim and offender will also have a bearing on any decision arrived at.

Police Cautions

11.6 The Home Office issues cautioning guidelines for offenders. If the defendant admits an offence cautioning will be the most common alternative to prosecution. Crown Prosecutors look at these criteria when considering the public interest; they should tell the police if they think that a caution is the most appropriate course of action for an offender.

Charging

11.7 Charges should be selected and preferred by the Crown Prosecutor, these should be selected to:

1: Reflect the serious nature of the offence
2: Ensure the court have adequate sentencing powers
3: Enable the case to be presented in a clear and precise way.

11.8 This can mean that the prosecutor may not continue with the most serious of charges, also that where duplicitous charges have been preferred by the police not all will be continued with. Decisions about which charge should be continued should not be made on the basis of the potential to 'plea bargain'.

Mode of Trial

11.9 The Crown Prosecution Service currently follows the guidelines set out in the 'National Mode of Trial Guidelines' issued by the Lord Chief Justice. It should never be the case that the mere need to expedite a trial should dictate where the trial should be held. Justice is the most important factor.

Guilty Pleas

11.10 Where a defendant offers to plead guilty to a lesser or different charge, the prosecutor must weigh the likely sentence and the probability of a successful prosecution, to ensure that any alternative charge reflects the seriousness of the circumstances. Crown Prosecutors must never accept a guilty plea solely on the grounds of convenience.

Restarting a Prosecution

11.11 There is a need for certainty in prosecution policy and the approach adopted to all defendants to criminal charges. Normally, where the prosecutor has informed the defendant that there will not be any action taken this must be the case unless:

– rare cases where a review of the original decision shows it was clearly wrong and should not be allowed to stand
– cases which are stopped to allow further and better evidence to become available. Where it is apparent that this is likely to occur, the prosecutor will normally inform the defendant of this possibility
– cases stopped for lack of evidence but where significant evidence is found at a later date.

DISCLOSURE OF EVIDENCE

12.1 There are two distinct types of disclosure, those of known and revealed facts upon which any prosecution is based, and those which are known but unused. This is further qualified by what is termed sensitive material and non-sensitive material.

12.2 When a police investigation begins, materials are collected which may or may not form part of the prosecution case to prove the guilt of a defendant. The very nature of any investigation is such that evidence will be collected which has no direct bearing on the prosecution's ability to prove a set of facts. The problem is that those facts may well support the defence assertions of innocence. Some evidence will contain facts which are inconclusive or misleading. An example is that of partial fingerprints found on a knife used to kill Adam. Bloggs when arrested had his fingerprints taken by the police for comparison. The fingerprint expert could not find sufficient detail on the fingerprint from the knife to prove who had held it when the fatal wound was inflicted. Although this evidence does not prove Bloggs guilty neither does it prove his innocence. It is a fact discovered during the investigation, of apparent irrelevance as it is inconclusive. However if the fingerprint expert is challenged on his evidence he might be able to say that of the five features found in the fingerprint from the knife, all five were found on the fingerprints of Bloggs. The evidence, although not provable in itself, provides corroboration of other assertions.

12.3 The provisions of disclosure becomes relevant during the investigation when considering pre-interview briefings for suspect's representatives, of known facts and evidence; also when after charge, decisions are to be made as to what is sensitive and should not normally be disclosed, and those details which may undermine the prosecution case within the unused materials. Police officers are now required to investigate offences rather than simply provide evidence to prosecute.

Pre-Interview Disclosure

12.4 Practically speaking, the defendant should have as much information as is available of what the officers investigating an offence wish to speak to him about including whether they have any statements or other evidence to justify the need for an interview. Most solicitors present during an interview will call the interview to a halt if they are 'ambushed' with facts and evidence unknown to them prior to the interview. This is especially true if the officer is making assertions for which he has no supporting statement or other evidence. The purpose of an interview is to get the suspect to account for a state of affairs that exist or facts which indicate guilt to some degree or other. Certain matters may result in the suspect simply refusing to answer questions, in which case the appropriate warnings should be given.

Post Charge Disclosure

12.5 When a person has been charged or reported for summons the decision as to what is to be revealed to the defence will depend on a decision made by the prosecutor. This decision in turn will depend on the information being submitted to him by the disclosure officer who in turn will depend upon the investigator to inform him about the evidence. The Criminal Procedure and Investigation Act 1996 (CPIA 96) creates a duty for the investigator of any crime to make reasonable enquires into the matter. This duty to make reasonable enquires is now a statutory requirement and will include making all such enquires as are reasonable and possible. In practical terms it will mean taking negative statements, or details of those who profess to have seen nothing, including those who are unwilling to say what they have seen, as well as taking statements from those who have seen something, especially those who provide first descriptions. The investigator may be called to court to account for what enquires were undertaken and why others were not. The emphasis is on the word reasonable. It would not be reasonable, for instance, to question an entire football ground full of supporters over a minor theft.

12.6 Primary disclosure under Section 3 CPIA 96 dictates that the prosecutor must disclose any evidence not previously disclosed to the defence which may undermine the prosecution case, or give a statement to the effect that all evidence has been disclosed and that there is no evidence which could undermine the prosecution case. This amounts to a certification that there is no such evidence known or available.

12.7 This legislation will impact on the procedures of police officers investigating any offence.

The Criminal Procedure and Investigations Act 1996 applies in circumstances where:

a) A person is charged with a summary offence in respect of which he or she pleads not guilty and the court proceeds to summary trial.

b) A person has attained the age of eighteen, is charged with an offence which is triable either-way, he or she pleads not guilty, and the court proceeds to summary trial.

c) A person aged under eighteen is charged with an indictable offence for which he or she pleads not guilty and the court proceeds to summary trial.

Disclosure is required also where regardless of the plea of the accused:

a) A person is charged and indicted for trial on that offence.

b) A person is charged with an indictable offence for trial under transfer to Crown Court by notice of transfer (serious or complex fraud).

c) Where a person is charged with an indictable offence for trial, and notice of transfer is served on the magistrates to transfer the case to Crown Court (certain offences involving children).

d) A charge of a summary offence is included under a bill of indictment (e.g. common assault).

e) There is a bill of indictment charging an offence to be dealt with at Crown Court (this is known as a voluntary bill of indictment).

This means that disclosure is effective for the prosecution in all cases where the defendant has pleaded not guilty at both magistrates and Crown Courts.

12.8 The Act also applies where there has not yet been a formal investigation into an offence [Section 9(4) Criminal Procedure and Investigations Act 1996]. For the purposes of the Act a criminal investigation is an investigation which police officers or other persons have a duty to conduct with a view to it being ascertained, whether a person should be charged with an offence or whether a person charged with an offence is guilty of it. This could affect courts of enquiry such as a coroner's court, where enquires are made into the cause of a person's death.

Explanation

The fact that the Act applies even where a formal investigation has not yet commenced means that any evidence which may be relevant to an impending investigation should be retained for disclosure.

12.9 The effect of the primary disclosure by the prosecutor is that the defence then have to respond with a 'statement of defence' under Section 5. This statement of defence is mandatory for all matters committed to trial at Crown Court, or dealt with by way of indictment under Section 1 of the Act. However defence statements are only subject to voluntary disclosure under Section 6 of the Act when proceedings are at the magistrates' court.

Defence Statement

Section 5(6) Criminal Procedure and Investigations Act 1996 states that for the purposes of this Section a 'defence statement' is a written statement:

a) setting out in general terms the nature of the accused's defence

b) indicating the matters on which the defence take issue with the prosecution, and

c) setting out, in the case of each matter, the reason why he takes issue with the prosecution.

Section 5(7) provides that if the defence statement discloses an alibi the accused must give particulars of the alibi including:

a) the name and address of any witness the accused believes is able to give evidence in support of the alibi, if the name and address are known to the accused when the statement is given

b) any information in the accused's possession which might be of material assistance in finding such a witness, if his name or address is not known to the accused when the statement is given.

Explanation

The defence statement should be in such terms as allow the prosecutor to determine what matters are at issue, which witnesses will be required, and such evidence of alibi as may require to be tested.

12.10 At the magistrates' court there is provision for voluntary disclosure by the accused and in time it will be seen whether or not this works in practice. There is a danger that even when a formal defence statement has been served, a different barrister or defence team may see an alternative or additional line of defence not included in the statement. How the courts will deal with the dilemma of a defendant facing a custodial sentence but for the appropriate defence, remains to be seen. If, as before, where the defence have been allowed on occasions to provide last minute alibi evidence, it is undoubted that similar latitude will be required for defence statements. There is provision for a sanction by the court, which may draw the failure of the defence to comply with the defence statement and alibi to the notice of the jury if the case gets that far. If the prosecution fail to comply evidence may be excluded.

12.11 Disclosure by the prosecutor remains a continual requirement throughout the prosecution process. Police forces and the Crown Prosecution Service have a joint policy which details how un-used materials will be dealt with.

12.12 The disclosure of unused materials will depend upon the category that they fall into, sensitive or non-sensitive. If the materials fall into the sensitive category they may be subject of a claim by the prosecution of public interest immunity from disclosure. Public Interest Immunity covers all materials which affect the security of state.

12.13 There is a code of practice issued under Section 23(1) of the Criminal Procedure and Investigations Act 1996, which gives definitions of the persons and materials to which the Act applies. It also specifies how these should be dealt with.

Definitions in Relation to the Interpretation of the Act

Criminal Investigation

12.14 Is an investigation conducted by police officers with a view to it being ascertained whether a person should be charged with an offence, or whether a person charged is guilty of it. This will include:

- investigations into crimes that have been committed
- investigations whose purpose is to ascertain whether a crime has been committed, with a view to the possible institution of criminal proceedings; and
- investigations which begin in the belief that a crime may be committed, for example when the police keep premises or individuals under observation for a period of time, with a view to the possible institution of criminal proceedings.

Charging
Charging a person with an offence includes prosecution by way of summons.

Investigator
An investigator is any police officer involved in the conduct of criminal investigation. All investigators have a responsibility for carrying out the duties imposed on them under this code, including in particular, recording information, and retaining records of information and other material.

Officer in Charge of the Investigation
Is the police officer responsible for directing a criminal investigation. He is also responsible for ensuring that proper procedures are in place for the recording of information, and retaining records of information and other material, in the investigation.

The Disclosure Officer
Is the person responsible for examining material retained by the police during the investigation; revealing material to the prosecutor during the investigation and any criminal proceedings resulting from it, and certifying that he has done this, and disclosing material to the accused at the request of the prosecutor.

The Prosecutor
Is the authority responsible for the conduct of criminal proceedings on behalf of the Crown. Particular duties may in practice fall to individuals acting on behalf of the prosecuting authority.

Material
Is material of any kind, including information and objects which are obtained in the course of a criminal investigation and which may be relevant to the investigation.

Relevant Material
Material may be relevant to an investigation if it appears to an investigator, or to the officer in charge of an investigation, or to the disclosure officer, that it has some bearing on any offence under investigation or any person being investigated, or on the circumstances of the case, unless it is incapable of having any impact on the case.

Sensitive Material
Is material which the disclosure officer believes after consulting the officer in charge of the investigation, it is not in the public interest to disclose.

Primary Prosecution Disclosure
References to primary prosecution disclosure are to the duty of the prosecutor under Section 3 of the Act to disclose material which is in his possession or which he has inspected in pursuance of this code. and which in his opinion might under-mine the case against the accused.

Secondary Prosecution Disclosure
References to secondary prosecution disclosure are to the duty of the prosecutor under Section 7 of the Act to disclose material which is in his possession or which he has inspected in pursuance of this code, and which might reasonably be expected to assist the defence disclosed by the accused in a defence statement given under the Act.

Disclosure to a Person

References to the disclosure of material to a person accused of an offence include references to the disclosure of material to his legal representative.

Police Officers

References to police officers and to the chief officer of police include those employed in a police force as defined in Section 3(3) of the Prosecution of Offences Act 1985.

General Responsibilities Arising Under the Rules

Investigator

12.15 The functions of the investigator, the officer in charge of an investigation and the disclosure officer are separate. Whether they are undertaken by one, two or more persons will depend on the complexity of the case and the administrative arrangements within each police force. Where they are undertaken by more than one person, close consultation between them is essential to the effective performance of the duties imposed by this code.

Chief Officer of Police

Is responsible for putting in place arrangements to ensure that in every investigation the identity of the officer in charge of an investigation and the disclosure officer is recorded.

Officer in Charge of an Investigation

May delegate tasks to another investigator or to civilians employed by the police force, but he remains responsible for ensuring that these have been carried out and for accounting for any general policies followed in the investigation. In particular, it is an essential part of his duties to ensure that all material which may be relevant to an investigation is retained, and either made available to the disclosure officer or (in exceptional circumstances) revealed directly to the prosecutor.

Conduct of the Investigation

The investigator should pursue all reasonable lines of inquiry, whether these point towards or away from the suspect. What is reasonable in each case will depend on the particular circumstances. If the officer in charge of an investigation believes that other persons may be in possession of material that may be relevant to the investigation, and if this has not been obtained already, he should ask the disclosure officer to inform them of the existence of the investigation and to invite them to retain the material in case they receive a request for its disclosure. The disclosure officer should inform the prosecutor that they may have such material. However, the officer in charge of an investigation is not required to make speculative enquires of other persons: there must be some reason to believe that they may have relevant material. That reason may come from information provided to the police by the accused or from other inquiries made or from some other source. If, during a criminal investigation, the officer in charge of an investigation or disclosure officer for any reason no longer has responsibility for the functions falling to him, either his supervisor or the police officer in charge of criminal investigations for the police force concerned must assign someone else to assume that responsibility. That person's identity must be recorded, as with those initially responsible for these functions in each investigation.

Explanation

Where an investigation takes place the identity of the disclosure officer must be recorded, it is the responsibility of the officer in charge of the investigation to do this and if there are any changes in the details of the disclosure officer these must also be recorded. In major enquires the disclosure officer may be the exhibits officer, but in smaller enquires could be the same officer as the investigator.

Recording of Information

12.16 If material which may be relevant to the investigation consists of information which is not recorded in any form, the officer in charge of an investigation must ensure that it is recorded in a durable or retrievable form (whether in writing, on video or audio tape, or on computer disk). Where it is not practicable to retain the initial record of information because it forms part of a larger record which is to be destroyed, its contents should be transferred as a true record to a durable and more easily-stored form before that happens. Negative information is often relevant to an investigation. If it may be relevant it must be recorded. An example might be a where details are obtained of persons who initially make negative statements at the scene of a crime, e.g. where a fight takes place in premises, details may be obtained of those who say they saw nothing, such negative information may reveal details of those who later can be questioned further, or who may change their view of what information they can supply. Where information which may be relevant is obtained, it must be recorded at the time it is obtained or as soon as practicable after that time. This includes, for example, information obtained in house-to-house enquiries, although the requirement to record information promptly does not require an investigator to take a formal statement from a potential witness where it would not otherwise be taken.

Explanation

Documents, information and objects should be preserved for evidential purposes in the most suitable form for production if required to the court. This will include photostats of originals, copies in a presentable form, copy computer printouts etc.

Collection and Retention of Material

12.17 There is a continuing duty to retain all material connected with a criminal investigation in a manner in which it can be inspected or produced. This is subject to review after conclusion of the case when the rules relating to retention periods apply. It should be remembered that some of the evidence may form part of an innocent party's or victim's personal belongings, or be records which are required for the operation of their businesses. As such, after conclusion of cases these should be returned to their rightful owners in accordance with the retention period rules *(see below)*.

12.18 The investigator must retain material obtained in a criminal investigation which may be relevant to the investigation. This includes not only material coming into the possession of the investigator (such as documents seized in the course of searching premises) but also material generated by him (such as interview records, notes made in preparation for such interviews etc). Material may be photographed, or retained in the form of a copy rather than the original, if the original is perishable, or was supplied to the investigator rather than generated by him and is to be returned to its owner. Where material has been seized in the exercise of the powers of seizure conferred by the Police and Criminal Evidence Act 1984, the duty to retain it under the code is subject to the provisions on the retention of seized material in Section 22 of that Act. If the officer in charge of an investigation becomes aware as a result of developments in the case that material previously examined but not retained (because it was not thought to be relevant) may now be relevant to the investigation, he should, wherever practicable, take steps to obtain it or ensure that it is retained for further inspection or for production in court if required. The duty to retain material includes in particular the duty to retain material falling into the following categories, where it may be relevant to the investigation:

- crime reports (including crime report forms, relevant parts of incident report books or police officers' notebooks)
- custody records
- records which are derived from tapes of telephone messages (for example 999 calls) containing descriptions of an alleged offence or offender
- final versions of witness statements (and draft versions where their content differs from the final version), including any exhibits mentioned (unless these have been returned to their owner on the understanding that they will be produced in court if required)
- interview records (written records, or audio or video tapes, of interviews with actual or potential witnesses or suspects)
- communications between the police and experts such as forensic scientists, reports of work carried out by experts, and Schedules of scientific material prepared by the expert for the investigator, for the purposes of criminal proceedings
- any material casting doubt on the reliability of a confession
- any material casting doubt on the reliability of a witness
- any other material which may fall within the test for primary prosecution disclosure in the Act.

The duty to retain material falling into these categories does not extend to items which are purely ancillary to such material and possess no independent significance (for example, duplicate copies of records or reports).

Periods for Retention of Materials Prior to Disposal After Investigation Completion

12.19 All material which may be relevant to the investigation must be retained until a decision is taken whether to institute proceedings against a person for an offence. If a criminal investigation results in proceedings being instituted, all material which may be relevant must be retained at least until the accused is acquitted or convicted or the prosecutor decides not to proceed with the case. Where the accused is convicted, all material which may be relevant must be retained at least until:

- the convicted person is released from custody, or discharged from hospital, in cases where the court imposes a custodial sentence or a hospital order
- six months from the date of conviction in all other cases
- If the court imposes a custodial sentence or hospital order and the convicted person is released from custody or discharged from hospital earlier than six months from the date of conviction, all material which may be relevant must be retained at least until six months from the date of conviction
- If an appeal against conviction is in progress when the release or discharge occurs, or at the end of the period of six months specified, all material which may be relevant must be retained until the appeal is determined
- If the Criminal Cases Review Commission is considering an application at that point in time, all material which may be relevant must be retained at least until the Commission decides not to refer the case to the Court of Appeal, or until the court determines the appeal resulting from the reference by the Commission.

Material need not be retained by the police if it was seized and is to be returned to its rightful owner.

Preparation of Material for Prosecutor

12.20 The officer in charge of the investigation, the disclosure officer or an investigator may seek advice from the prosecutor about whether any particular item of material may be relevant to the investigation. Material which may be relevant to an investigation, which has been retained in accordance with the code, and which the disclosure officer believes will not form part of the prosecution case, must be listed on a Schedule. Material which the disclosure officer does not believe is sensitive must be listed on a Schedule of non-sensitive material. The Schedule must include a statement that the disclosure officer does not believe the material is sensitive. Any material which is believed to be sensitive must be either listed on a Schedule of sensitive material or, in exceptional circumstances, revealed to the prosecutor separately.

Preparation of Schedule

The disclosure officer must ensure that a Schedule is prepared in the following circumstances:
- the accused is charged with an offence which is triable only on indictment
- the accused is charged with an offence which is triable either way, and it is considered either that the case is likely to be tried on indictment or that the accused is likely to plead not guilty at a summary trial
- the accused is charged with a summary offence, and it is considered that he is likely to plead not guilty.

Explanation

If the suspect is charged with an offence, for which it is suspected he will plead not guilty or is charged with an indictable offence a Schedule will be required.In practice it may be simpler to prepare a Schedule for all suspects who are charged.

The disclosure officer need not initially have to prepare a Schedule in the following circumstances:
- In respect of either way and summary offences, a Schedule may not be needed if a person has admitted the offence, or if a police officer witnessed the offence and that person has not denied it
- If it is believed that the accused is likely to plead guilty at a summary trial, it is not necessary to prepare a Schedule in advance. (If however contrary to this belief, the accused pleads not guilty at a summary trial, or the offence is to be tried on indictment, the disclosure officer must ensure that a Schedule is prepared as soon as is reasonably practicable after that happens).

Explanation

A Schedule is not required if a guilty plea at magistrates, is the anticipated result of charging the suspect.

Schedule Preparation

The disclosure officer should ensure that each item of material is listed separately on the Schedule:
- Is numbered consecutively.
- The description of each item should make clear the nature of the item and should

contain sufficient detail to enable the prosecutor to decide whether he needs to inspect the material before deciding whether or not it should be disclosed.

In some enquiries it may not be practicable to list each item of material separately. For example, there may be many items of a similar or repetitive nature. These may be listed in a block and described by quantity and generic title. Even if some material is listed in a block, the disclosure officer must ensure that any items among that material which might meet the test for primary prosecution disclosure are listed and described individually.

Sensitive Material

12.21 The disclosure officer must list on a sensitive Schedule any material which he believes it is not in the public interest to disclose, and the reason for that belief. The Schedule must include a statement that the disclosure officer believes the material is sensitive. Depending on the circumstances, examples of such material may include the following, (this is not an exhaustive list):

- material relating to national security
- material received from the intelligence and security agencies
- material relating to intelligence from foreign sources which reveals sensitive intelligence gathering methods
- material given in confidence
- material which relates to the use of a telephone system and which is supplied to an investigator for intelligence purposes only
- material relating to the identity or activities of informants, or under-cover police officers, or other persons supplying information to the police who may be in danger if their identities are revealed
- material revealing the location of any premises or other place used for police surveillance, or the identity of any person allowing a police officer to use them for surveillance
- material revealing, either directly or indirectly, techniques and methods relied upon by a police officer in the course of a criminal investigation, for example covert surveillance techniques. or other methods of detecting crime
- material whose disclosure might facilitate the commission of other offences or hinder the prevention and detection of crime
- internal police communications such as management minutes
- material upon the strength of which search warrants were obtained
- material containing details of persons taking part in identification parades
- material supplied to an investigator during a criminal investigation which has been generated by an official of a body concerned with the regulation or supervision of bodies corporate or of persons engaged in financial activities, or which has been generated by a person retained by such a body
- material supplied to an investigator during a criminal investigation which relates to a child or young person and which has been generated by a local authority social services department, an Area Child Protection Committee or other party contacted by an investigator during the investigation.

In exceptional circumstances, where an investigator considers that material is so sensitive that its revelation to the prosecutor by means of an entry on the sensitive Schedule is inappropriate, the existence of the material must be revealed to the prosecutor separately. This will apply where compromising the material would be likely to lead directly to the loss of life, or directly threaten national security. In such circumstances, the responsibility for informing the prosecutor lies with the investigator who knows the detail of the sensitive material. The investigator should act as soon as is reasonably practicable after the file containing the prosecution case is sent to the prosecutor. The investigator must also ensure that the prosecutor is able to inspect the material so that he can assess whether it needs to be brought before a court for a ruling on disclosure.

Revelation of Material to Prosecutor

12.22 The disclosure officer must give the Schedules to the prosecutor. Wherever practicable this should be at the same time as he gives him the file containing the material for the prosecution case (or as soon as is reasonably practicable after the decision on mode of trial or the plea where a Schedule was not prepared because a guilty plea was anticipated). The disclosure officer should draw the attention of the prosecutor to any material an investigator has retained (whether or not listed on a Schedule) which may fall within the test for primary prosecution disclosure in the Act. and should explain why he has come to that view. At the same time the disclosure officer must give the prosecutor a copy of any material which falls into the following categories (unless such material has already been given to the prosecutor as part of the file containing the material for the prosecution case):

- records of the first description of a suspect given to the police by a potential witness, whether or not the description differs from that of the alleged offender
- information provided by an accused person which indicates an explanation for the offence with which he has been charged
- any material casting doubt on the reliability of a confession
- any material casting doubt on the reliability of a witness
- any other material which the investigator believes may fall within the test for primary prosecution disclosure in the Act.

If the prosecutor asks to inspect material which has not already been copied to him, the disclosure officer must allow him to inspect it. If the prosecutor asks for a copy of material which has not already been copied to him, the disclosure officer must give him a copy. However, this does not apply where the disclosure officer believes, having consulted the officer in charge of the investigation, that the material is too sensitive to be copied and can only be inspected. If material consists of information which is recorded other than in writing, whether it should be given to the prosecutor in its original form as a whole by way of relevant extracts recorded in the same form, or in the form of a transcript, is a matter for agreement between the disclosure officer and prosecutor.

The Continuing Duty of the Disclosure Officer

12.23 At the time a Schedule of non-sensitive material is prepared, the disclosure officer may not know exactly what material will form the case against the accused, and the prosecutor may not have given advice about the likely relevance of particular items of material. Once these matters have been determined, the disclosure officer must give the prosecutor, where necessary an amended Schedule listing any additional material which:

- may be relevant to the investigation
- does not form part of the case against the accused
- is not already listed on the Schedule, and
- he believes is not sensitive.

After a defence statement has been given, the disclosure officer must look again at the material which has been retained and must draw the attention of the prosecutor to any material which might reasonably be expected to assist the defence disclosed by the accused; and he must reveal it to him as earlier stated. Section 9 of the Criminal Procedure and Investigations Act 1996 imposes a continuing duty on the prosecutor, for the duration of criminal proceedings against the accused, to disclose material which meets the tests for disclosure (subject to public interest considerations). To enable him to do this, any new material coming to light should be treated in the same way as the earlier material.

Disclosure Officer's Certificate

12.24 The disclosure officer must certify to the prosecutor that to the best of his knowledge and belief, all material which has been retained and made available to him has been revealed to the prosecutor in accordance with this code. He must sign and date the certificate. It will be necessary to certify not only at the time when the Schedule and accompanying material is submitted to the prosecutor, but also when material which has been retained is reconsidered after the accused has given a defence statement.

Explanation

Throughout the progress of a case there is a need for the disclosure officer to continually review the need to disclose the relevant materials, and review whether others have become pertinent or not. This is especially important if and when the defence statement has been served upon the prosecutor

Disclosure of Material to Accused

12.25 If material has not already been copied to the prosecutor, and he requests its disclosure to the accused on the ground that:
   – it falls within the test for primary or secondary prosecution disclosure, or
   – the court has ordered its disclosure after considering an application from the accused,
the disclosure officer must disclose it to the accused.

If material has been copied to the prosecutor, and it is to be disclosed, whether it is disclosed by the prosecutor or by the disclosure officer is a matter of agreement between the two of them. The disclosure officer must disclose material to the accused either by giving him a copy or by allowing him to inspect it. If the accused person asks for a copy of any material which he has been allowed to inspect, the disclosure officer must give it to him, unless in the opinion of the disclosure officer, is either not practicable (for example because the material consists of an object which cannot be copied, or because the volume of material is so great), or not desirable (for example because the material is a statement by a child witness in relation to a sexual offence). If material which the accused has been allowed to inspect consists of information which is recorded other than in writing, whether it should be given to the accused in its original form or in the form of a transcript, is a matter for the discretion of the disclosure officer. If the material is transcribed, the disclosure officer must ensure that the transcript is certified to the accused as a true record of the material which has been transcribed. If a court concludes that it is in the public interest that an item of sensitive material must be disclosed to the accused, it will be necessary to disclose the material if the case is to proceed. This does not mean that sensitive documents must always be disclosed in their original form: for example, the court may agree that sensitive details still requiring protection should be blocked out, or that documents may be summarised, or that the prosecutor may make an admission about the substance of the material under Section 10 of the Criminal Justice Act 1967.

Explanation

Sensitive materials may be edited, subject to the court's approval, so that the information contained is available as required to show proof of a point at issue, but that the sensitive parts of the document or thing are not disclosed.

Keynote Cases

13.1 Case One: Hearsay
Subramaniam v Public Prosecutor of Malaya [1956] 1 WLR 965

Problem
What is a hearsay statement?

Circumstances
This case arises from a period during which emergency powers had been sought and granted for the purpose of preventing terrorism during the Malayan uprising. The possession of firearms and ammunition were prohibited. The accused was charged with unlawful possession of ammunition. His defence was that he had been captured by terrorists and was acting under duress. The trial judge had refused to allow evidence of what had been said by the terrorists to the defendant as such statements are hearsay and inadmissible unless the terrorists gave evidence. An appeal was made to the Privy Council.

Decision
Evidence of a statement made to a witness may or may not he hearsay. It will be hearsay if the purpose of the statement is to prove the truth of the statement's content. It is not hearsay and is admissible if it is given to prove that a statement was made.

Comment
It is too simplistic to describe hearsay as, 'what a witness has heard another person, not the defendant, say.' Such evidence will be hearsay, and generally inadmissible where the purpose is to prove that truth of what the other person said. It will not amount to hearsay, when the purpose is to prove that the fact that the other person did say it.

13.2 Case Two: Hearsay
R v Woodcock (1789) I Leech 500

Problem
When making a dying declaration, must the deceased have made a statement acknowledging the fact that he was dying, or will the jury be able to infer knowledge of the nearness of death from other facts.

Circumstances
The accused was charged with murdering his wife. She made a statement implicating him at the time when her death was inevitable as a result of severe head injuries. She died within

forty-eight hours of making the statement. Although seriously injured she remained coherent almost until her death, she never made any statement which could be said to be in recognition that she was dying, or that she had a settled and hopeless expectation of death. The question of whether this could be imputed from her injuries and attendant facts was left for the jury.

Decision

A jury may take all factors into account to draw an inference that the deceased had a settled expectation of death.

Comment

There are many cases which take the opposing view from that in this case, that the dying person must show clear understanding that he is dying, and that the statements made clearly display this expectation of death and relate to its cause.

13.3 Case Three: Documentary Hearsay
R v Spiby [1990] Crim LR 199

Section 69(1) Police and Criminal Evidence Act 1984

Problem

If the court is considering the evidence provided by a machine must the person producing it be able to prove the machine was working properly if the machine acts automatically when printing its results?

Circumstances

Spiby was tried for smuggling drugs. He had visited France on numerous occasions, but on one visit had used a hotel in Cherbourg. Whilst at the hotel he had made some telephone calls to others involved. The telephone system at the hotel automatically produced a printout giving the time of the call, the duration and the number called. The prosecution sought to have this admitted in evidence but did not have the engineer for the phone system. They had called in evidence the hotel manager who admitted that he was not an expert with regard to the phone system. He could not product a certificate to show that the telephone was working properly. The recorder ruled that the printout could be admitted as real evidence. Spiby appealed on the grounds that the ruling was incorrect. It was held on appeal that the telephone printout being automatic was very similar to the operation of a thermometer, or camera. and although there is a risk of error in the program of the telephone system that is very similar to a thermometer being badly calibrated. The evidence of an automatic machine was to be treated as real evidence provided the machine could be shown to be reliable in its operation. An automatic machine was viewed as being one which operated without the intervention of the human mind.

Decision

Evidence in the form of a printout relating to its performance, from an automatic machine which operates without human intervention, may be admissible as real evidence. This means that the rules governing documentary evidence, and those relating to documents produced by a computer, do not apply.

Comment

If there had been some human involvement in the operation of the hotel telephone system, such as a receptionist having to enter certain details which might then appear on the printout, the printout might then not be regarded as real evidence, but as documentary evidence, subject to the requirements of Section 23, Criminal Justice Act 1988 and Section 69 Police and Criminal Evidence Act 1984.

13.4 Case Four: Similar Fact Evidence
R v Smith (1915) 11 Cr App R 229

Problem
If it is suspected that a person has committed the same or basically similar offences before, part of which can be proved by other evidence, will that evidence be admissible to prove the offence charged?

Circumstances
Smith was accused of the murder of his wife. Evidence was given to the court that he had gone through a marriage ceremony with the deceased, he had then taken out a life insurance policy for which he would be the beneficiary. The deceased was found to be dead in the bath. Smith had sent for the doctor and informed him that the deceased had previously suffered from epileptic fits. The bathroom door was unlocked or incapable of being secured from within. At the trial, evidence as adduced that Smith had two previous wives, each of whom had died in the bath. On each prior occasion Smith had taken out insurance on their lives, he had also called out local doctors and informed them that the deceased had suffered from epilepsy. In each case it was discovered that the bathroom doors were either not locked or were incapable of being locked. The effect of this evidence was such that coincidence could be ruled out, the chances of such strikingly similar circumstances occurring were almost nil, the cases were 'strikingly similar' The courts accepted the evidence as evidence of similar fact which would otherwise be inadmissible.

Decision
To be acceptable as evidence to negate the defence of accident or rebut lack of intention, evidence of similar fact is admissible but only if it is so 'strikingly similar'.

Comment
In these circumstances the evidence of prior instances is amazingly similar. The credibility of the evidence is such that if admitted, juries will be compelled to convict. For this reason judges will not admit similar fact evidence unless it is so similar as to be strikingly similar.

13.5 Case Five: Similar Fact Evidence
Noor Mohamed v R [1949] AC 182

Problem
How similar must the evidence be to show similar facts and circumstances exist in order to make evidence of other similar events admissible?

Circumstances
A defendant was charged with murder. At trial evidence was admitted to the effect that the defendant's first wife had died from a suspected overdose of cyanide. It was suggested to the court that in the instant case the possibility of two wives both committing suicide using similar means

was very unlikely. Convicted at first instance, Mohammed appealed. On appeal the court held that the evidence relating to the cause of death for the first wife was weak, its link to the second wife's death was tenuous at best and therefore should not have been admitted as similar fact.

Decision
To be admissible as similar fact evidence the circumstances must be 'strikingly similar'.

Comment
This confirms the position as set out in *R v Smith*, but in these circumstances the evidence ought not to have been admitted. This case emphasises the extent to which the evidence must reveal striking similarity before it can be properly admitted.

13.6 Case Six: Identification
R v Turnbull and Others [1976] 3 All ER 549

Problem
How can evidence of identification be judged to make it acceptable to the court, what factors must be considered?

Circumstances
Raymond Turnbull and Joseph Camelo were tried and convicted of conspiracy to burgle. They had been stopped and checked by police officers a short distance from the scene of an attempted burglary, they were in a van similar to that used by the offenders and had in their possession house breaking implements. Convicted, they appealed. The Court of Appeal led by Lord Widgery CJ said that whenever a case against an accused depends wholly or substantially on the correctness of one or more identifications of the accused which the defence disputes, the judge should warn the jury of the special need for caution. It seems appropriate to acknowledge the dangers of visual identification and to bring this to the attention of the jury. In addition he should instruct them as to the reason for the need for such a warning and make some reference to the possibility that a mistaken witness can be a convincing one and a number of such witnesses can all be mistaken. If the identification evidence is poor the judge should withdraw the case from the jury. Provided this is done in clear terms the judge need not use any particular form of words. Secondly the judge should direct the jury to examine closely the circumstances in which the identification by each witness came to be made. The matters to be considered by a court in weighing up the value of identification evidence are set out in paragraph 6.1 of this chapter.

Decision
Judges must instruct juries of the dangers of eyewitness identifications, informing the jury of the factors which may or may not be relevant to the particular case under consideration.

Comment
This case highlights the problems of trusting eyewitness testimony without corroborating evidence.

13.7 Case Seven: Identification
R v Kitchen [1994] Crim LR 684

Problem
If a person is known to have been in an area where a crime occurs and that person is tenuously

suspected of committing a crime can photographs be shown to the witnesses, or must the officers wait until he had been apprehended so that formal procedures can take place?

Circumstances

A police officer thought he saw a man Kitchen whom he knew was an escapee from prison. A search of the area failed to locate Kitchen. A short time later a robbery occurred in the area. The police officer obtained photographs of Kitchen to show the staff at the attacked premises. Kitchen was identified. The question for the court was whether at the time of showing photographs to the witnesses, Kitchen was known as a suspect, and available for formal identification procedures.

Decision

To be available the suspect must be capable of being arrested within a relatively short time. To be known as a suspect requires more than a policeman's hunch. In these circumstances the police officer had seen the suspect in the area a few hours prior to the crime, his suspicions at that time however did not amount to sufficient evidence upon which to base an arrest. However, once the witness had seen a photograph of Kitchen he was immediately identified. At this time he became a suspect and there was sufficient evidence upon which to arrest. Turning to the showing of photographs, the court viewed this as being necessary to prevent months of diverted policing activity, where the witness's ability to identify the suspect could be tested via photographs. The conflict between paragraphs 2.1 and 2.8 of Code D must be considered as requiring the suspect to be both a) known as a suspect with sufficient evidence to warrant arrest and b) available to be arrested within a relatively short period. Thus showing the photographs was not a breach of the Codes of Practice.

Decision

'Known and available', is a complete phrase, the suspect must be both known and available for formal procedures, otherwise the police may show photographs to test a witness's ability to identify a suspect. A person becomes a 'suspect' when there is sufficient evidence to arrest him on suspicion of having committed a crime.

Comment

The court offered no guidance as to the precise meaning of 'relatively short time'. In the absence of a definitive ruling, it will remain a question of fact, to be considered in the circumstances of any particular case.

Chapter 8: Assaults

1 COMMON ASSAULT
Criminal Justice Act 1988 Section 39

1.1 Terms Used
'Common assault and battery shall be summary offences ...'
The Act declares **assault** and **battery** to be offences, but does not describe them. To understand the terms, we must look to common law. However, while there are case decisions which provide a clear description of each of the terms, in practice 'assault' is often used to describe what is in fact 'battery'. There are a number of offences having assault or battery as an element, distinguished by degree of injury caused, intent, method, etc.

1.2 Assault
An assault is any act which:
- intentionally or recklessly
- causes another to apprehend
- immediate and unlawful personal violence
  (Keynote Case: Fagan v Metropolitan Police Commissioner (1968)).

1.2.1 *Explanation*
Intentionally or recklessly: The offender must mean to do what he does (intent) or is reckless as to the result of his action. If the act was accidental, then there would not be an assault.

Causes another to apprehend: The assault may be complete without actual violence being applied to the victim, so long as the victim fears that he is going to suffer immediate and unlawful violence. However, words alone will not amount to an assault; for a threat of violence to be an assault there must be more than mere words and the offender must be in a position to carry out the threat. Waving a stick at someone from the other side of a river while offering to 'knock your head in' will probably not amount to assault because the stick-waver is not in a position to carry out the threat. Pointing a gun at the same person could be an assault because the ability exists to carry out the threat.

Immediate: A threat to act violently at some time in the future will not amount to an assault; the victim must fear that the violence will be applied immediately.

Unlawful: It is lawful to apply force, or offer to do so, in certain circumstances, for example in order to prevent crime or carry out a lawful arrest. The police dog handler who calls upon a fleeing criminal to 'stand still or I will release the dog' is intentionally causing the criminal to apprehend immediate violence, but will not be guilty of an assault because the violence threatened is not unlawful.

1.3 Battery
Battery means the actual application of unlawful force to another. This is in contrast to the meaning of 'assault' which may be complete upon there being a threat of violence.

1.3.1 *Explanation*

Although the terms 'assault' and 'battery' have distinct meanings, assault for practical purposes is generally synonymous with the term 'battery' and is used to mean the actual or intended use of unlawful force. There are numerous offences where 'assault' is used, meaning 'assault or battery', e.g. assault occasioning actual bodily harm, assault with intent to resist arrest. In each of these cases, the assault could be a threat of violence rather than an actual battery, e.g. by the victim receiving an injury while trying to escape from the threatened violence. However, it is much more likely in practice that actual bodily harm will result from an actual application of force rather than a threat of it. So, in the wording of the offence, the term assault is taken to include battery.

1.4 Which to Charge?

When charging an offence of common assault, either 'assault' or 'battery' should be charged, but not both, even if the evidence clearly points to both having been committed (*DPP v Taylor and Little* (1992)). To take account of the fact that in practical terms, 'assault' will usually include 'battery', the judgment in *DPP v Taylor and Little* suggests that where a person is charged with common assault involving an assault and a battery, the charge should be 'assault by beating'.

1.5 Certificate of Dismissal

When a person is charged with assault or battery and the court dismisses the complaint either because it finds the case not proved or considers it to be so trifling as not to merit punishment, the court shall issue a certificate to the accused. When such a certificate has been issued, or when the accused has been found guilty and has discharged any penalty and/or satisfied any costs, the accused shall not be liable in any court, criminal or civil, in relation to that assault or battery.

2 DEFENCES TO ASSAULT

For an assault to amount to an offence, the violence offered or applied must be 'unlawful'. Violence applied in the following cases will not be unlawful.

2.1 Consent

The victim may consent to force being used, but this does not extend to situations where the act done is itself unlawful. Thus, a martial arts instructor may apply force to a volunteer member of the class when demonstrating a hold; a boxing match involves two people who consent to applying force to each other. Consent will not be a defence where there is an intention to do actual bodily harm for no good reason, in circumstances which are against the public interest, as in duelling, a fight in the street, etc. What is 'against the public interest' will depend on the circumstances of the particular case. *(Keynote Cases: Attorney General's Reference (No. 6 of 1980) (1981); R v Brown and others (1993); R v Wilson (1996))*

2.2 Lawful Correction

A parent or teacher may administer force on a child as punishment for misbehaviour but such correction must be reasonable and moderate, taking into account the age and health of the child, and any instrument used must be 'proper'. There are statutory restrictions on corporal punishment in schools (Education (No. 2) Act 1986).

2.3 **Self-defence**

Reasonable force may be used in defence of one's self, a member of one's family, or even a complete stranger if that person is being attacked unlawfully (*R v Duffy* (1967)). However, force used in self-defence will be justified only if faced with immediate apprehended attack and the force used is no more than is reasonably necessary in the circumstances (*Attorney General's Reference (No. 2 of 1983)* (1984)).

In considering whether use of force was justified, whether there was an opportunity to retreat is a factor to consider, but the lack of such opportunity is not essential for the plea of self-defence to succeed. Where a person is threatened 'he does not have to take to his heels and run but he must demonstrate by his actions that he does not want to fight' (*R v Julien* (1969); *R v Field* (1972)).

Force may be used in defence of property, provided the degree of force is reasonable *(Keynote Case: Taylor v Mucklow (1973))*.

2.4 **Prevention of Crime**

A person may use such force as is reasonable in the circumstances, in the prevention of crime or in effecting or assisting in the lawful arrest of an offender or suspected offender, or of a person unlawfully at large (Criminal Law Act 1967, Section 3). What is reasonable will vary with circumstances. In extreme cases, to kill the offender may be reasonable, as when armed police shoot an armed criminal. To shoot at a burglar who is trying to escape would not be reasonable. *(Keynote Case: Taylor v Mucklow (1973))*

3 ASSAULT OCCASIONING ACTUAL BODILY HARM
Offences Against the Person Act 1861 Section 47

3.1 **Offence**

A person commits an offence if he assaults another person so as to cause actual bodily harm.

3.1.1 *Explanation*

Actual bodily harm: This means any hurt or injury calculated to interfere with the health or comfort of the victim. It need not be permanent nor amount to grievous bodily harm (*DPP v Smith* (1960)). The degree of injury lies somewhere between common assault and grievous bodily harm or wounding. As well as physical injury, actual bodily harm may include injury to a person's state of mind, for the time being , i.e. there is no necessity that the harm be permanent (*R v Miller* (1954)). The making of silent telephone calls, which causes psychiatric injury may amount to inflicting bodily harm, and therefore amount to an assault (*R v Ireland, R v Burstow* (1997)).

3.1.2 *Arrest*

The offence carries a maximum possible sentence of five years' imprisonment, so is an arrestable offence.

4 WOUNDING WITH INTENT
Offences Against the Person Act 1861 Section 18

4.1 **Offence**

The offence is committed where a person:

- unlawfully and maliciously
- by any means whatsoever
- wounds or causes grievous bodily harm to any other person
- with intent
- either to do grievous bodily harm to any person
- or to resist or prevent the lawful apprehension or detainer of any person.

4.1.1 *Explanation*

Unlawfully: The offence will not be committed where the action is lawful, e.g. where one of the defences detailed above applies.

Maliciously: Means an awareness that some harm may be caused. Whilst this could amount to an actual intention to do the sort of harm which was done, it is not necessary that the offender should have foreseen the full seriousness of his actions. Foreseeing that minor harm may result will do (*R v Mowatt* (1968)).

Whether a person intends or foresees the likelihood that harm will be caused is a matter for the court to decide. However, this decision must be reached having regard to Section 8 Criminal Justice Act 1967, which lays down a subjective test, related to an individual accused. He shall not be held to have acted maliciously solely because what happened was the natural and probable consequence of his actions; the court must decide whether he intended or foresaw the consequences by reference to all the evidence, including the accused's own characteristics.

By any means whatsoever: This phrase means that the commission of the offence is not limited to situations where force is applied directly to the victim. The usual example quoted where the accused does not come directly into contact with the victim, is where the victim, in an effort to escape from the accused, suffers some injury, e.g. by jumping from a window. This was held to amount to an offence under Section 18 (*R v Coleman* (1920)).

Wounds or causes grievous bodily harm: To constitute a wound the whole of the skin must be broken. Grievous bodily harm means serious bodily injury (*DPP v Smith* (1960)). Thus, a wound need not be serious, and is not necessarily the same as grievous bodily harm. A deep cut could amount to a wound, and would be enough for the offence to be committed **provided** it was inflicted with the intention either to do grievous bodily harm, i.e. a more serious injury than was actually caused, or with intent to resist or prevent an arrest.

With intent: There must be evidence of the intention of the accused, either to cause grievous bodily harm or to prevent or resist arrest, etc.

Any person: The offence will be committed where a wound or grievous bodily harm is inflicted on 'any person' with intent to cause grievous bodily harm to 'any person' or to prevent the lawful arrest, etc, of 'any person'. Thus, the person actually injured need not be the intended target of violence; likewise the offender need not be seeking to prevent his own arrest, he could be trying to prevent someone else being arrested.

Prevent or resist the lawful apprehension or detainer: The archaic language of 1861 will be covered for the most part by the phrase 'lawful arrest', but there are powers to detain a person without arresting him to which this offence could also apply, e.g. powers to stop and search a person under the Police and Criminal Evidence Act 1984. The arrest or detaining must be lawful.

4.1.2 *Arrest*

This is an arrestable offence.

5 UNLAWFUL WOUNDING
Offences Against the Person Act 1861 Section 20

5.1 Offence
A person will commit an offence who:
- unlawfully and maliciously
- wounds or inflicts grievous bodily harm on any person
- with or without weapon or instrument.

5.1.1 *Explanation*
This is similar to the offence under Section 18, above, but there is no requirement for an intent. The term 'maliciously' has to be considered however, to determine whether the accused intended or foresaw that some harm might result from his actions.

5.1.2 *Arrest*
This is an arrestable offence.

6 ASSAULT WITH INTENT TO RESIST ARREST
Offences Against the Person Act 1861 Section 38

6.1 Offence
The offence is committed where someone:
- assaults any person
- with intent to resist or prevent the lawful apprehension or detainer of himself or of any other person
- for any offence.

6.1.1 *Explanation*
Assault: The degree of injury is not specified; here the term 'assault' would include 'battery'.

Any person: The offence may be considered where the person assaulted is neither a constable acting in the execution of her duty, nor a person assisting a constable in that duty. An assault on a store detective, security guard or other person seeking to carry out a 'citizen's power of arrest' would be covered by this provision.

Apprehension or detainer for any offence: There will be no offence under this Section if someone is assaulted while seeking to exercise a power to detain to search, for example.

7 ASSAULT ON POLICE
Police Act 1996 Section 89

7.1 Offence
A person commits an offence who:
- assaults a constable
- in the execution of his duty
- or assaults a person assisting a constable in the execution of his duty.

7.1.1 *Explanation*

Assault: This is dealt with in paragraph 1.2 above.

Constable: Knowledge that the person attacked is a police officer is not necessary. Thus, it is not essential to show that the constable was in uniform or was otherwise identifiable as such. However, a genuine mistake as to the character of the person, e.g. a genuine and reasonable belief that the person was a criminal about to assault the accused, would be highly relevant in considering a plea of self-defence (*Kenlin v Gardiner* (1966)).

Execution of her duty: There is no simple rule-of-thumb which may be used to determine whether a constable is acting in the execution of her duty in any particular set of circumstances. A duty may be one which is imposed by statute on a constable, e.g. assisting a licensee to expel a disorderly person from licensed premises. Along with duties there may be powers, e.g. to stop a motor vehicle which is on a road. However, unjustifiable use of such powers may be unlawful and outside the scope of the constable's duty. There are other tasks which a constable may perform which are lawful, but which she has no duty to do, such as helping to unlock a car in which a motorist has left the keys. An examination of some of the more prominent cases may help to give some idea of the scope and limits of a constable's lawful duties. These may be considered with regard to:

- What was the constable doing?
- Where was the constable doing it?

What was the constable doing?: When a police officer puts his hand on a person's shoulder, not to arrest that person but to detain him for further conversation against that person's will, the detention will be unlawful so the constable is not in the execution of his duty (*Ludlow v Burgess* (1971)). Taking hold of a person's arm, not to arrest him but to detain him for questioning, is a technical assault and the constable doing so will not be in the execution of his duty (*Kenlin v Gardiner* (1966)).

However, in circumstances where a constable approached a man who had been seen arguing with a woman, to check him out in case he was following the woman, it was held that this was within the scope of lawful duties, because the constable was seeking to preserve the peace or prevent crime. No physical force was used, unlike the cases quoted in the preceding paragraph (*Weight v Long* (1986)). However, another 'hand on the arm' case may be distinguished from the above. A police officer who takes hold of a man's arm, **not to arrest or detain him**, but to draw his attention to what is being said to him, can be regarded as acting within the execution of his duty. It is for the court to decide whether the physical contact goes beyond what is acceptable merely for the purpose of trying to attract his attention; if it goes on too long it could be regarded as seeking to detain (*Mepstead v DPP* (1996)).

When a police officer has reasonable grounds for anticipating that a breach of the peace is a real possibility, he is acting in the execution of his duty in taking action to prevent such a breach (*Piddington v Bates* (1960)).

Seeking to detain a damaged car for examination in a case of suspected dangerous driving, when there was no power to detain it, was not in the performance of lawful duty (*R v Waterfield and Lynn* (1964)). In this case, the car was driven at a constable who stood in its path, and was forced to jump out of the way. The charge of assault police was dismissed, but a charge of dangerous driving was upheld.

Where was the constable doing it?: A constable will not be in the execution of her duty if she is on premises as a trespasser. *(Keynote Case: Great Central Railway Company v Bates (1921))*

This may be contrasted with circumstances where police officers went to a shop where a burglar alarm had been activated. It was held that the installation of a burglar alarm linked to police headquarters gave implied authority to police officers to enter to investigate when the alarm was off. *(Keynote Case: Kay v Hibbert (1977))*

Police officers made enquiries at a house where a party was in progress and were invited in by one man who went to find the owner of the house. Another guest at the party then told the officers to leave, but they did not do so on the ground that they had been invited in. They were then assaulted. It was held that when a guest at a house invited police officers to enter, he may be presumed to have the authority of the owner of the house to issue such invitation. The police officers were therefore not trespassers at the time they were assaulted, but were in the execution of their duty *(Jones and Jones v Lloyd* (1981)).

A woman and a companion were seen by police officers, apparently loitering or soliciting for the purposes of prostitution. As the officers approached, the woman walked up the steps to the front door of her house. A constable followed and caught up with her as the woman opened her front door. He called to her that he was arresting her and followed her into the hall where a struggle ensued. It was held that the constable was not in the execution of his duty because the power of arrest for soliciting for prostitution, which is not an arrestable offence, does not carry with it a power to enter premises *(R v McKenzie and Davis* (1979)).

Person assisting a constable: An assault upon a person who is assisting a constable will also be an offence under Section 89. The same consideration applies – whether the constable was acting in the execution of her duty at the time.

8 ASSAULTS ON OTHER SPECIFIED OFFICEHOLDERS

8.1 Prisoner Custody Officers
Criminal Justice Act 1991 Section 90

8.1.1 *Offences*
Assault: A person commits an offence who assaults a prisoner custody officer acting in pursuance of his duties.

Obstruction: A person commits an offence who resists or wilfully obstructs a prisoner custody officer acting in pursuance of her duties.

8.1.2 *Explanation*
Pursuance of duties: A prisoner custody officer engaged on escort duties shall not be regarded as 'in pursuance of those duties' unless he is readily identifiable as such, by means of uniform, badge or otherwise.

8.2 Court Security Officers
Criminal Justice Act 1991 Section 78

8.2.1 *Offences*
Assault: Any person who assaults a court security officer in the execution of his duties, commits a summary offence.

Obstruction: A person commits an offence who resists or wilfully obstructs a court security officer in the execution of her duty.

8.2.2 *Explanation*

Court security officer: Persons may be employed as court security officers in magistrates' courts.

Execution of duty: A court security officer has powers to search persons seeking to enter the court premises, and to exclude or eject persons in the interests of good order.

A court security officer will not be regarded as acting in the execution of his duty unless he is readily identifiable as such, whether by means of wearing a uniform, badge, or otherwise.

8.3 **Clergyman**
Offences Against the Person Act 1861 Section 36

8.3.1 *Offence*

It is an offence for a person:
- to obstruct by threats or force or strike or offer violence to
- a clergyman or other minister
- celebrating divine service or otherwise officiating in a church, chapel, meeting house
- or at a lawful burial in a churchyard or burial place.

8.4 **Other Office Holders**

There are other offences of assault on holders of specific offices, e.g. on a magistrate. In the majority of cases of assault, it will be more appropriate to charge an offence of causing actual bodily harm, common assault, etc.

9 **OTHER ASSAULTS**

Most assaults, for practical purposes, may be placed into one of the categories already dealt with – actual bodily harm, unlawful wounding, wounding or G.B.H. with intent, assault police, etc. The principal legislation on assaults, the Offences Against the Person Act 1861, provides for all sorts of eventualities, with offences described by method used, result and/or intention. Some of these are now described briefly.

9.1 **Attempt to Strangle**
Offences Against the Person Act 1861 Section 21

9.1.1 *Offence*

The offence is committed where a person:
- attempts to choke, suffocate or strangle another person
- or by any means calculated to choke, suffocate or strangle, attempts to render another person unconscious, insensible or incapable of resistance
- with intent in either case to enable himself or someone else to commit an indictable offence, or to assist another to do so.

9.1.2 *Explanation*

Such a charge could be of practical value in a case where no injury was actually caused, provided that the intention to commit some other indictable offence could be proved.

9.2 **Administering Stupefying Drug**
Offences Against the Person Act 1861 Section 22

9.2.1 *Offence*
The offence is committed when a person:
- unlawfully applies, administers to or causes to be taken by someone, or attempts so to do
- any chloroform, or other stupefying or overpowering drug, matter or thing
- with intent to enable himself or another to commit an indictable offence, or to assist someone else to do so.

9.2.2 *Explanation*
This is similar to the Section 21 offence, but is even more specific than the 'any means' phrase used in that Section, and is thus likely to be of even less practical value. (Note also the similar offence provided in Section 4 Sexual Offences Act 1956, of administering drugs to a woman with intent to facilitate sexual intercourse (Chapter 10, paragraph 4).

9.3 **Administering Poison so as to Endanger Life**
Offences Against the Person Act 1861 Section 23

9.3.1 *Offence*
A person commits an offence who:
- unlawfully and maliciously
- administers to, causes to be administered to or to be taken by another person
- any poison or other destructive or noxious thing
- with the result that the person's life is endangered or grievous bodily harm is thereby inflicted on him.

9.3.2 *Explanation*
Poison: The term 'poison' is taken to mean something which is a recognised poison, whereas 'noxious thing' means something which may be harmful, either because it is inherently harmful, or because of the quantity in which it is taken.

Result: With this offence it is the result which counts – for the offence to be complete the victim must suffer serious harm, or his life must be endangered, whether or not the accused intended this to happen. Contrast this with the following offence, when it is the intention which matters, not the result.

9.4 **Administering Poison with Intent**
Offences Against the Person Act 1861 Section 24

9.4.1 *Offence*
A person commits an offence who:
- unlawfully and maliciously
- administers to, causes to be administered to or to be taken by another person
- any poison or other destructive or noxious thing
- with intent to injure, aggrieve or annoy such person.

9.4.2 *Explanation*
Action taken: The *actus reus* is the same as for the previous offence – unlawfully administering,

causing to administered or to be taken by another any poison or other destructive or noxious thing.

With intent: For the offence to be committed there has to be an intention to injure, aggrieve or annoy.

Consider Mary who sprinkles weedkiller on her husband's cornflakes in the morning, because she believes this will induce diarrhoea, thus causing him annoyance. Assuming that the weedkiller may rightly be described as a 'noxious thing', as soon as he eats the cornflakes, the offence under Section 24 will be complete because Mary had the necessary intention. Whether the weedkiller actually has the desired effect is irrelevant. However, if the weedkiller actually has a more serious effect than Mary intended, and he suffers so badly that his life is in danger for a time, the offence under Section 23 is made out, even though Mary did not intend to cause serious harm.

9.5 Explosives
There are several related offences involving use of explosives which are dealt with in Chapter 15.

9.6 Use of Dangerous Substances, etc
Offences Against the Person Act 1861 Section 29

9.6.1 *Offence*
An offence is committed where someone:
- Sends to, delivers to, or causes to be taken or received by any person any dangerous or noxious thing; or
- Put or lays somewhere, or casts, throws at or otherwise applies to a person any corrosive fluid or destructive or explosive substance;

With the intention in any of these cases:
- to burn, maim, disfigure, disable or cause grievous bodily harm to any person
- whether any bodily injury results or not.

9.6.2 *Explanation*
The style of the legislators in 1861 was to put down a large number of alternatives, so that there are numerous ways in which a charge could be worded. The necessary elements of an offence under this Section are:

An action: send to, deliver to, throw at, etc.

A substance: noxious thing, corrosive fluid, etc.

An intent: to maim, disfigure, etc.

The offence could be considered as an alternative to, say, an attempt at a Section 18 assault, where the offender throws a jug of acid at his intended victim, but his aim is bad.

9.7 Furious Driving
Offences Against the Person Act 1861 Section 35

9.7.1 *Offence*
The offence is committed when someone:
- having charge of any carriage or vehicle

- by wanton or furious driving or racing
- or by other wilful misconduct or neglect
- does or causes to be done any bodily harm to any person.

9.7.2 *Explanation*
The practical value of this offence will be limited, since offences of dangerous driving or dangerous cycling are more likely to be charged under the Road Traffic Act. Furious driving of a horse and cart would amount to this offence, but is not an everyday occurrence.

9.8 Endangering Railway Users
There are offences involving intent to injure or endanger persons using railways. These are dealt with in Chapter 14, along with other offences relating to railways.

10 TORTURE
Criminal Justice Act 1988 Section 134

10.1 Offences
i) A person commits an offence if:
   - in the United Kingdom or elsewhere
   - whatever his nationality
   - being a public official or a person acting in an official capacity
   - he intentionally inflicts severe pain or suffering on another person
   - in the performance or purported performance of his official duties.

ii) A person commits an offence (who is **not** a public official nor a person acting in an official capacity):
   - if in the United Kingdom or elsewhere
   - whatever his nationality
   - he inflicts severe pain or suffering on another:
        at the instigation, or with the consent or acquiesence of a public official or person acting in an official capacity;
        and the said official is performing or purporting to perform his offical duties when he instigates the commission of the pain or suffering, or consents to or acquiesces in it.

10.1.1 *Explanation*
Public official or person acting in an official capacity: This is a wide term and would include, for example, a police officer. References to elsewhere than the United Kingdom indicate that the actions of, say, members of the Armed Forces, would also be covered by this legislation.

Other person: Someone who is not a public official, nor acting in an official capacity may commit the offence, but only if he is acting in conjunction with someone who is.

Intentionally: It will not be enough that pain was inflicted accidentally, or even recklessly; there needs to be an intention to do so.

Severe pain or suffering: The pain or suffering may be mental or physical. Thus, a threat to inflict severe physical pain may be enough to cause severe mental pain or suffering. It is immaterial whether the pain or suffering is caused by an act, e.g. an assault, or by omission, e.g. deliberately neglecting to provide food.

10.2 Defence

A person will have a defence to a charge under this Section if he proves that he had lawful authority, justification or excuse for his conduct. The Section offers no guidance as to what may amount to lawful authority, justification or excuse.

Keynote Cases

11.1 *Fagan v Metropolitan Police Commissioner* [1968] 3 All ER 442

Problem

Meaning of 'assault'.

Circumstances

Fagan was directed by a police officer to move his car. In the course of doing so, a wheel of the car went on to the officer's foot. It was accepted that he had not driven on to the officer's foot deliberately, but when told what had happened Fagan refused to move the car. He was charged with assault police.

Decision

The crux of the argument was whether the criminal intent (*mens rea*) could come after the action (*actus rea*). The finding of the court was that where the action was still continuing (the wheel is resting on the officer's foot) when the *mens rea* is formed (Fagan decides that he is not going to move the car) then the crime may be committed. During the deliberations, the court pronounced a definition of assault, viz.

'Any act which intentionally or possibly recklessly causes another person to apprehend immediate and unlawful personal violence'.

Comment

It is not the point about intention coming after action which is important, for such circumstances would be fairly rare in practice, but the definition of assault set out by the court during the course of deliberation. This is now the widely accepted description of an assault.

11.2 *Attorney General's Reference (No. 6 of 1980)* [1981] QB 715

Problem

Assault – defence of 'consent'.

Circumstances

Two men agreed to settle their differences by fighting in the street. One of them was charged with an offence of causing actual bodily harm to the other.

Decision

Whereas it is recognised as a defence to assault, that the victim consented to the violence inflicted on him, there will be an exception to this where the public interest requires it. In this particular case the fight was in public, but it is not in the public interest for people to try to cause actual bodily harm to each other for no good reason, in public or in private.

(There is another argument, which the court considered, that fighting in the street amounts to a breach of the peace and is therefore unlawful, but in the end settled for the public interest principle.)

Comment
One person may inflict harm on another, with consent, during the course of properly organised sport, surgery, etc without an offence of assault being committed. The question whether such harm is against the public interest will serve to clarify whether the defence of 'consent' is available to a person charged with an assault.

11.3 *R v Brown and others* [1993] 2 All ER 75

Problem
Assault, the defence of 'consent'.

Circumstances
A number of appeals were considered where persons had been convicted of offences of causing actual bodily harm and wounding, arising from homosexual sado-masochistic practices involving injuries inflicted with consent, for the gratification of the person inflicting the pain and injury (the sadist) and of the victim (the masochist).

Decision
The fact that the victim gives consent is a defence to a charge of actual bodily harm or unlawful wounding. The decision of the court was that such activities, involving actual bodily harm and wounding are unlawful, notwithstanding consent because public policy requires that society be protected against a cult of violence.

Comment
This and the previous case decision are entirely compatible; consent will be no defence to a charge of deliberately inflicting actual bodily harm, or more serious injury, without good reason. However, the decision should be considered in the light of the circumstances – sado-masochism and a 'cult of violence'. Compare the decision with that in *R v Wilson* (below), in which it is made clear that not every case of actual bodily harm, deliberately inflicted, will be unlawful despite the victim having given consent.

11.4 *R v Wilson* [1996] 3 WLR 125

Problem
Assault, the defence of 'consent'.

Circumstances
Wilson used a hot knife to brand his initials on his wife's buttocks. He did this at his wife's instigation; she wanted him to tattoo his name on her breasts, because '...I love you enough to have your name on my body...'. He did not know how to do a tattoo and did not want to mark her breasts, so between them, they came up with the idea of using a hot knife on her buttocks. He was charged with an offence of assault occasioning actual bodily harm. A defence plea of

consent was rejected by the trial judge on the ground that the decision in *R v Brown and others* (above) had to be followed, that consent is no defence where actual bodily harm is deliberately inflicted for no good reason.

Decision

In the Court of Appeal it was held that the decision in *Brown* did not have to be followed in the present case. In *Brown* there was torture and violence of an extreme sort. In this case, Wilson was not seeking to cause injury to his wife, but to assist her in acquiring a 'desirable piece of personal adornment', akin to having nostril or tongue pierced for insertion of a ring. In the *Brown* case, the judges made reference to tattooing as an example of harm being inflicted which was not unlawful if the victim gave consent. Consensual activity between husband and wife should not normally be a matter for criminal investigation, let alone prosecution. Wilson's appeal was allowed.

Comment

The decisions in *R v Brown* and in *Attorney General's Reference (No. 6 of 1980)* were that consent was no defence to the deliberate infliction of actual bodily harm where this was against the public interest. In this case, what Wilson did was not against the public interest, indeed what a husband and wife get up to in private is a matter for them. This is not to say that a wife could consent, e.g. to having very serious harm inflicted on her. The court suggested that individual cases should be decided on their own merits.

11.5 *Taylor v Mucklow* [1973] Crim LR 750

Problem

What is 'reasonable' in relation to lawful use of reasonable force to prevent crime.

Circumstances

The defendant used an airgun to threaten a person who was causing criminal damage. He was charged with an offence and pleaded that the action he took was reasonable, to prevent crime. He was convicted by the justices and appealed.

Decision

It is lawful to use such force as is reasonable in the circumstances, in the prevention of crime, or in the lawful arrest of a suspected offender, or person unlawfully at large. It is a matter for the justices to decide in any case whether force used is reasonable in the circumstances. In this case, the justices decided that the force used was not reasonable, and the appeal judges found no reason to interfere with that decision.

Comment

Whether force used is reasonable will be a matter for the magistrates or jury to decide in any particular case. In this particular case, the judges queried whether the use of a loaded firearm is ever likely to be reasonable.

11.6 *Great Central Railway Company v Bates* [1921] 3 KB 578

Problem

When is a constable in the 'execution of his duty'?

Circumstances

A constable, in the course of his duties, entered a warehouse after dark, having found the door open, to check if everything was in order. He fell into an unfenced pit and suffered serious injury.

Decision

It was held that the constable had no legal right to enter, being neither an 'invitee' or a 'licensee', and did not suspect a crime had been committed. To quote from the judgment, 'It appears to be very important that it should be established that nobody has a right to enter premises except strictly in accordance with authority.'

Comment

This was not a criminal case, but a civil one relating to the injured officer's injuries and pension rights. However, the question as to whether a constable is in the execution of his lawful duty, is fundamental in cases involving assault police and a number of the cases quoted as examples in the text revolve around whether a constable has a right to be on premises.

11.7 *Kay v Hibbert* [1977] Crim LR 226

Problem

Constable in execution of his duty when on premises.

Circumstances

Kay was the proprietor of a shop fitted with a burglar alarm connected to the police. Sergeant Hibbert and another officer entered the premises upon the alarm being activated. There they met Kay, whom they did not know and who ordered them to leave his shop. The officers declined to leave until satisfied as to Kay's identity. Kay then assaulted Sergeant Hibbert and was convicted of assaulting a constable in the execution of his duty.

Decision

On hearing Kay's appeal the court held that the burglar alarm being connected to police headquarters gave implied authority for police officers to 'enter to investigate' when the alarm went off. The officers in this case had therefore entered as 'licensees' (the term used in *Great Central Railway Company v Bates*, above) and a reasonable time must be allowed for them to investigate before that licence is revoked.

Comment

In this case, it was proper that the officers satisfied themselves that Kay was lawfully on the premises. However, if they had stayed after doing so, they would then have been trespassers and no longer in the execution of their duty.

Chapter 9: Homicide and Related Matters

1 MURDER
Common Law

1.1 Offence
A person is guilty of murder who:
- being of sound memory and discretion
- unlawfully kills
- a reasonable creature in being
- under the Queen's peace
- with malice aforethought, expressed or implied.

1.1.1 *Explanation*
Of sound memory and discretion: A person will not be guilty of murder who is insane. In some circumstances a person's mental state may lead to his being found guilty of manslaughter rather than murder *(see paragraph 4.1.2).*

Unlawfully: In some circumstances, use of force may be lawful, even in the extreme case where the result proves fatal. Lawful use of force is discussed in Chapter 8.

Kills: The action of the accused need not be the sole or even most substantial cause of death, but the contribution to the death must be more than minimal. If death follows treatment for an original injury caused by the accused and the main cause of death arises from the treatment, this may still amount to murder. *(Keynote Case: R v Cheshire (1991))*

Even if medical treatment for injuries is shown to be negligent, the accused may still be liable for the subsequent death of the accused, providing that the treatment was not such as to be considered 'abnormal' (*R v Smith* (1959)). The refusal by the victim on religious grounds to have a blood transfusion after being stabbed will not absolve the accused. 'A person who uses violence has to take his victim as he finds him... the stab wound was an operative cause of death.' (*R v Blaue* (1975)). Where competent and careful medical treatment involves use of a life support machine, switching it off will not exonerate the defendant from responsibility for the death where the defendant's actions continue to be an operating cause of death (*R v Malcherek, R v Steel* (1981)).

Reasonable creature in being: The victim must be an independent, living being at the time of death if murder is to be made out. A child in the womb is not 'a reasonable creature in being', but death after birth caused by injuries received while still in the womb may amount to murder.

However, for murder there must be an intention to harm the victim. Where an attack on a pregnant woman causes her baby to be born prematurely and it later dies due to its prematurity, the attacker may be guilty of manslaughter, but not murder, in the absence of evidence of intention to harm the foetus (*Attorney General's Reference (No. 3 of 1994)* (1997)).

Difficulty may arise following an abortion or premature birth, as to whether a foetus may be the victim of murder. It has been held that a foetus at between 18 and 21 weeks of development was not capable of being born alive (*C and Another v S and Another* (1987)), while a foetus capable, if born, of breathing through its own lungs without connection to its mother, was 'capable of being born alive' (*Rance v Mid Downs Health Authority* (1991)).

Under the Queen's peace: The killing of a person within any of Her Majesty's territories may amount to murder. Excluded would be e.g. an alien enemy engaged in hostile operations against the Crown.

With malice aforethought, expressed or implied: Expressed malice means an intention to kill. Implied malice means an intention to do grievous bodily harm. If the only intention which can be proved is to cause a lesser degree of injury, this will be insufficient to support a charge of murder (*R v Moloney* (1985)).

2 INCITEMENT TO MURDER
Offences Against the Person Act 1861 Section 4

2.1 Offence
It is an offence to:
- solicit, encourage, persuade, endeavour to persuade, or propose to someone
- to murder another person
- whether that person is a citizen of Her Majesty or not and whether or not within H.M.'s jurisdiction.

2.1.1 *Explanation*
Home or abroad: The offence is contrary to the law of this country, irrespective of the nationality of the murder victim, and irrespective of where it is proposed the murder should occur.

3 THREATS TO KILL
Offences Against the Person Act 1861 Section 16

3.1 Offence
It is an offence:
- without lawful excuse
- to make to another person a threat
- intending that the other would fear it would be carried out
- to kill that or a third person.

3.1.1 *Explanation*
Intention: The essence of the offence is not that the offender should intend to carry out the threat, nor even that the threat is believed, but that the offender intends that the person to whom the threat is made should take it seriously.

That or a third person: The person to whom the threat is made need not be the person whose life is threatened.

4 MANSLAUGHTER
Manslaughter is an unlawful killing which does not amount to murder. There is a variety of reasons why a particular killing may not amount to murder, and these may be divided into two categories – **voluntary** and **involuntary** manslaughter.

4.1 **Voluntary Manslaughter**

The killings which fall into this category have the murder ingredient of malice aforethought and the defendant would be guilty of murder, were it not for special circumstances relating to his state of mind at the time of the killing. These special circumstances will come under one of three headings and it should be noted that these are defences to a charge of murder, not distinct offences.

4.1.1 *Provocation*

This is conduct which:
- would cause a reasonable person
- and actually did cause the accused
- a sudden and temporary loss of self-control so that he was not the master of his own mind.

Provocation may arise from things done, things said, or a combination. There are two questions for a court to consider:
- Would things said or done cause a reasonable person to lose self-control?
- Did what was said or done cause the defendant to lose self-control?

Regard must be had to the time which elapses between the provocation and the killing. *(Keynote Case: R v Ahluwalia (1992))*

4.1.2 *Diminished Responsibility*

This arises when the accused is suffering from such abnormality of mind as substantially impaired his mental responsibility for his acts or omissions at the time of the killing. Such abnormality may be due to arrested or retarded development of mind, or induced by disease, injury or inherent cause (Homicide Act 1957).

4.1.3 *Drink, Drugs, etc*

Only those causes of abnormality of mind mentioned will give rise to the defence of diminished responsibility. Other reasons for impairment of control, such as jealousy, anger or the effect of drink or drugs would not fall within the meaning of diminished responsibility. However, when abuse of drink or drugs had reached the stage where (a) the brain was damaged so as to result in gross impairment of judgment and emotional response or (b) the accused's use of alcohol or drugs is involuntary because he can no longer resist the impulse to take the drink or drug – then the defence of diminished responsibility could apply (*R v Tandy* (1989)).

4.1.4 *Suicide Pact*

A person will be guilty of manslaughter and not murder if he kills another (or is a party to someone else doing so) while acting in pursuance of a suicide pact between himself and the person killed. A 'suicide pact' is defined as:
- a common agreement between two or more persons
- having for its object the death of them all
- whether or not each is to take his own life.

However, nothing done by a person entering into such a pact will be treated as being 'in pursuance of the pact' unless when he does it he has the settled intention of dying as a result (Homicide Act 1957).

Thus, if Jill is in severe pain from a terminal illness and she and Jack agree that he will administer a fatal dose of pills to her, this is not a suicide pact because the agreement is not that they **both** should die. If Romeo and Juliet agree that they shall both die, he killing her then himself, but before killing her he changes his mind and decides not to kill himself, he will not then be acting in pursuance with a suicide pact when he kills her.

4.2 Involuntary Manslaughter

As the name implies, involuntary manslaughter arises where there is no 'malice aforethought' to kill or to cause injury, but death arises:
- from an unlawful act in a way which carries an obvious risk of injury to someone else; or
- by recklessness or gross negligence in performing a duty or in carrying out some lawful act.

4.2.1 *Unlawful and Dangerous Act*

To establish this form of manslaughter it must be shown that the accused carried out some act which was itself unlawful, quite apart from any death which resulted. The accused must actually have done something; it will not amount to involuntary manslaughter if death arises as a result of omitting to do something. **However**, there is no need to show that the accused himself foresaw the actual danger. If the jury is satisfied that sober and reasonable people would have foreseen the danger the accused may be convicted (*DPP v Newbury, DPP v Jones* (1977)). That the accused mistakenly believes that what he was doing was not dangerous, will be irrelevant (*R v Ball* (1989)).

An act which is lawful does not become 'unlawful' for the purposes of manslaughter merely because of the negligent manner in which it is carried out. Thus, a person who causes another's death by careless driving will not necessarily be guilty of manslaughter (*Andrews v DPP* (1937)).

4.2.2 *Recklessness or Gross Negligence*

Manslaughter arising from recklessness or gross negligence may be split into two categories:
- where a person has a duty towards the person who died
- where a person is carrying out a lawful act but does so in a reckless or negligent way.

Death arising from a breach of that duty will be manslaughter if there is a breach of duty resulting in death and the accused can be shown to have been grossly negligent. Mere carelessness is not enough. *(Keynote Case: R v Adomako (1994))*

Cases of manslaughter by persons having a duty towards others have typically included medical staff, train drivers, persons responsible for operating machinery, etc.

Carrying out an otherwise lawful act in a reckless or negligent way so as to cause someone's death may involve, for example, using a firearm, or driving a vehicle.

4.2.3 *Death Arising from Driving a Vehicle*

Undoubtedly the most common way of killing another person involving some degree of negligence in the latter half of the 20th Century has been by use of a mechanically-propelled vehicle. The offence of causing death by dangerous driving will normally be charged where a driver of a mechanically-propelled vehicle causes another person's death by driving dangerously on a road or other public place (Road Traffic Act 1988, Section 1). However, the fact that there is a statutory offence does not mean that the common law offence of manslaughter cannot be charged in relation to a death arising from the driving of a mechanically-propelled vehicle. In one case, the extradition to the United States was sought of a British driver involved in a road accident in California in which a child cyclist died. The charge in California was one of manslaughter. Her counsel argued that in this country she could not have faced a manslaughter charge arising from the same circumstances, because the correct charge would be one under Section 1, Road Traffic Act 1988 (causing death by (dangerous) driving). The House of Lords ruled that manslaughter was still available as a charge in appropriate cases (*Government of U.S.A. v Jennings* (1983)).

However, if manslaughter is to be charged rather than Section 1, the level of risk of causing death arising from the defendant's driving must be **very high**. In addition, only one of the offences may be charged at court; the prosecution may not put manslaughter and Section 1 as alternatives, for the jury to make a choice (*R v Seymour* (1984)).

5 INFANTICIDE
Infanticide Act 1938

5.1 Offence
The offence may be committed:
- by a woman
- who by any wilful act or omission
- causes the death of her child, being under the age of 12 months
- and at the time of that act or omission the balance of her mind was disturbed
- by reason of not having fully recovered from the effects of giving birth to the child
- or from the effect of lactation consequent upon the birth of her child.

In such as case, the offence committed by the woman will be infanticide and not murder.

5.1.1 *Explanation*
Her child being under the age of 12 months: The death must relate to the woman's own child, during the first year of its life. If she killed someone else, say another of her children, or her mother-in-law, due to the balance of her mind being disturbed as a result giving birth, this would not amount to infanticide. Instead, the defence of diminished responsibility would lie.

Effects of giving birth or of lactation: The cause of the mental disturbance in the woman must be directly due to the effects of childbirth or of the production of milk following the birth.

Not murder: Infanticide may be raised as a defence to a charge of murder, or infanticide may be the offence charged. This differs from the situation with diminished responsibility which is raised as a defence to murder, rather than manslaughter being the charge.

6 CHILD DESTRUCTION
Infant Life (Preservation) Act 1929 Section 1

6.1 Offence
The offence is committed by any person who:
- with intent to destroy the life of a child capable of being born alive
- by any wilful act
- causes the child to die before it has had an existence independent of its mother.

6.1.1 *Explanation*

Comparison with other offences: Infanticide involves the killing of a child under 12 months, the death of which would be murder, but for the mental state of the mother. The victim of murder must be 'a reasonable creature in being' which means a human being who has had its own separate existence *(see paragraph 1.1.1)*. The offence of abortion *(see paragraph 7 below)* relates to the destruction of a foetus which is not 'a reasonable creature in being'. Child destruction is designed to cover a situation somewhere between abortion and murder, although in some circumstances abortion and child destruction may well both apply.

Intent: The accused's intention to kill the child must be proved.

Capable of being born alive: Evidence of pregnancy of 28 weeks or more shall be *prima facie* proof that the child was capable of being born alive (Section 1(2)). Medical evidence may be brought to rebut this presumption, by showing either that a child of less than 28 weeks' gestation was capable of being born alive, or conversely that the child in excess of 28 weeks could not have been born alive.

Existence separate from its mother: There are circumstances in which the offences of abortion and child destruction could apply equally, once a child is capable of being born alive. It will be a matter for a court to decide whether the stage of 'separate existence' had been achieved, but a child who had, for example, only partly emerged into the world, could be the victim of this offence. An attack on a woman resulting in the death of her unborn child, capable of being born alive, may also be child destruction, so long as the requisite intent can be proved.

6.2 **Good Faith**

There is a proviso that a person will not be guilty of child destruction if the act which destroyed the life of the child was done in good faith for the purpose only of preserving the life of the mother. This proviso is unusual in that it is **not** a defence for the accused to raise; rather, the accused will be guilty only if the prosecution proves that the act was **not** done in good faith to save the mother.

7 **ABORTION**
Offences Against the Person Act 1861 Sections 58, 59

7.1 **Offences**

There are three separate offences related to unlawfully acting to cause a miscarriage in a woman. The three offences are:

a) Committed by a woman who:
  – being with child
  – with intent to procure her own miscarriage
  – unlawfully administers to herself any poison or other noxious thing
  – or unlawfully uses on herself any instrument or other means whatsoever.

b) Committed by any other person who:
  – with intent to procure the miscarriage of any woman
  – whether or not she be with child

- unlawfully administers to her or causes to be taken by her any poison or other noxious thing
- or unlawfully uses any instrument or other means whatsoever.

c) Committed by a person who:
- unlawfully supplies or procures
- any poison or other noxious thing
- or instrument or other thing whatsoever
- knowing that the same is intended to be unlawfully used or employed with intent to procure the miscarriage of any woman
- whether or not she be with child.

7.1.1 *Explanation*

With child: For the woman who tries to procure her own miscarriage, she must be pregnant before she can be guilty of the offence. For any other person to commit the offence of abortion or of supplying the wherewithal, the offence will be committed whether the woman involved is pregnant or not.

With intent to procure: For the offences of abortion, the offence will be complete if something is done with the intention of procuring a miscarriage, irrespective of whether a miscarriage results or not. One of the aims of the legislation is to prevent harm arising from unlawful operations on women. Clearly, harm may result from administering poison or using instruments, whether the object of ending the pregnancy is secured or not.

Poison: This is anything which is recognised as being a poison, and applies whatever the quantity administered or taken. Thus, if a substance is listed in relevant regulations as a poison, it does not matter whether the amount administered is too small to cause any real harm, nor does its likely effect have to be that it may result in a miscarriage. One of the aims of the legislation is to protect the health of women, and administering poison is not conducive to good health.

Noxious thing: The term means something which is harmful to the woman in the quantity in which it is administered. It may be something which is usually harmful, such as petrol, or something which, not necessarily harmful in usual dosage, is harmful because of the quantity taken, e.g. a whole bottle of rum.

Instrument or other means: An instrument could be any item. e.g. inserted into the woman in an effort to cause a miscarriage. 'Other means' could include, e.g. massage or immersion in very hot water.

Knowing that the same is intended: To be guilty of supplying the means for an abortion, the accused must know that what he supplies is intended to be used unlawfully with intent to procure a miscarriage. Even if the intention is never carried out, the offence of supplying or procuring will be complete.

7.2 **Lawful Abortion**

Unlawful abortion is less common than used to be the case, when legal abortions were available only in 'life threatening' cases. Now, an abortion will be lawful where two registered medical practitioners (i.e. properly qualified doctors) are of the opinion, formed in good faith that continuation of the pregnancy would involve risk and the pregnancy is terminated by a doctor.

'Risk' includes to the life, physical or mental health of the woman, or her family, or that the child if born would be physically or mentally handicapped.

8 CONCEALMENT OF BIRTH
Offences Against the Person Act 1861 Section 60

8.1 Offence
Where a woman is delivered of a child:
- every person who by any secret disposition of the dead body of the child
- endeavours to conceal the birth of the child
- shall commit an offence
- whether the child died before, at the time of or after its birth.

8.1.1 *Explanation*
Every person: The offence may be committed by the mother or by anyone else.

Secret disposition/to conceal the birth: It may well be the case that an unmarried mother, for example, wishes to conceal the fact that she has given birth to a baby, or to conceal the fact of birth from her own relatives. With this in mind, she may dispose of the body in a place where it is likely to be found, but which cannot be connected with herself, such as a public toilet. This is not sufficient for the offence; the intention must be to conceal the fact of birth from the world at large, by disposing of the body in a place where it is not likely to be found.

Dead body of the child: For the offence to be committed, there must be evidence that the child was capable of being born alive. Thus, the secret disposal of the child's remains after an unlawful abortion may or may not amount to this offence, depending on what stage of development had been reached.

Time of death: This offence involves a dead baby, irrespective of how the baby came by its death, or whether it died before, during or after birth. If the death arose from some unlawful cause, another offence may also be committed.

9 COMPLICITY IN SUICIDE
Suicide Act 1961 Section 2

9.1 Offence
A person commits an offence who:
- aids, abets, counsels or procures
- the suicide of another person
- or the attempt by another to commit suicide.

9.1.1 *Explanation*
This offence differs from that of manslaughter by means of suicide pact. The latter arises where a person kills another person in circumstances where they have both agreed to die. For complicity in suicide, the 'victim' kills himself or attempts to do so and the offender aids, abets, counsels or procures the killing or attempt.

Keynote Cases

10.1 *R v Cheshire* [1991] 3 All ER 670

Problem
In murder the accused's actions need not be the sole cause of death.

Circumstances
During an argument the accused shot the victim causing serious injury. The injured man was operated on at hospital and a tube inserted into his windpipe to assist breathing. The tube remained in place for several weeks and the injured man developed a chest infection and other complications, arising from the operation to insert the tube. Some two months after the shooting he died from cardio-respiratory failure due to breathing difficulties stemming from the tracheotomy. At the murder trial, defence evidence was given that the injuries received from the shooting were no longer life-threatening at time of death, and that death arose from the negligent failure of medical staff to treat the deceased properly.

Decision
The Appeal Court held that it was not the function of a jury to examine separate causes of death, to decide which was the most significant. If the accused's actions could fairly be said to have made a significant contribution to the victim's death, then a charge of murder could be upheld.

Comment
There is no need for the prosecution to prove that the actions of a person accused of murder were the sole or even the main cause of death of the victim. What has to be shown is that those acts contributed significantly to the death, even if there is negligence in the medical treatment given before death.

10.2 *R v Adomako* [1994] 3 All ER 79

Problem
The essential ingredients for involuntary manslaughter by breach of duty.

Circumstances
The defendant was an anaesthetist in charge of a patient during an operation. A tube became disconnected, leading to the oxygen supply to the patient being cut off, causing the patient to suffer cardiac arrest. The defendant tried to resuscitate the patient but failed to notice that the tube was disconnected. The patient died and the defendant was convicted of manslaughter. On appeal, the House of Lords upheld the conviction.

Decision
The House of Lords upheld the finding of the Court of Appeal that there were three essential elements required for manslaughter by breach of duty:
- proof of the existence of a duty
- breach of that duty causing death
- gross negligence.

Negligence would be gross negligence sufficient to warrant a criminal conviction in **any** of the following cases:

1) An inattention or failure to avoid a serious risk which went beyond mere inadvertence, in a matter falling within the defendant's duty.
2) An indifference to an obvious risk of injury to health.
3) Actual foresight of a risk together with a determination to run that risk.
4) An appreciation of the risk, plus a determination to avoid it, but coupled with such a high degree of negligence in avoiding it as to warrant conviction.

Comment

Where a person is prosecuted for manslaughter arising from a breach of duty, a very high degree of negligence is called for to secure a conviction. The four examples of gross negligence amount to a range of awareness of risk: (1) failure to avoid risk; (2) indifference to an obvious risk; (3) seeing that there is a risk but nevertheless going on to take it; (4) seeing a risk, seeking to avoid that risk, but being highly negligent in doing so.

10.3 *R v Ahluwalia* [1992] 4 All ER 889

Problem

What has to be proved for provocation to be established as a defence to murder.

Circumstances

The appellant was an Asian woman who had suffered violence and abuse from her husband over many years of marriage. Treatment included threats to kill her, and the open flaunting of an affair he was having with another woman. One evening they argued and the husband went to bed after threatening to beat her next morning. The appellant set fire to the husband's bedroom using petrol, and the husband died from burns. At her trial for murder, the judge directed the jury that the defence of provocation was available only if there had been a sudden and temporary loss of control as a result of acts which would have caused a reasonable person, having her characteristics as a married Asian woman, to lose her self control. She was convicted of murder and appealed. The grounds for appeal included a contention that the history of violence and humiliation at the hands of her husband amounted to provocation; an additional feature not put to the jury by the judge was that she suffered from 'battered woman syndrome'.

Decision

The court held:

- provocation as a defence to murder has to be founded on a sudden and temporary loss of self control
- this defence would not be ruled out simply because of a 'delayed reaction', i.e. a gap in time between the actions amounting to provocation and the killing, so long as it could be proved that there was the requisite sudden and temporary loss of control at the time of the killing. The longer the delay, and the stronger the evidence of deliberation on the part of the accused, the more likely that the defence of provocation would fail.
- Characteristics relating to the mental state or personality of the accused, as well as to physical characteristics, could be taken into account in determining whether a reasonable person with the same characteristics as the accused would have lost self-control in the face of the provocation endured by the accused.

Comment

There is a view that the law relating to provocation is unfair to a woman who retaliates after suffering ill-treatment over a long period, at the hands of her male partner. This decision allows that there may indeed be a delayed reaction, but the loss of self-control arising from the provocation must still be 'sudden' and 'temporary'. The more preparation there is, or other evidence of deliberation, and the longer the delay, the less easy it will be to convince the court that the loss of self-control on the part of the 'battered woman' arose suddenly at the time of the killing.

Chapter 10: Sexual Offences

1 **RAPE**
Sexual Offences Act 1956 Section 1

1.1 **Offence**
The offence is committed when:
- a man
- has sexual intercourse
- whether vaginal or anal
- with a person who at the time does not consent
- and at the time the man knows that the person does not consent to it
- or is reckless as to whether the person consents to it.

1.1.1 *Explanation*
Man: Only a male can commit this offence.

Sexual intercourse: The act of sexual intercourse is complete upon proof of penetration (of the vagina or anus) by the male organ; it is not necessary to prove 'emission of seed' (i.e. ejaculation), the slightest degree of penetration will be enough. Thus, rape must involve penetration by the penis; insertion of some other object into the victim's body would not amount to sexual intercourse, so would not constitute rape.

Person: The victim of rape may be a woman, with the intercourse being by way of vagina or anus, or a man, where there is of course only one option.

At the time does not consent: The act of sexual intercourse continues until withdrawal of the penis. Thus, where the defendant was not aware of a lack of consent at the time of penetration, but did realise thereafter, he was guilty of rape by continuing with the act of intercourse (*Kaitamaki v R* (1984)).

Consent: There will be no consent when a victim submits to intercourse through force, fear or fraud. Neither is there consent if intercourse takes place when the victim is unable to decide whether to consent or not, e.g. because he or she is asleep or intoxicated.

Force: Clearly, if the offender overcomes his victim by force, there is no consent.

Fear: If the victim submits because of threats or through fear of being subjected to violence, there is equally no consent. Just because the victim does not struggle or resist, does not mean that consent is given. In this context, 'fear' relates to fear of immediate physical force. (Where threats relate to something other than immediate physical violence, there may be an offence of procuring a woman by threats.)

Fraud: For an offence of rape to be committed by means of consent obtained by fraud, the fraud must relate to the nature of what is taking place, or to the identity of the person who is committing it. The following examples serve to explain 'fraud':
- If a man obtains consent to intercourse by impersonating a woman's husband, this will not amount to a valid consent, so the man will commit rape (Sexual Offences Act 1956, Section 1(3)). This statutory provision is restricted to impersonation of a husband, it does not extend to impersonation of e.g. a

> boyfriend. However, the Court of Appeal has indicated that any fraud as to the identity of the man engaging in sexual intercourse should invalidate consent and constitute rape, whether the man be impersonating a husband, co-habitee or lover. *(Keynote Case: R v Linekar (1995))*
> - Where a prostitute consents to intercourse on promise of payment, but the man intends at the time not to pay, this is not 'fraud' for the purposes of rape. The woman was not deceived as to the nature of what was taking place, i.e. she consented to the act of sexual intercourse with the man. *(Keynote Case: R v Linekar (1995))*

At the time the man knows: Whether there was knowledge that there was no consent will be a matter for the jury, based on the evidence. A genuine belief, even if mistaken, that there was consent, will mean that the offence is not committed.

'The presence or absence of reasonable grounds for such a belief is a matter to which the jury should have regard in conjunction with any other relevant matters in deciding whether he so believed' (Sexual Offences (Amendment) Act 1976, Section 1(2)).

Or is reckless as to whether the person consents: Recklessness involves the accused being indifferent to the feelings and wishes of the victim and giving no thought to the possibility that she might not be consenting. *(Keynote Case: R v Satnam, R v Kewal (1984))*

1.1.2 *Arrest*
Rape is a serious arrestable offence.

2 PROCURING A WOMAN BY THREATS
Sexual Offences Act 1956 Section 2

2.1 **Offence**
It is an offence for a person:
- to procure a woman
- by threats or intimidation
- to have sexual intercourse in any part of the world.

2.1.1 *Explanation*
Person: The offence may be committed by a man or a woman; it need not be the man who intends to have the sexual intercourse, who commits the offence of procuring.

Procure: The offence is not complete until the sexual intercourse takes place (*R v Johnson* (1964)).

Woman: The victim must be a woman; there is no homosexual element in this offence as there is in rape.

Threats or intimidation: This is a lesser offence than that of rape. A man may be guilty of rape if he uses force or a threat of bodily injury to overcome the victim's resistance. For this offence, the threat will not be of bodily injury, but could be of anything which the woman would consider detrimental; e.g. threatening to tell her husband that she was having an affair or threatening to sack her from her job.

Sexual intercourse: For an explanation of this term, see the comments relating to rape, above.

Anywhere in the world: It is something of an anomaly that whereas the offence will not be complete until sexual intercourse takes place, it is considered to be committed in this country if the procuring takes place here. It is immaterial where in the world the sexual intercourse occurs.

3 PROCURING A WOMAN BY FALSE PRETENCES
Sexual Offences Act 1956 Section 3

3.1 Offence
It is an offence for a person:
- to procure a woman
- by false pretences or false representations
- to have sexual intercourse in any part of the world.

3.1.1 *Explanation*
False pretences or false representations: The offence differs in only one respect from the offence of procuring by threats or intimidation.

For a man to commit rape as a result of obtaining the victim's consent by fraud, the fraud must relate to the nature of what is taking place, or to the identity of the person engaging in sexual intercourse. This lesser offence involves obtaining the woman's consent to intercourse by some false pretence which falls short of that required for rape. There will be limits in practice on what may be prosecuted; for example if a single man says to a woman, 'I will marry you next week if you agree to sex tonight,' the chances of a prosecution are remote. All the man has to say is that he has changed his mind. If, however, a man who is already married says the same thing, there is evidence of a false representation because he is implying that he is free to marry.

4 ADMINISTERING DRUGS TO FACILITATE INTERCOURSE
Sexual Offences Act 1956 Section 4

4.1 Offence
It is an offence for a person:
- to apply or administer to or cause to be taken by a woman
- any drug, matter or thing
- with intent to stupefy or overpower her
- so as thereby to enable any man to have unlawful sexual intercourse with her.

4.1.1 *Explanation*
Person: The ultimate aim is to enable a man to have sex with the woman, but the offence may be committed by a man or a woman; if by a man, he need not be the one with whom the intercourse is intended.

Supply, administer, cause to be taken: These terms would include, not only circumstances where a person directly applied the drug to the woman, e.g. by injecting it, but also circumstances where the substance is placed where the woman will take it, e.g. by putting it in her drink.

Drug, matter or thing: It does not necessarily have to be a recognised drug, it could be anything which is intended to stupefy or overcome the woman, such as putting neat alcohol in her orange juice.

With intent to stupefy or overpower: The offence is complete when the drug etc, is administered; there is no requirement (as there is with the offences of procuring by threats or false pretences) for the sexual intercourse to be completed or even attempted. Indeed, if the intended sexual intercourse does take place, this could well amount to an offence of rape, since the woman may not be in a fit state to give or withhold consent.

If the intention is to drug the victim so that several men may have sexual intercourse with her the offence is committed only once, by the person administering the drug.

It is not essential that the substance involved has the desired effect; the offence will be complete once the substance is administered or applied with the required intent.

Unlawful sexual intercourse: The term 'unlawful' refers to sexual intercourse outside marriage; somewhat confusingly, it does not mean that the sexual intercourse is necessarily against the law. If an offence requires 'unlawful sexual intercourse' it means that a man cannot commit that offence against his wife. An offence of rape, for example, requires only 'sexual intercourse', so a man could be guilty of raping his wife. Since the term here is 'unlawful sexual intercourse' a person cannot commit the offence by giving a woman a drug so as to facilitate the woman's husband having sexual intercourse with her.

5 UNLAWFUL SEXUAL INTERCOURSE WITH GIRL UNDER 13 YEARS
Sexual Offences Act 1956 Section 5

5.1 Offence
The offence will be committed where:
- – a man
- – has unlawful sexual intercourse with a girl under the age of 13 years.

5.1.1 *Explanation*
Unlawful sexual intercourse: This refers to sexual intercourse outside marriage. If some circumstances arose where a girl under 13 was married, e.g. from a country where such marriages were allowed, the husband would not commit this offence by having sexual intercourse with his young wife.

The fact that the girl consents to intercourse is no defence; indeed, if she did not consent, the offence would be rape.

5.1.2 *Arrest*
The offence carries a maximum sentence of life imprisonment and is therefore an arrestable offence. It is also a serious arrestable offence.

6 UNLAWFUL SEXUAL INTERCOURSE WITH GIRL UNDER 16 YEARS
Sexual Offences Act 1956 Section 6

6.1 Offence
This is similar to the previous offence committed where a man has unlawful sexual intercourse with a girl under the age of 16 years.

6.1.1 *Explanation*
Unlawful sexual intercourse: As for the previous offence, this refers to intercourse outside marriage. A man will have a defence if he has gone through a ceremony of marriage with the girl – which will be invalid because she is under the age to marry (also 16) – but he believes her to be his wife and has reasonable cause for that belief (Section 6(2)).

6.2 **Further Statutory Defence**
A man will not be guilty of the offence if:
- he is under the age of 24 years
- has not previously been charged with a like offence
- believes the girl to be aged 16 or over
- and has reasonable cause for that belief.

Man under 24: The defence is available only to young men. Perhaps the legislators felt that it is morally wrong and therefore undeserving of a defence, for older men to be involved with girls who turn out to be under 16, even if genuinely believed to be older.

Not previously charged: This means charged before a court, not charged by police.

Like offence: Means an offence under this Section, or an attempt to commit one. Thus a charge of, say, indecent assault on a 15 year old girl, would not be a bar to using this defence because indecent assault is not a like offence.

Believes with reasonable cause: It is not sufficient for the man to say he believed the girl to be of age; there must be reasonable cause for this belief.

Note: These defences apply only to the offence involving a girl under 16; they do not apply to the more serious offence of having intercourse with a girl under 13 years of age.

7 UNLAWFUL SEXUAL INTERCOURSE WITH A WOMAN WHO IS A DEFECTIVE
Sexual Offences Act 1956 Section 7

7.1 **Offence**
It is an offence for a man to have unlawful sexual intercourse with a woman who is a defective.

7.1.1 *Explanation*
Defective: The term means 'mental defective' – which in turn means a person suffering from 'severe mental impairment' – which in turn means a state of arrested or incomplete development of mind including severe impairment of intelligence and social functioning, which may be associated with abnormally aggressive or seriously irresponsible conduct.

Thus, the term 'defective' does not relate to a psychopathic disorder which might affect a previously healthy person, but to someone who has never achieved normal mental maturity (Mental Health Act 1983, Section 1).

7.2 **Defence**
A man will not be guilty of the offence if he did not know and had no reason to believe that the woman was a defective.

8 UNLAWFUL SEXUAL INTERCOURSE WITH A WOMAN MENTAL PATIENT
Mental Health Act 1959 Section 128

8.1 Offence
1) It is an offence for:
   - a man
   - who is an officer, manager, on the staff of or otherwise employed in a hospital or mental nursing home
   - to have unlawful sexual intercourse with a woman who is for the time being receiving treatment for mental disorder in that hospital or nursing home.

2) It is also an offence for such a man to have unlawful sexual intercourse:
   - on premises of which the hospital or nursing home forms a part
   - with a woman who is for the time being receiving such treatment there as an out-patient.

8.1.1 *Explanation*
The man: Only a man who is connected with the hospital or nursing home can commit the offence. It is not intended that a woman who is for the time being suffering from mental illness should include celibacy as part of her treatment; rather that such a woman should be protected from exploitation by male staff at the place where she receives treatment.

The woman: She is a person currently receiving treatment for 'mental disorder' – which means any mental illness, arrested or incomplete development of mind, psychopathic disorder or any other disorder or disability of the mind. The disorder may be of a temporary nature; it may also include incomplete development of the mind, but not to such an extent as to render the woman a 'defective'.

Knowledge: For the man to be guilty, he must know that the woman suffers from mental disorder.

The venue: If the woman is receiving treatment as an in-patient, then the offence may be committed anywhere; the man could for example take the woman away from the hospital premises on a day's outing, and have unlawful sexual intercourse away from the premises.

If, however, the woman is receiving treatment as an out-patient, the offence will be committed only when the intercourse takes place on premises of which the hospital or home forms a part. For example, the woman attends every Tuesday for treatment; a male member of staff commits the offence if he has unlawful sexual intercourse with her at the hospital – on Tuesday or any other day. However, if he arranges to meet the woman away from the hospital for intercourse, he will not be guilty.

9 OFFENCES BY OCCUPIERS AND MANAGERS OF PREMISES
Sexual Offences Act 1956 Sections 25, 26, 27

9.1 Offences
There are three offences which may be committed in connection with premises where offences are committed involving unlawful sexual intercourse. These offences correspond to the offences of unlawful sexual intercourse involving a girl under 13/girl under 16/mental defective.

1) It is an offence for any person:
   - who is the owner or occupier of any premises or who is involved in the control or

management of premises
- to induce or knowingly suffer a girl under 13
- to resort to or be on those premises for the purpose of having unlawful sexual intercourse with men or with a particular man (Section 25).

2) Same wording as above – but relates to girl under 16 (Section 26).

3) Same wording again but relates to a woman who is a defective (Section 27).

9.1.1 *Arrest*
The first of these offences, relating to a girl under 13, carries a maximum sentence of life imprisonment, so is an arrestable offence.

9.2 **Defence**
A person will not be guilty of the third offence if he did not know and had no reason to believe that the woman was a defective.

10 **PROCURING A DEFECTIVE**
Sexual Offences Act 1956 Section 9

10.1 **Offence**
It is an offence for any person:
- to procure a woman who is a defective
- to have unlawful sexual intercourse in any part of the world.

10.1.1 *Explanation*
Person: The offence may be committed by a male or female; if by a male, he need not be the person to have the unlawful sexual intercourse with the woman.

Defective: This term is explained at Paragraph 7.1.1.

Procure: For the offence to be complete, the unlawful sexual intercourse must take place. However, the offence will be committed and triable in this country, if the woman is 'obtained' here, wherever in the world the unlawful sexual intercourse may occur.

10.2 **Defence**
The same defence applies as in the case of other offences relating to defectives – the person will not commit the offence if he did not know and had no reason to suspect her to be a defective

11 **PROCURING A WOMAN UNDER THE AGE OF 21**
Sexual Offences Act 1956 Section 23

11.1 **Offence**
An offence is committed by any person:
- who procures a woman under the age of 21 years
- to have unlawful sexual intercourse anywhere in the world
- with a third person.

11.1.1 *Explanation*

Third person: The person procuring and the person engaging in the unlawful sexual intercourse must be different people. The third person need not commit any criminal offence. The rest of the offence is similar to that of procuring a defective.

12 INCEST BY A MAN
Sexual Offences Act 1956 Section 10

12.1 Offence
It is an offence for a man:
- to have sexual intercourse with a woman
- whom he knows to be
- his mother, sister, daughter or granddaughter.

12.1.1 *Explanation*

The woman: The span is from one generation older (mother) to two generations younger (granddaughter). The term 'sister' includes half-sister. Any relationship mentioned will apply even though it cannot be traced through 'lawful wedlock', i.e., an illegitimate daughter is still a daughter. With the increased numbers of people establishing 'partnerships' without going through a wedding ceremony, this provision is increasingly relevant. However, adoption does not found a relationship for the purposes of incest (Adoption Act 1976, Section 47).

Knowledge: For the man to be guilty, he must know that the woman is related to him to the relevant extent. Thus, for example, where a brother and sister are separated at a young age, and meet many years later, the offence of incest would not arise if the man was not aware that she was his sister.

Consent: The offence is committed whether the girl consents or not. However, if the intercourse takes place without consent, an offence of rape would be committed in addition to incest.

12.1.2 *Arrest and Sentence*
If the girl is under 13, the offence carries a maximum of life imprisonment; otherwise the maximum sentence is 7 years. (This is compatible with the sentence for having unlawful sexual intercourse with a girl under 13 who is not a relative, the maximum for which is life imprisonment.) The offence is arrestable, by virtue of the maximum sentence. If the girl is under 13, it is a serious arrestable offence.

13 INCEST BY A WOMAN
Sexual Offences Act 1956 Section 11

13.1 Offence
It is an offence for a woman aged 16 years or over:
- to permit a man whom she knows to be her grandfather, father, brother or son
- to have sexual intercourse with her
- by her consent.

13.1.1 *Explanation*
The woman: To commit the offence the woman must be 16 or over. If she is under that age,

she is a victim of unlawful sexual intercourse, so it is logical that she should not at the same time be regarded as a criminal.

The man: The relationships are the corresponding ones to those in the offence of incest by a man. The same considerations apply, in relation to half-sister/brother, adoption and illegitimacy.

Permit/consent: Why is it necessary to use both these words? A woman may permit the man to have intercourse, e.g. because she has been threatened. This is not enough; for her to be guilty of incest she must consent to the intercourse. Mere submission is not enough.

13.1.2 *Arrest*
The offence carries a maximum punishment of seven years' imprisonment so is an arrestable offence.

14 INCITING A GIRL UNDER 16 TO HAVE INCESTUOUS SEXUAL INTERCOURSE
Criminal Law Act 1977 Section 54

14.1 Offence
It is an offence for a man:
- to incite to have sexual intercourse with him
- a girl under the age of 16 years
- whom he knows to be his granddaughter, daughter or sister.

14.1.1 *Explanation*
Incite: Incitement includes soliciting, urging or encouraging the other to commit the crime. Incitement is complete, whether or not the end result is achieved. Thus, this offence is complete as soon as the man urges, encourages, etc, the girl. If he actually succeeds in persuading her and intercourse takes place, the full offence of incest will be committed.

Under 16: It is an offence at common law to incite a person to commit a criminal offence. However, common law does not cover a situation where a girl under 16 is persuaded to indulge in incest, because she would not thereby commit a crime. Thus, this offence is provided to deal with the man who seeks to have his evil way with his sister, daughter or granddaughter. If a man incites his 17 year old daughter to commit incest with him, he commits the offence at common law, of inciting her to commit a crime; if the girl is under 16, then this offence will apply.

The woman: The relationships are the same as for the full offence of incest, with the exception of the mother, who will not be under 16 in any case. The same comments apply, in respect of half-brother/sister and illegitimacy.

15 OFFENCES INVOLVING BUGGERY
Sexual Offences Act 1956 Section 12

15.1 Buggery
This is unnatural sexual intercourse, by anus or vagina, not the way nature intended, which is a male and female having intercourse per vagina. The possibilities include:

- man having intercourse with a woman per her anus
- man having intercourse with another man, per anus
- man having intercourse with an animal, per the animal's vagina or anus
- man or woman having intercourse with a male animal where the animal's organ penetrates the human vagina or anus.

Other forms of unnatural intercourse, e.g. oral sex, is **not** buggery. Buggery is an indictable offence at common law. Where both parties consent to buggery, the recipient commits an offence, as well as the 'donor'.

Statutory offences of buggery (with the corresponding maximum sentences) are:
- with a person under 16 or with an animal (life imprisonment)
- with a person who does not consent (life imprisonment)
- with the consent of a person who is aged 16 but under 18 years (five years)
- any other case (two years).

Buggery involves 'sexual intercourse' but this does not have to be 'unlawful sexual intercourse', i.e. a husband and wife may commit the offence. Where the buggery is without consent, this will amount to rape.

15.2 Assault with Intent to Commit Buggery
Sexual Offences Act 1956 Section 16

It is an offence for a person to assault another person with intent to commit buggery.

15.3 Lawful Acts
Sexual Offences Act 1967 Section 1

An act of buggery by one man with another man shall not be unlawful if:
- both parties have attained the age of 18 years; **and**
- both parties consent; **and**
- it takes place in private.

15.3.1 *Explanation*
In private: An act of buggery will not be regarded as being 'in private' if more than two persons take part or are present or it takes place in a lavatory to which the public have or are permitted access, on payment or otherwise.

Although this provision states that a public lavatory will not be private, this is not the only example of what is not private. Whether a particular location is 'private' will be a matter for the court to decide. *(Keynote Case: R v Reakes (1974))*

15.4 Defective
A man who is suffering from severe mental handicap cannot give consent to homosexual acts. 'Severe mental handicap' means a state of arrested or incomplete development of mind which includes severe impairment of intelligence and social functioning (Sexual Offences Act 1967, Section 1(3), (3A)).

The parallel defence applies as in the case with offences involving female defectives – the accused will not be guilty if he proves that he did not know and had no reason to suspect the man to be suffering from severe mental handicap.

15.5 **Mental Patients**

The provisions of Section 128, Mental Health Act 1959, which make it unlawful for managers and staff of mental homes, etc, to have unlawful sexual intercourse with women patients, shall apply equally to acts of buggery and gross indecency with male mental patients (Sexual Offences Act 1967, Section 1(4)).

15.6 **Procuring an Act of Buggery**
Sexual Offences Act 1967 Section 4

15.6.1 *Offence*

A man will commit an offence who:
- procures another man to commit an act of buggery with a third man
- even though that act of buggery is lawful.

15.6.2 *Explanation*

It is one thing for a homosexual man to meet another man and invite him to engage in lawful acts in private. However, it is not lawful for a man to find a sexual partner for a third man, whether what they intend to do would be lawful or not.

16 OFFENCES INVOLVING GROSS INDECENCY
Sexual Offences Act 1956 Section 13

16.1 **Offence**

It is an offence for a man:
- to commit an act of gross indecency
- with another man
- whether in public or private
- or to be a party to the commission of such an act by one man with another man
- or to procure same.

16.1.1 *Explanation*

Man and man: The offence may be committed only by men; there is no equivalent offence for women.

Gross indecency: The legislation does not define what is meant by the term. However, case law offers some guidance.

Gross indecency involves more than one person consenting and participating. *(Keynote Case: R v Preece and Howells (1976))*

Two men masturbating each other would clearly amount to an act of gross indecency, but there need not necessarily be physical contact between the two men involved (*R v Hunt* (1950)). Thus, if two men were standing facing each other, each masturbating himself, but acting in concert, this could amount to an act of gross indecency, whereas two customers in an 'adult movie' cinema who happened to be sitting in adjoining seats, each masturbating himself, but not acting together, would not be guilty of the offence. (If one man touches another in an indecent manner without the other's consent, it would amount to indecent assault.)

Party: A man may be a party to an offence committed by others if he, e.g., encourages the act or agrees to watch others performing such an act.

Procure: For the offence of procuring to be complete, the act of gross indecency must be completed. A man may be guilty of procuring another man to commit an act of gross indecency with himself, unless the act of gross indecency is lawful (*R v Jones* (1896)).

It will amount to an offence, however, for a man to procure another man to commit an act of gross indecency with a third man – even though that act of gross indecency is itself lawful (Sexual Offences Act 1967, Section 4).

16.2 Lawful Acts

The same provisions apply to acts of gross indecency between consenting adults in private, as apply to acts of buggery *(see paragraph 15.3 above)*.

16.3 Mental Patients

The provisions of Section 128, Mental Health Act 1959, which make it unlawful for managers and staff of mental homes, etc, to have unlawful sexual intercourse with women patients, shall apply equally to acts of gross indecency between male staff and male mental patients (Sexual Offences Act 1967, Section 1(4)).

16.4 Arrest

Where a man who is aged over 21 years commits an act of gross indecency with a person who is under the age of 18 years, he shall be liable to a possible maximum sentence of five years' imprisonment, making this an arrestable offence. For any other combination of ages, the maximum sentence is two years, so there is no specific power of arrest.

17 INDECENT ASSAULT ON A WOMAN
Sexual Offences Act 1956 Section 14

17.1 Offence

It is an offence for:
- a person
- to make an indecent assault on a woman.

17.1.1 *Explanation*

Person: The offence may be committed by any person, man or woman.

Indecent assault: An indecent assault is an assault accompanied by circumstances of indecency on the part of the prisoner (*Beal v Kelley* (1951)).

The term assault, dealt with more fully in Chapter 8, need not always include actual application of force by the offender on the victim. If there is a threat or offer of violence apprehended by the victim, then an assault may be made out. This principle applies also to indecent assault, e.g. where a man walks towards a woman in the confined space of a railway carriage, making an indecent suggestion. 'An assault can be committed without touching a person... if a man walks towards a woman with his person exposed and makes an indecent suggestion to her, that can amount to an assault.' *(Keynote Case: R v Rolfe (1952))*

One case which serves to illustrate the meaning of the term is that of *Fairclough v Whipp* (1951) *(Keynote Case)* where the absence of any hostile act or threat by the accused led to his acquittal on a charge of indecent assault. This case led in due course to the enactment of the offence of indecency with children to cater for circumstances not amounting to indecent assault.

Consent: There will not be an indecent assault if the woman consents to what takes place. If the woman is under 16 years of age, consent is no defence. (There is an exception where a girl under 16 has entered a marriage, invalid because of her age; her 'husband' will not commit indecent assault in respect of anything done with her consent if he believed her to be his wife and had reasonable cause for that belief.)

Similarly, if the woman is a mental defective, consent is no defence. However, a person will not be guilty of indecent assault on a defective who gives her consent if he did not know and had no reason to believe that she was a defective.

17.1.2 *Arrest*
The standard maximum penalty for the offence is 10 years' imprisonment making it an arrestable offence. However, if circumstances of gross indecency are involved, it becomes a serious arrestable offence (Police and Criminal Evidence Act 1984, Section 116(2)).

18 INDECENT ASSAULT ON A MALE
Sexual Offences Act 1956 Section 15

18.1 Offence
It is an offence:
- for a person
- to make an indecent assault on a man.

18.1.1 *Explanation*
Person: The offence may be committed by a man or by a woman.

Indecent assault: The *actus reus* is the same as for indecent assault on a woman.

Consent: There is no offence committed where the subject consents, but a boy under 16 or a mental defective cannot give valid consent. In the case of a defective, the same defence applies, a person will not be guilty if he did not know and had no reason to suspect him to be a defective.

In a case where a woman engages in sexual activity with a boy under 16, she may well commit an offence of indecent assault. There is, of course, no offence of unlawful sexual intercourse with a boy under 16, equivalent to that which a man may commit against a young girl.

18.1.2 *Arrest*
The maximum penalty is 10 years and it is an arrestable offence. If circumstances of gross indecency are involved, it becomes a serious arrestable offence (Police and Criminal Evidence Act 1984, Section 116(2)).

19 INDECENCY WITH CHILDREN
Indecency with Children Act 1960 Section 1

19.1 Offence
A person will be guilty of an offence who:

 — commits an act of gross indecency
 — with or towards
 — a child under the age of 14 years
 — or who incites a child under that age to such an act with himself or another.

19.1.1 *Explanation*
Gross indecency: This term is not defined but would include such actions as touching sex organs. However, mutual participation is not a required ingredient, as is the case when male homosexuals are involved. This legislation was enacted as a direct result of the case of *Fairclough v Whipp* (1951) *(Keynote Case)*, where the accused's action in inviting a young girl to touch his penis was held not to amount to indecent assault, through lack of a hostile act towards the girl.

With or towards: An act of gross indecency with or towards a child will amount to the offence. If the accused's behaviour involves a 'hostile act', then an indecent assault would also be committed. 'With or towards' indicates that there need not be joint participation by the offender and by the child, as is required for an offence of gross indecency between male homosexuals.

Incites – with himself or another: The circumstances of *Fairclough v Whipp* would amount to the offender inciting the child to commit the act with himself. The offence would equally be committed where the offender incited the child to engage in gross indecency with a third person. If the third person is an adult, he or she will also be guilty of the offence. The third person may be another child; there are cases recorded where the offender incited children to behave indecently towards each other, he deriving perverted satisfaction from looking on.

19.1.2 *Arrest*
Under the provisions of Section 52, Crime (Sentences) Act 1997, the maximum sentence for this offence is increased from 2 years to 10 years' imprisonment, thus making it an arrestable offence.

20 OFFENCES INVOLVING CHILDREN ABROAD

20.1 Conspiracy and Incitement
Sexual Offences (Conspiracy and Incitement) Act 1996

The intention in this Act is to curtail the activities of persons who arrange to go abroad to engage in sexual activity with children. Thailand and Indonesia are countries which have acquired a reputation as places for 'paedophile tourists'. Briefly, any conspiracy or incitement relating to a person going abroad to commit certain specified sexual offences may be dealt with in England and Wales as conspiracy or incitement.

20.2 Offences with Children Outside the United Kingdom
Sex Offenders Act 1997

20.2.1 *Offence*
Sex Offenders Act 1997 Section 7 and Schedule 2

A person will be guilty of a sexual offence under the law in England and Wales if:
 — he commits an act in a country or territory outside the United Kingdom

- which constituted an offence under the law in force in that country or territory
- and would constitute a sexual offence to which this Section applies if it had been done in England and Wales.

20.2.2 *Explanation*

Person: For a person to be guilty of an offence under these provisions, he must be a British citizen, or a resident in the United Kingdom. It is not the intention that any paedophile from anywhere in the world may end up in a UK court.

Offence in that country: The fact that an act carried out in a foreign country amounts to an offence in that country will be taken to be satisfied unless the defence requires the prosecution to prove this fact. In the Crown Court, the judge (i.e. not the jury) will decide whether this is satisfied.

Sexual offence in England and Wales: These provisions apply to acts which would amount to the following offences if committed in this country *(all contrary to the Sexual Offences Act 1956, except where stated)*:
- rape (Section 1)
- unlawful sexual intercourse with a girl under 13 (Section 5)
- unlawful sexual intercourse with a girl under 16 (Section 6)
- buggery (Section 12)
- indecent assault on a girl (Section 14)
- indecent assault on a boy (Section 15)
- assault with intent to commit buggery (Section 16)
- indecency with a child (Indecency with Children Act 1960, Section 1)
- offence involving indecent photographs of children (Protection of Children Act 1978, Section 1).

Age of victim: These provisions apply only where the victim is under the age of 16 years at the time of the offence. In some cases, the victim will necessarily be under 16, e.g. indecency with children applies to children under 14. However, a person who rapes a woman aged, say, 21, in a foreign country will not find himself in court under these provisions when he comes home.

20.2.3 *Scotland and Northern Ireland*

There are provisions for a person to be tried in a court in Scotland or Northern Ireland for acts committed outside the United Kingdom. The lists of sexual offences to which the provisions apply differ to take account of the differences in law in Scotland and Northern Ireland.

21 ANONYMITY OF VICTIMS OF SEXUAL OFFENCES
Sexual Offences (Amendment) Acts 1976 and 1992

21.1 Introduction

The 1976 Act makes provision in relation to rape offences, while the 1992 Act contains parallel provisions in respect of other sexual offences, see list below. For the purposes of the 1976 Act a 'rape offence' includes rape, attempted rape, and procuring or inciting rape. Anonymity was first granted to women victims of rape offences and later extended to victims

of almost all other sexual offences. The provisions now apply to male and female victims of such offences. There are four aspects to the provisions:
- the extent of anonymity, with exceptions
- when the provisions start to apply
- the offences to which the provisions apply
- who may commit offences by breaching the provisions, and associated defences.

21.2 Extent of Anonymity
Neither the name nor the address of the victim:
- nor a still or moving picture of the victim shall
- during that person's lifetime
- be published in England and Wales in a written publication available to the public
- or be included in a radio or television programme for reception in England and Wales
- if that is likely to lead to members of the public identifying the person as an alleged victim of such an offence.

21.2.1 *Explanation*
Picture: This means any likeness however produced. It would include a photograph, a sketch, or any other form of likeness.

Written publication: Includes a film soundtrack or other record in permanent form. It does not include an indictment or other document prepared for use in legal proceedings.

21.2.2 *Exceptions*
There are two categories of exceptions to the anonymity provisions:
- by reason of the offence
- and by order of the court.

1) **Offences of incest and buggery:** When a man has intercourse with a woman relative over 16 years with her consent, so that both commit an offence of incest, the woman will not enjoy anonymity. Her status is regarded as that of a co-defendant, rather than as a victim. Similarly, when a man has sexual intercourse with another person with consent which amounts to unlawful buggery, the second person does not enjoy a victim's anonymity.

2) **By court order:** The court may order that anonymity restrictions be lifted upon application of the defence on the grounds that publicity is required to bring forward a potential witness and without the publicity, the defence will suffer detriment.

   Additionally, a court may order the lifting of restrictions during a trial, in the public interest.

21.3 Start of Anonymity
The provisions apply after an allegation has been made that a man or woman has been the victim of a relevant offence, whether the allegation is made by the victim or by another person, **or** after a person has been accused of such an offence.

Accused: A person is 'accused' once an information is laid alleging that he committed the offence, or he appears before a court charged with the offence. In most cases, the anonymity provisions will be triggered by the allegation being made, since this will usually come before court proceedings are started against the accused.

21.4 Offences Covered

The provisions apply to most sexual offences and to others with sexual elements:
- rape
- most of the offences under the Sexual Offences Act 1956, such as the various offences of procuring a woman for unlawful sexual intercourse (USI), USI with under-age girls or mental defective, administering drugs to facilitate intercourse, incest, buggery, assault with intent to commit buggery, indecent assault
- intercourse with mental patients
- indecency with children
- inciting a girl under 16 to engage in incest
- conspiracy to commit any of these offences, attempting to commit such, or inciting another to do so.

21.5 Offences

An offence will be committed when material is published or included in a relevant programme. The following will commit an offence:
- where publication is in a newspaper or periodical – *any proprietor, editor or publisher*
- where the matter is published in any other form – *the person responsible for publishing it*
- where the matter is included in a relevant programme – *any company (body corporate) which provides the service in which the programme is included*
- *and any person having functions in relation to the programme which correspond to the functions of a newspaper editor.*

21.5.1 *Explanation*

A report is published in the Daily Bugle identifying a woman as the victim of an indecent assault. These details are then taken up by the local television company and broadcast in the early evening news. The following persons would be liable:
- owner of the Daily Bugle
- the editor of the Daily Bugle
- the television company
- the television news editor.

The following would not be liable:
- the newspaper reporter who wrote the story
- newsagents who sold the paper
- the television news reader
- the camera operator and other staff of the television company.

21.6 Defences

There are two defences available. The first does not apply to a rape offence but applies to other sexual offences covered by the 1992 Act:
- the person charged will have a defence if he proves that at the time of the alleged offence he was not aware and did not suspect nor had reason to suspect, that the publication or programme in question included the matter in question

- the accused shall have a defence if he proves that the victim of the alleged sexual offence had given written consent to the appearance of the material in that publication or programme.

However, this defence will not apply if it is proved that any person interfered unreasonably with the peace or comfort of the person giving consent with intent to obtain it.

Thus, if a freelance journalist harasses the victim of a sexual offence, with the intention of getting the victim to consent to details being published, and the victim eventually signs a consent form, the subsequent appearance of the details in the Daily Bugle will lead to offences being committed and the 'written consent' defence will not apply.

21.7 **Prosecution of Offences**

The consent of the Attorney General is required before proceedings may be instituted for these offences.

22 NOTIFICATION OF NAME AND ADDRESS OF SEX OFFENDER
Sex Offenders Act 1997

22.1 **Notification Requirements**
Sex Offenders Act 1997 Section 1

22.1.1 *Persons to Whom Requirements Apply*
A person will become subject to the notification requirements if:
- after the commencement of these provisions, he is convicted of a sexual offence to which this part of the Act applies, or he has admitted such an offence and is cautioned in respect of it by a constable in England, Wales or Northern Ireland; or
- at the time of commencement, he has been convicted of a sexual offence to which this part of the Act applies, but has not yet been sentenced in respect of it; or
- at the time of commencement he is serving a sentence of imprisonment or detention, or is subject of a community order, in respect of a sexual offence to which this part of the Act applies; or
- at the time of commencement he is subject of supervision, having been released from prison after serving the whole or part of a sentence in respect of such an offence.
- In the case of a person convicted (or found not guilty by reason of insanity, etc) who is under 18 (under 16 in Scotland) on the relevant date, the court may direct that a person having parental responsibility for the youth be authorised to comply with the notification requirements on his behalf until he reaches that age.

(The provisions apply also to a person who, rather than being convicted, has been found not guilty by reason of insanity, or has been found to be unfit to plead; or who, instead of being sentenced to imprisonment or detention, is detained in hospital or has been made subject of a guardianship order.)

22.1.2 *Applicable Period*
The requirements shall apply for a period the length of which depends on the punishment:

Sentence	*Applicable period*
1) Life imprisonment, or a sentence of 30 months or more	Indefinite period
2) Admitted to hospital, subject to a restriction order	Indefinite period
3) Sentence of more than 6 months but less than 30 months	10 years
4) Imprisonment for 6 months or less	7 years
5) Admitted to hospital not subject to a restriction order	7 years
6) In any other case	5 years

In the case of a person who is under 18 years of age on the relevant date, the indefinite period remains, for (1) and (2), but 10 years, 7 years and 5 years are reduced to half those periods.

22.1.3 *Explanation*

Persons to whom restrictions apply: These provisions apply only to a person convicted after this part of the Act comes into force, or who is still 'in the system' on that date, i.e. he has been convicted but has not yet been sentenced, he is still serving a sentence or subject of a community order, or he has been released after serving (part of) a custodial sentence and is still subject to supervision. It is not intended that every person ever convicted of a sexual offence going back over the years, should be subject to this legislation.

Imprisonment or detention: The provisions apply not only to prison sentences, but to detention in a young offenders' institution, secure training orders, detention under provisions relating to Scotland and Northern Ireland, custodial orders and sentences of detention by military courts.

Escape, bail, etc: A person who is unlawfully at large, absent without leave, absent with leave, or on bail pending an appeal, on the date of commencement of the provisions will be deemed to be serving a sentence, etc.

Community order: This term includes a community service order, probation order, or curfew order (Criminal Justice Act 1991, Schedule 2).

Relevant date: The period during which the requirements apply commence on the date of conviction, caution or finding of insanity etc. In the case of a police caution, the police must inform the offender that the offence is one to which these provisions apply, and complete a certificate.

Person under 18: If the person convicted (or found to be unfit to plead, etc) by a court is under 18, the responsibility for notifying details to the police may be passed to someone having parental responsibility for the young person. This arrangement requires a direction from the court; police have no power to pass responsibility in this way when a young person is dealt with by way of caution.

22.2 **Notification**
Sex Offenders Act 1997 Section 2

22.2.1 *Initial Notification*

A person subject to the notification requirements shall:
- before the end of a period of 14 days from the relevant date
- notify the police
- of his date of birth, his name, and where he uses one or more other names, each of those names
- and his home address on the relevant date.

22.2.2 *Subsequent Notification*

A person subject to notification requirements shall:
- before the end of a period of 14 days beginning with
- his using a name which has not been notified to the police; or
- any change of his home address; or
- his having resided at or stayed at, for a qualifying period, any premises in the United Kingdom the address of which has not been notified to the police
- notify the name or address to the police.

22.2.3 *Explanation*

Relevant date: As explained in the preceding paragraph, this is the date of conviction, or caution or finding of insanity, etc.

Notify police: A person will comply with the requirement if he goes to a police station in the police area in which his home is situated, and gives oral notification to any police officer or other authorised person there (e.g. a member of civilian support staff authorised to deal with such matters). Alternatively, the person may send written notification to any police station in the area where his home is situated. It will not be sufficient to stop a police officer in the street and recite the details to her, nor to tell the cleaner who is polishing the glass at the entrance to the police station.

The police must give the person a written acknowledgement, whether the notification was oral or in writing. The acknowledgement will be in a form stipulated by the Home Secretary.

Home address: A person's home address will be either the address of his sole or main residence in the United Kingdom, or if he does not have such residence, premises in the United Kingdom which he regularly visits.

14 day period: For the purpose of calculating the 14 day period, any time shall be disregarded when the person concerned is:
- outside the United Kingdom, or
- detained in hospital, or
- in custody by order of a court, or
- serving a custodial sentence.

If Smith is sentenced to imprisonment upon conviction for a relevant offence, it would not be sensible to require him to notify his home address to the police while he is still in prison. In such a case, he would have to do so within 14 days of his release from prison. Note that only time in custody by order of a court falls not to be counted. If Smith is arrested by police after coming out of prison and held in custody over the weekend to appear in court on Monday, his time spent in police cells still counts towards the 14 days. (Indeed, he has the ideal opportunity to notify the police while at the police station.)

Qualifying period: Any stay at premises in the United Kingdom for a period of 14 days, or for two or more periods in any period of 12 months which in aggregate amount to 14 days, means that the address of those premises has to be notified. If a person with a conviction for a sexual offence goes off to a hotel in Brighton for three weeks' holiday, or goes there regularly over the course of a year, the police have to be told. However, if the same person goes to different hotels, or different seaside resorts, never staying for more than 13 days in any one place, a requirement to notify would not arise.

22.3 **Offences to Which Requirements Apply**
Sex Offenders Act 1997 Schedule 1

22.3.1 *Sexual Offences*
For the purposes of the requirements, a sexual offence will include any of the following *(contrary to the provisions of the Sexual Offences Act 1956 unless stated)*:

1) rape (Section 1)
2) intercourse with a girl under 13 (Section 5)
3) intercourse with a girl under 16 (Section 6)
4) incest by a man (Section 10)
5) buggery (Section 12)
6) indecency between men (Section 13)
7) indecent assault on a woman (Section 14)
8) indecent assault on a man (Section 15)
9) assault with intent to commit buggery (Section 16)
10) causing or encouraging offences against a girl under 16 (Section 28)
11) indecency with a child (Indecency with Children Act 1960, Section 1)
12) offences involving indecent photographs of children (Protection of Children Act 1978, Section 1)
13) possession of indecent photograph of a child (Criminal Justice Act 1988, Section 160)
14) unlawful importation of indecent photographs of children (Customs and Excise Management Act 1979, Section 170)
15) inciting a girl under 16 to have incestuous intercourse (Criminal Law Act 1977, Section 54).

22.3.2 *Exceptions to the List of Offences*
There are a number of exceptions to the basic list. These include:

– offender under 20 years of age – the offences at (3) *sexual intercourse with a girl under 16*, (5) *buggery* and (6) *indecency between men*
– victim or other party over 18 years of age – all of the offences (4) to (10) inclusive.

However, even if the victim is aged 18, offences of indecent assault, (7) and (8) on the list, will not be excepted if the offender receives a sentence of 30 months' imprisonment or more (or is placed in a hospital subject to a restriction order).

22.3.3 *Explanation*
The effect of the legislation, taking account of the offences and the exceptions, is to focus on the most serious sexual offences – rape and indecent assaults which warrant sentences of 30 months or more – and those committed against persons under 18. In certain cases, offences committed by persons under 20 are also excepted.

22.3.4 *The United Kingdom Outside England and Wales*
The list of offences and exceptions differs to take account of the law in Scotland and Northern Ireland. A person convicted of a sexual offence in one country in the United Kingdom will be required to notify the police when he lives elsewhere in the kingdom.

There is provision in the Act for the requirement to notify the police to be extended at some future date to take in the Channel Islands and the Isle of Man (Section 9).

22.4 **Failure to Comply with Notification Requirements**
Sex Offenders Act 1997 Section 3

22.4.1 *Offence*

A person commits an offence who:
- fails without reasonable excuse to comply with notification requirements, or
- in purported compliance with the requirements, notifies to the police any information which he knows to be false.

22.4.2 *Explanation*

Failure to notify: The offence is committed on the day on which a person first fails to comply with the requirement to notify, and continues to be committed throughout the period during which the failure continues. However, the person may be prosecuted only once for the same failure.

Venue for prosecution: Proceedings for an offence of failure to notify, or of giving false information, may be commenced in any court having jurisdiction in an area where the offender resides or is found. This gets round any problem of deciding where the offender was when he first committed the offence, or which police force should deal with the matter.

Parental responsibility: In a case where a court has directed that the notification requirement in respect of a convicted person under 18 (16 in Scotland) be passed to a person having parental responsibility for the young person, liability for an offence shall also rest with that adult.

Keynote Cases

23.1 *R v Linekar* **[1995] 3 All ER 69**

Problem

The meaning of the term 'fraud' in the context of committing rape by obtaining consent to sexual intercourse by fraud.

Circumstances

The defendant met a woman who was soliciting as a prostitute and he agreed to pay her £25 in return for sexual intercourse. The act of sexual intercourse then took place, and the defendant thereafter refused to pay the agreed sum. The woman complained of rape. The prosecution suggested that since the consent to intercourse was given solely for payment, if the defendant intended not to pay, he had obtained that consent by fraud, the consent was therefore invalid, and the defendant was guilty of rape.

Decision

The Court of Appeal held that what matters for an offence of rape is not whether the defendant uses fraud, but whether the victim consents. In this context, 'consent' means consent to sexual intercourse with that particular man. The fact that the defendant in this case may have employed fraud to convince the woman that he would pay for sex, does not alter the fact that she consented to having sexual intercourse with him.

The court cited examples which would amount to rape, where the fraud was such that the woman did not actually consent to sexual intercourse with the man concerned:
- representing the act as a surgical operation (*R v Flattery* (1877))

– the victim agreed to physical manipulation to improve her singing voice (*R v Williams* [1923]).

Comment
It will be in only very rare cases that consent to sexual intercourse obtained by fraud will amount to rape. If the victim realises that what he or she is agreeing to is sexual intercourse with the particular man concerned, then rape will not be made out.

23.2 *R v Satnam, R v Kewal* (1984) 78 Cr App R 149

Problem
The meaning of 'reckless' as it applies in the offence of rape.

Circumstances
The two defendants persuaded a 17 year old woman to accept a lift in a car driven by one of them. During the time the woman was in the car, sexual intercourse took place between her and the two men. The woman claimed she had been raped; the men did not deny that sexual intercourse had taken place, claiming that this was with the consent of the woman. It was admitted by the defendants that there had been some show of reluctance on the part of the woman, to the extent that during one of the acts of intercourse, one of the defendant's held her while the other had intercourse. It was claimed that the defendants believed she was consenting. The points at issue related to whether the men believed the woman was consenting to intercourse, or were reckless as to the fact that there was no consent.

Decision
Two grounds for appeal were placed before the Court of Appeal:
– whether a mistaken belief that the victim is consenting affords a defence to a charge of 'reckless rape'
– whether it is necessary for a defendant to be actually aware of the possibility that the victim is not consenting before he can be held to be reckless.

The court held that a man is reckless if either:
– he was indifferent and gave no thought to the possibility that the victim might not be consenting in circumstances where, if any thought had been given to the matter, it would have been obvious that there was a risk of there not being consent; or
– he was aware of the possibility that he or she might not be consenting, but went ahead regardless of whether there was consent or not.

Comment
The offence of rape is committed where the victim does not consent to the sexual intercourse which takes place, and at the time the offender knows that there is no consent or is reckless as to whether there is.

The finding in this case is that either the man recognises that there is a risk that the victim is not consenting, but goes ahead anyway – or, he gives no thought to the fact that such a risk might exist, when if some thought had been given to this matter, it would have been quite obvious that there was a risk that consent was lacking.

Thus, in terms of the two questions put to the court, the answer to the first is – if the man's belief is genuinely held, he is not guilty, but in deciding whether his belief is genuine, regard should be had to the circumstances. To the second question the answer is – no, it is not necessary for the defendant to be aware of the possibility that consent is lacking. If he does not give any consideration to the question, he may still be reckless if such a risk was obvious from the circumstances, had he bothered to consider them.

23.3 *R v Reakes* [1974] Crim LR 615

Problem
The meaning of the term 'in private' as it relates to homosexual acts which may be lawful.

Circumstances
The defendant was charged with an offence of buggery against another man. The act took place in a yard which was enclosed, with a gate leading from a public road. It happened at 1.00am and the yard was unlit. In the yard was a toilet used by customers from two adjacent restaurants and the employees of a taxi firm. The defendant knew about the toilet having used it himself a short time previously and having seen others use it.

Decision
The Court of Appeal upheld the direction given by the trial judge to the jury on the meaning of 'in private'. When considering whether a place was 'in private' the jury should consider all the surrounding circumstances – the time of night – the nature of the place – and matters such as lighting – and to consider the likelihood of anyone else coming upon the scene.

Comment
It will be a matter for the court to consider in each individual case whether homosexual acts are lawful by reason of their taking place 'in private'. The test is 'What are the chances of someone else coming across the scene?'

23.4 *R v Preece, R v Howells* (1976) 63 Cr App R 28

Problem
For an act of gross indecency between men, does there have to be more than one man present and participating?

Circumstances
Two men were in adjacent cubicles in a public toilet. Preece was masturbating while Howells watched through a hole in the partition between the cubicles. While Preece's behaviour could clearly be described as amounting to gross indecency, the question arose as to whether Howells, by merely watching, could be said to be engaged in gross indecency.

Decision
The Court of Appeal decided that the offence of gross indecency required two men present and participating. If one man behaved in a grossly indecent way in the presence of another man, intending the other to see him, because that gives him pleasure, if the second man is not a party to this, e.g. he finds it disgusting, the offence of gross indecency will not be committed. For the offence of gross indecency, there must be two men participating; there need not however be any physical contact.

Comment

If one man masturbates himself in the view of another, who is a party to the actions of the first, each deriving pleasure from what takes place, this will amount to the offence. There must be two persons involved.

23.5 *R v Rolfe* (1952) 36 Cr App R 4

Problem

Whether physical contact is required to constitute indecent assault.

Circumstances

The defendant entered a railway carriage compartment in which a woman was the only other passenger. The defendant undid his trousers, exposed himself and walked towards the woman, inviting her to have sexual intercourse with him. The defendant denied touching the woman.

Decision

The Court of Appeal commented on the fact that 'assault' is often confused with 'battery'. Assault may be committed without touching the victim. Walking towards the woman while making the indecent suggestion was sufficient to amount to a hostile act accompanied by circumstances of indecency.

Comment

The terms 'assault' and 'battery' are dealt with in Chapter 8. This case confirms that an assault does not require physical contact, but may be complete if there is a threat or offer of violence, perceived by the victim. Here, in the confined space of the railway carriage compartment, the action of the man in walking towards the woman with his person exposed, was threatening and amounted to an assault.

23.6 *Fairclough v Whipp* (1951) 35 Cr App R 138

Problem

Whether inviting another person to touch one's self amounts to a hostile act and therefore an assault, for the purposes of the offence of indecent assault.

Circumstances

The defendant, Whipp, was standing on the bank of a canal urinating, when several young children walked by. Whipp, with his person exposed said to a nine year old girl, 'Touch it'. The girl then touched his penis. He then left the scene. He was charged with an indecent assault on the girl.

Decision

The Court of Criminal Appeal agreed that an assault could be committed without the actual application of violence, e.g. by a threat of violence (agreeing with the decision in *Rolfe* (above)). However, when one person invites another to touch him, this cannot amount to an assault on the second person because there is no 'hostile act'.

Comment

The Court, in upholding the magistrates's decision to dismiss the charge of indecent assault, commented that it would be a very good thing if Parliament passed an Act providing punishment for indecent conduct in the presence of children. The result was the Indecency with Children Act 1960, which does not say much for Parliament's speed of the response, but the behaviour of Whipp would now amount to an offence under that Act.

Chapter 11: Abduction and Kidnapping

1 INTRODUCTION

Offences of kidnapping or abduction involve taking and/or holding a person, usually against that person's will, but in some cases against the will of some other person. The specific offence committed depends on, for example, the age of the victim, whether the victim is a woman or the intention of the offender.

2 KIDNAPPING

2.1 Offence

Kidnapping is the common law offence committed by:

- stealing and carrying away
- or secreting
- any person of any age of either sex
- against that person's will.

2.1.1 *Explanation*

Elements of offence: There are four factors involved in the offence of kidnapping:

- there is a taking or carrying away by one person of another
- the taking or carrying away must be by force or fraud
- it must be without the consent of the victim
- it must be without lawful excuse.
  (Keynote Case: R v D (1984))

Force or fraud: Use of force to kidnap someone needs no explanation. Fraud would be involved when, for example, the victim went along willingly as a result of being told a false story, such as, 'Come with me, your father sent me to fetch you.'

Without consent: The fact that the offender and victim are married does not excuse the offender. 'The notion that a husband, without incurring punishment, can treat his wife with hostile force is obsolete, and if that force results in carrying her away from the place where she wishes to remain, then this amounts to the offence of kidnapping' (*R v Reid* (1972)).

Lawful excuse: A constable arresting someone for an offence, or a social worker taking a child into care, may well take a person by force against that person's will, but will not commit the offence because there is a lawful excuse for the action.

2.1.2 *Arrest*

Kidnapping is a serious arrestable offence.

3 CHILD ABDUCTION

The Child Abduction Act 1984 creates offences concerning the abduction of persons under 16 years of age. There are two distinct offences to consider – one which may be committed by a person 'connected with' the child, the other which may be committed by someone who is **not** the child's mother (or father in some cases), guardian or person having legal custody.

3.1 Person Connected with Child
Child Abduction Act 1984 Section 1

3.1.1 *Offence*
The offence is committed when:
- a person connected with a child under 16
- takes or sends the child out of the United Kingdom
- without the appropriate consent.

3.1.2 *Explanation*
Connected with: A person is connected with a child if he or she:
- is the parent or guardian, or
- if the parents were not married at the time of the child's birth, there are reasonable grounds for believing that he is the father; or
- has custody of the child; or
- is the person in whose favour there is a residence order in respect of the child.

To commit the offence one has to be connected with the child, so the offence will commonly arise in cases where the custody of a child is in dispute, e.g. because the parents are estranged.

Takes or sends: A person will 'take' a child if he causes or induces the child to accompany himself or someone else. Whether the child goes willingly is immaterial.

Out of the United Kingdom: There are some exceptions, e.g. when the child is out of the country for less than one month.

Without appropriate consent: This means with consent of either a court or of each of the mother, the father if he has parental responsibility, the guardian, the person having custody or the person in whose favour there is a residence order, as the case may be.

Exceptions: A person will not commit the offence if:
- he believes that consent was given or would have been; or
- consent was unreasonably refused; or
- he was unable to communicate with a person whose consent was required despite taking all reasonable steps to do so.

Note: This legislation caters for situations where a child is removed from the UK, and other countries have similar legislation. Under the terms of international agreement, a court in a country which is a signatory to the agreement will order a child to be returned to the country where it was usually domiciled, pending custody proceedings. Cases appear in the Press from time to time, where a British parent, usually a mother, is ordered by a court to return her child to a foreign country pending custody proceedings in that country.

3.2 Person Not Connected with the Child
Child Abduction Act 1984 Section 2

3.2.1 *Offence*
The second offence is committed by a person who is not connected with a child who without lawful authority or reasonable excuse takes or detains a child under 16 so as **either** to remove him from the lawful control of anyone having such control **or** so as to keep him out of lawful control.

3.2.2 *Explanation*

Not connected: To commit this offence the offender must not fall into one of the following categories:

- the mother of a child
- the father if the parents were married at the time of the child's birth
- the child's guardian or a person having custody or the person named in a residence order.

Takes or detains: As is the case with the other offence, 'takes' includes causing or inducing the child to go.

3.3 Differences Between the Two Offences

3.3.1 *Offender*

The first offence can only be committed by a person connected with the child, the second can be committed by anyone who is not so connected. The 'connected' person must take the child outside the United Kingdom for the offence to be completed; the 'unconnected' only has to remove or keep the child out of lawful control for what may be only a brief period, for the offence to be made out.

Both offences may be committed at the same time. For example, Smith and his wife are separated, wife has custody of their child, Smith wants to take child from wife; Smith hires Jones to collect child from school, deliver him to Smith at airport; Smith then takes child to Australia. Smith will commit the first offence, Jones the second.

Note: In these circumstances Smith and Jones could also commit the offence of kidnapping at common law. Where the offender is connected with the victim who is under 16, the consent of the Director of Public Prosecutions is required to proceed on a charge of kidnapping (Child Abduction Act 1984, Section 5).

3.3.2 *Prosecution*

Where a child is taken away by a parent or guardian, etc, in breach of a court order, this should normally be dealt with as a contempt of court, rather than by prosecuting for kidnapping or child abduction. *(Keynote Case: R v D (1984))*

4 ABDUCTION OF WOMEN

4.1 Girl Under 16
Sexual Offences Act 1956 Section 20

4.1.1 *Offence*

It is an offence for a person:
- without lawful authority or excuse
- to take an unmarried girl under 16
- out of the possession of her parent or guardian
- against **his** will.

4.1.2 *Explanation*

Take: For an abduction to be made out, it must be shown that there is a substantial interference with the parent-child relationship. There need not be any force involved. The girl need not be taken unwillingly; it will be enough to show that the accused used persuasion or assisted the girl in some way to leave her parent. The popular image of the youth placing a ladder against the girl's window for her to climb down and elope with him actually featured in one old case, where this degree of assistance towards the girl's leaving home was held to amount to a 'taking' (*R v Robins* (1884)).

Out of possession: There is no need to show that the 'taking' is intended to be permanent. Persuading a girl to spend a few nights away from her home would suffice for the offence to be made out. Even more telling is the case decision where the accused was convicted after the girl left home in order to marry the accused and returned within a matter of a couple of hours.

Against his will: Whatever the feelings of the girl in the matter, the taking of her must be against the wishes of the parent or guardian.

4.2 **Girl Under 18**
Sexual Offences Act 1956 Section 19

4.2.1 *Offence*
It is an offence for a person:
- to take an unmarried girl under the age of 18 years
- out of the possession of her parent or guardian
- against his will
- if she is taken with the intention that she shall have unlawful sexual intercourse with men or with a particular man.

4.2.2 *Explanation*
Unlawful sexual intercourse: This term refers to sexual intercourse outside marriage. The term 'unlawful' in this context does not necessarily mean that the sexual intercourse will amount to a crime in itself.

Man or men: It must be proved that the offender intended at the time of taking the girl, that she should have unlawful sexual intercourse with one or more men, but it is not necessary that he intended to be that man or one of them. The other elements of the offence are the same as for the preceding one.

4.3 **Woman Who is a Defective**
Sexual Offences Act 1956 Section 21

4.3.1 *Offence*
It is an offence for a person:
- to take a woman who is a defective
- out of the possession of her parent or guardian
- if she is so taken with the intention that she shall have unlawful sexual intercourse with men or with a particular man.

4.3.2 *Explanation*
This offence is very similar to that involving a girl under 18.

Defective: The term refers to a person suffering from severe subnormality to such an extent that she is incapable of leading an independent life or of guarding herself against serious exploitation.

4.4 **Woman of Any Age**
Sexual Offences Act 1956 Section 17

4.4.1 *Offence*
It is an offence for a person:
- to take away or detain a woman
- against her will
- with the intention that she shall marry or have unlawful sexual intercourse with that or any other person
- if she is so taken or detained by force
- or for the sake of her property or expectation of property.

4.4.2 *Explanation*
Take away or detain: The victim may be taken away against her will, or she may go willingly then be detained against her will.

Against her will: This differs from the other abduction offences which may be committed even if the girl is a willing participant. In this case, the woman must be taken or detained against her wishes.

Marry or have unlawful sexual intercourse: It need not be the person who takes or detains the woman who intends to marry her or have unlawful sexual intercourse with her, but it must be shown that the offender intended, at the time of taking or detaining her, that she would marry or have sex outside marriage with some man.

Force: It may be that force is used to take or detain the woman against her will. However, she could be detained without use of force, e.g. by denying her access to clothing. If force is not used, then the offender must have her wealth or expectation of wealth in mind.

For the sake of property/expectation of property: 'Expectation of property' relates to property of a person of whom the woman is next-of-kin.

It may be fairly rare for a man to hold a woman against her will, in order to persuade her to marry him, so that he can get his hands on her father's money when he dies. It is perhaps easier to visualise circumstances where a man holds a woman by force, intending to have unlawful sexual intercourse with her.

5 **WARRANT TO SEARCH FOR ABDUCTED WOMAN**
Sexual Offences Act 1956 Section 43

5.1 **Grounds for Issue**
A magistrate may issue a warrant to search premises where there is reasonable cause to suspect:

1) That a woman is detained there in order that she may have unlawful sexual intercourse with men or with a particular man; **and**
2) **Either**:
   - she is detained against her will, or

- she is under 16, or
- she is a defective, or
- she is under 18 and is detained against the will of her parent or guardian.

5.2 Powers Under the Warrant

The warrant authorises a constable:

- to enter the premises specified in the warrant, using force if necessary
- to search for the woman
- and take her to a place of safety.

5.2.1 *Explanation*

The information to obtain the warrant may be laid by the woman's parent, relative or guardian, or by any other person who appears to the magistrate to be acting in the woman's interests. The person laying the information **shall** accompany the police who execute the warrant, if that person so wishes – **unless** the magistrate who issues the warrant directs otherwise (in other words, the police have no say in whether the other person accompanies them).

Keynote Cases

6.1 *R v D* (1984) 79 Cr App R 313

Problem

What constitutes the common law offence of kidnapping?

Circumstances

The case arose from a marriage between a New Zealand man and a British mother. A child of the marriage was born in New Zealand. The family were living in England when the marriage broke up and the mother and child went to live with the mother's relatives. The mother obtained a High Court order making the child a ward of court, to prevent the father taking her out of the country. There then followed two incidents in which the father took the child from the mother using force and threats of violence. On the first occasion he took the child, then aged two years, to New Zealand and the mother regained custody after a court case there. On the second occasion the father took the child, now aged 5 years, to Ireland, but was subsequently arrested on warrant. He was charged with a number of offences, including two counts of kidnapping. The Court of Appeal allowed the father's appeal against conviction, on the grounds that a father could not be guilty of kidnapping his own child under the age of 14 years. The Crown appealed to the House of Lords.

Decision

The House of Lords found that there were four ingredients in the offence of kidnapping:

1) Taking and carrying away of one person by another

2) by force or by fraud

3) without the consent of the person so taken

4) and without lawful excuse.

There is no reason why a father may not be guilty of kidnapping his own child.

With regard to 'consent', it is necessary to prove, even in the case of a child, that there is no consent. If the child is very young, this may be inferred from its age; for an older child, it is left as a matter of fact for the jury, whether the child has sufficient intelligence and understanding to give consent.

It was held also that where parents snatch their own children in defiance of a court order, the matter should normally be dealt with as a contempt of court, rather than by criminal prosecution.

Comment

In a case where the child is old enough to understand, and does consent to go with a parent, the offence of kidnapping will not be committed. However, the offence(s) of child abduction involve lack of consent of the person having custody, rather than of the child.

Chapter 12: Prostitution and Brothels

1 PROSTITUTION/COMMON PROSTITUTE

1.1 Meaning

The term 'common prostitute' may be defined as:

- a woman
- who offers her body commonly for lewdness
- for payment in return.
  (*R v De Munck* (1918))

1.1.1 *Explanation*

Woman: There have been a number of changes in recent years in relation to sexual offences, aimed apparently at sex equality. For example, the offence of rape, for centuries confined to female victims, may now be committed against a man. There is an offence committed by a person who lives on the earnings of a 'male prostitute'. However, the traditional description of a common prostitute remains as it has been for so long that prostitution is often referred to as 'the oldest profession'. The term 'common prostitute is confined to women' (*DPP v Bull* (1994)).

Commonly: This implies that the woman does not confine herself to one man. If a wealthy man sets his mistress up in a flat and pays all her household expenses in return for her sexual favours, this will not make her a common prostitute.

Lewdness: The woman does not necessarily have to offer full sexual intercourse for her to be a prostitute. Other acts, such as 'massage' may amount to acts of lewdness.

Payment: However free a woman may be with her sexual favours, she will not be regarded as a prostitute unless she accepts payment.

1.2 Unlawful Aspects of Prostitution

Prostitution is not in itself against the law and it is not an offence for a woman simply to act as a prostitute. The law does prohibit women importuning clients in a street or public place. The offence is punishable only with a fine, but the police engage in an officially sanctioned cautioning scheme before prostitutes go to court. More severe penalties await persons who encourage women to act as prostitutes, who live off the earnings of a prostitute, or who have a part in running premises where two or more women engage in prostitution (a brothel). Women who become prostitutes do so in response to demand for their services. The law therefore seeks to discourage the clients by making it an offence for a man to solicit women for prostitution in the street.

2 SOLICITING

Street Offences Act 1959 Section 1

2.1 Offence

It is an offence for:

- a common prostitute
- to loiter or solicit

- in a street or public place
- for the purposes of prostitution.

2.1.1 *Explanation*

Common prostitute: The offence can be committed only by women. The equivalent offence for a male is soliciting or importuning in a public place for an immoral purpose.

Loiter or solicit: It has been held that 'solicit' involves the physical presence of the woman and activity on her part which amounts to importuning prospective clients. A woman who places an advertisement in a public place, but is not present there herself, is not soliciting (*Weisz v Monahan* (1962)).

However, a woman was held to be soliciting in the street, when she sat in a window overlooking the street, wearing a miniskirt and a low cut top, and bathed in red light. The court found that there was 'active solicitation in the form of attracting the attention of prospective men customers' (*Behrendt v Burridge* (1976)). This decision was in line with an earlier case in which the court found that 'it can matter little whether the prostitute is soliciting while in the street or is standing in a doorway, on a balcony or at a window...; in each such case her solicitation is projected and addressed to someone in the street' (*Smith v Hughes* (1960)).

Street or public place: The term 'street' is defined in the Act as:
- any bridge, road, lane, footway, court, alley or passage; whether a thoroughfare or not; which is for the time being open to the public; and the doorways or entrances of premises abutting on a street; and any ground adjoining and open to a street (Street Offences Act 1959, Section 1(4)).

One may imagine those responsible for drafting the legislation trying to cover all eventualities, by asking 'Where might a prostitute loiter in an effort to attract passing men? – in a shop doorway, down an alley, in a pedestrian subway, on waste ground next to the road, etc.'

The meaning of 'street' is further extended to include on a balcony overlooking the street (*Smith v Hughes* (1960)), as well as in the window of a house, as mentioned above.

The term 'public place' is not defined in the same way, but is taken to include any place to which the public has access, whether or not by right, including a place where there is public access temporarily.

Purposes of prostitution: This term means acts of lewdness, commonly offered for payment, in accordance with the meaning of the term common prostitute.

3 ARREST AND PROSECUTION
Street Offences Act 1959 Section 1(3)

3.1 Power of Arrest

A constable may arrest without warrant anyone whom he finds in a street or public place and suspects with reasonable cause to be committing this offence.

3.2 Cautioning Procedures

The Home Office have laid down a procedure of cautions to be followed before a woman found committing the soliciting offence is prosecuted. Although this procedure is not set out in legislation, it is officially recognised in the Act, by the provision of a procedure whereby a woman may appeal against a caution.

3.2.1 *First Occasion*

On the first occasion that a woman is seen apparently loitering or soliciting in a street or public place for the purposes of prostitution, the constable who suspects her should call upon another officer, so that the two of them may be satisfied that she is indeed committing the offence, before approaching her. She should then be offered the services of social workers or other advice, and cautioned. The precise action to be taken by police officers at this stage may vary from force to force, and will be contained in local procedures.

3.2.2 *Second Occasion*

On the second occasion, the same procedure is followed. Details of cautions must be entered in a register at the police station.

3.2.3 *Third Occasion*

On the third occasion that the woman is seen apparently soliciting, the same procedure is followed, in that two officers maintain observations to confirm that she is soliciting. On this occasion, however, there is no third caution; she may be arrested for the offence.

3.2.4 *Record of Cautions*

There is no provision for a national register of cautions; that is to say, if a woman, having received her first caution in one part of the country, moves elsewhere and is found soliciting, there is no procedure for discovering the existence of the first caution; it is likely that she would receive a 'first caution' in the new area. Once the woman is convicted, of course, details of the conviction will be available nationally, so there is no reason why the cycle of two cautions plus a conviction need be repeated.

3.2.5 *Appeal Against Caution*

The only part of the cautioning procedure set out in statute is that which provides for an appeal against caution by a woman who claims that she was not loitering or soliciting for the purposes of prostitution. If a woman is aggrieved by being cautioned, she may raise her objection with the police who may then reconsider the matter. However, the formal procedure allows the woman – within 14 days of receiving the caution – to apply to magistrates' court for an order to have the caution expunged. The court, unless satisfied beyond reasonable doubt by police evidence that she was in fact loitering or soliciting for the purposes of prostitution, shall grant the order to have the caution deleted from the record (Street Offences Act 1959, Section 2).

4 SOLICITING OF WOMEN BY MEN
Sexual Offences Act 1985 Sections 1, 2

4.1 **Offences**

There are two offences which a man may commit:
1) In a street or public place:
   - he persistently solicits
   - a woman or different women
   - for the purpose of prostitution (Section 2(1)).
2) Either from a motor vehicle while it is in a street or public place:
   - or in a street or public place while in the immediate vicinity of a motor

vehicle that he has just got off or out of
- solicits a woman or different women
- persistently
- or in such circumstances as to cause annoyance to the woman (or women) solicited or nuisance to other persons in the neighbourhood (Section 1(1)).

4.1.1 *Explanation*

With or without motor vehicle: The *actus reus* for the first offence would cater for a man on foot (men 'cruising' through red light districts by dumper truck or pedal cycle (i.e. these are not motor vehicles) would also be catered for but are not seen as a major problem), and the crucial element is 'persistence'. The man in a motor vehicle, seen as a greater problem than a man on foot, may commit the offence by persistence or by causing annoyance.

Man: The offences may be committed only by men. Thus, a woman who goes round looking for a prostitute on behalf of a man would not commit either of these offences.

Street or public place: The meaning of the term 'street' in the Act is exactly the same as that in the Street Offences Act 1959. The term 'public place' is not defined, but the meaning may be taken as the same as in the 1959 Act *(see paragraph 2.1.1 above)*.

Persistently solicits: The term 'persistently' means that there must be a degree of repetition. To approach one woman on one occasion would not be enough, but to approach at least two different women, or to approach the same woman more than once, would satisfy this element. In a case involving a male importuning males, it was held that two actions of importuning on the same night were just enough to establish persistence (*Dale v Smith* (1967)).

Purpose of prostitution: This means for the purpose of obtaining her services as a prostitute (Section 4(1)).

Motor vehicle: This has the same meaning as in the Road Traffic Act 1988, and the use of the phrase 'out of or off' clearly allows for motor cycles and the like, as well as cars, lorries, etc.

Immediate vicinity: There is no definition of what amounts to 'immediate vicinity'. It will be a matter to be determined from the evidence in any each individual case. If there is doubt, it may be prudent to consider the Section 2 offence, which does not require the presence of a motor vehicle.

Annoyance: This is one element which widens the scope of the 'motor vehicle' offence compared to the other. If there is evidence that one woman, approached only once, is annoyed by that approach, the offence is made out, without the need for proof of persistence. This would cater for a situation where a woman who is not a prostitute is mistaken for one by a kerb crawling man, to her annoyance.

Nuisance: Whatever the feelings of the woman who is approached, evidence of nuisance to persons in the neighbourhood will be enough. If prostitutes gather in a neighbourhood, attracting kerb crawlers, the prostitutes will not be annoyed by an approach, but that approach may be a regarded as a nuisance by persons in the neighbourhood. The magistrates may take their own knowledge of the area into account when determining whether a defendant's actions are likely to have caused nuisance to other persons in the neighbourhood, without any direct evidence from such a person that nuisance was actually caused (*Paul v DPP* (1989)).

5 MAN SOLICITING FOR AN IMMORAL PURPOSE
Sexual Offences Act 1956 Section 32

5.1 Offence
It is an offence for a man:
- persistently
- to solicit or importune
- in a public place
- for immoral purposes.

5.1.1 *Explanation*
Man: This offence cannot be committed by a woman, only by a male.

Persistently: This term is not defined in the legislation, but one approach only would appear not to amount to 'persistently', giving the word its usual meaning. The explanation given in *paragraph 4.1.1* above applies for this offence also.

Solicits or importunes: As with soliciting by a common prostitute, physical presence is required. Thus, to display an advertisement in public to the effect that one is available as a male prostitute, will not amount to soliciting (*Burge v DPP* (1962)).

Immoral purpose: To solicit a common prostitute has been held not to amount to this offence, hence the provision of specific offences covering such activity. However, to solicit young girls would be 'for an immoral purpose' (*R v Dodd* (1977)). Homosexual activity which is not in itself unlawful may amount to an immoral purpose; it is proper to leave it to the jury to decide whether a purpose is 'immoral' in any particular case (*R v Ford* (1978); *R v Gray* (1982)). Such conduct may also involve an offence of procuring an act of buggery or gross indecency *(for details of these offences, see Chapter 10).*

6 MAN LIVING ON IMMORAL EARNINGS OF PROSTITUTION
Sexual Offences Act 1956 Section 30

6.1 Offence
It is an offence for a man:
- knowingly
- to live wholly or in part
- on the earnings of prostitution.

6.1.1 *Explanation*
Man: The offence can be committed only by a male. A woman may commit the offence of exercising control over a prostitute *(see below)*.

Knowingly lives on: The Act gives a considerable amount of guidance on what is required to prove the offence. The accused will be presumed to be knowingly living on the earnings of prostitution unless he proves otherwise if:
- he lives with or is habitually in the company of a prostitute; or
- he exercises control, direction or influence over a prostitute's movements in a way which shows he is aiding, abetting or compelling her prostitution with others. (The phrase 'with others' is necessary, otherwise every one of the prostitute's clients could

come within the scope of this provision.)

Thus, the burden of proof shifts to the accused, if the prosecution produces evidence:
- either that he is living with the prostitute in question
- or is habitually in her company
- or may be shown to influence her movements to such an extent as to be assisting or compelling her to be a prostitute.

A period of surveillance may be effective in producing such evidence.

However, the presumption of guilt holds only for so long as it takes the defence to rebut it. A successful prosecution therefore would require more evidence, e.g. evidence that his expenditure far outweighed legitimate earnings from employment, social benefits, etc.

Earnings of prostitution: In its most straightforward form, the offence may be committed by a man who takes a proportion of a prostitute's earnings. However, it will be sufficient if it is shown that the accused is paid by a prostitute for goods or services supplied to her which he would not supply were she not a prostitute (*Shaw v DPP* (1961)).

If a landlord charges rent for a room to a woman who uses the room for the purposes of prostitution, he need not be guilty, merely by knowing that she is a prostitute; but if he charges an inflated rent, then he falls within the scope of the test outlined above – he is paid for supplying the room at an inflated rate, which he would not do were she not a prostitute (*R v Thomas* (1957)).

Other cases leading to decisions that men have lived on the earnings of prostitution include:
- taxi drivers plying for hire to take prostitutes to their clients (*R v Farrugia, Borg, Agius and Gauchi* (1979))
- accepting payments from prostitutes to publish their advertisements (*Shaw v DPP* (1961)) *(Keynote Case: Some of these earlier cases were considered in R v Stewart (1986))*

The offence may still be committed notwithstanding that payment is not made by the prostitute herself but by her customers, but there is a need to establish a close connection in such cases, between the payment and the exercise of control or influence over the prostitute. Where a man sold to other men, details which he had compiled of women who were prostitutes he was held not to be living on immoral earnings because the money he obtained from the men could not be considered to be the earnings of prostitution. The situation may have been different had there been evidence of his exercising some degree of control over the prostitutes (*R v Ansell* (1975)).

6.2 Warrant to Arrest
Sexual Offences Act 1956 Section 42

6.2.1 *Grounds for Issue*

A magistrate may issue a warrant upon information on oath:
- that there is reasonable cause to suspect
- that any house or part of a house is being used by a woman for the purposes of prostitution, and
- that a man residing in or frequenting the house is living wholly or partly on her earnings.

6.2.2 *Powers Under the Warrant*

The warrant will authorise a constable:
- to enter and search the house, and
- arrest the man.

7 WOMAN EXERCISING CONTROL OVER PROSTITUTE
Sexual Offences Act 1956 Section 31

7.1 **Offence**
It is an offence for a woman:
- for the purposes of gain
- to exercise control, direction or influence over a prostitute's movements
- in a way which shows she is aiding, abetting or compelling her prostitution.

7.1.1 *Explanation*
Woman: The offence is committed only by a female and although similar in some respects to the offence which may be committed only by a man – that of living on the earnings of prostitution – is significantly different.

Purposes of gain: It will not amount to the offence for a prostitute to persuade another woman to work as a prostitute, from the motive, e.g. of having someone to talk to while they stand in the street waiting for customers. The motive must be that of gain, so the offence in this respect, is closely related to that which a man may commit.

Control, direction or influence: There must be more than mere 'encouragement', there must be an element of compulsion or persuasion. *(Keynote Case: R v O (1983))*

8 PROCURING A WOMAN FOR PROSTITUTION, ETC
Sexual Offences Act 1956 Section 22

8.1 **Offences**
There are three distinct offences. In each case, the offence may be committed by any person, man or woman:
- to procure a woman to become a common prostitute in any part of the world
- to procure a woman to leave the United Kingdom intending her to become an inmate of, or frequent a brothel elsewhere
- to procure a woman to leave her usual place of abode in the United Kingdom intending her to become an inmate of or frequent a brothel in any part of the world, for the purposes of prostitution.

8.1.1 *Explanation*
To become a common prostitute: For the first offence it must be proved that the woman was not a prostitute before being procured.

Leave the United Kingdom: It is a necessary element of the second offence that the woman leaves the UK.

Intending: It is a requirement in offences of procuring, that the end result actually occurs for the procuring to be complete, e.g. procuring for unlawful sexual intercourse is complete when the intercourse takes place. Note carefully the wording of the second offence; it is complete when the offender obtains the woman's exit from the UK with the intention that she shall enter or frequent a brothel in another country. Whether she actually arrives at the foreign brothel is immaterial.

Inmate of or frequent: It need not necessarily be the intention, for the second offence to be committed, that once in the brothel, the woman should offer herself for unlawful sexual intercourse. Although this is the primary purpose of a brothel, presumably it would suffice if the intention was that she should become a cook or cleaner in the brothel. Contrast this with the third offence.

Brothel: A brothel is a place where persons of opposite sexes resort for the purposes of unlawful sexual intercourse, and at least two women must offer their services. It is not necessary that they be prostitutes (*for a fuller explanation see paragraph 12 below*).

Leave her place of abode: For the third offence to be committed, it is not necessary that the woman leaves the country (as is the case in the preceding offence), but that she leaves her usual address; she could for example move from one town to another, or from her own home to inhabit a brothel at another address in the same town.

Intending: For the third offence, as for the second, the offence is complete as soon as the woman leaves her usual place of abode and the necessary intention is in the offender's mind.

Purposes of prostitution: Compare this element of the third offence with that in relation to the preceding offence. This offence will **not** be committed if the intention is that the woman enters a brothel to become the cook there. The intention must be that she frequents or inhabits a brothel for the purposes of prostitution.

9 ENCOURAGING PROSTITUTION, ETC OF GIRL UNDER 16 YEARS
Sexual Offences Act 1956 Section 28

9.1 Offence
It is an offence:
- for a person who is responsible for a girl under 16 years
- to cause or encourage
- her prostitution or the commission of an offence of unlawful sexual intercourse or indecent assault upon her.

9.1.1 *Explanation*
Responsible for: There are three categories of person who may be responsible for a girl, and a person may fall into more than one of these at the same time. The three are:
- parent or guardian
- any person who has possession or control of the girl or to whose charge she has been committed by the parent or guardian
- any person having custody or charge of her.

Cause or encourage: Mere inactivity, such as not acting to prevent indecent assault taking place, may amount to 'encouraging'. Thus where a 14 year old girl was baby-sitting the male householder was guilty of this offence when he allowed the girl to drink alcohol, and did not intervene when his male friend indecently assaulted the girl in his presence. For the purposes of the offence, the householder was found to be 'responsible for' the girl while she was in his house (*R v Drury* (1974)).

The Act provides that a person will be deemed to have caused or encouraged what occurred (prostitution, unlawful sexual intercourse or indecent assault) if he knowingly allowed her to consort with, or to enter into or continue in the employment of any prostitute or person of known immoral character (Section 28(2)).

For example, Mary knows that her friend Jane has convictions for soliciting for prostitution, but nevertheless allows her daughter Sharon to spend time in the sauna club which Jane now runs. If Sharon is indecently assaulted by a customer of the sauna club, Mary will be **deemed** to have caused or encouraged the indecent assault by allowing her daughter to consort with Jane. Jane in turn may also commit the offence, as the person given charge of the girl by her mother, if there is evidence of her causing or encouraging the indecent assault.

Prostitution: For the meaning of this term, see *paragraph 1.1* above.

Unlawful sexual intercourse, indecent assault: 'Unlawful sexual intercourse' means intercourse outside marriage. An indecent assault is an assault accompanied by circumstances of indecency. Consent is no defence to a charge of indecent assault, where the victim is under 16 years of age.

10 CAUSING OR ENCOURAGING PROSTITUTION OF A DEFECTIVE
Sexual Offences Act 1956 Section 29

10.1 Offence
It is an offence for a person to cause or encourage the prostitution in any part of the world of a woman who is a defective.

10.1.1 *Explanation*
Defective: The term means 'mental defective' – which in turn means a person suffering from 'severe mental impairment' – which in turn means a state of arrested or incomplete development of mind including severe impairment of intelligence and social functioning. Put simply, a defective is someone who has never achieved normal mental maturity (Mental Health Act 1983, Section 1).

11 LIVING ON THE EARNINGS OF MALE PROSTITUTION
Sexual Offences Act 1967 Section 5

11.1 Offence
The offence is committed by a man or a woman:
  - who knowingly
  - lives wholly or partly
  - on the earnings of prostitution of another man.

11.1.1 *Explanation*
Man or woman: Whereas there are two separate offences relating to living on or making gain from the activities of a woman prostitute, when it comes to males who sell their bodies, the offence of living on such earnings is the same for men and women.

Knowingly lives on: There has to be knowledge on the part of the accused as to how the man in question came by his earnings. There is no corresponding provision to that for a man living on the earnings of a woman prostitute, where in certain circumstances, the onus of proof shifts to the accused.

Prostitution: Although it is established that only a woman may be regarded as a 'common prostitute', the law does recognise that males who offer their bodies for sexual purposes for payment may be equally vulnerable to exploitation. To provide a sanction against such exploitation, an offence of living on the immoral earnings of a male 'prostitute' is provided.

12 BROTHELS

12.1 Meaning of Term

Traditionally, a brothel was a place where men and women resorted, to engage in heterosexual activity. More recently, the meaning has been extended by statute to cover premises where men go, to engage in homosexual practices.

In heterosexual terms a brothel is a place:
- where persons of opposite sexes resort
- where the women offer themselves in physical acts of indecency
- for the sexual gratification of men.

12.1.1 *Explanation*

Women: There must be more than one woman, for premises to be a brothel (*Singleton v Ellison* (1895)). Where a team of prostitutes used premises, employing receptionists, but with only one of the prostitutes present there on any given day, this was held to amount to a brothel (*Stevens and Stevens v Christy* (1987)).

It is not necessary to prove that the women are known prostitutes, nor that payment is made. *(Keynote Case: Kelly v Purvis (1983))*

If premises are split into a number of separate rooms, each room being used by only one woman to carry out her trade as a prostitute, this does not preclude the whole of the premises being regarded as a brothel (*Abbott v Smith* (1964)). In contrast, where different floors of a building were let to different prostitutes, the building was held not to amount to a brothel because the lettings were separate (*Strath v Foxon* (1956)).

Whether premises or part of premises amount to a brothel is a matter of fact for the court to decide in any particular case (*Donovan v Gavin* (1965)).

Women offer themselves: Premises where men offered themselves to women customers would not constitute a brothel.

Acts of indecency: It is not necessary that the full act of sexual intercourse should take place. Evidence of masturbation of the men by the women would be enough.
(Keynote Case: Kelly v Purvis (1983))

12.2 'Homosexual' Brothels
Sexual Offences Act 1967 Section 6

For the purposes of offences relating to brothels, premises are to be treated as a brothel if persons resort to them for the purpose of lewd homosexual practices in circumstances in which resorting thereto for lewd heterosexual practices would have led to them being regarded as a brothel.

12.3 Keeping a Brothel
Sexual Offences Act 1956 Section 33

12.3.1 *Offence*

It is an offence for a person to keep a brothel or to manage or act or assist in the management of a brothel.

12.3.2 *Explanation*

Manage: This means to take an active part in running the business. The accused does not have to be the owner of the business, he or she may well act for someone else, but there must be evidence that the role played in running the brothel is more than a menial one (*Abbott v Smith* (1964)).

A woman who worked as a prostitute in a brothel would not necessarily be guilty of assisting in its management. If, however, she not only performed sexual acts with clients, but also negotiated the nature of the acts and the terms of payment for such acts, she would be assisting in the management (*Elliott v DPP* (1989)).

12.4 **Offence by Landlords, etc**
Sexual Offences Act 1956 Section 34

12.4.1 *Offence*
It is an offence:
  – for the landlord or lessor of any premises or his agent
  – to let the whole or part of the premises with the knowledge that it is to be used, in whole or part, as a brothel
  – or where the whole or part of the premises is used as a brothel, wilfully to be a party to that use continuing.

12.4.2 *Explanation*
Landlord or lessor: This refers to the owner of the property or the person who has the lease. The offence is committed when this person lets out the premises to someone else.

Agent: The offence may equally be committed by the person who lets out premises when acting as the agent for the landlord or lease holder. This would cover a situation where, for example, the landlord had no knowledge of who was the tenant of his premises, but left the letting to an estate agent.

Knowledge that it is to be used: This caters for the situation where the landlord, agent, etc, is aware in advance of the use to which the premises are intended to be put, but lets them out nevertheless.

Wilfully... use continuing: When the premises are let out the landlord may have no knowledge at the time of the letting that the premises are to be used as a brothel. Indeed, there need not be any such intention; the use as a brothel may well come long after the premises are first let out. In this case the offence will be committed when the landlord, etc becomes aware that the premises are being used as a brothel, and takes no action, but wilfully allows such use to go on.

12.5 **Offence by Tenant**
Sexual Offences Act 1956 Section 35

12.5.1 *Offence*
It is an offence for the tenant or occupier or person in charge of premises knowingly to permit the whole or part of the premises to be used as a brothel.

12.5.2 *Explanation*
Tenant, occupier, person in charge: The tenant will be the person to whom the premises are let. The terms 'occupier' and 'person in charge' are not defined in the legislation, but should pose few problems in practice.

Knowingly: There has to be knowledge on the part of the accused that the premises are being used as a brothel.

Permits: There is no need to show that the tenant, occupier or person in charge played any part in keeping or managing the brothel. To allow the activity to go on will be enough.

Prevention of further offences: There are additional provisions relating to the action of a landlord or lessor, in a situation where a tenant or occupier of premises is convicted of this offence. Briefly, if the landlord is aware of the first conviction of the tenant or occupier, he will be liable in certain cases, if there is a further conviction for a similar offence, for failing to take action, either to get rid of the tenant or to prevent a recurrence.

12.6 Detention of Woman in Brothel
Sexual Offences Act 1956 Section 24

12.6.1 *Offence*
It is an offence:
1) to detain a woman on premises:
   - against her will
   - with the intention that she shall have unlawful sexual intercourse with men or with a particular man, or
2) to detain a woman against her will in a brothel.

12.6.2 *Explanation*
Detain on premises: When a woman is on premises for the purposes of unlawful sexual intercourse, or is in a brothel, a person will be deemed to detain her if, with the intention of compelling or inducing her to remain there, he either withholds her clothes or any other item of her property or threatens her with legal action if she should leave with any item of clothing provided by him.

Thus, 'detain' may involve, as well as physical restraint or locked doors, the removal of the woman's clothes, or threatening her with court if she makes off with any clothing provided by or on behalf of the accused.

The complementary provision is that a woman will not be liable in legal proceedings, criminal or civil, in respect of any clothing which she needed in order to leave the premises.

Against her will: There must be evidence that the woman was detained on the premises against her will. Persuading or inducing her to stay (other than by threats or removing her property) would not be enough.

12.6.3 *Warrant to Search for Detained Woman*
Sexual Offences Act 1956 Section 43
If it is believed a woman is detained on premises in circumstances which would amount to an offence under Section 24, a warrant may be obtained to search for and remove her. This offence also applies where other offences of abduction are involved. Further details relating to such a warrant are contained in *Chapter 11, paragraph 5.*

12.7 Miscellaneous Offences
Licensing Act 1964 Section 176

12.7.1 *Licensed Premises*
The holder of a justices' liquor licence will commit an offence if he allows the licensed premises to be used as a brothel.

12.7.2 *Child or Young Person*
Children and Young Persons Act 1933 Section 3
It is an offence for a person having custody, charge or care of a child or young person aged 4 years or over but under 16 years, to allow that child or young person to reside in or frequent a brothel.

13 PROSTITUTES ON PREMISES
Sexual Offences Act 1956 Section 36

13.1 Offence
It is an offence:
- for the tenant or occupier of premises
- knowingly to permit the whole or part of the premises
- to be used for the purposes of habitual prostitution.

13.1.1 *Explanation*
Habitual prostitution: The offence is virtually identical to that of a tenant or occupier permitting premises to be used as a brothel. The significant difference is that for this offence there is no need to prove that the premises amount to a brothel. Thus, a tenant or occupier who allows a single prostitute to use premises for the purposes of her trade, would commit the offence.

If the prostitute used the premises on a few occasions only, this might not amount to 'habitual'; the term is not defined in the legislation.

13.2 Prostitutes in Licensed Premises
Licensing Act 1964 Section 176

13.2.1 *Offence*
It is an offence:
- for the holder of a justices' liquor licence
- knowingly to allow the licensed premises
- to be the habitual resort or meeting place of reputed prostitutes.

13.2.2 *Explanation*
The offence is committed whether the purpose of their meeting there is prostitution or not, but this does not prevent the licensee from allowing them to stay for the purpose of having reasonable refreshment.

In short, the licensee must not allow his premises to be the place where prostitutes habitually gather, but this is not to say that women who happen to be prostitutes cannot go into licensed premises for a drink.

A similar provision applies to the premises of a licensed late night refreshment house (Late Night Refreshment Houses Act 1969, Section 9).

Keynote Cases

14.1 *R v Stewart* (1986) 83 Cr App R 327

Problem

When will a man who receives payment from a prostitute in return for supplying her with goods or services be considered to be living on the earnings of prostitution?

Circumstances

The accused was charged with a number of counts of living on the earnings of prostitution, based on letting of flats owned by companies in turn owned by himself. Not all the flats which his companies owned were let to prostitutes but a number were; the prostitutes did not live on these premises but used them only for work. The prosecution evidence was that the flats were let at up to eight times the normal rent, and that he was seen to visit the flats at times when the prostitutes who rented them were 'open for business'. The defence denied that the rents were unusually high, claiming that the main prosecution witness was lying. The accused claimed that he made efforts to rid his properties of known prostitutes. The accused appealed against conviction, one of the main grounds being that the judge had failed to direct the jury adequately on the question of whether letting a flat at a normal rent could constitute the offence.

Decision

Summarising earlier decisions, the court held that deriving part of one's livelihood from the earnings of a prostitute, by supplying a prostitute with goods or services, did not necessarily amount to an offence. There has to be some closer connection with the trade of prostitution, and the court favoured the word 'parasite' as a useful starting point for describing an offender. In considering whether a supply of goods or services amounts to the offence, factors to be taken into account will include:
- the scale of the supply
- the price charged
- the nature of the goods or services.

It is not possible to say in advance what will or will not amount to the offence, but the jury should consider the extent to which the supplier is participating in the prostitute's business, e.g. selling her groceries is hardly participating in her business, but publishing her advertisements would be.

When it comes to letting premises, the fact that the rent is not exorbitant is not the only factor to be considered. Thus, if the prostitute did not live there, but used the premises solely for prostitution, or if the landlord equipped the premises in a particular manner, whether he took steps to remove prostitutes from the premises – these and other factors need to be considered. Knowledge that his tenant is a prostitute will not, alone, be sufficient.

Comment

Although several cases are referred to in the text, giving examples of what may or may not amount to living on immoral earnings, the judgment in this case emphasises that there are no hard and fast rules. The circumstances of each case should be left to the court to decide, based on determining to what degree the accused is involved in the prostitute's trade.

14.2 *R v O* [1983] Crim LR 401

Problem
Interpretation of the term 'exercising control, direction or influence' for the purposes of the offence committed by a woman under Section 31, Sexual Offences Act 1956.

Circumstances
Two women, X and O, lived together as lesbian lovers. There was evidence that O regularly drove X to the premises from which she worked as a prostitute, placed advertisements for X's services and was seen to escort a customer into the premises. On one occasion she was heard encouraging X to work hard to keep up O's standard of living.

Decision
The defence submitted that while there may be evidence of 'encouragement' of X by O, the term 'influence' used in the offence amounted to more than mere encouragement. The word 'influence' must be construed *ejusdem generis* with the words 'control' and 'direct'. This submission was accepted by the court and O was found to have no case to answer, in the absence of evidence that she had persuaded or compelled X to work as a prostitute.

Comment
This is a Crown Court case and therefore does not have the same weight as a decision of a higher court. However, the decision illustrates the difference between the offences which may be committed by a man and by a woman. A man may be guilty of living on immoral earnings, upon evidence, e.g. that he lived with a prostitute. For a woman to commit the corresponding offence, there must be clear evidence of control, direction or influence amounting to more than mere encouragement, of a woman to work as a prostitute.

14.3 *Kelly v Purvis* (1983) 76 Cr App R 165

Problem
Whether for premises to amount to being a brothel, it is necessary that full sexual intercourse takes place there, or whether acts of prostitution without full intercourse will be enough.

Circumstances
The defendant, a woman, was charged with being concerned in the management of a brothel. The charge related to premises licensed by the local authority as a massage parlour at which massage by female masseuses was available to male clients. For extra fees, additional services were available – manual masturbation of the client's penis, £15 – the same performed 'topless', £20 – and with the masseuse naked, £25. The defendant performed these services as a masseuse, and sometimes acted as receptionist. The stipendiary magistrate dismissed the charge on the ground that the premises did not amount to a brothel unless full sexual intercourse was offered. The prosecution appealed by way of case stated to the Divisional Court.

Decision
The court was asked to decide on the question, 'Whether for the purposes of a charge of being concerned in the management of a brothel, it was necessary to show that normal sexual intercourse took place there, or was it sufficient to prove that acts amounting to prostitution took place, provided by more than one woman. The court reviewed a number of cases relating

to the terms 'prostitute' and 'brothel' and found:

- The term 'prostitute' means a woman who offers her body commonly for lewdness and includes offering herself as a participant in physical acts of indecency for the gratification of men. That the women were prostitutes by dint of masturbating their customers was not in dispute.
- On a charge of assisting in the management of a brothel, it is not essential that there is evidence of normal sexual intercourse taking place on the premises. It is sufficient to prove that more than one woman offered herself as a participant in physical acts of indecency for the sexual gratification of men.

As an aside, the court drew attention to the compatibility of these findings with the provisions of Section 6, Sexual Offences Act 1967, which states that premises will be a brothel if persons resort there for lewd homosexual practices in circumstances in which to resort there for lewd heterosexual practices would amount to its being a brothel.

In the course of its deliberations, the court considered the case of *Winter v Wolfe* (1931), a case which involved women and men meeting regularly to engage in sexual intercourse in premises near Cambridge. In that case, the women were found not to be prostitutes because they were not paid. The Divisional Court in that case found:

- It is not necessary, for the purpose of deciding whether premises amount to a brothel, that the women are known to the police as prostitutes
- It is not necessary, for the purposes of premises being classed as a brothel, for women to receive payment for sexual intercourse.

Comment

Just as a woman who offers her body for acts of lewdness for payment may be a common prostitute without engaging in full sexual intercourse, so the premises where two or more women are involved in such acts may amount to a brothel without full sexual intercourse taking place there.

Taking account of the findings in this case and those in the *Winter v Wolfe* case to which the court made reference, premises will amount to a brothel in any of the following sets of circumstances:

- acts of prostitution, not amounting to full sexual intercourse, take place. An essential element of 'prostitution' being that the prostitutes are paid
- illicit sexual intercourse takes place there, involving more than one woman, even though the women are not known as prostitutes and are not paid
- whatever applies to heterosexual situations to render premises a brothel will be true equally of premises where homosexual behaviour goes on.

Chapter 13: Property Offences

THEFT

1.1 Theft is defined by Section 1(1) of the Theft Act 1968. The words of the Section including 'dishonesty', 'appropriation', 'property', 'belonging to another' and 'with the intention of permanently depriving the other of it' are defined and further explained by Sections 2 to 6.

Section 1 Theft Act 1968

(1) A person is guilty of theft if he dishonestly appropriates property belonging to another, with the intention of permanently depriving the other of it; and thief and steal shall be construed accordingly.

(2) It is immaterial whether the appropriation is made with a view to gain, or is made for the thief's own benefit.

(3) The five following Sections of this act shall have effect as regards the interpretation and operation of this Section, (and, except as otherwise provide by this act , shall apply only for the purposes of this Section).

Section 2 'Dishonesty'

(1) A person's appropriation of property belonging to another is not regarded as dishonest:
   a) if he appropriates property in the belief he has in law the right to deprive the other of it, on behalf of himself or a third person; or
   b) if he appropriates the property in the belief that he would have the other's consent if the other knew of the appropriation and the circumstances of it; or
   c) (except where the property came to him as a trustee or personal representative) if he appropriates the property in the belief that the person to whom the property belongs cannot be discovered by taking reasonable steps.

(2) A person's appropriation of property belonging to another may be dishonest, not withstanding that he is willing to pay for the property.

Section 3 'Appropriation'

(1) Any assumption by a person of the rights of an owner amounts to an appropriation, and this includes, where he has come by the property (innocently or not) without stealing it, any later assumption of a right to it by keeping it or dealing with as owner.

(2) Where property or a right or interest in property is or purports to be transferred for value to a person acting in good faith, no latter assumption by him of rights which he believed himself to be acquiring shall by reason of any defect in the transferor's title amount to theft of the property.

Section 4 'Property'

(1) Property includes money and all other property, real or personal, including things in action and other intangible property.

(2) A person cannot steal land, or things forming part of land and severed from it by his directions, except in the following cases, that is to say:

a) when he is a trustee or personal representative, or is authorised by power of attorney or as liquidator of a company, or otherwise, to sell or dispose of land belonging to another, and he appropriates the land or anything forming part of it by dealing with it in breach of the confidence reposed in him; or

b) when he is not in possession of the land and appropriates anything forming part of the land by severing it or causing it to be severed; or

c) when, being in possession of the land under a tenancy, he appropriates the whole or part of a fixture or structure let to be used with the land.

For the purposes of this subsection 'land' does not include incorporeal hereditaments; 'tenancy' means a tenancy of years or any less period and includes an agreement for such a tenancy, but a person who, after the end of a tenancy remains in possession as statutory tenant or otherwise, is to be treated as having possession under tenancy, and 'let' shall be construed accordingly.

(3) A person who picks mushrooms growing wild on any land, or who picks flowers or fruit or foliage from a plant growing wild on any land, does not (although not in possession of the land) steal what he picks, unless he does it for reward or for sale or other commercial purpose.

For the purpose of this Section 'mushroom' includes any fungus, and 'plant' includes any shrub or tree.

(4) Wild creatures, tamed or untamed, shall be regarded as property; but a person cannot steal a wild creature not tamed or ordinarily kept in captivity, or the carcass of such a creature, unless either it has been reduced into possession by or on behalf of another person and possession of it has not since been abandoned, or another person is in the course of reducing it into possession.

Section 5 'Belonging to another'

(1) Property shall be regarded as belonging to any person having possession or control of it, or having any proprietary right or interest (not being an equitable interest arising only from an agreement to transfer or grant an interest).

(2) Where property is subject to a trust, the person to whom it belongs shall be regarded as including any person having a right to enforce the trust, and an intention to defeat the trust shall be regarded accordingly as an intention to deprive of the property any person having that right.

(3) Where a person receives property from or on account of another, and is under an obligation to the other to retain and deal with that property or its proceeds in a particular way, the property or proceeds shall be regarded (as against him) as belonging to the other.

(4) Where a person gets property by anther's mistake, and is under an obligation to make restoration (in whole or in part) of the property or its proceeds or of the value thereof, then to the extent of that obligation the property or proceeds shall be regarded (as against him) as belonging to the person entitled to restoration, and an intention not to make restoration shall be regarded accordingly as an intention to deprive that person of the property or proceeds.

(5) Property of a corporation sole shall be regarded as belonging to the corporation notwithstanding a vacancy in the corporation.

Section 6 'With the intention of depriving the other of it'

(1) A person appropriating property belonging to another without meaning the other permanently to lose the thing itself is nevertheless to be regarded as having the intention of permanently depriving the other of it if his intention is to treat the thing as his own to dispose of regardless of the others rights; and a borrowing or lending of it may amount to so treating it, but only if the borrowing or lending is for a period and in circumstances making it equivalent to an outright taking or disposal.

(2) Without prejudice to the generality of subsection (1) above, where a person, having possession or control (lawfully or not) of property belonging to another, parts with the property under a condition as to its return which he may not be able to perform, this (if done for purposes of his own and without the other's authority) amounts to a treating property as his own to dispose of regardless of the others rights.

Explanation

1.2 The definition of theft contained in Section 1(1) is further defined and explained by Sections 2–6. Terms such as 'dishonestly' and 'permanently deprive' have the same meanings in other offences under the Act, such as obtaining property by deception.

1.3 In order to commit theft there is a need for an act, and an intention, in legal parlance 'actus reus' and 'mens rea'. The actus reus of theft is the appropriation.

1.4 The unauthorised usurpation of the rights of another will amount to theft (*R v Morris* [1983]). The most obvious examples of appropriation are the typical thefts where a person takes another's property and leaves the scene. Where a person removes goods from a shelf in a store with the dishonesty required, he could be said to be usurping the rights of the owner and so be guilty of theft. What externally appears as an incomplete act could possibly be theft. Practically however, there will always be problems adopting this approach as proving the necessary intention will be difficult. Looking at the act from the outside, you cannot show the apparently innocent act to be dishonest.

1.5 Appropriation can occur after the defendant has come into lawful possession of property. An example of this would be where a person is loaned articles. Failure to return the goods when requested, or selling the goods would amount to an appropriation. If the person who has possession of the goods does anything which amounts to taking the rights of the owner, that will be an appropriation. Any possible doubts are dispelled by the words in the Section:

> 'Where he has come by the property (innocently or not) without stealing it, any later assumption of a right to it by keeping it or dealing with it as owner.'
>
> Section 3(1) Theft Act 1968

1.6 A person can even appropriate without taking possession of goods. If a defendant purports to be the owner of goods, then sells or disposes of the goods to an innocent third party who then removes the goods, this will be theft. The goods will have been appropriated by the defendant. There will of course also be other offences such as deception, and perhaps practically it would be better to charge deception. The point however is that the appropriation takes place even though the defendant has never actually possessed the goods in question. In the case of *R* *v Bloxham* (1943) a defendant sold, or at least agreed to sell a refrigerator, a price was settled and he received the money for it. The refrigerator belonged to his employer, Bloxham never had possession of the refrigerator. Under the law at the time, Bloxham was not guilty (of larceny) but under the Theft Act if he intended to deliver the refrigerator he would be guilty. It could be said the there would be a difficulty in proving the intention to permanently deprive, this may however not be so as Section 6(1) is satisfied by the phrase 'to treat the thing as his own to dispose of'.

1.7 Where a defendant has some limited authority to deal with another's property then he may appropriate by dealing with the property in excess of his authority (*Pilgrim v Rice-Smith* [1977]). If a member of staff at a supermarket under-priced goods then sold them to a someone with whom he had colluded then appropriation occurs when the goods are under-priced. This point is taken further in *R v Morris (see keynote case)*. In these circumstances the customer would also possibly be handling stolen goods, although the part played by him in the theft would make that a more appropriate charge. In the case of *R v Bhachu* (1976) a dishonest cashier in collusion with a customer, undervalued goods by ringing them up at a lower price than the authorised price. The court considered that the appropriation took place when the customer put the goods in the basket to leave the store. It seems however, from the decision in *R v Morris*, that the cashier actually appropriated the goods when deliberately undervaluing them. It follows that that the customer could have been handling the stolen goods.

1.8 Almost every handler and receiver of stolen goods commits theft. They appropriate in that they usurp the rights of the owner and have an intention to deprive or treat the property as their own, and there must be dishonesty otherwise handling could not occur. At times it may be simpler to prove theft than attempt to prove handling.

1.9 Section 3(2) provides the innocent purchaser of stolen goods with a defence to theft:
  'Where property or a right or interest in property is or purports to be transferred for
  value to a person acting in good faith, no later assumption by him of the rights which
  he believed himself to be acquiring shall by reason of any defect in the transferor's title,
  amount to theft of the property'.

1.10 This Section exempts people from liability for theft in circumstances where they purchase goods in good faith and pay a fair price. Even if the person later discovers that the property is indeed not his of right and that he had in fact purchased stolen property, provided he is not dishonest he still does not commit theft. What then of the person who innocently purchases stolen property then makes an innocent gift of the property to another? If the receiver of the gift discovers that the goods are stolen and then assumes the rights of the owner, he is guilty of theft. He has not given value for them and his appropriation is dishonest so Section 3(2) will not protect him. If a person assumes rights over and above which he believed himself to get he may commit theft. Suppose Arthur finds a ring in circumstances where the lawful owner cannot reasonably be found, Arthur then gives the ring to Betty who knows of the circumstances in which the ring was found. If then Betty discovers the identity of the loser of the ring, the keeping of the ring under such circumstances would amount to appropriation and possibly theft. Arthur however, not commit theft, or rather he would have a defence were he charged with the offence.

1.11 The question, whether appropriation is a continuing matter or takes place at a moment in time, is difficult. There are three views about the nature of appropriation ('The Law of Theft' J. C. Smith p28).

(1) 'That it continues so long as the thief continues to exert the right of an owner over property'.

Certain provisions of the Act appear to rule out this view. Under Section 8, for an offence of robbery to be committed, violence or threats must be used 'immediately before or at the time' of stealing, implying that the action of stealing is not a continuing process.

(2) 'That appropriation is an instantaneous act, not continuing beyond the instant at which it is done'.

This proposition is that there is an instant in time when the theft takes place and after that the property is stolen. This view is supported by the case of *R v Pitham and Hehl* (1976) where a defendant stole property by selling it to a third party; The court held that the appropriation took place at the moment in time when invitation to sell was given. The second defendant was convicted of receiving, this not being in the course of the theft. The thief made the invitation to sell and at that moment in time committed theft as the appropriation was completed. The receiver agreeing to purchase at almost the same time was appropriating, but not in the course of theft.

(3) 'While theft is committed at the instant that the defendant does any act amounting to an assumption of the rights of an owner, appropriation continues for the duration of the 'transaction' of which it forms part'.

Common sense suggests that once an act of theft has taken place, what the thief does with the property thereafter is fairly immaterial; he has usurped the owner's rights, intending that the owner shall be permanently deprived of the property. The element of appropriation may be regarded as lasting for so long as it takes for the thief to assume the rights of the owner. In practical terms, in a case of a shoplifting, for example, this would be from the time the thief picked up goods, intending to leave the store without paying, to the moment he left the store. This view is supported by *R v Hale* (1978) *(keynote case)* where the court held that appropriation was a matter of fact for the jury to decide, when it was that the defendant had finished the appropriation.

1.12 The entire question of appropriation is now settled law as a result of the case of *R v Morris* [1983] *(see keynote case)*. The crux of this case is that any adverse act which is a usurpation of the rights of the owner of property will be an appropriation, and that there is no necessity to prove that all the rights of the owner have been appropriated. This case views the appropriation as continuing whilst the defendant usurped the rights of the owner, by doing the act of changing labels.

1.13 It must be borne in mind that although 'appropriation' is the principal element of the actus reus of theft, behaviour needs to be viewed in the light of the intent with which it is done to discover whether an appropriation has occurred. In *R v Morris* it was said that label switching with mischief as the intention, rather than theft in mind, would not be an appropriation. In order to have an appropriation there must be some proof of intention, not necessarily at that time but possibly later when the defendant does something knowingly which usurps the rights of the owner. This will of necessity require some form of act or omission. Practically, problems will arise where the act itself possibly was two quite opposite interpretations, one being innocent the other being dishonest. It will be a question of fact for the jury to decide which the suspect had in mind when the act was completed.

1.14 Theft can be committed only in respect of property belonging to another. Where one person has rights in property, and another has similar but greater rights in the same property, an owner could possibly be guilty of theft of his own property, by excluding the rights of the other. An example given by J C Smith is that of a person who pledges his watch for security on a loan but takes it back without repaying the loan and without consent. This would be theft. It appears strange that the owner, having a better right to the possession of the property, is under these circumstances liable for theft if he is dishonest. Where property belongs to more than one person, it may be easier to understand how one could deprive the others of it. For example, four men keen on water sports purchase jointly a boat. Each has rights to use the boat, but if one dishonestly excluded the others from use of the boat, by selling it or exchanging it for another unsuitable boat, he could be guilty of theft even though he is an owner. If Arthur loans a lawn mower to Brian, and Brian then gets his servant Cyril to mow the lawn, Arthur remains the owner, Brian has possession of it, and Cyril has control. If a defendant then steals the mower all three would be able to complain of theft.

1.15 Property also includes equitable interests. If Timothy has possession of a painting, for a child Celine, if a thief then takes the painting, he will have stolen from both Timothy and Celine. If Timothy makes an unauthorised sale of the painting he will be guilty of theft from Celine despite being in law the owner of the property. The only equitable interests not covered are 'equitable interests arising only from an agreement to transfer or grant an interest'. Section 5(2) provides.

> 'Where property is subject of a trust, the person to who it belongs shall be regarded
> as including any person having a right to enforce the trust, and an intention to defeat
> the trust shall be regarded accordingly as an intention to deprive of the property any
> person having that right.'

1.16 A trustee is one who holds ownership of property for another. An example would be if a house(property) is subject of a will, and grandfather decided in his will that his house would belong to the first born in the blood line of the eldest in each generation, for the duration of their life-time but not before the death of the previous generation's first born. The eldest child, would become the trustee and take possession of the house, the first born of the next generation of the family would then have a right in equity to the house but could not live there until the present occupant dies. In this example the person living in the house would have possession and ownership, but could not sell without breaking the trust. To do so would then deprive others of their rights in equity and would amount to theft. In basic terms then a trustee is one who has legal rights to property but is prevented from dealing with the property as his own by the rules of the trust set up to control the property. Trusts have many common rules but there is a need to know which rules apply to a particular trust before you can discover whether or not a trust has been broken.

1.17 Possession and ownership can be difficult concepts to separate. In *R v Cullen* (unreported no. 968/C/74 of 1974) a man gave his mistress money to pay certain debts. She spent the money on herself. The Court of Appeal held this to be a plain case of theft, not as Cullen had claimed just a domestic arrangement in which she had rights in the property. The importance of the Cullen case is that where a person is given strict instructions to deal with property in accordance with those instructions, theft may occur where the instructions are not followed.

1.18 Having discussed at some length appropriation, the actus reus of theft, we must discuss dishonesty, the mens rea. There has been considerable debate about how dishonesty should be interpreted, both as a word and as a moral standard. Academic writers have discussed whether the dishonesty should be an objective standard of the general public which should then be imposed on the understanding of the defendant, or whether the subjective standard of the defendant alone should be the test.

1.19 Section 2 of the Theft Act 1968 sets out circumstances under which an appropriation of property will not be held to be dishonest. Firstly, that the accused had a belief he had a right in law to deprive the other of it (Section 2(1)(a) Theft Act 1968). Generally, this defence puts the onus on the prosecution to show that the belief was not merely a mistake. This causes problems where the defendant takes property in the moral belief that he has a right. The Section clearly states that the defendant must have ' a belief that he has in law the right'. What then of a starving person who takes food, claiming that the alternative may have been collapse from lack of nourishment. There is currently no common law to defend such action but clearly this is a question of fact for the jury to decide on the evidence. The second strand is subsection 2(1)(b) 'he appropriates property believing that the owner would have consented had he known the circumstances'. This would cover a situation where, at the scene of a road accident for example, a person grabs a fire extinguisher from the cab of an unattended lorry in order to extinguish flames in a burning car. It may be reasonable to believe that the lorry driver would have consented to her fire extinguisher being used had she been aware of the circumstances. The third strand to Section 2 subsection 2(1)(c) 'the person to whom the property belongs cannot be discovered even after taking reasonable steps,' is intended to deal with the finder of property. This is a question of the defendant's belief not merely reasonable belief of a third party. It is a very subjective test about the particular finder. He maybe guilty of theft however if he later discovers the owner of the property and fails to return it (Section 3(1) Theft Act 1968).

1.20 There can be dishonesty where a person is willing to pay (Section 2(2) Theft Act 1968). The commonly quoted example is that of a person in need of milk who takes a bottle from the doorstep of another without lawful authority but leaves the money to pay for it. This is not to say, however, that a willingness to pay should always be disregarded when considering a defence that a person was 'not dishonest'. If the evidence clearly points to a willingness to pay, this may prove that the defendant thought that the owner would have consented had he known of the appropriation and of the circumstances of it *(Boggeln v Williams, keynote case)*. Returning to the classic milk float example, if David approaches Charlie's milk float, takes a bottle of milk, leaving the money on the seat, David may well claim that he assumed that Charlie would have agreed to this transaction had he known of it. This raises the defence under Section 2(1)(b), and does not rely on the fact that willingness to pay is no defence.

1.21 The matter of how to view dishonesty was to some extent clarified by *R v Feely* [1973] *(see keynote case)* when the Court of Appeal held that in each case it is a matter for the jury to decide, not only what the defendant's state of mind was, but also, subject to Section 2, whether that state of mind is to be categorised as dishonest.

> 'Jurors, when deciding whether an appropriation was dishonest can be reasonably
> expected to, and should, apply the current standards of ordinary decent people. In
> their own lives they have to decide what is and what is not dishonest. We can see no
> reason why, when in a jury box, they should require the help of a judge to tell them
> what amounts to dishonesty.'

This however is not the current, or rather the complete definition of how dishonesty is to be viewed. The problem with the Feeley guidance is that jurors and magistrates could quite easily come to different decisions based upon their dealings with the ordinary man. The Feeley direction was used as the basis for guidance handed down by the Court of Appeal in *R v Ghosh*

[1982] *(see keynote case)* where the court stated that the appropriate test for dishonesty is the two stage test:

i)   Was what was done dishonest according to the ordinary standards of reasonable and honest people?
    If no, the defendant is not guilty. If yes:
ii) Did the defendant realise that reasonable and honest people regard what he did as dishonest?
    If yes, he is guilty, if no he is not guilty.

This two stage test allows an objective test of dishonesty setting the standard as being the 'reasonable and honest person'. This is then made subjective by comparison with the defendant's own beliefs, in that his beliefs are compared with, 'did he realise how the reasonable and honest man viewed his actions'.

1.22 The last part of the initial definition of theft is 'the intention of permanently depriving the other'. Apart from the offences of unauthorised taking of a motor vehicle and removal of articles from public places, the borrowing of property does not amount to an offence. If you used your neighbour's horse for the afternoon, fully intending to return it, you would not commit theft. There may be a tortious action for civil trespass. Section 6 does give some examples of what intention to deprive can be. A person appropriating property belonging to another without meaning the other permanently to lose the thing is nevertheless to be regarded as having the intention to permanently deprive the other of it if his intention is to treat the thing as his own to dispose of regardless of the others rights. Borrowing and lending of it may amount to so treating it if, but only if, the borrowing or lending is for a period and in circumstances making it equivalent to an outright taking or disposal (Section 6(1) Theft Act 1968).

1.23 Parting with property subject of conditions as to its return may also be theft (Section 6(2) Theft Act 1968). This would cover cases where a person lawfully in possession of property belonging to another, pawns it. 'Where a person, having possession or control of property belonging to another, parts with the property under a condition as to its return which he may not be able to perform, this (if done for purposes of his own and without the other's lawful authority) amounts to treating the property as his own to dispose of, regardless of the other's rights'. Whatever his good intentions when putting the property in pawn, when the time comes to redeem it, he may not have sufficient funds to do so.

1.24 A person may or may not be guilty of theft, who 'borrows' another person's property, then later abandons it. If the circumstances are such that there is a strong likelihood of the property being restored to the owner, it will be difficult to prove an 'intention to permanently deprive'. The owner of an abandoned motor vehicle, for example, may be easily traced – hence the provision in the Theft Act of an offence of unlawfully taking a conveyance, to cater for circumstances in which theft cannot be proved. However, if a man picks up an umbrella from the coat stand in a restaurant, because it is raining outside, and later leaves it on a bench in the railway station, the circumstances of his abandoning the umbrella may be regarded as an intention that the owner will not retrieve it, and so he commits theft. In each case, it will be a matter of fact for the court to decide, from the defendant's actions, what he intended or did not intend.

ROBBERY

2.1 *Section 8 Theft Act 1968*

(1) A person is guilty of robbery if he steals, and immediately before or at the time of doing so, and in order to do so, he uses force on any person or puts or seeks to put any person in fear of being then and there subjected to force.

2.2 The main elements of the offence are theft and the use of force to achieve it. The word 'force' in the definition is meant to provide a wider meaning than the word 'violence'. Where a person, with intent to steal, makes threats then grasps the handle of a hand bag and tugs at it he may be guilty of robbery. There is a need to distinguish between force directed at property rather than at the person who has possession of it. If the force is directed at property and there is no threat of force to the person, or actual application of force, there will only be a theft, not robbery.

2.3 Thus where a person, unaware of what is happening, has a bag snatched from the arm there can be no robbery, merely theft. There must be knowledge on the part of the victim prior to the act of stealing, of some threat of force or the application of force against the person. However, an attempt to put a person in fear will suffice, e.g. waving a knife in the face of a blind person, who is unaware that the robber is trying to frighten him. The offender has sought to put someone in fear of being then and there subject to force.

2.4 Force used against any person would constitute robbery only if the intention is to commit theft. If Cynthia, walking down the street, is approached by Bobby who intends to steal her bag. Albert seeing this steps in to stop the theft, Bobby throws Albert to the ground and them grabs Cynthia's handbag and runs off. Bobby will have committed robbery. Cynthia will be the victim although the actual application of force is against Albert. The threat of force must however be towards someone then and there, this implies presence and understanding of the potential threat. A threat against a third party not able to hear the threat would not suffice. If Bobby stops Cynthia in the street and threatens her that he will hit Albert next week if she does not hand over her bag. this will not suffice for robbery. Section 8 requires that a threat for the purposes of robbery shall be 'of being then and there being subjected to force'. Similarly, if Albert is standing some distance away, a threat to assault Albert there and then will not be enough, because Bobby is not seeking to put Albert in fear. Such circumstances may, instead, reveal an offence of blackmail *(see paragraph 15)*.

2.5 Problems have occurred where force is used to make an escape after the theft. This revolves around the question of when the theft is completed. A person may be guilty of robbery if during the course of committing theft he uses force on any person. Bobby is about to leave a shop with goods not paid for, when he knocks over the store detective and makes his escape. It will be a question of degree as to whether theft and assault or robbery has occurred. In *R v Hale* (1978) *(see keynote case)* the court held that it is a matter of fact for a jury to decide when the theft is complete, and that the time of the theft includes the removing stolen goods from the premises. Where a clear dividing line between the theft and later application of force can be found, it is appropriate to charge theft and assault. Where a mere threat has been used after the theft this will not normally constitute robbery.

2.6 Where a person is assaulted and the intention of the offender is to commit robbery, but no theft takes place, the offence of assault with intent to rob is committed (Section 8(2) Theft Act 1968). Subsection 8(2) states that a person guilty of robbery, or of an assault with intent to rob, shall on conviction be liable to imprisonment for life. These are therefore arrestable offences.

BURGLARY

3.1 *Section 9 Theft Act 1968*

(1) A person is guilty of burglary if:
   a) he enters any building, or part of a building, as a trespasser, and with intent to commit any such offence as is mentioned in subsection (2) below; or
   b) having entered any building or part of a building as a trespasser, he steals or attempts to steal anything in the building or that part of it, or inflicts or attempts to inflict on any person therein any grievous bodily harm.

(2) The offences related to in subsection (1)(a) above are offences of stealing anything in the building or part of a building in question, of inflicting on any person therein any grievous bodily harm or raping any person therein, and of doing unlawful damage to the building or anything therein.

(3) A person guilty of burglary shall on conviction on indictment be liable to imprisonment for a term not exceeding:
   a) where the offence was committed in respect of a building or part of a building which is a dwelling, fourteen years
   b) in any other case ten years.

(4) Reference in subsection (1) and (2) above to a building, and the reference in subsection (3) above to a building which is a dwelling, shall apply also to an inhabited vehicle or vessel, and shall apply to any such vehicle or vessel at times when the person having habitation in it is not there as well as at times when he is (Theft Act 1968 Section 9 as amended by Section 26 of the Criminal Justice Act 1991).

Explanation

3.2 Burglary falls into two clear parts, one entering as a trespasser intending to commit the offences of theft, rape, damage or grievous bodily harm, the other having entered as a trespasser, steals or inflicts grievous bodily harm. The difference lies in the intention when entering as a trespasser.

There is no distinction in law between a burglary where forcible entry is made, and one where the burglar walks through an already open door. Whether the offence is committed by day or by night, whether the attacked building is a dwelling or not, are immaterial in establishing guilt. However, these are factors which may be taken into account in determining mode of trial (and eventual sentence).

A person who is lawfully in one part of a building, may become a trespasser when he enters another part of the same building. This may be so where a person goes behind the counter in a shop (*R v Walkington* (1979)). It will clearly assist in determining whether there is a trespass, if there is a barrier of some sort, making it clear that an invitation to enter one part does not extend to the other.

To be guilty of burglary, the accused must be a trespasser from the outset, i.e., he enters as a trespasser with intent, or having entered as a trespasser he there commits. A person who enters premises lawfully, then becomes a trespasser by exceeding the scope of that invitation, will not be guilty of burglary if he steals property in the premises prior to leaving.

3.3 The person must be a trespasser at the time of entry to commit burglary. In *R v Jones*

[1976] it was held that a person who knowingly enters in excess of authority, under circumstances where he must realise that it is in excess of authority, or being reckless as to whether he is exceeding that authority, will be a trespasser. The intention to commit crime may occur at a later stage, 'having entered as a trespasser'. The fact that the original intention is not completed will not defeat the Section. If a person goes behind the counter of a shop and has the intention of stealing from the till, then arrives at the till to find it empty, he will still have committed burglary (*R v Walkington* [1979]), although where entry is with intent to commit crime this must be clearly evident. It must also be considered, when deciding on suitable charges, that some of the offences which a burglar may intend to commit when entering a building, carry heavier penalties than does burglary. Rape and wounding with intent, for example, carry maximum sentences of life imprisonment.

Aggravated Burglary

3.4 *Section 10 Theft Act 1968*

(1) A person is guilty of aggravated burglary if he commits any burglary and at the time has with him any firearm or imitation firearm, any weapon of offence, or any explosive, and for this purpose:
   a) 'firearm' includes an airgun or air pistol, and 'imitation firearm' means anything which has the appearance of being a firearm, whether capable of being discharged or not; and
   b) 'weapon of offence' means any article made or adapted for use for causing injury to or incapacitating a person, or intended by the person having it with him for such use; and
   c) 'explosive' means any article manufactured for the purpose of producing a practical effect by explosion, or intended by the person having it with him for that purpose.

(2) A person guilty of aggravated burglary shall on conviction on indictment be liable to imprisonment for life.

Explanation
3.5 This may be referred to as being burglary with the 'WIFE', **w**eapon of offense, **i**mitation **f**irearm, firearm or **e**xplosive.

The offence is committed where a person has the necessary article with him **at the time of committing a burglary**. There are of course, two principal ways in which the offence of burglary may be committed – by entering a building as a trespasser with intent to commit one of the specified offences (Section 9(1)(a)); or having entered as a trespasser, going on to commit a relevant offence (Section 9(1)(b)). In the former case, the burglary is committed at the time the offender enters with the requisite intent; in the latter case, the burglary is complete when the relevant offence is committed. If a person is not in possession of a weapon of offence when he enters a house as a trespasser, but picks one up once inside, he may be guilty of aggravated burglary if the charge is of the 'having entered, there did steal'; he had the weapon at the time of stealing whatever it was that he stole from the house *(see R v O'Leary (1986) and R v Kelly (1993) – keynote cases)*. It is not necessary to prove that there is an intention to use the firearm, imitation firearm, weapon of offence or explosive during the course of the burglary, merely that he had it with him at the time, as per *R v Stones* [1989] *(see keynote case)*. Where a burglar had an offensive weapon with him for personal security from someone other than the victim of the burglary he would still be guilty under Section 10(1).

REMOVAL OF ARTICLES FROM PUBLIC PLACES

4.1 This provision caters for circumstances which do not amount to theft because of the absence of an intention permanently to deprive the owner of her property. There was a famous incident some years before the passing of the Theft Act 1968, when a man removed a very valuable painting from a major gallery and kept it for some time. When he was eventually prosecuted, the only charge which would stand was one of causing damage to the frame. Now, he could be charged with this offence.

Section 11 Theft Act 1968

(1) Subject to subsections (2) and (3) below, where the public have access to a building in order to view the building or part of it, or a collection or part of a collection housed in it, any person who without lawful authority removes from the building or its grounds the whole or part of any article, displayed or kept for display to the public in the building or that part of it or its grounds shall be guilty of an offence.

For this purpose 'collection' includes a collection got together for a temporary purpose, but references in this Section to a collection do not apply to a collection made or exhibited for the purpose of effecting sales or other commercial dealings.

(3) It is immaterial for the purposes of subsection (1) above, that the public's access to a building is limited to a particular period or particular occasion; but when anything removed from the building or its grounds is there otherwise than forming part of, or being on loan for exhibition with, a collection intended for permanent exhibition to the public the person who removes it does not thereby commit an offence under this Section unless he removes it on a day when the public have access to the building as mentioned in subsection (1) above.

(3) A person does not commit an offence under this Section if he believes that he has lawful authority for the removal of the thing in question or that he would have it if the person entitled to give it knew of the removal and the circumstances of it.

(4) A person guilty of an offence under this Section shall on conviction on indictment be liable to imprisonment for a term not exceeding five years.

Explanation

4.2 Taking things from public displays without the intention of permanaently keeping them gives the taker a defence, in that he could not be guilty of theft or burglary. As the only viable alternative is a civil action for trespass to goods, this offence bridges the gap. It is effectively theft without the need to permanently deprive.

Access only to the grounds of a building is not sufficient, if this offence is to be committed a person will be liable for removal of an article displayed in the grounds of a building, only if the building itself is open to the public. The building may be either open or closed to the public when the removal occurs provided it is a permanent exhibition. Permanent exhibition means available rather than on display. Any article forming part of collection being kept at a building whether on display or not to the public could be subject of this Section. Things which are brought in temporarily or intermittently, such as paintings at an art gallery which are rotated into display and storage, would be covered (*R v Durkin* [1973]).

4.3 A person removing articles not part of the exhibition, or from the grounds of the building may still be liable for theft dependent on the circumstances. If the removal is for purposes of sale and disposal then burglary or theft would be the appropriate charge. This Section is designed to deal only with the person whose intent is to keep the article for a period of time, intending that it shall be returned in due course.

UNAUTHORISED TAKING OF A CONVEYANCE

5.1 The offence set out in the original Section 12 of the Theft Act 1968 has been amended several times, by the Criminal Justice Act 1982, the Police and Criminal Evidence Act 1984 and the Aggravated Vehicle Taking Act 1992. The Police and Criminal Evidence Act made the offence one which is designated arrestable by virtue of Section 24(2). The further amendment under the Aggravated Vehicle Taking Act 1982 was due to the prevalence of dangerous driving by persons stealing cars, and the fact that the unauthorised taking charge of, often did not reflect the seriousness of offences committed. There is no need to show an intention to permanently deprive, although if the vehicle is abandoned in certain circumstances, or its identity changed, theft may have occured. Where the offender attempts to steal a car or anything contained in or on it, the offence of vehicle interference may be considered under the Criminal Attempts Act 1981.

Section 12 Theft Act 1968

(1) Subject to subsection (5) and (6) below, a person shall be guilty of an offence if, without having the consent of the owner or other lawful authority, he takes any conveyance for his own or another's use, or knowing that any conveyance has been taken without such authority, drives it or allows himself to be carried in or on it.

(2) A person guilty of an offence under subsection (1) above shall be liable on summary conviction to a fine, or imprisonment not exceeding six months, or both.

(3) Subsection 3 has been repealed.

(4) If on trial of an indictment for theft, the jury are not satisfied that the accused committed theft, but it is proved that the accused committed an offence under subsection (1) above, the jury may find him guilty of the offence under subsection (1) and if he is found guilty of it, he shall be liable as he would have been liable under subsection (2) above on summary conviction.

(5) Subsection (1) above shall not apply in relation to pedal cycles; but, subject to subsection (6) below, a person who, without having the consent of the owner or other lawful authority, takes a pedal cycle for his own or another's use, or rides a pedal cycle knowing it to have been taken without such authority, shall on summary conviction be liable to a fine.

(6) A person does not commit an offence under this Section by anything done in the belief that he has lawful authority to do it, or that he would have had the owner's consent if the owner knew of his doing it and the circumstances of it.

(7) For the purposes of this Section:
   a) 'conveyance' means any conveyance constructed or adapted for the carriage of a person or persons whether by land, water or air, except that it does not include a conveyance constructed or adapted for use only under the control of a person not carried in or on it, and 'drive' shall be construed accordingly; and
   b) 'owner', in relation to a conveyance which is the subject of a hiring agreement or hire-purchase agreement, means the person in possession of the conveyance under that agreement.

Explanation

5.2 The offender must be shown to have taken the vehicle, or been carried in it knowingly without the consent of the owner.

The fact that consent to borrow a vehicle has been obtained by false pretences need not invalidate that consent In *R v Peart* (1970), Peart was lent a van to drive to a nearby town, a condition being that it was returned by a given time. In fact, Peart had no intention of going to the nearby town, but drove a lot further and made no effort to return the van on time. His conviction was quashed on appeal. Similarly, the consent of a hirer to the hire of a vehicle will not be invalidated by the fact that the hirer gives incorrect details as to driving licence and identity (*Whittaker v Campbell* (1984)). For the purpose of the Section, a person who has possession of a vehicle under a hire purchase agreement is treated as the owner. The possession of a vehicle recently taken will provide evidence of similar weight to that of recent possession in theft, i.e. that the person in possession had in fact taken the vehicle. It is necessary to show that the conveyance taken without authority has be moved in order to show that it has been taken. To this end, there is need to show movement however minimal (*R v Bogachi* [1973]). It is not necessary to show the conveyance was moved in its own element (*R v Pearce* [1973]). An inflatable dingy loaded onto a trailer and driven away could be unauthorised taking of a conveyance. The word 'drive' is construed as controlling the movement of the conveyance. This can mean many different types of control dependent upon the type of conveyance taken. A horse will not be in itself a conveyance for the purposes of this Section, even if a halter and bridle are attached (*Neal v Gribble* [1978]).

Section 12A Theft Act 1968
(as amended by the Aggravated Vehicle Taking Act 1992)

(1) Subject to subsection (3) below a person is guilty of aggravated vehicle taking if:
    a) he commits an offence under Section 12(1) above (in this Section referred to as the basic offence) in relation to a mechanically propelled vehicle; and,
    b) it is proved that, at any time after the vehicle was unlawfully taken (whether by him or another) and before it is recovered, the vehicle was driven, or injury or damage was caused, in one or more of the circumstances set out in paragraphs (a) to (d) of subsection (2) below.

(2) The circumstances referred to in subsection (1) (b) above are:
    a) that the vehicle was driven dangerously on a road or other public place
    b) that, owing to the driving of the vehicle, an accident occurred by which injury was caused to any person
    c) that, owing to the driving of the vehicle, and accident occurred by which damage was caused to any property, other than that vehicle
    d) that damage was caused to the vehicle.

(3) A person is not guilty an offence under this Section if he proves that, as regards any such proven driving, injury or damage as is referred to in subsection (1)(b) above, either:
    a) the driving, accident or damage, referred to in subsection (2) above occurred before he committed the basic offence; or
    b) he was neither in nor on nor in the immediate vicinity of the vehicle when that driving, accident or damage occurred.

(4) A person guilty of an offence under this Section shall be liable on conviction on indictment to imprisonment for a term not exceeding two years or, if it is proved

that, in circumstances falling within subsection (2)(b) above, the accident caused the death of the person concerned, five years.

(5) If the person who is charged with an offence under this Section is found not guilty of that offence but it is proved that he committed the basic offence, he may be convicted of the basic offence.

(6) If by virtue of subsection (5) above a person is convicted of a basic offence before the Crown Court, that court shall have the same powers and duties as a magistrates' court would have in convicting him of such an offence.

(7) For the purposes of this Section a vehicle is driven dangerously if:
   a) it is driven in a way which falls below what would be expected of a competent and careful driver; and
   b) it would be obvious to a competent and careful driver that driving the vehicle in that way would be dangerous.

(8) For the purposes of this Section a vehicle is recovered when it is restored to its owner or other lawful possession or custody; and in the subsection 'owner' has the same meaning as Section 12 above.

5.3 *Explanation*

Vehicle: Whereas any conveyance may be the subject of an offence of taking a conveyance, only if the conveyance concerned is a mechanically-propelled vehicle, may the offence of aggravated vehicle taking be charged.

Driven dangerously: This term has the same meaning as in Section 2A Road Traffic Act 1988, which defines the offence of dangerous driving.

Relevant period/defence: The 'aggravating factor', be it dangerous driving, damage, etc, must occur between the time the vehicle was unlawfully taken and the time it was recovered. It may be, for example, that children damage a car which has been abandoned in the street after having been taken unlawfully. The offender who took the vehicle will be liable for the aggravated offence because of the damage, unless **he proves** that he was neither in the vehicle nor in the immediate vicinity of it when the damage occurred. Likewise, in the case of a car which has been unlawfully taken and which has already suffered damage at the hands of the 'taker', another youth who drives the car or allows himself to be carried will not be guilty of aggravated vehicle taking if he proves that the damage occurred before he committed the basic offence.

Mode of trial: The offence is triable either way. However, where damage is the aggravating factor, and the cost of repairing the damage does not exceed the limit at which an offence of criminal damage may be tried on indictment, the aggravated vehicle taking is likewise confined to magistrates' court.

ABSTRACTING ELECTRICITY

6.1 Whilst abstracting electricity is a criminal offence, the majority of offences are committed by householders who will be liable for a debt which can later be recovered by the supplier of the electricity. However the offence is subject of imprisonment not exceeding five years on first conviction on indictment.

Section 13 Theft Act 1968

A person who dishonestly uses without due authority, or dishonestly causes to be wasted or diverted, any electricity, shall on conviction on indictment be liable to imprisonment for a term not exceeding five years.

Explanation

6.2 The use of the electricity is dishonest, or dishonestly wasted or diverted.

Dishonesty for the purposes of this Section means exactly the same as in Section 2, the test being partly objective then subjective.

THEFT OF MAIL

7.1 Section 14 Theft Act 1968

(1) Where a person:
    a) steals or attempts to steal any mail bag or postal packet in the course of transmission as such between places in different jurisdictions in the British postal area, or any of the contents of such a mail bag or postal packet; or
    b) in stealing or with intent to steal any such mail bag or postal packet or any of its contents, commits any robbery, attempted robbery or assault with intention to rob;

then notwithstanding that he does so outside England and Wales, he shall be guilty of committing or attempting to commit the offence against this Act as if he had done so in England or Wales, and he shall accordingly be liable to be prosecuted, tried and punished in England or Wales without proof that the offence was committed there.

(2) In subsection (1) above the reference to different jurisdictions in the British postal area is to be construed as referring to the several jurisdictions of England and Wales, of Scotland and Northern Ireland, of the Isle of Man and of the Channel Islands.

(3) For the purposes of this Section mail bag includes any article serving the purpose of a mail bag.

Explanation

7.2 Mail is conveyed throughout the several parts of the United Kingdom, and if an item of mail is stolen in transit, it may not be possible to determine at what point on its journey the theft occurred. Since the law relating to theft, governed in England and Wales by the Theft Act 1968, is different in Scotland, for example, problems could arise when was sought to prosecute for theft of mail. The Act provides that any theft of mail, or attempted theft, or similar robbery offences, may be tried in England and Wales, whether or not the offence actually took place there. (These provisions do not extend to take in countries further afield.)

CRIMINAL DECEPTION

8.1 There are various offences involving deception, under the 1968 and the 1978 Theft Acts. These are considered together, since 'deception' is a common element, and for ease of comparison.

8.2 The offences covered are:

a) Obtaining property by deception, Section 15 Theft Act 1968.
b) Obtaining a pecuniary advantage by deception, Section 16 Theft Act 1968
c) Procuring the execution of a valuable security by deception, Section 20(2) Theft Act 1968.
d) Obtaining services by deception, Section 1 Theft Act 1978
e) Securing remission of a liability by deception, Section 2(1)(a) Theft Act 1978
f) Inducing a creditor to wait for or forgo payment by deception, Section 2(1)(b) Theft Act 1978.
g) Obtaining an exemption from or abatement of liability by deception, Section 2(1)(b) Theft Act 1978.
h) Obtaining a money transfer by deception, Section 15A Theft Act 1968 (as added by the Theft (Amendment) Act 1996).

8.3 Common elements in these offences include 'obtain', 'any deception', 'dishonestly'. Note that the terms 'obtain, 'procure', 'secure' and 'induce' all have similar meanings as they appear in the several offences.

8.4 It must be proved that the false statement made actually deceived the complainant and caused him to act in the way he did. If the complainant is not deceived (*R v Light* (1915)), or he would have acted in that way anyway (*R v Edwards* [1978]), there can be no offence. The same would apply if the victim did not rely on the false statement, or had arrived at the decision to follow the course of action suggested, through his own observations and conclusions. If the statements or representations made to induce the victim to follow a particular course of action are not communicated or for some reason although given are not received, the offender cannot be guilty. He may however be guilty of attempt (Section 1(1) Criminal Attempts Act 1981, *R v Laverty* [1970]).

8.5 The onus is on the prosecution to prove that the representation whether, verbal, written or other communication, operated on the complainant's mind to induce him to do an act which he otherwise would not have done. This may be proved by other matters and evidence, or inferences from other facts. There have been cases which are difficult to reconcile with these basic guidelines, but they may be explained as being very individual and decided on their own facts. In *R v Laverty* [1970], a case brought under Section 15 of the Theft Act 1968, a defendant changed the number plate of a car and sold it. When heard at court, it was originally considered that the defendant had impliedly made a representation that the car was the original car to which the number plates had been assigned. On appeal against conviction it was held that it was not proved that the deception had operated on the buyer's mind. This case highlights the problems of proving deceptions. It was necessary for the prosecution to show that the purchaser had bought the car because of some representation made by the seller which was untrue. In these circumstances the indictment would have been better worded that the seller represented he had a right to sell the car. The representation that it was something which it was not did not affect the buyer's desire to purchase. The car's original numbers plates were substituted to defeat identification by the police and the true owner, rather than to induce a sale. The deception must be shown to induce, procure, obtain or secure the action alleged. The victim must be seen to have been deceived by the offender.

8.6 It is an important element of any deception offence that someone must be deceived by a falsehood to do something which he otherwise would not have done. It follows that it would be impossible to deceive a machine. The law makes no differentiation between a person who puts a foreign coin into a machine to obtain goods and one who inserts an implement such as a screwdriver. Both of these circumstances are treated as theft, a dishonest action to appropriate property.

8.7 Section 15(4) Theft Act 1968 provides:

'For the purposes of this Section deception means any deception (whether deliberate or reckless, by words or conduct as to fact or as to law, including a deception as to the present intentions of the person using the deception or any other person'

This definition applies to both the 1968 and 1978 Theft Acts.

8.8 There must be some proof that the statement or representation made either expressly or impliedly was false. If a statement is true there can be no deception, although there may be an attempted deception dependent on the circumstances. It matters not that the maker of the statement believed that he was telling falsehoods. A good example of this principle in action is in the case of *R v Mandry and Wooster* [1973]. Street traders were arrested for selling bottles of perfume for twenty five pence, claiming in their spiel that the same perfume could be brought along the road at major stores for two guineas. The defendants were charged with deception offences in relation to this claim. In evidence the police officers stated that they had checked with some stores and could not find the perfume priced at two guineas. During cross examination the officers stated they had not checked Selfridges. The defence however did not bring evidence to show that the perfume could be purchased at any store. The defendants, having been convicted, appealed on the grounds that their statements could have been true. The trial judge quite rightly could not direct the jury that it would be impossible for the police to check every store. The defendants were quite right that they could call evidence to show that the statement made by them was true, but in this case had not done so, so the conviction was upheld. The importance of this point is that where reasonable enquires have been made to show that the statement is untrue the onus then falls to the defence to prove the accuracy of its own claim in defence.

8.9 A statement may be deliberately false, as when a person tells a lie. However, a statement made recklessly may also be enough to amount to a dishonest deception. For example, to say, 'This ring is made of gold', when this is known to be untrue, may supply the 'deception' element in an offence, when the statement induces someone to part with money for the worthless ring. If, however, the seller is not sure what it is made of, but still says, 'This ring is made of gold.' he may be equally liable in that, not being sure of the facts, he carries on to make the statement, being reckless as to the truth of what he says. There must however, be some 'adverse act' on the part of the accused. *(Dip Kaur v Chief Constable of Hampshire (1981) – keynote case)*. If a person misunderstands what another has said, through no fault of that other person, there will be no criminal deception.

8.10 The test of recklessness in these circumstances is generally that of the *R v Caldwell* [1981] type:

'where there is an obvious risk, and the defendant has not given any thought to the possibility of there being such a risk, or having realised there is a risk, nevertheless carries on to take it'.

This test must be applied to statements and representations made, or implied by words or conduct of the suspected offender. A representation implied may be from a simple thing such as wearing a badge which implies you are a member of a particular group which is entitled to certain discounts, when in fact you are not. There is no need for actual statements to cause a deception, the mere pretext of being what one is not is a deception.

8.11 *Section 15 Theft Act 1968*

(1) A person who by any deception dishonestly obtains property belonging to another, with the intention of permanently depriving the other of it, shall on conviction on indictment be liable to imprisonment for a term not exceeding ten years.

(2) For the purposes of this Section a person shall be treated as obtaining property if he obtains ownership, possession or control of it, and 'obtains' includes obtaining for another or enabling another to obtain or retain.

(3) Section 6 (Theft Act 1968) shall apply for the purposes of this Section, with the necessary adaptation of the reference to appropriating, as it applies to Section 1 (Theft Act 1968).

(4) For the purposes of this Section 'deception' means any deception (whether deliberate or reckless) by words or conduct as to fact or law, including a deception as to the present intentions of the person using the deception or any other person.

8.12 *Explanation*

Deception, recklessness, etc: Many of the elements of the offence have been dealt with in preceding paragraphs. Some additional observations are made here. An excessively high quotation for work to be done will not, generally, amount to a deception, but may do in circumstances where a duty of care lies (*R v Silverman* (1987)).

Ownership, possession or control: For the offence to be complete, it matters not whether the victim is deceived into giving up all rights in his property, or in fact expects them to be returned at some point in future. An offender who hands over a counterfeit £50 note to pay for goods deceives the seller into giving ownership. The person who says to the car saleswoman, 'I am interested in this car, may I take it for a short test drive?' has obtained possession when he is allowed to drive the car off the forecourt; he has not obtained ownership, because the saleswoman expects him to return with the car in a short time.

This distinction relating to what is obtained is of interest when considering whether an offence of obtaining property by deception may also amount to theft. The offender, having deceived the owner, is given the property. At the moment when the deceiver accepts the property, intending to permanently deprive the owner of it, he has appropriated it. If he has obtained ownership in the property, he is appropriating his own property, it has ceased to 'belong to another', so he will not commit theft. If however, he has obtained only possession or control, the item which he appropriates is still property belonging to another, so an offence of theft, as well as one of obtaining by deception, is committed. In practice, only one offence would be charged, and this is more likely to be theft, obviating the need to prove the element of deception.

Modern technology: There cannot be deception of a machine, and this has caused problems where money is frequently transferred electronically using modern technology. Cases such as those of *R v Halai* (1993) and *R v Preddy* (1996) highlighted the problems, arising from a charge of theft or of obtaining by deception, where an electronic transfer of money was made. Accordingly, Section 15A has been added to the 1968 Act by the Theft (Amendment) Act 1996. Under these provisions, an offence will be committed where, by any deception:

i) There is a money transfer of a type where one account is debited and another is credited, and the credit results from the debit (or vice versa)

ii) It does not matter that the amounts differ, or how the transfer of monies is carried out, ie, by cheque, debit, or even if either or both accounts become overdrawn

iii) An account is one either kept with a bank or a person carrying on a deposit taking business for the purpose of the Banking Act 1987.

8.13 Obtaining a pecuniary advantage by deception has caused problems for the courts, the nature of the offences being so complex that in 1978 a further Theft Act was passed which repealed parts of Section 16. Further offences were then enacted to resolve the situation.

Section 16 Theft Act 1968

(1) A person who by any deception, dishonestly obtains for himself or another any pecuniary advantage shall on conviction be liable to imprisonment for a term not exceeding five years.

(2) The cases in which a pecuniary advantage within the meaning of this Section is to be regarded as obtained for a person are cases where:
   i)   he is allowed to borrow by way of overdraft; or
   ii) he is allowed to take out any policy of insurance or annuity contract, or obtains an improvement of the terms on which he is allowed to do so; or
   iii) he is given an opportunity to earn remuneration or greater remuneration in an office or employment; or
   iv) he is given an opportunity to win money by betting.

(3) For the purposes of this Section 'deception' has the same meaning as in Section 15.

Explanation

There is no need to prove that the victim of the deception suffered loss to prove this offence (*R v Kovacs* [1974]). There must be causal link between the deception and the advantage gained. The victim of the deception could be an agent of the company which suffer the loss. For example, the offender attends his bank and falsely represents to the manager that he has just been employed in a senior managerial post and needs to have an overdraft to purchase new clothes to attend work. The manager relying on this statement gives an overdraft facility which otherwise he would not have done. It is later discovered that there is no job, merely that the offender wished to take his family on holiday. The offender commits this offence when the overdraft facility is granted, he does not necessarily have to use the facility (*R v Watkins* [1976]).

VALUABLE SECURITIES

9.1 Section 20 Theft Act 1968

(2) A person who dishonestly, with a view to gain for himself or another, or with intent to cause loss to another, by any deception, procures the execution of a valuable security shall on conviction on indictment be liable to imprisonment for a term not exceeding seven years, and this subsection shall apply in relation to the making, acceptance, endorsement, alteration, cancellation, or destruction in whole or part of a valuable security, and in relation to the signing or sealing of any paper or other material in order that it may be made or converted into, or used or dealt with as, a valuable security as if that were the execution of a valuable security.

(3) For the purposes of this Section 'deception' has the same meaning as in Section 15 and 'valuable security' means any document creating, transferring, surrendering or releasing any right to, in or over property, or authorising the payment of money, or delivery of such property, or evidencing the creation, transfer, surrender, or release of any such right, or payment of money or delivery of any property, or the satisfaction of any obligation.

9.2 *Explanation*

Procure: The term means to bring about or cause (*R v Beck* (1985)).

Execution: This means to give effect to or carry out the terms of the document in question. It is not confined to signing or doing something else on the face of the document. Persuading a bank to make payment on a cheque is to procure its execution (*R v Kassim* (1991)).

Gain and loss: These terms are defined in:

Section 34, Theft Act 1968

(2) For the purposes of this Act:
   a) 'gain' and 'loss' are to be construed as extending only to gain or loss in money or other property, but as extending to any such gain or loss whether temporary or permanent; and:
      i) 'gain' includes a gain by keeping what one has, as well as a gain getting what one has not; and,
      ii) 'loss' includes a loss by not getting what one might get, as well as a loss by parting with what one has.

9.3 The Theft Act 1978 was drafted to deal with the problems caused by the courts interpretation of Section 16(1)(a) of the 1968 Act.

Section 1 Theft Act 1978

(1) A person who by any deception dishonestly obtains services from another shall be guilty of an offence.

(2) It is an obtaining of services where the other is induced to confer a benefit by doing some act, or causing or permitting some act to be done, on the understanding that the benefit has been or will be paid for.

Explanation

In the ordinary course of business there will only be liability if the service given is ordinarily one which would be expected to be paid for. The provision of a service which is ordinarily not paid for or charged would not be such as to sustain a charge under this Section.

The Evasion of Liability by Deception

9.4   *Section 2 Theft Act 1978*

(1) Subject to subsection (2) below, where a person by any deception:
   a) dishonestly secures the remission of the whole or part of any existing liability to make a payment, whether his own liability or another's; or
   b) with intent to default in whole or in part on any existing liability to make payment, or with intent to let another do so, dishonestly induces the creditor or any person claiming payment on behalf of the creditor to wait for payment (whether or not the due date for payment is deferred) or to forgo payment; or
   c) dishonestly obtains any exemption from or abatement of liability to make payment; he shall be guilty of an offence.

(2) For the purposes of this Section 'liability' means legally enforceable liability; and subsection (1) shall not apply in relation to a liability that has not been accepted or established to pay compensation for a wrongful act or omission.

(3) For the purposes of subsection (1)(b) a person induced to take in payment a cheque or other security for money by way of conditional satisfaction of a pre-existing liability is to be treated not as being paid but as being induced to wait for payment.

(4) For the purposes of subsection (1)(c) 'obtains' includes obtaining for another or enabling another to obtain.

Explanation

There are a number of ways in which this offence may be committed. The common elements are a deception, and a liability to pay.

Existing liability: The first two subsections deal with situations where some property or a service has already been obtained and deception is then applied in respect of paying for it. This is in contrast to Section 15 of the 1968 Act or Section 1 of the 1978 Act, where the deception is applied to obtain the property or service in the first place. A person may commit the offence in relation to someone else's debt. For example, Mary forges an entry in her daughter's rent book, and deceives the landlord into thinking that the daughter paid last week's rent.

A liability to pay must be one which is legally enforceable. Gambling debts, or payment for the services of a prostitute, are examples of liabilities which are not enforceable in the courts.

Remission: This amounts to 'getting off' making payment, either wholly or in part. The example of Mary and the rent-book (above) is one of obtaining a remission of the whole of the week's rent. A customer orders goods and pays a deposit of £100 When the goods are delivered, he pays the outstanding balance, but by altering the receipt to indicate that the deposit was £1000, he thereby obtains a remission to the amount of £900 of the total bill.

Inducement to wait: It is not sufficient, that a debtor uses deception to persuade the creditor to wait until next week for a payment which is due today. This must be linked with an intention to make default in all or a part of the liability to pay. Returning to Mary and the rent-book, if Mary tells the landlord a false sob-story about her daughter being short of money this week, thus persuading him to wait until next week for the rent, this will amount to the offence only if she intends that some or all of the amount due will not be paid.

Bouncing cheques: Section 2(3) specifically provides that if a person is induced to accept a cheque or other security for money, as conditional satisfaction of an existing liability to pay, he will regarded as having been induced to wait for payment. This provision cuts short any legal debate as to what offence may be committed in such a case. When a person buys goods in a shop, handing over a stolen cheque in payment, this will amount to obtaining property by deception. Where, however, a debt has already been incurred, e.g. when a person comes to pay his hotel bill at the end of a week's stay, using a stolen cheque will be regarded as dishonestly inducing the hotel company to wait for payment.

Exemption or abatement of liability: In subsection (1)(c), the word 'existing' does **not** qualify the word 'liability'. The offence may therefore be committed, when dishonest action is taken in advance of a liability becoming due for payment, as well as after it has become due.

Making Off Without Payment

9.5   *Section 3 Theft Act 1978*

(1) Subject to subsection(3) below, a person who, knowing that payment on the spot

for any goods supplied or service done is required or expected from him, dishonestly makes off without having paid as required or expected and with intent to avoid payment of the amount due shall be guilty of an offence.

(2) For the purpose of this Section 'payment on the spot' includes payment at the time of collecting goods on which work has been done or in respect of which service has been provided.

(3) Subsection (1) above shall not apply where the supply of the goods or the doing of the service is contrary to the law, or where the service done is such that payment is not legally enforceable.

(4) Any person may arrest without warrant anyone who is or whom he, with reasonable cause, suspects to be, committing or attempting to commit an offence under this Section.

Explanation

Payment on the spot: This offence relates strictly to 'no credit' situations where payment is made at the time goods or services are supplied, whether by cash, cheque or plastic. Restaurants and self-service petrol stations are where the bulk of these offences are perpetrated.

Makes off: Making off necessarily involves leaving the scene giving rise to the liability or where payment is due (*R v Brooks* (1983)). There is no element of deception necessary, no subtlety required, no plausible story from an expert con-man; running off will be enough.

Intent to avoid payment: The intention to avoid payment must be a permanent one, not merely an intention to delay or defer payment (*R v Allen* (1985)). If, for example, a customer in a restaurant realises that he has left his wallet at home and, to cover his embarrassment, runs out of the restaurant without paying, he will not commit the offence if he intends to return next day to pay, or to send a cheque by post. In practice, an intention to make permanent default may be difficult to prove. Lapse of time may be a significant factor, if an accused claims that he intended to pay eventually.

Punishments for the 1978 Theft Act Offences

9.6 *Section 4 Theft Act 1978*

(1) Offences under this Act shall be punishable either on conviction on indictment or on summary conviction.

(2) A person convicted on indictment shall be liable:
   a) for an offence under Section 1 or Section 2 of this Act, to imprisonment for a term not exceeding five years; and
   b) for an offence under Section 3 of this Act, to imprisonment for a term not exceeding two years.

(3) A person convicted summarily of any offence under this Act shall be liable, a) to imprisonment for a term not exceeding six months; or b) to a fine, or to both.

FALSE ACCOUNTING

10.1 *Section 17 Theft Act 1968*

(1) Where a person dishonestly, with a view to gain for himself or another, or with intent

to cause loss to another:

a) destroys, defaces, conceals or falsifies any account or any record or document made or required for any accounting purpose; or

b) in furnishing information for any purpose produces or makes use of any account, or any such record or document as aforesaid, which to his knowledge is or may be misleading, false or deceptive in a material particular,

he shall, on conviction on indictment, be liable to imprisonment for a term not exceeding seven years.

(2) For the purposes of this Section a person who makes or concurs in making in an account or other document an entry which is or may be misleading, false or deceptive in a material particular, or who omits or concurs in omitting a material particular from an account or other document, is to be treated as falsifying the account or document.

Explanation

Gain or loss: An offender may be seeking gain for himself, or may be doing something in order that someone else may profit. Alternately, the object may be malice, with an intention that another shall suffer loss. A supermarket employee may ring up lower prices on the till when a relative goes through the check-out, with a view to gain for that relative. The employee may, however, under-charge every customer with a view to his employer suffering a loss as a result.

Destroy, deface, etc: There are a number of ways in which accounts may be 'doctored' for dishonest purposes. Invoices may be destroyed or hidden, receipts may be altered, etc. The Section provides that involvement in making a misleading entry, or omitting to make an entry will be regarded as 'falsifying'. The supermarket employee, unable to ring up incorrect prices because of new bar code technology on his till, may instead by-pass the bar code reader with a number of the items in his mother's basket. This amounts to omitting a material particular from his mother's bill, so he is regarded as having falsified the till roll.

Account, record, document: This will include a taximeter or a turnstile meter (*Edwards v Toombs* (1983). An application for a personal loan is a document for the purposes of this Section (*Attorney General's Reference (No 1 of 1980)* (1981)).

Accounting purpose: The document or record must have been made, or must be required, for some purpose related to accounting. However, the material particulars in question need not themselves be required for accounting purposes (*R v Mallett* (1978)).

THE DOCTRINE OF RECENT POSSESSION

11.1 Possession of stolen property recently after a theft is deemed to be proof if not rebutted that a person committed either theft or is a handler of stolen property. Proof must be given that the property was recently stolen, and the court may convict the person in the absence of a reasonable explanation of either theft or handling, whichever the court decides is more appropriate (*R v Seymour* (1954)). For the time elapsed since the theft to be designated to be recent depends upon the type of property involved and the ability to sell or exchange goods. A person in possession of a debenture bond has been held to be in recent possession up to four months after the theft (*R v Livock* (1914)), but not eight months for a bale of silk (*R v Marcus* (1923)), or six months for a horse (*R v Cooper* (1852)). A short period of twenty minutes after the theft will suffice (*R v Proctor* (1923)).

LIABILITY OF COMPANIES FOR OFFENCES OF DECEPTION AND FALSE ACCOUNTING

12.1 *Section 18 Theft Act 1968*

(1) Where an offence committed by a body corporate under Section 15, 16 or 17 of this Act (Theft Act 1968) is proved to have been committed with the consent or connivance of any director, manager, secretary or other similar officer of the body corporate, or any person who was purporting to act in any such capacity, he as well as the body corporate shall be guilty of an offence, and shall be liable to be proceeded against and punished accordingly.

(2) Where the affairs of a body corporate are managed by its members, this shall apply in relation to the acts and defaults of a member in connection with his functions of management as if he were a director of the body corporate.

Explanation

The effect of this Section is to make both companies, and any officers of companies, liable for acts of deception if committed to further the aims of the company.

FALSE STATEMENTS BY COMPANY DIRECTORS

13.1 *Section 19 Theft Act 1968*

(1) Where an officer of a body corporate or unincorporated association (or person purporting to act as such) with intent to deceive members or creditors of the body corporate or association about it's affairs, publishes or concurs in publishing a written statement or account which to his knowledge is or may be misleading, false or deceptive in any material particular, he shall on conviction on indictment be liable to imprisonment for a term not exceeding seven years.

(2) For the purposes of this Section a person who has entered into a security for the benefit of a body corporate or association is to be treated as a creditor of it.

(3) Where the affairs of a body corporate or association are managed by its members, this Section shall apply to any statement which a member publishes or concurs in publishing in connection with his functions of management as if he were an officer of the body corporate or association.

Explanation

This Section is designed to prevent companies from issuing false statements about their trading positions to the members or investors.

SUPPRESSION OF DOCUMENTS

14.1 *Section 20 Theft Act 1968*

(1) A person who dishonestly, with a view to gain for himself or another, or with intent to cause loss to another, destroys, defaces or conceals any valuable security, any will or other testamentary document or any original document belonging to, or filed or

deposited in, any court of justice or any government department, shall on conviction on indictment be liable to imprisonment for a term not exceeding seven years.

Explanation

14.2 Section 20(1) is designed to prevent persons from hiding or destroying documents relating to the ownership of property. The subsection deals with all documents required for registration of rights, and specifically includes documents required by government departments. The intention must always be shown to be dishonest, with a view to gain or to cause another to loss. Gain and lose are defined earlier in this chapter *(see paragraph 9.2)*.

BLACKMAIL

15.1 *Section 21 Theft Act 1968*

(1) A person is guilty of blackmail if, with a view to gain for himself or another, or with intent to cause loss to another, he makes any unwarranted demand with menaces; and for this purpose a demand with menaces is unwarranted unless the person making it does so in the belief:
   a) that he has reasonable grounds for making the demand; and
   b) that the use of the menaces is a proper means of reinforcing the demand.

(2) The nature of the act or omission demanded is immaterial, and it is also immaterial whether the menaces relate to action to be taken by the person making the demand.

(3) A person guilty of blackmail shall on conviction on indictment be liable to imprisonment for a term not exceeding fourteen years.

Explanation

The words gain or loss are to be interpreted as per Section 34(2)(a) *(see paragraph 9.2)*. A person makes a demand when he utters any threatening words verbally. Where the threat is contained in a letter, the threat is made at the time the letter is posted. If the letter is posted in England intended for a victim abroad, the offence is completed as soon as the letter is posted (*Treacey v DPP* [1971]). Menace is not limited to threats of violence, it can mean any action which is or would be considered to be detrimental or unpleasant to the person to whom they are addressed, even if the accused is entitled to carry it out (*Thorne v Motor Trade Association* [1973]). A threat to injure a man's property may be an offence within the meaning of this Section. The language used may by such as to appear only a request. It need not necessarily be a specific demand, a request giving conditions for completion may be evidence of the demand. Words or conduct may be menaces if they are likely to affect the mind of the victim who is reasonably strong minded so as to make him accede to the demands when he would not otherwise have done so. It is not necessary that the intended victim himself should be put in fear or be alarmed (*R v Garwood* [1987]).

OFFENCES IN RELATION TO STOLEN PROPERTY

16.1 It has long been acknowledged that if there were no people to receive stolen goods then very few thefts would take place. The Theft Act 1968 created sixty four ways by which a person could be involved with stolen property which would render him liable to prosecution.

Section 22 Theft Act 1968

(1) A person handles stolen goods if, otherwise than in the course of stealing, knowing or believing them to be stolen goods, he dishonestly receives the goods, or dishonestly undertakes or assists in their retention, removal, disposal or realisation by or for the benefit of another person, or if he arranges to do so.

(2) A person guilty of handling stolen goods shall on conviction on indictment be liable to imprisonment for a term not exceeding fourteen years.

Explanation

16.2 Goods obtained dishonestly by deception or by blackmail are to be treated as if stolen by burglary or theft (Section 24 Theft Act 1968). If a thief handles goods that he has stolen subsequent to the theft he could possibly be guilty of both theft and handling, but these would normally be considered to be alternative charges (*R v Dolan* [1976]). A person should be treated as 'knowing or believing goods to be stolen'; 'knowing' if he has first hand knowledge that they were stolen, 'belief' is the state of mind where a defendant says to himself 'I cannot say that they are stolen, but there can be no other reasonable conclusion in the light of the circumstances, in the light of all that I have heard or seen' (*R v Hall* (1985).

16.3 Guilty knowledge of the fact that the handler knew or believed the goods to be stolen must exist at the moment when the goods are received (*Atwal v Massey* [1971]). If this is not the case however, a later assumption of the rights of the owner occurring when the defendant discovers the fact that the goods are actually stolen is a later assumption of the rights of the owner and may amount to appropriation for theft. So the subsequent dishonesty in keeping the goods would possibly render the person, when his knowledge or belife about the origin of the goods changes, guilty of theft.

16.4 A person who buys goods for value with no reason to believe they are stolen, will not be guilty of handling stolen goods if he later finds out that they are stolen , and sells them on (*R v Bloxham* (1983)). However, if he explains the situation to friends, who then help him to dispose of the goods, they may be guilty of handling, by assisting in the disposal, realisation, etc, for his benefit.

SPECIAL EVIDENTIAL RULE FOR THEFT OR HANDLING STOLEN GOODS

17.1 The Theft Act 1968 brought into effect certain provisions designed to make the proof of guilty knowledge and dishonesty easier in the case of repeat offenders. It also clarified the procedural actions possible to ensure consistency in the interpretation of various Sections. Section 27(3)(a) and (b) provide support for prosecutions in proving knowledge or belief that goods handled were in fact stolen. The provisions apply only to cases brought on indictment to Crown Court and not to summary cases dealt with at magistrates' court. The purpose of this Section is to assist in proving guilty knowledge. It would be improper for the prosecution to do other than provide the information of the prior conviction and possession (*R v Fowler* [1987]).

Section 27 Theft Act 1968

(1) Any number of persons may be charged in one indictment, with reference to the same theft, with having at different times or at the same time handled all or any of the stolen goods, and the persons so charged may be tried together.

(2) On the trial of two or more persons indicted for jointly handling any stolen goods the jury may find any of the accused guilty if the jury are satisfied that he handled all or any of the stolen goods, whether or not he did so jointly with the other accused or any of them.

(3) Where a person is being proceeded against for handling stolen goods (but not for any offence other than handling stolen goods) , then at any stage of the proceedings, if evidence has been given of his having or arranged to have in his possession the goods the subject of the charge, or of his undertaking or assisting in, or arranging to undertake or assist in, their retention, removal, disposal or realisation, the following evidence shall be admissible for the purpose of proving that he knew or believed the goods to be stolen goods:
   a) evidence that he has had in his possession, or has undertaken or assisted in the retention, removal, disposal or realisation of, stolen goods from any theft taking place not earlier than twelve months before the offence charged; and
   b) (provided that seven days notice in writing is given to him of the intention to prove the conviction) evidence that he has within the five years preceding the date of the offence charged been convicted of theft or of handling stolen goods.

Explanation

Special evidence – (1) evidence of previous occasion: So-called 'special evidence' may be given by the prosecution to support a charge of handling stolen goods, to show that the accused knew or believed the goods in question to be stolen goods. This evidence may be given only after evidence of the actus reus of the offence, i.e. that the accused had received the goods, assisted in their disposal, etc, for the benefit of another, or arranged to do so. In other words, once evidence has been given of all the other elements required to prove the offence, the special evidence may be given to help prove the required guilty knowledge. The first sort of special evidence is that set out in Section 27(3)(a), that the accused has had dealings with stolen goods from any theft taking place within the 12 month period prior to the date of the offence currently charged. For example, Walter has a second-hand shop, buying and selling a wide range of household goods. Police find in his stock, a video recorder which came from a recent burglary. Walter admits to having bought this but denies knowing or believing that it was stolen. There being no evidence of guilty knowledge, the police take no further action. A few months later, police find a stolen stereo system in Walter's shop; again Walter says he neither knew nor suspected that the stereo system was stolen. This time, evidence of his having received the stolen video recorder may be brought by the prosecution, to support the allegation that Walter knew or suspected that the stereo system was stolen, subject to the proviso that not more than 12 months elapse between the theft of the video and the police finding the stereo system in his shop.

Special evidence (2) – previous convictions: The second sort of special evidence, in support of the contention that the accused did in fact know or believe that goods were stolen goods, is evidence of his previous convictions. The general principle is that a defendant's bad character cannot be given in evidence to show that he is guilty on this occasion; these provisions allow for such evidence, to support the claim that he had guilty knowledge in relation to stolen goods. Returning to Walter and the stolen video recorder found in his shop, if he has been convicted in the preceding five years of an offence of theft or of handling stolen goods, this could have been given in evidence to support a charge of handling the video recorder. Only a conviction for theft or handling will do; if an accused has been convicted of fraud, rape or other crime, such convictions will have no relevance.

Evidence of previous convictions may not be given unless the accused has had at least seven days written notice of the intention to prove his conviction(s).

STATUTORY DECLARATION
Theft Act 1968 Section 27(4)

18.1 In any proceedings for theft of anything in the course of transmission (whether by post or otherwise), or for the handling of stolen goods from such a theft, a statutory declaration made by any person that he had dispatched or received or failed to receive any goods or postal packet, or that any goods or postal packet when dispatched or received by him were in a particular state or condition, shall be admissible as evidence of facts stated in the declaration, subject to the following conditions:

a) a statutory declaration shall only be admissible where and to the extent to which oral evidence to the like effect would have been admissible in the proceedings; and

b) a statutory declaration shall only be admissible if at least seven days before the hearing or trail a copy of it has been given to the person charged, and he has not, at least three days before the hearing or trial or within such further time as the court may in special circumstances allow, given the prosecutor written notice requiring the attendance at the hearing or trial of the person making the declaration.

SCOPE OF OFFENCES INVOLVING HANDLING STOLEN GOODS

19.1 Problems will occur where goods are stolen in another jurisdiction and brought to England or Wales, systematic thefts across Europe for example where the offenders did all the arranging England and the property came here for onward transmission. This occurred in the case of *R v Ofori and Tackie* [1994] *(see keynote case)*. Provisions to deal with stolen property handled by persons in England and Wales is contained in Section 24 of the Act.

Section 24 Theft Act 1968

(1) The provisions of this Act relating to goods which have been stolen shall apply whether the stealing occurred in England or Wales or elsewhere , and whether it occurred before or after the commencement of this Act, provided that the stealing (if not an offence under this Act) amounted to an offence where and at the time when the goods were stolen; and references to stolen goods shall be construed accordingly.

(2) For the purposes of those provisions references to stolen goods shall include, in addition to the goods originally stolen and parts of them (whether in the original state or not):

a) any other goods which directly or indirectly represent or have at any time represented the stolen goods in the hands of the thief as being the proceeds of any disposal or realisation of the whole or part of the goods stolen or of goods so representing the stolen goods; and

b) any other goods which directly or indirectly represent or have at any time represented the stolen goods in the hands of a handler of the stolen goods or any part of them as being the proceeds of any disposal or realisation of the whole or part of the stolen goods handled by him or of goods representing them.

(3) But no goods shall be regarded as having continued to be stolen goods after they have been restored to the person from whom they were stolen or to other lawful possession

or custody, or after that person and any other person claiming through him have otherwise ceased as regards those goods to have any right to restitution in respect of the theft.

(4) For the purposes of the provisions of this Act relating to goods which have been stolen (including subsection (1) and (3) above) goods obtained in England and Wales or elsewhere either by blackmail or in the circumstances described in Section 15(1) of this Act shall be regarded as stolen; and 'steal', 'theft' and 'thief' shall be construed accordingly.

Explanation

Stolen in another country: The term 'stolen goods' apply to goods obtained by theft, deception or blackmail, all offences contrary to the Theft Act 1968, which does not apply to countries other than England and Wales. To cater for persons in England and Wales who dishonestly deal with property stolen in another country, Section 24(1) provides that the term 'stolen goods' shall include goods stolen anywhere, whether or not in England and Wales. This is subject to the proviso that the manner of acquiring the goods amounted to a criminal offence in the country concerned. If Bell obtains a quantity of whisky in Scotland, by means which in England would amount to an offence of obtaining property by deception, and which amount to a criminal offence in Scots law, then brings the whisky to England to sell to dishonest traders, the whisky will be 'stolen goods' for the purposes of offences of handling. Common sense tells us that the Scots probably regard theft or fraudulent obtaining of whisky as very serious crimes, but such an assumption will not suffice. The prosecution must prove that the manner of obtaining goods in the other country amounted to a criminal offence in that country at that time (*R v Oforie and Tackie* [1994] – *keynote case*).

Stolen goods exchanged for other goods: Section 24(2) provides that other goods which represent the proceeds of the original stolen goods, as proceeds of the disposal or realisation of the original stolen goods or of goods representing them, shall in turn be regarded as 'stolen goods'. This provision requires careful consideration, especially with regard to the phrases 'in the hands of the thief or a handler' and 'or of goods representing them'. Consider Albert who steals jewellery and sells most of it for £2000, but retains one ring which he gives to Bertha. The ring is part of the original stolen goods, but the £2000 also becomes stolen goods, representing the proceeds of disposal of the original, in the hands of the thief, Albert. If Albert then gives £500 to his brother, Charlie, the latter may be guilty of an offence of handling stolen goods, assuming that he is dishonest and is aware of how Albert came by the money. Charlie then buys a leather jacket with the money; the jacket becomes 'stolen goods' as representing the proceeds of disposal of goods representing the original stolen goods, in the hands of a handler (Charlie). Charlie gives the leather jacket to his friend, Dave, who exchanges it for a CD player. If Dave nether knows nor suspects that the jacket is 'stolen goods', he will not be guilty of handling the jacket, and the CD player will not be 'stolen goods' because it does not represent the proceeds of disposal in the hands of a handler. In other words, the 'chain' is broken when stolen goods come into the hands of someone who is neither a thief nor a handler.

Stolen goods recovered: Goods which have been 'stolen goods' shall cease to be regarded as such once they have been recovered - by the victim of the theft, or into other lawful possession. Money stolen in a robbery will become ' stolen goods' for the purposes of offences of handling, but will cease to be regarded as such once the police recover the stolen money. This has practical implications where stolen goods are discovered, hidden for example, and police lie in wait, hoping to arrest the thief when she returns to collect the property. If the thief has left the property to be collected by a handler, the latter may be guilty of the offence by having arranged to receive the stolen goods, but it will not be sufficient to prove handling, for the police to give evidence that they saw him pick up the stolen property; the property, having been recovered by the police, has ceased to be 'stolen goods'.

ADVERTISING REWARDS

20.1 There is a need to prevent thefts of property designed merely for re-sale to the loser. To prevent this from becoming a frequent method of obtaining reward for illegal acts the Theft Act 1968 incorporated a Section which prohibited the offering or rewards with 'no questions asked' for return of property. The mere offer of such a reward is sufficient to breach the Section. There is no need to prove intention to defeat the Theft Act legislation, i.e., the offence is one of strict liability requiring no proof of 'mens rea'.

Section 23 Theft Act 1968

Where any public advertisement of a reward for the return of any goods which have been stolen or lost uses any words to the effect that no questions will be asked, or that the person producing the goods will be safe from apprehension or inquiry, or that any money paid for the purchase of goods or advanced by way of loan on them will be repaid, the person advertising the reward and any person who prints or publishes the advertisement shall on summary conviction be liable to a fine not exceeding level 3 on the standard scale.

Keynote Cases

21.1 Case One: Theft
R v Morris [1983] 3 All ER 288

Problem
When does appropriation take place?

Circumstances
Morris had gone to a supermarket, taken goods from the shelves and changed the price tags for those of a lesser price. At the cash till he was asked for the lower price. The question for the House of Lords on appeal was; 'if a person has substituted on an item of goods displayed in a self service store a price label showing a lesser price than the original price, then takes it to the till and pays the lesser price, is there at any stage a dishonest appropriation? If so, when does the dishonest appropriation occur?'

The answer to this question is put in the following terms 'there is a dishonest appropriation for the purposes of the Theft Act 1968 where by the substitution of a price label showing a lesser price on goods for one showing greater price, a defendant either by that act alone, or by that in conjunction with another act or acts (whether done before or after the substitution of the labels) adversely interferes with or usurps the rights of the owner to ensure that the goods concerned are sold and paid for at the greater price.

Decision
Appropriation occurs where a person adversely interferes with or usurps the rights of the owner of goods.

Comment

An adverse act against the rights of the owner where dishonest intention can be proved is sufficient to complete the offence of theft. It is important to distinguish this case from that of *Dip Kaur v Chief Constable of Hampshire* [1981] *(see below)*. There is in the case some consideration of other circumstances; what for instance of the shopper who quite innocently knocks a bottle of spirits from a shelf and it breaks, that would not be appropriation; so there must be an element of mens rea required at the time of appropriation which can be inferred from the acts undertaken. There is also consideration that if the act is such that the store keeper would have consented to it, or using a negative test, not objected to the way in which the goods were treated prior to be taken to the till, then this would not be appropriation. It was also decided that the defendant need not have taken all the owner's rights in goods but merely some of those rights. Otherwise, to commit theft the offender would have had to completely exclude the owner from all rights in the goods, including ownership.

21.2 Case Two: Theft
Dip Kaur v Chief Constable of Hampshire [1981] 2 All ER 430

Problem

How is dishonesty interpreted where no overt act is done to disguise facts?

Circumstances

A woman shopping for shoes found a pair where the price tags on the soles were different, one being for £6.99 the other £4.99. She took the shoes to the till and was charged £4.99. She made no attempt to conceal the price tags nor any attempt to remove the higher priced tag. Convicted at first instance of theft, Dip Kaur appealed on the grounds that there was no dishonesty or appropriation until after the sale had been completed. The conviction was quashed on appeal.

Decision

There must be an adverse act to show appropriation which is in itself dishonest.

Comment

This case shows no adverse action against the goods, Dip Kaur had not altered the price, she had not therefore 'usurped the rights of the owner'. The contract of sale was therefore complete at the time of sale so she could not be said to have appropriated the goods at any stage. She merely entered into a contract to purchase and had done so at the lower price.

21.3 Case Three: Theft
21.3 *R v Robinson* [1977] CLR 173

Problem

Can threats to recover a debt be a defence to theft?

Circumstances

Robinson was owed some money by the wife of an acquaintance. Together with two others Robinson approached the acquaintance and threatened him with the knife to obtain the money owed. A fight began during which a five pound note fell from the pocket of the acquaintance. Robinson grabbed the money. Robinson was charged with robbery, but this was later reduced to theft and he was convicted. Robinson appealed on the grounds that he had an honest belief that he was entitled to the money.

The conviction was quashed. All that was required was for the defendant to show he had an honest belief that he was entitled to the money, not that he was entitled to take it in a particular way.

Decision
If the defence shows that the defendant has a reasonable belief that he has in law a right to deprive the other of the property he will have a defence to a charge of theft (Section 2(1)(a) Theft Act 1968).

Comment
The argument in this case was complicated by the fact that the original charge was one of robbery. If the use of force is ignored and the appropriation of the property considered in isolation the defence afforded by Section 2(1)(a) becomes apparent. Possibly other charges may have been appropriate under public order legislation.

21.4 **Case Four: Theft**
R v Ghosh **[1982] 2 All ER 689**

Problem
Can a belief that a debt was owed allow a defendant to misrepresent the facts to ensure he gets paid what he believes is due to him. Is his behaviour dishonest, and how can dishonesty be checked?

Circumstances
The defendant in this matter was a consultant surgeon working on a locum basis performing operations for a hospital. The charges alleged that he had falsely represented that he had himself carried out a surgical operation to terminate a pregnancy, or that money was due to himself or an anaesthetist for such an operation, when in fact the operation had been carried out by someone else, and/or under the National Health Service provision. The actual charges were, attempting to procure the execution of a cheque by deception, attempting to obtain money by deception, and obtaining money by deception.

His defence was that there was no deception, that the sums paid to him were due for consultation fees which were legitimately payable under the regulations, or else were the balance of fees properly payable. In other words, that there was nothing dishonest about his behaviour on any of the counts, because he was owed the money for other matters arising from his dealings with the hospital.

The jury's decision when convicting on all counts was that he had falsely represented that he had carried out a surgical operation and had intended to dishonestly obtain money thereby; he had falsely pretended that an operation had been carried out under the National Health Service; he had falsely pretended that the money was due to an anaesthetist; that he had obtained money by falsely pretending that an operation had been carried out on a fee paying basis when in fact it had been conducted under the terms of the National Health Service.

Ghosh appealed on the grounds that the judge had misdirected the jury on the matter of dishonesty, by saying, 'Now, finally dishonesty. There are, sad to say, infinite categories of dishonesty. It is for you today, having heard what you have, to consider contemporary standards of honesty and dishonesty in the context of all you have heard. I cannot really expand on this too much, but probably it is something rather like getting something for nothing, sharp practice, manipulating systems and many other matters which come to your mind.' The appeal was dismissed.

Decision
In determining whether the prosecution has proved that the defendant was acting dishonestly, a jury must first of all decide whether according to the ordinary standards of reasonable and honest people what was done was dishonest. If it was not dishonest by those standards, that is the end of the matter and the prosecution fails. If it was dishonest by those standards, then the jury must consider whether the defendant himself must have realised that what he was doing was by those standards dishonest.

Comment
In most cases, where the actions are obviously dishonest by ordinary standards there will be no doubt about it, it will be obvious that the defendant himself knew his actions to be dishonest. It is dishonest for a defendant to act in a way which he knows ordinary people consider dishonest, even if he asserts or genuinely believes that he is morally justified in acting as he did. Robin Hood, or those ardent anti-vivisectionists who remove animals from laboratories, are acting dishonestly, even though they may consider themselves morally justified, because they know that ordinary people would consider their actions to be dishonest.

21.5 Case Five: Theft
Boggeln v Williams [1978] 2 All ER 1061

Problem
Can reconnecting the electricity supply through a meter amount to abstraction of electricity or is this merely a civil debt?

Circumstances
Boggeln had his electricity supply disconnected for failing to pay the bill. When the electricity suppliers came to disconnect his supply, he said he intended to reconnect himself. Boggeln knew how to bypass the meter but did not do so. He reconnected the supply via the meter. At his initial trial he was charged and convicted with abstracting electricity. Boggeln appealed on the basis that he was not dishonest, he had informed the electricity board of his intention to reconnect the supply and that he fully intended to pay for the electricity. If he been dishonest he could have reconnected the supply without it going through the meter.

The appeal was heard by the Crown Court which accepted the argument of the defence that he was not dishonest, and that the presence of dishonesty was a question of fact to be answered subjectively in the light of his state of mind when he reconnected the electricity. The prosecution appealed to the Court of Appeal.

At the Court of Appeal it was held that despite Section 2(2) of the Theft Act 1968 stating 'a persons appropriation of property belonging to another may be dishonest not withstanding that he is prepared to pay' dishonesty is a question of fact, and this relates to the defendant's state of mind. The Crown Court was entitled to find that the defendant was not dishonest.

Decision
Dishonesty is a question of fact, applying the test from Ghosh. It is the defendant's state of mind, and how he understands how everyone else would view his actions.

Comment
Boggeln had reconnected through the meter and whilst he was using electricity he was actually incurring a debt. He was not diverting around the meter and did acknowledge that he owed for the electricity. Although he may have committed an act of damage he was not acting in a manner the jury thought was dishonest.

21.6 **Case Six: Theft**
R v Feeley [1973] 1 All ER 341

Problem
How can a jury be guided on the question of dishonesty?

Circumstances
Feeley was employed as the manager of a betting office. It was a practice that from time to time employees of the betting office had 'borrowed' monies from the till leaving a note as an 'IOU'. The practice, although not officially acknowledged, was tolerated by senior managers. The company decided that this practice should stop and circulated to all managers that it would no longer tolerate any cash deficiencies in the till. The practice of borrowing money was to stop immediately. About a month later Feeley borrowed a sum of money from the till and left an 'IOU' note. A short time later, a matter of days, he was transferred to another branch, without opportunity to repay the 'IOU'. The police were contacted and Feeley arrested. He stated that he had 'borrowed' the money from the float and fully intended to repay it, also that he was owed money by his employers plus commission which more than covered the deficiency. The initial trail was at the Crown Court. The judge did not direct the jury to decide whether Feeley actions had been shown to be dishonest by the prosecution but said, 'If someone does something deliberately knowing that his employers are not prepared to tolerate it, is that not dishonest?' The jury decided it was and convicted. Feeley appealed.

On appeal it was held that whether or not the defendant is dishonest is a matter of fact for the jury to decide, and dishonesty is an ordinary word for the jury to decide upon its meaning. The conviction of Feeley was quashed, the appeal court deciding that the most important part of the jury's decision about dishonesty had been taken for it (by the judge).

Decision
Dishonesty is a state of mind. It is a question of fact for the jury to decide what the defendant thought about his actions, and they should be directed as such.

Comment
Whether or not Feeley was dishonest depends on how the practice was carried on within the company, whether or not he felt what he did was dishonest. The most appropriate test for dishonesty is that of the case of Ghosh which adds to the Feeley test of what the defendant thought, consideration of how he would see that others view his actions.

21.7 Case Seven: Theft
R v Ofori and Tackie (1994) 99 Cr App R 223

Problem
Can a court in England be informed of matters outside the jurisdiction of the court and make a finding on such matters?

Circumstances
The defendants in this matter made various rental agreements at travel agents in England, by the use of false documentation, to hire vehicles at various destinations throughout Europe. The vehicles were collected as arranged and driven back the England where it had already been arranged to ship the vehicles to West Africa. The problem with the case was the jurisdiction of the court to deal with the matters. The defendants were charged with numerous different charges of conspiracy to steal, but also two counts of handling stolen property. The defence submitted that the court in England had no jurisdiction to hear the matters. At trial the judge ruled that there was jurisdiction and subsequently the defendants pleaded guilty to some of the charges. Both defendants then appealed.

The appeal was allowed on the grounds that the prosecution had not proved that the obtaining of the cars was an offence in the jurisdictions where the original obtaining had taken place. Section 24(1) Theft Act 1968, which gives the court jurisdiction to deal with allegations of handling stolen property in England and Wales, states 'The provisions of this Act relating to goods which have been stolen shall apply whether the stealing occurred in England or Wales or elsewhere, and whether it occurred before or after the commencement of this Act, provided that the stealing (if not an offence under this Act) amounted to an offence at the time the goods were stolen'. Such a question cannot be taken as judicial notice and must be proved to the court, nor can the court take into account any rebuttable presumption on the basis that there is a similar offence to theft in the jurisdictions concerned (Belgium and Germany).

Decision
Section 24(1) Theft Act 1968 can only give the courts of England and Wales jurisdiction for handling stolen goods if the goods have been first shown to be stolen, or subject of an equivalent offence in the jurisdiction where they are obtained.

Comment
On the basis of this ruling, had evidence been available at the initial trial that the property was subject of theft, or an equivalent offence in either Germany or Belgium then the appeal would have failed. In this instance the failure was to provide the evidence of a similar offence in the penal codes of the countries concerned.

21.8 Case Eight: Aggravated Burglary
R v Kelly [1993] JP 845

Problem
Is the use of an ordinary everyday tool as an offensive weapon sufficient to aggravate a simple burglary into aggravated burglary, or must the offender enter with an instrument which is a weapon of offence per se?

Circumstances

Kelly burgled a private dwellinghouse, he used a screwdriver he had brought with him to force and entry. Whilst making a search of the premises for goods to steal, he was disturbed by the occupant. Kelly made threats and used the screwdriver to hold the occupants at bay whilst he stole the video recorder. Kelly was caught leaving the premises with the stolen goods.

Kelly was prepared to plead guilty to burglary but not guilty to aggravated burglary. Kelly was convicted and appealed that he did not have with him at the time of entry an offensive weapon.

Kelly's conviction was sustained. The only question for the court was whether or not a screwdriver, which is not an offensive weapon per se, could be treated as an offensive weapon. In this case, the relevant time at which the prosecution had to prove that Kelly had with him an offensive weapon was when he stole (this indicates that the original charge was that having entered as a trespasser stole under 9(1)(b)) and before he threatened the occupants. In effect Kelly had to have used it to force entry as a tool, and once that was complete, changed his view of it to being a weapon. The court were satisfied that this is what had occurred and the conviction was upheld.

Decision

Where a person uses an article which is not in itself a weapon of offense per se, there is need to show that having entered he has with him an article which he views as an offensive weapon.

Comments

As is explained (at paragraph 3.5), to prove aggravated burglary, it must be shown that the weapon of offence was in possession of the burglar at the time he committed the burglary. Whether the burglary involves entry with intent to commit a specified crime, or committing a relevant crime, having entered, is crucial. A criminal who enters with intent to commit rape, then picks up a knife, intending to use it to threaten and injure the victim, will not commit aggravated burglary because he did not have the weapon with him at the time the burglary offence was completed.

21.9 Case Nine: Aggravated Burglary Offensive Weapon
R v O'Leary [1986] 82 CA Rep 341

Problem

At which stage of the offence must the weapon be in the possesion of the offender?

Circumstances

In the early hours of the morning O'Leary forced his way into a house. Once inside he grabbed a knife and went upstairs where he was confronted by the occupiers. During the ensuing fight all three were injured, O'Leary demanded cash and jewellery, this was given to him and he left. Charged with aggravated burglary O'Leary submitted that he was not guilty because he had not entered with the knife, although he accepted he had committed burglary. Convicted, O'Leary appealed.

On appeal it was stated that the offender must have with him the weapon of offence at the time at which he actually stole. In this case O'Leary still had the knife in his hand so he was guilty and the appeal was dismissed.

Decision
Possession of the weapon of offence must be at the same time as the theft for aggravated burglary to be committed.

Comment
This case appears to clarify the situation as far as offensive weapons are concerned.

21.10 Case Ten: Aggravated Burglary
R v Stones [1989] 1 WLR 156

Problem
Is the mere possession of a weapon of offence sufficient or must it have been brandished as such?

Circumstances
Stones and others were seen loading goods from a burglary into a car. They ran off and Stones was caught nearby. He was found to be in possession of a household knife which he stated was for personal protection against some local youths who had been trying to catch him. He was charged with aggravated burglary and convicted. He appealed on the grounds that the only reason he had the knife with him was for personal protection and not for use in the burglary. The conviction was upheld on the basis that the mere possession of the weapon aggravated the offence, it did not require any particular intention to use the weapon.

Decision
Mere possession of an offensive weapon is sufficient to convict under Section 10(1) Theft Act 1968.

Comment
The purpose of Section 10(1) is to prevent burglars going armed to cause injury. The fact that he had the weapon with him without the intention to injure someone is sufficient. The possibility that he might be tempted to use it if challenged is the mischief that the Section is aimed at.

21.11 Case Eleven: Robbery
R v Hale (1978) 68 Cr App R 415 CA

Problem
Is appropriation a continuing process for the purpose of robbery?

Circumstances
Hale and another went to the house of their victim. Hale put his hand over the victim's mouth in an attempt to quieten her. The woman screamed and this was heard by a neighbour who phoned to see if all was in order. Under threats from Hale the victim told the neighbour that she was all right and not to worry. Hale and his accomplice again demanded to know where the money was kept in the house, and before leaving tied up their victim threatening her not to call the police until at least five minutes after they had left. Both men were charged with robbery. The judge directed the jury that they had to be sure that force had been used against the victim to obtain property, and that the offenders had obtained property dishonestly. Hale was convicted and appealed. On appeal the court held that appropriation was a continuing process. At all relevant

times during this incident Hale was in the process of appropriating property for the purposes of theft, he was in fact in the act of stealing. The actions of putting his hand over her face, and tying her up both amounted to use of force to facilitate theft.

Decision
Physical force, or assault on a person is sufficient to sustain a conviction for robbery. Appropriation continues for the period of the material time taken to complete the theft.

Comment
It will be a matter for common sense to realise at what stage a crime is completed, a matter of fact for a jury to decide.

21.12 Case Twelve: Burglary to Commit Rape
R v Collins [1972] 2 All ER 1105

Problem
Is an invitation to enter premises, even where this is obtained by mistake, sufficient to negate a charge of burglary?

Circumstances
After going out for a few drinks one night Collins decided he wanted sexual intercourse. On passing a house with the bedroom light on, he put a ladder to the window. Having climbed the ladder he found a naked girl asleep inside. He climbed down the ladder undressed himself then ascended the ladder again and pulled himself up onto he window sill. The girl, waking, saw Collins and mistaking him for her boyfriend, beckoned him in. They then had sexual intercourse after which she realised her mistake and the police were called. Collins was arrested and later charged with burglary with intent to rape. He was convicted and appealed.

On appeal the direction of the judge to the jury was considered. The jury had been told to consider if they were satisfied that Collins had entered the room as a trespasser, with intent to commit rape, and that entry as a trespasser depended upon whether the entry was intentional or reckless. The Court of Appeal decided that the conviction could not stand. The true question for the jury was whether at the time of entry Collins knew that he was not welcome. Also to be considered, was whether he was inside or outside the window when he was beckoned in. The Crown had not established this. The jury needed to have considered whether Colins's entry into the premises was that of a trespasser.

Comment
The importance of this decision is that entry with intent to commit rape is required under Section 9(1)(a) for the offence to be complete.

Chapter 14: Criminal Damage and Related Offences

DESTROYING OR DAMAGING PROPERTY
1.1 *Section 1 Criminal Damage Act 1971*

(1) A person who without lawful excuse destroys or damages any property belonging to another intending to destroy or damage such property or being reckless as to whether such property would be destroyed or damaged shall be guilty of an offence.

(2) A person who without lawful excuse destroys or damages any property, whether belonging to himself or another:
   a) intending to destroy or damage any property or being reckless as to whether any property would be destroyed or damaged; and
   b) intending by the destruction or damage to endanger the life of another or being reckless as to whether the life of another would thereby be endangered;
   shall be guilty of an offence.

(3) An offence committed under this Section by destroying or endangering property by fire shall be charged as arson.

Explanation
Section 1(1) covers damage to another's property, Section 1(2) covers damaging anyone's property including your own whereby danger is caused to life, Section 1(3) covers damage caused by fire.

1.2 A person will not be guilty of causing criminal damage contrary to this Section if he damages his own property and the intention is to make a claim against his insurance company by fraud.

1.3 The damage committed need not be permanent, it could entail the reduction of value of an item or its impairment for use (*Roe v Lingerlee* [1986]). Impairment of usefulness does not require breaking, cutting or removal of a part. It has been held (*R v Whiteley* (1991)) that damage itself does not have to be tangible if the property which is damaged is tangible.

Note: The *Whiteley* case involved a computer 'hacker' who altered information on a computer disk so as to impair the operation of the computer. He was convicted of causing criminal damage, by alteration of the magnetic particles on the computer disk. However, under the provisions of the Computer Misuse Act 1991, which post-dates the Whiteley decision, any modification of the contents of a computer shall not be regarded as criminal damage, unless the modification impairs the physical condition of the computer or its storage medium. Whiteley would now be more likely to be charged with offences under the Computers Misuse Act, rather than with criminal damage *(see Chapter 37)*.

1.4 A person will be guilty of recklessly destroying or damaging property belonging to another under Section 1(1) above, if it can be shown that he committed an act which creates an obvious risk that property would be destroyed or damaged and when he commits that act he either gives no thought to the possibility of there being a risk, or, having recognised that was such a risk he carried on regardlessly (*R v Caldwell* [1981] – *see keynote case*).

1.5 What then of a person who causes damage to another's property to recover his own property. This situation was considered in *Lloyd v DDP* [1991] *(keynote case)*. Lloyd had parked his car on another's property and a wheel clamp was attached to it by the landowner's representative. Lloyd broke the wheel clamp to get his car back and he was convicted of criminal damage.

THREATS TO DESTROY OR DAMAGE PROPERTY
Section 2 Criminal Damage Act 1971
2.1 A person who without lawful excuse makes to another a threat, intending that that other

would fear it would be carried out:

    a) to destroy or damage any property belonging to that other or a third person; or

    b) to destroy or damage his own property in a way which he knows is likely to endanger the life of that other person or a third person;

shall be guilty of an offence.

Explanation

2.2 The offence is committed where a threat is made to commit damage, where the person making the threat intends that it shall be taken seriously. Whether the person making the threat intends to carry it out, or whether the person to whom it is made takes it seriously, are irrelevant. Thus, when Jack says to Jill, 'I'm going to burn your house down', the following are possible alternative situations:

    i)   Jack intends to frighten Jill, by her taking the threat seriously; Jill is frightened

    ii)   Jack intends to frighten her by her taking the threat seriously; she thinks he is joking

    iii)   He is joking; she takes the threat seriously, and is frightened

    iv)   He is joking; she thinks he is joking, and does not take the threat seriously.

    Jack will commit the offence in cases (i) and (ii), because he intends that Jill will take his threat seriously. He does not commit the offence in (iii) even though Jill is frightened by his threat. This is not to say that Jack may not commit some other offence, if the circumstances are right, e.g. harassment.

POSSESSING ARTICLES WITH INTENTION TO DESTROY OR DAMAGE

3.1 *Section 3 Criminal Damage Act 1971*

    A person who has anything in his custody or under his control intending without lawful excuse to use it or cause or permit another to use it:

    a) to destroy or damage any property belonging to some other person; or

    b) to destroy or damage his own or the users property in a way which he knows is likely to endanger the life of some other person;

    shall be guilty of an offence.

Explanation

3.2 For the offence to be proved, there must be proof of intention; possession alone is not enough to convict. The accused may intend to use the article herself, or her intention may be that someone else will use it to commit damage.

    It is not necessary to show an intention to commit an offence of damage in the immediate future; the intention may be to use it at some time in the future (*R v Buckingham* (1975)).

PUNISHMENT FOR DAMAGE OFFENCES

4.1 *Section 5(1) Criminal Damage Act 1971*

    (1) A person guilty of arson under Section 1 above or of an offence under Section 1(2) above (whether arson or not) shall on conviction on indictment be liable to imprisonment for life.

    (2) A person guilty of any other offence under this Act shall on conviction on indictment be liable to imprisonment for a term not exceeding ten years.

Explanation

4.2 For the majority of the offences under the Act, the maximum punishment is 10 years imprisonment, making them all arrestable offences.

    However, for an offence under Section 1 of causing damage involving use of fire, i.e., arson, the maximum is life imprisonment. Likewise, for an offence under subsection 1(2), i.e., criminal damage with intention to endanger life, or with recklessness as to whether life may be endangered, the maximum is life imprisonment.

LAWFUL EXCUSE

5.1 Throughout the Act the phrase 'lawful excuse' appears. Lawful excuse is defined as:

Section 5(2) Criminal Damage Act 1971

(1) This Section applies to any offence under Section 1(1) above and any offence under Section 2 and 3 above other than one involving a threat by the person charged to destroy or damage property in a way which he knows is likely to endanger the life of another or involving an intent by the person charged to use or cause or permit the use of something in his custody or under his control so as to destroy or damage property.

(2) A person charged with an offence to which this Section applies shall, whether or not he would be treated for the purposes of this Act as having a lawful excuse apart from this subsection, be treated for those purposes as having a lawful excuse:

   a) if at the time of the act or acts alleged to constitute the offence he believed that the person or persons whom he believed to be entitled to consent to the destruction of or damage to the property in question has so consented, or would have so consented to it if they had known of the destruction or damage and its circumstances; or

   b) if he destroyed or damaged or threatened to destroy or damage the property in question or, in the case of a charge of an offence under Section 3 above, intended to do so to protect property belonging to himself or another or a right or interest in property which was or which he believed to be vested in himself or another, and at the time of the act or acts alleged to constitute the offence believed:

      i) that the property, right or interest was in immediate need of protection; and

      ii) that the means of protection adopted or proposed to be adopted were or would be reasonable having regard to the circumstances.

5.2 *Explanation*

Scope of defences (subsection 5(1)): A defence provided by this Section may be pleaded to a charge under Section 1 (causing damage), Section 2 (threats to cause damage) or Section 3 (possession with intent), **excluding** any offence which involves an element of endangering life. Thus, an accused may claim a 'lawful excuse' for threatening 'to burn your house down while you are away on holiday', but not if the threat is to 'burn your house down with you in it.'

Consent: A woman in a state of self-induced intoxication, mistakenly caused damage to the wrong house, believing it to be her own. It was held that she had a defence (*Jaggard v. Dickinson* (1980)).

Reasonable means: It is a matter of fact in any particular case, whether the actions of the accused, in damaging another's property in order to safeguard his own, were reasonable in the circumstances. It is first, a subjective test of what the accused believed to be the state of affairs at the time, then an objective test, whether his actions were reasonable had the circumstances been as the accused believed them to be (*R v Hunt* (1978)). In this regard, at common law a person is entitled to defend her own property from threat, and any action taken will be considered on its merits in the prevailing circumstances (*Goodway v Beecher* (1951)).

In R v Hill *(keynote case)* the defendant argued that her possession of a hacksaw blade with intent to cut through the fence at a defence establishment was done in order to prevent a greater harm. Her claim to a defence under this Section failed.

PROPERTY

6.1 *Section 10 Criminal Damage Act 1971*

(1) In this Act 'property' means property of a tangible nature, whether real or personal, including money and:

   a) including wild creatures which have been tamed or are ordinarily kept in captivity, and any other wild creature or their carcasses if, but only if, they have been reduced into possession which has not been lost or abandoned or are in the course of being reduced into possession; but

b) not including mushrooms growing wild on any land or flowers, fruit or foliage of a plant growing wild on any land.

For the purposes of this subsection 'mushroom' includes any fungus and 'plant' includes and shrub or tree.

(2) Property shall be treated for the purposes of this Act as belonging to any person:

a) having custody or control of it;

b) having in it any proprietary right or interest (not being an equitable interest arising only from an agreement to transfer or grant an interest); or

c) having a charge on it.

(3) Where property is subject of a trust, the persons to whom it belongs shall be so treated as including any person having a right to enforce the trust.

(4) Property of a corporation sole shall be so treated as belonging to the corporation notwithstanding a vacancy in the corporation.

6.2 *Explanation*

The provisions as to what will or will not amount to 'property' for the purposes of offences under the Act, are similar to those relating to property which may be subject of theft. For further details, see Chapter 13.

OTHER DAMAGE OFFENCES

Damage Endangering Ships

7.1 Where a person does an act causing damage such as to endanger the safety of a ship, he will be guilty of an offence.

Section 12 Aviation and Maritime Security Act 1990

(1) Subject to subsection (6) below, it is an offence for any person unlawfully and intentionally:

a) to destroy or damage any property to which this subsection applies, or

b) seriously to interfere with the operation of any such property;

where the destruction, damage or interference is likely to endanger the safe navigation of any ship.

(2) Subsection (1) above applies to any property used for the provision of maritime navigation facilities, including any land, building or ship so used, and including any apparatus or equipment so used, whether it is on board ship or elsewhere.

(3) Subject to subsection (6) below, it is also an offence for any person intentionally to communicate any information which he knows to be false in a material particular, where the communication of the information endangers the safe navigation of any ship.

(4) It is a defence for a person charged with an offence under subsection (3) above to prove that, when he communicated the information, he was lawfully employed to perform duties which consisted of or included the communication of information and that he communicated the information in good faith in performance of those duties.

(5) Except as provided by subsection (6) below, subsections (1) and (3) above apply whether any such act as is mentioned in those subsections is committed in the United Kingdom or elsewhere and whatever the nationality of the person committing the act.

(6) For the purposes of subsections (1) and (3) above any danger, or likelihood of danger to the safe navigation of a warship or any other ship used as a naval auxiliary or in customs or police service is to be disregarded unless:

    a) the person committing the act is a United Kingdom National, or

    b) his act is committed in the United Kingdom, or

    c) the ship is used in the naval or customs service of the United Kingdom or in the service of any police force in the United Kingdom.

(7) A person guilty of an offence under this Section is liable on conviction on indictment to imprisonment for life.

7.2 *Explanation*

Intentionally: In contrast to an offence of causing criminal damage intentionally or recklessly, here the accused's actions have to be intentional. If a drunken youth on a cross-channel ferry smashes a navigation light, he may commit this offence if it is proved that he intended to cause the damage. If there is insufficient evidence of intent, but it can be proved that he was reckless, the proper charge will be one of criminal damage.

Likely to endanger safe navigation of any ship: It is not enough to prove that the accused caused damage to equipment on a ship; the likelihood of the damage resulting in danger to the safe navigation of that or any other ship must be proved.

Land, building, etc: These provisions are not limited to damage caused on board ship, but extend to damage to any facilities or equipment connected with safe navigation of shipping. This would include buoys, lighthouses, shore-based communications equipment, HM Coastguard premises, etc.

Liability outside this country: The net effect of subsections (5) and (6) is that actions carried out in any part of the world may be tried as offences in the United Kingdom, **except** in a case where – the offender is not a UK citizen – and the actions are taken outside the United Kingdom – and the likely danger is to a ship used by a foreign navy, customs service or police force. The practical effect of this is that if a foreign ship enters a UK port with a person on board who has endangered the safety of the vessel while on the high seas, the matter could be dealt with in this country (unless the ship is being used for foreign naval, customs or police purposes).

7.3 **Exhibiting False Signals to Shipping**
Malicious Damage Act 1861, Section 47

7.3.1 *Offence*

A person commits an offence who:

    i) unlawfully:

        – masks, alters or removes any light or signal

        – or exhibits any false light or signal

        – with intent to bring any ship, vessel or boat into danger; or

    ii) unlawfully and maliciously:

        – does anything

        – tending to the immediate loss or destruction of any ship, vessel or boat.

7.3.2 *Explanation*

Whereas offences under the Aviation and Maritime Security Act 1990 may involve causing damage so as to endanger shipping, these provisions relate to interfering with lights and signals with intent, or doing anything at all which tends to the immediate loss or destruction of any ship. One might be forgiven for asking why all offences involving danger to shipping was not brought together into the 1990 Act, but such is not the way with our legislators. Most of the

1861 Act has been repealed, principally by the Criminal Damage Act 1971, but odd Sections remain in force, preserving as they do the archaic language of the mid 19th century.

7.3.3 *Arrest and Punishment*
These offences carry a maximum possible sentence of life imprisonment and are therefore arrestable offences.

7.4 Removal of Buoys
Malicious Damage Act 1861, Section 48
7.4.1 *Offence*
A person commits an offence who:
- unlawfully and maliciously
- cuts away, casts adrift, removes, alters, sinks or destroys
- or does any act with intent to cut away, etc
- or in any other manner damages or conceals
- any boat, buoy, buoy rope, etc
- used or intended for the guidance of seamen or the purposes of navigation.

7.4.2 *Explanation*
An offence under this Section may also amount to an offence under the 1990 Act (above) if it involves intentional damage. However, an offence need not involve damage, and the term 'maliciously' includes recklessness as well as intention.

7.4.3 *Arrest and Punishment*
These offences carry a maximum possible sentence of seven years' imprisonment and are therefore arrestable offences.

7.5 Damage or Danger on Railways
Malicious Damage Act 1861, Sections 35, 36
7.5.1 *Offence*
A person commits an offence who shall:
- unlawfully and maliciously
- put, place, throw, etc, upon or across any railway, any wood, stone or other matter
- or do or cause to be done any other matter or thing
- with intent to obstruct, upset, overthrow, injure or destroy
- any engine, tender, carriage or truck using the railway (S 35).

Also, a person commits an offence who:
- by any unlawful act
- or by any wilful omission or neglect
- obstructs or causes to be obstructed (or aids or assists therein)
- any engine or carriage using a railway (S 36).

7.5.2 *Explanation*
Unlawfully and maliciously: The 'in phrase' of 1861, it appears in almost every offence in this Act and in the Offences Against the Person Act of the same year. Briefly, action which is intentional or reckless will give rise to the offence.

Wood, stone, etc: The offence will be committed where anything is placed on or across a railway line with the intent to obstruct, de-rail, damage, etc, any engine, carriage etc.

Do or cause to be done..: There are other ways of obstructing, etc, a train, without actually placing a physical barrier across the line, for example, seeking to loosen a rail. Whatever the method chosen, if the intent is there, the offence will be committed.

Obstruction: The offence under Section 36 may arise from an unlawful act, or from some wilful omission or neglect. There is no requirement to prove an intention to obstruct a train. For example, a farmer has fields on either side of a railway line with a level crossing for access. If he stops his tractor on the crossing, to go back to close a gate, thus causing an oncoming train to be obstructed, he will commit this offence. He is liable because of his wilful neglect.

7.5.3 *Arrest and Punishment*
The offences under Section 35 are triable either way, but when tried on indictment carry a maximum possible sentence of life imprisonment. They are therefore arrestable offences. The offence under Section 36, which may arise through neglect rather than intent, carries a maximum of two years imprisonment. There is no specific power of arrest for this offence.

7.6 **Throwing Stones on the Railway**
British Transport Commission Act 1949, Section 56
7.6.1 *Offence*
A person commits an offence who:
  - unlawfully
  - throws, causes to strike or to fall on, against, at or into
  - any engine, tender, truck, motor or carriage
  - or any works or apparatus
  - used upon a railway or siding, or belonging to or used by a railway undertaking
  - any stone, matter or thing likely to cause injury or damage.

7.6.2 *Explanation*
Stone, matter or thing: The provisions encompass any missile or other thing, being thrown at, causing to strike against, etc.

Engine, truck... apparatus: The offence may involve not only engines and other components of trains, but equipment and apparatus used in connection with a railway, such as signals, points, overhead cables, etc, Common occurrences of the offence include throwing stones at passing trains, and dropping objects from bridges onto overhead cables or trains.

Likely to cause damage or injury: The missile or other item must be likely to cause damage to property or injury to persons. Given the speed and nature of rail traffic, injury or damage may be caused by quite small, lightweight objects.

7.7 **Actions Likely to Injure Rail Users**
Offences Against the Person Act 1861, Sections 32, 33
7.7.1 *Offences*
A person will commit an offence who shall:
  - unlawfully and maliciously
  - put or throw across any railway any wood, stone or other matter
  - or do or cause to be done any other thing
  - with intent
  - to endanger the safety of any person travelling on the railway (S 32).
Also a person will commit an offence who shall:
  - unlawfully and maliciously
  - throw or cause to fall or strike against, etc
  - any engine, truck, carriage or tender used on a railway
  - with intent
  - to injure or endanger the safety of a person in or upon such engine, truck, etc, or in a train of which it forms part (S 33).

7.7.2 *Explanation*

Action: The two offences differ in respect of the actions required to commit them. Briefly, the first involves placing something on the line, the second, throwing something at a train.

Intent: The wording differs only slightly between the two offences, in the first, the intent is to endanger safety, in the second, to injure or endanger safety. The reason for the different wording can only be guessed at – after all, how does one injure someone safely?

Comparison with damage offences: The offences are very similar in wording to the offences of causing damage or danger, and throwing stones, outlined above. These two offences are dealt with here, rather than with other offences against the person (in chapter 8), for ease of comparing the several offences involving railways.

7.7.3 *Arrest and Punishment*

These offences carry a maximum possible sentence of life imprisonment and are therefore arrestable offences.

8 CONTAMINATION OF GOODS

Public Order Act 1986 Section 38

8.1 Offence

A person commits an offence who with the intention:

  a) of causing public alarm or anxiety, or
  b) of causing injury to members of the public consuming or using the goods, or
  c) of causing economic loss to any person by reason of the goods being shunned by members of the public, or
  d) of causing economic loss to any person by reason of steps taken to avoid any such alarm or anxiety, injury or loss:
   – contaminates or interferes with goods
   – or makes it appear that goods have been contaminated or interfered with
   – or places goods which have been contaminated or interfered with in a place where goods of that description are consumed, used, sold or otherwise supplied.

8.1.1 *Explanation*

Intention: There are four separate intentions, any one of which will constitute the mens rea for the offence. An offence may involve more than one of these, as where a person sprinkles flour over fresh fruit in a supermarket, and leaves leaflets bearing the message 'Contaminated with rat poison', the intentions being to alarm customers, to stop them buying the fruit, and to cause the management to destroy the fruit in order to allay public anxiety.

Action: There are three different actions, any one of which may form the actus reus of the offence. In theory, the four intentions and three actions give a possible 12 ways of committing the offence, but one combination is not viable – to make it appear that goods have been contaminated with the intention of causing injury.

Goods: The term 'goods' includes natural and manufactured substances, whether or not incoprporated in or mixed with other goods. The term is not restricted to goods intended for human consumption.

In a place...: One way of committing the offence is to place contaminated items in a place where such items are eaten, sold, supplied, etc. It will presumably not be an offence, therefore, to place a cabbage which has been interfered with in a baker's shop, since cabbages are not sold or supplied there.

8.2 **Threats**
It is an offence for a person:
- with any of the intentions mentioned at (a), (c) or (d) in paragraph 8.1
- to threaten that he or another will do any of the actions mentioned there
- or claim that he or another has done any such act.

8.2.1 *Explanation*
Intention: One cannot intend to injure someone by making threats, so intention (b) is not included, for the purposes of this offence.

Will do/has done: The offence may be committed, either by claiming that an offence of contamination has been carried out, or threatening that such action will be taken in future.

8.3 **Possession of Articles**
A person commits an offence if:
- with a view to the commission an offence of contamination of goods
- he has in his possession
- materials to be used for contaminating or interfering with goods, or making it appear that they have been contaminated or interfered with, or
- goods which have been contaminated or interfered with, or which appear to have been contaminated or interfered with.

8.3.1 *Explanation*
Future offence: This offence relates to the commission of an offence of contamination, not to an offence which has been committed in the past.

Materials: Any material to be used to contaminate goods, or to make it appear that they have been contaminated, will do, for this offence to be committed.

Goods themselves: One of the ways of committing the main offence, is by putting items which have been contaminated, or which appear to be, in a place where such goods are eaten, sold, etc. Being in possession of a jar of jam which has had broken glass put in it, intending to place the jar on a shelf full of jars of jam in a shop, will amount to this offence.

8.4 **Arrest**
These are arrestable offences.

Keynote Cases

9.1 **Case One: Property**
   ***R v Whiteley* [1991] Crim LR 436**
Problem
What if the property has been rearranged rather than broken, but in so doing the information held on the material has been destroyed?

Circumstances
Whiteley was a computer hacker who obtained unauthorised access to a computer network. He used and deleted files within that system. It was argued on Whiteley's behalf that it is impossible to damage what is effectively two separate entities, the computer disc and the magnetic particles on the disc. All that he had done was rearrange the particles, none had been damaged or destroyed, nor had the surface of the computer disc which held the magnetic particles. These particles are so small that they cannot be seen easily even with the help of a microscope.

These arrays of magnetic particles held patterns which were intangible and could not be damaged under the provisions of subsection's 1 and 10. Whiteley was convicted and appealed.

The appeal was dismissed on the basis that Section 10 does not state that damage to tangible property has to be tangible in itself. The fact that the damage could not be perceived by human senses without operating the computer, does not detract from the fact that Whiteley had intentionally and unlawfully altered the particles to impair the usefulness of the disc to the owner of it.

Decision
That damage is done to an article need not be capable of being perceived by human senses. If it impairs the function of the article, it must be treated as damage even if it is repairable.

Comment
The Computer Misuse Act 1990 now provides that modifications to the programming (software) content of a computer, not affecting the physical condition of the computer or its storage medium, shall not amount to criminal damage. The relevance of this case decision is that damage itself does not have to be tangible, so long as the property damaged is itself tangible (for details of the Computer Misuse Act 1990, see Chapter 37).

9.2 Case Two: Section 5(2) Defence
8.2 *R v Hill* [1988] TLR October 6th
Problem
How remote does the fear of greater damage have to be to provide a defence?

Circumstances
Hill was arrested in possession of a hacksaw blade at a political rally near to a major defence establishment. She claimed that she had the blade to get into the establishment to prevent a greater harm to mankind by the use of weapons within the premises. She claimed a defence under Section 5(2) effectively that if she caused minimal damage, a greater harm would be avoided to her and others. She was convicted at first instance and appealed.

On appeal the court confirmed the conviction saying that the trial judges summing of the case had been properly given. The jury had been directed to consider objectively whether Hill had intended to protect her own or other's property by her actions. The conclusions, that the action was merely part of a political campaign, and that the causative relationship between the acts and alleged protection were tenuous and nebulous, were correct. The test of immediacy of protection applies; there must be some threat of damage which is imminent for the defendant to have a claim that her action was for protection of property belonging to her or another.

Decision
The use of the defence under Section 5(2) of the Criminal Damage Act 1971 requires some imminent danger to property before it will apply.

Comment
The case highlights the need for there to be a real and present threat of damage to property to allow or justify causing damage to prevent a greater harm. An example would be causing damage to gain entry to premises to fight a fire believed to have broken out there.

9.3 Case Three: Damage to Recover Own Property
Lloyd v DPP [1991] TLR 28th June
Problem
Will a person be liable, who causes damage in order to recover his own property?

Circumstances

Lloyd had parked his car in a private parking area, there were notices stating that cars left without authority would be clamped and that release of the vehicles could be obtained on payment of £25. When Lloyd returned to his vehicle he found that it had been clamped and he was unable to move. He decided to break the locks holding the clamp and extricated his vehicle. Lloyd was convicted of causing criminal damage.

Lloyd's appeal was dismissed. An earlier, unrelated case, Stear v Scott was indistinguishable. The court were bound by the decision that where someone brought his chattel (car) onto another's land by trespass he had no right to use force where another means of recovery was available. If Lloyd had wished to argue the issue of the legality of wheel clamping and trespass to his car he should have paid the £25 charge and then taken a civil case on trespass to property at county court for a ruling.

Decision

The use of force (cutting locks on clamps) is not justified in a dispute over whose property was being trespassed against, (land or car). The correct course is to take the matter to civil court.

Comments

Trespass to property is a tort, or civil wrong. Any action done against a person's right to treat his own property in a way he would wish amounts potentially to trespass to property. The criminal law also protects property from intentional damage; preferably the two should be kept distinct, but there may be some overlap. Even if the police decide not to proceed with a case of damage to property, the owner still has a right to seek damages (financial compensation) in the civil courts. This decision is the opposite of that of the Scottish Courts, where the immobilisation of a car has been held to be appropriation for theft *(see Black v Carmichael [1992])*.

9.4 Case Four: Intention and Recklessness
R v Caldwell [1981] 1 All ER 961
Problem

What is recklessness for criminal damage?

Circumstances

Caldwell had been working at a hotel and had been upset by the manager. In a drunken state he set fire to a room to get back at his employer. He was indicted on two counts of causing damage, one of which included endangering life or being reckless as to whether life would be endangered. Caldwell had said that at the time he was so drunk he could not remember thinking whether anyone was in the hotel or not, it simply did not cross his mind. At his first trial the recorder directed the jury that self induced drunkenness was no defence. Caldwell was convicted on count one which included the more serious offence of endangering life. He appealed. At the appeal court the decision on count one was reversed as the direction on self induced drunkenness was incorrect.

This unfortunately left the law in a difficult state as regards self induced drunkenness and recklessness. Both issues were then subject of appeal to the House of Lords on the following grounds:

'Whether evidence of self-induced intoxication can be relevant to the following questions:
a) Whether the defendant intended to endanger the life of another; and
b) Whether the defendant was reckless as to whether the life of another would be endangered, within the meaning of Section 1(2)(b) of the Criminal damage Act 1971.'

In relation to the first part of the question as relates to drunkenness and intention Lord

Diplock stated, (he was supported in this statement by the majority of the other Law Lords):

    a) ' if the charge of an offence under Section 1(2) was so framed as to charge the defendant only with intending by the destruction or damage to endanger the life of another, evidence of self induced intoxication can be relevant to his defence; but

    b) if the charge is, or includes a reference to his being reckless as to whether the life of another would thereby be endangered, evidence of self intoxication is not relevant.'

The second part of the question is what would amount to recklessness:

    'if it can be shown that he committed an act which creates an obvious risk that property would be destroyed or damaged and when he commits that act he either gives no thought to the possibility of there being a risk, or, having recognised that was such a risk he carried on regardlessly'.

The appeal was dismissed.

9.5 Case Five: Recklessness and Intention in Attempt Cases
Attorney General's Reference (No3 1992) [1992] TLR 18th November
Problem

Where an attempt occurs, what is required to prove the mens rea for damage?

Circumstances

A petrol bomb was thrown at a car, with the intention of setting fire to it. There were persons in the car at the time. Although the petrol bomb was thrown, no damage was caused. The defendant was charged with an offence of attempting to commit aggravated arson (i.e. attempting to cause damage by fire, being reckless as to whether life would thereby be endangered). The defendant was discharged at Crown Court on the grounds that, for an attempt to commit the aggravated damage offence, there was a need to prove an intention to endanger life; an intention to cause damage coupled with recklessness as to whether life was thereby endangered was not sufficient *mens rea* for the attempt. The Attorney General referred the case to the Court of Appeal on the point of law, whether an attempt to commit a crime is made out when recklessness, rather than intent, is proved.

    The Court of Appeal held that it was sufficient to prove recklessness on the part of a defendant as to whether life would be endangered. For the full offence of aggravated damage, the prosecution had to prove that the defendant damaged property whilst in a state of mind where he was reckless as to whether the life of another would be endangered. Here, although the damage to property was intended but not achieved, the mental state of the defendant contained everything required to render him guilty of the full offence. Comment was passed that the mens rea for rape and attempted rape were also the same (as in *R v Khan* [1990]).

Decision

If recklessness is sufficient for mens rea in the full offence of damage with intent to endanger life, as with rape and attempt rape where recklessness occurs as to consent, both the attempt and the full offence are satisfied by the same reckless state of mind.

Comment

This decision clarifies the mental state required for offences of attempt where recklessness is required rather than intention.

Chapter 15: Explosives

Note: It has been decided to deal with all offences involving explosives in one chapter, rather than splitting them into offences against people and offences against property. Such crimes are likely to come to notice as a result of a loud bang (or, preferably, by the discovery of an unexploded device) rather than by the criminal announcing his motive. Once the dust has settled, read through this chapter to identify offences committed.

1 UNLAWFUL USE AND POSSESSION OF EXPLOSIVES
Explosive Substances Act 1883

1.1 Introduction
The Act provides for a range of offences, from causing an explosion, through attempting to do so, to possession under suspicious circumstances.

1.2 Causing an Explosion
Explosive Substances Act 1883 Section 2

1.2.1 *Offence*
A person commits an offence who:
  - in the United Kingdom or (being a citizen of the United Kingdom or Colonies) in the Republic of Ireland
  - unlawfully and maliciously
  - causes by any explosive substance an explosion
  - of a nature likely to endanger life or cause serious injury to property
  - whether any injury to person or property has actually been caused or not.

1.2.2 *Explanation*
UK or Ireland: When an explosion occurs in this country, the nationality of the criminal is immaterial. However, a citizen of this country (or any of the Colonies, not that there are many of those left) will also be liable in this country for an offence committed in the Irish Republic.

Unlawfully and maliciously: A demolition contractor would be acting lawfully in blowing up a derelict building; otherwise, there are few examples of lawful explosions likely to cause injury or damage. 'Maliciously' means an awareness that some harm may be caused. Whilst this could amount to an actual intention to do the sort of harm which was done, it is not necessary that the offender should have foreseen the full seriousness of his actions. Foreseeing that minor harm may result will do (*R v Mowatt* (1968)).

Whether a person intends or foresees the likelihood that harm will be caused will be a matter for the court to decide. However, this decision must be reached having regard to Section 8, Criminal Justice Act 1967, which lays down a subjective test, related to an individual accused. He shall not be held to have acted maliciously solely because what happened was the natural and probable consequence of his actions; the court must decide whether he intended or foresaw the consequences by reference to all the evidence, including the accused's own characteristics.

Explosive substance: The term is defined in the Act as including:
- any materials for making any explosive substance
- any apparatus, machine, implement or materials used or intended to be used or adapted, for causing or aiding in causing any explosion in or with an explosive substance
- also any part of such apparatus, machine or implement.

There must be evidence of adaptation or intent, otherwise innocent articles such as bags of fertiliser or alarm clocks would fall within the scope of explosive substance.

Causes an explosion: For this offence to be committed, there must be an explosion. It must be substantial enough to be likely to endanger life or cause serious damage.

Whether... or not: Although the offence will not be committed unless there is a substantial explosion, there is no need that anyone is thereby endangered or that any damage is caused.

1.2.3 *Arrest*
This offence carries a maximum of life imprisonment and is a serious arrestable offence for the purposes of the Police and Criminal Evidence Act 1984.

1.3 **Attempt or Intention to Cause Explosion**
Explosive Substances Act 1883 Section 3

1.3.1 *Offence*
A person commits an offence who:
- in the United Kingdom, or (he being a citizen of the United Kingdom or Colonies) in the Republic of Ireland
- unlawfully and maliciously:
  a) does any act with intent to cause, or conspires to cause:
    - by any explosive substance
    - an explosion of a nature likely to endanger life or to cause serious injury to property
    - in the United Kingdom or the Republic of Ireland; **or**
  b) makes or has in his possession or under his control an explosive substance:
    - with intent by means thereof
    - to endanger life or cause serious injury to property
    - or to enable any other person to do so
    - whether in the United Kingdom or the Republic of Ireland
    - whether any explosion takes place or not and whether any injury to person or property is actually caused or not.

1.3.2 *Explanation*
Does with intent: This offence falls one step short of that under Section 2, in that there is no necessity that an explosion occurs. To do something with intent to cause the explosion, or to conspire to do so, will amount to an offence.

Makes... possession or control... enable another: A series of people could commit the offence in sequence. The first person makes up an explosive substance, a second has possession or control while delivering it to a third who places the explosive intending to blow up some property.

1.3.3 *Arrest*

This offence carries a maximum of life imprisonment and is therefore an arrestable offence.

1.4 **Suspicious Circumstances**
Explosive Substances Act 1883 Section 4

1.4.1 *Offence*

A person commits an offence who:
- makes or knowingly has in his possession or under his control
- any explosive substance
- under such circumstances as to give rise to reasonable suspicion that he is not making it or does not have possession or control of it for a lawful object
- unless he can show that he did make, have or control it for a lawful object.

1.4.2 *Explanation*

Lawful object: The lawful purpose need not be one which is lawful in this country; it may be a purpose which is lawful in the country where it is intended to use the explosive substance. *(Keynote Case: R v Berry (1984))*

Unless he can show: Once the prosecution is able to establish reasonable ground to suspect that the explosive is not intended for a lawful use, the onus is then on the accused to show some lawful object for making the explosive substance, or having possession or control over it, as the case may be.

1.4.3 *Arrest*

This offence carries a maximum of 14 years' imprisonment and therefore is an arrestable offence.

1.5 **Aid and Abet Offences**
Explosive Substances Act 1883 Section 5

1.5.1 *Offence*

A person will be liable who:
- within Her Majesty's dominions or (being a subject of Her Majesty) without
- by supply of or solicitation for money
- or providing premises or supplying materials
- or in any manner whatsoever
- procures, counsels, aids, abets or is an accessory to the commission of any crime under this Act.

1.5.2 *Explanation*

Here and abroad: A person of any nationality may be liable for actions in this country. A citizen of this country may be liable in our courts for actions abroad.

Money, premises, materials: Anyone who, by giving assistance or material, or who procures, etc, in any other way, will be liable.

1.5.3 *Arrest*

For an offence under this Section a person is liable to the same punishment as for the principal offender. Therefore this is an arrestable offence, like those mentioned above.

1.6 Powers of Entry, Search and Seizure

In relation to all the crimes under the 1883 Act, the powers given to police under Sections 73 – 75 of the Explosives Act 1875 shall apply *(see paragraph 3)*.

2 INJURY, INTENTION TO CAUSE INJURY
Offences Against the Person Act 1861

2.1 Introduction

There are several related offences involving use of explosives, each offence requiring one or more of the ingredients – explosion, bodily injury caused, or intention to cause bodily injury by use of explosives.

2.2 Cause Serious Injury by Explosives
Offences Against the Person Act 1861 Section 28

2.2.1 *Offence*

The offence is committed by a person who:
- unlawfully and maliciously
- by the explosion of any gunpowder or other explosive substance
- burns, maims, disfigures, disables or does any grievous bodily harm to any person.

2.2.2 *Essential Ingredient(s)*

An explosion and injury.

2.3 Explosions, Dangerous Substances, etc
Offences Against the Person Act 1861 Section 29

2.3.1 *Offence*

The offence is completed when someone:
- unlawfully and maliciously
- causes gunpowder or other explosive substance to explode
- with intent to burn, maim, disfigure, disable or cause grievous bodily harm to anyone
- whether any bodily injury is caused or not.

2.3.2 *Essential Ingredient(s)*

Explosion and intent.

2.4 Placing Explosives with Intent to Injure
Offences Against the Person Act 1861 Section 30

2.4.1 *Offence*

The offence is committed where a person:
- unlawfully and maliciously
- places or throws in, into, upon, against or near any building, ship or vessel
- any gunpowder or other explosive substance
- with intent to do bodily injury to anyone
- whether or not any explosion takes place or whether any injury is caused or not.

2.4.2 *Essential Ingredient(s)*
Intention to cause bodily injury.

2.5 **Explanation**
Seriousness: The three offences form a progression in seriousness of consequence – causing injury by an explosion, causing an explosion with intent to injure, and finally placing explosives with intent to injure without an explosion necessarily occurring.

Unlawfully and maliciously: This element appears also in the 1883 Act *(for explanation see paragraph 1.2.2)*.

Arrest: All are arrestable offences.

3 POLICE POWERS OF SEARCH AND SEIZURE

3.1 **With Warrant**
Explosives Act 1875 Section 73

3.1.1 *Grounds for Issue*
A magistrate may issue a warrant upon information on oath:
- that there are reasonable grounds for believing
- that an offence with respect to an explosive has been or is being committed
- in any place (whether a building or not, carriage, boat or ship).

3.1.2 *Powers Under the Warrant*
The warrant will authorise a constable:
- to enter the place at any time (including Sunday)
- using force if necessary
- examine the place and search for explosives therein
- and take samples of any explosive or ingredients of an explosive.

3.2 **Superintendent's Written Order**
Explosives Act 1875 Section 73

A superintendent or other police officer of equal or higher rank:
- may issue a written order giving the same authority as a warrant
- if the case is one of emergency
- **and** delay in obtaining a warrant would be likely to endanger life.

3.3 **Explanation**
Grounds for issue: The same grounds apply to a written order as to a warrant; the superintendent or above must be satisfied (but not by information on oath, obviously) that there is reason to believe an offence involving an explosive is being or has been committed.

Offence: These provisions apply to any offence with respect to an explosive, under whatever Act.

Written order: A senior police officer may issue a written order only if both conditions are met, that the situation is one of emergency and that delay would endanger life. The term 'emergency' is not defined; the delay factor may vary depending on the time of day.

3.4 Power to Search – Explosives in Transit
Explosives Act 1875 Section 75

3.4.1 *Powers*
1) A chief officer of police:
   - for the purpose of seeing whether provisions relating to the conveyance, loading, unloading and importation of explosives are being complied with
   - may enter, inspect and examine any wharf, carriage, ship, store, etc
   - where there is reason to suppose an explosive to be
   - but not so as to obstruct the work or business concerned.

2) If an offence is discovered, there is a power to seize, detain and remove the explosive and the carriage, boat, etc, concerned.

3) There is a further power to stop any ship or carriage – other than a railway carriage – to inspect it if there is reason to believe the case is one of emergency.

3.4.2 *Explanation*
Chief officer of police: Presumably the chief officer may take along some officers of lower rank to assist.

Provisions relating to... explosives: It is unlikely that many chief officers of police will wish to go into a firework factory to see whether safety regulations are being complied with, a task better left to qualified inspection people. However, these powers may be useful in an emergency situation or where criminal offences are suspected.

Extent of powers: Every officer acting under this Section shall have the same powers as under a warrant *(see paragraph 3.1.2)*.

3.5 Seizure and Detention of Explosives
Explosives Act 1875 Section 74

3.5.1 *Powers*
1) Where any constable:
   - has reasonable cause to believe that any explosive or ingredient of an explosive, or substance, found by her is liable to forfeiture under this Act
   - she may seize and detain it until a magistrates' court has ruled on whether it is liable to forfeiture.

2) The officer seizing the explosive may require the occupier of the place where it is found either to keep it there, or to move it in a manner and to such a place as is least likely to endanger the public.

3) Where the matter appears to be urgent, involving serious public danger, a superintendent or above may cause it to be destroyed or rendered harmless.

4) If a person fails to comply with police instructions, or tampers with, alters etc any seized item, he will commit an offence.

3.5.2 *Explanation*
Explosives may be more safely dealt with by experts than by police officers, but these powers could be useful in emergency situations, for example, the power to require that the explosive should remain where it is, not to be tampered with.

Keynote Cases

4.1 *R v Berry* [1984] 3 WLR 1274

Problem
The meaning of 'lawful object' and the burden of proof thereof, in relation to possession of an explosive substance in suspicious circumstances, contrary to Section 4, Explosive Substances Act 1883.

Circumstances
The accused had produced a quantity of timing devices which were intended to be supplied to customers in the Middle East. There was prosecution evidence which was not refuted, that the devices were for use in making time-bombs. The accused's defence was that although there may be no lawful use for such devices in this country, 'lawful object' could include a use which was lawful abroad; and, the prosecution had not proved that there was no such lawful use in the countries to which the devices were intended to be sent.

Decision
The court accepted that 'lawful object' could refer to a purpose which was lawful in another country although not lawful here. However, the onus is clearly placed on the defence to show what the lawful object is. The onus is not on the prosecution to show that there are no possible lawful uses of such a device in a foreign country.

Comment
Once it is established that the accused has made or knowingly has possession of an explosive substance in suspicious circumstances, the onus is then on the defence to show that he had the substance for some lawful purpose.

This case involved timing devices, a reminder that the term 'explosive substance' extends beyond substances which are explosives in themselves, to include equipment to be used in conjunction with explosives to cause explosions.

In this case, the accused had made a number of timing devices, and there was clear evidence that the purpose of these devices was for use in making bombs. However, it is for the accused to show that there was a lawful object.

Chapter 16: Public Order Offences

1 BREACH OF THE PEACE
Common Law

1.1 Introduction
The law has for centuries provided a means of dealing with a person who might breach the peace, but 'breach of the peace' is not an offence as such, in that there is no penalty which may be imposed for causing a breach of the peace. Today, statutes provide a number of offences which may attract a fine or prison sentence, etc, but breach of the peace remains worth considering, not least for the power of arrest which goes with it.

1.2 Meaning of Terms
'The Peace', or as it is more usually referred to, 'the Queen's Peace', means the normal peaceful state of society, in which each of us is able to go about our business without unjustified interference from others. A breach of the peace arises when:
- harm is actually done to a person; or
- harm is caused to a person's property in his presence; or
- harm is **likely** to be done to a person, or to his property in his presence; or
- a person is in fear of suffering harm, to himself or to his property in his presence.
 (Keynote Case: R v Howell (1981))

A breach of the peace may arise if any of these alternatives occur in a private place, as well as in a public place.

1.3 Power of Arrest
The power of arrest provides, not only for a present breach of the peace, but also for one which has happened in the past, or may happen in the future, in that any person – constable or other citizen – may arrest for a breach of the peace where:
- a breach of the peace is committed in his presence; or
- a breach of the peace has already been committed and he reasonably believes that there is a threat of its being renewed; or
- although a breach of the peace has not yet been committed, he reasonably believes that a breach will be committed in the immediate future by the person to be arrested.
 (Keynote Case: R v Howell (1981))

The power of arrest may well be available for breach of the peace where arrest for a statutory offence is not available. As a means of 'defusing' a conflict situation, a constable may have to resort to this power.

1.4 Procedure After Arrest
A person arrested for a breach of the peace may not be charged with or prosecuted for breach of the peace as an offence. Instead, he must be brought before a magistrates' court where he may be **bound over** to keep the peace. This means that he has to enter into a recognisance, with or without sureties, to keep the peace, or to be of good behaviour. When there has been a breach of the peace, this procedure is intended as a means of preventing a recurrence.

1.5 **Bail**

Under the provisions of the Police and Criminal Evidence Act 1984, bail may be granted by police to a person who has been arrested for an offence. Such person may be bailed to court after charge, or to return to the police station at a later date. A person arrested for a breach of the peace will not be eligible for bail, not having been arrested for an offence. From a practical point of view, on a Saturday night it may be preferable to arrest a person for one of the several statutory public order offences, then charge and bail him, than arrest him for breach of the peace and keep him in custody all weekend.

2 **RIOT**
Public Order Act 1986   Section 1

2.1 **Offence**

The offence is committed where:
  - 12 or more persons who are present together
  - use or threaten unlawful violence
  - for a common purpose
  - and the conduct of them (taken together) is such as would cause a person of reasonable firmness present at the scene
  - to fear for his personal safety
  - then any of these persons who uses unlawful violence for the common purpose is guilty of riot.

2.1.1 *Explanation*

Riot is at the top of a scale of public order offences which are distinguished by the number of offenders involved and the degree of violence used or threatened.

Present together, common purpose: The 12 or more people must be together for a purpose. If six people are threatening violence for one purpose, and six for some other reason, this would not amount to a riot.

The common purpose may be inferred from the conduct of the persons gathered (Section 1(3)). Thus, where a crowd of football supporters are surging down the street shouting threats towards a group of rival supporters, this conduct may give rise to the inference that the common purpose is to attack the rival fans.

Conduct taken together: This recognises that whereas one individual's threats on his own may not be enough to frighten a reasonably firm person, the effect of a crowd acting in a threatening manner is quite different.

Would cause: The law provides that for the purposes of a prosecution, there is no need for any person of reasonable firmness actually to be present at the scene or even be likely to be there (Section 1(4)). If 20 people are gathered outside a house threatening to cause injury to the occupier, the fact that the house is empty at the time will not amount to a defence.

Fear for personal safety: The fear must be for the safety of a person. Thus, if threats are directed towards damaging property, it could be that there is no riot, but it is the perception of those witnessing the behaviour which counts. It would not absolve an accused from guilt if he said, 'Perhaps people were frightened but they should not have been because we only intended to smash up the pub, not to hurt anyone.'

Unlawful violence: The violence threatened or used must be unlawful. Twenty bailiffs threatening to smash the door down to evict trespassers from premises under the terms of a court order would rightly claim that the violence threatened was not unlawful. Likewise, police officers may have cause to threaten violence in certain circumstances, e.g. by displaying banners or giving verbal warnings during a public disorder situation, but so long as the violence proposed is no more than is required to effect an arrest or prevent a crime, this element of riot will be missing.

Use or threaten violence: It may assist understanding to consider two distinct elements – when there is 'a riot' – and who commits the offence. The riot will occur when there are at least 12 people present together who use or threaten unlawful violence for a common purpose in a way which would cause fear in a reasonable person. The threat of violence will go towards creating 'a riot', but the offence will not be committed unless one of the number actually uses unlawful violence.

If 20 people threaten violence and one person actually uses violence, then that one person commits the offence of riot, so long as the common purpose, etc, can be proved; the fact that the others are present making threats provides some of the essential elements for the offence, for without their threats there would be no riot.

It is not necessary that 12 or more persons use or threaten violence simultaneously. In the extreme example, if there were 12 people who took it in turns to shout threats, one at a time, this would be enough to satisfy this element (Section 1(2)).

The term 'violence' is not restricted to violence directed against a person, but may include violence towards property, i.e. causing or intended to cause damage.

In addition, the term is not restricted to conduct causing or intended to cause injury or damage, it will also include other violent conduct, such as throwing a stone capable of causing injury but which falls short (Section 8).

2.2 **Public or Private**

The offence of riot may take place in a private as well as in a public place.

2.3 **Guilty of Riot**

A person will be guilty of the offence if he actually uses unlawful violence for the common purpose. For an accused to be guilty of riot it must be proved either:

– it was that person's intention to use that violence; **or**
– he was aware that his conduct may be violent.

2.4 **Intoxication**
Public Order Act 1986 Section 6(5)

When a person's awareness is impaired by intoxication – he shall be taken to be aware to the same extent as he would had he not been intoxicated – unless he shows – either that his intoxication was not self-induced – or that it was caused solely by a substance taken or administered in the course of medical treatment.

Thus, if an accused claims he was not aware that his conduct may be violent because he had consumed 12 pints of lager, or that his 6 pints had affected him more than usual because of the medicine prescribed for him, he will be deemed to have been aware that his conduct may be violent to the same extent as he would have been aware if sober. However, if he shows that someone 'spiked' his drink, or that his condition was solely due to abnormal reaction to medication, he may have a defence.

2.5 Power of Arrest

Riot is an arrestable offence.

2.6 Consent to Prosecute

By its very nature, the offence of riot arises in what are sure to be confused and confusing circumstances. The evidence has to be that, amid a large number of people using or at the very least, threatening, violence, the accused used violence for the common purpose. In many cases, evidence will be more readily forthcoming for a lesser offence. Perhaps for these reasons, the consent of the Director of Public Prosecutions is required to prosecute riot.

3 VIOLENT DISORDER
Public Order Act 1986 Section 2

3.1 Offence

Where 3 or more persons who are present together:
  - use or threaten unlawful violence
  - and the conduct of them (taken together) is such as would cause a person of reasonable firmness present at the scene to fear for his personal safety
  - each person using or threatening unlawful violence is guilty of the offence of violent disorder.

3.1.1 *Explanation*

3 or more: For this offence, the degree of violence required is slightly less than for riot, and fewer people are required. In terms of numbers, this offence may be looked on as a 'mini-riot'.

Present together: The people concerned must be together. However, there is no need for a common purpose as was the case for riot. As with riot, the offence may be committed in a private or a public place.

Use or threaten: It is immaterial whether the persons concerned use or threaten violence simultaneously or not.

Guilty of violent disorder: To be guilty of riot, a person actually has to use unlawful violence; for this offence it suffices that there is a threat, not necessarily use, of unlawful violence. 'Violence' may be to person or property, as for riot. The provision concerning awareness and intoxication apply, as in the case of riot.

Power of Arrest: Violent disorder is an arrestable offence.

4 AFFRAY
Public Order Act 1986 Section 3

4.1 Offence

A person commits the offence of affray:
  - if he uses or threatens unlawful violence towards another
  - and his conduct is such as would cause a person of reasonable firmness present at the scene to fear for his personal safety.

4.1.1 *Explanation*

This offence moves down in terms of participants, but the violence required is more restricted in scope than for riot or violent disorder.

Use or threaten: For the purposes of affray, a threat cannot be by words alone (Section 3(3)). A threat could be a combination of actions and words, or actions alone.

If two or more persons are involved, and use or threaten unlawful violence, it is the conduct of them taken together which has to be considered.

Violence towards another: For the purposes of affray, violence does not include violence towards property, as it does with riot and violent disorder.

Guilty of affray: The provisions relating to awareness and intoxication apply to affray, as to riot and violent disorder.

4.1.2 *Power of Arrest*

A constable may arrest without warrant anyone she reasonably suspects is committing an affray.

5 COMPARISON OF RIOT, VIOLENT DISORDER AND AFFRAY

The three offences of riot, violent disorder and affray are compared on the table (below) to highlight differences and similarities.

Attribute	**Riot**	**Violent Disorder**	**Affray**
Minimum number	12	3	1
Present together	Yes	Yes	n/a
Common purpose	Yes	not required	n/a
Unlawful violence	person or property	person or property	personal only
Reasonable person	need not be present	need not be present	need not be present
Those guilty	actually use violence	use or threaten violence	use or threaten violence
Awareness/ Intoxication	provisions apply	provisions apply	provisions apply
Private or public	Yes	Yes	Yes
Arrest	Arrestable offence	Arrestable offence	Statutory power

6 THREATENING BEHAVIOUR
Public Order Act 1986 Section 4

6.1 Offence
A person commits an offence who either:

1) uses threatening, abusive or insulting words or behaviour towards another person; or
2) distributes or displays to another person any writing, sign or other visible representation which is threatening, abusive or insulting with intent either:
   - to cause that person to believe that immediate unlawful violence will be used (against himself or another) by any person; or
   - whereby that person is likely to believe that such violence will be used; or
   - to provoke the immediate use of unlawful violence by that person or another; or
   - whereby it is likely that such violence will be provoked.

6.1.1 *Explanation*
Towards another person: The behaviour, or display must be directed at someone. Thus, the offence would not be committed by a man walking down an empty street waving a banner with insulting words on it.

Neither will the offence be committed when threatening words are spoken to one person but the threat is directed towards another person, who is not within hearing of the words (*Atkin v DPP* (1989)).

However, there is no requirement that the person against whom the accused's attention is directed should feel abused, threatened or insulted (*Parkin v Norman* (1982)).

Threatening, abusive or insulting: The word 'insulting' is to be given its every day meaning, it would be unwise to seek to lay down positive rules for the recognition of insulting behaviour (*Brutus v Cozens* (1972)).

Conduct may be insulting even though it is not aimed at a particular person, if in fact it could be insulting to any member of the public who might see it (*Masterson and Another v Holden* (1986)).

Intent to cause/likely to cause: The wording of the offence, in its combination of 'intention and/or likely to' etc can be confusing. Consider the offence in stages:

Stage 1 the accused **either** intends his words, behaviour or display to be threatening, abusive or insulting **or** he is aware that it may be threatening, abusive or insulting.

Stage 2 he then **either** intends one of the two results (to cause fear of violence or to provoke another person to violence) **or** such a result is likely from what the accused does (Section 6(3)).

Thus, the offence may include – intention plus intention – intention plus likelihood – awareness plus intention – or awareness plus likelihood.

Immediate unlawful violence: Each of the three words in this phrase needs to be considered:

Immediate: This does not have to be instantaneous, but must be shortly afterwards (*R v Horseferry Road Metropolitan Magistrate (ex parte Siadatan)* (1991)). Thus, if the intention is to put the victim in fear of being assaulted at some future date, this will not be 'immediate' for the purposes of the Section.

Unlawful: As in the case of the other offences outlined in preceding paragraphs, the violence (intended or likely) to be feared or caused must be unlawful, so a threat of lawful violence, e.g. by a police officer in respect of an arrest, or by a person in self-defence, need not be unlawful.

Violence: As for the offences of riot and violent disorder, this includes violence towards property, as well as towards a person (Section 8).

6.2 **Place Committed**

The offence may be committed in public or in private, but there is one important exception – no offence is committed where the words or behaviour are used or the writing, etc, distributed or displayed by a person inside a dwelling – and the other person (to whom it is directed) is also inside the same or another dwelling (Section 4(2)).

Thus, a person leaning out of the window of his flat, shouting threats at a neighbour standing in the doorway of another flat, will not commit the offence. Likewise, a dispute between two people in the same dwelling will not give rise to this offence.

For this purpose 'dwelling' means any structure or part of a structure occupied as a person's home or as other living accommodation (but will not include any part of a structure not so occupied), and extends to a tent, caravan, vehicle, vessel or other temporary or movable structure (Section 8).

A threat made by one 'stop the by-pass protestor' from his tree house to another protestor in his tent on the ground below, would not give rise to this offence because both are in their 'dwellings'.

6.3 **Arrest**

A constable may arrest without warrant anyone whom he reasonably suspects is committing the offence (Section 4(3)). This power to arrest will not apply once the person has ceased to commit the offence. However, if a resumption of the offence was feared, the power to arrest for breach of the peace might be appropriate.

6.4 **Power to Enter and Search**

The power given to constables under Section 17 of the Police and Criminal Evidence Act 1984, to enter and search premises to arrest persons suspected of arrestable or certain other offences, applies to this offence. This power is set out in more detail in *Chapter 4, paragraph 2.10* but, briefly, empowers a constable to enter and search any premises for the purposes of arresting a person for this offence, if the constable has reasonable grounds for suspecting that person to be there.

7 **CAUSING HARASSMENT, ALARM OR DISTRESS**
Public Order Act 1986 Section 4A

7.1 **Offence**

A person commits the offence if:
- with intent to cause a person harassment, alarm or distress
- he uses threatening, abusive or insulting words or behaviour
- or he uses disorderly behaviour
- or displays any writing, sign or other visible representation which is threatening, abusive or insulting
- thereby causing that or another person harassment, alarm or distress.

7.1.1 *Explanation*

With intent: In contrast to the offence under Section 4, this offence will not be committed just because an offender's behaviour is likely to cause distress, etc; there must be an intention to do so.

Harassment, alarm or distress: In the absence of any statutory definition or case decisions, these words may be interpreted as amounting to something less than the fear of immediate violence which is required for the Section 4 offence. Harassment could arise from continuously calling a person by derogatory names; distress could be caused by making a person the target for insulting language.

Threatening, abusive or insulting: These terms are the same as those used in the Section 4 offence, above.

Disorderly behaviour: This would allow for a wide range of behaviour, not necessarily falling within the meaning of 'threatening, abusive or insulting'.

Thereby causing: Not only must there be an intention to cause alarm, harassment or distress, that intention must also be achieved for the offence to be complete.

That or another person: Whilst there must be a result as well as an intention, the two elements may relate to different people. Thus, if the offender uses insulting words with the intention of causing distress to Smith, but actually causes distress to Jones, the offence is complete.

7.2 **Place Committed**

The offence may be committed in a private as well as in a public place. However, the proviso concerning dwellings applies, as it does for the Section 4 offence *(see paragraph 6 above).*

7.3 **Arrest**

A constable may arrest without warrant a person whom she reasonably suspects is committing this offence (Section 4A(4)).

7.4 **Defences**

There are two defences provided by Section 4A(3). The accused will have a defence if he proves:
  - that his conduct was reasonable; or
  - that he was inside a dwelling – and had no reason to believe that the words or behaviour used, or writing, etc, displayed would be heard or seen by a person outside that or any other dwelling.

In short, the defence is that the accused thought he was not committing the offence because he was within the scope of the 'dwelling' exception.

8 **DISORDERLY CONDUCT**
Public Order Act 1986 Section 5

8.1 **Offence**

The offence is committed when a person:
  - uses threatening, abusive or insulting words or behaviour

- or uses disorderly behaviour
- or displays any writing, sign or visible representation which is threatening, abusive or insulting
- within the hearing or sight of a person who is likely to be caused harassment, alarm or distress thereby.

8.1.1 *Explanation*

Uses words or behaviour or displays sign, etc: These terms are the same as in the Section 4A offence.

Harassment, alarm or distress: Again, these are the same terms as in Section 4A.

Person likely to be caused: It may be that the behaviour of the accused is such that most people would be likely to be distressed. Likewise, it may be that there is something about the behaviour or words used which would render a particular person more likely than others to become distressed. In either case, if someone likely to be affected by the words or behaviour is in sight or earshot, the offence will be complete.

A constable may be a person likely to be caused, harassment, alarm or distress for the purposes of this offence (*DPP v Orum* (1988)). This is important because it means that a police officer may warn a person as to conduct, and subsequently arrest a person, even though no member of the public is present.

8.2 **Place Committed**

The 'dwelling exception' applies to this offence as it does to those under Sections 4 and 4A.

8.3 **Awareness**

A person will not commit the offence unless:
- he intends his words, behaviour, writing, etc, to be threatening, abusive or insulting, or his behaviour to be disorderly, as the case may be; or
- he is aware that it may be.

In considering whether a defendant was aware that his behaviour, etc, may be threatening, abusive or insulting, the court is right to apply a subjective test, rather than an objective one. In other words, it is whether the defendant was actually aware which matters, not whether, in the circumstances, a reasonable person would have been aware. *(Keynote Case: DPP v Clarke and others (1992))*

8.4 **Intoxication**

For the purposes of assessing the awareness of an accused, the provisions relating to intoxication apply to this offence as to others under the Act *(see paragraph 2.4 above)*.

8.5 **Arrest**

(Section 5(4).)

8.5.1 *Two Stage Power*

There is a statutory power to arrest which is in two stages, an unusual feature.

A constable may arrest without warrant a person who:

- engages in offensive conduct which a constable warns him to stop
- then engages in further offensive conduct immediately or shortly after the warning.

8.5.2 *Explanation*

A constable: It is important to note that 'a' constable may give the warning to stop and then 'a' constable may arrest. This means that it may be the same constable who warns and then arrests, or that two separate police officers may be involved.

Offensive conduct: This an all-embracing term meaning conduct which the constable reasonably suspects amounts to the offence. The 'conduct' on the second occasion need not be of the same nature as the 'conduct' on the first occasion (Section 5(5)).

Thus, a constable may warn a youth for use of insulting words within the hearing of a person likely to be caused distress, then arrest the youth for using disorderly behaviour after the warning.

8.6 **Defences**

The accused has three possible defences available. He may prove:
- his conduct was reasonable; or
- he was inside a dwelling and had no reason to believe that his words, behaviour, writing, etc, would be heard or seen by a person outside that dwelling; or
- he had no reason to believe that there was any person within sight or hearing who was likely to be caused harassment, alarm or distress.

The first two of these are also available to someone accused of an offence under Section 4A.

In considering whether a defendant's behaviour is reasonable, the test to be applied by the court is an **objective** one, i.e. whether in the circumstances the defendant's behaviour, etc, may be regarded as 'reasonable', rather than a **subjective** test, taking account of whether the defendant himself regarded his actions as reasonable. *(Keynote Case: DPP v Clarke and others (1992))*

9 **STIRRING UP RACIAL HATRED**
Public Order Act 1986 Sections 18 – 23

9.1 **Introduction**

There are three offences concerned with stirring up of racial hatred – the first relates to words and behaviour, the second to distributing written material, the third to being in possession of material, written or recorded.

9.2 **Threatening, Abusive or Insulting Words or Behaviour, etc**
Public Order Act 1986 Section 18

9.2.1 *Offence*

A person who:
- uses threatening, abusive or insulting words or behaviour
- or displays any written material which is threatening, abusive or insulting
- commits an offence if
- he intends thereby to stir up racial hatred
- or having regard to all the circumstances, racial hatred is likely to be stirred up thereby.

9.2.2 *Explanation*

Threatening, abusive or insulting: These terms appear in other offences under the Act *(see above)*.

Intends or in the circumstances... is likely: When the prosecution seeks to prove not that the accused intended to stir up racial hatred, but that in the circumstances, such a result was the likely outcome of his actions, if the accused is to be guilty, it must be proved that he was aware that his words, behaviour or written display might be threatening, abusive or insulting. Thus, for the offence to be complete, the offender must either intend his actions to be abusive, threatening or insulting, or be aware that they might be.

Racial hatred: Means hatred against any group of people in Great Britain defined by reference to their colour, race, nationality (including citizenship), or ethnic or national origins (Section 17).

Written material: Includes any sign or other visible representation (Section 29).

9.3 **Publish or Distribute Written Material**
Public Order Act 1986 Section 19

9.3.1 *Offence*

A person will commit an offence if:
- he publishes or distributes written material
- which is threatening, abusive or insulting
- and **either** he intends thereby to stir up racial hatred
- **or** having regard to all the circumstances racial hatred is likely to be stirred up.

9.3.2 *Explanation*

Publish or distribute: This is confined to publishing or distributing to the public or to a Section of the public (Section 19(3)).

What amounts to 'public' is a matter of fact in any particular case. What the law used to be is useful in considering this aspect. Under the equivalent legislation prior to 1986, there was specific provision that publication by a member of a group or organisation to other members of the same group was not publication to 'the public'. Since 1986, this has no longer been a proviso. This does not necessarily mean that distribution of material by a group member to other members will be deemed to amount to distribution for the purposes of the offence; it does, however, indicate that members of a group may amount to a 'Section of the public' for the purposes of the offence.

What is clear is that publication or distribution of material to a few people will not amount to a distribution or publication to 'the public or a Section of the public'. In a case where a person left racially-offensive material at the front door of the house of a Member of Parliament, this was held not to amount to an offence, even though three other members of the MP's family saw the material. Four members of the same family, therefore, do not amount to 'a Section of the public' (*R v Britton* (1967)).

Threatening, abusive, insulting/racial hatred: These terms have the meanings described in the other offences above.

Written material: This will include any sign or other visible representation (Section 29).

9.3.3 *Defence*

An accused will have a defence if:

- he is not shown to have intended to stir up racial hatred
- and he proves that he was not aware of the content of the material and did not suspect, nor had any reason to suspect that it was threatening, abusive or insulting (Section 19(2)).

Thus, the defence will not be available where the accused is shown to have intended to stir up racial hatred, only in a case where it is shown that in the circumstances, racial hatred was likely to be stirred up. The onus is on the defence to prove, not only that the accused was not aware of the content of the material he had distributed or published, but that he did not suspect and had no reason to suspect, that it was threatening, abusive or insulting.

9.3.4 *Restriction on Proceedings*
The consent of the Attorney General is required before proceedings may be instituted for this offence (Section 27).

9.4 **Possession of Written or Recorded Material**
Public Order Act 1986 Section 23

9.4.1 *Offence*
A person commits an offence if:
- he has in his possession
- written material or a recording of visual images or sounds
- which is threatening, abusive or insulting
- with a view to (i) in the case of written material, its being displayed, published, distributed or included in a programme service, or (ii) in the case of a recording, its being distributed, shown, played or included in a programme service, whether by himself or another
- **and** either he intends racial hatred to be stirred up thereby
- or having regard to all the circumstances, racial hatred is likely to be stirred up thereby.

9.4.2 *Explanation*
The offence may be seen as having four elements:
1) Possession of material
2) The material is threatening, abusive or insulting
3) The accused has it with a view to publishing, showing it, etc
4) Either he intends by its being shown, etc, that racial hatred will be stirred up, or that would be the likely outcome of its being shown, etc.

Possession: This comes a stage before the offence under Section 19, in that the material has not been published or distributed, but the accused has it with a view to doing so.

Written or recorded: The Section 19 offence deals only with written material, which is defined as including any visible representation. This offence extends to recordings of sounds or visual images.

Publish, show, etc: The terms include some which are relevant to a recording, such as 'play'.

Programme service: Briefly, this means any television or sound broadcast, or any other service consisting of sending sounds or visual images by means of a telecommunications system (Broadcasting Act 1990, Section 201).

Intended/likely: Regard may be had to the display, etc which the accused had in view or which it may reasonably be inferred he had in view (Section 23(2)).

9.4.3 *Defence*
An accused will have a defence:
- if he is not shown to have intended to stir up racial hatred
- and he proves that he was not aware of the content of the material or recording and did not suspect, nor had any reason to suspect that it was threatening, abusive or insulting (Section 19(2)).

The defence will not be available where the accused is shown to have intended to stir up racial hatred, only in a case where it is shown that in the circumstances, racial hatred was likely to be stirred up. The onus is on the defence to prove, not only that the accused was not aware of the content of the written material or recording which he had distributed, played, etc, but that he did not suspect and had no reason to suspect, that it was threatening, abusive or insulting.

9.4.4 *Restriction on proceedings*
The consent of the Attorney General is required before proceedings may be instituted for this offence (Section 27).

9.5 **Distribute, Show or Play Recordings**
Public Order Act 1986 Section 21

9.5.1 *Offence*
This offence is committed by any person who:
- distributes, shows or plays a recording of visual images or sounds
- which are threatening, abusive or insulting
- either when he intends thereby to stir up racial hatred
- or whereby, having regard to all the circumstances, racial hatred is likely to be stirred up.

9.5.2 *Explanation*
Distribute, show, play: These terms refer to a distribution, showing or playing to the public or a Section of the public.

9.5.3 *Defence*
The same defence applies as for the offence of possession in Section 23 *(paragraph 9.4.3 above)*.

9.5.4 *Cable Broadcasts*
Cable broadcasting is not covered by Section 21, but is catered for separately in Section 22.

9.6 **Public Performance of a Play**
Public Order Act 1986 Section 20

9.6.1 *Offence*
If a public performance of a play is given:
- which involves the use of threatening, abusive or insulting words or behaviour
- any person who presents or directs the play will commit an offence if
- he intends thereby to up racial hatred
- or, having regard to all the circumstances, racial hatred is likely to be stirred up thereby.

9.6.2 *Explanation*

Public performance: This does not include a rehearsal, or a recording.

10 POLICE POWERS IN ANTICIPATION OF VIOLENCE
Criminal Justice and Public Order Act 1994 Section 60

Note: These provisions have been amended by Section 8 of the Knives Act 1997, which has not yet been brought into force. The words in italics indicate the amendments.

10.1 Authorisation

A police officer of the rank of *inspector or above*:
- may give an authorisation to exercise powers to stop and search vehicles
- where he reasonably believes that
- incidents involving serious violence may take place in a locality in his area and it is expedient to do so to prevent their occurrence; or
- *that persons are carrying dangerous instruments or offensive weapons in any locality in her police area, without good reason.*

The original provision gave power to a superintendent or above to give an authorisation, with a chief inspector or inspector able to do so when a superintendent was not readily available.

If an officer of the rank of inspector gives such an authorisation she must, as soon as practicable, cause an officer of the rank of superintendent or above to be informed.

The authorisation must be in writing, signed by the officer giving it and specifying the grounds on which it was given, the locality in which and period during which the powers may be exercised.

10.2 Area

It is for the authorising officer to determine the geographical area to which the authorisation will apply. He may wish to take account of factors such as:
- the nature and venue of the anticipated incident or activity
- the numbers of people who may be in the immediate area of any possible incident
- their access to surrounding areas
- the anticipated level of violence.

The authorising officer shall not set a geographical area wider than that he believes necessary for the purpose of preventing anticipated violence (PACE Codes of Practice (1997 edition), Code A, Section 1.8 and Note for Guidance 1G).

10.3 Time Period

The authorisation shall include the period of time during which the powers may be exercised. This period shall not exceed 24 hours in the first instance. It is for the authorising officer to determine the time period – and he should set the minimum period he considers necessary to deal with the risk of violence (PACE Codes of Practice (1997 edition), Code A, Section 1.8 and Note for Guidance 1F).

If it appears to an officer of the rank of superintendent that having regard to the offences which have, or are reasonably suspected to have been committed in connection with any activity falling within the authorisation that it is expedient to extend the period of the authorisation he may authorise that it continues for a further period of up to six hours *(24 hours)* (Section 60(3)).

Such a direction, to extend the period, may be given only once. If powers are required thereafter, a fresh authorisation will be needed (Code A, Note for Guidance 1F).

Note 1: The extension may be authorised by any officer of the rank of superintendent.

Note 2: The fact that offences involving serious violence have been committed, will be grounds for extending the period of the authorisation, as will offences which are reasonably suspected to have been committed. So, for example, when it is anticipated that two rival groups intend to engage in serious violence in an area, leading to an authorisation being made, if there are reasonable grounds to suspect that offences have occurred even though none have been reported to the police, this will afford grounds for extending the period of the authorisation.

10.4 **The Powers**

10.4.1 *Police Powers*

An authorisation confers power on any constable in uniform:
  – to stop any pedestrian and search him or anything carried by him for offensive weapons or dangerous instruments
  – to stop any vehicle and search the vehicle, its driver and any passengers for offensive weapons or dangerous instruments.

10.4.2 *Explanation*

Offensive weapon: This has the same meaning as in Section 1, Police and Criminal Evidence Act 1984, i.e. any article made or adapted for use for causing injury to persons, or intended by the person having it with him, for such by himself or someone else.

Dangerous instruments: These are instruments which have a blade or are sharply pointed (Section 60(11)).

Carrying: A person carries a dangerous instrument or offensive weapon if he has it in his possession.

Vehicle: The powers apply to ships, aircraft and hovercraft, as they do to vehicles. 'Vehicle' includes a caravan.

Reasonable suspicion not required: Code A of the PACE Codes of Practice applies to the exercise of these powers to stop and search (Codes of Practice (1997 Edition), Code A, Section 1.5(b)).

However, in exercising these powers, a constable may stop any person or vehicle and make any search he thinks fit – whether or not he suspects that the person or vehicle is carrying offensive weapons or dangerous instruments.

Thus, although Code A applies to the exercise of these powers, the provisions in that Code relating to 'reasonable suspicion' need not apply.

Power to seize articles: A constable may seize anything which she discovers during a search conducted under these provisions, which is a dangerous instrument or which she reasonably suspects to be an offensive weapon.

10.5 Record of Search

When a vehicle is stopped by a constable under this Section the driver will be entitled to obtain a written statement that the vehicle was stopped under the powers conferred by this Section. The driver must make application for this statement not later than 12 months from the day the vehicle was stopped.

A person who is searched may similarly make application for a written statement. The statement which the person searched or driver who is stopped may apply for contains only the fact of the stop; there are no details of the constable carrying out the stop, the grounds for making it, etc. However, there is a requirement to supply certain information verbally before a search, such as the officer's name, the station he is attached to, the object of the search and the grounds for making it (Codes of Practice (1997 Edition), Code A, Section 2.4).

11 PUBLIC PROCESSIONS AND ASSEMBLIES
Public Order Act 1986 Sections 11 – 14

11.1 Advance Notice to Police of a Public Procession
Public Order Act 1986 Section 11

11.1.1 *Written Notice*
Written notice must be given to the police of any proposal to hold a public procession, intended:
- to demonstrate support for, or opposition to the views or actions of any person or body of persons;
- to publicise a cause or campaign
- to mark or commemorate an event.

11.1.2 *Explanation*
Public procession: Is a procession in a public place.

Public place: This is any highway, and any other place to which the public or a section of the public have access at the material time, whether on payment or otherwise, as of right, or by virtue of expressed or implied permission.

Written notice: The notice must specify the date, time and proposed route of the procession, together with the name and address of the organiser, or one of the organisers. There is a requirement that the notice be delivered to a police station in the area where it is proposed the procession will start, not less than six clear days before the date of the procession, or as soon as is reasonably practicable.

11.1.3 *Exceptions*
There are exceptions to these requirements:
- where it is not reasonably practicable to give any advance notice of the procession
- or where the procession is one commonly or customarily held in the police area
- or where it is a funeral procession organised by a funeral director in the normal course of business.

11.1.4 *Offence*
If a public procession is held each of the persons organising it will commit an offence if:
- the requirements as to notice have not been satisfied

– or the date it is held, the time it starts or its route differ from the details specified on the written notice.

11.1.5 *Defence*

A person accused of such an offence will have a defence if he proves:
- that he did not know of and neither suspected nor had reason to suspect the failure to give notification, or change in date, time or route; or
- where the offence arises from a difference in the date, time or route – that the difference arose from circumstances outside his control or from something done with the agreement or at the direction of a constable.

11.2 Police Powers to Impose Conditions on Public Processions
Public Order Act 1986 Section 12

11.2.1 *Grounds for Imposing Conditions*

If the senior police officer:
- having regard to the time, place, circumstances or route
- reasonably believes that a proposed public procession
- may result in serious public disorder, damage to property or serious disruption to the life of the community; or
- that the purpose of the organisers is the intimidation of others with a view to compelling them not to do something they have a right to do, or to do something they have a right not to do;

the officer may give directions imposing conditions on the persons organising or taking part in the procession.

The conditions may be such as appear to her necessary to prevent such disorder, damage, disruption or intimidation. They may include conditions as to the route of the procession or prohibiting it from entering any public place specified.

11.2.2 *Senior Police Officer*

There are two categories of senior police officer:
- in the case where persons are assembling with a view to taking part in a procession, it is the most senior in rank of the police officers present at the scene
- in any other case it means – the chief officer of police who may delegate his functions to an assistant chief constable or assistant commissioner.

11.2.3 *Directions About Conditions*

When the chief officer of police gives directions under this Section, they must be in writing. However, there is no requirement that they be in writing when they are given by the senior police officer present where people are assembling.

11.2.4 *Offences*

There are three offences which may be committed:
- by a person who organises a public procession – and knowingly fails to comply with a condition imposed by the police
- by a person who takes part in a public procession – and knowingly fails to comply with such a condition;

- by a person who – incites another person to commit the second offence, i.e. as a person taking part in a procession.

11.2.5 *Defence*
In respect of the first two offences listed above, i.e. organiser or person taking part in breach of a condition, the accused will have a defence if he proves that the failure to comply with the condition arose through circumstances beyond his control.

11.2.6 *Power to Arrest*
A constable in uniform may arrest without warrant anyone he reasonably suspects is committing an offence under this Section.

11.3 **Powers to Prohibit Public Processions**
Public Order Act 1986 Section 13

11.3.1 *Grounds for Police Action*
If at any time the chief officer of police reasonably believes that:
- because of particular circumstances existing in any district or part of a district
- the power under Section 12 to impose conditions will not be sufficient to prevent the holding of public processions there resulting in serious public disorder
- she may apply to the council of that district for an order prohibiting public processions.

The application should specify a period not exceeding three months, and whether it should apply to all public processions, or of classes specified.

11.3.2 *Local Authority Action*
The council with the consent of the Secretary of State may make an order – either in the terms of the application or with modifications approved by the Secretary of State.

11.3.3 *London*
The Commissioner of the Metropolis or of the City of London will make application direct to the Secretary of State, without going through a local authority.

11.3.4 *Chief Officer of Police*
The chief officer may delegate his functions under this Section, to assistant chief constable or assistant commissioner.

11.3.5 *Offence*
There are three offences which may be committed, corresponding to those under Section 12:
  i) a person who organises a public procession – knowing that it is prohibited;
  ii) a person who takes part in a public procession – knowing that it is prohibited;
  iii) a person who incites another to commit the offence (at (ii)) of taking part in a public procession knowing it to be prohibited.

11.3.6 *Power to Arrest*
A constable in uniform may arrest without warrant anyone he reasonably suspects is committing an offence under this Section.

11.4 **Police Powers to Impose Conditions on Public Assemblies**
Public Order Act 1986 Section 14

11.4.1 *Public Assembly*
There are powers open to a senior police officer, to impose conditions on a public assembly, very similar to those which allow for conditions to be imposed on a public procession. The conditions may relate to the venue, the maximum duration and the maximum number of people who may attend. A 'public assembly' is defined as:
- an assembly of 20 or more persons
- in a public place
- which is wholly or partly open to the air (Section 16).

11.4.2 *Offences*
There are offences and power to arrest, similar to those under Section 12.

12 **PUBLIC ORDER ACT 1936**

12.1 **Introduction**
This legislation was enacted to deal with public disorder arising from political meetings, associated mainly with fascist activity in this country, at the same time that fascists were gaining in influence in Germany. Over the 60 years since the Act was passed, much of it has been replaced, but some of its provisions remain in force.

12.2 **Political Uniforms**
Public Order Act 1936 Section 1

12.2.1 *Offence*
A person commits an offence who:
- in any public place or at any public meeting
- wears a uniform
- which signifies his association with any political organisation.

12.2.2 *Explanation*
Public meeting: This is a meeting held for the purpose of discussing matters of public interest. It may be held in a public place, or in a private place if members of the public are admitted.

Public place: This means any highway and any other premises or place to which at the material time the public has or is permitted access, on payment or otherwise (Section 9).

Uniform: Although the Act defines 'public place' and 'public meeting', no definition is offered there of 'uniform' or 'political'. A uniform may consist of a particular article of clothing worn by each member of a group to signify that they are together and in association (*O'Moran v DPP* (1975)). The *O'Moran* case involved persons wearing black berets and other items, to signify association with the IRA.

Political organisation: Many organisations which have uniforms are clearly NOT political – such as the Scouts, Guides, Salvation Army, local brass band, etc, There is no guidance in the Act as to what will or will not amount to a political organisation.

12.2.3 *Arrest*
Public Order Act 1936 Section 7(3)

A constable may arrest without warrant any person he reasonably suspects to be committing an offence under Section 1.

12.2.4 *Exception*
A chief officer of police with the consent of the Secretary of State may make an order permitting the wearing of political uniforms at a ceremonial, anniversary or other special occasion.

12.2.5 *Restriction on Prosecution*
The consent of the Attorney General is required, for the continuance of the prosecution of a person charged with this offence.

12.3 **Quasi-Military Organisations**
Public Order Act 1936 Section 2

12.3.1 *Offence*
It shall be an offence for a person to take part in the control or management of, or be involved in the training of members of any association organised, trained or equipped for the purpose of enabling them to be employed:
- to usurp the functions of the police or of the armed services; or
- for the use or display of physical force in promoting any political object, or to arouse reasonable apprehension that such is their purpose.

12.3.2 *Restriction on Prosecution*
The consent of the Attorney General is required before a prosecution may be instituted.

12.3.3 *Stewards at Meetings*
Nothing in this Section is to be construed as preventing the employment of a reasonable number of stewards to assist in preserving order at a public meeting held on private premises – or their being supplied with badges or other distinguishing signs.

13 **PUBLIC MEETINGS**
Public Meeting Act 1908 Section 1

13.1 **Offence**
A person commits an offence who:
- at a lawful public meeting
- acts in a disorderly manner
- for the purpose of preventing the transaction of the business for which the meeting was called
- or incites another person to do so.

13.1.1 *Explanation*
Preventing the transaction of the business: Disorderly conduct at a meeting will not in itself amount to an offence, it must be shown that the purpose of that conduct was to prevent the business of the meeting being conducted.

It is one thing to 'heckle' a speaker at a meeting, quite another to be disruptive to such an extent that the speaker is unable to continue.

13.1.2 *Police Powers*
If a constable:
- reasonably suspects a person of committing an offence under this Section
- **and** if requested to do so by the chairman of the meeting
- the constable may require that person to declare to him immediately his name and address
- if that person refuses or fails so to declare his name and address or if he gives a false name and address he shall commit an offence.

The power does not go on to provide for arrest or expulsion from the meeting of the offender, but a situation where an offence is committed and the name and address are not known to the constable does open up the prospect of use of the general power to arrest under Section 25, Police and Criminal Evidence Act 1984.

13.4 Election Meetings
Representation of the People Act 1983 Section 97

This Section makes provisions, virtually identical to those under the Public Meeting Act 1908. The provisions relate to lawful public meetings which are either - political meetings held in a parliamentary constituency in the run up to an election – or meetings with reference to a local government election held in the area of the election.

The offences and police powers are the same as those under the Public Meeting Act 1908.

14 DISORDER IN A POST OFFICE
Post Office Act 1953 Section 65

14.1 Offence
A person commits an offence who:
- wilfully obstructs or molests, or incites someone else to obstruct or molest, a person engaged in the business of the Post Office in the execution of his duty
- or whilst in any post office or other premises belonging to or used with a post office, obstructs the course of business of the Post Office.

14.1.1 *Requirement to Leave and Police Powers*
Any person engaged in the business of the Post Office may require a person guilty of an offence under the Section to leave the post office or other premises:
- if that person refuses or fails to comply with the requirement he shall commit an offence
- and may be removed by any person engaged in the business of the Post Office
- and any constable **shall** on demand, remove or assist in removing such person.

14.1.2 *Explanation*
P(p)ost O(o)ffice: The Post Office is an organisation; a post office is a place where the public go to do business with the Post Office.

Wilfully: To commit an offence, the person's actions must be deliberate and intentional, as opposed to accidental or inadvertent. Two people standing in the post office queue chatting, may well obstruct the business of the Post Office, but will not necessarily commit an offence.

Obstruct: This need not amount to physical obstruction. Anything which makes it more difficult for a person to carry out his duties may amount to obstruction.

Require to leave/removal: The requirement to leave must be made by an employee or agent of the Post Office. Such a person, but not necessarily the same one who made the requirement, may then remove a person who refuses or fails to go. A constable must lend a hand if called on to do so.

Keynote Cases

15.1 *R v Howell* (1981) 73 Cr App R 31

Problem: i) When is a breach of the peace committed?

ii) Is there a power to arrest a person upon reasonable belief that he will commit a breach of the peace in the immediate future, although he has not yet done so?

Circumstances

Police were called to a street in Coventry in the early hours of the morning after complaints of noise from a party being held at a house in the street. The appellant, Howell, was one of a number of youths in the street who were advised by police, either to disperse or to go back into the house. After a conversation with two constables, one of them went to arrest Howell, who then violently assaulted the officer. He was charged with assault occasioning actual bodily harm and convicted at Crown Court. He appealed on grounds which included one that his arrest was unlawful because no breach of the peace had been proved against him.

Decision

In reaching its decision, the Court of Appeal defined a breach of the peace as occurring when:
   – harm is actually done to a person; or
   – harm is caused to a person's property in his presence; or
   – harm is likely to be done to a person, or to his property in his presence; or
   – a person is in fear of suffering harm, to himself or to his property in his presence.

The Court of Appeal considered case decisions and other sources relating to the power to arrest for breach of the peace. Whereas there was general agreement that a citizen, including a constable, has a power to arrest when:
   – a breach of the peace is committed in his presence; or
   – a breach of the peace has already been committed and he reasonably believes that there is a threat of its being renewed,

the Court held that the power to arrest extended to circumstances in which:
   – although a breach of the peace has not yet been committed, he reasonably believes that a breach will be committed in the immediate future by the person to be arrested.

Lord Justice Watkins, in reading the judgment, said:

'The public expects a policeman, not only to apprehend the criminal, but to do his best to prevent the commission of crime, to keep the peace. To deny him therefore, the right to arrest a person who is reasonably believed to be about to commit a breach of the peace would be to disable him from preventing that...'.

Comment

In this case, although Howell was not shown to have committed a breach of the peace prior to his arrest, if the constable had the belief, honestly held and based on reasonable grounds, that a breach of the peace was imminent, then his arrest of Howell was lawful.

15.2 *DPP v Clarke and Others* (1992) 94 Cr App R 359

Problem

In relation to a charge under Section 5, Public Order Act 1986, should the court apply an objective or a subjective test in determining:

1) whether the accused was 'aware' that his conduct may be insulting, etc; and
2) whether the accused's conduct was reasonable.

Circumstances

A number of people were engaged in a demonstration outside the premises of a private health clinic where lawful abortions were carried out. The demonstrators, who were opposed to abortion, were acting in a manner described as peaceful and not disorderly, but several of them did display pictures of an aborted foetus. Police Constable Brown warned a number of them not to display this picture and eventually arrested four of them who continued to do so after being warned. The basis of the prosecution case was that the pictures of the aborted foetus were 'abusive' and 'insulting'. PC Brown gave evidence that, as a father, he found the pictures 'insulting' to him and felt 'abused' by them. He also found the pictures 'distressing'. Each of the defendants claimed that they did not intend their conduct to be threatening, abusive or insulting, that they were not aware that their conduct might be threatening, abusive or insulting, and that their conduct was reasonable.

The magistrates found:

- that the pictures were abusive and insulting
- that Police Constable Brown was a person likely to be caused harassment, alarm or distress
- that he was in fact caused alarm and distress
- and that the defendants' conduct was not reasonable.

However, the charges were dismissed because the magistrates found that the defendants did not intend the pictures displayed to be threatening, abusive or insulting and were not aware that they might be. The prosecution appealed by way of case stated to the Divisional Court.

Decision

The decision of the Court relates to two aspects of the offence under Section 5:

- Before a person is guilty of the offence, he must either intend his conduct to be threatening, abusive or insulting, or be aware that it may be. In the absence of evidence of intent, the prosecution has to prove that the accused was 'aware' of the possible nature of his conduct. The finding of the Court was that the test of whether an accused was 'aware' that his conduct may be threatening, abusive or insulting, is a subjective one; i.e. whether he was 'aware' or not should be decided by reference to the state of mind of that person. If the evidence indicates that he was not 'aware' then he will not be guilty, even though the circumstances are such that most other reasonable people would have been 'aware' in the same circumstances.

- A person will have a defence to the charge if he proves that his conduct was reasonable. The test for deciding whether in any particular case the accused's conduct was reasonable is an objective one; i.e. reasonableness must be decided by objective standards of reasonableness. An accused's conduct will not be reasonable just because he genuinely believes it to be reasonable. If it is apparent, applying ordinary standards of behaviour, that it is not reasonable, then the defence will not succeed.

Comment

If a person arrested for a Section 5 offence claims that he was not aware that his conduct may be threatening, etc, what is relevant is what he thinks. His state of mind may be judged by reference to the whole of the evidence, including his own. The burden of proving that he was aware rests with the prosecution. This case will have implications for a police officer seeking to gather sufficient evidence to charge a person, if that person claims that he was not 'aware' that his conduct may be abusive, threatening or insulting.

Note: That the fact that a police officer was the person who found the behaviour of the defendants to be 'abusive', 'insulting' and 'distressing' was accepted by the courts, thus following the decision in DPP v Orum (referred to at paragraph 8.1.1).

Chapter 17: Tresspass, Raves, Use of Force to Enter Property

1 ENTRY TO PREMISES USING VIOLENCE
Criminal Law Act 1977 Section 6

1.1 Offence
An offence is committed when someone:
- without lawful authority
- uses or threatens violence
- for the purpose of securing entry to premises for himself or another
- where there is someone present on the premises at the time who is opposed to the entry which the violence is intended to secure
- and the person using or threatening violence knows that this is the case.

1.1.1 *Explanation*
Without lawful authority: This offence does not require trespass by the offender, who may well be a person entitled to possession of the premises in question. However, the fact that a person has an interest in any premises, or a right to possession or occupation shall not amount to lawful authority for the use or threat of violence by him or by anyone else, for the purpose of securing his entry into those premises.

The proper course of action would be through the courts, not by 'taking the law into one's own hands'. However, violence may be used or threatened by or on behalf of a displaced residential occupier or protected intending occupier *(see paragraph 2.1.1 below)* for this purpose.

Violence: The term includes violence towards property, as well as personal violence. A threat to 'break the door down if you don't open it' would be a threat of violence for the purposes of this offence.

Premises: This term means any building, any part of a building under separate occupation, any land ancillary to a building or the site comprising any building or buildings together with land ancillary thereto (Section 12(1)).

Thus, if a factory site, college, council offices or whatever, consist of a number of buildings set in grounds, a person would commit this offence by using violence to gain entry to the grounds, e.g. by breaking down a fence, without necessarily reaching any of the buildings.

Person present/offender knows: The offence will be committed only if there is someone in the premises who does not want the other person to gain entry **and** the person using or threatening the violence knows that this is the case. In a case where the owner of a building threatens violence against people who had been in the building as squatters, he will not commit the offence if they have already left, even though he thinks they are still there. Again, the owner of the building will not commit the offence if, believing the squatters to have left, he breaks down a barricaded door, to find they are still there.

1.1.2 *Arrest*
A constable in uniform may arrest without warrant any person who is, or whom he suspects with reasonable cause to be, guilty of this offence.

*Note: That the term used in the power to arrest is 'guilty', rather than 'committing'.
Thus, the power to arrest may be exercised after the offender has finished committing
the offence.*

2 OCCUPATION OF RESIDENTIAL PREMISES AS A TRESPASSER
Criminal Law Act 1977 Section 7

2.1 Offence
The offence is committed by any person who:
- is on premises as a trespasser
- after having entered as a trespasser
- who fails to leave the premises on being required to do so
- by or on behalf of a displaced residential occupier or protected intending occupier of those premises.

2.1.1 *Explanation*
Trespasser: A person does not cease to be a trespasser merely because he is allowed time to leave the premises (Section 12(7)).

If any person is on premises by virtue of any title, licence or consent deriving from a trespasser, he shall himself be treated as a trespasser. In other words, if one trespasser invites another person to share his 'squat', the second person is also a trespasser, despite the invitation to enter (Section 12(6)).

Having entered as a trespasser: This offence will not be committed by a person who enters premises lawfully, then later becomes a trespasser, e.g. by staying there against the wishes of the occupier.

Displaced residential occupier: This means anyone who was occupying premises as a residence immediately prior to being excluded from the premises, or from access thereto. This person will continue to be a displaced residential occupier for so long as he remains excluded, either by the original trespasser, or by any subsequent trespasser (Section 12(3)).

However, a person who is himself residing in premises as a trespasser does not become a displaced residential occupier by reason of himself becoming excluded by another trespasser (Section 12(4)).

Protected intending occupier: A person is a protected intending occupier who is either:
- someone who himself has a freehold interest in property, or a leasehold interest with at least two years to run; or
- a person with a tenancy or a licence to occupy the premises granted by someone who has either a freehold interest or a leasehold interest with at least two years still to run; or
- someone who has a tenancy or a licence to occupy the premises granted by an authority, such as a housing authority.

And in either case:
- he requires the premises for his own occupation as a residence
- and he is excluded from occupying the premises by a person who entered the premises or any access thereto as a trespasser
- and he has a 'statement' of the type specified in the Act, setting out details of his interest, tenancy, etc (Section 12A).

Thus, a person does not become a protected intending occupier as soon as he finds himself excluded from the place in which he was intending to live; he must first acquire the 'statement' which confirms his status.

Access: A person may be a displaced residential/protected intending occupier if a trespasser excludes him from access to the premises, or from the premises themselves. 'Access' to premises means any part of any site or building within which the premises are situated which constitutes an ordinary means of access to those premises, whether or not this is its sole or primary use (Section 12(1)).

Thus, if a group of protestors trespass in a garden of a house, intending to prevent the occupier getting into the house, they could commit the offence by trespassing in the access to the house, even though they are not in the house itself. The fact that the garden is not there solely or primarily as an access to the house does not matter, so long as it amounts to an ordinary means of access to it.

2.1.2 *Arrest*
A constable in uniform may arrest without warrant anyone who is, or whom he with reasonable cause suspects to be guilty of the offence (Section 7(6)).

2.2 **Defences**
A person charged with this offence will have a defence if he proves:
  - that the premises in question are, or form part of, premises used mainly for non-residential purposes **and** that he was not in any part of the premises used wholly or mainly for residential purposes (Section 7(3)); or
  - that he believed the person requiring him to leave the premises was not a displaced residential occupier, a protected intending occupier, or a person acting on behalf of one of these (Section 7(2)).

The first defence will apply to prevent this legislation being used against persons trespassing on say, office premises which happen to have a caretaker's flat incorporated, so long as the trespassers stay away from that flat.

The second defence depends on what the accused genuinely believes. In the case of the protected intending occupier, the possession of the 'statement' and the fact that this was brought to the accused's attention may be good evidence for countering this defence.

3 **TRESPASS WITH A WEAPON OF OFFENCE**
Criminal Law Act 1977 Section 8

3.1 **Offence**
A person commits an offence who:
  - while he is on any premises as a trespasser
  - having entered as such
  - has with him on the premises without lawful authority or reasonable excuse
  - any weapon of offence.

3.1.1 *Explanation*
Premises: This means any building, any part of a building under separate occupation, any

land ancillary to a building or the site comprising any building or buildings together with land ancillary thereto (Section 12(1)).

Thus, if a factory site, college, council offices or whatever, consist of a number of buildings set in grounds, a person will commit this offence as soon as he enters the grounds as a trespasser with a weapon of offence.

While on: To commit the offence, the accused must have entered the premises as a trespasser, but he need not have had the weapon of offence with him at the time of entering. The offence will be committed whenever he has a weapon of offence with him while trespassing on the premises.

Weapon of offence: This means any article made or adapted for causing injury to a person or incapacitating a person or intended for such use by the person having it with him.

An article 'made' for causing injury would include a police truncheon or a bayonet; one made for incapacitating a person would include a set of handcuffs. An article is adapted if, having been made for some purpose other than to cause injury or to incapacitate a person, it is altered in some way so as to render it suited to such purpose, e.g. a screwdriver sharpened to a point with tape wrapped round the handle.

Any article, however innocent its proper function, may be carried with the intention that it shall be used to injure or incapacitate without any adaptation. Obviously, it will be necessary for the prosecution to prove that the accused had such intention. A baseball bat is made for use in a game of baseball, but may be carried with intent to use it to injure someone. A length of rope has many uses, but may be intended for use for incapacitating a person.

Lawful authority or reasonable excuse: There may not be too many occasions when a trespasser could claim some lawful authority for being in possession of an offensive weapon on premises. The usual examples applicable to having an offensive weapon in a public place, e.g. a police officer carrying a truncheon, tear gas, etc, hardly seem appropriate to an offence which involves entering premises as a trespasser.

For the related offence of being in possession of an offensive weapon in a public place, without lawful authority or reasonable excuse, it has been held that having a knife for self-defence only, on the off-chance of being attacked, does not amount to a reasonable excuse (*Evans v Hughes* (1972)).

3.1.2 *Arrest*
A constable in uniform may arrest without warrant anyone who is, or whom he with reasonable cause suspects to be guilty of the offence (Section 7(6)).

4 TRESPASS ON PREMISES OF A FOREIGN MISSION
Criminal Law Act 1977 Section 9

4.1 Offence
A person commits an offence who enters or is upon specified premises as a trespasser.

4.1.1 *Explanation*
Enters or is upon: Unlike the offences in the preceding paragraphs, which entail being on premises as a trespasser, having entered as such, this offence may be committed either by entering as a trespasser, or by being there as such.

Specified premises: Such premises include those of a diplomatic mission, those of a consular post, and the private residence of a person who is a diplomatic agent or who is entitled to diplomatic immunity.

The great majority of 'specified premises' are no doubt in the Metropolitan Police District, but there are some, Consulates for example, in other parts of the country. That particular premises are 'specified premises' will most likely be known to police officers in the locality, who should be aware of the elements which make up this offence.

4.1.2 *Arrest*

A constable in uniform may arrest without warrant anyone who is, or whom he with reasonable cause suspects to be guilty of the offence (Section 7(6)).

4.2 **Defence**

A person will have a defence if he proves that he believed that the premises were not 'specified premises'.

5 **OBSTRUCTION OF COURT OFFICERS**
Criminal Law Act 1977 Section 10

5.1 **Offence**

A person commits an offence if he:
- resists or intentionally obstructs
- an officer of a court engaged in executing process issued by the High Court or a county court
- for the purpose of enforcing a judgment or order for the recovery of or possession of any premises.

5.1.1 *Explanation*

Officer of a court: This means a sheriff, sheriff's officer, bailiff, other county court officer, etc.

Process for recovery of premises, etc: The provisions relate only to cases where it is alleged that the premises are occupied solely by persons who entered into or remained on premises without licence or consent. Specifically excluded is a case where the persons on the premises are former tenants, remaining after termination of the tenancy.

Basically, the offence applies if the persons on the premises are there as trespassers, never having had any valid consent for being there. It clearly applies to any case where the persons have already committed an offence under Section 7 of the Act.

5.1.2 *Arrest*

A constable in uniform may arrest without warrant anyone who is, or whom he with reasonable cause suspects to be guilty of the offence (Section 7(6)).

5.2 **Defence**

The accused will have a defence if he proves that he believed that the person he was resisting or obstructing was not an officer of the court.

6 INTERIM POSSESSION ORDER – TRESPASS OFFENCES
Criminal Justice and Public Order Act 1994 Sections 75, 76

6.1 Offence
When an interim possession order has been made, and served in the laid down manner, then a person will be liable for an offence if he:
  i) Is present on the premises as a trespasser during the currency of the order unless either:
     – he leaves the premises within 24 hours of the service of the order and does not return; or
     – a copy of the order was not fixed to the premises in accordance with the rules of court.
  ii) Having been in occupation of the premises when the order was served:
     – left the premises
     – then re-enters as a trespasser or attempts to do so
     – after the expiry of the order but within one year of the day it was served.

6.1.1 *Explanation*
Interim possession order: For the purposes of these provisions, an 'interim possession order' is an order made by a court to start court proceedings for the recovery of premises occupied by trespassers.

Trespasser: For the purposes of these offences, a person who is in occupation of premises at the time of service of the interim possession order shall be treated as being present as a trespasser.

6.1.2 *Arrest*
A constable in uniform may arrest without warrant anyone who is, or whom he reasonably suspects to be guilty of one of these offences.

7 COLLECTIVE TRESPASS – POLICE POWERS TO REMOVE
Criminal Justice and Public Order Act 1994 Section 61

7.1 Police Power
In certain circumstances, police have power to require trespassers to leave land. The senior police officer present at the scene may direct persons to leave land if he reasonably believes that:
  – two or more persons are trespassing on land; and
  – that they are there for the common purpose of residing there for any period; and
  – that reasonable steps have been taken by or on behalf of the occupier of the land to ask them to leave; and

that any of those persons have:
  – either caused damage to the land or to property on it; or
  – have used threatening, abusive or insulting words or behaviour towards the occupier, a member of his family, his employee or his agent; or
  – those persons have between them six or more vehicles on the land.

The direction to leave may be made to those persons or to any one of them and includes a direction to remove any vehicles or property they have with them on the land.

7.1.1 *Explanation*

Senior police officer: This could be a police constable or a chief constable, or officer of any rank between, but it is only the senior officer present who has the power.

Once the senior police officer has given the direction to leave, this may be communicated to the person(s) concerned by any constable at the scene.

At an incident involving a large number of trespassers, for example, the officer who gives the direction does not have to convey it personally to each of the trespassers for it to become effective. The other constables present may take a hand in communicating the direction to leave to those to whom it applies.

Trespasser: When the senior police officer reasonably believes that the persons were not originally trespassers but have become so, then before he may exercise the power to direct any of them to leave, he must reasonably believe that the ground for doing so – damage, threatening, abusive or insulting words or behaviour, or the presence of six or more vehicles – were satisfied **after** they became trespassers.

Thus, if Farmer Jones gives a group of travellers permission to stay on his land for a while, then changes his mind and asks them to leave because one of them has threatened Mrs. Jones, this does not give a police officer grounds for directing them to leave. They are now trespassers but the threatening words or behaviour occurred before they became trespassers.

In a case where there is more than one occupier, to become a trespasser involves trespassing against all the occupiers. If one of the occupiers gives permission for the 'visitors' to be on the land, against the wishes of the other occupiers, they will not be trespassers.

Common purpose of residing: The senior police officer must reasonably believe that the persons on the land have the common, i.e. shared, intention of residing on the land for a period. The length of the period is not specified, so may be fairly short.

The fact that a person has a home elsewhere does not preclude him from being regarded as having the purpose of staying on land for a time.

Land: This does not include buildings, so there is no police power to direct 'squatters' to leave premises.

However, buildings which are farm buildings or scheduled monuments are included. 'Land' does not include a highway, in most cases, but the following 'highways' are included – footpath, bridleway, byway, road used as public path, cycle track.

Common land is included for the purposes of the offence. References to the 'occupier' of the land will extend to the 'commoners', i.e. the persons who have rights in relation to common land. Where there is public access to common land, the 'occupier' will be taken to be the local authority.

Note: Where there are a number of commoners, it only needs one to give permission, for the persons on the land not to be trespassers – see the explanation of 'trespasser', above.

Vehicle: This includes any vehicle, whether in a fit state for use on roads or not. It extends to any chassis or body, with or without wheels which appears to have formed part of a vehicle, as well as any load carried by such a vehicle, or anything attached to it. Last but not least, 'vehicle' includes a caravan.

Damage: For the purposes of the offence, 'damage' will include depositing any substance capable of polluting the land. For example, a trespasser who allows his van to remain on the land leaking engine oil would be guilty of causing damage.

7.1.2 *Offence*
A person commits an offence if:
- knowing that a direction has been given
- which applies to him
- he fails to leave the land as soon as practicable
- or having left, he then enters the land as a trespasser within a period of three months.

For this purpose the three months begins on the day the direction to leave was given.

7.1.3 *Power of Arrest*
A constable in uniform may arrest without warrant a person whom he reasonably suspects to be committing one of the offences.

Note: that the power to arrest applies to a person who is committing an offence. If a person returned to land within three months of being directed to leave, he could be arrested while he remained on the land as a trespasser. However, once he left the land again, the power to arrest would no longer apply.

7.1.4 *Defence*
The accused will have a defence to the offences of failing to leave, or returning within three months, if he shows:
- either that he was not trespassing on the land
- or that he had a reasonable excuse for failing to leave, or for returning within the three month period.

7.2 Police Power to Seize and Remove Vehicles
Criminal Justice and Public Order Act 1994 Section 62

If a direction to leave land has been given under Section 61, and a constable reasonably suspects that a person to whom the direction applies has either:
- failed to remove from the land any vehicle which appears to the constable to belong to him or to be in his possession or under his control; or
- entered the land as a trespasser with a vehicle within the period of three months from the date the direction was given;

then the constable may seize and remove that vehicle.

7.2.1 *Explanation*
This power will enable police to clear a site of apparently abandoned vehicles after a direction to leave has been given. However, where a person returns to the same land as a trespasser within three months, the police have the power to seize and remove his vehicle as soon as he brings it on to the land.

8 Powers in Relation to Raves
Criminal Justice and Public Order Act 1994 Section 63

8.1 Power to Give Direction
In respect of any land in the open air:
- if a police officer of at least the rank of superintendent
- reasonably believes that:

    i) two or more persons are making preparations for holding a gathering there; or

    ii) ten or more persons are waiting for a gathering to begin there; or

    iii) ten or more persons are attending a gathering which is in progress there;

she may give a direction that:

- those persons
- and any others who come to prepare, to wait for or to attend the gathering
- are to leave the land
- and remove any vehicles or other property which they have with them on the land.

8.1.1 *Explanation*

Gathering: The Section applies to a gathering:

- on land in the open air
- of 100 or more persons
- whether trespassers or not
- at which amplified music is played during the night (with or without intermissions)
- and by reason of its loudness, its duration and the time at which it is played
- it is likely to cause serious distress to the inhabitants of the locality.

The event will continue to amount to such a 'gathering' during intermissions in the music. However, where an event is held over several days, it will amount to a 'gathering' only during the periods when amplified music is played at night (with or without intermissions).

This means that there will be a 'gathering' in existence when amplified music is played at night, including during the time when the music has stopped for a while. When the event continues over several days, it will cease to be a 'gathering' during the daytime, but it will resume its existence as such when amplified music is played at night and during any intermissions in the music during that night.

Rave: The term 'rave' has come to mean a gathering of large numbers of people, usually late at night, or overnight, dancing to a particular style of music. The Act recognises the term 'rave' in the heading covering Sections 63–66, but the word does not appear in the actual Sections themselves.

Superintendent: In contrast to the power to direct collective trespassers to leave, which may be given by a police constable if she is the senior police officer present, a direction under this Section has to be given by a police officer of at least superintendent rank.

However, once the direction has been given by the officer of the requisite rank, it may be communicated to the persons to whom it applies by any constable present at the scene. This helps preserve the superintendent's vocal cords, and precludes anyone putting forward a defence that he did not hear the superintendent give the direction.

As a further safeguard, to cater for, e.g. the person who puts his fingers in his ears to avoid hearing what a constable may be saying, a person shall be treated as having had the direction communicated to him if reasonable steps have been taken to bring it to his attention.

Person to whom direction may apply: A direction may be given to persons who are present with the permission of the occupier of the land, as when a farmer hires out a field for a rave. However, the following persons will be exempt:

- the occupier of the land, or any member of his family
- the occupier's employee or agent
- any person whose home is on the land.

Numbers of persons: For there to be a 'rave', at least 100 persons must be present. However,

the Act recognises the need to 'nip in the bud' a potential gathering before large numbers of people turn up. Therefore a direction may be given to:
- two or more people making preparations
- ten or more waiting for the event to start
- ten or more who are actually taking part in the gathering.

Land in the open air: Includes any land which is partly open to the air.

Music: This is defined as sound wholly or predominantly characterised by the emission of a succession of repetitive beats. This provision will preclude a defence succeeding which is based on a 'Call that music?' argument.

Vehicle: This extends to any vehicle, whether in a fit state for use on roads or not. It extends to any chassis or body, with or without wheels which appears to have formed part of a vehicle, as well as any load carried by such a vehicle, or anything attached to it. Last but not least, 'vehicle' includes a caravan.

8.2 Licensed Event
A direction may not be given in relation to a gathering held under the auspices of an entertainment licence granted by a local authority.

8.2.1 *Offence*
A person commits an offence if:
- knowing that a direction has been given which applies to him
- he fails to leave the land as soon as reasonably practicable
- or having left, enters the land again within a period of seven days from the day the direction was given.

The period during which return to the land is prohibited is far shorter than the three month period applicable to collective trespass.

8.2.2 *Arrest*
A constable in uniform may arrest without warrant a person whom he reasonably suspects to be committing one of the offences.

The power to arrest applies to a person who is committing an offence. If a person returned to land within seven days of being directed to leave, he could be arrested while he remained on the land. However, once he left the land again, the power to arrest would no longer apply.

8.2.3 *Defence*
An accused will have a defence if he shows that he had a reasonable excuse for failing to leave as soon as reasonably practicable, or for returning within seven days, as the case may be.

8.3 Power to Seize Vehicles and Sound Equipment
If a direction to leave land has been given under Section 63:
- a constable may seize and remove any vehicle or sound equipment from the land in question
- if he reasonably suspects that a person to whom the direction applies has either:
  i) failed to remove from the land the vehicle or sound equipment which appears to the

constable to belong to him or to be in his possession or under his control; or

ii) entered the land as a trespasser with a vehicle or sound equipment within the period of seven days from the day the direction was given.

8.3.1 *Forfeiture of Sound Equipment*
Criminal Justice and Public Order Act 1994 Section 66

When a person is convicted of an offence under Section 63 and the court is satisfied that any sound equipment seized from him (or which was in his possession or under his control at the relevant time) has been used at the gathering, the court may make an order of forfeiture in respect of that equipment.

Equipment so forfeited then passes into police possession and may be disposed of.

8.4 **Power to Enter Land**
Criminal Justice and Public Order Act 1994 Section 64

If a police officer of at least the rank of superintendent reasonably believes that circumstances exist in relation to any land which would justify the giving of a direction under Section 63, he may authorise any constable to enter the land without warrant, for any of the following purposes:

– to ascertain whether those circumstances exist
– to exercise any power conferred on a constable by Section 63
– to exercise power to seize vehicles or sound equipment.

8.4.1 *Explanation*
This power assists police in exercising other powers in relation to raves. For example, if there is reason to believe that a group of people on land are making preparations to hold a gathering, this power enables the police to go on to the land to check whether this is the case, and if so whether there are grounds for giving them a direction to leave. Similarly, if it is believed that persons have returned to the land during the seven days after a direction has been given, a superintendent or above may authorise officers to enter the land to arrest those persons and seize vehicles or sound equipment.

9 POWERS TO STOP PERSONS GOING TO A RAVE
Criminal Justice and Public Order Act 1994 Section 65

9.1 **Police Power**
If a constable in uniform reasonably believes that a person is on his way to a gathering to which Section 63 applies (i.e. a rave) in relation to which a direction under Section 63 is in force, the constable may:

– stop that person; and
– direct her not to proceed in the direction of the gathering.

This power may be exercised only within five miles of the boundary of the site of the gathering.

9.1.1 *Exemptions*
The following persons may not be made subject to the power to divert persons away from a gathering:

- the occupier of the land on which the gathering is sited, or any member of his family
- the occupier's employee or agent
- any person whose home is on the land where the gathering is sited.

9.1.2 *Offence*

A person commits an offence who, knowing that a direction under this provision has been given to him, fails to comply with it.

9.1.3 *Arrest*

A constable in uniform who reasonably suspects that a person is committing this offence may arrest him without warrant.

The constable making the arrest need not be the same one who gave the direction to the offender. Although the power to arrest is restricted to a person who is committing the offence, it does afford the police considerable scope in preventing persons getting to the rave. For example, a person within the 'five mile exclusion zone' is directed to stop and not to proceed to the site of the gathering. The person duly turns away, apparently complying with the direction. If the same person is seen later, still within the five mile zone and heading in the direction of the gathering, this may give rise to the suspicion that he is committing the offence of failing to comply with the direction, so opening up the prospect of arrest.

10 DISRUPTIVE TRESPASSERS
Criminal Justice and Public Order Act 1994 Section 68

10.1 Offence of Aggravated Trespass

A person commits the offence of aggravated trespass if:
- he trespasses on land in the open air
- and in relation to any lawful activity which persons are engaging in or are about to engage in on that or on adjoining land in the open air
- he does anything intended by him to have the effect:
   i) of intimidating those persons or any of them, so as to deter them or any of them from engaging in that activity; or
   ii) of obstructing that activity; or
   iii) of disrupting that activity.

10.1.1 *Explanation*

Distinction from other offences: In recent years there has been a rise in incidents in which a group of protesters seek to prevent other persons taking part in an activity which is not against the law. Examples include hunt saboteurs seeking to prevent a fox hunt taking place, or those seeking to prevent a by-pass or motorway extension being built. The law has always made provision for dealing with people whose activities lead to damage being caused or violence threatened. Where the protesters are 'peaceful', e.g. climbing trees to prevent their being felled, offences such as violent disorder or breach of the peace are not appropriate. Hence, these provisions were brought in for dealing with trespassing on land to disrupt lawful activity.

Lawful activity: An activity will be lawful if persons are able to engage in it on the land on that occasion without committing an offence and without themselves trespassing.

Land: Land does not include a highway, in most cases, but the following 'highways' are included – footpath, bridleway, byway, road used as public path, cycle track.

Note: A highway is a way over which the public have a right to pass. A new by-pass or stretch of motorway will not become a highway until such time as it is opened to the public.

Engaging in or about to: The offence may be committed by persons who seek to prevent an activity starting, or to put a stop to something which has started. For example, if members of a fox hunt are gathering prior to setting off, the activities of hunt saboteurs may amount to this offence, well before any fox appears on the scene.

Adjoining land: If the offenders trespass on one area of land, they may commit the offence even though the activity they are seeking to disrupt is on another area of land, so long as the two areas adjoin. Thus, if demonstrators invade the depot of a construction company, in an effort to dissuade the company from building a road some miles away, the offence will not be committed.

10.1.2 *Arrest*
A constable in uniform may arrest without warrant a person whom he reasonably suspects is committing this offence.

The power to arrest is restricted to 'is committing', so that if a constable saw a person in the street who some time earlier had been committing the offence, the power to arrest would no longer apply.

11 DIRECTIONS TO DISRUPTIVE TRESPASSERS
Criminal Justice and Public Order Act 1994 Section 69

11.1 Power to Give Direction
The senior police officer present at the scene may direct persons (or any of them) present to leave land if he reasonably believes:
  - that a person is committing, has committed or intends to commit the offence of aggravated trespass; or
  - that two or more persons are trespassing on land in the open air with the common purpose of intimidating persons so as to deter them from engaging in lawful activity or of obstructing or disrupting a lawful activity;

11.1.1 *Explanation*
Communicating the direction: Once the senior police officer present has given the direction, it may be communicated to the persons concerned by any constable at the scene.

11.1.2 *Offence*
A person commits an offence who:
  - knowing that a direction under this Section has been given, which applies to him:
    i) fails to leave the land as soon as practicable; or
    ii) having left, enters again as a trespasser within the period of three months beginning with the day the direction is given.

11.1.3 *Arrest*

A constable in uniform may arrest without warrant a person whom he reasonably suspects is committing this offence.

11.1.4 *Defence*

It will be a defence for the accused to prove that he was not trespassing on the land or that he had a reasonable excuse for failing to leave as soon as practicable (or for returning within three months, as the case may be).

12 TRESPASSORY ASSEMBLIES
Public Order Act 1986 Sections 14A, 14B, 14C

12.1 Introduction

These Sections give a procedure whereby a chief officer of police may apply to the local authority for an order to prohibit a large gathering of trespassers, and provide for offences and police powers to deal with persons who attend a prohibited gathering.

12.2 Prohibition of an Assembly

If a chief officer of police for an area outside London:
- reasonably believes that an assembly is intended to be held
- on land to which the public has no right of access or only a limited right of access
- and that the assembly:
  i) is likely to be held without the permission of the occupier of the land or is to be conducted in such a way as to exceed the limit's of the occupier's permission, or of any public right of access; **and**
  ii) may result in serious disruption to the life of the community or, where the land or a monument or building on it is of historical, architectural, archaeological or scientific significance, in significant damage to the land, building, etc,
  then she may apply to the local authority for an order prohibiting all trespassory assemblies in the authority area, or in part of it. The local authority may then make an order (subject to amendment by the Secretary of State).

London: In respect of the Metropolitan Police and City of London police areas, the commissioner would make application for an order direct to the Secretary of State.

12.2.1 *Explanation*

Assembly: This means a gathering of 20 or more persons.

Land: The provisions apply only to land in the open air.

Land with limited public access: A road or highway would fall into this category, albeit these are generally regarded as public places. However, members of the public do not have unlimited rights on a highway; generally, there is a right to pass and re-pass, and to do anything incidental thereto. There does not exist a lawful right to hold an assembly of 20 or more persons on the highway *(Keynote Case: DPP v Jones and another (1997))*. A gathering of people on a road or highway may well amount to a trespassory assembly.

12.2.2 *Effect of Order*

If an order is made, it will have the effect of prohibiting any assembly which is held on land where there no public access, or only a limited right of access, without permission of the occupier, or so as to exceed the limits of his permission, or the limits of any public right of access.

The order may prohibit such assemblies for a period not exceeding four days, and the area of the prohibition shall not be greater than that of a circle with a five mile radius from a specified centre.

Thus, the chief officer of police may apply for an order because of reason to believe that a trespassory assembly is to be held at a particular time in a particular place. The effect of the order will be to prohibit any such assembly for up to four days, within five miles of a specified centre.

12.3 **Police Powers to Direct Persons Away from Assembly**

If a constable in uniform reasonably believes:
- that a person is on his way to an assembly
- in an area where a prohibition order is in force
- which assembly the officer reasonably believes is likely to one prohibited by that order
- he may:
  - i)   stop that person; and
  - ii) direct him not to proceed in the direction of the assembly.

This power may be exercised only within the area to which the prohibition order applies.

12.3.1 *Offences*

There are several offences which a person may commit once a prohibition order has been made:
- to organise an assembly, the holding of which he knows to be prohibited
- take part in an assembly which he knows to be prohibited
- incite a person to take part in an assembly which that person knows to be prohibited
- fail to comply with a direction from a constable which he knows has been given to him.

12.3.2 *Arrest*

A constable in uniform may arrest without warrant anyone he reasonably suspects to be committing any of these offences.

Keynote case

13.1 *Director of Public Prosecutions v Jones and another* **[1997] 2 All ER 119**

Problem

Whether a gathering of persons on a highway may be capable of amounting to a 'trespassory assembly', or whether there is a right in law for members of the public to hold a peaceful assembly, which does not amount to an obstruction, on the highway.

Circumstances

A group of persons held a peaceful, non-obstructive demonstration on part of the public highway near Stonehenge, in an area which at that time was covered by an order made under

Section 14A, Public Order Act 1986, prohibiting trespassory assemblies. The police judged the gathering to amount to such an assembly, asked the demonstrators to disperse, and then, when they refused to disperse, arrested them. The defendants were convicted at magistrates' court and appealed against their conviction. At Crown Court their appeals were allowed, the Court accepting a defence submission, that an assembly on the highway was lawful as long as it was peaceful and did not cause an obstruction. The prosecution appealed by way of case stated to the Queen's Bench Divisional Court.

Decision

The Court held that there was no right in law for members of the public to hold a peaceful, non-obstructive assembly on the public highway. It is accepted that a right of passage and re-passage will include matters incidental thereto, such as passing the time of day. Holding a demonstration on the highway, peaceful or not, had nothing to do with the right to pass by. Holding a gathering may well not amount to an offence of obstruction of the highway, but that is a different matter from establishing a right to hold an assembly. The Court allowed the prosecution appeal and the convictions were restored.

Comment

For a gathering to amount to a trespassory assembly, it must:
- be held on land where there is no public right of access, or only a limited right of public access; and
- it is held without permission of the occupier of the land, or so as to exceed the limits of the occupier's permission, or so as to exceed any public right of access.

There is another characteristic which turns a gathering into a trespassory assembly, that it may result in serious disruption to the community or serious damage to significant land or buildings.

This decision confirms that a highway is a place where there is a limited public right of access, in that the public have a right to pass and re-pass, and to do other things incidental to that passage or re-passage. There is no right to hold an assembly on the highway, to do so exceeds the public right of access, and may give rise to a trespassory assembly, if the element of possible serious disruption or damage is present.

Chapter 18: Prevention of Terrorism

1 INTRODUCTION

1.1 Terrorism

'Terrorism' means the use of violence for political ends including the use of violence for the purpose of putting the public or a section of the public in fear.

Terrorism is usually taken to include acts of violence such as setting off explosive devices, shootings, etc, where the motive is political, rather than the usual criminal motives of financial gain or revenge. Acts of terrorism will always amount to criminal offences and will be prosecuted as such. Legislation dealing specifically with terrorism provides for offences relating to membership and organisation of terrorist organisations, fund raising and other assistance for terrorism, as well as providing police powers. For offences arising from setting off bombs, using firearms, etc, one looks to the criminal law which applies to everyone, politically motivated or otherwise.

1.2 Types of Terrorism

Legislation recognises two sorts of terrorist activity:
- that connected with the affairs of Northern Ireland
- terrorism related to the affairs of any other part of the world, which is **not** connected solely with the affairs of any other part of the United Kingdom.

Thus, a bombing campaign by animal rights activists, or by a group claiming independence for Wessex, for example, would not be classed as terrorism, but acts related to Middle Eastern politics would.

1.3 Legislation

The principal legislation dealing with terrorism is the Prevention of Terrorism (Temporary Provisions) Act 1989. References to legislation in this chapter will be to this Act unless otherwise indicated. Additional powers are provided by the aptly named Prevention of Terrorism (Additional Powers) Act 1996.

There are special provisions in the Codes of Practice to the Police and Criminal Evidence Act 1984, dealing with the detention and interviewing by police of terrorist suspects.

2 PROSCRIBED ORGANISATIONS

2.1 List of Organisations

The Act lists a number of organisations which are proscribed. The Home Secretary is given power to add further organisations to the list. The organisations which are proscribed include the Irish Republican Army (IRA), both Provisional and Official wings, and the Irish National Liberation Army (INLA). (Schedule 1)

2.2 'Organisation'

Includes any association or combination of persons.

2.3 **Membership and Support**
Prevention of Terrorism (Temporary Provisions) Act 1989 Section 2

2.3.1 *Offence*
A person commits an offence if he:
   i) belongs to or professes to belong to a proscribed organisation
   ii) solicits or invites support for a proscribed organisation, other than support
       with money or other property
   iii) arranges or assists in the management of, or addresses any meeting of three or more
        persons whether or not it is a meeting to which the public are admitted, knowing that
        the meeting is:
        – to support a proscribed organisation, or
        – is to further the activities of such an organisation, or
        – is to be addressed by someone who belongs to or professes to belong to such
          an organisation.

2.3.2 *Explanation*
Member: This offence does not require any direct involvement in an act of terrorism, but is committed by being a member, or merely by claiming to be a member of a proscribed organisation.

Support: Soliciting support is confined to support other than in money or property; financial support is dealt with separately *(see below)*.

Meeting: Being concerned in the arrangements for a meeting, or addressing a meeting, which is in support of a proscribed organisation, is covered by this Section. The meeting need not be large – three persons amount to a 'meeting' – and it need not be a public meeting.

Profess to belong: It will be for a court to decide whether a person's actions amounted to 'professing to belong' to a proscribed organisation. The simplest form of 'professing to belong' would be a statement or claim to be a member. However, giving an interview or addressing a meeting in such a way as to suggest that one was a member, may also amount to 'professing to belong'. A person may be convicted of the offence even though he denies that he is or has been a member.

2.3.3 *Arrest*
These are arrestable offences and will be serious arrestable offences for the purposes of Sections 56 and 58 of the Police and Criminal Evidence Act 1984 (right to have someone informed of arrest, right to legal advice).

2.3.4 *Defence*
It will be a defence to a charge of being a member of a proscribed organisation, for the accused to prove:
   – that the organisation was not proscribed when he joined it; **and**
   – that since he joined he has not taken part in any of its activities while it has
     been proscribed.

In this context 'joined' refers to the only or last occasion on which he joined. Thus, a person who joined a proscribed organisation before it became proscribed, ceased to have membership, then re-joined while it was proscribed, could not avail himself of this defence.

2.4 **Contributions**
Prevention of Terrorism (Temporary Provisions) Act 1989 Section 10

2.4.1 *Offence*
It will amount to an offence for someone to:
   i) solicit or invite another person
      – to give, lend or otherwise make available
      – whether for consideration or not
      – any money or other property
      – for the benefit of a proscribed organisation.

   ii) give, lend or otherwise make available:
      – whether for consideration or not
      – money or other property
      – for the benefit of such organisation.

   iii) receive, accept, use or have possession of:
      – money or other property
      – whether for consideration or not
      – for the benefit of such organisation.

   iv) enter into or be concerned in an arrangement:
      – whereby money or other property
      – is, or is to be, made available for the benefit of such organisation.

2.4.2 *Explanation*
Solicit, give, receive, etc: The offence covers the various stages, which may be in the following order:
   – asking for
   – making arrangements
   – giving
   – receiving
   – having possession of.

Money or other property: This Section covers the aspects of support for a proscribed organisation which are specifically excluded from the scope of Section 2.

Benefit of a proscribed organisation: In each case, the donation is, or is to be for the benefit of one of the listed organisations.

For consideration or not: Put simply, 'consideration' is something in return. The inclusion of this term means that it is not merely donations or gifts which are covered, but extends the scope of the Section in two ways:
   – to cover, e.g. a commercial transaction, such as the sale of weapons;
   – where a person buys something, and the money is to go towards a proscribed organisation, the equivalent of an 'IRA flag-day'.

2.4.3 *Arrest*
These are arrestable offences and will be serious arrestable offences for the purposes of Sections 56 and 58 of the Police and Criminal Evidence Act 1984 (right to have someone informed of arrest, right to legal advice).

2.4.4 *Defence*
Prevention of Terrorism (Temporary Provisions) Act 1989 Section 12

1: It will be a defence for a person to prove that he did not know and had no reasonable cause to suspect that the money or other property was for the benefit of a proscribed organisation or, in the case of arrangements, that these related to such an organisation.

2: A person will not commit an offence under this Section if he is acting on the instructions of a constable or if he discloses suspicions about the arrangements to a constable, on his own initiative and as soon as is reasonable for him to do so.

3: It is a further defence to a charge under this Section to prove that he intended to disclose his suspicions to a constable and there was reasonable excuse for his failure to do so as soon as was reasonable.

2.5 Display of Support in Public
Prevention of Terrorism (Temporary Provisions) Act 1989 Section 3

2.5.1 *Offence*
A person will be guilty of an offence who:
- in a public place
- wears any item of dress or wears, carries or displays any article
- in such a way or in such circumstances
- as to arouse reasonable apprehension that she is a member or supporter of a proscribed organisation.

2.5.2 *Explanation*
Public place: Public place includes any highway, or any other place to which at the material time, the public have or are permitted to have access, whether on payment or otherwise. This offence cannot therefore be committed in private. Contrast this with the provisions under Section 2, relating to meetings, which extend to meetings held in private.

Wears or carries: This offence may be compared with that of wearing an article of political uniform, under Section 1, Public Order Act 1936 *(see Chapter 16)* which is similar. Indeed, the case decision referred to in relation to that offence relates to the wearing of articles associated with the IRA (*O'Moran v DPP* (1975)). This offence is wider in scope, covering the carrying of articles, e.g. banners, as well as the wearing of uniform.

Reasonable apprehension … member or supporter: For the offence to be complete, the circumstances must give rise to a reasonable belief that the person wearing or carrying the article(s) in question is a member or supporter of a proscribed organisation. Whether the alleged offender professes to be such is not what has to be proved.

3 CONTRIBUTIONS TO TERRORISM
Prevention of Terrorism (Temporary Provisions) Act 1989 Section 9

3.1 Offences
Offences under this Section may be considered as being **receiver** or **donor** offences.

3.1.1 *'Receiver' Offences*
A person commits an offence if he:
  i) solicits or invites any other person to give, lend or otherwise make available, whether for consideration or not, any money or other property; or
  ii) receives or accepts from any other person, whether for consideration or not, any money or other property; or
  iii) uses or has possession of, whether for consideration or not, any money or other property:
    – intending that it shall
    – or having reasonable cause to suspect that it may
    – be applied or used for the commission of, in furtherance of, or in connection with acts of terrorism to which this Section applies.

3.1.2 *'Donor' Offences*
A person commits an offence who:
  i) gives, lends or otherwise makes available, whether for consideration or not, any money or other property; or
  ii) enters into or is otherwise concerned in an arrangement whereby money or other property is to be made available to another person:
    – knowing or having reasonable cause to suspect
    – that it will or may be applied or used for the commission of, in furtherance of, or in connection with acts of terrorism to which this Section applies.

3.2 **Explanation**
Acts of terrorism: Whereas Section 10 deals with contributions to proscribed organisations, this Section caters for contributions towards acts of terrorism. This distinction recognises several factors, e.g:
  – a donation towards the funds of a proscribed organisation may not be applied directly towards an act of terrorism; it could, for example, be used to fund propaganda activity;
  – an act of terrorism connected with Northern Ireland need not be the work of a proscribed organisation, but could be the work of an individual or a group of persons not amounting to a proscribed organisation;
  – the law is directed at other acts of terrorism, not related to Northern Ireland.

Consideration or not: As is the case for offences under Section 10, the Section will cover commercial or other transactions where something is given in exchange for the money or property handed over.

Give, lend, etc: The offences are not limited to situations where money or property is handed over permanently. Lending an article, or allowing someone else to use property, would equally come within the scope of this Section.

Acts... to which the Section applies: The Section applies to two broad categories of terrorism:
  – acts of terrorism connected with the affairs of Northern Ireland;
  – any other acts of terrorism **not** connected solely with the affairs of any other part of the United Kingdom. An act may be covered by this provision even though it is done outside the United Kingdom, but only if it amounts to an offence triable in the United Kingdom.

Thus, an act of terrorism relating to Northern Ireland, or an act of terrorism relating to some foreign country would fall within the scope of this Section. In the latter case, the act of terrorism may be committed here, such as setting off a bomb near an embassy in London, as an action connected with Middle East politics. A donation towards an act of terrorism to be committed abroad would also be covered if the intended act of terrorism amounted to an offence which would be triable in this country.

What will not be covered is a donation, or soliciting donations, etc, for criminal acts relating solely to matters in any part of the United Kingdom outside Northern Ireland. The activities of Welsh or Scottish nationalist extremists, for example, do not come within the scope of this legislation.

3.3 **Arrest**

These are arrestable offences and will be serious arrestable offences for the purposes of Sections 56 and 58 of the Police and Criminal Evidence Act 1984 (right to have someone informed of arrest, right to legal advice).

3.4 **Defence**

The same defence applies to offences under this Section as applies under Section 10, relating to disclosure to a constable, or action taken on the instructions of a constable.

4 **RETENTION OR CONTROL OF FUNDS**
Prevention of Terrorism (Temporary Provisions) Act 1989 Section 11

4.1 **Offence**

A person commits an offence if:
- he enters into or is otherwise concerned in an arrangement
- whereby the retention or control by or on behalf of another person of terrorist funds is facilitated
- whether by concealment, removal, transfer to nominees or otherwise.

4.1.1 *Explanation*

Behalf of another: The offence is not concerned with the person who has control of the funds, but with the person who helps in the arrangements.

Terrorist funds: Briefly, this means funds which may be used in connection with acts of terrorism – or the proceeds either of acts of terrorism or of activities aimed at furthering such acts – or the funds of a proscribed organisation.

Acts of terrorism: This is not confined to acts connected with the affairs of Northern Ireland, but extends to acts of terrorism relating to the affairs of areas outside the United Kingdom.

4.1.2 *Arrest*

These are arrestable offences and will be serious arrestable offences for the purposes of Sections 56 and 58 of the Police and Criminal Evidence Act 1984 (right to have someone informed of arrest, right to legal advice).

4.1.3 *Defences*

1: A person will have a defence to a charge under this Section if he proves that he did not know and had no reason to suspect that the arrangement related to terrorist funds.

2: The same defence applies to offences under this Section as applies under Section 10, relating to disclosure to a constable, or action taken on the instructions of a constable.

5 EXCLUSION ORDERS
Prevention of Terrorism (Temporary Provisions) Act 1989 Sections 5 – 8

5.1 Scope of Exclusion Orders
The Home Secretary may make an order prohibiting a person from being in or entering Great Britain if satisfied that the person:
- is or has been concerned in the commission, preparation or instigation of acts of terrorism; or
- is attempting or may attempt to enter Great Britain with a view to being concerned in such activity.

There is a similar power to exclude a person from Northern Ireland (Section 6).

The Home Secretary may also exclude a person who is **not** a British citizen from the United Kingdom (Section 7).

A person who is a British citizen cannot be made the subject of an order excluding him from Great Britain if – he is ordinarily resident there – and has been so for the previous three years. (A corresponding provision relates to excluding a person from Northern Ireland who is normally resident there.)

5.1.1 *Explanation*
British citizen: A British citizen cannot be the subject of orders excluding him from Great Britain and from Northern Ireland, at the same time. In other words, a British citizen has to be allowed to live somewhere in either Britain or Northern Ireland.

Acts of terrorism: The provisions relating to exclusion orders apply to acts of terrorism connected with the affairs of Northern Ireland, only.

5.2 Offences Relating to Exclusion Orders
Prevention of Terrorism (Temporary Provisions) Act 1989 Section 8

5.2.1 *Offences*
1: A person who is the subject of an exclusion order commits an offence if he fails to comply with the order after becoming liable to be removed from Great Britain or from Northern Ireland or the United Kingdom, as the case may be.

2: A person commits an offence who is knowingly concerned in arrangements to secure or facilitate the entry into Great Britain (etc, as the case may be) of a person whom he knows or has reasonable grounds to believe is an excluded person.

3: A person commits an offence if he knowingly harbours such a person.

5.2.2 *Arrest*

These are arrestable offences and will be serious arrestable offences for the purposes of Sections 56 and 58 of the Police and Criminal Evidence Act 1984 (right to have someone informed of arrest, right to legal advice).

6 OFFENCES AGAINST PUBLIC SECURITY
Prevention of Terrorism (Temporary Provisions) Act 1989 Section 16A

6.1 Possession of Articles

6.1.1 *Offence*

A person commits an offence if:
  - he has any article in his possession
  - in circumstances giving rise to reasonable suspicion that the article is in his possession
  - for a purpose connected with the commission, preparation or instigation of acts of terrorism.

6.1.2 *Proof*

Where evidence is given that at the time of the alleged offence:
  - the accused and the article in question were both on premises; **or**
  - the article was on premises of which the accused was the occupier, or which he habitually used, other than as a member of the public
  - the court may accept that as sufficient evidence of his possession of the article at that time
  - unless it is further proved that he did not at that time know of its presence, or if he did know, that he had no control over it.

For these purposes, the Section applies to vehicles, vessels and aircraft, as it does to premises.

6.1.3 *Defence*

The accused will have a defence if he proves that at the time of the alleged offence the article in question was not in his possession for a purpose relating to acts of terrorism.

6.1.4 *Explanation*

Acts of terrorism: The acts of terrorism covered by the Section are those relating to Northern Ireland affairs, and also those relating to areas outside the United Kingdom.

Proof: If the accused and the article are found on the same premises, he may be deemed to be in possession of it. Similarly, if the article is found in premises where the accused occupies or which he habitually uses, he will be deemed to be in possession of the article. As far as habitual use is concerned, this does not apply to premises which he habitually uses as a member of the public. Thus, if an article was found in Fred's favourite pub, the assumption that Fred had possession of the article will not be made.

The onus will be on the accused to prove either that he did not know the article was there, or if he did know, that he had no control over the article.

Defence: It will be for the prosecution to prove that the accused had possession of the article in such circumstances as to give rise to reasonable suspicion that he had it for the purposes of terrorism. The onus is then on the accused to prove that he did not have it for such a purpose.

6.1.5 *Arrest*
This is an arrestable offence.

6.2 Collection of Information
Prevention of Terrorism (Temporary Provisions) Act 1989 Section 16B

6.2.1 *Offence*
A person commits an offence if:
- without lawful authority or reasonable excuse
- proof of which lies on him:
    i) he collects or records information of such a nature as is likely to be useful to terrorists in planning or carrying out any act of terrorism; or
    ii) he has in his possession any record or document containing such information.

6.2.2 *Explanation*
Records information: This means recording it by photography or by any other means.

Acts of terrorism: The acts of terrorism covered by the Section are those relating to Northern Ireland affairs, and also those relating to areas outside the United Kingdom.

6.2.3 *Arrest*
This is an arrestable offence.

7 DISCLOSURE OF INFORMATION
Prevention of Terrorism (Temporary Provisions) Act 1989 Section 18

7.1 Failure to Disclose Information About Offences

7.1.1 *Offence*
A person commits an offence if:
- he has information
- which he knows or believes might be of material assistance:
    i) in preventing the commission by another person of an act of terrorism connected with the affairs of Northern Ireland; or
    ii) in securing the apprehension, prosecution or conviction of another person for an offence involving committing, preparing for or instigating such an act;
- and he fails without reasonable excuse to disclose that information as soon as reasonably practicable to a constable.

7.1.2 *Explanation*
He knows or believes: It must be shown that the accused knew or believed his information to be material; it is not sufficient that someone else thinks the information is useful.

By another person: The information must relate to someone else committing an offence. The accused cannot be prosecuted for failing to incriminate himself.

Affairs of Northern Ireland: The offence is restricted to acts of terrorism connected with Northern Ireland; it does not extend to other acts of terrorism.

Disclose as soon as reasonably practicable: For the purposes of charging the accused, the offence may be treated as having been committed in any place where the accused is or has been at any time since he first knew or believed that his information might be of material assistance.

7.1.3 *Arrest*
This is an arrestable offence.

7.2 **Failure to Disclose Information About Funds**
Prevention of Terrorism (Temporary Provisions) Act 1989 Section 18A

7.2.1 *Offence*
A person commits an offence if:
- he knows or suspects that another person is providing financial assistance for acts of terrorism; and
- the information or matter on which that knowledge or suspicion is based comes to his attention in the course of his trade, profession, business or employment; and
- he does not disclose the information or other matter to a constable as soon as is reasonably practicable after it comes to his attention.

7.2.2 *Explanation*
In the course of trade, etc: The offence will be committed only by a person who comes by it in the course of his business, employment, etc. The provision is aimed at accountants, financial advisers, etc, and their staff, who may gain knowledge about a client's payments to a terrorist organisation, for example.

Restriction on disclosure: Disclosure of information under these provisions will **not** amount to a breach of any restriction under any other legislation, code of professional conduct, etc, which may apply. Thus, an accountant would not be liable to disciplinary proceedings by an association of which she is a member, for disclosing confidential information about a client's affairs.

Exemption: A legal adviser is exempt from the requirement under this Section to disclose information to the police.

7.2.3 *Arrest*
These are arrestable offences.

7.3 **Unlawful Disclosure of Information**
Prevention of Terrorism (Temporary Provisions) Act 1989 Section 17

7.3.1 *Offence*
A person commits an offence if:
- knowing or having reason to believe
- that a constable is acting or proposing to act in connection with a terrorist investigation:
  - i) he discloses to another person information or any other matter likely to prejudice the investigation; or
  - ii) he falsifies, conceals, destroys or disposes of, material which is or is likely to be relevant in the investigation, or causes or permits someone else to falsify, conceal, destroy or dispose of it.

7.3.2 *Explanation*

The offence caters for situations where a person acts in a manner likely to hamper an investigation into terrorism, which is actually underway, or which is likely to start.

7.3.3 *Defence*

A person will have a defence to a charge under this Section if he proves:
- that he did not know and had no reason to suspect that his disclosure was likely to prejudice an investigation; or
- he had lawful authority or reasonable excuse for making his disclosure; or
- he had no intention of concealing information from anyone who might carry out an investigation.

7.3.4 *Exemptions*

The following persons will be exempt from liability in respect of any disclosure they make:

- a professional legal adviser in the course of giving legal advice to a client, or to any person in connection with (possible) proceedings;
- a constable or other person in respect of anything done by him while acting in connection with the enforcement of the Act or of other legislation relating to terrorism.

7.3.5 *Arrest*

This is an arrestable offence.

8 POLICE POWERS OF ARREST AND SEARCH

8.1 Powers of Arrest

Prevention of Terrorism (Temporary Provisions) Act 1989 Section 14

8.1.1 *Powers*

1: A constable may arrest without warrant a person whom he reasonably suspects to be guilty of an offence under:

Section 2:   proscribed organisation – membership, fund raising, meetings, etc
Section 8:   breach of exclusion order
Section 9:   fund-raising for acts of terrorism
Section 10:   fund-raising for proscribed organisation
Section 11:   retention, etc of funds

2: A constable may arrest without warrant a person whom he reasonably suspects to be subject to an exclusion order.

3: A constable may arrest without warrant anyone whom he reasonably suspects is or has been concerned in the commission, preparation or instigation of acts of terrorism.

8.1.2 *Explanation*

Use of this power: Most of the offences for which this Section provides a power of arrest are in themselves arrestable offences. However, special provisions apply to persons arrested under Section 14, exempting their detention from some of the provisions of PACE and the Codes of Practice. Most important, are the provisions relating to time limits on detention, reviews and tape recording of interviews *(see paragraph 9 below)*.

Acts of terrorism: The acts of terrorism referred to are those as defined in Section 9, i.e. relating to matters outside the United Kingdom, as well as to the affairs of Northern Ireland.

8.2 Power to Stop and Search a Person
Prevention of Terrorism (Temporary Provisions) Act 1989 Section 15(3), (4), (5)

8.2.1 *Stop and Search*
In any of the circumstances in which a constable has power to arrest a person under Section 14, she may also:
  - for the purpose of ascertaining whether a person has in his possession any document or other article
  - which may constitute evidence that he is a person liable to arrest
  - stop that person and search him.

8.2.2 *Search After Arrest*
Where a constable has arrested a person under Section 14 – for any reason other than for the commission of a criminal offence – he, or any other constable may search him for the purpose of ascertaining whether he has in his possession any document or other article which may constitute evidence that he is a person liable to arrest.

8.2.3 *Explanation*
Gender: A search under these powers must be carried out by a person of the same sex as the person being searched.

PACE: Such searches are governed by the provisions of the Police and Criminal Evidence Act 1984 and Code A of the Codes of Practice.

Arrest other than for an offence: There are powers under Section 14 to arrest a person who is subject to an exclusion order, or against whom the Home Secretary is considering making such an order, and for that person to be detained while procedures are gone through which will or may, in due course, lead to his being excluded from Great Britain (or the United Kingdom, as the case may be).

8.3 Identification of Persons Arrested
Prevention of Terrorism (Temporary Provisions) Act 1989 Section 15(9)

Where a person has been detained under Section 14, any constable may take all such steps as may be reasonably necessary for photographing, measuring or otherwise identifying that person.

Fingerprints and other samples may be taken in terrorist cases, not only if a person is reasonably suspected of involvement in a particular offence, but also to determine whether a person is or has been involved in terrorism. The relevant provisions of Code D of the Codes of Practice will apply to the taking of fingerprints and other samples in such cases, **except** that the prints and samples need not be destroyed afterwards (Code D, Section 1.16).

8.4 Powers to Search
Prevention of Terrorism (Temporary Provisions) Act 1989 Section 15(1)

8.4.1 *Warrant to Search for Person*
If a magistrate is satisfied that there are reasonable grounds for suspecting:
- that a person whom a constable believes to be liable to arrest under Section 14 on suspicion of being involved in acts of terrorism
- is to be found on any premises
- she may issue a warrant authorising any constable to enter those premises
- for the purpose of searching for and arresting that person.

8.4.2 *Warrant to Search for Evidence*
Prevention of Terrorism (Temporary Provisions) Act 1989 Schedule 7, paragraph 2

Grounds for Issue
A magistrate may on application made by a constable issue a warrant if satisfied that:
- a terrorist investigation is being carried out, and
- that there are reasonable grounds for believing that there is on premises specified in the application
- material which is likely to be of substantial value (whether by itself or together with other material) to the investigation.

Conditions for Issue
The issue of a warrant is subject to **any one** of a number of conditions being satisfied. The conditions are:
- that it is not practicable to communicate with any person entitled to grant access to the premises
- that while it is practicable to communicate with a person entitled to grant access to the premises, it is not practicable to communicate with anyone entitled to grant access to the material
- that entry to the premises will not be granted unless a warrant is produced
- that the purpose of the search may be frustrated or seriously prejudiced unless a constable arriving at the premises can secure immediate entry.

Powers Under the Warrant
The warrant will authorise a constable:
- to enter the premises specified in the warrant
- to search the premises
- to search any person found there
- to seize and retain anything found there, or on any person found there, other than items subject to legal privilege
- if the constable has reason to believe that it is likely to be of substantial value to the investigation (by itself or together with other material) AND that it is necessary to seize it to prevent its being concealed, lost, damaged, altered or destroyed.

A search of a person under the warrant must be carried out by a person of the same sex as the person being searched. (The material must not include items subject to legal privilege or excluded material or special privilege material.)

8.4.3 *Search Warrant – Non-Residential Premises*
Prevention of Terrorism (Temporary Provisions) Act 1989
Schedule 7, paragraph 2A

Application for Warrant
Upon application by an officer not below the rank of superintendent a magistrate may issue a warrant upon being satisfied:
– that there is a terrorist investigation being carried out; and
– that there are reasonable grounds to believe that there is material likely to be of substantial value to the investigation
– in one or more premises specified in the application which must not be used wholly or mainly for residential purposes.

The material must not include items subject to legal privilege or excluded material or special privilege material.

Powers Under the Warrant
Once the warrant is issued any constable may:
– enter the specified premises
– search them
– and search any person in them
– and seize and retain anything found, other than items subject to legal privilege.

Before seizing any item however, the constable must be satisfied that there is reason to believe:
– that the item is likely to be of substantial value to the investigation; and
– that it is necessary to seize it to prevent its being concealed, lost, damaged or altered.

Note: A warrant under this Section must be executed within 24 hours of being issued.

8.4.4 *Police Written Order to Search*
Prevention of Terrorism (Temporary Provisions) Act 1989
Schedule 7, paragraph 7

If a police officer of the rank of at least superintendent:
– has reasonable grounds for believing
– that the case is one of great emergency
– and that in the interests of the State immediate action is necessary
– she may give a written order signed by her to any constable
– and this written order will then give the same authority as a warrant, either under paragraph 2, or paragraph 2A.

When such an authority is issued, the case will be reported to the Secretary of State as soon as may be.

8.5 **Power to Stop and Search Vehicles**
Prevention of Terrorism (Temporary Provisions) Act 1989 Section 13A

8.5.1 *Authority to Exercise Powers*
Where it appears to a police officer of or above the rank of commander (Metropolitan or City of London) or assistant chief constable (any other police area):

- that it is expedient to do so in order to prevent acts of terrorism
- she may give an authorisation that powers to stop and search vehicles and persons in them shall be exercisable
- at any place within that police area, or a specified locality in that area
- for a specified period, not exceeding 28 days.

If it appears to an officer of the said rank that the exercise of the powers ought to continue beyond the period specified she may from time to time authorise a further period, not exceeding 28 days.

It is for the authorising officer to set the minimum period considered necessary to deal with the risk of terrorism. A direction to extend the period may be given once only. Thereafter further use of the powers requires a fresh authorisation (PACE Code of Practice A, Note for Guidance 1F).

The authorising officer determines the geographical area in which the use of the powers are to be authorised. The area should not be set wider than is believed necessary for the purpose of preventing anticipated terrorism. Thus the area, like the time period, should be set at the minimum considered necessary (PACE Code of Practice A, Note for Guidance 1G).

8.5.2 *Powers to Search*

The powers under this Section are given to a constable in uniform and authorise him:
- to stop any vehicle
- to search any vehicle, its driver or any passenger for articles of a kind which could be used for a purpose connected with the commission, preparation or instigation of acts of terrorism.

8.5.3 *Explanation*

Reason to search: In the exercise of these powers a constable may stop any vehicle or person and make any search he thinks fit whether or not he has any grounds for suspecting that the vehicle or person is carrying articles of that kind.

However, Code A of the Codes of Practice applies even though reasonable suspicion is not a prerequisite of the exercise of these powers. Powers should be used responsibly by those who exercise them and by those who authorise their use. Every police officer should take care to ensure that the selection and treatment of those searched is based upon objective factors, not upon personal prejudice. Any person searched should be treated courteously and considerately (PACE Code of Practice A, Note for Guidance 1A).

Vehicles: The powers apply equally to stop and search of ships and aircraft as it does to vehicles.

Acts of terrorism: The acts of terrorism referred to are those as defined in Section 9, i.e. relating to matters outside the United Kingdom, as well as to the affairs of Northern Ireland.

8.5.4 *Offence*

A person commits an offence if he:
- fails to stop, or to stop a vehicle, as the case may be when required to do so by a constable in the exercise of these powers
- wilfully obstructs a constable in the exercise of these powers.

8.5.5 *Record of Search*

When a vehicle is stopped by a constable under these powers the driver will be entitled to obtain a written statement that the vehicle was stopped under these powers if he applies for it within the period of 12 months from the day the vehicle was stopped. Likewise, a pedestrian who is stopped will also be entitled, if he applies, to receive a written statement.

8.6 Powers to Search Pedestrians
Prevention of Terrorism (Temporary Provisions) Act 1989 Section 13B

8.6.1 *Written Authorisation*
When an officer of specified rank:
  - believes that it is expedient to do so in order to prevent terrorist acts
  - he may authorise within his police area, or part of it
  - use of powers to stop and search pedestrians.

Such authorisation may be given orally or in writing, but if given orally must be confirmed in writing as soon as is practicable.

The Home Secretary must be informed that the authorisation has been given, and may cancel or confirm it. If he does not confirm it within 48 hours of its being given, it ceases to have effect. If he does confirm it, it will remain in force for the time he specifies, being not longer than 28 days.

The 'specified rank' is the same as for vehicle stops, i.e. commander or above in the Metropolitan and City of London, assistant chief constable or above elsewhere.

8.6.2 *Powers*
An authorisation gives power to a uniformed constable:
  - to stop any pedestrian
  - to search him or anything carried by him
  - for articles which could be used to commit, prepare for or instigate acts of terrorism.

The power may be exercised whether or not there is reasonable grounds for suspecting the presence of such articles.

In exercising the power a constable may not require a person to remove in public any item of clothing other than headgear, footwear, outer coat, jacket or gloves.

8.6.3 *Offence*
It is an offence for a person to fail to stop when required to do so, or wilfully to obstruct a constable in the exercise of these powers.

8.6.4 *Stop Record*
A person who has been stopped under these powers is entitled to a written record to the effect that he was stopped, if he applies within 12 months.

8.7 Police Cordons
*Prevention of Terrorism (Temporary Provisions) Act 1989
Section 16C and Schedule 6A*

8.7.1 *Authority for Cordon*
Where it appears to a police officer not below the rank of superintendent:

- to be expedient to do so in connection with a terrorist investigation
- he may authorise a cordon to be imposed on a specified area, which must be within the police area for which the authorising officer acts.

Authority for a cordon may be given orally or in writing; if given orally it must be confirmed in writing as soon as practicable.

8.7.2 *Urgent Cases*

In a case of urgency, a police officer below the rank of superintendent may give an authorisation. A superintendent or above must be notified as soon as is reasonably practicable, and that officer may then, in writing, confirm the authorisation or cancel it.

8.7.3 *Duration*

An authorisation must specify the period for which it is to remain in force, not exceeding 14 days. The authorisation may be extended, by a superintendent or above, for further periods, but the total from start to finish must not exceed 28 days.

8.7.4 *Marking a Cordon*

A cordoned area must be marked, as far as reasonably practicable, using 'police tape' or other appropriate means. ('Police tape' means plastic or other tape which is generally used by the force concerned for keeping the public out of somewhere.)

8.7.5 *Powers Inside Cordons*

A constable **in uniform** may:
- order a person to leave any premises which abut the cordoned-off area, or are wholly or partly inside the area
- order any person in the area to leave it immediately
- order the driver or other person in charge of a vehicle in the area to move it from the area immediately
- prohibit or restrict any pedestrian or vehicular access to the area.

Any constable may:
- move a vehicle from one place to another in a cordoned-off area, or
- remove a vehicle from that area.

8.7.6 *Offences*

A person commits an offence who:
- fails to comply with an order from a constable in uniform
- contravenes any prohibition or restriction on entry to a cordoned-off area
- wilfully obstructs a constable in the exercise of these powers.

8.7.6.1 *Defence*

It will be a defence to show lawful authority or other reasonable excuse for one's actions.

8.7.7 *Written Authority to Search Within Cordon*

A superintendent or above may give a written order to search premises wholly or partly within a cordoned-off area if he has reasonable grounds for believing that material of substantial evidential value to a terrorist investigation is there.

Such a written authority gives a constable powers to:
- enter the premises
- search the premises and any person found there
- seize and retain anything found reasonably believed to be of substantial evidential value
- if it is reasonably believed that seizure is necessary to prevent the item being concealed, lost, damaged, altered or destroyed.

Entry and search may be at any time while the area remains cordoned off, and may be on more than one occasion.

Power to search a person does not extend to requiring him to remove clothing in public, other than headgear, gloves, footwear, outer coat or jacket.

8.7.8 *Offence*

A person commits an offence who wilfully obstructs, or seeks to frustrate the object of a search made under a written authority.

8.7.8.1 *Defence*

It will be a defence to show lawful authority or other reasonable excuse for one's actions.

8.8 Additional Powers to Control Traffic
Prevention of Terrorism (Temporary Provisions) Act 1989 Section 16D

8.8.1 *Written Authorisation*

If it appears to the appropriate officer (commander, assistant chief constable, or above):
- to be expedient to do so for the purpose of preventing terrorist acts
- he may give an authorisation relating to specified roads or parts of roads, for a specified period, being roads or parts of roads within that officer's police area.

The specified period must not exceed 28 days, but a further period of up to 28 days may be authorised subsequently.

The authorisation may be given orally or in writing, but if given orally, must be confirmed in writing as soon as practicable.

8.8.2 *Powers*

An authorisation will give any constable the power to prohibit or restrict persons from leaving vehicles in any specified road or part of a road.

The powers may be exercised by placing appropriate traffic signs.

8.8.3 *Offences*

1: A person commits an offence who leaves a vehicle, or allows it to remain at rest, on a road in contravention of such prohibition or restriction.

2: A person commits an offence who, being the driver or other person in charge of a vehicle, and having allowed that vehicle to remain on a road in contravention of a prohibition or restriction made under this provision, fails to move it when ordered to do so by a constable **in uniform**.

8.8.4 *Defence (or non-defence)*

1: It is a defence to either offence, for a person to show that he had lawful authority or reasonable excuse.

2: The fact that a person holds a current disabled person's badge does not exempt him from any of these prohibitions or restrictions, nor does the holding of such a badge constitute lawful authority or reasonable excuse.

9 PACE AND THE CODES OF PRACTICE

9.1 Application of Codes

The provisions of the Police and Criminal Evidence Act 1984 and the Codes of Practice apply to the investigation of terrorist matters and treatment of persons stopped, searched or detained in relation to the prevention or investigation of terrorism and terrorist offences, as they do to persons being dealt with in relation to other aspects of criminal law. However, there are a number of special provisions in the Act and Codes relating to terrorism, summarised below.

9.2 Exercise of Powers to Stop and Search

Before carrying out a search of a person or vehicle, a police officer is required to give his name and other details to the person to be searched, or the person in charge of the vehicle to be searched. If not in uniform, the officer is also required to show his warrant card. In the case of a search linked to the investigation of terrorism, in giving information and in showing his warrant card, the officer is not obliged to give his name (Code A, Section 2.5).

Where a search record is completed following a search being carried out, the identity of the officer making the search should be included in the record. Where the search was linked to the investigation of terrorism, the officer's name should not be included in the search record; instead, his warrant or other identification number, together with his station, should be recorded (Code A, Section 4.5).

An application for a warrant requires the authority of an officer of at least the rank of inspector. In the case of an application for a warrant under Schedule 7, the authority required is that of a superintendent or above (Code B, Section 2.4).

When a warrant is executed and there is someone on the premises, the officer in charge is required to provide details to that person, including her name, and if not in uniform, to show her warrant card. When the search is linked to the investigation of terrorism, she need not give her name in doing so (Code B, Section 5.5).

When a warrant is executed at premises which are not occupied, the officer in charge should leave copies of the warrant and of the Notice of Powers and Rights, endorsed with her name. In the case of a searched linked to terrorism, her warrant or identification number, not her name, should be endorsed (Code B, Section 5.8).

When premises have been searched under a warrant, the names of the officers who executed it have to be endorsed on the back of the warrant, together with other details. In the case of enquiries linked to terrorism, the officers' warrant or identification numbers, together with their duty stations, shall replace their names (Code B, Section 7.2).

When premises occupied by a person arrested for an arrestable offence are to be searched under the provisions of Section 18 of PACE the authority of an officer of the rank of inspector or above is required. In giving the authority, and in endorsing the custody record, where the case is linked to the investigation of terrorism, the authorising officer should use his warrant or other identification number, not his name (Code B, Section 3.3).

9.3 Treatment of Detained Persons

For the purposes of Code C, a person taken to a police station after being arrested under the provisions of Section 14, e.g. as the subject of an exclusion order, will be regarded as a person in police custody (Code C, Section 1.11).

In any case where an officer's name or signature is required to be entered on a custody record, either as authority for some action, or the signing of any other entry, if the person is detained under the provisions of the Act, the officer's warrant or identification number, together with her duty station, should be entered, not her name (Code C, Sections 2.1, 2.6).

A number of rights may be delayed if an officer of the rank of superintendent or above has reasonable grounds to believe that the exercise of any such right:
- will lead to interference with the gathering of information about the commission, instigation or preparation of acts of terrorism; or
- by alerting any person will make it more difficult to prevent an act of terrorism, or to secure the apprehension, prosecution or conviction of any person in connection with the commission, instigation or preparation of an act of terrorism (Code C, Annex B).

The rights which may be delayed are:
- the right to have a nominated person notified of his whereabouts under Section 56 of PACE
- to send a letter and to be allowed to speak on the telephone for a reasonable time (Code C, Section 5.6). Note: The denial of this right may be authorised by an inspector or above if satisfied that the conditions set out in Annex B apply
- the right to consult a solicitor in accordance with Section 58 of PACE. In this case, an interview may be conducted before the detained person has had access to legal advice (Code C, Section 6.6).

The rights may be delayed only for so long as is necessary and in no case beyond 48 hours from the time of arrest. If the grounds for delay cease to apply, the detained person must be offered the opportunity to exercise the rights as soon as practicable.

Special mention is made of the importance of clean bedding and a varied diet in the case of a person detained under the provisions of the Act, who is likely to be in custody for a longer period than other detained persons (Code C, Note for Guidance 8B).

9.4 Reviews and Time Limits on Detention
Prevention of Terrorism (Temporary Provisions) Act 1989
Section 14 and Schedule 3

The provisions of Section 40 of PACE, giving time limits on detention and arrangements for reviews, do not apply to a person arrested under Section 14 of the Act. The following apply instead:
- a person arrested shall not be detained under that power for more than 48 hours after his arrest

- the Secretary of State may extend the period of 48 hours but any further period of detention shall not exceed 5 days in all; application must be made to the Secretary of State when an extension is sought after the first 48 hours
- the first review of detention shall be carried out as soon as practicable after the start of that detention
- subsequent reviews shall be carried out at intervals of not more than 12 hours
- once an application has been made for an extension, no further review shall be held.

The review officer must be one who has not been directly involved in the case. For any review carried out within the first 24 hours of a person's detention, she must be an officer not below the rank of inspector. For subsequent reviews she must be an officer not below the rank of superintendent.

Schedule 3 provides for matters to be taken into account by the review officer, postponement of reviews, representations by the detained person and others, and records of reviews. These are all largely similar to the corresponding provisions of Section 40 of PACE and of Code C of the Codes of Practice.

9.5 Tape Recording of Interviews

Tape recording is not required of an interview with a person arrested under certain provisions of the Act, or who is being questioned about an offence where there are reasonable grounds to suspect that it is connected with terrorism or was committed in pursuance of the objectives of an organisation engaged in terrorism (Code E, Section 3.2).

This applies to terrorism connected with the affairs of Northern Ireland and also to terrorism relating to parts of the world outside the United Kingdom (Code E, Note for Guidance 3G).

When it only becomes clear during an interview which is being tape recorded that the person being interviewed may have committed such an offence, the interviewing officer should turn off the tape recorder (Code E, Note for Guidance 3H).

Chapter 19: Football and Related Matters

1 DESIGNATED SPORTING EVENTS

1.1 Introduction

For several decades now, disorder among spectators at football matches has been a problem in Britain. More recently, bad behaviour has spread to the followers of certain other sports, much of the cause being seen as over-indulgence in alcohol.

1.2 Scope of Legislation

Four principal areas of legislation seek to address these problems:
- restriction on the possession and consumption of alcohol at certain sporting events
- the creation of offences relating specifically to spectators at association football matches
- provisions for preventing convicted hooligans attending future soccer matches
- restrictions on the unofficial sale of tickets by 'ticket touts'.

1.3 Meaning of Terms

These provisions will usually apply to **designated sporting events** held at a **designated sports ground** during the **period of the designated sporting event**. Although restriction on alcohol could be applied to other sports, the overwhelming thrust of the legislation is aimed at association football.

Designated sporting event: This means an event which has been designated, or is of a class designated by the Home Secretary. Generally, Football League matches, Scottish and Welsh League matches, the several European competition matches and international matches held at designated sports grounds will be designated sporting events.

Designated sports ground: Is any place used for sporting events and where accommodation is provided for spectators – which has been designated, or is of a class designated by the Home Secretary.

Period of a designated sporting event: The term usually means the period:
- commencing two hours before the start of the event, or two hours before the advertised start time, in a case where the start has been delayed
- ending one hour after the end of the event.

For example, a designated soccer match is due to start at 3pm, and end at 4.45pm. The start is delayed for 30 minutes, 5 minutes injury time is played and the game ends at 5.20pm. The designated period of the event will be from 1.00pm to 6.20pm, i.e. from two hours before it was advertised to start until one hour after it actually finished.

If a designated match is not played at all on the day it should, the period shall be:
- from two hours before the advertised start time
- until one hour after the advertised start time, being a total period of three hours.

This provision would cater for a situation where the ground starts to fill up in anticipation of the kick-off, then for some reason the game is postponed or cancelled before it starts. The restrictions have already started to be applied, offences committed etc, and this may continue for up to an hour after the time the game should have started.

Individual events: Although any professional soccer match in Great Britain is likely to be a designated sporting event, so may some other events. When arrangements are made to police a sporting event, it is likely that the fact that the event is 'designated' will be mentioned in briefings.

It is important to take account of the fact that an event held outside England and Wales may be of significance to police officers, because part of the legislation deals with offences which may be committed on trains and other vehicles taking spectators to a designated event.

2 CONTROL OF ALCOHOL AND OTHER ARTICLES
Sporting Events (Control of Alcohol etc) Act 1985

2.1 Possession on Trains and Coaches and Minibuses
Sporting Events (Control of Alcohol etc) Act 1985 Sections 1, 1A

2.1.1 *Public Service Vehicles*
An offence will be committed by a person:
- if he is the operator or the servant or agent of the operator
- or if he is the person to whom a vehicle is hired, or the servant or agent of such
- who knowingly
- causes or permits intoxicating liquor to be carried on the vehicle.

2.1.2 *Minibuses*
An offence will be committed in the case of a minibus, by a person who is:
- the driver of the vehicle; or
- its keeper, or the keeper's servant or agent; or
- the person to whom it is made available (by hire, loan or otherwise), or his servant or agent
- who knowingly
- causes or permits intoxicating liquor to be carried on the vehicle.

2.1.3 *Public Service Vehicles, Railway Passenger Vehicles and Minibuses*
An offence will be committed by a person who:
- while on the vehicle has intoxicating liquor in his possession; or
- while on the vehicle is drunk.

2.1.4 *Explanation*
When offence may be committed:
Section 1 applies to:
- a vehicle which is a public service vehicle or railway passenger vehicle
- which is being used for the principal purpose of carrying passengers for the whole or part of a journey to or from a designated sporting event.
Section 1A applies to:
- a motor vehicle which is not a public service vehicle
- but is adapted to carry more than eight passengers
- which is being used for the principal purpose of carrying **two or more** passengers for the whole or part of a journey to or from a designated sporting event.

For ease of reference, such a vehicle will be referred to in this chapter as a minibus, which is the name commonly applied to such vehicles. This term may have a more precise meaning where it appears in other legislation.

Public service vehicle: Basically, this means a motor vehicle which is licensed and operated for the carriage of passengers for payment, excluding taxis.

Operator: The operator is the person for whom the driver of a public service vehicle works (or the driver himself, if he is self-employed). The operator may commit an offence, as can an employee or agent of the operator. Note that there is no corresponding liability placed on the operator of a railway, or on railway employees if alcohol is carried on railway passenger vehicles.

Hired/made available: In the case of a public service vehicle, offences may be committed by a person to whom the vehicle is hired (or an employee or agent of that person). In the case of a minibus, this liability applies to anyone to whom the vehicle has been made available. This recognises that a minibus may be borrowed, as well as hired, whereas one does not expect a bus to be lent out by its operator.

Two or more passengers: Although a minibus is a motor vehicle adapted for more than eight passengers, it does not have to be full. Two passengers are enough to bring it within the scope of these restrictions.

Driver: The driver of a minibus may be liable. There is no mention of 'driver' in relation to public service vehicles, but the driver is likely to be the employee or agent of the operator, and liable as such.

Knowingly: For the offence to be committed the offender must know that there is intoxicating liquor on board. The prosecution will have to prove this point, so evidence will be required, e.g. that cans or bottles were clearly visible.

Principal purpose: The vehicle must be mainly used to carry persons on the way to or back from a designated sporting event, but this need be for only part of the journey, e.g. on a minibus taking fans to an airport, to fly to a European Cup match.

However, if a scheduled service bus or train happens to be full of football supporters going to a match, this does not bring it within the scope of the Act, since the principal purpose is to provide a scheduled public service.

Note: Some scheduled trains operate on football match days with intoxicating liquor not available from the buffet car. This is due to the train operator seeking to avoid trouble from football fans; it does not necessarily mean that the train is one to which the Act will apply.

2.1.5 *Police Powers*
Sporting Events (Control of Alcohol etc) Act 1985 Section 7

- A constable may stop a public service vehicle or minibus to which these provisions apply:
  i) and may search that vehicle or a railway passenger vehicle
  ii) if he has reasonable grounds to suspect that an offence under these provisions is being or has been committed in it.
  It is perhaps sensible that there is no power to stop a train, but a train may be searched.
- A constable has power to search a person whom he has reasonable grounds to suspect is committing or has committed an offence under the Act.

– A constable may arrest a person whom he has reasonable grounds to suspect is committing or has committed an offence under the Act.

Note: The powers to search require reasonable suspicion and are subject to the provisions of Code A of the PACE Codes of Practice.

The powers to search a person and to arrest suspected offenders apply to all the offences under the Act, not just to those involving intoxicants on trains and buses.

2.2 Alcohol and Containers at Sports Grounds
Sporting Events (Control of Alcohol etc) Act 1985 Section 2

2.2.1 *Offences*
1: A person commits an offence if:
   – he has in his possession
   – intoxicating liquor
   – or an article to which this Section applies
   – during the period of a designated sporting event
   – while he is in an area of a designated sports ground from which the event may be directly viewed; or
   – while he is entering or trying to enter a designated sports ground.

2: A person commits an offence who:
   – is drunk during the period of a designated sporting event
   – while in a designated sports ground
   – or while entering or trying to enter such a ground.

2.2.2 *Explanation*
Article: The Section applies to any article capable of causing injury to a person struck by it, which is:
   – any bottle, can or other portable container, or part of one (including one which is crushed or broken), and
   – which is for holding any drink, and
   – which is of a kind which, when empty, is normally discarded or returned to, or left to be recovered by the supplier.

A vacuum flask or hip flask would not fall into this description, but a drinks can (discarded when empty), a returnable bottle (increasingly rare these days) or a milk bottle (left to be recovered by the supplier) would. The article must be capable of causing injury, so certain drinks containers, e.g. of paper or cardboard, may not come within this description. Containers for medicines are exempt.

Period of designated sporting event: This term is dealt with in *paragraph 1.3* above. However, see the reference to 'from which the event may be directly viewed', below.

From which the event may be directly viewed: There is no complete ban on alcohol in designated sports grounds, indeed many have bars and there are provisions for these *(see paragraph 2.4 below)*. The ban is on bringing one's own supply into the ground, or being in possession of it in a part of the ground from which there is a direct view of the pitch.

Special provision is made for an area of the ground from which there is a direct view, but which is not open to the public, such as the directors' box or executive boxes leased out to companies. In such an area, the 'period of the designated event' is reduced to a period 15 minutes before the start or advertised start of the event, to 15 minutes after the end of the event. This affords the privileged few some 2 1/2 hours of additional 'drinking time' before and after the match.

2.2.3 *Police Powers*
Sporting Events (Control of Alcohol etc) Act 1985 Section 7

1: A constable has power to search a person whom he has reasonable grounds to suspect is committing or has committed an offence under the Act.

Note: The power to search requires reasonable suspicion and is subject to the provisions of Code A of the PACE Codes of Practice. This power is not to be confused with searches conducted as a routine measure of persons seeking entry to a designated sports ground. Nothing in Code A affects the routine searching of persons entering a sports ground or other place ~~with their consent as a condition of entry~~ (Code A, Note for Guidance 1D). 'Agree to be searched or you're not coming in', applies at many football grounds, pop music concerts etc.

2: A constable may arrest a person whom he has reasonable grounds to suspect is committing or has committed an offence under the Act.

2.3 **Possession of Fireworks etc**
Sporting Events (Control of Alcohol etc) Act 1985 Section 2A

2.3.1 *Offence*
A person commits an offence who:
  - at any time during the period of a designated sporting event
  - when he is in an area of a designated sports ground from which the event may be directly viewed, or
  - when he is entering or trying to enter the ground
  - has in his possession an article or substance to which this Section applies.

2.3.2 *Explanation*
Article or substance: The Section applies to possession of any of the following items:
  - any firework
  - any article or substance the main purpose of which is the emission of a flare for the purposes of signalling or illumination (as opposed to heating or ignition) or the emission of smoke or a visible gas.

In particular, this includes distress flares, fog signals and articles intended as fumigators for testing pipes. It does not include matches, cigarette lighters or heaters.

In some cases, it will be clear that an article is prohibited, e.g. a marine distress rocket. In other cases, something of an expert knowledge may be required to determine whether an article is a flare for the purposes of illumination or a flare for the purposes of ignition.

Designated period: As in the case of having alcohol or drinks containers, this offence is committed during the period of the designated sporting event.

Area ... directly viewed: It would be more sensible for the ban on these items to apply anywhere in the ground, but such is not the case. In the case of intoxicants, it is an offence to have them when coming into the ground or when in an area from which the event may be directly viewed. This allows for the possession of drinks and drink containers in other parts of the ground, which is understandable. It does not appear logical however, to apply the same rules to the possession of fireworks and flares. Is there an intention that a football ground may have a flare shop or a firework display area out of sight of the pitch?

2.3.3 *Defence*
A person will have a defence to a charge under this Section if he proves that he had the item with lawful authority.

2.3.4 *Police Powers*
The same powers of search and arrest apply to this offence as to others under the Act.

2.4 Supply of Alcohol in Designated Sports Grounds
Sporting Events (Control of Alcohol etc) Act 1985 Section 3

2.4.1 *Permitted Hours*
Where there are licensed premises or a registered club within the area of a designated sports ground, the permitted hours shall not include any part of the period of a designated sporting event at that ground.

Many football grounds have social club facilities for supporters or restaurants open to the public. The effect of this restriction is that intoxicants may not be supplied in such premises during the period of a designated sporting event, i.e. two hours before it starts to an hour after it finishes. However... read on.

2.4.2 *Exemption Orders*
A magistrates' court may make an order – to include part of designated period within the permitted hours – and the order may include conditions which will apply to the sale and supply of intoxicants during that period. (These conditions may be in addition to, or may vary, existing conditions already attached to the licence or registration certificate.)

Note: An exemption order may not apply to any part of the ground from which the designated sporting event may be directly viewed. So, if a football ground has a licensed restaurant open to the public, magistrates may make an order allowing alcoholic drinks to be served during all or part of the period of a designated sporting event, but not if the restaurant overlooks the pitch. However... read on.

2.4.3 *Private Facilities*
The 'period of a designated sporting event' is reduced in relation to executive boxes, etc, to which the public are not admitted *(see paragraph 2.2.2 above)*.

2.4.4 *Police Powers*
Sporting Events (Control of Alcohol etc) Act 1985 Sections 3(7) and 6

This is the third stage of the sequence 'close the bar – open it again – close it again', i.e. there is a general ban on supply of alcohol during the designated period – magistrates may grant an exemption order – then the police may step in.

There are two distinct powers:
1: An inspector or above:
   – may give a written notice, under which an exemption order will cease to have effect, or will be modified on the grounds that:

- the sale and supply of intoxicants under the exemption order is likely to be detrimental to the orderly conduct or safety of spectators at the event, **and**
- it is impracticable for an application to be made to a magistrates' court for a variation of the exemption order in respect of that event (Section 3(7)).

2: A constable in uniform:
- during the period of a designated sporting event
- may require any person having control of a bar in the designated sports ground to close and to keep it closed to the end of that period
- if it appears to him that the supply of intoxicating liquor at any bar within the ground is detrimental to the orderly conduct or safety of spectators (Section 6).

2.4.5 *Explanation*

Written notice: The situation in which such a notice may be issued would be one where time was too short to go to magistrates' court, but there was sufficient time for a notice to be prepared and served. Service is on a nominated person, i.e. a person pre-designated to receive it.

Order to close bar: This would apply in a more immediate situation than one where a written notice might be considered. Such an order may be made when the period of the designated event has already started. The order is given to the person having control of that bar, who need not be the licensee.

Constable in uniform: The power to close a bar may have to be exercised as a last-minute action, to avert imminent disorder, or danger. Hence the power is given to any constable in uniform. However, Home Office advice is that a decision whether to close a bar will require considerable care. An 'experienced' officer should be consulted if possible.

2.4.6 *Offences*

1: A person in charge of a bar who fails to comply with a requirement to close it commits an offence, unless he shows that he took all reasonable steps to comply (Section 6(2)).

2: Where intoxicating liquor is sold or supplied at a time excluded from permitted hours by virtue of Section 3, or in contravention of conditions imposed under the Section, then a licensee, officer of a registered club, or other person who knows or believes the sale or supply to be outside the permitted hours will commit an offence under Section 3, rather than under the appropriate Section of the Licensing Act 1964 (Section 3(10)).

One effect of this provision is that the statutory power of arrest under this Act applies, as it does to all offences under the Act *(see paragraph 2.2.3)*.

2.4.7 *Not an Offence*

When a person consumes intoxicating liquor at a time which is outside permitted hours because of the effect of a written notice from an inspector or above, the person will not commit an offence of consuming outside permitted hours under the Licensing Act 1964, unless he knows or has reason to believe that the time is now outside permitted hours (Section 3(11)).

Put simply, if the licensee or some other person fails to comply with a police written notice not to supply intoxicants, the licensee, etc, will commit an offence, but the customers will not be liable for drinking, unless it is shown that they knew or had good reason to believe that the permitted hours were in abeyance at that time.

2.4.8 *Arrest*
The statutory power to arrest, applies to these offences as to others under the Act.

2.5 **Police Power of Entry**
Sporting Events (Control of Alcohol etc) Act 1985 Section 7

A constable may:
- at any time during the period of a designated sporting event at any designated sports ground
- enter any part of that ground
- for the purpose of enforcing the provisions of the Act.

3 OFFENCES AT FOOTBALL MATCHES
Football (Offences) Act 1991

3.1 **Meanings of Terms**

3.1.1 *Designated Football Match*
The legislators might have seen fit to make the term mean the same as that of 'designated sporting event' under the 1985 Act, but such is not the case. A football match is a designated one if:

1: It is either:
- a UEFA competition match; or
- it involves a team from the Football League or the F.A. Premier League; or
- it involves a team from a club in a country or territory outside England and Wales; or
- it involves a team representing a country or territory; **and**

2: It is played at a sports ground which, at the time:
- is designated under the Safety of Sports Grounds Act 1975; or
- is occupied by a club which at the time is in the Football League or the F.A. Premier League.

The description allows for quite a few permutations, but put simply, a football match involving a League or Premier League side on their ground, will be a designated match.

3.1.2 *Period of the Designated Match*
The period during which offences may be committed is the same as the provision under the 1985 Act, i.e. from two hours before the start (or advertised start time, if the kick-off is delayed) to one hour after the end of the match.

If the match is not played on the advertised day, the designated period is also the same as in the 1985 Act – i.e. from two hours before the advertised start until one hour after that time, a total of three hours.

3.2 **Offences**

3.2.1 *Throwing Objects*
Football (Offences) Act 1991 Section 2

It is an offence for a person at a designated football match:

- without lawful authority or lawful excuse
- to throw anything at or towards:
  i) the playing area; or
  ii) any area adjacent to the playing area to which spectators are not generally admitted; or
  iii) any area in which spectators or other persons are or may be present.

3.2.2 *Chanting*
Football (Offences) Act 1991 Section 3

It is an offence for a person at a designated football match:
- to take part in chanting
- of a racialist or indecent nature.

3.2.3 *Pitch Invasion*
Football (Offences) Act 1991 Section 4

A person commits an offence at a designated football match who:
- without lawful authority or lawful excuse (the onus of proving which is on him)
- goes on to the playing area
- or any area adjacent to the playing area to which spectators are not generally admitted.

3.2.4 *Explanation*
Throw: The offence is completed by throwing an object. There is no need to prove that it was directed at anyone, that it hit anyone, or even that it was capable of causing injury.

Are or may be present: If an object is thrown towards an area where persons may be present, it matters not that there is no one in the area at the time.

Chanting: This means the repeated uttering of words or sounds in concert with one or more others. There must be an element of repetition, words may be used, but a sound such as a 'chimpanzee' type grunt, may equally amount to chanting. The offender has to be acting together (the word 'concert' does not imply any musical element!) with at least one other person.

Racialist nature: Means that the chanting consists of or includes matter which is threatening, abusive or insulting to a person by reason of his colour, race, nationality, citizenship or ethnic or national origins.

3.2.5 *Arrest*
Although these offences carry less than five years' imprisonment, they are all arrestable offences, the Police and Criminal Evidence Act 1984 having been amended to include them as such.

4 EXCLUSION AND RESTRICTION ORDERS

4.1 Types of Order
An exclusion order applies to prevent a person attending certain football matches in this country. A restriction order is aimed at preventing a person travelling to a football match outside England and Wales.

4.2 **Exclusion Orders**
Public Order Act 1986 Section 30

4.2.1 *Prescribed Football Match*
The effect of the order is to exclude that person from entering premises for the purpose of attending a football match there. An exclusion order shall apply to a prescribed football match which means:
 – one involving a Football League or F.A. Premier League side; or
 – one which is an international match; or
 – one which is a UEFA cup, European Cup Winners' Cup or European Champion Clubs' Cup.

4.2.2 *Relevant Offences*
Public Order Act 1986 Section 31

A exclusion order may be made by a court, in addition to a sentence, before which a person is convicted of one of a number of offences. An offence is a relevant one if it fulfils one or more of the following conditions:
 – it was committed during the period relevant to a prescribed football match, while the accused was at, or was entering, leaving, trying to enter or trying to leave the football ground
 – the offence involved:
    i) the use or threat of violence and occurred when the accused and/or the victim was going to or from a soccer match, or
    ii) criminal damage or threat of damage while the accused was on such a journey, or
    iii) racial hatred (Sections 17-29, Public Order Act 1986) or an offence under Section 5 of this Act
 – the offence was one involving alcohol on a train, bus, coach or minibus, etc, going to or from a designated soccer match (Sections 1, 1A, Sporting Events (Control of Alcohol etc) Act 1985).

4.2.3 *Explanation*
Offence: The offence is 'relevant' if only one of these conditions is met, so any offence committed in a football ground during the relevant period could in theory lead to an exclusion order, even something as minor as dropping litter.

Relevant period: This is the same as for the control of alcohol legislation, basically two hours before the start to one hour after the finish; the provisions for delayed and postponed matches are the same *(see paragraph 1.3 above)*.

Journey to or from: Includes any breaks in the journey. Thus, a supporter travelling back from an away match who stops overnight en route may commit a relevant offence during the course of that evening, albeit some distance from the football ground and some time after the match has finished.

4.2.4 *Grounds for Making Exclusion Order*
The court may make an exclusion order if satisfied that the making of such an order in relation to the accused will help prevent violence or disorder at or in connection with prescribed football matches.

4.2.5 *Offence*
A person commits an offence who enters premises in breach of an exclusion order.

4.2.6 *Arrest*
A constable may arrest without warrant a person whom he reasonably suspects has entered premises in breach of an exclusion order.

4.2.7 *Duration of Order*
The period of time over which an order shall have effect is decided by the court. If the period is greater than one year, the convicted person may at any time apply to the court to have the order terminated.

4.3 Restriction Orders
Football Spectators Act 1989

4.3.1 *Designated Football Match*
There are two sorts of 'designated match', those inside England and Wales, and those in other countries:

1: In England and Wales a designated match is one played:
   – at Wembley Stadium
   – at the National Stadium, Cardiff
   – or at any sports ground registered with the Football League or the F.A. Premier League.

2: Outside England and Wales it is one:
   – involving a national side (England or Wales)
   – or one involving a club in the Football League or the F.A. Premier League
   – or one involving a club playing in a UEFA competition.

4.4 Convictions
Football Spectators Act 1989 Section 15 and Schedule 1

A restriction order may be made in addition to any punishment when a person is convicted of one of a list of 'football related' offences. These include:
   – all offences under the Football (Offences) Act 1991
   – offences under the Sporting Events (Control of Alcohol, etc) Act 1985
   – any offence involving violence, threat of violence, harassment, alarm, distress or racial hatred or violence or damage or threat of damage to property – committed during the relevant period of a designated match, while at, entering or leaving the ground, or on the journey to or from the match
   – offences of drunkenness, including drink drive offences committed while on a journey to or from a designated match.

4.4.1 *Relevance of Offence*
In a case where an offence is committed away from a football ground, i.e. on a journey to or from the game, the court in making an order, must make a 'declaration of relevance'. The prosecution must give notice to the accused before the court date, of an intention to seek such a declaration. The relevance of the offence for these purposes is therefore a matter which might usefully be included in a file going to the Crown Prosecution Service.

4.4.2 *Grounds for Making Order*

A court may make an order if satisfied that – in relation to the accused – it would help to prevent violence or disorder at or in connection with designated football matches.

4.5 **Effect of Order**
Football Spectators Act 1989 Section 16

A person subject to an order must report:
- in the first instance, to a police station specified in the order, within five days of the order being made
- on subsequent occasions, to any police station in England or Wales at the time or between the times specified in a notice which he may receive.

The notices are issued by the Football Spectators Restriction Orders Authority, on the occasion of designated matches outside England and Wales. By having to present himself at a police station in compliance with the notice, the person is prevented from travelling abroad to the match.

4.5.1 *Duration of Order*

A restriction order will last:
- in the case of a person sentenced to an immediate term of imprisonment, for five years, taking effect from the date of his release;
- in any other case for two years.

4.5.2 *Appeal and Exemption*

There is a provision whereby the person subject to the order may apply for its termination. Application must be made to the court after one year. There is also provision for an exemption to be granted in respect of a reporting requirement on any particular occasion, where the applicant is able to show that there are special circumstances, and because of those circumstances, he would not in any case attend the football match in question.

4.5.3 *Offence*

It is an offence for a person without reasonable excuse, to fail to report to a police station as required by an order.

5 **TICKET TOUTS**
Criminal Justice and Public Order Act 1994 Section 166

5.1 **Purpose**

One aspect of crowd control at soccer matches is regulation of the sale of tickets. This allows organisers to segregate rival fans within the ground, refuse the sale of tickets to known troublemakers, etc. Such strategies may come to nought if tickets are sold by unauthorised sellers. In addition, the activities of ticket touts may lead to disorder or obstruction, arising from the touting of tickets in the vicinity of the ground, and by encouraging persons without tickets to turn up in the hope of being able to obtain some. Stolen and/or forged tickets being identified at the turnstiles provides further potential for disorder.

5.1.1 *Offence*

It is an offence:

– for an unauthorised person
– to sell or offer or expose for sale a ticket for a designated football match:
   i) in any public place or place to which the public have access; or
   ii) in any other place, in the course of a trade or business.

5.1.2 *Application*

The provisions of the Section will apply to such matches or categories of matches as the Secretary of State shall designate, by order, being a match for which 6,000 or more tickets are issued for sale.

5.1.3 *Explanation*

Unauthorised: A person is unauthorised unless she is authorised in writing to sell tickets for the match by the home club or by the match organisers. There should be little difficulty in most cases, in deciding whether a person selling tickets is authorised to do so.

Ticket: This includes anything purporting to be a ticket. The effect of this is that a person selling forged tickets would be liable under this Section, in addition to any other liability, for offences of forgery, obtaining property by deception, etc. The claim 'I'm not guilty of touting tickets because they weren't genuine tickets', will not succeed.

Designated football match: This has the same meaning as under the Football (Offences) Act 1991 *(see paragraph 3.1.1 above)*.

Specified matches: The provisions will apply to such matches or categories of match as designated by the Home Secretary in an order. The matches must be ones for which at least 6,000 tickets are available for sale.

A certificate, signed by an authorised official, shall be conclusive evidence of the fact that at least 6,000 tickets are offered for sale.

5.2 **Police Powers**

5.2.1 *Arrest*

Offences under this Section, although punishable only with a fine, are inserted into Section 24(2) of the Police and Criminal Evidence Act 1984, and are therefore arrestable offences.

5.2.2 *Search*
Police and Criminal Evidence Act 1984 Section 32

Section 32, which gives a constable power to search premises after a person has been arrested for evidence of the offence for which he was arrested, shall extend to give a constable power:
– to enter and search any vehicle
– which the constable has reasonable grounds to suspect
– was being used for any purpose connected with this offence.

A person touting tickets near a football ground may well not keep too many tickets or cash about his person, for fear of becoming the victim of theft. This power allows police, once a person has been arrested for the offence, to enter and search any vehicle which a constable has reason to suspect was being used by the tout, for evidence, such as cash or tickets.

Chapter 20: Labour Law

1 INTRODUCTION

1.1 Historical Context

There have been numerous examples over many decades, of violence associated with trade disputes. This has continued to be the case up to recent times, with the Miners' Strike and events at Wapping in the mid-1980's as two notable examples. Legislation has had two effects – first to render strikes less frequent by requiring that a ballot be held before a strike can be held, secondly by limiting the scope of pickets to travel from place to place for the purpose of picketing. It is noteworthy that these laws are matters for civil not criminal courts. As far as the criminal law is concerned, there are no offences which relate exclusively to trade disputes; the one offence which may be associated closely with a trade dispute, intimidation with a view to compelling someone to do or not to do something, is equally applicable to non-industrial situations.

1.2 Right to Strike

The requirement for a union to hold a ballot before calling its members out on strike does not affect an individual's right to refrain from working. Any breach of contract arising from such action would be a matter for the civil not criminal law. There are notable exceptions to this, of which the Police Service is an example. Intimidation of a worker to return to work when he is on strike is equally a crime as when the object is to force him to strike.

1.3 Right to Picket

Picketing, in the context of labour law, is the activity whereby persons on strike seek to persuade those not on strike to support them, by joining the strike, by declining to deliver materials to the strikers' work place, etc. There is no general right to picket in this country. Picketing, or in the words of the legislation 'besetting the place where a person works' may amount to a crime if done 'with a view to compelling' a person to do or not to do something. The law does allow for peaceful picketing by a limited category of persons, but it may be argued that even this does not amount to a 'right to picket' since police may limit numbers of pickets in order to avoid an anticipated breach of the peace.

1.4 Civil Law

The principal legislation governing labour relations is the Trade Union and Labour Relations (Consolidation) Act 1992, commonly referred to as TULR(C)A. Reference is made here to but two of its many Sections. Much of the rest of TULR(C)A is concerned with civil law, and some mention needs to be made of the civil side, in order to place in context Sections 220 and 241 which are referred to below.

The organiser of industrial action such as a strike will normally commit a number of torts. (A 'tort' is a wrong at civil law for which the person wronged may take court action.) Such torts may include – inducing another to break a contract of employment – interfering with a trade or business – trespass – conspiracy, etc. The terms 'wrongfully' and 'lawfully' as they appear in Sections 220 and 241 may be taken as referring to whether there is a liability at civil law, rather than at criminal law.

1.5 **Public Disorder**

There are three elements to consider in relation to the public order aspects of labour law:
- offences involving intimidation, etc
- peaceful picketing
- the application to trade disputes of the criminal law generally.

2 **PEACEFUL PICKETING**

Trade Union and Labour Relations (Consolidation) Act 1992 Section 220

2.1 **What is Peaceful Picketing?**

2.1.1 *Activity*

It is lawful for a person:
- in contemplation or furtherance of a trade dispute to attend
- for the purpose **only** of peacefully obtaining or communicating information
- or peacefully persuading any person to work or to abstain from working.

2.1.2 *Who May Do It?*

A person may attend for that purpose:
- at or near his own place of work;
- as an official of a trade union, at or near the place of work of a member of the union:
  i) whom he represents and
  ii) whom he is accompanying.

2.1.3 *Explanation*

Lawful: The Section describes what may be done lawfully, as peaceful picketing. Here, the term 'lawful' means that the activities of pickets will be exempt from civil action for tort. If pickets remain within what is permitted under this Section they will commit no crime. Conversely, if they commit a crime they have gone beyond what is allowed by the Section. There is an intermediate stage, where pickets go beyond what is permitted by the Section but do not commit any crime. In such cases, it is not a matter for police to become involved in obtaining evidence for the civil court or in assisting employers to do so.

At or near: A picket is permitted to attend at or near his place of work. 'At' implies that he may attend on the public road at the gate, entrance etc. The fact that there is a lawful right to attend on the highway at the gate, has implications for a possible offence of obstructing the highway, in that such use of the highway may be reasonable, and not amount to obstruction.

Pickets can picket 'near' their workplace where it does not abut the public highway, e.g. where the premises are on an industrial estate, and the picket line is at the entrance to the estate.

However, 'at or near' does not include 'in or on'. The Section does not allow pickets the right to act as such on private property (*British Airports Authority v Ashton* (1983)).

Place of work: There are two aspects of the meaning of 'place of work' which require further explanation:
1: If a person normally works otherwise than at one place – or at a place so located that attendance there for the purposes of peaceful picketing is not practicable – then for the purposes of this Section his 'place of work' shall be any premises of his employer from

which he works or from which his work is administered.

This allows for a situation where a person may work out of a number of different sites, or he may not work from any premises of his employer. Examples would include a bricklayer, who reports each day to whatever building site he is working on at that time, or a maintenance engineer who goes around his employer's branches repairing machinery as defects arise. Such a worker could lawfully picket any of the employer's premises from which he usually works, or the premises from which his work is administered.

Also catered for is a worker who normally works from a place where it is impracticable to attend for the purposes of peaceful picketing. An oil platform in the middle of the North Sea would pose some problems for even the most determined picket, so workers from there would be allowed to picket instead the premises from where their work is administered.

2: If a worker is not in employment and either his last employment was terminated in connection with a trade dispute or the termination of his employment was one of the factors giving rise to a trade dispute – then his former place of work in relation to that dispute shall be treated as his place of work for the purposes of this Section.

This proviso caters for the situation where someone's dismissal is one of the factors giving rise to industrial action, or who is dismissed after becoming involved in an industrial dispute. It is not uncommon for colleagues to strike after a worker is dismissed, e.g. following disciplinary action or as a result of compulsory redundancy. Likewise, workers are sometimes dismissed for refusing to give up industrial action.

There are three limitations on a dismissed worker being allowed to picket at his former place of work:
– He may do so if he is **not in employment**. Once he gets another job, his right to picket at his previous place of work ends.
– He may picket at his last place of work, so if he gets another job, then ceases that employment, his right to picket is not revived.

Where an employer dismisses workers in connection with a trade dispute then closes the place where they used to work, moving his operations to a different site, the dismissed workers have no lawful right to picket at that site because they never worked there. In one case, the employers sacked many print workers and moved production to Wapping. The sacked printers were held not to have a right peacefully to picket at Wapping because they had never worked there (*News Group Newspapers Ltd v Sogat 82 (No. 2)* (1987)).
– He may picket in relation to that trade dispute. For example, if Fred is sacked and his colleagues strike to get him re-instated, Fred may join the pickets while he remains out of work. If this strike is settled, then a short time later the workers strike again for some other reason, Fred, even though still without a job, would not be allowed to join the pickets, because the picketing is not in connection with the dispute which arose from his dismissal.

Union official: A person who is an official of a trade union may have been elected or appointed to represent only some of its members. For example, an official may be a branch secretary, or a shop steward at a particular site. In such a case, the official may picket while accompanying one of the members whom he represents, while that member is picketing lawfully. The branch secretary could not lawfully join pickets in the area of another branch of the union.

If an official is elected or appointed to represent all union members, e.g. as a national official, then he may accompany any of those members while they are peacefully picketing.

In contemplation or furtherance of a trade dispute: Peaceful picketing, as provided for in Section 220, is lawful only in relation to a trade dispute. Persons who picket a hamburger shop as part of an 'animal rights' protest, or an abortion clinic as part of an anti-abortion demonstration, cannot claim to have a lawful right to do so, because their action will not amount to 'peaceful picketing' under Section 220. Contrast this with the provisions of Section 241 (below).

It must be emphasised that the importance of Section 220 is primarily to afford workers and their union officials freedom from civil action during a trade dispute. Picketing which does not fall within what is allowed by the Section, either because it is not in connection with a trade dispute, or because some of those picketing are not workers from that site, may render those involved liable to civil action, but need not involve criminal offences.

The attendance on picket lines of 'flying pickets' or 'secondary pickets', i.e. persons who are not workers from that site, may well give rise to criminal offences, especially where the numbers involved are large, but not necessarily so if they continue to act peacefully.

3 INTIMIDATION
Trade Union and Labour Relations (Consolidation) Act 1992 Section 241

3.1.1 *Offence*
A person is guilty of an offence who:
  - wrongfully and without legal authority
  - with a view to compelling another person
  - to abstain from doing something he has a legal right to do
  - or to do an act he has a legal right to abstain from doing
  - does one of six actions specified.

These are:
  - uses violence to or intimidates that person, or his wife or children
  - injures that person's property
  - hides any tools, clothes or other property owned or used by that person or deprives him of or hinders him in the use thereof
  - persistently follows that person about from place to place
  - follows that person with two or more others in a disorderly manner in or through any street or road
  - watches or besets the house or other place where that person lives, works, carries on business or happens to be, or the approach to any such house or place.

3.1.2 *Explanation*
Wrongfully and without legal authority: In this context 'wrongfully' refers to a liability in civil law. This element must be present if one of the six actions is to amount to the offence. Anything other than peaceful picketing as provided for in Section 220 will be 'wrongful and without legal authority'.

With a view to compelling: The term implies something stronger than merely persuading, amounting to compulsion. In a case not involving a trade dispute, demonstrators opposed to abortion picketed a clinic where abortions were carried out. Their intention was to dissuade women attending there not to have their pregnancies terminated. The evidence was that they held up pictures of dead babies and displayed plastic models of a foetus. Despite this and the shouting of words such as 'You are evil and God will punish you', and despite evidence that some women attending the clinic were distressed by the behaviour of the accused, the magistrates were satisfied that there had been no intention to prevent women from having abortions, merely to persuade them not to (*DPP v Fidler* (1992)).

To do or not to do: In terms of a trade dispute, the offence may be thought of primarily as committed by strikers seeking to compel those still working to refrain from working. The offence could equally arise where persons at work and at risk of suffering loss of earnings because of a strike by others, sought to compel the strikers to go back to work, when they had every right to refrain from working.

The offences are not limited however, to situations involving trade disputes. The intention could equally be to persuade a woman not to have an abortion, people not to eat beefburgers or lorry drivers not to drive their vehicles loaded with live calves on to cross-Channel ferries.

Use violence or intimidates: 'Violence' needs little explanation. 'Intimidation' includes frightening a person by a show of force or violence, or a threat of force or violence. The Court of Appeal has held that 'intimidate' in this context must be given its every day meaning. Without seeking to give an exhaustive definition it would include 'putting persons in fear by the exhibition of force or violence, or the threat of force or violence, and this is not limited to violence or threats of violence against the person' (*R v Jones and Others* (1974)).

Injures property: Criminal damage to property with a view to compelling the victim to do or not to do something will be an offence. A threat to damage property would amount to intimidation.

Hides tools, etc: Hiding tools, equipment or clothing required by a person to do his job would be covered by this provision. Whereas damage is restricted to damage caused to the person's own property, 'hiding or hindering' extends to items belonging to or used by the person in question. Dropping protective clothing into a vat of oil would hinder a person in the use of that clothing, and could also give rise to the offence under the 'criminal damage' provision if the clothing was owned by that person, rather than by his employer.

Persistently follows: For the offence to be made out by this action, there is no need for the 'following' to be through a street, the following is from 'place to place'. This need not be in a public place, but could be e.g. in a factory or other private place. The term 'persistently' denotes some element of carrying on for a period of time. There is no minimum period or minimum distance laid down, for a following to be 'persistent'.

Thomasson was engaged to work at a mill to replace a worker who was on strike. Smith followed him as he left the mill one evening; when Thomasson crossed the street, Smith did likewise. He followed him along two streets, close behind him, although no words were spoken. Magistrates convicted Smith on the ground that he persistently followed Thomasson and the Queen's Bench Division upheld that conviction (*Smith v Thomasson* (1890)).

Follows with two or more in disorderly manner: In this case, there is no requirement for 'persistence'. The following must be in a street or road, there must be at least two other persons involved with the accused, and there must be an element of disorderly conduct. The disorderly conduct need not necessarily include violence or a threat. Pickets spoke to two workers who continued to work through a strike, seeking to persuade them not to send mail on behalf of the employers. When the two drove off, they were followed by the strikers in two or three cars. The accused and others then persistently overtook the workers on a motorway, slowing down in front of them to impede their progress. The accused was convicted on two counts, by 'persistently following' and by 'following with two or more others in a disorderly manner', The manner of driving on the motorway was held to be disorderly (*Elsey v Smith* (1983)).

Watches or besets: Peaceful picketing under the terms of Section 220 extends only to a place of work. To 'watch or beset' any other premises with a view to persuading someone to come out on strike would render the 'besetters' liable to civil action. To amount to an offence under this Section, such action would have to be done with a view to 'compelling' the person concerned. If pickets stand quietly outside a person's house, seeking peacefully to persuade him to join a strike, or in a non-industrial context, demonstrate peacefully outside the house of a research scientist against her use of animals in the laboratory, this will not be peaceful picketing within the meaning of Section 220, but will not necessarily amount to any criminal offence.

3.1.3 *Arrest*
A constable may arrest without warrant anyone she reasonably suspects is committing an offence under this Section.

Note: The power is to arrest a person whom the constable suspects 'is committing' the offence. There is no power to arrest after the behaviour giving rise to the offence has ceased.

4 OTHER ASPECTS OF LAW AS THEY RELATE TO TRADE DISPUTES

4.1 Range of Offences
While peaceful picketing is limited to obtaining or communicating information, or peaceful persuasion, the intention of pickets may be to obstruct the entrance to premises to prevent persons or vehicles from entering, to threaten, to cause damage, etc. Such action may amount to an offence of intimidation, but this does not rule out other offences being considered. Obstruction of the highway, breach of the peace, other public order offences, assault and criminal damage are among those which have arisen in disputes in the past.

4.2 Obstruction of the Highway
The action of peacefully communicating information to a lorry driver who has come to deliver goods to a factory, may necessarily involve some degree of obstruction of a highway. While Section 220 allows that it is lawful to 'attend' for the purpose of peacefully communicating or persuading, there is no right beyond attendance, i.e. there is no right to stop people in order to communicate with them or to obstruct the highway by engaging in conversation with a lorry driver.

It is an offence wilfully to obstruct the free passage along a highway without lawful authority or reasonable excuse. There must be proof that the use of a highway, to amount to unlawful obstruction, is unreasonable. 'It depends on the circumstances, including the length of time the obstruction continues, the place, the purpose and whether it does in fact cause an actual as opposed to a potential obstruction' (*Nagy v Weston* (1965)).

Standing on the highway in reasonable numbers and in an orderly manner does not necessarily amount to an unlawful obstruction of the highway, whether in connection with a trade dispute or not.

Therefore, if pickets do speak to a lorry driver at the factory gate for a reasonable time for information to be communicated there need not be an offence of obstruction committed. There may come a time when the lorry driver has heard all she wants to hear and has decided to continue with her delivery. If pickets continued to obstruct the highway thereafter, this would amount to an offence of unlawful obstruction. Pickets may well be off the carriageway, at the gates to premises, but if the queue of vehicles waiting to enter blocks back on to the highway, unlawful obstruction would arise.

If the intention of the pickets is to obstruct, rather that to persuade, then the question of 'reasonable use' does not arise. A picket tried to persuade a lorry driver not to enter a building site. When the driver was not persuaded the picket stood in front of the lorry. He was convicted because his intention was to obstruct not to persuade (*Broome v DPP* (1974)).

Note: Obstruction of the highway is dealt with more fully in Chapter 46.

4.3 **Obstruct Police**

The offence of obstruction of the highway is very often linked to that of obstructing a constable in the execution of his duty. The constable asks pickets to move because they are obstructing the highway; by refusing to move, they obstruct the constable. The common law offence of public nuisance may arise where there is obstruction of the highway. *(Keynote Case: Tynan v Balmer (1967))*

4.4 **Breach of the Peace**

A constable has powers to limit the numbers of pickets in a particular place where there is reasonable cause to fear disorder. *(Keynote Case: Piddington v Bates (1960))*

Not every public disturbance amounts to a breach of the peace. A breach of the peace will arise where:
 – harm is actually done to a person; or
 – harm is caused to a person's property in his presence; or
 – harm is likely to be done to a person, or to his property in his presence; or
 – a person is in fear of suffering harm, to himself or to his property in his presence.

The term is discussed more fully in *Chapter 16.*

4.5 **Public Nuisance**

To cause a public nuisance is a common law offence. It may be defined as an unlawful act which endangers lives, safety, health, property or comfort of the public – or whereby the public are obstructed in the exercise or enjoyment of any right common to all Her Majesty's subjects.

A nuisance is a public nuisance if within the neighbourhood it materially affects the reasonable comfort and convenience of life of a class of citizens. Whether the number affected is enough to amount to a 'class' is a question of fact (*Attorney General v PYA Quarries Ltd* (1957)). An obstruction of the highway may be a public nuisance if the public are prevented from freely, safely and conveniently passing along the highway.

The obstruction must be unlawful and unreasonable. Mass picketing will be a public nuisance, especially if accompanied by scenes of violence. In the newspaper industry dispute at Wapping in the mid-1980's, besides pickets at the premises affected, there were daily attendances of demonstrators, often in large numbers, with frequent rallies, marches and other demonstrations. A number of employees were assaulted or intimidated, with damage caused to vehicles.

In connection with this dispute it was held that picketing, marches and demonstrations ceased to be lawful if there was unreasonable obstruction of the highway amounting to a public nuisance (*News Group Newspapers Ltd and Others v Society of Graphical and Allied Trades '82 and Others (No. 2)* (1987)).

On a smaller scale, unreasonable use of the highway may amount to a public nuisance. *(Keynote Case: Tynan v Balmer (1967); Hubbard and Others v Pitt and Others (1975))*

5 NUMBERS OF PICKETS

5.1 Code of Practice

There is a Code of Practice relating to picketing issued under Section 203 of TULR(C)A which, while not of itself creating any liability, seeks to set the standard of good industrial relations. The code provides that 'in general the number of pickets does not exceed six at any entrance to or exit from a workplace; frequently a smaller number will be appropriate' (paragraph 51).

5.2 Police Power to Limit Numbers

It is not a matter for the police to seek to enforce this Code. The police power to regulate numbers of pickets is governed by the reasonable apprehension that a breach of the peace may occur. A number of pickets greater than six may not give cause to fear a breach of the peace, whereas a lesser number may do. *(Keynote Case: Piddington v Bates (1960))*

Keynote Cases

6.1 *Tynan v Balmer* [1967] 1 QB 91

Problem

Whether peaceful picketing will amount in all circumstances to a lawful use of the highway.

Circumstances

A strike was in progress involving draughtsmen at a factory; the strike is reported as having been well-managed and lacking in disturbance or bad temper. In particular, the strikers had maintained friendly relations with police. Constables saw the defendant leading a group of about 40 pickets, moving in a circle at the front entrance, the circle extending on to the highway. The defendant was asked by a constable to stop the pickets from circling. He refused saying he was challenging the authority of the police and intended to make it a test case. He was arrested and charged with wilful obstruction of a constable in the execution of his duty, contrary to what is now Section 89, Police Act 1996.

Decision

He was convicted, the court finding:
- that the circling action would hinder rather than facilitate the pickets communicating information, so that their powers of persuasion would be nil

— the object of the pickets by the circling action was to seal off the area so as to bring traffic to a standstill.

The defendant appealed, but the conviction was upheld. The court held that since part of the objective was to seal off the highway to stop vehicles, the conduct was a nuisance at common law and amounted to unreasonable use of the highway. The law (now Section 220) did not render picketing a lawful use of the highway in all circumstances, so that the pickets' action could be the subject of interference by the police.

Comment

The judgment recognises that some potential obstruction of the highway may arise from the presence of pickets, but this need not be unreasonable. Once the obstruction goes beyond what is reasonable, the police have a lawful right to intervene.

Although the police decided that the pickets were causing unreasonable obstruction, the arrest was not for obstructing the highway, but for obstructing a constable, by not acceding to his request to stop what they were doing.

The court found that the action, in obstructing the highway, amounted to a public nuisance at common law.

There is no comment from the court on whether a charge of obstructing the highway, obstructing a constable, or public nuisance is to be preferred in any particular circumstances. In some cases, it may be the only appropriate charge *(see comments to Piddington v Bates, below)*.

6.2 *Piddington v Bates* [1960] 3 All ER 660

Problem

Whether a constable is acting within the execution of his duty in seeking to limit the numbers of pickets present at a place during a trade dispute.

Circumstances

Bates, a chief inspector, went to factory premises in Islington where eight employees out of a total staff of 24 were working. There were two entrances to the premises, the front entrance some six feet wide, the rear 11 feet wide. Some 18 men, most of them wearing picket badges arrived. Two pickets went to the front, four to the rear entrance, while others patrolled the street nearby. Another police officer told Piddington that two pickets were enough at each entrance. Chief Inspector Bates then spoke to the pickets at the rear and two of them moved away. Piddington then appeared, asking where the rear entrance was. Bates told Piddington that two pickets were enough. Piddington insisted on joining the pickets there, saying, 'I can stand by the gate if I want to... If you don't want me to you'd better arrest me'. He then pushed past the chief inspector and was arrested. He was charged with obstructing a constable in the execution of his duty, and convicted at magistrates' court.

Decision

The defence appealed on two grounds:
- that there must be more than a mere 'possibility' of a breach of the peace, for a police officer to have a lawful right to interfere with the numbers of pickets
- that a breach of the peace could not reasonably have been anticipated, given that there was no obstruction of the street, no intimidation, nor any threat of violence.

The court held that in the circumstances, where some 18 people had arrived in two vehicles, the police were fully entitled to think there was a real danger of something more than the peaceful communication of information, or peaceable persuasion. A police officer charged with the duty of preserving the peace must be left to take such steps as, on the evidence before him, he thinks are proper. This does not mean that there should be a rule about two pickets being allowed at a particular door, but in the circumstances of this case, there was nothing wrong with the decision that two pickets were sufficient.

Comment

In this case, the charge was of obstructing a police officer in the execution of his duty. Since there was no evidence that the defendant or any of the other pickets were guilty of a breach of the peace, obstruction or other offence, any other charge would have been inappropriate. The police acted to prevent an offence, rather than dealing with one when it arose.

The effect of the decision is that the police may take action to limit numbers of pickets, if a police officer has reason to believe that a breach of the peace is likely to occur unless such action is taken. There is no formula which may be applied to arrive at a proper number of pickets; it is a matter for the police officer concerned, taking account of the prevailing circumstances.

Chapter 21: Firearms – Certificates and Dealers

1 INTRODUCTION

1.1 Firearm Control

There are strict controls on the purchase, possession and use of firearms in this country. The principal form of control is by issue of certificates to people who have 'Section 1 firearms' or 'shotguns'. Persons who deal in firearms as a business of manufacturing, repairing or selling them, have to be registered as firearms dealers.

1.2 Police Role

The controlling agency with powers to issue certificates and register dealers is the chief officer of police for the police area in which a person lives, or in the case of a dealer, where he has his business premises. The Home Office oversees the police exercise of these functions and will issue advice from time to time on such matters as whether a particular item is or is not a firearm, and what conditions should normally be imposed on firearms dealers.

1.3 Appeal
Firearms Act 1968 Section 44

A decision by a chief officer of police in respect of a firearm or shotgun certificate, whether it be imposition of extra conditions, refusal to grant or renew a certificate, or revocation of one, may be subject of an appeal to Crown Court.

1.4 Legislation

The principal legislation is the Firearms Act 1968. References in this chapter are to this Act unless stated. Account is taken of the changes brought about by the Firearms (Amendment) Act 1997 and the Firearms (Amendment) (No. 2) Act 1997.

2 MEANING OF TERMS

2.1 Firearm
Firearms Act 1968 Section 57

A firearm is a lethal barrelled weapon of any description from which any shot, bullet or other missile can be discharged and includes:
  - any prohibited weapon, whether it is such a lethal weapon or not
  - any component part of such a lethal or prohibited weapon
  - any accessory to such a weapon, designed or adapted to diminish the noise or flash caused by firing the weapon.

2.1.1 *Explanation*

Lethal: The term means capable of causing injury to a person which may result in death. (*Read v Donovan* (1947)). Death or serious injury does not have to be the probable result of being hit by a missile from a weapon. An air rifle firing darts or pellets may not be likely to kill a person, but if fired from close range and the missile hit the eye, it could cause death. This will be enough to make it 'lethal' for the purpose of being a firearm.

Barrelled: To amount to a firearm, it must have a barrel. A crossbow or a powerful catapult may be lethal weapons which fire missiles, but will not be firearms unless they have a barrel from which the missile is discharged, i.e. fired.

Some weapons may be a firearm in every respect, except that the 'barrel' is solid, not capable of discharging a missile. If a gun may be easily converted, by drilling out the barrel, it will be regarded as a firearm (*Cafferata v Wilson* (1936)). If conversion of the gun would be difficult, it should not be treated as a firearm; a starting pistol is likely to fall into this category.

Prohibited weapon: *See paragraph 2.2 below.* It should be noted that a prohibited weapon will be classed as a firearm even though it is not lethal. This would include a gun designed for firing non-lethal gas canisters.

Component part: This is regarded as meaning a working part, as opposed to an 'optional extra' or accessory. A telescopic sight has been held not to be a component (*Watson v Herman* (1952)).

Accessory: An accessory which is designed to lessen the noise or flash caused by firing a weapon, commonly referred to as a 'silencer' will be classed as a firearm in its own right. Like component parts, such accessories will be subject to the restrictions which apply to lethal barrelled weapons.

Not firearms: The following are not regarded as firearms, in the view of the Home Office:
nail guns; alarm guns (operated by trip wires which set off small explosive charges); most rocket signal devices (but note that a **Very** pistol has been held to be a firearm (*Read v Donovan* (1947)); devices for firing a rescue line to save life, e.g. to put a line aboard a ship; equipment used by bird-ringers to fire nets to trap birds.

2.2 **Prohibited Weapon**
Firearms Act 1968 Section 5

2.2.1 *Other Than Handguns*
Certain types of firearms may not be made, traded in, or be in a person's possession without authority of the Home Secretary. These are referred to as prohibited weapons. Certain types of ammunition are also prohibited.

The following are some examples, but the list is not exhaustive:
- any firearm from which two or more missiles can be discharged without repeated pressure on the trigger, e.g. a machine gun
- certain self-loading or pump action rifles and other guns
- rocket launcher or mortar (excluding one for signalling, firing flares or line throwing)
- any weapon of whatever description designed or adapted for the discharge of any noxious liquid, gas or other thing (such a weapon need not have a barrel)
- any firearm which is disguised as another object
- expanding ammunition
- exploding ammunition or military armour piercing ammunition.

Water pistols filled with ammonia have been held not to be adapted for the discharge of noxious liquid, and therefore did not amount to prohibited weapons (*R v Titus and Others*

(1971)). Likewise, a detergent bottle filled with acid was held not to be a prohibited weapon (*R v Formosa* (1991)). Whereas the mere filling of a water pistol with a noxious liquid may not amount to adaptation, in other circumstances an object such as a water pistol may well be adapted to become a prohibited weapon.

2.2.2 *Small Firearms (Commonly Called Handguns)*

The following type of firearm will be a prohibited weapon:
- any firearm which either has a barrel less than 30 centimetres in length or is less than 60 centimetres in length overall, except
- an air weapon, a muzzle-loading gun or a firearm designed as signalling apparatus.

2.2.3 *Explanation*

Length: In measuring the length of a firearm, any detachable, folding, retractable or other movable butt-stock shall be disregarded. The prohibition of small firearms is intended to prevent access to the sorts of firearms used in the Dunblane incident in 1996. It would obviously defeat the purpose, of preventing possession of easily concealed guns, if a gun larger than the stated maximum could then be made smaller by removing or folding the stock. For this reason, when measuring a firearm, any such stock is disregarded.

Muzzle-loading gun: This refers to a gun designed to be loaded at the muzzle end of the barrel or chamber, with a loose charge and a separate ball or other missile.

2.3 Imitation Firearm

An imitation firearm is anything which has the appearance of being a firearm (other than certain prohibited weapons) whether or not it is capable of discharging any shot, bullet or other missile. Certain criminal offences may be committed by having possession of an imitation firearm.

However, if an imitation firearm is readily convertible into a firearm, it may be regarded as a 'firearm' rather than as an 'imitation firearm' for most of the purposes of the Act. It will be regarded as easily convertible if:
- it can be converted without any special skill; and
- the work to convert it does not require any specialised tools or equipment (Firearms Act 1982, Section 1).

2.4 Ammunition

This means any ammunition for any firearm and also includes grenades, bombs and similar missiles whether capable of use with a firearm or not. Ammunition includes prohibited ammunition.

2.5 Section 1 Firearm/Ammunition
Firearms Act 1968 Section 1

There are three broad categories of firearm (with corresponding ammunition):
- Section 1 firearms
- shotguns
- and air weapons.

Section 1 of the Act details the types of firearm and ammunition for which a firearm certificate

is required. This applies to every firearm and ammunition, except:
- a shotgun, as defined below
- an air gun, air rifle or air pistol, not being of a type declared especially dangerous
- cartridges containing five or more shot, none of which exceeds .91 cm (.36 inches) diameter
- ammunition for an air weapon
- blank cartridges not more than 2.54 cm (1 inch) diameter.

2.5.1 *Explanation*
Every firearm which is not a shotgun or an air weapon will be covered by the requirements of Section 1, relating to firearm certificates. These will include:
- rifles, equipment for slaughtering animals
- certain flare and signalling instruments, etc.

2.6 **Shotgun**
A shotgun is a smooth bore gun (not being an air gun) which:
- has a barrel not less than 60.96 cms (24 inches) in length; and
- has a bore not exceeding 5.08 cms (2 inches) in diameter
- either has no magazine attached, or has a non-detachable magazine which can hold not more than two cartridges.

Any smooth bore gun which has a barrel shorter than the minimum, or of greater diameter than the maximum given above, or which has a magazine outside the scope of that given, will not be a shotgun for the purposes of the Act, and will be subject to the need for a firearms certificate.

2.7 **Air Weapon**
An air weapon is an air rifle, air gun or air pistol not of a type declared to be specially dangerous under rules made by the Home Secretary.

Whereas other types of firearm rely on an explosive charge to propel the bullet or other missile out of the barrel, in an air weapon a blast of air, created by a spring being released (or some other means) propels the missile. This results in air weapons being far less powerful than other types of firearm. However, if a particular model is more powerful than usual, exceeding limits laid down in the Firearms (Dangerous Air Weapons) Rules 1969, a firearm certificate will be required. The measure of the power of an air weapon is the kinetic energy of the missile on leaving the muzzle of the gun. This may be determined by use of special equipment.

A firearm which operates by means of a gas may not amount to an air weapon, so a certificate would be required. However, if the gas used is compressed carbon dioxide, the weapon will be regarded as an air weapon (Firearms (Amendment) Act 1997, Section 48).

2.8 **Antique Firearm**
An antique firearm is exempt from all the provisions of the Act (Section 58(2)). Unfortunately, there is no explanation in the Act as to what is meant by 'antique'. Whether a firearm is 'antique' is a matter for the court to decide in any particular circumstances (*Richards v Curwen* (1977)).

However, the following, based on case decisions and Home Office advice, apply:

- a modern reproduction of an old firearm is **not** an antique;
- if a firearm is used, e.g. an old muzzle-loader used for shooting at targets, rather than being kept merely for its ornamental value, it should not be regarded as an antique. The exemption does not apply to ammunition, so the fact that ammunition is held for a firearm might indicate that it is not held as an ornament.

Note: The provisions of Section 7, Firearms (Amendment) Act 1997 (relating to pre-1919 firearms) do not affect these provisions.

2.9 Possess/Purchase/Acquire/Transfer

Possession: In relation to possession of a Section 1 firearm or shotgun without a certificate, possession means more than physically having the gun with one. A person who spends the week in the city, and keeps a shotgun in her country cottage which she visits at weekends, will have possession of the shotgun on Monday as well as on Saturday. *(Keynote Case: Sullivan v Earl of Caithness (1975))*

However, 'possession' may also include having physical custody of the firearm without having ownership in it (*Hall v Cotton and Treadwell* (1986)).

Purchase: This term is not defined in the Act, so it should be given its normal meaning.

Acquire: This means to hire, borrow or accept as a gift.

Transfer: The term includes to let on hire, give, lend or part with possession. There may be transfer when a firearm is passed to another for a temporary period without ownership being passed to that person (*Hall v Cotton and Treadwell* (1986)).

3 FIREARM CERTIFICATES

3.1 Possession without a Certificate

3.1.1 *Offence*
Firearms Act 1968 Section 1

A person commits an offence who:
  i) has in his possession
    - or purchases or acquires
    - a Section 1 firearm or ammunition
    - without holding a firearm certificate currently in force
    - or otherwise than as authorised by his certificate;
  ii) has in his possession or purchases or acquires
    - Section 1 ammunition
    - in quantities in excess of those authorised in his certificate.

3.1.2 *Arrest*
The offences carry a maximum sentence of five years' imprisonment so are arrestable offences.

3.1.3 *Aggravated Offence*
When the offence arises through the conversion into a Section 1 firearm of something which was not a firearm, or of a shotgun by shortening its barrel to less than 24 inches, the offence is committed in aggravated form, and the maximum sentence rises to seven years' imprisonment.

3.2 **Grant of Certificate**
Firearms Act 1968 Section 27

A firearm certificate shall be granted by the chief officer of police if she is satisfied that the applicant:
- is fit to be entrusted with a Section 1 firearm, and is not a person prohibited from possession of such
- has a good reason for having in his possession, or for purchasing or acquiring the firearm or ammunition in respect of which the application is made
- in all the circumstances, can be permitted to have the firearm or ammunition in his possession without danger to public safety or to the peace.

3.2.1 *Explanation*
Good reason: This means that:
- the type of firearm must relate to the proposed use (e.g. a large calibre rifle is not the type of firearm required for rabbit shooting)
- the numbers of firearms should be limited, so it should not be necessary to have more than one of a particular type
- it should not be necessary to have a firearm for self-protection.

Prohibited: A person may be prohibited from possessing firearms by a court after a conviction or as a result of having served a sentence of imprisonment.

3.3 **Content of Firearm Certificate**
A firearm certificate should contain the following details:
- the nature and number of the firearms to which it relates
- their identification numbers, if known
- the quantities of ammunition which may be purchased or acquired
- the conditions which apply.

Thus, a firearm certificate may cover more than one firearm, but it does not cover 'any firearm'; the specific firearms must be identified individually in the certificate. If the holder wants to buy a new one, sell an existing one, or whatever, application must be made for the changes to be considered and, if approved, for the certificate to be amended.

In the case of a proposed purchase, the identification number of the firearm may not be known when application is made, but may be completed later, if approval to buy is granted.

3.4 **Conditions Attached to a Firearm Certificate**
There are certain standard conditions which apply to all firearm certificates. In addition, the chief officer of police may impose other conditions, upon first grant or on renewal. The conditions may be varied at any time, by written notice, requiring the holder to surrender the certificate for alteration. The standard conditions are:
- i) the certificate must be signed in ink upon receipt
- ii) any change of permanent address must be notified without delay
- iii) the firearms and ammunition covered by the certificate must at all times (except when (iv) below applies) be stored securely so as to prevent unauthorised access, as far as reasonably practicable
- iv) when the firearm(s) or ammunition is in use, being cleaned, repaired, in transit, etc,

reasonable precautions must be taken for their safe custody

v) any theft or loss in Great Britain of a firearm or ammunition covered by the certificate must be reported at once to the chief officer of police who issued the certificate (Firearms Rules 1989).

3.4.1 *Offence*
Firearms Act 1968 Section 1(2)

A person will commit an offence if she fails to comply with the conditions subject to which a firearm certificate is held.

3.4.2 *Punishment*

Failure to comply with the conditions attached to a firearm certificate is punishable as a summary offence, maximum six months' imprisonment and/or a fine.

4 SHOTGUN CERTIFICATES

4.1 Offence
Firearms Act 1968 Section 2

It is an offence for a person:
- to have in his possession or to purchase or acquire
- any shotgun
- without holding a shotgun certificate.

4.2 Grant

A shotgun certificate shall be granted (or renewed) if the chief officer of police is satisfied that the applicant can be permitted to possess a shotgun without danger to public safety or to the peace. One shall not be granted or renewed if the chief officer of police:
- has reason to believe that the applicant is prohibited from possessing a shotgun; or
- is satisfied that the person does not have a good reason for possessing, purchasing or acquiring a shotgun.

4.2.1 *Explanation*

Ammunition: There is no need to hold a certificate to possess shotgun ammunition, provided it is of the sort to which Section 1 does not apply, nor is there any limit on how much shotgun ammunition a certificate holder may have at any one time.

However, a shotgun certificate has to be produced when buying ammunition, to show that one has a valid reason for having it (Firearm (Amendment) Act 1988, Section 5).

Good reason: The general principle governing the grant of shotgun certificates is that one should be granted unless there is a good reason not to do so, whereas a firearm certificate should not be granted unless there is a good reason for the applicant having firearms.

An intention to use a shotgun for sporting or competition purposes, or for shooting vermin, shall be regarded as a good reason. The fact that a person does not intend to use the shotgun himself nor to lend it to anyone else to use shall not be a ground for refusing an application (Section 28(1B)).

Chief officers are advised that a criminal conviction need not in itself be a ground for refusing an application, but convictions for certain offences may well be. A police force may well have a general policy in relation to applications, but this should be flexible.

4.3 Content of Shotgun Certificate

A shotgun certificate will specify the descriptions of the shotguns to which it relates, together with their identification numbers, if known. There is no limit on the number of shotguns which may be held under one certificate, providing they are all listed.

4.4 Conditions

The same standard conditions apply to the grant of a shotgun certificate as to a firearm certificate. No other conditions may be imposed. This differs from the situation with a firearm certificate, where the police may impose additional conditions.

4.5 Offence
Firearms Act 1968 Section 2(2)

A person will commit an offence if she fails to comply with the conditions subject to which a shotgun certificate is held.

5 AUTHORITY FOR PROHIBITED WEAPONS
Firearms Act 1968 Section 5

5.1 Home Secretary's Authority

5.1.1 *Offence*
A person commits an offence who:
- has in his possession or purchases or acquires
- any prohibited weapon or prohibited ammunition
- without a written authority from the Secretary of State.

5.1.2 *Conditions*
Conditions may be imposed upon the grant of an authority to secure that the prohibited weapon or ammunition will not endanger public safety or the peace.

5.1.3 *Offence*
It is an offence to fail to comply with any of the conditions attached to a written authority.

5.2 Exemptions from Need for Home Secretary's Authority
Firearms (Amendment) Act 1997 Sections 2 – 8

Although falling within the description of a prohibited small firearm, the following will not be subject to the need for an authority from the Secretary of State, in relation to sale, transfer, purchase, acquisition and/or possession, where this is authorised by a firearm certificate (or is subject to an exemption from the need for a certificate):
- a slaughtering instrument
- a firearm for use only in connection with the humane killing of animals
- a shot pistol subject to a condition on the firearm certificate that it is to be used only

in connection with shooting vermin
- a firearm for use in starting races at an athletic meeting
- a firearm acquired as a trophy of war before 1946
- a firearm of a type authorised by regulations, being manufactured before 1919 and for which ammunition is not readily available, subject to a condition in the firearm certificate that it is kept or exhibited as part of a collection
- a firearm which is of historical importance, particular rarity, aesthetic quality or technical interest, subject to a condition in the firearm certificate that it is kept and used at a place designated by the Secretary of State
- a firearm, weapon or ammunition designed or adapted for tranquillising or otherwise treating any animal, with a condition on the firearm certificate restricting its use to that purpose.

5.3 **Expanding Ammunition**
Firearms Act 1968 Section 5A(4)

Expanding ammunition was added to the list of prohibited ammunition by the Firearms (Amendment) Act 1997. However, an authority from the Secretary of State is not required when such ammunition is held under a firearm certificate (or visitor's firearm permit) subject to a condition that it is used only for:
- the lawful shooting of deer
- shooting of vermin, or of other wildlife in connection with estate management
- humane killing of animals
- shooting of animals for protection of other animals or humans.

Firearms dealers and their staff may deal with expanding ammunition in the course of the business.

5.4 **Firearm Certificate for Prohibited Weapon**

A prohibited weapon or prohibited ammunition will fall within the scope of Section 1 and will be subject to the need for a firearm certificate.

When a person who is in possession of a Home Secretary's authority applies for a firearm certificate for prohibited weapons or ammunition, the police may not refuse to grant the certificate. Conversely, if a person who already has a prohibited weapon or ammunition, applies for a certificate but does not have a written authorisation, he should be required to surrender the weapon or ammunition forthwith.

6 **REVOCATION OF CERTIFICATES**

6.1 **Grounds for Revoking a Certificate**

6.1.1 *Firearm Certificate*
Firearms Act 1968 Section 30A

A firearm certificate may be revoked by the chief officer of police for the area where the holder resides if the chief officer:
- has reason to believe that the holder is of intemperate habits or unsound mind or is otherwise unfitted to be entrusted with a firearm
- has reason to believe that the holder can no longer be permitted to have a firearm or

ammunition to which the certificate relates in his possession without danger to public safety or to the peace
- is satisfied that the holder no longer has a good reason for possessing, purchasing or acquiring the firearm or ammunition which he is authorised by virtue of the certificate to possess, purchase or acquire
- is satisfied that the holder is prohibited by the Act from possession of a Section 1 firearm.

A certificate may also be revoked if the holder fails to comply with a written notice to surrender the certificate, e.g. for alteration to the conditions under which it is held.

6.1.2 *Partial Revocation of Firearm Certificate*
Firearms Act 1968 Section 30B

The chief officer of police for the area where the holder of a firearm certificate lives may partially revoke the certificate, i.e. in relation to any firearm or ammunition to which the certificate refers, if satisfied:
- that the holder no longer has a good reason for having in his possession, or purchasing or acquiring, the firearm or ammunition to which the partial revocation relates.

If a certificate authorises the holder to have several firearms and/or to purchase and hold different sorts of ammunition, revocation would remove the right to possess any of them, whereas partial revocation would be directed at one or more of them.

6.1.3 *Shotgun Certificate*
Firearms Act 1968 Section 30C

A shotgun certificate may be revoked by the chief officer of police for the area in which the holder lives if satisfied that:
- the holder is prohibited from possessing a shotgun; or
- he cannot be permitted to possess a shotgun without danger to public safety or to the peace.

6.2 Notice of Revocation
When police revoke a certificate, the holder is sent a written notice, requiring her to surrender her certificate.

6.2.1 *Offence*
A person who has received notice that her certificate has been revoked will commit an offence by failing to surrender the certificate to the chief officer of police within 21 days of the notice.

If she appeals against the decision to revoke the certificate, this 21-day period is held in abeyance until the appeal has been dealt with.

6.3 Surrender of Weapons
Firearms Amendment Act 1988 Section 12

When a certificate is revoked (other than for failure to hand it over for alteration) written notice may be given to the holder requiring him to surrender forthwith the certificate and any firearms or ammunition in his possession to which the certificate relates. In such a case, the foregoing provisions, allowing 21 days etc, will not apply.

7 MISCELLANEOUS PROVISIONS RELATING TO CERTIFICATES

7.1 Spent Convictions

An applicant for the grant, renewal or variation of a certificate is obliged to reveal details of all convictions when he makes application. Failure to give details, including any spent convictions, may be a proper ground for refusing the application.

7.2 No Certificate

The offence of possession without a certificate is an absolute offence, i.e. the prosecution have to prove possession, but do not also have to prove *mens rea* that the accused knew he did not have a certificate (*R v Hussain* (1981)).

7.3 False Statements

It is an offence for a person knowingly or recklessly to make a statement false in any material particular for the purpose of securing for himself or another person the grant, renewal or variation of a certificate or permit under the Act (Sections 7, 9, 13, 26, 29).

7.4 Conversion of Firearms and Shortening Shotguns
Firearms Act 1968 Section 4

7.4.1 *Conversion*

It is an offence for any person:
- other than a registered firearms dealer
- to convert into a Section 1 firearm
- anything which, though having the appearance of a firearm
- is so constructed as to be incapable of discharging a missile through its barrel.

Note: that the article which is turned into a firearm had the appearance of a firearm to start with. This offence is not meant to cover a person who makes his own firearm by clever use of assorted bits of scrap metal (this is not to say that to make such a firearm will not be an offence; however, it will not be this offence). Taking a replica firearm or a starting pistol with a solid barrel and making it capable of firing a bullet, would constitute the offence.

7.4.2 *Shorten Shotgun*

It is an offence for any person:
- to shorten the barrel of a shotgun to less than 24 inches
  (or as metrication so succinctly puts it, 60.96 centimetres).

However it will not be an offence for a registered firearms dealer to shorten a shotgun barrel in the course of repairing a shotgun, so long as the barrel when the repair is finished is restored to a length of at least the 24 inch (60.96 cm) minimum.

Note: A registered firearms dealer may lawfully convert a replica into a Section 1 firearm; not even a dealer may lawfully shorten the barrel of a shotgun, other than temporarily during a repair, because the law does not recognise any legitimate use for a shortened shotgun.

7.4.3 *Arrest*

These offences carry a possible maximum of seven years' imprisonment so are arrestable offences.

7.4.4 *Firearm Certificate*

A replica converted so as to become a firearm, or a shotgun with a barrel of less that 24 inches, will become a Section 1 firearm. There will not be a certificate for such a firearm, because the police would not issue one, so an offence of possession without a firearm certificate will arise. This offence will be committed in an **aggravated** form when it arises from unlawful conversion or shortening of a shotgun, and as such attracts an increased maximum sentence (seven years rather than five years' imprisonment).

7.5 **Register of Certificate Holders**
Firearms (Amendment) Act 1997 Section 39

A central register is to be established of all persons:
  – who have applied for a firearm certificate or shotgun certificate, or
  – to whom a certificate has been granted, or
  – whose certificate has been renewed.

Each person on the register will have an identifying number. The register will be kept on computer with on-line access to all police forces.

8 EXEMPTIONS FROM THE NEED FOR CERTIFICATES

8.1 Complete Exemption

8.1.1 *Extent of Exemption*
There are a number of 'complete exemptions' – i.e. exemption in respect of purchase, acquiring or possessing a Section 1 firearm or shotgun, as the case may be, without the relevant certificate. Other exemptions will usually be for 'possession only', although there are some exceptions to this.

8.1.2 *Registered Firearms Dealer*
Firearms Act 1968 Section 8

A registered firearms dealer or his employee may, without holding a certificate, possess, purchase, acquire any firearm or ammunition in the normal course of that business without holding a certificate.

8.1.3 *Miniature Rifle Range*
Firearms Act 1968 Section 11(4)

A person carrying on a miniature rifle range or shooting gallery, which is restricted to the following types of firearms, may possess, purchase or acquire firearms or ammunition for use at the range.

The range or shooting gallery must be one at which only air weapons or miniature rifles not exceeding .23 in calibre (.58 cm) are used, and the exemption will apply only to such rifles and ammunition for them.

Note: The air weapons must not be ones which fall into the 'specially dangerous' category, otherwise they would require firearm certificates.

8.1.4 *Crown Servants*
Firearms Act 1968 Section 54

(i) Purchase or acquire: A person who is in the service of H.M. The Queen who is duly authorised in writing may purchase or acquire firearms or ammunition for the public service without holding a certificate. For these purposes, a member of a police force will be regarded as a Crown servant.

(ii) Possess: A Crown servant (including a member of a police force) may possess firearms and ammunition without a certificate in the course of official duties.

The soldier on duty on Salisbury Plain with his rifle, the constable in her armed response vehicle with police issue firearms, do not need certificates. When it comes to a member of the police force going to buy firearms or ammunition, or a commissioned officer buying his own sidearm for use on duty, then a written authority from a senior officer would be required.

8.1.5 *Museum Firearm Licence*
Firearms (Amendment) Act 1988 Section 19

A museum firearm licence may be granted in respect of items held by a museum, or which a museum wishes to purchase or acquire, which will replace a firearm certificate, shotgun certificate or authorisation for prohibited weapons.

A museum firearm licence is issued by the Home Secretary, after consultation with the local police as to safety and security arrangements. The Home Secretary may revoke the certificate, again after consultation with the police, if there is a danger to public safety or the peace, or if any member of staff of the museum is convicted of a relevant offence, etc.

Offences may be committed, of making false statements to secure the grant or renewal of a licence, or arising from failure to comply with any conditions on the licence.

8.2 Exemptions for Possession

8.2.1 Police Permit
Firearms Act 1968 Section 7

Police may issue a permit to a person resident in the police area authorising him to have possession of a firearm and ammunition without a certificate in accordance with the terms of the permit.

A permit may cover possession of a Section 1 firearm or ammunition, or a shotgun. A permit is issued to cover temporary possession in special circumstances, usually while steps are taken to dispose of the firearm. Disposing of the property of a bankrupt or a deceased person, are typical examples.

8.2.2 *Auctioneer, Delivery, Storage*
Firearms Act 1968 Section 9

(i) A person carrying on business as an auctioneer, carrier or warehouseman, or an employee of such, may have possession of a firearm or ammunition without a certificate, in the normal course of that business.

The terms 'carrier' and 'warehouseman' are somewhat dated; 'courier', 'next-day delivery', 'secure storage', are some of the more modern equivalents.

(ii) The offence of selling or transferring a firearm or ammunition which requires a certificate to a person who doesn't have one will not be committed by a carrier or warehouseman, or employee, delivering in the ordinary course of business.

(iii) An auctioneer who sells by auction, or possesses, offers or exposes for auction, any such firearm or ammunition will not commit the offence of trading in firearms without being registered as a firearms dealer IF he has obtained a police permit authorising this.

In summary, storage and delivery is covered by the exemption but auctioning of firearms or ammunition requires a police permit.

8.2.3 *Animal Slaughter*
Firearms Act 1968 Section 10

(i) Licensed slaughter person: A person who is licensed (under the appropriate legislation) to slaughter animals, may possess a slaughtering instrument and ammunition for it, in any slaughter house or knacker's yard where he is employed.

8.2.3.1 *Explanation*

This is very restrictive in that it applies only to a licensed person for possession of a specified type of firearm and ammunition in the premises where he is employed.

Basically, a slaughterhouse is where animals are killed for human consumption, a knacker's yard is for dealing with animals not for human consumption. A slaughtering instrument is a firearm specially designed or adapted for the instantaneous slaughter of animals, or instantaneous stunning of them with a view to slaughter (Section 57(4)).

(ii) The proprietor of a slaughterhouse or knacker's yard, or a person appointed by him to take charge of slaughtering instruments and ammunition may possess them at the premises – for the purpose of storage or safe-keeping.

The difference between this and the previous exemption is that the proprietor or person appointed by him to look after the equipment does not have to be a licensed slaughterer; the exemption covers storage and safe-keeping, not use.

Both these exemptions cover possession on the premises only. Purchase of an instrument or ammunition, or taking it out of the premises, e.g. to deal with an injured animal, will require a firearm certificate, but these are usually issued free of charge for these purposes.

8.2.4 *Shooting for Sport*
Firearms Act 1968 Section 11(1)

A person may have possession of a firearm or ammunition without a certificate if he has possession under the instructions from, and they are for the use of, another person who owns the firearm or ammunition and who holds a certificate.

Again, a very restrictive exemption, because the gun bearer must be carrying the weapon or ammunition for the person to whom they belong, for that person's own use, and under his direction.

8.2.5 *Athletic Meeting*
Firearms Act 1968 Section 11(2)

A person may without a certificate, have possession of a firearm at an athletics meeting for the purpose of starting races at that meeting. The exemption does not cover ammunition, but in most cases the ammunition used, if it is blank, not exceeding 1 inch (2.54 cm) diameter will not require a certificate *(see paragraph 2.5 above).*

Neither does the exemption cover possession away from the athletics meeting, so the person bringing the firearm to and from the venue will need a certificate. (A starting pistol is also exempt from the need for authority as a prohibited weapon.)

Note: Many starting pistols will not be classed as firearms at all, if they are not capable of discharging a missile and would not easily be converted to do so.

9.2.6 *Cadet Corps*
Firearms Act 1968 Section 11(3)

A member of an approved cadet corps may have a firearm or ammunition without a certificate when engaged as a member of such – in drill or target practice or related activity.

This allows for members of the Sea Cadet Corps, Army Cadets, Air Training Corps, etc, whose organisation and officers are closely connected with the respective branches of H.M. Forces, to train with firearms.

8.2.7 *Miniature Rifle Range*
Firearms Act 1968 Section 11(4)

A person who is using such a rifle at the range or gallery is exempt from the need for a certificate, for possession of the rifle and ammunition. An exemption applies to a person running a miniature rifle range or shooting gallery, to buy, acquire or possess rifles not exceeding .23 inch (.58 cm) calibre *(see paragraph 8.1.3).* This exemption covers the customers there.

8.2.8 *Borrowing a Firearm*

Shotgun
Firearms Act 1968 Section 11(5)

A person does not have to hold a shotgun certificate to borrow a shotgun from the occupier of private premises and to use it on those premises in the occupier's presence.

This is very restrictive in that the shotgun cannot be used anywhere else other than the premises of the person whose gun it is. In addition, it can be used only in the presence of the occupier. If a landowner lends a shotgun to a visitor to use on his land, it will not be sufficient for the visitor to go off with the estate gamekeeper; the landowner herself would have to be present before the visitor qualified for this exemption.

Section 1 Firearm
Firearms (Amendment) Act 1988 Section 16(1)

A person who does not hold a certificate:
  – who is aged 17 or over

- may borrow a rifle from the occupier of private premises
- and use it on those premises
- in the presence either of the occupier or of his employee
- if the occupier or employee who is there holds a firearm certificate for that rifle and any conditions on the certificate are complied with.

This is also very restrictive; it is limited to a rifle, so any other type of firearm is not included. Although it would allow the guest to go off shooting with the gamekeeper, which is not allowed with a borrowed shotgun, the gamekeeper would have to have a certificate for that rifle.

Although ammunition is not referred to directly in the exemption, the fact that 'use' of the rifle is covered, implies that possession of sufficient ammunition for that purpose is also catered for.

8.2.9 *Clay Pigeon Shooting*
Firearms Act 1968 Section 11(6)

This exemption applies to a person using a shotgun at a time and place approved by the chief officer of police for shooting at artificial targets.

The exemption applies only at a place and on an occasion approved by the police. If a clay pigeon club is used by certificate holders, a visitor wishing to 'have a go' on an occasion which was not police-approved would have to rely on the private premises exemption, by borrowing a shotgun from the occupier of the site.

8.2.10 *Rifle Clubs*
Firearms (Amendment) Act 1988 Section 15

These provisions apply to a rifle club approved by the Secretary of State. A member of such a club may possess a firearm or ammunition without a certificate when engaged in or in connection with target shooting as a member of the club.

The approval for the club may restrict activity to target shooting with specified types of firearms. These arrangements shall apply equally to a muzzle-loading pistol club.

8.2.10.1 *Explanation*
In an approved rifle club, the conditions attached to approval may allow for members to use firearms without certificates, e.g. by borrowing each other's rifles.

8.2.11 *Visitors to Britain*
Firearms (Amendment) Act 1988 Section 17

1: The holder of a visitor's firearm (or shotgun) permit may:
   - have possession of any firearm; or
   - possess, purchase or acquire Section 1 ammunition; or
   - (in the case of a shotgun permit) possess, purchase or acquire shotguns.

   A permit does not allow a visitor to purchase or acquire a Section 1 firearm.

2: An application for a visitor's permit is made not by the visitor herself, but by a person resident in this country, to the police for the area where he lives. The chief officer of police may grant a permit to the visitor if satisfied that she is visiting or intending to visit the country and has a good reason for possessing a firearm or possessing, buying, etc, ammunition or a shotgun, as the case may be.

A permit shall not be granted if there is reason to believe that the visitor is prohibited from possessing firearms or shotguns, or that her possession thereof would represent a danger to public safety or to the peace.

8.2.12 *Export by Visitor*
Firearms (Amendment) Act 1988 Section 18

A person who has not been in Great Britain for more than 30 days in the last 12 months may, without holding a certificate, purchase a firearm from a registered firearms dealer, if the firearm is bought solely to be exported from Great Britain without first coming into that person's possession.

This exemption is restricted to the visitor buying the firearm; it then has to be sent out of the country, he cannot have possession of it in order to take it home himself.

8.2.13 *Theatre, Films, etc*
Firearms Act 1968 Section 12

1: A person taking part in a performance or rehearsal, for theatre or film, may have possession of a firearm without a certificate during and for the purpose of the performance, rehearsal, etc.

2: The Home Secretary may issue an authorisation under Section 5, for the possession of prohibited weapons, for a theatrical, film, etc production. The authorisation will allow the person in charge, plus selected persons taking part in the performance, to possess prohibited weapons for the purposes of the performance or rehearsals.

The exemption is with respect to possession for the purposes of the performance or rehearsal; someone will need a certificate to fetch and carry the firearms before and after, and to buy them in the first place. The exemption does not extend to ammunition; there are limits on realism in the theatre!

8.2.14 *Boats and Planes*
Firearms Act 1968 Section 13

This exemption allows for firearms which are kept on ships (which may be weapons or some sort of signalling device) and aircraft or at airports (being signalling apparatus only) and ammunition. The exemption allows a person:
- to have possession of a firearm or ammunition on board a ship, or signalling apparatus and its ammunition on board an aircraft, or at an airfield – as part of the equipment of that ship, aircraft or airfield
- remove signalling apparatus or its ammunition which is part of an aircraft's equipment, from one aircraft to another on an airfield, or between an aircraft and a storage place at an airfield, or to keep equipment in that storage place
- subject to a police removal permit having been issued, move a firearm to or from a ship, or signalling apparatus to or from an aircraft or airfield, to or from a place and for a purpose, specified in the permit.

The net effect of the exemption is to allow firearms to be kept on board ship as part of a ship's equipment; to allow signalling equipment to kept on aircraft and airfields, and to be moved around an airfield or between aircraft there. However, when it is necessary to take the weapons or equipment away from the ship, or away from the airfield, e.g. for sale or repair, a police permit is required.

A permit issued under this Section may be issued by a constable, it need not be issued by the chief officer of police. The purpose of moving the firearm must be stated on the permit.

The officers authorised to issue such permits and the procedures for doing so, may vary from force to force.

8.2.15 *Proof Houses*
Firearms Act 1968 Section 58

A proof house is a place where guns (or more specifically gun barrels) are tested during manufacture, to ensure that they are sufficiently strong and not likely to burst apart when fired. A barrel when proofed is stamped, rather in the way that gold is hall-marked (there are proof houses in London and in Birmingham).

A person is exempt from the need for a certificate when in possession of a firearm at, or going to or from, a proof house.

8.2.16 *Northern Ireland Certificate*
Firearms Act 1968 Section 15

A person who holds a Northern Ireland firearm certificate authorising him to possess a shotgun is exempt from the need for a shotgun certificate in Britain

8.3 Police Powers

8.3.1 *Certificates*
Firearms Act 1968 Section 48

A constable may demand:
- from a person whom he believes to be in possession of a Section 1 firearm or ammunition, or of a shotgun
- production of his firearm or shotgun certificate, or its equivalent under the law of another EC country.

If the person fails to produce a certificate or other EC document, or to allow the constable to read it, or to show that he is exempt from the need for a certificate, the constable may:
- seize and detain the firearm
- and require the person immediately to give his name and address.

It is an offence for a person to fail or refuse to give his correct name and address when required to do so. There is no power of arrest for the offence, but lack of a name and address opens up the prospect of an arrest under the Police and Criminal Evidence Act 1984 general power.

8.3.2 *Approved Rifle Clubs*
Firearms Act 1968 Section 15

A constable or civilian officer:
- who is authorised in writing by the chief officer of police

- may enter any premises occupied or used by the club
- upon production of his written authority, if required
- and inspect the premises and anything on them
- to ascertain whether the provisions of the Section, and any limitations contained in the Home Secretary's approval/licence and any regulations are being complied with.

The power shall include a power to require any information kept on computer and accessible from the premises, to be available for inspection in a visible and legible form.

Offence
A person commits an offence who intentionally obstructs a constable or civilian officer in the exercise of these powers.

8.3.3 *Search Warrant*
Firearms Act 1968 Section 46

Grounds for issue: A magistrate may issue a warrant if satisfied on information on oath that there is reasonable ground for suspecting:
- that an offence relevant for the purposes of this Section, has been, is being or is about to be committed; or
- that, in connection with a firearm, imitation firearm or ammunition, there is a danger to public safety or to the peace.

Powers under the warrant: A warrant will authorise a constable or a civilian officer:
- to enter at any time the premises or place named in the warrant, using force if necessary
- search the premises or place and any person found therein
- seize and detain anything which he may find there, or on a person there, in respect of which or in connection with which he has reasonable grounds for suspecting:
  - i) that a relevant offence has been, is being or is about to be committed there, or
  - ii) in connection with a firearm or ammunition, there is a danger to public safety or to the peace.

Explanation
Relevant offence: Every offence under the 1968 Act is a relevant offence except:
- any offence relating specifically to air weapons; and
- an offence under Section 22(3) (person under 15 having an assembled shotgun).

Danger: A warrant may be obtained on the ground that there is a danger, either to safety or to the peace, arising from a firearm, imitation, or ammunition. Any number of situations could give rise to a fear of danger – e.g. a certificate holder is believed to be mentally ill, someone has been threatened with a gun, etc. An imitation firearm may not be a source of risk to safety, but it could give rise to a risk of disturbance to the peace.

Computer information: The powers of a constable or civilian officer to seize and detain items found on the premises, shall include a power to require information kept on computer and accessible from the premises, to be produced in a form in which it is visible, legible and in which it can be taken away, i.e. as a computer print-out.

Civilian officer: A civilian officer is a person who is directly employed by the police.

Offence: A person commits an offence who intentionally obstructs a constable or civilian officer in the exercise of her powers under this Section.

9 FIREARMS DEALERS

9.1 Meaning

A firearms dealer is any person who by way of trade or business, manufactures, sells, transfers, repairs, tests or proves Section 1 firearms or ammunition, or shotguns (Section 57(4)).

9.2 Registration

9.2.1 *Offence*
Firearms Act 1968 Section 3(1)
A person commits an offence by acting as a firearms dealer without being registered (maximum sentence five years' imprisonment, therefore it is an arrestable offence).

9.2.2 *Register*
Firearms Act 1968 Section 33
The chief officer of police keeps a register of all firearms dealers with business premises in that police area, together with details of all such premises.

9.2.3 *Certificate*
A certificate of registration is issued to a registered firearms dealer. The certificate is valid for a period of three years, after which it has to be renewed.

9.2.4 *Conditions*
Conditions may be imposed by police on a dealer's registration. Conditions may be varied or added to at any time, for which purpose the chief officer of police may require the dealer to deliver the certificate for amendment.

The Home Office has produced a list of 'standard conditions' which police are advised should be imposed wherever practicable. These relate in the main, to security measures, such as keeping guns in locked racks, having display windows lit at night, etc.

9.3 Refusal of Registration
Firearms Act 1968 Section 34

9.3.1 *Grounds for Refusal*
The chief officer of police may refuse an application for the registration of a person as a dealer or of particular premises, on grounds that:
- he is not satisfied that the applicant will carry on business as a dealer, to a substantial extent or as an essential part of another business.
(In other words, a person will not be registered as a dealer merely to allow him to take advantage of that status, e.g. being able to hold weapons without a firearm certificate.)
- the person is disqualified by a court from being registered
- the applicant cannot be allowed to carry on business as a firearms dealer without danger to public safety or to the peace

    – in the case of premises, that a dealer's business cannot be carried on from here without danger to public safety or to the peace.

9.3.2 *Prohibited Weapon*

If a person is authorised by the Home Secretary to deal in prohibited weapons, the police may not refuse an application (or afterwards may not remove his name from the register) on the grounds of danger to public safety or to the peace.

9.4 Removal from Register
Firearms Act 1968 Section 38

9.4.1 *Grounds for Removal*

A person's name (or as the case may be, a place of business) may be removed from the register on any of the following grounds:

    – the person is no longer carrying on business, or no longer has a place of business in that police area

    – failure to comply with any condition in force

    – he cannot be permitted to continue in business, or cannot be permitted to continue to carry on business at that particular place, without danger to public safety or to the peace

    – failure to apply for a new registration certificate when the old one expires

    – the dealer wishes his name to be removed from the register.

9.4.2 *Procedure*

In some cases, the dealer has to be given prior notice of an intention to remove his name from the register. In every case, once the name has been removed, the dealer must be notified in writing of this fact, and is required to surrender his certificate within 21 days. Failure to surrender the certificate is an offence.

9.5 Registration Offences
Firearms Act 1968 Section 39

There are several offences related to registration:

    – being a registered firearms dealer, carries on business at a place not entered in the register

    – failure to comply with a condition of registration

    – knowingly or recklessly making a statement which is false in a material particular, for the purpose of procuring registration for one's self or another, or for procuring the registration of a place of business.

9.6 Records of Transactions
Firearms Act 1968 Section 40

9.6.1 *Keeping Records*

A firearms dealer has to keep a register of transactions and must enter therein specified details relating to transactions involving Section 1 firearms and ammunition, and shotguns. He is not required to keep details relating to air weapons or to ammunition not covered by Section 1.

Entries in the transaction register must be made within 24 hours. However, in the case of the sale or transfer of a firearm or ammunition, if the customer is not known to him, the dealer must obtain sufficient details to identify the customer, and enter these details immediately.

The transaction register must be kept for a period of at least five years from the date of any transaction.

9.6.2 *Police Powers*
The dealer must allow a constable or a civilian authorised in writing by the chief officer of police, and who must produce that authority on demand, to enter and inspect the stock. The register must be produced if required. If the register is kept by means of computer, a copy of the information comprised in that register must be produced in visible and legible form, in which it can be taken away (in plain language, a print-out must be made available).

9.6.3 *Offences*
1: Failure to comply with a requirement to keep a register and to make the necessary entries.

2: Failure to comply with a requirement to allow an authorised constable or civilian officer to inspect the stock, or to produce the register.

3: Knowingly or recklessly make an entry in the register false in a material particular.

10 REQUIREMENTS RELATING TO CERTIFICATES, SALE, ETC

10.1 Purpose
There are a number of requirements relating to the sale, transfer, etc, of firearms to ensure that possession is restricted to certificate holders and registered firearms dealers.

10.2 Dealings with Person who Does Not Hold Certificate
Firearms Act 1968 Section 3

A person commits an offence who:
- sells or transfers a Section 1 firearm or ammunition or shotgun;
- undertakes to repair, test or prove a Section 1 firearm or shotgun

to or for a person who does not produce a certificate or prove he is exempt, and who is not a registered firearms dealer (arrestable offence).

10.3 Transfer of Section 1 Firearms
Firearms Act 1968 Section 42

A person who sells, lets on hire or lends a Section 1 firearm or ammunition to the holder of a firearm certificate, shall comply with any condition on that certificate.

10.4 Transfers to be in Person
Firearms (Amendment) Act 1997 Sections 32, 33

In Great Britain:
- if a Section 1 firearm or ammunition is sold, let on hire, lent or given; or
- a shotgun is sold, let on hire, lent or given or lent:

for a period of more than 72 hours to a person who is neither a registered firearms dealer nor a person entitled to purchase or acquire the same without a certificate (or visitor's permit) then the following conditions must be observed:

1: The transferee must produce to the transferor the certificate or permit entitling him to purchase or acquire the firearm or ammunition in question.

2: The transferor must comply with any instructions contained in the certificate or permit which is produced.

3: The handover from transferor to transferee must be in person, they must both be there.

4: Within seven days each party to the transfer must give notice containing required details to the chief officer of police who granted his certificate or permit (unless the transfer related only to ammunition).

10.4.1 *Offence*
Failure to comply with any of these conditions is an offence, punishable with:
five years' imprisonment if it involves a Section 1 firearm or ammunition; six months in the case of a shotgun. In the former case, therefore, it is an arrestable offence.

10.5 **Notification of Loss etc**
Firearms (Amendment) Act 1997 Section 34

When in Great Britain any firearm to which a firearm or shotgun certificate (or a visitor's certificate or permit) relates:
- is de-activated or destroyed
- or lost (whether by theft or otherwise)
- the certificate holder who was last in possession of the firearm
- shall within seven days, give notice of that fact, by registered post or recorded delivery
- to the chief officer of police who granted the certificate or permit.

10.5.1 *Offence*
Failure without reasonable excuse to give the required notice is an offence, punishable with:
five years' imprisonment if it involves a Section 1 firearm; six months in the case of a shotgun. In the former case, therefore, it is an arrestable offence.

10.6 **Notification Relating to Firearms Outside Great Britain**
Firearms (Amendment) Act 1997 Section 35

When a firearm or shotgun to which a firearm or shotgun certificate relates is transferred, destroyed, lost, etc, outside Great Britain, written notice must be given to the chief officer of police who issued the certificate.

In this case, notice has to be given, by registered post, recorded delivery, or appropriate foreign equivalent, within 14 days of the event.

10.6.1 *Offence*
Failure without reasonable excuse to give the required notice is an offence, punishable with:

five years' imprisonment if it involves a Section 1 firearm; six months in the case of a shotgun. In the former case, therefore, it is an arrestable offence.

10.7 Falsehood and Personation
Firearms Act 1968 Section 3(5)

A person commits an offence who:
- with a view to buying, acquiring, or having repaired or proved any Section 1 firearm or ammunition, or shotgun
- produces a false certificate or one containing a false entry
- or personates a person to whom a certificate has been issued
- or makes any false statement (arrestable offence).

10.8 Pawnbroker
Firearms Act 1968 Section 3(6)

It is an offence for a pawnbroker to take in pawn any Section 1 firearm or ammunition, or any shotgun.

10.9 Sale, etc to Person Drunk or of Unsound Mind
Firearms Act 1968 Section 25

It is an offence for a person to sell or transfer, or test, repair or prove, a Section 1 firearm or ammunition, or shotgun, to or for a person whom he knows or has reason to believe is drunk or of unsound mind.

Keynote Case

11.1 *Sullivan v Earl of Caithness* (1975) 62 Cr App R 105

Problem
What amounts to 'possession' in relation to firearms and firearm certificates.

Circumstances
The Earl of Caithness lived in Oxfordshire and was the owner of certain guns which he kept at his mother's apartment in Surrey. The Earl failed to renew his firearm certificate in respect of the guns and was prosecuted for having firearms in his possession without a certificate, contrary to Section 1, Firearms Act 1968. The defence put forward to the magistrates was that he was not 'in possession' of the firearms because he lived in one county, while the firearms were in another. He was acquitted and the prosecution appealed.

Decision
The Queen's Bench held that a person may be in possession of a firearm even though the person and the firearm are in different places. Indeed the application form for a certificate asks for the applicant's home address and for the address at which the firearm is to be kept, implying that 'possession' was never intended to equate with actual physical custody.

Comment

In a later case, in which this one was considered, the court held that temporary custody of a firearm could also amount to 'possession' (*Hall v Cotton and Treadwell* (1986)). Thus, more than one person may have possession of the same firearm at the same time.

The term 'has with him' is used in several offences involving criminal use of firearms. This is much more restricted in meaning than 'possession', and would not arise when the accused and the firearm were in different counties. For a discussion on 'has with him' *see the Keynote Cases in Chapter 22.*

Chapter 22: Firearms – Restrictions on Use

1 INTRODUCTION

1.1 Restrictions on Possession and Use of Firearms and Crossbows

There are restrictions placed on where firearms may be possessed, carried and used, depending on the nature of the place and the age of the person involved. These restrictions are quite separate from requirements for a certificate; a person cannot walk down the street carrying a loaded shotgun, even though he has got a certificate for the gun.

Whereas certificates are required only for Section 1 firearms and ammunition, and shotguns, restrictions are placed on possession and use not only of these but of air weapons and crossbows also. The principal legislation dealing with firearms is the Firearms Act 1968.

2 AGE RESTRICTIONS
Firearms Act 1968 Sections 22, 23, 24

2.1 Purchase or Hire – Minimum Age 17

2.1.1 *Offences*

1: It is an offence for a person under the age of 17 years to purchase or hire any firearm or ammunition.

2: It is an offence for any person to sell or let on hire any firearm or ammunition to a person under 17.

2.1.2 *Explanation*

Purchase, hire, etc: Persons under the age of 17 may possess firearms, and receive them as gifts, in some circumstances; indeed they may be granted certificates. This provision is intended to prevent the young person acquiring her own without the involvement of an adult.

Any firearm or ammunition: The reference is to 'any' firearm or ammunition, so includes air guns, air gun ammunition and other items for which no certificate is needed.

2.2 Have Air Weapon – Minimum Age 14 (or 17)

2.2.1 *Offences*

1: It is an offence:
  – for a person under the age of 14 years
  – to have with him an air weapon or ammunition for an air weapon.

2: It is an offence:
  – for a person under 17 years
  – to have with her in a public place an air weapon
  – except an air gun or air rifle, so covered with a securely fastened gun cover that it cannot be fired.

3: It is an offence:

– for a person to make a gift of an air weapon or ammunition for one
– to a person under the age of 14.

4: It is an offence:
– for a person to part with possession of an air weapon or ammunition for one
– to a person under the age of 14.

2.2.2 *Explanation*

Under 14: For a person under 14, the ban on possession applies anywhere, public or private, and includes ammunition as well as air weapons.

Aged 14 – 16: For a person aged 14, but under 17, possession in a private place is allowed. In a public place, possession of an air pistol is unlawful. An air rifle or an air gun may be carried, so long as it is kept fastened in a cover, so that it cannot be fired.

Have with him: This means having it physically in possession, or immediately available. *(Keynote Case: R v Kelt (1977))*
   A firearm some 50 yards away in a locked car has been held to be 'accessible'. *(Keynote Case: R v Pawlicki and Swindell (1992))*
   The term is much more restricted in meaning than 'possession' *(see paragraph 4.2.2 below)*.

2.3 **Have Assembled Shotgun – Minimum Age 15**

2.3.1 *Offences*

1: It is an offence:
– for a person under 15 to have with him an assembled shotgun
– except while under the supervision of a person aged 21 or over
– or while the shotgun is so covered with a securely fastened gun cover that it cannot be fired.

2: It is an offence:
– for a person to make a gift of a shotgun or ammunition for one
– to a person under the age of 15.

2.3.2 *Explanation*

Place: There is no distinction here between a private place and a public one.

Under 15: A person under 15 may not buy or hire a shotgun and may not receive one a gift. She could have one with her, if it was lent to her. Being under 15, she may walk about with the parts to a shotgun, so long as it is not assembled. If it is assembled, she must be under the supervision of a person aged 21, or the shotgun must be in a gun cover.

Aged 15 – 16: If the youth is 15 or 16 years old, she may have an assembled shotgun, with no adult companion and without it being in a gun cover. The same youth could not however, have an uncovered air rifle or air gun in public, nor could she have an air pistol, covered or not.

2.4 **Possess Section 1 Firearm – Minimum Age 14**

2.4.1 *Offences*

1: It is an offence:

– for a person under the age of 14 years
– to have in his possession any firearm or ammunition to which Section 1 applies.

2: It is an offence:
– for a person to make a gift of or lend to
– a person under the age of 14 years
– any Section 1 firearm or ammunition.

3: It is an offence:
– for a person to part with possession of a Section 1 firearm or ammunition
– to a person under 14.

2.4.2 *Explanation*

Whereas a shotgun cannot be passed as a gift to a person under 15, but could be lent, the situation with a Section 1 firearm or ammunition is that lending one to, or even parting with possession of it to a person under 14, is forbidden.

2.5 Exceptions

2.5.1 *Air Weapon*

1: A person under 14 may have an air weapon or ammunition while he is under the supervision of a person aged 21 or over.

This allows for having the air weapon in a private place; or having an air rifle or air gun in a public place, in a gun cover. (Having an uncovered air gun or air rifle, or an air pistol in public, being under 17, is a separate offence, not covered by this exception.)

However, if the air weapon is used on premises under this exception, the youngster using it, and the adult supervisor, will each commit an offence, if the air weapon is used for firing a missile beyond those premises. 'Premises' includes land (Section 57(4)).

'Use' does not have to be intentional. If the person under 14 is firing at a target in the garden, supervised by his 21 year old uncle, and unintentionally, by bad aim or whatever, fires a pellet into next-door's garden, the uncle and the nephew each commit an offence.

2: It will be an exception to both offences (person under 14, person under 17 in a public place) to have an air weapon or ammunition while:
– at a shooting gallery (where no firearms other than air weapons and rifles up to .23 inch (.58 cm) calibre are used; or
– as member of an approved rifle club.

2.5.2 *Section 1 Firearms*

A person under 14 will not commit an offence by having possession of a Section 1 firearm or ammunition in the following cases; likewise any other person will not commit the offence of parting with possession of the Section 1 firearm or ammunition to the child (each of the cases is one where a person may have possession of a Section 1 firearm or ammunition without a certificate, and are dealt with in detail in *Chapter 21*):
– carrying a firearm or ammunition for another for sporting purposes
– as a member of an approved cadet corps
– at a shooting gallery or miniature rifle range
– as a member of an approved gun club.

2.6 Defence

A person will have a defence to a charge of selling, presenting as a gift, parting with possession, etc, to person under a relevant age of a particular type of firearm or ammunition if he proves that:
- he believed the young person to be over the relevant age
- and that he had reasonable grounds for that belief.

2.7 Summary

Age	Section 1 (incl ammo)	Shotgun	Air Weapon
under 14	cannot possess except ①②③④ ❷❸❹ except ①②⑤	cannot have assembled ⑤⑥ ❷ (incl ammo)	cannot have with him, except ⑤ ❷❹ except ⑤
14 years *under 15*	cannot buy or hire ❶		cannot buy or hire (incl. ammo) cannot possess air gun or air rifle in public, except ③④⑥ cannot possess air pistol in public, except ❶③④
15 years *under 17*		cannot buy or hire (incl ammo) ❶	

Key

Exceptions:
① Carry for another for sporting purpose.
② Member of approved cadet corps.
③ At shooting gallery or miniature rifle range.
④ Member of approved gun club.
⑤ Supervised by a person aged 21 or over.
⑥ Securely fastened in gun cover so that it cannot be fired.

Offences committed by person other than the juvenile concerned:
❶ Sell or let on hire to (including ammunition).
❷ Make gift of (including ammunition) to.
❸ Lend to.
❹ Part with possession of to.

3 OFFENCES ARISING FROM POSSESSION OF A FIREARM OR AMMUNITION (WITHOUT ANY OTHER CRIMINAL INTENT)

3.1 In a Public Place

3.1.1 *Offence*
Firearms Act 1968 Section 19

A person commits an offence who:

- without lawful authority or reasonable excuse (proof of which lies with him)
- has with him in a public place:
  - i) a loaded air weapon; or
  - ii) a loaded shotgun; or
  - iii) any other firearm, loaded or not, together with ammunition suitable for use in such a firearm.

3.1.2 *Explanation*

Burden of proof: When it is shown that the defendant had a shotgun or air weapon with him in a public place, there is no need for the prosecution to prove that he knew it was loaded. If the defendant knows he has 'something' with him, it then is an offence of absolute liability as far as the state of the firearm is concerned. 'I thought is was unloaded' will not constitute a defence (*R v Harrison* (1996)).

Lawful authority: A police officer or member of the Armed Forces would have lawful authority to have firearms in a public place in the course of their duties. The fact that one holds a valid shotgun certificate does not amount to lawful authority (*Ross v Collins* (1982)).

These provisions are quite distinct from provisions relating to certificates or minimum ages. A person aged 15 years or over may have an assembled shotgun in a public place, but if the gun is loaded he commits this offence.

Reasonable excuse: There are a number of case decisions on what is **not** a reasonable excuse; what does constitute one will be a matter for the court to decide.

Where a builder and customer were in dispute over an unpaid bill, the builder started to knock down the extension he had completed at the customer's house. Seeking to prevent damage to his property was held not to amount to a reasonable excuse for the customer to be standing in the road with a loaded air rifle threatening to shoot the builder. (*Taylor v Mucklow* (1973) – this is a *Keynote Case in Chapter 8*, in relation to use of reasonable force to prevent a crime or detain a criminal.)

Has with him: This term is discussed in *paragraph 2.2.2 above.*

Public place: This means any highway and any other premises or place to which at the material time the public have, or are permitted to have, access on payment or otherwise (Section 57(4)).

The space behind a counter in a shop has been held to be a public place for these purposes (*Anderson v Miller* (1976)). In this case the court found that the whole of the shop area was one place, even though separated into two parts by a counter. This decision should be taken as applicable only to the offence in question. Under other legislation, behind the counter may be regarded as not public, e.g. for an offence under the Theft Act 1968, a person going behind the counter as a trespasser may commit burglary.

Loaded: A shotgun or air weapon is considered loaded if there is ammunition in the chamber or barrel, or in any magazine or other device in such as position that ammunition can be fed into the chamber or barrel by operation (manual or automatic) of some part of the weapon.

In the case of an air weapon, it may be considered loaded, even if the necessary compression of air needed to fire it is not present. An air rifle, for example, usually has a spring which is released by squeezing the trigger. After firing, the spring has to be reset, by pulling a lever, or some similar action. The effect of this provision is that such a weapon may still be considered 'loaded' even if the spring has not yet been reset (Section 57(6)).

With suitable ammunition: In the case of an air weapon or shotgun, this has to be loaded for the offence to be made out. In the case of a Section 1 firearm, it is enough that a person has the firearm in public and also has ammunition with him, suitable for use in that firearm. Thus, a gamekeeper might lawfully walk down the road carrying his unloaded shotgun, with a full ammunition belt round his waist. If the same gamekeeper had a .22 rifle, then either he does not carry any .22 ammunition at the same time, or he is prepared to persuade a court that he has a 'reasonable excuse' for doing so in public.

3.1.3 *Arrest*
In the case of a shotgun or Section 1 firearm, the offence is triable either way and is an arrestable offence (maximum sentence 7 years' imprisonment on first conviction). If the offence arises from possession of a loaded air weapon, this is triable summarily only so is not an arrestable offence.

3.2 **Trespass with a Firearm**
Firearms Act 1968 Section 20

3.2.1 *Offences*
1: A person commits an offence if:
   - while he has a firearm or imitation firearm with him
   - he enters or is in any building or part of a building as a trespasser
   - and without reasonable excuse (onus of proof lies on him).

2: A person commits an offence if:
   - while he has a firearm or imitation firearm with him
   - he enters or is on any land as a trespasser
   - and without reasonable excuse (onus of proof lies on him).

3.2.2 *Explanation*
Imitation firearm: The offence may be committed even if the article the trespasser has with him is only an imitation.

Enters or is in/on: The offence would be committed if a person went on to land or entered a building, with a firearm. He would also commit the offence if he did not have a firearm until after he started trespassing, e.g. if he picked up the firearm in the building, or if he met a friend while trespassing on land, who passed him the firearm.

Part of a building: As is the case in burglary, a person may be a trespasser when he moves from a part of a building where he is not trespassing, to another part where he has no right to be.

Land: For the purposes of this Section 'land' includes water.

3.2.3 *Arrest*
Trespassing in a building with a Section 1 firearm or shotgun is an arrestable offence, carrying a possible maximum of 7 years' imprisonment when tried on indictment.

Trespassing on land whatever the type of firearm, or trespassing in a building with an air weapon or imitation firearm, will give rise to summary offences; they are not arrestable offences.

3.3 **Drunk in Possession of Loaded Firearm**
Licensing Act 1872 Section 12

3.3.1 *Offence*
A person commits an offence who is drunk when in possession of a loaded firearm.

3.3.2 *Explanation*

The offence is not restricted to any particular type of firearm, so would include air weapons. 'Loaded' is dealt with at *paragraph 3.1.2 above.*

3.3.3 *Arrest*

Any person may arrest someone found committing the offence. The 'any person' powers are open to the police, but Home Office advice is that a constable should exercise this power only if the general arrest conditions under Section 25 of the Police and Criminal Evidence Act 1984 are satisfied. Since one of the general arrest conditions is a belief that arrest is necessary to prevent the offender causing physical injury to anyone, arrest may very well be justified for this offence.

3.4 Firearms and Highways

3.4.1 *Offence*
Highways Act 1980 Section 161

A person commits an offence who:
- without lawful authority or excuse
- discharges any firearm within 50 feet of the centre of a highway which consists of or comprises a carriageway
- and as a consequence, a user of the highway is injured, interrupted or endangered.

3.4.2 *Explanation*

Lawful authority or excuse: Shooting a runaway heifer, or putting down an animal injured in a road accident, are examples of lawful authority or excuse.

Any firearm: Would include an air weapon.

Highway consists of or comprises a carriageway: A highway is any road or other way over which the public has a right to pass. A public footpath is a highway, as is the M1 motorway; the difference is that the M1 comprises a 'carriageway', i.e. a way for vehicles, whereas a footpath does not. The offence would not be committed by discharging a firearm within 50 feet of the centre of a footpath.

Consequence: The offence is not complete by discharging the firearm, there must be evidence that another user of the highway is endangered, injured or interrupted. If an airgun pellet nicks a highway user's ear, causing him to throw himself flat on the ground for fear of being shot, he could be said to have suffered all three consequences – injury, danger and interruption of his progress along the highway.

4 CRIMINAL USE AND POSSESSION OF FIREARMS

4.1 Introduction

The offences dealt with above, arise from possession of a firearm, in a particular place, or because it is loaded, or because of a person's age. The following offences arise when persons have firearms for use in committing crimes such as robbery or assault. In addition, there are restrictions on a person possessing a firearm after release from prison.

4.2 Possession with Intent to Injure

4.2.1 *Offence*
Firearms Act 1968 Section 16

It is an offence for a person:
- to have in his possession any firearm or ammunition
- with intent by means thereof to endanger life
- or to enable anyone else by means thereof to endanger life
- whether or not any injury has been caused.

4.2.2 *Explanation*

Possession: This term is wider in meaning than 'has with him' *(see paragraph 2.2.2 above)*. A person may have a firearm in his possession even though it is not readily accessible to him. *(Keynote Case in Chapter 21: Sullivan v Earl of Caithness (1975))*

Any firearm or ammunition: To endanger life, you need a real firearm and ammunition for it. Thus, an imitation firearm will not be enough for this offence to be committed. However, if the intention is only to frighten someone, an imitation may well suffice *(see below)*.

Endanger life: There must be evidence of this intention, using the firearm or ammunition concerned. The accused may have possession, intending that someone else would use the firearm or ammunition to endanger the life of a third person.

Anyone else: The 'anyone else' has to be identified if a prosecution is to succeed. In a case where a person had a large number of firearms and supplied guns unlawfully to others, it was not sufficient to amount to this offence that he intended to supply a firearm to a person who might use it to endanger life. In a criminal venture of this kind, it is likely that some of those supplied will use the firearm to endanger life, but for the defendant to be convicted of this offence, the evidence must be specific (*R v Jones* (1996)).

Injury or not: Since the essence of the offence is possession with intent to endanger life, the phrase 'whether any injury has been caused or not' appears somewhat superfluous but it does serve to emphasise the point that the *actus reus* is possession.

4.2.3 *Arrest*
This is a serious arrestable offence.

4.3 Possession with Intent to Cause Fear of Violence

4.3.1 *Offence*
Firearms Act 1968 Section 16A

It is an offence for a person:
- to have in his possession any firearm or imitation firearm
- with intent by means thereof to cause
- or to enable another person by means thereof to cause
- any person to believe that unlawful violence will be used against him, or against another person.

4.3.2 *Explanation*
Firearm or imitation: The criminal use offences differ slightly from one another in what is

required, whether it be a firearm, ammunition and/or imitation firearm. Logic usually applies, in that the item required for the offence to be committed is related to the intention or use. To endanger life requires a firearm and ammunition, so possession of either gives rise to the Section 16 offence. To frighten someone does not require ammunition, or even a real firearm; a firearm or imitation will do.

Possession with intent: As with the previous offence, the *actus reus* is possession, there is no need for the firearm to be used to frighten someone.

Believe unlawful violence will be used: The offence is committed where a person has the firearm or imitation with the intention that it shall be used to make someone believe that unlawful violence will be used. Whether the firearm is used to frighten, and if so, whether it does actually frighten the victim, is not relevant.

Another person: The intention may be that two people are involved, or that three or four are. The person with the firearm may intend to use it to make the victim think violence is going to be used against him; the person with the firearm may intend to pass it to his 'hit-man' to use it to make the victim believe he is to be subjected to violence; or the intention may be that the 'hit-man' uses it to make e.g. a husband believe that violence will be used against his wife.

4.3.3 *Arrest*
This is a serious arrestable offence.

4.4 Use Firearm with Intent to Resist Arrest

4.4.1 *Offence*
Firearms Act 1968 Section 17(1)

A person commits an offence who:
- – makes use of or attempts to make use of
- – a firearm or imitation firearm
- – with intent to resist or prevent the lawful arrest or detention of himself or another.

4.4.2 *Explanation*
Makes or attempts: Pointing a gun at a police officer would be 'making use' of it. Trying to grab it out of the glove compartment as police officers were seizing hold of the accused to arrest him, would be 'attempting to make use' of it.

Firearm or imitation: Once again, it is logical to have imitation firearms included, since one of these could be pointed at the police officer to prevent her from making an arrest.

In relation to this offence, 'firearm' does not include component parts or silencers, i.e. it is restricted to whole lethal barrelled weapons. Similarly, 'imitation' means something that looks like a lethal barrelled weapon (Section 17(4)).

Intent to resist or prevent: Whether the criminal succeeds in resisting or preventing an arrest is not relevant; there has to be evidence of his intention to do so. The words 'resist' and 'prevent' should be given their everyday meanings, in the absence of any relevant case law.

If the accused says, 'I was going to give myself up, I just wanted to impress my mates first by pointing the imitation firearm at the police', then his intention was to resist arrest. The fact that he did not intend to avoid arrest permanently will not be a defence.

Lawful arrest or detention: The Section does not restrict what the arrest or detention may be for. It does not have to be, for example for an arrestable, recordable or imprisonable offence. Indeed, the arrest does not have to be for an offence at all. An arrest following a positive breath test, or of a person liable to be excluded under prevention of terrorism legislation, is not an arrest for an offence, but will be an 'arrest' for the purposes of this Section.

The arrest or detention does have to be lawful, before this offence arises. Using a firearm to prevent an unlawful arrest may well give rise to another firearms offence, but not to this one.

Self or another: The accused may be seeking to resist or prevent his own arrest, or that of some other person.

4.4.3 *Arrest*
This is a serious arrestable offence.

4.5 **Possession when Committing/Arrested for First Schedule Offence**
4.5.1 *Offence*
Firearms Act 1968 Section 17(2)

It is an offence for a person:
  - to have in his possession any firearm or imitation firearm
  - at the time of committing or at the time he is arrested for any First Schedule offence
  - unless he shows that he had possession of it for a lawful object.

4.5.2 *Explanation*
Possession: This is discussed at *paragraph 4.2.2 above.*

Firearm or imitation: The purpose of the Section is to provide a sanction against criminals who carry firearms in a situation where they may be used in the furtherance of crime. Since many crimes 'benefit' from involving an imitation firearm just as much as a real one, the Section applies to imitations.

As in the case of use of a firearm with intent to resist arrest, the term 'firearm' here does not include component parts of firearms.

Schedule 1: Schedule 1 to the Act lists the Offences to which Section 17(2) applies. These offences are:
  1: Criminal damage (Criminal Damage Act 1971, Section 1).
  2: Any of the following under the offences Against the Person Act 1861 – Section 47 assault (actual bodily harm); Section 20 assault (wounding or grievous bodily harm); Section 38 assault (assault with intent to resist arrest); Section 21 (garotting); Section 22 (unlawful use of drugs); Section 30 (explosives); Section 32 (endangering railway passengers).
  3: Abduction of children (Child Abduction Act 1984).
  4: Any of the following under the Theft Act 1968 – theft, robbery, burglary, blackmail, taking a conveyance.
  5: Assault on a constable in the execution of his duty (Police Act 1996, Section 89) assault on a prisoner custody officer (Criminal Justice Act 1991, Section 90); assault on a secure training centre custody officer (Criminal Justice and Public Order Act 1994, Section 13).
  6: Any of the following under the Sexual Offences Act 1956 – Section 1 (rape); Sections 17, 18, 20 (abduction of women).

7: Aid and abet any of the above offences.

8: Attempt to commit any of the above offences.

Unless... lawful object: The onus of proof is on the accused, to show that at the time of committing, or at the time of his arrest, for a Schedule 1 offence, he had possession of the firearm or imitation for some lawful purpose. For example, Mellors, a gamekeeper, is at work, using a shotgun to shoot foxes when he gets into an argument with a farmer. He then assaults the farmer causing him actual bodily harm. Next day, while he is on his employer's land shooting rabbits, police arrive to arrest him for the assault. The possession of the shotgun by Mellors has nothing to do with the assault, so he will not be guilty if he shows he had the shotgun at that time of committing the assault and again at the time of being arrested for it, for a lawful purpose. Likewise, Webley is at the funfair, spending the proceeds of a burglary, when police arrest him as he is trying to win a cuddly toy by shooting at ping pong balls with an air rifle.

4.5.3 *Arrest*
This is an arrestable offence.

4.6 Have Firearm with Criminal Intent

4.6.1 *Offence*
Firearms Act 1968 Section 18

It is an offence for a person:
- to have with him a firearm or imitation firearm
- with intent to commit an indictable offence
- or with intent to resist arrest, or prevent the arrest of another
- in either case while he has the firearm / imitation with him.

4.6.2 *Explanation*
Firearm or imitation firearm: Even if the article the accused has with him is only an imitation, he may still commit the offence.

Have with him: This is discussed at *paragraph 2.2.2 above* and means having it physically in possession, or immediately available. *(Keynote Cases: R v Kelt (1977), R v Pawlicki and Swindell (1992))*

Intent to commit indictable offence: An indictable offence is one triable on indictment at Crown Court. It may be triable on indictment only, as in serious crimes such as rape, robbery or murder; or it may be an 'either way' offence such as theft, triable either at magistrates' court or at Crown Court.

The intention need not be to commit the indictable offence in the immediate future. An intention to commit the offence at some time in the future when the occasion arises will be enough for this offence to be committed (*R v Bentham, Baillie and Simpson* (1973)).

Resist or prevent arrest: The intention may be to resist one's own arrest or prevent someone else being arrested.

While he has the firearm with him: It is not required that there is an intention to use the firearm for the purpose of committing the offence or resisting the arrest. However, if a person is carrying a firearm (which he has no intention of using) while he intends to commit a crime, the risk of his resorting to its use is far greater than if he was not carrying it in the first place. It is to discourage the criminal use of firearms that the legislation is aimed.

Proof: The Section provides that:
  - proof that the accused had a firearm or imitation firearm with him
  - plus proof that he had the necessary intention, to commit an indictable offence, or to resist or prevent an arrest
  - shall be evidence that he intended to have it with him while doing so (Section 18(2)).

The fact that Sykes has a gun in his pocket and that he intends to rob a post office does not necessarily mean that he intends to have the gun with him during the robbery, and it is going to be difficult for the prosecution to prove that he does so intend. The effect of subsection 2 is that once the first two elements are proved, they become evidence of the third element.

Note: That proofs of having the firearm plus intent will be 'evidence', not 'proof'. It will still be open for the defence to bring evidence to rebut that evidence.

4.6.3 *Arrest*
This is a serious arrestable offence.

4.7 Possession After Conviction

4.7.1 *Offence*
Firearms Act 1968 Section 21

There are two separate prohibitions on possession of firearms by a person who has served a custodial sentence, dependent on the length of that sentence.

1: A person who has been sentenced to a 'long custodial sentence' shall not at any time have a firearm or ammunition in his possession.

2: A person who has been sentenced to a 'short custodial sentence' shall not at any time have a firearm or ammunition in his possession during a period of five years from the date of his release.

4.7.2 *Explanation*
Long sentence: The terms 'long/short custodial sentence' do not appear in the Act, but are used here to make for ease of explanation. The term 'long custodial sentence' means – life imprisonment, preventive detention, or a sentence of three years or more of imprisonment, corrective training, youth custody, etc.

Short sentence: This means a term of imprisonment, youth custody, etc of three months or more but less than three years.

Sentenced: It is the length of the sentence which is relevant, not how long the person actually serves of that sentence. Anyone sentenced to a term of imprisonment of up to two years, will normally serve only half that period. Thus, someone given a sentence of five months will actually serve less than three months, but the prohibition still applies because his sentence was 'three months or more'.

Date of release: In the case of a person sentenced to imprisonment which is partly served and partly suspended, the date of release is the date on which he completes that part of the sentence which he has to serve in prison.

In the case of a sentence which is wholly suspended, the prohibition will not apply (*R v Fordham* (1969)). Put simply, the date of release is the date he walks out of prison, whether on licence, parole, completion of his sentence, whether it be partly suspended, etc. If he never went inside because his sentence was suspended, then the ban on his having firearms does not apply. (The situation is virtually the same for a secure training order (for persons aged 12–14, half the sentence spent in detention, half under supervision), in that the date he finishes the detention phase is the date of release.)

Firearm or ammunition: Includes any firearm or ammunition, so even airgun pellets are banned.

Scotland and Northern Ireland: A sentence in Scotland counts as a sentence for the purposes of the ban on possession in England and Wales.

If a person is prohibited from possession of a firearm or ammunition under the corresponding provisions of the law in Northern Ireland, that prohibition shall apply in Great Britain also (subsection 3A).

4.7.3 *Arrest*
The offence carries a maximum sentence of five years' imprisonment, so is an arrestable offence.

4.7.4 *Other Prohibitions*
1: Children and young persons convicted of serious crime may be detained in secure accommodation under the provisions of the Children and Young Persons Act 1933. A person so detained may be released on licence, and a prohibition on possession of firearms or ammunition will apply during the period of that licence.

2: It may be a condition of a probation order or of a recognisance to keep the peace or be of good behaviour, that the person concerned shall not possess a firearm during the period of that order or recognisance.

In either of these cases, it will be an offence under this Section to possess a firearm or ammunition during the relevant period. Thus, a person subject of a probation order which includes a condition that he shall not possess a firearm while on probation, faces a possible five years in prison for breaking that condition.

4.7.5 *Removal of Prohibition*
A person prohibited from possession under any of the provisions of this Section may apply to Crown Court for removal of the prohibition.

4.7.6 *Sale, etc to Prohibited Person*
A person commits an offence who:
  – sells or transfers a firearm or ammunition
  – or repairs, tests or proves same
  – for a person whom he knows or has reasonable grounds for believing to be prohibited under this Section from possessing a firearm or ammunition (subsection 5).

4.7.7 *Arrest*
This offence also carries a five year maximum sentence, so is an arrestable offence.

5 POLICE POWERS

5.1 Stop and Search
Firearms Act 1968 Section 47

5.1.1 *Exercise of Power*
1: If a constable has reasonable cause to suspect a person:
   - of having a firearm with or without ammunition, with him in a public place; or
   - to be committing or to be about to commit elsewhere than in a public place, any 'relevant offence'
   - then the constable may require that person to hand over the firearm or any ammunition for examination **and**
   - the constable may search that person, and detain him for the purpose of doing so.

2: If a constable has reasonable cause to suspect:
   - that there is a firearm in a vehicle in a public place
   - or that a vehicle is being used or is about to be used in connection with the commission elsewhere than in a public place of a 'relevant offence'
   - then he may search that vehicle and for the purposes of doing so may require the driver or person in control to stop the vehicle.

3: For the purposes of exercising these powers, the constable may enter any place.

5.1.2 *Explanation*
Have with him: This term is discussed at *paragraph 2.2.2 above.* Note that whereas 'have with him' may include when a firearm is in a vehicle, there is power to search a vehicle as well as a person.

Firearm or ammunition: Having any ammunition, without a firearm, may give rise to the offence.

Public place: The constable does not need reason to believe that any offence arises from the person having the firearm or ammunition with him, possession in a public place affords ground for exercise of these powers.

Relevant offence: The offences which are relevant are:
   Section 18:   have firearm with intent to commit indictable offence or resist arrest
   Section 20:   trespass in building or on land with firearm

5.1.3 *Offence*
Firearms Act 1968 Section 47(2)

A person commits an offence if he fails to hand over a firearm for examination when required to do so by a constable in exercise of these powers.

5.2 Production of Certificates
Firearms Act 1968 Section 48

A constable may demand:
   - from a person whom he believes to be in possession of a Section 1 firearm or ammunition, or of a shotgun

- production of his firearm or shotgun certificate (or its equivalent under the law of another EC country)
- If the person fails to produce a certificate or to allow the constable to read it or to show that he is exempt from the need for a certificate
- the constable may seize and detain the firearm
- and require the person immediately to give his name and address.

It is an offence for a person to fail or refuse to give his correct name and address when required to do so.

5.3 Search Warrant
Firearms Act 1968 Section 46

Grounds for issue: A magistrate may issue a warrant if satisfied on information on oath that there is reasonable ground for suspecting:
- that an offence relevant for the purpose of this Section, has been, is being or is about to be committed; or
- that, in connection with a firearm, imitation firearm or ammunition, there is a danger to public safety or to the peace.

Powers under the warrant: A warrant will authorise a constable or a civilian officer:
- to enter at any time the premises or place named in the warrant, using force if necessary
- search the premises or place and any person found therein
- seize and detain anything which he may find there, or on a person there, in respect of which or in connection with which he has reasonable ground for suspecting:
  a) that a relevant offence has been, is being or is about to be committed there, or
  b) in connection with a firearm or ammunition, there is a danger to public safety or to the peace.

5.3.1 *Explanation*
Relevant offence: Every offence under the 1968 Act is a relevant offence except:
- any offence relating specifically to air weapons; and
- an offence under Section 22(3) (person under 15 having an assembled shotgun).

Danger: A warrant may be obtained on the ground that there is a danger, either to safety or to the peace, arising from a firearm, imitation or ammunition. Any number of situations could give rise to a fear of danger – e.g. a certificate holder is believed to be mentally ill, someone has been threatened with a gun, etc. An imitation firearm may not be a source of risk to safety, but it could give rise to a risk of disturbance to the peace.

Computer information: The powers of a constable or civilian officer to seize and detain items found on the premises, shall include a power to require information kept on computer and accessible from the premises, to be produced in a form in which it is visible, legible and in which it can be taken away, i.e. as a computer print-out.

Civilian officer: A civilian officer is a person who is directly employed by the police.

Offence: A person commits an offence who intentionally obstructs a constable or civilian officer in the exercise of her powers under this Section.

5.4 Seizure of Forfeited Firearms
Firearms Act 1968 Section 52

When a person:
  - is convicted of an offence involving firearms (other than one of the offences mentioned as exceptions in the preceding paragraph)
  - is convicted of a crime and receives a custodial sentence
  - is subject of a condition that he shall not possess, carry or use a firearm, as part of a probation order, bind over, etc

then the court may order forfeiture of any firearms or ammunition found in his possession, and may also cancel any firearm or shotgun certificate which he holds.

A constable may seize and detain any firearm or ammunition which may be the subject of such a forfeiture order.

6 TIME LIMIT ON PROSECUTION OF OFFENCES
Firearms Act 1968 Section 51

6.1 Extended Time Limit
Summary proceedings are normally subject to a six month time limit, in that the prosecution has to commence proceedings within six months of the date the offence is committed. In the case of offences under the Act, the time limit for summary prosecution is four years.

6.2 Exceptions
The exceptions to this (i.e. six months still applies) are the same as those relating to a search warrant – possession of assembled shotgun by person under 15, and any offence specifically related to air weapons.

6.3 Authority to Prosecute
Only proceedings instituted by or on behalf of the Director of Public Prosecutions may be commenced after the usual six month period.

7 CROSSBOWS
Crossbows Act 1987

7.1 Introduction

7.1.1 *Meaning of Term*
There is no definition of the term 'crossbow' in the Act, so the dictionary definition will have to do. A crossbow may be described as a bow fixed across a stock, with a groove for the arrow and a mechanism for drawing and releasing the string *(Concise Oxford Dictionary)*.

7.1.2 *Explanation*
Relevant points about the description are:
  - a crossbow has a stock, like a shotgun or rifle, enabling it to be held steady for aiming
  - there is a mechanism for drawing it, making the crossbow capable of considerable power, without having to rely on the strength of the user

    — there is a groove for the arrow – if there was barrel instead of a groove, the crossbow would be a firearm.

7.1.3 *Low Powered Crossbow*

Because a crossbow can be lethal and discharges a missile, there is a need for some control, but this is by no means as extensive as that applying to firearms, being confined to restrictions on persons under 17 years of age having them. The Act does not concern itself with very low-powered crossbows, those with a draw weight of less than 1.4 kilograms.

7.2 **Offences**

7.2.1 *Selling to a Person Under 17*
Crossbows Act 1987 Section 1

A person commits an offence who:
    — sells or lets on hire
    — a crossbow or part of a crossbow
    — to a person under the age of 17 years
    — unless he believes him to be 17 or older **and** has reasonable grounds for that belief.

7.2.2 *Buying*
Crossbows Act 1987 Section 2

A person commits an offence who:
    — being under the age of 17 years
    — buys or hires
    — a crossbow or part of a crossbow.

7.2.3 *Possession*
Crossbows Act 1987 Section 3

A person commits an offence who:
    — being under the age of 17 years
    — has with him
    — a crossbow which is capable of discharging a missile
    — or parts of a crossbow which together (without any other parts) can be assembled to form a crossbow capable of discharging a missile
    — unless he is under the supervision of a person aged 21 years or older.

7.3 **Explanation**

Sell/buy/let/hire: There is no offence committed by lending or giving a crossbow as a gift to a person under 17; what is unlawful is for the young person to acquire his own without reference to an adult.

Belief over 17: A person will not commit the offence of selling or letting, if he believed the young person to be 17 or over, but for this claim to succeed, there must be some reasonable ground for such a belief. 'I know he looks no older than 12 but I thought he was 17', will not in itself be enough to avoid conviction.

Part of a crossbow: The offences of selling, buying and hiring extend to parts of a crossbow as well as whole ones, otherwise shopkeepers could sell them in two separate boxes, without breaking the law. When it comes to possession however, for the young person to commit the offence she must be in possession, either of a whole crossbow capable of firing a missile, or of enough of the bits needed to make up a crossbow capable of discharging a missile.

Supervision: Possession will be lawful if the young person is 'under the supervision' of a person aged 21 or over. This implies more than merely 'accompanied by'. While there is no specific offence of failing to exercise supervision, the adult person might be liable for aiding or abetting any crime committed by the young person arising from irresponsible use of the crossbow.

7.4 Police Powers
Crossbows Act 1987 Section 4

7.4.1 *Search*
If a constable suspects with reasonable cause that:
- a person under 17 is committing or has committed an offence of unlawful possession of a crossbow or enough parts to make one capable of firing a missile
- the officer may
- search that person for a crossbow or part of one
- search any vehicle, or anything in a vehicle, in or on which the constable reasonably suspects there is a crossbow or part of one connected with that offence.

7.4.2 *Stop to Search*
For the purpose of a search, the constable may detain the person or vehicle. For that purpose, the constable may enter any land – except a dwelling house.

7.4.3 *Seizure*
The constable may:
- seize and retain for the purposes of proceedings for an offence
- anything she finds in the course of a search
- which appears to her to be a crossbow or part of one.

Keynote Cases

8.1 *R v Kelt* [1977] 3 All ER 1099

Problem
The distinction between the terms 'have with him' and 'possess' for the purposes of firearms offences.

Circumstances
Kelt took part in a robbery and police recovered a 'robber's kit' which included a gun and other equipment used in the robbery. Some months later police searched Kelt's house and in the kitchen found another 'robber's kit', which included a gun and ammunition. Kelt was charged with an offence under Section 18 of the Firearms Act 1968, having a firearm with him with intent to commit an indictable offence.

At the trial the judge directed the jury that as the accused knew the gun was in the kitchen, and the kitchen was under his control, he 'had the firearm with him' for the purposes of the offence. Kelt appealed.

Decision

The Court of Appeal held that in the several offences of criminal use of firearms, there was a distinction between 'possession' and 'have with him'. For the latter there had to be established a close physical link and immediate control over the firearm. However, it was not necessary to show that the accused was carrying the firearm.

Comment

Whereas 'have with him' requires a close physical link and immediate control, 'possession' requires neither of these. *See the Keynote Case of Sullivan v Earl of Caithness in Chapter 21. For more on 'close physical link' see Pawlicki, below.*

8.2 *R v Pawlicki and Swindell* [1992] 3 All ER 902

Problem

Whether a person 'has with him' a firearm when it is in a locked car some 50 yards away.

Circumstances

Pawlicki and Swindell allegedly having agreed to commit a robbery at the premises of an auctioneer, Pawlicki drove a car to the premises. He parked it and locked it; inside were three sawn-off shotguns and other articles suitable for use in a robbery. Pawlicki went into the premises where he met Swindell. They were then arrested by police who were 'acting on information received'. They were convicted of an offence under Section 18 of the Firearms Act 1968, of having a firearm with them with intent to commit an indictable offence. They appealed on the ground that 'have with them' meant immediately available, which was not the case when the car was 50 yards away.

Decision

The Court of Appeal found that the element of closeness and accessibility of the firearm had to be judged in a common sense way. It was the intention of the criminal to commit a crime, rather than the exact distance, which was relevant. It was sufficient that the guns were readily available to them at the time they were about to commit the offence.

Comment

The foregoing case, of *R v Kelt*, was referred to by the Court of Appeal. The two decisions are quite compatible. Whether a person has a firearm with him will be a matter of whether it is readily accessible (a close physical link), but this need not be within arm's reach.

Chapter 23: Bigamy

1 This is the criminal offence which is committed when a man or woman marries more than once. The original offence is set out in the Offences Against the Person Act 1861, but this has been subject to amendment (Schedule 3 Criminal Justice Act 1925, Section 1 Criminal Justice Act 1948).

Section 57 Offences Against The Person Act 1861

Whosoever being married, shall marry any other person during the life of the former husband or wife, whether the second marriage shall have taken place in England or Ireland or elsewhere shall be guilty of an offence, and being convicted thereof shall be liable to imprisonment for any term not exceeding seven years.

Provided that nothing in this Section contained shall extend to any second marriage contracted elsewhere than in England and Ireland by any subject of Her Majesty, or to any person marrying for the second time, whose husband or wife shall have been continually absent from such a person for the space of seven years then last past, and shall not have been known by such a person to be living within that time or shall extend to any person who, at the time of such second marriage, shall have been divorced from the bond of the first marriage, or to any person whose former marriage shall have been declared void by the sentence of any court of competent jurisdiction.

Explanation

2 The offence is stated in the first paragraph, the second half is the defence of not having seen the former spouse for a period in excess of seven years. Over the years there have been many infamous cases of alleged bigamy. It is a matter for the defendant to prove any defence upon which he relies. In *R v Thomson* (1906) the defendant claimed that his first marriage was void as at the time the woman whom he married was already married and had a husband living. The court stated that the onus on the prosecution was to prove that the defendant had undergone more than one marriage where one was within the currency of another. Once this had been done it is for the defendant to prove his defence.

3 For evidential purposes the marriages are to be strictly proved. Production of certificates and proof of the identity of those taking part will be required. The validity of the second marriage is immaterial to the offence (*R v Allen* (1872)). Where a man underwent a ceremony to marry his wife's niece, which is prohibited by affinity and would have been void, he would still be liable for the offence of bigamy.

4 The English courts have jurisdiction to try cases of bigamy committed in a foreign jurisdiction (*R v Earl Russell* [1901]). Proof will be required of the first and second ceremonies, expert evidence will be required to prove the validity of the ceremonies. It is not necessary to show on the indictment that the defendant is a subject of Her Majesty. Bigamy is an either-way offence and the circumstances of the offence must be taken into account when deciding on mode of trial. The Court of Appeal in *R v Crowhurst* [1979] held that for bigamy the sentence must vary in accordance with the circumstances of the case. Where there is a deception of the innocent party, with some injury resulting, an immediate custodial sentence was necessary, the length depending on the gravity of the injury suffered.

Chapter 24: Obscene Publications

1.1 The purpose of the legislation in relation to obscene publications is protection of those who do not wish to be have offensive materials displayed openly before them, also to restrict access to those who have attained the age of discretion. As time progresses the level of publication which is deemed automatically to be obscene gets less and less, this reflects the liberalisation of society.

1.2 The protection of children from harmful publications is one aim of legislation. Some offences infrequently used although still law include the Children and Young Persons (Harmful Publications) Act 1955 which covers the type of materials which should not be shown to children.

CHILDREN AND HARMFUL PUBLICATIONS
Section 1 Children and Young Persons (Harmful Publications) Act 1955

This Act applies to any book, magazine or other like work which is of a kind likely to fall into the hands of children or young persons and consists wholly or mainly of stories told in pictures (with or without the addition of written matter), being stories portraying:
— the commission of crimes; or
— acts of violence or cruelty; or
— incidents of a repulsive or horrible nature;

in such a way that the work as a whole would tend to corrupt a child or young person into whose hands it might fall.

Explanation
2.1 For the purpose of this legislation the definition of child is under fourteen years of age, and young person is under eighteen years of age.

Section 2 Children and Young Persons (Harmful Publications) Act 1955

(1) A person who prints, publishes, sells or lets on hire a work to which this Act applies, or has any such work in his possession for the purpose of selling it or letting it on hire, shall be guilty of an offence and liable, on summary conviction to imprisonment for a term not exceeding four months and or a fine;

   Provided that, in any proceedings taken under this subsection against a person in respect of selling or letting it on hire, it shall be a defence for him to prove that he had not examined the contents of the work and had no reasonable cause to suspect that it was one to which this Act applies.

(2) A prosecution for an offence under this Section shall not, in England or Wales, be instituted except by, or with the consent of, the Attorney General.

Explanation
2.1.1 Simple possession of 'horror comics' will not be unlawful; the legislation is aimed at those who trade in such publications, by producing, selling or hiring them. The defence, that he had not examined the work, and had no reason to believe that it was one to which these provisions apply, is not open to someone accused of printing or publishing it.

2.2 The Act also contains provisions for the application of a warrant (Section 3) to search for articles involved in the making of such articles, or the articles themselves, but this requires the consent of the Attorney General before even an application for a warrant may be made. Further provisions under Section 4 prohibit the importation of such materials, and the means for production of them. Importation is an offence under the Customs and Excise Management Act 1979.

OBSCENE ARTICLES

2.3 The extent to which an article is regarded as obscene will vary according to the tastes and preferences of individuals. To bring some degree of objectivity into what is very much a matter of subjective judgement, the law provides a test of obscenity.

The 'Obscenity Test'
Section 1 Obscene Publications Act 1959

(1) For the purposes of this Act an article shall be deemed to be obscene if its effect or (where the article comprises two or more distinct items) the effect of any one of its items is, if taken as a whole, such as to tend to deprave and corrupt persons who are likely, having regard to all relevant circumstances, to read, see or hear the matter contained or embodied in it.

(2) In this Act 'article' means any description of article containing or embodying matter to be read or looked at or both, any sound record, and any film or other record of a picture or pictures.

(3) For the purposes of this Act a person publishes an article who:
   a) distributes, circulates, sells, lets on hire, gives, or lends it, or who offers it for sale or for letting on hire; or
   b) in the case of an article containing or embodying matter to be looked at or a record, shows, plays or projects it.

(4) For the purposes of this Act a person also publishes an article to the extent that any matter recorded on it is included by him in a programme included in a programme service.

(5) Where the inclusion of any matter in a programme so included would, if that matter were recorded matter, constitute the publication of an obscene article for the purpose of this Act by virtue of subsection (4) above, this Act shall have the effect in relation to the inclusion of that matter in that programme as if it were recorded matter.

(6) In this Section 'programme' and 'programme service' have the same meaning as in the Broadcasting Act 1990.

2.4 Section 1(1) sets out the basic 'test of obscenity' the key phrase is 'tending to corrupt and deprave' persons who are likely to have access to it. This refers to the effect on the mind, it can include emotions and need not have an overt or open manifestation by way of physical sexual activity (*DPP v Whyte* [1972]). The proposition that those who read and were addicted to these types of books are incapable of being further depraved is false, and as such people would be capable of being further depraved as a result of access to such material. The application of the test depends on the publication itself, the intention of the publisher is irrelevant (*R v Shaw*

[1961]). There are two offences:
- to publish an obscene article, whether for gain or not
- to have possession of an obscene article, for publication for gain for one's self or another.

Publication with a View to Gain

2.5 *Section 29 Obscene Publications Act 1959 as amended by Sections 28, 53 and Schedule 13 of the Criminal Law Act 1977, Schedule 1 Cinematography (Amendment) Act 1982, and Schedule 2 Cinemas Act 1985*

(1) Subject as hereinafter provided, any person who, whether for gain or not, publishes an obscene article or who has an obscene article for publication for gain (whether gain for himself or gain to another) shall be liable.

The punishment is up to six months and or a fine on summary conviction and up to three years and or a fine on indictment. There is a limitation for proceedings which is up to two years after the commission of the offence. Prosecutions can only be by or with the consent of the Director of Public Prosecutions. The existence of provision to prosecute for public nuisance at common law is specifically withdrawn (Section 4 Obscene Publications Act 1959). There is a defence under Section 2(5), a person cannot be convicted of an offence under Section 2 if he proves that he had not examined the article in respect of which he is charged and had no reasonable cause to suspect that it was such that his publication of it would make him liable to be convicted of an offence. By virtue of Section 3 the courts can issue a warrant to enter and search premises, stalls or vehicles where it is suspect that obscene articles are stored. This however must be on behalf of or authorised by the Director of Public Prosecutions.

2.6 There has been much controversy about what is or is not in the interests of the public. The defence of possession of obscene articles for publication in the public interest was included in the 1959 Act. The defence covers the interests of furthering science, learning, art or literature and allows for the introduction of expert evidence of opinion.

Defence to Obscenity 'The Public Good'
Section 4 Obscene Publications Act 1959
as amended by Section 53Criminal Law Act 1977

(1) Subject to subsection (1a) of this Section, a person shall not be convicted of an offence against Section two of this Act, and an order for forfeiture shall not be made under the foregoing Section, if it is proved that the publication of the article in question is justified as being for the public good on the ground that it is in the interests of science, literature, art or learning, or of other objects of general concern.

(1a) Subsection (1) of this Section shall not apply where the article in question is a moving picture film or soundtrack, but:
   a) a person shall not be convicted of an offence against Section 2 of this Act in relation to any such film or soundtrack, and
   b) an order for forfeiture of any such film or soundtrack shall not be made under Section 3 of this Act;
   if it is proved that publication of the film or soundtrack is justified as being for the public good on the ground that it is in the interests of drama, opera, ballet or any other art, or of literature or learning.

(2) It is hereby declared that the evidence of experts as to the literary, artistic, scientific or other merits of an article may be admitted in any proceedings under this Act either to establish or to negative the said ground.

(3) In this Section 'moving picture soundtrack' means any sound record designed for playing with a moving picture film, whether incorporated in the film or not.

Explanation

2.7 The 1959 Obscene Publications Act was amended by the 1964 Act, the amendment was designed to resolve a defence successfully used to defeat a charge of possession with a view to publication. A person shall be deemed to have an article for publication for gain if with a view to such publication he has the article in his ownership, possession or control (Section 1(2) Obscene Publications Act 1964). The 1964 Act created the offence of having in possession an obscene article for publication (Section 1(1) Obscene Publications Act 1964). Other changes clarified and broadened the definition of materials which could be considered as being obscene, to include materials used to produce obscene publications, 'anything which is intended to be used, either alone or as one of a set, for the reproduction or manufacture therefrom of articles containing or embodying matter to be read, looked at or listened to, as if it were an article containing or embodying that matter so far as that matter is to be derived from it or the set'.

Subsections (5) and (6) of Section 2 of the 1959 Act are also amended to read (Section 1(3) Obscene Publications Act 1964):
- he shall not be convicted of that offence if he proves that he had not examined the article and had no reasonable cause to suspect that it was such that having it would make him liable to be convicted of an offence against that Section; and
- the question whether the article is obscene shall be determined by reference to such publication for gain of the article as in the circumstances may be reasonably be inferred he had in contemplation and to any further publication that could reasonably be expected to follow from it, but not to any other publication.

2.8 The publication of obscene materials does not include displays not for gain. This omission was covered in 1981 by the Indecent Displays (Control) Act. This does not however cover private displays for individuals.

Control of Indecent Displays
Section 1 Indecent Displays (Control) Act 1981

(1) If any indecent matter is publicly displayed the person making the display and any person causing or permitting the display to be made shall be guilty of an offence.

(2) Any matter which is displayed in or so as to be visible from any public place shall, for the purposes of this Section, be deemed to be publicly displayed.

(3) In subsection (2) above 'public place', in relation to the display of any matter, means any place to which the public have or are permitted to have access (whether on payment or otherwise) while that matter is displayed except:
   a) a place to which the public are permitted to have access only on payment which is or includes payment for that display; or
   b) a shop or any part of a shop to which the public can only gain access by passing beyond an adequate warning notice;

but the exclusion contained in paragraphs (a) and (b) above shall only apply where a person under the age of 18 years are not permitted to enter while the display in question is continuing.

(4) Nothing in this Section applies to any matter:
  a) included by any person in a television broadcasting service or other television programmed service (within the meaning of Part I of the Broadcasting Act 1990);
  b) included in the display of an art gallery or museum and visible only from within the gallery or museum;
  c) displayed by or with the authority of, and visible only from within a building occupied by the Crown or any local authority; or
  d) included in any performance of a play (within the meaning of the Theatres Act 1968; or
  e) included in a film exhibition as defined in the Cinemas Act 1985:
    i) given in a place which as regards that exhibition is required to be licensed under Section 1 of that Act, or, by virtue of Sections 5,7, or 8 of that Act is not required to be licensed; or
    ii) which is an exhibition to which Section 6 of that Act applies given by an exempted organisation as defined in subsection (6) of that Section.

(5) In this Section 'matter' includes anything capable of being displayed, except that it does not include an actual human body or any part thereof ; and in determining for the purpose of this Section whether any display is indecent:
  a) there shall be disregarded any part of that matter which is not exposed to view; and
  b) account may be taken of the effect of juxtaposing one thing with another.

(6) A warning notice shall not be adequate for the purposes of this Section unless it complies with the following requirements:
  a) The warning notice must contain the following words, and no others:
  'Warning
  Persons passing beyond this notice will find material on display which they may consider indecent.No admittance to persons under 18 years of age.'
  b) The word 'warning' must appear as a heading.
  c) No pictures or other material shall appear on the notice.
  d) The notice must be so situated that no one could reasonably gain access to the shop or part of the shop in question without being aware of the notice and it must be easily legible by any person gaining such access.

Explanation

2.9 The Act declares that the public display of indecent matter or the causing or permitting of an indecent public display is an offence. It will be a public display if the public can view it, or it is visible from any public place. The prime purpose of this Act is to prevent adult shops from openly displaying goods and wares in a way which could upset or offend members of the public. It is for this reason that closed, or limited access displays are allowed.

2.10 Where a police officer has reasonable grounds to believe an offence has been committed and indecent materials have been displayed he may seize the article or articles (Section 2(2) Indecent Displays (Controls) Act 1981). Where in England and Wales, a justice of the peace is satisfied by information on oath that there are reasonable grounds for believing that an offence under this Act has been or is being committed on any premises, may issue a warrant authorising entry to premises by force if required, to seize any article reasonable believed to have been used to commit and offence (Section 2(3) Indecent Displays (Controls) Act 1981 as amended by Schedule 7 Police and Criminal Evidence Act 1984).

2.11 A person convicted of an offence under this Act is liable to a fine not exceeding the statutory maximum (as set by Section 32 Magistrates' Courts Act 1980) on summary conviction, on indictment up to two years imprisonment and a fine.

2.12 The taking of indecent photographs of children became a public concern during the 1970's, the growth and openness of paedophile organisations bringing such matters to the general attention of government. To prevent the abuse of children in this way legislation was passed which prohibits the taking of indecent photographs of children.

Indecent Photographs of Children
Section 1 Protection of Children Act 1978

(1) It is an offence for a person:
   a) to take, or permit to be taken, any indecent photograph of a child (meaning in this Act a person under the age of 16); or
   b) to distribute or show such indecent photographs; or
   c) to have in his possession such indecent photographs; or
   d) to publish or cause to be published any advertisement likely to be understood as conveying that the advertiser distributes or shows such indecent photographs, or intends to do so.

(2) For the purposes of this Act, a person is to be regarded as distributing an indecent photograph if he parts with possession of it to, or exposes or offers it for acquisition by, another person.

(3) Proceedings for an offence under this Act shall not be instituted except by or with the consent of the Director of Public Prosecutions.

(4) Where a person is charged with an offence under subsection (1)(b) or (c), it shall be a defence for him to prove:
   a) that he had a legitimate reason for distributing or showing the photographs or (as the case may be) having them in his possession; or
   b) that he had not himself seen the photographs and did not know, nor had any cause to suspect, them to be indecent.

Explanation

There is a common defence theme in most obscene publication law, that is that the defendant had not seen, and had no reason to examine the articles. Also the possession by those lawfully required to examine them, such as police officers, customs officials, etc, acting in the course of their duties will not be unlawful.

2.13 The 1978 Act was aimed at those who take indecent photographs of children or are in some way engaged in the distribution or trading in such photographs. Simply to possess such photographs, with no intent to circulate them, was not unlawful under the Act, but is now catered for under the Criminal Justice Act 1988, section 160. The age of the child is important, the defendant must also have deliberately taken the photograph. The decision as to whether the photograph is indecent will be judged by applying the normal and recognised standards of propriety. In any proceedings under the Act a child will be taken as having at the material time been under 16 if it appears so from the evidence taken as a whole (Section 2(3) Protection of Children Act 1978). On application to a magistrate by evidence on oath constables may obtain a warrant to search for and seize evidence. The justice may issue a summons to require the person from whom the indecent photographs were seized, to give him opportunity to say why such photographs should not be destroyed.

2.14 The offences relating to the taking of photographs are either-way offences, on indictment they carry a maximum of three years imprisonment or a fine or both, on summary conviction imprisonment for up to six months and or a fine not to exceed one thousand pounds. They are designated arrestable offences under the Police and Criminal Evidence Act 1984.

Pseudo-Photographs

2.15 The legislation has been amended to take account of modern technology, by providing that offences relating to photographs may also be committed by making, distributing, etc. a pseudo-photograph. This term is defined as an image, whether made by computer graphics or otherwise, which appears to be a photograph. If the impression given by a pseudo photograph is that the person shown is a child, the pseudo-photograph shall be regarded as being of a child, even though some of the physical attributes appear to be of an adult.

References to a photograph or pseudo-photograph shall include negatives or copies of such, as well as data stored on a computer disc, or by other electronic means, capable of conversion into a photograph or pseudo-photogrph.

Possessing Indecent Photographs of Children
Section 160 Criminal Justice Act 1988

2.16 (1) It is an offence for a person to have any indecent photograph of a child (meaning in this Section a person under the age of 16) in his possession.

(2) Where a person is charged with an offence under subsection (1) above, it shall be a defence for him to prove:
   a) that he had a legitimate reason for having the photograph in his possession; or
   b) that he had not himself seen the photograph and did not known, nor had any cause to suspect, it to be indecent; or
   c) that the photograph was sent to him without any prior request made by him or on his behalf and that he did not keep it for an unreasonable time.

(3) A person shall be liable on summary conviction of an offence under this Section to a fine not exceeding level five on the standard scale.

Explanation
Possession: The original legislation catered for persons involved in the taking or trading of indecent photographs of children, but simple possession was not an offence before 1988.

Defence: There will not, one supposes, be too many examples of 'legitimate' reason as a defence. Not having looked at the photo, and having no reason to suspect it to be what it is, is a defence which appears in other areas of law relating to illicit documents. Finally, a person who receives unsolicited photographs will have a defence, so long as he does not hang on to them for too long before getting rid of them.

Chapter 25: Communications

POST

1.1 There are a number of offences which can be committed is relation to the post, many are confined to the conduct of staff employed to deliver post and messages.

Improper Disclosure of Information
Section 45 Telegraph Act 1863

> If any person in the employment of the company, wilfully or negligently omits or delays to transmit or deliver any message; Or by any wilful or negligent act or omission prevents or delays the transmission or delivery of any message; Or improperly divulges to any person the purport of any message he commits an offence.

1.2 This offence is a summary offence for which a fine not exceeding level three can be imposed. The change of message switching systems to electronic mail and decrease in the use of telegrams make this one of the rarer offences. Reference to 'company' in this offence is now accepted as being, the Post Office, and includes British Telecom (Schedule 4 Post Office Act 1969, as amended by Schedule 3 Part II British Telecommunications Act 1981).

1.3 Even in the mid-nineteenth century, considerable financial advantage could be derived from intercepting or disclosing details from items sent by post. To deter Post Office staff from indulging in such practices, an offence was created:

Section 20 Telegraph Act 1868

> Any Person having official duties connected with the Post Office, or acting on behalf of the Postmaster General, who shall, contrary to his duty, disclose or in any way make known or intercept the contents or any part of the contents of any telegraph message, or message entrusted to the Postmaster General for the purpose of transmission, shall in England be guilty of an offence.

1.4 This offence is triable either-way (Section 17 and Schedule 1; 18-21 (procedure) and 32 (penalty) Magistrates' Courts Act 1980), upon conviction on indictment the maximum penalty is one years' imprisonment. Reference to the Postmaster General is the same as the Post Office authority.

Sending by Post of 'Noxious' or 'Dangerous' Packets

1.5 The sending of postal packages which contain dangerous or noxious substances is subject of legislation prohibiting such behaviour without proper authority. Authority enables the proper shipment of substances under control and with reasonable safety precautions.

Section 11 Post Office Act 1953

> (1) A person shall not send or attempt to send or procure to be sent a postal packet which:
>   a) save as the authority may either generally or in any particular case allow, enclose any explosive, dangerous, noxious or deleterious substances, any filth, any sharp instrument not properly protected, any noxious living creature, article or thing

whatsoever which is likely to injure either other postal packets in the course of conveyance or a person engaged in the business of the postal authority; or

b)   encloses any indecent or obscene print, painting, photograph, lithograph, engraving, cinematography film, book, card or written communication, or any indecent or obscene article whether similar to the above or not; or

c)   has on the packet, or on the cover thereof, any words, marks or designs which are grossly offensive or of an indecent or obscene character.

(2) If any person acts in contravention of the foregoing subsection, he shall be liable on summary conviction to a fine not exceeding the statutory maximum or on conviction on indictment to imprisonment not exceeding twelve months.

1.6 For the purposes of Section 11(1)(b) the question of what is or is not obscene is a matter for the jury to decide on the basis of the evidence before them. The word obscene does not have the same variable meaning as under the Obscene Publications Acts, a single standard is to be applied and will not vary according to the addressee (*Kosmos Publications Ltd v DPP* [1975]). The full offence may committed, not only by sending an item by post, but also by attempting to send it. This being so, it matters not whether the item actually arrives at its destination, or whether in fact, it is even accepted for posting by a member of staff of a post office.

Grossly Offensive or Indecent Post
1.7 *Section 1 Malicious Communications Act 1988*

(1) Any person who sends to another person:
a)   a letter or other article which conveys:
i)   a message which is indecent or grossly offensive
ii) a threat; or
iii) information which is false and known or believed to be false by the sender; or

b)   any other article which is, in whole or part, of an indecent or grossly offensive nature,

is guilty of an offence if his purpose, or one of his purposes, in sending it is that it should, so far as falling within paragraph (a) or (b) above, cause distress or anxiety to the recipient or to any other person to whom he intends that it or its contents or nature should be communicated.

(2) A person is not guilty of an offence by virtue of subsection (1)(a)(ii) above if he shows:
a)   that the threat was used to reinforce a demand which he believed he had reasonable grounds for making; and
b)   that he believed that the use of the threat was a proper means of reinforcing the demand.

Explanation
Message or information: There are three sorts of message or information which may be involved in the offence – an indecent or grossly offensive message, a threat, or information which is false and which the sender knows or believes to be false. An example of the latter would be sending a letter telling the recipient that a close relative had died; however the scope for falsely telling someone something which will upset them, is very wide indeed. Note that where the accused believes information to be false, it must indeed be false for the offence to be committed. If he sends information which he thinks is false, but which is actually correct, the offence will not be committed.

Offensive article: The item sent need not consist of information, if by its nature, it is indecent or grossly offensive. An example would be sending pigs trotters to a person of Jewish faith.

Distress or anxiety: The accused's purpose, or one of her purposes, in sending the message or article, is to cause distress or anxiety. This may be directed at the person receiving the letter or article, or the intention may be to cause the distress to someone else, to whom the accused intends that the letter or article, or its contents or nature shall be communicated. For example, a man writes to his ex-girlfriend's doctor falsely claiming that he is suffering from AIDS and that she will now be infected. He commits the offence if his intention is that the doctor will convey this information to the girl, thus causing her distress or anxiety.

Defence: Where the offence arises from making a threat, the accused will have a defence if he shows (a) that the threat was used to reinforce a demand which he believed he had reasonable grounds for making; **and** (b) that he believed that the use of the threat was a proper means of reinforcing that demand. If the owner of property writes to the tenant, threatening to have him evicted unless he pays the overdue rent, this defence may be open.

Note: That the defence applies only if the offence involves a threat; the landlord seeking payment of rent would not be justified in sending indecent or offensive messages.

TELEPHONES

2.1 The provision of controls to prevent abuse of the telephone systems is contained in the 1984 Telecommunications Act, the main control on abuse being the provisions of Section 43. The Section should deal with most if not all nuisance callers using the public phone systems.

Threatening Phone Calls
Section 43 Telecommunications Act 1984

(1) A person who:
   a) sends, by means of a public telecommunications system, a message or other matter that is grossly offensive or indecent, obscene or menacing in character; or
   b) sends by those means, for the purpose of causing annoyance, in convenience or needless anxiety to another, a public message that he knows to be false or persistently makes use for that purpose of a public telecommunications system;

   shall be guilty of an offence and liable on summary conviction to a fine not exceeding level three on the standard scale.

2.2 This offence is a summary one, carrying a relatively small fine as maximum punishment. Whilst this may be adequate for dealing with a person responsible for one or two offences, it may be inappropriate for dealing with someone who has made a large number of, say, obscene calls over a period of time. In such a case, an alternative charge of public nuisance may be considered (see *R v Norbuty* (1978)). If a number of calls are made to an individual victim, an offence of harassment may be committed (see Chapter 39).

Phones, Avoiding Payment for Use
2.3 *Section 42 Telecommunications Act 1984*

(1) A person who dishonestly obtains a service to which this subsection applies with intent

to avoid payment of any charge applicable to the provision of that service shall be guilty of an offence and liable:

a) on summary conviction to imprisonment for a term not exceeding six months or a fine not exceeding the statutory maximum or to both;

b) on conviction on indictment to imprisonment for a term not exceeding two years or a fine or both.

Bomb Hoaxes

2.4 *Section 51 Criminal Law Act 1977*
as amended by Section 26 of the Criminal Justice Act 1991

(1) A person who:

a) places any article in any place whatever; or

b) dispatches any article by post, rail or any other means whatever of sending things from one place to another;

with the intention (in either case) of inducing in some other person a belief that it is likely to explode or ignite and thereby cause personal injury or damage to property is guilty of an offence.

In this subsection 'article' includes substance.

(2) A person who communicates any information which he knows or believes to be false to another person with the intention of inducing in him or any other person a false belief that a bomb or other thing is liable to explode or ignite is present in any place or location whatever is guilty of an offence.

(3) For a person to be guilty of an offence under subsection (1) or (2) above it is not necessary for him to have any particular person in mind as the person in whom he intends to induce the belief mentioned in that subsection.

(4) A person guilty of an offence under this Section shall be liable to:

a) on summary conviction to imprisonment for a term not exceeding six months or to a fine not exceeding the statutory maximum or both;

b) on conviction on indictment, to imprisonment for a term not exceeding seven years.

2.4.1 *Explanation*

Places or sends: There are two distinct categories of offence. The first, in sub-section 1, deals with packages, dummy devices, etc. left somewhere, or sent by post or other means. In each case, the intention is to make someone believe that the package is a 'bomb'.

Explode or ignite: The term 'bomb' does not appear in the legislation. However, something which is likely to explode or ignite and thereby cause injury to a person or damage to property, may commonly be described as a 'bomb'.

Communicates information: The second category of offence does not involve dummy bombs, but arises when a person communicates information which she knows or believes to be false, intending to induce a false belief in another person that there is a 'bomb' somewhere. The intention may be to induce that belief in the person to whom the communication is made, or in a third person. The offender must know or believe the information she is passing to be false; thus, if a phone call is received by the receptionist at an office, to the effect that there is a bomb in the building, the receptionist will not be liable when he passes that information on, if he believes it to be true.

Arrest and Punishment: The offence is triable either way; if tried on indictment, the maximum punishment is 7 years imprisonment, making it an arrestable offence. The potential severity of this sentence reflects the considerable disruption which hoax bomb calls may cause.

Unlawful Interception of Communications
Interception of Communications Act 1985

2.5 *Offence*
Interception of Communications Act 1985 Section 1

A person commits an offence who:
- intentionally
- intercepts a communication in the course of transmission
- by post or by other means of public telecommunications system.

2.5.1 *Exceptions*
- the interception has been authorised by a warrant by the Secretary of State
- there is reasonable grounds to believe that a person receiving or sending the communication has consented to the interception
- the communication is intercepted for purposes connected with the provision of postal or public telecommunication services or with the enforcement of law relating to their use
- in the case of radio, the communication is intercepted with the authority of the Secretary of State (for the purposes of licences or of the prevention or detection of interference with radio).

2.5.2 *Explanation*
Intentionally intercepts: No offence is committed where, for example, a person overhears a telephone conversation because of a 'crossed line'.

Consent: A person will not commit the offence if he has reason to believe that one of the parties to the communication, the sender or the receiver, has consented to its interception. For example, a person who is the victim of a blackmailer, may consent to all telephone calls coming in to her telephone, to be intercepted. There is provision in Section 9 of the Act, for information obtained by unauthorised interception to be excluded from evidence in court proceedings. This has recently been subject of judicial review (*R v Rasool, R v Choudhary* (Times Law Reports, 17.2.97) when it was decided that this provision did not prevent evidence being admissible when one of the parties involved had consented to the interception.

Warrant: The Home Secretary may issue a warrant allowing interception of post or telecommunications:
  i) in the interests of State security
  ii) for the purpose of preventing or detecting serious crime
  iii) for the purpose of protecting and securing the economic well-being of the State.
  Before issuing such a warrant, the Home Secretary must consider whether there is an alternative method of securing the information which is sought, and whether an interception is necessary.

Provision...enforcement: The law allows interception for purposes connected with the provision of services. This would allow, for example, a telephone company to monitor calls from time to time to check on quality. Similarly, for the purpose of enforcing the prohibition on sending obscene material by post, officials of the Post Office may have to intercept a package in transit.

Radio: ...or to use the phrase used in the legislation – wireless telegraphy, is controlled by the Home Secretary, who may give authority to intercept transmissions, for purposes connected with licensing, or to prevent or detect interference with radio transmissions. For example, unauthorised or 'pirate' radio transmitters may interfere with licensed radio transmissions. Interception of the unauthorised signals is necessary to trace the location of the transmitter.

Chapter 26: Misuse of Drugs

1 CLASSIFICATION OF DRUGS

1.1 Drug

A dictionary definition of a drug is – a medicinal substance, or one which has a narcotic, stimulant, or hallucinogenic effect, especially if it is addictive. A drug therefore affects the body in some way; the law is concerned principally with those which have a harmful effect, either directly or by causing a person to behave in a way which may be harmful to himself or others.

1.2 Legislation

The principal legislation as far as the criminal law is concerned is the Misuse of Drugs Act 1971.

1.3 Classification

Drugs covered by the Act are placed in one of three classes, according to how harmful they are perceived to be, to the individual abuser or to society in general. Classification affects maximum sentences for offences arising from misuse of drugs.

1.3.1 *Class A*

Examples include heroin, cocaine, diamorphine and opium. Maximum sentence, e.g. for unlawful importation – life imprisonment; for unlawful possession – seven years.

1.3.2 *Class B*

Examples include cannabis and cannabis resin, amphetamine and codeine. Maximum sentence, e.g. unlawful importation – 14 years; unlawful possession – five years.

1.3.3 *Class C*

Examples include bromazepam, diazepam and prazepam. Maximum sentence, e.g. for unlawful importation – 5 years; unlawful possession – two years.

1.4 Cannabis

Cannabis is derived from cannabis plants and may be used in vegetable or resin form. In this Act 'cannabis' means any plant of the genus (a Latin word for family of plants) Cannabis or any part of such plant, **excluding**:
- cannabis resin
- the mature stalk of a plant
- fibre produced from a mature stalk
- seed from the plant.

1.4.1 *Cannabis Resin*

Means the separated resin, crude or purified, from any plant of the genus Cannabis.

2 IMPORTATION AND EXPORTATION
Misuse of Drugs Act 1971   Section 3
Customs and Excise Management Act 1979   Sections 50, 68 and Schedule 1

Section 3 provides that the unlawful import or export of controlled drugs will amount to offences under the 1979 Act. Whatever the class of drug involved, these are all arrestable offences.

3 UNLAWFUL PRODUCTION
Misuse of Drugs Act 1971   Section 4(2)

3.1 Offence
A person commits an offence who:
- unlawfully
- produces a controlled drug
- or is concerned in its production.

3.2 Explanation
Unlawfully: There are circumstances in which the production of drugs will be lawful, otherwise drug companies and pharmacists would be out of business. The regulations governing the lawful production of drugs is outside the scope of this book.

Produce: The term is defined as applying to manufacture, cultivation or any other method of production (Section 37). Whether it is turning out ecstasy tablets in a laboratory, or drying cannabis leaves grown in the greenhouse, both will amount to the production of a controlled drug.

There is no 'possession' of a controlled drug when one has possession of a naturally occurring material which contains a drug which has not been separated out (*DPP v Goodchild* (1978)). There have been several case decisions relating to 'magic mushrooms', a naturally occurring material which contains one form of a hallucinogenic Class A drug, psilocin. 'Preparation' of these mushrooms would include drying them and crushing them to powder (*R v Cunliffe* (1986)), or bagging and freezing them for later use (*Hodder v DPP, Matthews v DPP* (1990)).

Concerned in: There must be some evidence of participation in the process of production. Merely hiring out a laboratory, or allowing another to use one's kitchen, will not amount to 'being concerned in' (*R v Farr* (1982)).

3.3 Arrest
This is an arrestable offence for all classes of drug.

4 CULTIVATION OF CANNABIS
Misuse of Drugs Act 1971   Section 6(2)

4.1 Offence
It is an offence for a person:
- unlawfully
- to cultivate
- any plant of the genus Cannabis.

4.2 **Explanation**

Unlawfully: A licence may be obtained from the Home Office, authorising the cultivation of cannabis. Without a licence, cultivation will be unlawful. In particular, there is no exemption which allows a property officer employed by the police to tend a cannabis plant on the window of the detained property store, in order that it may be available as an exhibit in a court case in a few months time.

Cultivate: To 'cultivate' requires some degree of looking after the plant. If seed thrown out for the birds happens to sprout and a cannabis plant is the result, this will not necessarily amount to cultivation. Plants grown in pots on a windowsill are being 'cultivated' (*Tudhope v Robertson* (1980)).

The prosecution do not have to prove that the defendant knew it was cannabis. If the prosecution proves 'cultivation', it is then for the defence to prove ignorance that it was a cannabis plant (*R v Champ* (1982)).

Comparison with production offence: Since 'cannabis' includes all parts of the plant except mature stalk and seed, it follows that growing cannabis plants amounts to an offence of producing a controlled drug.

(The reason for there being a separate offence is that the definition of 'cannabis' used not to include immature plants, so cultivation of young plants did not amount to production of a controlled drug.)

5 **UNLAWFUL SUPPLY**
Misuse of Drugs Act 1971 Section 4(3)

5.1 **Offence**
A person is guilty of an offence if he:
- supplies
- offers to supply
- is concerned in supplying
- or is concerned in offering to supply
- a controlled drug to another person.

5.2 **Explanation**
Unlawfully: There are provisions which allow for the lawful supply of drugs, otherwise the doctor who prescribes a drug and the pharmacist dispensing it would be guilty of being concerned in an offer to supply, and supplying, respectively.

Supply: 'Supply' includes 'distribute' (Section 37), there is no requirement that there be a sale of the drug. If one youth collects money from his friends and goes off to buy drugs to be shared out among them, when he returns and dishes the drugs out to those who have subscribed, he will be guilty of 'supplying'.

Neither is 'supply' confined to handing it over. To inject a drug into an addict would amount to a supplying. However, it will not be supplying to inject the addict's own drug into her; if she is already in possession of it, another person cannot then be guilty of supplying it to her (*R v Harris* (1968). Supply means a transfer of physical control from one person to another, whether or not there is a transfer of ownership (*R v Delgado* (1984)).

To amount to 'supply', the drug must be passed for the benefit of the recipient; giving it to someone for safekeeping, intending to retrieve it later will not amount to a 'supply' on behalf of the person who originally has it (*R v Maginnis* (1987)). Conversely, the person who is looking after the drug DOES commit the offence of supply when he returns it to its owner, because he is handing it over for that person's benefit. The following example illustrates these points:

> Jack and Jill are in a café when officers of the police drug squad enter. Jack is a known drug dealer and expects to be searched, so he hands over drugs in his possession to Jill, to keep until the police have gone. The ruse works, Jill is not searched, so when the police leave, she returns the package of drugs to Jack. Jack is not guilty of an offence of supply to Jill, but she does commit an offence of supplying when she returns them to Jack.

Concerned in: The term has the same meaning here as in relation to being concerned in production – there must be evidence of some active involvement.

6 POSSESSION
Misuse of Drugs Act 1971   Section 5(2)

6.1 Offence
A person commits an offence who:
- unlawfully
- has a controlled drug in her possession.

6.2 Explanation
Unlawfully: As well as the obvious examples of lawful possession, relating to production and dispensing of drugs in connection with human or veterinary medicine, the following may lawfully possess a controlled drug in each case, while in the course of official duties:
- a constable
- a person working for the Post Office (Royal Mail, etc), or in the business of a carrier
- officer of Customs and Excise
- person working at a forensic science laboratory
- person taking a drug to an authorised person.
  (Misuse of Drugs Regulations 1985)

Possession: Possession includes control. To return to the example of Jack and Jill in the café (*paragraph 5.2*), when Jack hands a drug to Jill for safekeeping, she will then have possession of it, but he will still have possession, also.

For possession, there must be an element of knowledge, or at least suspicion that one has possession of a controlled drug. When Jack passes the package to Jill, if she is aware that it contains drugs, she is 'in possession'; if she has grounds for believing it to contains drugs, she will be in possession. However, if she does not know that there are drugs in the package, she will not be guilty of possession.

In one case, a van driver collected two packages, one containing perfume, the other a large amount of a controlled drug. He claimed that he thought both packages contained perfume. He was held not to be 'in possession' because he did not know that the second package contained drugs (*Warner v Metropolitan Police Commissioner* (1969)).

Even a small amount of a drug may give rise to an offence of unlawful possession, there is no requirement that it be a 'usable amount'. When the quantity concerned is very small, there must be sufficient for the accused to be aware that he had it. If traces of the drug could be detected only by forensic examination, the offence would not be made out, but this is based on knowledge of possession not 'usability'. *(Keynote Case: R v Boyesen (1982))*

More than one person may have possession of the same drug at the same time.

6.3 Defence
Misuse of Drugs Act 1971 Section 5(4)

There are two statutory defences to a charge of unlawful possession.

6.3.1 *Prevent Offence*
The accused will have a defence if he proves that:
- knowing or suspecting it to be a controlled drug
- he took possession of it for the purpose of preventing another person from committing or continuing to commit an offence relating to that drug
- **and** as soon as possible after taking possession of it he took all reasonable steps
- to destroy the drug
- or to deliver it to a person lawfully entitled to take custody of it.

6.3.2 *Delivery*
The accused will have a defence if he proves that:
- knowing or suspecting it to be a controlled drug
- he took possession of it for the purpose of delivering it to a person lawfully entitled to take custody of it
- and that as soon as possible after doing so he took all reasonable steps to deliver it to the custody of such a person.

6.3.3 *Explanation*
Knowing or suspecting: These defences do not rely on a claim of ignorance as to the nature of the substance or the fact that it was in one's possession. They are intended for a person who is seeking to remove a drug from circulation. There are other defences which are based on lack of knowledge *(see paragraph 12)*.

Why two defences?: In the first defence, there is only one set of circumstances leading to taking possession of the drug – someone else is committing or will commit an offence. In the second, there could be lots of different scenarios, leading to the defendant deciding to take possession – he found it in the street, he bought from a dealer to gain evidence of an offence, or, as in the first case, he took it to prevent someone else continuing to commit an offence. In short, the circumstances of the first defence are catered for in the second, so why have two?

A possible answer is that in the first defence, the intention is either to destroy the drug, or to hand it over; in the second, the intention must be to hand it over. If a parent, for example, finds cannabis in her son's bedroom, she may take possession of it to prevent him continuing to commit the offence of unlawful possession. If only the second of the two defences was available, the mother would have to hand it over, to the police for example. Recognising that the finder may not want to get the drug offender into trouble, the first defence affords the finder the lawful option of destroying the drug.

In other circumstances however, such as when a licensee finds drugs stuffed down the back of a seat in her pub, it is in the interests of society that she hands the drugs over, not that she destroys possible evidence.

Person lawfully entitled...: Some of these are listed at *paragraph 6.2*. In most circumstances a police officer would be the most appropriate recipient.

Applicability: These defences may be pleaded only in answer to a charge of unlawful possession contrary to Section 5(2). They do not apply to any other charge, such as cultivating cannabis or possession with intent to supply.

6.4 Arrest

Where the drug concerned is a Class A drug or a Class B drug, unlawful possession is an arrestable offence (7 years and 5 years respectively). Unlawful possession of a Class C drug carries a maximum of two years' imprisonment, so is not an arrestable offence.

7 POSSESSION WITH INTENT TO SUPPLY
Misuse of Drugs Act 1971 Section 5(3)

7.1 Offence

A person commits an offence who:
- has a controlled drug in his possession
- whether lawfully or not
- with intent to supply it unlawfully to another.

7.2 Explanation

Lawfully or not: A youth visits his doctor and is prescribed pills which contain a controlled drug. He obtains them from the chemist with the intention of selling them to a friend who is addicted to the drug. He has possession lawfully, because the pills were prescribed for him by his doctor.

Intent: The offence is complete when the offender has possession of drugs intending to supply them unlawfully to someone else. There is no need for the unlawful supply to take place, so in the example of the youth who obtains his prescribed pills from the chemist, he would commit the offence as soon as he had both the possession of the pills and the intention to supply them unlawfully to his friend.

In practice, there will need to be evidence of the intention to supply to another. If a person is arrested in possession of a large quantity of a drug, especially if it is split into individual small 'wraps', this would be useful evidence that he had it for other than personal use.

7.3 Arrest

This is an arrestable offence, whatever the class of drug involved. Maximum sentences are, for Class A – life imprisonment, for Class B – 14 years, for Class C – 5 years.

8 USE OF PREMISES
Misuse of Drugs Act 1971 Section 8

8.1 Offence

A person commits an offence who:

- being the occupier or being concerned in the management of premises
- knowingly permits or suffers
- any of the following activities to take place on the premises, viz:
  i) producing or attempting to produce a controlled drug
  ii) supplying, offering, or attempting to supply or offer, a controlled drug to another
  ii) preparing opium for smoking
  iv) smoking cannabis, cannabis resin or prepared opium.

8.2 Explanation

Occupier: A Cambridge University student claimed that he was not the 'occupier' of his room in his college because it belonged to the college and college staff retained a right to enter. The court held that 'occupier' is not restricted to someone having legal possession but will include someone entitled to have exclusive possession of the premises, in occupation so as to have control over what goes on there (*R v Tao* (1976)).

Two young women, staying in their parents' house while the parents were on holiday were held not to be 'occupiers' (*R v Mogford* (1970)).

Concerned in the management: Management means management of the activity on those premises, so a person needs to have some control over what goes on there to be 'concerned in the management' (*Sweet v Parsley* (1970)).

There is no necessity that such a person has a legal right to be in the premises. Two men ran a card school in the basement of a house in Dalston, although they had no right to be in the premises. They were convicted of knowingly allowing the supply of a controlled drug there and appealed on the ground that, as trespassers, they were not 'concerned in the management'. The court held that if a person is on premises as a trespasser or squatter, but nevertheless controls what goes on there, he may be liable (*R v Josephs and Christie* (1977)).

Premises: This term is not defined in the Act. It is not necessarily synonymous with 'building', so would presumably include land in the curtilage of a building, such as the grounds of a house.

Knowingly: The prosecution must prove that the accused knew what was going on. A person may be regarded as having 'knowledge' if he shuts his eyes to the obvious (*Westminster City Council v Croyalgrange Ltd* (1986)). Likewise, where a person deliberately refrains from asking questions, the answers to which he might not care for.

Permits: Before one may 'permit' an activity to take place, one must know about it. However, the principles stated above, closing one's eyes to the obvious, etc, will apply.

The term connotes knowledge or grounds for reasonable suspicion on the part of the occupier that the premises will be used for the particular purpose and 'an unwillingness on his part to take the means available to him to prevent it' (*Sweet v Parsley* (1970)).

Before one can 'permit' one must be in a position to forbid the activity. In the case of a corporate body, there will be no liability for permitting unless the activity was known to someone in the organisation who is at director or company secretary level in the company. The fact that an employee knows, even if he is a manager, will not be sufficient for the company to be liable (*Tesco Supermarkets v Nattrass* (1972)).

Activity: The offence is committed only in relation to permitting or allowing certain activities to take place. It is not an offence under Section 8 to allow a person on premises, e.g. to inject himself with heroin.

9 USE OF OPIUM
Misuse of Drugs Act 1971 Section 9

9.1 Offences
A person will commit an offence who:
- smokes or otherwise uses prepared opium
- frequents a place for the purpose of opium smoking
- has in his possession:
  i) any pipes or other utensils made or adapted for use in connection with the smoking of opium:
     - which have been used in that connection, either by him, or with his knowledge and permission
     - or which he intends to use or permit others to use in that connection; or
  ii) any utensils which have been used by him or with his knowledge and permission in connection with the preparation of opium for smoking.

9.2 Explanation
Opium: Opium, a Class A drug, has been used (and abused) for considerably longer than most other drugs in circulation today. The use of opium may involve rather more preparation and use of equipment than is the case with, say, cannabis. Whether opium users sitting round in groups in 'opium dens' smoking is a widespread phenomenon is doubtful, but the Act caters for it with these offences.

Smoke or use: There are offences relating to production, supply and possession of controlled drugs, but this Section provides that it is an offence to use opium. There are no corresponding offences relating to use of other drugs.

Frequents: This term has been taken to mean either returning to the same place on a number of occasions (*Clark v R* (1884)) or loitering long enough to achieve one's purpose (*Goundry v Police* (1955)).

Place used for the purpose: A place is not 'used for the purpose' just because someone happens to smoke a controlled drug there. There would have to be some evidence of going to that place for the purpose of smoking opium. If a tenant of premises on an isolated occasion, smoked opium in his flat, this would not necessarily mean that he frequented the flat for that purpose (*Sweet v Parsley* (1970)).

Made or adapted: For the offence to be committed in relation to items used in connection with the smoking of opium, there must be evidence that the items are made or adapted for that purpose. The offence would not be committed by having possession of an ordinary tobacco pipe with no adaptation. (Whether an ordinary pipe could be used without adaptation for smoking opium, is another matter.)

When it comes to items used for preparing opium, there is no element in the offence of 'made or adapted' so the offence may arise from possession of any article which has been used previously, for use in the smoking of the drug.

10 ARTICLES FOR ADMINISTERING OR PREPARING DRUGS
Misuse of Drugs Act 1971 Section 9A

10.1 Offences
A person commits an offence who:

1: Supplies or offers to supply:
   - any article which may be used or adapted (whether by itself or in combination with any other article(s))
   - in the administration by a person of a controlled drug to himself or to another
   - believing that the article (or the article as adapted) is to be so used, in circumstances where the administration is unlawful.

2: Supplies or offers to supply:
   - any article which may be used to prepare a controlled drug for administration by any person to himself or another
   - believing that the article is to be so used in circumstances where the administration will be unlawful.

10.2 Explanation
Article: An offence will not arise when the article supplied is a hypodermic syringe or a part of one. This exception is included for health reasons, in an effort to prevent the spread of disease arising from drug abusers sharing needles. If a local council, for example, offers free needles, believing that they will be used by heroin addicts, in an attempt to cut down on sharing or repeated use of the same syringes, this will not amount to an offence.

Belief: Not only must the article be capable of being used for administering or preparing the drug, but the accused must believe that the article will be used for that purpose. In the case of a pipe which has been made for the purpose of smoking opium, for example, the offence would not be committed where the supplier believed that the person receiving it intended to keep it as an ornament.

Unlawful: **any** administration of a controlled drug will be unlawful for the purposes of these offences, **except**:
   - when the administration of a drug by one person to another does not amount to an offence of unlawful supply
   - when the administration of a drug by a person to himself does not amount to an offence of unlawful possession.

11 OFFENCES ABROAD
Misuse of Drugs Act 1971 Section 20

11.1 Offence
A person commits an offence in the United Kingdom who:
   - assists in or induces the commission
   - in any place outside the United Kingdom
   - of an offence punishable under the provisions of a corresponding law in force in that place.

11.2 **Explanation**

Offence... in that place: Anyone who is involved in drugs offences in foreign countries may be dealt with for an offence here. However, the action in which the accused is involved must amount to a drugs offence in the foreign country. If, say, possession of cannabis is not unlawful in a particular country, anyone who induces another person to possess cannabis there will not be liable under this provision.

12 **STATUTORY DEFENCES**
Misuse of Drugs Act 1971 Section 28

12.1 **Applicability**
The defences may be pleaded in respect of any of the following offences:
- unlawful production (Section 4(2))
- unlawful supply (Section 4(3))
- unlawful possession (Section 5(2))
- possession with intent to supply (Section 5(3))
- cultivation of cannabis (Section 6(2)).

12.2 **Lack of Knowledge of Fact**

12.2.1 *Defence*
It will be a defence for the accused to prove that:
- he neither knew nor suspected, nor had reason to suspect
- the existence of some fact alleged by the prosecution
- which it is necessary for the prosecution to prove if he is to be convicted of the offence charged.

12.2.2 *Explanation*
Know or suspect: It is not enough for the accused to prove that he did not know of some fact, he must also show that he did not suspect its existence. For example, Damien is aware that Nigel is carrying a package containing cannabis. They leave the car to go into a pub. Police then find the package in the glovebox of the car. Damien's defence is that he did not know that Nigel had placed a quantity of cannabis in the glovebox of Damien's car. However, if Damien had realised that Nigel was no longer carrying the package of cannabis, and suspected that he had slipped it into the glovebox, the defence may not succeed.

Prosecution evidence: For a person to be guilty of an offence involving 'possession' it is necessary to prove that the accused knew he had control of the drug *(see paragraph 6.2)*. The fact that the accused may plead as a defence, that he was unaware of some fact, does not mean that the prosecution no longer has to prove, in a case involving possession, that the defendant knew he had possession of a drug. It is not sufficient for the prosecution to prove that the accused had the drug, leaving the onus on him to prove that he did not know he had it (*R v Ashton-Rickardt* (1977)).

12.3 **Lack of Knowledge of Controlled Drug**

12.3.1 *Defence*
Where in proceedings for an offence:

- it is necessary for the prosecution to prove that the substance involved in the offence was a particular controlled drug
- and it has been proved that it was that drug
- the accused will have a defence if he proves
- either that he neither believed nor suspected, nor had reason to believe or suspect, that the substance was a controlled drug
- or that he believed the substance was a controlled drug of a description such that, had it in fact been that drug, he would not have committed an offence.

But the accused shall not escape conviction by reason only of proving:
- that he neither believed nor suspected, nor had reason to believe or suspect
- that the substance was the particular controlled drug in question.

12.3.2 *Explanation*

If a person is charged with unlawful possession of, say, heroin and the prosecution proves that what he had was heroin, the accused will have a defence if he proves:
- that he thought the substances was icing sugar and had no reason to believe it to be a controlled drug
- or that he thought it was a controlled drug which he could lawfully possess, e.g. the doctor had prescribed it for him.

What will not amount to a defence is if he claims that he thought it was some other controlled drug, not the one subject of the charge.

13 POLICE POWERS
Misuse of Drugs Act 1971 Section 23(2)

13.1 Without Warrant

13.1.1 *Powers*

If a constable has reasonable grounds to suspect that a person is in unlawful possession of a controlled drug, she may:
- search that person and detain him for the purpose of doing so
- search any vehicle or vessel in which she suspects the drug may be found, and for that purpose require the person in charge of the vehicle or vessel to stop it
- seize and detain for the purposes of proceedings under the Act anything found in the course of a search which appears to the constable to be evidence of an offence under the Act.

13.1.2 *Explanation*

Vehicle or vessel: Vessel includes a hovercraft.

Person in charge: The constable may require the person in charge of the vehicle or vessel to stop it for the purposes of a search. This is not dependent on the person in charge being suspected of any offence. For example, if a constable has reason to suspect that Nixon is in unlawful possession of a drug and she sees Nixon getting on to a bus, she may require the bus driver to stop the vehicle while she searches it.

13.2 **With a Warrant**
Misuse of Drugs Act 1971   Section 23(3)

13.2.1 *Grounds for Issuing Warrant*
A magistrate may issue a warrant if satisfied on information on oath that there is reasonable ground to suspect:
- that any controlled drug is unlawfully in some person's possession on any premises
- or that a document directly or indirectly relating to an unlawful transaction or dealing, is in a person's possession on any premises.

13.2.2 *Powers Under the Warrant*
The warrant will authorise any constable acting for the police area in which the premises in question are situated:
- at any time or times within one month from the date of the warrant
- to enter the premises named in the warrant, if need be by force
- to search the premises
- to search any person found therein
- and if there is reasonable ground for suspecting that an offence under the Act has been committed in respect of any controlled drugs found there,
- or if there is reason to believe that any document found there is a document relating to an unlawful transaction
- to seize and detain such drugs or document.

13.2.3 *Explanation*
Unlawful possession: The warrant may be issued if there is ground to suspect someone has possession of a controlled drug in contravention of the Act or of any regulations made under it.

Unlawful transaction: The documents in respect of which a warrant may be issued are any documents relating to or connected with a transaction or dealing which was an offence (or an intended transaction which would amount to an offence if carried out), being either an offence under this Act in the United Kingdom, or if carried out abroad, an offence under the corresponding law in force in that place.

Thus, documents relating to a proposed purchase of drugs in a foreign country will be covered by these provisions, as long as what is proposed will be against the law in the country concerned. 'Corresponding' means law relating to the control of drugs.

Premises and persons: The powers to search, and the power to seize what is found as a result, extend to people found on the premises as well as to the premises themselves.

13.3 **Entry to Premises of Producer or Supplier**
Misuse of Drugs Act 1971   Section 23(1)

13.3.1 *Power*
A constable has power:
- to enter the premises of a person carrying on a business as a producer or supplier of controlled drugs
- and there to demand production of and inspect any books or documents relating to dealings in such drugs
- and to inspect stocks of drugs.

13.3.2 *Explanation*

Exercise of this power is usually restricted in a police force to a small number of officers, experienced in drug-related matters, who carry out inspections, e.g. of chemists' shops.

The power to enter premises of suppliers and producers may also be exercised by persons authorised to do so by the Home Secretary.

13.4 Offences Relating to Powers
Misuse of Drugs Act 1971 Section 23(4)

1: A person commits an offence if he:
   - intentionally
   - obstructs a constable
   - in the exercise of her powers under this Section.

2: In relation only to the power to enter the premises of a producer or supplier of drugs, it is an offence:
   - to conceal from a constable or other person exercising these powers, any book, document, drugs, etc
   - or without reasonable excuse fail to produce any book or document required to be produced in the exercise of these powers.

14 DRUG TRAFFICKING
Drug Trafficking Act 1994

14.1 Confiscation Orders

14.1.1 *Purpose*

Illegal trade in controlled drugs generates vast sums of money. Those involved then use complex 'money laundering' procedures to move these profits between countries and to disguise their ill-gotten source. The purpose of the Act is to make provision whereby persons convicted of drug trafficking offences may be deprived of the proceeds of their crimes.

14.1.2 *Making an Order*

An order may be made:
   - by the Crown Court
   - when a person who has been convicted of a drug trafficking offence
   - appears before the court for sentence
   - and the court considers that he has benefitted from drug trafficking.

If the court considers that he has so benefitted, then before sentencing him, it shall determine an amount to be recovered and order him to pay it.

14.2 Drug Trafficking Offence

14.2.1 *In England and Wales*

The term includes any of the following offences, if committed in England and Wales:
   - the production, supply, import, export, of a controlled drug
   - the transport or storage of a controlled drug, or the use of a ship for illicit traffic in drugs.

14.2.2 *Anywhere*

The term also includes entering into or being concerned in any arrangement, in this country or elsewhere, whereby:

- retention or control by or on behalf of another person of the other person's proceeds of drug trafficking is facilitated
- proceeds of drug trafficking by another person are used to secure funds for that person or to acquire investments for that person's benefit.

14.2.3 *Explanation*

There are two distinct categories of drug trafficking offence – those directly related to dealing in drugs, committed in England and Wales; and activities carried out for the benefit of another, whereby the proceeds of drug trafficking are realised or invested, anywhere in the world.

14.3 **Procedures for Enforcing a Confiscation Order**

14.3.1 *Assessment of Proceeds*

In assessing the total proceeds a person has accrued from drug trafficking, the court may assume that all payments, property, etc made to or received by the person during the period of six years prior to proceedings being started against him, are the proceeds of drug trafficking. From this starting point, the court will then deduct anything in respect of which the assumption appears to be incorrect.

14.3.2 *Police Powers*

When a person is prosecuted for drug trafficking offences, the task of assessing the assets which may be liable to confiscation is likely to be carried out by someone with training and skills in doing so. The following provisions are available to assist in assessing amounts and in enforcing a confiscation order.

Seize cash (without warrant): A constable (or customs officer) may seize cash which is being imported into or exported from the United Kingdom if:

- there is reason to believe that it represents someone's proceeds of drug trafficking
- or that it is intended for use in drug trafficking.

Cash so seized may be held for up to 48 hours in the first instance. Application may be made to a magistrate for an order to hold the money for up to three months. Further orders may be made, but the maximum period the cash may be kept is two years, unless a forfeiture order is made by a court, or proceedings are commenced to which the cash relates.

Order of judge to make material available: A constable may apply to a circuit judge for an order to make material available for the purposes of an investigation into drug trafficking. Such an order may require a person having material in his possession, to allow a constable to have access to it, or to produce it to the constable for him to take away.

Search warrant: A circuit judge may, on the application of a constable, issue a warrant to search premises in connection with a drug trafficking investigation.

Grounds for issue: The judge may issue the warrant if she is satisfied either that an order to produce material has not been complied with or that, for specified reasons, it is not appropriate or practicable to issue such an order.

Powers under the warrant: The warrant will authorise the constable:

- to enter and search the premises specified
- seize and retain any material (other than privileged or excluded material) likely to be of substantial value to the investigation.

14.4 Offence in Relation to Investigations
Drug Trafficking Act 1994 Section 58

14.4.1 *Offence*
A person commits an offence who:
- knowing or suspecting that an investigation into drug trafficking is taking place
- makes any disclosure which is likely to prejudice the investigation.

14.4.2 *Exception*
This does not prevent a professional legal adviser disclosing information in relation to giving legal advice, or to any other person disclosing information in relation to legal proceedings – so long as this is not done in furtherance of a criminal purpose.

14.4.3 *Arrest*
This is an arrestable offence, carrying a five year maximum prison sentence.

15 INTERNATIONAL CO-OPERATION
Criminal Justice (International Co-operation) Act 1990

15.1 Drugs and Other Substances
The purpose of the Act is to make provision for this country to co-operate with others in controlling unlawful trade not only in controlled drugs, but also in substances which are not drugs in themselves, but which may be used in drug manufacture.

15.2 Offences
The Act provides for offences in relation to import and export of specified substances, and for use of ships for illicit traffic in controlled drugs.

15.3 Enforcement

15.3.1 *Non-Police Agencies*
The Act gives powers of arrest to Customs and Excise officers and to members of H.M. Forces in U.K. territorial waters and, in certain circumstances, outside the limits of those waters.

15.3.2 *Police Powers*
A constable, along with a Customs and Excise officer and others, is an 'enforcement officer' for the purposes of powers to stop and search ships. Briefly, these powers include a power:
- to stop and board a ship and require it to be taken into port
- search a ship and its cargo
- arrest without warrant persons suspected of certain offences under the Act
- use reasonable force for the purpose of exercising these powers.

Keynote Cases

15.1 *R v Boyesen* [1982] AC 768

Problem

Whether for the purposes of an offence involving unlawful possession of a controlled drug, the minimum quantity of the drug had to be a 'usable' amount.

Circumstances

Boyesen was found by police to be in possession of a small metal tin in which was a plastic bag containing traces of a brown substance. This was found to be cannabis resin, and he was charged with possession of five milligrams of same. At Crown Court the prosecution suggested that he was guilty because the drug was visible to the naked eye and was measurable. The defence suggested that for the offence to be made out, the quantity of the drug had to be sufficient to be useable in a way which the law was intended to prohibit. He was convicted but won his appeal at the Court of Appeal. The prosecution then appealed to the House of lords.

Decision

Their Lordships found for the prosecution, declaring that the test of usability was wrong in law. It was not the quantity of the drug which mattered, but whether the accused was in possession of it. Possession involves a physical control and custody, and a knowledge that one has such control and custody. The quantity would be relevant only if the amount was so minute that the court, on the basis of common sense, could not be satisfied that the accused knew that he had it.

Comment

If traces of a drug were detectable only by forensic examination, for example, traces found on the blade of a knife or on clothing, then it would be difficult to show that the accused knew he had possession of it. However, as in this case, where the traces are visible and the accused knew what the traces were, this was sufficient to convict him. The fact that there was not enough cannabis to gather up for smoking, did not alter the fact that the accused had it in his possession.

Chapter 27: Bribery and Corruption in Public Office

1.1 There are several Acts of Parliament which are specifically aimed at controlling the abuse of public power for personal gain. The first piece of legislation we will deal with is the Public Bodies Corrupt Practices Act 1889 which deals with gifts, loan and general preferential treatment of persons in public office. A further topic dealt with in this chapter is corrupt practices in elections, and election campaigns for public office.

Section 1 Public Bodies Corrupt Practices Act 1889

(1) Every person who shall by himself or by or in conjunction with any other person, corruptly solicit or receive, or agree to receive, for himself, or for any other person, any gift, loan, fee, reward, or advantage whatever as an inducement to, or reward for, or otherwise on account of any member, officer, or servant of a public body as in this Act defined, doing or forbearing to do anything in respect of any matter or transaction whatsoever, actual or proposed, in which the said public body is concerned, shall be guilty of a misdemeanour.

(2) Every person who shall by himself or by or in conjunction with any other person corruptly give, promise, or offer any gift, loan, fee, reward, or advantage whatsoever to any person, whether for the benefit of that person or another person, as an inducement to or reward for or otherwise on account of any member, officer, or servant of any public body as in this Act defined, doing or forbearing to do anything in respect of any matter or transaction whatsoever, actual or proposed, in which such a public body as aforesaid is concerned, shall be guilty of a misdemeanour.

Explanation

Section 1(1) deals with those who corruptly solicit or receive, Section 1(2) deals with those who corruptly offer, give or promise rewards for doing or not doing something which would normally be expected of them in that office.

1.2 The word corruptly denotes that the person making the offer does so deliberately and with the intention that the person to whom it is addressed should enter into a corrupt bargain as in *R v Smith* [1960] *(see keynote case)*. Reward covers receipt of past favours done without prior agreement, the offence lies not in the showing of favour but in accepting a reward for doing so (*R v Parker* [1985]). The words 'doing forbearing to do' are equally applicable to past conduct as to future conduct (*R v Andrews Weatherfoil Ltd* [1972]).

1.3 The law relating to the differences between felonies and misdemeanours has been abolished (Criminal Law Act 1967 Section 1), both are now referred to as being offences.

PENALTIES FOR CORRUPT PRACTICES

2.1 The 1889 Act sets out periods of disqualification from office as well as the punitive terms of sentence by way of fine or imprisonment.

Section 2 Public Bodies Corrupt Practices Act 1889

(1) Any person on invocation for offending as aforesaid shall, at the direction of the court before which he is convicted:

a) be liable:

   i) on summary conviction, to imprisonment for a term not exceeding six months, or to a fine not exceeding the statutory maximum, or both; and

   ii) on conviction on indictment, to imprisonment for a term not exceeding seven years or to a fine, or both; and

b) in addition be liable to be ordered to pay to such body, and in such a manner as the court directs, the amount or value of any gift loan fee, or reward received by him or any part thereof; and

c) be liable to be adjudged incapable of being elected or appointed to any public office for five years from the date of conviction; and

d) in the event of a second conviction of a like offence he shall be, in addition to the foregoing penalties, be triable to be adjudged to be for ever incapable of holding public office, and to be incapable for five years of being registered as an elector, or voting at any election either of members of parliament or of members of any public body, and the enactment's for preventing the voting and registration of persons declared by reason of corrupt practices to be incapable of voting shall apply to a person adjudged in pursuance of this Section to be incapable of voting; and

e) if such a person is an officer or servant in the employ of any public body upon such conviction he shall, at the discretion of the court, be liable to forfeit his right and claim of compensation or pension to which he would otherwise have been entitled.

Explanation

The penalties for corrupt practices are quite simple, the person on first conviction is banned from public office for up to five years also fined and/or imprisoned for six months at Magistrates or seven years if on indictment at Crown Court. A further conviction however renders the person liable to be banned from voting in any elections for up to five years, and banned from public office for life as well as a fine or imprisonment. For public servants a further penalty of losing their employment and any rights in compensation for loss of employment and all pension entitlements makes the punishment for corruption very severe.

RESTRICTIONS ON PROSECUTIONS

3.1 Section 4 of the Act imposes the limitation on proceedings for offences under Section 1 as requiring the authority of the Attorney General, or Solicitor General for England and Wales.

INTERPRETATION OF THE WORDING OF THE ACT

Section 7 Public Bodies Corrupt Practices Act 1889

4.1 In this Act:

The expression 'public body' means, any council or county council of a city or town, any council of a municipal borough, also any board, commissioners, select vestry, or other body which has power to act under and of any Act relating to local government, or the public health, or to poor law or otherwise to administer money raised by rates in pursuance of any public general Act, but does not include any public body as above defined existing elsewhere than in the United Kingdom;

The expression 'public office' means any office or employment of a person as a member, officer, or servant of such a public body;

The expression 'person' includes a body of persons, corporate or incorporate;

The expression 'advantage' includes any office or dignity, and any forbearance to demand any money or money's worth or valuable thing, and includes any aid, vote, consent, or influence, or pretended aid, vote, consent, or influence, and also includes any promise or procurement of any agreement or endeavour to procure, or the holding out of any expectation of any gift, loan, fee, reward, or advantage, as before defined.

Explanation

4.1.1 The term 'public body' relates to all forms of local government organisation, health authorities and the like. Later amendments hacve taken account of such as the Civil Aviation Authority, a body not catered for in an act of Parliament of 1889. Persons concerned my hold office on such a body, e.g. an elected representative, or be an employee. The term 'advantage' is not confined to monetary considerations, but extends to votes, influence, help or promises thereof.

CORRUPTION INVOLVING THIRD PARTIES OR AGENTS

5.1 The Public Bodies Corrupt Practices Act 1889 was designed to deal with the main offenders in public bodies who got involved in corruption. It did not however deal with third parties or agents acting for those persons, this oversight was repaired by the passing of the Prevention of Corruption Act 1906.

Section 1 Prevention of Corruption Act 1906

(1) If any agent corruptly accepts or obtains, or agrees or attempts to obtain, from any person, for himself or another person, any gift or consideration as an inducement or reward for doing or forbearing to do, or for having after the passing of this Act done or forborne to do, any act in relation to his principal's affairs or business, or for showing of forbearing to show favour or disfavour to any person in relation to his principal's affairs or business; or

If any person corruptly gives or agrees to give or offers any gift or consideration to any agent as an inducement or reward for doing or forbearing to do, or for having after the passing of the Act done or forborne to do, any act in relation to his principal's affairs or business, or for showing or forbearing to show favour or disfavour to any person in relation to his principal's affairs or business; or

If any person knowingly gives any agent, or if any agent knowingly uses with intent to deceive his principal, any receipt, account, or other document in respect of which his principal is interested, and which contains any statement which is false or erroneous or defective in any material particular, and which to his knowledge is intended to mislead the principal;

he shall be guilty of a misdemeanour, and shall be liable to:
a) on summary conviction, to a term of imprisonment not exceeding six months, or a fine not exceeding the statutory maximum, or to both; and

b) on conviction on indictment, to a term of imprisonment not exceeding seven year or to a fine, or both.

(2) For the purposes of this Act the expression 'consideration' includes valuable consideration of any kind; the expression 'agent' includes any person employed by or acting for another; and the expression 'principal' includes employer.

(3) A person serving under the Crown or under any corporation or any borough county, or district council, or any board of guardians, is an agent within the meaning of this Act.

5.2 Problems arose in practice in proving the intentions of those involved in order to secure convictions for offences of corruption. Further legislation proved necessary, making provision for a rebuttable presumption, that payment made to the holder of public office was corrupt.

Section 2 Prevention of Corruption Act 1916

Where in any proceedings against a person for an offence under the Prevention of Corruption Act 1906, or the Public Bodies Corrupt Practices Act 1889, it is proved that any money, gift, or other consideration had been paid or given or received by a person in the employment of Her Majesty or any Government Department or public body by or from a person, or agent of a person, holding or seeking to obtain a contract from Her Majesty or any Government Department or public body, the money, gift, or consideration shall be deemed to have been paid or given and received corruptly as such inducement or reward as is mentioned in such Act unless the contrary is proven.

Explanation

5.3 When a payment of money has been made it is then upon the defendant to show that it was not a corrupt transaction (*R v Evans-Jones* (1923)). The expression 'public body' also refers to any body which has statutory or public duties to perform where those duties are to carry out transactions for the benefit of the public and not for private gain (*DPP v Manners* [1977]) *(see keynote case)*.

Keynote Cases

6.1 **Case One: Corruptly**
R v Smith **[1960] 2 QB 423**

Problem
How will the courts interpret the word 'corruptly'?

Circumstances
Smith was charged with an offence under Section 1(2) of the Public Bodies Corrupt Practices Act 1889. It was alleged that Smith had made an offer to the Mayor of Castleford of a gift in order that the Mayor should use his influence in favour of the Smith with dealings involving the borough council. Smith admitted at the trial that he had made the offer of the gift to the mayor, but contended that the offer was not a genuine one, but was made with the intention to show corrupt practice and expose corruption which he had considered existed at that time, and had the Mayor accepted the offer he would have exposed him, also that in fact he did not seek any favours. The trial judge had directed the jury that the motive behind the offer was irrelevant and 'corruptly' for the purposes of this Section

meant, 'with the intention of corrupting the person to whom the offer was made'. Smith was convicted and appealed.

On appeal the Queens Bench decide that the judge had quite correctly summed the matter up and Smith was guilty. The word corruptly as used in the Act denoted that the person making the offer did so deliberately and with the intention that the person to whom it was addressed should enter into a corrupt bargain.

Decision
Corruptly means that regardless of the motives involved, any offer made with the intention of getting someone else to accept it, even if only to test their scruples is an offer which could corrupt another. The purpose of the legislation was to prevent offers from or solicitation of corrupt practice.

Comments
On the basis of this decision anyone who attempts to disclose corruption by making 'agent provocateur' approaches would be guilty of 'corruption' regardless of the motives. The mere offer of a gift, reward or favour would suffice to complete the offence.

6.2 Case Two: Employers
DPP v Manners [1977] 1 All ER 316

Problem
What scope is given to the meaning of the word employer or public body?

Circumstances
Manners and another had been convicted of offences against Section 1(1) of the Prevention of Corruption Act 1906, in that they accepted a gift to show favour to a firm of contractors in relation to some building work to be completed by Manners' employers the North Thames Gas Board. The jury were directed that within the meaning of the Prevention of Corruption Acts 1889 and 1906 Manners' employers were a 'public body'. Manners appealed on the ground that his employers were not a public body. The Court of Appeal dismissed the appeal but allowed the matter to go before the House of Lords on the point of law regarding public bodies.

It was held that the expression 'public body' in Section 7 of the Public Bodies Corrupt Practices Act 1898 and Subsections 2(b) and 4(2)(c) of the Prevention of Corruption Act 1916 is not restricted to local authorities but refers to any body which has public or statutory duties to perform and which perform those duties and carry out their transactions for the benefit of the public and not for private profit.

Decision
A public body is one which performs its duties by or for the public benefit.

Comments
It is quite possible that the result would be different now that the public utilities are privately owned and run for private profit, rather than from public funds for public benefit.

Chapter 28: Forgery and Counterfeiting

1.1 The principal legislation, the Forgery and Counterfeiting Act 1981, deals with two topics:
- forgery, which is making false documents, etc, for dishonest purposes; and
- counterfeiting, which is also making false documents, but the documents concerned are bank notes.

Older legislation, the Forgery Act 1861, has been replaced almost entirely; remaining provisions include offences of forgery of birth certificates and related items, and acknowledging bail for someone else.

FORGERY
Forgery and Counterfeiting Act 1981 Section 1

2.1 A person is guilty of forgery if he makes a false instrument, with the intention that he or another shall use it to induce somebody to accept it as genuine, and by reason of so accepting it to do or not to do some act to his own or any other persons prejudice.

Explanation
2.2 The various terms which appear in the wording of the offence are dealt with in some detail in Sections 8–10 of the Act (see paragraph 8 of this chapter). Briefly, to be false, a document must tell a lie about itself. If a garage proprietor makes out a test certificate for a car which he has not examined, completing all the details and signing it, the certificate will not be a forgery, because it does not purport to be something it is not (there will of course, be an offence committed under road traffic legislation). If, however, an apprentice mechanic makes out a test certificate for a friend's car, and signs it in the name of an authorised examiner, the certificate will be a forgery because it purports to be signed by someone who did not sign it (see keynote case *R v Warneford and Gibbs* (1994)).

The intention of the person making the false document must be to induce someone to accept it as genuine and thereby to do something to his own or someone else's detriment. For example, forging a payment note which will entitle the bearer to collect goods from the pick-up point in the furniture warehouse, is intended to induce staff to hand over goods to their employer's detriment. An action which is to the forger's own detriment is not covered (*R v Utting* (1987)).

COPYING A FALSE INSTRUMENT
Forgery and Counterfeiting Act 1981 Section 2

3.1 It is an offence for a person to make a copy of an instrument which is, and which he knows or believes to be, a false instrument, with the intention that he or another shall use it to induce somebody to accept it as a copy of a genuine instrument, and by reason of so accepting it to do or not to do some act to his own or anothers prejudice.

USING A FALSE INSTRUMENT
Forgery and Counterfeiting Act 1981 Section 3

4.1 It is an offence for a person to use an instrument which is, and which he knows or believes to be, false, with the intention of inducing somebody to accept it as genuine, and by reason of so accepting it to do or not to do some act to his own another person's prejudice.

USING A COPY OF A FALSE INSTRUMENT
Forgery and Counterfeiting Act 1981 Section 4

5.1 It is an offence for a person to use a copy of an instrument which is, and which he knows or believes to be, a false instrument, with the intention of inducing someone to accept it as a copy of a genuine instrument, and by reason of so accepting it, to do some act to his own or another's prejudice.

Explanation
5.1.1 The offences under Sections 3 and 4 are virtually identical. the difference is that the former involves use of a false instrument; the latter entails use of a copy of such. Sections 1 and 2 dealt with making false instruments, or copying same, in each case, intending that they should be used dishonestly. These offences move to the next stage, the actual use of the false instrument or copy of one. The disqualified driver who produces a forged driving licence in order to obtain a hire car will commit the Section 3 offence. If she uses a photocopy of a forged licence, the offence under Section 4 will be committed.

MONEY ORDERS, SHARE CERTIFICATES, PASSPORTS AND OTHER DOCUMENTS

6.1 *Forgery and Counterfeiting Act 1981 Section 5*

(1) It is an offence for a person to have in his custody or under his control an instrument to which this Section applies which is, and which he knows to be, false, with the intention that he or another shall use it to induce somebody to accept it as genuine, and by reason of so accepting it to do or not to do some act to his own or any other persons prejudice.

(2) It is an offence for a person to have in his custody or under his control without lawful authority or excuse, an instrument to which this Section applies which is, and which he knows or believes to be , false.

(3) It is an offence for a person to make or have in his custody or under his control a machine or implement, or paper or any other material, which to his knowledge is or has been specifically designed or adapted for the making of an instrument to which this Section applies, with the intention that he or another shall make an instrument to which this Section applies which is false and that he or another shall use the instrument to induce somebody to accept it as genuine, and by reason of so accepting it to do or not to do some act to his own or any other persons prejudice.

(4) It is an offence for a person to make or have in his custody or under his control any such machine, implement, paper or material, without lawful authority or excuse.

(5) The instruments to which this Section applies are:
   a) money orders;
   b) postal orders;
   c) United Kingdom postage stamps;
   d) Inland Revenue Stamps;
   e) share certificates;
   f) passports and documents which can be used instead of passports;
   g) cheques;
   h) travellers cheques;
   k) cheque cards;
   l) credited copies relating to an entry in a register of births, adoptions, marriages or deaths and issued by the Registrar General, the Registrar General of Northern Ireland, a registration officer or a person lawfully authorised to register marriages;
   m) certificates relating to entries in such registers.

(6) In subsection 5(e) above 'share certificate' means an instrument entitling or evidencing the title of a person to a share or interest:
   a) in any public stock, annuity, fund or debt of any government or state, including a state which forms part of another state; or,
   b) in any stock, fund or debt of a body (whether corporate or incorporated) established in the United Kingdom or elsewhere.

Explanation

Offences: The section goes through a series of offences, in decreasing degrees seriousness, from possession of a false instrument with intent to use, to possession of a false instrument, possession of implements, intending to make and use, and finally, possession of materials without lawful excuse.

Instruments: The section provides a comprehensive list of documents which have some monetary value, or prove entitlement to something of value – plus passports.

PUNISHMENT

7.1 The penalties for the offences created under Sections 1 to 5 of this are specified by Section 6 *(below)*, the powers of search and forfeiture by Section 7 *(below)*.

Forgery and Counterfeiting Act 1981 Section 6

(1) A person guilty of an offence under this part of this act shall be liable on summary conviction to:
   a) a fine not exceeding the statutory maximum; or,
   b) to imprisonment for a term not exceeding six months; or,
   c) both.

(2) A person guilty of an offence to which this subsection applies shall be liable on conviction on indictment to imprisonment for a term not exceeding ten years.

(3) The offences to which subsection (2) above applies are offences under the following provisions of this part of this Act:
   a) Section 1;

b) Section 2;
c) Section 3;
d) Section 4;
e) Section 5(1); and
f) Section 5(3).

(4) A person guilty of an offence under Section 5(2) or (4) above shall be liable on conviction on indictment to imprisonment for a term not exceeding two years.

(5) In this Section 2 statutory maximum, in relation to a fine on summary conviction means the prescribed sum, within the meaning of Section 32 of the Magistrates' Courts Act 1980.

Powers of Entry and Search Under Warrant
7.2 *Forgery and Counterfeiting Act 1981 Section 7*

(1) If it appears to a justice of the peace, from information given to him on oath, that there is reasonable cause to believe that a person has in his custody or under his control:
   a) anything which he or another has used, whether before or after the coming into force of this Act, or intends to use, for the making of any false instrument or copy of a false instrument, in contravention of Sections 1 or 2 above; or,
   b) any false instrument or copy of a false instrument which he or another has used, whether before or after the coming into force of this Act, or intends to use , in contravention of Section's 3 or 4 above; or,
   c) any thing custody or control of which without lawful authority or excuse is an offence under Section 5 above,

the justice may issue a warrant authorising a constable to search for and seize the object in question, and for that purpose to enter any premises specified in the warrant.

Explanation
7.2.1 The warrant, when issued, will authorise a search, but only for the items specified. The application for the warrant will therefore have to include some detail as to the nature of the false instrument, copy, etc. which the search is intended to discover. Anything which has been used, or is intended shall be used, in the commission of any of the offences contained in Sections 1 – 5, may be the subject of a warrant.

INTERPRETATION OF WORDING

Instrument
Forgery and Counterfeiting Act 1981 Section 8

8.1 (1) Subject to subsection (2) below, in this part of this Act 'instrument' means:
   a) any document, whether of a formal character or informal character;
   b) any stamp issued or sold by the Post Office;
   c) any Inland Revenue stamp; and
   d) any disc, tape, sound track or other device on or in which information is recorded or stored by mechanical, electronic or other means.

(2) A currency note within the meaning of part II of this Act is not an instrument for the purposes of this part of the Act.

(3) A mark denoting payment of postage which the Post Office authorise to be used instead an adhesive stamp is to be treated for the purposes of this Act as if it were a stamp issued by the Post Office.

(4) In this Part of this Act 'Inland Revenue stamp' means a stamp defined in Section 27 of the Stamp Duties Management Act 1891.

'False' and 'Making'
Forgery and Counterfeiting Act 1981 Section 9

(1) An instrument is false for the purposes of this Act:
  a) if it purports to have been made in the form in which it is made by a person who did not in fact make it in that form; or,
  b) if it purports to have been made in the form in which it is made on the authority of a person who did not in fact authorise its making in that form; or
  c) if it purports to have been made in terms in which it is made by a person who did not in fact make it in those terms; or
  d) if it purports to have been made in the terms of which it is made on the authority of a person who did not in fact authorise its making in those terms; or,
  e) if it purports to have been altered in any respect by a person who did not in fact alter it in that respect; or,
  f) if it purports to have been altered in respect on the authority of a person who did not in fact authorise the alteration in that respect; or
  g) if it purports to have been made or altered on a date on which, or at a place which, or otherwise in circumstances in which, it was not in fact made or altered; or,
  h) if it purports to have been made or altered by an existing person but if he did not in fact exist.

(2) A person is to be treated for the purposes of this Part of this Act as making a false instrument if he alters an instrument so as to make it false in any respect (whether or not it is false in some other respect apart from its alteration).

'Prejudice' and 'Induce'
Forgery and Counterfeiting Act 1981 Section 10

(1) Subject to subsection (2) and (4) below, for the purposes of this Part of this Act, an act or omission intended to be induced is to a person's prejudice if, and only if, it is one which, if it occurs:
  a) will result:
    i) in his permanent or temporary loss of property; or,
    ii) in his being deprived of an opportunity to earn remuneration or greater remuneration; or,
    iii) in his being deprived of an opportunity to gain financial advantage otherwise than by way of remuneration; or
  b) will result in somebody being given an opportunity:
    i) to earn remuneration or greater remuneration from him; or

ii) to gain financial advantage from him otherwise than by way of remuneration;

c) will be the result of his having accepted a false instrument as genuine, or a copy of a false instrument as a copy of a genuine one, in connection with his performance of any duty.

(2) An act which a person has an enforceable duty to do and an omission to do an act which a person is not entitled to do shall be disregarded for the purposes of this Part of this Act.

(3) In this Part of this Act references to inducing somebody to accept a false instrument as genuine, or a copy of a false instrument as a copy of a genuine one, include references to inducing a machine to respond to the instrument or copy of a genuine instrument or, as the case may be, a copy of a genuine one.

(4) Where subsection (3) above applies, the act or omission intended to induced by the machine responding to the instrument or copy shall be treated as an act or omission to a person's prejudice.

(5) In this Section 'loss' includes not getting what one might get as well as parting with what one has.

Explanation

Instrument: The term includes any sort of document, with stamps getting a special mention, lest they be considered not to be documents. Note that the definition recognises modern versions of 'information technonolgy'. A currency note is not an instrument for these purposes, but there are other offences relating specifically to currency notes.

Make, false: Section 9 provides a comprehensive list of what amounts to making an instrument false. The fact that an instrument may already be false in some respect, will not absolve from guilt someone who alters it so as to make it false in some other way.

Prejudice: It may be supposed that forged instruments are most likely to be used for dishonest financial gain, but section 10 also provides that apart from gain and loss, the term will also cover a situation where the opportunity is gained to earn money, e.g., by producing false references to get a job. Note that in many situations where a forged instrument is actually used, other offences, especially under the Theft Acts, will also be committed. A person will also be 'prejudiced' when he is induced to accept a false instrument or copy of one in connection with his duty. Use of a forged identity card, to get past the security officer at the gate, would be covered by this provision, without there being any financial motive involved.

Induce: The term will normally apply to a situation where a person is led to doing something as a result of accepting a forgery as genuine. However, section 10(3) extends the meaning of 'induce' to making a machine do something as a result of accepting a forgery. A forged credit or cash-card may be intended for use in automatic cash dispensers, for example.

OFFENCES IN RELATION TO CURRENCY

Counterfeiting Coins and Notes

9.1 *Forgery and Counterfeiting Act 1981 Section 14*

(1) It is an offence for a person to make a counterfeit of a currency note or protected coin, intending that he or another person shall pass or tender it as genuine.

(2) It is an offence for a person to make a counterfeit of a currency note or of a protected coin without lawful authority or excuse.

Explanation

The main offences in relation to currency are contained in Section 14, the simple offence of making counterfeit currency, firstly to intend its use as genuine, and secondly just to make counterfeit currency without lawful authority. The penalties for these offences are contained in Section 22 (see later).

PASSING COUNTERFEIT CURRENCY COINS AND NOTES

10.1 *Forgery and Counterfeiting Act 1981 Section 15*

(1) It is an offence for a person:
   a) to pass or tender as genuine any thing which is, and which he knows or believes to be, a counterfeit of a currency note or of a protected coin; or,
   b) to deliver to another any thing which is, and which he knows or believes to be such a counterfeit, intending that the person to whom it is delivered or another shall pass or tender it as genuine.

(2) It is an offence for a person to deliver to another, without lawful authority or excuse, any thing which is, and which he knows or believes to be, a counterfeit of a currency note or any protected coin.

Explanation

10.1.1 A key phrase in these offences is 'knows or believes'. The fact that a person is found trying to pass counterfeit currency does not not necessarily mean that he is guilty – he may claim that he is a victim, having been passed a 'dud' note. The fact that he has a suitcase full, may assist the prosecution case, but it will be for the prosecution to prove that the accused 'knew or believed' the notes or coins to be counterfeit.

CUSTODY AND CONTROL OF COUNTERFEIT CURRENCY NOTES AND PROTECTED COINS

11.1 *Forgery and Counterfeiting Act 1981 Section 16*

(1) It is an offence for a person to have in his custody or under his control any thing which is , and which he knows or believes to be, a counterfeit of a currency note or of a protected coin, intending either to pass or tender it as genuine or to deliver it to another with the intention that he shall pass or tender it as genuine.

(2) It is an offence for a person to have in his custody or under his control, without lawful authority or excuse, any thing which is, and which he knows or believes to be, a counterfeit of a currency note or protected coin.

(3) It is immaterial for the purposes of subsections (1) and (2) above that a coin or note is not in a fit state to be passed or tendered, or that the making of a counterfeiting of a coin or note has not been finished or perfected.

Explanation

11.1.1 These offences come a stage earlier than those under Sction 15, involving possession with intent, to deliver, to pass, etc. As well as having to prove that the accused knew or believed the items were counterfeit, the prosecution also have to prove his intent.

A coin or note does not have to be finished, or in a fit state to be passed, for these offences to be committed.

POSSESSION OF IMPLEMENTS OR MATERIALS TO MAKE COUNTERFEITS
12.1 *Forgery and Counterfeiting Act 1981 Section 17*

(1) It is an offence for a person to make, or to have in his custody or control, any thing which he intends to use, or to permit any other person to use, for the purpose of making a counterfeit of a currency note or of a protected coin with the intention that it be passed or tendered as genuine.

(2) It is an offence for a person without lawful authority or excuse:
   a) to make; or,
   b) to have in his custody or under his control,

any thing which, to his knowledge, is or has been specially designed or adapted for the making of a counterfeit of a currency note.

(3) Subject to subsection (4) below, it is an offence for a person to make, or to have in his custody or under his control, any implement which, to his knowledge, is capable of imparting to any thing a resemblance:
   a) to the whole or part of either side of a protected coin; or,
   b) to the whole or part of the reverse of the image on either side of a protected coin.

(4) It shall be defence for a person charged with an offence under subsection (3) above to show:
   a) that he made the implement or as the case may be, had it in his custody or under his control, with the written consent of the Treasury; or,
   b) that he had lawful authority otherwise than by virtue of paragraph (a) above, or a lawful excuse, for making it or having it in his custody or control.

Explanation

The section creates offences relating to three categories of object which may be used in the making of counterfeit notes or coins:
   i) something intended for use
   ii) something specially designed or adapted for use
   iii) something capable of being used.

An offence may be committed where an article is intended to be used to check the quality of counterfeit notes; the scope of the section is not limited to articles which are essential for the production of counterfeit currency (keynote case – *R v Maltman* (1994)).

MAKING BRITISH CURRENCY NOTES
13.1 *Forgery and Counterfeiting Act 1981 Section 18*

(1) It is an offence for any person, unless the relevant authority has previously consented in writing, to reproduce on any substance whatsoever, and whether or not on the correct scale, any British currency note or any part of a British currency note.

(2) In this Section:
'British currency note' is any note which:
a) had been lawfully issued in England and Wales, Scotland or Northern Ireland; and
b) is or has been customarily used as money in the country where it was issued; and
c) is payable on demand; and
'the relevant authority', in relation to a British currency note of any particular description, means the authority empowered by law to issue notes of that description.

13.2 Making any form of copy of a note is an offence, this is regardless of the size of the copy unless there is written consent. In such event the person making the copy would undoubtedly be able to show the written proof of his defence.

IMITATION BRITISH COINAGE
14.1 *Forgery and Counterfeiting Act 1981 Section 19*

(1) It is an offence for a person:
a) to make an imitation British coin in connection with a scheme intended to promote the sale of any product or the making of contracts for the supply of any service; or
b) to sell or distribute imitation British coins in connection with any such scheme, or to have imitation British coins in his custody or under his control with a view to such sale or distribution,

unless the Treasury have previously consented in writing to the sale or distribution of such imitation British coins in connection with that scheme.

(2) In this Section:
'British coin' means any coin which is legal tender in any part of the United Kingdom, and 'Imitation British coin' means any thing which resembles a British coin in shape, size and substance of which it is made.

IMPORTATION AND EXPORTATION OF COUNTERFEITS
Forgery and Counterfeiting Act 1981 Section 20

15.1 The importation, landing or unloading of a counterfeit of a currency note or of a protected coin without the consent of the treasury is hereby prohibited.

Forgery and Counterfeiting Act 1981 Section 21

(1) The exportation of a counterfeit of a currency note or of a protected coin without the consent of the Treasury is prohibited.

(2) A counterfeit of a currency note or of a protected coin which is removed to the Isle of Man from the United Kingdom shall be deemed to be exported from the United Kingdom:

a) for the purposes of this Section; and,

b) for the purposes of the Customs and Excise Acts, in their application to the prohibition imposed by this Section.

15.2 It was necessary to prevent counterfeits from being laundered via the Isle of Man into and out of the United Kingdom, subsection (2) of Section 21 specifically deal with this problem. Otherwise all importation or exportation of counterfeit currency, either in notes or coins is prohibited.

PENALTIES FOR OFFENCES UNDER THE FORGERY AND COUNTERFEITING ACT 1981

16.1 *Forgery and Counterfeiting Act 1981 Section 22*

(1) A person guilty of an offence to which this subsection applies shall be liable:
   a) on summary conviction:
      i) to a fine not exceeding the statutory maximum; or
      ii) to imprisonment for a term not exceeding six months; or
      iii) to both; and
   b) on conviction on indictment:
      i) to a fine; or
      ii) to imprisonment for a term not exceeding ten years; or
      iii) to both.

(2) The offences to which subsection (1) applies are offences under the following provisions of this part of this Act:
   a) Section 14(1);
   b) Section 15(1);
   c) Section 16(1); and,
   d) Section 17(1).

(3) A person guilty of an offence to which this subsection applies shall be liable:
   a) on summary conviction to:
      i) to a fine not exceeding the statutory maximum; or
      ii) to imprisonment for a term not exceeding six months; or
      iii) to both; and,
   b) on conviction on indictment:
      i) to a fine; or,
      ii) to imprisonment for a term not exceeding two years; or,
      iii) to both.

(4) The offences to which subsection (3) above applies are offences under the following provisions of this Part of this Act:
   a) Section 14(2);
   b) Section 15(2);
   c) Section 16(2);
   d) Section 17(2); and,
   e) Section 17(3).

(5) A person guilty of an offence under Section 18 or 19 shall be liable to:

a) on summary conviction, to a fine not exceeding the statutory maximum; and

b) on conviction on indictment, to a fine.

16.2 For the purposes of this punishment Section the words statutory maximum mean the maximum that magistrates are at that time empowered to make as a fine under Section 32 and 143 of the Magistrates' Courts Act 1980. It is also worthy of note that in each Section the secondary offence carries the lesser sentence.

POWERS TO ENTER AND SEARCH

17.1 If it appears to a magistrate, from information on oath, that there is reasonable cause to believe that a person has in his custody or under his control:

- any thing which is a counterfeit of a currency note or of a protected coin, or which is an unlawfully made reproduction; or
- any thing which he or another has used or intends to use, for the making of any such counterfeit or reproduction

the justice may issue a warrant authorising a constable to search for and seize the object in question, and for that purpose to enter any premises specified in the warrant.

A court may subsequently order forfeiture and disposal of any such article seized by police, whether under a warrant or otherwise.

INTERPRETATION

18.1 Section 27 of the Forgery and Counterfeiting Act 1981 sets out the meaning of the words 'currency note' and 'protected coin' as:

any note which:

a) has been lawfully issued in England and Wales, Scotland, Northern Ireland, and any of the Channel Islands, the Isle of Man or the Republic of Ireland; and,

b) is or has been customarily used in the country where it was issued; and,

c) is payable on demand; or,

any note which:

d) has been lawfully issued in some country other than those mentioned in paragraph (a) above; and,

e) is customarily used as money in that country.

protected coin:

a) is customarily used as money in any country; or,

b) is specified in an order made by the Treasury for the purposes of this Part of this Act.

18.2 The word 'counterfeit' is a little more complex and is covered by:

Forgery and Counterfeiting Act 1981 Section 28

(1) For the purposes of this Part of this Act a thing is counterfeit of a currency note or of a protected coin:

a) if it is not a currency note or a protected coin but resembles a currency note or protected coin (whether on one side only or on both) to such an extent that it is reasonably capable of passing for a currency note or protected coin of that description; or

b) if it is a currency note or protected coin which has been so altered that it is reasonably capable of passing for a currency note or protected coin of some other description.

(2) For the purposes of this Part of this Act:
   a) a thing consisting of one side only of a currency note, with or without the addition of other material, is a counterfeit of such a note;
   b) a thing consisting:
      i) of parts of two or more currency notes; or
      ii) of parts of a currency note, or of parts of two or more currency notes, with the addition of other material, is capable of being a counterfeit of a currency note.

(3) References in this Part of this Act to passing or tendering a counterfeit of a currency note or protected coin are not to be confined to passing or tendering it as legal tender.

Explanation

Note: There is a small distinction between the bank notes from countries of the British Isles, and those from elsewhere. A note from this country, Channel Islands, Isle of Man or Irish Republic is covered if it has been used as money, even if it is no longer used, so long as it remains payable on demand. When a type of note ceases to be used, there is usually a period during which such notes may be changed at a bank. For foreign notes, only those types still being used in their country of origin, may be subject of counterfeiting offences in this country.

Coin: Coins from any country may be subject of offences, with no distinction drawn between British coins and foreign ones. For an offence to be committed, the coin must be of a type currently in use.

Counterfeit: The better the quality of a dud note or coin, the more easy it will be to pass it as genuine. The law however, does not require perfection; a note or coin will be counterfeit if it resembles a genuine one to such an extent that it is reasonably capable of passing as genuine.

Also, it is enough if it meets this standard on one side only. For example, a good one-sided photocopy of a £10 note may be considered a counterfeit. It's chances of being accepted as genuine may be enhanced by handing it over folded up.

A genuine note or coin may be a counterfeit if it is altered to represent a note or coin of a different description. Two pennies, glued together, may make a counterfeit £1 coin.

FORGERY AND FRAUD INVOLVING VEHICLE DOCUMENTS

19.1 It is an offence to forge or alter certain documents required to be kept in relation to motor vehicles. The documents and the manner in which they cannot be altered are set out in:

Vehicle Excise and Registration Act 1994 Section 44

It is an offence for any person to forge or fraudulently, use, alter, lend, or allow to be used by another person any vehicle licence, trade licence, trade plate, registration mark, registration document, or document in the form of a licence issued to the driver of an exempt vehicle.

19.2 An intention to deprive some other person by deceit of some economic value or advantage or to inflict economic harm is not necessary for this offence. The only intention required is to stop some official doing his or her duty (*R v Mcrae* [1995]) *(see keynote case)*. This offence carries a maximum sentence on indictment of two years imprisonment, or a fine, or both.

Goods Vehicles (Licensing of Operators) Act 1995 Section 38

(1) A person is guilty of an offence if, with intent to deceive, he:
   a) forges, alters, or uses a document, or other thing to which this Section applies; or
   b) lends to or allows to be used by, any other person a document or other thing to which this Section applies; or,
   c) makes or has in his possession, any document or other thing so closely resembling a document or other thing to which this Section applies as to be calculated to deceive.

(2) This offence applies to the following documents and other things, namely:
   a) any operators licence; or,
   b) any document, plate, mark or other thing by which, in pursuance of regulations, a vehicle is to be identified as being authorised to be used, or as being used, under an operators licence; or,
   c) any document evidencing the authorisation of any person for the purpose of Section 40 (inspection and maintenance provisions of the same legislation) and Section 41 (power to seize documentation under same legislation).
   d) any certificate of qualification under Section 49 (qualifications of examiners under the same legislation); and
   e) any certificate or diploma such as those which show:
      i) he has demonstrated that he possessed the requisite skills by passing a written examination organised by an approved body and is the holder of a certificate to that effect issued by that body; or
      ii) he is the holder of any other certificate of competence, diploma or other qualification recognised by the Secretary of State.

Explanation

To 'forge' means to make a false document in order that it may be passed as genuine. As in the case of offences under the Forgery and Counterfeiting Act, a document is false if it tells a lie about itself. It is not enough that it is a document which contains false information (see keynote case – *Warneford v Gibbs*).

TRADE MARKS

20.1 The counterfeiting of 'brand' name goods has become big business. Fashions within society tend to make goods of greater value if they have the trade mark than if they do not. The Trade Marks Act 1994 deals with goods which are subject of counterfeiting. Frequently officers will come into contact with offenders selling counterfeit goods at car boot sales, or in the street as itinerant street sellers. Frequently the sellers having been released from custody during an investigation will fail to reappear and will be difficult to trace. The Trade Marks Act 1994 gives the police and trading standards officers power to deal with the counterfeit goods by forfeiture.

20.2 Section 97 gives power to the police or trading standards department to make application to court for the forfeiture of goods seized which came into possession during the investigation of a relevant offence. The power of forfeiture applies to all goods which, or, the packaging of which, bears a sign identical to or likely to be mistaken for a registered trade mark, or materials bearing such a sign and intended to be used for labelling or packaging goods, as a business paper in relation to the goods, or for advertising goods, or articles specifically designed or adapted for making copies of such a sign.

20.3 If the goods are counterfeit, even if there is no prosecution a court order can be obtained for forfeiture. The majority of offences dealt with under the Trade Marks Act 1994 will be enforced by trading standards officers, police officers may however become involved in circumstances where they are preventing a breach of the peace, or verifying names and addresses. Section 92 of the Trade Marks Act 1994 deals with the unauthorised use of trade marks.

Keynote Cases

21.1 *R v Warneford and Gibbs* **[1994] Crim LR 753 CA**

Problem
Is a proper document which contains false information a forgery, or is the offence one of deception under the Theft Acts.

Circumstances
The accused were tried for offences relating to use of forged instruments, involving false employment references which were used to obtain mortgages. The references showed that the defendants had worked for a company for a period of time, and were issued by the person in the company who normally dealt with such matters. In fact, the defendants had not worked for the company, but the references were then used in support of mortgage applications. The defence claimed that the references were not forged, because the person who purported to have made the documents did in fact make them. They were convicted at first instance, but the convictions were overturned on appeal.

Decision
To amount to a forgery, a document must tell a lie about itself; it is not what it purports to be. In this case, the employment references were what they purported to be. The fact that they contained false information did not make them forgeries.

Comment
There are various offences which will be committed in circumstances such as these, where documents are used which contain false information. In a case such as this, where a mortgage is obtained, the new offence of obtaining a credit transfer by a deception, under Section 15A of the Theft Act 1968, appears appropriate.

20.2 *R v Maltman* **[1994] TLR 28.6.94**

Problem
If a thing as defined by Section 28 is not necessary to make a forgery but merely to check its accuracy, will it fall into the category of things' which it is illegal to possess.

Circumstances
Maltman was found in possession of two chromolins for both sides of a United States of America fifty dollar note. A chromolin is a type of photograph used to check the accuracy of

the printing plate by comparison methods. Maltman was charged with Section 17(1) of the 1981 Forgery and Counterfeiting Act, in that he had possession and control of 'any thing' which he intended to use for making counterfeit currency notes. The US $50 bills were currency notes for the purposes of Section 17 Forgery and Counterfeiting Act 1981.

Maltman was convicted and appealed on the grounds that the chromolins were not articles which were necessary for the production of counterfeit currency notes. The purpose was to use them to check on the quality of the counterfeits produced. As such, they could not be said to be 'anything intended for use for the purpose of making a counterfeit currency note'.

Decision
The appeal was dismissed, the court deciding that the term 'any thing' must be given its wider meaning, to include everything involved in the process of counterfeiting. This would extend to anything used to check on the process, whether or not essential to that process.

Comment

This could include innocuous things such as the water for cleaning the plates after printing, provided the necessary intention could be proved.

20.3 *R v Macrae* (1995) 159 JP 359 CA

Problem
For an offence of forgery to be made out, is gain an essential element?

Circumstances
The defendant sent off a valid application form, together with the appropriate sum, in order to obtain a renewal of his vehicle excise licence. In order to avoid being stopped by police while waiting for the new licence to arrive, he photocopied the old licence and changed details on it, to display on the vehicle. He was convicted of forgery of an excise licence and appealed.

Decision
The court decided that the offence of forgery was complete, when the defendant made the false licence intending to use it to induce a police officer to accept it as genuine and thereby to do some act to his prejudice – i.e. fail to take steps to report the defendant for an offence of failing to display a current excise licence. The decision was based upon the provision in Section 10(1) Forgery and Counterfeiting Act 1981, that a person acts to his prejudice if he accepts a false instrument as genuine in the performance of any duty.

Comment
For a person to suffer prejudice as a result of accepting a forged instrument as genuine, does not necessarily involve economic loss.

Chapter 29: Public Justice

ESCAPE FROM LAWFUL CUSTODY

Common Law Offences

Common Law Escape

1.1 The common law offence of escape is committed by:

1) the custodian who negligently or voluntarily allows a prisoner, lawfully in his custody on a criminal charge, to escape

2) the prisoner who, whether innocent or not, escapes from lawful custody without use of force

3) any person who aids the prisoner to escape.

Prison Breach

1.2 A person commits this offence who escapes from lawful custody by use of any force, whether he is in a prison, private house, or any other place where he is under lawful arrest.

Explanation

Custodian: The custodian may be a police or prison officer, a prisoner custody officer, or anyone else who has lawful custody. If the custodian is negligent, he will be liable for allowing the escape.

Use of force: The offence of escape is committed when no force is used, so a custodian will not be liable if the prisoner used force on him. Prison breach involves use of some force, whether on property or on a person. If the prisoner jumps over a wall or goes through an unlocked door, he has not used force, so the correct charge would be escape rather than prison breach.

Prison: The word 'prison' is misleading, since prison breach need not be from a prison at all.

Statutory Offences

Facilitate Escape from Prison
Section 39 Prison Act 1952

1.3 Any person who aids any prisoner in escaping or attempting to escape from a prison or who, with intent to facilitate the escape of any prisoner, conveys anything into a prison or to a prisoner, sends anything (by post or otherwise) into a prison or to a prisoner or places any thing anywhere outside a prison with a view to its coming into the possession of a prisoner, shall be guilty of an offence and liable to imprisonment for a term not exceeding ten years.

Harbour Escaped Prisoner
Section 22 Criminal Justice Act 1961

1.4 Any person who knowingly harbours a person who has escaped from a prison or other institution to which Section 39 of the Prison Act 1952 applies, or who having been sentenced in any part of the United Kingdom or in any of the Channel Islands or the Isle of Man to imprisonment or detention, is otherwise unlawfully at large, or gives to any such person any assistance with intention to prevent, hinder or interfere with his being taken into custody shall be liable:

   a) on summary conviction to a term not exceeding six months imprisonment, or a fine not exceeding the statutory maximum, or both.
   b) on conviction on indictment, to imprisonment for a term not exceeding ten years or to a fine, or both.

Explanation

Harbour: This means actually providing shelter or refuge, it is not enough merely to assist or support an escaped prisoner (*Darch v Weight* (1984)). The offence of harbouring may not be committed in respect of a person who escapes from police custody while being taken to a remand centre (*Nichol v Carton* (1985)).

Power to Detain Escaped Prisoner
Section 49(1) Prison Act 1952

1.5 Any person who, having been sentenced to imprisonment, custody for life or youth custody, or ordered to be detained in a detention centre or a young offenders institution, or having been committed to a prison or remand centre, is unlawfully at large, may be arrested by a constable without warrant and taken to the place in which he is required in accordance with the law to be detained.

   This Section includes children and young persons who have been detained in accordance with the directions of the Secretary of State by virtue of Section 67 of the Criminal Justice Act 1967.

Taking Liquor or Tobacco into Prison
Section 40 Prison Act 1952

1.6 Any person who contrary to the regulations of a prison brings or attempts to bring into the prison or to a prisoner any spirituous or fermented liquor or tobacco, or places any such liquor or tobacco anywhere outside the prison with intent that it shall come into the possession of a prisoner, and any officer who contrary to those regulations allows any such liquor or any tobacco to be sold or used in the prison, shall be liable on summary conviction to imprisonment for a term not exceeding six months, or a fine not exceeding level three on the standard scale, or both.

PRISONER CUSTODY OFFICERS AND COURT SECURITY

2.1 Prisoner Custody Officer

The contracting out of escorting duties, private contracted out prisons and court escort and security duties has brought about many changes in the way both the prison and police services deal with prisoners on remand and awaiting court. The control of these functions is subject of legislation under the Criminal Justice Act 1991, Sections 80 – 92 as amended by the Criminal Justice and Public Order Act 1994, ss. 93 – 95.

Role of a Prisoner Custody Officer

Legal Status

2.2 Between 1992 and 1997 those functions formerly carried out by police and prison officers, of escorting persons in custody between police stations, courts and prisons, were contracted out to private companies. The running of a number of prisons is also contracted out. The contractors employ 'prisoner custody officers' (PCO) to carry out the roles formerly performed by police and prison officers. A PCO is certificated as such by the Home Office, after having been vetted as suitable, and having undergone an approved training course. The certificate may qualify a PCO:

    i) to carry out duties both in a prison and in a court escort role; or

    ii) to carry out court escort duties only.

2.3 It is stressed that prison and prisoner escort duties are 'contracted out', not 'privatised'. The Home Office retains responsibility for all prisons and for monitoring the performance of the private contractors.

Contact with Police and Legal Profession

2.4 Police officers, especially custody officers, will have dealings with PCO's from time to time when prisoners are collected from or taken to police stations. Legal representatives will likewise have contact with them at courts, when arranging to interview clients before or after their court appearances. An outline of the powers and duties of a PCO is therefore given here, to facilitate an understanding of how the roles of lawyer, constable and PCO inter-relate. A police presence at a court may be required, e.g. when there is reason to believe that there may be disorder. PCO's have limited powers, and no more than a citizen's powers of arrest. Current Home Office arrangements exclude court escort PCO's from dealing with Category 'A' prisoners, who will continue for the time being to be escorted in magistrates' court by police officers, and by prison officers at Crown Court.

2.5 PCO's are instructed that, in police premises, they will always carry out any instructions of a police custody officer. It is important that any instruction given by a police custody officer is valid. It would not be proper, for example, to instruct PCOs not to search a prisoner being handed over to their custody, since the PCO is empowered to search that prisoner when it appears to be necessary to do so.

Powers and Duties

Powers

2.6 A PCO engaged in prisoner escort duties has the following powers:

    i) to search any prisoner whose delivery or custody he is responsible for;

    ii) to search any other person who is in or is seeking to enter any place where a prisoner is or is to be held, and may search any article in that person's possession;

Duties

2.7 A PCO's duties in respect of a prisoner for whose delivery or custody he is responsible include:

    i) to prevent escape;

    ii) to prevent or detect and report on, unlawful acts or attempts by prisoners;

    iii) to ensure good order and discipline;

    iv) to attend to prisoners' well-being;

    v) to carry out the directions of a court as to a prisoner's treatment.

In particular, a PCO shall carry out any lawful direction:

    vi) of a magistrates' court to search a prisoner (in respect of money found on a defaulter).

    vii) of a Crown Court to search a person before the court.

Use of Force

2.8 In carrying out these duties and in the exercise of the powers, a PCO may use reasonable force where necessary.

Explanation

Search of Prisoners

2.9 A PCO may search a prisoner when it appears necessary to do so in the interests of security, good order or discipline. The search shall be conducted in as seemly a manner as is consistent with discovering anything concealed, and this may necessitate a strip search. The operating procedures laid down by the Home Office for PCO's carrying out a strip search accord with those contained in Code C of the PACE Codes of Practice. There is no provision for PCO's to carry out an intimate search.

Search Other Persons

2.10 A PCO may search any person in a place where a prisoner is, or who is seeking to meet with a prisoner. This extends to solicitors and others who wish to consult with or otherwise have contact with a prisoner at court – including police officers. In such cases, there is no power to require removal of clothing, other than an outer coat, jacket or gloves. Any bag or other article being carried by the person seeking access to the prisoner may also be searched.

Unlawful Acts

2.11 A PCO has a duty to report unlawful acts and attempts by a prisoner. Unlawful acts commonly committed by prisoners in court cells include criminal damage, assault on staff or on other prisoners, and unlawful possession of drugs or other articles, often as the result of efforts by friends and relatives to pass items to a prisoner in the court room. Criminal activity may well be reported to police for further investigation.

Good Order and Discipline

2.12 Persons remanded in custody by a court to go to prison are subject to the Prison Rules, so may be dealt with by the governor when they arrive at prison, for disciplinary offences committed at court or en route to the prison. A matter may amount both to a crime and to a disciplinary offence, e.g. assault on a member of staff or on another prisoner. In such a case, if the matter has been reported to the police, the prison governor will adjourn the disciplinary proceedings until the result of the police enquiry is known.

Court Security

2.13 A PCO has no responsibility for court security, other than in relation to prisoners, or for keeping order on the public benches.

Protection for Prisoner Custody Officers (PCO's)

Assault

2.14 A person commits an offence who assaults a PCO acting in pursuance of his duties.

Obstruction

2.15 A person commits an offence who resists or wilfully obstructs a PCO acting in pursuance of his duties.

Pursuance of Duties

2.16 A PCO engaged on escort duties shall not be regarded as 'in pursuance of those duties' unless he is readily identifiable as such, by means of uniform, badge or otherwise.

Prison Controllers and Escort Monitors

Prison Controller

2.17 In a prison run by the Prison Service, the governor is responsible for the management of the prison and for enforcing discipline. The governor or her deputy adjudicates at discipline hearings and awards punishments to prisoners found guilty of breaches of Prison Rules. In a contracted out prison, the day-to-day running of the prison, including the maintenance of good order and discipline, is a matter for the contractor company. However, responsibility for adjudicating at discipline hearings and for awarding punishment, remains with the Prison Service, in the person of the prison Controller. Controllers are governor grades from the Prison Service, responsible for monitoring the contractor's performance and those of the prison PCO's. A complaint made against a prison PCO will be investigated by the Controller. In serious cases, the Controller may suspend a PCO pending the outcome of an enquiry, but has no disciplinary responsibility for PCO's.

Escort Monitors

2.18 Each escort area has Escort Monitors who are Prison Governor grades, responsible to the Home Office for monitoring the performance of the contractor companies and their escort PCO's. Any complaint made against a PCO will be investigated by the Escort Monitor. A complaint may be made by a prisoner, or by any other person, such as a solicitor. In serious cases, a Monitor may have a PCO suspended from duty pending the investigation of a complaint. However, unlike a prison controller, an escort monitor has no disciplinary responsibility for prisoners.

Complaints Against Prisoner Custody Officers

Disciplinary Procedures

2.19 There are no formal disciplinary procedures which apply to PCO's as there are for police and prison officers. A PCO may be dealt with by his/her employers for breaches of discipline in accordance with company procedures. In the case of serious allegations, an escort PCO may be suspended from office by the Escort Monitor.

Complaints Received by Police Officers

2.20 Any complaint made to police against a PCO should be passed on to the Escort Monitor or to a manager of the contractors, in accordance with any force procedures there may be in this regard.

Wrongful disclosure of information

Offence

2.21 A person will commit an offence who:
- is employed or has been employed in pursuance of prisoner escort arrangements or at a contracted out prison
- whether as a PCO or otherwise

- who discloses any information acquired in the course of her employment and relating to a particular prisoner
- otherwise than in the course of duty or as authorised by the Home Secretary.

Explanation

'Is or has been employed': The ban on revealing information goes on without time limit, after a person has ceased to be employed in the contracted out sector.

'PCO or otherwise': The offence may be committed by any person employed in connection with prisoner escorts or in contracted out prisons. This would include clerical, catering and medical staff, etc, as well as PCO's.

'Course of employment ... particular prisoner': Information gained other than in the course of employment, e.g. by reading a newspaper, is not subject to this restriction. For the offence to be committed, the details disclosed would have to relate to a prisoner; details of e.g. working practices or relating to another employee would not give rise to an offence.

Court Security Officers

Legal Status

2.22 A committee for a petty sessions area (or in some cases, the local authority) may appoint court security officers for courts in that area.

Powers and Duties

Duties

2.23 The duties of a court security officer are:
   i) to maintain order at the court house to which he is for the time being assigned;
   ii) to carry out any instructions of a magistrate or magistrates' clerk at the court-house. (This includes instructions from any person on the clerk's staff, authorised in this respect by the clerk.)

Powers

2.24 A court security officer when acting in the execution of his duty, has the following powers:
   i) search any person who is in or who is seeking to enter the court house, and search any article in such person's possession;
   ii) exclude or remove from the court-house any person who refuses to permit such a search;
   iii) exclude or remove from the court-house any person who refuses to surrender any article in his possession which the officer reasonably believes may jeopardise the maintenance of order in the court-house;
   iv) exclude or remove any person from the court-house, or restrain a person in the court-house, when it is reasonably necessary to do so in order to:
       - maintain order therein
       - enable court business to be carried out without interference or delay
       - secure his own or some other person's safety.

Use of Force

2.25 In carrying out these duties and in exercise of the powers, a court security officer may use reasonable force where necessary.

Explanation

'**Execution of duty'**: A court security officer will not be regarded as acting in the execution of his duty unless he is readily identifiable as a court security officer, whether by means of wearing a uniform, badge, or otherwise.

'**Search'**: Power to search does not authorise the officer to require removal of clothing, other than an outer coat, jacket or gloves.

'**Prisoner custody officers'**: The role of a court security officer is to maintain order; that of a PCO is to prevent escapes and look after prisoners. The two roles are distinct and should not be confused.

Protection of Court Security Officers

Assault

2.26 A person commits an offence who assaults a court security officer acting in the execution of his duties.

Obstruction

2.27 A person commits an offence who resists or wilfully obstructs a court security officer acting in the execution of his duties.

Pursuance of Duties

2.28 A court security officer engaged on escort duties shall not be regarded as 'in the execution of those duties' unless he is readily identifiable as such, by means of uniform, badge or otherwise.

PERJURY

3.1 *Offence*
Perjury Act 1911 Section 1

(1) If any person lawfully sworn as a witness or as an interpreter in a judicial proceeding wilfully makes a statement material in that proceeding, which he knows to be false or does not believe to be true, he shall be guilty of perjury.

(2) The expression 'judicial proceedings' includes a proceeding before any court, tribunal or other person having by law power to hear, receive, and examine evidence on oath.

(3) Where a statement made for the purposes of a judicial proceeding is not made before the tribunal itself, but is made on oath before a person authorised by law to administer an oath to the person who makes the statement, and to record or authenticate the statement it shall, for the purpose of this Section, be treated as having been made in a judicial proceeding.

(4) A statement made by a person lawfully sworn in England for the purposes of a judicial proceeding:
   a) in another of Her Majesty's dominions; or
   b) in a British tribunal lawfully constituted in any place by sea or land outside her Majesty's dominions ; or

c) in a tribunal of any foreign state,

shall for the purposes of this Section, be treated as a statement made in a judicial proceeding in England.

(5) Where, for the purposes of a judicial proceeding in England, a person is lawfully sworn under the authority of an Act of Parliament:

a) in any other part of Her Majesty's dominions; or,

b) before British tribunal or a British officer in a foreign country, or within the jurisdiction of the Admiralty of England;

a statement made by such a person so sworn as aforesaid (unless the Act of Parliament under which it was made otherwise specifically provides) shall be treated for the purposes of this Section as having need made in the judicial proceeding in England for the purposes whereof it was made.

(6) The question whether a statement on which perjury is assigned was material is a question of law to be determined by the court of trial.

3.2 *Explanation*

Lawfully sworn: The offence is committed only in respect of 'sworn' evidence, however the oath may have been administered. For these purposes, a witness who has not taken an oath, e.g because he has no religious belief, but has instead affirmed, will be regarded as being on oath.

Wifully: The statement must be made deliberately, not by mistake.

Does not believe: To be guilty, the witness must know that what he is saying is false, or at least believe that it is not true.

Material: The statement must be 'material' , i.e. relevant, of significance.

Judicial proceedings: The offence of perjury is not confined to a court of law. There are other venues where evidence may be given on oath.

3.3 Unsworn Evidence of a Child
Perjury Act 1911 Section 1(a)

If any person, in giving testimony (either orally or in writing) otherwise than on oath, where required to do so by an order under Section 2 of the Evidence (Proceedings in Other Jurisdictions) Act 1975, makes a statement:

a) which he knows to be false in a material particular; or,

b) which is false in a material particular and which he does not believe to be true,

he shall be guilty of an offence and shall be liable on conviction on indictment to a term not exceeding two years and a fine or both.

3.4 Subornation of Perjury
Perjury Act 1911 Section 7

The Perjury Act 1911 contains a number of other provisions making it a serious offence to knowingly give false information on oath for the purposes of registering births, deaths, marriages and the registering of any false certificate or information relating to such a certificate which relates to a profession or calling (Section 6 Perjury Act 1911). Perhaps the widest of the offences is that of aiding or abetting.

(1) Every person who aids, abets, counsels, procures or suborns another person to commit an offence against this Act shall be liable to be proceeded against, indicted, tried and punished as if he were the principal offender.

(2) Every person who incites another person to commit an offence against this Act shall be guilty of an offence.

3.5 There is a requirement for corroboration (Section 13 Perjury Act 1911) to prove any offence under the Perjury Act. This can be by two witnesses, or by a witness and other supporting evidence.

ASSISTING OFFENDERS

Perverting The Course Of Justice

4.1 This common law offence is triable only on indictment – which gives an indication of how seriously is regarded any attempt to interfere with the course of justice. The elements of the offence are:
- a course of justice has been embarked on;
- the defendant is shown then to have intentionally interfered with the administration of justice in that case;
- in an effort to prevent it from taking its natural course to its normal conclusion.

Examples include:
  i) a motorist drank beer after telling his mother to obstruct and delay police, so that he might evade breath test procedures (*R v Britton* (1973)).
  ii) use of improper means in an attempt to persuade witnesses from giving evidence (*R v Thomas and Ferguson* (1979)).
  iii) assisting someone wanted by police to evade arrest. However, there is a substantive offence of assisting an offender *(see below)*.

If the only basis of the prosecution case amounts to perjury or providing false information, then attempting to pervert the course of justice should not be charged (*Tsang Ping-nam v R* (1982)). Attempting to pervert the course of justice is a substantive offence; it would be wrong to charge as an offence under the Criminal Attempts Act 1981 (*R v Williams* (1991)).

Assisting Offenders

4.2 *Criminal Law Act 1967 Section 4*

(1) Where a person has committed an arrestable offence, any other person who, knowing or believing him to be guilty of the offence, or some other arrestable offence, does without lawful authority or reasonable excuse any act with intent to impede his apprehension or prosecution shall be guilty of an offence.

(1a) In this Section and Section 5 below 'arrestable offence' has the meaning assigned to it by Section 24 of the Police and Criminal Evidence Act 1984.

4.3 If an offender is found not guilty of committing the original offence indicted, he may be convicted of this offence. This means that a person charged with a co-defendant for an offence of theft could be convicted under Section 1 if cleared of involvement in the actual crime, if it could be shown that he did something to impede the prosecution of the other offender. No action can be taken by way of prosecution for an offence under Section 1 without the consent of the Director of Public Prosecutions (Section 4(1) Criminal Law Act 1967). There is a complex scale of possible punishments which rely upon the original offence and its punishment. If the original offence is liable to a fixed term of imprisonment, the maximum imprisonment for this offence is ten years; if the maximum for the original offence is fourteen years then this offence carries seven years imprisonment; if it is an offence for which the original offender is liable to ten years imprisonment then this offence carries a term of five years; in any other case the offence carries a maximum sentence of three years. There is no need to prove that the offender knew the identity of the person he was assisting (*R v Brindley, R v Long* [1971]). This offence will be triable either-way if the original offender's offence was triable either-way.

Concealing or Giving False Information
4.4 *Criminal Law Act 1967 Section 5*

(1) Where a person has committed an arrestable offence, any other person who, knowing or believing that the offence or some other arrestable offence has been committed, and that he has information which might be of material assistance in securing the prosecution or conviction of an offender for it, accepts or agrees to accept for not disclosing that information any consideration other than the making good of the loss or injury, shall be liable on conviction on indictment to imprisonment for two years.

(2) Where a person causes any wasteful employment of the police by knowingly making to any person a false report tending to show that an offence has been committed, or to give rise to apprehension for the safety of any persons or property, or tending to show that he has information material to any police enquiry, he shall be liable on summary conviction to imprisonment for not more than six months, or to a fine of not more than level four on the standard scale or both.

(3) No proceedings shall be instituted for an offence under this Section except by or with the consent of the Director of Public Prosecution.

Explanation
Concealing information: There are two distinct offences, one of concealing information, the other of wasting police time. The essential feature of the first of these is that a person accepts or agrees to accept some consideration, in return for not disclosing information about an arrestable offence. An exception will be where the consideration amounts to making good of loss or injury suffered as a result of the arrestable offence in question. If a householder catches a youth damaging his fence, he will not commit this offence if he accepts money from the youth's father, just sufficient to cover the cost of repairs to the fence. However, if Green knows that his colleague, Brown, has been stealing from their employer, he will be liable if he accepts something of value from Brown, in return for saying nothing about the theft.

Wasting police time: To commit this offence, a person must cause wasteful employment of police resources by knowingly making a false report to any person. A person who hears a car back-firing and calls the police to say that a shot has been fired will not commit the offence because he has not knowingly made a false report. The false report need not be made to the police directly, it will suffice that it is made to some other person, who may then be the one who contacts the police.

There are three categories of false report which may give rise to the offence:

i) to show that an offence has been committed, e.g., the person who falsely reports his car stolen, after being himself involved in a non-stop accident;

ii) so as to give rise to fears for the safety of any person or property; an example may be a man who reports his wife missing from home, when in fact he knows that she has gone off with her boyfriend. A hoax bomb call would fall into this category, but such an offence carries a far heavier maximum penalty, so it is unlikely in practice, that such an instance would be prosecuted as wasting police time.

iii) tending to show that one has information material to a police enquiry, e.g. calling the police falsely to report a sighting of a missing person, or claiming to know who has committed a particular crime.

Limitation on prosecution: For both these offences, the consent of the Director of Public Prosecutions is required before proceedings may be instituted. In practical terms, for the offence of wasting police time, there needs to be proof of the amount of time wasted, and there is a limit on the number of hours wasted, below which a prosecution will not be authorised.

Chapter 30: Aliens

1.1 The rights of people to freely move from one country to another are as a matter of necessity controlled. If there were no controls certain countries with welfare rights, social services and other state benefits would be swamped by those who have none. These essential services and the host countries would not be able to cope.

1.2 Legislation separates those who are visitors, with visitation rights, those who are visitors with working rights and those who have a right of abode. Each of these classes of person is clearly defined by the Immigration Act 1971. Section 1 of the Act sets out the intention of the legislation which is to allow those who have a right of abode to be free to come and go without hindrance. Those not having that right may enter, live and work by permission under the Act and be regulated by conditions as to their stay and requirement to leave.

THE RIGHT OF ABODE

2.1 *Immigration Act 1971 Section 2 (as substituted by the Section 39 of the British Nationality Act 1981 and Section 3 of the Immigration Act 1988)*

(1) A person is under this Act to have the right of abode in the United Kingdom if:
   a) he is a British citizen; or,
   b) he is a Commonwealth citizen who:
      i) immediately before the commencement of the British Nationality Act 1981 was a Commonwealth citizen having a right of abode in the United Kingdom by virtue of Section 2(1)(d) or Section 2(2) of this Act as then in force; and,
      ii) has not ceased to be a Commonwealth citizen in the meanwhile.

(2) In relation to Commonwealth citizens who have the right of abode in the United Kingdom by virtue of subsection 1(b) above; this Act, except this Section and Section 5(2) shall apply as if they were British Citizens, and in this Act (except as just mentioned) 'British citizens' shall be construed accordingly.

Explanation

On the basis of Section 2(2)(b) above, Commonwealth citizens to whom this subsection applies to will be treated as if they are British citizens. Persons who are connected with the British Isles for various reasons are automatically British citizens. The British Nationality Act 1981 redefined rights of abode (now as above) giving three distinct types of citizenship:

   a) British citizenship's for people closely connected with the United Kingdom, the Channel Islands and the Isle of Man.
   b) British Dependent Territories citizenship for people connected with dependencies.
   c) British Overseas citizenship's for those citizens of the United Kingdom and Colonies who do not acquire either of the other citizenship's at commencement.

REGULATION AND CONTROL OF ALIENS

3.1 Everyone who does not have British citizenship is subject of control and regulation as to their ability to enter the United Kingdom. The 1971 Immigration Act has now been amended to include changes made by the British Nationality Act 1981 and the Immigration Act 1988.

Immigration Act 1971 Section 3 (as amended by Section 39 and Schedule 4 of the British Nationality Act 1981, Section 3 and Schedule to the Immigration Act 1988)

(1) Except as otherwise provided by or under this Act, where a person is not a British citizen:
  a) he shall not enter the United Kingdom unless given leave to do so in accordance with this Act;
  b) he may be given leave to enter the United Kingdom (or, when already there, leave to remain in the United Kingdom) either for a limited or for an indefinite period;
  c) if given a limited leave to enter or remain in the United Kingdom, it may be given subject to conditions restricting his employment or occupation in the United Kingdom, or requiring him to register with the police or both.

(2) The Secretary of State may lay before Parliament rules laid down by him as to the practice to be followed for regulating entry and stay in the United Kingdom.

(3) In the case of a limited leave to enter or remain in the United Kingdom:
  a) a person's leave may be varied, whether by restricting, enlarging or removing the limits on its duration, or by adding varying, or revoking conditions, but if the limit on its duration is removed, any conditions attached to the leave shall cease to apply; and,
  b) the limitation on and any conditions attached to a person's leave (whether imposed originally or on a variation) shall, if not superseded, apply also to any subsequent leave he may obtain after an absence from the United Kingdom within the period limited for the duration of the earlier leave.

(4) A person's leave to enter or remain in the United Kingdom shall lapse on his going to a country or territory outside the common travel area (whether or not he lands there), unless within the period for which he had the leave he returns to the United Kingdom in circumstances in which he is not required to obtain leave to enter; but, if he does so return, his previous leave (and any limitation on it, or conditions attached to it) shall continue to apply.

(5) A person who is not a British citizen shall be liable to deportation from the United Kingdom:
  a) if, having only limited leave to enter or remain, he does not observe a condition attached to the leave or remains beyond the time limited by the leave; or,
  b) if the Secretary of State deems his deportation to be conducive to the public good; or
  c) if another person to whose family he belongs is or has been ordered to be deported.

(6) Without prejudice to the operation of subsection (5) above, a person who is not a British citizen shall be liable to deportation from the United Kingdom if, after he has attained the age of seventeen, he is convicted of an offence for which he is punished with imprisonment and on his conviction is recommended for deportation by a court empowered by this Act to do so.

(7) Where it appears to Her Majesty proper to do so by reason of restrictions or conditions imposed on British citizens, British Dependant Territories citizens or British Overseas citizens when leaving or seeking to leave any country or the territory subject to government by any country, Her Majesty may by Order in Council make provision for prohibiting persons who are nationals or citizens of that country and are not British citizens from embarking in the United Kingdom, or from doing so elsewhere than at a port of exit, or for imposing restrictions or conditions on them when embarking or about to embark in the United Kingdom; and Her Majesty may also make provisions by Order in Council to enable those who are not British citizens, to be, in such cases as may be prescribed by the Order, prohibited in the interests of safety from embarking on a ship or aircraft specified or indicated in the prohibition.

(8) When any question arises under this Act whether or not a person is a British citizen, or is entitled to any exemption under this Act, it shall lie on the person asserting it to prove that he is.

(9) A person seeking to enter the United Kingdom and claiming to have a right of abode there shall prove that right by means of either:
   a) a United Kingdom passport describing him as a British citizen, or as a citizen of the United Kingdom and Colonies having the right of abode in the United Kingdom; or,
   b) a certificate of entitlement issued by or on behalf of the Government of the United Kingdom certifying that he has such a right of abode.

3.2 For obvious reasons persons temporarily arriving with no intention of staying in the United Kingdom, such as aircrews and sailors who will be leaving within seven days are exempt from requiring permission to embark. This is subject to the stringent provision that they are neither subject of a deportation order nor have been refused leave to enter the United Kingdom. Such persons may be required to undergo examination at the request of an immigration officer.

3.3 Persons entering the United Kingdom other than from areas within the common travel area must obtain leave to enter. Ships and aeroplanes bringing in passengers may do so only at approved locations where the passengers and crew will be subject of immigration control.

3.4 Where a person enters the United Kingdom under limited leave, restrictive conditions can be placed upon him. Conditions can include the length of stay, requirement to register with the police, not to undertake employment. Immigration officers may also require the person to report to the Medical Officer of Health for a medical examination.

3.5 The 'common travel area' is defined (Section 1(3) Immigration Act 1971 as amended) as being the United Kingdom, Channel Islands, the Isle of Man and the Irish Republic. As a general rule persons arriving from the European Economic Community States are allowed leave to enter and remain usually for up to six months without employment restrictions, upon presentation of their relevant and valid identification papers.

3.6 The powers to grant leave to enter are given to immigration officers, as are powers of detention and examination of suspected illegal immigrants (Section 4(1) and 4(2) Immigration Act 1971 as amended). The Secretary of State has authority to make regulations regarding the registration of persons given leave to enter the United Kingdom.

Immigration Act 1971 Section 4

(3) The Secretary of State may by regulations made by statutory instrument, which shall be subject of annulment in pursuance of a resolution in either House of Parliament, make provision as to the effect of a condition under this Act requiring a person to register with the police; and the regulations may include provision:

  a) as to officers of police by whom registers are to be maintained, and as to the form and content of the registers;

  b) as to the place and manner in which anyone is to register and as to the documents and information to be furnished by him, whether on registration or on any change of circumstances;

  c) as to the issue of certificates of registration and as to the payment of fees for certificates of registration.

The regulations may require anyone who is for the time being subject to such a condition to produce a certificate of registration to such persons and in such circumstances as may be prescribed by the regulations.

3.7 The administration and control of persons having been granted leave to enter the United Kingdom is quite complex. Persons entering the United Kingdom via the 'common travel area' will be expected to have had their passports stamped with the port of entry and any relevant restrictions as to the stay noted. Part of the restrictions may be a requirement to register with the police in the area where they intend to stay.

Regulation 5 Immigration (Registration with Police) Regulations 1972

(1) An alien shall attend at the office of the appropriate registration officer and furnish that officer such information, documents and other particulars (including a recent photograph) relating to him as are required by that officer for the purposes of the local register kept by him or for the issue of a certificate of registration to the alien.

(2) Without prejudice to the generality of paragraph (1) an alien attending as aforesaid shall either:

  a) produce to the appropriate registration officer a passport furnished with a photograph of himself or some other documents satisfactorily establishing his identity and nationality; or,

  b) give to that officer a satisfactory explanation of the circumstances which prevent him from producing such a passport or document.

3.8 Having registered as required the person must report any change of address within seven days, other changes in circumstances must be reported within eight days. An alien for the purposes of this legislation is a person who is not a Commonwealth citizen, a British citizen or a citizen of the Republic of Ireland. Having registered with the local police an alien may be required to produce his certificate of registration to any constable or immigration officer.

Regulation 11 Immigration (Registration with Police) Regulations 1972

(1) On the making of any alteration or addition to the local register, the registration officer may require the alien concerned to produce his certificate of registration in order that any necessary amendment may be made thereto.

(2) Any immigration officer or constable may:

  a) require an alien to whom these regulation apply, forthwith, to either produce a certificate of registration or to give to the officer or constable a satisfactory reason for his failure to produce it;

b) where the alien fails to produce a certificate of registration in pursuance of such a requirement (whether or not he gives a satisfactory reason for his failure), require him, within the following 48 hours, to produce a certificate of registration at a police station specified by the officer or constable,

so however, that a requirement under sub-paragraph (b) to produce a certificate of registration at a police station shall have effect in substitution for the requirement under sub-paragraph (a) so as to cause that previous requirement to cease to have effect.

3.9 Failure to produce the certificate or comply with any regulation made under the provisions of Section 4(3) of the Immigration Act 1971 is an offence (Section 26(1)(f) Immigration Act 1971 as amended). Persons who enter the United Kingdom illegally commit offences as do those who aid and assist them.

CRIMINAL OFFENCES IN RELATION TO ILLEGAL ALIENS

4.1 A person who illegally enters the United Kingdom commits an offence. The power of arrest mentioned in Section 24 (below) is one of the preserved powers under Section 26 of the Police and Criminal Evidence Act 1984.

Immigration Act 1971 Section 24

(1) A person who is not a British citizen shall be guilty of an offence punishable on summary conviction with a fine of not more than level 4 on the standard scale, or with imprisonment for not more than six months, or both, in any of the following cases:

a) if contrary to the Act he knowingly enters the United Kingdom in breach of a deportation order without leave;

b) if, having only a limited leave to enter or remain in the United Kingdom, he knowingly either:

i) remains beyond the time limited by the leave; or,

ii) fails to observe a condition of the leave;

c) if, having lawfully entered the United Kingdom without leave he remains without leave beyond the time allowed;

d) if, without reasonable excuse, he fails to observe any restriction imposed upon him under Schedule 2 of this Act to report to a Medical Officer of Health, or to attend, or submit to a test or examination, as required by such an officer;

e) if, without reasonable excuse he fails to observe any restriction placed upon him under Schedule 2 or 3 to this Act as to residence, as to his employment or occupation or as to reporting to the police or to an immigration officer;

f) if he disembarks in the United Kingdom from a ship or aircraft after being placed on board under Schedule 2 or 3 to this Act with a view to his removal from the United Kingdom;

g) if he embarks in contravention of a restriction imposed by or under an Order in Council.

(1A) A person commits an offence under subsection (1)(b)(i) above on the day when he first knows that the time limited by his leave has expired and continues to commit it throughout any period during which he is in the United Kingdom thereafter; but a person shall not be prosecuted under that provision more than once in respect of the same time limited leave.

(2) A constable or immigration officer may arrest without warrant anyone who has, or whom he, with reasonable cause, suspects to have, committed or attempted to commit an offence under this Section other than an offence under subsection (1)(d) above.

(3) The extended time limit for prosecutions which is provided for by Section 28 below shall apply to offences under subsection (1)(a) and (c) above.

(4) In proceedings for an offence against subsection (1)(a) above of entering the United Kingdom without leave:

a) any stamp purporting to have been imprinted on a passport or other travel document by an immigration officer on a particular date for the purposes of giving leave shall be presumed to have been duly so imprinted, unless the contrary is proved;

b) proof that a person had leave to enter the United Kingdom shall lie on the defence if, but only if, he is shown to have entered within six months before the date when the proceedings were commenced.

4.2 Assisting the entry of or harbouring illegal entrants is an offence.

Immigration Act 1971 Section 25

(1) Any person knowingly concerned in making or carrying out arrangements for securing or facilitating the entry into the United Kingdom of anyone whom he knows or has reasonable cause for believing to be an illegal entrant shall be guilty of an offence, punishable on summary conviction with a fine of not more than the statutory maximum or with imprisonment for not more than six months, or with both, or on conviction on indictment with a fine or with imprisonment for not more than seven years, or with both.

(2) Without prejudice to subsection (1) above, a person knowingly harbouring anyone whom he knows or has reasonable cause for believing to be either an illegal entrant or a person who has committed an offence under Section 24(1)(b) or (c) above, shall be guilty of an offence, punishable on summary conviction with a fine of not more than level five on the standard scale, or with imprisonment for not more than six months, or with both.

(3) An immigration officer may arrest without warrant anyone who has, or whom he , with reasonable cause, suspects to have, committed an offence under subsection (1) above.

(4) The extended time limit for prosecutions which is provided for by Section 28 below shall apply to offences under this Section.

(5) Subsection (1) above shall apply to things done outside as well as to things done in the United Kingdom where they are done:

a) by a British citizen, a British Dependant Territories citizen, or a British Overseas citizen;

b) by a person who under the British nationality Act 1981 is a British subject; or

c) by a British protected person (within the meaning of that Act)

4.3 Where a person is convicted of an offence under Section 25 of the Immigration Act 1971 the court has powers to make orders of forfeiture (Section 25(6) – (8) Immigration Act 1971 as amended) on any transportation methods used to convey illegal entrants, and can order ships, vessels, etc, to be forfeited. There is no break when committing the offence of making or assisting an illegal entry then harbouring, the offence is a continuing one. Harbouring means giving shelter. A husband may be guilty of harbouring his wife (*R v Mistry* [1980]). The offence of assisting in the entry of an illegal entrant is arrestable by virtue of the sentence, whereas harbouring is only a summary offence. Failure to comply with the provisions of regulations made with regard to immigration will also give liability to offences.

Immigration Act 1971 Section 26

(1) A person shall be guilty of an offence punishable on summary conviction with a fine of not more than level four on the standard scale or with imprisonment for not more than six months, or with both in any of the following cases:

a) if, without reasonable excuse, he refuse or fails to submit to examination under Schedule 2 of this Act;

b) if, without reasonable excuse, he refuses or fails to furnish or produce any information in his possession or control, which he is on examination under that Schedule required to furnish or produce;

c) if on any such examination or otherwise he makes or causes to be made to an immigration officer or other person lawfully acting in the execution of this Act a return, statement or representation which he knows to be false or does not believe to be true;

d) if without lawful authority, he alters any certificate of entitlement, entry clearance, work permit or other document issued or made under or for the purposes of this Act, or uses for the purposes of this Act, or has in his possession for such use, any passport, certificate of entitlement, entry clearance, work permit or other document which he knows or has reasonable cause to believe to be false;

e) if, without reasonable excuse he fails to complete and produce a landing or embarkation card in accordance with any order under Schedule 2 to this Act;

f) if, without reasonable excuse, he fails to comply with any requirement of the regulations or of an order;

g) if, without reasonable excuse, he obstructs an immigration officer or other person lawfully acting in the execution of this Act.

(2) The extended time limit for prosecutions which is provided for by Section 28 below shall apply to offences under subsection (1)(c) and (d) above.

4.4 For the purposes of Section 26 above reference to 'other person lawfully acting' under subsection (g) does not include a constable (*R v Gill* [1976]) investigating a suspected illegal entry.

4.5 Person controlling aircraft and ships can also be guilty of offences in relation to the embarkation and disembarkation of passengers.

Immigration Act 1971 Section 27 (as amended by Sections 38 and 46 of the Criminal Justice Act 1982, and SI 1990/2227)

A person shall be guilty of an offence punishable on summary conviction with a fine of not more than level four on the standard scale, or with imprisonment for not more than six months, or with both, in any of the following cases:

a) if, being the captain of a ship or aircraft:
   i) he knowingly permits a person to disembark in the United Kingdom when required under Schedule 2 or 3 to this Act to prevent it, or fails without reasonable excuse to take steps he is required by or under Schedule 2 to take in connection with the disembarkation or examination of passengers or for furnishing a passenger list or particulars of the crew; or,
   ii) he fails, without reasonable excuse, to comply with any direction given him under Schedule 2 or 3 with respect to the removal of a person from the United Kingdom;
b) if, as owner or agent of a ship or aircraft:
   i) he arranges, or is knowingly concerned in any arrangements for the ship or aircraft to call at a port other than a port of entry contrary to any provision or Schedule 2 to this Act;
   ii) he fails, without reasonable excuse, to take any steps required by an order under Schedule 2 for the supply to passengers of landing or embarkation cards; or,
   iii) he fails, without reasonable excuse, to make arrangements for the removal of a person from the United Kingdom when required to do so by directions given under Schedule 2 or 3 to this Act;
c) if, as owner or agent of a ship or aircraft or as a person concerned in the management of a port, he fails without reasonable excuse, to take any steps required by Schedule 2 in relation to the embarkation or disembarkation of passengers where a control area is designated;
d) if, as the Concessionaires:
   i) they fail without reasonable excuse, to make arrangements for the removal of a person from the United Kingdom when required to do so by directions given under Schedule 2 to this Act; or,
   ii) they fail, without reasonable excuse, to observe any condition or restrictions notified to them under Schedule 2 to this Act in relation to controlled areas.

Explanation

4.6: Only certain sea-ports and air-ports are designated for the landing of persons in this country. In order that proper control may be exercised by immigration authorities, the onus is placed on captains, owners and agents of ships and aircraft, to ensure that requirements laid down in the Act are complied with. Offences arise if, for example, a ship or aircraft calls at a port other than a port of entry, if a passenger list is not produced, if landing cards are not provided for passengers, etc.

4.7: Provision is made for proceedings for an offence under the Act to be commenced after the end of the usual six-month limitation on summary proceedings. Proceedings may be commenced within two months of the discovery of sufficient evidence to justify prosecution, subject to an over-riding limitation of three years from the date the offence was committed.

DEPORTATION

5.1 The rules about deportation are contained in Section 3(5) for illegal entrants, and those who overstay, and Section 3(6) for those who not being British citizens are over seventeen and are convicted of an offence punishable by imprisonment before a court competent to order their deportation.

Immigration Act 1971 Section 3

(5) A person who is not a British citizen shall be liable to deportation from the United Kingdom:

    a) if, having only limited leave to enter or remain, he does not observe a condition attached to the leave or remains beyond the time limited by the leave; or

    b) if the Secretary of State deems his deportation to be conducive to the public good; or

    c) if another person to whose family he belongs is or has been ordered to be deported.

(6) Without prejudice to the operation of subsection (5) above, a person who is not a British citizen shall be liable to deportation from the United Kingdom if, after he has attained the age of seventeen, he is convicted of an offence for which he is punished with imprisonment and on his conviction is recommended for deportation by a court empowered by this Act to do so.

5.2 There are many issues which can complicate immigration matters. Some persons may claim asylum, others may have complex family ties which make the claiming of rights to British citizenship difficult to comprehend. In all such cases the immigration authorities will be able to deal with the person concerned. In the event of the immigration authorities making requests for police officers to conduct enquires for them, these enquires should be conducted with tact and courtesy as quickly as is possible under the prevailing circumstances.

Chapter 31: Elections

VOTING

1.1 In many countries in the world which aspire to democracy, the right which lies at the very heart of representative democracy – that of a free vote – is often denied the citizens, by use of force, destruction of ballot boxes, bribery, etc. In the United Kingdom, the procedures for running elections, including the holding of pre-election meetings, the amounts which candidates may spend, and the smooth, peaceful running of polling stations, are catered for by statute. The majority of the legislation is contained in the Representation of the People Acts 1983 and 1985.

1.2 Now that this country is part of the European Community, we have the opportunity to vote in elections for the European Parliament. These elections are further controlled by the provisions of the European Assemblies Elections Act 1987.

OFFENCES

2.1 Personation is an offence whereby a person pretends to be someone else so that he can then excercise that person's right to vote.

Representation of the People Act 1983 Section 60

(1) A person shall be guilty of a corrupt practice if he commits, or aids, abets, counsels, or procures the commission of, the offence of personation.

(2) A person shall be deemed to be guilty of personation at a parliamentary or local government election if he:
   a) votes in person or by post as some other person, whether as an elector or as proxy and whether that person is living or dead or is a fictitious person; or,
   b) votes in person or by post as proxy:
      i) for a person whom he knows or has reasonable grounds for supposing to be dead, or to be a fictitious person; or,
      i) when he knows or has reasonable grounds for supposing that his appointment as proxy is no longer in force.

(3) For the purpose of this Section, a person who has applied for a ballot paper for the purpose of voting in person, or who has marked, whether validly or not, and returned a ballot paper issued for the purpose of voting by post, shall be deemed to have voted.

2.2 To prove personation there is a need to prove identity which may cause problems as the only evidence is frequently a voting slip simply marked with an X. Evidence may be available from a witness who is able to identify someone as being a person who had attended earlier to vote as someone else. The offence of a person who has already had a postal vote voting again in person may be easier to prove. A proxy is where a person nominates someone else to take his vote for him, proxy votes are usually requested where the person wishing to vote will be unavailable for some reason and is unable to use a postal vote. Postal votes are available for people who cannot get to the polling station.

Representation of the People Act 1983 Section 61

(1) A person shall be guilty of an offence if:
  a) he votes in person or by post, whether as an elector or as a proxy , or applies to be treated as an absent voter or to vote by post as proxy, at a parliamentary or local government election, knowing that he or the other person to be appointed is subject to a legal incapacity to vote.
  b) he applies for the appointment of a proxy to vote for him at a parliamentary or local government election, knowing that he or the person to be appointed is subject of a legal incapacity to vote; or,
  c) he votes, whether in person or by post, or applies to vote by post, as proxy for some other person, at a parliamentary or local government election, knowing that that person is subject of a legal incapacity to vote.

For the purposes of this subsection references to a person being subject to a legal incapacity to vote do not, in relation to things done before polling day at the election or first election at or for which they are done, include his being below voting age if he will be voting age on that day.

(2) A person shall be guilty of an offence if:
  a) he votes as elector otherwise than by proxy either:
    i) more than once in the same constituency at any parliamentary election, or more than once in the same electoral area at any local government election; or,
    ii) in more than one constituency at a general election, or in more than one electoral area at an ordinary election of councillors for a local government area which is not a single electoral area; or,
    iii) in any constituency at a general election, or in any electoral area at such an ordinary election as mentioned above, when there is in force an appointment of a person to vote as his proxy at the election in some other constituency or electoral area; or,
  b) he votes as elector in person at a parliamentary or local government election at which he is entitled to vote by post; or,
  c) he votes as elector in person at a parliamentary or local government election knowing that the person appointed as his proxy at the election either has already voted in person at or is entitled to vote by post at the election; or,
  d) not being a service voter, he applies for a person to be appointed as his proxy to vote for him at parliamentary election without applying for the cancellation of a previous appointment of a third person then in force or without withdrawing a pending application for such an appointment.

(3) A person shall be guilty of an offence if:
  a) he votes as a proxy for the same elector either:
    i) more than once in the same constituency at any parliamentary election, or more than once in the same electoral area at any local government election; or,
    ii) in more than one constituency at a general election, or in more than one electoral area at an ordinary election of councillors for a local government area which is not a single electoral area; or,
  b) he votes in person as proxy for an elector at a parliamentary or local government election at which he is entitled to vote by post as proxy for that elector; or,
  c) he votes in person as a proxy for an elector registered as a service voter at a

parliamentary or local government election knowing that the elector is entitled to vote by post at the election; or,

(4) A person shall also be guilty of an offence if he votes at a parliamentary election in any constituency as proxy for more than two persons of whom he is not the husband, wife, parent, grandparent, brother, sister, child or grand-child.

(5) A person shall be guilty of an offence if he knowingly induces or procures some other person to do an act which is, or but for that other person's want of knowledge would be, an offence by that person under the foregoing subsections of this Section.

(6) For the purposes of this Section a person who has applied for a ballot paper for the purpose of voting in person, or who has marked, whether validly or not, and returned a ballot paper issued for the purpose of voting by post, shall be deemed to have voted, but for the purpose of determining whether an application for a ballot paper constitutes an offence under subsection (4) above, a previous application made in circumstances which entitle the applicant only to mark a tendered ballot paper shall, if he does not excercise that right, be disregarded.

(7) An offence under this Section shall be an illegal practice, but, a candidate shall not be liable, nor shall his election be avoided, for an illegal practice under this Section of any agent of his other than an offence under subsection (5) above.

2.3 The various combinations of voting more than once other than by proxy properly authorised are dealt with by Section 61. The legislation is complicated because of the need to make it possible for everyone who is not disqualified from voting to vote. Similar rules apply to the voting process to the EEC.

European Assemblies Elections Act 1978 Section 4 (double voting)

(1) Without prejudice to any enactment relating to voting offences as applied by regulations under this Act to elections of representatives to the Assembly held in the United Kingdom, a person shall be guilty of an offence if, on any occasion when under Article 9 elections to the Assembly are held in all the member States, he votes otherwise than as a proxy more than once in those elections, whether in the United Kingdom or elsewhere.

(2) The provisions of the Representation of the People Act 1983 as applied by regulations under this Act shall have effect in relation to an offence under this Section as they have effect in relation to an offence under Section 61(2) of that Act (double voting); and without prejudice to the generality of the foregoing provision, Section 61(7) of that Act (which makes such an offence an illegal practice but allows any incapacity resulting from conviction to be mitigated by the convicting court) and Section 178 of that Act (prosecution for offences committed outside the United Kingdom) shall apply accordingly.

Explanation
2.4: There are a number of ways in which a person may be guilty of 'illegal practice', which are not gone into in detail here. Examples include tampering with nomination papers or ballot papers, and breach of official duty. One illegal practice – disorderly conduct at an election meeting – is considered below. Many are summary offences only; tampering with papers is triable either way, with a maximum sentence of two years' imprisonment. Thus, none of these are arrestable offences.

KEEPING THE PEACE DURING ELECTIONS

Disorderly Conduct at an Election Meeting
Representation of the People Act 1983 Section 97

Offence
3.1.1 A person shall be guilty of an illegal practice if at a lawful public meeting to which this section applies, he acts or incites others to act, in a disorderly manner for the purpose of preventing the transaction of the business for which the meeting was called.

The section applies to a political meeting held in a constituency in the run up to a parliamentary election in the constituency, or to a meeting held in an electoral area in connection with a local government election in that area.

Police Action
3.1.2 If a constable reasonably suspects any person of committing this offence:
  - and if requested to do so by the chairman of the meeting
  - she may require that person immediately to declare to her his name and address.
  - if that person refuses or fails to declare his name and address, or gives false details, he commits a further offence.

There is no specific power to arrest for this offence, but the absence of correct details of name and address, does open up the prospect of an arrest under the general power to arrest provided by Section 25 of the Police and Criminal Evidence Act 1984.

Explanation
3.1.3 The wording of the offence and of the police powers are identical to those in Section 1 of the Public Meeting Act 1908. The 1908 Act covers any public meeting, whereas these provisions relate specifically to election meetings.

Keeping Order in Polling Stations
Representation of the People Act 1983 Schedule 1, paragraphs 32, 33

Presiding Officer's Powers and Duties
3.2.1 It is the presiding officer's duty to keep order in his polling station. He shall regulate the numbers of voters to be admitted at the same time and must exclude all other persons, except:
  - candidates and their agents
  - polling agents and clerks allocated to that polling station
  - companions of blind voters
  - constables on duty there.

Police Power and Duty
3.2.2 If a person misconducts himself in a polling station or fails to obey the presiding officer's lawful orders:
  - then by the presiding officer's order
  - he may immediately be removed from the polling station
  - by a constable in or near that station (or by any other person authorised in writing to do so by the returning officer).

A person so removed may not, without the permission of the presiding officer, enter the polling station again that day.

A person may, if so removed, if charged with the commission of an offence in the polling station, be dealt with as a person arrested without warrant for an offence.

These powers shall not be exercised so as to prevent a person from voting.

Explanation

Presiding/returning officer: There is one returning officer for each constituency in a Parliamentary election (or council area for a local government election). This person, who is usually the chief executive of the council for that area, is in charge of all the arrangements for the election. At each polling station there is a presiding officer, assisted by a clerk or clerks, responsible for running that polling station.

Constable on duty: The presiding officer shall not admit a constable to the polling station unless:
 – the constable is on duty there
 – or it is her own polling station (so she is allowed to vote)
 – or she has a certificate which allows her to vote there.

A constable may obtain a certificate if her duties preclude her from visiting her own polling station to vote. She may then surrender the certificate at another polling station, and vote there. The net effect is that a constable does not have a carte blanche power to enter polling stations.

Removal from polling station: A constable may act to remove a person, only on the order of the presiding officer. This would not preclude the constable exercising another power to arrest, e.g. for a public order offence. However, in such a case, it would be prudent to consider the proviso to the power to remove – that the power should not be used so as to prevent a person casting his vote.

Offence...arrest: When a person is removed from a polling station, proceedings for an offence in the polling station may or may not follow; the constable may, for example, release the person once he calms down, and the presiding officer may then allow him back in. However, if a charge does follow, the person may be treated as a person arrested for an offence. The practical effect of this is that, although a person being removed is not being arrested, he may subsequently be treated as an arrested person; in particular the provisions of the Police and Criminal Evidence Act 1984 and the Codes of Practice thereto, shall apply.

European elections: These provisions apply to elections for the European Parliament, as well as to UK elections.

Challenge of Voter
Representation of the People Act 1983 Schedule 1, paragraph 36

Challenge
3.3.1 If at the time a person applies for a ballot paper for the purpose of voting in person (or after he has applied for one and before he has left the polling station):
 – a candidate or his election or polling agent declares to the presiding officer that he has reasonable cause to believe that the person has committed an offence of personation, and
 – that he undertakes to substantiate this in court, the presiding officer may use the police powers that follow in paragraph **3.3.2**.

Police power

3.3.2 Subject to the conditions outlined in paragraph **3.3.1**, the presiding officer may:
- order a constable to arrest that person, and the presiding officer's order shall be sufficient authority for the constable to act.

However, a person against whom a declaration is made shall not be prevented from voting. A person so arrested shall be treated as a person arrested without warrant for an offence. In particular, the provisions of the Police and Criminal Evidence Act 1984 and the Codes of Practice thereto, shall apply.

Explanation

Personation: This offence involves voting, or applying for a ballot paper, as someone else. These provision will apply when a person asks for a ballot paper, and one of the candidates in that election, or a candidate's agent, claims to the presiding officer that the person is posing as someone else.

Left the polling station: Once the person has left the polling station, these provisions will cease to apply.

Prevent from voting: Even though a challenge is made, the person must be allowed to vote. Thus, a constable who carries out an order to arrest the person, must ensure that the person, although arrested, has the opportunity to vote.

European elections: These provisions apply to elections for the European Parliament, as well as to U.K. elections.

Chapter 32: The Police

INTRODUCTION

Control of Police Forces

1.1 Police forces in England and Wales are subject to a mix of local and central control; the former should make individual forces responsive to local needs, the latter is to provide central services, identify and disseminate best practice, and ensure efficiency. The chief officer (the commissioner in the Metropolitan and City of London areas, the chief constable elsewhere) is responsible to the police authority for the effective running of his or her police force. The police authority, composed of local councillors and other community representatives (the Home Secretary is the police authority for the Metropolitan Police Service), has to provide sufficient resources to enable the chief officer to run the force. The police authority obtains just under half the money from local authorities in the police force area.

Central control is exercised by means of inspections conducted by Her Majesty's Inspectors of Constabularies. Rather more than half the money required to run a police force comes from central government funds. In an extreme case, the government may withhold funding if, following an inspection, a force is considered not to be run efficiently.

Office of Constable

1.2 Members of police forces, of whatever rank, all hold the office of 'constable'. Although a police officer is subject to the direction and control of officers of higher rank, he is not an employee. As an office holder, he is responsible for exercise of his powers. When various aspects of law, applicable to employees, are to be applicable to constables, special provision has to be made. For example, the Police Act 1996 provides that a chief officer is liable for the wrong-doing of officers in her force, as an employer is responsible for those of his employees. (see paragraph 7) Further control on an individual constable's exercise of his powers is provided by a detailed discipline code and a comprehensive procedure for the investigation of complaints from members of the public.

COMPLAINTS AGAINST THE POLICE

2.1 Where a complaint is received about a police officer, the first and overriding requirement is the preservation of evidence. The chief officer of police for the area in which the complaint is made has a responsibility to ensure that any steps that appear desirable for the purpose of obtaining or preserving evidence are taken. Once this has been done the chief officer must determine if he is the appropriate authority to deal with the complaint. If not, he must send the complaint to the appropriate authority to deal with it, and he must notify the person by whom or on whose behalf the complaint was made that he has done this. The 'appropriate authority' is the chief officer (ie, the chief constable or commissioner). However, if the officer complained of is above the rank of superintendent, the police authority is the appropriate authority.

2.2 The standard complaints procedure for recording and investigation of matters not to be referred to the Police Complaints Authority is set out in Section 69 of the Police Act 1996:

Police Act 1996 Section 69

(1) If a chief officer of police determines that he is the appropriate authority in relation to a member of a police force:
   a) whose conduct is the subject of a complaint, and
   b) who is not a senior officer (above the rank of superintendent),
   he shall record the complaint.

(2) After recording a complaint under subsection (1), the chief officer of police shall consider whether the complaint is suitable for informal resolution and may appoint a member of his force to assist him.

(3) A complaint is not suitable for informal resolution unless:
   a) the member of the public concerned gives his consent, and
   b) the chief officer of police is satisfied that the conduct complained of, even if proved, would not justify criminal or disciplinary proceedings.

(4) If it appears to the chief officer of police that the complaint is suitable for informal resolution, he shall seek to resolve it informally and may appoint a member of his force to do so on his behalf.

(5) If it appears to the chief officer of police that the complaint is not suitable for informal resolution, he shall appoint a member of his own or some other force to investigate it formally.

(6) If, after attempts have been made to resolve a complaint informally, it appears to the chief officer of police:
   a) that informal resolution of the complaint is impossible, or
   b) that the complaint is for some other reason not suitable for informal resolution,
   he shall appoint a member of his own or some other force to investigate it formally.

(7) A member of a police force may not be appointed to investigate a complaint formally if he has previously been appointed to act in relation to it under subsection (4).

(8) If a chief officer of police requests the chief officer of police of some other force to provide a member of that force for appointment under subsection (5) or (6), that chief officer shall comply with the request.

(9) Unless the investigation is supervised by the Authority under Section 72, the investigating officer shall submit his report on it to the chief officer of police who appointed him.

Explanation

It is the duty of the police authority in the case of a senior officer, or the chief officer otherwise, to record the complaint and to cause it to be investigated. If satisfied that even if proven the complaint would not warrant discipline or criminal proceedings then the police authority or chief officer have discretion to deal with it appropriately (Section 68(2) Police Act 1996). This option includes the informal disposal of complaints. In any other case, the appropriate authority must appoint someone to investigate the complaint, in which case that person should not be of a lower rank than that of the person subject of the complaint. Unless the enquiry is one requiring the supervision of the Police Complaints Authority, the investigating officer will report to his chief officer (Section 68(6) Police Act 1996).

2.3 There is an important distinction to be drawn between force internal discipline procedure and the requirement of legislation. In many cases force policy will mirror the requirements of the Act. Occasionally however there may be minor differences where additional requirements are made before informal resolution can take place. Throughout the Police Act 1996 reference to 'appropriate authority' means chief officer of police or police authority, and 'Authority' means the Police Complaints Authority. This is a little confusing in Section 70 where the requirement is for mandatory referral of some complaints.

Police Act 1996 Section 70

(1) The appropriate authority:
   a) shall refer to the Authority:
      i) any complaint alleging that the conduct complained of resulted in the death of, or serious injury to, some other person, and
      ii) any complaint of a description specified for the purposes of this Section in regulations made by the Secretary of State, and
   b) may refer to the Authority any complaint which is not required to be referred to them.

(2) The Authority may require the submission to them for consideration of any complaint not referred to them by the appropriate authority; and the appropriate authority shall comply with any such requirement not later than the end of the period specified for the purposes of this subsection in regulations made by the Secretary of State.

(3) Where a complaint falls to be referred to the Authority under subsection (1)(a), the appropriate authority shall refer it to them not later than the end of the period specified for the purposes of this subsection (i) or, as the case may be, (ii) of that subsection in regulations made by the Secretary of State.

Explanation

2.4 The senior police officer making the initial investigation decision about a complaint may decide that due to the gravity of the matter complained of, or the exceptional circumstances of the incident complained of, that the investigation should be overseen or referred to the Police Complaints Authority. There need not be a formal complaint in relation the matter, the provision applies to situations where a member of a police force may have committed a disciplinary or criminal offence such as would justify disciplinary proceedings (Section 71 Police Act 1996). There are some matters where the Police Complaints Authority must supervise the investigation;

Police Act 1996 Section 72

(1) The Authority shall supervise the investigation of:
   a) any complaint alleging that the conduct of a member of a police force resulted in the death of, or serious injury to, some other person,
   b) any other description of complaint specified for the purposes of this Section in regulations made by the Secretary of State, and,
   c) any complaint which is not within paragraph (a) or (b), and any matter referred to the Authority under Section 71, if the Authority determine that it is desirable in the public interests that they should do so.

(2) Where the Authority have made a determination under Section 1(c), they shall notify it to the appropriate authority.

(3) Where an investigation is to be supervised by the Authority, they may require:

a) that no appointment is made under Section 68(3) or 69(5) unless they have given notice to the appropriate authority that they approve the person whom the authority propose to appoint, or

b) if such an appointment has already been made and the authority are not satisfied with the person appointed, that:

   i) the appropriate authority, as soon as is reasonably practicable, select another member of a police force and notify the Authority that it proposes to appoint him, and

   ii) the appointment is not made unless the Authority give notice to the appropriate authority that they approve that person.

Explanation

The Police Complaints Authority shall supervise investigations involving death or serious injury, any complaint falling within the scope of regulations made by the Home Secretary, and any other where the Authority considers that they should do so, in the public interest.

A chief officer may refer a matter to the PCA, where it is decided that there are exceptional circumstances, or the matter is considered grave. There need not be a compliant from the public, for a matter to be referred; it may be that it appears that a member of the force has committed a criminal or disciplinary offence, although no complaint has been received.

Where the PCA supervise an investigation, the chief officer may be required to appoint another investigating officer, even though one has already been appointed.

2.5 At the conclusion of the investigation a report must be submitted to the Police Complaints Authority who will review the investigation and make recommendations as to the outcome. Criminal proceedings cannot be instigated until the Authority have made an 'appropriate statement' about the conduct of the complaint investigation and their recommendations as to disposal of the matter investigated.

Informal Resolution of Complaints

2.6 The chief officer may if it appears to him that a complaint is suitable to be resolved informally, and that even if proven is unlikely to result in formal discipline or criminal proceedings, appoint an officer to informally resolve the matter. The person making the complaint must be consulted and must consent to informal resolution, and should be consulted about the appropriate method of resolving the complaint. It may be that all the complainant wanted was for suitable advice to be given to the officer. It may be that a training need is identified and that suitable arrangements for such training will resolve the complaint. Such matters would be communicated to the complainant.

2.7 If the complaint cannot be informally resolved, the investigating officer must report accordingly and a formal investigation must be conducted. The officer who was responsible for the attempted informal resolution must not be the investigating officer in the formal investigation. A complainant is entitled for a period of up to three months, should he or she apply, to a copy of the informal resolution.

2.8 Statements made by officers for the purpose of informal resolution of complaints cannot be later used for any subsequent, criminal, civil, or disciplinary proceedings unless the statement consists of or includes admissions to matters which do not fall within the scope of informal resolution (Section 86 Police Act 1996).

THE POLICE DISCIPLINE CODE

3.1 The police discipline code is set out in regulations made under the Police Act 1996. The code contains a list of discipline offences which may be committed by a constable acting in his capacity as such. It is anticipated that new discipline regulations will be made during 1998.

3.2 The punishments which may be imposed upon a police officer found guilty of a disciplinary offence are, in ascending order of severity:
- caution
- reprimand
- fine
- reduction in rate of pay for a period up to 12 months
- reduction in rank
- requirement to resign
- dismissal.

A chief constable may impose any of these punishments. However, his deputy may take a disciplinary hearing, in which case dismissal and requirement to resign are not available as possible punishments. In practice, if a case is thought to be serious enough to warrant either of these two punishments, in the event of the accused officer being found guilty, it will be heard by the chief constable. A chief constable may ask the chief officer of another force to hear a case where he has some interest in the case, or is a witness.

3.3 An officer convicted of a disciplinary matter before the deputy chief constable has a right of appeal to the chief constable. The chief constable under such circumstances cannot increase the penalty imposed by his deputy. Disciplinary proceedings against officers of chief constable or assistant chief constable rank are dealt with by the police authority and Secretary of State.

Offences Contained In The Discipline Code

Discreditable Conduct
3.4 May be committed by an officer who acts in a manner prejudicial to discipline or reasonably likely to bring discredit on the reputation of the force or service in general.

Explanation
It covers conduct on and off duty. It will mainly involve disorderly or similar behaviour.

Misconduct Towards Another Member of the Police Service
3.5 This offence covers circumstances of abusive or oppressive conduct and incidents of minor assault towards another member of the service.

Disobedience to Orders
3.6 Where an officer without good and sufficient cause:
  i) disobeys, or neglects to carry out any lawful order, written or otherwise,
  ii) fails to comply with a code of practice in force under Section 66 of the Police and Criminal Evidence Act 1984,
  iii) contravenes any provision of the Police Regulations containing restrictions on the private lives of police officers, or requiring notification of a business interest.

Explanation

The phrase 'good and sufficient cause' may allow for a constable to use some initiative, where for example, circumstances have changed since he was given an order. The offence may be committed, whether an order is written or verbal, and whether it is disregarded deliberately or by neglect. The PACE Codes of Practice are regarded as 'orders' for these purposes.

Neglect of Duty

3.7 Where an officer, without good and sufficient cause:
  i) neglects or omits to attend to or carry out with due promptitude and diligence anything which it is his duty as a member of a police force to attend to or carry out; or
  ii) fails to work his beat in accordance with orders, or leaves the place of duty to which he has been ordered, or having left his place of duty for an authorised purpose fails to return thereto without undue delay; or
  iii) is absent without leave from, or is late for, any duty; or
  iv) fails to properly account for, or to make a prompt and true return of, any money or property received by him in the course of duty.

Explanation

This offence covers a variety of acts and omissions. It may arise from simply neglecting to do something which, as part of his duties, the officer should have done. It may be serious, if what was neglected was very important. Turning up a few minutes late for duty may not warrant discipline proceedings, but going absent without leave for several weeks is a different matter. In a case where a constable fails to deal properly with money or other property, there may be theft or dishonesty involved. Even if there is no dishonest intent, merely neglect, this discipline offence will be committed.

Falsehood or Prevarication

3.8 Is committed by any member of a police force who:
  i) knowingly, or through neglect, makes any false, misleading or inaccurate oral or written statement or entry in any record or document made, kept or required to be kept for police purposes; or
  ii) either wilfully and without proper authority, or through lack of due care, destroys or mutilates any record or document made, kept or required for police purposes; or,
  iii) without good and sufficient cause alters, erases or adds to any entry in such a record or document; or
  iv) has knowingly, or through neglect, made any false, misleading or inaccurate statement in connection with his appointment to the police force.

Explanation

The phrase 'falsehood or prevarication' implies dishonesty or untruthfulness, which may well be involved, but the offence also covers such actions as carelessly throwing away a document which should have been kept, or putting inaccurate details in the found property register. The offence extends to giving inaccurate details relating to one's recruitment. This would provide a possible means of terminating the services of an officer who was accepted into the force on the basis of false details given at the time he joined the force.

Improper Disclosure of Information

3.9 Committed where a member of a police force:

i) without proper authority communicates to any person any information which he has in his possession as a member of a police force; or

ii) makes any anonymous communication to any police authority, or any member of a police force; or,

iii) without proper authority makes representation to the police authority or the council or district comprised in the police area with regard to any matter concerning the force; or,

iv) canvasses any member of that authority or of such council with regard to any such matter.

Explanation

The unauthorised disclosure of information may amount to a criminal offence, e.g., under the Data Protection Act, but will amount to a disciplinary offence whether the information has come from a computer or not. This offence may have serious consequences, e.g., where a criminal is informed of intended police action, or the name of an informant is passed. There is also an 'internal' element, covering the sending of anonymous letters to another member of the force, or to a member of the police authority, and making unauthorised representations to the police authority or to a local authority. Thus, letting the police authority have her views on the latest cut in the police budget, may land a constable in trouble.

Corrupt and Improper Practice

3.10 Is committed by a member of a police force who:

i) in his capacity as such, and without the consent of the chief officer of police or the police authority, directly or indirectly solicits or accepts any gratuity, present or subscription; or,

ii) places himself under a pecuniary obligation to any person in such a manner as might affect his properly carrying out his duties as a member of the force; or,

iii) improperly uses, or attempts to use, his position as a member of the force for his private advantage; or,

iv) in his capacity as a member of the force, and without the consent of the chief officer of police, writes, signs or gives a testimonial of character or other recommendation with the object of obtaining employment for any person or of supporting an application for the grant of a licence of any kind.

Explanation

The term 'corruption' implies bribery, and a disciplinary offence under this heading may well involve something as serious as taking money from criminals or others, in return for favours. The offence also covers accepting gifts, seeking advantage by reason of being a police officer, or getting into someone's debt in circumstances which may affect the performance of one's police duties.

For a company to offer 'special rates for police officers' is an acceptable marketing strategy, but for a constable to seek free admission to an event, or a special price for goods, on the basis of his being the local beat officer, is not acceptable. There is a significant difference between a constable buying a car on hire purchase and borrowing money from a local criminal. Police officers are frequently asked to provide a reference for an acquaintance or relative who is seeking a job; to do so in the capacity of a member of the force, is not permitted, other than with the consent of the chief officer.

Abuse of Authority

3.11 Is committed where a member of the police force treats anyone, with whom he comes into contact during the execution of his duties, in an oppressive manner, and in particular where he:

i) without good and sufficient cause conducts a search, or requires any person to submit to any test or procedure, or makes an arrest; or,

ii) uses any unnecessary violence towards any prisoner or other person with whom he may be brought into contact during the execution of his duty; or,

iii) is abusive or uncivil to any member of the public.

Explanation

Police officers have extensive powers, to stop persons and vehicles, to search people and places, and to arrest. In every case, there has to be reasonable grounds for exercising a power, otherwise this offence may be committed. Police officers do sometimes have to use violence, as illustrated by their carrying truncheons, gas canisters, or even guns. Any undue use of force is covered by these provisions. Members of the public may be uncivil towards police officers, but reciprication is not permitted.

Note that abuse of authority extends to dealings with fellow officers, as well as with members of the public.

Racially Discriminatory Behaviour

3.12 This offence is committed where a member of a police force:

i) while on duty, on the grounds of another person's colour, race, nationality, or ethnic or national origins, acts towards that other person in a way involving abuse of authority (as above); or

ii) in any other way, on any of those grounds, treats improperly a person with whom he may be brought into contact while on duty.

Explanation

This offence will include any behaviour motivated by a person's nationality, colour, etc, be it abuse of authority or any other action. The behaviour may be directed towards any person with whom the officer concerned comes in contact while on duty, including other police officers or members of civilian support staff, as well as persons in custody and members of the public.

Neglect of Health

3.13 Where a member of a force neglects, without good and sufficient cause, to carry out the instructions of a medical officer appointed by the police authority or, while absent from duty on account of sickness, commits any act or adopts any conduct calculated to retard his return to duty.

Explanation

This could include failing to take prescribed medicines, taking part in sports or activities which will possibly cause further injury or prevent recovery from the ailment which necessitates the original absence due to sickness.

Improper Dress or Untidiness

3.14 This offence is committed where without good and sufficient cause a member of a police force while on duty, or off duty in uniform in a public place, is improperly dressed or is untidy in appearance.

Explanation

This offence may be regarded as less serious than some of the others, since it does not involve deceitfulness, dishonesty, abusiveness or discriminatory behaviour. If an officer is off duty, the offence may be committed only in a public place, when the officer is in uniform. This implies that if the officer is on duty, untidiness may give rise to the offence, whether she is in a public place or not, whether in uniform or not.

Note the phrase 'without good and sufficient cause'; scruffy dress may well be justified when an officer is keeping observations or otherwise working in plain clothes.

Drunkenness

3.15 Where a member of a police force renders himself unfit for duties which he is, or will be, required to perform, or which he may reasonably foresee having to perform.

Explanation

There are three possible ways in which a member of a police force may commit this offence:
  i) becoming unfit for duties he is required to perform, e.g. by getting drunk while on duty
  ii) becoming unfit for duties which he will be required to perform, e.g., stopping off at the pub before going on duty, and getting drunk
  iii) becoming unfit for duties which he may reasonably forsee having to perform, as when an officer who, although not on duty, is on call, and who has so much to drink that he will be unfit for duty if he is called upon.

Drinking on Duty or Soliciting Drink

3.16 Where a member of a police force, while on duty, without proper authority, drinks, or receives from any other person, any intoxicating liquor, or, while on duty, demands or endeavours to persuade any other person to give him, or to purchase or obtain for him, any intoxicating liquor.

Entering Licensed Premises

3.17 Is committed where a member of a police force, while on duty, or off duty but wearing uniform, enters, without good and sufficient cause, any premises in respect of which a licence or permit has been granted in pursuance of the law relating to liquor licensing or betting and gaming or of the law regulating places of public entertainment.

Explanation

The two offences of drinking on duty and entering licensed premises cater for situations where an officer has not yet got to the stage of being unfit for duty. Drinking intoxicating liquor amounts to an offence if done 'without proper authority'. Such authority may be given specifically by an officer of higher rank on a particular occasion, or may be implied generally from the nature of the duty being performed, e.g., a C.I.D officer going to a pub to meet an informant.

To enter licensed premises becomes an offence if done without good or sufficient cause. The law does not require a constable to have reasonable suspicion that an offence is being committed, before exercising a power to enter a pub, betting office or cinema (during the hours it is open); entry may be made to ensure that the relevant law is being complied with. This does not mean that these powers may be exercised indiscriminately. In particular, nipping into the cinema to watch the latest film, or into the betting office to place a bet, will give rise to this offence. The offence may be committed while off-duty, if wearing uniform.

Being an Accessory to a Disciplinary Offence

3.18 This offence is committed by a member of a police force who, incites, connives at, or is knowingly an accessory, to any offence against discipline.

Explanation

A police officer who helps a colleague to commit an offence against discipline may well commit an additional substantive offence. For example, trying to cover for another officer's absence from a place of duty may involve committing the offence of falsehood. Being aware that a colleague has committed an offence is not enough for an officer to be liable, but any encouragement or assistance given, may give rise to liability for being an accessory.

Criminal Conduct

3.19 This offence is committed where a member of a police force is found guilty by a court of law of any criminal offence.

Explanation

If a member of a police force uses an unnecessary degree of force to effect an arrest, he may be liable for a criminal offence of assault, as well as for a disciplinary offence of abuse of authority. The principle, that he should not be placed in 'double jeopardy' *(see paragraph 4, below)*, means that if the officer is convicted at court of an offence of assault, he will not also be proceeded against for abuse of authority. However, he will be liable for the discipline offence of criminal conduct. Other criminal convictions which will normally lead to proceedings under this provision will include offences involving dishonesty, or drink-drive offences.

The practical purpose in having such a discipline offence, is that the services of an officer may be dispensed with whose conduct renders him unfitted to continue in office.

DOUBLE JEOPARDY

Liability of Police Officers for Criminal and Disciplinary Offences
Police and Criminal Evidence Act 1984 Section 104

4.1 Where a member of a police force has been convicted or acquitted of a criminal offence, he shall not be liable to be charged with any offence against discipline which is in substance the same as the offence of which he has been convicted or acquitted. This shall not apply to the discipline offence of being found guilty of a criminal offence.

Explanation

The 'no double jeopardy' rule applies only to disciplinary proceedings for an offence which is the same in substance as the criminal offence. This would not rule out proceedings for other disciplinary matters. For example, an officer who is charged with a criminal offence arising from an incident which takes place while he is away from his place of duty, may be dealt with for neglect of duty, for leaving his place of duty. Discipline offences of falsehood or prevarication may be committed in an effort to conceal involvement in a criminal offence.

Statements Made During Informal Resolution

4.2 The Police and Criminal Evidence Act 1984 goes on to provide that any statement made by a person for the purpose of informal resolution of a complaint against police, shall not be admissible in any subsequent criminal, civil or disciplinary proceedings.

However, there is an important exception – a statement will not be rendered inadmissible if it consists of or includes an admission relating to a matter which does not fall to be resolved informally. For example, a member of the public complains that P.C. Smith was rude to him when he called at his house earlier that day. The complainant agrees to an informal resolution of the complaint and the inspector sees PC Smith. The officer then says to the inspector, 'He was rude to me, but I got my own back, I left a big scratch on his antique table on the way out'. Clearly, the criminal offence of causing damage is not suitable for informal resolution, and the admission made by PC Smith may be used in evidence in subsequent proceedings.

REPRESENTATION AT DISCIPLINARY AND OTHER PROCEEDINGS

Police Act 1996 Section 84

5.1 (1) A member of a police force of the rank of superintendent or below may not be dismissed, required to resign or reduced in rank by a decision taken in proceedings under regulations made in accordance with Section 50(3)(a) unless he has been given an opportunity to elect to be legally represented at any hearing held in the course of those proceedings.

(2) Where a member of a police force makes an election to which subsection (1) refers, he may be represented at the hearing, at his option, either by counsel or by a solicitor.

(3) Except in a case where a member of a police force of the rank of superintendent or below has been given an opportunity to elect to be legally represented and has so elected, he may be represented at the hearing only by another member of a police force.

(4) Regulations shall specify:
   a) a procedure for notifying a member of a police force of the effect of subsections (1) and (3) above.
   b) when he is to be notified of the effect of those subsections, and,
   c) when he is to give notice whether he wishes to be legally represented at the hearing.

(5) If a member of a police force:
   a) fails without reasonable cause to give notice in accordance with the regulations that he wishes to be legally represented, or
   b) gives notice in accordance with the regulation that he does not wish to be legally represented, he may be dismissed, required to resign or reduced in rank without his being legally represented.

Explanation

5.2 The financial consequences of any of the three most severe punishments – dismissal, requirement to resign, or reduction in rank – may be far more severe than any financial penalty likely to be imposed in a criminal court. It is reasonable, therefore, that an officer facing the possibility of such a punishment should be given the opportunity to be legally represented at the disciplinary hearing. If, for some reason, the officer concerned was not given such an opportunity, then none of these punishments may be imposed.

An officer to whom these provisions apply, may elect instead to be represented by a member of a police force, either someone from his own force, or an officer from another force.

APPEALS

6.1 As with most quasi-judicial functions carried out by tribunals there is a right of appeal from the decision of disciplinary hearings. If the chief officer for an area has delegated his power to hear a disciplinary matter to a deputy the first line of appeal is to the chief officer. Where the original hearing was before the chief officer the procedure is for a hearing before an appeals tribunal.

Police Act 1996 Section 85

(1) A member of a police force who is dismissed, required to resign, or reduced in rank by a decision taken in proceedings under regulations made in accordance with Section 50(3) may appeal to a police appeals tribunal against a decision except where he has a right of appeal to some other person; and in that case he may appeal to a police appeals tribunal from any decision of that other person as a result of which he was dismissed, required to resign or reduced in rank.

(2) Where a police appeals tribunal allows an appeal it may, if it considers that it is appropriate to do so, make an order dealing with the appellant in a way:
   a)   which appears to the tribunal to be less severe than the way in which he was dealt with by the decision appealed against, and,
   b)   in which he could have been dealt with by the person who made that decision.

(3) The Secretary of State may make rules as to the procedure on appeals to police appeals tribunals under this Section.

(4) Rules made under this Section may make provisions for enabling a police appeals tribunal to require any person to attend a hearing to give evidence or to produce documents, and may in particular, apply subsections (2) and (3) of Section 250 of the Local Government Act 1972 with such modifications as may be set out in the rules.

Composition of an Appeals Tribunal
Police Act 1996 Schedule 6

6.2 Where the appellant is an officer of the rank of superintendent or below, the appeal tribunal will consist of four members appointed by the relevant police authority, as follows:
   i)   a person from a list of legal practitioners nominated by the Lord Chancellor, being a barrister or solicitor of at least 7 years standing;
   ii) a member of the police authority; (in the case of the Metropolitan Police Service, where the Home Secretary is the police authority, a person nominated by the Home Secretary);
   iii) a person from a list held by the Home Office of chief officers of police, or persons who have been chief officers during the previous five years;
   iv) a retired police officer who held an 'appropriate rank'. This means, when the appellant is a superintendent, a retired superintendent; in any other case, a retired officer of the rank of police constable through to chief inspector.

Procedures at Appeals Tribunal

6.3 With the agreement of both parties, the tribunal may reach a decision without a hearing, both parties being given the opportunity to make written or oral submissions.

If there is a hearing, the appellant shall have the right to be present and may be represented by a barrister, solicitor or member of a police force.

The decision of the tribunal shall have the effect of substituting the original decision. If an officer was dismissed, for example, and the tribunal decision is to reinstate him, his pensionable service shall be treated as continuous from the date of the original hearing.

LIABILITY OF CHIEF CONSTABLES FOR OFFICERS' ACTIONS

7.1 *Police Act 1996 Section 88*

(1) The chief officer of a police area shall be liable in respect of the torts committed by constables under his direction and control in the performance or purported performance of their functions in like manner as a master is liable in respect of torts committed by his servants in the course of their employment, and accordingly shall in respect of any such tort be treated for all purposes as joint tortfeasor.

Explanation

7.2 Under civil law, an employer is liable for the torts (wrong-doing) of his employee who is acting in the course of his employment, and employer and employee may be sued jointly for damages. A police officer is not an employee, but the holder of the office of constable; however, this provision allows for the chief officer of police to be sued in civil court, as if he was the employer of constables in his force. A chief officer will be liable in respect of:

i) a member of that police force
ii) a special constable appointed for that police area
iii) a constable for the time being required to serve in that police area,
    e.g., under mutual aid.

7.3 The purpose of the provision is to enable a person who is entitled to damages for, say, unlawful arrest, to sue the police as an organisation, with adequate funds, rather than suing the individual constable alone, who may not have sufficient funds to pay the damages awarded.

To this end, the police authority must pay out of the police fund costs and damages awarded against the chief officer, or any sum agreed as an 'out-of-court' settlement, together with costs incurred by the chief officer.

The police authority may pay out of the police fund, to such extent as appears to be appropriate, the corresponding sums in respect of an individual constable's liabilities.

For example, Smith sues the chief constable and PC Wesson, for unlawful arrest and assault, arising from his having been arrested by PC Wesson, and is awarded damages and costs. The police authority must pay on behalf of the chief constable. Whether or to what extent the authority pays on behalf of PC Wesson is a matter for the authority. The decision may, for example, be influenced by whether the officer is seen as having acted in good faith, or whether his behaviour was clearly wrong in making the arrest.

RESTRICTIONS ON THE PRIVATE LIVES OF POLICE OFFICERS

8.1 A number of general restrictions were imposed on police officers by the 1987 Police Regulations; these are listed under Schedule 2:

i) A member of a police force must at all times abstain from any activity which is likely to interfere with the impartial discharge of his duties, or which is likely to give rise to the impression amongst members of the public that it may so interfere.
In particular, a member of a police force must not take any active part in politics.

ii) A member of a police force shall not reside at premises which are not for the time being approved by the chief officer.

iii) A member of a police force must not without previous consent of the chief officer of police receive a lodger in a house or quarters with which he is provided by the police authority, or sub-let any part of the house or quarters.

iv) A member of a police force must not, unless he has previously given notice to the chief officer of police, receive a lodger in a house in which he resides and in respect of which he receives a rent allowance, or sub-let any part of the house.

v) A member of a police force must not wilfully refuse or neglect to discharge any lawful debt.

Explanation

8.2 It is considered essential in this country, that the Police Service is seen as impartial, especially with regard to politics. Note that a police officer must refrain from any activity which is likely to give rise to the impression that it may interfere with his impartiality, whether it actually so interferes or not.

It is not incurring debt which is frowned upon, but wilfully refusing or neglecting to pay one's debts.

Non-compliance

8.3 Failure to observe any of these restrictions will constitute the disciplinary offence of disobedience to orders.

INCOMPATIBLE BUSINESS INTERESTS

Meaning of 'Business Interest'

9.1 A member of a police force is considered to have a business interest if:

i) he holds any office or employment for gain, or carries on any business;

ii) his spouse (not being separated from him) or any member of his family who lives with him, keeps a shop or like business at any premises in that police area;

iii) his spouse (not being separated from him) or any member of his family who lives with him, holds, or has a pecuniary interest in, any licence or permit relating to liquor licensing, refreshment houses, betting and gaming, or places of entertainment.

Explanation

9.1.1 A member of family is the officer's spouse, parent, son, daughter, brother or sister. The officer will have a business interest if he has some other employment, apart from the police force, or if he runs a business. If a member of the family living with him has an interest in a licence, whether in the force area or elsewhere, this will also amount to a business interest.

Thus, if the daughter of the manager of a cinema wants to join the police service, she will have to declare a business interest – or leave home! A family-run shop will amount to a business interest only if it is within the force area.

Declaring a Business Interest

9.2 If a member of a police force has or proposes to have a business interest (by herself or through a member of her family living with her) she must forthwith give written notice of that interest to the chief officer of police. The chief officer must then decide whether the business interest is compatible with that officer remaining a member of the force. The chief officer must then give written notice of that decision.

If the decision is that the business interest is incompatible, the officer may appeal to the police authority, and in due course, to the Home Secretary.

If the officer does not appeal, or does not win her appeal, the chief officer may, subject to the approval of the police authority, dispense with her services. Before giving approval, the police authority must give the officer an opportunity to make representations.

Explanation

9.2.1 The fact that the officer's husband is proposing to open a newsagents shop may well be seen as compatible with her continuing to serve, whereas her announcement that she has taken a part-time job as a bouncer in a nightclub may not be viewed favourably.

Note that, whereas in disciplinary proceedings, the chief officer alone makes the decision to dispense with an officer's services, here the approval of the police authority is required.

Failure to declare business interest

9.2.2 An officer who has a business interest, e.g., part-time employment, and who fails to declare it commits the disciplinary offence of disobedience to orders.

JURISDICTION OF CONSTABLES
Police Act 1996 Section 30

Regular Officers

10.1 A member of a police force shall have all the powers and privileges of a constable throughout England and Wales and the adjacent United Kingdom waters.

Special Constables

10.2 A special constable appointed for a police area shall have all the powers and privileges of a constable:

   i) in the case of a police area other than the City of London, in any other police area contiguous to that police area;
   ii) in the case of the City of London, in the metropolitan police district, and in any area contiguous to that district.

Explanation

Powers: A special constable has all the powers to arrest, search, enter premises, stop vehicles, etc, which a regular police officer has.

Privileges: This term is not defined in the Act; what it means is anyone's guess.

Extent of jurisdiction: Apart from certain cross-border powers, a member of a police force has powers throughout England and Wales. A special constable has powers only in the area for which he is appointed and in adjoining police areas.

The City of London, with an area of less than 700 acres, and entirely surrounded by the metropolitan police district, is a special case. City special constables have jurisdiction in those areas which adjoin the metropolitan police district, as well as in that district.

OFFENCES RELATING TO POLICE OFFICERS AND POLICE UNIFORM

Obstruction
Police Act 1996 Section 89(2)

11.1 A person commits an offence who:
- resists or wilfully obstructs
- a constable in the execution of his duty
- or a person assisting a constable in the execution of his duty.

Explanation
Wilfully obstruct: Obstruct means to do some act which makes it more difficult for the police to carry out their duty. This could include shouting a warning to the licensee of a pub, suspected of serving drinks after closing time, that the police were about to enter, thus giving the licensee time to remove any evidence of an offence (see keynote case *Hinchcliffe v Sheldon* (1955)).

The term 'wilfully' means, not only intentionally, but without lawful excuse. Where a constable asked a man for his name and address, when there was no power to require those details, the man was not guilty of obstruction by refusing to give them, although by so refusing, he clearly made it more difficult for the officer to carry out his duty (*Rice v Connolly* (1966)).

Execution of duty: This term is dealt with in Chapter 8, in relation to the offence of assaulting a constable.

Impersonating a Police Officer
Police Act 1996 Section 90 (1)

11.2 A person commits an offence who:
- with intent to deceive
- impersonates a member of a police force or a special constable
- or makes a statement or does any act calculated falsely to suggest that he is such.

Explanation
Intent to deceive: Intent is a necessary element in the offence. It is not enough that a person is mistakenly thought to be a constable, if he had no intention to deceive someone. There must be an actual intention to be taken for a constable; mere recklessness is not enough.

Calculated to suggest: A statment may be direct and unambiguous, such as 'I am a police officer.' The offender's conduct may suggest that he is a constable, without him saying so directly, e.g., by asking a motorist to produce his driving licence.

Wear Article of Police Uniform
Police Act 1996 Section 90(2)

11.3 A person commits an offence who:
- not being a constable
- wears any article of police uniform
- in circumstances where it gives him an appearance so nearly resembling that of a member of a police force
- as to be calculated to deceive.

Explanation
Article of police uniform: The term includes any article of uniform, any distinctive mark or badge, and any identification document, e.g., a warrant card, usually issued to members of police forces or special constables. The term extends also to anything having the appearance of such item of uniform, badge, document, etc. Thus, it will be no defence for an accused to claim that the uniform he was wearing was not police uniform, because he made it himself.

Calculated to deceive: This term means 'likely to deceive' and does not require any intent or recklessness on the part of the accused (*Turner v Shearer* (1973)).

For example, persons employed by a security company may be issued with uniforms so as to give them an appearance resembling police officers. For the offence to be committed, there is no need to prove an intention that the security guards should look like constables.

Possession of Article of Police Uniform
Police Act 1996 Section 90(3)

11.4 A person commits an offence who:
- not being a member of a police force or a special constable
- has in his possession any article of police uniform
- unless he proves:
  - i) that he obtained possession of the article lawfully; **and**
  - ii) that he had possession of it for a lawful purpose.

Explanation
Article of uniform: This has the same meaning as for the offence of wearing uniform, above.

He proves: The burden of proof is on the accused, to show not only that he obtained possession lawfully, but also that he has it for a lawful purpose. A person who hires a uniform from a costume shop, intending to use it to impersonate a police officer will satisfy the first requirement but not the second. Wearing a costume on stage or at a fancy dress party is likely to be lawful.

Causing Disaffection
Police Act 1996 Section 91

11.5 A person commits an offence who:
- i) causes, attempts to cause or does some act calculated to cause disaffection amongst members of any police force; or

ii) induces or attempts to induce or does an act calculated to induce any member of a police force to withhold his services.

Explanation

Member of a police force: Here, the term includes special constables, as well as regular officers. It is not necessary to show that the accused's efforts were directed at any particular member of the force.

Keynote Case

12.1 *Hinchcliffe v Sheldon* [1955] 3 All ER 406

Problem

The meaning of the tem 'obstruct' for the purposes of the offence of obstructing a constable in the execution of his duty.

Circumstances

The appellant, the son of the licensee of a public house, returned there one night, at about 11.17pm, to find police officers outside, who wanted to enter because they suspected the licensee of committing offences of supplying liquor outside permitted hours. The appellant shouted a warning to the licensee who did not open the door to the police until 11.25pm. No evidence of any offence was found. The appellant was convicted of wilfully obstructing a constable in the execution of his duty and appealed. The ground for appeal was that he could not commit the offence of obstructing a constable unless it was shown that the licensee had committed an offence. (Note: in the 1950's permitted hours probably ended at 10.30pm, with 10 minutes drinking up time; nowadays at 11.17pm on a weekday, there would still be a few minutes drinking up time remaining.)

Decision

The court held that 'obstructing' meant making it more difficult for the police to carry out their duties. It was the duty of the police to enter the licensed premises if they thought it likely that an offence was being committed. Since the appellant made it more difficult for the police to enter the premises, he was guilty of the offence.

Comment

Other similar examples would include a person warning motorists of a police speed check ahesad, not with a view to persuading motorists to observe the law, but to make it more difficult for the police to detect offences.

Chapter 33: Armed Forces

1 ARMED FORCES – CRIMINAL AND DISCIPLINE OFFENCES

1.1 Discipline

Members of Her Majesty's forces are subject to military, naval and air-force laws which do not apply to persons outside the armed forces, and may be dealt with by service tribunals for breaches of that law. In the case of desertion or being absent without leave, service personnel may be arrested by the police, taken before a magistrates' court and remanded to service custody. For the most part, however, discipline matters will be dealt with entirely by the service authorities.

1.2 Criminal Offences

In all but the most serious cases (murder, manslaughter, aid and abet suicide, rape, treason), service tribunals may try service personnel for criminal offences committed on or off duty. Short sentences of imprisonment will be served in a service establishment but a longer sentence will be served in a civil prison.

When a member of H.M. Forces comes to police attention as having committed a criminal offence, it will be a matter for the police to decide whether the accused should be dealt with in the ordinary courts or be handed over to the service to be dealt with by a service tribunal.

1.3 Families/Visiting Forces

In certain cases, civilian support staff and members of families of service personnel may be dealt with by service tribunals, when posted abroad.

There are special provisions relating to criminal offences committed in this country by members of the armed forces of another country. These provisions are not dealt with in this book.

1.4 Legislation

There are separate Acts of Parliament relating to each of the three services. The Army Act 1955 and the Air Force Act 1955 contain virtually identical provisions, with the same Section numbers applying to each. The Naval Discipline Act 1957 contains many similar provisions.

For ease of reference, terms such as 'soldier' which appear in the Army Act may be used to include members of the other services of corresponding rank.

2 ABSENTEES AND DESERTERS

2.1 Power to Arrest
Army Act 1955, Air Force Act 1955 Section 186
Naval Discipline Act 1957 Section 105

2.1.1 *Without Warrant*

A constable may arrest any person whom he has reasonable cause to suspect of being an officer, warrant officer, non-commissioned officer or soldier of the regular forces who has deserted or who is absent without leave.

When no constable is available, any officer, warrant officer, non-commissioned officer or soldier of the regular forces or any other person may arrest a person whom he has reasonable cause to suspect has deserted or is absent without leave.

2.1.2 *On Warrant*
Any person having authority to issue a warrant for the arrest of a person charged with a crime on being satisfied on evidence on oath:
- that there is or is reasonably suspected of being within his jurisdiction
- a member of the regular forces who has deserted or is absent without leave or is reasonably suspected of such
- may issue a warrant authorising his arrest.

2.1.3 *Subsequent Action*
A person arrested under these provisions shall be taken before a magistrates' court as soon as is practicable.

2.1.4 *Explanation*
Person having authority: Usually, a magistrate will issue a warrant (or a judge in the case of someone who fails to appear at Crown Court).

Member of regular forces: All ranks are covered, whether officer, warrant officer, non-commissioned officer or other rank. The various ranks are specified in the power of arrest to make the contrast with other powers to arrest contained in the Acts, where an officer may be arrested only by another officer. If the officer is suspected of being a deserter or absentee, he may be arrested by any member of the armed forces if there is no police officer around to do so.

Warrant: A magistrate may issue a warrant for the arrest of a suspected absentee/deserter. This is not to be confused with a warrant issued by the armed services *(see paragraph 3.1 below)*.

Magistrates' court: A person who is arrested with or without warrant, must appear before a magistrates' court. If, however, he surrenders himself voluntarily to the police, he may be dealt with differently, as outlined below.

2.2 **Procedure for Dealing with Absentees and Deserters**

2.2.1 *Following Arrest*
Army Act 1955, Air Force Act 1955 Section 187
Naval Discipline Act 1957 Section 109

When the arrested person appears before magistrates and admits that he is a deserter or absentee, the court may remand him in custody to be handed over to service custody. If he does not admit to being absent or a deserter, the court shall consider the evidence, akin to considering a plea of 'not guilty' to a charge. The court will then either remand the person in custody if satisfied that he is absent or a deserter, or if not so satisfied, release him.

When a court remands a person in custody as an absentee or deserter, a certificate will be prepared, signed by a magistrate, containing details of his arrest. This certificate may then be admitted in evidence in subsequent proceedings, such as a court-martial.

Note: A person will not be handed over to service custody if he is in custody for some other reason, e.g. if he has been arrested for a crime.

2.2.2 *Surrender to Police*
Army Act 1955, Air Force Act 1955 Section 188
Naval Discipline Act 1957 Section 108

A person may surrender to police, either at a police station, or to a constable, who must then take him to a police station. The custody officer at that station, if satisfied that the person is illegally absent, may then either hand him directly over to a service escort, or bring him before a magistrates' court, as for a person arrested. If the person is handed directly to a service escort, the custody officer must prepare a certificate, setting out the circumstances of his surrender to the police, akin to the certificate prepared by a magistrates' court.

Note: In certain cases the service authorities may decide not to send an escort, but to trust the absentee to make his own way back to his unit or station. In such a case, action should be taken in accordance with the next paragraph.

2.2.3 *Unable to Return to Unit*
When a member of H.M. Forces informs police that he is without the means to return to his unit, e.g. he has lost his rail ticket, action should be taken as follows:
- if there is any service establishment, or a careers information office, in the area, he should be referred there
- if there is no such establishment or it is closed or otherwise unable to assist, and his own unit is more than 10 miles away, he should be given a rail warrant (once he has been established as bona fide)
- if his own unit is within 10 miles, he should be told to make his own way there.

3 OTHER POWERS TO ARREST SERVICE PERSONNEL

3.1 Service Warrants
Army Act 1955, Air Force Act 1955 Section 190A
Naval Discipline Act 1957 Section 103

A warrant may be issued by the service authorities, for the arrest of a member of the services who is alleged to have committed an offence for which he may be dealt with by the services. The warrant authorises police to arrest the person concerned and to hand him over to service custody. A person arrested under this procedure is not taken before a magistrates' court.

When police hand over a person arrested under such a warrant, the officer who causes him to be handed over (usually the custody officer) will sign a certificate giving details of the arrest, including whether the person was wearing any service uniform at the time of arrest.

Note: Such a warrant could be issued in respect of an absentee or deserter. The Army and Royal Air Force do not usually do so, but the Royal Navy do. If an absentee is arrested under a warrant issued by the Royal Navy, he would not have to be taken before a magistrates' court.

3.2 Arrest of Person Unlawfully at Large
Army Act 1955, Air Force Act 1955 Section 190B
Naval Discipline Act 1957 Section 104

A constable may arrest without warrant a person who is unlawfully at large having been sentenced by service authorities to imprisonment or detention.

4 JURISDICTION IN RELATION TO OFFENCES COMMITTED BY SERVICE PERSONNEL

4.1 Liability for 'Civil Offences'
Army Act 1955, Air Force Act 1955 Section 70
Naval Discipline Act 1957 Section 42

It is an offence against these Acts for a person subject to them to commit any 'civil offence', i.e. any offence contrary to the criminal law of this country, on or off duty, at home or abroad. This provision gives service courts jurisdiction over all criminal offences committed by service personnel.

4.1.1 *Exceptions*
A service court does not have jurisdiction to try any of the following offences:
- treason
- murder
- manslaughter
- rape
- aid and abet suicide (not a complete list).

4.2 Decision on Jurisdiction

4.2.1 *Who Decides?*
When a member of H.M. Forces comes to police attention as having committed an offence, it will be a matter for the chief officer of police to decide whether the accused should be charged and appear before the ordinary courts, or instead handed over to the service authorities to be dealt with by service tribunals. It is advised that the police should consult with the accused's commanding officer when making the decision.

Any decision has to take account of the fact that a person arrested without warrant and charged with an offence must be brought before a magistrates' court, as required under Sections 46 of the Police and Criminal Evidence Act 1984.

4.2.2 *Guiding Principles*
In making a decision as to jurisdiction, the police should take account of the following principles:
- an offence which affects the person or property of a civilian should normally be dealt with in the criminal courts; one which does not affect civilians should normally be left to a service tribunal. It should be noted that traffic offences such as dangerous driving pose a danger to the public and should normally go to the ordinary courts
- as far as practicable, police should not charge a person who is about to be sent overseas, since this may prevent him joining his unit
- if the offence was committed while on duty and amounts to a breach of duty, the matter should go to a service tribunal even though the property of a civilian was involved
- the matter should go to a service tribunal if the offence was committed on service premises, involved the person or property of a civilian to a minor extent only, and could be dealt with summarily by the accused's commanding officer
- service courts have jurisdiction only in respect of persons subject to naval, military or air force law. Therefore if a member of H.M. Forces commits an offence jointly with a civilian, they should appear together before a criminal court – unless the identity of

the civilian is not known, in which case this factor may be left out of the decision making process.

A case may involve several of the above factors; these are guiding principles, by no means guaranteed to provide a clear cut answer in every case.

5 OFFENCES BY CIVILIANS

5.1 Pretending to be a Deserter
Army Act 1955, Air Force Act 1955 Section 191
Naval Discipline Act 1957 Section 96

5.1.1 *Offence*
A person commits an offence who:
- in the United Kingdom or any colony
- falsely represents himself to be a deserter from the regular forces
- to any military, naval, air-force or civil authority.

5.1.2 *Explanation*
Home or abroad: For a person abroad, to pretend to be a deserter may be seen as a way of obtaining a free flight home. Why anyone should want to commit the offence in this country is a puzzle. It is one thing to make 'Walter Mitty' false claims of wartime exploits, but to claim to be a deserter...?

Military... or civil authority: A person would commit the offence who goes to a service establishment or to the police, for example, falsely claiming to be a deserter. This offence may be a useful alternative to one of 'wasting police time'.

5.2 Procuring or Assisting Desertion
Army Act 1955, Air Force Act 1955 Section 192
Naval Discipline Act 1957 Section 97

5.2.1 *Offence*
A person commits an offence who (anywhere in the world):
- procures or persuades any member of the regular forces to desert or absent himself without leave; or
- knowing that such person is about to desert or go absent without leave, assists him in so doing; or
- knowing a person to be a deserter or absentee from the regular forces, procures, persuades or assists him to remain a deserter or absentee, or assists in his rescue from custody.

5.2.2 *Explanation*
Three phases: The offence may be committed before a member of the regular forces deserts or goes absent – by procuring or persuading him to do so; during the time he is deserting – by assisting him to do so; or afterwards – by procuring, assisting or persuading him to remain absent.

Knowing: For the offence to be committed, there must be knowledge that the person is deserting or has deserted, etc. To stop for a soldier hitching a lift outside camp, dropping him at the bus station, will not render the motorist liable if he did not know that the soldier was in the process of going AWOL.

5.3 Unauthorised Use of or Dealing in Decorations
Army Act 1955, Air Force Act 1955 Section 197

5.3.1 *Offence – Unauthorised Use*

A person commits an offence who:
- without authority, uses or wears any decoration, badge, wound stripe, or emblem authorised by the Defence Council
- uses or wears any decoration, badge, etc, so nearly resembling any such real one as to be calculated to deceive
- falsely represents himself to be a person who is or has been entitled to use or wear such decoration, badge etc.

5.3.2 *Offence – Dealing in Decorations*

A person commits an offence who:
- purchases or takes in pawn any military, naval or air-force decoration
- awarded to any member of H.M. Forces
- or solicits or procures any person to sell or pledge such decoration, or acts for any person in so doing
- unless he proves that at the time of the alleged offence the person to whom the decoration was awarded was dead or had ceased to become a member of those forces.

5.3.3 *Explanation*

Unauthorised use: There are three ways in which this offence may be committed:
- by unauthorised use of an actual decoration, badge, etc
- by using or wearing something which looks so much like a real one as to be likely to deceive
- and by falsely claiming to be entitled to use or wear such item.

Badge, emblem, etc: This Section does not prohibit the wearing of ordinary regimental badges, or of brooches or ornaments representing them.

Purchase or take in pawn: There would be no offence committed by a person who accepted a decoration as a gift.

Dead or no longer serving: The offence is committed only in respect of persons who are still serving. There is a thriving trade in medals, with prestigious ones such as the Victoria Cross selling for very large sums of money. Once the recipient has left the services or has died, there is nothing wrong in such trade.

Chapter 34: Children

1 INTRODUCTION

1.1 Protection of Children

The law seeks to protect children by providing for cruelty and neglect to be criminal offences. Employment of children, or their use in show-business, is restricted by national laws and council by-laws. If the standard of care a child is getting is below acceptable standards, the police and local authority staff may step in and institute court proceedings to have the child brought into local authority care.

1.2 Offences Involving Children

In addition to dealing with cruelty, welfare and employment, this chapter also covers legislation relating primarily to children, covering matters such as the sale of tobacco or supply of solvents to young people. There are references to young people in many areas of legislation, as a minor element of various aspects of the law. These are to be found in the same chapters as the rest of that subject. For example, references to children in pubs or betting shops appear in the chapters on liquor licensing and betting, respectively.

1.3 Legislation

The Children and Young Persons Act 1933 deals with offences of cruelty, neglect, exposing a child to danger, and a number of miscellaneous matters. The principal legislation covering care and custody is the Children Act 1989. Other legislation includes the Children and Young Persons Act 1969 and the Intoxicating Substances (Supply) Act 1985.

2 MEANING OF TERMS

2.1 Classification by Age

2.1.1 *Child*

For the purposes of the Children and Young Persons Act 1933, a child is a person under the age of 14 years. In the Children Act 1989, a child is anyone under 18 years of age.

2.1.2 *Young Person*

A young person is a person who has reached the age of 14 years and is under 18 years old. This is applicable to the Children and Young Persons Act 1933, but has no relevance for the 1989 Act. Indeed the distinction has little relevance for the former Act. Although the eponymous 1933 Act deals with persons under 18 years old, various offences relate to other ages. For example, an offence of cruelty under Section 1 of that Act, may be committed only against a person under 16, and many of the other provisions also relate to persons under that age.

Note: For convenience, the term 'child' will be used in the text to denote a 'child or young person'.

2.1.3 *Determination of Age*

A person attains a given age on her birthday. Thus, if Jade was born on 14 July 1983, then at a minute before midnight on 13 July 1997 she was 13 years old; after midnight she is 14.

2.1.4 *Defences*
Children and Young Persons Act 1933 Section 99

If an offence under the 1933 Act, is committed against a child or against a young person, it will not be a defence where the victim is thought to be a child, to prove that she is in fact a young person, or vice versa.

Some offences may arise where a person is 'apparently' under a particular age, e.g. selling fireworks to a person apparently under 16. It will be a defence to prove that the person was actually over that age (even though the person did look younger, and even though the accused thought he was under age).

2.2 **Place of Safety**

This term appears in the Acts and means any local authority or other home, any police station, hospital, surgery or any other suitable place, the occupier of which is willing temporarily to receive a child. A constable has powers in certain circumstances to take a child to a place of safety. This would normally be a police station in the first instance, but from there the youngster could go to a council home, or to the home address of foster parents. Any of these would be a 'place of safety'.

2.3 **Refuge**
Children Act 1989 Section 51

Certain premises operate as places where children at risk may stay. Such premises operate under a government certificate as a 'refuge'.

2.4 **Guardian**

This will include any person who, in the opinion of the court which is dealing with the matter, has the care of a child for the time being.

2.5 **Parental Responsibility**
Children Act 1989 Section 2

More than one person may at the same time have parental responsibility for a person under 18. Where the child's mother and father are married (to each other) at the time the child is born, then each will have parental responsibility. If the parents are not married to each other at the time of the child's birth, then the mother, but not the father, will have parental responsibility. The father, or another person, may acquire parental responsibility through the courts.

2.6 **Authorised Person**
Children Act 1989 Section 31

For the purposes of applying to a court for a care order, etc, an 'authorised person' is the NSPCC or any of its officers, any body authorised to take such proceeding, and any officer of such a body.

3 **CRUELTY**
Children and Young Persons Act 1933 Section 1

3.1 **Offence**
The offence will be committed:
- by a person who has attained the age of 16 years
- who has responsibility for a child under that age
- who wilfully
- assaults, ill-treats, neglects, abandons or exposes the youngster, or causes or procures such treatment
- in a manner likely to cause unnecessary suffering or injury to health (physical or mental).

3.2 **Explanation**
16 years: The offence arises only when the accused is 16 or over and the victim is under 16. Thus, a 15 year old baby-sitter could not be charged with cruelty to a child left in her care.

Responsibility: This includes a person who:
- has parental responsibility; or
- is otherwise legally liable to maintain the child; or
- has care of the child, e.g. a baby-sitter.

Wilfully: The action must be deliberate and intentional or reckless. Cruelty may arise from an act or an omission, i.e. doing something, or failing to do something. In either case, the action or the failure has to arise from more than mere ignorance. Thus, if a parent fails to obtain medical help, to be guilty of neglect it must be shown that the parent was aware of the risk to the child's health. A genuine lack of awareness that the child needed medical treatment, through stupidity, inadequacy, etc, will be a defence (*R v Sheppard and Another* (1980)).

Assault: This has the usual meaning, i.e. any act which intentionally or recklessly causes another to apprehend immediate and unlawful personal violence. No particular level of injury is required to constitute an assault, but to amount to cruelty, it must be likely to cause unnecessary suffering or injury. A common assault will not amount to cruelty if it is not likely to cause the required suffering or injury to health.

Ill-treat: Means a continuous course of misconduct.

Neglect: This is a lack of care to the standard a parent would be expected to give. Without affecting the generality of the meaning of neglect, the Section does provide specific instances which will be deemed to amount to neglect in a manner likely to cause injury to health. These are:
- where the parent, guardian or other person legally liable to maintain the child fails to provide adequate food, clothing, medical aid or lodging for the child, or being unable to do so, has failed to take steps to procure it, by applying for social security benefits, etc
- where a child under the age of three years dies of suffocation (not caused by disease or by having something stuck in its airways) while in bed with a person over 16 who was under the influence of drink when he went to bed.

The first of these demonstrates that the parent or other person responsible for a child has a responsibility to provide the child with food, clothing, somewhere to live and medical care. If unable to provide these things herself, the responsible person must take steps to get them, by applying for welfare benefits or whatever.

The second was presumably enacted to meet a perceived need at the time. Whether this is still a common cause of death in toddlers is not known.

In failing to obtain medical treatment, more so than in failing to feed or clothe, the element of 'wilfulness' requires careful consideration. A parent may genuinely not realise how ill a child is; failure to call a doctor may well be due to ignorance, whereas failure to feed a child for several days can hardly be put down to 'oversight'.

Abandons: This means leaving the child to its fate *(see also the separate offence of 'abandoning' at paragraph 3.3 below).*

Exposes: Means exposing the child to the risk of unnecessary suffering or injury to health. There is no need to show that the exposing arose from an intention that the child should suffer, but the element of 'wilfulness' will have to be made out for the offence to be complete, i.e. there is an awareness of the risk, or ignorance of the risk arising from recklessness.

Note: that there is no strict demarcation between 'assault', 'ill-treat' and 'neglect'. The treatment of a child could amount to one or more of these.

3.3 Abandoning a Child
Offences Against the Person Act 1861 Section 27

3.3.1 *Offence*
It is an offence for a person:
  – to abandon or expose
  – a child under the age of two years
  – whereby the child's life is endangered or its health is, or is likely to be, permanently injured.

3.3.2 *Explanation*
The offence differs from that of cruelty, not in what is done – to abandon or expose the child – but in the result of the action. Danger to the child's life or permanent damage to health is somewhat more than the 'unnecessary suffering or injury to health' required for cruelty. The age of the victim, under two years, indicates that the offence is aimed to protect children who are too young to take even the most elementary action to save themselves from being 'abandoned or exposed'.

3.3.3 *Arrest*
This is an arrestable offence.

4 MISCELLANEOUS OFFENCES

Note: The first five topics listed below have been traditionally referred to as the '5 B's' – Brothels, Begging, Burning, Booze and 'Baccy.

4.1 Brothels
Children and Young Persons Act 1933 Section 3

4.1.1 Offence
A person who has responsibility for a child aged four or over but under 16 commits an offence by allowing that child to reside in or frequent a brothel.

4.1.2 *Explanation*
Brothel: The meaning of 'brothel' is discussed in Chapter 12; briefly it is a place where persons go to indulge in heterosexual or male homosexual activity.

Reside or frequent: For the offence to be committed, it is not enough that the child is in the brothel for a visit; he must live there or go there frequently.

4.2 **Begging**
Children and Young Persons Act 1933 Section 4

4.2.1 *Offence*
An offence is committed by a person who:
- – causes or procures a child under 16 to be in a street, premises or place
- – or who having responsibility for such a child allows him to be in a street, premises or place
- – for the purpose of begging, receiving alms or inducing the giving of alms
- – whether or not there is any pretence at singing, playing, performing or selling anything.

4.2.2 *Explanation*
Offender: There are two categories of offender, a person who actively causes or procures the child to be somewhere for the purposes of begging, and someone who has responsibility for the child, who allows him to be there for that purpose. Each could commit the offence in respect of the same child at the same time.

Begging/receiving/inducing: The child may be begging on her own, may be holding the cup for donations on behalf of someone else who is begging, or may simply be there to look pathetic, starved or whatever, so as to evoke sympathy and induce passers-by to contribute.

Singing, selling, etc: A pretence at busking, selling articles, etc, will not necessarily afford a defence. What amounts to 'pretence' is not clear. If there is a genuine effort to perform or sell something, this will not constitute begging.

However, a child under 16 may not be employed in street trading, which includes musical and other performances, so even if the playing or selling is not a pretence, it may still be unlawful *(see paragraph 6.1.2 below)*.

4.3 **Burning**
Children and Young Persons Act 1933 Section 11

4.3.1 *Offence*
The offence may be committed by a person:
- – who has attained the age of 16 years
- – who has responsibility for a person under 12 years
- – where:
    - i) he allows the child to be in a room containing an open fire grate, or a heating appliance liable to cause injury by contact; and
    - ii) the fire or heater is not sufficiently protected to guard against the risk of the child being burned or scalded; and
    - iii) the responsible person does not take reasonable precautions to guard against that risk; and

iv) as a result the child is killed or suffers serious injury.

4.3.2 *Explanation*

Offender: To be liable for the offence, a person must be 16 or over and must have had responsibility for the child who is burned or scalded.

Under 12: Presumably, a child aged 12 or over should have enough common sense not to touch a fire.

Room: This is an offence committed in a building. It will not arise where a child is burned at a barbecue or bonfire.

Guarded/precautions: There are two separate elements; first the fire or heater is not guarded so as to prevent the risk of burning; secondly, this being so, the offender does not take any reasonable precautions to guard against the risk.

The result: This could not be described as a preventive measure; the offence will be complete only if the child suffers death or serious injury by being burned or scalded on the fire or heater in question.

4.4 Intoxicating Liquor
Children and Young Persons Act 1933 Section 5

4.4.1 *Offence*
An offence is committed by any person who:
- gives or causes to be given
- to a child under the age of five years
- any intoxicating liquor
- except upon the order of a qualified medical practitioner
- or in the case of sickness, apprehended sickness or other urgent cause.

4.4.2 *Explanation*

Offender: The offence may be committed by anyone; there is no requirement that the offender has responsibility for the child at the time.

Intoxicating liquor: This has the same meaning as in the Licensing Act 1964. This is significant because that definition excludes any alcoholic spirits or wine which seems to be intended for use as a medicine rather than as a beverage.

Except: Giving the young one intoxicants on the order of a doctor, or because he is sick, or it is thought he is going to be ill, will not amount to an offence. Considering that preparations which are primarily intended to be medicines are not deemed to be 'intoxicating liquor' in any case, one may well be puzzled as to what sort of illness is to be treated effectively by giving a four year old an alcoholic beverage.

4.5 Tobacco
Children and Young Persons Act 1933 Section 7

4.5.1 *Offence*
A person commits an offence who:
- sells

- tobacco or cigarette papers
- to a person under the age of 16 years
- whether for her own use or not.

4.5.2 *Explanation*
Sells: It will not be an offence to give a child tobacco, only to sell it.

Tobacco or cigarette papers: Cigarettes and cigars are 'tobacco', the offence is not confined to loose tobacco. Snuff, chewing tobacco and any other tobacco products are all within the meaning of 'tobacco'. Selling cigarette papers alone, without tobacco, will amount to the offence. There can be few alternative uses for cigarette papers, so if a youngster seeks to buy some, the law assumes he has managed to get his hands on some tobacco.

Own use or not: The shopkeeper will not have a defence if he claims he thought the cigarettes were 'for her mum', even if that is the case.

4.5.3 *Defence*
A person will have a defence if he proves that he took all reasonable precautions and exercised all due diligence to avoid committing the offence.

4.5.4 *Unpackaged Cigarettes*
Children and Young Persons (Protection from Tobacco) Act 1991 Section 3

4.5.5 *Offence*
It shall be an offence for a person:
- carrying on a retail business
- to sell cigarettes to any person
- other than in pre-packaged quantities of ten or more in their original packaging.

4.5.6 *Explanation*
Offender: The offence may be committed only by a person carrying on a retail business, so for a youth to buy a packet of cigarettes then sell them individually to persons under 16, would amount to the Section 7 offence, above, but not to this offence.

To any person: Although the law is aimed at preventing the sale of cigarettes to children, mainly by unscrupulous keepers of small shops, willing to sell individual cigarettes, the offence is actually committed irrespective of the age of the customer.

Cigarettes: Cigars are commonly sold individually; the restriction applies only to cigarettes.

Original package: This means the package in which the cigarettes were supplied for retail sale by the wholesaler or importer. It will not be lawful for a retailer to re-package cigarettes, even if the packets contain ten or more.

4.5.7 *Police Powers*
Children and Young Persons Act 1933 Section 7(3)

It is the duty of a constable in uniform:
- to seize any tobacco or cigarette papers in the possession of any person apparently under the age of 16 years
- whom she finds smoking in any street or public place.

4.5.8 *Explanation*

Duty: The term 'duty' implies that the officer has no discretion.

Uniform: The officer must be in uniform to have this power.

Smoking: The power may be exercised only when the person is actually smoking. The fact that a child has cigarettes in her possession without smoking does not give a constable the right to seize them.

4.6 **Cigarette Machines**
Children and Young Persons Act 1933 Section 7(2)

4.6.1 *Court Order*

It is one thing to control the sale of tobacco across the counter, but the law also seeks to prevent youngsters obtaining cigarettes from machines.

If a complaint is made to a magistrates' court and it is proved to the satisfaction of the court that any automatic machine for the sale of tobacco kept on any premises has been used by any person under the age of 16 the court may make an order.

4.6.2 *Effect of Court Order*

The order may be directed to the owner of the machine or to the person on whose premises the machine is kept to take such precautions as are specified in the order to prevent the machine being used by persons under 16 **or** to remove the machine within a specified time.

4.6.3 *Offence*

Failure to comply with the order, either by not taking the specified precautions, or by failing to remove the machine within the stipulated time period, renders the person against whom the order is made liable to a fine.

4.7 **Education**
Children and Young Persons Act 1933 Section 10

4.7.1 *Offence*

A person is guilty of an offence who:
  – habitually wanders from place to place
  – with a child of compulsory school age
  – unless he proves that the child is not being prevented from receiving an education suitable to his age, ability and aptitude.

4.7.2 *Prosecution*

This offence would be prosecuted by the local authority. However, it may come to police notice when dealing with persons with no fixed address.

5 **SALE OF SOLVENTS, ETC**
Intoxicating Substances (Supply) Act 1985

5.1 **Offence**

It is an offence for a person to supply or offer to supply a substance which is not a controlled drug:

- to a person under the age of 18, whom he knows or has reasonable cause to believe, to be under that age; or
- to a person who is acting on behalf of a person under 18, whom he knows or has reasonable cause to believe, is so acting;

if he knows or has reason to believe that the substance or its fumes will be or are likely to be inhaled by the person under 18 for the purpose of causing intoxication.

5.2 **Explanation**

Supply or offer: The offence does not depend on a 'sale', so there is no need to show that money changed hands. An offer to supply completes the offence, even if the actual supply does not take place. If a person over 18 buys a solvent from a shop, for a person under that age to use for 'sniffing', the shopkeeper may commit the offence by supplying to someone acting on behalf of an under-age person, and the buyer will then commit the offence by supplying to the youngster, in each case, providing the 'knowing or believing' element is proved.

Other than controlled drug: If the substance concerned is a controlled drug, then drugs legislation provides the sanctions against unlawful possession and supply.

Knows or believes: The person supplying the substance must know or have reasonable cause to believe two distinct facts:
- that the person being supplied (or the person for whom someone else is acting) is under 18; and
- that the substance is to be used by a person under 18 to cause intoxication.

Thus, if an adult buys glue to give to a youngster, so that she may build a model aircraft, the shopkeeper will not be liable, even if he knows that the customer is acting on behalf of a person under 18, and the adult will not be liable for supplying the glue to the child, because neither has reason to believe that the glue will be used for causing intoxication.

This does leave considerable scope for the supply of such substances without an offence being committed. For example, a shopkeeper may sell glue to a person whom he knows to be under age; unless it is proved that the shopkeeper knew or had reason to believe that the youngster was going to sniff the fumes from the glue, he will not be guilty of the offence.

Inhaled... intoxication: There are many products, produced and sold for legitimate purposes, which may be used, by sniffing the fumes or in some other way, for inducing a feeling of intoxication. Paint, glue and butane gas are a few examples. Unfortunately, such abuse of solvents, as well as leading to undesirable behaviour due to intoxication, may have side effects which cause permanent physical damage.

Possession: There are no offences comparable to those under misuse of drugs legislation, of possession, or possession with intent to supply. The restrictions are solely on supply or offer to supply.

5.3 **Defence**

A person accused of an offence will have a defence if she proves:
- that she was herself under 18 at the time she supplied (or offered) the substance; **and**
- that she was not acting in the course or furtherance of a business.

This defence is not open to a young shop assistant, for example, who supplies or offers a substance in the course of the shop business. It does, however, remove liability from a person under 18 who offers a substance to another youngster, perhaps in the course of sharing it among members of a group. However, if one of that group is over 18, he will commit the offence by offering the substance to someone under that age.

6 EMPLOYMENT OF CHILDREN

6.1 Employment Generally
Children and Young Persons Act 1933 Section 18 – 21

6.1.1 *Basic Restrictions*

Section 18 provides a number of restrictions on employing children of compulsory school age (currently up to 16, but attendance may be compulsory until the end of a term after the 16th birthday). In addition, local authorities have by-laws which impose further restrictions. A breach of Section 18 or of local by-laws is an offence under the Act. The offence is committed by the employer, not by the child. (However, a child may be personally liable for an offence of engaging in street trading.)

The basic restrictions are that a child of compulsory school age shall not be employed:
  – while under the age of 13 years
  – before the close of school on a day on which he is required to attend school
  – before 7.00 am or after 7.00 pm on any day
  – for more than two hours on any day he is required to attend school
  – for more than two hours on a Sunday
  – to lift, carry or move anything so heavy as to be likely to cause injury.

(Local by-laws may allow for a child under 13 to be employed by her parent(s) in light horticultural work.)

6.1.2 *Street Trading*

No child of compulsory school age shall engage in or be employed in street trading. However, a local authority may make by-laws allowing a child aged 14 or over to be employed by his parents in street trading, subject to restrictions in those by-laws.

6.1.3 *Explanation*

Employed: A child who assists in a trade or occupation which is carried on for profit shall be deemed to be employed, even though she does not get paid. This means that a child assisting in the family shop, for example, will be employed, whether she is paid or not. At the same time, a child assisting without payment in some non-profit making venture, such as selling programmes for the village fete, will not be 'employed'.

A chorister who is taking part in a religious service, or a rehearsal for a service, will not be employed, even if he is paid. The 12 year old boy treble, paid for singing in the church choir at a wedding on Saturday afternoon will not render the vicar liable for employing a child under 13.

Restrictions: Only on Saturdays and during school holidays, may a child be employed for more than two hours a day. A common breach of the restrictions is by the newsagent who allows his delivery boys and girls to start work before 7.00 am. Many 'free' newspapers are sent to the home addresses of the children who deliver them. To comply with the law the publishers should seek to prevent the children from working later than 7.00 pm.

Street trading: This includes offering for sale newspapers, flowers, etc, singing, playing or performing for profit, shoe cleaning and other like services – carried on in a street or public place. Delivering goods from a van is **not** street trading (*Stratford Co-operative Society v East Ham Corporation* (1915)).

6.1.4 *Police Power to Enter*
Children and Young Persons Act 1933 Section 28(1)

Police may apply to a magistrate for an **order** on the ground that there is reason to believe restrictions on employment, under the Act or a local by-law, are being contravened in respect of a child.

The order will empower a constable:
- at any time within 48 hours of the order being made
- to enter any place where it is believed the child is employed
- and to make enquiries therein.

It is an offence for any person to obstruct a constable in the exercise of these powers, or to refuse to answer, or give false answers to, enquiries authorised under the order.

Note: This is called an 'order', not a 'warrant'; unlike a warrant, the order does not give power to force entry, nor to search, merely to enter and make enquiries.

6.2 **Performing and Entertainment**

6.2.1 *Theatrical Performances*
Children and Young Persons Act 1963 Sections 37, 38

There are restrictions on the employment of children in theatres, broadcasting and rehearsals. These restrictions relate to hours of employment, and provision of opportunity for education. These are matters for local authorities. However, there is a police power to enter premises *(see below)*.

6.2.2 *Dangerous Performances*
Children and Young Persons Act 1933 Sections 23, 24

A child under 16 may not take part in a dangerous performance or one involving acrobatics or contortion. A child under 12 years of age may not be trained to take part in such performances. For a child from the age of 12 onwards, a licence may be obtained from the local authority to enable the child to be trained for such performances. Again, there is a police power to enter premises.

6.2.3 *Police Powers to Enter*
Children and Young Persons Act 1933 Section 28(2)

There are two provisions whereby police may enter premises:
- where it is believed that a child is taking part in a performance, or being trained in a dangerous performance, in contravention of the restrictions in the Act (e.g. without a licence) a magistrate may issue an order, under the same provisions as apply to unlawful employment
- any constable may enter (without warrant or order) any broadcasting studio or film

studio where children are performing or rehearsing, or any place where a child is being trained under licence for a dangerous performance, and make enquiries about this child.

In each case, it is an offence to obstruct a constable, or refuse to answer or give false answers to, any enquiries.

6.2.4 *Performing Abroad*
Children and Young Persons Act 1933 Section 25

A person under the age of 18 may not be taken out of this country for the purpose of performing except under the authority of a licence issued by a magistrate at Bow Street Magistrates' Court, or by certain other magistrates.

A copy of the application is sent to the police force local to where the young person concerned lives. A police officer of the rank of inspector or above must then make enquiries into the circumstances and prepare a report for the magistrate, which will be taken into account when a decision is made whether or not to grant the licence.

In this context, playing football or other sport is included in 'performing', so a trip abroad by a professional soccer club, for example, may lead to a licence being sought in respect of a young player.

7 SAFETY AT ENTERTAINMENTS
Children and Young Persons Act 1933 Section 12

7.1 Provision of Attendants
Where an entertainment is held in a building, for children or at which the majority of the audience will be children, and more than 100 children attend, there must be sufficient trained adult attendants to control entry and exit and prevent overcrowding.

7.2 Liability
The person providing the entertainment has the responsibility of ensuring there are sufficient attendants. The occupier of a building who lets it out for payment for such an entertainment also has a responsibility for ensuring that attendants are provided.

7.3 Police Powers
A constable has power to enter a building where she has reason to believe such an entertainment is taking place or is about to take place, for the purpose of ensuring that these requirements are being complied with.

7.4 Prosecution
If the premises where the entertainment is held is a cinema or somewhere with an entertainments licence in force, the local authority should prosecute. If the premises are not licensed for entertainment, prosecution is a matter for the police (through the Crown Prosecution Service).

8 CARE OF CHILDREN
Children Act 1989

8.1 Introduction

When a child (under the 1989 Act, this means a person under 18) is not receiving proper care from his parent or whoever else is supposed to look after him, then the police, the local authority and magistrates' court may become involved, and the child made subject of a court order. Under such an order, a child may continue to live at home under council supervision, or may be removed to accommodation provided by the council.

At a stage between a lack of care being identified and the matter being dealt with at court, emergency measures may be taken, which often involve the police.

8.2 Local Authority Responsibility
Children Act 1989 Sections 20–21

A local authority has a responsibility to provide accommodation for any child in need in its area, who appears to require accommodation. In the case of a child who is 16 or over, accommodation must be provided if the authority consider that her welfare will be seriously prejudiced unless accommodation is provided.

The local authority must provide accommodation when requested to do so for a child:
- who is in police protection *(see paragraph 8.5 below)*; or
- who has been refused bail by a custody officer, and is to be kept in custody (Police and Criminal Evidence Act 1984, Section 38(6)).

8.3 Care or Supervision Order
Children Act 1989 Section 31

A local authority or an authorised person may make application to a court in respect of a child, for an order:
- either placing the child in the care of a local authority; or
- putting the child under the supervision of a local authority or of a probation officer.

An order may be made on grounds:
- that the child is suffering or is likely to suffer significant harm; **and**
- the harm or likelihood of it is attributable either to the care the child is receiving or is likely to receive if the order is not made, or
- the child is beyond parental control.

An order cannot be made in respect of a child who has reached the age of 17 years, or 16 years in the case of a child who is married (16 being the minimum age for a legal marriage). This does not mean to say that a care order which is in force does not continue past the child's 17th birthday.

8.4 Emergency Protection Order
Children Act 1989 Section 44

8.4.1 *Application*

An application for such an order may be made to a court in respect of a child. It will usually be granted where there is a need for action to be taken, but there is insufficient information available at that stage to support an application for a care order.

The application may be made by a local authority, an authorised person or by any person. A 'designated police officer' may make an application in certain circumstances *(see paragraph 8.5.5 below)*. The order may be granted by the court:

- if the application is made by a local authority or by an authorised person, on the grounds that the authority or authorised person is making enquiries into the child's welfare, access to the child is being unreasonably denied, and such access is required as a matter of urgency
- whoever makes the application, if there is reason to believe that the child is likely to suffer significant harm:
  i) either if he is not removed to accommodation provided by the applicant
  ii) or if he is removed from where he now is.

8.4.2 *Explanation*

Access denied: A local authority may be making enquiries, in order to decide whether an application needs to be made for a care order. An authorised person, e.g. an officer of the NSPCC, may be making enquiries because there is reason to believe a child is at risk of harm. In either case, if access to the child is denied and is felt to be required urgently, an emergency protection order may be applied for.

Removal: The other ground for making an order is that there is reason to believe the child is likely to be harmed, either if he is not removed to other accommodation, or if he is removed from where he now is. In the first case, it may be that the child will be at risk if he stays at home. In the second case, the child may, for example, be ill in hospital, and the purpose of the emergency order is to prevent the child being removed from there.

8.4.3 *Effect of the Order*

This follows from the ground for granting it. An order may:

- require a person who is in a position to do so to produce the child to the applicant (i.e. where access has been denied); or
- authorise the removal of the child to accommodation provided by the applicant; or
- authorise the prevention of the child's removal from hospital or other place where he was being accommodated.

In addition, the order gives the applicant parental responsibility for the child.

8.4.4 *Disclosure of Information*
Children Act 1989 Section 48(1)

The court making an emergency protection order may include a requirement that a person disclose to the applicant any information he may have as to the child's whereabouts.

8.4.5 *Entry to Premises and Warrant*
Children Act 1989 Section 48

1: An emergency protection order may authorise the applicant to enter premises specified in the order, and search for the child to whom the order relates.

2: Where a person seeking to exercise powers under an emergency protection order has been refused access to premises, or access to the child, or it is likely that access will be denied, a magistrate may issue a warrant.

The warrant will authorise any constable to assist the person in the exercise of the powers under the order. When the warrant is being executed, the constable doing so may be accompanied by the applicant (if that person so wishes and the court does not direct otherwise), and by a doctor, nurse or health visitor (if the court allows and the constable so wishes).

8.5 Police Protection
Children Act 1989 Section 46

8.5.1 *Police Power*
Local authority or NSPCC officers may not act without a court order, but police officers have powers to take a child into their keeping in an emergency. Where a constable has reasonable cause to believe:
- that a child would otherwise be likely to suffer significant harm
- he may remove the child to suitable accommodation and keep him there
- or take such steps as are reasonable to prevent the child's removal from a hospital or other place where he is being accommodated.

A child in respect of which this power is used is deemed to be under **police protection**.

8.5.2 *Explanation*
Significant harm: 'Harm' means ill-treatment, impairment of health or impairment of physical, intellectual, emotional or mental development. 'Ill-treatment' may be physical or non-physical and includes sexual abuse (Section 31(9)).

'Significant' means important, considerable or worthy of comment, and a child's development may be compared to that of a similar child.

Remove or prevent removal: The power is similar to the authority of an emergency protection order, in that a child may be taken away from a situation which is likely to result in harm to him. Conversely, if taking the child away would be likely to cause harm, such as where a parent decides against medical advice to remove the child from hospital, then the constable has power to prevent this.

Suitable accommodation: A constable's choice of accommodation may be limited, usually to a police station. Once there, steps should be taken to have the child moved to a refuge or to local authority accommodation.

8.5.3 *Subsequent Action*
The constable who takes a child into police protection must, as soon as practicable after doing so, take the following action:
- tell the local authority (for the area where the child was found) what steps have been taken, what steps are proposed, and the reasons for them
- tell the local authority (for the area where the child usually lives) of the child's whereabouts
- inform the child (if she appears capable of understanding) of the steps which have been taken, steps proposed to be taken, and the reasons
- take practicable steps to find out how the child feels about it
- inform the child's parents, any other person with parental responsibility, and any

person with whom the child was living, of the action taken, the reasons for it
and the steps which may be taken
- in a case where the child was removed from somewhere, arrange for the child
to be moved to a refuge, or to local authority accommodation
- arrange for the case to be looked into by a 'designated officer'.

8.5.4 *Designated Officer*

The chief officer of police for an area has to designate certain officers for the purposes of
carrying out the role of looking into the circumstances of a child who has been taken into
police protection. From training and experience, a designated officer should be better able to
carry out this task than an officer who does not specialise in such matters.

The role of the designated officer is:
- to enquire into the child's case
- after completing the enquiry, release the child from police protection **unless** he
considers that there is still reason to believe that the child would be likely to suffer
significant harm if released
- to do what is reasonable in the circumstances in the interests of the child's welfare,
especially taking account of the length of time the child will be under police protection
*Note: Neither the constable taking the child into police protection, nor the designated
officer, shall at any stage have 'parental responsibility' for the child.*
- to allow such contact with the child as the designated officer considers is reasonable,
and is in the child's interest (and this may be no contact). Contact may be by:
i) the child's parents
ii) any other person having parental responsibility
iii) a person with whom the child was living before being taken into police protection
iv) certain other persons who have a right to contact
v) or someone acting on behalf of any of these (e.g. a solicitor).

8.5.5 *Emergency Protection Order*

The designated officer may make application to a court for an emergency protection order on
behalf of the local authority (the one for the area where the child usually lives). The application
may be made whether the authority knows of the application or agrees to it, or not.

8.5.6 *Duration of Protection and of Police Responsibility*

A child may not be kept in police protection for longer than 72 hours. The duties of the
designated officer shall be carried out by the local authority once a child is transferred to local
authority accommodation.

8.6 Abduction of Child in Care

8.6.1 *Offence*
Children Act 1989 Section 49

A person commits an offence who:
- knowingly
- and without lawful authority or reasonable excuse:
i) takes a child to whom the provisions apply, away from the responsible person; or
ii) keeps such child away from the responsible person; or

iii) induces, incites or assists the child to run away or stay away from the responsible person.

8.6.2 *Explanation*

Child: The Section applies to a child who (in care) is the subject of an emergency protection order or who is in police protection.

Responsible person: This means any person who has responsibility for the child under the (emergency) care order, or while the child is in police protection, as the case may be.

Knowingly: To commit the offence, the accused must be aware that the child is one to whom the Section applies. Thus, if a man persuades a girl to go to his flat rather than home, for him to commit this offence it must be proved that he knew she was subject of a care order, etc.

Lawful authority or reasonable excuse: The onus will be on the accused to show that he had some such authority or excuse.

Takes or keeps: The use of the two words caters for situations where the child either is already with the responsible person, or away from that person at the time. If an estranged father sneaks into the grounds of the children's home where his son has been placed in council care, and removes him, he is guilty of 'taking'. If the father instead was to prevent the boy returning to the children's home after visiting him, then he would be guilty of 'keeping him away'.

Induces, incites or assists: The offence will be committed by a person who persuades or helps the child to run away or stay away.

8.6.3 *Recovery Order*
Children Act 1989 Section 50

If a court has reason to believe that a child has been abducted from care, or has run away, is staying away or is missing, a recovery order may be issued. The application may be made by any person who has parental responsibility for the child under a care (or emergency care) order; in the case of police protection, the application must be made by the designated officer.

8.6.4 *Effect of Order*

A recovery order:
- directs any person who is in a position to do so, to produce the child on request to an authorised person
- authorises removal of the child by an authorised person
- requires any person with information as to the child's whereabouts to disclose that information when asked by a constable or by a court officer
- authorises a constable to enter any premises specified in the order to search for the child, using force if necessary.

8.6.5 *Offence*

A person commits an offence if he intentionally obstructs an authorised person seeking to exercise the power under a recovery order, to remove a child. It is only this aspect of the order which gives rise to an offence. It will not be an offence, for example, to refuse to give information when required.

8.7 Attendance at Care Proceedings
Children Act 1989 Section 95

8.7.1 *Court Order*

When a court is dealing with an application for an order relating to a child, the court may direct that the child concerned attends court at some stage. If such a direction has not been complied with, or the court feels that it would not be complied with, then an order may be made:

– for a person in a position to do so, to bring the child to court
– for a person reasonably believed to have information about the child, to disclose that information to the court
– for a constable to enter and search premises specified in the order if there is reason to believe the child may be found there, to take charge of the child and to bring her to court.

8.8 Search Warrant
Children Act 1989 Section 102

8.8.1 *Application for Warrant*

There are a number of enactments which give power to certain persons in respect of children, and these are listed in Section 102. For example, to inspect premises where child minding is carried on, to check on arrangements for privately fostered children and to examine independent schools which offer residential accommodation.

These are not police matters but become so when the person concerned is refused entry to premises or access to the child, or refusal is likely. On these grounds, application for a warrant may be made.

8.8.2 *Powers Under Warrant*

The warrant:
– authorises a constable to assist the person applying for the warrant in the exercise of whatever the powers are – using reasonable force if necessary;
– may direct that the constable may choose to take a doctor, nurse or health visitor along. This is a matter for the police officer's choice.

8.8.3 *Explanation*

The warrant differs from most others in that it does not actually give police power to take specific action. It does, however, authorise the police to use force if necessary, to assist the person who applied for the warrant. Thus, if a local authority officer has power to make enquiries, e.g. in relation to a child-minder, but has been prevented from doing so, by being refused access to premises, the warrant allows a constable to use force to enter the premises when assisting the council officer.

9 ARREST OF CHILD ABSENT FROM CARE
Children and Young Persons Act 1969 Section 32

9.1 Police Power

A constable anywhere in the United Kingdom or Channel Islands may arrest without warrant a child or young person (i.e. under the age of 18) who is absent without consent of the responsible person, from:

- a place of safety where he has been placed after being arrested on warrant, being subject of a supervision order
- from local authority accommodation where he is required to live under a supervision order; or
- from accommodation where he has been remanded by a court, awaiting trial or following conviction.

9.2 Explanation

This power to arrest relates only to youngsters who have been through the criminal justice system, being under a supervision order, awaiting trial or having just been tried. If a child has run off from a place where he was living subject of a care order, this power of arrest will not apply. Instead, a police officer should consider power to take a child into police protection.

10 EXCLUSION REQUIREMENT
Children Act 1989 Sections 38A, 44A

10.1 Court Powers

When a court makes an interim care order or an emergency protection order, in respect of a child, the court may include in the order an **exclusion requirement** subject to certain conditions being satisfied. These conditions are:

- there is reasonable cause to believe that if a particular person (the 'relevant person') is excluded from the dwelling house in which the child lives, the child will cease to suffer, or cease to be likely to suffer, significant harm, or (in relation to an emergency protection order only) enquiries will cease to be frustrated
- another person living in the dwelling house is able and willing to give the child the care which it would be reasonable to expect a parent to give the child
- that other person consents to the inclusion of the exclusion requirement.

10.2 Effect of Exclusion Requirement

An exclusion requirement may be one or more of the following:

- a requirement that the relevant person leave the dwelling house in which he is living with the child
- a provision prohibiting the relevant person from entering the dwelling house in which the child lives
- a provision excluding the relevant person from a defined area in which the dwelling house where the child lives is situated.

10.3 Arrest

10.3.1 *Power to Arrest*

The court may attach a power of arrest to an exclusion requirement. If a power of arrest is attached, a constable may arrest without warrant any person whom he has reasonable cause to believe to be in breach of the requirement.

10.3.2 *Action After Arrest*

There is no provision for police bail for a person arrested under these provisions. A person who has been arrested must be brought before the relevant judicial authority (magistrates' court which made the order, or a judge of the court, if the order was made other than by magistrates) within 24 hours of his arrest. The only exclusion from reckoning the 24 hours will be Sundays, Christmas Day or Good Friday. The court or judge may deal with the matter, or remand the arrested person, in custody or on bail.

10.4 Explanation

Conditions: One of the conditions before an exclusion requirement may be made is that there is another person (a parent or someone else) who is able and willing to care for the child, and who agrees to the exclusion. If a man who lives with a mother and her child has been abusing a child, the mother may well be able and willing to care for the child, but her agreement is required before an exclusion requirement is made.

Extent of exclusion: The requirement may be that the relevant person leaves the child's home, if he is living there, or that he does not enter it, or that he stays out of an area around the house. Any one, two or all of these may be included.

Duration of requirement: The exclusion requirement may be for a shorter period than the order to which it is attached. The power of arrest may be for a shorter period than the exclusion requirement. It is essential therefore, before arresting a person for breach of a requirement, that a police officer should make certain that a power to arrest is still in force.

Domestic incidents: These provisions are similar to those under a non-molestation order, details of which are included in *Chapter 35 (Domestic Violence)*.

Chapter 35: Domestic Violence

1 INTRODUCTION

1.1 Court Orders

There are provisions under two different pieces of legislation, for court orders to be made in an effort to prevent violence by one member of a family against other family members. An order may restrict access to the family home or contact with members of the family. Failure to comply with an order may be dealt with by the courts. In a case involving violence or apprehension of violence, police may be given powers to arrest a person in breach of an order and bring him before the court.

1.2 Domestic Incidents

Police are frequently called to incidents involving violence or other disturbance between members of a family. A significant proportion of homicides involve a perpetrator who is known to the victim; the vast majority of incidents do not involve homicide, but research shows that incidents tend to increase in severity of violence over time. The victim is usually the woman in a partnership, but may also be a child or children in the household.

2 MAGISTRATES' COURT ORDERS
Domestic Proceedings and Magistrates' Courts Act 1978

2.1 Grounds for Issue
Domestic Proceedings and Magistrates' Courts Act 1978 Section 16

An order under this Act may be granted by a magistrates' court to one partner in a marriage (the applicant), against the other partner (the respondent). The court may grant the order if satisfied:
- that the respondent has used or threatened violence against the person of the applicant or a child of the family
- and that it is necessary that an order is made for the protection of the applicant or a child of the family.

2.2 Requirements of Order

An order may contain one or more of the following requirements:
- that the respondent shall not use or threaten violence against the person of the applicant
- that the respondent shall not use or threaten violence against the person of a child of the family

and in certain cases, any of the following:
- that he shall leave the matrimonial home
- prohibiting him from entering the matrimonial home
- that he shall permit the applicant to enter the matrimonial home
- that he shall not incite or assist any other person to use or threaten violence against the person of the applicant or child of the family.

2.3 Power of Arrest
Domestic Proceedings and Magistrates' Courts Act 1978 Section 18

2.3.1 *Grounds for Attaching Power to Arrest*
In granting an order, the magistrates may attach a power of arrest if:
 - satisfied that the respondent has physically injured the applicant or a child of the family
 - and consider that he is likely to do so again.

2.3.2 *When Arrest May be Made*
A constable may arrest a person under this provision if she has reasonable cause to believe him to be in breach of an order, by reason of:
 - his use of violence towards the applicant or a child of the family
 - or his entry into the matrimonial home.

2.3.3 *Duration of Power to Arrest*
The power to arrest may be of shorter duration than the order itself. Research shows that violence towards an applicant or child is unlikely outside the first three months of the order being made. To this end, the High Court has recommended that any power to arrest attached to an order should be limited to no more than three months, unless a court is satisfied that a longer period is necessary (*Practice Note* (1981)).

2.4 Explanation
Marriage: These provisions relate only to married people and their children. The applicant for the order is one of the partners to the marriage. Persons who co-habit without being married may seek relief under the provisions of the Family Law Act 1996 *(see below)*.

Requirements of order: The two basic requirements, one or both of which may be applied, are that the respondent will not use or threaten violence against the applicant and/or a child of the family. Any of the other requirements may also be applied on grounds relating to a previous history of violence.

Arrest: A power of arrest may be attached to the order only if the respondent has physically injured the applicant or child of the family in the past and it is likely that he will do so again. The power of arrest may be exercised if the respondent breaches the order, but this applies only to certain of the requirements. He may be arrested if he breaches a requirement not to **use** violence, or not to enter the matrimonial home. If he breaches another requirement, e.g. not to threaten violence, or that he shall leave the family home, such a breach will not give ground for arrest.

Duration of power: A power to arrest attached to an order may well be of shorter duration than 12 months. To enable the police to exercise powers to arrest, while avoiding unlawful arrests, court clerks send copies of orders containing arrest powers to police stations, in accordance with local arrangements. The police are then responsible for keeping these, weeding out when a power to arrest expires, and ensuring that officers attending an incident of domestic violence are given accurate information as to whether a power to arrest exists.

3 NON-MOLESTATION ORDERS
Family Law Act 1996

3.1 Issue of Order
Family Law Act 1996 Section 42

The High Court or a county court may issue such an order:
- upon the application of a person 'associated with the respondent', whether in the course of other family proceedings or not;
- in the course of family proceedings to which the respondent is a party, even though no application has been made.

A court which has made an emergency protection order under Section 44, Children Act 1989, which includes an exclusion requirement, may also make a non-molestation order.

Any person 'associated with the respondent' may make an application. A child under 16 requires leave of the court to make an application.

3.2 Requirements of Order
The order may contain one or both of the following:
- prohibiting the respondent from molesting another person who is associated with the respondent
- prohibiting the respondent from molesting a relevant child.

3.3 Occupation Order
Family Law Act 1996

An occupation order may be issued under one of several provisions of the Act, providing for one or other of the parties to proceedings to occupy the family home. A power of arrest may be attached to such an order, as is the case with a non-molestation order.

3.4 Power of Arrest Included in Order
Family Law Act 1996 Section 47

3.4.1 *Ground for Attaching Power of Arrest*
A court which makes a non-molestation or occupation order:
- shall attach a power of arrest
- if it appears to the court that the respondent has used or threatened violence against the applicant or a relevant child
- unless satisfied that in all the circumstances of the case, the applicant or child will be adequately protected without such power of arrest.

3.4.2 *When an Arrest May be Made*
The power of arrest may be attached to **one or more** of the provisions of the order. A constable may arrest without warrant a person whom she has reasonable cause for suspecting to be in breach of a provision to which a power of arrest is attached.

3.4.3 *Duration of Power to Arrest*
The power of arrest may only remain in force for a relatively short period *(see paragraph 2.3.3).*

3.5 Explanation

Connected with the respondent: A person is 'connected' with another if:
- they are or have been married
- they are or have been co-habiting
- they live or have lived in the same household
  (excluding where one or other is a lodger, employee, tenant, etc)
- they have agreed to marry, whether or not the agreement has been terminated
- they are related.

  Note: In the case of an agreement to marry, the 'connection' does not extend more than three years from the ending of the agreement.

Co-habiting: This term refers to a man and a woman who, not being married, are living together as man and wife. Thus, the Act does not cater for single-sex couples.

Relevant child: This term is fairly wide in scope, encompassing any of the following:
- a child who is living with either party to the proceedings
- a child who might reasonably be expected to be living with one or other of the parties to the proceedings
- any child whose interests the court considers are relevant.

Non-molestation: This is less specific than 'use or threaten violence' which may appear in an order under the 1978 Act. The order may be general as to 'molestation' and/or include reference to specific acts.

Arrest: Whereas under the 1978 Act, a power to arrest may be attached to an order only if the respondent has caused injury in the past, under this legislation the power to arrest may be attached if the respondent has previously used or threatened violence.

One similarity between the two sets of provisions is that the power to arrest does not necessarily attach to each and every one of the provisions of an order. A respondent may be liable for failing to comply with the requirements of an order, without being liable to arrest.

4 ARREST ON WARRANT
Domestic Proceedings and Magistrates' Courts Act 1978 Section 18(4)
Family Law Act 1996 Section 47(8)

When a court has made an order but has not attached a power of arrest, if at any time the applicant considers that the respondent has failed to comply with the order she may apply to the court for a warrant to arrest the respondent. If granted, the warrant gives the police power to arrest the respondent.

5 PROCEDURE ON ARREST

5.1 Police Action

When a person has been arrested for breach of an order (under either Act) he must be brought before the relevant judicial authority (magistrates' court, county court judge or High Court judge, depending on which court made the order) within 24 hours beginning with the time of his arrest (the only exclusions from reckoning the 24 hours will be Christmas Day, Good Friday and Sundays).

There is no provision for police bail for a person arrested for breach of an order.

5.2 **Action by the Court**
The relevant judicial authority may deal with the breach, or remand the respondent. The High Court and county courts are given the same powers as a magistrates' court to remand a respondent in such cases (Family Law Act 1996, Schedule 5). Remand may be on bail, with or without conditions. Remand in custody may be to prison (usually for not more than eight days), or to police custody for not more than three days.

6 POLICE ACTION UPON BREACH OF AN ORDER

6.1 **Action for Breach**
If an arrest has been made for breach of an order, the police are responsible for bringing the respondent before the court. The applicant should be informed of arrangements, in order that appropriate action may be taken. However, it is not a police responsibility to institute court proceedings for breach of an order. Indeed, in many cases, a breach of a provision of an order will not lead to arrest, because there is no power to arrest for breach of that provision.

6.2 **Arrest for Another Offence**
If there is a breach of a provision which has attached to it a power to arrest, it is **not compulsory** that the police arrest for the breach. If there is a breach of an order, together with a criminal offence such as an assault, it will be a matter for the police to decide whether to arrest and charge for the crime, or to arrest for breach of the order and take the respondent before a court within 24 hours. If the criminal offence is proceeded with, the applicant should be advised that it is open to her to institute action for the breach of the order.

6.3 **Proceedings for Criminal Offence**
The Home Office has issued detailed advice to police forces on procedures for dealing with incidents of domestic violence, including the need to liaise closely with the Crown Prosecution Service and other agencies, from the time of the incident to subsequent court proceedings. In particular, the Crown Prosecution Service should be advised without delay in any case where a witness, usually the victim, expresses reluctance to give evidence, through fear or other reason.

In a case where the victim of violence confirms that the complaint is true but does not want to give evidence, the Crown Prosecution Service will consider whether the victim's statement may be used in evidence under Section 23, Criminal Justice Act 1988. This provides that a statement may be admitted in evidence in criminal proceedings if the person who made it does not give oral evidence through fear. In an Appeal Court judgment relating to a woman victim of serious violence jailed for refusing to give evidence, the judges expressed the hope that greater use would be made of Section 23 procedures in cases where victims were too frightened to give evidence (*R v Holt, R v Bird* (1996)).

Chapter 36: Equal Opportunities

1 INTRODUCTION

1.1 Purpose of Legislation

Equal opportunities legislation is intended to stop persons being treated less favourably than others on grounds of:

- sex or marital status (Sex Discrimination Acts 1975 and 1986)
- race, colour, nationality, ethnicity or national origins (Race Relations Act 1976)
- physical or mental impairment (Disability Discrimination Act 1995).

1.2 Matters Affected

The Acts deal with discrimination in the following areas:

- employment
- education
- goods, facilities, services and premises
- barristers.

1.3 Legal Proceedings

In relation to employment, an aggrieved person may have recourse to an industrial tribunal. Proceedings in relation to other areas will lie in the ordinary civil courts.

2 SEXUAL DISCRIMINATION

2.1 Discrimination

2.1.1 *Against Women*
Sex Discrimination Act 1975 Section 1

A person discriminates against a woman in any circumstances relevant for the purposes of the Act if:

- on the grounds of sex he treats her less favourably than he treats or would treat a man, of the same marital status, or
- he applies to her a requirement or condition which applies or would apply equally to a man, but:
    i) which is such that the proportion of women who can comply with it is considerably smaller than the proportion of men who can comply with it; **and**
    ii) which he cannot show to be justifiable irrespective of the sex of the person to whom it is applied; **and**
    iii) which is to the woman's detriment because she cannot comply with it.

2.1.2 *Against Men*
Sex Discrimination Act 1975 Section 2

The above provisions are to be read, with appropriate modification, as applying equally to discrimination against men.

2.1.3 *Against Married People*
Sex Discrimination Act 1975 Section 3

A person discriminates against a married person of either sex in relation to employment if:
- on the grounds of his or her marital status he treats that person less favourably than he treats or would treat an unmarried person of the same sex; or
- he applies to that person a requirement or condition which he applies equally to an unmarried person, but:
  i) which is such that the proportion of married persons who can comply with it is considerably smaller than the proportion of unmarried persons of the same sex who can so comply; **and**
  ii) which he cannot show to be justified irrespective of the marital status of the person to whom it is applied; **and**
  iii) which is to that person's detriment because he or she cannot comply with it.

2.1.4 *Explanation*
Purposes of the Act: It must be understood that the Sex Discrimination Act (and the other two Acts) do not cover every aspect of human relations, but only those specified – employment, supply of goods and services, etc.

Less favourably: In relation to employment, discrimination may arise in a number of ways *(set out in paragraph 6)*. One of these is that, on the grounds of a person's sex, he is subjected to a 'detriment'. This need not be any more serious than 'putting under a disadvantage'. *(Keynote Case: Ministry of Defence v Jeremiah (1979))*

Considerably smaller proportion: When the discrimination is indirect – by applying a condition to men and women equally – it must be that a **considerably** smaller proportion of one sex is unable to comply. To apply a height limit of 5 ft 5 in, for example, would lead to a considerably greater proportion of women than men being unable to meet the requirement.

Justified: Some jobs, by their nature, demand a degree of physical strength more likely to be found in a man than a woman. If a job entails carrying a hod full of bricks up a ladder, there is nothing wrong with testing applicants, to see whether they can do the job. Male as well as female applicants may fail; what would be unlawful would be to advertise the job as only open to male applicants (to advertise for a man may be in order in the case of a 'genuine occupational qualification'; *see below*).

Cannot comply: A woman cannot take action for discrimination arising from an unjustified requirement, unless she herself suffers detriment by being unable to comply with it. If a strength test is given to applicants for a job, but is not justified, a woman who actually passes the test has not been discriminated against.

It is not whether it is theoretically possible for women to meet a requirement to the same extent as men can, but whether in practice they are able to do so. In a case where a job was advertised as being open to persons between the ages of 17 1/2 and 28 years, this was held to discriminate against women, not because there were less women than men in that age group, but because a significant proportion of women between those ages were not available for work, being engaged in having and bringing up children. Women returning to work after starting a family were too old, and were therefore discriminated against (*Price v Civil Service Commission and others* (1978)).

Pregnancy: Arrangements for a woman to be treated more favourably than a man, in relation to pregnancy, will not be regarded as sex discrimination. If, for example, pregnant employees are taken off regular duties and given less strenuous work, this will not be regarded as sex discrimination against males.

Married people: There is no provision for unmarried persons to take action if they are treated less favourably than married persons.

2.2 **Genuine Occupational Qualification**
Sex Discrimination Act 1975 Section 7

It will not be unlawful to discriminate against women in the field of employment where being a man is a 'genuine occupational qualification'. Strength and stamina is specifically excluded as being such a qualification, but preference may be shown to a man on grounds such as decency, e.g. where the job involves physical contact, or being in the presence of men in states of undress.

3 **RACIAL DISCRIMINATION**

3.1 **Discrimination**
Race Relations Act 1976 Section 1

A person discriminates against another in any circumstances relevant for the purposes of any provisions of the Act if:
- on racial grounds he treats that other person less favourably than he treats or would treat other persons; or
- he applies to that person a requirement or condition which he applies or would apply equally to persons not of that racial group, but:
  - i) which is such that the proportion of persons of the same racial group who can comply with it is considerably smaller than the proportion of persons not of that racial group who can comply with it; **and**
  - ii) which he cannot show to be justifiable irrespective of the colour, race, nationality or ethnic or national origins of the person to whom it is applied; **and**
  - iii) which is to the detriment of that person because he cannot comply with it.

3.1.1 *Explanation*
Provisions of the Act: The Act covers the same aspects of human relations as does the Sex Discrimination Act.

Racial grounds, racial group: Racial grounds means grounds of colour, race, nationality or ethnic or national origins. A racial group is a group of persons defined on any of these grounds.

'Nationality' refers to citizenship of a particular state, while 'national origins' refer to a person's connections by birth to a particular group who could be described as a 'nation'. Ethnic origin is not used solely with reference to race, but may take account of history or culture.

A person may belong to more than one group. The fact that a racial group comprises two or more distinct racial groups does not prevent it from being considered as one racial group for the purposes of the Act.

Can comply: Whether a person can comply with a particular condition is not a question of whether he can comply in theory, but whether he can comply with it consistent with the culture of the racial group to which he belongs. If it is a condition of a job that women employees wear short skirts, there is no physical reason why a woman from a particular group cannot wear a skirt. However, if to do so goes against the traditions of her racial group, then it may be said that she cannot comply with the condition.

Comparison with sex discrimination: The wording of the provisions under the two Acts is very similar, providing for direct discrimination and indirect, by imposing unjustifiable conditions.

3.2 **Genuine Occupational Qualifications**
Race Relations Act 1976 Section 5

Preference may be shown to members of a particular racial group in the field of employment when being a member of that group is a genuine occupational qualification. Such a qualification may arise in relation to acting, photographic modelling, etc, and also:
  – in situations such as a restaurant, where a member of a particular group is required for authenticity. A restaurant specialising in Thai, Chinese or Bangladeshi food may therefore employ staff from the appropriate racial groups
  – where the job involves provision of personal welfare services to members of a racial group and those services can be provided most effectively by a person from that racial group.

In all cases, these provisions will not apply if the employer already has sufficient employees of that racial group who are capable of performing the role and whom it would be reasonable to employ in that role without undue inconvenience.

4 **VICTIMISATION AND HARASSMENT**

4.1 **Victimisation**
Sex Discrimination Act 1975 Section 4
Race Relations Act 1976 Section 2

A person will discriminate against another person for the purposes of sex discrimination or racial discrimination, if he treats the person victimised less favourably by reason of that person having brought proceedings for discrimination, given evidence in such proceedings, made an allegation of discrimination, or by reason of the discriminator knowing or suspecting that the person victimised intends to do so.

4.2 **Harassment**
Sex Discrimination Act 1975 Section 6(2)
Race Relations Act 1976 Section 4(2)

Sexual and racial harassment in the work place feature in many reports of proceedings at industrial tribunals. Harassment is not catered for as a separate provision of the legislation, but is one aspect of subjecting an employee to a detriment. Allowing working conditions made unpleasant by the attitudes or actions of other employees, especially where the employer does not seek to remedy the situation, could amount to subjecting the employee to a detriment.

5 DISABILITY DISCRIMINATION

5.1 Discrimination in Employment
Disability Discrimination Act 1995 Section 5

An employer discriminates against a disabled person if:
- for a reason which relates to that person's disability
  - i) he treats him less favourably than he treats or would treat someone to whom such reason does not or would not apply; **and**
  - ii) he cannot show that this treatment is justified; or
- he fails to comply with a duty to make adjustments, **and** he cannot show that his failure to comply with that duty is justified.

5.1.1 *Explanation*
Disabled person: A 'disabled person' is a person with a disability. Disability in turn, means a physical or mental impairment which has a substantial and long-term adverse effect on the person's ability to carry out normal day-to-day activities (Section 1).

Treatment justified: Whereas there are very few occasions when less favourable treatment will be justified on grounds of sex or race (genuine occupational qualifications) the law recognises that less favourable treatment of a disabled person on account of his disability may be justified for reasons related to the job in question. For less favourable treatment to be justified, it must be shown that the reason for the treatment is 'both material to the circumstances of the particular case and substantial' (Section 5(3)).

Duty to make adjustments: When any arrangements made by an employer, or any physical feature of the employer's premises, places a disabled person at a substantial disadvantage in comparison to non-disabled persons, the employer has a duty to take reasonable steps to make adjustments. Such adjustments may be physical adjustments to the premises or to equipment, alterations to working hours, giving additional training or granting time off for treatment or training, etc (Section 6).

In considering whether it is reasonable for an employer to take a particular step, account may be taken of cost, the employer's financial resources and the practicability of that step.

6 AID, INSTRUCT OR INDUCE DISCRIMINATION

6.1 Aid an Unlawful Act
Sex Discrimination Act 1975 Section 42
Race Relations Act 1976 Section 33
Disability Discrimination Act 1995 Section 57

A person who knowingly aids another person to do some act which is unlawful by any of the three Acts shall be treated as doing an unlawful act of like description.

However, a person shall not be liable for aiding an unlawful act if he has acted in reliance on a statement made by the other person that because of any provision of the relevant Act, his action would not be unlawful.

6.2 **Instruction to Discriminate**
Sex Discrimination Act 1975 Section 39
Race Relations Act 1976 Section 30

It is unlawful for a person:
- who has authority over another person **or**
- in accordance with whose wishes the other person is accustomed to act
- to instruct him to do any act which is unlawful by virtue of either Act
- or to procure or attempt to procure the doing by him of such an act.

6.3 **Pressure to Discriminate**
Sex Discrimination Act 1975 Section 40

It is unlawful to induce, or attempt to induce, a person to discriminate against a person on grounds of sex or marital status by:
- providing or offering to provide her with any benefit
- or subjecting or threatening to subject her to any detriment.

6.4 **Inducement to Discriminate**
Race Relations Act 1976 Section 31

It is unlawful to induce, or attempt to induce, a person to discriminate against a person on grounds of race.

6.5 **Explanation**
Aid unlawful act: There is provision in each of the three Acts for a person to be liable for aiding another person to contravene the Act.

Reliance on statement: Where one person tells another that an action will not amount to unlawful discrimination by virtue of the law, the second person will not be liable for aiding the first to discriminate, if he relies on what the first person has told him. Note that this defence applies only where it is the person who is being helped to discriminate who makes the statement which the second person relies on.

Instruction to discriminate: There is no corresponding provision in relation to discrimination against disabled people. The person giving the instruction may be in a formal position of authority, e.g. of higher rank or grade, or it may be that the one person usually acts in accordance with the other's wishes, e.g. where both persons are at the same level in an organisation, but the one who has been there a lesser amount of time usually does what her longer serving colleague says.

Pressure or induce: For whatever reason, the unlawful actions of inducing or attempting to induce a person to discriminate on grounds of sex or race, differ in wording. Under the Sex Discrimination Act, the type of inducement is specified – an offer of some benefit or a threat of something detrimental. Under the Race Relations Act, the type of inducement is not specified.

7 EMPLOYER'S AND EMPLOYEE'S LIABILITY FOR UNLAWFUL DISCRIMINATION
Sex Discrimination Act 1975 Section 41
Race Relations Act 1976 Section 32
Disability Discrimination Act 1995 Section 58

7.1 Employer's Liability
Anything done by a person in the course of his employment shall be treated for the purposes of any of the three Acts as done by his employer as well as by him, whether or not it was done with the employer's knowledge or approval. Corresponding provisions apply where a person acts as another person's agent.

7.2 Employer's Defence
An employer will have a defence in respect of liability for acts of his employee, if he proves that he took such steps as were reasonably practicable to prevent the employee from doing that act, or from doing acts of that sort in the course of his employment.

7.3 Employee's Liability
Where an employer is liable for the actions of his employee, the employee will be liable for having aided the employer to commit the unlawful act *(see paragraph 6.1)*. If the employer successfully pleads the employer's defence, this does not alter the employee's liability for aiding the employer.

Thus, an employee who carries out an act of unlawful discrimination will render the employer liable. However, the employee is in turn liable for aiding the employer, and will be treated for the purposes of the respective Acts as equally liable. If the employer then escapes liability by pleading the defence, the employee, the cause of the problem, is left to 'carry the can'. Corresponding provision is made for persons acting as agents to others.

7.4 Police and Government

7.4.1 *Sex or Race Discrimination*
Sex Discrimination Act 1975 Section 17
Race Relations Act 1976 Section 16

For the purposes of these two Acts, a constable is regarded as an employee. This provision is made because a constable (of a 'Home Office' police force) is regarded as the holder of an office, not as an employee. A constable is treated as an employee by specific provision in other legislation (e.g. in the Police Act 1996, for the purposes of civil action being taken against police). Crown service is also regarded as employment.

7.4.2 *Disability Discrimination*
Disability Discrimination Act 1995 Section 64

There is no provision for service as a constable to be regarded as employment under this legislation. Therefore, chief officers do not have to offer employment as constables to disabled persons, nor do adjustments have to be made to buildings, equipment or procedures, to enable disabled persons to function as constables.

7.4.3 *Stated Exemptions*

Service as a member of a fire brigade (as a firefighter), as a prison officer, as a member of the Armed Services and as a constable in certain police forces (Ministry of Defence Police, British Transport Police, United Kingdom Atomic Energy Authority Constabulary, Royal Parks Constabulary) is exempt from the employment provisions of the Disability Discrimination Act. Thus, for example, the working practices of the Royal Marines or the firefighters of London Fire Brigade do not have to be altered to take account of disabled people, but provision will still have to made under that Act for disabled persons in clerical and support roles.

8 POSITIVE ACTION
Sex Discrimination Act 1975 Sections 47 – 49
Race Relations Act 1976 Sections 35 – 38

So-called 'positive discrimination', e.g. discriminating in favour of a racial group or gender so as to increase the proportion of that group or gender in a particular area of work, is unlawful. However, it is lawful to offer training designed to improve the opportunities of a group or gender to qualify for jobs in areas where members of that group or gender are under-represented.

Keynote Cases

9.1 *Ministry of Defence v Jeremiah* [1979] 3 All ER 833

Problem

1: Whether paying men extra to do a 'dirty' job which women employees were not required to do, is discrimination against men.

2: To what extent the interests of safety and 'chivalry' will amount to valid reasons for treating female employees differently from male employees.

Circumstances

In a workshop, men and women were employed as 'examiners'. From time to time examiners were required to perform a particular task which meant working in dirty and unpleasant conditions, and necessitated wearing protective clothing. Only male employees were chosen for this work, for which they were paid an enhancement. Male employees complained of discrimination, in that women were not required to carry out this unpleasant work. The employers contended that there was no discrimination because the men were paid extra to perform the task. Further, it was claimed, the fact that protective clothing had to be worn, and provision had to made for showers afterwards, made it undesirable that women should be asked to perform the work.

Decision

The court held that:
- Whether women objected to carrying out the work, and whether or not there were facilities for them to do so, was irrelevant. If the men had been placed at a disadvantage compared to the women, there was discrimination.
- The fact that men were paid extra for doing the work did not remove the detriment against them. Employers cannot 'buy the right to discriminate'.

- The fact that arrangements are made in the interests of good administration, safety or chivalry, should not be regarded as a defence to discrimination in favour of women employees. The court does not have to consider whether the employer is acting in a manner hostile to the interests of his employees, in deciding whether there is discrimination.

Comment

The case raises several important issues:

- Lack of facilities is no excuse for discrimination. If there are, for example, no showers or toilet facilities for women, this is no excuse for not employing women there.
- An employer's motive for discriminating is not relevant. It makes no difference that the employer thinks he is acting in the best interests of the employee.
- An earlier decision involving the concepts of safety and chivalry, is cast into doubt. In the earlier case (*Peake v Automotive Products Ltd* (1978)), women workers were allowed to leave work a few minutes earlier than men, to avoid them being injured in the rush through the factory gates when the men came out. The earlier decision was that this was not discriminatory, being in the interests of safety, courtesy and chivalry.

Chapter 37: Data Protection

1 INTRODUCTION

1.1 Scope
The law on data protection is intended to prevent the misuse of information about people, stored on computers. Information which is not personal or which is not on a computer or other automatic equipment, is not subject to protection.

1.2 Legislation
The law is the Data Protection Act 1984. Also included in this chapter are the provisions of the Computer Misuse Act 1990, dealing with unauthorised access to computer systems and the Police Act 1997, relating to criminal record certificates.

1.3 Data Protection Register
The operation of the legislation is overseen by the Data Protection Registrar. In the Register are entered details of each 'data user' *(see note below)* together with details of:
- a description of the personal data held by the data user
- the purpose(s) for which the data are held
- the source of the data
- the person(s) to whom it is intended the data may be disclosed.

  † *A person may be registered as falling into one of three descriptions:*
  - *a data user*
  - *a person carrying on a computer bureau*
  - *or a person who does both.*

1.4 Enforcement
Data users must adopt procedures which comply with the 'Data Protection Principles'. Failure to comply with these principles may lead to the Data Protection Registrar issuing an enforcement notice requiring a user to comply. Failure to respond to a notice may then lead to a prosecution.

There are a number of offences which may be committed by data users. Employees and agents of data users may also be liable when offences are committed. The Registrar may apply for a search warrant in order to gather evidence of offences.

1.5 Meaning of Terms
Data Protection Act 1984 Section 1

Data: 'Data' means information recorded in a form in which it can be processed by equipment operating automatically or in response to instructions given for that purpose.

Note: The word 'data' is the plural of 'datum', meaning an item of information; thus 'data' is a number of items of information. 'Data' is used, correctly, in the plural in the Act. However, it is conceded (Concise Oxford Dictionary) that 'data' is commonly used as a term in the singular, denoting information.

Personal data: These are data consisting of information which relates to **living** individuals who can be identified from that information (on its own or together with other information held by the data user).

Exception: Data used only to prepare the text of documents will not be classed as 'data' because the operation of preparing the text of documents is not regarded as data processing. Thus, letters prepared in a word-processing package on a computer may contain personal details but such details will not be considered to be 'data' for the purposes of the Act.

The term 'personal data' will include expressions of opinion about an individual, but will not include any indication of the intentions of the data user in respect of that individual.

Thus, 'I think Smith is incompetent in his current job' is part of the personal data relating to Smith, whereas, 'I intend to move Smith out of the department before June' will not be regarded as personal data.

Data user: A data user is a person who holds personal data.

Computer bureau: A person carries on a computer bureau for the purposes of the Act if he provides others with services in respect of data, e.g. processes data for data users, or allows data users to have use of his equipment on which to process their data.

Data subject: A data subject is a person in respect of whom personal data are held.

Disclosure: Where the identification of an individual depends partly on data and partly on other information held by the data user, those data are not regarded as disclosed unless the other information is also disclosed. For example, personal details of employees are held on computer, each employee being identified by a 'roll number' rather than by name; their names are kept on a separate list. There will be no 'disclosure' of the personal details, unless the list of names is also disclosed.

2 DATA PROTECTION PRINCIPLES
Data Protection Act 1984 Schedule 1

2.1 First Principle

Principle: The information to be contained in personal data shall be obtained, and personal data shall be processed, fairly and lawfully.

Explanation: In determining whether information is obtained fairly, regard will be had to the method used to obtain it, in particular whether anyone from whom it was obtained was deceived or misled. Whereas subterfuge may well be used to gather information in the course of investigating a crime, if any such information is used to compile personal data, a breach of this principle may arise.

2.2 Second Principle

Principle: Personal data shall be held only for one or more specified and lawful purposes.

Explanation: The purpose for which a particular data application is held will be specified in the registration. To hold data for some other purpose, or to hold data in an application which is not registered, will contravene this principle.

2.3 **Third Principle**

Principle: Personal data held for any purpose(s) shall not be used or disclosed in a manner incompatible with such purpose(s).

Explanation: There are two distinct aspects here – use and disclosure. If a police officer keeps a computer list of neighbourhood watch members and supplies their names and addresses to a salesman for security locks, both the use and the disclosure of the data will be in breach of this principle.

2.4 **Fourth Principle**

Principle: Personal data held for any purpose(s) shall be adequate, relevant and not excessive in relation to such purpose(s).

Explanation: It is not in keeping with this principle to have personal details which are not needed for the purpose for which the data are held. In the case of the example of the list of neighbourhood watch members, name, address and telephone number would be essential; religion, whether married or merely living together, etc, are not relevant, and to keep such information would be excessive.

2.5 **Fifth Principle**

Principle: Personal data shall be accurate and, where necessary, kept up-to-date.

Explanation: This principle has particular relevance for criminal intelligence and other police systems. Implicit in the principle is the need for procedures for reviewing and updating entries on a regular basis.

2.6 **Sixth Principle**

Principle: Personal data kept for any purpose(s) shall not be kept longer than are necessary for such purpose(s).

Explanation: If a person's details are held on a police computer as a result of that person having been the victim of a crime, for how long should it be necessary to retain those details? Questions such as these are addressed in a code of practice which has been agreed between police forces and the Registrar.

2.7 **Seventh Principle**

Principle: An individual shall be entitled:
  – at reasonable intervals and without undue delay and expense:
    i) to be informed by any data user whether she holds personal data of which that individual is the subject; and
    ii) to have access to any such data held by a data user; and
  – where appropriate, to have such data corrected or erased.

Explanation: A person is entitled to ask whether a data user has data relating to that person. If that is the case, the person is entitled to have access to those details and to require that if they are no longer required, or if they are not accurate, that they be deleted or put right. This right is widely exercised in respect of credit ratings, but applies equally to police systems (subject to exemptions – *see below*).

Note: that access does not have to be instant or free, but it must be provided within a reasonable period, which is laid down in the Act as no more than 40 days. The fee which may be charged must not exceed the maximum specified in regulations made under the Act.

2.8 Eighth Principle

Principle: Appropriate security measures shall be taken against unauthorised access to, or alteration, disclosure or destruction of personal data, and against their accidental loss or destruction.

Note: This principle applies, as do all the others, to data users. It is, however, the only one which applies to persons carrying on computer bureaux, who do not hold data themselves, but provide processing services or equipment to data users.

Explanation: It is not only for the convenience of the data user, that steps have to be taken to prevent unauthorised access to or tampering with personal data; this principle also seeks to safeguard the data subject. Accidental loss or destruction must also be catered for, so a prompt such as, 'Are you sure you want to delete this file?' would go some way towards a system meeting this requirement. Implicit in this principle is the need for codewords, restriction of access to offices where computers are housed, provision for disposal of confidential waste, etc. The nature of the security provisions required will be determined taking account of the nature of the personal data and the harm which may be caused by unauthorised disclosure, accidental destruction, etc.

3 OFFENCES

Data Protection Act 1984 Sections 5, 6

3.1 Any Person

A person commits an offence who:
- in connection with an application for registration
- knowingly or recklessly
- furnishes the Registrar with false or misleading information.

3.2 Not Registered

A person commits an offence who:
- holds personal data
- without being registered for the time being as a data user.

3.3 Registered Data User

A person who is a registered data user will commit an offence if:
- knowingly or recklessly
- he does any of the following:
    i) holds personal data of any description other than that specified in the entry
    ii) holds any such data, or uses data held by him, for any purpose(s) other than is described in the entry
    iii) obtains such data, or information to be contained in the data, to be held by him from any source which is not described in the entry
    iv) discloses such data held by him to any person who is not described in the entry; or

v) directly or indirectly transfers such data held by him to any country or territory outside the United Kingdom other than one named or described in the entry.

3.4 **Servant or Agent**

When a data user is in breach of the requirements (ii) – (v) of the preceding paragraph, any person who:

- being the servant or agent of the registered person
- knowingly or recklessly
- uses, discloses or transfers data in breach of any of the requirements (ii) to (v)
- will commit an offence.

3.5 **Procure Disclosure**

A person commits an offence who:

- procures the disclosure to him of personal data
- the disclosure to him being in breach of the restrictions on disclosure
- and he knows or has reason to believe that this is the case.

3.6 **Sell Data**

A person commits an offence who:

- sells personal data the disclosure of which he has unlawfully procured
- or offers to sell personal data which have been, or are subsequently unlawfully procured by him
- the offence applies equally to information extracted from personal data.

3.7 **Explanation**

Knowingly or recklessly: This element is missing from the offence of holding data without being registered. To be guilty of an offence a registered data user must know he is contravening one or other of the restrictions, or at least be reckless as to the possibility.

The various ways in which offences may be committed correspond closely to the Data Principles. If a data user has effective procedures in place to effect compliance with the Principles, it is less likely that he will be found to have contravened them knowingly or recklessly, and more likely that the fault will lie with an agent or employee.

Servant or agent: For the purposes of the Act the constables under the direction and control of a chief officer of police shall be treated as his servants. Similar provisions apply to a body of constables maintained other than by a police authority, e.g. British Transport Police. A Government Department shall not be liable to prosecution under the Act, but Crown servants shall be treated as servants of Government departments and may be liable for offences.

Procure disclosure: Any person who procures the disclosure of personal data in circumstances amounting to a breach of restrictions, i.e. not being a person described in the register as someone to whom that data may be disclosed, will commit an offence if she knows or has reason to believe that disclosure to her amounts to a contravention of the law. It is not necessary that the person making the disclosure is himself guilty of an offence, e.g. he may have been misled into disclosing the data, rather than having done so 'knowingly or recklessly.'

A police officer, or anyone else carrying out an enquiry, who procures the wrongful disclosure of information may commit this offence. However, there is an exemption where information is required for the purposes of preventing or detecting crime *(see 'paragraph 5)*.

Sell or offer: Once a person has committed an offence by procuring improper disclosure, he will commit a further offence if he sells that data or offers them for sale. Offering to sell data which are thereafter procured unlawfully will likewise be an offence.

For these purposes, an advertisement that personal data are or may be for sale will be regarded as an offer to sell.

4 DATA SUBJECT'S ACCESS TO DATA
Data Protection Act 1984 Section 21

4.1 Right of Access
A person shall be entitled:
 – to be informed by a data user whether the data held by that user includes personal data relating to that person; and
 – to be supplied by the data user with a copy of the information constituting such data.

4.1.1 *Explanation*
Request: A data user does not have to respond to a request unless it is in writing. A fee may be chargeable (maximum fee prescribed by the Act). The data user must respond within 40 days from the time he is satisfied as to the identity of the person making the request.

Information: When information is supplied, if it is supplied in terms which are not intelligible without explanation, then an explanation of those terms must be supplied also.

Data identifying another person: The data user does not have to comply with the request if to do so necessitates identifying someone else, unless that second person has consented to the first person having the information.

Court order: If a data user fails to comply with a request for information, the person concerned may obtain an order from the High Court or a county court, requiring the data user to comply.

4.2 Compensation and Rectification
Data Protection Act 1984 Sections 22 – 24

4.2.1 *Compensation*
A data subject who suffers damage by reason of inaccuracy of data held by a data user shall be entitled to compensation from the data user for that damage and for any distress caused as a result. Compensation may similarly be claimed following loss or destruction of data or unauthorised disclosure. Proceedings are taken in the High Court or a county court.

Compensation may not be claimed for distress alone, but if damage results to the data subject, the compensation may be for distress as well as for the damage.

4.2.2 *Rectification and Erasure*
When a person claims compensation, the court which hears the matter may order that the data to which the claim relates be rectified or erased, as appropriate.

5 EXEMPTIONS

5.1 Prevention and Detection of Crime, etc
Data Protection Act 1984 Section 28

5.1.1 *Extent of Exemption*
This exemption applies to:
- subject access
- non-disclosure provisions.

5.1.2 *When Exemption Applies*
The exemption applies:
- in relation to the prevention or detection of crime
- or the apprehension or prosecution of offenders
- in any case in which the application of the provisions would prejudice the purpose(s) for which the data is held.

5.1.3 *Explanation*
Extent: The effect of the exemption is that a data subject may lawfully be refused access to data about himself, and that a data user may lawfully disclose personal data to a person who is not listed in the registration as a person to whom the data may be disclosed, e.g. the police.

Prejudice: It is not sufficient for the exemption to apply, that police are seeking to detect crime or arrest an offender; it must be shown that if the subject was allowed access, or if a data user refused to disclose information to the police, the purpose (detection of crime, etc) would be prejudiced.

If an active criminal is subject of an intelligence gathering operation with a view to obtaining sufficient evidence to arrest and prosecute him, it would clearly be prejudicial to the operation to allow him access to data on the criminal intelligence computer. It would not be prejudicial to allow access to Police National Computer details of his previous convictions, so access to these could not be denied under this provision. When police seek details of the finances of a crime suspect from his bank, the bank manager will not release details as a matter of course; an investigating officer will have to satisfy the bank manager that she will be protected by the exemption when she releases personal data.

5.2 National Security
Data Protection Act 1984 Section 27

5.2.1 *Extent of Exemption*
The exemption extends to the whole of the Act, including the need to register.

5.2.2 *When Exemption Applies*
The exemption applies when necessary for the purposes of safeguarding national security.

5.3 Domestic or Recreational Purposes
Data Protection Act 1984 Section 33

5.3.1 *Extent of Exemption*
The exemption applies to most of the Act, including registration, subject access and action for damage arising from inaccurate, etc, information.

5.3.2 *When Exemption Applies*
This exemption applies to:
- personal data held by a person relating only to the management of her personal, family or household affairs, or for her recreational purposes
- personal data relating to members of a members' club
- data held for the purposes of distributing articles or information, consisting only of names and addresses, or other information necessary for effecting distribution.

5.3.3 *Explanation*
Personal, family, etc: The effect of this exemption is that the Registrar does not chase after individuals who keep names and addresses of friends and acquaintances on a home computer or in a personal organiser. This does not, however, allow for an individual to keep applications relating to other matters, such as his employment, without registration.

Club: It is a condition of this exemption that a member must have been asked whether he has any objection to his data being kept, and that he has not objected.

Distribution: In the case of a list kept for distribution of articles, there are two conditions which must be met if the exemption is to apply – that the persons concerned have been asked and do not object – and that the information is not disclosed without their consent.

5.4 Other Exemptions

5.4.1 *Taxation*
This exemption is similar to that relating to crime investigation.

5.4.2 *Health and Social Work*
There are limited exemptions to subject access rights.

5.4.3 *Court Orders*
There is exemption from the non-disclosure provisions where disclosure is required by law or by order of a court.

5.4.4 *Life and Limb*
There is exemption from the non-disclosure provisions where disclosure is urgently required for preventing injury or damage to someone's health.

5.4.5 *Other Exemptions*
Among other exemptions are:
- details of salaries, pensions, purchase, sales and other business records
- examination marks
- data relating to judicial appointments or where a claim of legal professional privilege could be made
- data held for carrying out research or for preparing statistics.

6 COMPUTER MISUSE
Computer Misuse Act 1990

6.1 Hacking

Some expert people are able to gain unauthorised access to computer systems, despite sophisticated security, in ways which are unfathomable to those of us whose computing skills are stretched to the limit getting our own machines to work properly. The 1990 Act creates offences in relation to the activities of these 'hackers', and to anyone else who seeks to gain unauthorised access to a computer system. Such activity may or may not also involve a breach of data protection legislation.

6.2 Offences

6.2.1 *Unauthorised Access*
Computer Misuse Act 1990 Section 1

A person commits an offence if:
 - he causes a computer to perform any function with intent to secure access to any program or data held in any computer; and
 - the access he intends to secure is unauthorised; and
 - he knows at the time he causes the computer to perform the function that this is the case.

6.2.2 *Unauthorised Access with Intent*
Computer Misuse Act 1990 Section 2

A person commits an offence who:
 - commits an offence under Section 1 (unauthorised access)
 - with intent either
 - to commit an offence to which this Section applies
 - or to facilitate the commission of such an offence, by himself or another.

Section 2 applies to any offence:
 - the sentence for which is fixed by law; or
 - the sentence for which on first conviction may be five years' imprisonment.

6.2.3 *Unauthorised Modification of Computer Material*
Computer Misuse Act 1990 Section 3

A person commits an offence if:
 - he does any act which causes an unauthorised modification of the contents of any computer; and
 - at the time he does the act he has the requisite intent; and
 - at the time he does the act he knows that any modification he intends to cause is unauthorised.

The 'requisite intent' is an intent to cause a modification to the contents of the computer and by so doing:
 - to impair the operation of any computer, or
 - to prevent or hinder access to any computer, or data held in any computer, or
 - to impair the operation of any such program or the reliability of any such data.

6.2.4 *Explanation*

Intent... any computer: A person may commit an offence, under Section 1 (unauthorised access) or Section 3 (unauthorised modification) with intent to access or modify **any** computer, program or data. For example, a hacker may cause his own computer to perform a function, such as dialling large amounts of telephone numbers, with intent to gain unauthorised access to any program or data held on any computer. He does not have to have any particular program or any specific computer in mind. Similarly, a person who distributes a floppy disk containing a 'computer virus' (a program which will cause other programs to malfunction), will commit an offence under Section 3 without there being a need to prove that he intended the disk to be loaded into a specific computer.

Knowledge: To commit the offence, the person must know at the time of carrying out the necessary action, that the access or modification he intends is not authorised.

Intent to commit offence: The offences to which Section 2 relates may at first sight appear to be equivalent to arrestable offences. Indeed, any offence for which the sentence is fixed by law (murder) or for which a person may on first conviction receive a sentence of five years, will be an arrestable offence. However, those offences which are arrestable offences even though the maximum sentence is less than five years (such as taking a conveyance, possession of an offensive weapon) will not amount to an offence to which Section 2 relates.

The offences for which unauthorised access to a computer is most likely to be part of the preparation, such as theft, obtaining property by deception, false accounting, etc, all carry a possible five year sentence.

Further offence: For the purposes of an offence of obtaining unauthorised access with intent to commit a further offence, it is immaterial whether the further offence is to be committed at the same time as the unauthorised access, or on some future occasion. In order to make preparation to carry out a fraud, a criminal may well seek to gain unauthorised access to a computer some time before carrying out the fraud.

Unauthorised modification: To amount to the offence under Section 3, the intended modification must be a detrimental one – to impair the operation of a computer or of a program, or of data reliability, or to hinder access to any program or data. If a well meaning employee makes some modification to her employer's computer system intending to improve it, she will not commit the offence, even if her efforts cause chaos.

Temporary or permanent: An offence under Section 3 may arise whether the intended modification is to be temporary or permanent.

Criminal damage: Any modification to the contents of a computer shall **not** be regarded as an offence of criminal damage, unless the modification impairs the physical condition of the computer or its storage medium – i.e. disk, etc (Section 3(6)).

6.3 Comparison with Data Protection Offences

A person who has authority to access a computer system will not be guilty of an offence under Sections 1 or 2, if he accesses the system to extract information which he then intends to use for an unauthorised or unlawful purpose. Police officers who secured access to a police computer, to use the information therein for non-police purposes, were not guilty of gaining unauthorised access. The improper use of data is covered by the Data Protection Act 1984 (*DPP v Bignell and Another* (1997)).

6.4 **Sentence and Arrest**

An offence under Section 1, of unauthorised access, carries a maximum sentence of six months' imprisonment, and there is no statutory power of arrest for the offence. Offences under Sections 2 and 3 are triable either way; on indictment the maximum sentence is five years' imprisonment, making these arrestable offences.

6.5 **Search Warrant**
Computer Misuse Act 1990 Section 14

6.5.1 *Grounds for Issue*

A circuit judge may issue a warrant, if satisfied by information on oath from a constable that there are reasonable grounds for believing:
- that an offence under Section 1 has been or is about to be committed in any premises; and
- that evidence that such an offence has been or is about to be committed is in those premises.

6.5.2 *Powers Under the Warrant*

The warrant will authorise a constable:
- to enter and search the premises, using such reasonable force as is necessary
- to seize any article he reasonably believes is evidence that an offence under Section 1 has been or is about to be committed.

In addition the warrant may authorise persons to accompany any constable executing the warrant.

6.5.3 *Explanation*

Circuit judge: Most warrants are issued by magistrates; in this case only a circuit judge will do.

Offence under Section 1: The warrant applies only to an offence under Section 1. This is logical since offences under Sections 2 and 3 are arrestable offences, so carrying with them powers to search for evidence under the Police and Criminal Evidence Act 1984.

Other persons may accompany: The warrant may authorise other persons to accompany police executing the warrant. This would allow for the presence of, say, a computer expert, necessary in some cases, given the highly technical nature of some computer systems.

Premises: The term 'premises' includes any land, building, movable structure, vehicle, vessel, aircraft or hovercraft.

Excluded material: The warrant does not authorise searching for privileged, excluded or special procedure material.

7 CERTIFICATES OF CONVICTIONS AND CRIMINAL RECORDS
Police Act 1997 Part V

Note: at time of publication, this legislation is not yet in force – awaiting commencement date.

7.1 **System for Issue of Certificates**

A certificate will be issued by the Secretary of State, upon application by any individual, but in certain cases, the application must be countersigned by a registered person. In each case, the applicant must pay the appropriate fee. The certificate will either give details of the applicant's criminal record, or state that there is no such detail on record. There are different sorts of certificates, containing differing levels of detail. The primary purpose of such certificates is to provide prospective employers with a check on the background of job applicants. This extends to unpaid work, e.g. as a youth leader, as well as to paid employment.

These provisions are quite distinct from the rights of a data subject to be supplied with details of the data relating to him kept by a data user.

7.2 Criminal Conviction Certificate
Police Act 1997 Section 112

7.2.1 *Content*
A criminal conviction certificate gives details of every conviction of the applicant which is recorded on central records, excluding any 'spent conviction'.

7.2.2 *Counter-Signature*
There is no need for an application for a criminal conviction certificate to be countersigned.

7.3 Criminal Record Certificate
Police Act 1997 Sections 113 and 114

7.3.1 *Content*
A criminal record certificate gives details of the applicant recorded in central records which relate to convictions, including spent convictions, and cautions.

7.3.2 *Counter-Signature*
An application must be:
- counter-signed by a registered person, or
- in relation to Crown employment, be accompanied by a statement by a Minister of the Crown.

7.3.3 *Purpose*
The application must be accompanied by a statement, by the registered person or by the Minister, as appropriate, to the effect that it is required in relation to an 'exempted question', which may be asked, in accordance with the provisions of the Rehabilitation of Offenders Act 1974.

7.4 Enhanced Criminal Record Certificate
Police Act 1997 Sections 115 and 116

7.4.1 *Content*
An enhanced criminal record certificate will contain details relating to the applicant:
- which are recorded in central records, of convictions, including spent convictions, and cautions
- any relevant details provided to the Secretary of State by a relevant police force.

7.4.2 *Counter-Signature*
An application for an enhanced criminal record certificate must be:
- countersigned by a registered person, or
- be accompanied by a statement from a Minister of the Crown.

7.4.3 *Purpose*

The application must be accompanied by a statement, by the registered person or by the Minister, as appropriate, to the effect that it is required in relation to an 'exempted question', which may be asked, in accordance with the provisions of the Rehabilitation of Offenders Act 1974.

The exempted question must relate to considering the applicant's suitability for certain posts, paid or unpaid, or for certain licences, etc, including:

- a position involving training, caring for, supervising or being in charge of persons aged under 18
- certain positions, set out in regulations, relating to the care or supervision of persons aged 18 or over
- matters relating to fostering children
- judicial appointments
- applications for certain certificates or licences relating to gaming or lotteries.

7.4.4 *Enhanced Criminal Record Certificate – Information Supplied*

In addition to supplying an enhanced criminal record certificate to the applicant, the Secretary of State will also send a copy of the certificate to the registered person, together with certain additional information, not included in the certificate.

7.5 **Explanation**

Level of detail: The three types of certificate give increasing levels of detail. If a person has no convictions or cautions, and no details are recorded about him by a police force, then a 'statement', that there are no details known, would result from an application for any of the three types of certificate. If a person has received a police caution, or has only a spent conviction, this would lead to a statement of no convictions if he applied for a criminal conviction certificate, but would be revealed if the application was for one of the other two types.

Registered person: A 'registered person' may be:

- a body
- the holder of an office; or
- an individual who employs others in the course of business.

In each case, the Secretary of State before registering the person or body, must be satisfied that the applicant is likely to ask 'exempted questions', or to countersign applications on behalf of someone who does.

Exempt question: Under the provisions of the Rehabilitation of Offenders Act 1974, a person is not obliged to answer questions about spent convictions he may have, except in relation to applications for certain sorts of employment or licences. Thus, questions may be asked, and must be answered, relating to a spent conviction, when applying for registration as a veterinary surgeon, accountant, chemist, etc, or for a job as a traffic warden, magistrates' clerk or prison officer.

If a man applies for a job as a car park attendant at a supermarket, the employer may well require him to apply for a criminal conviction certificate and to produce it at an interview. The man does not need any counter-signature for his application. The employer would not be entitled to ask the prospective car park attendant about spent convictions, and would not be entitled to require him to show one of the other types of certificate. If a person seeks a post as a magistrates' clerk, she may be asked to apply for a criminal record certificate, and her application will have to be countersigned.

Information from police: An enhanced criminal record certificate will include information supplied by a 'relevant police force', in addition to details of convictions and cautions. The meaning of 'relevant police force' will be set out in regulations. A police force will be paid a fee for supplying such information. This could be information kept in criminal intelligence files, for example.

Additional information: A chief officer of police, in supplying information for an enhanced certificate, should indicate what matters ought not to be included in the certificate, in the interests of the prevention or detection of crime. This is similar to the provisions of the Data Protection Act, that a data subject does not have to be given information relating to ongoing crime enquiries. However, the police may also indicate what information, which ought not to be included on the certificate, may be disclosed to the authorised person without harming the interests of the prevention or detection of crime.

7.6 Identification of Applicant
Police Act 1997 Section 119

The Secretary of State may refuse to issue a certificate unless the application is accompanied by satisfactory evidence of the identity of the applicant. In particular, the applicant may be required to have his fingerprints taken, for which another fee may be charged.

7.7 Offences

7.7.1 *Deceit and False Statements*
Police Act 1997 Section 123

A person commits an offence who, with intent to deceive:
- makes a false certificate; or
- alters a certificate; or
- uses a certificate relating to another person in a way which suggests it relates to him; or
- allows a certificate which relates to him, to be used by another person in a way which suggests it relates to that other person.

A person also commits an offence who:
- knowingly makes a false statement
- for the purpose of obtaining, or enabling another to obtain, a certificate.

7.7.2 *Improper Disclosure of Information*
Police Act 1997 Section 124

A number of offences are provided under this Section, which may be committed by members, employees etc, of bodies following an application for a criminal record certificate or enhanced criminal record certificate. It will not be unlawful for information to be disclosed to an employee who requires it in the course of his duties, but improper disclosure by that person in turn, will amount to an offence.

Chapter 38: Mental Health

1 INTRODUCTION

1.1 Compulsory Hospital Admission

A person cannot be forced to enter hospital for removal of tonsils or to have an artificial hip fitted. However, when it comes to mental illness, there are provisions for compulsory admission to hospital, and these provisions bring with them terms such as 'custody', 'detention', 'escape' more commonly applied to criminals. Police officers and others have powers to detain mental patients in certain circumstances. A person may also be detained in a mental hospital as a result of a court order, before sentence having been found guilty, in lieu of a sentence, or having been ruled unfit to plead to a criminal charge. A person serving a prison sentence after conviction may be moved into a hospital and detained there for treatment.

1.2 Approved Social Worker
Mental Health Act 1983 Section 145

The term 'approved social worker' means a local authority social services officer appointed to act as an approved social worker for the purposes of the legislation. Put simply, an approved social worker has undergone special training in dealing with mentally-ill people and will usually be involved with police and doctors in making arrangements for such a person's admission to a hospital.

2 MENTALLY DISORDERED PERSON IN PUBLIC PLACE
Mental Health Act 1983 Section 136

2.1 Police Powers
If a constable finds:
- in a place to which the public have access
- a person who appears to her to be suffering from mental disorder
  and to be in immediate need of care or control
- the officer may if she thinks it necessary to do so in the interests of that person
  or for the protection of other people
- remove that person to a place of safety.

2.2 Subsequent Arrangements
A person removed to a place of safety under this Section may be:
- detained there for a period not exceeding 72 hours for the purpose of enabling him to be
- examined by a registered medical practitioner
- and interviewed by an approved social worker
- and of making any necessary arrangements for his treatment and care.

2.2.1 *Explanation*
Grounds for detaining: The policy of demolishing Victorian mental hospitals and returning former patients to care in the community has led to a large increase in the number of persons

who appear to be mentally ill, who come to the notice of the police. The fact that a person appears to be mentally ill is not sufficient ground to detain him. The constable must also be satisfied that the person is in immediate need of care and control and that his detention is necessary, for that person's own protection or for the protection of other people.

Place of safety: For the purposes of this Section, the term includes a police station, social services residential accommodation, a mental nursing home or residential home, or any other suitable place the occupier of which is willing temporarily to receive the patient.

Note: That for the purposes of persons detained under other provisions, 'place of safety' includes a prison (paragraph 3.1.3). Here, 'place of safety' encompasses a different list so there is no question of taking a mentally-ill person from a public place straight to prison.

Reason for detaining: The purpose of detaining the person is for a doctor and approved social worker to make an expert assessment of the person's condition, to confirm whether what 'appears to the constable' to be the case is actually so. If it is decided that further treatment is required, detention may continue (but not beyond the original 72 hours) until arrangements are made.

3 CUSTODY
Mental Health Act 1983 Section 137

3.1 Legal Custody

3.1.1 *Patient Deemed to be in Legal Custody*
Any person who is required or authorised under the Act to be conveyed to any place, to be detained or kept in custody in a place of safety or other place where he is taken (e.g. in connection with an enquiry) shall while he is being so conveyed, detained or kept be deemed to be in legal custody.

There are various provisions whereby a person may be detained in a hospital, and powers to re-take him if he absconds or goes absent without leave. This Section caters for persons being taken to or from a place of safety or other place. There is a specific power to re-take a person who absconds from 'legal custody' as it is here defined.

3.1.2 *Powers of a Constable*
A constable or any other person taking a person into custody under the provisions of the Act or conveying or detaining such a person shall for these purposes have all the powers, authorities, protection and privileges which a constable has in the area for which he acts.

3.1.3 *Explanation*
Legal custody: When a person is detained at a police station under these provisions, he will be subject to the provisions of Code C of the Codes of Practice to the Police and Criminal Evidence Act 1984. The Code provides for care and treatment of detained persons. (The provisions of PACE relating to reviews of detention do not apply, however.)

Place of safety: In this Section, 'place of safety' means any police station, prison or remand centre, or any hospital the managers of which are willing temporarily to receive the patient.

3.2 Powers to Convey Patients
Mental Health Act 1983 Section 40

In certain circumstances a Crown Court or magistrates' court may make a hospital order in relation to a person who appears before the court, for that person either to be examined as to his mental health, or to receive treatment. A hospital order shall be sufficient authority for a constable, approved social worker or any other person directed to do so by the court, to convey the patient to the hospital specified in the order within a period of 28 days.

Thus, the hospital order takes the place of what would be a commitment warrant if the person was being remanded to prison.

4 PATIENT UNLAWFULLY AT LARGE

4.1 Power to Re-take Patients

There are a number of provisions which allow for a patient who is unlawfully at large to be re-taken (or arrested) by the police or other persons. In some cases, the power to re-take lasts only for a relatively short period, related to the maximum time the patient was liable to be detained in the first place.

4.2 Person Liable to be Detained in Hospital
Mental Health Act 1983 Section 18(1)

When a person who is liable to be detained in hospital:
- goes absent without leave
- fails to return after a period of leave of absence or upon being recalled
- or absents himself without permission from where he is supposed to stay during leave of absence

he may be taken into custody and returned to the hospital or other place by:
- a constable
- an approved social worker
- hospital staff or other person authorised by the hospital management.

4.3 Person Subject of Guardianship Order
Mental Health Act 1983 Section 18(3)

When a person who is subject of a guardianship order absents himself without leave from the place where he is required to reside he may be taken into custody and returned to that place by:
- any constable
- staff of social services
- or any person authorised by the guardian or by social services.

4.4 Person Remanded for Medical Report or Medical Treatment
Mental Health Act 1983 Sections 35(10), 36(8), 38(7)

If an accused person who has been remanded by a court to a hospital for a medical report, or by a Crown Court for treatment, absconds either from the hospital or while being conveyed to or from, he may be arrested without warrant by any constable.

4.5 Person in Legal Custody
Mental Health Act 1983 Section 138

If a person who is in legal custody (as the term is defined in Section 137 – *see paragraph 3.1*)

escapes he may be re-taken by:
- by any constable
- by the person who had his custody immediately before he escaped
- by any approved social worker
- by any person who could have re-taken him under Section 18 had he gone absent without leave *(see paragraphs 4.2, 4.3).*

4.6 Time Limits on Powers to Re-take Patients

In relation to the several powers to re-take patients detailed above, the power may not extend beyond the period for which the person concerned was liable to be detained.

For example, a person liable to be re-taken under Section 18(1) *(paragraph 4.2)* may not be re-taken after six months have expired. A person detained by the police having been found in a public place, may be kept for up to 72 hours in a place of safety. If he escapes during this time, the power to re-take him expires when the 72-hour period ends.

5 OFFENCES RELATING TO MISSING MENTAL PATIENTS
Mental Health Act 1983 Section 128

5.1 Persons Liable to be Detained or Subject of Guardianship

A person commits an offence who:
- in relation to a person who is liable to be detained in hospital or who is subject of a guardianship order
- induces or knowingly assists that person to absent himself without leave.

5.2 Person in Legal Custody

A person commits an offence who:
- in relation to a person in legal custody under Section 137
- induces or knowingly assists that person to escape.

5.3 Harbouring a Missing Patient

A person commits an offence who:
- in relation to a patient who is absent without leave or otherwise at large and liable to be re-taken
- knowingly harbours the patient
- or gives him any assistance
- with intent to prevent, hinder or interfere with his being taken into custody or returned to the hospital or other place where he ought to be.

6 SEARCH WARRANTS
Mental Health Act 1983 Section 135

6.1 Patient Liable to be Taken into Custody

6.1.1 *Grounds for Issue*

A magistrate may issue a warrant if it appears on information on oath:

- laid by a constable
- that there is reasonable cause to believe that a patient who is liable to be taken into custody or re-taken under this Act (or under corresponding provisions for Scotland)
- is to be found on any premises (within the magistrate's jurisdiction)
- and that admission to the premises has been refused or a refusal is apprehended.

6.1.2 *Powers Under the Warrant*
The warrant will authorise any constable:
- to enter the premises if need be by force
- and remove the patient.

6.1.3 *Accompanying the Police*
In the execution of such warrant, the constable **may** be accompanied by a registered medical practitioner and/or a person authorised under the Act to take or re-take the patient.

6.2 Concern for Welfare

6.2.1 *Grounds for Issue*
A magistrate may issue a warrant if it appears on information on oath:
- laid by an approved social worker that in any place within the magistrate's jurisdiction
- there is reasonable cause to suspect that a person believed to be suffering from mental disorder
- has been or is being ill-treated, neglected or kept otherwise than under proper control
- or being unable to care for himself is living alone there.

6.2.2 *Powers Under the Warrant*
The warrant will authorise a constable:
- to enter premises specified in the warrant in which the person is believed to be, if need be by force
- and if thought fit, remove the person to a place of safety with a view to making arrangements for his treatment or care.

6.2.3 *Accompanying the Police*
In the execution of this warrant the police **shall** be accompanied by a registered medical practitioner and by an approved social worker.

6.2.4 *Detention*
A person removed to a place of safety may be detained there for a period not exceeding 72 hours.

6.3 Explanation
Application for warrant: In the case of a patient liable to be taken or re-taken, the application is made by the police. In the welfare situation, the application is made by an approved social worker. In either case, the warrant is issued to the police to do the 'strong-arm' bit.

Accompanying: When the warrant is issued on welfare grounds upon application by an approved social worker, the police who execute the warrant must be accompanied by an approved social worker (not necessarily the same one who made the application) and by a doctor. The patient's condition may not be sufficiently serious to justify that person's removal to a place of safety; the decision can be made by the experts, rather than by the police. In the case of the person liable to be taken or re-taken, the decision that he shall be detained has already been made. The history may indicate that a doctor should accompany the police, and the Section allows for this. In addition, the presence of a person authorised to take or re-take a patient may be helpful. This would allow, for example, a member of staff of the hospital a patient has escaped from, to accompany the police.

Place of safety: For the purposes of this Section, the term includes a police station, social services residential accommodation, a mental nursing home or residential home, or any other suitable place the occupier of which is willing temporarily to receive the patient.

7 ILL-TREATMENT OF MENTAL PATIENTS
Mental Health Act 1983 Section 127

7.1 Offences
1: A person will commit an offence who:
  - being on the staff, otherwise employed in, or a manager of a hospital or mental nursing home
  - ill-treats or wilfully neglects a person receiving treatment for mental disorder as an in-patient
  - or, on those premises, ill-treats or wilfully neglects a person receiving such treatment as an out-patient.

2: A person will commit an offence who:
  - ill-treats or wilfully neglects a mentally-disordered person
  - who is subject to his guardianship under the Act
  - or who is otherwise in his custody or care (whether by virtue of a legal or moral obligation or otherwise).

7.1.1 *Explanation*
Staff: The first offence may be committed only by a member of staff or manager of a hospital or mental nursing home. The offence would cover a situation where evidence of some other offence, e.g. assault, was lacking.

In-patient/out-patient: The victim may be an in-patient, in which case the ill-treatment or neglect may occur on or off the hospital premises. If the victim is an out-patient, the ill-treatment has to occur on the premises. Thus, if a patient attends every Tuesday for treatment, the offence may only be committed while he is on the hospital premises.

Otherwise in custody or care: The offence may be committed by any person who has custody or care of a mental patient for any period of time. This may be legal custody, as when a constable or approved social worker is escorting a patient to hospital. The 'custody' may, however, have no legal status, as where a neighbour looks after a mentally-disordered person while the parent with whom he lives is out.

7.2 Restriction on Prosecution
Proceedings may not be instituted for any offence under this Section, other than by or with the consent of the Director of Public Prosecutions.

Chapter 39: Harassment

1 PROTECTION FROM HARASSMENT

1.1 Harassment of Another

1.1.1 *Offence*
Protection from Harassment Act 1997 Sections 1, 2

A person commits an offence who:
- pursues a course of conduct
- which amounts to harassment of another
- and which he knows or ought to know amounts to harassment of the other person.

1.1.2 *Explanation*
Conduct: Speech may amount to 'conduct'.

Course of conduct: There must be conduct on at least two occasions before there can be said to be a 'course of conduct'.

Harassment: Harassing a person includes alarming that person or causing him distress.

Ought to know: A person 'ought to know' that his conduct amounts to harassment of another if a reasonable person in possession of the same information would think the course of conduct amounted to harassment of the other person. Since a person who harasses another may well be a very unreasonable person, this provision removes a need to establish an awareness in the accused of the effect his conduct is having on the victim.

Public order offences: The Public Order Act 1986 provides offences of a broadly similar nature, relating to causing alarm and distress. Such an offence is likely to arise as a result of conduct on one occasion, and to obtain a conviction based on one occasion, the offender's conduct would have to be overtly distressing or alarming. For the offence to be committed under this Act, the conduct of the offender may at first sight, appear harmless. For example, walking past the house where the victim lives, or standing outside her place of work, may not appear too distressing. When such behaviour is repeated, on many occasions over a period, it may indeed be seen as harassing.

1.1.3 *Exemption*
An offence will not be committed if a person shows that his course of conduct:
- i) was pursued for the purpose of preventing or detecting crime; or
- ii) was pursued under any enactment or rule of law or to comply with any condition or requirement imposed by any person under any enactment; or
- iii) in the particular circumstances was reasonable.

An active criminal may well feel harassed if he realises he is under surveillance every time he sets out to plan his next robbery, but the officers concerned will not be liable for an offence, their purpose being to prevent or detect crime. Bailiffs seeking to regain possession of a building acting under a court order will likewise not be guilty of harassment of the person in the building.

A private 'detective' may well seek to follow and/or photograph a person involved in court proceedings, e.g. in a divorce case, or where the person is claiming damages for alleged injuries. If this causes harassment, it will be for the 'detective' to show that his conduct was reasonable in the circumstances.

1.1.4 *Arrest*

The offence carries a maximum sentence of six months' imprisonment and/or a fine. However, it is included as an arrestable offence under the provisions of Section 24(2) of the Police and Criminal Evidence Act 1984.

1.2 **Breach of Injunction**
Protection from Harassment Act 1997 Section 3

1.2.1 *Proceedings in Civil Court*

An actual or anticipated course of conduct amounting to harassment may be the subject of a claim in civil proceedings by the person who is or may be the victim, in the High Court or a county court. As well as awarding damages, the court may grant an injunction in order to restrain the defendant from pursuing any conduct which amounts to harassment.

1.2.2 *Offence*

When an injunction has been granted, the defendant will commit an offence if:
- without reasonable excuse
- he does anything which he is prohibited from doing by the injunction.

1.2.3 *Warrant for Arrest*

If the plaintiff (i.e. the victim of the actual or anticipated harassment) considers that the defendant has done anything which he is prohibited from doing by the injunction, he may apply to a judge (of the High Court or a county court, dependent on which court granted the injunction) for the issue of a warrant for the arrest of the defendant.

1.2.4 *Arrest Without Warrant*

The offence of doing anything in breach of an injunction is triable either way; on indictment it is punishable with a maximum of five years' imprisonment, making it an arrestable offence.

1.2.5 *Explanation*

Civil remedies: A person who causes harassment to another, e.g. by 'stalking' the victim over a period of time, may well prove determined and not put off by an appearance in a magistrates' court. The civil route offers the opportunity to the victim to obtain damages, which may be substantial, as well as an injunction.

Arrest warrant: One may wonder why there is provision for a warrant to be issued to arrest a defendant for breach of an injunction, when that breach amounts to an arrestable offence. One advantage for the victim of having the option to apply for a warrant lies in the nature of the conduct which may amount to harassment. Any single action may appear relatively harmless when looked at on its own; it may be necessary to consider a course of conduct over a period of time, to appreciate that harassment is taking place. A complaint to the police may not lead to an arrest, if the officer concerned is unaware of the history and therefore shies away from making an arrest, having doubts as to the existence of 'reasonable grounds for suspecting that an arrestable offence has been committed'.

1.3 Causing Fear of Violence
Protection from Harassment Act 1997 Section 4

1.3.1 *Offence*
A person commits an offence:
- whose course of conduct causes another to fear
- on at least two occasions
- that violence will be used against him
- if he knows or ought to know that his conduct will cause the other so to fear on each of those occasions.

1.3.2 *Exemption*
An offence will not be committed if a person shows that his course of conduct:
- i) was pursued for the purpose of preventing or detecting crime; or
- ii) was pursued under any enactment or rule of law or to comply with any condition or requirement imposed by any person under any enactment; or
- iii) was reasonable for the protection of himself or another, or for the protection of his or another's property.

1.3.3 *Explanation*
Ought to know: The person whose course of conduct is in question ought to know that it will cause another to fear violence will be used against him on any occasion if a reasonable person in possession of the same information would think that the course of conduct would cause the other so to fear on that occasion. This provision, the same as for the offence of harassment, relieves the prosecution of having to prove that a defendant, who may be a person of unreasonable character, was aware of the effect of his actions.

Exemptions: A police officer may have cause to make a person fear that violence will be used against him, e.g. when making an arrest, but will not be liable if acting to prevent or detect crime. Protection of a person or of property will also afford an exemption.

1.3.4 *Arrest*
The offence is triable either way; on indictment it carries a maximum of five years' imprisonment, so is an arrestable offence.

1.3.5 *Alternative conviction*
When a person is charged on indictment with this offence, the jury may find him guilty instead of an offence of harassment contrary to Section 2. In such a case, although harassment is solely a summary offence, the Crown Court may sentence the defendant, and will be restricted to the same maximum punishment as a magistrates' court.

1.4 Restraining Orders
Protection from Harassment Act 1997 Section 5

1.4.1 *Making a Restraining Order*
When a person is convicted of an offence under Section 2 (harassment) or Section 4 (causing fear of violence), the court may, in addition to any sentence, make an order under this Section.

The order may prohibit the defendant from doing anything described in the order, with a view to protecting the victim of the offence or any other person mentioned in the order, from further conduct which amounts to harassment or will cause fear of violence.

The order may have effect for a specified period, but there is no limit to how long this period may be. The prosecutor, the defendant or any other person mentioned in the order may apply to the court which made the order, for it to be varied or discharged.

1.4.2 *Offence*
A person commits an offence who:
- without reasonable excuse
- does anything which he is prohibited from doing by an order under this Section.

1.4.3 *Arrest*
The offence is triable either way, and on indictment is punishable with a maximum of five years' imprisonment, so is an arrestable offence.

1.4.4 *Explanation*
A restraining order is similar to an injunction and affords the criminal courts the opportunity to seek to prevent further incidents.

1.5 Exemption for Action Taken on Behalf of the Crown
Protection from Harassment Act 1997 Section 12

If the Secretary of State certifies that, in his opinion anything done by a specified person on a specified occasion was done on behalf of the Crown and related to:
- national security, or
- the prevention or detection of serious crime, or
- the economic well-being of the United Kingdom
the certificate is conclusive evidence that the Act does not apply to any conduct of that person on that occasion.

This provision bears some similarity to the exemptions provided under Sections 2 and 4 – conduct being pursued to prevent or detect crime, etc. The distinction is that under Sections 2 and 4, the onus is on the person accused to show that the exemption applies to him. Here, the Secretary of State issues a certificate, which effectively avoids the matter having to be further examined by the court.

1.6 Restriction on Use of Harassment Law

The essence of the offence of harassment, carrying out a course of conduct which amounts to harassment of another, may lead to a charge for this offence being considered in a wide variety of circumstances. The primary purpose in enacting the legislation was to give protection to individuals suffering at the hands of so-called 'stalkers', where existing laws were deemed inadequate. The Act was not intended to be used to restrict persons exercising their right to protest about a matter of public interest. The Court of Appeal has indicated that the Act should not be used to deal with persons engaged in political protest or public demonstrations (*Huntingdon Life Sciences Ltd v Curtin and Others* (1997)).

2 **HARASSMENT OF TENANTS**

2.1 **Introduction**

A person who pays rent for premises which are occupied as a dwelling has certain rights, such as freedom from being arbitrarily evicted by the landlord. When the owner of premises wants to have a tenant evicted, court proceedings will normally have to be taken to do so lawfully. A property owner who seeks to 'persuade' a tenant to give up occupancy by applying pressure is likely to commit a criminal offence. People who live in caravans on certain sites have a similar degree of protection from eviction and harassment.

2.2 **Unlawful Eviction**
Protection from Eviction Act 1977 Section 1(2)

2.2.1 *Offence*

A person shall be guilty of an offence who:
- unlawfully deprives the residential occupier of premises
- of his occupation of the premises or of part thereof
- or attempts to do so
- unless he proves that he believed and had reasonable cause to believe
- that the residential occupier had ceased to reside there.

2.2.2 *Explanation*

Residential occupier: This means a person occupying premises as a residence, whether by a contract, or some lawful right to remain there or which restricts the right of others to recover possession of the premises.

These provisions do not extend to premises rented as a shop or office. Usually, there will be an agreement or contract relating to the tenancy, but if an agreement has come to an end and some legal provision allows the occupier, for example, to remain until court proceedings are taken to evict him, he would still be regarded as a residential occupier.

Premises: The term 'premises' may include a caravan and the land on which it stands (*Norton v Knowles* (1967)). This case related to a caravan in which a person had lived on a plot of land for some ten years, with the permission of the owner of the land. The decision does not necessarily apply to every caravan in which someone happens to live.

Reason to believe: The accused will not be guilty if she proves, not only that she believed the tenant had left, but that there was good reason for such belief. If the tenant disappears, taking all his possessions and owing several weeks rent, the landlord has good reason to think that the tenant is not coming back.

2.3 **Harassment of Residential Occupiers**

2.3.1 *Offence*
Protection from Eviction Act 1977 Section 1(3)

A person commits an offence who:
- with intent to cause the residential occupier of premises
- either to give up occupation of the premises or part thereof
- or to refrain from exercising any right or pursuing any remedy in respect of the premises or part thereof

- does acts likely to interfere with the peace or comfort of the residential occupier or members of his household
- or persistently withdraws or withholds services reasonably required for the occupation of the premises as a residence.

2.3.2 *Explanation*

Intent: To be liable, the accused must have the required intent at the time of carrying out the acts of harassment.

Premises or part: It is not necessary that the accused should intend the resident to go away. If the resident, for example, occupies two floors in the building and the accused harasses him to move out of one of the floors, the offence may be committed.

Right or remedy: It may be, for example, that the owner of premises is obliged as part of a tenancy agreement, to keep the premises in good repair. If the tenant then threatens legal action to force the owner to carry out repairs, the owner would commit the offence by harassing the tenant to persuade him not to go to court.

Interfere with peace or comfort: This could be anything from actual threats, to playing loud music late at night. The acts may be directed at the residential occupier or at any other member of his household. Not allowing tenants to use a lavatory close to their rooms has been held to be interference with their peace and comfort, even though there were other lavatory facilities elsewhere in the building, albeit not so convenient (*R v Burke* (1990)).

Withhold services: Services such as water, electricity and gas are those which are required in order to live in a reasonable degree of comfort. If any of these are withheld persistently, i.e. on a number of occasions, this will amount to harassment.

2.4 **Prosecution of Offences**

2.4.1 *Local Housing Authority*

The local housing authority is the body authorised to take proceedings for offences under the Act.

2.4.2 *Police Action*

Complaints of unlawful eviction or harassment may come to the attention of police who, although they will not institute proceedings, should take action as follows:
   i)   in a dispute between a landlord and tenant, or if it seems that an offence may have been committed, make such enquiries as are possible there and then;
   ii) if these enquiries indicate a likely offence, warn the landlord of the provisions of the Act and of the possibility that he may be prosecuted;
   iii) send a full report of the incident to the local housing authority;
   iv) inform the tenant in writing that his complaint has been passed to the housing authority.

2.5 **Caravans**
Caravan Sites Act 1968

Very similar provisions apply to persons who reside on caravans on authorised sites. There are two offences as there are in relation to premises, unlawful eviction and interfering with peace and comfort.

Chapter 40: Liquor Licensing

1 SYSTEM OF LICENSING

1.1 Licensing Justices

Before a person may lawfully sell intoxicating liquor (alcoholic drink) by retail, she must obtain a licence to do so. The body responsible for issuing licences in an area is a group of magistrates, drawn from those who sit at the local magistrates' court, known as the licensing justices. They deal with the issue of new licences, transfer from one licensee to another, or from one set of premises to another, and may impose conditions.

The licensing justices renew licences at their main sitting each year, called the annual general licensing meeting (more commonly called the brewster sessions). They also sit on at least four other occasions during the year, every six to eight weeks or so, at transfer sessions.

Some matters are too urgent to wait for the next sitting of the licensing justices, such as when a licensee walks out and the owners of the pub want to appoint a new manager quickly, or when permission is sought for premises to be open late one night to cater for a special occasion such as a wedding. In such cases application may be made to the ordinary magistrates' court, where such business will usually be dealt with before the criminal matters for that day.

A liquor licence is required only for sale of intoxicating liquor by retail. If sale is wholesale, then a justices' licence is not required, and there will be no restrictions on when business may be done, i.e. permitted hours will not apply. To amount to 'wholesale', the transaction must involve at least nine litres (or one case of 12 bottles) of wine or spirits, or at least 20 litres (or two cases) of beer (Alcoholic Liquor Duties Act 1979, Section 65).

The principal legislation is the Licensing Act 1964, and all references to legislation are to this Act unless stated.

1.2 Types of Licences (permanent)

1.2.1 *On Licence*

Permits the sale and supply of intoxicants for consumption on or off the licensed premises. This type of licence will be held by pubs, restaurants, etc where customers stay on the premises to drink, but drinks may also be taken away.

1.2.2 *Off Licence*

As the name implies, this licence authorises sale and supply of intoxicating liquor for consumption off the licensed premises only. Supermarkets, wine merchants and, of course, your neighbourhood 'off-licence' operate under this type of licence; any consumption in the premises, or even nearby, may render the licensee liable for an offence *(see paragraph 1.5.7)*.

1.2.3 *Full or Restricted*

A licence may be a full licence, which authorises the sale of all types of alcoholic drink, e.g. spirits, wines, beer, cider, or it may be restricted to one or more of these categories. Such a restriction would normally be at the request of the applicant, rather than being imposed by the justices.

1.2.4 *Restaurant or Residential Licence*
An on-licence may be restricted to certain categories of customer, e.g. persons having meals, or persons resident on the licensed premises. These are dealt with in more detail at *paragraph 8*.

1.2.5 *Licence with Conditions*
The justices may impose conditions when they grant a licence. Conditions may, for example, limit sale of liquor to certain groups of persons, such as members of a club.

1.2.6 *Offence*
Licensing Act 1964 Section 161(1)

If the holder of a justices' on-licence knowingly sells or supplies intoxicating liquor for consumption on the premises, to a person not permitted to consume it there under conditions attached to the licence, he shall commit an offence.

1.2.7 *Canteens, Messes, etc*
Certain premises may be authorised by the Secretary of State for the sale of intoxicants, and these are not licensed premises, nor have the police any powers in respect of such premises. Examples include messes on armed forces bases and other government establishments. Generally, there will be one such 'canteen' in each police force area, usually the Police Club at force headquarters, where the hours of opening and rules of conduct for the premises will be approved by the chief officer of police.

1.2.8 *Seamen's Canteens*
Licensing Act 1964 Section 148

A licence may be issued by the licensing justices to premises approved (by the Department of Transport) as a canteen for seamen. To qualify as a seamen's canteen, food and beverages, other than intoxicating liquor, must be available for sale.

The licence will authorise supply for consumption on the premises only, there must be no off-sales. Such premises will be licensed premises, so permitted hours, etc, will apply as they apply in other licensed premises.

1.2.9 *Ships, Planes and Trains*
Licensing Act 1964 Section 199

Intoxicating liquor may be lawfully sold and supplied without a licence:
- on a ship or aircraft travelling within the United Kingdom or to other countries
- on a train, in a carriage where passengers may also be served with food. On a train with a trolley service, this may be every carriage.

1.2.10 *Theatres*
A justices' licence is not required for the sale and supply of intoxicants in premises licensed as a theatre under the provisions of the Theatres Act 1968.

However, the holder of the theatre licence must notify the clerk to the licensing justices of his intention to sell intoxicating liquor. The premises will then be treated as 'licensed premises' for all the purposes of the Act. (However, the holder of the theatre licence is not regarded as the holder of a justices' licence, and is therefore unable to apply for, e.g. a special hours certificate (*R v South Westminster Licensing Justices, ex parte Raymond* (1973)).

1.2.11 *Registered Clubs*

A registered club is one which is restricted, generally, to members and their guests, where the profits from the supply of intoxicating liquor goes to the membership as a whole, rather than as gain to a private individual or company. Such clubs are not governed by the licensing justices, but by the magistrates in ordinary magistrates' courts. These are dealt with in more detail later in the chapter.

1.3 Licences and Other Authorities to Sell (temporary)

1.3.1 *Occasional Licence*

An occasional licence will be granted to the holder of a justices' on-licence, authorising him to sell intoxicating liquor at a place other than his own licensed premises, for a period which may be one day only, or may extend to a maximum of three weeks. Examples when an occasional licence would be appropriate include a function in the village hall or the beer tent at an agricultural show. The hours during which the licence will operate will be specified in the licence. Occasional licences are granted by ordinary magistrates at magistrates' courts, not by the licensing justices.

1.3.2 *Occasional Permission*
Licensing (Occasional Permissions) Act 1983

Whereas an occasional licence will enable the holder of a justices' licence to sell intoxicating liquor in a place which is not normally licensed, an occasional permission serves the same purpose but will be granted to an officer of an organisation not carried on for the purposes of private gain. This enables, for example, a Parent Teacher Association to sell drinks at a function in the school hall without having to operate under an occasional licence through a local licensee, who may want to charge higher prices and keep the profits. A maximum of 12 occasional permissions may be granted to an organisation in any 12 month period. Occasional permissions are granted by the licensing justices.

1.3.3 *Protection Order*
Licensing Act 1964 Section 10

A protection order is granted by the ordinary magistrates, not by the licensing justices, because application may have to be made at very short notice. The order authorises a person to sell intoxicants at particular premises, and has the effect of a temporary licence. An order may be granted to a person who intends to apply for a licence at the next transfer sessions, or may be granted, e.g. to the owner of the premises when the licensee is disqualified, to enable the business to be carried on until the licence may be transferred to a new licensee.

1.3.4 *Death or Bankruptcy*

If a licensee dies, or is declared bankrupt and therefore is unable to continue as a licensee, the licensee's personal representative may carry on the business as if a protection order had been obtained (but without the need to apply for one) (Section 10).

1.4 Application for Licences

When an application is made for the grant or transfer of a justices' licence, for an occasional licence, occasional permission or protection order, the application has to be made to the clerk to the licensing justices (or magistrates' clerk, as the case may be) in accordance with specified procedures, within set time limits. A copy of the application is sent to the chief officer of police for the area. The police then are responsible for looking into the background of the applicant, in order to decide whether or not to oppose the application. Some applications have to be advertised in the local papers and objections may be made by members of the public.

In certain cases, if application is made in sufficient time, and there are no objections, the application may be granted without a hearing.

The licensing justices, as well as granting new licences and renewing expiring ones, may also grant an application for transfer or removal of a justices' licence.

A transfer is when a licence is passed from the previous holder to a new applicant. A removal is when the licence is passed from the old licensed premises to a new set of premises.

1.5 Offences Relating to Licences

1.5.1 *Selling Without a Licence*
Licensing Act 1964 Section 160(1)

There are two offences to consider which may be committed by persons who sell intoxicating liquor without a licence:
- by a person who sells or exposes for sale by retail any intoxicating liquor without being the holder of a justices' licence (or canteen or occasional licence) authorising that sale
- by a person who holds a justices' licence (or a canteen licence, occasional licence or occasional permission) who sells or exposes for sale by retail any intoxicating liquor at a place other than that at which the licence (or permission) authorises sale of that liquor.

1.5.2 *Occupier of Premises*
Licensing Act 1964 Section 160(2)

If one of the above offences is committed on premises, by selling intoxicating liquor without a licence, then the occupier of the premises will also be liable for an offence if it is proved that he was privy or consenting to the sale.

1.5.3 *Explanation*
Sale: A group of drunken men leaving licensed premises at 1.00 am has been held to be evidence of sale or supply outside permitted hours. Where five men, three of whom were drunk, were found sitting round a table in licensed premises, there being glasses of spirits on the table, this was held to be evidence of consumption of liquor after hours, even though no drinking was actually seen to take place.

Where there is evidence that a transaction in the nature of a sale took place, this shall be evidence of a sale, without the need for evidence that money changed hands (Section 196(1)). Payment in advance, before attending an event at which intoxicants were provided, has been held to be a sale (*Doak v Bedford* (1964)). Payment of an admission charge to include a 'free drink' has been held to amount to a sale (*DPP v McVitie* (1996)).

Expose for sale: The offences are complete without a sale taking place, if the liquor is on display for sale. Evidence, e.g. of price lists, fresh glasses available or a till, would all help to strengthen the prosecution case that the liquor was there to be sold.

Privy or consenting: It is not enough to convict the occupier of premises, to show that she had knowledge of unlawful sale of intoxicants. There has to be evidence of her agreement or encouragement.

1.5.4 *Credit Sales*
Licensing Act 1964 Section 166

Sale or supply in licensed premises or in a registered club of intoxicating liquor for consumption on the premises, and consumption of the liquor is subject to the requirement that it must be paid for at the time of sale or supply.

1.5.5 *Exception*
1: When the liquor is for consumption with a meal, and is to be paid for together with the meal.

2: When the liquor is supplied for consumption by a resident or his guest and is to be paid for together with his accommodation.

1.5.6 *Explanation*
The habit of waiters and bar staff in continental Europe, of serving drinks all night and only giving you the bill at the end of the evening, is not followed in this country because it would be unlawful.

Although intoxicating liquor is technically considered not to be 'sold' in a registered club, but rather being a distribution to a member of what he already partly owns, nevertheless he has to pay for that 'distribution' at the time, just as he would have to pay in a pub.

1.5.7 *Off-Licence Offences*
Licensing Act 1964 Section 164

There are two categories of offence which may be committed in relation to an off-licence:

1: When a person has bought intoxicating liquor at premises where the licence does not cover consumption on the premises (i.e. an off-licence) if he then drinks that liquor:
   – in the licensed premises
   – or in premises adjoining or nearby which belong to the licensee, or are under his control or used with his permission
   – or on a highway adjoining or near to those premises

   the licensee shall be guilty of an offence if it is proved that the drinking was with his privity or consent.

2: The licensee commits an offence if:
   – he takes, or causes someone else to take, intoxicating liquor from his premises
   – with intent to evade the terms of the licence
   – and for the purpose of its being sold elsewhere on his behalf or for his benefit or profit.

   If liquor is taken for the purpose of being consumed in a tent, shed or building belonging to the licensee, or hired, used, etc by him, the burden of proving that he did not intend to evade the terms of his licence shall rest with him.

1.5.8 *Explanation*
The aim of these provisions is to prevent off-licences being turned into pubs. Not only is it

unlawful for the licensee to allow customers to drink alcohol on the premises, but if there is any other building nearby in which the licensee has an interest, or if he connives at drinking on the highway outside his premises, he will be liable. There must be proof of the licensee's 'privity or consent'; the fact that he has placed a table and chairs on the pavement outside his shop would be evidence of this.

Likewise, having intoxicants taken to other premises or even a tent, from the off-licence, may be unlawful. It was not unknown, before occasional permissions were invented, for organisations, such as a parents' group having a fund-raising dance, to obtain the intoxicants from an off-licence on a sale-or-return basis, probably in breach of this provision, this being more profitable than having the holder of an on-licence come along with an occasional licence.

1.6 Delivery from Vehicles
Licensing Act 1964 Section 163

1.6.1 *Pre-Ordered Liquor*
A licensee may deliver intoxicating liquor to a customer if it has been ordered in advance, but the Act does not allow liquor to be touted round to be offered for sale on the doorstep, or for extra to be carried which has not been ordered. The milkman may be asked for 'an extra pint today', but the licensed grocer may not.

This Section covers deliveries made from any van, barrow or other vehicle, or any basket or other receptacle. Presumably, the amount of liquor which the licensee or his assistant is able to carry in his arms without using a basket or receptacle is considered unworthy of attention.

1.6.2 *Delivery Records*
Before any intoxicating liquor is despatched for delivery to a customer by way of sale, details have to be entered in:
- a day book kept on the premises from which the liquor is despatched; and
- in a delivery book or invoice carried by the person making the delivery.

The details required are:
- a description of the liquor
- the quantity
- price
- name and address of the customer.

1.6.3 *Police Powers*
A constable may require to examine any van, barrow, vehicle, basket, etc, used in the course of delivery of intoxicating liquor, and may also examine the delivery book or invoice, and the day book kept at the licensee's premises.

1.6.4 *Offences*
The licensee, himself or by his servant or agent, will commit an offence by:
- carrying any liquor for delivery, details of which are not entered in the day book and in the delivery book/invoice
- delivering by sale to any address not entered in the books
- refusing to allow a constable to examine the vehicle or receptacle being used to carry the liquor, or to examine the books.

1.6.5 *Defence*
When a licensee is charged with an offence arising from the action of his servant or agent, he shall not be guilty if he proves that the offence was committed without his knowledge or consent.

1.6.6 *Exception*
This Section does not cover trade deliveries to licensed premises and clubs, so a police officer has no power to stop the brewery lorry on its way to deliver to a pub, to examine the load or invoices.

2 MEANING OF TERMS

2.1 Intoxicating Liquor
Licensing Act 1964 Section 201(1)

2.1.1 *Meaning*
Whatever popular terms are used:
- booze, the hard stuff, alcohol, etc
- the official term is intoxicating liquor.

This term is defined as:
  spirits, wine, beer, cider, and any fermented, distilled or spirituous liquor, but does not include:
- any liquor not exceeding 0.5 per cent alcohol at time of sale (or supply)
- perfume
- certain flavouring essences
- spirits or wine medicated so as to be intended for use as a medicine rather than as a beverage.

2.1.2 *Explanation*
Thus, 'low alcohol' beer at or just under 1 per cent alcohol will still be intoxicating liquor. When a bartender serves a shandy, by mixing beer and lemonade, this is regarded as the sale of two separate items – beer and lemonade – so if the original beer is stronger than 0.5 per cent alcohol, there is a sale of intoxicating liquor even if the resultant mixture is below that strength (*Hall v Hyder* (1966)). However, where a pre-prepared shandy, in a can or bottle, is below the alcohol level it will not amount to intoxicating liquor.

2.2 Licensed Premises
Licensing Act 1964 Section 200

This term means the premises for which a justices' licence or an occasional licence is in force, and is not limited, e.g. to the bars and lounges, but would include other areas of the premises. The term has relevance in relation to certain offences, e.g. being drunk on licensed premises, and is much wider in scope than 'bar'.

2.3 Bar
Licensing Act 1964 Sections 201, 171

2.3.1 *Meaning*
A bar is part of licensed premises exclusively or mainly used for the sale **and** consumption

of intoxicating liquor. The term 'bar' is very important in relation to offences arising from drinking by persons under 18, employment of persons under 18, and children under the age of 14.

The term 'bar' applies in a place operating under an occasional permission, as it does in licensed premises.

2.3.2 *Not a Bar*

To amount to a bar, the part of licensed premises concerned must be used for the sale and the consumption of intoxicating liquor. A counter in a passageway where drink is sold, but drinking is not permitted, will not be a bar because it is used for sale but not for consumption. A 'family room' in a pub, where drinks may be consumed, but where there is no counter and no waiter service will not be a bar because there is no sale of intoxicating liquor in that room.

2.3.3 *Exclusion for Table Meals*

Specifically excluded from the meaning of 'bar', even though there is sale and consumption of intoxicants there, is part of the premises set aside for the service of 'table meals'. This part of licensed premises will not amount to a 'bar' if the following conditions are satisfied:
   - that part of the premises is usually set aside for the service of table meals
   - it is not used for the sale and supply of intoxicating liquor, other than to persons having table meals there
   - the intoxicating liquor is for consumption by those persons as ancillary to their meals.

2.3.4 *Explanation*

Set aside: The place where meals are served does not necessarily have to be a separate room but that part of the premises does have to be set aside from parts where people may have a drink without eating. Many pubs serve food without having separate facilities; others have a separate 'restaurant'. The test is, 'May someone who is not having a table meal, be served with intoxicating liquor in that part of the premises?' If the answer is 'Yes', then the part of the premises will not benefit from this exception and will be a bar.

Table meals: There are two aspects to 'table meal':
   - what is a 'table meal'?
   - what is a 'meal'?

A table meal is a meal eaten by a person seated at a table, counter or other structure which serves as a table, but which is not used by persons eating there who are not seated. Consider a room where there is a counter with stools for persons who are served food. Providing everyone who is served food is sitting on the stools, then the counter will be a 'table' and they will be having table meals. However, if when the room gets crowded, some people are served food while standing at the counter, the counter will not be a 'table' and none of the meals will be table meals, and the room will be a bar.

A meal must amount to 'substantial refreshment' and whether this criterion is satisfied is a question for the court to decide in any particular case. A substantial sandwich accompanied by beetroot and pickles, eaten at a table has been held to be a table meal (*Timmis v Millman* (1965)).

Ancillary: The intoxicating liquor is supplied as an 'add on' to the meal. The intention is that the meal is the more significant, with the drink being secondary. However, this is not to say that the intoxicants may be consumed only along with food. An apéritif served before the meal, not necessarily while sitting down, wine with the table meal, and a brandy afterwards, may all be 'ancillary' to the meal.

2.4 Liability of Licensee

A licensee, generally speaking, is liable for what goes on in her licensed premises. If an employee of the licensee sells intoxicants in breach of a condition on the licence, or sells to a person under 18, the licensee may be liable. However, if the employee is acting contrary to instructions, or outside the scope of what he is employed to do, the licensee will not, generally, be liable. *(Keynote Case: Vane v Yiannopoullos (1965))*

If a licensee goes off on holiday, or for some other reason leaves the premises in charge of an employee, the licensee will be responsible for the actions of that person. The licensee is responsible for how the premises are run, and cannot escape that liability by leaving another person in charge (*R v Winson* (1968)).

In some cases, for example in relation to selling to a person under 18 by an employee, the licensee will have a defence if he proves that he took all reasonable steps to avoid such offences being committed.

3 REGISTERED CLUBS

3.1 Registration System

3.1.1 *Meaning of 'Club'*

A 'club' may be defined as an association of persons pursuing a common object or purpose. When those persons decide that their pursuit of the common object will be enhanced by being able to drink intoxicants, they may seek to obtain a justices' licence for the club premises, or instead, they may seek registration. While licences are handled by the licensing justices, registration is dealt with by the ordinary bench of magistrates.

3.1.2 *Conditions for Registration*
Licensing Act 1964 Section 41

In a registered club, the profits from the supply of intoxicants go to the benefit of the members as a whole. The qualifications for registration are:
- there must be at least two days elapse between a person being nominated for membership and being admitted as a member
- the club should have at least 25 members and be conducted in good faith
- supply of intoxicating liquor to members on the premises shall be by the club only
- purchase and supply of intoxicants shall be controlled by an elective committee of the members
- no person shall derive private gain from the purchase or supply of intoxicants, other than gain which goes to members as a whole.

3.1.3 *Police Objections*
Licensing Act 1964 Section 44

The police may object to the grant or renewal of a club's registration on the grounds that:
  i) any of the conditions for registration are not met

ii) the premises are not suitable

iii) there is disorderly conduct or habitual disregard of club rules

iv) there is habitual use of the club premises for indecent displays, frequent drunkenness, etc.

Items (i), (iii) and (iv) will also be grounds for a police application to have a club's registration revoked.

3.1.4 *Police Power of Entry*
Licensing Act 1964 Section 45

The premises of a registered club are private and police generally have no power to enter. (There is an exception in the case of a club with a special hours certificate – *see paragraph 9.3*) However, since police may object to the grant of a club registration on the ground that the premises are unsuitable, it seems reasonable that police should have an opportunity to look at the premises.

Accordingly, on first application for registration, a constable who is authorised in writing by the chief officer of police, may inspect the premises within 14 days of the application for registration. The chief officer should not issue such authority unless in her opinion special reasons exist making the inspection necessary. The constable must produce his written authority if required to do so. It is an offence for a person to obstruct a constable in the exercise of this duty.

3.1.5 *Club Rules*

A registered club will have a set of rules governing how the club should be run. The magistrates will take account of the rules when considering an application for registration; habitual disregard of the rules is one of the grounds for revocation or objection to renewal of the registration. The following provisions apply to club rules:

- certain matters must be contained in the rules, such as arrangements for the annual general meeting (Schedule 7)
- on first application, a set of the rules must be included with the application. On renewal, any changes to the rules since the last application must be included, for the attention of the magistrates
- written notice of any change in the rules must be sent to the chief officer of police and to the local authority (Section 48).

There need be nothing in the rules relating to the supply of intoxicants to persons under 18, and there is no law against such supply, but whether magistrates would tolerate habitual supply to young persons is doubtful. They might for example, consider that this amounted to the premises being run in a 'disorderly manner', a ground for refusal of renewal of registration.

3.1.6 *Supply to Non-Members*

In a registered club, for the most part, intoxicants may be supplied only to members and their guests. It is not unusual for the rules to limit the number of times in a year that a particular individual may be signed in as a guest. When a member is supplied with intoxicants and hands over money, this is not regarded as a 'sale' but as a supply from the stock of intoxicants which the club has already purchased on behalf of the membership. Thus, there is no question of 'selling without a licence'.

The club rules may allow for the sale of intoxicants to non-members in certain circumstances, and if done in accordance with the rules, this will not be regarded as a 'sale'. Some examples

which may typically appear in club rules are:
- – the function room is available to non-members for wedding receptions, parties, etc, with persons attending such functions being able to buy drinks
- – on a limited number of occasions per year, dances are held which are open to the public
- – persons attending sporting events held on the club pitches may buy drinks before and after a sporting event
- – during December, the club dining room is open to non-members for Christmas lunches.

3.1.7 *Magistrates' (dis)approval*
The rules, although they have to be submitted to the magistrates upon application for grant or renewal of registration, are a matter for the club. However, the extent to which the rules allow for sales to non-members may be taken into account by the magistrates in deciding whether a club is 'conducted in good faith', one of the conditions for registration (Section 49(2)).

3.2 Licensed Clubs
If a club cannot meet the conditions for registration, especially that relating to no private gain, then it may operate as a licensed club (often referred to as a proprietary club) under a justices' licence. Such a club will be a licensed premises in all respects, with a licensee. (The only relaxation of the law governing licensed premises, is that in a licensed club certain notices relating to extensions to hours do not have to be displayed.)

The licensing justices may impose conditions on the licence, such as limiting sale and supply of intoxicants to members and their guests, 48 hours to elapse between nomination and admission as members, etc.

4 PERMITTED HOURS

4.1 General Licensing Hours
Licensing Act 1964 Section 60

4.1.1 *Effect of Hours*
The Act lays down the general licensing hours, being the periods during which intoxicating liquor may be sold, supplied and/or consumed on licensed premises. These hours apply throughout the country, but the licensing justices have limited scope for varying these hours for their particular district.

There is provision for licensed premises to be closed on Sundays in parts of Wales, where a referendum has been held in this regard (there are no such areas at present).

4.1.2 *For On-Licences*
1: On weekdays, other than Good Friday and Christmas Day, 11 am to 11 pm.

2: On Good Friday and on Sundays (except Christmas Day), 12 noon to 10.30 pm.

3: On Christmas Day, 12 noon to 3 pm and 7 pm to 10.30 pm.

The licensing justices may, if satisfied that the needs of the district make it desirable, modify the weekday hours to start earlier than 11.00 am, but not earlier than 10.00 am. What the requirements of a district may be which are satisfied by opening the pubs up to an hour earlier is a matter for conjecture.

4.1.3 *For Off-Licences*

1: On weekdays, from 8.00 am until the end of general permitted hours (i.e. 11.00 pm).

2: Sundays, Christmas Day, Good Friday, the same as for on-licences.

Thus, if you go into your local supermarket during the week, the shelves stocking wines, beers, etc, are available from 8.00 am, but on Sundays and Good Friday, these shelves will be roped off or covered over until 12 noon.

4.1.4 *Off-Sales Department of Pub*
Licensing Act 1964 Section 86

Some premises with an on-licence have a separate department for off-sales. Upon application by the licensee, the justices may insert a condition in the licence, allowing that part of the premises to operate under off-licence permitted hours, i.e. to be open from 8.00 am on weekdays. This is subject to:
- the premises being structurally adapted for off-sales
- their being used only for off-sales
- there being no internal communication for customers between that part and the rest of the premises, i.e. there has to be a separate entrance.

4.1.5 *For Registered Clubs*
The hours are:

1: On every day, except Christmas Day, the general licensing hours for on-licences for the district.

2: On Christmas Day, hours as fixed under the rules of the club and notified to the magistrates' clerk, subject to the following constraints:
- start no earlier than 12 noon
- finish no later than 10.30 pm
- no more than 6 1/2 hours in total
- break in the afternoon of at least 2 hours, and the period 3.00 pm to 5. 00 pm to be included in this break
- no more than 3 1/2 hours after 5.00 pm.

What this amounts to is not hugely significant; whereas on Christmas Day evening, licensed premises may open between 7.00 pm and 10.30 pm, a registered club may open as early as 5.00 pm, providing it closes correspondingly early. The insignificance of this provision becomes even more marked when one considers that most pubs and clubs do not open at all on the evening of Christmas Day.

4.1.6 *Registered Club – Special Occasion*
Licensing Act 1964 Section 39(3)

On a special occasion, a registered club may use premises other than its registered premises.

The only restrictions are:
- persons other than members and their guests must be excluded from the premises
- intoxicating liquor is supplied only for consumption on the premises.

The advantages are:
- there is no need to apply to the magistrates for permission, so the club decides what is a 'special occasion'
- permitted hours do not apply, since the premises are not licensed, nor are they part of the club's registered premises
- this does not affect the club's registered premises, which may be open as usual for those members who are not attending the special event.

4.1.7 *Offence*
Licensing Act 1964 Section 59(1)

An offence is committed by a person who, other than during permitted hours:
- himself, or through his servant or agent, sells or supplies intoxicating liquor to another person on licensed premises or the premises of a registered club; or
- consumes in or takes from any licensed premises or registered club, any intoxicating liquor.

4.1.8 *Occasional Licence*
There is something of an anomaly in relation to premises operating under an occasional licence, in that offences of sale and consumption after permitted hours do not apply. If an occasional licence is granted for a period of say, one evening, then any sale after the end of the period specified in the licence will amount to an offence of selling without a licence. However, if the licence extends over several days, any sale outside the specified times during that period of days will not be selling without a licence; nor is there an offence of selling outside permitted hours. Police action in such a situation is to gather the evidence of late drinking and use it as grounds to object to any future application by that licensee for an occasional licence.

4.1.9 *Explanation*
Licensee and servant: A licensee commits an offence if he sells or supplies intoxicating liquor outside permitted hours. The licensee will also be responsible for her employee or agent who does so. However, this liability extends only to an employee's action in the course of employment, so if a member of staff sells intoxicants outside hours, without the knowledge of the licensee, and contrary to instructions, the licensee may not be liable.

Customer: The customer who is drinking on the licensed premises or in a registered club, or who takes intoxicants away from the premises outside permitted hours commits an offence. Note that the offence committed by the licensee is that of sale or supply. If a customer is drinking after the end of permitted hours, having bought the drink before closing time, he will commit an offence, but the licensee will not. However, the licensee may be liable for aiding and abetting the customer to commit this offence.

4.1.10 *Occasional Permission*
The hours for which an occasional permission is valid will be specified in the permission itself. A constable may require production of an occasional permission and the holder of it will commit an offence if she fails to produce it within a reasonable time.

4.2 Exceptions to Serving After Time, etc
Licensing Act 1964 Section 63

4.2.1 'Drinking-Up Time'

No offence is committed by a person who consumes intoxicants, or who takes away intoxicants from the premises, during the first 20 minutes after the end of permitted hours. This exemption applies only to the consumption or taking away, not to the sale or supply, so the drink must have been bought and supplied before the end of permitted hours.

Note: Intoxicants taken away must not be in an open vessel, so if you want to walk out of the pub with a jug or glass of beer, do so before the end of permitted hours.

4.2.2 Extra Drinking Up Time with Food

Consumption (but not taking out) is allowed during the first 30 minutes, rather than 20, in the case of a person having a meal, providing the liquor was supplied as ancillary to that meal.

Note: The extra drinking-up time applies when eating a 'meal', it does not have to be a table meal. Thus, a person standing at the bar eating a pie and chips, for example, may continue to wash the food down with a drink for up to half an hour after closing time.

4.2.3 Residents

Intoxicants may be sold or supplied to and consumed by a person on premises where he is residing, and a resident may also take intoxicants from licensed premises, outside permitted hours. This will apply, for example, to hotel guests.

The person who carries on or is in charge of the business is regarded as 'resident' for these purposes even if she does not live on the premises. Thus, the manager of a hotel may live elsewhere, but may still have a drink there outside permitted hours, as a resident.

4.2.4 Friend of Resident

A person may be supplied with and may consume intoxicating liquor on licensed premises outside permitted hours if he is a private friend of a resident and *bona fide* entertained at the resident's expense.

Thus, not only may a resident have intoxicants for himself outside permitted hours, but he may also buy for friends who are not resident there.

Whether a person is a 'private friend' is a matter of fact for the court to decide in any particular case. A business acquaintance may well fall into the category of 'private friend', and there is no requirement that the resident should have known his 'friend' for any length of time.

4.2.5 Employees

A person who is employed on the licensed premises for the purpose of the business carried on by the licensee may be supplied with and may consume intoxicants outside permitted hours if the drink is supplied at the expense of the employer, or of the person running the business.

This would enable, for example, the staff of a restaurant to have a drink at their employer's expense at the end of the evening, outside permitted hours. The distinction between 'employer or person running the business' allows for persons not working directly for the licensee, e.g. agency staff, to be included.

4.2.6 *Trade Supplies*
Permitted hours do not restrict sale and supply to the trade, or to a mess or registered club.

4.2.7 *Other Supply*
Intoxicants which are ordered for consumption off the premises may be despatched outside permitted hours. This would have to involve delivery to the customer, it does not authorise the customer to take the intoxicants away from the premises himself.

4.3 International Airports
Licensing Act 1964 Section 87

4.3.1 *Exemption from Permitted Hours*
At certain airports, permitted hours shall not apply in licensed premises within the 'examination station' defined for the purposes of Customs and Excise. This is the part of the airport, commonly referred to as 'air side' where only passengers and authorised persons are allowed. Licensed premises in the parts of the airport accessible to the non-passenger public will be governed by normal permitted hours.

These provisions apply only in specified airports, which include most of the ones used for international scheduled and/or charter flights in this country.

4.3.2 *Seaports, Hoverports and Channel Tunnel*
Similar provisions exist in relation to certain hoverports, and the Channel Tunnel terminal, and to approved seaports (Section 86A).

4.4 Vineyards
Licensing Act 1964 Section 87A

The effects of global warming may have some way to go before this country is seen as a serious rival to Bordeaux as a wine producing region. Nevertheless, there are vineyards in England and there is provision to vary the permitted hours at on-licensed premises which form part of a vineyard. The licensing justices may grant an application to vary the hours if satisfied that the sale of intoxicants is ancillary to the business of producing wine from grapes grown at that vineyard.

5 VARIATIONS AND EXTENSIONS TO PERMITTED HOURS

5.1 Introduction
There are various means by which the general permitted hours may be extended, in cases where the intoxicants are deemed to be secondary to some other delight, such as food, entertainment, dancing or a combination of these. In recent years, there has been a relaxation of restrictions on permitted hours, so that some of these variations are less significant than was the case when permitted hours finished earlier, with a lengthy break in the afternoon. These variations may be granted by the licensing justices after application by the licensee, or by the magistrates upon application by the secretary of a registered club.

5.2 Extension with Meals
Licensing Act 1964 Section 68

5.2.1 *Requirements*
Premises are:
- structurally adapted
- bona fide used or intended for use
- for the purpose of habitually providing substantial refreshment
- to which the sale and supply of intoxicating liquor is ancillary.

5.2.2 *Effect*
The effect on permitted hours is in two parts:

1: Lunch time – this provision used to be very significant when there was an afternoon break in permitted hours, but there is now a break only once a year, on Christmas Day. The effect is to allow intoxicants to be sold, supplied and consumed during the period between the first and second parts of permitted hours on Christmas Day, i.e. the premises may be 'open all day'.

2: Evening – the extension adds one hour to permitted hours, i.e. from 11.00 pm to 12 midnight, hence the popular name for this provision – supper hour extension.

5.2.3 *Restrictions*
During the extended hours, i.e. Christmas Day afternoon and the extra hour at night, intoxicants may not be supplied to all the customers. The only customers to benefit from the extended hours are those who:
- are having table meals
- in part of the premises usually set aside for the service of such meals
- where the intoxicants are ancillary to the meal.

5.2.4 *Explanation*
Food: Before an extension is granted, the premises must be structurally suitable for supply of 'substantial refreshment' on a regular basis. This may be an intended use, in the case of premises where such refreshment has not been supplied before.

Set aside: Table meals should be in part of the premises 'set aside' for such. In this context 'set aside' means used for a significant period during general permitted hours. It will not do for the licensee, to allow customers to sit at tables drinking all night, then at 11.00 pm, to insist that they eat something in order to enjoy another hour of drinking.

Drinking until: With permitted hours extended to midnight, and with there being 30 minutes of drinking-up time allowed with a meal, customers may effectively continue drinking until 12.30 am (half an hour earlier on Sunday, Good Friday, Christmas Day).

5.3 Extended Hours Order
Licensing Act 1964 Section 70

5.3.1 *Requirements*
Such may be granted in respect of premises in which:
- an extension for meals (supper hour extension) is already in force
- the premises are structurally adapted

- and bona fide used or intended to be used
- for habitually providing musical or other entertainment, as well as substantial refreshment
- with the supply of intoxicating liquor being ancillary to the entertainment and refreshment.

5.3.2 *Effect*

The effect of the order is to extend the permitted hours on weekdays, to 1.00 am. The magistrates or licensing justices may fix a time earlier than 1.00 am (or may limit the order to particular days of the week or times of the year) taking account of circumstances, including the comfort and convenience of persons in neighbouring premises.

5.3.3 *Restrictions*

The extra period of permitted hours will not apply:

- to any part of the premises not habitually set aside for entertainment and refreshment
- to sale or supply for consumption off the premises
- on any day when there in no entertainment
- after the entertainment or the provision of substantial refreshment has ended.

In addition, the order does not allow for a person to be served intoxicants who is admitted to the premises after midnight or within a half hour of the end of the entertainment, except with a table meal.

5.3.4 *Explanation*

Part of premises: The extended hours may apply to the whole of the premises or only to part, depending to what extent the premises have been structurally adapted for entertainment and refreshment.

Entertainment: What amounts to 'entertainment' may be a matter of personal taste, but the law requires that it must be by a person actually present and performing, so satellite television, or records will not do.

Food: It is important to note that whereas entertainment and substantial refreshment have to be habitually provided on the premises, there is no restriction on who may be provided with intoxicants. With a supper hour extension, only people having table meals could be served drinks during the extended hour. Here, there is no requirement that a customer be served any substantial refreshment, **except** in the case of late-comers, when a person admitted to the premises after midnight, or within 30 minutes of the entertainment being due to finish, if this is earlier, not being allowed intoxicants unless he has a table meal. Someone who came into the premises earlier may continue ordering intoxicants after midnight and have nothing to eat.

5.4 Special Hours Certificate
Licensing Act 1964 Sections 76 – 78

5.4.1 *Requirements*

A special hours certificate may be granted in respect of licensed premises where:

- a licence allowing music and dancing (i.e. a music and dancing licence in London, an entertainment licence elsewhere) is in force for the premises;
- the whole (or part) of the premises is structurally adapted and bona fide used or intended for use
- for habitually providing

- music and dancing
- and substantial refreshment
- to which the sale of intoxicating liquor is ancillary.

5.4.2 *Registered Club*

For a registered club, instead of a music and dancing or entertainment licence, the club has to have a 'certificate of suitability' which is granted by the magistrates. The reason for the difference is that a licence applies to premises open to the public; since a registered club is not open to the public it does not require a licence.

Note: For premises under construction, a provisional special hours certificate may be granted if, when finished, the premises will be 'structurally adapted' etc.

5.4.3 *Effect*

The certificate will extend permitted hours on weekdays until 2.00 am next day, at the latest (3.00 am in parts of the Metropolitam Police District). The justices may specify a time before 2.00 am but no earlier than midnight, when permitted hours shall end.

5.4.4 *British Summer Time*

On the morning that summer time begins, the permitted hours are extended to 3.00 am (or by an extra hour in premises where the hours end at some time between 1.00 am amd 2.00 am). This compensates for the fact that the clock officially goes forward at 1.00 am which becomes 2.00 am summer time, by allowing the extra hour which would otherwise be lost (Section 76(2A)).

The certificate may have limitations attached, limiting its effect:
- to certain hours of the day
- days of the week
- or times of the year.

Note: A special hours certificate actually provides an alternative set of permitted hours for the premises, rather than just an extension of the general licensing hours. Therefore, the magistrates or licensing justices may vary the time at which the premises open (Chief Constable of West Midlands v Marsden (1995)).

5.4.5 *Restrictions*

The following restrictions apply:
- on any day when the music and dancing ends before midnight, permitted hours must end at midnight
- on a day when the music and dancing finishes sometime between midnight and 2.00 am, permitted hours must end when the music and dancing end.

5.4.6 *Explanation*

Use of facilities: The premises have to provide facilities for people to dance and partake of substantial refreshment, but there is no requirement that customers have to make use of these facilities before being served with intoxicating liquor. However, if it can be shown that on the whole, the intoxicants have ceased to be ancillary to the other facilities, this could be a ground for revoking the special hours certificate *(see paragraph 5.7.3)*.

Part of premises: The certificate may apply to the whole of the premises or only to part, depending to what extent the premises have been structurally adapted for dancing and refreshment. For example, a large pub may have a 'night club' facility in one room, with only that room having the special hours certificate.

Music: There is no requirement that the music be provided by musicians actually present and playing live, as there is with an entertainment extension order. Thus, disco music will be sufficient.

5.5 Special Order of Exemption
Licensing Act 1964 Section 74

5.5.1 *Requirements*
This may be granted upon application of a licensee or secretary of a registered club for a special occasion.

5.5.2 *Effect*
The effect is to extend the permitted hours for the period specified in the order.

Note: The special event giving rise to the order may be held in one part of the premises only, but the effect of the order is to extend the hours for the whole of the licensed premises. The licensee may be asked to give an undertaking to limit sale and supply during the extra time allowed, to persons attending the special occasion. If he fails to do so and serves his other customers who are not attending the function, he will not commit any offence, but the magistrates may well decide to refuse any future application for a special order of exemption by that licensee, on the ground that he had failed to observe the spirit of the law.

5.5.3 *Explanation*
Duration: Unlike the various extended hours described in the preceding paragraphs, a special order of exemption applies as a 'one-off' to mark an event. The usual application will be to extend the permitted hours after 11.00 pm on the occasion of some special event.

Special occasion: What amounts to a special occasion is a question of fact for the magistrates to decide. To some extent, this allows magistrates considerable scope for personal whim. Whereas there may be general agreement that an 18th or 21st birthday party is 'special', some magistrates may not agree that a 40th or 50th is worthy of late drinking.

Application: Application is made to a magistrates' court, not to the licensing justices, who may meet too infrequently to deal with such matters. There is provision for the police to object to the application. In the City of London and the Metropolitan Police District, application is made to the Commissioner.

5.6 General Order of Exemption
Licensing Act 1964 Section 74

5.6.1 *Requirements*
This order will be granted to the holder of a justices' on-licence by the licensing justices, or the secretary of a registered club by the magistrates, if they are satisfied:
- that the making of the order is desirable
- for the accommodation of a considerable number of people

- attending a public market
- or following a particular trade or calling.

5.6.2 *Effect*

The effect of the order is to add specified hours to the permitted hours for those premises, on certain days of the week, or generally. This is not a 'one-off' as with a special order of exemption, but of a more permanent nature.

5.6.3 *Explanation*

Scope: There was perhaps more scope for a general order of exemption when there was a lengthy break in permitted hours in the afternoon. A common application was to extend the afternoon permitted hours in a town where farmers attended in large numbers on market day. However, there is still scope for opening early in the morning in the vicinity of a wholesale market, for example, where people attend from the early hours. At the other end of the day, there may be scope for extending permitted hours to allow shift workers at a factory to enjoy a drink after work.

Notice: The licensee of premises where such an order is in force shall have a sign displayed on the premises, giving details of the effect of the order. The requirement for a notice does not apply to clubs.

5.7 Revocation of Order, etc

5.7.1 *Police Application*

When an extended hours order or a special hours certificate has been granted in respect of licensed premises or a registered club, by the licensing justices or a magistrates' court respectively, the police may apply to those justices or magistrates to have it revoked.

5.7.2 *Revocation of Extended Hours Order*
Licensing Act 1964 Section 73(4)

The licensing justices or magistrates' court may revoke an extended hours order if satisfied upon application by the chief officer of police for the area:
- that the premises have not been used for the purpose for which the order was granted (i.e. habitually providing entertainment and substantial refreshment to which intoxicants are ancillary); or because of
- disorderly or indecent conduct in the premises; or
- because the premises have been ill-conducted; or
- because of the conduct of persons going there and annoyance resulting or likely to result to persons in premises in the neighbourhood.

5.7.3 *Revocation of Special Hours Certificates*
Licensing Act 1964 Section 81

The chief officer of police for the area may apply for revocation of a special hours certificate on the grounds that:
  i) the premises have not been used for the purpose for which the certificate was granted (music and dancing, etc); or
  ii) a person has been convicted of an offence on the premises (or in the part covered by

the certificate) of selling or supplying intoxicants outside permitted hours

iii) on the whole, the customers who go there during the extra hours provided under the certificate (i.e. after the end of the general licensed hours) do so for the intoxicating liquor rather than for the music and dancing or for obtaining refreshments other than intoxicants

iv) it is expedient to revoke the certificate because of the occurrence of disorderly or indecent behaviour in the premises or in the part to which the certificate relates.

The justices (magistrates' court) may revoke the certificate – or, in the case of the ground for revocation being (i), (ii) or (iii) – may impose limitations as to times of day when the certificate shall have effect.

5.7.4 *Police Application for Limitations*
Licensing Act 1964 Section 81A

The chief officer of police for the area may make application to have limitations attached to particular times of the day, or vary any such limitation.

5.8 **Display of Notices**
Licensing Act 1964 Section 89

On licensed premises where the permitted hours have been modified, the licensee has to display a notice in a conspicuous part of the premises detailing the effect of the modification.

This applies to:
- extension with meals (Section 68)
- extended hours order (Section 70)
- special hours certificate (Section 76)
- general order of exemption (Section 74)
- variation for vineyards (Section 87A).

6 RESTRICTIONS RELATING TO YOUNG PEOPLE

6.1 **Young People in a 'Bar'**
In relation to children and persons under 18, the meaning of the term 'bar' becomes very significant. Children under 14 years of age may not be present in a 'bar', with certain exceptions. Persons under 18 may not consume intoxicants in a 'bar', but may do in other parts of licensed premises. In certain circumstances, 16-year olds may buy intoxicating liquor for themselves – but not in a 'bar'.

6.2 **Persons Under 14**
Licensing Act 1964 Section 168

6.2.1 *Offences*
1: The licensee shall not allow a person under the age of 14 years to be in a bar of the licensed premises during permitted hours.

2: Any other person commits an offence if he causes or procures, or attempts to cause or procure, a person under 14 to be in the bar of licensed premises during permitted hours.

6.2.2 *Defences*

If a person under 14 is in the bar of licensed premises during permitted hours, the licensee will not be guilty of an offence if he proves, either:

- that he exercised all due diligence to prevent a person under 14 being admitted to the bar; or
- that the person under 14 had apparently reached that age.

6.2.3 *Exceptions*

These provisions do not apply in the case of a person under 14 being in a bar during permitted hours if:

- she is the child of the licensee; or
- she resides on the premises but is not employed there; or
- she is in the bar solely for the purpose of passing to or from some other part of the premises, there being no other convenient means of access; or
- the bar is in a railway refreshment room or some other premises constructed, fitted and intended for use for some purpose to which the justices' licence is merely ancillary; or
- the provisions relating to children's certificates apply (see below).

6.2.4 *Explanation*

During permitted hours: There is no restriction on children being in a bar outside permitted hours.

Cause or procure: Anyone, such as a parent, who brings, or attempts to bring the child into the bar will be liable.

Due diligence: The licensee is liable if he **allows** the child to be in the bar. If he takes reasonable steps to keep children out, e.g. by giving clear instructions to his staff, then he will have a defence, as he will if the child looks to be 14 or over.

Exceptions: The licensee's own child may be in the bar, but this does not extend to, e.g. the child's school friends, or cousins. Any other child resident on the premises may also be in the bar, except in the unlikely event of the child being an employee. If, for example, a pub had a restaurant (which was not a bar), but to reach the toilets, one had to go through the bar, a child going to or from the toilet would be covered by the exceptions while passing through the bar.

6.3 Children's Certificates
Licensing Act 1964 Section 168A

6.3.1 *Application*

A licensee may apply to the licensing justices for a children's certificate for any area of the premises which is part of or comprises a bar. The effect of such a certificate is to allow children under 14 years to be present in that area, which may or may not be the whole of the bar.

6.3.2 *Requirements*

The justices may grant the application if satisfied:

- that the area in question constitutes an environment in which it is suitable for persons under 14 to be present; and
- that meals, and beverages other than intoxicating liquor will be available for sale and consumption in that area.

6.3.3 *Display*

The licensee has to display a notice in a conspicuous place in the area in question, stating that a children's certificate is in force, explaining the effect of the certificate, and specifying any conditions attached to it. Failure to display this notice is an offence.

6.3.4 *Effect*

The effect of a children's certificate is to make it lawful for children under 14 to be:

- in the specified area (not necessarily the whole bar)
- during a certain period of permitted hours
- subject to certain conditions.

6.3.5 *Conditions*

The conditions in which it is lawful for a child under 14 to be in the area covered by the children's certificate are:

- the child is in the company of a person aged 18 years or over; and either
- the certificate is operational; or
- no more than 30 minutes have elapsed since the certificate ceased to be operational **and** either the child or a person in whose company she is, is eating a meal bought during the period when the certificate was operational.

6.3.6 *Explanation*

Period of operation: The certificate will operate during a certain period, which need not be the whole of permitted hours; the licensing justices may feel that children under 14 should be home in bed long before 11.00 pm.

Eating: Although the provision of meals and non-alcoholic drinks is a requirement before a certificate will be issued, there is no requirement that a child has to be given a meal or a drink during the time that the certificate is in operation. It would be lawful therefore, if an adult was drinking intoxicants while the accompanying child had nothing.

Eating-up time: Just as there is 'drinking-up time' at the end of permitted hours, so there is 30 minutes allowed after a certificate ceases to be operational when the child may still be in that area of the bar, but only if the child or someone else in the party is still eating food bought when the certificate was operational. Note that this is time allowed to finish a meal **not** time allowed to finish a drink. This means that if the certificate ceases to be operational at, say, 9.00 pm, children may remain in the children's area of the bar until 9.30 pm, so long as someone in the party is still eating.

6.4 Restrictions on Persons Under 18
Licensing Act 1964 Section 169

6.4.1 *Purchasing Intoxicants*

There are three offences to consider:

1: A person under the age of 18 shall not:
- in licensed premises
- buy or attempt to buy any intoxicating liquor.

2: The licensee or his servant:
- in licensed premises

- shall not sell intoxicating liquor to a person under the age of 18.

3: The licensee shall not:
  - knowingly allow another person to sell intoxicating liquor to a person under 18
  - in licensed premises.

6.4.2 *Drinking Intoxicants*
There are three offences which may be committed:

1: By a person under the age of 18 who:
  - consumes intoxicating liquor
  - in a bar.

2: By a person who:
  - buys or attempts to buy intoxicating liquor
  - for consumption by a person under 18
  - in a bar.

3: By a licensee or her servant who:
  - knowingly allows a person under 18
  - to consume intoxicating liquor in a bar.

6.4.3 *Off-Sales*
There are three offences which may be committed in relation to off-sales:

1: A licensee or his servant shall not:
  - knowingly deliver intoxicating liquor
  - for consumption off the premises
  - to a person under 18
  - except where the delivery is made at the residence or place of work of the purchaser.

2: The licensee shall not:
  - knowingly allow another person to make such a delivery.

3: A person shall not:
  - knowingly send a person under the age of 18
  - to obtain intoxicating liquor sold in licensed premises for consumption off the premises
  - whether the liquor is to be obtained from the licensed premises or from somewhere else from which it is delivered.

6.4.4 *Employment of Person Under 18 in a Bar*
Licensing Act 1964 Section 170

Offence: A licensee shall be liable if:
  - a person under 18 is employed in any bar of licensed premises
  - at a time when the bar is open for the sale or consumption of intoxicating liquor.

6.4.5 *Sales by a Person Under 18*
Licensing Act 1964 Section 171A

In an off-licence, or in the off-sales department of other licensed premises, the licensee shall not allow a person aged under 18 to make a sale of intoxicating liquor for consumption off the premises unless that sale is approved by the licensee herself, or by someone over 18 acting on her behalf.

A practical example of this in operation is when the young check-out operator at the supermarket seeks the approval of the supervisor before passing the bottle of wine or six-pack of beer across the barcode reader.

The need for a salesperson under 18 to seek approval before making a sale also applies in the case of sale by wholesale (Section 181A).

6.4.6 *Exceptions*
Buying: A person who is aged 16 or over may purchase beer, porter, cider or perry for consumption with a meal in part of the premises usually set aside for meals which is not a bar.

Off-sales: The offences of supplying, or sending a person under 18 for intoxicants, will not be committed in respect of a person who is employed as a messenger to deliver intoxicating liquor.

Employment:
1: A person aged 16 years or over may be employed in a bar as part of an approved training scheme.

2: A person will not be regarded as 'employed' in a bar if in the course of his employment elsewhere in the premises, he enters the bar for the purpose of giving or receiving a message, or for passing to or from another part of the premises, there being no other convenient means of access.

3: The restriction will not apply at a time when the bar is set aside, and it is usually set aside at that time, for the service of table meals, with intoxicants being supplied only as ancillary to such a meal.

6.4.7 *Defences*
1: When a person is charged with an offence of selling to a person under 18, by reason of his own act, he will have a defence if he proves that he exercised all due diligence to avoid committing such an offence **or** that he had no reason to suspect the person of being under 18.

2: When a licensee is charged with the offence of selling to a person under 18, by reason of the action of someone else, he shall have a defence if he proves that he exercised all due diligence to avoid committing the offence.

6.4.8 *Explanation*
Selling: There is no need to prove 'knowingly' for the offence of selling to a person under 18; i.e. it does not have to be proved that the offender knew the customer to be under 18.

The licensee may commit this offence by selling directly to the young person, or he may be guilty of the offence through the action of a member of his staff.

Although the offence may be committed even without knowledge that the customer was under 18, the offender does have a possible defence. For example, if people who look as if they may be under age have to produce an identity card or other proof of age before being served, the licensee or his staff may well be able to prove that they exercised all due diligence in seeking to avoid selling to a person under age.

Knowingly: For the offences of allowing an under-age person to consume in a bar, or delivering intoxicants, it must be proved that the licensee or his employee knew the person to be under 18.

Consuming: Whereas offences of buying/selling to a person under 18 may be committed in any part of licensed premises, offences involving the young person consuming relate only to a bar. There is nothing unlawful about an adult buying intoxicants and giving them to a child in a restaurant, family room or other part of licensed premises which is not a bar (provided, that is, the child is aged five or over – *see Chapter 34 on Children*).

16-year old buying: The exception which allows a 16-plus year old to buy, is restricted to 'long drinks', i.e. beer or cider. (Porter is a type of beer, perry is like cider, but made from pears not apples.) For spirits and wine, they have to be 18. The drinks may not be bought in a bar, and must be for taking with a meal.

Employed in a bar: A person will be 'employed' by the person for whom he works, even if he does not get paid.

Wholesalers: While sales by wholesale are not subject to the restrictions of permitted hours, the offences of selling intoxicating liquor to a person under 18, or a person under that age buying or attempting to buy, apply equally to supply by wholesale as to supply in licensed premises.

6.4.9 *Occasional Permissions*
The following offences relating to persons under 18 apply in premises operating under an occasional permission, as they do on licensed premises:
- allowing to consume in a bar
- the holder of the permission knowingly allowing a person to sell to a person under 18
- person under 18 buying or attempting to buy
- buying or attempting to buy for person under 18 to consume in a bar
- allowing a person under 18 to sell or serve intoxicating liquor.

The exception allowing a person aged 16 to buy beer, cider or perry to have as ancillary to a meal, applies.

6.5 **Police Powers to Confiscate Intoxicating Liquor**
Confiscation of Alcohol (Young Persons) Act 1997 Section 1

6.5.1 *Police Requirement to Surrender Liquor*
Where a constable reasonably suspects that a person in a relevant place is in possession of intoxicating liquor, and that either:
- he is under the age of 18; or
- he intends that any of the liquor should be consumed by a person under 18 in that or any other relevant place; or
- a person under the age of 18 who is, or who has recently been, with him has recently consumed intoxicating liquor in that or any other relevant place.

The constable may require him:
- to surrender anything in his possession which is, or which the constable reasonably believes to be, intoxicating liquor
- and to state his name and address.

The constable who imposes the requirement shall inform the person of his suspicion, and that failing without reasonable excuse to comply with the requirement is an offence.

6.5.2 *Offence*
A person commits an offence who:
- without reasonable excuse
- fails to comply with a requirement imposed on him.

6.5.3 *Arrest*
A constable may arrest without warrant a person who fails to comply with a requirement imposed on him.

6.5.4 *Disposal of Surrendered Material*
A constable may dispose of anything surrendered to him under these provisions in such manner as he considers appropriate.

6.5.5 *Explanation*
Relevant place: This is defined as any public place, other than licensed premises, or any place which is not a public place, to which the person has unlawfully gained access. 'Public place' is defined in turn as any place to which at the material time the public has access, on payment or otherwise, as of right or by virtue of permission, expressed or implied.

A bus shelter, a public park or a cinema will all be 'relevant places', as will be a school playing field or other place where the person concerned has no right to be, accessed by climbing over the fence. These provisions do not extend to licensed premises, where the person under 18 may well be entitled to drink, e.g. in the restaurant.

Intends the liquor should be consumed: This provision caters for a situation where, for example, one older person in a group of under-18's goes into the off-licence to buy the drink for the others.

Recently consumed: The preceding provisions cater for current and future possession by a person under 18. Here, the police may deal with recent past consumption. For example, a constable sees a group of youths, most of whom are under 18. One youth, who is over 18, is holding two opened cans of lager. If the constable has reason to believe the youngsters have recently consumed some of the lager, the power exists to require that the cans are surrendered.

Warning: When a constable imposes a requirement, she must state the grounds for suspicion, i.e. one of those listed at paragraph 6.5.1, and that failure to comply is an offence. Although it does not specifically say so in the Act, presumably a failure to give this warning will be a bar to a successful prosecution for failure to comply.

Reasonable excuse: To commit the offence, the person must fail to comply without a reasonable excuse. What amounts to 'reasonable excuse' will be a matter of fact for the court to decide in any particular case.

Disposal: If a person complies with a requirement to hand over intoxicating liquor, it is a matter for the constable as to how that liquor is then disposed of. No doubt the constable's force procedures will prohibit him from drinking it himself, but such a method of disposal would not be contrary to this legislation.

7 DRUNKENNESS AND DISORDER

7.1 General
Since the primary effect of intoxicating liquor is to intoxicate, it is hardly surprising that the Act contains provisions to deal with drunks and disorderly conduct.

7.2 Drunks on Licensed Premises
Licensing Act 1964 Sections 172, 173

7.2.1 *Selling*
The holder of a justices' licence shall not sell intoxicating liquor to a drunken person.

7.2.2 *Helping the Drunk to Get Drink*
There are two offences:
- committed by any person who, in licensed premises, procures or attempts to procure intoxicating liquor for consumption by a drunken person
- committed by any person who aids a drunken person in obtaining or consuming intoxicants in licensed premises.

7.2.3 *Explanation*
Selling: The offence is committed only by the licensee. However, the offence is one of absolute liability, which means there is no need to prove guilty knowledge on the part of the licensee. It matters not whether the licensee or any of his employees realised that the customer was drunk. If the drunk is served by a member of staff, that person may be guilty of aiding and abetting the licensee to commit the offence.

Procuring: For the offence of procuring or attempting to procure for a drunk, the procuring must take place on licensed premises, but the drunken person for whom the drink is intended need not be on licensed premises. Thus, the offence would be committed by the person who went into the off-licence to buy booze for the drunk who was outside in the street.

7.2.4 *Permit Drunkenness, etc*
The holder of a justices' licence shall not permit drunkenness, or any violent, quarrelsome or riotous behaviour on the licensed premises.

Again, this offence may be committed only by the licensee, and since it is not an offence of absolute liability, there needs to be some knowledge on his part that there is a drunk, or quarrelsome person on the premises. However, the licensee may be liable for the acts of his servants *(see explanation of liability at paragraph 2.4).*

7.3 Power to Deal with Drunk, etc Person
Licensing Act 1964 Section 174

7.3.1 *Licensee*
The licensee may refuse to admit or may expel from licensed premises any person who is drunken, violent, quarrelsome or disorderly – or whose presence in the licensed premises would subject the licensee to a penalty under this Act.

7.3.2 *Constable*
A constable is **required** to assist a licensee, his servant or agent in expelling such a person from the licensed premises, and may use such force as is reasonable for the purpose.

7.3.3 *Offence*
A person who is liable to be expelled from licensed premises under this provision commits an offence if she fails to leave when requested to do so by the licensee, his servant or agent, or by a constable.

7.3.4 *Explanation*
Power to expel: Since the licensee will be liable if he allows drunks or violent, etc, persons to remain on his premises, it is only right that he should have a power to remove them.

Constable: A constable has no choice in whether or not she assists in removing such persons from licensed premises, she must assist if required to do so by the licensee or his staff. However, since the power to expel, using force if required, arises when the miscreant has refused to leave on request, it is sensible that a constable should make such a request, or hear it made by the licensee or his staff, before using force.

Subject licensee to a penalty: As well as drunks and persons behaving violently, etc, a licensee must keep certain other persons out of his premises, such as prostitutes, in certain circumstances *(see paragraph 7.6)*, or persons under 14 out of a bar.

7.4 Occasional Permissions
The following provisions apply in premises operating under an occasional permission as they do in licensed premises:
- the holder of the permission shall not sell to a drunken person;
- the holder shall not permit drunkenness, nor riotous, quarrelsome or violent conduct on the premises
- procuring or attempting to procure intoxicating liquor for a drunken person
- aiding a drunken person to obtain or consume intoxicating liquor on the premises
- the right to refuse admission, or to expel from the premises any person who is violent, quarrelsome, etc
- the obligation placed on a constable to assist in expelling a person from the premises if called on
- the offence of failing to leave when required to do so by the holder of the permission, by his agent or by a constable.

7.5 Other Drunkenness Offences

7.5.1 *Found Drunk*
Licensing Act 1872 Section 12

A person commits an offence if he is found drunk in any highway or other public place, whether a building or not, or in any licensed premises.

7.5.2 *Power to Arrest*
Licensing Act 1902 Section 1

There is no power of arrest simply for being drunk in public, but there is a power to arrest if the drunken person appears to be incapable of taking care of himself. The power to arrest is given to any person. This is usually referred to by police as 'drunk and incapable' although the incapability does not give rise to a separate offence.

A constable should not exercise an 'any person' power to arrest unless conditions for the PACE general power to arrest are satisfied. In the case of a person incapably drunk, injury to himself would be a likely ground for arrest.

7.5.3 *Drunk and Disorderly*
Criminal Justice Act 1967 Section 91

A person who, in any public place while drunk, is guilty of disorderly behaviour may be arrested without warrant by any person. Again, before a constable exercises this power of arrest, one of the general arrest conditions should be satisfied.

7.5.4 *Drunk in Charge*
There are several offences arising from being in charge of someone or something while drunk:
- on a highway or other public place, drunk in charge of carriage, horse, cattle or steam engine (Licensing Act 1872, Section 12)
- on a highway or other public place, or on licensed premises, drunk in charge of a child apparently under the age of seven years (Licensing Act 1902, Section 2)
- drunk in charge of a loaded firearm (Licensing Act 1872, Section 12).

7.5.5 *Explanation*
Carriage: Will include pedal cycles and mechanically-propelled vehicles (the specific mention of steam engine reflects the age of the legislation). However, in the case of a mechanically-propelled vehicle, the offender should be dealt with under road traffic legislation, which provides more appropriate penalties, including disqualification.

Cattle: This includes pigs and sheep, which information may prove useful, even though flocks of sheep wandering uncontrolled along the highway with a drunken shepherd in tow may not be a common sight.

Firearm: The term includes airgun. This offence is not confined to public places.

Under seven: If the child appears to be under the age of seven years, she will be deemed to be under that age until the contrary is proved.

Arrest: These offences all carry an 'any person' power to arrest *(see comment at paragraph 7.5.2)*.

7.6 **Prostitutes**
Licensing Act 1964 Section 175

A licensee commits an offence if he knowingly allows the licensed premises to become the habitual resort or meeting place of reputed prostitutes. This does not preclude prostitutes being allowed to remain on the premises long enough to obtain reasonable refreshment. It is a separate offence for a licensee to permit the licensed premises to be used as a brothel *(see Chapter 12)*.

7.7 **Constables**
Licensing Act 1964 Section 178

7.7.1 *Offences*
The holder of a justices' licence will commit an offence if:
- he knowingly suffers a constable to remain on licensed premises while on duty, except for the purpose of the execution of the officer's duty; or
- he supplies any liquor or refreshment to a constable on duty, whether by gift or sale, except with the authority of the constable's superior officer; or
- he bribes or attempts to bribe any constable.

7.7.2 *Explanation*
Knowingly: For the purposes of the first offence, it has to be proved that the licensee knew that the person was a constable and that she was on duty. The word is omitted from the second offence, but this is not an offence of absolute liability, so a licensee would have a defence if he showed that he did not know that the person was a constable or that she was on duty.

Liquor or refreshment: The second offence is not confined to intoxicating liquor, it would apply to the supply of any refreshment.

7.8 **Exclusion Orders**
Licensed Premises (Exclusion of Certain Persons) Act 1980

7.8.1 *Court Power to Make Order*
When a person is convicted before a court of a relevant offence, the court may make an exclusion order. A relevant offence will be any offence committed on licensed premises involving violence or an offer of violence. The exclusion order may be for a period between three months and two years, as specified by the court.

7.8.2 *Effect*
The offender will commit an offence if he enters the licensed premises specified in the order except with the express consent of the licensee, his servant or agent. The licensed premises may be those where the offence was committed, or any other licensed premises specified by name and address in the order. The clerk to the court should send a copy of the order to the licensee of the premises concerned.

7.8.3 *Power to Expel*
The licensee or his servant or agent may expel from licensed premises any person who has entered, or whom he reasonably suspects has entered, in breach of an exclusion order.

A constable **shall** on demand of the licensee, his servant or agent, help to expel from the premises any person whom the constable reasonably suspects of having entered in breach of such an order. These powers are in addition to any other powers which exist to deal with persons on licensed premises.

7.8.4 *Explanation*
Specified premises: For an exclusion order to be effective, the offender has to be known and recognised by staff in the licensed premises concerned. This will not be the case if the court includes too many premises in the order, e.g. all the licensed premises in the county/city. In any

case, the requirement to include addresses of premises, and for individual licensees to receive copies of the notice, should deter courts from making the exclusion too widespread. An order specifying all licensed premises in the County of Norfolk was commented on by the High Court as being too wide. It is better to confine the order to specific premises (*R v Grady* (1990)).

Police to help: Note that while there is a duty, not an option, for a constable to assist in expelling an excluded person, the constable must have reason to suspect that the person is in breach of an exclusion order. This may involve a few enquiries at the scene for the officer to satisfy herself on this point, before helping to expel a person, rather than just taking the licensee's word for it that the person is excluded.

7.9 Restriction Order
Licensing Act 1964 Section 67A

7.9.1 *Grounds for Making an Order*
The licensing justices may make a restriction order in respect of licensed premises in their district, on the grounds:
  - that it is necessary and desirable to make an order
  - to avoid or reduce disturbance of or annoyance to residents, persons working in the neighbourhood, schools, etc
  - or to avoid or reduce disorderly conduct in the premises or their vicinity by persons resorting there.

7.9.2 *Application for an Order*
Application may be made by the chief officer of police, a local resident, person in charge of a local business, or head teacher of a local school.

7.9.3 *Effect*
The effect of a restriction order will be to remove from the permitted hours (i.e. close the premises for the sale and supply of intoxicating liquor), a period specified in the order, which may be between 2.30 pm and 5.30 pm on weekdays and 3.00 pm and 7.00 pm on Sundays and Good Friday.

The order may have effect on certain days of the week only, or every day, throughout the year, or at specified times of year. For example, if the complaint of disturbance came from a head teacher, it may be reasonable to expect that the order would apply Monday-Friday during school terms.

7.9.4 *Why These Hours?*
This provision was brought in at the same time as permitted hours were extended by removing the break in the afternoon, which had always been a feature of on-licence hours. To appease those who foresaw pubs being open all day as heralding the end of civilisation as we knew it, restriction orders offered the means of restoring the status quo, i.e. if a pub being open all day led to rowdiness, the justices could take steps to restore the afternoon break.

8 RESTAURANT AND RESIDENTIAL LICENCES
Licensing Act 1964 Section 94

8.1 Part IV Licence
While the licensing system seeks to regulate the retail sale of intoxicating liquor, including by

limiting the numbers of on- and off-licences in an area, there may be less likelihood of opposition if the licence restricts the category of customer. There are three types of restricted licence, commonly referred to as Part IV licences, because they are provided for in Part IV of the Act:
- restaurant licence
- residential licence
- combined (restaurant and residential) licence.

8.2 Restaurant Licence

8.2.1 Qualifications
May be granted for premises structurally adapted and bona fide used or intended for use:
- for habitually providing one or both of the customary main meals of the day, at midday or in the evening.

8.2.2 Restrictions
Intoxicating liquor may be sold or supplied only to persons taking table meals there – for consumption by them as ancillary to such meals.

8.2.3 Permitted Hours
The permitted hours will be the same as for other on-licensed premises, with the exception that the hours extend to cover the afternoon break on Christmas Day. This is, in effect, the afternoon part of an 'extension with meals' and comes automatically with a restaurant licence. If the licensee wants the benefit of the 'supper hour extension', i.e. the extra hour at night, then he would have to make application *(see paragraph 5.2)*.

8.2.4 Explanation
Midday/evening: Some restaurants are open all day, some are open at lunch-time, but closed in the evening; others do not open until evening. A restaurant licence may be granted for any of these, but will not be granted for premises which do not serve table meals.

Ancillary: Intoxicating liquor may be supplied only to persons eating a table meal in the restaurant. There must be no off-sales. In addition, a customer who goes to collect a 'take away' should not be asked, 'Would you like a drink while you're waiting?'.

8.3 Residential Licence

8.3.1 Qualifications
May be granted in respect of premises:
- bona fide used or intended to be used
- for habitually providing for reward
- board and lodging including breakfast and at least one other of the customary main meals of the day.

8.3.2 Restrictions
Intoxicating liquor may be sold only to residents, and supplied to residents or their private friends bona fide entertained by them at their own expense. In addition, the intoxicating liquor may be supplied only:
- for consumption on the premises, or

> – consumption off the premises with a meal supplied at the premises but to be eaten off the premises.

8.3.3 *Permitted Hours*

There is no restriction on when a resident may be served with intoxicants, i.e. he does not have to have a table meal. Since only residents and their bona fide guests will be served, permitted hours have no relevance, residents and guests being included in the exceptions to permitted hours *(see paragraph 4.2.3)*.

8.3.4 *Explanation*

Bed, breakfast and...: For premises to qualify for a residential licence, there must be offered bed, breakfast and at least one other meal, i.e. lunch and/or evening meal. There is no requirement that a resident shall have dinner or lunch before qualifying for a drink, so long as this facility is on offer.

Off-sales: Intoxicants are for consumption on the premises, or off the premises to accompany a meal supplied from there, e.g. a picnic lunch.

8.4 **Combined Licence**

8.4.1 *Qualifications*

To qualify for a combined licence, the premises must meet the requirements both for a restaurant licence and for a residential licence. There will be two distinct categories of customer:
- those who patronise the restaurant only; and
- those who are residents.

8.4.2 *Explanation*

Premises operating under a combined licence will not be able to offer all the facilities which could be offered by a hotel with a full on-licence, i.e. no public bar, no off-sales.

8.5 **Matters Common to all Part IV Licences**

8.5.1 *Water*

It is an implied condition that suitable beverages other than intoxicating liquor, including water, should be available.

8.5.2 *Offence*
Licensing Act 1964 Section 161(2)

The holder of a Part IV licence commits an offence if he:
- knowingly
- permits intoxicating liquor sold under the licence
- to be consumed on the premises by persons to whom he is not permitted to sell it.

8.5.3 *Explanation*

To commit the offence, the license holder must knowingly permit the consumption. This applies only to liquor sold under the licence, so if a friend of a resident brings a bottle of whisky into a guest house, for himself to drink in the resident's room, no offence would be committed because the whisky has not been sold under that licence.

8.5.4 *Grounds for Refusal to Grant a Licence*

There are a number of grounds on which the grant of a Part IV licence may be refused. The grounds for refusal are:

- the applicant for the licence is not aged 18 years or over, or is not a fit and proper person
- the premises do not meet the requirements for the particular licence, or are not suitable
- within the preceding 12 months the premises were ill-conducted under a justices' licence or a refreshment house licence; that was forfeit, or that certain conditions relating to a Part IV licence were not met
- in relation to a restaurant or combined licence, meals supplied to restaurant customers were generally not table meals
- that sale or supply of intoxicants is by a self-service method
  (note, there is no objection to food or soft drinks being self-service)
- that a large proportion of the persons using the premises are under 18 years of age, and not accompanied by persons aged 18 or over who pay for them.

Note: There is nothing unlawful in persons under 18 going to a restaurant for a meal, or even buying a beer to go with the meal, if they are aged 16 or over. However, if a large proportion of the customers are under 18, not hosted by an adult, this will be a ground for refusing the licence.

9 POLICE POWERS OF ENTRY WITHOUT WARRANT
Licensing Act 1964 Section 186

9.1 Purpose

The reason for a constable exercising a power to enter licensed premises (or the premises of a registered club in limited cases) is for the purpose of preventing or detecting the commission of any offence against the Act.

9.2 Licensed Premises

9.2.1 *When Power May be Exercised*

A constable may enter licensed premises or a licensed canteen (excluding premises operating under an occasional licence):

- at any time during permitted hours and during the 30 minutes after the end of permitted hours; **and**
- at any time outside those hours when he suspects with reasonable cause that an offence under the Act is being or is about to be committed there.

9.2.2 *Occasional Licence*

The power to enter premises operating under an occasional licence is limited to the hours during which the licence is in force. Once the effect of the licence has ended for that day, there is no power to enter without warrant. (See comment at *paragraph 4.1.8* re the serving of drinks after time where an occasional licence is in force.)

9.2.3 *Occasional Permission*

There is a corresponding power to enter premises operating under an occasional permission. The power applies only during the hours specified in that permission.

9.2.4 *Explanation*

No suspicion: A constable may enter licensed premises during permitted hours (and during the half-hour afterwards, except in the case of an occasional licence) to check whether offences are being committed and to prevent their commission.

Suspicion: If the constable has reason to suspect an offence is being committed or is about to be, he may enter at other times. For example, there is reason to believe liquor is being served in the Red Lion pub at 2.00 am; acting on that suspicion, a constable may go in.

Occasional licence: Once an occasional licence ceases to have effect, the premises concerned will no longer be covered by a licence, so there is no power to enter there, once the hours specified on the licence have ended.

Occasional permission: The power to enter the premises applies only during the hours specified in the permission. There is a power to require the holder to produce the permission for examination, but if a constable suspects that intoxicants are being served after the occasional permission has ceased to have effect, there is something of a problem. Once the period has expired, there is no longer a power to enter the premises, and no power to require the holder to produce the permission. In such circumstances, initiative is called for.

9.3 **Registered Club**

9.3.1 *Limit on Power to Enter*

In the case of a registered club for which a special hours certificate is in force, a constable has a power to enter for the purpose of preventing or detecting any offence under the Act, during the period from 11.00 pm to 30 minutes after the end of the permitted hours.

9.3.2 *Explanation*

The period during which the police may enter is, in effect, the extra hours which the special hours certificate provides. Under a special hours certificate, the permitted hours end at 2.00 am or such earlier time as the magistrates may set when granting the certificate, so police may exercise the power to enter up to 2.30 am, at the latest (one hour later in parts of London).

Note: There is no power to enter outside this period, as there is for licensed premises. If offences are suspected, a warrant will have to be obtained.

9.4 **Offence**

Any person who:
- – by himself
- – or by any person acting in his employment or with his consent
- – refuses admission to a constable with a lawful right to enter
- – shall commit an offence.

To rebut any defence that the persons inside were not aware that a constable was seeking to exercise his power to enter, the officer should announce that he is a constable and that he wants to come in.

10 WARRANTS

10.1 Types of Warrant

There are two warrants which police may apply for under the Act – one relating to registered clubs – the other in respect of premises where it is suspected intoxicants are sold by retail without a licence. This second might also, in certain circumstances, relate to a registered club. (A third warrant, relating to parties organised for gain, is dealt with at *paragraph 11.6.*)

10.2 Registered Club
Licensing Act 1964 Section 54

10.2.1 *Grounds for Issue*

A magistrate may issue this warrant, upon being satisfied upon information on oath that there is reasonable ground to believe either:

- that there is ground for cancelling in whole or part a club's registration certificate, and that evidence of this is to be obtained at the club premises; or
- that intoxicating liquor is sold or supplied by or on behalf of a club in club premises not covered by a registration certificate or justices licence, or is kept in any club premises for sale or supply in contravention of the part of the Act relating to sale and supply in club premises.

10.2.2 *Powers Under the Warrant*

The warrant will authorise a constable at any time or times within one month of issue of the warrant:

- to enter any of the club premises, using force if need be
- search the premises
- and seize any documents relating to the business of the club.

10.3 Sale Without a Licence
Licensing Act 1964 Section 187

10.3.1 *Grounds for Issue*

A magistrate may issue the warrant upon being satisfied on information on oath that there is a reasonable ground for believing:

- that intoxicating liquor is sold by retail, or exposed or kept for sale by retail
- at any place in the area where it may not lawfully be sold by retail.

10.3.2 *Powers Under the Warrant*

The warrant will authorise a constable at any time or times within one month of the date of issue of the warrant:

- to enter the premises named in the warrant, using force if necessary
- search the place for intoxicating liquor
- seize any intoxicating liquor which a constable reasonably supposes is there for the purpose of unlawful sale
- and seize the vessels containing such liquor (designed to counter the 'Merchant of Venice' defence).

10.3.3 *Additional Power*

If intoxicating liquor has been seized, a constable has power to require any person found in the place to give his name and address.

10.3.4 *Offences*
There are two offences which may be committed, if intoxicating liquor has been seized, but not otherwise:

1: Any person found in the place shall commit an offence:
 – unless he proves he was there for a lawful purpose.

2: Any person required by a constable to give his name and address will commit an offence if:
 – he refuses to give his details; or
 – he gives false details; or
 – he gives details and the constable has reasonable grounds to believe the name or address he has given is false; and
 – he then refuses to give a satisfactory answer to any question put to him by the constable to verify the details he has given.

11 PARTIES ORGANISED FOR GAIN
Licensing Act 1964 Section 84

11.1 Regular Events
If persons meet regularly at a place and consume intoxicating liquor, they may be regarded by the law as a 'club' and be registered if the qualifications for registration are satisfied; on the other hand, there may be offences of selling without a licence. The Act caters specifically for one type of gathering, where parties are held on a regular basis outside permitted hours, with intoxicants being supplied, and there being some element of gain involved.

11.2 Party

11.2.1 *Meaning of Terms*
A party will be fall within the scope of these provisions if:
 – intoxicating liquor is supplied
 – before the beginning or after the end of the general licensing hours
 – at a party organised for gain
 – held on premises kept or habitually used for such parties
 – where intoxicating liquor is consumed.

11.2.2 *Exception*
There is an exception for any party held on licensed premises, licensed canteen, mess, premises covered by an occasional licence, or registered club.

11.3 Offences
The following are offences which may be committed in respect of such a party:
 – supply intoxicating liquor at the party
 – being the occupier of premises, permits them to be used for a party where intoxicants are unlawfully supplied
 – being concerned in the organisation of a party, permits any person to supply or consume intoxicating liquor unlawfully
 – consume intoxicating liquor at the party

- being the holder of a liquor licence, delivers intoxicating liquor to premises
  kept or habitually used for such parties, before the beginning or after the end
  of the general licensing hours.

11.4 Explanation

Outside permitted hours: For the party to be unlawful, intoxicants must be supplied and consumed before the beginning or after the end of the general licensing hours for the district. At, say, 12.30 am, licensed premises and clubs may be open, under special hours certificates, extended hours orders, etc. However, the general licensing hours finished at 11.00 pm (weekdays) so supply or consumption at a party after this time will be unlawful.

Kept or habitually used: The arrangements for the party will only be unlawful if the premises where it is held are kept or habitually used for such parties. A 'one-off' will not be unlawful.

Organised for gain: Here, 'gain' does not necessarily mean making a profit. A party is deemed to have been organised for gain if:
- any pecuniary advantage accrued or was intended to accrue from holding the party,
  to any person concerned in its organisation;

But in determining the question of pecuniary advantage, no account shall be taken of any expenditure incurred in connection with the party.

Thus, if a party is intended to make a profit for the organisers, e.g. by charging admission, by selling beer, etc, but it incurs a loss because not enough people turn up, it falls within the scope of the Section because a pecuniary advantage was intended to accrue.

On the other hand, if the organiser charges for beer or food, or whatever, with the price intended just to cover costs without making a surplus, this is still 'organised for gain' because the expenditure must not be considered when looking for pecuniary advantage.

Residents: For the purposes of deciding whether there is a party organised for gain, the presence in the premises of a person who is resident there shall be disregarded. Thus, for example, if all the persons seen being supplied with drinks actually lived in the premises, there would be no unlawful party (Section 84(6)).

Exception: Any profits made or intended to be made by an organiser of the party from any gaming taking place at the party shall not be counted towards 'pecuniary advantage', so long as the arrangements for the gaming gave the organiser only the same chance of winning as anyone else.

Concerned in the organisation: A person is deemed to be concerned in the organisation of a party if she:
- took any part in getting the party assembled; or
- acted as host, or assisted the host, at the party.

11.5 Search Warrant
Licensing Act 1964 Section 85

11.5.1 *Grounds for Issue*
A magistrate may issue a warrant if satisfied upon information on oath that there is reasonable ground to believe premises in that area are kept or habitually used for the holding of parties where the provisions of Section 84 are contravened.

11.5.2 *Powers Under the Warrant*

The warrant will empower a constable at any time or times within a month from the issue of the warrant:

— to enter the premises using force if necessary
— search for, seize and remove any intoxicating liquor found there, which the constable has reason to suppose is on the premises for the purpose of unlawful supply and consumption.

11.5.3 *Additional Power*

If intoxicating liquor is so seized, then any person found on the premises, on being required by a constable, shall give his name and address.

11.5.4 *Offence*

A person commits an offence if, having been so required to give his name and address:

— refuses to give his details; or
— gives a false name or address.

11.5.5 *Forfeiture*

If any person is convicted of an offence under Section 84 relating to the premises where intoxicating liquor has been seized, then the liquor and the containers it is in, shall be forfeited.

Note: The power to seize liquor does not specifically refer to the containers, as is the case with a warrant under Section 187, but it is implied that the power to seize the liquor extends to the containers, given that both may be forfeited by the court.

Keynote Case

12.1 *Vane v Yiannopoullos* [1965] AC 486

Problem

Whether when an employee does something, the knowledge is imputed to the employer who is then liable.

Circumstances

Yiannopoullos was the holder of a justices' on-licence with a condition attached that intoxicants were supplied only to persons ordering meals. A waitress employed by him had been instructed not to serve drinks to persons not ordering meals. However, on one occasion when he was in another part of the restaurant, the waitress served drinks to two persons who did not order a meal. Yiannopoullos was charged with knowingly selling intoxicants on the licensed premises to persons to whom he was not, under the conditions of the licence, allowed to sell. The case went through to the House of Lords.

Decision

The prosecution contended that he was liable for the acts of the waitress since he had delegated to her the authority to sell intoxicants, so that her knowledge was imputed to him. It was held that Yiannopoullos was not liable because he had not delegated responsibility for running the premises to the waitress.

A distinction is drawn between two situations:

- where the licensee retains responsibility for running the premises, he will not be liable for the actions of his employee, done without his knowledge;
- when the licensee delegates all responsibility to his servant he has vicarious liability for acts done without his knowledge by that servant.

Comment

A licensee has responsibility for the running of his licensed premises. He cannot avoid that responsibility by going off and leaving someone else in charge; he will be responsible for any misdeeds of that person. However, when the licensee is himself in charge, he will not be responsible for an action of his employee, done without his knowledge, where the offence requires knowledge on his part.

Chapter 41: Places of Entertainment

1 INTRODUCTION

1.1 Safety

The law seeks to regulate places of entertainment, primarily for safety reasons. The police, the local authority and the fire brigade all have extensive powers to enter and inspect premises, and to make objection to applications for licences. Local authority and fire brigade powers are not included here.

1.2 Raves

In recent years the phenomenon of 'raves' has become a problem, with large numbers of young people turning up at a location to be entertained by loud music for several hours. Where such events are held on unlicensed premises, there may be offences in relation to entertainment licences; in the open air this will not be the case, but these events usually involve serious disturbance to persons in the neighbourhood with the likelihood of safety risks to those attending. Police powers and related offences in relation to raves are dealt with as public order matters in *Chapter 17*.

2 ENTERTAINMENT LICENCES
Local Government (Miscellaneous Provisions) Act 1982

2.1 Requirement

An entertainment licence is required for any place where entertainment is provided consisting of:
- public dancing or music or public entertainment of a like kind
- a sporting event to which the public are invited as spectators.

This legislation applies only outside Greater London. Arrangements for London are dealt with at *paragraph 3*.

Many licences will be in force on a permanent basis, and are renewable. However, a licence is still required for a place where an entertainment is held on one occasion only.

A licence is required for public entertainment only. However, an entertainment does not cease to be 'public' merely because persons attending have to buy tickets 24 hours in advance (*Lunn v Colston-Hayter* (1991)).

A local authority may also require licences for certain entertainments which are not open to the public, but which are promoted for private gain (Private Places of Entertainment (Licensing) Act 1967).

2.2 Exceptions

2.2.1 *General Exceptions*

The requirement for an entertainment licence does not apply to:
- music in a place of public religious worship, or at a religious service or meeting

- entertainment or sporting event at a pleasure fair
- an entertainment taking place wholly or mainly in the open air
- a sporting event which is not the main use of the place where it is held (in certain circumstances).

2.2.2 *Liquor Licensed Premises*
Licensing Act 1964 Section 182

On premises licensed for the sale and supply of intoxicating liquor, no entertainment licence is required for:
- any radio or television broadcast
- music and singing only, provided by either recorded music, or not more than two performers, or a combination of first one, then the other.

Thus, a disc jockey playing records in a pub may fall within the exception, but if the customers dance to the music, this goes beyond 'music and singing only' and an entertainment licence would be required.

2.3 **Entertainment on Private Land**
A local authority **may**, if it chooses to implement the provisions, require a licence to be held in respect of an entertainment:
- held wholly or mainly in the open air
- on private land
- where the entertainment is musical to a substantial degree
- to which the public are admitted on payment or otherwise.

If the local authority does adopt these provisions, there will be exceptions for any religious event, and for certain other events such as garden fetes and exhibitions.

2.4 **Suitability and Conditions**
When application is made for the grant or renewal of an entertainment licence, the applicant must notify the chief officer of police (as well as the local authority and the fire authority).

The local authority, in deciding whether to grant the application, will then take account of any observations made by the police or the fire authority. The local authority may make regulations which lay down standard conditions for entertainment licences; every licence issued by that authority will then be subject to these conditions. A licence will specify the hours during which it shall have effect.

2.5 **Offences**
Local Government (Miscellaneous Provisions) Act 1982 Schedule 1, paragraph 12

There are two offences to consider in relation to the use of a place for an entertainment of the sort which requires a licence.

2.5.1 *Licence in Force*
Where the conditions attached to an entertainment licence are breached, an offence will be committed by:
- the licence holder

– any other person who, having reason to believe that the place would be used in this way, allowed it to be used or let it out.

2.5.2 *No Licence*
Where an entertainment is held at a place where there is no licence in force, an offence will be committed by:
– any person concerned in the organisation or management of the entertainment
– any other person who, having reason to believe that the place would be used in this way, allowed it to be used or let it out.

2.5.3 *Exception*
When a licence is in force in respect of liquor licensed premises and a special order of exemption is in force there on a particular occasion, entertainment may go on after the end of the hours allowed by the entertainment licence, until the end of the hours permitted by the special order of exemption, without the licence holder being liable for breaching the terms of the entertainment licence (Schedule 1, paragraph 13).

2.5.4 **Defence**
A person accused of any of these offences will have a defence if he proves that he took all reasonable precautions and exercised all due diligence to avoid an offence being committed.

2.6 **Police Powers of Entry**
Local Government (Miscellaneous Provisions) Act 1982 Schedule 1, paragraph 14

2.6.1 *Licence in Force*
When a constable has reason to believe:
– that an entertainment (of a sort requiring a licence) is being or is about to be given
– in any place for which a licence is currently in force
– he may enter with a view to seeing whether the terms and conditions of the licence are being complied with.

2.6.2 *Licence or No Licence*
A constable may be granted a warrant by a magistrate, to enter a place where he has reason to believe that any offence – breach of conditions, or running an entertainment on unlicensed premises – is being committed.

2.6.3 *Refusal to Admit*
Any person who without reasonable excuse, refuses to admit a constable to enter and inspect the premises when exercising powers with or without warrant, shall be guilty of an offence.

2.7 **Misuse of Drugs in or Near Premises**
Local Government Act (Miscellaneous Provisions) Act 1982 Schedule 1
as amended by the Public Entertainments Licences (Drug Misuse) Act 1997

2.7.1 *Police Reports*
The chief officer of police may send a report to a local authority responsible for the issue of an entertainment licence in respect of a particular place:
– stating that there is a serious problem relating to the supply or use of controlled drugs

at the place, or at any place nearby which is controlled by the licence holder; and
- giving reasons for the police view that there is such a problem.

Acting on the police report, the local authority may:
- refuse an application for the renewal or transfer of the entertainment licence; or
- revoke the entertainment licence; or
- impose terms, restrictions or conditions on the holding of the licence.

In each case, the local authority may take the action on the ground that they are satisfied this action will significantly assist in dealing with the problem.

2.7.2 *Court Action*

When the holder of an entertainment licence is convicted of an offence of failing to comply with the terms, conditions or restrictions on the licence, the court may revoke the licence if satisfied:
- that there is a serious problem relating to the supply or use of controlled drugs at the place, or at any place nearby which is controlled by the licence holder; and
- to revoke the licence will significantly assist in dealing with the problem.

2.7.3 *Explanation*

Immediate action: A local authority has power to revoke an entertainment licence when the holder is convicted of an offence relating to the licence, but it will usually be some time after an offence is committed before such action is taken. With these amendments, as soon as police identify a drugs problem and report on it, with supporting evidence, the local authority may act to close the place down – so long as it is satisfied that this will significantly assist in dealing with the drugs problem.

Proof in court: When a court is considering whether to revoke a licence, the standard of proof that there is a drugs problem will be the civil one, 'on the balance of probabilities', rather than the criminal one, 'beyond reasonable doubt'.

Appeal: When a local authority, acting on a police report, revokes a licence or imposes conditions, the action has effect immediately. The holder of the licence may within the following 21 days make representations to the authority, seeking to reverse the action. The authority must consider any representations made and either confirm the original decision, or reverse it.

When a court revokes a licence, the usual appeals procedure applies. The court may however, if satisfied that it would be unfair not to do so, order that the licence shall remain in force until an appeal is heard.

3 LICENCES IN GREATER LONDON
London Government Act 1963

3.1 Types of Licence

3.1.1 *Music and Dancing*

A music and dancing licence is required for any premises (whether or not licensed for liquor) used for the purposes of public dancing or music, or public entertainment of a like kind.

The exception, allowing for recorded music or up to two live performers in liquor licensed premises, applies *(see paragraph 2.2.2)*.

3.1.2 *Indoor Sports*

A licence is required for any premises used for a sporting event to which the public are invited as spectators. The same exceptions apply as in the case of an entertainment licence, namely to events at a pleasure fair, or in certain cases when the sporting event is not the main use of the premises.

3.1.3 *Boxing and Wrestling*

A licence is required for any public boxing or wrestling contest or display held wholly or mainly in the open air.

Exceptions include:
- by a travelling showman at a pleasure fair
- by a school
- by the Boy Scouts or other non-profit making organisation.

3.1.4 *Occasional Licence*

Licences granted on a permanent basis are renewable, usually annually, but an application may be made for a licence for one or more events.

3.2 **Suitability and Conditions**

When an application is made for the grant, transfer or renewal of a licence, the commissioner of police (of the Metropolis or of the City, as the case may be) must be notified, and the council will then take into account any police representations when considering the application.

The council granting licences may make regulations and these will then apply to every licence of that sort granted by that council.

3.3 **Offences**
London Government Act 1963 Schedule 12, paragraph 10

The offences which may be committed are the same as for entertainment licences, and the provisions relating to liquor licensed premises with a special order of exemption also apply in London *(see paragraphs 2.5.1 – 2.5.4)*.

3.4 **Police Powers**
London Government Act 1963 Schedule 12, paragraph 12

3.4.1 *Licence in Force*

A constable may:
- at all reasonable times
- enter premises for which a licence is in force
- at which he has reason to believe
- an entertainment or sporting event (of a sort requiring a licence) is being or is about to be given
- with a view to seeing whether the terms and conditions of the licence are being complied with.

3.4.2 *Licence or No Licence*

A constable may be granted a warrant by a magistrate, to enter a place where he has reason to believe that any offence – breach of conditions, or running an entertainment on unlicensed premises – is being committed.

3.4.3 *Refusal to Admit*
Any person who refuses to admit a constable to enter and inspect the premises when exercising powers with or without warrant, shall be guilty of an offence.

3.4.4 *Power to Seize Equipment*
A constable who enters premises under a warrant may seize and remove any apparatus, equipment or other article reasonably believed to relate to an offence.

Note: This power to seize articles may not extend to certain outer London boroughs.

3.5 Misuse of Drugs in or Near Premises
London Government Act 1963 Schedule 12
as amended by the Public Entertainments Licences (Drug Misuse) Act 1997

Identical provisions are made for Greater London as for other areas, for a local authority acting on police reports, to revoke an entertainment licence or impose extra conditions, as a means of addressing a serious drugs problem. Likewise, a court may revoke a licence when the holder of it is convicted of certain offences. These provisions are dealt with at *paragraph 2.7* above.

4 THEATRES

4.1 Licences
Theatres Act 1968 Section 12

4.1.1 *Requirement*
No premises may be used for the public performance of a play unless a licence has been granted for it.

4.1.2 *Suitability*
The local authority may grant or renew a theatre licence, subject to such conditions and restrictions as it thinks fit. A licence may be transferred from one person to another.

An applicant for the grant, transfer or renewal of a licence shall send a copy of that notice to the chief officer of police for the area.

4.1.3 *Offences*
Theatres Act 1968 Section 13

1: No licence: If a public performance of a play is given without a licence then an offence will be committed by:
   - any person concerned in the organisation or management of that performance
   - any other person who knew or had reason to believe the play would be performed and who allowed the premises to be used or made them available.

2: Licence conditions: Breach of any condition or restriction on the licence will lead to an offence being committed by:
   - the licence holder

– any other person who allowed the premises to be used or made them available, knowing or having reason to believe that the conditions or restrictions would be contravened.

4.1.4 *Defence*
The licence holder will have a defence if he proves that the contravention took place without his consent and connivance and that he exercised all due diligence to prevent it.

4.1.5 *Explanation*
Play: Involves, wholly or in part, one or more persons actually present and performing and is either:
– a ballet; or
– a dramatic piece in which the whole or most of the performance involves speech, singing or action.

Thus, opera, mime, and a panto on ice would all come within the meaning of a play, as well as what would be referred to in common parlance as a 'play' (Section 18).

Premises: The term includes a place, so a play does not have to be in a building to fall within the scope of the Act.

Public performance: Includes any performance:
– in a public place
– which the public or a Section of the public are allowed to attend, on payment or otherwise
– (in an area where the local authority have so determined) promoted for private gain, whether open to the public or not.

4.2 Offences Arising from Performances

4.2.1 *Obscene Performances*
Theatres Act 1968 Section 2

4.2.2 *Offence*
An offence will be committed by any person:
– who presents or directs (whether for gain or not)
– an obscene performance of a play
– in private or in public.

4.2.3 *Defence*
A person may claim a defence of 'public good' on the grounds that the performance was given in the interest of drama, art, etc. The opinion of experts as to the literary or artistic merits of a play may be submitted in evidence, by defence or prosecution.

4.2.4 *Exception*
This offence will not be committed where the performance was in a private dwelling on a domestic occasion.

4.2.5 *Breach of the Peace*
Theatres Act 1968 Section 6

Offence: A person will commit an offence who:

- presents or directs a public performance of a play (whether for gain or not)
- involving the use of threatening, abusive or insulting words or behaviour
- having done so with the intent to provoke a breach of the peace
- or whereby a breach of the peace was likely to be provoked.

4.2.6 *Exceptions*
Theatres Act 1968 Section 7

Neither of these offences will be committed where the performance in question is given solely or primarily as a rehearsal, or to allow the performance to be recorded or broadcast.

However, if it is shown that persons attended the performance other than those who had to be there for the purposes of the performance, e.g. the cast plus camera crew, etc – then the onus will be on the defence to show that it was given 'solely or primarily' for one of those purposes.

4.2.7 *Consent to Prosecute*
The consent of the Attorney-General is required before a prosecution may be instituted for one of these offences.

4.2.8 *Evidence*
When a performance of a play is based on a script, a copy of that script may be submitted in evidence, and the performance will be taken to have been performed according to the script, unless the contrary is shown (Section 9).

4.3 Police Powers

4.3.1 *To Copy Scripts*
Theatres Act 1968 Section 10

If a police officer of the rank of superintendent or above has reasonable cause to believe:
- that an offence (under Sections 2 or 6) has been committed by any person in respect of a performance of a play
- or that a performance of a play is to be given which is likely to involve such an offence being committed by any person
- then the officer may make a written order in relation to that person and that performance.

Such an order may require the person named in it to produce an actual script (if one exists) and to afford the officer the opportunity to have it copied.

4.3.2 *Offence*
A person who fails without reasonable excuse to comply with the requirement of a written order commits an offence.

4.3.3 *Entry Without Warrant*
Theatres Act 1968 Section 15(3)

Any constable may:
- at all reasonable times

- enter any licensed premises where he has reason to believe a performance of a play is being or about to be given
- and inspect the premises with a view to seeing whether the terms and conditions of the licence are being complied with.

If the constable is not in uniform he must produce some authority (such as a warrant card), if required. If he is in uniform he does not have to do so.

4.3.4 *Entry with a Warrant*
Theatres Act 1968 Section 15(1)

Grounds for issue: A magistrate may issue a warrant if satisfied upon information on oath that there is reasonable ground to suspect:
  i) either that a performance of a play is to be given on premises, in respect of which an offence is likely to be committed under Section 2 (obscene performance) or Section 6 (threatening behaviour, etc); or
  ii) that the performance is, or is to be on premises which are not licensed.

Powers under the warrant: The warrant will authorise a police officer at any time within a month of the issue of the warrant to enter the premises and:
  - either attend the performance, if the warrant was issued on ground (i)
  - or inspect the premises, if the warrant was issued on ground (ii).

4.3.5 *Offence*
Theatres Act 1968 Section 15(5)

These powers may be exercised also by authorised officers of the local authority and/or the fire authority. It will be an offence under the Act to obstruct either of them in the exercise of these powers, but there is no corresponding provision for obstructing a police officer. Presumably, the legislators felt that the police already had available the offence of obstructing a constable in the execution of her duty.

4.3.6 *Explanation*
Present or direct: A person may be guilty of directing a performance of a play even though she is not present at the performance. An actor will not be guilty of presenting or directing a performance simply because he takes part in it. However, an actor who performs in a way not as directed (i.e. he 'ad libs') may be guilty of 'directing'.

Private or public: As far as an offence involving an obscene performance is concerned, this may arise from a performance held in public or in private. An offence involving threatening, etc, behaviour will arise only if the performance is in public.

5 HYPNOTISM
Hypnotism Act 1952

5.1 Control of Entertainment Involving Hypnotism

5.1.1 *Conditions*
Hypnotism may be regulated by means of conditions imposed by the local authority on an entertainment or music and dancing licence.

5.1.2 *Offences*

1: It will be an offence for any person to give an exhibition of hypnotism on a living person, to which the public are admitted on payment or otherwise, unless the place where it is given is licensed for entertainment, or as a theatre under the Theatres Act 1968, or the performance has been authorised by the local authority (Section 2).

2: It will be an offence for a person at a demonstration or performance involving hypnotism to which the public are admitted, to demonstrate or use in the performance, a person under the age of 18 years, unless he proves that he had reasonable cause to believe the person to be over 18 (Section 3).

5.1.3 *Exceptions*

This legislation does not affect any demonstration or performance of hypnotism for scientific or research purposes or for the treatment of mental or physical disease (Section 5).

5.2 Police Powers
Hypnotism Act 1952 Section 4

Any constable may enter any premises where any entertainment is held if he has reason to believe that anything is being done which is or may be in contravention of this Act.

This gives a power to enter unlicensed premises without a warrant, in contrast to powers to enter under other entertainments law.

6 CINEMAS
Cinemas Act 1985 Section 1

6.1 Cinema Licences

6.1.1 *Requirements for Licence*
No premises shall be used for a 'film exhibition' unless licensed for that purpose. A licence is issued by the local authority, who may impose conditions and restrictions, including conditions relating to children being allowed in when certain types of film are being shown.

6.1.2 *Application for Licence*
When an application is made for the grant, renewal or transfer of a licence, the applicant must notify the chief officer of police of the application. In considering the application, the local authority shall consult and have regard to any observations made by the police.

6.1.3 *Children's Shows*
Cinemas Act 1985 Section 2

In addition to a licence, a 'consent' is required from the local authority when a film exhibition is to be given wholly or mainly for children.

6.1.4 *Exemptions*
Cinemas Act 1985 Sections 5 – 8

A licence will not be required for a film exhibition in the following cases:
  – in a private dwelling house, where the public are not admitted; or

- in a place where the public are not admitted, or are admitted without payment, or the show is given by an organisation which has a certificate from the Home Secretary.

And in either case, the show is not promoted for private gain **or** the sole purpose is to demonstrate a product, advertise, inform, educate or instruct:
- where the premises are used not more than six times a year for film exhibitions, and notice has been given to the local authority, fire authority and police;
- where the show is to be given in a movable building or structure, for which a licence is in force in another local authority area, so long as the local authority, police and fire service are notified in advance.

6.1.5 *Explanation*

Film exhibition: A film exhibition is an exhibition of moving pictures, but excludes the simultaneous reception and showing of programmes included in a programme service. A 'programme service' is, briefly, a television or sound broadcast. The word 'simultaneous' is important. If a television broadcast was recorded and shown later, this could amount to a film exhibition.

A video game is not a film exhibition. A distinction is made between 'moving pictures' and objects moving across the screen of a video monitor (*British Amusement Catering Trades Assoc. v Westminster City Council* (1989)).

No private gain: Certain film shows of an educational nature, or advertising a product may be given without a licence, subject to certain conditions.

Occasional or travelling shows: If premises are used only a handful of times in a year (or a handful plus one to be precise) a licence will not be required so long as the local council and the fire brigade have been notified. The same applies to a film show given in a temporary structure, so long as a licence is held in another local authority area. Whether any 'travelling cinemas' still operate in Britain is another matter.

6.1.6 *Offences*
Cinemas Act 1985 Section 10

An offence will be committed if:
- premises which are not licensed are used for a film exhibition which requires a licence
- a children's film exhibition is held in premises for which no 'consent' has been granted
- conditions or restrictions on a licence or consent are not complied with
- regulations relating to safety in cinemas are not complied with.

The following persons may be liable for these offences:
- any person concerned in the organisation or management of the event
- the holder of the licence if the premises are licensed
- any other person who allowed the premises to be used or let them or made them available for use, knowing or having reason to suspect that they would be used in breach of the Act.

6.1.7 *Defence*

A person will have a defence if he proves that he took all reasonable precautions and exercised all due diligence to avoid an offence being committed.

6.2 Regulations and Conditions

6.2.1 *Regulations*
Cinemas Act 1985 Section 4

The Home Secretary may make regulations concerning the health and welfare of children attending film exhibitions. These regulations contain comprehensive provisions, much of them concerned with safety and fire precautions. Among the regulations are the following provisions:
- the licensee or some other responsible person nominated in writing by the licensee, being over the age of 21, must be present and in charge of the premises whenever the public are allowed in
- attendants shall be instructed in safety precautions
- no child under the age of five years to be admitted unless in the charge of a person aged 16 or over
- a child under 12 shall not be admitted after 7.00 pm to a showing of a film which has been shown earlier than 7.00 pm on that day, unless in the charge of a person aged 16 or over
- where the film show is wholly or mainly for children under 16, attendants have to be provided as follows:
  i) on the lowest floor, at least one attendant for every hundred (or part of a hundred) persons under 16
  ii) on upper floors at least one for every 50 or part of 50
  iii) in each case there being at least as many attendants as there are exits.

Cinematograph (Safety) Regulations 1955; Cinematograph (Children) (No 2) Regulations 1955.

6.2.2 *Conditions and Restrictions*
The local authority may impose conditions and restrictions when granting a licence. To assist local authorities, the Home Office has produced 'model conditions', which may or may not be adopted by a particular authority. Some of these are:
- apart from newsreels, and subject to the permission of the local authority, films must be classified by the British Board of Film Classification, as 'U', 'PG', '15' or '18' and young people may be admitted only in accordance with these classifications, i.e. no one under the age of 18 years or 15 years respectively to be admitted when a film classified as '18' or '15' is to be shown
- the local authority may alter any film classification with which it does not agree
- standing in gangways is not permitted
- exit doors must be clearly marked as such, available for use at all times and kept free of obstruction
- exit doors should be fitted with no fastenings other than automatic bolts. The local authority may authorise other devices to be fitted when the premises are not open to the public, but they must be removed before the public are allowed in
- the licensee shall maintain good order. As soon as he becomes aware of any indecent conduct taking place, he shall inform the police.

6.3 Police Powers
Cinemas Act 1985 Section 13

6.3.1 *Without Warrant*
A constable may enter and inspect a licensed cinema in which he has reason to believe a film

exhibition is being or is about to be given, with a view to seeing whether the relevant provisions are being complied with. This power also extends to premises used occasionally and to movable buildings.

Because each local authority imposes its own conditions, it will be necessary for a police officer seeking to exercise powers of inspection, to know what conditions apply before doing so.

6.3.2 *Search Warrant*
A constable, if authorised by a search warrant issued under this Section, may enter and search any premises in respect of which he has reason to believe an offence under the Act is being, has been or is about to be committed. Having entered under the warrant, the constable may then seize and remove any equipment or other thing whatsoever found there which he has reason to believe relates to such an offence.

6.3.3 *Offence*
Any person who intentionally obstructs a constable in the exercise of these powers will commit an offence.

7 ENTERTAINMENT FOR CHILDREN
Children and Young Persons Act 1933 Section 12

7.1 Provision of Attendants
When a person, in any building, provides entertainment for children or at which the majority of persons attending will be children under the age of 14 years and the number of children exceeds 100, he must provide attendants.

The attendants must be sufficient to control movement in the building, take reasonable precautions for the safety of the children and to prevent more people being admitted than can be properly accommodated. This requirement does not apply to an entertainment held in a private dwelling house (more than 100 children in one house!).

7.2 Offence
If these provisions are not met, then an offence will be committed by:
 – the person providing the entertainment; and
 – the occupier of the building who:
   i) for hire or reward
   ii) allows the building to be used for the entertainment and
   iii) fails to take reasonable steps to ensure that attendants are provided as required.

7.3 Police Powers
A constable may enter any building in which he has reason to believe an entertainment of this sort is being or is about to be provided, for the purpose of seeing that these provisions are being carried out.

7.4 Explanation
How many attendants?: No numbers are laid down for attendants, as is the case in relation to film shows for children. Instead the term 'sufficient' is used.

Private and public: These provisions, including the police power to enter, are not restricted to public entertainments or licensed cinemas. A private party on private premises will equally require attendants. However, the provisions do not apply to an entertainment held in a private dwelling house.

8 LATE NIGHT REFRESHMENT HOUSES AND NIGHT CAFÉS
Late Night Refreshment Houses Act 1969
London Local Authorities Act 1990

8.1 Introduction
The 1969 Act provides for the licensing of cafés open late at night. However, the 1990 Act may be adopted by any London Borough (not applicable in the City of London), the effect of which is to replace the former Act in that area.

8.2 Late Night Refreshment House

8.2.1 *Meaning*
Late Night Refreshment Houses Act 1969 Section 1

This is any premises (house, room, shop or building) kept open for public refreshment, resort and entertainment, at any time between 10.00 pm and 5.00 am.

8.2.2 *Requirement for Licence*
Late Night Refreshment Houses Act 1969 Section 2

Such premises may not operate except under a licence issued by the local authority. It is an offence for a person to keep a late night refreshment house which is not licensed.

8.2.3 *Exemption*
A late night refreshment house is not required for liquor licensed premises which do not stay open later than 30 minutes beyond the end of evening permitted hours for those premises.

8.2.4 *Explanation*
Refreshment, resort and entertainment: The Act suffers from the archaic language of legislation from a hundred years earlier. The word 'entertainment' is particularly misleading; what the law is aimed at is what is generally known as a 'café'. A structure with a hatch through which the public could be served has been held not to amount to a late night refreshment house (*Bucknell, Frank and Son Ltd v London Borough of Croydon* (1973)). However, where food or drink is provided in premises and customers stay there to consume it, even though there are no chairs to sit on, this has been held to require a licence.

Liquor licence: If the premises operate under a liquor licence, and do not stay open for longer than 30 minutes (which is drinking up time for someone having food there) after the end of permitted hours, a late night refreshment house licence is not required. The permitted hours referred to are the hours for those premises, which may involve some extension to the hours, e.g. under a special hours certificate. However, if a pub or restaurant continued to serve meals and other non-alcoholic refreshments into the early hours, after permitted hours were ended, a licence under this Act would be required. Many restaurants remain open into the early hours of the morning.

8.2.5 *Restricted Hours*
Late Night Refreshment Houses Act 1969 Section 7

The local authority may impose a condition on a licence, if satisfied that it is desirable to do so to avoid unreasonable disturbance to residents of the neighbourhood. The condition may specify a period of time during which the premises shall not be open to the public. This period may start no earlier than 11.00 pm and extend no later than 5.00 am.

8.2.6 *Offence*
If premises are open in contravention of a restriction, the licensee shall be guilty of an offence.

8.2.7 *Charges and Touting*
Late Night Refreshment Houses Act 1969 Section 8

The local authority may impose conditions on a licence for the purposes of preventing people from being misled as to charges. These conditions may apply between 10.00 pm and 5.00 am and may:
- require charges to be displayed on a notice where they may be seen by a person before entering the premises; and
- prohibit anyone touting for custom outside or in the immediate vicinity of the premises.

8.2.8 *Offence*
If any such condition is not complied with, the licensee and any other person who is knowingly responsible, will commit an offence.

8.2.9 *Preservation of Order*
Late Night Refreshment Houses Act 1969 Section 9

The licensee of a late night refreshment house shall not knowingly permit unlawful gaming, or prostitutes, thieves or anyone who is drunk or disorderly to assemble at or remain in the premises.

8.2.10 *Offence*
The licensee commits an offence if he fails to comply with this requirement.

Any one who is riotous, drunk, quarrelsome or disorderly in the premises may be requested to leave by the manager, member of staff or by a constable.

A person who has been required to leave under this Section will commit an offence if he refuses or neglects to leave.

8.2.11 *Police Powers*
Late Night Refreshment Houses Act 1969 Section 10

To enter: A constable may at any time he thinks fit enter the premises of a licensed late night refreshment house.

8.2.12 *Offence*
The licensee or any other person employed by him or acting on his behalf, will commit an offence by failing or refusing to admit a constable on demand.

To expel: A constable **must** on the demand of the manager, occupier, member of staff or agent of the manager or occupier, assist in expelling from the premises any person who is drunk, riotous, quarrelsome or disorderly.

8.2.13 *Explanation*

Den of thieves: The provision that the licensee shall not allow 'prostitutes or thieves' to assemble on his premises is a relic of 19th century legislation. It would not be practicable for a café proprietor to bar a person from coming in for a coffee solely because he knew the customer to have a conviction for theft. A similar provision in respect of liquor licensed premises, allows that prostitutes may wish to use a pub for reasonable refreshment. Although this Act does not contain that proviso, it seems sensible to distinguish between a situation where known prostitutes gather for a drink and a sandwich, and one where prostitutes congregate in a café in order to meet potential clients there.

Power to enter: There are no 'permitted hours' for late night refreshment houses as there are for liquor licensed premises, so a constable's power to enter is not limited by reference to certain times of day. A constable may enter 'at any time he thinks fit'. There is no power to force an entry, so it would not be sensible to seek to go in when the premises are in darkness and locked, unless there was reason to believe that there was someone on the premises aware of the officer's desire to enter.

Police to assist: A constable does not have an option, whether or not to assist in expelling someone from the premises. If the licensee or a member of staff require the constable to help, then she must do so. However, before doing so, it will be wise for the officer to satisfy herself that the person to be expelled does fall into one of the categories – drunk, riotous, quarrelsome or disorderly – otherwise the expulsion may not be lawful.

8.3 Night Cafés in London

8.3.1 *Meaning of Term*
London Local Authorities Act 1990 Section 4

A night café is any premises:
  - kept open for public refreshment at any time between 11.00 pm and 5.00 am; or
  - used by a club or other organisation which if they were open to the public, would come under the preceding description; or
  - any premises where meals or refreshments are supplied between midnight and 5.00 am, exclusively for consumption off the premises.

But does not include premises:
  - in respect of which there is in force a liquor on-licence, during the permitted hours of such licence and for 30 minutes after the end of the permitted hours
  - for which there is in force a theatre licence, a cinema licence, music and singing or entertainment, etc, licence – during the hours permitted by the licence
  - used wholly or mainly as ancillary to a bona fide hotel, guest house, etc
  - used exclusively and bona fide by a registered or licensed club for sale or supply of intoxicating liquor, or a club provided by the borough council
  - used by a club or organisation:
    i) which is a registered charity
    ii) as a gym, swimming baths or for playing sports or games

iii) as a factory or office canteen
iv) comprised in London Regional Transport, Heathrow Airport or a
railway undertaking.

8.3.2 *Requirement for Licence*
London Local Authorities Act 1990 Section 6

Premises shall not be used as a night café except in accordance with a licence granted by the borough council. The council may apply restrictions and conditions to a licence covering such aspects as fire safety, maximum number of customers at any one time, opening hours with a view to minimising nuisance to neighbours, etc. The council may make regulations prescribing standard conditions for all night cafés in its area, so that any licence will be granted subject to those standard conditions.

A licence normally lasts for one year, but the council may issue an 'occasional night café licence' to cover one or more specific occasions.

An applicant for the grant, renewal or transfer of a licence must send a copy of the application to the Commissioner of Police, and the council will consult with the police before deciding whether to grant the application, having regard to any observations the police may make.

8.3.3 *Grounds for Refusal*
London Local Authorities Act 1990 Section 8

Among the grounds for refusal of an application, many relate to fire safety, which would be a matter for the London Fire Brigade to make recommendations on. The following are grounds for refusal on which police recommendations may focus:

- there is likelihood of nuisance being caused due to the conduct, management or situation of the premises, the nature of the locality or the use of other premises in the vicinity
- the persons concerned or proposed to be concerned in the management are not fit and proper persons
- the applicant has in the past five years been convicted of an offence relating to night cafés.

8.3.4 *Explanation*

Club or public: The requirement for a licence applies to a club as well as to premises open to the public. This serves to prevent any attempt to evade the requirement for a licence, by having some spurious requirement for membership. However, if an establishment is genuinely run as a gym, sports club, etc, it will be exempt.

Other licence: Since the purpose of the legislation is very much the same as that relating to places of entertainment, theatres, etc – i.e. to provide for public safety and to ensure that the people running such places are suitable – a night café licence is not required if some other licence is in force for premises, unless the premises stay open beyond the hours allowed by that other licence.

Works canteens: Where the premises are used exclusively as a canteen for workers on a site, or maintained by one of the specified transport industry bodies, it will be exempt.

8.3.5 *Offences*
London Local Authorities Act 1990 Section 15

A person will commit an offence if he:
- uses premises as a night café without a licence
- permits premises to be used, knowing or having reason to suspect that they are not licensed
- as the licensee or person concerned in the management of premises which are licensed, uses them in breach of terms, conditions and restrictions attached to the licence.

8.3.6 *Police Power of Entry*
London Local Authorities Act 1990 Section 17

Any police officer may at all reasonable times:
- enter, inspect and examine any premises
- which he has reasonable cause to believe are being used as a night café without a licence
- or are being used in breach of conditions or restrictions on a licence
- and while on the premises may do all that is reasonably necessary for determining whether an offence has been committed.

8.3.7 *Offence*
Any person who intentionally obstructs a constable in the exercise of these powers commits an offence.

9 SEX ESTABLISHMENTS
Local Government (Miscellaneous Provisions) Act 1982 Schedule 3

9.1 Local Authority Licence
A local authority may choose to adopt the relevant legislation, to enable it to control sex establishments in its area by means of licensing. A 'sex establishment' is a sex cinema, sex shop (or in London only, a sex encounter establishment).

Nothing in these provisions affects laws relating to obscenity or indecency; the fact that a licence may be in force does not afford a defence to a charge of such a nature.

9.2 Meaning of Terms

9.2.1 *Sex Cinema*
A sex cinema means any premises, vehicle, vessel or stall used to a significant extent for showing moving pictures concerned primarily with the portrayal of sexual activity, sexual organs, or intended to stimulate sexual activity.

There are exemptions in respect of private dwelling houses, licensed cinemas and certain non-commercial film shows.

9.2.2 *Sex Encounter Establishment*
This means premises at which:
- performances are given by persons present and performing, wholly or mainly amounting to the sexual stimulation of customers; or

- services are given which do not constitute sexual activity, by people with no clothes on or who expose their breasts, genitals or excretory organs; or
- entertainment is provided by persons without clothes, or who so expose themselves; or
- not being a sex cinema, pictures are shown by any means, the main purpose being to stimulate or encourage sexual activity.

And in each case, the activities are not unlawful.

There are exemptions in the case of a private dwelling house or any premises which operates under a theatre licence, cinema licence or music and singing, etc, licence (Greater London Council (General Powers) Act 1986, Section 12).

9.2.3 *Sex Shop*
A sex shop is any premises, vehicle, vessel or stall used for a business which involves a significant degree of buying, selling, hiring, showing or demonstrating any 'sex article' or anything else use in or for encouraging sexual activities.

9.2.4 *Sex Article*
A sex article is anything for use in connection with sexual activity or for encouraging or stimulating same, including books or sound or visual recordings.

9.2.5 *Explanation*
Application of law: The law applies in an area only if the local authority chooses that it shall.

Obscenity: The fact that an establishment has a licence does not allow for activity which might otherwise be unlawful. For example, offences relating to indecent photographs of children will remain offences, and no licence under these provisions will alter that.

Sex encounter establishment: The proviso about lawfulness applies equally in these establishments. Activity which amounts to prostitution will not be lawful and will therefore not be permitted under a licence. Services supplied by people with breasts exposed means that a 'topless bar', for example, would be a sex encounter establishment.

9.3 Licences

9.3.1 *Issue*
The local authority may issue, renew and transfer licences for sex establishments. A licence may have conditions or restrictions attached. A copy of an application for the grant, renewal or transfer of a licence shall be sent to the chief officer of police. The local authority shall take account of any observations made by the police in deciding whether to grant an application. The local authority shall send a copy of each licence to the chief officer of police

9.3.2 *Waiver*
A local authority may decide to waive the need for a licence in certain cases. This waiver may be revoked at any time.

9.3.3 *Exempt*
A licence is not required in relation to the sale, supply or demonstration of articles related to birth control.

9.4 Offences

There are a number of offences which may arise:

- a person knowingly uses, or causes or permits the use, of premises as a sex establishment without a licence
- the licensee employs a person who is disqualified
- the licensee, his servant or agent, without reasonable excuse knowingly contravenes or permits someone else to contravene any term, restriction or condition applying to the licence
- a person makes a false statement in relation to an application
- the licensee without reasonable excuse knowingly permits a person under 18 to enter, or employs someone in the establishment whom he knows to be under 18
- the licensee fails to keep a copy of his licence and any standard conditions applying to it, exhibited in the premises.

9.4.1 *Explanation*

Disqualified: A licence may be revoked by the council if a person is convicted of an offence. When a licence is revoked, the holder of the licence is disqualified for a period of 12 months, from holding a licence in that local authority area but not in any other.

9.5 Police Powers

9.5.1 *Entry without Warrant*

Any constable may, at any reasonable time, enter and inspect any licensed sex establishment with a view to determining whether any of the following offences are being committed:

- failing to comply with conditions, terms or restrictions on the licence
- employing a disqualified person, or a person under 18
- allowing a person under 18 on to the premises.

9.5.2 *Entry with Warrant*

If a constable is authorised to do so by a warrant issued by a magistrate, he may enter and inspect a sex establishment (whether licensed or not) if he has reason to suspect that an offence relating to such has been, is being or is about to be committed in relation to it.

9.5.3 *Demand Name and Address*

If a constable has reasonable cause to suspect that a person has committed an offence in relation to a sex establishment, he may require that person to give his name and address. Failure or refusal is an offence.

9.5.4 *Exception*

This provision does not apply to an offence of making a false statement relating to an application, or failing to display the licence on the premises.

9.5.5 *Offence*

A person shall commit an offence if, without reasonable excuse, he refuses to permit a constable to exercise any of these powers.

10 SAFETY AT SPORTS GROUNDS
Safety of Sports Grounds Act 1975

10.1 Certificates
The local authority will issue a safety certificate in respect of any sports ground in its area designated by the Secretary of State. The local authority must send a copy of an application for the grant, renewal or transfer of a safety certificate to the chief officer of police, and must consult the police in relation to terms or conditions to be applied.

10.2 Police Power to Inspect
Safety of Sports Grounds Act 1975 Section 11

A person authorised by the chief officer of police, on production of his written authority if required, may:
- enter a sports ground at any reasonable time
- make such inspection and enquiries as are considered necessary for the purposes of the Act
- examine and take copies of records of attendance, and of records of maintenance and safety.

10.2.1 *Offence*
A person commits an offence who wilfully obstructs someone in the exercise of these powers, or fails without reasonable excuse to answer questions put by such person in the exercise of these powers.

10.3 Police Attendance
Safety of Sports Grounds Act 1975 Section 2(2A)

A condition attached to a safety certificate may be that there must be police officers in attendance when events are held there. If there is such a condition, it must contain wording to the effect that the extent to which police officers are deployed will be a matter for the chief officer of police.

10.4 Prohibition Notice
Safety of Sports Grounds Act 1975 Section 10

The local authority has power to serve a prohibition notice in a situation where it is believed spectators would be at serious risk if admitted to the sports ground, pending repairs or alterations.

10.5 Explanation
Interested parties: Representatives of the police, the local authority, the housing authority, fire service and relevant government department, all have power to enter and inspect the premises. Power to examine maintenance records, for example, is far more likely to be of interest to those from the other bodies, than to the police.

Offences: There are a number of offences which may be committed by those responsible for running a designated sports ground, such as admitting spectators when there is no certificate in force, or which is outside the scope of the certificate.

Prohibition notice: The holder of the safety certificate may take action in a magistrates' court for an order to lift the prohibition notice. If the notice is lifted in this way, the police, among others, may appeal to a Crown Court, to have the prohibition re-imposed. Although the local authority serve the prohibition notice in the first place, it is quite possible that the police would have been involved in advising the authority on the need for the prohibition.

Chapter 42: Betting, Gaming and Lotteries

1 INTRODUCTION

1.1 Purpose of Legislation

The law addresses itself to three forms of gambling, placing controls on each, presumably in an effort to regulate what is seen by some as somewhat immoral, or at least undesirable conduct, and to save from themselves those who would over-indulge. These restrictions do not prevent the Exchequer from being one of the major 'winners', with substantial cuts from the revenues of the National Lottery and football pools, and expensive excise licences required for gaming machines.

1.2 Meaning of Terms

1.2.1 *Betting*

The term is not defined in legislation. According to the dictionary (*Concise Oxford*) it is the staking of money, etc, on the outcome of an unpredictable event. Who or what will win horse or dog races, football and other sports matches, or even general elections, are all 'unpredictable events', despite the major industry generated by those who seek to predict the outcome. A 'bet' as to which horse won the Derby in 1903, or whether the Nile is longer than the Mississippi, will not fit this definition of betting, because these are not unpredictable outcomes.

What is defined by statute is that betting does **not** include any bet or stake made in the course of or incidental to any gaming (Betting, Gaming and Lotteries Act 1963, Section 55). Thus, if card players 'bet' on which of them will be the first to draw the ace of diamonds during a game of cards, this is 'gaming', not 'betting'.

1.2.2 *Gaming*

This is defined in legislation as the playing of a game of chance for winnings in money or money's worth – whether any person playing the game is at risk of losing any money or money's worth or not. If players were to be offered the 'free' opportunity of winning prizes by taking part in a game of chance without having to risk a stake themselves, this would still amount to 'gaming' (Gaming Act 1968, Section 52).

The term 'game of chance' does not include any athletic game or sport, but it will include a game of chance and skill combined or a pretended game of chance and skill combined. It is possible for a person, by skill, to win more often than not at backgammon, cribbage, or poker, but winning still depends on the throw of the die or the shuffle of the cards or dominoes.

1.2.3 *Lottery*

A lottery is the distribution of prizes by lot or chance. A lottery will not be controlled by law unless the participants have paid for their ticket or chance. However, tickets given 'free' with something which is bought, will be considered as being paid for. This is why the 'No envelope' is included in the junk mail when books or magazines are offered for sale; there is an opportunity to take part in the 'prize draw' without having to buy anything, so removing the scheme from the controls on lotteries.

A lottery is unlawful unless it fits into one or other of the different types laid down in the Lotteries and Amusements Act 1976. However, if a lottery amounts to gaming, it is controlled as 'gaming', not as a lottery. The Gaming Act 1968 (Section 52(3)) declares that if a winner is determined by more than three determining factors, this is gaming, not a lottery. Consider bingo, which involves drawing numbers as in a lottery, to decide who wins prizes. Bingo is gaming, because a house, line, or whatever, involves having more than three numbers chosen. (On this basis the National Lottery, although it is a lottery, is also actually gaming, because some of the winners are decided by drawing more than three numbers. However, the National Lottery Act specifically states that the National Lottery is **not** gaming.)

2 BETTING

2.1 Control of Betting

2.1.1 *Extent of Controls*
The law seeks to control betting in four areas:
- who may carry on a business involving taking bets
- betting on premises
- betting in the street or a public place
- involvement of young people in betting.

2.1.2 *Betting Licensing Committee*
Just as there is a committee of local magistrates appointed to deal with liquor licensing, so there is a corresponding committee for betting matters. The committee issues permits for bookmakers and agents, and licences for betting offices.

2.2 Bookmakers
Betting, Gaming and Lotteries Act 1963 Section 55

2.2.1 *Meaning of Term*
A bookmaker is a person who whether on his own account or as the servant or agent of someone else, carries on a business of receiving or negotiating bets, whether regularly or occasionally, or by way of business is held out to be a person who receives or negotiates bets.

Note: a bookmaker may also be involved in 'pool betting' (e.g. football pools) which is not dealt with in this book.

A person shall not act as a bookmaker on his own account unless he is the holder of a bookmaker's permit, issued by the betting licensing justices (Section 2).

2.2.2 *Offence*
It is an offence to act as a bookmaker without being the holder of a bookmaker's permit.

2.2.3 *Application for Permit*
Betting, Gaming and Lotteries Act 1963 Schedule 1

When application is made for the grant or renewal of a bookmaker's permit, a copy of the application has to be sent to the chief officer of police for the area. The application may be refused on a number of grounds, including that the applicant is not a fit and proper person, or that the applicant is acting as a 'front' for someone else who will run the business, to whom a permit would not be granted. A permit may be granted to a limited company, as well as to an individual.

2.2.4 *Production to Police*
Betting, Gaming and Lotteries Act 1963 Section 2(3)

If the holder of a bookmaker's permit fails to produce it for examination when required to do so by a constable, he shall be guilty of an offence.

2.2.5 *Bookmaker's Agents*
Betting, Gaming and Lotteries Act 1963 Section 3

A bookmaker may appoint agents to transact bets on his behalf, subject to the following conditions:
  – the agent must be 21 or over;
  – he is authorised in writing by the bookmaker;
  – the bookmaker has a current bookmaker's permit;
  – the bookmaker keeps a register, showing the details of every person authorised to act as his agent.

An agent may be appointed by the bookmaker without reference to magistrates. However, if the bookmaker wants an agent to hold a betting office licence on the bookmaker's behalf, a betting agency permit must be obtained.

2.2.6 *Betting Agency Permit*
Betting, Gaming and Lotteries Act 1963 Section 9

A person who acts as an agent for a bookmaker and who seeks to obtain a betting office licence must first of all obtain a betting agency permit from the betting licensing justices. The holder of a betting agency permit may, in turn, appoint agents, subject to the same conditions as apply to the holder of a bookmaker's permit.

2.2.7 *Explanation*
Own behalf: A person needs a bookmaker's permit only if he acts as a bookmaker on his own behalf. If a person deals with betting as an agent for a bookmaker, he need not have any formal authority from the justices, unless he wants to apply for a betting office licence, in which case he first needs to obtain a betting agency permit.

2.2.8 *Police Powers*
A constable may require an authorised agent to produce his written authority, or the holder of a betting agency permit to produce that permit, for inspection. Likewise, the constable may require to inspect the register containing the details of agents. Refusal to produce or permit inspection, or failure to do so without reasonable excuse, is an offence.

2.3 **Premises**
Betting, Gaming and Lotteries Act 1963 Section 1

2.3.1 *Unlawful Betting*
With exceptions, it is generally unlawful to use premises for the purposes of betting. Offences may be committed by any person who:

   i) uses premises for the purpose of effecting betting transactions with a person or persons resorting there

   ii) causes premises to be so used by another

   iii) knowingly permits premises to be so used by another

   iv) for any purpose connected with the effecting a betting transaction, resorts to premises which are being used unlawfully for carrying out betting transactions.

2.3.2 *Evidence*

In respect of the offence of resorting to premises ((iv) above), proof that a person was on the premises while they were being used for unlawful betting shall be evidence that he resorted there for such a purpose unless he proves that he was there for bona fide purposes not connected with betting.

2.3.3 *Exceptions*

The following will be among exceptions:

   – in a licensed betting office

   – at an approved horse racing or dog racing track, subject to conditions

   – premises used to receive coupons etc, in connection with pool betting run by a registered pools promoter

   – all the persons involved, including the person taking bets, either live or work on those premises (or on premises of which those premises form part)

   – all the persons involved are holders of bookmakers' permits or are acting on behalf of such.

2.3.4 *Explanation*

Premises: This will include any place, not just a building, and will include a vessel.

Resorting: This means actually going to the premises. To telephone a place is not to resort there, so placing bets by telephone to a bookmaker's office is not resorting there and the bookmaker will not be using the premises unlawfully because he is not effecting a betting transaction with a person resorting there.

Evidence: If a person is on premises while those premises are being used for unlawful betting, the onus will be on the person to prove he was there for some valid reason, not connected with betting. For example, if police raid a pub where bets are being collected and paid out unlawfully, every person in the pub will be liable for the offence of resorting there for the purposes of betting; it will be for an individual to show that he was there merely to have a quiet pint, and that he had not gone there to place a bet or receive winnings, etc.

Lives or works: Betting is not unlawful where everyone concerned, the person collecting the bets and the punters, all live or work on those premises. This is where the need for a bookmaker's agent arises, because an authorised bookmaker may appoint as his agent, a person who works in a factory to collect bets from other workers in that factory. If this agent does his business in the works canteen, this will be in order since the canteen forms part of the larger premises, where he and all the people placing bets, work. Similar provisions would apply to halls of residence at a college, or to a barracks, etc.

All bookmakers: If all concerned are holders of permits, or their representatives, no offence will be committed. This allows for a gathering of bookmakers where, for example, one with a small business may place bets with a bigger operator, to cover bets he has himself taken from customers.

2.4 Licensed Betting Offices
Betting, Gaming and Lotteries Act 1963 Section 10

2.4.1 *Management of Licensed Betting Offices*
A licensed betting office should be run in accordance with rules which are intended to ensure the orderly behaviour of clients. In recent years these rules have been relaxed considerably, allowing facilities such as refreshments and televisions, which were strictly forbidden until relatively recently.

2.4.2 *Offence*
A licensed betting office shall be run in accordance with the rules. If any rule is contravened the licensee **and** any servant or agent of the licensee responsible for breaking the rule, will be guilty of an offence.

2.4.3 *Defence*
If the licensee is charged and the offence was the fault of his agent or servant, he will have a defence if he proves that the contravention of the rule took place without his consent or connivance **and** that he exercised all due to diligence to prevent it.

2.4.4 *Maintaining Order*
The licensee, his servant or agent may refuse to admit or may expel from the premises any person who is drunken, violent, quarrelsome or disorderly, or whose presence on the premises would subject the licensee to a penalty.

If any person liable to be expelled under this provision fails to leave when requested to do so by the licensee, his servant or agent, or by a constable he shall be guilty of an offence.

2.4.5 *Police Powers*
Any constable may enter a licensed betting office for the purpose of ascertaining whether it is being run in accordance with the rules.

2.4.6 *Offence*
Any person who obstructs a constable in the exercise of these powers will commit an offence.

A constable may on the request of the licensee, his servant or agent help to expel from the licensed premises any person who is liable to be expelled under this Section and may use such force as is required to do so.

2.4.7 *Explanation*
Liability for breach of rules: If any of the rules governing the management of a licensed betting office are broken, the licensee will be liable. If the breach of the rule was due to the fault of an employee or agent of the licensee, that person will also be liable. If the licensee is charged solely because he is the licensee, i.e. it was the fault of his employee or agent, then he will have a defence, but he has to prove not only that he did not know about the rule being broken, but that he did not consent to it being broken and had taken every care to ensure that rules were kept.

Presence... liable to a penalty: An example of a person whose presence would make the licensee liable to a penalty is a person under the age of 18 years; a person apparently under that age shall not be allowed to remain on the premises.

Power to eject: The power given to the licensee and employees to eject a person from the premises is in addition to and does not affect any other right to refuse admission or expel a person from premises.

Police powers: The power of entry is not limited to certain hours, as is the case for premises licensed in respect of intoxicating liquor.

A constable called upon to assist in expelling someone from a licensed betting office **may** assist, whereas there is no choice in relation to liquor licensing, where a constable **shall** assist if called on to do so.

2.4.8 *The Rules*
Some of the rules are quite detailed and specific. Some of the rules, more relevant for ensuring the orderly conduct of the premises are:

1: A licensed betting office shall be closed on Christmas Day and Good Friday. Certain other days may also be prescribed for the premises to be closed. On any day, the premises shall not be open earlier than 7.00 am. During the months of April to August, they must close no later than 10.00 pm; at other times of the year they must not be open later that 6.30 pm.

2: No person apparently under the age of 18 years, or who is known to somebody connected with the business who is there, to be under that age, shall be admitted to or allowed to remain on the premises. (It will be a defence to show that a person apparently under 18 was in fact 18 or over.)

   A notice or notices, to the effect that persons under 18 will not be admitted, must be displayed conspicuously, near the entrance and preferably in a window so it may be read from outside.

3: There must be no direct access (except for staff) between the premises and any other premises open to the public, such as a shop.

4: There are restrictions on the use of broadcasting equipment on the premises, and these even detail the maximum size of television screen allowed.

   Basically, information relating to sporting events and betting may be broadcast. There is a private sound system which is available in betting offices, giving details of races. If a visual system is used, i.e. television, only a public broadcast is allowed, or one which may be received in any licensed betting office. In other words, there is no scope for showing satellite television broadcasts at selected sites only.

5: Except for broadcasts as permitted in accordance with (4) above, no music, dancing or entertainment shall be provided on the premises. However, advertisements which are included as incidental to a broadcast of a sporting event will be permitted.

6: Drinks and refreshments may be provided, subject to the following restrictions:
   - intoxicating liquor is not permitted
   - only pre-packaged food is allowed, such as sandwiches, biscuits, snacks, etc.

2.5 Betting in Public

2.5.1 *Offence*
Betting, Gaming and Lotteries Act 1963 Section 8

It is an offence for any person:

    – to frequent or loiter in a street or public place

    – for the purposes of bookmaking, betting, agreeing to bet, receiving, settling or paying out bets.

2.5.2 *Exception*

An exception exists in relation to any ground used for the purposes of a racecourse for horse racing, or adjacent land, on a day when horse racing is taking place on the racecourse.

2.5.3 *Police Power*

When a person is found committing the offence, a constable may seize and detain any books, cards, papers or other articles relating to betting found in his possession. These items may then be liable to forfeiture by a court.

2.5.4 *Explanation*

Street: Includes any road, alley, passageway, etc, whether a thoroughfare or not, and any doorway, entrance or land abutting and open to a street.

Frequent: Means continuous or repeated presence in a place (*Nakhla v R* (1975)).

2.6 **Young Persons**

2.6.1 *Offences*
Betting, Gaming and Lotteries Act 1963 Section 22

A person will commit an offence who:
    1: has any betting transaction with a young person
    2: receives or negotiates a bet through a young person
    3: employs a young person in a licensed betting office
    4: employs a young person in effecting any betting transaction
    5: for the purposes of earning commission, reward or profit
        – he sends or causes to be sent
        – to a person whom he knows to be under the age of 18 years
        – any advertisement, letter, circular or other document
        – which invites or may be reasonably implied to invite the person receiving it
        – to make a bet or become involved in a betting transaction
        – or to apply for information or advice about betting or information about a sporting event or other event on which betting is generally carried on.

2.6.2 *Exceptions*

Employing a young person to effect a betting transaction by post, or in carrying any communication relating to a betting transaction, to be sent by post.

2.6.3 *Explanation*

Young person: For the purposes of this legislation, a 'young person' is a person:
    – under the age of 18 years, whom the offender knows or ought to know, to be under that age; or
    – a person apparently under that age.
    However, in the case of a prosecution arising from dealings with a person apparently under 18, it shall be a defence to prove that he had actually attained that age.

Employing, etc: Virtually the only way a person under 18 may be lawfully engaged in transacting bets, is when the betting is carried out by post. As well as it being unlawful to employ a young person in connection with betting, it is also an offence to enter into a betting transaction with a person under 18.

Note: There is no liability attached to the young person in, say making a bet while under 18, as there is with the corresponding provisions of liquor licensing law, when it is an offence for a person under 18 to buy or attempt to buy intoxicants in licensed premises.

Advertising: There are two provisions which assist in the prosecution of a person for this offence:

1: If any such document refers to a person as someone to whom payment may be made or from whom information may be obtained, relating to betting that person shall be deemed to have sent the document or to have caused it to be sent:
   - unless he proves
   - that had not consented to being named in the document
   - and he was not a party to its being sent
   - and he was wholly ignorant of its being sent.

2: If such a document is sent to a person under 18 at a university, college or place of education the person sending it shall be deemed to have known that the recipient was under 18, unless he proves that he had reasonable grounds for believing that person to be 18.

It is not enough for the person named in a leaflet to deny having sent the leaflet out; the burden of proof will be on him to show that it was sent out without his knowledge or involvement.

Similarly, if the leaflet is sent to a young person at a school or college, the onus of proving that he had good reason to believe the recipient to be over 18 will rest with the defendant.

2.7 Search Warrant
Betting, Gaming and Lotteries Act 1963 Section 51

2.7.1 *Grounds for Issue*
A magistrate may issue a warrant if satisfied upon information on oath that there is reasonable ground for believing that an offence under the Act is being, has been, or is about to be committed on any premises.

2.7.2 *Powers Under the Warrant*
The warrant will empower a constable:
   - to enter the premises, using force if need be, and search them
   - seize and remove any document, money, valuable thing, instrument or anything else whatsoever found on the premises which a constable has reason to believe may be required as evidence of a betting offence
   - search any person found on the premises whom the constable has reasonable cause to believe to be committing or to have committed such an offence.

3 GAMING
Gaming Act 1968

3.1 Scope of Act
The law seeks to control gaming by means of restrictions on amounts of stake money involved, size of prizes, methods and rules of games, where gaming may take place and who may take

part. The Act is divided into four parts:

Part I: deals with gaming at premises which are **not** licensed or registered under the Act
Part II: caters for premises which **are** licensed or registered for gaming
Part III: gaming by means of machines
Part IV: miscellaneous provisions, including gaming at non-profit entertainments.

3.2 **Part I**

3.2.1 *Premises*
This part of the Act does not deal with gaming in licensed or registered premises. Since gaming in public places is severely limited, what does this leave? The answer is – gaming in a works canteen, in a hostel, in a social club, or any other premises not licensed or registered for gaming.

3.2.2 *Restrictions*
Gaming Act 1968 Section 2

Gaming carried out under Part I is restricted, in that **none** of the following must apply to it:
- the game involves playing or staking against a bank, whether or not the bank is held by one of the players
- the nature of the game is such that the chances are not equally favourable to all players
- the nature of the game is such that the chances in it lie between a player or players and some other person and the chances are not as favourable to the players as to that other person.

3.2.3 *Exception*
None of these restrictions shall apply to gaming which takes place on a 'domestic occasion' in a private dwelling house, or in a hostel, hall of residence, etc, which is not carried on by way of trade or business and where the persons taking part are exclusively or mainly residents or inmates at those premises.

3.2.4 *Explanation*
Banker games: Under Part I, a banker game will not be lawful, even when the bank may pass from one player to another with all of them having an equal chance to be the banker. It is not the intention here to explain how certain games are played; suffice it to say that in a game such as pontoon, players stake against the bank, and in the event of a player's and the banker's cards having the same value, the banker wins. Thus the banker has an advantage.

The third restriction, relating to one person having more favourable chances than other players, caters for any variation on the 'banker' theme.

Unequal chances: In a game of bingo, the fact that one player has several cards does not contravene the 'equal chances' rule (*Rogers v Cowley* (1962)). This seems a logical conclusion, since each card may be considered as a separate 'player'. Similar logic would apply to any gambling, where a person may place several stakes, e.g. at roulette or even in a lottery, where the person who buys a fistful of tickets expects to have a greater chance of winning than the person who buys only one.

Exception: There are a number of points to note relating to the exception:
- It does not extend to premises carried out for trade or business, such as a hotel. Thus

all the three restrictions will apply if a number of hotel residents gather in a bedroom for a spot of gambling.
- For the exception to apply, it is not necessary that **all** the gamblers are resident on the premises, so long as they are **mainly** residents. Contrast this with the corresponding provision relating to betting, where betting on premises is lawful if every person involved is resident on the premises.

3.2.5 *Charges and Levies*
Gaming Act 1968 Sections 3, 4

There are further restrictions on Part I gaming in that:
- there must be no payment required to take part, other than the money or money's worth which is staked on the game
- and there must be no levy charged on any of the stakes or on any of the winnings.

For the purposes of determining whether a levy has been paid, it is immaterial whether the levy is compulsory, customary or voluntary.

3.2.6 *Explanation*

There is a ban on any organiser of the gaming making money by charging an entry fee or having a cut of the stakes or winnings. A fee charged for admission to premises will be considered to be a charge to take part in gaming. When tokens (or chips) are sold to players and then redeemed at a lower rate than that at which they were issued, this will amount to a 'levy'.

Exception: Any payment which is a subscription for membership (a 'joining fee') or is a quarterly or half-yearly instalment of an annual subscription shall not be regarded as a charge to take part in gaming, provided the club is not of a temporary nature and the membership concerned is not a temporary membership. The Act specifically mentions 'quarterly or half yearly' instalments, so any instalment on, say a monthly or weekly basis, would be regarded as a charge for taking part in gaming.

There are further exceptions relating to small charges at clubs, and to events involving gaming at events which are held other than for private gain, i.e. fund-raising events and the like (Sections 40, 41).

3.2.7 *Gaming in Public*
Gaming Act 1968 Section 5

It is an offence for any person to take part in gaming (to which Part I applies) in any street or in any other place to which the public have access, on payment or otherwise.

For these purposes, 'street' has the same meaning as for betting in the street (paragraph 2.5.4), viz. it includes alleys, passageways, doorways abutting the street, etc.

There is an exception in the case of certain games played in liquor licensed premises.

3.2.8 *Gaming in Pubs, etc*
Gaming Act 1968 Section 6

The ban on gaming in a public place does not apply to gaming in premises for which a justices' on-licence is in force (other than a Part IV licence, i.e. a restaurant, residential or combined

licence), so long as gaming is limited to:
- dominoes and cribbage; plus
- any other game which the licensing justices may have authorised for particular premises, upon application made by the licensee.

3.2.9 *Restriction*
Licensing justices may make an order in respect of any premises in the district imposing restrictions on the playing of dominoes, cribbage or any other game which they may have authorised which they consider necessary in order to secure that gaming does not take place:
- for high stakes; or
- so as to amount to an inducement to people to go there primarily for the purpose of taking part in gaming.

3.2.10 *Offence*
A person under 18 shall commit an offence if he takes part in such gaming. The licensee or his employee will commit an offence if he knowingly allows a person under 18 to take part in such gaming.

3.2.11 *Explanation*
Dominoes and cribbage: These traditional pub games may be played on on-licensed premises without any authority being required from anyone.

This does not extend to premises operating under a restaurant, residential or combined licence. However, an area restricted to residents has been held not be to be a public place in any case (*Bytheway v Oakes* (1965)), so the net effect of this is to stop dominoes and crib being played for money in a licensed restaurant.

Other games: The licensee may make an application for an order allowing other games to be played on the premises.

Restrictions: The licensing justices may impose conditions and restrictions, whether on dominoes and cribbage alone, or when other games are authorised. These may be imposed to stop gaming for high stakes, or to stop the gaming being the main attraction.

3.2.12 **Offences**
Gaming Act 1968 Section 8

When any gaming takes place in contravention of restrictions (banker games, etc) or where there is a charge to take part or a levy applied offences will be committed by the following:
- any person concerned in the organisation or management of the gaming
- any person who allows any premises, vessel or vehicle to be used for unlawful gaming, knowing or having reason to suspect that the premises, etc, was to be used for that purpose
- any person who lets, hires or otherwise makes available any premises, vehicle or vessel to any of the organisers, knowing or suspecting that unlawful gaming was to be carried on there.

Vessel includes any raft or other apparatus floating on water. **Vehicle** includes a railway carriage, an aircraft on the ground, or a hovercraft on or off the ground.

3.2.13 *Gaming at Entertainments*
Gaming Act 1968 Section 41

There is provision for gaming to take place at fêtes, dances, etc, subject to the following conditions:
- all the proceeds, less reasonable expenses, must go to purposes other than private gain
- restrictions on banker games, unfair chances, etc, shall apply
- stakes and prizes are small and subject to laid down limits
  (which may be varied by regulations).

The 'wheel of fortune', 'roll a penny', etc, at the school fair or village carnival will be catered for by these provisions. There are similar provisions relating to gaming machines at such entertainments *(see paragraph 3.8.8)* and 'amusements with prizes' which may involve lotteries and/or gaming *(see paragraph 4.8)*.

3.3 **Control of Premises Licensed Under Part II**

3.3.1 *Issue of Licences*
Licences are issued by the betting licensing committee, the panel of magistrates who deal with bookmakers' permits and betting office licences. The committee sits on a number of occasions throughout the year and may issue new licences, renew, cancel or transfer existing ones. A licence is issued to a person in respect of particular premises and may be transferred from one person to another.

3.3.2 *The Gaming Board*
Gaming Act 1968 Section 10 and Schedule 1

The Gaming Board for Great Britain is body set up to keep under review the extent and character of gaming in Great Britain and the provision of gaming facilities. Members of the Board are appointed by the Home Secretary. The Board employs inspectors who have powers to enter and inspect licensed premises.

3.3.3 *Certificate of Consent*
Gaming Act 1968 Schedule 2, paragraph 3

Before an application is made to the justices for the grant or transfer of a licence, the applicant must have a 'certificate of consent' to make that application, from the Gaming Board. In considering an application for a certificate, the Board may have regard to whether the applicant is likely to run gaming on the premises properly, and without disorder or disturbance, taking account of the applicant's character, reputation and financial standing.

A certificate of consent is not required to apply for renewal of a licence, but notice of the application for renewal must be sent to the Gaming Board, who may raise an objection with the justices.

3.3.4 *Certificate of Approval*
Gaming Act 1968 Section 19

Before a person may have a contract to work in a specified capacity in premises licensed for gaming, she must have a 'certificate of approval' issued by the Gaming Board. This applies to persons employed:
- to take part in gaming as a player, by holding the bank *(see paragraph 3.4.4 below)*

- to operate or handle any apparatus, cards, tokens or other articles used in the gaming
- to issue, receive or record cash, tokens or cheques which are winnings or losses
- to watch the gaming or the performance of any person carrying out duties.

3.4 Licences Restricted to Clubs
Gaming Act 1968 Section 12

3.4.1 *Who May Obtain a Licence*
A licence is granted to an applicant (who may be an individual or a company) in respect of particular premises, but the licence must contain the name of a 'club', and persons wishing to take part in gaming at the premises have to join the club. This applies whether the premises provide full casino facilities, or are restricted to bingo.

3.4.2 *Who May Take Part*
A person will be eligible to take part in gaming as a member of the club if at least 48 hours have elapsed since he applied for membership. In addition, a person may take part in gaming if he is a bona fide guest of a member who is himself eligible to take part in the gaming.

A person shall not cease to be regarded as a bona fide guest solely by reason of being required to pay a charge to take part in the gaming, where such a charge is lawful in licensed premises.

3.4.3 *Who May Not Take Part*
A person may not take part in gaming:
- who is not present himself on the premises at the time; or
- who is playing on behalf of someone else who is not present; or
- who is the holder of the licence, or a person acting on his behalf or who is employed on the premises.

3.4.4 *Exception*
The ban on the licensee or an employee taking part does not apply where the game involves a bank and that person is holding the bank or has a share in it. This explains why an employee needs a certificate of approval to take part in gaming as a player, even though an employee is not allowed to take part as a player – *see paragraph 3.3.4 above*. In practice, under regulations covering gaming on licensed premises, the bank may be held by or on behalf of the licensee and no one else *(see paragraph 3.6.1)*.

3.4.5 *Persons Under 18*
Gaming Act 1968 Section 17

A person under the age of 18 may not be in any room in registered or licensed premises while gaming takes place in that room.

3.4.6 *Special Provisions for Bingo Clubs*
Gaming Act 1968 Section 20

When a club is restricted by the licence to playing bingo only, the following modifications shall apply:
Person must be present: Allowance is made for 'simultaneous bingo', where persons

in different bingo clubs throughout the country may be linked together to play a game where the prizes are much higher than would be possible or allowed in any one of them. So long as the players are present in one or other of the clubs taking part, they will be deemed to be 'present'.

Eligible member: In a bingo club the time between applying for membership and being eligible to play is reduced from 48 to 24 hours.

Persons under 18: A person under 18 may be present in a room where bingo is being played, so long as that person does not play.

3.5 Control of Premises Registered for Gaming

3.5.1 *Qualification for Registration*
Gaming Act 1968 Schedule 3, paragraph 7

A club or miner's welfare institute may be registered for gaming under Part II of the Act. Premises licensed for gaming have to have a 'club' which patrons have to join before being able to take part in gaming there. However, a club which is registered under the Act is different, and not unlike a club which is registered for the supply of liquor. To qualify for registration the club must meet the following conditions:
  - it is a bona fide members club
  - it has at least 25 members
  - it is not of a temporary character
  - the principal purpose for which it is established is **not** gaming, **unless** that gaming consists of bridge, whist or both bridge and whist.

3.5.2 *Explanation*
Club: Whereas, the 'club' element on premises licensed for gaming is to provide a means of recording membership and to prevent persons being able to walk straight in off the street and start gambling, for registered premises the club is established for some purpose more important than the gaming which takes place there.

Bridge and whist: A club may qualify for registration if it is primarily for members to play bridge or whist. Otherwise, the club must be set up for reasons not related to gambling.

3.5.3 *Role of Justices*
The body responsible for registration is the betting licensing committee, the same as for licensed premises. This is in contrast to the situation with liquor licensing, where the licensing justices deal with licensed premises, but the general body of magistrates deals with registered clubs.

In most respects, apart from the absence of Gaming Board certificates, applications for registration are treated in the same way as applications for licences.

3.5.4 *Role of Gaming Board*
There are no certificates of consent or approval required in respect of a registered club or institute. However, copies of applications for registration or for the renewal of a registration certificate have to be sent to the Gaming Board, which may make an objection to the application being granted. Gaming Board inspectors have no power to enter registered premises to inspect them *(see paragraph 3.9)*.

3.5.5 *Who May Take Part in Gaming*

On registered premises, virtually the same as for licensed premises, a member shall be eligible to take part in gaming once 48 hours have elapsed since he applied for or was nominated for membership. A bona fide guest of an eligible member may also take part in gaming. However, in contrast to the situation in licensed premises, a person will not be regarded as a bona fide guest if he himself makes any payment to take part, other than by way of his stake.

3.5.6 *Who May Not Take Part*

As in the case of licensed premises, a person may not take part in gaming on registered premises unless he is actually present. A person who is actually present may not take part in gaming on behalf of a person who is not present.

3.6 Games Which May be Played in Licensed or Registered Premises

3.6.1 *Equal Chances, etc*
Gaming Act 1968 Section 13

The basic rule is that any gaming in licensed or registered premises must conform to the restrictions about equal chances, no banker games, etc, which apply to Part I gaming *(see paragraph 3.2.2)*.

However, regulations made under the Act then allow a relaxation of these restrictions in respect of certain games. These regulations, which may set out detailed rules and set the odds for various outcomes, are not covered here.

In addition, gaming which does not conform to these restrictions and which is limited to small prizes may take place on licensed premises (Section 21).

3.6.2 *Charges and Levies*
Gaming Act 1968 Sections 14, 15

Whereas no charges for taking part, or levies on stakes or winnings are permitted under Part I, such charges may be made in registered or licensed premises, again controlled by detailed regulations.

3.7 Offences Under Part II
Gaming Act 1968 Section 23

3.7.1 *Persons Liable*
In the event of a breach of any of the provisions of Part II, or of regulations relating to gaming on registered or licensed premises, the following person(s) shall be liable for an offence:
- the holder of the licence, for licensed premises
- every officer of the club or institute, in respect of registered premises
- every person concerned in the organisation or management of the gaming, for registered or licensed premises.

3.7.2 *Defence*
A person liable for an offence will have a defence if he proves:
- that the contravention occurred without his knowledge; and
- that he exercised all reasonable care to ensure that the contravention would not occur.

3.7.3 *False Statements*

It is an offence for a person, intentionally or recklessly, to make a false statement with a view to obtaining a certificate of approval from the Gaming Board, for himself or another.

3.8 Gaming with Machines (Part III)

3.8.1 *Gaming Machine*
Gaming Act 1968 Section 26

Part III applies to any machine:
  - constructed or adapted for playing a game of chance by that machine
  - and which has a slot or similar for insertion of cash or tokens.

Thus, a roulette wheel is a machine for playing a game of chance, but is not covered by Part III because one does not put money into it.

3.8.2 *Exception*

An 'amusement only' machine, which is one where the prize is either a free go, or cash or tokens which amounts to your stake money or less, is not covered by Part III.

3.8.3 *'Jackpot' Machines*
Gaming Act 1968 Section 31

On premises which are licensed or registered for gaming, not more than two gaming machines may be available. The following restrictions apply:
  - the charge for playing is by coin(s) inserted in the machine, and this charge must not exceed the maximum set out in regulations
  - the only prizes allowed are by way of coins delivered from the machine itself, and there is a maximum amount which may be paid as one prize
  - there must a notice on the machine or in the premises, giving details of the minimum percentage of stake money which the machine is designed to pay out, and the values of the prizes which may be won.

3.8.4 *Explanation*

Stake and prize: The maximum amount which may be charged for one play of the machine, and the maximum amount of the top prize (commonly called the 'jackpot') are laid down in regulations and change on a regular basis.

Coins only: Only coins, not tokens, may be used in these machines. Any prize must be paid out from the machine; it is not lawful for any other prize to be awarded.

3.8.5 *Machines with Smaller Prizes*
Gaming Act 1968 Sections 32, 34

A request may be made in respect of licensed premises, for authority to have a larger number of machines paying out smaller maximum prizes, instead of the maximum two 'jackpot' machines.

Such a request may be made, for example, in relation to a bingo club, where a large number of members are likely to be present at the same time; a larger number of machines would afford more 'amusement' to the members (and more profits to the licensee). These arrangements apply only to licensed premises, not to registered ones.

3.8.6 *Machines on Other Premises*

In addition, such machines giving small prizes may also be used:
- on premises covered by a permit issued by the local authority
- at a pleasure fair, where the main attraction is amusements provided other than by these gaming machines.

Machines seen in cafés, for example, will be covered by a local authority permit. A local authority permit may not be issued for premises which are registered or licensed for gaming.

3.8.7 *Prizes*

Prizes which may be won on these machines include:
- small money prizes, the maximum being laid down in regulations
- tokens to exchange for a non-monetary prize of a value somewhat larger (but not large) than the maximum money prize
- tokens for further plays of the machine.

3.8.8 *Fêtes, Entertainments, etc*
Gaming Act 1968 Section 33

Gaming machines may be used on premises which are not licensed or registered, subject to the following conditions:
- the machines are part of an entertainment, such as a dinner dance, fête, etc
- the whole of the proceeds of the entertainment, not just the proceeds from any gaming machines, after deducting any expenses, go to purposes other than private gain, i.e. the event is raising funds for some cause or other
- the opportunity to win prizes, whether by gaming or by lotteries, shall not be the main attraction at the event.

(For gaming at such events, other than with machines, *see paragraph 3.2.13*)

3.8.9 *Supply and Operation of Machines*
Gaming Act 1968 Sections 27, 28, 36

The following aspects of dealing in and operating gaming machines are controlled in an effort to keep the gaming machine business free of criminal elements:
- any person who sells or supplies machines must be in possession of a certificate from the Gaming Board (subject to exceptions, such as selling to another trader, dealing in amusement-only machines etc)
- any person running a business in maintaining gaming machines must have a certificate from the Gaming Board
- any arrangement for the supply or maintenance of a machine must not involve consideration of the extent to which or the manner in which the machine is used – in plain words, there must be no 'profit-share' for the person supplying or maintaining the machine
- money may be removed from a machine:
  i) on licensed premises by the licensee or his employee
  ii) on registered premises by a member or officer of the club or by a club employee. Any arrangement whereby, e.g. the maintenance engineer, emptied the machine, would not be lawful.

3.8.10 *Offences Under Part III*
Gaming Act 1968 Section 38

Persons liable: In the event of a breach of any of the provisions of Part III, or of regulations relating to gaming machines, the following person(s) may be liable for an offence:
- the holder of the licence, for licensed premises
- every officer of the club or institute, in respect of registered premises
- every person concerned in the organisation or management of an entertainment where there is unlawful use of machines
- any person who allows a machine to be used unlawfully on premises
- selling or supplying or maintaining a machine in breach of restrictions, e.g. without holding a Gaming Board certificate.

3.8.11 *Defence*
A person liable for an offence will have a defence if he proves:
- that the contravention occurred without his knowledge; and
- he exercised all reasonable care to ensure that the contravention would not occur.

3.9 **Powers to Enter and Inspect Premises**
Gaming Act 1968 Section 43

3.9.1 *Police Powers*
A constable may at any reasonable time enter licensed premises and while there may:
- inspect the premises and any machine, equipment, book or document which she reasonably requires to inspect for the purpose of discovering whether any offence has been committed under the Act or regulations
- take copies of any such book or document, or any entry in it
- if information which she reasonably requires is contained in a computer and the computer is accessible from the premises, require the information to be produced in a visible and legible form in which it can be taken away.

These powers may also be exercised by a Gaming Board inspector, who has extra powers as well.

3.9.2 *Offence*
The holder of the licence will commit an offence if he or a person acting on his behalf:
- fails without reasonable excuse to admit a constable who demands admission to exercise her powers
- fails without reasonable excuse to permit the constable, on demand, to inspect the premises or equipment
- upon being required to do so by the constable, fails without reasonable excuse to produce any book or document under his control which the constable reasonably requires to inspect, or to permit the officer to take copies
- fails without reasonable excuse to obtain a computer print-out if required.

3.9.3 *Explanation*
Licensed premises: There are no powers to enter registered premises without a warrant, but there is a power to require information *(see paragraph 3.9.4)*.

Purpose of inspection: Police powers are limited to looking for breaches of the Act and regulations, so there would be power to inspect a roulette wheel, for example, but not a coffee machine.

Document: The licence holder has to produce any book or document under his control. He could not be required to produce records which were kept elsewhere, e.g. at head office.

Computer records: The power to require details from a computer record applies only to information accessible from those premises. If the computer terminal there was used merely as a means of sending information elsewhere, the licence holder may not be required to produce information. In simple language, the constable may require a print-out, so there has to be a printer there before she may have the information.

Offence: Only the licensee will be responsible for the offence, whether the person 'obstructing' the inspection is the licensee himself or someone acting on his behalf. If any other person sought to keep the constable from going into the premises, for example one of the members, an offence of obstructing a constable in the execution of her duty could be considered.

3.9.4 *Written Notice*
The chief officer of police may serve a written notice on the licensee of licensed premises or on the chairperson or secretary of a registered club or institute, requiring him:
- within a reasonable time
- to produce books or documents for inspection
- or to provide information about the premises
- as may reasonably be required for the purpose of deciding whether any breach of the Act or regulations is being or has been committed.

3.9.5 *Search Warrant*

Grounds for Issue:
A magistrate may issue a warrant upon being satisfied on information on oath:
- that there are reasonable grounds to suspect that an offence under the Act is being, has been or is about to be committed on any premises.

Powers Under the Warrant:
A constable acting under the warrant may:
- enter the premises using force if necessary and search them
- seize and remove any document, money, valuable thing or instrument found there, which he reasonably believes is required as evidence of an offence under the Act
- require a computer print-out of any information on a computer accessible from the premises which he reasonably believes is required as evidence
- search any person found on the premises whom he reasonably believes is committing or has committed an offence under the Act there.

3.9.6 *Offence*
If the premises searched under a warrant are licensed under the Act, then the licensee will commit an offence if he or someone acting on his behalf fails without reasonable excuse to produce a computer print-out when required to do so under the warrant.

4 LOTTERIES

4.1 Lawful Lotteries

The law provides that all lotteries are unlawful, except those which comply with certain specified requirements. The principal legislation is the Lotteries and Amusements Act 1976, and all references relating to lotteries are to this Act unless otherwise stated.

The Act specifies four types of lottery which may be lawful:
- small lottery
- private lottery
- society lottery
- local lottery.

The National Lottery is not dealt with here (apart from mention of an offence, *see paragraph 4.2.5*), nor is another type of lottery, an 'art union' lottery, which involves a group of people clubbing together to buy a work of art then drawing lots to see which of them gets it.

4.2 Unlawful Lotteries
Lotteries and Amusements Act 1976 Sections 1, 2

4.2.1 *Examples of 'Lottery'*

Any lottery which does not amount to gaming is unlawful, unless provided for under the Act.

The following case decisions have contributed to the meaning of the term 'lottery':
- It is not necessary that money paid by participants should be used to fund prizes. There will be a lottery whenever prizes are distributed by chance and participants have to make a payment to take part. Thus, where people buying cigarettes could win money prizes by discovering combinations of numbers printed inside the packets, there is a lottery, even though the cigarettes did not cost any more than normal (*Imperial Tobacco Co v Attorney General* (1980)).
- When prizes are offered in conjunction with the sale of books, this will not amount to an unlawful lottery when the opportunity to enter the draw is not dependent on whether a person buys books *(Keynote Case: Reader's Digest Assoc Ltd v Williams (1976))*.
- Where there is a scheme which involves a player being selected by pure chance, then having to exercise some degree of skill to confirm his right to a prize, the two elements have to be separated, and the first part will be regarded as a lottery – the right to go on to the second stage will be regarded as having value and will be a 'prize' in itself (*DPP v Bradfute and Associates Ltd* (1967)).

4.2.2 *Explanation*

Not gaming: If a lottery is promoted in accordance with the rules for one of the four sorts of lotteries provided in the Act – **and** every winner is identified by not more than three determining factors, the event will not amount to gaming. If there are more than three determining factors, e.g. the holder of a card with four numbers on, then it will be gaming *(see paragraph 1.2.3)*.

No purchase necessary: Prizes are frequently offered to promote the sale of goods. However, the opportunity to win must not be given only to those who buy, because this is seen as paying to have the chance of winning. Some companies which operate by mail order offer two envelopes in which to return prize draw tickets, a 'Yes' envelope for those who wish to buy, a 'No' envelope for those who wish to enter the draw without buying.

Packets of crisps (up to £100,000 if you find the lucky token in your packet), cans of drinks and even toilet rolls, have all been marketed in circumstances appearing to resemble the Imperial Tobacco case referred to above. The small print on the packaging will, however, give details of how one may have an opportunity to win a prize without buying the product.

4.2.3 *Offences Arising from an Unlawful Lottery*

The following are among offences which may be committed in connection with the promotion of an unlawful lottery:

- print tickets for the lottery;
- sell or distribute tickets or chances, offer or advertise tickets or chances for sale or distribution
- have possession of tickets or chances for sale or distribution
- print, publish, distribute or have possession of, for publication or distribution, any advertisement for the lottery, any other material about the draw likely to attract people to the lottery or any list or part-list of winners
- use premises, or cause or knowingly permit them to be used, for the purposes of the lottery
- bring, or invite anyone to send into Great Britain any ticket or advertisement for the lottery, for sale or distribution
- send or attempt to send out of Great Britain any money or valuable thing representing the proceeds of sale of a ticket, or any document relating to the sale or distribution or containing details of people who hold tickets or chances
- cause or procure anyone else to do any of the aforementioned acts.

4.2.4 *Defence*

A person will have a defence to a charge of printing, possession of or distribution of tickets, documents or advertisements if he proves that the lottery would not be conducted in Great Britain and that none of the tickets, advertisements, etc would be distributed in this country.

4.2.5 *False Representations as to the National Lottery*
National Lottery, etc, Act 1993 Section 16

A person commits an offence who:

- advertises or offers the opportunity to take part in any lottery, competition or other game
- giving a false indication that it is a lottery forming part of or connected with the National Lottery.

4.2.6 *Explanation*

Money: The term includes cash, cheques, money orders, etc.

Ticket: This includes anything which is evidence of a person having a claim to take part in the lottery.

Printing: This includes writing or any other means of producing visible words. Thus, any electronic means of sending visible words would be included.

Purpose of sale or distribution etc: It will not be an offence to bring into the country, a ticket one has bought abroad for one's self , e.g. in a German state lottery, providing there is no intention to sell or distribute the ticket here. Similarly, it will not be an offence to have a list of prize winners in a foreign lottery, so long as there is no intention of publishing that list to other people.

Send money out: It is not unknown for residents in Britain to receive by post tickets for a German state lottery, or an Irish lottery. It will not be an offence to buy these tickets and send the money for them to an address abroad, because the money is not the proceeds of 'sale or distribution', provided, of course, that the recipient has not sold the tickets on to someone else.

Defence: It is not the intention that the legislation should prevent printers in this country from earning a crust and contributing to Britain's export drive, by printing tickets or other material for a lottery to be held in some foreign country, so long as the lottery is not promoted here and none of the material is distributed in Great Britain.

4.3 Small Lotteries
Lotteries and Amusements Act 1976 Section 3

4.3.1 *When/Where*
A small lottery may be held as incidental to an entertainment such as a jumble sale, fête, dinner, sporting event, etc. A tombola stall at a fête or a raffle after a dinner may be held as a small lottery.

4.3.2 *Conditions*
The following conditions apply for the small lottery to be lawful:
- the whole of the proceeds of the entertainment, not just the proceeds of the lottery, must be devoted to purposes other than private gain, after deduction of reasonable expenses
- there shall be no money prizes
- the amount of money which may be deducted from the proceeds to buy prizes is limited to a maximum amount, set out in regulations
- all sales of tickets or chances, and the declaration of the result of the lottery must take place only during the entertainment and on the premises where it is being held
- facilities for taking part in a lottery and/or other lotteries or gaming shall not be the only or main attraction to attend the entertainment.

4.3.3 *Offence*
If any of the conditions relating to a small lottery are breached, every person concerned in promoting or conducting the lottery shall be guilty of an offence, unless he proves:
- that the contravention occurred without his knowledge or connivance; **and**
- that he exercised all due diligence to prevent it.

4.3.4 *Explanation*
Private gain: A raffle held at a charity soccer match could come within the definition of a small lottery, but one held at, say, a professional league match could not, because the proceeds of the whole event, not just the lottery, must go elsewhere than to private gain.

Prizes: Cash prizes are not allowed. In addition, the amount of money which the promoters are allowed to deduct for buying prizes is very limited. There is, however, no limit on the value of prizes, so a prize could be quite valuable, if it has been donated.

Inducement to attend: The idea is that the lottery is an incident at the entertainment, rather than the lottery, or any gaming being the main attraction.

4.4 **Private Lottery**
Lotteries and Amusements Act 1976 Section 4

4.4.1 *When/Where*
A private lottery is one which is promoted for:
- members of a society established and conducted for purposes not connected with betting, gaming or lotteries; or
- persons who all work on the same premises; or
- persons who all live on the same premises.

4.4.2 *Conditions*
The following conditions apply, if a private lottery is to be lawful:
- the promoter(s) is one of the persons for whom the lottery is promoted, and, in the case of a society, is authorised in writing as a promoter by the governing body of the society
- sale of tickets is confined to those for whom the lottery is promoted **and**, in the case of one promoted by a society, to any other person on the society's premises
- the whole of the proceeds of the lottery, after deduction of expenses for printing and stationery, shall be devoted either – to buying prizes for the lottery – or in the case of a society, to the purposes of the society and/or to buying prizes
- the lottery may not be advertised, except on the premises of the society, or where the persons live or work, as appropriate. Such notice or advertising as is contained on a ticket is also allowed
- the price of each ticket or chance shall be the same, and that price shall be stated on each ticket
- each ticket shall bear the name and address of the promoter, and details of who is eligible to buy a ticket
- any prize must be delivered only to the person to whom the ticket or chance was sold, and this fact shall be stated on each ticket
- a ticket or chance will not be issued except by way of sale, and must be paid for in full at the time of sale
- no ticket money is to be returned whatever the circumstances
- tickets must not be sent through the post.

4.4.3 *Offence*
If any of the conditions of the lottery is broken, an offence will be committed by:
- each and every one of the promoters; and
- any other person who was responsible for breaking the condition.

However, a promoter will have a defence if he proves that the contravention occurred without his consent or connivance and that he exercised all due diligence to prevent it.

4.4.4 *Explanation*
No outsiders: The whole of the lottery, i.e. the promotion of it and the sale of tickets or chances, must be confined to the eligible group, as must any notices or advertisements about the lottery. However, tickets may be sold for a lottery organised by a society to persons who are on the society's premises. This concession does not apply to a lottery organised for persons who live or work on the same premises.

Ticket or chance: There are various requirements relating to tickets, e.g. having details on them, etc, but there need not in fact be any tickets. For example, numbers are written on lined paper, and the names óf persons buying chances entered against the respective numbers. Winners are then chosen, e.g. by picking numbered balls out of a bag, by a random number programme on a computer, or whatever (this applies equally to a small lottery).

Society: For the purposes of this type of lottery, every local or affiliated branch of a society shall be treated as a separate society. If a national organisation wants to run a lottery across the country, then a private lottery is not the type to choose.

Prizes: In marked contrast to the situation with a small lottery, where only a limited amount of the proceeds may be spent on prizes, with this lottery, **all** the proceeds, apart from printing costs must, in the case of persons who live or work together, or may, in the case of a society, be spent on prizes. It will not be lawful for everyone who works in an office building, for example, to run a private lottery to raise money for a charity.

Same price, full price: 'Twenty five pence each or five for a £1' may help boost sales of tickets, but is not lawful. Neither is it lawful for the promoters to issue 'free' tickets, or allow credit sales.

4.5 Society Lottery
Lotteries and Amusements Act 1976 Section 5

4.5.1 *Where/When*
A society lottery is one which is promoted on behalf of a society which exists wholly or mainly for one or more of the follow purposes:
- charitable purposes
- participation in or support for sporting, athletic or cultural activities
- any other purpose which is not for private gain and which is not for the purposes of a commercial undertaking.

4.5.2 *Conditions*
The following conditions apply, for a society lottery to be lawful:
- The society is registered for the purpose of lotteries, either with the local authority in whose area the head office of the society is situated, or with the Gaming Board. Whether registration is with the local council or with the Gaming Board depends on the amount of money to be raised, either from a single lottery, or over a year from a number of lotteries run by the society.
- The lottery must be promoted in accordance with a scheme approved by the society and in accordance with regulations. These regulations, which apply also to local lotteries, are dealt with at *paragraph 4.7.1* below.
- The whole of the proceeds of the lottery, less expenses and the cost of prizes, shall be devoted to the purposes of the society.
- The society does not hold lotteries more frequently than is allowed by law.

4.6 Local Lotteries
Lotteries and Amusements Act 1976 Section 6

4.6.1 *When/Where*
A local lottery is one promoted by a local authority.

4.6.2 *Conditions*
The lottery must:
- be promoted in accordance with a scheme approved by the local authority
- be registered with the Gaming Board
- not be held more frequently than allowed by law.

4.7 **Matters Relating to Society and to Local Lotteries**

4.7.1 *Regulations for Society and Local Lotteries*
The Lotteries Regulations 1993

There are numerous regulations governing society and local lotteries, some of which are of an administrative nature. Some of the requirements are:
- tickets not to be sold by anyone under 16 years of age
- no sale of tickets in a street (but an exception is made in respect of a kiosk in a street)
- no sale of tickets by means of any machine
- the name of the local authority with whom a society is registered, or the authority promoting a local lottery, shall appear on every ticket.

4.7.2 *Offences*
If any of the conditions of the lottery is broken, then an offence will be committed by:
- the promoter; and
- any other person who was responsible for breaking the condition.

However, a promoter will have a defence if he proves that the contravention occurred without his consent or connivance and that he exercised all due diligence to prevent it.

4.7.3 *Lottery Managers*
Lotteries and Amusements Act 1976 Section 9A

No person shall manage a society lottery or a local lottery unless that person is one of the following:
- a member or employee of the society or the local authority by which the lottery is promoted
- a person certified as a lottery manager under the Act, or an employee of a certified person.

In addition, a society lottery may be managed by a limited company which is owned by that society.

4.7.4 *Explanation*
Society and local lotteries may generate very large sums of money, leading to many of them being run by experienced, professional managers. This provision ensures that if the manager of the lottery is not a member or employee of the organisation promoting the lottery, then she must be certificated by the Gaming Board.

4.8 **Amusements with Prizes**
Lotteries and Amusements Act 1976 Sections 15 and 16

Provision is made for amusements with prizes:
- at entertainments where the proceeds go to other than private gain; and

– at certain commercial entertainments, such as fun fairs.

These provisions are very similar to those which relate to gaming and the use of gaming machines in such circumstances *(see paragraphs 3.8.6, 3.8.8)*.

4.9 **Search Warrant**
Lotteries and Amusements Act 1976 Section 19

4.9.1 *Grounds for Issue*
A magistrate may issue a warrant if satisfied on information on oath that there is reasonable ground for suspecting:
– that an offence under the Act has been, is being or is about to be committed on any premises (and here 'premises' includes 'place').

4.9.2 *Powers Under the Warrant*
A constable is authorised under the warrant:
– to enter the place specified in the warrant, using force if necessary, and search it
– seize and remove any document, money, valuable thing, instrument or whatever, found there which the constable has reason to believe may be required as evidence of an offence under the Act
– search any person found on the premises whom he has reasonable cause to believe to be committing or to have committed any such offence.

4.10 **Prize Competitions**
Lotteries and Amusements Act 1976 Section 14

4.10.1 *Offence*
A person commits an offence who:
– conducts in or through any newspaper
– or in connection with a trade or business or the sale of any article to the public
– any competition in which prizes are offered:
   i) for the forecast of the result of a future event; or
   ii) for the forecast of the result of a past event, the result of which is not yet ascertained or is not yet generally known; or
   iii) where success in the competition does not involve a substantial degree of skill.

4.10.2 *Explanation*
These provisions seek to control competitions which offer prizes, from becoming simply a form of gaming or a lottery. Thus a competition which offers a prize for putting a cross on a photograph to indicate where the soccer ball is, would be unlawful if it was merely a forecast of where the ball actually was when the photograph was taken (past event, outcome not generally known). If, however, the position of the ball is decided by an 'expert' using skill and judgement, and the competitors likewise exercise skill in placing their crosses, the competition will be lawful (*News of the World Ltd. v Friend* (1973)).

Keynote Case

5.1 *Reader's Digest Association v Williams* [1976] 3 All ER 737

Problem

Whether a prize draw associated with the marketing of books for sale will amount to an unlawful lottery.

Circumstances

The Reader's Digest Association sent literature to people, offering books for sale and at the same time offering tickets or numbers in a prize draw. The draw documents could be returned to the Association, either in a 'YES' envelope, signifying a desire to buy the book(s) being offered, or in a 'NO' envelope, indicating that the person did not want to receive the book(s) even on approval. The Association was prosecuted for promoting an unlawful lottery, i.e. one which did not fall into any of the several categories authorised under the relevant legislation. On the facts given to the court, some 4.7 million sets of prize draw entries and book order forms were sent out, of which approximately half were returned. One third of these, 856,000 were returned in 'YES' envelopes, while close to 1.6 million 'NO' envelopes came back.

Decision

The Queen's Bench Division pointed out that there are three elements of a lottery:
- distribution of prizes
- this is done by means of a chance; and
- participants, or a substantial number of them, make a payment in return for having the chance of a prize.

The court ruled that because the chances of success in the draw were exactly the same, whether one returned the 'NO' envelope, or the 'YES' one, those who returned the latter were not actually paying anything to participate in the draw. The third element required for a lottery was therefore absent, so the scheme was not a lottery.

Comment

The fact that there were twice as many 'NO' envelopes as 'YES' ones in this case is not of enormous significance in relation to the decision of the court. If the prospects of a prize are the same whether one has the books being offered for sale or not, then in the words of the Lord Chief Justice, 'there is absolutely no such contribution that I can see payable in return for obtaining a chance'.

When prizes are offered in relation to the sale of products, e.g. 'Look under the lid of the can to see if you have won £10,000', then the opportunity to have a chance of winning a prize by writing to a given address without actually buying a can in the first place, brings the promotion into the same category as the Reader's Digest one. The phrase 'No purchase necessary' is usually displayed somewhere on the product concerned and on advertisements.

Chapter 43: Animals

1 CRUELTY TO ANIMALS

1.1 Meaning of Animal
Protection of Animals Act 1911 Section 15

Animal: Means any 'domestic animal' or any 'captive animal'. However, 'animal' is confined to vertebrates (i.e. animals with backbones). Thus, lobsters, insects, spiders and other invertebrates are not animals for these purposes.

Domestic animal: The term includes horses, cattle, dogs, cats, ducks, hens and any other animal of whatever kind or species, whether with four legs or not, which is tame, or which has been or is being tamed, to serve some purpose for the use of man.

Captive animal: This means any animal – not being a domestic animal – including any bird, fish or reptile which is in captivity or confinement, or which is maimed, pinioned or subject to any device for the purpose of preventing or hindering its escape.

1.1.1 *Explanation*

Sufficiently tamed: An animal which is not sufficiently tamed to serve some purpose for humans, will not be a domestic animal. A pet dog may be tame so that anyone may approach it. A bull may not be tame to the same extent, but it may be sufficiently tamed to serve its purpose, i.e. it can be handled by people who take proper precautions and know what they are doing. Both will be domestic animals. Any animal which is undergoing a process to make it sufficiently tame will also fall into this category.

Captive animal: A pet parrot which says 'Pretty Polly' and sits on its owner's shoulder will be a domestic animal. A parrot in a large enclosure in a zoo will be a captive animal. If an animal is in a cage, it is clearly captive. However, geese on a lake may have their feathers clipped, so that they are unable to fly away, i.e. they are 'maimed'. For a wild animal to be termed a captive animal, a period of time must elapse during which it is under human control. During a stag hunt, the stag went under the wheels of a lorry and was dragged out by hunt staff, taken into a nearby enclosure where it was killed. The time taken to extricate and kill the animal was about 10 minutes. It was held on these facts, that a temporary inability to get away did not render the stag a 'captive animal', so the manner of its being killed could not be subject of a prosecution for cruelty to an animal (*Rowley v Murphy* (1964)).

What other sort is there?: If an animal is not a domestic one and is not captive then it is a wild animal which is not captive, such as the squirrels eating the bird seed in your garden, or the mole tunnelling under your lawn. To treat wild animals or birds in a cruel manner will not attract a prosecution under this Act. However, wild mammals are protected against cruel treatment *(see paragraph 3 of this chapter)* and there are other provisions, dealt with in Chapter 44, which protect badgers, various species of birds, rare bats, toads, etc.

1.2 **Offence of Cruelty**
Protection of Animals Act 1911 Section 1

1.2.1 *Offence*
The offence of cruelty may be committed in a number of ways. The person causing or procuring the cruel treatment commits an offence, as in most cases does the owner of the animal who permits the treatment to take place. The ways in which the offence may be committed are:

i)   cruel treatment – e.g. beating, kicking, overloading, torturing or terrifying the animal.

ii) wantonly or unreasonably doing or omitting to do something so as to cause unnecessary suffering;

iii) carrying or conveying the animal so as to cause unnecessary suffering;

iv) subjecting the animal to an operation which is performed without due care and humanity;

v)   administering injurious poison or drugs without reasonable cause or excuse;

vi) tethering any horse, ass or mule so as to cause unnecessary suffering.

1.2.2 *Exceptions*
There are a number of activities which may be lawful in relation to persons inflicting pain or suffering on animals. The use of animals in experiments (vivisection) may be carried out by licensed persons; the slaughter of animals by ritual methods, e.g. by cutting throats, will be lawful if certain conditions are met.

1.2.3 *Fighting or Baiting*
A person will also be guilty of the offence of cruelty if he is involved in fighting or baiting an animal in any of the following ways:

i)   cause, procure or assist at fighting or baiting the animal;

ii) keep, use or manage premises or place for that purpose, or assist in doing so;

iii) permit the premises or place to be kept, used or managed for that purpose;

iv) receive, or cause or procure another person to receive, money for admission to such place.

1.2.4 *Other Offences Related to Fighting*
It is also an offence for a person:

i)   without reasonable excuse, to be present when animals are placed together for the purpose of their fighting each other (Section 5A);

ii) publishes or causes to be published an advertisement for a fight between animals – knowing or believing that it is such an advertisement (Section 5B).

1.2.5 *Explanation*
Present: There is no need to prove that the person is taking part in organising the animal fight, or even that he is a spectator. If he is present the onus is on him to show that he has a reasonable excuse for being there.

Knowing or believing: The prosecution has to prove knowledge on the part of the accused. There is case law to the effect that closing ones eyes to the obvious may be taken as 'knowledge', so an advertisement which is couched in language suggesting that a dog fight is to be held, even though this is not stated in so many words, may give rise to this offence.

1.2.6 *Cockfighting*

Although the 1911 Act caters for the fighting or baiting of any animal, there is additional provision relating to the fighting of domestic fowl. The Cockfighting Act 1952 provides that a person shall be guilty of an offence:

- if he has in his possession any instrument or appliance designed or adapted for use in connection with the fighting of any domestic fowl
- if the court is satisfied that he had it in his possession for the purpose of using it or permitting it to be used for this purpose.

1.2.7 *Abandonment of an Animal*
Abandonment of Animals Act 1960 Section 1

A person will be deemed to be guilty of an offence of cruelty to an animal if:
- being the owner or person in charge or control of an animal
- he abandons it, permanently or not, without reasonable cause or excuse
- or being the owner causes or procures such
- in circumstances likely to cause it unnecessary suffering.

1.2.8 *Explanation*

Unnecessary suffering: Suffering is 'unnecessary' if it could be terminated or alleviated by some reasonably practical measure (*RSPCA v Isaacs* (1994)).

Owner permits: An owner will be deemed to have permitted cruelty to his animal if he failed to exercise reasonable care and supervision to protect the animal. Thus, the owner may be guilty of permitting by neglect, as well as when he deliberately allows his animal to be treated cruelly. When an owner is guilty of permitting cruelty by reason only of failing to exercise reasonable care and supervision, he will be liable to a fine only, whereas the usual sentence is a fine and/or imprisonment. This is significant in relation to the power of arrest *(see paragraph 1.3.1)*.

Abandonment: An animal may be abandoned permanently, e.g. by leaving a litter of kittens in a sack in a dustbin, or temporarily, e.g. going off on holiday and leaving a dog without enough food. There has to be a physical leaving of the animal unattended in circumstances likely to cause suffering (*Hunt v Duckering* (1993)).

1.2.9 *Miscellaneous Animal Protection Measures*

There are numerous measures aimed at protecting animals, wild and domestic, in specific ways. The manner in which farm animals are transported is governed by detailed regulations; there are laws relating to the use of poisons and traps; the use of dogs to pull carts is unlawful. These matters are not dealt with in this book.

1.3 **Police Powers**
Protection of Animals Act 1911 Section 12

1.3.1 *Arrest*

A constable may arrest without warrant:
- any person whom he has reasonable cause to believe is guilty of an offence under the Act
- which is punishable by imprisonment without the option of a fine
- whether on his own view

- or upon information from another person who must give his name and address to the constable.

1.3.2 *Take Charge of Animal, etc*

When a constable arrests someone under this power, who is in charge of a vehicle or animal, the officer (or another constable) may take charge of that vehicle or animal and safeguard it until the court proceedings are over (or until a court directs otherwise). Police costs, including any veterinary costs, are recoverable from the arrested person.

1.3.3 *Explanation*

On his own view or...: A constable may act upon what another person has told him, provided he obtains that person's name and address before arresting the suspect. This would not give a person such as an officer of the RSPCA the right to detain a suspected offender and hand him over to the police, the officer would have to pass the information to the police for them to carry out the arrest.

Option of a fine: The power to arrest applies to any offence under the Act for which a prison sentence is a possible punishment. If the offence is punishable only with a fine (not counting the possibility of being imprisoned for non-payment of a fine) then the power to arrest does not apply. Most of the offences under the Act are imprisonable; a notable exception is where an owner permits cruelty, by failing to exercise care and supervision *(see paragraph 1.2.8)*.

Safeguard animal or vehicle: This provision caters for a situation where, for example, a person in charge of a horse and cart is arrested for cruelty to that animal. In more up-to-date terms, it would also apply to the situation where the driver of a cattle truck was arrested for cruelty to animals on that truck. The law does not offer suggestions as to how a constable might cope with his irate inspector when he arrives at the police station with a truckload of sheep which have to be looked after.

1.3.4 *Power to Enter Knacker's Yard*
Protection of Animals Act 1911 Section 5

Any constable shall have the right to enter a knacker's yard:
- at any time by day, or at any time when business is, or appears to be or is usually carried on there
- for the purpose of examining whether there is or has been any contravention of provisions of this Act.

1.3.5 *Offence*

A person commits an offence who refuses to permit a constable to enter premises in exercise of this power, or who obstructs or impedes her in her duty in this respect.

1.3.6 *Prosecution*

For the purposes of a prosecution for an offence of cruelty, the knacker shall be deemed to be the owner of any animal delivered to him, to a person on his behalf or to his yard.

1.3.7 *Explanation*

A knacker is a person who deals in and slaughters animals not for human consumption.

2 INJURED ANIMALS
Protection of Animals Act 1911 Section 11

2.1 Meaning of Animal
For the purposes of this provision, an 'animal' is restricted to the following:
- horse
- mule
- ass
- bull (in turn extends to all cattle)
- sheep
- goat, or
- pig.

2.2 Police Powers
The powers given to the police to deal with ill or injured animals may be considered in stages.

2.2.1 Initial Police Action
If a constable finds an animal so diseased, so severely injured or in such physical condition, that in her opinion it is not possible to move it without causing cruelty, having regard to the means available, she shall, if the owner is not there or if he refuses to consent to its destruction, call a veterinary surgeon, if there is one within a reasonable distance.

2.2.2 Vet Says 'Slaughter'
If the vet then **certifies** that the animal is in such condition that it would be cruel to keep it alive, it shall be lawful for the constable, without the consent of the owner, to slaughter the animal or cause or procure it to be slaughtered in a manner which inflicts as little suffering as possible. If the animal is slaughtered on a public highway, the constable may also arrange removal of the carcase.

2.2.3 Vet Says 'No' to Slaughter
If the vet certifies that the animal may be moved without cruelty, it will be the duty of the person in charge of it to arrange its removal. If he fails to do so, the constable may without that person's consent, cause the animal to be moved forthwith.

2.2.4 Costs
Any costs incurred by the police, including vet's and slaughtering fees, may be recovered from the owner of the animal through the civil courts.

2.3 Explanation
Purpose: This provision relieves the police of the risk of being sued by the owner of a valuable animal, either when the owner does not agree, or is not present to agree, to its being slaughtered.

Animal: Perhaps the animal most frequently encountered in an injured state on Britain's roads is the dog. Dogs and cats are not included in the definition of 'animal' for these purposes.

Certificate: Before a constable arranges for an animal to be slaughtered or moved without the owner's consent, she must ensure that the veterinary surgeon records his decision in writing.

3 CRUELTY TO WILD MAMMALS

3.1 Offence
Wild Mammals (Protection) Act 1996 Section 1

A person commits an offence if he treats any wild mammal in one of the following ways, with intent to inflict unnecessary suffering. Treatment specifically mentioned includes:
- mutilates
- kicks
- beats
- nails or impales
- stabs
- burns
- stones
- crushes
- drowns
- drags
- asphyxiates.

3.2 Exceptions
Wild Mammals (Protection) Act 1996 Section 2

A person will not commit an offence under the Act by doing any of the following:
  i)   attempting to kill a wild mammal as an act of mercy, when he must show that it was so seriously disabled, otherwise than by his unlawful act, that it had no reasonable chance of recovering;
 ii)   killing in a reasonably swift and humane manner, if he shows that the wild mammal had been injured or taken in the course of lawful shooting, hunting, coursing or pest control;
iii)   making lawful use of any poison or noxious thing on a wild mammal;
 iv)   making lawful use of any snare, trap, gun, dog or bird for the purpose of taking or killing a wild mammal;
  v)   doing anything which is lawful under any other legislation.

3.3 Explanation
Wild mammal: A wild mammal is any mammal which does not fall within the meaning of 'domestic animal' or 'captive animal' under the Protection of Animals Act 1911.
Note: That the legislation covers only mammals, it does not extend to birds, fish or reptiles.

Treatment with intent: Rather than using a more general term, such as 'ill-treats', the Act has a list of 12 different ways of being cruel to a wild mammal. These appear to cover most eventualities. Whatever the treatment, it must be done with an intention to inflict unnecessary suffering before the offence is complete.

Act of mercy: Putting an injured animal out of its misery is one of the exceptions, provided the animal's condition did not arise through the unlawful act of the person concerned. Thus, a youth throws a stone at a squirrel, intending to hit it and causing it injury. If he then kicks it to put it out of its suffering, he commits the offence twice, first by throwing the stone (one of the 12 ways), then by kicking it (another listed method), and in the second instance cannot claim the exception. A motorist who accidentally runs over a badger and then seeks to end its suffering may claim the exception because his action which caused its condition was not unlawful.

Hunting, snaring, poisoning, etc: The exceptions reflect the various ways in which humans seek to kill wild animals. Providing the action is lawful, whether it be hunting, shooting or whatever, killing an injured animal, or using poison, will not amount to an offence under this Act.

3.4 **Police Powers**

3.4.1 *Arrest*
Wild Mammals (Protection) Act 1996 Section 4

If a constable has reasonable ground for suspecting that a person has committed an offence under the Act and that evidence of the offence may be found on that person, or in or on a vehicle which he has with him, the constable may without warrant:
  i) stop and search that person;
  ii) stop and search any vehicle or article he has with him;
  iii) seize and detain for the purposes of proceedings anything which may be evidence of the commission of such offence, or which may be liable to be confiscated.

3.4.2 *Confiscation*
Wild Mammals (Protection) Act 1996 Section 6

In addition to any other punishment, a court on convicting a person of an offence under the Act, may order confiscation of any vehicle or equipment used in committing the offence. Thus, the police powers involve not only seizing evidence, but seizing anything else, such as a car, used in committing the offence.

4 **DISEASE CONTROL**
Animal Health Act 1981

4.1 **Introduction**

4.1.1 *Diseases*
There are many diseases to which farm animals may succumb, and there is a great deal of rules and regulations aimed at combating disease, preventing any outbreak from spreading, and dealing with dead or affected livestock. The disease which has hit the headlines in recent years is BSE, but an older generation of reader may remember outbreaks of foot-and-mouth disease, involving police standing guard on affected farms.

4.1.2 *Police Involvement*
Although enforcement of the complex regulations is largely a matter for local authority animal health inspectors and the Ministry of Agriculture, Fisheries and Food, the police have a part to play, with a number of powers, to stop vehicles, etc. There are also powers specific to the disease, rabies. It is a requirement of the Act that the police force for an area will execute and enforce the Act and every order (made under the Act) (Section 60(1)).

4.2 Discovery of Disease
Animal Health Act 1981 Section 15

When a person has in his possession or charge an animal affected with disease, he shall:
  i)   as far as practicable, keep that animal separated from unaffected animals; and
  ii) with all practicable speed notify a constable (in the area where the animal is).

The constable in turn must notify the appropriate person, in accordance with an order made under the Act.

4.2.1 *Offences*
A person will commit an offence if, contrary to these requirements, he:
  i)   fails to keep an animal separate; or
  ii) fails to notify a constable.

4.2.2 *Explanation*
Disease: This means one of the diseases to which the various orders made under the Act refer.
Note: There are separate provisions in respect of rabies – see paragraph 4.4.

Appropriate person: There will be a direction contained in an order made under the Act, as to whom police should notify.

4.3 Police Powers
Animal Health Act 1981 Section 60

4.3.1 *Stop and Search*
When a person is seen or found committing any offence against the Act, or is reasonably suspected of being engaged in committing such offence, a constable may, without warrant:
  i)   stop and detain that person; and whether so stopping or detaining the person or not:
  ii) stop, detain and examine any animal, vehicle, boat or thing to which the suspected offence relates; and
  iii) require it to be taken back forthwith to the place or district from which it was unlawfully removed;
  iv) execute and enforce any requirement to take something back.

The powers outlined above may also be exercised by any person whom a constable calls upon to assist him.

4.3.2 *Non-Police Enforcement*
The Act, most unusually, provides a power of arrest which a person who is **not** a police officer may exercise:

If any person obstructs or impedes, or assists in obstructing or impeding:
  –   an officer (who is not a constable) in the execution of any provision of this Act or an order made under it, or of a local authority regulation
  –   then the officer may arrest that person without warrant.

4.3.3 *Explanation*
Take back: A place where a particular disease has occurred may be cordoned off, with all movement of animals in or out of the place prohibited. A constable has power to turn back persons, vehicles, animals, etc. In addition to requiring a person to turn his cattle truck round,

a constable may actually enforce that requirement, i.e. have the vehicle taken back if the driver fails to co-operate.

Person assisting: A constable may call on another person to assist, in which case that person would be able to exercise the same powers. This would be useful in a remote rural area where a constable was acting without the assistance of other officers.

Arrest: The non-police power to arrest is a preserved power for the purposes of the Police and Criminal Evidence Act 1984. If a constable is obstructed or impeded while seeking to exercise these powers, this does amount to an offence under the Act, but there is no specific power of arrest.

Disposal of person arrested: A person arrested under this power shall be taken before a magistrates' court with all practicable speed, and may not be detained without warrant for longer than is necessary for this purpose. A person arrested under this provision may be given bail by police.

4.3.4 *Detained Vehicles and Vessels*
Animal Health Act 1981 Sections 65, 66

A Ministry inspector has power to order the detention of a vehicle or vessel in certain circumstances. A person will be guilty of an offence if, without lawful authority or reasonable excuse, he fails to allow an inspector to inspect a vehicle, vessel, place, etc, or obstructs or impedes him, or obstructs or impedes a constable in the execution of his duty, or assists someone else to do so.

Under these provisions, the non-police power to arrest could be exercised. A constable could consider using the general power under the Police and Criminal Evidence Act 1984 if he is obstructed.

4.4 **Provisions Relating Specifically to Rabies**

4.4.1 *Requirement to Notify Police*
Animal Health Act 1981 Section 15(2)

Any person who knows or suspects that an animal – whether in captivity or not – is affected by rabies, shall give notice of that fact to a constable, unless:
 – he is exempted (by an order made under the Act) from doing so; or
 – he reasonably believes that someone else has notified the police about that animal;
 and if the animal is in his possession or charge, he shall as far as practicable, keep it separate from other animals.

4.4.2 *Police Power to Arrest*
Animal Health Act 1981 Section 61

A constable may arrest without warrant any person whom he reasonably suspects to be in the act of committing or to have committed an offence relating to rabies prevention, consisting of any of the following:
 i) landing or attempted landing of an animal in Great Britain;
 ii) failure of a person in charge of a vessel or boat to discharge any obligation placed on him;
 iii) movement of an animal into, within or from an area declared to be infected with rabies.

4.4.3 *Police Powers of Entry and Search*
Animal Health Act 1981 Section 62

i) For the purpose of arresting a person for an offence under Section 61, a constable may enter, using force if necessary, and search any vessel, boat, aircraft or any other vehicle in which that person is or in which the constable reasonably suspects him to be.

ii) For the purpose of exercising any power given to a constable, relating to rabies prevention, to seize an animal or cause it to be seized, a constable may enter, using force if necessary, and search any vessel, boat, aircraft or any other vehicle in which there is or in which the constable reasonably suspects there to be an animal to which the power applies.

4.4.4 *Explanation*

Requirement to notify: In contrast to the situation for other diseases, the obligation to notify the police is not limited to a person who has charge of an animal. Any person who suspects that an animal, even a wild one, is suffering from rabies, has an obligation to report this to a constable, unless he has reason to believe someone else has done so (or unless he is exempt).

Arrest: This is a preserved power to arrest, under the provisions of the Police and Criminal Evidence Act 1984.

5 CONTROL OF DOGS

5.1 Introduction

Properly controlled, 'man's best friend' may be worthy of that title, but dogs can also pose a nuisance or danger, and the law seeks to address problem dogs in a number of ways, relating to those which:

i) stray;
ii) are on roads;
iii) pose a danger to people;
iv) chase farm animals;
v) are used as guard dogs.

5.2 Stray Dogs
Environmental Protection Act 1990 Sections 149, 150 and Dogs Act 1906

5.2.1 *Police or Council*

Looking after stray dogs, a responsibility of the police for many decades, has increasingly been seen as an unsuitable use of police officers, diverting resources from the primary responsibility of fighting crime. The aim of the 1990 Act is to have local authorities take over this responsibility, but at present, the police retain a parallel responsibility under the provisions of the 1906 legislation for dealing with stray dogs which come into police possession. A member of the public who finds a stray dog has an option, to hand it over to the police, or to the local authority.

5.2.2 *Police Involvement*

The relevant provisions of the 1906 Act are:

i) A constable has power under the Act to seize any dog he finds in a public place, or in a private place with the consent of the owner or occupier of that place, which he has reason to believe is a stray dog.

ii) A person finding a stray dog who takes it to a police station, may keep it, subject to giving his name and address to the police and obtaining a certificate. He must keep the dog for at least a month before seeking to dispose of it.

iii) If a found dog has a collar with the owner's address on, the police are required to notify the owner in writing that if he does not claim the dog within seven days, it will be sold or destroyed.

iv) Dogs in police care are kept for seven days. If claimed in that time, the owner is liable to pay a charge for its upkeep. After seven days an unclaimed dog may be sold or destroyed.

v) Police must keep a register of found dogs, making it available to the public to view.

5.2.3 *Local Authority Responsibilities*

The local authority shall appoint an officer to be responsible for stray dogs in the council's area. The provisions under this legislation are very similar to that under the 1906 Act. A significant difference is that the council's officer must if possible seize any dog he reasonably believes to be a stray in a public place, or in a private place with the consent of the owner or occupier of that place. This is in contrast to the constable's discretionary power to seize a stray dog. A member of the public finding a stray dog must either:

i) return it to its owner; or

ii) take it to the council officer; or

iii) take it to the police station nearest to where it was found.

The finder commits an offence by failing to do so.

5.2.4 *Explanation*

Police power to seize: There are occasions when it is appropriate for a constable to seize a dog which is apparently a stray, e.g. where the animal is running loose through heavy traffic and likely to cause an accident, or where it is a danger to the public. A constable has discretion whether to exercise this power, in contrast to the situation with the local authority officer, who must make an effort to catch any stray dog he comes across.

Offence: A person who 'finds' a stray dog must either return it to its owner, or take it to the police or local authority. Clearly, the law does not require a member of the public, under pain of prosecution, to take responsibility for every dog which passes by apparently without an owner. Rather, the intention is that a person shall not be entitled to keep for himself a dog which he finds; however if he does want to keep it, he may do so by giving his details to the police or council officer and agreeing to keep it for at least a month, to allow an opportunity for the loser to claim it back.

5.3 DOGS ON ROADS, ETC

5.3.1 *Requirement for Collar*
Control of Dogs Order 1992

Every dog which is on a highway or other public place must have a collar with the owner's address on it or on a disc or whatever attached to it.

5.3.2 *Exceptions*
There a number of exceptions, relating to what may be termed 'working dogs':
    i) hounds in a pack, dogs used for sporting purposes, or for catching vermin;
   ii) dogs being used for tending or herding sheep or cattle;
  iii) dogs being used by the police, Customs and Excise or H.M. Forces;
   iv) blind person's guide dog;
    v) dog being used for emergency rescue work.

5.3.3 *Offence*
An offence is committed by the owner or person in charge of a dog who without lawful authority or excuse causes or permits it to be on a highway or public place without the required collar.

5.3.4 *Designated Roads*
Road Traffic Act 1988 Section 27

A local authority has power to make an order designating roads in the council's area on which dogs must be kept on a lead at all times. The following provisions apply in relation to such orders:
    i) The council must consult the police before making an order.
   ii) Signs must be displayed on any stretch of road subject to such an order.
  iii) It is an offence for a person to cause or permit a dog to be on a designated road without being on a lead.
   iv) The order may allow for exceptions, and MUST make exceptions for dogs tending cattle or sheep, or being used for sporting purposes.

5.4 **Dangerous Types of Dog**

5.4.1 *Prohibited Dogs*
Dangerous Dogs Act 1991 Section 1

The Act prohibits persons from having possession or custody of dogs of certain types. The Act designates the following types as being prohibited:
    i) the type known as the pit bull terrier;
   ii) the type known as the Japanese Tosa;
  iii) any other type which the Home Secretary designates as being a type which appears to be bred for fighting, or having the characteristics of a dog bred for fighting.

The Home Secretary may make an order adding to or amending the list of types to which these prohibitions apply, under the 'fighting dog' provision. Types which have been added include the Dogo Argentino and the Fila Braziliero.

5.4.2 *Offences*
A person commits an offence if in relation to a dog of one of these types, he:
    i) has possession or control of such a dog, subject to certain exceptions;
   ii) breeds, or breeds from, such a dog;
  iii) sells or exchanges a dog, makes a gift of it, or offers, advertises or exposes it for such purpose;
   iv) as owner or person for the time being in charge of such a dog, allows it to be in a public place without being muzzled;

v) as owner or person in charge of it, allows it to stray, or as the owner, abandons it.

5.4.3 *Exception*
A person may have possession or control of such a dog subject to strict conditions:
i) the dog was born before 30 November 1991;
ii) the keeper of the dog has notified the police of the dog's name, address, age and gender;
iii) the dog has been neutered;
iv) there is third party insurance in respect of any injury the dog may cause;
v) a certificate of exemption has been issued, the terms of which must be complied with.

5.4.4 *Defence*
In relation to a charge of advertising a dog for sale, exchange or gift, a person will have a defence if he shows:
i) that he published the advertisement to the order of someone else, and did not himself devise the advertisement; **and**
ii) that he did not know, nor had reason to suspect that the advertisement related to a dog of a prohibited type.

5.4.5 *Sentence*
If the accused is able to prove only the first of these two facts, he will be liable to be convicted, but will not be liable to imprisonment as part of his sentence.

5.4.6 *Police Powers*
Dangerous Dogs Act 1991 Section 5

A constable (or authorised 'dog' officer of the local authority) may seize a dog which appears to him to be of a prohibited type which is in a public place:
i) at a time when possession or custody of it is unlawful; or
ii) it is not muzzled and kept on a lead (i.e. the offence at *paragraph 5.4.2 (iv)* is committed).

5.4.7 *Search Warrant*
Dangerous Dogs Act 1991 Section 5(2)

Grounds for issue: A magistrate may issue a warrant if he is satisfied on information on oath, either:
– that an offence under the Act is being or has been committed; **or**
– that evidence relating to the offence is to be found on any premises.

5.4.8 *Powers Under the Warrant*
A constable may enter the premises, using force if necessary, search them and seize any dog or other thing which is evidence of such an offence.

5.4.9 *Explanation*
Note that the grounds for issue of the warrant are separate; that an offence is being committed **or** (not **and**) that evidence may be found on the premises.

5.4.10 *Court's Powers*
Dangerous Dogs Act 1991 Section 4

When a person is convicted of an offence (under Section 1) relating to a dog of a prohibited type, the court **shall** (subject to the exception at *paragraph 5.4.12*) order the dog to be destroyed, and may also order the accused to be disqualified from having custody of a dog for a specified period of time.

If a dog has been seized by the police (or the local authority) but there is no prosecution, e.g. because the owner cannot be found, a magistrates' court before which the matter is brought **shall** (subject to the exception at *paragraph 5.4.12*) make an order for the dog's destruction.

5.4.11 *Explanation*

Type of dog: The word 'type' is not necessarily the same as the term 'breed'. It will be a matter for a court to decide whether, given evidence about the degree of resemblance of a particular dog to the physical characteristics associated with a particular breed, the dog in question is of that 'type'.

Burden of proof: In any proceedings where it is alleged that a dog is of a prohibited type, the onus is on the accused to adduce evidence that it is not of that type. The accused must give the prosecution 14 days' notice of an intention to adduce such evidence.(Section 5(5)).

Possession or control: The exceptions allow a dog to be kept which was born before a specified date, subject to being insured, neutered, etc. This provision will in due course cease to have any practical effect, as any dogs subject to it die of old age, but was brought in to cater for people who already had such dogs at the time the Act was brought into force.

Owner: When a dog is owned by a person under the age of 16 years, then the 'owner' for the purposes of this legislation shall be taken to be the head of the household of which the young person is a member (Section 6).

Lead and muzzle: References to a dog being on a lead mean that it is securely held on a lead by a person who is not less than 16 years old.

References to a dog being on a muzzle mean that the dog is securely fitted with a muzzle sufficient to prevent it biting any person (Section 7).

Police powers: A constable (or the council 'dog catcher') has power to seize a dog which is held unlawfully, or one held lawfully which is unmuzzled or off its lead in public.

Summary: In the few years after the Act came into force, newspapers had lots of stories of the sort involving 'dog seized by police when walking with its owner in the park, when the owner removed its muzzle for a moment to give it a biscuit – dog then spent months in kennels pining for its owner – then magistrates ordered it be destroyed, so owner appealed claiming it wasn't a pit bull terrier in any case ...'. When a dog is seized and the owner disputes that it is of one of the prohibited types, expert opinion is usually sought, and proceedings may proceed from a magistrates' court through the appeal system. The process may involve a dog being kept for considerable periods at police expense.

5.4.12 *Destruction Order – Court Discretion*
Dangerous Dogs Act 1991 Sections 4, 4A, as amended by Dangerous Dogs (Amendment) Act 1997

The requirement that a court **shall** order the destruction of a dog subject of an offence under Section 1 (prohibited breed) or an aggravated offence under Section 3 (dog dangerously out of control), need not apply if the court is satisfied that certain criteria apply, principally that the dog will not constitute a danger to public safety.

In addition, a court may make a 'contingent destruction order', providing that the dog shall be destroyed unless the owner keeps it under proper control and adheres to conditions, e.g. that it is always muzzled in specified places or that (in the case of a male dog) it is neutered.

5.5 **Dangerous Dogs**
Dogs Act 1871

5.5.1 *Procedure*
A dog may be dealt with by way of a 'complaint' to a magistrates' court. (A complaint is a procedure by which a court may hear evidence then make an 'order', as opposed to proceeding by 'information' which leads to a summons and hearing evidence of an offence.) If a court decides, having heard evidence, that a dog is 'dangerous', it may make an order – either that the dog be kept under control, or that it be destroyed. An order to keep a dog under control may specify what measures are to be taken, e.g. that it be kept on a lead, or that it be neutered.

5.5.2 *Dangerous*
The usual reason for a dog being declared dangerous is that it has attacked a person, but a dog may also be declared dangerous if it attacks other animals. In particular, a dog which has worried livestock may be dealt with as a dangerous dog *(see paragraph 5.7).*

5.5.3 *Additional Powers of Courts*
When a magistrates' court makes an order for the destruction of a dangerous dog, it may also:
   i) appoint a person to undertake its destruction;
   ii) order person who has custody of the dog to deliver it up for the purpose of destruction;
   iii) disqualify the owner from having custody of a dog for a specified period.

5.5.4 *Offences*
A person commits an offence who:
   i) fails to comply with an order, either to keep a dog under control, or to have it destroyed;
   ii) fails to comply with an order to deliver the dog up for destruction;
   iii) has custody of a dog when disqualified by order of a court.

5.6 **Dog Dangerously at Large**

5.6.1 *Offences*
Dangerous Dogs Act 1991 Section 3

   i) If a dog is dangerously out of control in a public place, then the owner of the dog **and** any other person who for the time being has charge of it, shall be guilty of an offence.
   ii) If a dog is allowed to enter a place which is not a public place, where it is not permitted to be, and while there it injures a person or there are reasonable grounds to believe it will injure a person, the owner or the person in charge of it if different, commits an offence.

5.6.2 *Aggravated Offence*
If the dog, while dangerously out of control or in the place where it should not be, injures any person, then the offence is committed in aggravated form.

5.6.3 *Explanation*
Dangerously out of control: A dog is dangerously out of control if:
- there are grounds for reasonable apprehension that it may injure any person
- whether or not it actually does so.

5.6.4 *Except*
A dog will not be regarded as dangerously out of control if it is being used for a lawful purpose by a constable or by a Crown servant.

5.6.5 *Defence*
When a person is charged with the first of these offences (i.e. in a public place), on the basis that he is the owner, while the dog was in charge of someone else, he will have a defence if he proves that at the material time it was in the charge of a person whom he reasonably believed to be a fit and proper person to have charge of it.

5.6.6 *Court Powers*
When a person is convicted of one of the offences, the court **may** order the destruction of the dog concerned, but if the offence is in the aggravated form, the court **must** order its destruction, subject to the exceptions at *paragraph 5.4.312* above. The court may also order that the accused be disqualified from having custody of a dog for a specified period.

5.6.7 *Offences*
A person will commit an offence who:
  i) has custody of a dog when disqualified by a court; or
  ii) fails to comply with a requirement to hand over a dog to a person appointed by a court to undertake its destruction.

5.6.8 *Police Powers*
Dangerous Dogs Act 1991 Section 5

A constable (or a local authority dog officer) may seize any dog in a public place which appears to him to be dangerously out of control.

5.6.9 *Warrant*
The warrant which may be issued under this Act applies equally to these offences as to offences involving prohibited types of dog *(see paragraph 5.4.1)*.

5.6.10 *Explanation*
Offences: The two offences, one in a public place, one in a private place where the dog is 'trespassing', are very similar, although the legislators for some obscure reason, have made the wording different. There is no reason why the phrase 'dangerously out of control' could not have been used for both. Note that a dog which attacks a person on private property where it has a right to be, e.g. in its owner's garden, will not give rise to an offence under the 1991 Act, although the dog could still be declared 'dangerous' under the 1906 Act.

Owner's liability: There is no need to prove that the owner or person in charge of a dog knew or intended that the dog was or was likely to be 'dangerously out of control'. The offence is one of strict liability. *(Keynote Case: R v Bezzina (and other cases) (1994))*

Public place: A public place means any street, road or other place whether or not enclosed, to which the public have a right to access or are permitted access on payment or otherwise. The term includes the common parts of a building comprising two or more dwellings. The reference to the common parts of buildings which contain several dwellings, takes the term 'public place' beyond its usual meaning, because the stairways, entrance halls etc in a block of flats would not normally be regarded as a public place.

Defence: An important distinction between the two offences is that for the 'public place' offence, the owner **and** the person in charge may commit the offence; with the 'private place' offence it is the owner **or** the person in charge of the dog who will be liable. The defence available to the owner in respect of the former offence, that he thought it was in the charge of a responsible person, does not apply to the second offence, indeed it is unnecessary, because it is the person in charge who will be liable, not the owner.

5.7 Dogs Worrying Livestock
Dogs (Protection of Livestock) Act 1953

5.7.1 *Offence*
If a dog worries livestock on agricultural land, then:
- the owner; and
- the person in charge of the dog at the time,
- will each be liable.

5.7.2 *Exception*
A person will not be liable if the livestock were trespassing on the land at the time and the dog is owned by the occupier of the land or by a person authorised by the occupier. However, this exception will cease to apply, if the person causes the dog to attack the livestock.

5.7.3 *Defence*
If a person is charged with the offence because he is the owner of the dog, he will have a defence if he proves that at the time the dog worried the livestock, it was in the charge of some other person whom he reasonably believed to be a fit and proper person to have charge of it.

5.7.4 *Meaning of Terms*
Livestock: This means cattle, sheep, pigs, goats, horses, donkeys, mules, and poultry (chickens, turkeys, geese and ducks) – in short, farm animals.

Agricultural land: Means land used for farming, grazing animals, poultry farming, market gardens, allotments, orchards, nursery grounds.

Worries: A dog worries livestock if it:
   i) attacks livestock; or
   ii) chases livestock in such a way as may reasonably be expected to cause injury or suffering, or, in the case of females, abortion, or loss of or diminution in their produce; or
   iii) not being on a lead or otherwise under close control, is in a field or enclosure in which there are sheep.

Chases: It is not necessary to show that the dog actually pursued the livestock. It will be sufficient if the dog runs among the livestock so as to cause them to panic and run (*Stephen v Milne* (1960)).

Exception: The last part, being at large in a field of sheep, does not apply to any of the following:
  - police dog
  - guide dog
  - trained sheep dog
  - working gun dog
  - hounds in a pack.

5.7.5 *Explanation*

Owner's defence: The owner will have a defence if he proves that someone whom he reasonably believed was a responsible person, was in charge of the dog at the time it worried livestock. There is no age stipulation here in determining who will be a 'responsible person', in contrast to the Dangerous Dogs Act 1991, where 'on a lead' means a lead held by a person aged 16 or over.

Agricultural land: As well as all sorts of farming and horticultural land, allotments are included. In some parts of the country, poultry and young pigs are reared on allotments. Grazing land is included, which could be a stretch of grass in an urban area where an itinerant scrap metal dealer tethers his horse.

Worries: The fact that 'worrying' includes attacking or chasing in a manner likely to cause injury, requires no explanation. As far as females are concerned, a pregnant sheep which has been chased by a dog may abort its unborn lamb, a cow may give less milk, or a hen may stop laying (diminution or loss of produce).

The third category of 'worrying' may arise with a dog which is quite docile and which makes no effort to chase after sheep. The sheep, being wary of dogs, may however, panic and run at the sight of a dog running loose in their field, and suffer injury as a result.

Note: that the exception for police dogs and other working dogs relates only to being loose in a field of sheep. A police dog handler will be liable if her dog injures or chases livestock.

5.7.6 *Police Power to Seize Dog*

When a dog is found on land:
  - which appears to a constable to be agricultural land
  - and the officer has reason to believe the dog has been worrying livestock there
  - and no person is present who admits to owning or being in charge of the dog
  - the constable may seize and detain it in order to find out who owns it.

5.7.7 *Search Warrant*

Grounds for issue: If a magistrate is satisfied on information on oath that there are reasonable grounds for believing:
  - that an offence under the Act has been committed and
  - that the dog in respect of which the offence was committed is to be found on specified premises he may issue a warrant.

Powers under the warrant: A constable is authorised to enter the premises specified in the warrant and search them in order to identify the dog.

Explanation: Provision for a warrant arrived in an amendment some 30 years after the Act was first passed, in response to problems which often arose in identifying the dog responsible for injuring a farmer's sheep, or whatever. The typical scenario would have a police officer accompanied by a witness to go to the house where the canine culprit was thought to be. The occupier would be asked to produce his dog, which the witness would then identify or not, as the case may be. (A dog's rights do not extend to be being placed with at least eight others of similar appearance.) If the occupier of the premises refused to produce the dog, the identification evidence would not be forthcoming, which in many cases made a prosecution very difficult. The amendment, providing for a warrant, seeks to overcome such problems.

5.7.8 *The Farmer's Rights*
Animals Act 1971 Section 9

A person may take action to protect livestock from the attentions of a dog and this may result in the dog being killed or injured, e.g. the farmer shoots it. There is a procedure for a person who takes such action to report the matter to the police. He will then have a defence to civil proceedings.

The defence: In civil proceedings for killing or injuring a dog, the defendant will have a defence if he proves:

i)   that he acted for the protection of livestock and was a person entitled to do so; and
ii) that within 48 hours of the incident, he gave notice of the matter to the officer in charge of a police station.

Notice to police: Notice may be given orally or in writing, and the following details should be recorded:

i)   by whom reported;
ii) by whom the killing/injury was done;
iii) when and where it happened;
iv) description of the dog;
v)   whether or not the owner of the dog has been notified;
vi) date and time notice given.

Explanation: The notice has to be given to 'the officer in charge of a police station', so it is not appropriate for the person making the report to stop a constable in the street to tell him about it. There is no bar on reporting the matter by telephone.

No further action is required of the police, once the details have been noted, but the record needs to be kept for production in civil proceedings if required. However, it would be eminently sensible for an entry in the 'Found Dog Register' to be made, cross-referenced to the details in the notice, lest the owner of the dog should enquire whether it has been found.

5.8 **Guard Dogs**
Guard Dogs Act 1975

5.8.1 *Requirement for Control*

a)   A person shall not use or permit the use of a guard dog at any premises unless:
i)   a handler capable of controlling the dog is present on the premises; and
ii) the dog is under the control of the handler at all times while being used as such
 – except when it is so secured that it cannot go freely about the premises.
b)   The handler of a guard dog shall keep the dog under his control at all times while it is being used as a guard dog on premises, except:
i)   when another handler has control of it; or
ii) when it is so secured that it not able to go freely about the premises.

c) A person shall not use or permit the use of a guard dog on premises unless a warning notice, clearly stating that a guard dog is present, is clearly displayed at each entrance to the premises.

5.8.2 *Offence*

A person commits an offence who fails to comply with any of these requirements.

5.8.3 *Explanation*

Dog secured: On first reading of requirement (a), above, it may be difficult to decide whether 'except when it is so secured...' applies only to when the dog is under the control of a handler, or to when a handler is present on the premises, also. Any doubt is clarified by a case decision, that if the dog is secured, there is no need for the handler to be present (*Hobson v Gledhill* (1978)). A judge in the case commented that 'the Act is ambiguous'.

Guard dog: This means a dog being used to protect premises, or property kept in premises, or to protect a person who is guarding the premises or property therein.

Premises: In turn, means land and buildings and parts of buildings, **except**:
    i)   agricultural land;
    ii) land within the curtilage of a dwelling house;
    iii) dwelling houses and...

Agricultural land: This has the same meaning as in relation to dogs worrying livestock *(see paragraph 5.7.5)*, i.e. it includes farm land, grazing land, allotments and orchards.

   Thus, the restrictions on guard dogs do not apply to a dog guarding any dwelling house or any agricultural land.

6 PET ANIMALS

6.1 Pet Shops
Pet Animals Act 1951 Sections 1, 4

No person may keep a pet shop unless it is licensed by the local authority for the area. The council may impose conditions. The purpose of licensing is to secure the welfare of the animals and to prevent spread of disease. Officers of the local authority may enter and inspect the premises of a licensed pet shop. It is an offence to keep a pet shop without a licence.

6.2 Restrictions on Sale of Pet Animals
Pet Animals Act 1951 Sections 2, 3

Sale in street: It is an offence for a person to carry on a business of selling animals as pets, in any street or public place, or from a stall or barrow in a market.

Sale to children: A person commits an offence who sells an animal as a pet to a person whom he has reasonable cause to believe to be under the age of 12 years.

Explanation: The offence of selling to a child under 12 may be committed by any person, anywhere. Sale in a street or market relates only to a person carrying on a business of selling pets.

6.3 Enforcement

There are no police powers under the Act. Any suspected offence should be reported to the local authority.

7 KEEPING DANGEROUS WILD ANIMALS
Dangerous Wild Animals Act 1976

7.1 Licence

Before a person may keep a dangerous wild animal, a licence to do so must be obtained from the local authority. The local authority should not grant a licence unless satisfied that the applicant is a suitable person, the animal will be kept secure, and that it is not against the public interest to grant the licence.

7.2 Dangerous Wild Animal

The legislation applies to animals of species specified in the Act, encompassing not only the more obviously 'dangerous' ones such as lions and bears, but also seals, monkeys, wild goats, etc.

7.3 Enforcement

There are no police powers under the Act. Any suspected offence should be reported to the local authority.

8 STRAYING ANIMALS
Highways Act 1980 Section 155

8.1 Offence

If any horses, cattle, sheep, goats or pigs:
-   are at any time found straying on or lying on or at the side of a highway
-   the person in whose possession they are shall be liable for an offence.

8.2 Exception

This does not apply on part of a highway passing over any common, waste or unenclosed land.

8.3 Liability for Costs

If straying animals are moved to a 'common pound' or to any other place, costs incurred may be recovered as a civil debt from the keeper of the stray animals.

8.4 Explanation

Animal: These provisions apply only to the usual sorts of farm animals. Cats, dogs, etc, are not included.

Impounding strays: Stray animals are a not uncommon source of problems, not only in rural areas, but in suburban areas too. Horses are often involved, and because of their speed, agility and nervousness, can pose a danger to traffic as well as being difficult to catch.

Once upon a time, every area had a 'common pound' with a 'pound keeper' where stray animals could be taken and looked after until claimed. Indeed, it remains an offence to release an animal from the pound without lawful authority or excuse, to deter the animal owner perhaps, who didn't want to pay the charges for his animals having been there.

Police officers dealing with stray animals may be tempted to put them in the nearest convenient field, but this could be unwise – damage may be caused to crops, or animals already there might be exposed to risk of disease. Permission of the owner of the land should be sought first.

Keynote Cases

9.1 *R v Bezzina, R v Codling, R v Elvin* [1994] 3 All ER 964

Problem
Whether a dog being dangerously out of control in a public place, leading to the owner or handler being liable, amounted to an offence of strict liability, or whether it was necessary to show *mens rea*.

Circumstances
The Court of Appeal dealt with three separate cases, each relating to a prosecution for being the owner of a dog which was dangerously out of control in a public place, contrary to Section 3(1) of the Dangerous Dogs Act 1991:

   i) Bezzina had been walking his dog off its lead when it bit a youth; his appeal was based on the contention that the judge was mistaken in having ruled the offence to be one of strict liability.

   ii) Codling was walking her dog on its lead when it bit another dog walker. Her ground for appeal was that there was no evidence that she had reason to believe that her dog might injure anyone.

   iii) Elvin had left two pit bull terriers in a garage, they got out and attacked a man. His ground for appeal was that, for the owner to be liable, it has to be shown that he caused or permitted the dog to be at large.

Legal Points
The court accepted that in criminal law, *mens rea* is an essential ingredient of every offence, **unless** some reason may be found for that not being necessary. Examples of where it is not necessary include matters of public health and safety, where a person who chooses to participate in an activity has an obligation to take all necessary measures to prevent harm to the public. It was clear from the wording of the Act and from that of its long title, that Parliament intended the offence in question to be one of strict liability. In Elvin's case, it was put forward that the injured man had let the dogs loose from the garage in the course of burglary. The court acknowledged that where a third party intervened to set a dog loose, there may well be a problem to be resolved. In this case, the court declined to consider those circumstances, finding that the garage where the dogs had been kept was not properly secure.

Comment
This case settles that there is no need to prove the owner of a dog to be 'blameworthy', e.g. by being negligent, if his dog is dangerously out of control in a public place. For example, if a dog

has never shown any sign of aggression, until the day it retaliates when a child pokes it with a stick, the owner may be liable even though she could not reasonably have foreseen that it would attack anyone.

Chapter 44: Wildlife Protection, Poaching and Fishing

1 INTRODUCTION

1.1 Scope of Legislation

Quite apart from cruel treatment of animals, the law seeks to protect wild animals and certain species of plants, in a series of enactments. These laws cover:
  i)   certain rare species of plants and animals;
  ii) birds and their eggs;
  iii) badgers and deer, these species being specifically catered for;
  iv) poaching laws, aimed not at protecting the animals for their own sake, but so as to ensure that they may be killed only by those authorised to do so;
  v)   fisheries law.

1.2 Close Season

In most cases, the law will prohibit the taking of the animal or plant concerned, then allow limited exceptions. For many species, there is a 'close season' when they are protected against all-comers, and an 'open season', when they may be killed (but only by those authorised to do so).

1.3 Police Powers

Police are given a fair number of powers under the various enactments; the wording of some of these, especially in the more recent legislation, is virtually identical, with power to stop vehicles, search vehicles and occupants, and seize evidence.

2 PROTECTION OF RARE SPECIES
Wildlife and Countryside Act 1981

2.1 Animals

2.1.1 *Protected Species*

Certain rare species of animal are protected and there are police powers to assist in detecting offences. The species concerned are listed in Schedule 5 to the Act, which has been amended by order on a number of occasions. The Schedule lists the species by their scientific (Linnaean) name; the common names include – otter, pine marten, most species of butterfly and moth, various species of bat, red squirrel, various snakes, dormouse, certain beetles, snails, whales, natterjack toad and the wart biter grasshopper ('common' is a relative term!). In case of doubt, refer to the up-to-date list.

2.1.2 *Offences*
Wildlife and Countryside Act 1981 Section 9

A person will commit an offence in relation to an animal of a protected species if she, intentionally:
  i)   kills, injures or takes the animal;
  ii) has possession or control of one, alive or dead;

iii) has possession or control of any part of one or of something derived from one;

iv) sells, offers or exposes for sale, has possession of or transports for the purpose of sale any animal, alive or dead, or any part or anything derived from one;

v) publishes or causes to be published an advertisement likely to be understood as conveying that she buys or sells such things or intends to do so;

vi) damages, destroys or obstructs access to any structure or place used by the animal for shelter or protection, or disturbs the animal while it is occupying a structure or place for that purpose.

2.1.3 *Attempts, etc*

A person will commit an offence who:

i) attempts to commit an offence contrary to Section 9;

ii) for the purposes of committing such an offence, has possession of anything capable of being used for doing so.

2.1.4 *Exceptions*
Wildlife and Countryside Act 1981 Section 10

A person will not commit an offence when:

i) he takes an animal of a protected species if he shows that the animal had been disabled other than by his unlawful act and that he took it solely to tend for it and then release it when it recovered;

ii) he kills an animal and shows that it was so seriously disabled other than by his unlawful act that there was no reasonable chance of its recovering;

iii) his unlawful action was the incidental result of a lawful action and could not reasonably have been avoided;

iv) being an authorised person he kills or injures such an animal and shows that his action was necessary to prevent serious damage to crops, livestock, fish or other property;

v) he is the holder of a licence issued by an authorised body, allowing specific activity, e.g. for purposes of scientific research.

2.1.5 *Explanation*

Offences: The actions which are unlawful cover killing or injuring animals of a protected species, as well as possession or trade in such, dead or alive. Interfering with the animal's nest or other place of shelter, or disturbing the animal in its lair will also amount to an offence.

Injured animal: It is not an offence to take in an injured animal to look after it until it recovers, or to kill one which is so badly injured that it is unlikely to recover. In each case, this is provided the person concerned did not cause the injury in the first place by some unlawful action. A motorist who accidentally runs over a red squirrel and then kills it to relieve its suffering will not be guilty because he did not act unlawfully to injure it.

Incidental to a lawful act: The builders who destroy the roosting site of a protected bat in the course of demolishing an old building will not commit an offence, so long as it is established that this could not be reasonably avoided. One may read of dormice or some other species being 'relocated' in the course of building a new road, this being action to 'reasonably avoid' killing the creatures in the course of road construction.

Authorised person: Only an 'authorised person' may kill protected species to protect crops, livestock, etc. The term includes the owner or occupier of land, persons having hunting, shooting or fishing rights on land, as well as persons having written authority from a local authority or other statutory body.

2.1.6 *Methods of Killing or Taking Wild Animals*
Wildlife and Countryside Act 1981 Section 11

Although the killing or taking of an animal may be lawful in certain circumstances, there are methods of doing so which are prohibited. These include using a live bird or mammal or a sound recording of one as a decoy, using a crossbow or explosives, setting certain types of snare, etc.

These prohibitions are not limited to the species specially protected by the foregoing provisions of the Act; some apply to all wild animals, other methods are prohibited in relation to certain listed species only.

2.2 **Plants**

2.2.1 *Protected Species*
The species of plants protected under this legislation is contained in Schedule 8. However, certain offences relate to **any** wild plant.

2.2.2 *Offences*
Wildlife and Countryside Act 1981 Section 13

The offences correspond closely to those involving protected animals, with terms such as 'kill' and 'injure' suitably adjusted. A person commits an offence who:
  i) intentionally picks, uproots or destroys any wild plant listed in Schedule 8;
  ii) not being an authorised person, intentionally uproots any wild plant **not** included in the Schedule;
  iii) sells, exposes for sale or has possession of or transports for the purpose of sale any wild plant, alive or dead, listed in Schedule 8, or any part of such a plant or anything derived from it;
  iv) publishes or causes to be published any advertisement likely to be understood as conveying that he buys, sells or intends to buy or sell any such protected plant, or part or derivative of one.

2.2.3 *Exception*
A person shall not be guilty of an offence if his unlawful act was incidental to a lawful operation and could not reasonably have been avoided.

2.2.4 *Explanation*
Intentionally: The offences require an element of *mens rea*. A person would not be guilty if he dug up a rare wild plant by accident.

Authorised person ... any wild plant: The term 'authorised person' has the same meaning as in relation to animals, i.e. the occupier of land, etc *(see paragraph 2.1.5)*. Quite apart from specially protected plants, a person who is not the occupier, etc, of land will commit an offence by uprooting **any** wild plant.

This provision is compatible with that in Section 4(3) of the Theft Act 1968, relating to plants growing wild. A person who is not in possession of some land will not commit theft by picking flowers, fruit or foliage **from** a plant growing wild on that land. Picking from a plant is not the same as uprooting the plant, the latter would not come within the exception to theft. In practice, it may be easier to prove the wildlife protection offence of intentionally uprooting, than to prove the several elements of theft.

Sale, advertising, etc: These offences correspond to those relating to protected species of animals.

Lawful operations: A person will not commit an offence who uproots, etc, a plant in the course of some lawful activity, so long as it is shown that the damage to the plant could not reasonably have been avoided. This corresponds precisely to the provision relating to animals *(see paragraph 2.1.5).*

2.3 **Introduction of New Species**
Wildlife and Countryside Act 1981 Section 14

2.3.1 *Animals*
A person commits an offence who:
- releases or allows to escape into the wild
- any animal which is not ordinarily resident in, or a regular visitor to Great Britain
- or which is of a species listed in (Schedule 9 to) the Act.

2.3.2 *Plants*
A person commits an offence who:
- plants or otherwise causes to grow in the wild
- any plant of a species listed (in Schedule 9 to) the Act.

2.3.3 *Defence*
A person shall have a defence if he proves that he took all reasonable steps and exercised all due diligence to avoid committing the offence.

2.3.4 *Explanation*
It is very often the case that a 'foreign' species of plant or animal introduced into this country has proved at best a 'pest' or at worst, has had serious effects on existing wildlife. It is not just a deliberate introduction which will amount to an offence, to allow an animal to escape, or to 'cause a plant to grow' will be sufficient.

These offences are ones to which police powers, with or without warrant, apply *(see paragraph 2.4).*

2.4 **Police Powers**
Wildlife and Countryside Act 1981 Section 19

2.4.1 *Without Warrant*
A constable who has reasonable cause to suspect that a person is committing or has committed an offence under this part of the Act may without warrant:
- i) stop and search that person;
- ii) search and examine anything he is then using or has in his possession;
- iii) seize and detain for the purposes of proceedings anything which may be evidence of such an offence or which may be liable to be forfeited *(see paragraph 2.6);*

iv) enter any land other than a dwelling house in order to exercise these powers, or to arrest a person for an offence. *(Note: The power to arrest would be the general arrest power under Section 25 of the Police and Criminal Evidence Act 1984, subject to the necessary conditions being satisfied.)*

2.4.2 *Search Warrant*
Grounds for issue: A magistrate may issue a warrant to a constable if satisfied upon information on oath that an offence (under the foregoing provisions of the Act) has been committed and that evidence of the offence may be found on certain premises.

Police powers: A constable may enter the premises and there search for the purpose of obtaining that evidence.

2.5 **Prosecution – Miscellaneous Provisions**
Wildlife and Countryside Act 1981 Section 20

The following may assist the prosecution when proceedings are taken for an offence:
  i) the animal or plant involved is presumed to have been a wild animal or plant, unless the contrary is proved;
  ii) proceedings for an offence of killing or taking a wild animal, or of picking, uprooting or destroying a wild plant, may be started within six months of the date on which sufficient evidence to warrant proceedings came to the knowledge of the prosecutor. (The usual time limitation on proceedings for a summary offence is six months from the date the offence was committed.)

2.6 **Forfeiture**
Wildlife and Countryside Act 1981 Section 21

The court before which a person is convicted of an offence:
  i) **Must** order the forfeiture of any animal, plant, etc, in respect of which the offence was committed.
  ii) **May** order the forfeiture of any vehicle, animal, weapon or other thing used to commit the offence.

Note: When exercising power to stop and search without warrant, a constable may seize any item liable to forfeiture.

3 PROTECTION OF BIRDS

3.1 **Extent of Protection**
Almost all wild birds are protected to a greater or lesser extent, along with their eggs and nests. The sight of pheasant, wild duck and other birds hanging up in a butcher's shop should serve as a reminder that not all species enjoy the same level of protection. Various Schedules to the Act list birds which may be killed outside their 'close season', those the killing of which will attract a higher penalty, etc.

3.2 **Offences**
Wildlife and Countryside Act 1981 Section 1

3.2.1 *All Birds*
It is an offence for any person – intentionally:
- i) to kill, injure or take any wild bird;
- ii) to take or destroy the egg of any wild bird;
- iii) to take, damage or destroy a wild bird's nest while it is in use or being built;
- iv) to have possession or control of any wild bird, dead or alive, any wild bird's egg, or part of such bird or egg, or of anything derived from such.

3.2.2 *Specially Protected Birds*
Birds listed in Schedule 1 are afforded additional protection in that:
- i) it is an offence for any person intentionally to disturb such a bird while building a nest or while it is in, on or near a nest containing an egg or young, or to disturb the dependant young of such a bird;
- ii) the offences detailed in the preceding paragraph carry a higher penalty if the bird concerned is of a species listed in Schedule 1.

3.2.3 *Sale and Advertising*
Wildlife and Countryside Act 1981 Section 6

There is a prohibition on having certain live wild birds for sale, or offering or exposing them for sale. In respect of birds on a different list, it is an offence to possess, offer for sale, etc, a dead wild bird.

3.3 **Exceptions and Licences**
Wildlife and Countryside Act 1981 Sections 2 and 16

3.3.1 *Lawful Killing*
There are various exceptions to the general prohibition on killing or taking wild birds, dependent on the species of bird, who is killing it and when. Licences may be granted to allow activities relating to scientific research, conservation, and a wide range of other actions which otherwise would be unlawful.

3.3.2 *Open Season*
It is no offence for any person to take or kill, attempt to take or kill, or injure during an attempt to do so, any wild bird of a specified sort (specified in Schedule 2, Part I) outside the close season for that bird.

3.4 **Defences**
Wildlife and Countryside Act 1981 Section 4

The following will be among defences to a charge of taking, killing, etc any wild bird, egg, etc:
- i) certain acts done under statutory provisions relating to agriculture or animal health;
- ii) for an authorised person to a charge of taking, killing, injuring or so attempting, any wild bird (other than one listed in Schedule 1), if he shows that it was necessary to do so to preserve public health, air safety, or prevent damage to crops, livestock, fisheries or inland waters;

iii) for any person to a charge of taking or attempting to take any wild bird, if he shows that the bird was disabled (other than by his unlawful act) and that the purpose of taking it was to tend it and then to release when it had recovered;

iv) similarly to (iii), it will be a defence to a charge of killing a wild bird to show that it was so severely injured (other than by his unlawful act) that there was no reasonable chance of its recovering;

v) on a charge of any unlawful act relating to wild birds, to show that the act was the incidental result of a lawful operation and could not reasonably have been avoided.

3.5 Explanation

Wild bird: Generally, a wild bird is one which ordinarily is a resident or a visitor to this country in the wild state. Domestic fowl are excluded as are – more significantly – game birds such as pheasant, partridge, grouse, etc.

Nest: Once a bird starts to build its nest, that nest is protected for so long as it is in use. The nest will cease to be protected once the bird has finished with it, when the young have fledged.

Close season: For certain species, a period is designated – the close season – during which it is not lawful to take, kill, etc, these birds. This is so that the species may breed and raise young free from the attentions of 'hunters'. The start and finish dates for close seasons vary according to species.

Exceptions: Among the exceptions allowing an authorised person to take or kill a wild bird are – public health, e.g. the local authority may try to keep down numbers of wild pigeons or starlings in a town centre – air safety, which caters for dealing with large birds at airports. Note that specially protected birds, listed in Schedule 1, may not be lawfully killed for these reasons.

Defences: Defences apply in relation to ill or injured birds, and to the unavoidable consequences of otherwise lawful actions, as they do to protected plants and animals (see paragraphs 2.1.4, 2.2.3).

3.6 Miscellaneous Provisions

3.6.1 Special Protection
Areas may be designated in which wild birds enjoy special levels of protection (Section 3).

3.6.2 Methods of Taking Birds
Various methods of taking or killing those wild birds which may be lawfully taken or killed, are banned. These include use of snares, hooks and lines, bird-lime, crossbows and bows, etc (Section 5).

3.6.3 Registration of Captive Birds
A person who keeps captive a bird of certain species (listed in Schedule 4) must register that fact in accordance with regulations. The measures are aimed at preventing the young of certain species, for example, birds of prey, being taken from the wild; only those born in captivity may be kept (Section 7).

3.6.4 Welfare of Captive Birds
A captive bird must be kept in a receptacle which is large enough to allow the bird to stretch its

wings freely. There are exceptions to this requirement, such as when the bird is being transported (Section 8(1), (2)).

3.6.5 *Shooting of Captive Birds*

It is unlawful to release captive birds for them to be shot immediately upon being released. Any person who organises, assists or takes part in an event of this nature will commit an offence, as will the owner or occupier of land who allows her land to be used for this purpose (Section 8(3)).

3.7 **Police Powers**

Police powers with and without warrant, apply in relation to wild birds as they do to protected species of plants and animals *(see paragraph 2.4)*.

3.8 **Prosecution and Forfeiture**

Provisions relating to the prosecution of offences, and courts' powers to order forfeiture of articles associated with offences, apply in relation to wild birds as they do to protected species of plants and animals *(see paragraphs 2.5 and 2.6)*.

4 **PROTECTION OF BADGERS**
Protection of Badgers Act 1992

4.1 **Purpose of Legislation**

The badger has over the centuries been subjected to 'badger baiting', by being dug out of the ground and having dogs set upon them, as a form of 'sport'. Now comparatively rare in many parts of the country, it is protected by its very own legislation.

4.2 **Offences, Defences, Exemptions**

4.2.1 *Kill, Injure, etc*
Protection of Badgers Act 1992 Section 1

1: It is an offence to wilfully kill, injure or take any badger or attempt to do so.

   Evidence: In proceedings, if there is evidence from which it could reasonably be concluded that at the material time the accused was attempting to kill, injure or take a badger, he shall be presumed to have been attempting to do so unless the contrary is shown.

   Exceptions: Action taken which the accused shows was necessary to prevent serious damage to land, crops, poultry or other property. However, this will not apply if it is shown that the accused could have applied for a licence to take badgers (or that an application for a licence had been turned down) (Section 7).

2: It is an offence to have possession or control of any dead badger, part of one, or anything derived from same.

   Defence: A person will have a defence if he shows that the badger had not been killed, or had not been killed unlawfully. It will be a further defence to show that the badger, etc, had been sold (to her or to someone else) and the buyer at the time of buying it had no reason to believe that the badger had been unlawfully killed.

Police power: If a person is found committing any of the offences under this Section on any land, any constable (or the owner or occupier of the land, or his employee) may require that person forthwith:

- to quit the land; and
- to give his name and address.

Failure to comply with either requirement is an offence.

4.2.2 *Explanation*

Evidence: If a person is doing something which may reasonably be seen as attempting to take a badger, the burden of proof switches to the defence to show that he was not doing so.

Exception: If there is time to apply for a licence but the accused has not done so (or if an application for a licence has been turned down) he will not escape liability on the grounds that he was seeking to protect crops, etc.

Part of, derived from: It is not only possession of a whole badger which is unlawful. Having part of one, such as a 'lucky' badger's foot, or of something derived from one, such as a brush made from badger bristles, may also give rise to an offence.

Unlawful possession: If a person is in possession of a badger which has not been killed, e.g. it died of natural causes, or if its killing did not amount to an offence under this Act or under the Badgers Act 1973, an offence of unlawful possession will not be committed. For example, a stuffed badger which last drew breath 50 years ago will not have been killed contrary to the 1973 Act, so it is not unlawful to have it.

It will be a further defence to show that the badger (or anything derived from a badger) had been bought by someone who had no reason to believe that it had been unlawfully killed.

4.2.3 *Cruel Treatment*
Protection of Badgers Act 1992 Section 2

A person commits an offence if he:
  i)   cruelly ill-treats a badger;
  ii) uses any badger tongs in the course of killing or taking a badger or attempting to do so;
  iii) unlawfully digs for any badger;
  iv) uses for the purpose of killing a badger, a firearm less powerful than certain specified limits.

Evidence: In proceedings for an offence of unlawfully digging for a badger, if there is evidence from which it could reasonably be concluded that at the material time the accused was digging for a badger, he shall be presumed to have been doing so unless the contrary is shown.

4.2.4 *Explanation*

Cruel treatment: It is now an offence to ill-treat any wild mammal (Wild Mammals (Protection) Act 1996 – *see Chapter 43*) but an ingredient of an offence under that Act is an intention to cause unnecessary suffering. The offence of ill-treating a badger continues to have relevance, where an intention to cause suffering cannot be proved.

Tongs: Badger tongs are long handled implements which enable the 'sportsman', having dug down into the badger's place of refuge, to grab hold of the animal without risk of being bitten.

Dig: Digging to get to a badger which has taken refuge underground is an offence. If a person is doing something which may reasonably be supposed to be digging for a badger, the burden of proof shifts to the defence to show that he was not doing so. Without this provision it could be very difficult to prove the offence, with stories being put forward such as, 'I was digging for worms to go fishing', 'I am an archaeologist'.

Firearm: If a firearm is to be used to kill a badger then it must be of a specified minimum gauge or power. This reflects the fact that a badger is quite a large and powerful animal; seeking to kill it with a firearm of insufficient power could result in unnecessary suffering.

4.2.5 *Interfering with Badger Setts*
Protection of Badgers Act 1992 Section 3

A person commits an offence if, otherwise than is lawful under the Act, he intentionally or recklessly:
   i) damages a badger sett or any part of it;
   ii) destroys a badger sett;
   iii) obstructs access to the sett, or to any of its entrances;
   iv) causes a dog to go into the sett;
   v) disturbs a badger when it is occupying a sett.

4.2.6 *Defences*
Protection of Badgers Act 1992 Section 8

The following will amount to defences:
   a) The accused shows that his action was necessary to prevent serious damage to land, crops, poultry or other property. However, this will not apply if it is shown that the accused could have applied for a licence to take badgers (or that an application for a licence had been turned down).
   b) Damaging a sett, obstructing it or disturbing a badger in it shall not be unlawful if the accused shows that his action was incidental to some lawful activity and could not reasonably have been avoided.
   c) Certain actions taken in connection with fox hunting shall afford a defence, so long as materials used to block entrances are removed afterwards. The hunt concerned must keep a register of persons authorised to carry out this activity.

4.2.7 *Explanation*
Sett: A badger's home, or sett, is usually a complex of underground tunnels with several entrances. However to avoid doubt the term is defined in the Act as – any structure or place which displays signs indicating current use by a badger.

Once a family of badgers have given up using a particular den, it will no longer be a 'badger's sett' for the purposes of the Act.

Protection of crops, etc: The defence that action was taken to protect crops, etc, will not apply if there was sufficient time to apply for a licence (or if an application for one had been turned down).

Lawful operation: The defence that a sett was damaged, obstructed, etc, as incidental to some lawful activity, such as road building, will hold only if it is shown that the damage to the sett could not reasonably have been avoided.

Fox hunting: Foxes have been known to take refuge in holes in the ground, rather than entering into the sporting spirit of the hunt by giving the hounds a good run. To prevent this, persons connected with a recognised hunt may lawfully obstruct entrances to a sett. This activity may be carried out only by authorised persons, subject to conditions.

4.2.8 *Sell or Possess a Live Badger*
Protection of Badgers Act 1992 Section 4

A person commits an offence if she:
   i) sells or offers for sale a live badger;
   ii) has a live badger in her possession or control.

4.2.9 *Exceptions (Section 9)*
   a) The badger is in her possession or control in the course of her business as a carrier.
   b) The animal has been disabled, other than by her action, it was taken solely for the purpose of tending it and it is necessary for her to have it for that purpose.

4.2.10 *Explanation*
Carrier: ParcelForce may not deal with many live badgers, but the Act does allow for this should the occasion arise.

Injured animal: A person may have possession of a live badger without committing an offence if it is injured and being looked after. This is subject to the provisos – that the injury was not caused by that person – and that it is necessary to be looking after it. The fact that a badger has some minor injury will not necessarily be a reason for a person keeping it, if it could recover just as well left to its own devices.

4.2.11 *Marking or Ringing*
Protection of Badgers Act 1992 Section 5

A person commits an offence if he marks, rings, tags or fixes a marking device to a badger, otherwise than in accordance with a licence.

4.2.12 *General Exceptions*
Protection of Badgers Act 1992 Section 6

A person will not commit an offence by reason of action taken for any of the following purposes:
   a) taking or attempting to take a badger which has been disabled (other than by the accused's action) solely for the purpose of tending it;
   b) the 'mercy' killing or attempted killing of a badger which appears to be so seriously injured or in such condition that it ought to be killed;
   c) the unavoidable killing or injuring of a badger as an incidental result of some lawful action.

4.3 Licences
Protection of Badgers Act 1992 Section 10

Licences may be granted to authorise taking, killing, keeping, etc, badgers for scientific purposes, for conservation and for a variety of other purposes.

4.4 Police Powers
Protection of Badgers Act 1992 Section 11

When a constable has reasonable grounds to suspect:
 – that a person is committing an offence under the Act
 – or has committed an offence under this Act or under the Badgers Act 1973
 – and that evidence of the offence is to be found on that person or on any vehicle or article he may have with him
 – the constable may without warrant:
   i)   stop and search that person;
   ii) search any vehicle or article he has with him;
   iii) seize and detain for the purposes of proceedings anything which may be evidence;
   iv) seize and detain anything which may be liable to forfeiture *(see paragraph 4.5)*.

4.4.1 *Explanation*
Badgers Act 1973: The 1973 Act was superseded by the 1992 Act but may still have relevance, e.g. a person killed a badger before 1992, thus committing an offence under the 1973 Act. The offence comes to light when a second person is found in possession of the stuffed body of the badger.

4.5 Forfeiture
Protection of Badgers Act 1992 Section 12

When a person is convicted of an offence under the Act, the court:
 – **shall** order forfeiture of any badger or badger's skin to which the offence relates;
 – and **may** order forfeiture of any weapon or article relating to the commission of the offence.

4.6 Offence Involving a Dog
Protection of Badgers Act 1992 Section 13

4.6.1 *Court Order*
When a person is convicted of an offence under Section 1, 2 or 3 (taking, killing, cruelty, interfering with a sett, etc) and a dog was used or was present at the time, the court may, in addition to any other punishment, make either or both of the following orders:
 i) an order for the destruction or disposal of the dog;
 ii) an order disqualifying the offender from having custody of a dog for a specified period.

4.6.2 *Offences*
The person against whom an order is made will commit an offence by failing to hand a dog over for destruction or disposal, or by having custody of a dog during the period when an order prohibits him from having one.

5 POACHING/GAME LAWS

5.1 Introduction

5.1.1 *Legislation*
Whereas legislation such as the Badgers Act is aimed at protecting wildlife, game laws seek to protect the rights of certain people to shoot or otherwise kill certain (edible) birds and

mammals. Much of the legislation has survived with little alteration since the first half of the 19th Century, so the language used is fairly archaic.

5.1.2 *Game*

What is meant by 'game' varies depending on the Act concerned. In the Night Poaching Act 1828, the term means hares, pheasant, partridge, grouse, heath or moor game, black game and bustards.

Whatever the bustard population may have been in 1828, the several species of bustard are not found in Britain on anything other than a 'rare visitor' basis. Parliament must have woken up to this fact, because the definition of game in the Game Act 1831 omits bustard from the list. However, as recently as 1960 bustards were reinstated as 'game', for whatever reason.

Later legislation gives various other definitions, but anything with fur or feathers which is reasonably tasty (but not too small – in this country it is not considered 'sporting' to shoot songbirds or grey squirrels, for example) is likely to be classed as fair game in some Act or other. The largest game of all, deer, is subject of separate legislation.

5.2 **Poaching by Day**

5.2.1 *Offences*
Game Act 1831 Sections 30, 32

There are three offences involving trespassing in pursuit of game, in ascending order of seriousness (as measured by the maximum fine):
  i)   A person commits an offence by trespassing in the daytime on any land in pursuit of game, woodcock, snipe or rabbits.
  ii) A person commits an offence if he is one of five or more persons who together trespass on land in the daytime in pursuit of game, woodcock, snipe or rabbits.
  iii) If five or more persons trespass in pursuit of game, etc, and any one of them is armed with a gun, then an offence will be committed by any one of them who uses violence, intimidation or menace in seeking to prevent some authorised person from exercising powers (to require them to leave, give name, etc) in respect of them.

5.2.2 *Exceptions*
Game Act 1831 Section 35

The following will not be liable for an offence:
  – anyone engaged in hunting with hounds who is in fresh pursuit of deer, hare or fox, started on other land;
  – lawfully appointed gamekeepers.

5.2.3 *Powers of Police and Others*
Game Act 1831 Sections 31, 31A

Who may exercise powers: The powers may be exercised by:
  – the occupier of the land and any person having a right to take game on the land;
  – any gamekeeper or employee of either of the aforesaid, or any other person authorised by them.

First stage: Any person found committing the offence of trespassing in pursuit of game

may be required:
- – to give his name and address; and
- – forthwith to quit the land;
- – hand over any game in his possession which appears to have been recently killed. If the person refuses to hand over such game, it may be seized from him (Section 36).

Second stage: A person who refuses to give his name and address, or who gives false details, or who wilfully continues on the land or returns to it, may be arrested.

5.2.4 Police Powers

Arrest: A constable has power at the 'first stage' only – to require a trespasser to quit the land and to give his name and address. A constable cannot exercise the subsequent power to arrest. However, the general power to arrest (Police and Criminal Evidence Act 1984) may well be available when, for example, a trespasser fails to give his name and address.

Search after arrest: Where a constable does arrest someone for one of these offences, under the PACE general power, any constable who made the arrest or was present, may search the arrested person and seize any game, rabbits, guns, snares, etc, Any items so seized may be forfeited by the court before whom the person is later convicted of a poaching offence, whether or not the item in question is connected with the offence for which the defendant is convicted (Section 4, Game Laws (Amendment) Act 1960).

Entry to land: A constable who has reasonable cause to suspect that a person is committing one of these offences on any land may enter the land for the purposes of:
- i)   exercising the 'first stage' power to require the suspect's name and address;
- ii) exercising the general power of arrest under Section 25, Police and Criminal Evidence Act 1984.

The power to enter land does not extend to land occupied by the Defence Ministry or certain other organisations (Section 2, Game Laws (Amendment) Act 1960).

5.2.5 *Explanation*

Daytime: The offences may be committed during the period from one hour before sunrise to one hour after sunset.

Trespasser: The Act specifically provides that permission from the occupier of the land shall **not** amount to a defence to 'trespass' in a case where the landlord or some other person has the right to kill game there. This measure appears to have been designed to keep the lower orders in their proper place – just because someone rents a field from the landowner does not mean he may allow his friends to hunt for rabbits there.

Action after arrest: If someone is arrested, e.g. for failing to give his name and address, he must then be brought before a magistrate within 12 hours; otherwise, he must be released, proceedings thereafter being by summons or warrant.

5.2.6 *Forfeiture of Vehicle*
Game Laws (Amendment) Act 1960 Section 4A

When a person is convicted of the offence of poaching in the company of others (i.e. being one of five or more), the court before which he is convicted may order the forfeiture of any vehicle:
- – belonging to him, or in his possession or under his control at the 'relevant time'

   — which the court is satisfied was used for committing or facilitating the commission of
   the offence.

5.2.7 *Explanation*

Relevant time: This means the time the vehicle was used to commit the offence or facilitate
its commission, **or** the time the summons was issued in respect of the offence.

Court order: This may be in addition to any other order or sentence the court may impose.
A vehicle which is forfeited shall be taken into police possession, when it is then subject to
the usual procedures for persons being able to lodge a claim, its being disposed of in due
course, etc.

5.3 Poaching at Night

5.3.1 *Offences*
Night Poaching Act 1828 Sections 1, 2, 9

A person will commit an offence if, by night:
    i) he unlawfully takes or destroys game or rabbits on any land;
    ii) unlawfully enters or is on any land with any gun, net or other device, for the purpose
        of taking or destroying game;
    iii) being one of three or more persons together unlawfully on land for the purpose of
        taking or destroying game or rabbits there, and any one of them is armed with a
        firearm, crossbow or offensive weapon;
    iv) having committed one of the above offences, assaults or offers any violence with any
        firearm, crossbow or offensive weapon towards any person authorised to arrest him.

5.3.2 *Explanation*

Night: This means the period from one hour after sunset to one hour before sunrise, which is
compatible with the meaning of 'day' in the 1831 Act.

Land: The offences may be committed on land, open or enclosed. The meaning of land was
extended by the Night Poaching Act 1844 to include any public road, highway or path, along
with gateways and entrances leading from land to roads. Having made it unlawful in 1828 for
hungry peasants to sneak onto land to take a rabbit or two, the landowners a few years later
closed the loophole which allowed for the game and rabbits to be taken on roads and highways.

5.3.3 *Power to Arrest*
Night Poaching Act 1828 Section 2

Who may exercise power: The power to arrest may be exercised by:
   — the owner or occupier of the land, or the lord of the manor;
   — a gamekeeper or employee of any of the aforesaid;
   — any person assisting the gamekeeper or employee.

*Note: Since the offence may be committed on roads and highways, when a person does commit the
offence on a road for example, the power to arrest is given to the owners, etc of land adjoining either
side of that road.*

Who may be arrested: Any person committing an offence of taking or destroying game or of
being on land for that purpose, either on that land, or anywhere else if there is a pursuit.

Action after arrest: The person making the arrest is required to hand the arrested person over to a 'peace officer' in order that he may then be taken before 'two justices'. Translating this into up-to-date terms, the person making the arrest should hand the offender over to the police in order that he may appear in a magistrates' court.

5.3.4 *Power to Seize Game*

The power to seize game may be exercised in respect of a person trespassing on land by night as well as by day *(see paragraph 5.2.3)*.

5.3.5 *Police Powers of Arrest and Search*

The police are given no specific power to arrest for these offences, but the general power to arrest under Section 25, Police and Criminal Evidence Act 1984 may be used in appropriate cases. If an arrest is made, any constable present at the arrest has a power to search for and seize game or poaching equipment. Items seized may then be ordered to be forfeited by a court before whom the arrested person is convicted of one of these offences, whether or not the item to be forfeited is connected with the offence for which the defendant is convicted (Section 4, Game Laws (Amendment) Act 1960).

Entry to land: The police power to enter land to carry out an arrest applies to these offences as it does to daytime poaching *(see paragraph 5.2.3)*.

5.4 **Possession of Game in Public Places**
Poaching Prevention Act 1862

5.4.1 *Purpose of this Act*

Earlier legislation catered for persons found on land by day or night but by the middle of the 19th Century police forces were well established, so this Act gives constables powers to deal with persons making their way home after a poaching expedition.

5.4.2 *Police Powers*
Poaching Prevention Act 1862 Section 2

A constable may:
   - in any highway, street or public place
   - search any person whom he has good cause to suspect
   - of coming from land where he has been unlawfully in pursuit of game (or other person aiding and abetting such) and of being in possession of any game unlawfully obtained, or of any gun, part of a gun, ammunition, nets, traps, snares or other devices used for killing or taking game
   - and the constable may also stop and search any cart or conveyance in which he has good reason to suspect such game, gun or device may be found, and may search anything carried by that person.

   If any such game, gun, device, etc, is found the constable may seize it.

5.4.3 *Offence*
Poaching Prevention Act 1862 Section 2

If anything is found as a result of a search, which is shown to be game unlawfully taken, or to be a gun or other article used in killing or taking game, the person concerned shall be liable to a fine.

5.4.4 *Explanation*

Grounds for suspicion: The fact that a person is a habitual poacher is not sufficient to afford grounds to stop and search him. Under the provisions of Code A of the PACE Codes of Practice, reasonable suspicion cannot be based on personal factors, such as previous convictions, alone (Code A, Section 1.7).

Coming from ... where he has been: A constable may stop and search a person whom she has reason to suspect has committed one of the offences relating to daytime or night-time poaching. The power does not extend to a person who may be on his way to do a spot of poaching, i.e. it is not a 'going equipped' or 'carrying with intent' provision.

Game: The term is similar in meaning to that in the earlier legislation – including hare, pheasant, partridge, grouse – but extends to woodcock, snipe, rabbits and the eggs of pheasant, partridge and grouse.

Seizure of articles: When police seize game, firearms or poaching equipment, a court before whom the person concerned is convicted of an offence may order the forfeiture of the seized items, whether or not the items were involved in the offence of which he is convicted.

6 **PROTECTION OF DEER**
Deer Act 1991

6.1 **Extent of Protection**

6.1.1 *Deer*
The legislation applies to deer of any species, wild or tame. There are several native British species – red, roe, fallow – and others which were brought in to ornament the parks of country houses and now breed in the wild, e.g. the muntjack. Some are now farmed for their meat. The term 'deer' also includes the carcase or part of a dead deer.

6.1.2 *Close Season*
There are different close seasons for different species. Poaching, i.e. unauthorised taking, is unlawful at any time; certain persons are authorised to take or kill deer outside the close season; in exceptional cases, deer may be killed during the close season.

6.2 **Poaching Offences**
Deer Act 1991 Section 1

6.2.1 *Trespass with Intent*
A person commits an offence who:
- enters any land without the consent of the owner or occupier, or other lawful authority
- in search or in pursuit of deer
- intending to take, kill or injure it.

6.2.2 *Taking or Chasing, etc*
A person commits an offence who, while on any land:
- and without the consent of the owner or occupier or other lawful authority
- intentionally takes, kills or injures any deer, or attempts to do so;
- searches for or pursues a deer with the intention of taking, killing or injuring it;
- removes the carcase of any deer.

6.2.3 *Defence*

A person will not be guilty of any of these offences if he acted in the belief:
- that he would have had the consent of the owner or occupier of the land had that person known of his action and the circumstances of it; or
- that he had some other lawful authority for his action.

6.2.4 *Powers of Authorised Person*

If an authorised person has reasonable cause to believe that someone is committing one of these offences, she may require that person:
- to give his full name and address; and
- to quit that land forthwith.

Failure to comply with such a requirement is an offence.

6.2.5 *Explanation*

Trespass: The first offence involves being on land without proper authority, intending to take, etc, any deer. To commit offences of actually taking, killing, pursuing etc, the offender need not necessarily be a trespasser. He could be on land quite lawfully; it is the taking or killing, etc, which is done without authority.

Authorised person: For the purposes of requiring a suspected poacher to give his details and leave, the term includes the owner or occupier of the land, any person authorised by the owner or occupier, or any person who has rights to take or kill deer on that land.

6.3 **Deer Not be Killed or Taken at Night**
Deer Act 1991 Section 3

6.3.1 *Offence*

A person will commit an offence if he takes or intentionally kills any deer during the period from one hour after sunset to one hour before sunrise.

6.3.2 *Exceptions*
Deer Act 1991 Sections 6, 8

No offence is committed of taking or killing a deer at night if the action is taken:
- to prevent suffering in the case of an injured or diseased animal;
- to prevent damage by pests under provisions relating to agriculture;
- under a licence issued under provisions relating to conservation.

6.3.3 *Explanation*

Intentionally: An offence arises from the intentional killing of a deer. Accidental killing, e.g. as a result of a collision with a motor vehicle, would not amount to an offence.

6.4 **Close Season**
Deer Act 1991 Section 2

6.4.1 *Offence*

It is an offence to take or intentionally kill a deer during the close season for that species.

6.4.2 *Exceptions*
A person will not be liable for an offence in respect of:
- the killing of farmed deer, by the keeper of those deer, his employee or agent;
- the shooting of deer on cultivated land, pasture or enclosed woodland, provided this is done by a specified class of person;
- anything which is an exception to taking or killing at night (*see paragraph 6.3.2*).

6.4.3 *Explanation*
Farmed deer: To amount to 'farmed', the animals must be kept in an enclosure and bear distinctive markings, identifying their owner.

Cultivated land: The exception in relation to cultivated land and enclosed woodland applies only if there is reason to believe that the action taken is necessary to prevent further serious damage to crops, timber, etc. The exception applies only to the occupier of the land, his family, employees and other authorised persons.

6.5 **Prohibited Weapons and Instruments**
Deer Act 1991 Sections 4, 5

6.5.1 *Offences*
The following will amount to an offence:
i) use for the purpose of killing or taking deer any trap, net, snare, or poisoned or stupefying bait;
ii) set any trap, snare, bait of such a nature and so placed as to be calculated to injure any deer coming in contact with it;
iii) use for the purpose of killing or taking deer any arrow, spear or similar missile, or any firearm of a specified type, or any missile (whether discharged from a firearm or not) carrying a poison or drug;
iv) use a mechanically-propelled vehicle for the purpose of driving deer;
v) shoot at deer from any mechanically-propelled vehicle;
vi) for the purpose of committing one of the foregoing offences, or an offence under Section 2, have possession of poisoned or stupefying bait, spear or similar missile or any drugged missile, or any firearm or ammunition.

6.5.2 *Exception*
The following will amount to exceptions:
i) anything which would otherwise amount to one of these offences will not be unlawful if it is done in relation to deer kept on enclosed land, with the written authority of the occupier of that land;
ii) using certain prohibited means to prevent suffering of an ill or injured deer;
iii) where there is a licence in force relating to the action taken.

6.5.3 *Explanation*
Specified firearm: This provision is intended to ensure that a firearm used to shoot deer is sufficiently powerful. Details are contained in a Schedule to the Act.

Possession: Possession of any of the prohibited articles, such as drugged bait, if for the purpose of taking or killing deer, will amount to an offence, as will possession of **any** firearm or ammunition, not merely the prohibited sort.

Enclosed herd: Where deer are usually kept in an enclosure, the occupier of the land may give written authority for otherwise unlawful means to be used to kill them.

6.6 Dealing in Venison
Deer Act 1991 Section 10

It is an offence for any person to deal in (i.e. buy, sell, offer to buy or sell, etc) venison, knowing or believing it to have come from a deer which has been unlawfully taken or killed.

6.7 Police Powers
Deer Act 1991 Section 12

6.7.1 *Arrest*
There is no power of arrest provided by the Act; none of the offences are arrestable ones. However, there may be circumstances where the general power of arrest under Section 25, Police and Criminal Evidence Act 1984 may be applied. The legislation caters for this eventuality by providing a power to enter land to carry out an arrest.

6.7.2 *Stop and Search*
A constable may, without warrant, when she has reason to suspect that a person is committing or has committed any offence against the Act:
  i) stop and search that person if she has reason to suspect that evidence of the offence may be found on him;
  ii) search and examine any vehicle, animal, weapon or other thing which the person has with him, on which the officer has reason to suspect evidence of the offence may be found;
  iii) seize and detain for the purpose of proceedings under the Act, anything which is evidence of the commission of an offence;
  iv) seize and detain anything which may be liable to forfeiture *(see below)*.

6.7.3 *Enter Land*
A constable may enter any land other than a dwelling house:
  – to carry out her powers to stop and search;
  – to arrest a person for an offence under the Act, using the PACE general power to arrest.

6.7.4 *Sale of Items Seized*
A constable may sell any deer or venison seized under the provisions of this Section. The proceeds of the sale may be detained and/or forfeited in the same manner as that which was sold.

Note: Police may not be held liable for failure to exercise the power to sell deer or venison.

6.8 Forfeiture
Deer Act 1991 Section 13

When a person is convicted of an offence under the Act, the court may order forfeiture of:
  – any deer or venison in respect of which the offence was committed, or which was found in the defendant's possession;

- any vehicle, animal, weapon or other thing used to commit the offence or which was capable of being used to take, kill or injure deer and which was found in the defendant's possession.

Under powers to stop and search, a constable has power to seize any item which is liable to forfeiture.

7 FISH
Salmon and Freshwater Fisheries Act 1975

7.1 Extent of Protection
The law is aimed at regulating fishing, prohibiting certain methods of taking fish, and protecting fishing rights. All freshwater fish, together with salmon, trout and eels (the latter three being found in salt and fresh water) are protected. The body primarily responsible for regulating fishing and enforcing the legislation is the Environment Agency.

7.2 Regulation of Fishing
Salmon and Freshwater Fisheries Act 1975 Sections 25 – 28

7.2.1 *Fishing Licence*
Before a person may fish, he must obtain a fishing licence. The licence will authorise him to fish for certain types of fish, using specified methods. An individual or organisation having exclusive rights to fish on a stretch of water may obtain a general licence; any person authorised in writing by the licence holder will then be entitled to fish there.

It is an offence for a person to fish without a licence, or other than in accordance with the terms of a licence.

7.2.2 *Production of Licence*
A constable or a water bailiff may require:
i) a person who is fishing;
ii) a person reasonably suspected of being about to fish;
iii) a person reasonably suspected of having fished in the last half hour;
to produce his fishing licence (or other authority to fish) and to state his name and address.

This power may also be exercised by anyone who himself holds a fishing licence for the area. He must produce his own licence as proof of his right to exercise the power.

7.2.3 *Failure to Produce*
A person commits an offence if he fails to produce his licence or other authority, or to give his name and address, when required. However, he will not be guilty of failing to produce if he produces the licence or other authority within seven days at an office of the Environment Agency.

7.2.4 *Explanation*
Effect of licence: A fishing licence is required for fishing in any water, whether the water is on private or public land, whether or not there are private fishing rights on that water. The grant of a licence does not amount to permission to enter private land; permission to fish on private water does not do away with the need for a licence.

General licence: An organisation with exclusive fishing rights on certain water may obtain a general licence from the Environment Agency, so that anyone then authorised to fish on that water will be covered by the licence. This facility enables, for example, a water company to sell tickets for a day or longer period, without the customers having to obtain their fishing licences separately. For the purposes of powers to require production, the ticket or permit will then be an 'other authority', to be produced on demand.

Reasonable cause to suspect: Production of a licence may be required of someone who appears to be about to fish, or to have fished in the preceding half hour. The fact that a person is setting up her rods would give rise to reasonable suspicion that she was about to fish; if she is seen coming away from the river carrying fishing tackle, it would not be unreasonable to presume that she had been fishing there in the last 30 minutes.

7.3 Water Bailiffs' Powers
Salmon and Freshwater Fisheries Act 1975 Sections 31 – 36

7.3.1 Specific Powers
A water bailiff is a person appointed as such by the Environment Agency. A bailiff has extensive powers to examine dams, weirs, waterways, fishing tackle, bait, containers for fish, boats, etc. There is power to enter land, other than a dwelling house, for the purpose of detecting offences. A bailiff may seize any fish, equipment, vessel or vehicle involved in an offence or liable to forfeiture by a court.

7.3.2 Court Order to Keep Observations
A magistrate may grant an order authorising a bailiff (or certain other persons) to enter and remain on land for a period of up to 24 hours, for the purpose of detecting suspected fishing offences.

7.3.3 Search Warrant
Grounds for issue: If a magistrate is satisfied that there is reason to suspect any offence against the Act has been committed on any premises or that there are any illegally taken fish or eels there, or any illegal nets or other equipment there, he may issue a warrant.

Powers under the warrant: The warrant may be issued to any water bailiff (or certain others connected with the water industry) or to a constable, giving authority to:
- enter the premises for the purpose of detecting any offences under the Act
- or to find fish, nets, etc
- to seize any fish suspected of having been taken illegally, as well as any illegal nets or equipment.

7.3.4 Night Fishing
If any person at night, i.e. from one hour after sunset to one hour before sunrise:
- illegally takes or kills any fish or eels;
- or has in his possession for the purpose of taking any fish or eel, any prohibited instrument;
- or is found on or near waters with intent illegally to take or kill fish or eels;
- that person may be arrested without warrant by a water bailiff, who must as soon as may be hand him over to the custody of a police officer.

7.3.5 *Bailiff's Powers as a Constable*

A water bailiff shall be *deemed to be a constable* for the purposes of enforcing the Act and any order or by-laws made under it. For that purpose a bailiff will have all the powers (and privileges whatever they may be) under common or statute law. This would, for example, enable a bailiff to use the general power to arrest for non-arrestable offences under Section 25 of the Police and Criminal Evidence Act 1984.

7.4 **Police Involvement**

7.4.1 *Specific Powers*

A constable has the same power as a water bailiff:
- – to require production of a fishing licence *(see paragraph 7.2.2)*;
- – to act under a search warrant *(see paragraph 7.3.3)*.

7.4.2 *Night Fishing*

When a bailiff detains a person for this offence, he must hand him over to the police as soon as practicable *(see paragraph 7.3.4)*.

7.4.3 *Power to Act as a Bailiff*

In relation to enforcement of fisheries legislation, the Environment Agency has statutory authority to hire the services of police officers, in the same way as police are hired to soccer clubs and the like. Any constable performing such duty will have all the powers of a water bailiff while doing so.

7.5 **Fishing on Private Waters**
Theft Act 1968 Schedule 1, paragraph 2

7.5.1 *Offences*

It is an offence for any person:
- – unlawfully
- – to take or destroy fish or attempt to do so
- – on water which is private property or on which there is a private right to fish.

The offence may be committed in two different ways, with different maximum punishments, and a power of arrest relating to the more serious:
i)   The less serious offence is committed by angling in the daytime. 'Angling' means fishing with a rod and line; 'daytime' means during the period from one hour before sunrise to one hour after sunset.
ii) The more serious offence is committed by any other form of fishing, i.e. other than by angling at any time, or by angling at night.

7.5.2 *Power of Arrest and Seizure of Tackle*

Any person may arrest without warrant a person who is, or whom he reasonably suspects is committing the more serious offence, i.e. there is no power to arrest for angling in the daytime.

Any person may seize from a person committing or reasonably suspected of committing **either** offence, anything which would be liable to forfeiture by a court.

7.5.3 *Forfeiture of Tackle*

If a person is convicted of an offence of unlawful fishing, the court may order forfeiture of anything he had with him for use in taking or destroying fish.

7.6 Handling Salmon in Suspicious Circumstances
Salmon Act 1986 Section 32

7.6.1 *Offence*

A person commits an offence if:
- at a time when he believes, or when it would be reasonable for him to suspect
- that a relevant offence has been committed in respect of a salmon
- he receives the salmon
- or undertakes or assists in its retention, removal or disposal by or for the benefit of another
- or arranges to do any of the above.

7.6.2 *Explanation*

Relevant offence: Relevant offences are those committed in England and Wales or Scotland involving taking, killing or landing a salmon.

Know or suspect: It does not have to be proved that the accused knew or suspected that a specific offence had been committed in respect of the salmon.

Receive, assist, arrange, etc: The actions which may give rise to an offence are very similar to those in the offence of handling stolen goods. Receiving the salmon one's self, doing something for the benefit of another person, or arranging to do any of these, may lead to the offence being committed.

7.6.3 *Defences*

A person will have a defence to a charge under this Section if:
  i) he shows that the salmon in question was not the proceeds of a relevant offence; or
  ii) his action was carried out in good faith for purposes relating to the prevention or detection of crime, or investigation or treatment of disease.

Chapter 45: Litter, Noise and Nuisance

1 LITTER

1.1 Litter in Public Places and Other Designated Areas

1.1.1 *Offence*
Environmental Protection Act 1990 Section 87

A person will be guilty of an offence who:
- throws down, drops or otherwise deposits
- anything whatsoever
- in, into or from any place to which these provisions apply
- and leaves it
- in such circumstances as to cause, contribute to, or tend or lead to the defacement by litter
- of any place to which these provisions apply.

1.1.2 *Exception*
No offence will be committed where the depositing and leaving was authorised by law or was done with the consent of the owner, occupier or other person or authority having control over the place in or into which the article was deposited.

1.1.3 *Explanation*
Applicable places:
  i) The offence may be committed in any public open space, which is any place:
  - to which the public are entitled to or permitted to have access
  - without payment
  - which is in the open air.
  A place will be in the open air if, although it is covered, it is open on at least one side.
  A bus shelter is an example of a place which is covered but open on at least one side.
  If the public have to pay to go in, as at a sports ground or zoo, this will not amount to a public open space.
  ii) The second category of place where the offence may be committed is any place:
  - on 'relevant land'
  - belonging to or under the control of one of a variety of bodies.

Relevant land: This means land which is open to the air, which is under the control of one of the specified bodies, and to which the public are entitled or permitted to have access, on payment or otherwise. Thus relevant land differs from a public open space to some extent, but being open to the air and the public having access (not necessarily as of right and not necessarily for free) remain common to both.

Note: However, in certain circumstances, land to which the public do not have access may be designated as 'relevant land'. This would allow, e.g. a railway embankment to become a place where it is unlawful to deposit litter, if to do so would lead to an unsightly mess, detracting from local amenity.

Specified body: The body in control of the relevant land will be one of the following:
- a principal litter authority, which basically means a local authority;
- the Crown;
- a designated educational institution, which includes universities, colleges and schools;
- a designated 'statutory undertaker', which has nothing to do with funerals, but means a body which operates some form of railway, tramway, road transport, canal, harbour, pier or airport.

In summary, the second category of place where an offence of dropping litter may take place would include a bus station, a canal towpath, a railway station platform, a university campus, etc, in each case, subject to the place being open to the air, but not necessarily wholly in the open air.

Designated litter control areas: A litter authority may designate places as 'litter control areas'.

In, into or from: The litter may be dropped 'in' the place by someone who is in there, it may be dropped 'into' from outside, or dropped outside the place 'from' it. As far as 'from' is concerned, the end result must be the defacement of, or tendency to deface, one of the specified places. Thus, to throw litter into a private garden from the street is throwing it 'from' a public open space, but will not lead to the defacement of a specified place.

Leaves: To 'leave' does not necessarily mean to abandon, intending never to return for the item. If an item is placed in a public open space for such a time and in such circumstances that it appears to have been left there, the offence may be committed even if the offender intends to remove it eventually. On the other hand, if the intention is to abandon the item, it may immediately be considered to have been 'left' (*Witney v Cattanach* (1979)).

Cause, contribute to...: It must be shown that leaving the item causes defacement by litter, or will tend to do so, or will contribute to such defacement. If lots of litter has already been dropped, it will not be a defence to claim that the extra bit makes no difference; it will 'contribute' to the defacement of the place.

1.1.4 *Fixed Penalty Notices*
There is provision for local authorities to enforce litter legislation by issue of fixed penalty notices to offenders. Such notices may be issued only by local authority personnel; there is no police involvement in such schemes.

1.2 Interfering with Litter Bins

1.2.1 *Offence*
Litter Act 1983 Section 5

A person commits an offence who:
- wilfully removes or otherwise interferes with
- a litter bin or notice
- placed by a local authority.

1.2.2 *Explanation*
Bin or notice: Local councils may provide litter bins for public use and may erect signs warning as to the consequences of dropping litter. Interfering with these will amount to an offence.

1.3 **Abandoning Vehicles and Other Articles on Land**

1.3.1 *Offence*
Refuse Disposal (Amenity) Act 1978 Section 2

A person commits an offence who without lawful authority abandons on any land in the open air, or on any land forming part of a highway:
  i) a motor vehicle or anything forming part of a motor vehicle, removed from it in the course of dismantling it on that land; or
  ii) anything other than a motor vehicle, which he brought to the land for the purpose of abandoning it there.

1.3.2 *Explanation*
These provisions cater for two rather more serious aspects of litter – the dumping of motor vehicles or bits of them, and taking articles on to land for the specific purpose of dumping them there.

Abandons: A person who leaves anything on land in such circumstances or for such period that he may reasonably be assumed to have abandoned it shall be deemed to have done so unless the contrary is proved (Section 2(2)). This provision is compatible with the court's finding in the case of *Witney v Cattanach (see paragraph 1.1.3)*.

Motor vehicle: The term includes the standard Road Traffic Act definition of motor vehicle – a mechanically-propelled vehicle intended or adapted for use on roads – but goes on:
  – whether it is in fit state for such use or not
  – and includes any trailer intended or adapted for use as an attachment to such a vehicle
  – any chassis or body, with or without wheels, appearing to have formed part of such vehicle or trailer
  – and anything attached to such a vehicle or trailer (Section 11).
  Thus, trailers, bits of motor vehicles or trailers, and accessories, all come within the scope of the legislation.

Brought to the land: The offence will be committed by a person who takes an old mattress or bags of rubbish out into the countryside and dumps same in a field or hedgerow, rather than going to the nearest council tip.
  A person who leaves anything on land in such circumstances or for such a period that he may reasonably be assumed to have brought it to the land for the purpose of abandoning it there will be deemed to have done so unless the contrary is shown. Thus, if a person is seen to dump an old sofa into a hedge in a country lane then drive off, he may be deemed to have taken the sofa there for the purpose of abandoning it there. The onus will then be on him to prove that he intended to return for it later.

1.3.4 *Removal of Abandoned Vehicles*
Refuse Disposal (Amenity) Act 1978 Section 3

A local authority has a duty to remove a motor vehicle in their area which has been abandoned without lawful authority on a highway or on any land in the open air. If the vehicle is in a poor condition, it may be removed with a view to having it destroyed. There are procedures to be fulfilled, including the fixing of a notice to the vehicle, before the removal is carried out.

The police have a discretionary power to remove vehicles in that a constable may remove a vehicle which appears to have been abandoned on a road or on land in the open air (Removal and Disposal of Vehicles Regulations 1986, Regulation 4).

Unless the police station has a particularly commodious yard, and crime figures are extremely low, it would seem sensible for a police officer to bring the presence of an abandoned vehicle to the attention of the local council, rather than spend crime-fighting time on such matters.

2 NOISE

2.1 Statutory Nuisances
Environmental Protection Act 1990 Sections 79 – 81

Complaints are often made by members of the public, of loud noise coming from premises, causing disturbance to neighbours. Such complaints may relate to noisy parties, but may also arise because of a continuously sounding burglar alarm.

The Act provides that certain matters which give cause for complaint are classed as 'statutory nuisances' and are to be dealt with by the local authority. These include noise coming from premises, and also include other sources of annoyance to neighbours, such as smoke, fumes, smells, etc. For any of these to amount to a statutory nuisance it must be a nuisance, or be prejudicial to health.

2.2 Duty of Local Authority
It is the duty of the local authority to take such steps as are reasonably practicable to investigate any complaint of statutory nuisance.

2.3 Abatement Notice

2.3.1 *Service of Notice*
When a local authority is satisfied that a statutory nuisance exists, or is likely to occur or recur in the area, it shall serve an 'abatement notice', requiring that the nuisance be abated and prohibiting its occurrence or recurrence. The notice is served on the person responsible for the nuisance, or if he cannot be found, on the owner or occupier of the premises.

2.3.2 *Offence*
A person who fails to comply with an abatement notice commits an offence.

2.4 Explanation

Local authority: In practice, a complaint of noise nuisance is more likely to be made to the police than to the local council. The local authority will probably have procedures for making an official available to respond to a serious complaint of noise passed to the authority by the police. The official will have equipment to measure noise levels, to decide whether service of an abatement notice is required. If the noise is emanating from a noisy party, for example, police may be in attendance on other grounds, e.g. because of potential for public disorder. Police may well assist the local authority representative in serving the abatement notice, e.g. by taking steps to ensure there is no breach of the peace.

Offence: The offence is one of failure to comply with the requirements of an abatement notice; making a lot of noise is not in itself an offence.

Premises: Statutory noise nuisance arises when there is noise from 'premises', but this is not confined to noise from a building because the term 'premises' includes land and vessels.

Noise: The noise may be from any source, except aircraft. Model aircraft, however, are included as a potential source of nuisance.

Several sources: Where more than one person is responsible for noise (or any other statutory nuisance), the procedure for serving an abatement notice shall apply to each of them, even though the noise made by any one of them would not in itself be enough to amount to a statutory nuisance. For example, if each of the 40 or so residents in a hostel plays his stereo with the window open, the aggregate noise amounting to a nuisance, an abatement notice may be served against each, even though the music from one stereo would not be a nuisance by itself.

2.5 Noise from Dwellings at Night
Noise Act 1996

2.5.1 *Council's Duty to Investigate Complaints*
Noise Act 1996 Section 2

In an area where the Act is in force, the local authority must investigate a complaint:
- from a person present in a dwelling
- during night hours
- that excessive noise is being emitted
- from another dwelling.

2.5.2 *Explanation*
Area where in force: The provisions of the Act apply only if the local authority resolves to adopt them. However, if an authority does investigate a complaint and finds that the offending dwelling is outside its area, i.e. just over the boundary, the council may nevertheless continue to deal with the matter.

Night hours: This means the period between 11.00 pm and 7.00 am.

Excessive noise: The Secretary of State advises local authorities on what are acceptable or unacceptable noise levels, and also approves equipment for measuring noise.

House-to-house: Complaints about noise from pubs or clubs, or a complaint from a tramp sleeping on a park bench, cannot be dealt with under this legislation. The person complaining must be in a dwelling house and the complaint must relate to noise coming from another dwelling house.

However, noise coming from a garden, yard, outhouse or other appendage to a dwelling house may be dealt with.

2.5.3 *Warning Notices*
Noise Act 1996 Section 3

A local authority officer may issue a warning notice to the effect that failure to reduce the level of noise may amount to an offence. The notice must specify:
- the time it is served

- the period during which an offence may be committed, which shall begin not earlier than 10 minutes from the time of the notice, and end at 7 am.

The notice may be served:
- on any person who is present at or near the offending dwelling who appears to be responsible for the noise; or
- if such a person cannot be identified, by leaving it at the offending dwelling.

2.5.4 *Offence*
Noise Act 1996 Section 4

If a warning notice has been served in respect of noise from a dwelling:
- and excessive noise is emitted from that dwelling during the period of the notice
- then any person who is responsible for that noise will commit an offence.

2.5.5 *Defence*
A person will have a defence if he proves that there was a reasonable excuse for causing the noise, allowing it to be caused, etc.

2.5.6 *Explanation*
Measuring the noise: The council official who serves a warning notice may do so without actually measuring the noise level, if satisfied that there is noise coming from a dwelling and it may exceed the permitted level. However, before a person commits an offence once the notice has been served, the noise level has to be measured.

Period of notice: The warning in the notice is that any more noise that night may amount to an offence. The period must start no sooner than 10 minutes from the time the notice is served, and ceases at 7am. This is very much a procedure for achieving a quick resolution of an immediate problem, but does not address a possible recurrence on a future date.

2.5.7 *Punishment*
An offence under Section 4 is triable summarily and punishable with a fine only. However, there is provision (Section 8) for council officials to offer fixed penalty notices. The rationale (according to *Hansard* reports of Parliamentary debate on the Noise Bill) was that issue of a fixed penalty notice 'on the night' may have an instant deterrent effect and lead to a speedy cessation of the noise nuisance.

2.5.8 *Powers of Entry and Seizure*
Noise Act 1996 Section 10

Certain powers apply if a warning notice has been served in relation to a particular dwelling and an officer of the local authority has reason to believe that excessive noise has been emitted from that dwelling during the period of the warning notice.

In such a case, an officer of the authority or any other person so authorised by that authority, may:
- enter the dwelling from which the noise is being or has been emitted;
- and seize and remove any equipment which it appears to him is being or has been used in the emission of the noise.

If entry to the premises is refused, or it is anticipated that there will be a refusal (or that a request for entry would defeat the object), application may be made to a magistrate for a warrant. A warrant authorises entry to premises using force if necessary. A person commits an offence who obstructs any person exercising powers under the Section.

2.5.9 *Explanation*

Grounds for exercise of powers: The circumstances in which the powers may be exercised are those in which an offence under Section 4 may be committed – further noise after a warning notice has been issued. However, there is no requirement that a prosecution should follow from a seizure of equipment; a council official might use powers to seize equipment instead of or in addition to reporting an offender or issuing a fixed penalty notice.

Other authorised person: Once an officer of the local authority has decided that grounds exist for exercising powers to enter and seize equipment, the powers may be exercised either by such an officer, or by some other person acting for the authority. A council may, for example, engage the services of a security company to assist its officers.

Noise is being or has been emitted: Once a council official is satisfied that noise has been emitted from a dwelling in breach of a warning notice, the power to enter and seize equipment continues even if the noise stops. If such was not the case, it would be a simple matter for the offenders to turn the volume down when the council official approached, then turn it up again when he had gone.

3 INJUNCTIONS AGAINST ANTI-SOCIAL BEHAVIOUR BY TENANTS
Housing Act 1996 Sections 152 – 158

3.1 Types of Injunction
The legislation provides for:
  i) a local authority to obtain an injunction against tenants of local authority residential premises, or persons in premises provided for homeless persons; and for such an injunction to have a power of arrest attached;
  ii) a power of arrest to be attached to an injunction against breach of the conditions of a tenancy, granted to a housing authority, housing trust or social landlord.

Any power of arrest attached to one of these injunctions will be exercisable by the police. It is probable therefore, that there will be discussion relating to the problem tenant between police and the housing people at some stage, perhaps prior to making application for a power of arrest to be attached, or after an injunction is granted.

3.2 Injunction Obtained by a Local Authority
Housing Act 1996 Sections 152

3.2.1 *Grounds for Granting the Injunction*
The High Court or a county court may grant an injunction to a local authority against a person on the grounds that:
  – that person has used or threatened violence against a person residing in, visiting, or otherwise engaging in lawful activity in residential premises; **and**
  – there is a significant risk of harm to that person or to a person of a similar description if the injunction is not granted.

3.2.2 *Scope of Injunction*
Such an injunction may prohibit a person:
- from engaging or threatening to engage in conduct likely to cause nuisance or annoyance to a person residing in, visiting or otherwise engaging in lawful activity in residential premises or in the vicinity of such premises;
- from using or threatening to use residential premises for immoral or illegal purposes;
- from entering residential premises or being found in the locality of such premises.

The injunction may have attached to it a power of arrest.

3.2.3 *Explanation*
Violence: Although the injunction may prohibit, for example, use of premises for immoral purposes or conduct likely to cause nuisance, one may be granted only if there has been violence used or threatened and there is significant risk of harm to a person if the injunction is not granted.

Person threatened etc: The person against whom violence is threatened, etc, must either live in residential premises, or be a visitor there, or be otherwise connected with such premises in some lawful way, e.g. calling to deliver goods.

Residential premises: The provisions apply to a dwelling house let by the local authority, or provided by the authority under arrangements for dealing with homelessness.

3.3 Injunctions for Breach of Terms of Tenancy
Housing Act 1996 Sections 153

3.3.1 *Scope of Injunctions*
This Section allows for a power of arrest to be attached to an injunction granted to a local housing authority, housing trust or social landlord in relation to a breach or anticipated breach of the terms of a tenancy. The effect of the injunction to which a power of arrest is attached is similar to that for one granted under Section 152.

3.3.2 *Grounds for Attaching Power of Arrest*
The High Court or a county court may attach a power of arrest to one or other of the provisions of one of these injunctions on the grounds that:
- the respondent (the person against whom the injunction is granted) or his tenant or lodger has used or threatened violence against a person residing in, visiting, or otherwise engaging in lawful activity in the locality; **and**
- there is a significant risk of harm to that person or to a person of a similar description if the power of arrest is not attached to one or more conditions of the injunction immediately.

3.3.3 *Explanation*
Whereas Section 152 makes provision for a specific sort of injunction, to which a power of arrest may be attached, this Section adds a provision allowing for a power of arrest in similar cases, to injunctions granted in relation to breach of the terms of a tenancy.

3.4 Arrest Provisions
Housing Act 1996 Sections 155

3.4.1 *Power of Arrest*
If a power of arrest is attached to one or more of the provisions of an injunction, a constable may

arrest without warrant a person whom he has reasonable cause for suspecting to be in breach of any such provision, or to be otherwise in contempt of court in relation to such a provision.

3.4.2 *Subsequent Police Action*
When a person is arrested, the police must:
  i) forthwith inform the person on whose application the injunction was granted;
  ii) bring the arrested person before the relevant judge within 24 hours of the time of the arrest.

A person brought before a judge may be remanded in custody or on bail if the matter is not resolved.

3.4.3 *Warrant for Arrest*
If an injunction does not have attached to it a power of arrest and the applicant considers that the respondent (the person against whom the injunction is granted) has failed to comply with one or other of the provisions, application may be made for a warrant to arrest the respondent.

3.4.4 *Explanation*
Otherwise in contempt of court: A constable may arrest, not only the respondent but any other person who is in contempt of court, e.g. a person who aids the respondent to breach the injunction.

Police action: The police must notify the person who applied for the injunction once an arrest has been made. It will then be a matter for that person, not for the police, to make arrangements for the court hearing and to present evidence to the judge.

Within 24 hours: A person arrested must be brought before the judge within 24 hours of his arrest, but this excludes Christmas Day, Good Friday or a Sunday.

3.4.5 *Duration of Power of Arrest*
Housing Act 1996 Section 157

When a court attaches a power of arrest to an injunction, the power may last for a shorter period than the injunction itself. The power of arrest may also be extended for a further period, or may be varied from time to time by the court. It is essential therefore that police, before making an arrest under one of these injunctions, ensure that a power of arrest exists at that time.

4 NUISANCE ON EDUCATIONAL PREMISES

4.1 Offence
Local Government (Miscellaneous Provisions) Act 1982 Section 40

A person commits an offence who:
  – without lawful authority
  – is present on premises to which these provisions apply
  – and causes or permits nuisance or disturbance
  – to the annoyance of persons who lawfully use the premises (whether such persons are present at the time).

4.1.1 *Explanation*

Without lawful authority: The offence may be committed only by someone who has no right to be on the premises. The teacher who finds children smoking in the toilets may well cause them some disturbance; they may regard the teacher as a nuisance, but neither the teacher nor the pupils will commit this offence.

Premises: The provisions apply to the premises of a school maintained by a local education authority, a grant-maintained school, or an institution maintained by a local education authority which provides further and/or higher education.

A grant-maintained school derives part of its funding from public funds and part from fees charged or other private sources. A school which derives no income from the public sector (e.g. a public school!) will not be covered by these provisions. An institution run by the local education authority which provides courses leading to a degree from an associated university would be covered, but not a university itself.

The offence may be committed anywhere on those premises, including playgrounds, playing fields and other premises for outdoor recreation.

Cause or permit: The offender may cause a nuisance by his own behaviour. He may also commit the offence by permitting nuisance, e.g. permitting his dog to foul a school playing field.

Annoyance: It is not enough for an offender to cause nuisance or disturbance, this must lead to someone being annoyed. Youths may shout and scream, amounting to a disturbance, but if there is no one there to be annoyed by it, the offence will not arise. The annoyance must be caused to a person who may lawfully use the premises.

Present or not: The person annoyed need not be present when the offender causes the nuisance. A dog may be allowed to foul the playing field one evening, the annoyance not arising until next day when a member of staff or a child stands in the mess.

4.1.2 *Police Powers*

A constable who:

- has reasonable cause to suspect that a person is committing or has committed this offence
- may remove that person from the premises.

This power may also be exercised by a person authorised in this regard by the local education authority.

There is no power to arrest for the offence; in appropriate circumstances the general power under Section 25, Police and Criminal Evidence Act 1984 may be considered.

Chapter 46: Highways

1 MEANING OF TERMS

1.1 Highway

A highway is a 'way' over which members of the public have a right to pass and repass. The 'way' could be:
- a footpath, where the public's right of access is restricted to those on foot;
- a bridleway, over which they may pass on foot or riding or leading a horse;
- a carriageway on which the public may pass in carriages, i.e. vehicles.

1.2 Consisting of or Comprising a Carriageway

A highway will normally include all the land from hedge to hedge, e.g. it may include a grass verge, a footpath and a carriageway. The phrase 'consisting of or comprising a carriageway' appears frequently in provisions relating to highways and means that the provisions do not apply to any highway which is not for vehicles. A highway with a carriageway and a footpath at the side will 'comprise a carriageway', an elevated section of road with no verge or footpath would 'consist of a carriageway'.

1.3 Legislation

The legislation is the Highways Act 1980.

2 OBSTRUCTION

2.1 Offence
Highways Act 1980 Section 137

A person is guilty of an offence who:
- without lawful authority or excuse
- wilfully obstructs the free passage along any highway.

2.1.1 *Explanation*

Lawful authority or excuse: Whereas a court may well find that circumstances amount to a lawful excuse for causing an obstruction of a temporary nature, there can be no lawful excuse for causing an obstruction intended to be permanent, as where a man erected a bollard on the footpath outside his shop to stop large vehicles mounting the kerb at that point.

Wilfully: A person is acting wilfully if she does something deliberately, of her own free will. She does not necessarily have to intend by her action to cause an obstruction. *(Keynote Case: Arrowsmith v Jenkins (1963))*

Obstruction: An obstruction involves an unreasonable use of the highway. Whether a particular use of the highway is unreasonable depends on the circumstances of the individual case. The place, the purpose of the use, the length of time it continued, will all be relevant. For example, a load of sand is dumped on the road outside a building site and workmen move the sand onto the site using wheelbarrows. Whether this amounts to an unlawful obstruction depends on whether the sand could have been dropped off the highway in the first place, how quickly the workmen moved to clear it, etc.

Where a person acts for the express purpose of causing an obstruction, e.g. by lying down in the carriageway as part of a protest, then the purpose of the action will be more significant than how long the obstruction lasts, in determining whether an offence is committed (*Nagy v Weston* (1965)).

An obstruction may be an actual or a potential one. For a potential one, there is no evidence that any particular user of the highway was obstructed, but the potential was there for this to occur if the obstruction was left long enough.

2.2 **Obstruction by a Vehicle**
Road Vehicles (Construction and Use) Regulations 1986, Regulation 103

It shall be an offence for a person in charge of a motor vehicle or trailer to cause or permit the vehicle to stand on a road so as to cause unnecessary obstruction.

2.2.1 *Explanation*
Vehicle: An obstruction arising from any source other than a motor vehicle or trailer will not amount to this offence but to one under the Highways Act.

Road: The term road will include every highway (where the public have a right to go), and goes on to include any other road to which the public has access, and any bridge over which such a road passes. Thus, if a road is not a highway but a private one which the public are allowed to use, this offence could arise from an obstruction there, but the Highways Act offence could not.

Stand: This offence will only arise if a motor vehicle or trailer is caused or permitted to 'stand' on a road. If a group of drivers decide to cause traffic chaos by driving very slowly on a highway, the Highways Act offence may be committed, but the Construction and Use offence would not.

2.3 **Common Law Nuisance**
The term 'common law nuisance' is applied to a variety of ways of obstructing a highway or rendering it dangerous. These provisions may apply in some cases where a charge for the statutory offence of obstruction is inappropriate. Some examples are:
   – to use vehicles of an unreasonable size or type, so as to damage the road surface, cause obstruction or excessive noise;
   – to use the highway other than for passage;
   – allowing a discharge across the highway arising from some activity off it, so as to endanger highway users (this would cover spillage on the road from premises or perhaps mis-hit golf balls);
   – putting on some event adjacent to the highway which causes crowds to gather so as to obstruct the highway. This would apply to people gathering on the highway, and not to queues waiting to enter or to people coming and going from an event.

2.3.1 *Offence*
A common law public nuisance amounts to an offence, triable summarily or on indictment.

3 MISCELLANEOUS OFFENCES
Highways Act 1980 Section 161 – 162

3.1 Deposit Something on Highway
A person commits an offence who:
- without lawful authority or excuse
- deposits anything whatsoever on any highway
- and in consequence thereof a user of the highway is injured or endangered.

3.2 Fires, Firearms, Fireworks
A person commits an offence who:
- without lawful authority or excuse
- lights a fire on or over any highway which consists of or comprises a carriageway
- or discharges any firearm or firework within 50 feet (15.24 metres) of the centre of such a highway
- and in consequence a user of the highway is injured, endangered or interrupted.

3.3 Play Game
It is an offence for a person:
- to play football or any other game on a highway
- to the annoyance of a user of the highway.

3.4 Offensive Matter
It is an offence for a person:
- without lawful authority or excuse
- to allow any filth, dirt, lime or other offensive matter or thing to run or flow onto a highway
- from any adjoining premises.

3.5 Rope, etc
A person will be guilty of an offence who:
- for any purpose places any rope, wire or other apparatus across a highway
- in such manner as to be likely to cause danger to persons using the highway
- unless he proves that he took all necessary means to give adequate warning of the danger.

3.5.1 *Explanation*
The several offences differ slightly in what constitutes each one. Most require that the offender acts 'without lawful authority or excuse'; the consequences of the action may be that injury is caused to a user of the highway, or obstruction or danger, or some combination of these elements.

4 SMOKE FROM FIRES
Highways Act 1980 Section 161A

4.1 Offence
A person commits an offence who:
- lights a fire on any land **not** forming part of a highway which consists of or comprises

a carriageway
- or directs or permits such a fire to be lit there
- and in consequence a user of any highway which consists of or comprises a carriageway
- is injured, interrupted or endangered
- by smoke from that fire or from another fire caused by the first one.

4.2 Defence

The accused shall have a defence in any proceeding for this offence if he proves:
- that at the time the fire was lit he was satisfied on reasonable grounds
- that it was unlikely that users of a highway consisting of or comprising a carriageway
- would be injured, interrupted or endangered by smoke from that fire or from any other fire caused by that fire; and
- either both before and after the fire was lit, he did all he reasonably could to prevent users of such a highway from being so injured, endangered or interrupted
- or he had a reasonable excuse for **not** taking such preventive measures.

4.2.1 *Explanation*

Land not forming: Lighting a fire within 50 feet (15 and a bit metres) from the centre of a highway is a distinct offence *(see paragraph 3.2)*. This offence relates to fires which are lit away from a highway which has a carriageway, which may be, e.g. in a field next to a road, or on land which has a footpath (i.e. a non-carriageway highway) running through it. Put simply, this provision is aimed at preventing road accidents caused by smoke billowing across a carriageway.

Injured, interrupted or endangered: If an accident does occur due to a cloud of smoke drifting over a carriageway then there is actual injury and/or interruption caused. However, danger to highway users will be enough, if the smoke is likely to cause an accident. If a driver has to brake sharply and slow down or stop, this would amount to 'interruption'.

Fire or another fire: Smoke may arise from the fire which the offender has lit or caused to be lit. However, if this fire spreads unintentionally and causes a second fire, it may be smoke from the second fire that gives rise to the offence.

Defence: There are two elements to the defence and both must be proved if the defence is to succeed:

i) First, the accused must show that at the time the fire was lit, he had good reason to believe that smoke from the fire would not cause a problem.

ii) Secondly, he has to show that from before the fire was lit, and at all times thereafter, he took all reasonable steps to prevent there being a problem. If the wind is blowing away from the highway when the demolition team set fire to a large pile of scrap timber on a building site, the first part of the defence will be satisfied. If the fire is then monitored, so that action may be taken should the wind direction change, the second part of the defence will also be satisfied.

As an alternative to showing that he took steps to monitor the fire, the accused may prove that he had a reasonable excuse for not doing so. Thus, the demolition contractor lit the fire when the wind was blowing away from the highway. He then slipped and cut himself, necessitating a trip to the hospital casualty department. While his injury was being treated, the wind changed. He will have a reasonable excuse for not taking reasonable steps to prevent smoke from the fire causing a problem.

4.3 **Stubble Burning Regulations**
Environmental Protection Act 1990 Section 152

The offence of allowing smoke from a fire to endanger carriageway users is not restricted to any particular sort of fire. However, one of the most common sources of such problems arises from farmers setting fire to straw and stubble after harvesting cereal crops. Nuisance and danger arising from such fires may affect other people and need not necessarily be confined to motorists. To combat this problem, there is power for regulations to be made prohibiting or restricting the burning of straw or stubble (or other crop residues) by farmers on agricultural land. These regulations are not dealt with in this book.

5 **BUILDERS' SKIPS**
Highways Act 1980 Sections 139 – 140A

5.1 **Control**
A builder's skip shall not be deposited on a highway without the permission of the highway authority. Remember that the 'highway' in the case of an ordinary road or street, will include pavements and verges as well as a carriageway. The local authority usually issue a form giving details of the permission, together with any conditions which may attach to the placing of the skip on the highway.

5.2 **Offences**
There are a number of offences which may arise in relation to skips on highways:
   i) a skip is placed on a highway without the required permission;
   In relation to a skip which has been placed with permission:
   ii) the skip is not properly lit during hours of darkness;
   iii) it does not bear the owner's name, plus either his address or telephone number, clearly and indelibly marked;
   iv) it is not removed as soon as practicable after it has been filled;
   v) there is a failure to comply with any conditions imposed by the highway authority in granting the permission.

5.3 **Liability**
Liability for an offence in relation to a skip falls on:
   – the owner of the skip **and** (**not or**)
   – any other person whose action or default gave rise to the offence.

A person who is charged with an offence because he is the owner, will have a defence if he proves:
   – that the offence arose due to the action or default of some other person; and
   – he had taken all reasonable precautions and exercised all due diligence to prevent the commission of such an offence by himself or anyone under his control.

5.4 **Obstruction or Lighting Offence**
The placing of a skip on a highway may cause an obstruction of the highway, or give rise to an offence involving lighting, not specifically related to builders' skips. In either case, a person charged with such an offence may put forward the defence detailed in the preceding paragraph, that someone else was to blame.

In addition, it will be a defence to a charge of obstructing the highway with a skip, to prove that the skip was placed with permission and that all the necessary requirements had been complied with.

5.4.1 *Explanation*

Skip: A builder's skip is defined as a container designed to be carried on a road vehicle and to be placed on a highway or other land for storage of builder's materials, or for the removal of rubble, rubbish, waste or earth.

Owner: The owner of a skip includes a person having possession of it under a hire-purchase agreement, or a hiring agreement of at least one month. If someone hires a skip for a few days to dispose of some rubbish, he will not be regarded as the owner. Liability for any offence will remain with the person hiring it out.

Without permission: If there is no permission for the skip to be placed on the highway, only one offence is committed. If that skip is then left for a time after it is full, or it does not have the owner's name on it, no further offence will arise because the other offences relate only to skips placed with permission.

Owner's details: The name of the owner must be indelibly marked on a skip, together with either his address or his telephone number. A telephone number on its own, written in chalk will not do.

Removal: The written permission from the highway authority will state the period during which the skip may remain in place. However, it must be moved as soon as practicable after it is full, however long it may be before the permission expires.

Conditions: The highway authority may place conditions on the grant of a permission, to cover such matters as – the siting of the skip – its size – that it be painted with reflective paint – the manner in which it is to be lit and guarded (e.g. by placing cones) – its removal.

Defence and liability: Any of the offences may be committed by the owner **and** by a person whose actual fault it was that the offence arose. The latter may be charged, even if the owner is not. This is a sensible provision, because there is little point in prosecuting the owner if it is clear that he is able successfully to plead the statutory defence.

5.5 **Police Powers**

There are powers available to a constable in uniform (which may also be exercised by a representative of the highway authority) to move or cause to be moved a skip which has been placed on a highway. These are:

i) A constable in uniform may require the owner of the skip to remove it, re-position it, or cause it to be removed or repositioned.

ii) If the owner having been required to remove it, etc, fails to do so as soon as practicable, he commits an offence.

iii) A constable in uniform may herself remove or reposition the skip or cause this to be done.

iv) If the police do have a skip moved, the chief officer of police must inform the owner if practicable.

v) If the owner cannot be traced, or has not recovered the skip within a reasonable time of being notified, the police may dispose of the skip and its contents.

vi) Any costs are recoverable as a civil debt. Any proceeds from disposal of the skip or its contents may be used to defray costs, with any surplus going to the skip owner or to the police fund.

5.5.1 *Explanation*

Reason for moving skip: One reason for having a skip moved may be that it is causing an obstruction, but there may be other reasons, and the law does not restrict police by specifying grounds on which the power to move a skip may be exercised. In particular, it should be noted that the police may require a skip to be moved even though there is a highway authority permission for it to be there. Apart from any road safety consideration, a police officer may require a skip to be moved, e.g. because it is near a football ground, trouble is expected at a forthcoming game and the bricks in the skip could be used as ammunition by rival fans.

Requirement of owner: The requirement must be made by the constable to the owner of the skip in person. If the owner is to be convicted of an offence of failing to comply with a requirement, a request by telephone is not good enough (*R v Worthing Justices, ex parte Waste Management Ltd* (1989)).

In practice however, a telephone call may well be all that is required; if a requirement made by telephone met with a refusal, a personal visit by a uniformed officer would then be necessary.

Remove or reposition: The requirement may be to take it away, or to move it to a different spot on the highway.

Constable may move it: A uniformed constable's power herself to have a skip moved is **not** dependent on first asking the owner to do so. It would be sensible in most cases, first to require the owner to move his skip, but there is no legal requirement for the police to do so before acting themselves.

Keynote Case

6.1 *Arrowsmith v Jenkins* [1963] 2 All ER 210

Problem

The meaning of the term 'wilfully' as it applies to an offence of causing an obstruction of the highway.

Circumstances

Arrowsmith addressed a public meeting in a street in Bootle for approximately 20 minutes. For the first five minutes the carriageway and pavements were completely blocked by the crowd of people gathered to listen to her. Then police cleared a way through the crowd for vehicles to pass, so that for the remainder of the meeting, the street was only partially obstructed. The charge was that without lawful authority or excuse she wilfully obstructed the free passage along the highway. She was convicted at a magistrates' court and her appeal went to the Queen's Bench Division.

Decision

Arrowsmith's appeal was based on the fact that public meetings had frequently been held in the same street in the past, and that she believed she had a lawful right to address a meeting there. The argument was that since she was not aware that what she was doing was unlawful, she did not have the *mens rea* necessary to commit the offence.

The court held that 'wilfully obstructs' does not mean that there is an intention to obstruct. If a person 'by an exercise of free will' does something which causes an obstruction, then the offence is committed. 'Wilfully' applies to the activity in which the accused is engaging, in this case, addressing a meeting; it does not have to be proved that she intended thereby to obstruct the highway.

Comment

In the appellant's submission it was suggested that the offence of obstruction required more than that 'the highway had in part been rendered less convenient or less commodious'. This phrase expresses fairly neatly the point that an obstruction of the highway does not have to amount to a blockage, so that highway users are unable to pass. A vehicle stopped on a wide street with plenty room for other vehicles to pass, may nevertheless constitute an obstruction.

Chapter 47: Knives and Offensive Weapons

1 INTRODUCTION

1.1 Aim of Legislation

There are a number of statutes which create offences aimed at preventing even more serious offences being committed. By making it an offence to carry a weapon, the law aims to prevent serious assaults being carried out. It is illegal for Bill Sykes to walk down the street carrying a jemmy and skeleton keys, in order that police may have a power to arrest him **before** he carries out any burglaries.

1.1.1 *Meanings of Terms*

The terms 'offensive weapon' and 'weapon of offence' appear in several statutes. The statutes quoted after each definition is by no means a complete list.

Offensive weapon: An offensive weapon is:
- any article made or adapted
- for causing injury to the person
- or intended by the person having it with him for such use by himself or another.

Prevention of Crime Act 1953, Section 1(4); Police and Criminal Evidence Act 1984, Section 1(9).

Weapon of offence: A weapon of offence is:
- any article made or adapted
- for use for causing injury to or incapacitating a person
- or intended by the person having it with him for such use by himself or another.

Theft Act 1968, Section 10; Criminal Law Act 1977, Section 8(2).

1.1.2 *Explanation*

Injury to a person: An offensive weapon is one for causing injury to a person; anything which is made, adapted or intended for use in causing injury to an animal or damage to property, is not included. The fact that a weapon was intended for use only in self-defence if attacked, does not alter the fact that it was intended for causing personal injury; it would still amount to an 'offensive' weapon although its intended purpose is 'defensive'.
(Keynote Case: Evans v Hughes (1972))

Incapacitate: A weapon of offence may be described as 'an offensive weapon, plus'. The additional element is that it may be used to incapacitate a person. Incapacity may be achieved by restraining a person's limbs, by rendering him unconscious or by otherwise placing a physical restriction on his ability to act freely.

Made: An article is 'made' for causing personal injury or for incapacitating a person, if it was manufactured for that purpose. A bayonet, a police truncheon or a hand grenade, are all made for the purpose of causing injury to a person. Handcuffs and a spray can of **mace** gas are examples of items made for incapacitating a person.

Adapted: An article is 'adapted' for causing injury to or for incapacitating a person if it was not manufactured in the first instance for such use, but has been adapted in such a way that it now serves this purpose. A screwdriver which has been sharpened to a point and has insulating tape wound round the handle to improve grip, has been adapted for causing injury. Many 'home made' weapons will fall into the 'adapted' category.

Intended: Many articles are capable of causing injury to people, or incapacitating them if used in a way which was not intended by the manufacturer. Knives have a wide variety of household, industrial and sporting uses, but many are bought and carried as offensive weapons. A baseball bat, a shotgun, a hockey stick and a spanner are all capable of causing injury and there are doubtless many examples of such use. A clothes line and a roll of masking tape are not made for the purpose of incapacitating a security guard, but may well be used for that purpose during a robbery.

An intention to use the article to cause injury is required. An intention to use it to frighten is not enough (*R v Edmonds, McGuiness and Salisbury* (1963)).

Proof of intent: The significance of the distinction between items made, adapted or intended is that the prosecution have to prove the intention to use an otherwise innocent item to cause someone injury or to incapacitate. This may not always be easy, and the law has recognised this fact to some degree, by stipulating that certain articles will be regarded as offensive weapons *per se*, such as flick knives *(Keynote Case: Gibson v Wales (1983))*, or a sword stick (*R v Butler* (1988)).

A rice flail has been found to be an offensive weapon, although this is not to say in another case, that evidence of such an instrument actually having been made for the purpose of flailing rice, rather than as a martial arts weapon, might lead to a different conclusion. The difficulty facing the defence would be that there is not a great deal of rice flailing carried on in this country (*Copus v Director of Public Prosecutions* (1989)).

Legislation has also been enacted, creating offences of carrying sharp or pointed articles in public places, or of trading in certain 'martial arts' instruments. This legislation avoids the need to prove that a diver's knife is an offensive weapon, leaving it up to the person carrying it to come up with a good reason for carrying such an item in the streets of, say, West Bromwich, where the risk of attack by a shark or giant octopus is fairly remote.

2 OFFENSIVE WEAPON IN A PUBLIC PLACE

2.1 Offence
Prevention of Crime Act 1953 Section 1

A person is guilty of an offence who:
- without lawful authority or reasonable excuse
- proof of which lies on him
- has with him
- in any public place
- any offensive weapon.

2.1.1 *Explanation*
Lawful authority: A soldier on duty carrying his rifle and bayonet as part of official duties would have lawful authority, as would a police officer carrying her pepper spray, extendable baton, and Heckler Koch. ''Lawful authority' is a reference to those people who from time to time carry an offensive weapon as a matter of duty' (*Bryan v Mott* (1975)).

Security guards at dance halls who carried truncheons as a 'deterrent' and as 'part of the uniform' were held not to have lawful authority and were convicted of the offence. Their appeal was dismissed, the Court of Appeal commenting that weapons must not be carried as routine or as part of a uniform (*R v Spanner, Poulter and Ward* (1973)).

Reasonable excuse: It is an a matter for the court in any particular case to decide whether an excuse is reasonable. The onus of proving an excuse to be reasonable lies with the defence. The offence is one of 'having with him' and the reasonable excuse relates to this. A man who had a knuckleduster and a truncheon in his car claimed that he carried these when he collected large sums of money from the bank for his employees' wages. He was not collecting money on the day he was stopped. The court held that collecting money from the bank may amount to a reasonable excuse at the time (but not necessarily, and the court offered no opinion on this since these were not the facts of the case) but could not amount to a reasonable excuse for having the weapons several days later (*Evans v Wright* (1964)).

In the same vein, where a man was using an air rifle at a shooting gallery, and turned it on a woman, shooting her in the hip, his conviction for carrying an offensive weapon was quashed on appeal. The offence is committed by having a weapon. The man had a reasonable excuse for having it; the fact that he then used the rifle unlawfully did not amount to the offence (*R v Jura* (1954)).

(Comment: On this reasoning, since an air rifle is not made or adapted for causing personal injury, perhaps the court should have considered whether in fact it could be described as an offensive weapon at all, rather than whether the accused had a reasonable excuse for having it *(see R v Dayle, below).*

Self-defence may be put forward but for this to amount to a reasonable excuse, there must be an anticipation of imminent attack. Carrying a weapon permanently to protect one's self against a possible attack would not amount to a reasonable excuse *(Keynote Case: Evans v Hughes (1972)).*

Has with him: This has a narrower meaning than 'possession' in that a person may have possession of an article even when he is some distance away from it. 'Has with him' denotes actually having it physically with him, or at least having it readily accessible *(Keynote Case in Chapter 22: R v Kelt (1977)).*

The phrase means **knowingly** has with him. A man was arrested in possession of a stolen van. In the back of the van were pickaxe handles bound with adhesive tape which the prosecution alleged were offensive weapons (adapted). The accused's defence was that he did not know they were in the van. He was convicted, the jury being directed that once evidence was given that he had an offensive weapon with him, the onus was on the defence to prove a reasonable excuse. The Court of Appeal allowed his appeal; the prosecution have to prove he 'knowingly' had the offensive weapon with him (*R v Cugullere* (1961)). However, if the accused had known that he had an offensive weapon with him, but had since forgotten, this would not affect the fact that he 'knowingly had it' (*R v McCalla* (1988)).

In any public place: In this context 'public place' means any highway and any other premises or place to which at the material time the public have or are permitted access, whether on payment or otherwise. If a person is in a private place with an offensive weapon but from the circumstances, the inference may be drawn that to get to where he is, he must have passed through a public place with the offensive weapon, he may be convicted (*R v Mehmed* (1963)).

Offensive weapon: *See paragraph 1.1.1 above.* Where an article which is not an offensive weapon, is picked up and used to cause injury, this does not necessarily prove that it is being carried with intent to be used as such. Thus, a car driver, confronted by occupants of another vehicle after a minor collision, who picked up a car jack from his vehicle was not guilty of having it with him with intent that it be used for causing injury (*R v Dayle* (1973)).

2.2 **Arrest**

The offence carries a maximum sentence of four years' imprisonment but is included in the Police and Criminal Evidence Act 1984 (Section 24(2)) as an arrestable offence (as amended by the Offensive Weapons Act 1996).

3 **ARTICLE WITH BLADE OR POINT IN PUBLIC**

3.1 **Offence**
Criminal Justice Act 1988 Section 139

A person commits an offence who:
- in a public place
- has with him
- an article to which this Section applies.

3.1.1 *Explanation*
Public place: Means any place to which at the material time the public have or are permitted to have access, whether on payment or otherwise.

Article: The Section applies to any article which has a blade or which is sharply pointed – except a folding pocket knife the cutting edge of the blade not exceeding 7.62 centimetres (3 inches).

A pocket knife will not be exempt however, if the blade locks in the open position and can be folded only when a release button is pressed. To be a 'folding' pocket knife it has to be immediately foldable at all times simply by the process of folding it (*Harris v DPP, Fehmi v DPP* (1993)).

3.2 **Defence**
It will be a defence for an accused to prove that he had good reason or lawful authority for having the article with him in a public place. For example, a person who proved that he had just purchased a set of kitchen knives and two pairs of knitting needles and was taking them home for domestic use, would probably escape conviction.

There is no limit on what may amount to good reason or lawful authority in any particular case, and without affecting this general defence, a person will have a defence if he proves that he had the article with him in a public place:
- for use at work
- or for religious reasons
- or as part of any national costume.

A male follower of the Sikh religion may carry a knife as part of that religion; a skean dhu (small knife) tucked into the top of a sock is part of Scottish highland dress. A more frequent use of the defence may arise in relation to tools being carried by a person for work.

3.3 **Arrest**
The offence carries a maximum sentence of two years' imprisonment but is included in the Police and Criminal Evidence Act 1984 (Section 24(2)) as an arrestable offence (as amended by the Offensive Weapons Act 1996).

4 WEAPONS ETC ON SCHOOL PREMISES

4.1 Offence
Criminal Justice Act 1988 Section 139A

A person shall commit an offence who:
- has with him on school premises
- an article to which Section 139 applies (article with a blade or point); or
- an offensive weapon as defined in Section 1, Prevention of Crime Act 1953 (article made, adapted or intended for causing injury to a person).

4.2 Defences

1: A person shall have a defence if he proves that he had good reason or lawful authority for having the article or offensive weapon with him on school premises.

2: Without affecting the generality of the meaning of 'good reason', it shall be a defence for the person to prove that he had the article or weapon in question:
- for use at work;
- for educational purposes;
- for religious reasons;
- as part of a national costume.

4.2.1 Explanation

Has with him: This is likely to have the same meaning as in the Prevention of Crime Act 1953 *(see paragraph 2.1.1)*.

School premises: A 'school' is an institution for providing primary or secondary education, but not one providing further or higher education. It matters not whether the school is a private one or a local authority one. A university or college for taking people above school age would not be a 'school' for these purposes.

'School premises' includes land such as playing fields used for the purposes of the school, but excludes any land occupied solely as a dwelling by an employee of the school. This means that a house occupied by a caretaker or a teacher is excluded, even though in the school grounds.

Good reason or lawful authority: The case decisions in relation to offensive weapons under the Prevention of Crime Act 1953 are likely to be relevant *(see paragraph 2.1.1)*. Note that the defence requires good reason or lawful authority not just for having the weapon or article with him, but for 'having it with him on the school premises'.

Specific reasons: The fact that there are four specific reasons which will amount to a defence – work, education, etc, does not affect the general nature of 'good reason or lawful authority'. The four specified ones are just a few of many possible reasons which there may be for having a weapon or article at school.

4.3 Arrest

The maximum sentences for the two offences, possession of an offensive weapon or of an article with a blade or point on school premises, are the same as for the corresponding offences of having those articles in a public place, i.e. four years in the case of an offensive weapon, two years for an article with a blade or point. Likewise, both are included in Section 24(2) of the Police and Criminal Evidence Act 1984, as arrestable offences.

4.4 **Police Powers to Search School Premises**
Criminal Justice Act 1988 Section 139B

4.4.1 *Grounds for Entering*
A constable may exercise these powers if he has reasonable grounds for believing that an offence under Section 139A is being or has been committed there.

4.4.2 *Powers*
The constable has the following powers:
- enter school premises
- search those premises and any person on those premises for an offensive weapon or an article with a blade or point
- seize and retain anything found during such search which he reasonably believes to be such a weapon or article
- use reasonable force if necessary, in exercising the powers.

5 SALE OF KNIVES TO PERSON UNDER 16

5.1 **Offence**
Criminal Justice Act 1988 Section 141A

It is an offence for a person to sell to a person under the age of 16 years any of the following articles:
  i) knife, knife blade or razor blade;
  ii) any axe;
  iii) any other article which has a blade or which is sharply pointed **and** which is made or adapted for use for causing injury to the person.

5.1.1 *Exceptions*
This Section does not apply to any flick knife, etc, or any prohibited martial arts article. (Such articles are subject of offences under other legislation – see below.) In addition, there is provision for an order to be made specifying other articles to be exempt from the Section.

5.2 **Defence**
A person charged with the offence will have a defence if he proves that he took all reasonable precautions and exercised all due diligence to avoid the commission of the offence.

5.2.1 *Explanation*
Sell: The offence arises only if an article is sold. This is not as extensive as say, restrictions on flick knives *(see paragraph 6 below)* where it is an offence merely to expose or offer an article for sale.

Knife, knife blade, etc: Note that there is no minimum length of blade, as is the case for an offence of having an article with a blade or point under Section 139 of the Act. Any knife, whether the blade folds, and whatever the length of the blade, is included. If a lad under 16 needs to shave, he will not be able to buy his own razor blades.

Other article: In the case of any other article with a blade or sharp point, it will come within the scope of the Section only if it is made or adapted for causing injury to a person. Thus, tools such as chisels and screwdrivers may be sold lawfully to persons under 16.

Defence: The onus of proving the defence lies on the accused. He has to show that he took all reasonable precautions, and exercised all due diligence to prevent an offence being committed. It will probably not be enough for the accused to say that he asked the customer her age, he will have to show that he took steps to obtain proof of age.

6 RESTRICTIONS ON OFFENSIVE WEAPONS

6.1 Flick Knives

6.1.1 *Offence*
Restriction of Offensive Weapons Act 1959 Section 1

It is an offence for a person:
- in relation to an article to which the Act applies
- to do any of the following:
    - manufacture
    - sell
    - hire
    - offer for sale or hire
    - expose or have possession of for the purpose of sale or hire
    - lend or give to any person.

The importation of such articles is also prohibited.

6.1.2 *Explanation*
Article: The Act covers:
i) Any knife which has a blade which opens automatically by hand pressure applied to a button, spring or other device in or attached to the handle. Such an article is sometimes known as a flick knife or flick gun.
ii) A knife with a blade which is released from the handle or sheath by the force of gravity or the application of centrifugal force and which, when released is locked into place by means of a button, spring, lever or other device. An article of this sort is sometimes known as a gravity knife.

The flick knife, being spring loaded, does not actually need a flick, but the gravity knife may well open upon a 'flick of the wrist' being applied. There are two elements in the description of the gravity knife – the blade opens by gravity or by centrifugal force – and once open, the blade locks in place.

Unlawful action: An offence is committed by a person who has these articles to pass on to others, or who does pass them on, by way of sale, hire, lending or giving away. A notable omission from the list is possession for one's own use. Whereas a number of legitimate users were identified when this legislation was first proposed, notably fishermen, the fact remains that trade in them is unlawful. Possession by a person in public is restricted by the fact that such an article has a blade and, more often than not, a point. In addition, a flick knife has been held to be an offensive weapon *per se*, i.e. made as an offensive weapon. *(Keynote Case: Gibson v Wales (1983))*

6.2 **Martial Arts Equipment**

6.2.1 *Offence*
Criminal Justice Act 1988 Section 141

A person commits an offence who in relation to a weapon to which this Section applies:
- manufactures
- sells
- hires
- offers for sale or hire
- exposes or has possession of for the purposes of sale or hire
- or lends or gives to any person.

The importation of such a weapon is prohibited.

6.2.2 *Explanation*
Unlawful action: The acts which constitute the offence are exactly the same as apply in the case of flick knives. Again, possession for personal use is absent from the list of offences.

Weapons to which applicable: There is a long list of weapons to which the Section applies, from the traditional knuckle duster to oriental items such as the *kusari gama* and the *manrikigusari*. A telescopic truncheon is included in the list, but see the defence, below (Criminal Justice Act 1988 (Offensive Weapons) Order 1988).

The Home Secretary specifies items to be placed on the list, by means of an order approved by Parliament. In such an order however, the Home Secretary may not specify anything which is a crossbow or which is subject of the Firearms Act 1968.

6.2.3 *Exception*
An item which is an antique is excepted from the restrictions. For these purposes 'antique' applies to something manufactured more than 100 years before the date of the alleged offence.

6.2.4 *Defence*
There are three defences to a charge under this Section:
  i) the accused was acting in relation to functions carried out by or on behalf of the Crown or of a visiting force;

  ii) the accused was acting only for the purpose of making the item available to a museum or gallery;

  iii) the accused was acting on behalf of a museum or gallery, is charged with hiring or lending the article, and proves that he had reason to believe that the person to whom the item was lent or hired would use it only for cultural, artistic or educational purposes.

6.3 **Search Warrant**
Criminal Justice Act 1988 Section 142

6.3.1 *Grounds for Issue*
A magistrate may issue a warrant upon application by a constable:
- if satisfied that there are reasonable grounds for believing that on the premises specified in the application are:

i) knives of the kind to which the Restriction of Offensive Weapons Act 1959 applies, i.e. flick knives, gravity knives; or

ii) weapons to which Section 141 applies, i.e. martial arts weapons; **or**

— that an offence under either of those two provisions has been or is being committed in relation to those premises.

6.3.2 *Police Powers Under the Warrant*

The warrant will authorise a constable to enter and search the premises, and to seize and retain anything in respect of which the warrant was issued.

7 COMBAT KNIVES

Knives Act 1997

7.1 Offences

7.1.1 *Marketing*
Knives Act 1997 Section 1

A person commits an offence who:
— markets a knife in a way which
— indicates or suggests that the knife is suitable for combat; or
— is otherwise likely to stimulate or encourage violent behaviour involving the use of the knife as a weapon.

7.1.2 *Publishing Marketing Material*
Knives Act 1997 Section 2

A person commits an offence who:
— publishes any written, pictorial or other material in connection with the marketing of any knife, and that material
— indicates or suggests that the knife is suitable for combat; or
— is otherwise likely to stimulate or encourage violent behaviour involving the use of the knife as a weapon.

7.1.3 *Explanation*
Market: A person markets a knife if he:
a) sells or hires it;
b) offers or exposes it for sale or hire; or
c) has it in his possession for the purpose of sale or hire. This Act is aimed at the persons who trade in knives, not at persons who buy or have possession.

Knife: Any instrument which has a blade or is sharply pointed will amount to a 'knife'.

Indicates or suggests: An indication or suggestion that a knife is suitable for combat may arise from a name or description applied to the knife, on the knife itself, on any packaging or on any advertisement which, expressly or by implication, relates to the knife. The name of the knife, e.g. 'Commando dagger' or other description, e.g. 'As issued to the SAS' will be a fairly clear and unambiguous indication that the knife is suitable for combat, but a suggestion that a knife may be suitable for fighting, even if not stated directly, will be enough.

Suitable for combat: This expression means that the knife is suitable for use as a weapon for inflicting injury on a person or causing a person to fear injury. This means that use for self-defence amounts to use for combat, e.g. 'Buy this and scare off a burglar' comes under causing a person to fear injury.

Violent behaviour: This expression means an unlawful act inflicting injury on a person or causing a person to fear injury.

Publication: A publication includes one in electronic form, and in the case of a publication produced from electronic data, any medium on which those data are stored.

Thus, any advertising of knives on the 'internet' or any computer disks for use in a word processor to produce such material, will fall within the scope of Section 2.

7.2 Defences

7.2.1 *Particular Uses*
Knives Act 1997 Section 3

A person will have a defence to either of the offences (marketing or publishing) if she proves:
  i) that the knife was marketed for use by the armed forces of any country, or as an antique or curio, or as falling into a category prescribed by regulations; and
  ii) it was reasonable for the knife to be marketed in that way; and
  iii) there were no reasonable grounds for suspecting that a person into whose possession the knife might come as a consequence of the way it was marketed or as a consequence of publication of material might use it for an unlawful purpose.

7.2.2 *Lack of Awareness*
Knives Act 1997 Section 4

A person will have a defence if he proves:
  − that he did not know or suspect, and had no reasonable grounds for suspecting
  − that the way in which the knife was marketed (or the material published, as the case may be)
  − amounted to an indication or suggestion that the knife was suitable for combat; or
  − was likely to stimulate or encourage violent behaviour involving the use of the knife as a weapon.

7.2.3 *Reasonable Precautions*
Knives Act 1997 Section 4(3)

A person will have a defence if he proves:
  − that he took all reasonable precautions and exercised all due diligence
  − to avoid committing the offence.

7.2.4 *Explanation*
Armed forces, curio, etc: If a firm in this country markets bayonets or other items of military hardware, for the armed forces of **any** country, this need not be unlawful, so long as it is reasonable to market the instrument in that way and there is no reason to believe that this form of marketing (or use of the marketing material in question) will lead to the product falling into 'the wrong hands'. Antique or curio would cover trade in items such as swords.

There is provision for the Home Secretary to bring in regulations specifying other items, apart from antiques and military knives, to come within the scope of this defence.

Lack of knowledge: The practical effect of the second defence is that the prosecution will have to prove, not only that the accused marketed the knife (or published material as the case may be) but that he had some degree of awareness as to the nature of the marketing or the material.

Reasonable precautions: This defence may apply to a situation where, for example, a person seeking to trade in knives engages another person to devise an adverting campaign, and that person fails to follow instructions as to the nature of advertising material.

7.3 Search Warrant
Knives Act 1997 Section 5

7.3.1 *Grounds for Issue*
A justice of the peace may issue a warrant on application by a constable if satisfied:
- that a person (the suspect) has committed an offence under Section 1 in relation to knives of a particular description (or under Section 2 in relation to particular material); and
- that knives of that description (or publications containing that material, as the case may be) and in the suspect's possession or under his control are to be found on particular premises.

7.3.2 *Powers under the Warrant*
A constable is authorised by the warrant:
- using reasonable force if necessary
- to enter those premises
- search for the knives (or publications)
- and seize and remove any he finds.

Any property seized may be retained until the conclusion of proceedings against the suspect.

7.4 Forfeiture of Knives and Publications
Knives Act 1997 Sections 6, 7

When a person is convicted of an offence, the court may order forfeiture of any knives or publications seized under a Section 5 warrant, or in the offender's possession or control at the time he was arrested for the offence, or at the time a summons was issued in respect of it.

Any property in respect of which a forfeiture order is made shall be taken into police possession, if not in their possession already.

There is provision for a court to grant a 'recovery order' to a person who applies to have the forfeited property. The Home Secretary may make regulations providing for the disposal of forfeited property remaining in police possession.

Keynote Cases

8.1 *Evans v Hughes* (1972) 56 Cr App R 813

Problem
i) Whether an article intended for use for self-defence only is an 'offensive' weapon.
ii) Whether fear of being attacked amounts to a reasonable excuse for having an offensive weapon in public.

Circumstances
Hughes was charged with having an offensive weapon with him in a public place without lawful authority or reasonable excuse, contrary to Section 1, Prevention of Crime Act 1953. The article concerned was a short metal bar, neither made nor adapted for causing injury, so it was necessary for the prosecution to show that it was an offensive weapon by reason of the accused's intention to use it as such. The accused admitted that he carried it because he had been attacked by three men one week previously, saying, 'If the blokes had attacked me again I would have used the iron bar on them'.

The magistrates dismissed the charge against Hughes, finding that the metal bar was not an offensive weapon because he carried it for self-defence, not for an aggressive purpose. They also found, that had it been an offensive weapon, he had reasonable cause to fear that he might be attacked, so had a reasonable excuse for having it. The prosecution appealed.

Decision
The court held:
i) The fact that the accused intended to use the metal bar only in self-defence did not alter the fact that he intended to use it for causing injury to the person. The fact that a person carrying a weapon intends only to use it defensively does not prevent it being an offensive weapon.

ii) An imminent fear of attack may amount to a reasonable excuse for carrying an offensive weapon for personal defence. This does not extend, however, to the permanent carrying of a weapon because of a continuing fear of attack. Someone who lives in constant fear of attack should make some other arrangements.

In this case, the period since Hughes had been attacked was eight days. The court felt that this was very much borderline, so left the magistrates' decision to stand, i.e. the prosecution appeal failed.

Comment
The divisional court cited a Scottish case, in which a taxi driver who carried a large cosh in his cab was convicted of having an offensive weapon. The fact that taxi drivers were sometimes attacked at night was not a reasonable excuse for carrying a weapon for self-defence on a permanent basis. As far as fear of imminent attack is concerned, to have a weapon for self-defence one or two days after having been attacked may be reasonable. To be carrying it some weeks later would not.

In another case cited during the appeal, a man was found to have offensive weapons in his car and claimed that he carried them for self-defence when he collected employees' wages from the bank. He was not collecting money from the bank on the day he was stopped, and leaving the items in his car for next week was held not to amount to a reasonable excuse (*Evans v Wright* (1964)).

8.2 *Gibson v Wales* (1983) 76 Cr App R 60

Problem

Whether a flick knife is an offensive weapon *per se* within the meaning of the Prevention of Crime Act 1953.

Circumstances

The respondent was seen by police officers showing to other youths a flick knife which he was carrying in his pocket. He was arrested for having an offensive weapon with him in a public place. The magistrates dismissed the charge, finding that a flick knife was not an offensive weapon *per se*, i.e. it was not manufactured or adapted for the purpose of being used to cause personal injury. There was no evidence that the accused had it with him with intention of using it for causing personal injury. The prosecution appealed by way of case stated, seeking a declaration from the court that a flick knife was an offensive weapon *per se*.

Decision

The court considered the fact that flick knives are the subject of the Restriction of Offensive Weapons Act 1959, which prohibits their manufacture, sale, etc, but not, significantly, mere possession. The court felt that an explanation for the omission of 'possession' from the 1959 Act was that possession of an offensive weapon in public was already an offence under the 1953 Act. On this reasoning, a flick knife would be an offensive weapon *per se*.

While allowing that a flick knife may well be used for quite innocent purposes, such as when a person had only one hand free and wished to use a knife, taking account of the dangerous nature of such a knife, and of the legislation passed by Parliament, a flick knife is an offensive weapon *per se*.

Comment

If an article is not an offensive weapon *per se*, then the onus is on the prosecution to prove that the accused had it with him for the purpose of using it to cause injury to the person. In the case of a flick knife, as a result of this decision, a person may be convicted of the offence without evidence being adduced of an intention to use the knife to cause injury.

Chapter 48: Going Equipped and Other Preventive Measures

1 GOING EQUIPPED FOR THEFT

1.1 Offence
Theft Act 1968 Section 25

A person commits an offence who:
- when not at his place of abode
- has with him
- any article for use in the course of or in connection with
- any burglary, theft or cheat.

1.1.1 *Explanation*
Place of abode: A person cannot commit this offence when at the place where he lives. In a case where items for use in a theft were found in a car, the accused put forward in defence that, having no settled address, he was living in his car at that time. The Court of Appeal, upholding the conviction held that 'place of abode' denoted a site and did not extend to a motor car (*R v Bundy* (1977)).

Has with him: This has a narrower meaning than 'possession' in that a person may have possession of an article even when he is some distance away from it. 'Has with him' denotes actually having it physically with him, or at least having it readily accessible *(Keynote Case in Chapter 22: R v Kelt (1977))*. The phrase means 'knowingly' has with him, so a person does not have an article with him unless he is aware of the fact.

Any article: There is no restriction on the sort of article covered by the offence, so long as it is for use in the course of or in connection with any of the crimes mentioned. 'In the course of' articles would include burglary tools, stocking masks or forged cheques. 'In connection with' would include items used in preparation – such as a forged reference as part of a fraud, or for use after the offence – such as a disguise.

In the course of or in connection with: The offence applies to having an article **for use**. The offence will not apply to an article which has already been used (unless of course, there is evidence of intention to use it again). The prosecution has to prove that at some time the accused had the article with him, for the purpose of being used, by himself or by someone else, for committing or in connection with committing, one of the specified crimes. However, the prosecution does not have to prove an intention to use the article in committing a specific offence. If it is proved that the accused had a knife with him to use to rob someone when the opportunity arose, this will suffice (*R v Ellames* (1974)).

The offence relates not only to use by the accused, but to use by someone else as well. If Bill has a knife intending that Ben shall use it when committing a robbery, then Bill commits this offence.

Where it is proved that a person had with him an article made or adapted for use in committing burglary, theft or cheat, this shall be proof that he has it with him for that purpose. This, in effect, shifts the burden of proof on to the defence once it has been established that the article was made or adapted for the relevant criminal use. A counterfeit credit card would probably fall into the 'made' category, but in practical terms, most burglary implements would not. A case opener, a screwdriver, or even a large bunch of car keys, all were made for legitimate purposes. 'Adapted' might include a half-tennis ball for opening a central locking car, or a wire coathanger adapted for removing a car radio.

Burglary, theft or cheat: Burglary requires no further elaboration. 'Theft' will include an offence of taking a conveyance (Theft Act 1968, Section 12(1)) and 'cheat' means an offence of obtaining property by deception (Theft Act 1968, Section 15).

1.2 Arrest

Although carrying a maximum of only three years' imprisonment, the offence is included in Section 24(2) of the Police and Criminal Evidence Act 1984 as an arrestable offence.

2 FOUND ON ENCLOSED PREMISES

2.1 Offence
Vagrancy Act 1824 Section 4

A person commits an offence who:
- is found in or upon
- any dwelling-house, warehouse, coach-house stable or outhouse
- or in any enclosed yard, garden or area
- for any unlawful purpose.

2.1.1 *Explanation*

Found in or upon: This has to be taken literally. If an alarm is set off at a house and Sykes is seen running away from the scene, he cannot be said to have been found 'in or upon' the house. This does not mean to say that he has to be detained inside the house. If he is seen in the house and runs off, to be arrested later, the offence may be made out. 'Found in' means that the accused was arrested in, or seen in or is otherwise proved to have been in the place concerned (*R v Lumsden* (1951)).

Type of building: The descriptions of the buildings reflects the era in which the Vagrancy Act was passed. There is no mention of hypermarkets, shopping malls or airports. Nevertheless the term 'warehouse' would cover many modern commercial buildings.

Enclosed yard, garden or area: The place where the offence may be committed has to be enclosed, but this does not necessarily mean that a fence or wall must have no breaks or gaps in it. The fact that access may be gained through an open gateway, for example, does not preclude the place from being 'enclosed' (*Goodhew v Morton* (1962)). The term 'area' may have a restricted meaning, referring to the basement space of a house. This was suggested in a case where it was held that a 'yard' does not mean a very large space, such as a railway siding a mile long and a quarter mile wide (*Knott v Blackburn* (1944)).

Unlawful purpose: This refers to a criminal purpose, not to a civil wrong such as trespass, nor an immoral purpose such as prostitution.

2.2 Arrest
Vagrancy Act 1824 Section 6

Any person may arrest without warrant a person found committing an offence under this Act.

This is one of the 'any person' powers of arrest preserved under the Police and Criminal Evidence Act 1984. Home Office advice is that a constable should use this power as she would the PACE general power, i.e. only when the general arrest conditions are satisfied.

3 VEHICLE INTERFERENCE

3.1 Offence
Criminal Attempts Act 1981 Section 9

A person is guilty of the offence who:
— interferes with a motor vehicle or trailer
— or with anything carried in or on a motor vehicle or trailer
— with the intention that he or another person
— will commit one of the specified offences.

3.1.1 *Explanation*

Specified offences: The offences in relation to which the interference takes place are:
i) theft of the motor vehicle or trailer concerned, or of part of it;
ii) theft of anything carried in or on the motor vehicle or trailer;
iii) an offence under Section 12(1), Theft Act 1968, i.e. taking a conveyance.

Thus, the interference could be with the intention of stealing the vehicle or trailer itself, stealing part of it, or something from it, or committing an offence of taking a conveyance.

Note: The offence of taking a conveyance is not restricted to taking the motor vehicle interfered with. If a motor vehicle or trailer had a conveyance, such as a car, as its load, then the intention could be to take that conveyance.

Interferes: This term is not defined, but any action could amount to interference if done with the necessary intent. Trying the door handles on a car, or sliding a steel ruler down between the window and the rubber seal, would be actions with an apparent intent to take a motor vehicle or steal something from it. Twisting a wing mirror or pushing a piece of potato up the exhaust would be interference but the necessary intent would be absent.

Where there is no evidence of the required intent, there may be an offence committed of 'tampering', contrary to Section 25, Road Traffic Act 1988.

Proof of intent: If it is shown that the accused intended to commit one of the specified offences, it is immaterial that it cannot be shown which one it was. For example, if a youth is seen to force the door of a car, lift the bonnet and start to 'hot wire' the ignition, this may be accepted as sufficient evidence that he intended either to steal the car or to take it without consent; there is no need to prove which of these offences he actually intended to commit.

Chapter 49: Selling and Collecting

1 INTRODUCTION

The need for some sort of control over people who knock on other people's doors has led to the law which requires that anyone wishing to go from house to house to sell goods has first to obtain a certificate from the police. There are controls on who may go around seeking donations to charity; begging in public places is unlawful, as is touting for trade for taxis. Anyone seeking to set up business as a scrap metal dealer, whether by going round the streets, or having a yard to which customers bring scrap metal, must register with the local council.

2 PEDLARS

2.1 Certificate Required
Pedlars Act 1871 Sections 2 – 5

The requirement for a pedlar's certificate extends to:
-   any hawker, pedlar, petty chapman, tinker, caster of metals, mender of chairs or other person
-   who without horse or other beast drawing or bearing burden travels and trades on foot
-   and goes from town to town or to other men's houses
-   carrying to sell, exposing for sale or procuring orders for goods, wares or merchandise
-   immediately to be delivered
-   or selling or offering for sale his skill in handicrafts.

2.1.1 *Offence*
It is an offence to act as a pedlar without a certificate.

2.2 Exempt
A certificate will not be required by any of the following:
-   commercial travellers and other persons selling to or seeking orders from dealers who buy to sell again
-   persons selling or seeking orders for books as agents authorised in writing by the publishers of such books
-   sellers of fish, fruit, vegetables or victuals
-   persons selling or exposing for sale goods in any legally established public mart, market or fair.

2.3 Explanation
Hawker, petty chapman, etc: The archaic terms of 125 years ago all amount to variations on a theme. 'Chapman' is another word for pedlar, a 'tinker' was a mender of kettles and pans. In essence, the provisions apply to anyone selling goods, or selling a skill. There may not be too many people knocking on doors offering to mend kettles or broken chairs, but offers to sharpen lawn-mowers or sell dish cloths are still made.

On foot, no horse: This may seem a strange provision, but there was other legislation at one time, covering the more up-market independent trader who may have had a horse. Note that Reliant vans and other motor vehicles do not feature, which is hardly surprising, given the date of the legislation.

House to house, town to town: A person who stays in one town and goes from house to house will fit the description. Travelling by van then selling goods from a portable stand is not acting as a pedlar (*Watson v Malloy* (1988)), but parking the van then going round houses on foot is.

Sale: Selling goods for charitable purposes rather than by way of trade will not be regarded as acting as a pedlar (*Gregg v Smith* (1873)). In this case, a number of women went round houses selling articles of clothing which they had made. Some of the money raised was used to buy materials to make more articles to sell, the profits going to charity. The court found that the women could not be said to be carrying on the trade of pedlar, because their fund raising activities could not be described as their trade. Whether this decision may be relied on by modern-day sellers of cheap household goods who donate a proportion of their earnings to charity, is another matter. However, since these people usually produce an identification card, perhaps the intention of the legislation is met without their having pedlars' certificates.

Immediately to be delivered: If a person is taking orders for goods which will be available at a later date, a pedlar's certificate is not required. Thus, the representatives of a well-known supplier of brushes and household wares do not have to register as pedlars.

Commercial travellers, book sellers: Since the purpose of the legislation is to prevent persons of bad character having an excuse for wandering round houses, it is reasonable that a person who is selling by wholesale, or someone having written authority from a book publisher, will be exempt from the need for a certificate. Whether there are many sales representatives going round on foot in any case, is doubtful.

Food sellers: 'Victuals' means any ingredient in food for humans.

2.4 Grant of Certificates

Granted by: The chief officer of police for the area in which the applicant has lived for at least one month previous to the application. If the chief officer of police refuses to grant a certificate, appeal lies to a magistrates' court.

Granted to: A person aged 17 or over – of good character – who intends in good faith to carry on the trade of pedlar.

Duration, extent: A certificate lasts for 12 months and authorises the holder to act as a pedlar within any part of the United Kingdom.

Offences: The offences which may be committed in relation to certificates are:
   i)   lends or transfers, borrows or makes use of a certificate;
   ii) makes a false representation with a view to obtaining a certificate;
   iii) forges or counterfeits a certificate, aids or procures the making of such, or travels with, produces or shows same.

2.5 Powers of Police and Others
Pedlars Act 1871 Section 19

2.5.1 *Production of Certificate*
A person acting as a pedlar must:

- at all times, on demand, produce and show his certificate and allow it to be read or a copy taken
- by a justice of the peace, constable, or any person to whom he offers his goods for sale or on whose private property he is found.

2.5.2 *Arrest*

If a person acting as a pedlar:
- refuses to show his certificate
- or has no certificate
- or prevents or seeks to prevent any opening or inspection of his bag, pack, case, etc

he commits an offence and may be arrested:
- by any person authorised to demand production of his certificate
- or on order or request of such person, by any other person.

2.6 **Endorsements and Forfeiture**

An offence under the Act is triable at a magistrates' court. The magistrates must endorse details of a conviction on the certificate.

Any court before which the holder of a pedlar's certificate is convicted of any offence **may** deprive the pedlar of his certificate. This applies to any offence, not just those relating specifically to pedlars.

If the conviction is for begging, the court **must** deprive him of the certificate.

3 **SCRAP METAL DEALERS**
Scrap Metal Dealers Act 1964

3.1 **Meaning of Terms**

Scrap metal dealer: A scrap metal dealer is a person who carries on a business which consists, wholly or partly, of buying and selling scrap metal.

Scrap metal: Scrap metal includes any old metal, any broken, worn out, defaced or partly manufactured articles made wholly or partly of metal, and any metallic wastes. This extends to old, broken, worn out or defaced tool tips or dies made of materials commonly known as 'hard metals', or of cemented or sintered metallic carbides.

3.1.1 *Explanation*

Buying and selling: A dealer is a person who buys **and** sells scrap metal.

Wholly or partly: Dealings in scrap metal need not be a person's only activity, for him to be regarded as a scrap metal dealer. He may for example, deal in all sorts of second-hand goods, including metals. Similarly, an object may amount to 'scrap metal' even though it is only partly made of metal. An old fridge will be classed as scrap metal, even though there is a fair amount of plastic in its construction.

Exception: A person will not be regarded as a scrap metal dealer who buys scrap metal for use only as a raw material for the manufacture of other articles, and does not sell scrap metal except as a by-product of that manufacture, or as a surplus bought and not required. Thus, a company which operates a foundry, turning out metal castings, will not be classed as a scrap metal dealer, even though it buys in scrap to be melted down and turned into castings, and sells off scrap castings or any surplus scrap which was not required for melting down.

3.2 Registration
Scrap Metal Dealers Act 1964 Section 1

A scrap metal dealer is required to register with the local authority in whose area he has a scrap metal store. Details to be registered include details of his name and address, and the address of his 'store' (place where he keeps scrap metal, commonly referred to a 'scrap yard'). If he does not have a store, he must register with the local authority for the area where he has a place of business, or where he lives.

3.3 Records to be Kept

3.3.1 *Dealer with a Store*
Scrap Metal Dealers Act 1964 Section 2

A registered scrap metal dealer is required to keep **two** sets of details for each scrap metal store:
  i) relating to scrap metals received there;
  ii) relating to scrap metal processed at or despatched from there.

These records may be kept in two books, one for each, or both sets of records may be kept in one book. However, there shall be no more than one book for each.

The details to be recorded are:
  i) In respect of metals received:
    – description and weight of metal
    – date and time received
    – name and address of person from whom received
    – price paid, if known at the time the entry is made OR the estimated value if the price is not known
    – registered number of any motor vehicle in which the scrap is delivered.
  ii) In respect of metals processed or despatched:
    – description and weight
    – date of processing or despatch
    – if processed, the process applied
    – if despatched on sale or exchange, name and address of person to whom despatched
    – if despatched on sale or exchange, the consideration (price, etc)
    – if not sold or exchanged, the estimated value immediately before process/despatch.

3.3.2 *Itinerant Dealer*
Scrap Metal Dealers Act 1964 Section 3

If a registered scrap metal dealer satisfies the local authority that he intends to trade as an 'itinerant' scrap metal dealer, he will be exempted from the need to keep full records, but will be required instead:
  i) to keep all receipts for metals sold, showing weight and aggregate price;
  ii) to keep such receipts for a period of two years;
  iii) to produce the receipts on demand for inspection.

3.3.3 *Explanation*

Books: The dealer's records must be kept in bound books, one for metals 'In' and one for metals 'Processed or Out'. Alternatively, both sets of records may be kept in one book. What is not permitted is to have more than one currently in use for either purpose.

Value: If the dealer is unable to state the price at time of receiving, or of despatching, metal, the estimated value is required.

Vehicle registration: When metal is brought to the yard in a vehicle, the registered number must be recorded – even though it is the dealer's own vehicle.

Itinerant: An itinerant is a person who goes from house to house collecting old or worn out objects. To cater for the dealer, such as a 'rag and bone man' who goes round the streets pushing a small hand-cart or old pram, there is provision for less detailed records to be kept. It would be unrealistic to expect such a dealer to have the names and addresses of everyone from whom he received a bit of scrap metal. Instead, the itinerant has to keep the receipts he receives when he sells the metal on.

3.4 **Restrictions After Conviction**
Scrap Metal Dealers Act 1964 Section 4

A court before whom a person is convicted of certain offences, may apply restrictions to the way in which that person carries on business as a scrap metal dealer.

3.4.1 *Relevant Offences*

The offences relevant for these purposes are:
  i) carrying on business as a scrap metal dealer without being registered;
  ii) being a registered scrap metal dealer, any offence under Section 2 (failing to keep required records);
  iii) being a registered scrap metal dealer, any offence which, in the opinion of the court, involves dishonesty.

3.4.2 *Restrictions*

The restrictions which may be imposed apply to any place occupied by the dealer as a scrap metal store and are:
  i) no metal to be received there between 6.00 pm and 8.00 am;
  ii) all scrap metal received there to be kept in the form in which it was received, for a period of 72 hours from time of receipt.

Such an order shall remain in force for a specified period set by the court, not to exceed two years. The dealer may, during the duration of an order, apply to the court which made it, for the order to be revoked.

3.5 **Dealing with a Person Under 16**

3.5.1 *Offence*
Scrap Metal Dealers Act 1964 Section 5

A scrap metal dealer will commit an offence who:
  – acquires any scrap metal from a person apparently under the age of 16 years
  – whether offered by that person on his own behalf or on behalf of another person.

3.5.2 *Defence*
An accused dealer will have a defence if he proves that the person was 16 years of age or over.

3.5.3 *Explanation*
Acquire: The dealer does not have to buy to commit the offence.

On behalf of: The offence is committed even if the young person is acting for someone over 16. 'My Dad said to give you this' will not amount to an excuse.

Defence: The offence is committed if the young person involved is 'apparently' under the age of 16. If a person is 14 and looks it, the offence is committed; if the person is 14 but looks 18, the offence would not arise; if the person is 16 but looks 14, the offence would be committed but the defence would be available.

3.6 Police Powers
Scrap Metal Dealers Act 1964 Section 6

3.6.1 *Enter and Inspect*
A constable shall have a right:
- at all reasonable times
  - i) to enter and inspect any place registered as occupied by a scrap metal dealer as a scrap metal store, or as a place occupied by him wholly or partly for the purposes of business;
  - ii) to require production of and inspect any scrap metal and any book which the dealer is required to keep, or any receipt required to kept under Section 3 (by an itinerant dealer);
  - iii) to take copies of or extracts from such book or receipt.

3.6.2 *With Warrant*
Grounds for issue: A magistrate may issue a warrant upon being satisfied on information on oath that admission to a specified place is reasonably required in order to secure compliance with the provisions of the Act, or to ascertain whether there is compliance.

3.6.3 *Powers Under the Warrant*
The warrant will authorise any person having a right of entry to that place to enter at any time within one month from the date of the warrant, using force if necessary.

3.6.4 *Offence*
A person commits an offence who:
- obstructs the exercise of any right of entry or inspection
- or who fails to produce a book or other document which a person has a right to inspect.

3.6.5 *Explanation*
Enter and inspect: The right to enter may be exercised by any constable, at any reasonable time. This would normally be when the premises are open. The right extends to inspection of metal and of records.

Warrant: There is no provision for force to be used when exercising a right to enter and inspect. A warrant will therefore be required in any case where entry has been, or may be, refused.

4 BEGGING

4.1 Offence
Vagrancy Act 1824 Section 3

A person commits an offence who:
- wanders abroad or places himself in a public place, street, highway, court or passage
- to beg or gather alms
- or who causes, procures or encourages a child to do so.

4.1.1 *Explanation*
Wanders, or places: The offence may be committed whether the person begging moves around, or places himself in a public place, street, etc.

Public place: Although generally having largely the same meaning across many statutes, there may be slight differences from one Act to another. In this case it means a place to which the public go, whether they have a right to go or not.

Beg: Workmen on strike soliciting money from the public has been held not to be begging (*Pointon v Hill, Boot v Hill* (1884)). In fact the case decision goes further than merely identifying persons on strike as not being beggars. The Queen's Bench took the view that to commit the offence one has to 'be deemed a person of idle and disorderly habits of life ... making it their habit and mode of life to ... beg'.

Thus, to secure a prosecution for begging will require more than evidence of seeking money on one occasion; there will have to be evidence that the accused has made it a habit to do so.

Cause: To cause implies some degree of control.

Procure: To procure that something happens involves some effort to see that it does. 'You procure a thing by setting out to see that it happens and taking the appropriate steps to produce that happening' (*Attorney-General's Reference No. 1 of 1975* (1975)).

Child to beg: The offence is committed when the child is caused, procured or encouraged to do the begging. This is very similar to the offence under the Children and Young Persons Act 1933, of causing, procuring or allowing a child to beg *(see Chapter 34)*.

Punishment: If the offence is one of causing, procuring or encouraging a child to beg, the maximum sentence is one month's imprisonment. Otherwise the maximum is a Level 3 fine.

4.2 Begging by Exposing Wounds
Vagrancy Act 1824 Section 4

A person commits an offence who:
- wanders abroad
- and endeavours to gather alms
- by exposure of wounds or deformities.
(Maximum punishment – three months' imprisonment.)

4.3 Power of Arrest
Vagrancy Act 1824 Section 6

Any person may arrest a person found committing any offence against the Act.

The Act provides that a person making an arrest shall 'forthwith take and convey him before some justice of the peace ... or to deliver him to any constable or other peace officer ... to be so taken and conveyed'. Magistrates may not take too kindly to members of the public dragging beggars into court, but it must be remembered that police forces and the Crown Prosecution Service did not exist in 1824.

In accordance with Home Office advice, a constable should not exercise this or any other 'any person' power of arrest unless general arrest conditions, as set out in Section 25, Police and Criminal Evidence Act 1984, are satisfied.

5 COLLECTIONS FOR CHARITY

5.1 Note on Current Legislation

Charitable collections are currently governed by the House to House Collections Act 1939, which, despite the title, also deals with street collections.

However, the Charities Act 1992 will repeal the 1939 Act on some date which is not yet fixed. It is envisaged that some current regulations, made under the 1939 Act, setting out detail in relation to charitable collections, will remain in force, unchanged.

5.2 Regulations

Regulations may be made governing such matters as applications for authority to hold collections, keeping of accounts, collector's badges, lower age limits for collectors, etc.

5.3 Unauthorised Use of Badges, etc

House to House Collections Act 1939 Section 5
To be replaced by:
Charities Act 1992 Section 74(1)

5.3.1 *1939 Act*

A person commits an offence who:
- in connection with an appeal made by him to the public with a representation that the appeal is for a charitable purpose
- displays or uses:
  i) a badge or certificate of authority which is not for the time being held by him in connection with a lawfully authorised collection, or
  ii) any badge or device, certificate or other document, so nearly resembling a prescribed badge or certificate as to be calculated to deceive.

5.3.2 *1992 Act*

The wording is virtually identical. The principal difference being in the last few words:
- '... as to be likely to deceive a member of the public'.

5.3.3 *Explanation*

Real or imitation: An offence is committed, either by using a real badge or certificate of authority, not in connection with the collection for which that badge or certificate was issued, or by using something which resembles a real badge or certificate.

5.4 **Police Powers**
House to House Collections Act 1939 Section 6
To be replaced by regulations made under:
Charities Act 1992 Section 74(2)

5.4.1 *1939 Act*
A constable may require any person whom he believes to be acting as a collector for the purposes of a collection for a charitable purpose:
    – to declare to her immediately his name and address
    – and to sign his name.

Failure to comply with this requirement is an offence.

5.4.2 *1992 Act*
Regulations may be made requiring a collector, on request, to permit his badge or certificate of authority to be inspected by:
    – a constable
    – a duly authorised officer of the local authority
    – or by the occupier of any premises visited by him in the course of the collection.

Failure to comply with any such requirement will be an offence.

6 **TAXI TOUTS**

6.1 **Offence**
Criminal Justice and Public Order Act 1994 Section 167

A person commits an offence who:
    – in a public place
    – solicits persons
    – to hire vehicles to carry them as passengers.

6.1.1 *Exceptions*
Public service vehicles: A person will have a defence if he shows that he was soliciting for passengers for public service vehicles with the authority of the PSV operator.

Shared taxis: No offence will be committed by a person who is soliciting persons to hire licensed taxis, in connection with an approved shared taxi scheme (set up under the provisions of Section 10, Transport Act 1985).

6.1.2 *Explanation*
Public place: A public place is defined as any highway, and any other premises or place to which at the material time the public have access, on payment or otherwise. This will include airports, railway stations, the foyer of a theatre, etc.

Solicit: To constitute soliciting, there need not be reference made to a specific vehicle. A person could commit the offence by soliciting for passengers for one vehicle or for any number. To display a sign on a vehicle, that it is for hire, will not constitute soliciting. Thus, the driver of a taxi does not commit the offence merely by having the 'for hire' sign illuminated.

As passengers: The provisions relate only to vehicles to be hired to carry people as passengers. Self-drive car hire is not included.

Chapter 50: Driving Offences

1 MEANINGS OF TERMS

1.1 Introduction

This section of the book deals with the law relating to road traffic, but is far from being a comprehensive guide to traffic law. There is a huge quantity of legislation, in the form of European law, regulations and rules, relating to the physical construction of vehicles, which is constantly changing, in response to technological progress and the unceasing demands of (mainly European) legislators and administrators for uniformity across the continent. In this and succeeding chapters, the principal offences are dealt with, together with the less technically based requirements in relation to construction, use, equipment and driving of vehicles.

In most traffic legislation, there is reference to one or other of the terms – motor vehicle – drive – road – so a clear understanding of the scope and meaning of these terms is essential. These terms contain, in turn, references to other terms which are also dealt with, e.g. 'road' refers to 'highway'.

1.2 Motor Vehicle
Road Traffic Act 1988, Section 192

A motor vehicle is defined as a **mechanically propelled vehicle** intended or adapted for use on roads. A mechanically propelled vehicle is one which may derive its motive power from some sort of engine, as opposed to a wheel barrow or pram (pedestrian powered), horse drawn carriage or dog-sled (pulled by an animal), or pedal cycle. A touring caravan or the trailer section of an articulated lorry will be a vehicle, but not a mechanically propelled one. Certain requirements apply to such trailers when they are used on roads. The engine of a mechanically propelled vehicle may be powered by internal combustion, steam or battery power. A moped has an engine which may be assisted by pedalling, but is still a mechanically-propelled vehicle.

Not every mechanically propelled vehicle will be a motor vehicle; only those intended or adapted for use on roads will be so regarded. A dumper truck is intended for use on a building site, a fork lift truck for use in a factory or warehouse. Vehicles of these types may be driven on roads for short distances, as where a fork lift truck is being used to unload a lorry outside premises, or a dumper truck is driven between separate areas of a building site. These are not motor vehicles, and so do not have to comply with requirements in respect of lights, brakes, seat belts, etc, and the driver will not require a driving licence, even when the vehicle is used on a road

A trials motor bicycle may not be intended for use on roads, and may therefore have no lights, its silencer may not conform to requirements for road vehicles, etc. However, if it is then adapted, by being fitted with lights and a proper silencer , so that it may be used on a road, it will become a motor vehicle, and will have to be registered, taxed, covered by insurance, etc. Conversely, where a person stripped out windows and interior fittings from a car, to use it for auto-cross racing, off roads, it did not cease to be a motor vehicle, just because the defendant did not intend to drive the car under its own power on roads. He was stopped on a road while the car was being towed by another vehicle. Since the car had been produced as a motor vehicle, intended to run on ordinary roads, it retained its character throughout, and did not cease to be a motor vehicle merely because its present owner saw no prospect of driving it on a road under its own power (*Nichol v Leach and Another* (1972)).

1.3 **Driver**
Road Traffic Act 1988, Section 192
The word driver (except for the purposes of Section 1 of the Road Traffic Act 1988, relating to the offence of causing death by dangerous driving) includes a separate person acting as steersman of a motor vehicle, as well as any other person engaged in driving the vehicle. This provision is of little practical relevance, since very few mechanically propelled vehicles will require a steersperson; an example may be a steam powered traction engine, where one person steers while another keeps an eye on the boiler and regulates the speed.

Case law provides examples of what is and what is not meant by 'driver' and 'driving'. There are three main criteria to be satisfied if a person is to be regarded as driving:
1. She has control over the movement of the vehicle, whether or not this movement is produced by means of the engine;
2. She has control over the direction of the vehicle, i.e. the steering;
3. What she is doing falls within the ordinary meaning of the word 'driving' (*Keynote case: R v MacDonagh (1974)*).

A person sitting behind the wheel of a car, steering it as it free-wheels down hill, satisfies all these criteria. Control over the movement may be achieved by applying the brakes. However, a person who releases the handbrake on a parked car and allows it to run down a hill, without getting into the car, is not driving (*R v Roberts* (1964)). Such a person may have started the car off, but does not thereafter meet any of the above criteria.

Two persons may be regarded as driving at the same time, as where a woman passenger leant across and took the steering wheel while her boyfriend was in the driver's seat operating the foot pedals. In this case, the woman was regarded as satisfying the three criteria, because she could reach the handbrake and ignition key, so being able to control the movement of the vehicle (*Tyler v Whatmore* (1976)).

A person may still be 'driving' although his motor vehicle is stopped and the engine switched off, depending on the reason for his ceasing to drive. If this reason is sufficiently connected with the actual driving, he may still be considered to be the driver; it is a question of fact in any particular case. Where the driver had stopped his car and had been sitting in the driving seat for 20 minutes, having a conversation with others in the car, he was held not to be driving. Holding a conversation was not something connected with the driving of the car (*Stevens v Thornborrow* (1969)). However, on appeal to the Queen's Bench, one of the judges pointed out that it should not be taken as a general rule, that in every case where a driver has been sitting in the driving seat for 20 minutes, he should be regarded as no longer 'the driver'. In many cases he will be still regarded as driving.

1.3.1 *Attempt to Drive*
Some offences may be committed when a person is attempting to drive, e.g. offences involving excess alcohol. Whether a person is 'attempting to drive' will be a question of fact for a court to decide in any particular case. An act which is merely preparatory to driving, such as opening the door of the vehicle, will not amount to an attempt to drive. However, if a person starts the engine and is trying to put the car in gear, but is stopped by police before he can drive off, or he is so drunk that he is unable to engage gear, this would amount to an attempt to drive.

1.4 **Road**
Road Traffic Act 1988, Section 192
The term road means any highway and any other road to which the public has access, including bridges over which a road passes.

In order to understand this definition, it is first necessary to consider the term highway. A **highway** is a way over which members of the public have a right to pass and re-pass. This term is dealt with in detail in Chapter 46, including the different sorts of highways – footpath, bridleway, carriageway. This raises the point that a motor vehicle being driven across country, e.g. along an old drove road which is subject to a public right of way, will have to be covered by insurance, and the driver will require to be licensed, because he is driving on a road.

A road which is not a highway, because the public do not have a right to pass along it, may still amount to a 'road' for road traffic law purposes, if the public are permitted access. Examples would include roads through an industrial estate, where all the land is privately owned. If only a restricted class of person is allowed access, e.g. friends driving along the driveway leading to a large house, the driveway is not one to which the public have access, so will not amount to a road.

Major car rallies may include sections over 'forest roads'. The manner in which cars are driven on these sections would amount to dangerous driving, except for the fact that the 'forest roads' are not roads, because members of the public do not have access.

The extent to which the ground over which vehicles may pass will amount to a road, has been considerably increased since a Court of Appeal ruling in 1996 *(Keynote case: Cutter v Eagle Star Insurance Co. Ltd)*. Prior to this decision, one of the required characteristics of a road was that it was an ordinary line of communication; on this basis, a particular car park may have been held not be a road, because it was not ordinarily used by persons to get from A to B. Now, the ruling is that any way used for the passage of vehicles will amount to a road, including areas of a public car park marked out for the passage of vehicles.

Additionally, a way from a car park to a parade of shops, regularly used by pedestrians, but not by vehicles, constitutes a road, provided the route is definable (*Clarke v Kato* (1996).

2 **DANGEROUS DRIVING**

2.1 **Offence**
Road Traffic Act 1988, Section 2
A person commits an offence who:
  – drives
  – a mechanically propelled vehicle
  – dangerously
  – on a road or other public place.

2.1.1 *Explanation*
Drives: This term is explained in paragraph 1.3.

Mechanically propelled vehicle: The offence is not confined to motor vehicles. The driver of a fork lift truck, motorway construction earth-mover, or other non-motor vehicle may be liable for driving dangerously.

Road or public place: The manner in which a person drives off-road in a public place may render him liable for this offence.

Drive dangerously: The Act assists in determining whether a person will be driving dangerously by providing guidelines:

1) A person will be regarded as driving dangerously if:
    i) the way he drives falls far below what would be expected of a competent and careful driver, **and**
       it would be obvious to a competent and careful driver that driving in that way would be dangerous; or
    ii) it would be obvious to a competent and careful driver that driving the vehicle in its current state would be dangerous.

2) The term 'dangerous' refers to danger either of injury to any person or of serious damage to property. This would include danger to a person in the offender's vehicle as well as to anyone else. So far as property is concerned, the danger must be of serious damage.

    Driving in excess of a speed limit may be a factor to take into account when determining whether driving was dangerous. However, a competent and careful driver would not drive along a motorway at 70 mph in thick fog, so prevailing conditions, as well as speed limits, may have to be considered.

3) In determining what would be expected of, or obvious to a competent and careful driver, regard may be had not only to the circumstances of which he would be expected to be aware, but also to any circumstances shown to have been within the knowledge of the accused. Thus, the accused is judged on what would have been obvious to a reasonable driver, even if it was not obvious to the accused, **plus** anything in the accused's own knowledge, even if that fact would not have been obvious to a competent driver unless he was specifically made aware of it.

4) Reference to the condition of the vehicle will include anything attached to or carried in or on the vehicle, and the manner in which it is attached or carried. Thus, an insecure load on a lorry could lead to the driver being charged with the offence, if this gives rise to danger of injury or serious damage (Road Traffic Act 1988, Section 2A).

3 CAUSING DEATH BY DANGEROUS DRIVING

3.1 Offence
(Road Traffic Act 1988, Section 1)
A person commits an offence who:
- causes the death of another person
- by driving
- a mechanically propelled vehicle
- dangerously
- on a road or other public place.

3.1.1 *Explanation*
Causes death: In many cases, the cause of death will clearly arise from the dangerous driving of the accused, e.g. where the victim is on a pedestrian crossing and the accused's vehicle,

being driven dangerously, collides with the victim. In some cases, there will be other factors leading to the death if the victim, such as pneumonia setting in when the victim is recovering from serious injury.

The dangerous driving need not be the only, or even the most substantial cause of death, but the relationship between the dangerous driving and the death must be more than merely trifling (the legal term for trifling is de minimis). For example, a person is injured in an accident and is being taken to hospital by ambulance when the ambulance is involved in an accident, resulting in the death of the injured person. It could be argued that had it not been for the first accident, the injured person would not have been in the ambulance, so would not have died. This connection, between the first accident and the death, is not enough for a driver in the first accident to be charged with this offence; the connection between his driving and the death of the victim is too remote.

Any person: The deceased person may be in another vehicle, be a pedestrian, or a passenger in the accused's vehicle; it matters not.

In almost all other respects, the elements of the offence are the same as for the offence of dangerous driving. The one exception is the meaning of the term 'driver'. As mentioned in paragraph 1.2 above, a steersman is not a driver for the purposes of this offence.

3.2 **Arrest and Sentence**
The offence is triable on indictment only and carries a maximum sentence of 10 years' imprisonment. It is a serious arrestable offence.

4 **CARELESS OR INCONSIDERATE DRIVING**

4.1 **Offence**
Road Traffic Act 1988, Section 3
A person commits an offence who:
 - drives
 - a mechanically propelled vehicle
 - on a road or other public place
 - without due care and attention
 - or without reasonable consideration for other persons using the road or public place.

4.1.1 *Explanation*
Due care and attention: There is no statutory definition of what constitutes driving without due care, as there is for dangerous driving. However, the standard of care required of a driver is an objective one, which does not take account of the skill or experience of the driver (*McCrone v Riding* (1938)). Thus, a learner driver, on her first driving lesson, is required to exercise the same degree of care and attention as an experienced driver.

A police officer responding to an emergency call is required to meet the same standards of care as any other person (*Wood v Richards* (1977)).

To give misleading signals, e.g. failing to cancel a left-turn indicator, amounts to careless driving (*Another v Probert* (1968).

Reasonable consideration: Lack of care and attention is overwhelmingly the way in which this offence is committed, but failing to give reasonable consideration will also give rise to the offence The usual example quoted is the driver who consciously drives through a puddle, so as to soak a pedestrian. A bus driver who drove his bus at high speed, taking a corner very sharply, so as to cause alarm and panic among his passengers, was convicted of driving without reasonable consideration for other road users.

Other persons using the road: This will include passengers in the vehicle being driven by the accused (*Pawley v Wharldall* (1966)).

5 EVIDENCE OF ALCOHOL CONSUMPTION

Offences involving alcohol and vehicles are quite distinct from offences of dangerous or careless driving. These are dealt with in Chapter 51. However, evidence of alcohol consumption may be given by the prosecution in cases of dangerous or careless driving, or of causing death by dangerous driving. The matter was considered in two cases, *R v McBride* (1961) and *R v Woodward* (1994). In the former case it was stated that:

'The question is, was the driver adversely affected by the alcohol, this fact is a circumstance relevant to the issue of whether he was driving dangerously. Evidence to this effect is of probative value, and is admissible in law – the mere fact that the driver had a drink is not of itself relevant – such evidence must tend to show that the amount of drink taken was such as would adversely affect the driver or, alternatively, that the driver was adversely affected. Secondly, the court has overriding discretion to exclude such evidence if, in the opinion of the court its prejudicial effect outweighs its probative value.'

For example, evidence that a driver had been seen in a pub drinking from a glass of beer a short time before she was involved in an accident would be likely to be excluded. It is prejudicial to the defendant, raising the possibility in the mind of the magistrates or jury that she may have been affected by alcohol, without in any way showing that she was so affected, or that she was likely to be affected.

6 DEFENCES

6.1 Automatism

Automatism refers to involuntary movement of a person's body. If such involuntary movement causes a driver to lose control of her car, she may have a defence to a charge involving dangerous or careless driving. This may arise from illness, such as a sudden seizure, fit or diabetic coma, or from some other cause such as being hit in the face by an object thrown at one's vehicle (*Hill v Baxter* (1958)).

It is an element of this defence that the cause was unforseen and could not have been predicted by the accused. For example, if a person suffers regularly from fits or loss of consciousness, it is reasonable to suppose that he may such an attack while driving. In such a case, he would not have the defence open to him. The burden of proof rests with the defence (*Moses v Winder* (1981)).

6.2 Mechanical Defect

This defence bears some similarity to that of automatism, in that it refers to loss of control, not of one's body, but of one's vehicle. A driver will have a defence to a charge involving dangerous or careless driving if he was deprived of control of his vehicle as a result of a mechanical defect.

The driver will only have the defence available if he did not know of the defect and it was not such that he should have discovered it by exercising reasonable care. For example, the defence of brake failure will not succeed if the accused knew that his brakes were faulty, or if the fault is one which should have been discovered had he carried out normal, routine maintenance of the vehicle.

The onus of proof is on the prosecution, but it is up to the accused to raise the defence (*R v Spurge* (1961)). Thus, if a driver, charged with dangerous driving after his car mounted the pavement and injured a pedestrian, claims that the accident arose because of faulty steering on his car, it will then be up to the prosecution to prove either that the accused knew of the defect, or that he should have discovered it had he taken steps to service the car.

Keynote Cases

7.1 *R v MacDonagh* [1974] 2 All ER 257

Problem
The meaning of the term 'drive'.

Circumstances
A police officer told MacDonagh to move his car, which was parked on a road, because it was causing an obstruction. MacDonagh was at that time disqualified from driving. Some 10 minutes later, the officer returned to find MacDonagh manoeuvring the car. MacDonagh appeared at Crown Court charged with driving while disqualified. There is some dispute as to the evidence, the police officer claiming that the engine was running, the defendant denying this. The recorder directed the jury that even if they accepted MacDonagh's version – that he had both feet on the ground, with his shoulder against the door pillar pushing the car, and one hand on the steering wheel – he might still be regarded as driving, being in control of the steering and propulsion of the vehicle. He was convicted and appealed.

Decision
The Court of Appeal held that MacDonagh was not driving. To constitute driving, a person must be in control of the steering, or be in the driving seat, and he must have something to do with the propulsion, although this may arise from the vehicle coasting downhill, or even being pushed by other persons. In summary, he must to a substantial effect be controlling the movement and direction of the car. The additional factor is that the person's activities must come within the ordinary meaning of the word 'driving'. A person who puts one foot into the car which he is pushing, the better to have access to the controls **may** be driving, but someone who has both feet on the ground clearly is not.

Comment
Whether a person is driving will be a matter of fact to be decided in any particular case, but the decision here sets out the three criteria to be satisfied. In the course of its deliberations, the Court of Appeal over-ruled an earlier decision, that a person behind the wheel of a broken down motor vehicle being towed by another, was not a driver (*Wallace v Major* (1946)). A person in such a position will clearly satisfy all three criteria.

7.2 *Cutter v Eagle Star Insurance Company Ltd* (1996) TLR 3 December 1996

Problem

To what extent will parts of a car park constitute a 'road' for the purposes of traffic law?

Circumstances

Cutter was injured while a passenger in a motor vehicle on a car park. His claim against the insurance company for damages for his injuries was turned down at Tunbridge Wells County Court, on the grounds that when Cutter suffered his injuries, the vehicle was not on a road. (As with most motor vehicle insurance, cover extended only to when the vehicle was on a road.) Cutter appealed and the matter was decided at the Court of Appeal.

Decision

Lord Justice Beldham took the view that a 'road' was any way used for the passage of vehicles. The legislation intended that the term would include not just highways, but other roads, provided the public had access. Because of the increase in the use of motor vehicles, the size of car parks generally had increased. Many were laid out with kerbs marking the areas on which drivers were expected to drive, giving an appearance more like that of a conventional road. The purpose of insurance was to enable persons injured by motor vehicles to obtain compensation. The meaning of 'road' should reflect this purpose. The question should not be, as in some earlier cases, 'Was the car park a road?', but rather 'Was there within the car park, a roadway?'.

In the present case, the car park was laid out with a way marked for the passage of vehicles, controlled by conventional road signs and markings. The risk of accidents occurring in the car park was just as great as on any other road. There were other situations in which vehicles may be driven over defined routes over open spaces, when attending a sporting event or other entertainment.

Comment

This decision will have a significant effect on the enforcement of traffic law in places which were not previously considered as roads. A route across a field used as a parking area on the day of the annual agricultural show or pop concert, will be a road, as will the marked out areas of a supermarket car park.

Note that 'road' is not confined to a way used for vehicles, the term equally applies to a footpath. A compatible decision to that in Cutter was reached in *Clarke v Kato* (1996), involving a route used only by persons on foot.

Chapter 51: Drink and Drugs

DRIVING OR BEING IN CHARGE WHILST UNDER THE INFLUENCE OF DRINK OR DRUGS
Road Traffic Act 1988 (as amended by Section 4 Road Traffic Act 1991) Section 4

1.1 (1) A person who, when driving or attempting to drive:
- a mechanically propelled vehicle
- on a road or other public place
- is unfit to drive through drink or drugs
- is guilty of an offence.

(2) Without prejudice to subsection (1) above, a person who, when in charge of a mechanically propelled vehicle which is on a road or other public place, is unfit to drive through drink or drugs is guilty of an offence.

(3) For the purposes of subsection (2) above, a person shall be deemed not to have been in charge of a mechanically propelled vehicle if he proves that at the material time the circumstances were such that there was no likelihood of his driving it so long as he remained unfit to drive through drink or drugs.

(4) The court may, in determining whether there was such a likelihood as is mentioned in subsection (3) above, disregard any injury to him and any damage to the vehicle.

(5) For the purposes of this Section, a person shall be taken to be unfit to drive if his ability to drive properly is for the time being impaired.

(6) A constable may arrest a person without warrant if he has reasonable grounds to suspect that that person is or has been committing an offence under this Section.

(7) For the purposes of arresting a person under power conferred by subsection (6) above, a constable may enter (if needed by force) any place where that person is or where the constable, with reasonable cause suspects him to be.

1.1.1 *Explanation*
Attempt to drive: The meaning of this term is dealt with in chapter 50. An attempt to drive while unfit will **not** constitute an attempt to commit the offence of driving whilst unfit; it is the full offence of attempting to drive while unfit.

In charge: Whether a person is in charge of a vehicle on a particular occasion will be a question of fact for the court to decide. Generally, a person who takes a vehicle out on a road will be 'in charge' of that vehicle until he has finished using it on that occasion. In the course of a journey there may be a progression through the stages – not in charge – in charge – attempting to drive – driving – in charge – not in charge. For most practical purposes, a person in charge may be standing beside his vehicle, or sitting in it. In theory, a person who is at home, in possession of the car keys, intending to use his car soon, will be 'in charge', but proving this intention is another matter. A number of questions may be asked, in seeking to determine whether a person is in charge:

- Where is the vehicle?
- How far is he from it?
- What is he doing at the relevant time?
- Is he in possession of a key for the vehicle?
- Is there evidence that he intends to drive or take control of the vehicle?
- Does any other person have any form of control over the vehicle?

A person who realises that he has had too much to drink, so curls up in the back seat of his car to sleep it off, may be liable for the 'in charge' offence if the car is on a road or public place.

Vehicle: This offence may be committed in relation to a mechanically propelled vehicle, it is not confined to motor vehicles.

Road: This term is dealt with in Chapter 50.

Unfit: Subsection (5) provides that a person is unfit to drive if her ability to drive properly is for the time being impaired. What amounts to 'impaired' will be a question of fact for the court to decide, on the evidence. There may be evidence from an eye-witness, as to the accused's condition, a doctor may give evidence as to the accused's ability to carry out certain tasks, and there may be evidence of the level of alcohol found in a specimen of blood or urine.

Through drink or drugs: The term 'drug' means any intoxicant other than alcohol. This would therefore include substances used for 'sniffing' if capable of causing intoxication, and drugs lawfully used, e.g. prescribed by a doctor, as well as drugs used unlawfully, such as cannabis or cocaine. Although the overwhelming majority of prosecutions relate to alcoholic drink, the offence may arise when a person's ability to drive is impaired by the affect of a drug. One of the simple ways of detecting that a person has been drinking alcoholic beverages is by smell. This, coupled with evidence of staggering and slurred speech, may be enough to secure a conviction.

Evidence of uncoordinated movement without a distinctive smell is unlikely to be sufficient to prove that a person is affected by a drug, and there are no readily-available devices for detecting cannabis, equivalent to breath-testing kits and analysis machines. Evidence from a medical practitioner will almost certainly be required, if use of drugs is suspected. A person who is suspected of having committed this offence may be required to provide specimens of breath, blood or urine *(see paragraph 4.1 below)*. If a doctor suspects that the person's condition is due to a drug, rather than to alcohol, the requirement to provide specimens may be restricted to blood or urine.

Defence: A person may be deemed not to have been 'in charge' if there was no likelihood of him driving while he remained unfit *(see paragraph 7.1 below)*.

DRIVING OR BEING IN CHARGE WITH AN ALCOHOL CONCENTRATION ABOVE THE PRESCRIBED LIMIT
Road Traffic Act 1988 Section 5

2.1 (1) If a person:
  a) drives or attempts to drive a motor vehicle on a road or other public place, or
  b) is in charge of a motor vehicle on a road or other public place
  after consuming so much alcohol that the proportion of it in his breath, blood or urine exceeds the prescribed limit he is guilty of an offence.

(2) It is a defence for a person charged with an offence under subsection (1)(b) above to prove that at the time he is alleged to have committed the offence the circumstances were such that there was no likelihood of his driving the vehicle whilst the proportion of alcohol in his breath, blood or urine remained likely to exceed the prescribed limit.

(3) The court may, in determining whether there was such a likelihood as is mentioned in subsection (2) above, disregard any injury to him and any damage to the vehicle.

2.1.1 *Explanation*

Drive/attempt to drive/road: The meanings of these terms are explained in Chapter 50.

In charge: This term is explained in paragraph 1.1.1 above.

Vehicle: Offences involving excess alcohol may be committed only in relation to motor vehicles. A person driving a mechanically propelled vehicle which is not intended or adapted for use on roads, will not be liable for these offences.

Prescribed limit: When a person consumes an alcoholic drink, the alcohol passes into the digestive system, then into the blood. Some of the alcohol passes from the blood into the air in the lungs, while some of it passes into the urine, as the body rids itself of it. There are therefore three different, but equivalent limits prescribed by law. An offence is committed when the level of alcohol in the body exceeds one of these limits. They are currently:
  i) 35 micrograms of alcohol in 100 millilitres of breath;
  ii) 80 milligrams of alcohol in 100 millilitres of blood;
  iii) 107 milligrams of alcohol in 100 millilitres of urine.

Defence: A person will be deemed not to be in charge while over the prescribed limit if it is proved that there was no likelihood of him driving whilst he remained over the limit *(see paragraph 7.1 below)*.

THE REQUIREMENT TO PROVIDE SAMPLES OF BREATH
Road Traffic Act 1988 Section 6

3.1 (1) Where a constable in uniform has reasonable cause to suspect:
  a) that a person driving or attempting to drive
    – or in charge of a motor vehicle
    – on a road or other public place
    – has alcohol in his body
    – or has committed a traffic offence
    – whilst that vehicle was in motion, or
  b) that a person has been driving or attempting to drive
    – or has been in charge of a motor vehicle
    – on a road or other public place
    – with alcohol in his body
    – and that that person still has alcohol in his body, or
  c) that a person has been driving or attempting to drive
    – or been in charge of a motor vehicle
    – on a road or other public place

    – and has committed a traffic offence
    – whilst the vehicle was in motion.

he may, subject to Section 9 of the Act, require him to provide a specimen of breath for a breath test.

(2) If an accident occurs:
    – owing to the presence of a motor vehicle
    – on a road or other public place
    – a constable may
    – subject to Section 9 of the Act
    – require any person
    – who he has reasonable cause to believe was
    – driving or attempting to drive
    – or in charge of the vehicle
    – at the time of the accident
    – to provide a specimen of breath for a breath test.

(3) A person may be required under subsection (1) or subsection (2) above to provide a specimen either at or near the place where the requirement is made or, if the requirement is made under subsection (2) above and the constable making the requirement thinks fit, at a police station specified by the constable.

(4) A person who, without reasonable excuse, fails to provide a specimen of breath when required to do so in pursuance of this Section is guilty of an offence.

3.1.1 *Explanation*

In uniform: For the purposes of subsection (1) – moving traffic offence or suspicion of alcohol – only a police officer in uniform may exercise the power to require a breath test. However, following an accident, any police officer, may exercise the power. Unless the point is challenged, a court is entitled to assume that the constable was wearing uniform (*Richards v West* (1980)). Failure to wear a helmet or cap will not mean that the officer is not in uniform (*Wallwork v Giles* (1970)).

Reasonable cause to suspect: Evidence should be given from which the court may assess whether there was good reason for requiring a breath test. The reasonable suspicion may include anonymous information (*DPP v Wilson* (1991)). When a police officer stopped a driver without suspecting that he had consumed alcohol, then formed the opinion that he had, the officer was entitled to require a specimen of breath (*DPP v McGladigran* (1991)).

Drive/attempt to drive/in charge: These terms have the same meanings as in relation to the offences under Sections 4 and 5, above.

Motor vehicle: Offences involving excess alcohol relate only to motor vehicles, not to mechanically propelled vehicles which are not motor vehicles. It is logical then, that breath tests may be required only in relation to motor vehicles.

Road or public place: A breath test may be required in respect of a motor vehicle in a public place as well as on a road. The car park of a public house which is open to the public will amount to a public place (or, perhaps to a road) while the public are allowed access. If there is a gate which is closed when the pub is closed, to keep people out, the car will no longer be a road or public place, so requirements for breath tests should no longer be made there.

Traffic offence: A requirement for a breath test may be made even where there is no ground for suspecting that a driver has alcohol in his body, if there is suspicion that he has committed a traffic offence while the vehicle was in motion (or in common parlance a 'moving traffic offence').The term 'traffic offence' will include most offences under the Road Traffic Act 1988 and the Road Traffic Offenders Act 1988, as well as some offences under other Acts. A full list is given in subsection 7(8). Remember that regulations are made under Acts, and a breach of say, lighting regulations, will be an offence under the Road Traffic Act 1988.

Offences relating to driving instruction or to registration and vehicle licensing are excluded, but most other offences, relating to vehicle documents, lights, construction and use, speed limits, etc, will be 'traffic offences'. Only offences involving moving vehicles qualify, so parking in the controlled area of a pedestrian crossing, or leaving a vehicle with the engine running, will not give grounds for a breath test.

Is driving/has been: A breath test may be required, based on reasonable suspicion, of a person who:

i) is driving, attempting to drive, or in charge of a motor vehicle;

ii) has been driving, attempting to drive in charge of a motor vehicle.

There is no time limit as to how long ago it is since the person may have been driving, and there are many examples of drivers being found to be well over the limit on the morning following a night of heavy drinking. However, the body does rid itself of alcohol over time, so there are limits in practice, after which to require a breath test will be a pointless exercise. Where the ground for the requirement is a suspicion of alcohol, the constable must suspect that the person still has alcohol in his body.

Accident: The term 'accident' is not defined in the Road Traffic Act 1988; all the Act does make provision for, is the action to be taken by a driver in relation to certain types of accidents, where injury or damage is caused to other people or their property. The term 'accident' has to be given its ordinary, popular meaning, and will include an incident where damage is caused deliberately to a vehicle (*Chief Constable of West Midlands Police v Billingham* (1979)).

A breath test may be required when an accident has occurred owing to the presence of a motor vehicle on a road or other public place. 'Owing to the presence' does not imply that it was the fault of the driver of that motor vehicle; it merely indicates that if the vehicle had not been there, it would not have been involved in the accident. For example, a pedestrian steps off the footpath into the path of a lorry and is knocked flying; the pedestrian is at fault, but the accident occurred 'owing to the presence' of the lorry on the road.

A breath test may be required when an accident has occurred, of a person whom the constable has reason to believe was driving, etc, at the time of the accident. There must have been an accident; mere reason to believe that there has been an accident is not enough. If a constable stops a car with damage to it, and the damage turns out to have occurred when the car was driven into the garage door on the owner's driveway, any breath test required on the basis that the constable believed the car to have been involved in an accident, will be unlawful. On the other hand, if a non-stop accident is reported and a constable stops a car which answers the description of the offending vehicle, a breath test may properly be required of the driver, based on reasonable cause to believe he was involved in the accident, even if it later transpires that he was not.

The fact that a person found near the scene of an accident, is the owner of a motor vehicle abandoned at the scene, gives rise to a reasonable belief that the owner was the driver at the time of the accident (*Baker v Oxford* (1980)).

Quantity and quality: The Act provides that a specimen of breath for a breath test will not be regarded as having been provided unless it is of sufficient quantity, and is given in such a way, as to enable the test to be carried out. (Section 11(3)) To give an accurate indication of the level of alcohol in the blood, breath must come from reasonably deep in the lungs. A short, shallow breath would not be sufficient, and would be regarded as a failure to provide.

Fail without reasonable excuse: The term 'fail' includes refuse. Failure is only reasonable if related to the person's physical or mental condition. The fact that a driver has a damaged lung, for example, or is suffering from injuries to his mouth, would afford a reasonable excuse. A claim that one has not had any alcoholic drink, or a request to wait until a solicitor arrives to advise on whether or not to give breath, will not amount to excuses sufficient to avoid committing the offence of failing to provide a specimen.

PROVISION OF SPECIMENS FOR ANALYSIS
Road Traffic Act 1988 Section 7

4.1 (1) In the course of an investigation into whether a person has committed an offence under Section 3A, 4 or 5 of this Act a constable may, subject to the following provisions of this Section and Section 9 of this Act, require him:
   a) to provide two specimens of breath for analysis by means of a device of a type approved by the Secretary of State, or
   b) to provide specimen of blood or urine for a laboratory test.

(2) A requirement under this Section to provide a specimen of breath can only be made at a police station.

(3) A requirement under this Section to provide a specimen of blood or urine can only be made at a police station or at a hospital, and it cannot be made at a police station unless:
   a) the constable making the requirement has reasonable cause to believe that for medical reasons a specimen of breath cannot be provided or should not be required, or
   b) at the time the requirement is made a device or a reliable device of the type mentioned in subsection (1)(a) above is not available at the police station or it is then for any reason not practicable to use the device there, or
   c) the suspected offence is one under Section 3A or 4 of this Act and the constable making the requirement has been advised by a medical practitioner that the condition of the person required to provide the specimen might be due to some drug;
   But may then be made notwithstanding that the person required to provide the specimen has already provided, or has been required to provide two specimens of breath.

(4) If the provision of a specimen other than a specimen of breath may be required in pursuance of this Section the question of whether it is to be a specimen of blood or urine shall be decided by the constable making the requirement, but if a medical practitioner is of the opinion that for medical reasons a specimen of blood cannot or should not be taken the specimen shall be that of urine.

(5) A specimen of urine shall be provided within one hour of the requirement for its provision being made and after the previous specimen of urine.

(6) A person who, without reasonable excuse, fails to provide a specimen when required to do so in pursuance of this Section is guilty of an offence.

(7) A constable must on requiring any person to provide a specimen in pursuance with this Section, warn him that a failure to provide it may render him liable to prosecution.

4.1.1 *Explanation*

Investigation: Specimens may be required for analysis whenever an investigation is being conducted into whether a person has committed an offence under Section 3A (cause death by careless driving), Section 4 (unfit through drink or drugs) or Section 5 (excess alcohol). A person may be arrested on suspicion of driving whilst unfit through drink, be required to give specimens for analysis, and end up being prosecuted for excess alcohol. Alternatively, evidence of the level of alcohol in a specimen of breath, blood or urine, may be used in a prosecution for driving whilst unfit.

An unlawful arrest does not invalidate subsequent requirements to provide specimens; what matters is whether police are investigating a relevant offence, not whether an arrest was lawful (*Hartland v Alden* (1987)).

Police station/hospital: There is no requirement that a person be under arrest when he is required to provide specimens for analysis. However, the requirement for breath specimens may be made only at a police station; for blood or urine, only at a police station or hospital.

Which sort?: At a police station, the first choice will be for breath, to be analysed there and then on an approved type of machine. Only in the circumstances set out in subsection (3), may a constable at a police station make a requirement for blood or urine, rather than for breath, viz. medical reasons, the breath-analysis machine not working properly, or not available, or a doctor has advised that drugs, rather than alcohol, may be involved.

Blood or urine may be required even though breath specimens have already been asked for, or provided. For example, a person appears to be intoxicated, provides breath specimens which show low alcohol content, a doctor then advises that the person's condition may be due to a drug. In such a case, blood or urine may then be required.

A blood sample may be used in evidence only if it has been taken by a doctor, and with the suspect's consent (Section 11(4)).

How many/how much?: Two specimens of breath are required; prosecution is based on the lower of the two readings. If the two readings are identical, the prosecution may be based on either (*R v Brentford Magistrates' Court, ex parte Clarke* (1987)).

Two specimens of urine are required, to be supplied within one hour of the requirement being made. The first is discarded, the second is used for laboratory analysis. In the case of blood or urine, part is sent for analysis, part given to the suspect, so that he may, if he wishes, have it analysed independently.

The requirement as to quantity and quality of breath, applies equally to specimens for analysis as it does to breath for a breath test *(see paragraph 3.1.1)*.

Choice – blood or urine: The police officer making the requirement will decide whether the specimen to be provided is to be of blood or urine. However, if a doctor advises that she is of the opinion that for medical reasons urine rather than blood should be required, the police officer has to require urine.

Before a constable decides which, of blood or urine, he will require, he must inform the person that blood or urine specimens will be required, tell him that the choice rests with the police, and ask the suspect if there is any reason why he cannot provide blood. There is no requirement to ask the suspect which of blood or urine he would prefer *(Keynote case: DPP v Warren (1992))*.

Warning: When requiring a specimen of breath, blood or urine for analysis, the constable making the requirement must warn the person that failure to provide the specimen(s) may render him liable to prosecution.

Fail without reasonable excuse: An agreement to provide a specimen, subject to a condition, is treated as a failure to supply. Usually, to be 'reasonable', there must be some medical reason for failing to supply a specimen. The fact that a person wanted to see a doctor and a solicitor and to make a complaint against police, did not amount to a reasonable excuse (*Chief Constable of Avon and Somerset v O'Brien* (1987)).

However, a foreigner with a limited command of English, was held to have a reasonable excuse when he claimed that he did not understand what was being required of him, or the consequences of failing to provide a specimen (*Beck v Sager* (1979)).

A person who provides one specimen of breath, but fails to provide a second should be prosecuted for failure to provide the specimens as required. He may not be charged with an excess alcohol offence based on the one specimen, because a prosecution has to be based on the lower of two specimens. Any evidence that indicates the level of alcohol consumed may be admitted with a view to deciding the seriousness of the punishment for an offence of failure to provide specimens; this could include evidence of the reading when only one specimen is provided (*Cracknell v Willis* (1987)).

4.2 Voluntary Specimens of Blood or Urine
Road Traffic Act 1988 Section 8

4.2.1 *Suspect's Choice*
If the specimen of breath with the lower proportion of alcohol contains no more than 50 micrograms of alcohol in 100 millilitres of breath, the person providing it may then claim that it should be replaced with a specimen of blood or urine. If such a specimen is provided, then neither specimen of breath shall be used.

4.2.2 *Police Choice*
Once the suspect has opted for the blood/urine alternative to breath, the choice as to whether it shall be blood or urine, rests with the constable. Although the police officer will make the decision, he must nevertheless tell the suspect of the alternative options, blood or urine (*DPP v Magill* (1988)) and then ask if there is any reason why he cannot give blood (Keynote case: *DPP v Warren* (1992)).

4.2.3 *Explanation*
The provision, allowing for a motorist to choose an alternative to breath samples, was intended to overcome suspicions when breath analysis machines were introduced, that the new technology might not be reliable. With a reading not too far above the limit, the opportunity to have a blood or urine sample analysed at a laboratory, would serve to forestall a defence claim that the machine produced inaccurate results.

The choice, whether stick with the breath specimen results or go for blood/urine, rests with the suspect, he may not be required to provide blood or urine (*Wakely v Hyams* (1987)).

HOSPITAL PROCEDURE
Road Traffic Act 1988 Section 9

5.1 (1) While a person is at hospital as a patient he shall not be required to provide a specimen of breath for a breath test or to provide a specimen for a laboratory test unless the medical practitioner in immediate charge of his case has been notified of the proposal to make the requirement; and:

a) if the requirement is then made, it shall be for the provision of a specimen at hospital, but

b) if the medical practitioner objects on the ground specified in subsection (2) below the requirement shall not be made.

(2) The grounds on which the medical practitioner may object is that the requirement or the provision of the specimen or, in the case of a specimen of blood or urine, the warning required under Section 7(7) of this Act, would be prejudicial to the proper care and treatment of the patient.

5.1.1 *Explanation*

Patient at hospital: Whether a person is a patient at a hospital is a question of fact for the court to determine in any particular case. A person remains a patient until his treatment is finished for that particular day. For example, a doctor tells a patient, 'The nurse will give you an injection. Sit in the waiting room for 15 minutes after the injection, then you can go.' The person will then remain a patient receiving treatment during the period he spends in the waiting room after the injection. If he decides to leave before the 15 minute period elapses, he will cease to be a patient at hospital at the time he walks out.

If the man steps outside for a cigarette, then comes back into the waiting room, he will still be a patient at hospital, while he remains in the grounds of the hospital.

Provision at hospital: A person at a hospital as a patient may not be required to go to a police station to give a specimen there; any requirement made must be for the specimen to be provided at the hospital. The requirement may be for breath for a screening breath test and/or blood or urine for analysis.

Consultation: The doctor in immediate charge of the patient is the one who must be consulted, and the consultation must be before any requirement is made of the patient.

Objection: The doctor may object on the ground that the patient's care and treatment will be adversely affected by any one of:

— the requirement to provide a specimen

— the provision of the specimen itself

— or the warning which must be given when blood or urine is required, i.e. that failure to provide may lead to prosecution.

POST PROCEDURE DETENTION OF SUSPECTS
Road Traffic Act 1988 (as amended by Schedule 4 Road Traffic Act 1991)
Section 10

6.1 (1) Subject to subsections (2) and (3) below, a person required to provide a specimen of breath, blood or urine may afterwards be detained at a police station until it appears to the constable that, were that person then driving or attempting to drive a mechanically propelled vehicle on a road, he would not be committing an offence under Section 4 or 5 of this Act.

(2) A person shall not be detained in pursuance of this Section if it appears to a constable that there is no likelihood of his driving or attempting to drive a mechanically propelled vehicle whilst his ability to drive properly is impaired or whilst the proportion of alcohol in his breath, blood or urine exceeds the prescribed limit

(3) A constable must consult a medical practitioner on any question arising under this Section whether a person's ability to drive properly is or might be impaired through drugs and must act on the medical practitioner's advice.

6.1.1 *Explanation*
Appears ... Section 4 or 5: Once a person being dealt with at a police station for a drink or drugs/vehicle offence has been dealt with, either by providing specimens or by failing to do so when required, he may be detained until such time as it appears to a constable (usually this will be the custody officer) that he is no longer unfit or over the limit. In other words, he may be detained until, if driving on a road or public place, he would no longer be committing an offence.

A simple method of determining this, where alcohol is suspected, is to administer screening breath tests until the appropriate result is achieved.

No likelihood of driving: If it appears that there is no likelihood of the detained person driving while he remains unfit or over the limit, there will be no power to detain him further. This will be a matter for the police officer's judgement, taking account of such factors as:
 – whether a friend or relative has taken control of the car keys
 – perhaps the detained person has agreed to leave his car at the police station until next day
 – whether he has access to another car
 – etc.

Drugs: If the detained person's condition is thought to be due to drugs, the opinion of a doctor should be sought, to advise on whether he is fit to be released.

DEFENCES
7.1 **Statutory Defences**
Road Traffic Act 1988 Sections 4(3) and 5(2)

7.1.1 *Unfit*
A person will be deemed not to have been in charge of a mechanically propelled vehicle if he proves that at the material time, the circumstances were such that there was no likelihood of his driving it so long as he remained unfit to drive through drink or drugs.

7.1.2 *Excess Alcohol*

It is a defence for a person charged with an offence of being in charge of a motor vehicle with alcohol in his body exceeding the prescribed limit, to prove that at the time of the alleged offence the circumstances were such that there was no likelihood of his driving the vehicle while the proportion of alcohol in his breath, blood or urine remained likely to exceed the prescribed limit.

7.1.3 *Injury or Damage*

The court, in determining the likelihood of a person driving while he remains unfit or over the limit, may disregard any injury to him or damage to the vehicle (Sections 4(4), 5(3)).

7.2 **Explanation**

Likelihood of driving: The purpose of legislating against a person being in charge of a vehicle with drink or drugs inside him, is because such a person may subsequently drive and become a source of danger to others. However, if that person is not likely to drive, thus is not likely to become danger, he will have a defence. A person drives to a party, realises that she has had too much to drink, so decides to sleep it off in the car. Whether she is likely to drive before becoming fit to do so, will depend on the circumstances. Has she left the keys with someone else? Is she in the driving seat, or in the back seat? The answers to these questions are not necessarily decisive; it will be a question of fact for the magistrates to decide.

Injury or damage: A driver is in the driving seat, in charge of his car on a road, unfit through drink, perhaps intending to drive in a few minutes. Another vehicle collides with the stationary car, resulting in the driver suffering a broken arm and his car being badly damaged. Clearly, the likelihood of his driving is non-existent, because he is injured and his car cannot be driven. However, if he is prosecuted for being in charge with excess alcohol or whilst unfit, the court **may** disregard his injuries and the damage to the car, in assessing the likelihood of his driving. The principle is that the accident was not part of his plans for the evening, so why should he benefit from it; he will be liable for his own actions, without regard to the intervening circumstances.

CAUSING DEATH BY CARELESS DRIVING WHILST UNDER THE INFLUENCE OF DRINK OR DRUGS

8.1 **Offence**
Road Traffic Act 1988 Section 3A

(1) A person commits an offence who:
   - causes the death of another person
   - by driving a mechanically propelled vehicle
   - on a road or other public place
   - without due care and attention
   - or without reasonable consideration for other persons
   - using the road or place, and:
     a) he is, at the time when he is driving, unfit to drive through drink or drugs, or
     b) he has consumed so much alcohol that the proportion of it in his breath, blood or urine at that time exceeds the prescribed limit, or

c) he is, within 18 hours after that time, required to provide a specimen in pursuance of Section 7 of this Act, but without reasonable excuse fails to provide it.

(2) For the purposes of this Section a person shall be taken to be unfit to drive at any time when his ability to drive properly is impaired.

(3) Subsection (1) (b) and (c) above shall not apply in relation to a person driving a mechanically propelled vehicle other than a motor vehicle.

8.1.1 *Explanation*

Driving/road/due care: These terms are explained in Chapter 51. The purpose of this provision is to cater for circumstances where a person has been killed by a vehicle, the way in which the vehicle was driven does not amount to dangerous driving, but there was carelessness, aggravated by drink or drugs, or a suspicion of drink having been consumed.

Unfit/over limit: For this offence to be committed, the circumstances must amount to the commission of one of the offences of driving whilst unfit (Section 4) or whilst over the limit (Section 5).

Failure to provide specimen for analysis: Apart from circumstances where the accused driver is unfit to drive through drink or drugs, or is over the alcohol limit, the offence will also be committed if, following the incident where he was driving, he fails, without good reason, to provide a specimen for analysis. The failure to provide must be within 18 hours of the driving incident. It is emphasised that this provision refers to a failure to provide specimens of breath, blood or urine for analysis, not to specimens of breath for a screening breath test.

Consider, for example, where Smith is driving his car when it is involved in an accident as a result of which a person dies. Smith has gone home. If police arrive at his house and he fails to take a breath test when lawfully required to do so, he will not commit the Section 3A offence at that stage. If Smith is arrested for failure to supply breath for a breath test, the offence is complete if he subsequently fails to give breath, blood or urine, as appropriate, at the police station.

Type of vehicle: The offence of driving whilst unfit may be committed by the driver of a mechanically propelled vehicle, whether or not this is a motor vehicle (for explanation of these terms, see Chapter 50). However, offences relating to levels of alcohol in the body, and provisions concerning specimens of breath, blood or urine, apply only to drivers of motor vehicles. Corresponding provisions apply in the case of this offence. The driver of a dumper truck who drives from the building site on to a road or public place may be liable for an offence of driving whilst unfit through drink or drugs (or for causing a death by careless driving whilst unfit), but may not be required to take a breath test, will not commit an offence of driving with excess alcohol, and will not commit a Section 3A offence by causing a death and being over the limit, or failing to provide specimens.

8.2 **Arrest and Punishment**

The offence carries a maximum sentence of 10 years' imprisonment. It is a serious arrestable offence.

POLICE POWERS OF ARREST AND OF ENTRY TO PREMISES

9.1 Unfit to Drive

9.1.1 *Arrest*
A constable may arrest a person without warrant whom she has reasonable cause to suspect:
- is committing
- or has been committing
- an offence under Section 4 (driving, attempting to drive or in charge whilst unfit to drive through drink or drugs) (Section 4(6))

9.1.2 *Entry*
For the purpose of arresting a person under this power, a constable may enter (by force if need be) any place where that person is or where the constable with reasonable cause, suspects him to be (Section 4(7)).

9.2 Breath Tests and Excess Alcohol

9.2.1 *Arrest*
A constable may arrest a person without warrant if:
a) as a result of a breath test, he has reasonable cause to suspect that the proportion of alcohol in that person's breath or blood exceeds the prescribed limit; or
b) that person has failed to provide a specimen of breath for a breath test in pursuance of this Section and the constable has reasonable cause to suspect that he has alcohol in his body.

However – a person may not be arrested by virtue of this power when he is at a hospital as a patient (Section 6(5)).

9.2.2 *Entry*
A constable may for the purpose, either:
i) of requiring a person to provide a specimen of breath for a breath test following an accident, in a case where he has reasonable cause to believe that the accident involved injury to another person; or
ii) of arresting a person under subsection (5), in such a case;
   enter (if need be by force) any place where that person is or where the constable with reasonable cause suspects him to be (Section 6(6)).

9.3 Explanation
Arrest for unfit: The arrest may be of a person whom a constable believes is committing the offence, or who has committed it, perhaps some time ago.

Arrest after breath test: The most likely reason for suspecting that a person is likely to be over the limit after a breath test, is that the test proves positive. If the person fails a requirement to give breath for a breath test, he may be arrested only if the constable has reason to suspect him of having alcohol in his body. The purpose of arrest is to require specimens of breath, blood or urine for analysis; if there is no reason to believe the driver has alcohol in his body, it is pointless pursuing the matter.

Consider two scenarios where a constable requires a breath test following a moving traffic offence, and the driver fails to supply breath for the breath test:

1   The driver refuses, without good reason, but there is no ground for believing he has alcohol in his body. He commits the offence of failing without reasonable excuse to give a specimen of breath for a breath test, but there is no power to arrest, because the officer has no reason to suspect he has alcohol in his body.

2   The driver suffers from chronic asthma and smells strongly of intoxicating liquor. He will not commit the offence of failing to give the breath specimen, because he has a reasonable excuse for not doing so, but he may be arrested because there is reason to suspect he has alcohol in his body.

The arresting officer need not be the same constable who administered the breath test, but must have been able to see the result of the test (*Knight v Taylor* (1979)).

Note: The term 'breath test' means a preliminary, screening breath test of the sort carried out using a hand-held device.

Entry: There is power to force entry to arrest a person for an offence of being unfit to drive, whatever the circumstances of the offence. With excess alcohol and breath tests however, the power of entry is limited to cases where there has been an accident which the constable concerned has reason to believe resulted in injury being caused to some person, other than the suspect. If Bell is stopped for a moving traffic offence, refuses to take a breath test, then runs into a nearby house and refuses to come out, there is no police power to force entry to arrest him for failing to take the breath test.

9.4 Cause Death by Careless Driving

The offence under Section 3A being a serious arrestable offence, there is no need for specific powers of arrest and entry.

EVIDENCE FOR OFFENCES UNDER SECTIONS 3A, 4 AND 5

10.1 Proportion of Alcohol or Drug
Road Traffic Offenders Act 1988 Section 15

Evidence of the proportion of alcohol or any drug in a specimen of breath, blood or urine provided by the accused shall in all cases (including cases where the specimen was not provided in connection with the alleged offence), be taken into account and, subject to subsection (3) below, it shall be assumed that the proportion of alcohol in the accused breath, blood or urine at the time of the alleged offence was not less than in the specimen.

That assumption shall not be made if the accused proves:
a)   that he consumed alcohol before he provided the specimen and:
    i)   in relation to an offence under Section 3A, after the time the alleged offence and
    ii)   otherwise, after he had ceased to drive, attempt to drive or be in charge of a vehicle on a road or other public place, and
b)   that had he not done so the proportion of alcohol in his breath, blood or urine would not have exceeded the prescribed limit and, if it is alleged that he was unfit to drive through drink, would not have been such as to impair his ability to drive properly.

10.1.1 *Explanation*

Proportion at time of offence: From the time of a driver's arrest to his supplying breath, blood or urine at a police station or hospital, may involve a period of at least an hour, perhaps considerably longer. To avoid any arguments about whether the level of alcohol in his blood was as high when he was driving as it was when the blood sample was taken, the law provides that the court will assume that at the time of the alleged offence, the alcohol level was at least as high as the level in the specimen provided for analysis.

Drinking after driving: The assumption will not be made, that the accused's alcohol level at the time of the offence was at least as high as that found in the specimen provided, if he proves:

i) that he consumed alcohol after he ceased to do what it was which is unlawful – drive, attempt to drive or be in charge of a motor vehicle on a road or public place – and before supplying the specimen; and

ii) that had it not been for this alcohol, he would not have been over the prescribed limit.

A driver may seek to take advantage of this provision, by deliberately drinking, e.g. after an accident. However, the so-called 'hip flask defence' may rebound on the driver. Consider the circumstances where police arrive at the scene of an accident, to see Haig standing by his car, drinking whisky from his hip flask. In such a case, Haig is still the driver, or at the very least, is in charge of his motor vehicle, so the whisky he has just drunk will only serve to increase the level of alcohol in any specimen which he subsequently provides.

A driver who attempts to drink after being stopped by police, may commit an offence of obstructing a constable in the execution of her duty, depending on the circumstances.

If police go to a house to require a person to take a breath test, e.g. after an accident or if there is reason to suspect that he has been driving with excess alcohol, and the person claims that he has just had a drink, the officers may take practical steps to rebut such a defence. For example, a request to see the glass, or the bottle, to estimate how much, if any, has been consumed, may yield valuable prosecution evidence.

10.2 **Provision of Specimen to Accused**
Road Traffic Offenders Act 1988 Section 15(5)

Evidence of the proportion of alcohol in a specimen of blood or urine will not be admissible in evidence for the prosecution, unless the specimen was divided into two parts at the time it was supplied, one part being the one used for evidence, the other part having been supplied to the accused.

The specimen need not have been divided in the presence of the accused (*DPP v Elstrob* (1992)), but it is good practice that this should be the case.

10.3 **Evidence by Certificate**
Road Traffic Offenders Act 1988 Section 16

10.3.1 *Analysis of Specimens*

Evidence of the proportion of alcohol or of a drug in a specimen of breath, blood or urine may (subject to conditions) be given by the production of a document or documents purporting to be whichever of the following is appropriate:

a) a statement automatically produced by the device by which the proportion of alcohol in a specimen of breath was measured, and a certificate signed by a constable that the statement relates to a specimen provided by the accused at the date and time shown in the statement (the certificate may or may not be contained in the same document as the statement);

b) a certificate signed by an authorised analyst as to the proportion of alcohol or of any drug found in the specimen of blood or urine identified in the certificate.

10.3.2 *Doctor's Evidence*

Evidence that a specimen of blood was taken from the accused with his consent by a medical practitioner may be given by production of a document purporting to certify that fact and to be signed by a medical practitioner.

10.3.3 *Copy to Accused*

A statement produced by a breath analysis device, together with the accompanying constable's certificate, will be admissible in evidence on behalf of the prosecution only if a copy was handed to the accused at the time when the document was produced, or has been served on him not later than seven days before the hearing.

Any other document is admissible as prosecution evidence only if it has been served on the accused not later than seven days before the hearing.

Any of these documents will not be admissible in evidence if the accused, not later than three days before the hearing (or within such further time as the court may in special circumstances allow) has served notice on the prosecution requiring the attendance at the hearing of the person by whom the document purports to be signed.

10.3.4 *Explanation*

Purpose: The purpose of these provisions is to allow evidence to be given of the amount of alcohol in a specimen, without analysts, doctors and police officers having to attend court to give evidence in person. However, if the defence do wish to cross-examine any of these professional witnesses, a request for the attendance in person of the witness may be made.

Breath analysis: When the proportion of alcohol in a specimen of breath is measured on a machine, the machine will produce a piece of paper with the alcohol level recorded thereon, together with the time and date. This piece of paper will usually allow for details to be included of the person supplying the specimen and of the police officer operating the machine. The police officer may then sign the document, certifying that the alcohol reading relates to the accused. Alternatively, the police officer's certificate may be on a separate piece of paper.

Blood or urine: The evidence of the doctor who took a blood specimen, and of the analyst who analysed a blood or urine specimen, may be in the form of a document, signed by that person.

Agreement of accused: Evidence in the form of a document will be admissible only if a copy has been served on the accused, at least a week before the court hearing. In the case of breath specimens, the copy or copies may be given to the accused at the time. The accused may then serve notice that he wants the witness to attend in person to give evidence. This notice should normally be given at least three days before the hearing, but the court may allow a later defence request for the witness to attend.

Keynote Case

11 *DPP v Warren* [1992] 4 All ER 865

Problem

To what extent should a person suspected of a drink/drugs driving related offence be involved in the decision as to whether a specimen required for laboratory examination be of blood or of urine?

Circumstances

Warren was stopped by police while driving his motor vehicle, arrested after a positive breath test, and taken to a police station where he subsequently provided two specimens of breath on an intoximeter. The police officer in charge then found that the intoximeter was not working properly, and told Warren that this was the case. The officer told Warren that he would require blood or urine for a laboratory test, that it was for him (the officer) to decide, and asked if there was any reason why a blood specimen should not be taken by a doctor. Warren replied 'No' and blood was subsequently taken which proved to contain a proportion of alcohol well over the limit. At magistrates' court, the defence claimed that Warren should have been given an opportunity to express a preference for blood or urine. The case was dismissed, the prosecution appealed to the Divisional Court, which upheld the magistrate's decision. The prosecution then appealed to the House of Lords.

Decision

In giving the judgement, Lord Bridge pointed out that the lower courts had followed previous court decisions, to the effect that, although the decision as to blood or urine rests with the police, a suspect should be given an opportunity to consider which sample he would prefer to give, and that the police officer should make the decision with knowledge of the suspect's preference.

The previous decisions however, were over-ruled. Where blood or urine was required under Section 7, subsections (3) and (4), e.g. breath analysis machine not working, drugs suspected, or specimens required at a hospital, the constable concerned should:
- tell the suspect why breath specimens cannot be taken or used;
- tell him that blood or urine will now be required;
- say that it is for the constable to decide which it is to be;
- tell the suspect that failure to provide may render him liable to prosecution;
- if the constable decides to require blood, then to ask the suspect if there is any reason why a specimen cannot or should not be taken by a doctor.

In a situation where the suspected driver has the opporrtunity to have his breath specimens replaced by blood or urine, because the lower of the two breath specimens gives a reading of not more than 50 milligrams of alcohol in 100 millilitres of breath, the constable must inform the driver:
- that the lower sample does not exceed 50 milligrams;
- that in those circumstances he is entitled to claim to have the breath replaced by blood or urine if he wishes;
- if he so elects, it will be for the constable to decide which it is to be;
- if the officer decides that the specimen shall be of blood, the driver's only right to object to giving blood and to request urine instead, will be for medical reasons, to be determined by the medical practitioner.

In neither case is there any need to invite the driver to express his preference for giving blood or urine.

Comment

The Act clearly leaves the choice, as to whether a specimen shall be of blood or urine, to the police, except when a doctor advises that, for medical reasons, it should be urine. However, the police officer should inform the suspect that she will request either blood or urine and ask whether, if she does choose blood, if there is any medical reason why he would not be able to give a blood specimen.

Earlier case decisions, to the effect that the suspect should be permitted to express a preference, are over-ruled.

Chapter 52: Construction and Use Regulations

INTRODUCTION

1.1 Regulations

There is a great deal of legislative requirements governing the manner of construction of vehicles used on roads, and the way in which they may be used. The current regulations are the Road Vehicles (Construction and Use) Regulations 1986. These are constantly being amended, in line with technical advances and pressures to improve road safety. This chapter is not intended to contain comprehensive detail of these requirements, most of which will be of direct concern only to qualified vehicle examiners, who may be called on to give expert evidence if required.

1.2 Type Approval

It is an objective of the European Community to achieve uniformity of traffic law throughout the Community. To this end, vehicle manufacturers now submit prototype vehicles for 'type approval'. If approval is given, vehicles conforming to a particular type may then be manufactured and used throughout Europe.

Any vehicle which conforms to a Community Directive will be exempt from the need to comply with the corresponding requirements of the Construction and Use Regulations.

1.3 Offences

1.3.1 *Breach of Regulations*

Regulations are made under the authority of an Act of Parliament, and any breach of the requirements of a regulation will amount to an offence under that Act. The Construction and Use Regulations are made under the authority of the Road Traffic Act 1988, which caters for three separate sets of offences:

i)   Section 41A: Contravenes or fails to comply with a requirement relating to brakes, steering gear or tyres, or uses, or causes or permits to be used, on a road a motor vehicle or trailer which does not comply with such a requirement.
     An offence under this Section is punishable with a fine and obligatory driving licence endorsement (3 penalty points).

ii) Section 41B: Contravention of any requirement relating to vehicle weight, relating to a goods vehicle or to a passenger vehicle for more than 8 passengers.
     An offence under this Section is punishable with a fine, but not with endorsement.

iii) Section 42: Contravention of any requirement of the regulations, not punishable under Sections 41A or 41B.
     An offence under this Section is punishable with a smaller maximum fine, but not with endorsement.

1.3.2 *Vehicle in Dangerous Condition*
Road Traffic Act 1988 Section 40A

A person is guilty of an offence if he uses, or causes or permits another to use, a motor vehicle or trailer on a road when:

a) the condition of the motor vehicle or trailer, or of its accessories or equipment, or
b) the purpose for which it is used, or
c) the number of passengers carried by it, or the manner in which they are carried, or
d) the weight, position or distribution of its load, or the manner in which it is secured;

is such that the use of the motor vehicle or trailer involves a danger of injury to any person.

1.3.3 *Type Approval*
Road Traffic Act 1988 Section 63

A person commits an offence who uses, or causes or permits to be used on a road a vehicle which appears not to comply with approval requirements, or to which is fitted a vehicle part which appears not to comply.

1.3.4 *Explanation*

Use: A person will use a vehicle on a road if he is the driver. However, the owner of the vehicle, who is not driving, will also use the vehicle in the following cases:

i) the vehicle is being driven by an employee of the owner, in the course of the owner's business;

ii) the owner is a passenger in the vehicle while it is being used for his purposes.

If Bates runs a business, and one of his vans is stopped while being driven on a road by one of his employees in the course of his employment, both the driver and Bates will be liable for 'using' the vehicle on a road, if any breaches of the regulations are discovered.

If Bates is then a passenger in his own car, being driven by a friend of his, e.g. taking Bates home after he has had too much to drink, both Bates and his friend will 'use' the car.

A vehicle may be used on a road for some purposes, even when it is not being driven there. In a case involving defective tyres, it was held that 'use' in the Construction and Use Regulations means 'have the use of', and a car kept on a verge for several months may be 'used' in that sense (*Eden v Mitchell* (1975)). This may be so even if it is not capable of being driven in its current state (*Elliot v Gray* (1960)).

Cause: If a person is to be liable for causing a vehicle to be used, it must be shown that he was in some position of authority over the person using the vehicle (*McLeod v Buchanan* (1940)). This will usually arise in an employment situation where a supervisor or manager instructs a driver to use a vehicle on a road. The owner would be liable for using the vehicle, so the person who 'causes' use will be likely to be someone else, acting with authority. In theory, the owner may also be liable for causing, but in practice, he would not be charged with both using and causing use.

Permit: If a person is to be guilty of permitting a vehicle to be used on a road with some defect, it must be shown that she was in a position to withhold consent for the vehicle to be used. The term differs from 'cause' however, in that there is no need to prove a compulsion on the driver to use the vehicle; the driver is in a position to decline the use of the vehicle.

Knowledge of defect: To be guilty of an offence of using a vehicle on a road with some defect, it is not necessary to prove that the accused knew of the defect. If the vehicle has a defective tyre, the user will be guilty of using the vehicle on a road with a defective tyre, whether on not he knew about the state of the tyre. However, for a person to be guilty of causing or permitting the vehicle to be used with a defective tyre, it must be shown that he was aware of the defect.

Consider the example of Hobart, who owns a number of goods vehicles, employing Foden as a depot manager. Baker, one of the employee drivers points out to Foden that a trailer on his lorry has a defective tyre. Foden instructs Baker to take the lorry and trailer out, and to have the tyre changed on his return. Hobart knows nothing of these circumstances.

In this case, Hobart and Baker will be liable for using the trailer with a defective tyre, Baker knowing of the defect, Hobart having no knowledge of it. Foden will be guilty of causing the trailer to be used with a defective tyre, so long as the prosecution is able to prove that he knew of the defect.

BRAKES

2.1 **Brakes, Maintenance**
Regulation 18

(1) Every part of every braking system and of the means of operation thereof fitted to a vehicle shall be maintained in good and efficient working order and be properly adjusted.

(1A) Without prejudice to paragraph (3), where a vehicle is fitted with an anti-lock braking system ('the ABS'), then while the condition specified in paragraph (1B) is fulfilled, any fault in the ABS shall be disregarded for the purpose of paragraph (1)

(1B) The condition is fulfilled while the vehicle is completing a journey at the beginning of which the ABS was operating correctly or is being driven to a place where the ABS is to undergo repairs.

(2) Paragraph (3) applies to every wheeled motor vehicle except:
  a) an agricultural motor vehicle which is not driven at more than 20 mph;
  b) a works truck; and
  c) a pedestrian controlled vehicle.

2.1.1 *Explanation*
Paragraph 3 of regulation 18 sets out braking efficiency requirements of the various classes of vehicles. To test the efficiency of brakes on a vehicle against the laid down requirements will require the services of a qualified vehicle examiner.

TYRES

3.1 **Mixing of Tyres, Types and Classes**
Regulation 26

(1) Save as provided in paragraph (5) pneumatic tyres of different types of structure shall not be fitted to the same axle of a wheeled vehicle.

(2) Save as provided by paragraphs (3) or (5), a wheeled motor vehicle having only two axles each of which is equipped with one or two single wheels shall not be fitted with:
  a) a diagonal-ply tyre or bias-belted tyre on its rear axle if a radial ply tyre is fitted on its front axle; or
  b) a diagonal-ply tyre on its rear axle if a bias belted tyre is fitted to the front axle.

(3) Paragraph (2) does not apply to a vehicle to an axle of which there are fitted wide tyres

not specially constructed for use on engineering plant or to a vehicle which has a maximum speed not exceeding 30miles per hour.

(4) Save as provided in paragraph (5) pneumatic tyres fitted to:
   a)   the steerable axles of a wheeled vehicle; or
   b)   the driven axle of a wheeled vehicle, not being the steerable axle;
   shall all be of the same type of structure.

(5) Paragraphs (1),(2), and (4) do not prohibit the fitting of a temporary use spare tyre to a wheel of a passenger vehicle (not being a bus) unless it is driven at a speed exceeding 50 mph.

(6) In this regulation 'Axles' include:
   i)   two or more stub axles which are fitted on opposite sides of the longitudinal axis of the vehicle so as to form:
      a)   a pair in the case of two stub axles; and
      b)   pairs in the case of more than two stub axles; and
   ii) a single stub axle which is not one of a pair;

3.1.1 *Explanation*

Diagonal ply tyres are commonly known as 'cross ply tyres'; a bias belted tyre is a cross ply tyre with a supporting belt of reinforcing directly below the tread patterning but built above the cord structure of the tyre. Radial ply tyres are probably most common on cars and light vans. The regulation makes it illegal to mix the types of tyre other than by having:
   a)   Cross-ply front and radials at the rear.
   b)   Cross-ply front and bias belted at the rear.
   c)   Bias-belted front and radials at the rear.

As a general rule when tyre types are mixed the radials tyres must always be on the rear axle.

Wide tyres are commonly found on the rear of large lorries, they have a tread width exceeding 300 mm and usually replace the twin rear tyres. It is unlawful to mix the tyres on the axles of a vehicle with more than one steering axle.

CONDITION AND MAINTENANCE OF TYRES

3.2 Defective and Unsuitable Tyres
Regulation 27

(1) Save as provided in paragraphs (2),(3) and (4), a wheeled motor vehicle or trailer a wheel of which is fitted with a pneumatic tyre shall not be used on a road, if:
   a)   the tyre is unsuitable having regard to the use to which the motor vehicle or trailer is being put or to the types of tyres fitted to its other wheels;
   b)   the tyre is not so inflated as to make it fit for the use to which the motor vehicle or trailer is being put;
   c)   the tyre has a cut in excess of 25mm or 10% of the Section width of the tyre, whichever is the greater, measured in any direction on the outside of the tyre and deep enough to reach the ply or cord;
   d)   the tyre has any lump, bulge or tear caused by separation or partial failure of its structure;

e) the tyre has any of the ply or cord exposed;

f) the base of any groove which showed in the original tread pattern of the tyre is not clearly visible;

g) either:

    i) the grooves or tread pattern of the tyre do not have a depth of at least 1mm throughout a continuous band measuring at least three-quarters of the breath of the tread and round the entire outer circumference of the tyre; or

    ii) if the grooves of the original tread pattern of the tyre did not extend beyond three-quarters of the breath of the tread, any groove which showed in the original tread pattern does not have a depth of at least 1mm; or

h) the tyre is not maintained in such condition as to be fit for the use to which the vehicle or trailer is being put or has a defect which might in any way cause damage to the surface of the road or damage to persons on or in the vehicle or to other persons using the road.

(2) Paragraph (1) does not prohibit the use on a road of a motor vehicle or trailer by reason only of the fact that the wheel of the vehicle or trailer is fitted with a tyre which is deflated or not fully inflated and which has any of the defects described in sub-paragraph (c),(d)or (e) of paragraph (1), if the tyre and the wheel to which it is fitted are so constructed as to make the tyre in that condition fit for use to which the motor vehicle or trailer is being put and the outer sides of the tyre are so marked as to enable the tyre to be identified as having been constructed to comply with the requirements of this paragraph.

(3) Paragraph (1)(a) does not prohibit the use on a road of a passenger vehicle (not being a bus) by reason only of the fact that a wheel of that vehicle is fitted with a temporary use spare tyre, unless the vehicle is driven at a speed in excess of 50 mph.

(4) a) Nothing in paragraph (1)(a) to (g) applies to:

    i) an agricultural motor vehicles that is not driven at more than 20 mph;

    ii) an agricultural trailer;

    iii) an agricultural trailed appliance; or

    iv) a broken down vehicle or a vehicle proceeding to a place where it is to be broken up, being drawn, in either case, by a motor vehicle at a speed not exceeding 20 mph.

b) Nothing in paragraph (1)(f) and (g) applies to:

    i) a three wheeled motor cycle the unladen weight of which does not exceed 102 kg which has a maximum speed of 12 mph; or

    ii) a pedestrian controlled works truck

c) Nothing in paragraph (1)(g) applies to a motor cycle with an engine size which does not exceed 50 cc.

Paragraphs (f) and (g) shall not apply to vehicles of the following description:

    i) passenger vehicles other than motor cycles constructed or adapted to carry no more than eight seated passengers in addition to the driver;

    ii) goods vehicles with a maximum gross weight which does not exceed 3500kg; and

    iii) light trailers not falling within sub-paragraph (ii);

first used on or after 3rd January 1933.

Instead, the tyres on these vehicles must meet the following requirements:

the grooves of the tread pattern of every tyre fitted to the wheels of these vehicles shall be of a depth of at least 1.6 mm throughout a continuous band comprising the central three-quarters of the breadth of the tread and round the entire circumference of the tyre.

(5) a recut pneumatic tyre shall not be fitted to any wheel of a motor vehicle or trailer if:
   a) its ply or cord has been cut or exposed by the recutting process; or
   b) it has been wholly or partially recut in a pattern other than the manufacturer's recut tread pattern.

(6) a) In this regulation:
   Breadth of pattern: means the breadth of that part of the tyre which can contact the road under normal conditions of use measured at 90 degrees to the peripheral line of the tread;
   Original tread pattern: means in the case of:
   - a re-treaded tyre, the tread pattern of the tyre immediately after it was retreaded;
   - a wholly recut tyre, the manufacturer's recut tread pattern;
   - a partially recut tyre, on that part of the tyre which has been recut, the manufacturer's recut tread pattern , and on any other part of the tread pattern of the tyre when the tyre was new
   Tie bar: means any part of the tyre moulded in the tread pattern of the tyre for the purpose of bracing two or more features of such tread pattern;
   Tread pattern: means the combination of plain surfaces and grooves extending across the breadth of the tread and round the entire outer circumference of the tyre but excludes any:
   i) tie bars or tread wear indicators;
   ii) features which are designed to wear out substantially before the rest of the pattern under normal conditions of use; and
   iii) other minor features; and
   Tread wear indicator: means any bar, not being a tie-bar, projecting from the base of a groove of he tread pattern of a tyre and moulded between two or more features of the tread pattern of the tyre for the purpose of indicating the extent of the wear of such a tread pattern.

   b) The references in this regulation to grooves are references:
   if a tyre has been recut, to the grooves of the manufacturers recut tread pattern; and, if a tyre has not been recut, to the grooves which showed when the tyre was new.

   c) A reference in this regulation to first use, shall in relation to a trailer, be construed as a reference to the date which is 6 months after the date of manufacture of the trailer.

3.2.1 *Explanation*

Unsuitable: A tyre may be considered defective taking account of the use to which the vehicle is being put, or to the nature of other tyres fitted. For example, if one of four tyres is of a different size to the other three, it may be regarded as defective.

Inflated: A tyre which is significantly over or under inflated may affect the handling of a vehicle; such a tyre may be considered defective.

Cuts, lumps, etc: There are many ways in which a tyre's physical condition may render it defective. A small cut will not suffice to make a tyre defective, but one longer than 10% of a particular section of the tyre, or deep enough to expose the fabric, will do.

Tread: There are minimum requirements for the depth of the tread pattern. There are two sets of requirements:

i) for passenger vehicles for not more than 8 passengers plus driver, for goods vehicles up to 3.5 tonnes maximum gross weight and for light trailers, there must be at least 1.6 mm of tread, over the entire central three-quarters of the tyre's circumference. This means that the tyre would be within the requirements if there was a band of not more than 1/8th of the width, on either side of the tyre, where the tread was worn down below 1.6 mm., so long as the tread was at least 1.6 mm over the rest of the width.

ii) for other classes of vehicle, a tyre will be defective if any part of the tread is worn completely smooth – in the words of the regulation, 'the base of any groove in the tread pattern is not clearly visible.' In addition, there must be at least 1 mm of tread across at least 3/4 of the breadth of the tyre, and round the entire circumference. Thus, if there is a band right round the tyre amounting to a quarter of the width, where the tread pattern is worn down to below 1 mm, the tyre may still be used. This is in contrast to the preceding requirement, that the 3/4 width of good tread should be the central portion.

Partly deflated tyre: Provision is made for use of a special type of tyre which may be used after it has suffered a puncture, so long as the tyre is clearly marked to the effect that it complies with this regulation.

Temporary use tyre: Some motor vehicles which are fitted with expensive wheels and tyres, have a spare wheel of lesser quality, intended for emergency use only, such as when one of the tyres is punctured. It will be lawful to use one of these, at speeds not exceeding 50 mph, but only on a passenger vehicle and then only provided it is not a bus.

Exemptions: There are various exemptions to one or other of the requirements of this regulation. for example, if a vehicle is being towed to a scrap yard, it may lawfully be towed there with defective tyres, so long as the speed does not exceed 20 mph.

STEERING GEAR
Regulation 29

4.1 All steering gear fitted to a motor vehicle shall at all times while the vehicle is used on a road be maintained in good and efficient working order, and be properly adjusted.

VISION

5.1 **Clear View**
Regulation 30

(1) Every motor vehicle shall be so designed and constructed that the driver thereof while controlling the vehicle can at all times have a full view of the traffic ahead of the motor vehicle.

(2) Instead of complying with the requirement of paragraph (1) a vehicle may comply with Community Directives.

(3) All glass or other transparent material fitted to a motor vehicle shall be maintained in such condition that it does not obscure the vision of the driver while the vehicle is being driven on a road.

5.2 Windscreen Wipers and Washers
Regulation 34

(1) Subject to paragraphs (4) and (5) every vehicle fitted with a windscreen shall, unless the driver can obtain an adequate view to the front of the vehicle without looking through the windscreen, be fitted with one or more automatic windscreen wipers capable of clearing the windscreen so that the driver had an adequate view of the road in front of both sides of the vehicle and to the front of the vehicle.

(2) Save as provided in paragraph (3), (4), and (5), every wheeled vehicle required by paragraph (1) to be fitted with a wiper or wipers shall also be fitted with a windscreen washer capable of cleaning, in conjunction with the windscreen wiper, the area of the windscreen swept by the wiper of mud or similar deposit.

(3) The requirement specified in paragraph (2) does not apply in respect of:
   a) an agricultural motor vehicle (other than a vehicle used on or after 1st of June 1986 which is driven at more than 20mph);
   b) a track laying vehicle;
   c) a vehicle having a maximum speed not exceeding 10mph; or
   d) a vehicle being used to provide a local service, as defined in the Transport Act 1985.

   Instead of complying with paragraphs (1) and (2), a vehicle may comply with the relevant Community Directive.

(6) Every wiper and washer fitted in accordance with this regulation shall at all times while a vehicle is being used on a road be maintained in efficient working order and be properly adjusted.

5.3 Explanation

Design: A motor vehicle must be built in such a way that the driver has a clear view of traffic ahead of the vehicle. In the case of a mechanical digger, for example, it would not be lawful for it to be designed in such a way that the driver's view ahead was obstructed by the bucket (or scoop).

Obscured vision: All glass or transparent material must be in such condition that it does not obscure the driver's view. This requirement relates to all the glass, not just that to the front. It is necessary therefore, that the side windows and rear windscreen should be free of frost, mud etc. The driver who, on a cold morning, clears only part of the front windscreen of frost or snow, is in breach of this regulation.

Wipers and washers: There is no stipulation as to how many wipers are required, some motor cars have only one. The wiper(s) must clear enough of the windscreen to give the driver a view to front of her vehicle and to both sides at the front. In addition to windscreen wipers, motor vehicles must also have washers to work in conjunction with the wipers.

These requirements relate only to the front windscreen; estates and hatchbacks usually have rear wipers and washers, but these are not required by law.

Maintenance: Windscreen wipers and washers must be kept in good working order. If the washer bottle is empty, the washers will not be in good and efficient working order.

SPEED INDICATOR INSTRUMENTS

6.1 Requirements for Speedometer
Regulation 35

(1) Save as provide in paragraphs (2) and (3), every motor vehicle shall be fitted with a speedometer which, if the vehicle is first used on or after 1st of April 1984, shall be capable of indicating speed in both miles per hour and kilometres per hour, either simultaneously or, by the operation of a switch, separately.

(2) Paragraph (1) does not apply to:
   a) a vehicle having a maximum speed not exceeding 25 mph;
   b) a vehicle which it is at all times illegal to drive at more than 25mph;
   c) an agricultural motor vehicle which is not driven at more than 20mph;
   d) a motor cycle first used before the 1st of April 1984 the engine of which has a cylinder capacity not exceeding 100cc;
   e) an invalid carriage first used before April 1984;
   f) a works truck first used before April 1st 1984;
   g) a vehicle first used before 1st October 1937; or
   h) a vehicle equipped with recording equipment which complies with Community Recording Equipment Regulations.

(3) Instead of complying with paragraph (1) a vehicle may comply with Community Legislation.

6.2 Clear View of Speedometer
Regulation 36

(1) Every instrument for indicating speed fitted to a motor vehicle:
in compliance with the requirements of regulation 35(1) or (3);
shall be kept free from any obstruction which might prevent its being easily read and shall at all material times be maintained in good working order.

(2) In this regulation 'all material times' means all times when the motor vehicle is in use on a road except when:
   a) the vehicle is being used on a journey which as a result of a defect, the instrument ceased to be in good working order; or
   b) as a result of a defect, the instrument has ceased to be in good working order and steps have been taken to have the vehicle equipped with all reasonable expedition, by means of repairs or replacement, with an instrument which is in good working order.

6.2.1 *Explanation*
Not required: If a vehicle is not capable of travelling at other than slow speeds, there is no need for a speedometer. The regulations are littered with dates, reflecting the continuous up-dating which goes on, to take account of changes in technical specification of vehicles.

Maintenance: A speedometer which is required to be fitted, must be maintained in good working order when the vehicle is in use on a road. If a speedometer is not required to be fitted, but is fitted anyway, e.g. on a vehicle which is incapable of exceeding 25 mph, there is no requirement that it shall be in good working order.

Exception: There are two defences to a charge of not having a working speedometer:
i) where the defect arose on the present journey, as where the driver says: 'It was working when I left home.';
ii) where arrangements are in hand to have the faulty instrument repaired or replaced as soon as practicable. (While the legislators persist in using phrases like 'with all reasonable expedition', prizes for use of clear English will surely continue to elude them.) Few garages will accept motor vehicles for repair there and then; an appointment may have to be made, and a replacement speedometer may have to be ordered.

FUEL TANKS
Regulation 39

7.1 (1) This regulation applies to every fuel tank which is fitted to a wheeled vehicle for the purpose of supplying fuel to the propulsion unit or to an ancillary engine or to other equipment forming part of the vehicle.

(2) Subject to paragraph (3) and (4), every fuel tank to which this regulation applies:
a) shall be constructed and maintained so that the leakage of any liquid from the tank is adequately prevented.
b) shall be constructed and maintained so that the leakage of vapour from the tank is adequately prevented; and
c) if it contains petroleum spirit and is fitted to a vehicle first used on or after 1st July 1973, shall be:
i) made only of metal; and
ii) fixed in such a position and so maintained as to be reasonably secure from damage.

(3) Notwithstanding the requirement of paragraph (2)(b), the fuel tank may be fitted with a device which by the intake of air or the emission of vapour, relieves changes of pressure in the tank.

7.1.1 *Explanation*
Wheeled vehicle: These provisions are not confined to motor vehicles; they would extend, for example, to the fuel tank for the refrigeration unit on a trailer.

Liquid or vapour: A piece of rag, stuffed into the filler pipe, to replace a missing cap, will not be sufficient to 'adequately prevent' leakage of vapour. It will be lawful if a fuel tank is fitted with a pressure-relief device, which may discharge vapour.

Petrol: If the tank is for petrol, rather than, say, diesel fuel, it must be made of metal and positioned and maintained so as to be reasonably secure from damage. A vehicle manufacturer is unlikely to build a car with the petrol tank under the rear bumper, but to do so would be in breach of this regulation.

EXHAUST NOISE, AND NOISY VEHICLES

8.1 Defective Exhaust
Regulation 54

(1) Every vehicle propelled by an internal combustion engine shall be fitted with an exhaust system including a silencer and the exhaust gases from the engine shall not escape into the atmosphere without first passing through the silencer.

(2) Every exhaust system and silencer shall be maintained in good and efficient working order and shall not be altered so as to increase the noise made by the escape of the exhaust gases.

8.2 Excessive Noise
Regulation 97

No motor vehicle shall be used on a road in such a manner as to cause any excessive noise which could have been avoided by the exercise of reasonable care on the part of the driver.

8.3 Engine Noise
Regulation 98

The driver of a vehicle shall, when the vehicle is stationary, stop the action of any machinery attached to or forming part of the vehicle, so far as may be necessary for the prevention of noise.

8.3.1 Exceptions
Exceptions are made:
  i)   when the vehicle is stationary owing to the necessities of traffic;
  ii) when it is necessary to have the machinery running to examine it in the case of failure or malfunction, or where the machinery is required for some purpose other than driving the vehicle;
  iii) in the case of a gas-propelled vehicle, where the machinery is connected with the production of the gas.

8.4 Warning Instrument

8.4.1 Requirement
Regulation 37

Every motor vehicle shall be fitted with a horn, not being a reversing alarm or two-tone horn.

8.4.2 Exceptions
A motor vehicle with a maximum speed not exceeding 20 mph; an agricultural vehicles, unless being driven at more than 20 mph.

In the case of a wheeled vehicle first used on or after 1 August 1973, the sound emitted by this horn shall be continuous and uniform, and not strident. A reversing alarm shall not be strident.

8.4.3 *Two Tone Horn, Siren, etc*
Regulation 37

No motor vehicle shall be fitted with a two-tone horn, siren, bell or gong.

Exceptions (emergency vehicles)
Vehicles used for police, fire brigade or ambulance purposes:
- fire salvage vehicles; local authority and Forestry Commission vehicles which are sometimes used for fighting fires;
- Ministry of Defence bomb disposal vehicles;
- Blood Transfusion Service vehicles;
- H.M. Coastguard emergency vehicles; RNLI vehicles used for launching lifeboats;
- Royal Air Force Mountain Rescue Service ;
- vehicles used for mine rescue purposes.

Exceptions (other)
i) A bell, gong or siren may be fitted to a motor vehicle to inform the public that goods are for sale from that vehicle.
ii) A bell, gong or siren may be fitted to a bus for the purpose of summoning help for the crew.
iii) A bell, gong or siren may be fitted to a motor vehicle, for the purpose of preventing theft or attempted theft of the vehicle or its contents.

However, in the case of bus alarms, and vehicle alarms since 1.10.82, they must be fitted with a device to cut the sound off after five minutes.

8.4.4 *Use of Audible Warning Instruments*
Regulation 99

i) An audible warning instrument shall not be sounded on a vehicle while it is stationary, except when there is danger from another moving vehicle on or near the road.

ii) The audible warning instrument shall not be sounded on a vehicle in motion on a restricted road between the hours of 11.30 pm and 7.00 am.

8.5 Explanation
Silencer: If there is a leak in the exhaust system between the engine and the silencer box, gases will escape before passing through the silencer. A hole in the tail pipe, after the exhaust fumes have passed through the silencer, will not give rise to an offence.

Maintenance: As with all the other components and instruments covered by the regulations, the exhaust system must be maintained in good working order. In addition, the system must not be altered so as to increase the noise level, e.g. by removing plates from inside the silencer box.

Excessive noise: The driver must take reasonable care to avoid excessive noise, if practicable. Unnecessary revving of the engine is avoidable, but this requirement is not confined to engine noise. A badly-packed load may give rise to noise which could be avoided.

Machinery: The machinery referred to in regulation 98 could be the engine of the motor vehicle, but there is no requirement to stop machinery when the vehicle is stopped in traffic, e.g. at traffic lights or in a queue of vehicles. Machinery may be kept running if it is being checked or repaired after a malfunction, or where the purpose of the machinery has nothing to do with driving the vehicle, e.g. a refrigeration unit, required to keep the load cool, or the machinery on a refuse collection lorry.

Uniform and continuous: A motor vehicle horn which plays a tune will not be lawful, because the sound is not uniform and continuous.

Strident: There is no definition of the term 'strident'; the dictionary defines the term as 'loud and harsh.'

Emergency vehicles: The use of sirens and two-tone horns is not restricted to public service fire brigades and ambulance services. A works fire engine, or an ambulance operated by a private company may also use such warning instruments. Use is not restricted to fire engines and ambulances; a car used by a fire brigade officer, or by an emergency doctor working for an ambulance service will come within the scope of 'vehicle used for fire brigade or ambulance purposes.'

Use of horn: If a vehicle is stationary, and the driver sees another car rolling down a slope towards him, it would be lawful in that situation to sound the horn, because of danger from another moving vehicle. A restricted road may be regarded as one which carries a speed limit of 30 mph.

DANGER TO ROAD USERS

9.1 Dangerous Condition
Road Traffic Act 1988 Section 40A

A person is guilty of an offence if he uses, or causes or permits another to use, a motor vehicle or trailer on a road when:
   a) the condition of the motor vehicle or trailer, or of its accessories or equipment, or
   b) the purpose for which it is used, or
   c) the number of passengers carried by it, or the manner in which they are carried, or
   d) the weight, position or distribution of its load, or the manner in which it is secured is such that the use of the motor vehicle or trailer involves a danger of injury to any person.

9.2 Maintenance so as not to Cause Danger
Regulation 100

(1) A motor vehicle, every trailer drawn thereby and all parts and accessories of such vehicles and trailers shall at all times be in such condition and the number of passengers carried by such vehicle or trailer, the manner in which any passengers are carried in or on such vehicle or trailer, and the weight, distribution, packing and adjustment of the load of such vehicle or trailer shall at all times be such, that no danger is caused or is likely to be caused to any person in or on the vehicle, trailer, or on the road.

(2) The load carried by a motor vehicle or trailer shall at all times be so secured, if necessary by physical restraint other than its own weight, and be in such a position, that neither danger nor nuisance is likely to be caused to any person or property by

reason of the load or any part thereof falling or being blown from the vehicle or by reason of any other movement of the load or any part thereof in relation to the vehicle.

(3) No motor vehicle or trailer shall be used for any purpose for which it is so unsuitable as to cause or be likely to cause danger or nuisance to any person in or on the vehicle or trailer or on a road.

9.3 Unroadworthy Vehicles and Parts
Road Traffic Act 1988 Sections 75 and 76

9.3.1 *Sell or Offer*
No person shall sell, supply, offer to sell or supply, or expose for sale a motor vehicle or trailer in an unroadworthy condition.

9.3.2 *Alterations*
No person shall alter a motor vehicle or trailer so as to render its condition if used on a road:
   i) unlawful by virtue of regulations relating to construction, weight or equipment; or
   ii) as would involve a danger of injury to any person.

9.3.3 *Vehicle Parts*
A person commits an offence who fits or causes or permits to be fitted a vehicle part to a vehicle, so that the use of the vehicle on a road would amount to a failure to comply with construction and use requirements, or would involve a danger of injury to any person.

An offence will also be committed by a person who supplies, or who causes or permits to be supplied, a vehicle part which he has reason to believe is to be fitted to a motor vehicle, or to a particular class of vehicle, or to a particular vehicle, if that part could not be so fitted without contravention of construction and use requirements, or so as to involve danger of injury to any person should the vehicle be used on a road.

9.4 Explanation
Repetition: There appears to be little difference between the provisions of Section 40A and those of regulation 100; the latter uses more words, to say basically the same. An offence under Section 40A carries obligatory endorsement of the defendant's driving licence, whereas failure to comply with regulation 100 does not.

Condition: Due to poor maintenance, poor quality or damage, the condition of the vehicle or any of its accessories, equipment or component parts, may be such that the use of the vehicle on a road is a source of danger. Inefficient brakes may amount to a breach of regulation 18 (see paragraph 2 above), but if the brakes are in very bad condition, a breach of Section 40A or of regulation 100 may also arise.

   To drive a mechanically propelled vehicle in a dangerous condition may also amount to an offence of dangerous driving *(see chapter 50)*.

Passengers: The number of passengers carried, or the manner in which they are carried, may give rise to danger. A small car with six or seven passengers crammed into it may be unstable; passengers sitting on seats which are not secured are likely to be injured in the event of sudden braking.

Load: A load may give rise to danger because of:

- its distribution, packing or adjustment, perhaps causing the vehicle to lean to one side, or to carry too much weight on one axle;
- its weight, too heavy for the vehicle to carry safely;
- not being properly secured, liable to fall off. The best evidence for an offence in this respect is that the load or part of it has actually fallen off, but an offence arises if it not properly secured, whether it falls off or not.

Unroadworthy: A vehicle will be unroadworthy if:

i) its use on a road in that condition would amount to a breach of regulations relating to brakes, steering gear, tyres, or the construction, weight or equipment of vehicles; or

ii) it is in such condition that its use on a road would involve danger of injury to any person.

Defences: A person will not be guilty of selling, etc. an unroadworthy vehicle or of altering a vehicle, if he proves:

i) the vehicle was supplied or altered for export from Great Britain; or

ii) that he had reason to believe that the vehicle or trailer would not be used on a road in Great Britain until it had been made roadworthy; or

iii) in the case of selling or exposing for sale, in the course of trade or business, if he also proves that he took all reasonable steps to ensure that a prospective customer would be aware, or an actual customer was aware, of the fact that its use in its current condition on a road in Great Britain would be unlawful.

Corresponding defences apply to fitting of defective vehicle parts.

MISCELLANEOUS 'USE' REQUIREMENTS

10.1 Parking on Nearside During Hours of Darkness
Regulation 101

(1) Save as provided in paragraph (2) no person shall except with the permission of a police officer in a uniform, cause or permit any motor vehicle to stand on a road at any time between sunset and sunrise unless the nearside of the vehicle is as close to the edge of the carriageway.

(2) The provisions of paragraph (1) do not apply in respect of any motor vehicle:

a) being used for the fire brigade, ambulance or police purposes if compliance with those provisions would hinder or be likely to hinder the use of the vehicle for the purpose for which it is being used on that occasion;

b) being used in connection with:

i) any building or demolition;

ii) the repair of any other vehicle;

iii) the removal of any obstruction to traffic;

iv) the maintenance, repair or reconstruction of any road; or

v) the laying, erection, alteration or repair in or near to any road of any sewer, main, pipe or apparatus for the supply of gas, water or electricity, of any telecommunication apparatus or of the apparatus of any electric transport undertaking;

if in any such case, compliance with those provisions would hinder or be likely to hinder the use of the vehicle for the purpose for which it was being used on that occasion;

  c) on any road which vehicles are allowed to proceed in one direction only;
  d) standing on part of a road set aside for the parking of vehicles or as a stand for hackney carriages or as a stand for buses or as a place at which such vehicles may stop for a longer time than is necessary for the taking up and setting down of passengers where compliance with those provisions would conflict with the provision of any order, regulation or bylaws governing the use of part of the road for that purpose.
  e) waiting to set down or pick up passengers in accordance with regulations made or directions given by the chief officer of police in regard to such setting down or picking up.

10.1.1 *Explanation*

Purpose: If a vehicle is parked on the nearside of the road, its reflectors, picked up in the lights of traffic on the same side of the road, give added warning of its presence, which would not be the case if the vehicle was parked on the off-side of the road. On a one-way street, the distinction between parking on the nearside or off-side is of no relevance, hence this is one of the exemptions.

Exemptions: Where it is necessary to stop a vehicle other than close to the nearside kerb, an exemption may be available. In most cases, the stationary vehicle will be well lit, perhaps with blue or amber beacon operating.

10.2 **Motor Cycle Foot Rests**
Regulation 102

If any person in addition to the driver is carried astride a two-wheeled motor cycle on a road (whether a sidecar is attached to it or not) suitable supports or rests for the feet shall be available on the motor cycle for that person.

10.2.1 *Explanation*

The pillion passenger on a motor bicycle must have available, somewhere to place her feet, as a safety measure. This applies whether or not there is a side-car attached to the motor bike, but does not apply to a motor cycle with more than two wheels.

10.3 **Unnecessary Obstruction**

No person in charge of a motor vehicle or trailer on a road shall cause or permit the vehicle to stand on a road so as to cause any unnecessary obstruction of the road.

10.3.1 *Explanation*

Stand: To amount to an unnecessary obstruction, the vehicle must be stationary. If a number of vehicles are driven very slowly, so as to hold up traffic, as part of a demonstration or protest, such action will not amount to a breach of this regulation.

Obstruction: It is not necessary, for the road to be blocked, to constitute an obstruction, anything which diminishes the capacity of the road may be enough. For further explanation, see Chapter 46, paragraph 2 – obstruction of a highway.

10.4 **Proper Control and Full View**
Regulation 104

No person shall drive or cause or permit any other person to drive a motor vehicle on a road if he is in such a position that he cannot have proper control of the vehicle or have a full view of the traffic ahead.

10.4.1 *Explanation*
There are a variety of ways in which a driver may be in breach of this regulation. Using one hand to hold a mobile phone is a comparatively modern example, while the young man driving with his left arm engaged in embracing a young woman in the passenger seat, probably dates from not long after the development of the internal combustion engine.

10.5 **Opening Doors Dangerously**
Regulation 105

No person shall open, or cause or permit to be opened any door of a vehicle on a road so as to injure or endanger any person.

10.5.1 *Explanation*
Person: This offence may be committed by a passenger in a vehicle, as well as by a driver. For example, the driver of a car opens the door , failing to see a cyclist coming up-from behind, causing injury to the cyclist. The nearside door, opened by a passenger, could similarly cause injury to a person on the pavement.

Injury or danger: Injury is not an essential element in an offence arising from breach of this regulation. A cyclist who spots the door opening in a parked car he is about to overtake, in time to take evasive action, may nevertheless have been endangered.

10.6 **Reversing**
Regulation 106

No person shall drive, or cause or permit to be driven a motor vehicle backwards on a road further than may be requisite for the safety or reasonable convenience of the occupants of the vehicle or other traffic, unless it is a road roller or is engaged in the construction, maintenance or repair of the road.

10.6.1 *Explanation*
Requisite: Very few drivers are capable of driving in reverse with the same degree of skill as they show when going forward. What will amount to an unreasonable distance will be a matter of fact for a court to decide in any particular case. A police officer in a car reversing along the hard shoulder of a motorway, to warn approaching drivers of a rapidly growing queue of traffic ahead, is doing what is 'requisite for the safety of other traffic.'

10.7 **Quitting and Setting**
Regulation 107

(1) Save as provided in paragraph (2), no person shall leave or cause or permit to be left on a road a motor vehicle which is not attended by a person licensed to drive it unless the

engine is stopped and any parking brake with which the vehicle is required to be equipped is effectively set.

(2) The requirement specified in paragraph (1) as to the stopping of the engine shall not apply in respect of a vehicle:

a) being used for ambulance, fire brigade or police purposes; or

b) in such a position and condition as not likely to endanger any person or property and engaged in an operation which requires the engine to be used to:

i)   drive machinery forming part of, or mounted on, the vehicle and used for purposes other than driving the vehicle; or

ii) maintain the electrical power of the batteries of the vehicle at a level required for driving that machinery or apparatus.

10.7.1 *Explanation*

Person licensed: The engine need not be switched off if there is a person with the motor vehicle who holds a licence to drive that class of vehicle.

Engine off and handbrake on: Both conditions must be complied with; if the handbrake is engaged but the engine is left running, or vice versa, the requirement has not been met.

This requirement is quite distinct from that of regulation 98 (above), which is to switch off any machinery in a stationary vehicle, to prevent undue noise.

10.8 **Televisions**
Regulation 109

(1) No person shall drive, or cause or permit to be driven, a motor vehicle on a road, if the driver is in such a position as to be able to see, whether directly, or by reflection, a television receiving apparatus or other cinematographic apparatus use to display anything other than information:

a) about the state of the vehicle or its equipment;

b) about the location of the vehicle and the road on which it is located;

c) to assist the driver to see the road adjacent to the vehicle; or

d) to assist the driver to reach his destination.

(2) In this regulation 'television receiving apparatus' means any cathode ray tube carried on a vehicle and on which there can be displayed an image from a television broadcast, a recording or a camera or computer.

10.8.1 *Explanation*

The driver: This is not a reference to the driver of any other vehicle; a television operating in a coach for the entertainment of passengers, may be visible to the drivers of vehicles which overtake the coach. What matters is that it should not be visible to the driver of the coach.

Television: The term is wider in meaning than merely sets for receiving television broadcasts, and will include video players, computer screens, or a screen for displaying images from a camera.

Exceptions: The exceptions allow for the use of traffic information displays, computerised navigation systems, e.g. displaying maps of the route, or video cameras to assist the driver to manoeuvre a large vehicle. If conventional instruments are replaced with displays on a screen, this will be permissible.

SEAT BELTS

11.1 **Fitting of Seat Belts**
Road Vehicles (Construction and Use) Regulations 1986 Regulations 46, 47

Seat belt anchorage points and seat belts are required in various classes of motor vehicles, with a plethora of starting dates ranging back as far as 1965 (anchorage points in motor cars). The most recent requirements relate to certain minibuses and coaches.

The earliest requirements for seat belts related to the driver's seat and one front passenger seat. Since 1 April 1987, additional belts have been required for other front seats and for rear seats. A seat belt is not required for every rear seat however. For example, a motor car with a rear seat designed for three persons, may have two lap-diagonal belts. Clearly, if there are three rear seat passengers in that car, one of them cannot wear a seat belt.

Seat belts, anchorage points and the bodywork around anchorage points must be maintained in good condition. Belts must be free of obstruction and accessible, without serious cuts.

11.2 **Wearing of Seat Belts**
Motor Vehicles (Wearing of Seat Belts) Regulations 1993

11.2.1 *Adults (Regulation 5)*
Subject to exceptions, a person aged 14 years or over, who is the driver, or passenger in the front or rear of a relevant motor vehicle being driven on a road, shall wear an adult seat belt.

Exceptions
1. A person holding a medical certificate;
2. A person using a vehicle constructed or adapted for the delivery of goods or mail, while engaged in making local rounds of deliveries or collections;
3. A driver performing a manoeuvre which includes reversing, and the qualified driver supervising a provisional licence holder who is doing so;
4. A person driving or riding in a vehicle used for police or fire brigade purposes, or for carrying a person in lawful custody (including a person who is in lawful custody);
5. The driver of a licensed taxi while it is being used for hire;
6. The driver of a private hire vehicle while it is being used to carry a passenger for hire;
7. A person riding in a vehicle being used under a trade licence, investigating or remedying a mechanical fault;
8. A disabled person wearing a disabled person's belt;
9. A person riding in a vehicle taking part in a procession, in certain circumstances;
10. In a case where no adult seat belt is available.

11.2.2 *Children (Regulation 6)*
The general rule is that a child may not travel in the front of a vehicle unless she is wearing a seat belt. The fact that there is no seat belt available for the child is not an excuse.

Where a child under 14 is in the rear of a motor vehicle and there is a seat belt fitted in the rear, the vehicle should not, without reasonable excuse, be driven on a road unless the child is wearing the seat belt.

Where a small child is in the rear of a passenger car and no seat belt is fitted in the rear, but there is a unoccupied seat in the front which has a seat belt fitted, the car must not, without reasonable excuse, be driven on a road.

Exceptions

Among the exceptions are taxis and hire cars with a partition separating the rear seats from the driver, a child aged under one year, in a carry cot which is restrained by suitable straps.

11.3 Offences
Road Traffic Act 1988 Sections 14, 15

11.3.1 *Adults*

If an adult fails to wear a seat belt, that person, and only that person, is guilty of an offence. No other person will be liable, e.g. for aiding and abetting.

11.3.2 *Children*

If a child is not wearing a seat belt when required, the driver of the motor vehicle shall be liable for an offence.

11.4 Explanation

Complexity: The Act and Regulations are quite detailed, not the easiest topic to understand. There are different requirements for different classes of vehicle, for persons of various ages, and for front and back seats. There are exemptions galore, with exceptions to exemptions. The treatment of the topic here is in fairly general terms.

Child, large or small: A child is a person aged under 14 years. A small child is one who is – under the age of 12 years **and** who is under 150 cm (approximately 5 feet) in height. A large child is one who is not a small child, e.g. 12 or 13 years old, or taller than 150 cm.

Appropriate seat belt: Generally, a seat belt will be appropriate:
   i)   for a child under 3 – if it is one prescribed for a person of that height and weight;
   ii) for a child aged 3 or more, if it is either a child restraint, or an adult belt;
   iii) for a person over 14, if it is an adult belt.

However, in a passenger car, light goods vehicle or small bus, a 'small child' in the back seat must wear a child restraint, not an adult belt – **unless** there is no child restraint available in the front or back. (Try explaining that to a parent who seeks advice!)

Not available: The Regulations contain detailed provisions as to whether a seat belt will be 'available' for a person to wear. It will not be available if, for example, another person is wearing it, if a person who holds a medical certificate is sitting in the seat fitted with the belt, or if a carry cot occupied by a child under 12 months is in the seat.

Medical certificate: A person will be exempt from the requirement to wear a seat belt if he holds a valid certificate, signed by a doctor, to the effect that it is inadvisable on medical grounds, for him to wear a seat belt. The holder of a certificate will not escape prosecution for failing to wear a seat belt, unless the certificate is produced to the police. Provisions for producing the certificate are similar to that for other traffic documents; if the certificate is not produced on demand, it must be produced, subject to exceptions, within 7 days at a nominated police station.

Chapter 53: Road Traffic Accidents

REPORTABLE ACCIDENT
Road Traffic Act 1988, section 170

1.1 Scope of Term 'accident'

(1) This Section applies in a case where, owing to the presence of a mechanically propelled vehicle on a road, an accident occurs by which:

   a) personal injury is caused to a person other than the driver of that mechanically propelled vehicle, or

   b) damage is caused:

      i) to a vehicle other than that mechanically propelled vehicle or a trailer drawn by that mechanically propelled vehicle , or

      ii) to an animal other than an animal in or on that mechanically propelled vehicle, or in a trailer drawn by it

      iii) to any other property constructed on, fixed to, growing in or otherwise forming part of the land on which the road in question is situated or land adjacent to such land.

1.2 Driver's Duties and Responsibilities

(2) The driver of the mechanically propelled vehicle must stop and, if required to do so by any person having reasonable grounds for so requiring, give his name and address and also the name and address of the owner and the identification marks of the vehicle.

(3) If for any reason the driver of a mechanically propelled vehicle does not give his name and address under subsection (2) above, he must report the accident.

(4) A person who fails to comply with subsection (2) and (3) above is guilty of an offence.

1.3 Injury Accidents

(5) If, in the case where this Section applies by virtue of subsection (1)(a) above, the driver of a motor vehicle does not at the time of the accident produce such a certificate of insurance or security, or other evidence, as is mentioned in Section 165(2) of this Act:

   a) to a constable, or

   b) to some other person who, having reasonable grounds for so doing, has required him to produce it.

(6) To comply with a duty under this Section to report an accident or to produce such a certificate of insurance or security, or other evidence, as is mentioned in Section 165(2)(a) of this Act, the driver:

a) must do so at a police station or to a constable, and

b) must do so as soon as is reasonably practicable and, in any case, within twenty-four hours of the occurrence of the accident.

(7) A person who fails to comply with a duty under subsection (5) above is guilty of an offence, but shall not be convicted by reason only of failure to produce a certificate or other evidence if, within seven days after the occurrence of the accident, the certificate

or other evidence is produced at a police station that was specified by him at the time when the accident was reported.

1.4 *Explanation*

Mechanically propelled vehicle: The duty to stop and report an accident is not confined to the drivers of motor vehicles; it applies equally in the case of a mechanically propelled vehicle which is not intended or adapted for use on roads. (For explanations of the terms 'motor vehicle' and 'mechanically propelled vehicle', see Chapter 50.)

Road: The scope of the term 'road' has been increased considerably, following case decisions in 1997. (For an explanation of the term, see chapter 50.)

Owing to the presence: This term does not imply that the driver of the vehicle has to be at fault, before he is required to stop, etc. There has to be some connection between the presence of that vehicle on the road and the accident. If the vehicle has collided with another vehicle, a person or some object, the connection is clear. Where, for example, a driver pulls out from a side road, forcing a vehicle on the main road to swerve and collide with a tree, the accident occurred owing to the presence of the first vehicle on a road, as well as of the second one. Where a vehicle is stationary on a road and a driver pulling over to the offside to pass the stationary car, misjudges his move and collides with an oncoming vehicle on its correct side of the road, one might argue that the accident would not have happened if the stationary car had not been there. An opposing argument would be that there are all sorts of manoeuvres which a driver is required to make in the course of journey, and that his accident was due to the presence only of the other two vehicles. When a passenger was injured when getting off a bus, this was held to be 'due to the presence' of the bus on the road. (*Quelch v Phipps* (1955)) Whether the 'owing to the presence' element is satisfied will be a question of fact in any particular case.

Accident: The term 'accident' is not defined in the Act, but has been described as 'an unintended occurrence which has an adverse physical result' (*R v Morris* (1972)).

A deliberate act resulting in damage to a motor vehicle has been held to be an 'accident'. (*Chief Constable of West Midlands Police v Billingham* (1979)).

Other person/vehicle: The accident will not impose duties on a driver if injury or damage is confined to that driver, to his vehicle, or to an animal carried in his vehicle or in a trailer drawn by it. This could lead to a situation where one driver in an accident is required to stop and report, another is not. Jill is driving her RangeRover, towing a horse box, past road works. She misjudges a gap and collides with a road roller. There is slight damage to her vehicle, she cuts her head and the horse falls over in the horse box, suffering injury. There is no damage whatsoever to the road roller. The driver of the road roller has a duty to stop and give details, etc, but no such duty falls on Jill because the injury and damage was confined to her, her vehicle and the horse in her trailer.

Animal: The term includes horse, cattle, ass, mule, sheep, pig, goat or dog. A notable exception, on the domestic animal front, is cat. The term does not include any wild animal; deer, foxes, rabbits, badgers and hedgehogs are involved in countless collisions on roads, but none of these accidents are 'reportable'.

Stop: The duty imposed on a driver to stop at the scene, involves more than a momentary stop. To be regarded as having stopped, the driver must remain there long enough, taking account of the circumstances, including the location and nature of the road, to afford a person having a right to require details, a reasonable opportunity to do so (*Lee v Knapp* (1966)).

A driver who has knocked over a keep left bollard at 3.00 am, will have discharged this duty as soon as it is apparent that there is no council employee in the vicinity, seeking details. A driver involved in a multi-vehicle, serious injury accident on a motorway, may be expected to wait rather longer.

If required: The driver must give all three sets of details, if required by someone having reason to ask. If the driver is asked only for some of this information, or is not asked for any, he will not be liable for his failure to give all of it. However, the fact that he has not may give rise to a duty to report to the police.

Report to police: A duty to report to the police arises only if a driver has not given his own name and address at the scene of the accident. If he has given his name and address, but was not asked for the vehicle owner's details, he has complied with the requirements at the scene, and does not thereafter have to report to the police. (A duty to report also arises if insurance is not produced in injury accidents – see **produce insurance**, below.)

The report to the police must be:

i) at a police station or to a constable. At a police station, the details may be taken, e.g. by a civilian enquiry officer, or by a constable. The report has to be AT a police station; reporting by telephone **to** a police station will not be good enough (*Wisdom v MacDonald* (1983)). Other than at a police station, the report must be made to a constable; it will not suffice to report details to a traffic warden in the street.

ii) as soon as practicable and in any case within 24 hours. The report has to be made as soon as practicable, taking account of the circumstances (*Britton v Loveday* (1981)). If the driver reports within 24 hours, but could have done so earlier, he has not complied with the requirement (*Bulman v Lakin* (1981)).

Offence: For a driver to be guilty of failing to stop or failing to report, *mens rea* must be proved; in other words, it must be proved that he was aware that an accident had occurred of a sort which gave rise to the duty to stop, etc (*Harding v Price* (1948)).

The duty to stop and give details if required, is one duty; whether the driver fails to do both, or whether he stops but fails to give details, will amount to one offence only. However, fail to stop and give details, and fail thereafter to report the accident to the police, amounts to two separate offences (*Roper v Sullivan* (1978)).

Produce insurance: The duty to produce insurance arises only in the case of an accident where injury is caused to a person (other than to that driver). If the insurance certificate or other document is not produced at the scene (to a constable or to a person have reason to require it), the driver must report the accident and produce his insurance to the police. The same time scales apply as in other cases where it must be reported, i.e. as soon as practicable, with a maximum limit of 24 hours.

However, if a driver reports an accident, but fails to produce the insurance document, she will escape prosecution, if she thereafter produces it at a police station specified by her at the time of reporting the accident, within 7 days of the accident. Note that this differs slightly from the usual conditions for production of driving licences and other documents – here, production has to be within 7 days of the accident, not 7 days of a police officer asking for the insurance to be produced; if the driver is on the limit of the 24 hour period for reporting the accident, this distinction may be relevant.

Chapter 54: Driving Licences

REQUIREMENT TO HOLD A DRIVING LICENCE

1.1 **Offences**
Road Traffic Act 1988 Section 87

(1) It is an offence:
- for a person to drive on a road
- a motor vehicle of any class
- otherwise that in accordance with a licence authorising him
- to drive a motor vehicle of that class.

(2) It is an offence:
- for a person to cause or permit
- another person to drive on a road a motor vehicle of any class
- otherwise than in accordance with a licence
- authorising that other person to drive a motor vehicle of that class.

1.1.1 *Explanation*
Class: There are currently some 23 categories and sub-categories of motor vehicles for driving licence purposes, these having been changed frequently over the years. When a person passes a driving test, the licence granted may well cover a number of these categories, dependent on what sort of vehicle she was driving when she took the driving test.

Offences: An offence is committed by a person who drives 'other than in accordance with a licence'. The popular description of this offence is 'no driving licence', but the proper wording reflects the fact that a person who commits the offence may hold a driving licence, but not for the class of vehicle in question.

A person who causes or permits another to drive otherwise than in accordance with a licence also commits an offence. This offence may well be committed by an employer.

PROVISIONAL LICENCES

2.1 **Scope of Provisional Licence**
Road Traffic Act 1988, Section 97

A provisional licence:
  i) shall not authorise a person under the age of 21 years, before he has passed a test of competence to drive a motor bicycle:
  a) to drive a motor bicycle without a side-car unless it is a learner motor bicycle (or it was first used before 1982 and it has a cylinder capacity not exceeding 125 cc); or
  b) to drive a motor bicycle with a side-car unless its power to weight ratio is within a specified limit.
  ii) shall not authorise a person, before he has passed a test of competence to drive, to drive a motor bicycle on a road unless he has successfully completed an approved training course, or is driving while undergoing training on such a course.

iii) in the case of a licence for a motor bicycle, shall be valid for a period of two years only. A new provisional licence shall not be issued to a person who was the holder of a previous licence which expired within the preceding 12 months.

2.2 Conditions
Motor Vehicles (Driving Licences) Regulations 1996, Regulation 15

Driving whilst the holder of a provisional licence requires certain conditions to be met in order to be lawful. These conditions fall basically into four sub headings:
a) Supervision
b) 'L' plates
c) Towing trailers
d) Motor cycles.

2.2.1 *Supervision*
A provisional licence holder shall not drive or ride a motor vehicle (not including a motor bicycle) otherwise than under the supervision of a qualified driver who is present with him in or on the vehicle. A qualified driver is a person who holds a full licence to drive the class of vehicle being used by the provisional licence holder, and, except in the case of a member of the armed forces of the Crown, the full licence holder must have held a licence for at least three years and must be aged over 21years. The supervisor may be liable if he fails to properly supervise. It is a question for the court to decide if a supervisor has failed in his duty, dependant upon the offences committed. A provisional licence holder is not required to be supervised:

(1) While undergoing a driving test;

(2) While driving an invalid carriage or motor tricycle under a specified unladen mass (500 kg) and designed not to exceed 50 kilometres per hour (just over 30 mph);

(3) While driving a motor vehicle which is – an agricultural tractor, road roller or tracked vehicle – and which is constructed or adapted to carry not more than one person;

(4) While riding a moped or a motor bicycle with or without sidecar;

(5) While driving a motor vehicle (subject to exceptions) on an exempted island.

2.2.2 *'L' plates*
Are required to be placed in such a manner as to be clearly visible to other person's using the road from within a reasonable distance from the front and back of the vehicle used by the provisional licence holder.

In Wales, there is an option to use 'D' plates instead of 'L' plates. This applies when a motor vehicle is used on a road in Wales, so a resident of Wales, taking a driving lesson near the border, would have to exchange the D plates for L plates, should he venture into England.

2.2.3 *Towing Trailers*
The holder of a provisional licence must not drive a motor vehicle which is being used to draw a trailer. This general rule is subject to exceptions, e.g. where the motor vehicle is an agricultural or forestry tractor.

2.2.4 *Motor Cycles*

A person may not hold a provisional driving licence for a motor cycle for more than two years. If she has not passed a test within that period, she will be barred from holding a provisional motor cycle licence for a period of 12 months. This measure is intended to prevent someone riding a motor cycle on a permanent basis, without ever reaching the standard necessary to pass a test and obtain a full licence.

There are restrictions placed on provisional licence holders, relating to the riding of certain categories of motor cycle, and to the carriage of passengers. The holder of a provisional licence shall not:

(1) Drive a moped, or a motor bicycle, with or without sidecar, while carrying on it another person;

(2) Drive a moped unless he is the holder of a valid certificate, signifying that he has completed a course of training;

(3) Drive a large motor bicycle otherwise than subject to the following:
   – under the direct supervision of a certified instructor, who is riding another motor bicycle
   – the instructor is supervising no more than two provisional licence holders
   – the instructor is in radio communication with the provisional licence holder (or using some other means of communication, in the case of a learner rider with hearing impairment) and – the learner rider and instructor are both wearing reflective or luminous garments.

2.3 Explanation

Supervised: A person supervising a provisional licence holder must hold a full licence for the class of vehicle concerned. In the case of a motor car a person aged 20 years may have held a full licence for 3 years, but will not be eligible as a supervisor, being under 21. A person who passes her test at the age of, say 20 years, will not be eligible to supervise until she has held a licence for a full three years. There is an exception in the case of members of H.M. forces.

A supervisor must do more than merely 'accompany' and may, in certain circumstances be liable for aiding and abetting an offence committed by the driver.

Exempt from supervision: A driving test examiner will invariably hold a full licence but his role is not to advise or offer guidance to the person undergoing the test. The purpose of the exemption is to free the examiner from liability as a supervisor, for any offence committed by the driver during the driving test.

One person: Clearly, if a motor vehicle is constructed to carry only one person, it cannot be used by a provisional licence holder plus a supervisor. In certain cases, the provisional licence holder may drive such a vehicle, e.g. a 3-wheel vehicle classed as a motor cycle, agricultural tractor, etc.

Motor bicycle: A motor bicycle has two wheels. It may have a sidecar attached, but is still regarded as a 'motor bike and sidecar', because if the sidecar was unbolted from it, the motor bike could be driven on its own. This is different from a motor tricycle, which will have a frame mounted on three wheels. The vehicle could not be used if one wheel was removed. A sidecar is any roadworthy attachment made or adapted for the carriage of goods or passengers (*Kenn v Parker* (1976)).

Large motor bicycle: A large motor bicycle is one which exceeds a specified power to weight ratio. There are different ratios for motor bikes with and without side-cars.

Learner motor bicycle: A learner motor bicycle is one which has:
  a) an engine capacity not exceeding 125 cc; and
  b) a maximum net power output of its engine not exceeding 11 kilowatts.

Motor bicycles – summary: The purpose for the various classifications of motor bicycles is to prevent young and inexperienced persons driving around on powerful machines capable of swift acceleration and high top speeds. A person under 21 may not drive a large motor cycle under any circumstances on a provisional licence; an older person may ride one only as part of supervised training. (Once the holder of a full licence, restrictions on large motor cycles still apply to a person under 21 – see Minimum Ages (below)). Before venturing on to a road unsupervised, the learner rider must successfully complete a course of training. Thereafter, she may ride only a learner motor bicycle, of relatively limited power. If the holder of a provisional licence does not pass a driving test for a motor bicycle during the two year duration of the licence, she must then wait 12 months before obtaining a renewal.

EYESIGHT
Road Traffic Act 1988 Section 96

3.1 (1) If a person drives a motor vehicle on a road:
  – while his eyesight is such (whether through a defect which cannot be or one which is not for the time being sufficiently corrected)
  – that he cannot comply with any requirements,
  – to eyesight prescribed under this Part of this Act,
  – for the purposes of tests of competence to drive,
  – he is guilty of an offence.

(2) A constable having reasonable cause to suspect that a person driving a motor vehicle may be guilty of an offence under subsection (1) above my require him to submit to an eyesight test for the purpose of ascertaining whether, using no other means of correction than he used at the time of driving, he can comply with the requirement concerned.

(3) If that person refuses to submit to the test he is guilty of an offence.

3.2 The standard for eyesight is set by the Motor Vehicles (Driving Licence) Regulations 1996, Regulation 67:

'Read in good daylight (with the aid of glasses or contact lenses if worn) a registration mark fixed to a motor vehicle and containing letters and figures 79.4 millimetres high at a distance of:
a) 20.5 metres, in any case except that mentioned below; and,
b) 12.3 metres, in any case of a driving test carried out on a vehicle of a class included in group K only (pedestrian controlled vehicles).

3.3 *Explanation*
Corrected: If a driver's eyesight is acceptable when he wears his spectacles, but he drives without them, then he is driving when his eyesight is 'not for the time being sufficiently corrected'.

Person driving: Police powers to require a person to take an eyesight test, apply only to a person who 'is driving'. A person who has been stopped by the police is still 'driving', but if, e.g. he has gone home after being involved in an accident and is in his house, he will probably no longer be 'driving'. (For more on the meaning of 'driving', see chapter 50.)

No other means of correction: A driver who was not wearing glasses when he was driving, may not put them on to undergo an eye-sight test.

Daylight: The police power to require a driver to undergo an eye-sight test will not apply during hours of darkness, or in bad visibility.

DISQUALIFICATION FROM HOLDING OR OBTAINING A DRIVING LICENCE

4.1 Disqualification by a Court
Road Traffic Offenders Act 1988 Sections 28 – 49

4.1.1 *Obligatory Disqualification*
When a person is convicted of an offence involving obligatory disqualification, the court must order him to be disqualified for such period not less than 12 months, as the court thinks fit, unless the court, for special reasons, thinks fit to order him to be disqualified for a shorter period, or not to order him to be disqualified.

4.1.2 *Discretionary Disqualification*
Where a person is convicted of an offence involving discretionary disqualification then (provided disqualification for 12 or more penalty points does not apply) the court may order him to be disqualified for such period as the court thinks fit.

4.1.3 *Disqualification for 12 Penalty Points*
Where a person is convicted of an offence involving discretionary disqualification and obligatory endorsement (or one involving obligatory disqualification where no order is made), then if the penalty points to be taken into account on that occasion number 12 or more, the court shall order the person to be disqualified for not less than the minimum period, unless the court is satisfied that there are grounds for mitigating the conviction, in which case the court may order disqualification for a shorter period, or order no disqualification.

The minimum period shall be:
   a) six months if no previous disqualification on the offender is to be taken into account;
   b) 12 months if one, and two years if more than one, such disqualification is to be taken into account.

4.1.4 *Criminal Cases*
A court may order a person to be disqualified who has been convicted of a criminal offence and the court is satisfied that a motor vehicle was used in the commission of crime. (Powers of Criminal Courts Act 1973, section 44)

4.1.5 *Explanation*
Obligatory/discretionary: The more serious motoring offences carry obligatory disqualification. These include causing death by dangerous driving and offences of driving or attempting to drive whilst unfit through drink or drugs, or with excess alcohol. Offences involving being in

charge of a motor vehicle whilst unfit or over the limit, together with a host of other offences, give the courts an option to impose disqualification as the court thinks appropriate.

Penalty points: When a person is convicted of two or more offences committed on the same occasion and involving obligatory endorsement, the number of penalty points to be attributed shall be the highest number which would be attributed on the conviction of one of them. Note that this applies to offences committed on the same occasion, not to offences where the convictions are on the same occasion. If a defendant is convicted of three offences of using a motor vehicle with a defective tyre (3 penalty points), and with speeding (3 – 6 points), all arising from the same occasion when he was stopped by police, the penalty points to be attributed will be between 3 and 6, dependent on how seriously the court views the speeding offence. A court may set aside this provision, but must state the reasons for doing so.

When a person is found guilty of an offence involving obligatory endorsement, the penalty points to be taken into account, in determining whether or not the total will now reach 12, are:

(i) those to be attributed to offences of which he is convicted on this occasion (but excluding any offence for which disqualification is being imposed); plus

(ii) any other penalty points endorsed on the counterpart of the licence on a previous occasion, but excluding:

   – any points in respect of an offence committed more than 3 years before the date of the current offence(s);

   – any points endorsed before a previous disqualification for having 12 or more points.

For example, Nixon is dealt with for an offence of speeding and for having defective brakes. The magistrates decide to disqualify him for two months for the speeding offence and attribute 3 points for the brake offence. His existing penalty points include – 10 for dangerous driving , four years ago; 3 for defective tyre, two years ago, and 5 for careless driving six months ago. However, when he was dealt with for the defective tyre, he was disqualified, having accrued 13 penalty points. None of these points, whether dating from more or less than three years ago, will count on this occasion, since they pre-date a previous disqualification. The speeding endorsement does not count either, because he being disqualified. His total to be considered is therefore – 5 for careless driving and 3 for the defective brakes, a total of 8, so no further disqualification order will be made on this occasion.

Minimum period: Obligatory disqualification is for a minimum period of 12 months. However this minimum period is increased to:

(i) two years, where the offence concerned is:
   – manslaughter
   – causing death by dangerous driving
   – causing death by careless driving while unfit, etc (under Section 3A Road Traffic Act 1988);

(ii) two years, where the defendant has had one or more periods of disqualification for a fixed period of 56 days or more, imposed in the three years preceding the date of the offence;

(iii) three years in a case where the conviction is for an offence:
   – of causing death by careless driving etc – driving or attempting to drive whilst unfit or with excess alcohol – or failing to provide breath, blood or urine for analysis in a case involving driving or attempting to drive; **and**

- in the 10 years preceding the date of the offence, the defendant has been convicted of such an offence.

When a person accrues 12 or more penalty points, the minimum period of disqualification goes up from six months, to one or two years if there are previous disqualifications to take into account. A period of disqualification will be taken into account if:

(i) it was for a fixed period of 56 days or more; and

(ii) it was imposed within three years of the date of committing the latest offence for which penalty points are attributed.

Shorter period: The court may impose a period of disqualification shorter than the minimum, which may be no disqualification at all, if, in the case of obligatory disqualification, there are special reasons, or in the case of 12 or more penalty points, there is mitigation.

Special reasons relate to the circumstances of the offence and not to the offender himself. Thus, the fact that the defendant has a previously unblemished record, or that disqualification will cause him serious hardship, will not be special reasons relating to the commission of the offence (*Whittall v Kirby* (1947)). An emergency situation, such as where an ambulance driver was taking an urgent case to hospital (*R v Lundt-Smith* (1964)) may give rise to special reasons. If a person's drinks have been 'laced' with something stronger, unknown to him, so that he had consumed more alcohol than he believed he had, this will amount to special reasons (*Williams v Neale* (1971)); *R v Shippam* (1971)). However, where a person suffered from a liver defect, causing his body to retain alcohol for longer than would normally be the case, this was something relating to the driver himself, not to the circumstances of the offence, so would not amount to special reasons (*R v Jackson* (1970)).

Note: When a person is convicted of an offence of aggravated vehicle taking (contrary to Section 12A Theft Act 1968), the fact that he did not drive the vehicle shall not be regarded as a special reason for not disqualifying him for the offence (Road Traffic Offenders Act 1988, Section 34(1A)).

Mitigation: A court may take personal factors into account, so as to mitigate the effect of a disqualification, arising from 12 or more penalty points. The fact that the offender lives in the countryside, with no public transport available, or that his employment involves driving, may be considered.

Reduced period: Provision is made for a person who attends a course, to have his period of disqualification reduced, upon successful completion of that course. The provisions may be implemented where the conviction is for an offence:

- of causing death by careless driving etc
- driving or attempting to drive whilst unfit or with excess alcohol
- or failing to provide breath, blood or urine for analysis in a case involving driving or attempting to drive; and

the court has ordered a period of disqualification of 12 months or more.

Till test is passed: In certain circumstances, a court may order a person who has been disqualified to remain disqualified until he passes a driving test. In certain cases, this may amount to an extended driving test.

4.2 **Disqualification by Age**
Road Traffic Act 1988 Section 101

(1) A person is disqualified for holding or obtaining a driving licence to drive a motor vehicle of a class specified in the following Table if he is under the age specified in relation to it in the second column of the table:

Class of motor vehicle	Age in years
1 Invalid carriage	16
2 Moped	16
3 Motor bicycle	17
Large motor bicycle	21
4 Agricultural or forestry tractor	16 or 17
5 Small vehicle	16 or 17
6 Medium sized goods vehicle	18 or 21
7 Other motor vehicle	18 or 21

4.2.1 *Explanation*

Motor bicycle: The minimum age for riding a large motor bicycle (defined in paragraph 2.3 above) is 21 years, unless the rider has passed a motor bicycle driving test (for other than a learner motor bicycle) and at least two years have elapsed since he passed that driving test. The minimum age for large motor bicycles is 18 for members of H.M. Forces riding Forces machines.

Tractors: The minimum age is generally 17 years, but may be 16 in cases where the driver has passed a test, and the tractor meets certain width limits.

Small vehicle: The general minimum is 17 years, but will be 16 in the case of certain persons suffering from disability, or where no trailer is drawn.

Medium sized goods vehicle: The general minimum is 18 years, but this becomes 21 if the vehicle is drawing a trailer over a certain weight.

Other: The general minimum for this class, which includes large goods and passenger carrying vehicles, is 21, but may be reduced to 18 in certain cases. These include some categories of ambulance, where the motor vehicle and its trailer do not exceed certain limits, and where the driver is registered on a large goods vehicle training agreement.

4.3 **Disqualification by Virtue of Duplicate Licence**
Road Traffic Act 1988 Section 102

A person is disqualified for obtaining a licence, authorising him to drive a motor vehicle, of any class, so long as he is the holder of another licence, authorising him to drive a motor vehicle of that class, whether the licence is suspended or not.

4.4 **Offence**
Road Traffic Act 1988 Section 103

A person commits an offence who – while disqualified from holding or obtaining a licence:
- obtains a licence; or
- drives a motor vehicle on a road.

4.4.1 *Explanation*

Guilty knowledge: The offence of driving whilst disqualified does not require *mens rea*. A person who genuinely but mistakenly believes that his period of disqualification has ended, will commit the offence if he drives a motor vehicle on a road.

Under age: A person who drives a motor vehicle while disqualified by reason of age for driving a vehicle of that particular class, will commit an offence, not of driving while disqualified, but of driving otherwise than in accordance with a licence.

4.5 **Arrest**
Road Traffic Act 1988 Section 103(3)

A constable in uniform may arrest without warrant any person driving a motor vehicle on a road whom she has reasonable cause to suspect is disqualified.

4.5.1 *Explanation*

Uniform: An officer keeping plain clothes observations on the car of a person suspected of driving whilst disqualified, will have no power to arrest that person should the suspect do so.

Driving: The power does not extend to attempting to drive, nor to having driven. If a constable sees a person driving whom he knows is disqualified, but is unable to stop that person's vehicle at the time, there is no power to arrest him later.

Disqualified: The power to arrest does not extend to a person disqualified by reason of age. To be liable to arrest, the person must have been disqualified by a court.

Chapter 55: Fixed Penalty Notices

PURPOSE OF FIXED PENALTY SYSTEM

1.1 Alternative to Court Appearance

A constable or, in respect of certain offences only, a traffic warden, may issue a fixed penalty notice when a person is suspected of committing one of a specified number of traffic offences, as an alternative to reporting the offender for prosecution. The recipient of the notice then has three alternatives open to him:

i) pay the amount of the fixed penalty within the time allowed, as an alternative to prosecution;

ii) fail to pay within the stipulated time, in which case the fixed penalty plus 50% is registered as a fine at magistrates's court, payment to be enforced as for any other fine;

iii) elect to appear in court, for the matter to be dealt with as for a summary offence. The motorist may wish to plead not guilty, and to dispute the evidence of the constable or traffic warden, or may wish to offer mitigation.

The option to appear in court takes cognisance of the principle that an accused person is innocent until found guilty by a court.

1.2 Types of Fixed Penalty Notices

A fixed penalty notice may be endorsable, or non-endorsable, dependent on whether or not the offence for which it is issued is one for which penalty points will be endorsed on the offender's driving licence. The procedures for each are different. For an endorsable offence, the driver must surrender his driving licence (and counterpart) to the police; the licence will then be forwarded to the magistrates' clerk, for the requisite penalty points to be endorsed on it. The driver will be issued with a receipt for his licence.

Provisions for local authority staff to issue notices in respect of breaches of parking regulations, or fixed penalty notices for noise or litter offences, are not considered here.

ENDORSABLE AND NON-ENDORSABLE

2.1 Endorsable or Non-endorsable Offence – Driver Present
Road Traffic Offenders Act 1988 Section 54

(1) This Section applies where in England or Wales, on any occasion a constable in uniform has reason to believe that a person he finds is committing or has on that occasion committed a fixed penalty offence.

(2) Subject to subsection (3) below, the constable may give him a fixed penalty notice in respect of the offence.

(3) Where the offence appears to the constable to involve obligatory endorsement, the constable may only give him a fixed penalty notice under subsection (2) above in respect of the offence if:

a) he produces his licence and its counterpart for inspection by the constable

b) the constable is satisfied, on inspecting the licence and its counterpart, that he would not be liable to be disqualified under Section 35 of this Act if he were convicted of that offence, and:

c) he surrenders his licence and its counterpart to the constable to be retained and dealt with in accordance with this Part of this Act.

(4) Where:

a) the offence appears to the constable to involve obligatory endorsement, and

b) the person concerned does not produce his licence and its counterpart for inspection by the constable

the constable may give him a notice stating that if, within seven days after the notice is given, he produces the notice together with his licence and its counterpart in person to an authorised person at the police station specified in the notice (being a police station chosen by the person concerned) and the requirements of subsection (5)(a) and (b) below are met he will then be given a fixed penalty notice in respect of the offence.

(5) If the person to whom the notice has been given under subsection (4) above produces the notice together with his licence and its counterpart in person to an authorised person at the police station specified in the notice within seven days after the notice was given to him and the following requirements are met, that is:

a) the authorised person is satisfied, on inspecting the licence and its counterpart, that he would not be liable to be disqualified under Section 35 of this Act if he were convicted of the offence, and:

b) he surrenders his licence and its counterpart to the authorised person to be retained and dealt with in accordance with this part of this Act

the authorised person must give him a fixed penalty notice in respect of the offence to which the notice under subsection (4) above relates.

2.1.1 *Explanation*

Type of offence: When the driver is present, the fixed penalty notice may be for an endorsable, or for a non-endorsable offence. An endorsable offence may **not** be dealt with by way of fixed penalty, if it appears to the constable that the penalty points to be endorsed for the current offence, added to the penalty points already endorsed on the offender's driving licence, will render him liable to disqualification. For example, a driver is stopped for exceeding a speed limit. If his licence already carries 9 or more penalty points, the 3 penalty points for the current speeding offence brings his total to 12 and renders him liable to disqualification. The matter must therefore go before the magistrates. (Note: speeding carries from 3 – 6 penalty points, but when dealt with by fixed penalty, the limit is 3.)

Endorsable offences: The most prevalent offences dealt with by way of fixed penalty are likely to be speeding, failing to conform to traffic lights or other traffic signs, and breaches of construction and use regulations relating to tyres, brakes or steering. Other breaches of construction and use regulations do not carry endorsement.

Constable in uniform: A constable must be in uniform before she may issue a fixed penalty notice to a driver.

On that occasion: A fixed penalty notice under this Section may be issued when the driver is committing, or where the constable suspects he has on that occasion committed a fixed penalty offence. There is no scope here, for a fixed penalty notice to be issued several days after the event.

Provisional fixed penalty notice: If a driver stopped for speeding, produces his driving licence and it does not bear nine or more penalty points already, the constable may issue an endorsable fixed penalty notice there and then. However, if the driver is unable to produce his licence, he may produce it within 7 days, at a police station which he specifies at the time. He will be issued with a **provisional** endorsable fixed penalty notice. If he then produces his licence and its counterpart together with the fixed penalty notice at the specified police station, the authorised person there will examine the licence, satisfy herself that here are less than nine penalty points on it, and convert the provisional notice into a **full** one, so long as the driver is willing to surrender his licence and counterpart.

Authorised person: A person may be authorised by or behalf of the chief officer of police for the area, to issue endorsable fixed penalty notices at a police station, by converting provisional notices into full ones. This allows for civilian enquiry counter clerks to be authorised for such tasks.

Multiple offences: There is no legal constraint on a motorist being issued with several fixed penalty notices on one occasion, but Home Office advice is that the procedure should not be used in this way. Whether to proceed by fixed penalty or by reporting for summons is always a decision for the constable concerned. If several offences are committed and the constable decides to issue a fixed penalty notice, he should do so for the one most serious offence only, and deal with the others by means of a verbal warning.

2.2 **Non-endorsable Offences – Driver Not Necessarily Present**
Road Traffic Offenders Act 1988 Section 62

(1) Where on any occasion a constable has reason to believe in the case of any stationary vehicle that a fixed penalty offence is being or has been on that occasion committed in respect of it, he may fix a fixed penalty notice in respect of the offence to the vehicle unless the offence appears to him to involve obligatory endorsement.

(2) A person is guilty of an offence if he removes or interferes with any notice fixed to a vehicle under this Section, unless he does so by or under the authority of the driver or person in charge of the vehicle or the person liable for the fixed penalty offence in question.

2.2.1 *Explanation*
Non-endorsable offences: Offences involving breaches of waiting regulations are non-endorsable, as are offences involving vehicle lighting. Clearly, an endorsable fixed penalty notice, full or provisional, may not be issued where the driver is not present, because there will be no opportunity to require him to produce his driving licence.

Interference: A fixed penalty notice gives a motorist the opportunity, if she wishes, to avoid prosecution by paying a fixed sum. If she wishes to rip up the notice and throw it in a litter bin, (or ask her passenger to do so) this is a matter for her; eventually, an increased sum will be registered as a fine, or she may appear in court to have her say. If any other person, without authority of the driver or person in charge of the vehicle or of the person liable for the fixed penalty, removes or interferes with a notice fixed to a vehicle, that person will commit an offence.

CONDITIONAL FIXED PENALTY NOTICES

3.1 Issue
Road Traffic Offenders Act 1988 Section 75

Where in England or Wales:

a) a constable has reason to believe that a fixed penalty offence has been committed, and

b) no fixed penalty notice in respect of the offence has been given under Section 54 of this Act or fixed to the vehicle under Section 62 of this Act

A notice under this Section may be sent to the alleged offender by or on behalf of the chief officer of police.

Where a person issues a conditional offer, he must notify the justices clerk, specified in it of its issue and its terms, and that clerk is referred to in this Section and Sections 76 and 77 as 'the fixed penalty clerk'.

A conditional offer must:

a) give such particulars of the circumstances alleged to constitute the offence to which it relates as are necessary for giving reasonable information about the alleged offence:

b) state the amount of the fixed penalty for that offence, and:

c) state that proceedings against the alleged offender cannot be commenced in respect of that offence until the end of the period of twenty-eight days following the date on which the conditional offer was issued or such longer period as may be specified in the conditional offer.

A conditional offer must indicate that if the following conditions are fulfilled, that is:

a) within twenty-one days following the date on which the offer was issued, or such longer period as may be specified in the offer, the alleged offender:

i) makes payment of the fixed penalty to the fixed penalty clerk, and:

ii) where the offence to which the offer relates is an offence involving obligatory endorsement, at the same time delivers his driving licence and its counterpart to that clerk, and:

b) where his licence and its counterpart are so delivered, that clerk is satisfied on inspecting them that, if the alleged offender were convicted of the offence, he would not be liable to be disqualified under Section 35 of this Act

any liability to conviction of the offence shall be discharged.

3.1.1 *Explanation*

Vehicles not stopped: Sections 54 and 62 (see above) provide for fixed penalty notices to be issued, either by giving one to a driver, or by leaving it on a stationary vehicle, in each case, on the occasion of the offence. New methods for detecting offences of speeding and failure to comply with traffic signals, involving cameras and other technology, have called for new procedures, whereby an offender may be issued with a fixed penalty notice some time after committing the offence.

Conditional offer: A document is sent to the registered keeper of the motor vehicle concerned, and this is called a 'conditional offer'. If the registered keeper was not the driver on the occasion of the offence, then he must give details of the driver, to end his involvement in the matter. The police will then issue a further 'conditional offer' to the alleged offender, who may in turn dispute that he was the driver. Eventually, if the system operates successfully, the person who was driving will receive a conditional offer.

If the recipient follows the laid down procedure, the document is converted, in effect, into a fixed penalty notice, and the matter may be dealt with, without further correspondence between the registered keeper and the police. This involves the offender paying the fixed penalty sum within 28 days and, in the case of an endorsable offence, surrendering his driving licence and counterpart to the magistrates' clerk.

If the clerk, upon examining the licence, finds that the offender will be liable to disqualification with the additional penalty points for the current offence, then the matter may not proceed by way of fixed penalty, but will have to be dealt with by the magistrates.

The driver has the option to have the matter dealt within court, rather than pay the fixed penalty.

Chapter 56: Lights on Vehicles

LAMPS AND MARKINGS REQUIRED

1.1 Scope of Regulations

The Road Vehicles Lighting Regulations 1989, made under the Road Traffic Act 1988, make provision for lights, reflectors and rear markings, to be fitted and used on vehicles when used on roads. Included, are provisions relating to warning beacons, (blue, amber, green and yellow) and other lamps of a special nature. The following are some of the terms used:

Obligatory: as far as it relates to lamps, reflectors, rear markings or devices, means those lamps, reflectors, rear markings or devices, the vehicle or its load are required by regulations to have.

Optional: used in the same context as regards lamps, reflectors, rear markings, or devices means such items with which the vehicle its load or equipment are not required to be fitted.

Hours of Darkness: means the period of time which elapses between half an hour after sunset and half an hour before sunrise.

1.2 The Maintenance of Lights and Marking Devices
Road Vehicles Lighting Regulations 1989 Regulation 23

(1) No person shall use, or cause or permit to be used, on a road a vehicle unless every lamp, reflector, rear marking and device to which this paragraph applies is in good working order and, in the case of lamps, clean.

(2) Save as provided in paragraph (3), paragraph (1) applies to:
   a) every:
      i) front position lamp
      ii) rear position lamp
      iii) headlamp
      iv) rear registration plate lamp
      v) side marker lamp
      vi) end-outline marker lamp
      vii) rear fog lamp
      viii) retro reflector, and
      ix) rear marking of a type
   with which the vehicle is required by these regulations to be fitted; and
   b) every:
      i) stop lamp
      ii) direction indicator
      iii) running lamp
      iv) dim-dip device
      v) headlamp levelling device
      vi) hazard warning signal device
   with which it is fitted.

(3) Paragraph (2) does not apply to:

a) a rear fog lamp on a vehicle which is a combination of vehicles any part of which is not required by these regulations to be fitted with a rear fog lamp

b) a rear fog lamp on a motor vehicle drawing a trailer

c) a defective lamp, reflector, dim-dip device or headlamp levelling device on a vehicle in use on a road between sunrise and sunset, if any such lamp, reflector or device became defective during the journey which is in progress or if arrangements have been made to remedy the defect with all reasonable expedition; or

d) a lamp, reflector, dim-dip device, headlamp levelling device or rear marking on a combat vehicle in use on a road between sunrise and sunset.

1.2.1 *Explanation*

Use, cause, permit: These terms are dealt with in detail in Chapter 52.

Various types: Front and rear position lamps are popularly referred to as 'side lights'. A dim-dip device allows headlamps to be used at reduced power as an alternative to front position lamps.

Must/may be fitted: It is understandable that obligatory lamps should be kept in working order, and clean. However, the same requirement applies to those lamps listed in paragraph (2)(b) of the regulation – stop lamps, direction indicators, etc – even though there may be no requirement for these to be fitted. The rationale is that if one of these lamps is working properly, but another is not, other road users may be misled, leading to risk of an accident, e.g. in the case of direction indicators.

Exemptions: An offence will not be committed where a lamp, etc, is defective between sunrise and sunset, if the defect occurred during the present journey, or if arrangements have been made to remedy the defect as soon as is practicable. For example, the headlamp on a car becomes defective at 11.00 am on Tuesday; the garage will obtain a replacement and fit it on Thursday morning. The car may be used on a road during the day until Thursday, but it may not be used during period that the headlamp has to be lit, i.e. between sunset and sunrise.

Other exemptions include the rear fog lamp on a motor vehicle towing a trailer, and lamps on military vehicles used during the day.

THE USE OF LIGHTS
Road Vehicles Lighting Regulations 1989 Regulation 24

2.1 **Position Lamps, etc**

(1) Save as provided in paragraphs (5) and (9) below, no person shall:
a) use, or cause to be used on a road any vehicle which is in motion:
 i) between sunset and sunrise, or
 ii) in seriously reduced visibility between sunrise and sunset; or
b) allow to remain at rest, or cause, or permit to be allowed to remain at rest on any road any vehicle between sunset and sunrise;
unless every front position lamp, rear position lamp, rear registration plate lamp, side marker lamp and end outline marker lamp with which the vehicle is required by these regulations to be fitted is lit and unobscured.

(2) Save as provided in paragraph (5) and (9) below, where a solo motor bicycle is not fitted

with a front position lamp, no other person shall use it, or cause or permit it to be used, on a road (other than when parked) between sunset and sunrise, or in seriously reduced visibility between sunrise and sunset, unless a headlamp shall be lit and unobscured.

(3) Save as provided by paragraph (5) and (9) below, no person shall allow to remain parked, or cause or permit to remain parked between sunset and sunrise:
   a) a motor bicycle combination which is required to be fitted only with a front position lamp on the sidecar; or
   b) a trailer to the front of which no other vehicle is attached and which is not required to be fitted with front position lamps
   unless a pair of front position lamps is fitted and kept lit and unobscured.

(4) Save as provided by paragraph (5) and (9) below, no person shall allow to remain parked or cause or permit to be allowed to remain parked between sunset and sunrise a solo motor bicycle which is not required to be fitted with a front position lamp, unless a front position lamp is fitted and kept lit and unobscured.

2.2 **Parking Without Lights**

(5) Paragraphs (1), (2), (3), and (4) shall not apply in respect of a vehicle of a class specified in paragraph (7) which is parked on a road on which a speed limit of 30 miles per hour or less is in force and the vehicle is parked:
   a) in a parking place for which provision is made, or which is authorised, or designated under the Road Traffic Regulation Act 1984, or which is set apart as a parking place under some other enactment or instrument and the vehicle is parked in a manner which does not contravene the provisions of any enactment or instrument relating to the parking place; or
   b) in a lay-by:
      i) the limits of which are indicated by a traffic sign, or
      ii) the surface of which is of a colour or texture which is different from that part of the carriageway of the road used primarily by through traffic; or
      iii) the limits of which are indicated by a continuous strip of surface of a different colour or texture from that of the surface of the remainder of the carriageway of the road; or
   c) elsewhere than in such a parking place or lay-by if:
      i) the vehicle is parked in one of the circumstances described in paragraph (8); and
      ii) no part of the vehicle is less than 10 m from the junction of any part of the carriageway of any road with that carriageway of the road on which it is parked whether that junction is on the same side of the road as that on which the vehicle is parked or not.

(7) the classes referred to in paragraph (5) above are:
   a) a motor vehicle being a goods vehicle the unladen weight of which does not exceed 1525 kg;
   b) a passenger vehicle other than a bus
   c) an invalid carriage; and
   d) a motor cycle or pedal cycle in either case with or without a sidecar
   in the case of (a)(b)(c) or (d) (above) not being:
      i) a vehicle to which a trailer is attached; or

    ii) a vehicle which is required to be fitted with lamps by regulation 21; or

    iii) a vehicle carrying a load, if the load is required to be fitted with lamps by regulation 21.

(8) The circumstances referred to in paragraph (5)(c) (above) are that:

    a) the vehicle is parked on a road on which driving of vehicles otherwise than in one direction is prohibited at all times and its left or near side is as close as may be and parallel to the left hand edge of the carriageway or its right offside is as close as may be and parallel to the right hand edge of the carriageway; or

    b) the vehicle is parked on a road on which such a prohibition does not exist and its left near side is as close as may be and parallel to the edge of the carriageway.

2.3 Exemptions

(9) Paragraphs (1), (2), (3), and (4) do not apply in respect of:

    a) a solo motor bicycle or a pedal cycle being pushed along the left hand edge of the carriageway; or

    b) a pedal cycle waiting to proceed provided it is kept to the left hand or near side edge of a carriageway; or

    c) a vehicle which is parked in an area on part of a highway on which roadwork's are being carried out and which is bounded by amber lamps and other traffic signs so as to prevent the presence of the vehicle, its load or equipment being a danger to persons using the road.

2.4 Explanation

Sunset and sunrise: Although the term 'hours of darkness' is defined in the regulations, for most purposes lights are required to be used for an hour longer than the hours of darkness. Going back some years, the regulations required lights to be used during hours of darkness; the requirements have changed for almost all purposes, but 'hours of darkness' still has relevance, e.g. in relation to use of dipped headlamps.

Position lamps, etc: These are required to be lit when vehicles are moving or stationary, between sunset and sunrise. They are also required in the daytime, in conditions of seriously reduced visibility, such as fog or snow.

Solo motor bicycle: Sub-paragraph (2) allows for a motor bike without a sidecar to have a headlamp instead of a front position lamp.

No front position lamp: Certain vehicles which do not need front position lamps, such as a solo motor bike, must have one fitted and lit, if it is parked on a road at night.

Parking without lights: Apart from vehicles parked in designated parking areas and lay-bys, smaller categories of vehicles may be parked without lights, subject to conditions:

    i) there is a speed limit of 30 mph or less on that road;

    ii) the vehicle is parked close to the nearside (or to either side in a one-way street) and parallel to the kerb;

    iii) every part of the vehicle is at least 10 metres from a junction, whether on the same or opposite side of the road.

2.5 **The Use of Dipped Beam Lights**
Road Vehicles Lighting Regulations 1989 Regulation 25

(1) Save as provided by paragraph (2), no person shall, use, cause, or permit to be used, on a road, a vehicle which is fitted with obligatory dipped beam headlamps unless every lamp is kept lit:

a) during the hours of darkness, except on a road which is a restricted road for the purposes of Section 81 of the Road Traffic Regulation Act 1984 by virtue of system of street lighting which is lit; and

b) in seriously reduced visibility.

(2) The provisions of paragraph (1) do not apply:

a) in the case of a motor vehicle fitted with one obligatory dipped-beam headlamp or a solo motor bicycle combination fitted with a pair of obligatory dipped beam headlamps, if a main beam headlamp or a front fog lamp, is kept lit; or

b) in the case of a motor vehicle, other than a solo motor bicycle, or motor bicycle combination, fitted with a pair of obligatory dipped beam headlamps if:

i) a pair of main-beam headlamps is kept lit; or

ii) in seriously reduced visibility, a pair of front fog lamps which is so fitted that the outermost part of the illuminated area of each lamp in the pair is not more than 400 mm from the outer edge of the vehicle is kept lit; or

c) to a vehicle being drawn by another vehicle, or

d) to a vehicle while being used to propel a snowplough; or

e) to a vehicle which is parked.

(3) For the purposes of this regulation a headlamp shall not be regarded as lit if its intensity is reduced by a dim-dip device.

2.5.1 *Explanation*

Hours of darkness: The period from a half hour after sunset to a half hour before sunrise, is relevant in relation to dipped headlamps, whereas most of the other requirements for lights apply from sunset to sunrise.

Restricted road: Briefly, this means a road subject to a speed limit of 30 mph or less. Thus, on a road which has a 30 mph (or perhaps 20 mph) speed limit and which has a system of street lights which are of the required standard, it will not be compulsory to use dipped headlamps. On any other road, during hours of darkness, dipped headlamps are required.

Bad weather: Dipped headlamps are also compulsory during conditions of seriously reduced visibility, e.g. snow or fog, and in such case, this applies irrespective of street lamps or speed limits.

Alternatives: It almost goes without saying, that an alternative to dipped headlamps, will be full-beam. In bad weather, a pair of front fog lamps, properly positioned, will do instead.

Dim-dip: On many modern motor vehicles, the front position lamps change to a dim version of the headlamps when the ignition is switched on. These dimmed dipped headlamps are not acceptable as dipped headlamps.

2.6 **Restrictions on Use**
Road Vehicles Lighting Regulations 1989 Regulation 27

No person shall use, or cause to be used, on a road any vehicle on which any lamp, hazard warning device of warning beacon of a type specified in column 1 of the Table below, to be used in a manner specified in column 2:

Type of lamp, hazard warning signal device, or warning beacon	Manner of use prohibited
Headlamps	a) used so as to cause undue dazzle or discomfort to other persons using the road. b) used so as to be lit when a vehicle is parked.
Front fog lamp	a) used so as to cause undue dazzle or discomfort to other persons using the road. b) used so as to be lit at any time other than in conditions of seriously reduced visibility. c) used so as to be lit when a vehicle is parked.
Rear fog lamp	a) used so as to cause undue dazzle or discomfort to the driver of a following vehicle. b) used so as to be lit at any time other than in conditions of seriously reduced visibility. c) save in the case of an emergency vehicle, used so as to be lit when the vehicle is parked.
Reversing lamp	Use so as to be lit except for the purpose of reversing the vehicle
Hazard warning signal device	Used other than for the purpose of: a) to warn persons using the road of a temporary obstruction when the vehicle is at rest; or b) on a motorway or unrestricted dual carriageway, to warn following drivers of a need to slow down due to temporary obstruction ahead; or c) in the case of a bus, to summon assistance for the driver or any person acting as a conductor or inspector on the vehicle
Warning beacon emitting blue light and special warning lamp	Used so as to be lit except: a) at the scene of an emergency; or ii) when it is necessary or desirable either to indicate to persons using the road the emergency purpose for which the vehicle is being used, or to warn persons of the presence of the vehicle or a hazard on the road.

Type of lamp, hazard warning signal device, or warning beacon	Manner of use prohibited
Warning beacon emitting amber light	Used so as to be lit except: a) at the scene of an emergency; b) when it is necessary or desirable to warn persons of the presence of the vehicle; and c) in the case of a breakdown vehicle, while it is being used in connection with, and in the immediate vicinity of, an accident or breakdown, or while it is being used to draw a broken-down vehicle.
Warning beacon emitting green light	Used so as to be lit except whilst occupied by a medical practitioner registered by the General Medical Council and used for the purposes of an emergency.
Warning beacon emitting yellow light	Used so as to be lit on a road.
Work lamp	a) used so as to cause undue dazzle or discomfort to the driver of any vehicle. b) used so as to be lit except for the purpose of illuminating a working area, accident, breakdown or works in the vicinity of the vehicle.
Any other lamp	Used so as to cause undue dazzle or discomfort to other persons using the road.

2.6.1 *Explanation*

Dazzle or discomfort: Headlamps and fog lamps must not be used so as to cause dazzle or discomfort to other road users. Failing to dip main beams would amount to doing so, as would having rear fog lamps operating on a clear night.

Headlamps: Headlamps must not be switched on when a motor vehicle is parked. 'Parked' is not the same thing as stationary, indicating that there is no need to turn headlamps off when temporarily stopped, e.g. at traffic lights.

Fog lamps: As with headlamps, these should be turned off when a vehicle is parked. They should also be turned off at all times, except during conditions of seriously reduced visibility. With more and more cars coming with front 'driving lamps' as part of their equipment, the habit seems to be growing, of using these lamps instead of headlamps. This may give rise to two offences – not having dipped headlamps in use when required – and using front fog lamps when visibility is not seriously reduced.

Hazard warning device: It is not lawful for hazard warning lights to be used to indicate that a broken down vehicle is being towed by another, a not-uncommon practice. Neither does their use afford immunity to fixed penalty notices for the driver who leaves his vehicle on double-yellow lines. Use on a moving vehicle is limited to dual carriageways and motorways, as a vehicle is slowing on the approach to stationary traffic ahead. They may also be used as part of an alarm system on a bus. When the hazard warning lamps are wired into the theft alarm on a vehicle, strictly speaking, an offence will be committed when the alarm is activated while the vehicle is on a road.

Blue lamps: The fitting and use of blue beacons and warning lamps are restricted to specified emergency vehicles – police, fire, ambulance, etc. The use on such vehicles is limited to occasions of emergency, to warn other road users of the presence of the vehicle on a road, or to warn of some hazard.

Amber beacons: In addition to their use in emergency situations, or on breakdown trucks at a breakdown or accident, or which are towing , use is also permitted when it is necessary or desirable to warn others of the vehicle's presence on as road. In some cases, such use is compulsory, e.g. slow moving vehicles on dual carriageways.

Green beacons: A vehicle being used by a doctor may have one of these operating in an emergency. Note that the doctor does not have to be the driver, so long as a doctor is using the vehicle.

In some areas, doctors have formed an emergency response service, to provide cover at scenes of accidents and other emergencies. Such a service may have use of a car fitted with blue lights and a siren, rather than with a green light only. In such a case, it is probable that this will be lawful because the vehicle is operated in conjunction with the ambulance service, not simply as a vehicle used by a doctor.

2.7 Lighting Offences

A person who fails to comply with any of the regulations stated by the Road Vehicle Lighting Regulations commits an offence under Section 42 of the Road Traffic Act 1988. Those regulations stipulating the requirements for lights on pedal cycles give rise to offences under Section 91 of the Road Traffic Offenders Act 1988.

Chapter 57: Traffic Control

TRAFFIC SIGNS

1.1 Introduction

Signs on or near roads fall into several categories, whether giving information, warning of possible hazard ahead, prohibiting some activity, or giving an instruction which drivers must comply with. A sign may consist of a piece of metal on a pole, or of yellow, red or white markings on the road surface or kerb.

The plethora of signs with which a road user is presented may be confusing, and in order to minimise that confusion, signs must conform to specifications laid down in regulations, governing size, shape and colour. A 'Stop' or 'No waiting' sign in Penzance should look exactly the same as one in Aberdeen, so that an offender cannot claim that he did not recognise the sign. (Indeed, most signs look the same across the European community.)

1.2 Meaning of Term 'Traffic Sign'
Road Traffic Regulation Act 1984 Section 64

In this Act 'traffic sign' means any object or device (whether fixed or portable) for conveying, to traffic on roads or any specified class of traffic, warnings, information, requirements, restrictions or prohibitions of any description:
a) specified by regulations; or
b) authorised by the Secretary of State,
and any line or mark on a road for so conveying such warnings, information,
requirements, restrictions or prohibitions.

It is assumed, unless evidence is given to the contrary, that any sign is lawfully placed and of the correct specification in terms of size and colour. If a sign is not lawful, in terms of its placing or description, then it will not be a traffic sign for the purposes of legislation.

1.3 Placing of Signs

A traffic sign may not be placed on or near a road unless such placing of the sign is authorised. The following are authorised to place traffic signs:
a) a traffic authority in respect of roads in their area;
b) a constable or other person authorised by the chief officer of police in certain circumstances;
c) any person in respect of a temporary obstruction.

1.4 Signs Placed by Police
Road Traffic Regulation Act 1984 Section 67

A constable, or person acting under the instructions (whether general or specific) of the chief officer of police, may place on a road, or on any structure on the road, traffic signs (of any size, colour and type prescribed or authorised under Section 64 of this Act) indicating prohibitions, restrictions or requirements relating to vehicular traffic, as may be necessary or expedient to prevent or mitigate congestion or obstruction of traffic, or danger to or from traffic, in consequence of extraordinary circumstances; and

The power to place signs conferred by this subsection shall include power to maintain a sign for a period of seven days or less from the time when it was placed, but no longer.

1.4.1 *Explanation*

Constable or other person: Signs may be placed by a police officer or by someone, such as a traffic warden or civilian van driver, under police instructions.

Prohibitions, restrictions, requirements: Police are not authorised to place signs giving information or warnings, such as 'slippery road surface' or 'sharp bend ahead'. The most common is 'Police – No Waiting', but any other sign of specified size, shape and colour, may be placed.

Congestion, obstruction, danger: Police signs may be placed only for one or other of the purposes of preventing or minimising one of these three effects.

Extraordinary circumstances: If heavy traffic routinely causes congestion at certain times of day, and it is decided that parking restrictions may alleviate the problem to some extent, this should be a matter for the highway authority, not for the police. Police action should be confined to situations which are not ordinary, such as a carnival procession, protest march, fun run, road accident, broken down lorry, etc.

Seven days: In the same vein, police signs may not be lawfully placed for a period longer than 7 days. There is however, no provision in law as to any interval which must elapse between one period of seven days and another.

1.5 **Signs Placed by Other Persons**
Traffic Signs (Temporary Obstructions) Regulations 1985

1.5.1 *Authority to Place Signs*
Regulation 8

Subject to the provisions of regulations 9,10 and 11, any person not otherwise lawfully authorised to do so is hereby authorised to place a traffic cone, traffic pyramid, traffic triangle or warning lamp on a road for the purpose of warning traffic of a temporary obstruction on any part of the road other than road works.

1.5.2 *Number and Type*
Regulation 9

(1) A traffic cone may be placed on a road by virtue of regulation 8 if it is placed in conjunction with at least three other traffic cones of a similar size, colour and type.

(2) A traffic pyramid may only be placed on a road by virtue of regulation 8 if it is placed in conjunction with at least three other traffic pyramids of similar size, colour and type.

(3) A warning lamp may only be placed on a road by virtue of regulation 8 if it is used in conjunction with a triangle, traffic cone or traffic pyramid. A warning lamp shall be placed in such a position that it does not obscure from the view of approaching traffic any part of the traffic triangle, traffic cone or traffic pyramid. Not more than one warning lamp shall be used with each.

1.5.3 *Position of Triangle*
Regulation 10
A traffic triangle placed on a road by virtue of regulation 8 shall be placed upright:
a) at least 45 metres away from any obstruction; and

b) in such a position that it will warn traffic approaching on the same side of the road as the obstruction.

1.5.4 *Position of Cones and Pyramids*
Regulation 11
Traffic cones and traffic pyramids placed on a road in accordance with regulation 9 shall be placed upright so as to guide traffic past the obstruction.

1.5.5 *Explanation*
Road works: These provisions are intended to allow an ordinary person to take steps to lessen the hazard arising from a temporary obstruction in the road, such as a broken down vehicle, a fallen tree or a pile of sand which has just been delivered. The regulations specifically exclude road works from their scope. Road works are covered by comprehensive legislation with which contractors must comply, which does not feature in this chapter.

Cone, pyramid, triangle, lamp: Cones and pyramids are similar – plastic objects, wider at the bottom to aid stability, for placing round an obstruction in the road. A triangle is a red, reflective, object, which usually folds up for storage. A warning lamp emits an orange light, and may be used in conjunction with a triangle, cones or pyramids.

Numbers: A triangle is intended for use on its own, but at least four cones or four pyramids should be used together. The four or more cones/pyramids should all be of similar size, colour and type. Warning lamps may be used only in conjunction with triangles, cones or pyramids. These lamps may be designed to fit into the top of a cone or pyramid, or they may be placed on the ground. There is no minimum number of lamps which should be used, but there should be no more than one for each triangle, cone or pyramid; a cone festooned with lamps, like a Christmas tree, is not permissible.

Position of triangle: The triangle must be placed so as to warn traffic approaching on the same side of the road as the obstruction. This does not necessarily mean that the triangle has to be on that side of the road; on a wide road, it may have to be, but on a narrow road, say approaching a bend, it may be advantageous to place the triangle on the opposite side, in a position where drivers approaching the obstruction may see it. There is no maximum distance within which the triangle must be placed, this will be dictated by common sense, but the minimum distance of 45 metres is intended to give approaching drivers sufficient time to react.

OBLIGATORY SIGNS

2.1 **Failure to Comply with a Traffic Sign**

2.1.1 *Offences*
A person who fails to comply with a traffic sign which indicates a prohibition, restriction or requirement, will commit an offence. Offences will fall into one of three categories:
i) Failure to comply with a sign which indicates a prohibition, restriction or requirement contained in a statute, as opposed to one in regulations or an order. Such an offence is

punishable under Section 36 of the Road Traffic Act, 1988;

ii) Failure to comply with a sign to which Section 36 specifically applies, by virtue of this being declared in legislation. This will include all the signs listed in Regulation 10 of the Traffic Signs Regulation and General Directions, 1994. Such an offence is also punishable under Section 36;

iii) Failure to comply with any sign not included in (i) or (ii). Such an offence is punishable by Section 91 of the Road Traffic Offenders Act, 1988.

2.1.2 *Distinction Between Section 36 and Section 91*

An offence punishable under Section 36 of the Road Traffic Act 1988, is subject to the requirement for a notice of intended prosecution. Police officers and anyone involved in the prosecution of traffic offences, will therefore require some knowledge of which traffic signs fall into which category.

2.1.3 *Regulation 10*

Some of the signs included in regulation 10, to which the procedure for notice of intended prosecution will apply are:

- Stop (and also a manually operated STOP board at road works)
- Give way
- No 'U' turn
- Keep left (or keep right) bollards
- Turn right only or turn left only
- Red traffic light
- No entry
- Double white line markings.
  (This is by no means a full list.)

2.2 **Requirement of 'Stop' and 'Give Way' Signs**
Traffic Signs Regulations 1994, Regulation 16

2.2.1 *Stop Sign*

This sign requires that:

i) every vehicle shall stop at the transverse line at the junction, or if that line is not visible, before entering the major road; and

ii) no vehicle shall proceed past the single transverse line into that road, or if that line is not visible, shall enter the major road, in such a manner or at such a time as is likely to cause danger to the driver of any other vehicle on the major road, or to cause the driver to change its speed or course so as to avoid an accident.

2.2.2 *Give Way Sign*

The requirement of a give way sign is the same as that contained in paragraph (ii) of the requirement of the stop sign.

2.2.3 *Explanation*

Difference: The stop sign requires that every vehicle entering a major road shall stop. Then the driver must do the same as at a give way sign, which is basically, stay there until the road is clear to pull out, With a give way sign, there is no need to stop if the major road is seen to be clear.

Transverse line: Stop and give way signs are accompanied by road markings, including a line across the nearside of the mouth of the junction. If this line is visible, it marks the limit beyond which the vehicle may not proceed until safe to do so. If it is not visible, e.g. due to snow, this does not invalidate the sign; in such a case, a driver must not enter the major road before it is safe to do so.

Change speed or course: In simple terms, this could be expressed as 'brake or swerve'. A stop or give way sign has not been complied with if a driver on the major road has to slow or swerve to avoid colliding with the car which has just emerged from the side road.

2.3 Requirement of Double White Line Markings
Traffic Signs Regulations 1994 Regulation 26

(1) A road marking for conveying the requirements specified in paragraph (2) and the warning specified in paragraph (5) shall be of the size, colour and type specified.

(2) The requirements conveyed by the road marking mentioned in paragraph (1) shall be that:
   a) subject to the provisions of paragraph (3), no vehicle shall stop on any length of road along which the marking has been placed at any point between two ends of the marking; and
   b) subject to the provisions of paragraph (4), every vehicle proceeding on any length of road along which the marking has been so placed that, as viewed in the direction of travel of the vehicle, the continuous line is on the left of a dotted line or of another continuous line, shall be so driven as to keep the first mentioned continuous line on the right hand or offside of the vehicle.

(3) Nothing in paragraph (2)(a) shall apply:
   a) so as to prevent a vehicle stopping on any length of road so long as may be necessary for the following purposes:
      i) to allow persons to board or alight from the vehicle.
      ii) to enable goods to be loaded onto or to be unloaded from the vehicle, or,
      iii) to enable the vehicle to be used in connection with:
         – any building or demolition work
         – the removal of any obstruction to traffic
         – the maintenance, improvement or reconstruction of that length of road; or
         – the laying, erection, alteration or repair in or near to that length of road of any sewer or of any main, pipe or apparatus for the supply of gas, water or electricity, or of any telecommunications apparatus.
   if the vehicle cannot be used for such a purpose without stopping on the length of road;
   b) so as to prevent the vehicle stopping in a lay-by;
   c) to a vehicle for the time being used for fire brigade, ambulance or police purposes;
   d) to a pedal bicycle not having a sidecar attached thereto, whether additional means of propulsion by mechanical power are attached to the bicycle or not;
   e) to a vehicle stopping in any case where the person in control of the vehicle is required by law to stop, or is obliged to do so in order to avoid an accident, or is prevented from proceeding by circumstances outside his control;

    f) to anything done with the permission or at the direction of a constable in uniform or in accordance with the direction of a traffic warden; or,

    g) to a vehicle on a road with more than one traffic lane in each direction.

(4) Nothing in paragraph (2)(b) shall be taken to prohibit a vehicle from being driven across, or so to straddle, the continuous line referred to in that paragraph, if it is safe to do so and if it is necessary to do so:

    a) to enable the vehicle to enter, from the side of the road on which it is proceeding, land or premises adjacent to the length of the road on which the line is placed, or another road adjoining that road;

    b) in order to pass a stationary vehicle;

    c) owing to circumstances outside the control of the driver;

    d) in order to avoid an accident;

    e) in order to pass a road maintenance vehicle which is in use, is moving at a speed not exceeding 10 miles per hour, and is displaying to the rear the (requisite) sign;

    f) in order to pass a pedal cycle moving at a speed not exceeding 10 miles per hour;

    g) in order to pass a horse that is being ridden or led at a speed not exceeding 10 miles per hour; or,

    h) for the purposes of complying with any direction of a constable in uniform or a traffic warden.

(5) The warning conveyed by the road marking mentioned in paragraph (1) shall be that no vehicle while travelling next to a broken line placed on the left of a continuous line should cross or straddle the first-mentioned line unless it is seen by the driver of the vehicle to be safe to do so.

2.3.1 *Explanation*

Double white lines: The road markings may consist of – two continuous lines along the middle of the carriageway – or a continuous and a broken line. The restrictions on crossing the lines differ, depending on whether the line nearer the vehicle is a continuous or a broken one.

Note that the double white lines need not necessarily be close together. They may be separated by an area of diagonal lines ('hatching').

Stopping: The general requirement is that no vehicle shall stop on any stretch of road on which there are double white line markings. Among the lengthy list of exemptions to this rule, note that those listed in paragraph (3)(a) of regulation 26 are subject to the proviso that they are exempt only if they cannot be used without stopping there. If the van used by the telephone repair people is parked on the road a few yards from a lay-by, then the driver may not be able to plead the exemption.

Crossing – continuous line: The rather complicated phrasing of paragraph (2)(b) amounts to a requirement that a driver shall not allow her vehicle to cross a continuous white line which is on her side of the road, whether the other line is a continuous or a broken one. The several exemptions listed in paragraph (4) are all subject to the proviso that the line may be crossed only if it is safe to do so and it is necessary to do so. The fact that a driver is pulling out to pass a stationary or slow moving vehicle, does not excuse him from doing so when there is a vehicle coming the other way.

Note that the exemptions do not afford the opportunity to pass just any slow moving vehicle. A cyclist travelling at 15 mph, or a tractor drawing a trailer at any speed, are not included.

Crossing – broken line: When a driver has a broken line nearer to him, and a continuous line further from him of the two, he may not cross or straddle the broken line unless he sees that it is safe to do so.

POLICE POWERS
3.1 **Direct Traffic**
Road Traffic Act 1988 Section 35

3.1.1 *Regulate Traffic*
(1) Where a constable is for the time being engaged in the regulation of traffic in a road, a person driving, or propelling a vehicle who neglects, or refuses:
   a) to stop the vehicle, or
   b) to make it proceed in, or keep to, a particular line of traffic, when directed to do so by the constable in the execution of his duty is guilty of an offence.

3.1.2 *Traffic Surveys*
(2) Where:
   a) a traffic survey of any description is being carried out on or in the vicinity of a road, and
   b) a constable gives to a person driving or propelling a vehicle a direction:
      i) to stop the vehicle
      ii) to make it proceed in, or keep to, a particular line of traffic, or
      iii) to proceed to a particular point on or near the road on which the vehicle is being driven or propelled

being a direction given for the purposes of the survey (but not a direction requiring any person to provide any information for the purposes of the survey), the person is guilty of an offence if he neglects or refuses to comply with the direction.

(3) The power to give such a direction as is referred to in subsection (2) above for the purposes of a traffic survey shall be so exercised as not to cause any unreasonable delay to a person who indicates that he is unwilling to provide any information for the purposes of the survey.

3.2 **Stop Vehicles**
Road Traffic Act 1988 Section 163

(1) A person riding a mechanically propelled vehicle on a road must stop the vehicle on being required to do so by a constable in uniform.

(2) A person driving a cycle on a road must stop the cycle on being required to do so be a constable in uniform.

(3) If a person fails to comply with this Section he is guilty of an offence.

3.3 **Pedestrians**
Road Traffic Act 1988 Section 37

Where a constable in uniform is for the time being engaged in the regulation of vehicular traffic in a road, a person on foot who proceeds across or along the carriageway in contravention of a direction to stop given by the constable in the execution of his duty, either to persons on foot or to persons on foot and other traffic, is guilty of an offence.

3.4 Scene of Fire
Fire Services Act 1947 Section 30(5)

The senior police officer present at any fire, or in the absence of any police officer the senior fire officer present, may close any street to traffic or may stop or regulate traffic in any street, whenever in the opinion of that officer it is necessary or desirable to do so for fire fighting purposes.

3.5 *Explanation*

Regulate traffic: There are countries where police officers regularly take up point in the middle of a busy junction and direct traffic. This practice gradually died out in Britain with the advent of traffic lights. The introduction of 'traffic signals out of order' signs further reduced the need for police officers to perform this task, so that a constable now is likely to regulate traffic only at the scene of an accident or other obstruction, or when controlling the exit from a car park at a race meeting, pop concert or the like.

The power to regulate traffic does not require that the officer wears uniform, but not to do so will only increase the hazard. The power to direct drivers extends to drivers of all vehicles, not just mechanically propelled ones, and to pedestrian controlled ones.

Surveys: Traffic surveys are held, usually by the highway authority, to gain information which will assist in future road planning. A constable has power to direct a driver to proceed to a point on or near the road, where the survey team are waiting with their clipboards and questionnaires. However, a driver may not be required to answer any questions. In addition, the police are required by the Section, not to cause undue delay to a driver who indicates that she does not want to answer questions.

Stop traffic: Regulating traffic involves controlling traffic in a particular place for a time. The power to stop may relate to one vehicle only, and the purpose in stopping it need have nothing to do with traffic flow. To exercise this power, the constable must be in uniform, and he may stop only a mechanically propelled vehicle or a pedal cycle; both these points are in contrast to the power to regulate traffic.

Pedestrians: Only when a constable is for the time being engaged in the regulation of vehicular traffic, may he give directions also to pedestrians. A pedestrian will commit an offence if he goes along or across the carriageway, when directed by the constable to stop.

Name and address: When a pedestrian commits the offence of failing to comply with a direction to stop, a constable may require that person to give his name and address. Failure to do so amounts to a further offence, and opens up the possibility of the constable being able to exercise the general power to arrest under Section 25 Police and Criminal Evidence Act 1984 (Road Traffic Act 1988, Section 169).

Fires: The powers at the scene of a fire are quite extensive, including the power to close off a road, as well as to regulate or stop traffic. Only if there is no police officer present, may a fire brigade officer exercise this power.

SCHOOL CROSSING PATROLS
Road Traffic Regulations Act 1984 Section 28

4.1 **Powers**

(1) When between the hours of eight in the morning and half past five in the afternoon a vehicle is approaching a place in the road where children on their way to and from school, or from one part of a school to another, are crossing or seeking to cross the road, a school crossing patrol wearing a uniform approved by the Secretary of State shall have power, by exhibiting a prescribed sign, to require the person driving or propelling the vehicle to stop it.

4.2 **Requirements on Drivers**

(2) Where a person has been required under subsection (1) above to stop a vehicle:
   a) he shall cause the vehicle to stop before reaching the place where the children are crossing or seeking to cross and so as not to stop or impede their crossing; and
   b) the vehicle shall not be put in motion again so as to reach the place in question so long as the sign continues to be exhibited.

(3) A person who fails to comply with paragraph (a) of subsection (2) above, or who causes a vehicle to be put in motion in contravention of paragraph (b) of that subsection, shall be guilty of an offence.

4.3 **Explanation**
Times, children, school: The power to stop traffic is limited to the period specified, there must be children, or at least one child, crossing or seeking to cross the road, and those children must be going to or from, or between parts of, a school. If a school crossing patrol stops traffic at 7.00 pm when children are on their way to a youth club, his signal to stop will not be lawful on two counts. A more common practice, is for the patrol to stop traffic when parents are returning from the school in the morning after depositing their off-spring, or on their way there in the afternoon to collect them. If there are no children in the group crossing the road, a signal to stop will not be lawful.

Uniform and sign: The size, shape, etc of these are set out in regulations, in common with traffic signs.

Stop/remain stopped: The requirement on the driver of a vehicle is to stop when the school crossing sign is exhibited and to remain stopped for so long as it remains exhibited. There are two ways in which a driver may commit an offence – by failing to stop, and by starting off again while the sign is still displayed.

5 PEDESTRIAN CROSSINGS
The Zebra, Pelican and Puffin Pedestrian Crossing Regulations 1997

5.1 **Types of Crossings**
The oldest, 'low-tech' type of crossing is the Zebra, so called for its black and white stripes, requiring only a couple of flashing orange beacons. The drawback with a Zebra crossing is that control is entirely in the hands (or feet) of the pedestrian; a steady stream of individuals may

unduly hold up traffic flow. To counter this problem, the Pelican was devised, complete with traffic light type signals, capable of limiting the time allocated to pedestrians to cross the road. The latest type, with more complex technology, is the Puffin (which does not have stripes like the bill of the seabird of that name), complete with 'pedestrian demand unit', intended to be more flexible that a Pelican, in respect of how much time is allocated to pedestrians to cross. A Puffin crossing is similar to a Pelican, but does not have a 'flashing amber' phase, when drivers may continue unless there is a pedestrian on the crossing.

In relation to crossings, the following should be noted:

i) **Limits of the crossing:** The edges or limits of a crossing will be marked with lines of studs, in accordance with the regulations, so as to establish what constitutes 'on the crossing'. In addition, crossings have 'stop' lines, over which vehicles must not proceed when stopped to allow pedestrians to cross.

ii) **Controlled area:** Each crossing has a controlled area, either side of it, marked in the specified fashion (zig-zag lines on the road) in which stopping and overtaking is restricted.

iii) **Central reservation:** Where there is a central reservation, a Zebra crossing in each carriageway will be treated as separate from the other, i.e. there are two crossings, not one extra-long one. In the case of a Puffin or Pelican crossing, a refuge or central reservation shall be treated as part of the crossing, unless there is a system of staggered crossings which operate independently of one another, in which case each will be treated as a separate crossing.

iv) **Driver:** For the purposes of these regulations, the term 'driver' includes a person riding on a motor cycle or pedal cycle, who is in charge of it.

5.2 Offences
Road Traffic Regulation Act 1984 Section 25

A breach of the requirements of a regulation, will amount to an offence under Section 25, punishable with a fine and, if the offence involves use of a motor vehicle, obligatory endorsement.

5.2.1 Stopping Vehicle on a Crossing
Regulation 18
The driver of a vehicle shall not cause the vehicle or any part of it to stop within the limits of a crossing, unless he is prevented from proceeding by circumstances beyond his control or it is necessary for him to stop to avoid injury or damage to person or property.

5.2.2 Stopping Vehicle in Controlled Area
Regulation 20
The driver of a vehicle shall not cause it or any part of it to stop in the controlled area of a crossing.

For the purposes of this regulation, the term 'vehicle' does not include a pedal cycle (whether or not motor assisted) which does not have a side-car.

5.2.3 Exceptions
Regulations 21, 22
a) If the driver has stopped to afford precedence to a pedestrian, either on a Zebra crossing, or on a Pelican crossing during the flashing amber phase;

b) If the driver is prevented from proceeding by circumstances beyond his control or it is necessary for him to stop to avoid injury or damage to person or property;

c) When the vehicle is used for police, fire brigade or ambulance purposes;

d) When the vehicle is stopped for so long as may be necessary for it to be used for the purposes of:
   – building, demolition or excavation;
   – removal of an obstruction to traffic;
   – road maintenance or road works;
   – work connected with sewage, water, gas, electricity or telecommunications;
   but only if the vehicle cannot be used for such purpose without stopping in the controlled area;

e) If the vehicle is a public service vehicle being used for a local service or to carry passengers at separate fares for hire or reward - provided that the vehicle has passed over the crossing, and is waiting to pick up or set down passengers;

f) If the driver stops the vehicle for the purposes of making a left or right turn.

5.2.4 *Explanation*
Precedence: It is self-evident that vehicles will have to stop in the controlled area when pedestrians are using a crossing in the way intended.

Roadworks etc: A vehicle may be stopped in the controlled area in connection with building work, digging holes, etc, but only if it cannot be used for that purpose without being stopped in the controlled area.

Buses: A bus may be stopped in the controlled area to set down or pick up passengers, but subject to two provisos:
   1 It is a local service, or otherwise is carrying passengers at separate fares, i.e. it is not being used for an excursion or outing, nor is it, e.g. a bus owned by a company, carrying its employees; and
   2 It is stopped on the far side of the crossing, not on the approach to it. The controlled area extends on both sides of the crossing on both sides of the road, to minimise congestion, and to ensure that drivers and pedestrians have a clear view of one another. The risk of an obstructed view is far less when a vehicle is stopped on the far side of the crossing, than when it is on the approach to it.

5.2.5 *Red Lights on Puffin and Pelican Crossings*
Regulation 23
A driver commits an offence if he fails to conform to the indication given by a red light displayed at a Puffin or Pelican crossing.

5.2.6 *Explanation*
A driver can be in no doubt of the need to stop when the Pelican lights are on red and someone is crossing the road. When however, a youth walking on the pavement presses the button as he walks past, not intending to cross the road, the red light which shows as a result, still has to be complied with.

5.2.7 *Overtaking in the Controlled Area*
Regulation 24

When a motor vehicle or any part of it is in the controlled area and travelling towards the crossing, the driver shall not cause any part of it:
a) To pass ahead of the foremost part of any other motor vehicle proceeding in the same direction;
b) To pass ahead of the foremost part of any vehicle which is stationary for the purposes of affording precedence to a pedestrian (on a Zebra or when the amber lights are flashing on a Pelican) or complying with the red lights at a Pelican or Puffin.

5.2.8 *Explanation*
Motor vehicle: Other regulations refer simply to 'vehicle', so include pedal cycles. Offences of overtaking are committed only by drivers of motor vehicles, and only in relation to overtaking other motor vehicles...

Other motor vehicle: When there are more than one other motor vehicle travelling towards the crossing, or stopped to let someone cross, or to comply with a red light, the ban on overtaking applies only to the foremost of these vehicles. Thus, where there are two lanes of traffic and several vehicles in the inside lane are slowing down or have stopped, the driver of a motor vehicle in the outside lane may overtake all of these, except the one at the front of that line.

5.2.9 *Precedence to Pedestrians*
Regulations 25, 26

The driver of a vehicle must accord precedence to a pedestrian who is on the carriageway within the limits of a crossing before the vehicle or any part of has entered the limits of the crossing if the crossing is:
i) A Zebra crossing which is not for the time being controlled by a constable in uniform or by a traffic warden;
ii) A Pelican crossing displaying the flashing amber signal.

These requirements are subject to the provisions relating to central reservations (see paragraph 5.1 above).

5.2.10 *Explanation*
On the carriageway: The requirement is that if a pedestrian steps on to the carriageway within the limits of a Zebra, or Pelican crossing during the flashing amber phase, before a vehicle reaches the limits of the crossing, the driver must give way to the pedestrian. In practice, a sensible pedestrian will wait until traffic stops before venturing into the carriageway, but by the strict letter of the law, the pedestrian could stand at the kerb all day and drivers would not be obliged to stop.

Police/traffic warden: If a constable in uniform, or a traffic warden is controlling traffic and pedestrians at a Zebra crossing, then the directions given by that officer or traffic warden take precedence over the requirements of these regulations.

Summary: To summarise the requirements of regulations 23, 25 and 26, a driver must stop:
a) In the case of a Puffin or Pelican crossing, when the red lights are showing;
b) In the case of a Zebra crossing, or a Pelican during the flashing amber phase, if a pedestrian steps into the carriageway on the crossing, before any part of the vehicle reaches the limits of the crossing.

5.2.11 *Pedestrians Not to Delay*
Regulation 19

No pedestrian shall remain on the carriageway within the limits of a crossing longer than is necessary for that pedestrian to pass over the crossing with reasonable despatch.

6 SPEED LIMITS

6.1 Types of Speed Limit
Road Traffic Regulation Act 1984

Speed limits may be established under various provisions of the Act:

Section 14 –   speed limits at road works.
Section 17 –   speed limits on motorways.
Section 81 –   speed limits on restricted roads.
Section 84 –   speed limits on other than restricted roads.
Section 86 –   speed limits applicable to different classes of vehicles.
Section 88 –   temporary speed limits.

6.1.1 *Explanation*

Restricted road: A restricted road is one which:
  i)   Has provided a system of street lighting furnished by street lamps placed not more than 200 yards apart; or
  ii) One which the traffic authority has directed is a restricted road; subject to (iii);
  iii) The traffic authority may direct that a restricted road shall cease to be a restricted road.

The general speed limit on a restricted road is 30 mph. The fact that lamp-posts render a road restricted, does away with the need for 30 mph speed limit signs on every street corner. The possibilities are:
  a) Street lamps not more than 200 yards apart, no signs – the 30 mph limit applies;
  b) Street lamps, as above, but the road has been declared not to be a restricted road – there must be signs (often on lamp posts) indicated another speed limit, or that there is no speed limit (diagonal black line in white circle);
  c) The system of lighting is not there, but it has been declared to be a restricted road - there must be '30 mph' signs not more than 200 yards apart.

Note: A motorway is not a restricted road, so do not expect to see 70 mph signs on lamp-posts on a motorway.

Other roads: Speed limits, e.g. of 40, 50 or 60 mph may be imposed on specified stretches of road. These will be denoted by large signs at the beginning and end of such a stretch of road, with smaller repeater signs along its length.

Classes of vehicle: Speed limits are specified for various classes of vehicles, for motorways, dual-carriageways and other roads. For example, for goods vehicles over a given gross weight, the limits are 60, 50 and 40 for motorways, dual carriageways and other roads, respectively. Where a road is subject to a speed limit, then whichever is the lower of the road's or the vehicle's limit will apply.

Temporary speed limits: The term 'temporary' is somewhat misleading. Temporary speed limits were introduced over 20 years ago (as a fuel-economy measure) of 50 mph on certain lengths of dual – or single carriageway; 60 mph on all other single carriageway roads and on some dual carriageways, and 70 mph on all other dual carriageways. These temporary limits still apply.

6.2 Speeding Offences
Road Traffic Regulation Act 1984 Section 89

A person who drives a motor vehicle on a road at a speed exceeding a speed limit shall be guilty of an offence (Speeding on a motorway is prosecuted as an offence under Section 17).

A person prosecuted for such an offence shall not be liable to be convicted solely on the evidence of one witness to the effect that, in the opinion of the witness, the defendant was driving the vehicle at a speed exceeding the specified limit.

If a person who employs other to drive motor vehicles on roads, publishes or issues any time-table or schedule, or directs that any journey or part of a journey is to be completed within a specified time, and it is not practicable in the circumstances for that journey or part of it to be completed in the specified time without breaking a speed limit, the publication or issue of the time-table or schedule, or the giving of the direction, may be produced as prima facie evidence that the employer procured or incited his employee drivers to commit such an offence.

6.2.1 *Explanation*
Evidence: The provision that a driver may not be convicted on one person's opinion, predates 1984 by a long way. A single witness may give evidence of distance and time, whence speed may be calculated, because this is not a matter of opinion. Similarly, evidence may be given of readings from mechanical and electronic instruments, such as speedometers, stop watches, radar devices, etc, without the need for corroboration. There is separate legislation covering the admission of evidence from devices such as speed cameras.

Employer's liability: If a time-table or instructions given to a driver by her employer means that a journey or part of one cannot be completed in the time required by that time-table or instruction without the driver breaking a speed limit, then the time-table or instruction may be used in evidence against the employer, for procuring or inciting the employee to commit an offence.

6.3 Exemption for Emergency Vehicles
Road Traffic Regulation Act 1984 Section 87

A speed limit will not apply in the case of a motor vehicle being used for police, fire brigade or ambulance purposes, if observing the speed limit would be likely to hinder its use for that purpose on that occasion. This has been held to include a situation in which a police officer, delayed by a vehicle breakdown, exceeded a speed limit in order not to be late for court where he was to give evidence (*Aitken v Yarwood* (1965)).

6.3.1 *Explanation*
Dangerous driving: This provision does not in any way affect a driver's liability for offences of dangerous or careless driving. A police motor cyclist on his way to an emergency, was in collision with a woman while travelling at 60 mph in a 40 mph limit. In civil court, it was held

that although travelling at this speed was not in breach of criminal law, as far as civil liability was concerned, the police driver owed exactly the same duty of care to the public as a civilian driver (*Gaynor v Allen* (1959)).

Chapter 58: Motor Cycles and Pedal Cycles

MOTOR CYCLES

1 Safety Helmets

1.1 Requirement for Safety Helmets
Motor Cycles (Protective Helmets) Regulations 1980 Regulation 4

(1) Save as provide in paragraph (2) below, every person driving or riding (otherwise than in a sidecar) on a motor bicycle when on a road shall wear protective headgear.

(2) Nothing in paragraph (1) above shall apply to any person driving or riding a motor bicycle if:
   a) it is a mowing machine
   b) it is for the time being propelled by a person on foot; or
   c) he is a follower of the Sikh religion while he is wearing a turban.

(3) In this regulation:

Motor bicycle: means a two wheeled motor cycle, whether having a side car attached thereto or not and for the purposes of this definition any wheels of a motor cycle shall, if the distance between the centres of the areas of contact between such wheels and the road surface is less than 460 millimetres, be counted as one wheel; and

Protective headgear: means headgear which:
   a) is either:
      i) a helmet bearing a marking applied by its manufacturer indicating compliance with the specifications contained in one of the British Standards mentioned is Schedule 2 (whether or not modified by any amendment), or,
      ii) a helmet of a type manufacturer for use by persons on motor cycles which by virtue of its shape, material and construction could reasonably be expected to afford to persons on motor bicycles a degree of protection from injury in the event of an accident similar to or greater than that provided by a helmet of a type prescribed by Regulation 5; and
   b) if worn with a chin cup attached to or held in position by a strap or other fastening provided on the helmet, is provided with an additional strap or other fastening (to be fastened under the wearer's jaw) for securing the helmet firmly to the head of the wearer; and,
   c) is securely fastened to the head of the wearer by means of the straps or other fastening provided on the headgear for that purpose.

1.1.1 *Explanation*

Motor bicycle: A motor cycle with two wheels is still a motor bicycle, if it has a side-car attached to it. The requirement to wear a crash helmet will apply to the driver and any pillion passenger on the motor bike itself, but not to a passenger in the side-car.

Headgear: A helmet which is manufactured to a specified standard, and bearing the appropriate standards marking, will satisfy the requirements of the regulations. A helmet which is not made to those standards will also suffice if:

i) it is made as a motor cycle helmet; and

ii) it will afford as least as much protection in the event of an accident as one which has been made to the specified standards.

Thus, a motor cycle helmet made in a foreign country will be acceptable if it is at least as strong as one made to the specified standards, but a helmet which was made, e.g. for military use, will not be acceptable no matter how much protection it affords.

Chin straps: To comply with the regulations, a helmet must be fitted with a strap which passes under the jaw, which must be fastened.

1.2 Liability for Offence
Road Traffic Act 1988 Section 16

A breach of the regulations amounts to an offence contrary to Section 36.

A person who drives or rides on a motor cycle in contravention of regulations under this Section is guilty of an offence; but notwithstanding any enactment or rule of law no person other than the person actually committing the contravention is guilty of an offence by reason of the contravention unless the person actually committing the contravention is a child under the age of sixteen years.

1.2.1 *Explanation*

If there are two people riding on a motor bicycle, the rider and a pillion passenger, whichever one is not wearing a proper helmet as required by the regulations, will be guilty of an offence. However, the other person on the machine will not be liable for aiding and abetting the offence, unless the offender is under the age of 16. Thus, where the pillion passenger is not wearing a helmet, she will be liable for the offence, whether she be over or under the age of 16. The rider of the motor bike will not be liable, if the passenger is 16 or over; if the passenger is aged under 16, he may be liable for aiding and abetting the passenger to commit the offence.

1.3 Sale of Protective Helmets for Motor Cyclists
Road Traffic Act 1988 Section 17

A person commits an offence who:
- sells or offers for sale a helmet
- as a helmet for affording protection for motor cyclists
- and the helmet is not of a type authorised under regulations.

1.3.1 *Explanation*

Export: No offence is committed where the accused proves that a helmet was sold or offered for sale, for export from Great Britain.

Sell: 'Sell or offer for sale' includes letting on hire or offering to let on hire.

2 Carriage of Persons on Motor Bicycles
Road Traffic Act 1988 Section 23

2.1 Offence

(1) No more than one person in addition to the driver may be carried on a motor bicycle.

(2) No person being carried on a motor bicycle in addition to the driver, shall be carried otherwise than sitting astride the motor bicycle, on a proper seat securely fixed to the machine, behind the driver's seat

(3) If a person is carried on a motor bicycle in contravention of these requirements, the driver commits an offence.

2.1.1 *Explanation*

Carry passenger: There may not be more than one passenger carried on a motor bicycle, i.e. on a motor cycle with two wheels. This does not prevent another passenger being carried in a side-car, because such a passenger will not be 'on' the motor bike. The passenger must be:

i) on a proper seat secured to the machine; a cushion tied to the mudguard is not good enough;

ii) astride the machine; sitting side-saddle will not do;

iii) behind the driver; not in front nor alongside.

There is no requirement that the passenger be facing forward.

PEDAL CYCLES

3 Offences Committed by Cyclists

3.1 Offences Corresponding to Those for Mechanically Propelled Vehicles

There are offences of dangerous and careless cycling, and of cycling while unfit, which correspond closely to equivalent offences which may be committed by the drivers of mechanically propelled vehicles:

i) Dangerous cycling
   Road Traffic Act 1988 Section 28
   A person who rides a cycle on a road dangerously commits an offence.

ii) Careless cycling
   Road Traffic Act 1988 Section 29
   A person commits an offence who rides a cycle on a road without due care and attention, or without due consideration for other road users.

iii) Cycling when unfit
   Road Traffic Act 1988 Section 30
   A person commits an offence who, when riding a cycle on a road or other public place, is unfit to ride through drink or drugs.

3.1.1 *Explanation*

Road: This term is explained in Chapter 50. Note that, whereas all the corresponding mechanically propelled vehicle offences may be committed on a road or other public place, dangerous or careless cycling may be committed only on a road.

Dangerous: This has the same meaning as in the offence of dangerous driving of mechanically propelled vehicles, under Section 2 of the Act (see Chapter 50). However, a person shall not be guilty of dangerous cycling because of the dangerous state of the cycle, as is a possibility with a mechanically-propelled vehicle.

Unfit: For cycling offences, the term 'unfit' means that the rider is under the influence of drink or a drug to such an extent as to be incapable of having proper control of the cycle.

There is no provision to breath test cyclists, nor is there a prescribed alcohol level, but neither are there for mechanically propelled vehicles which are not motor vehicles.

3.2 Carriage of Persons on Pedal Bicycles
Road Traffic Act 1988 Section 24

Not more than one person shall be carried on a road on a bicycle not propelled by mechanical power, unless it is constructed or adapted for the carriage of more than one person.

3.2.1 *Explanation*
Bicycle: A bicycle is a pedal cycle with two wheels, so there is no restriction on carrying several persons on a cycle with three or more wheels.

Constructed or adapted: A 'bicycle built for two' (to quote the words of the old song) may be used to carry more than one person.

Liability: To avoid argument as to who is the rider and who is the passenger, a person is 'carried' whether he is the rider or a passenger. Each of the persons being carried will be equally liable for the offence. Contrast this with the provisions relating to passengers on motor bikes, where any offence is committed by the driver only.

4 Brakes on Pedal Cycles
Pedal Cycles (Construction and Use) Regulations 1983

4.1 Requirements for Brakes
Regulations 7 – 9

   i)   Every pedal cycle shall be equipped with at least one braking system.
   ii) Every bicycle or tricycle with a saddle height of 635 millimetres or more (approximately 25 inches), and every cycle having four or more wheels:
       a) if it is so constructed that one or more of the wheels is incapable of rotating independently of the pedals – be equipped with a braking system operating on the front wheel, or at least two front wheels, if it has more than one; or
       b) otherwise it shall be equipped with two independent braking systems, one on the front wheel (or on at least two of them if it has more than one), and one operating on the rear wheel (or on at least two of them if it has more than one).

4.1.1 *Exceptions*
There are exceptions in relation to:
   – certain cycles manufactured before a specified date (1.8.1984),
   – a cycle which has pedals acting directly on a wheel, e.g. as on a penny-farthing,
   – cycles brought temporarily into Great Britain,
   – a goods tricycle, which may comply with somewhat different requirements.

In addition, these requirements do not apply to electrically assisted pedal cycles.

4.1.2 *Explanation*

Saddle height: The provision relating to saddle height means that the requirements apply to most cycles, excluding those in smaller child sizes.

Rotate independently: Some cycles are such that the back wheel goes round only when the pedals go round (so called 'fixed wheel'); stop pedalling and the rear wheel locks. On such a machine, there is no real need for rear brakes.

4.2 **Police Powers to Inspect Brakes**
Regulation 11

A constable in uniform is empowered to test and inspect the braking systems on a pedal cycle:
  i) on a road; or
  ii) on premises where the cycle is
    – within 48 hours of an accident in which the cycle has been involved
    – if the owner of the premises consents.

4.2.1 *Explanation*

Constable: The constable does not require any specific authority or training as a cycle examiner, but she must be in uniform in order to exercise these powers.

Consent: There is no requirement to obtain the consent of the owner of the cycle, whether the cycle is on a road or on premises, nor has the cycle owner an opportunity to defer a test, as has the owner of a motor vehicle in similar circumstances.

4.3 **Offences**
Regulations 10 and 12 and Road Traffic Act 1988 Section 81

4.3.1 *Ride*

No person shall ride, or cause or permit to be ridden, on a road a pedal cycle unless the braking system(s) required to be fitted are in efficient working order. (This does not apply to electrically-assisted pedal cycles.)

4.3.2 *Sell*

No person shall sell or supply, or offer to sell or supply a pedal cycle which does not meet the requirements of these regulations. (This applies to electrically assisted cycles.)

Exception

There is an exception in the case of a cycle which has no braking system and which is designed for off-road racing on enclosed tracks.

Chapter 59: Taxis and Private Hire Vehicles

TYPES OF TAXIS

1 Historical Development

1.1 London

The arrangements for regulating taxis in London differ from those in the rest of the country. The several London Hackney Carriage (or Carriages) Acts date from 1831, the principal legislation being the Metropolitan Public Carriage Act 1869. From the dates of this legislation, it is evident that the hackney carriages envisaged were horse drawn. The law still applies today, although the familiar 'black cab' has long since replaced the horse drawn cab. Legislation to control 'mini-cabs', more correctly called private hire vehicles, is currently in preparation.

Control in London is strict, with cabs of certain types only, and drivers having to pass an exacting knowledge test of the streets and buildings of the Metropolis. The material in the remainder of this chapter refers to the situation outside London.

1.2 Outside London

The Town Police Clauses Act 1847 empowered local authorities to licence hackney carriages in their areas. The Local Government (Miscellaneous Provisions) Act 1976 makes provision for local authorities to control the operation of hackney carriages and private hire vehicles.

2 Hackney/Private Hire

2.1 Hackney Cab
Town Police Clauses Act 1847 Section 38

A hackney carriage is defined as:
- a wheeled carriage, whatever its form or construction
- used for standing or plying for hire in any street within the prescribed distance
- having thereon the required plate.

2.2 Private Hire Vehicle
Local Government (Miscellaneous Provisions) Act 1976 Section 88

A private hire vehicle is:
- a motor vehicle constructed or adapted to seat fewer than nine passengers
- other than a hackney carriage, public service vehicle or London cab
- which is provided for hire with the services of a driver
- for the purposes of carrying passengers.

2.3 Explanation
Stand or ply: The essential difference between a hackney carriage and a private hire vehicle is that the former may be stationary in the street, on a taxi rank, or be driven around, seeking custom. A private hire vehicle must be booked in advance, perhaps by ringing the operator's

office. There has been considerable discord in some parts of the country, between the operators and drivers of the two different types, with allegations that at busy periods, private hire vehicles are parked near pubs and clubs, effectively standing for hire, taking business away from hackney carriages.

Prescribed distance: A hackney carriage may be used to look for business within the area prescribed by the council which issues the licence.

Fewer than nine, etc: The description of a private hire vehicle clearly designates what it is **not**, as well as what it is. It is not:

- a bus, because it carries fewer than nine passengers;
- a hackney carriage, and it is not allowed to be parked or driven around seeking passengers;
- a public service vehicle; a public service vehicle (in common parlance, a bus) usually carries passengers at separate fares. A private hire vehicle usually is hired out as a whole, the fare not being dependent on the number of passengers. A taxi may be used to carry passengers at separate fares in certain circumstances (Transport Act 1985, Sections 10 – 16).

It is:

- hired out with driver, to distinguish it from a self-drive hired car;
- for carrying passengers, to distinguish it from the light goods van, available with driver for moving goods.

HACKNEY CARRIAGES

3.1 Licensing and Control

3.1.1 *Licence*
Town Police Clauses Act 1847 Section 37

The council may licence to ply for hire within the prescribed distance, hackney coaches or carriages of any kind for the carriage of persons.

A licence is issued in respect of the vehicle, not its owner. If the vehicle changes hands, the new owner may apply to have her name entered on the licence.

3.1.2 *Conditions on Licence*
Local Government (Miscellaneous Provisions) Act 1967 Section 47

(1) A district council may attach to the grant of a licence of a hackney carriage under the Act of 1847 (Town Police Clauses Act 1847) such conditions as the district council may consider reasonably necessary.

(2) Without prejudice to the generality of the foregoing subsection, a district council may require any hackney carriage licensed by them under the Act of 1847 to be of such design or appearance or bear such distinguishing marks as shall clearly identify it as a hackney carriage.

(3) Any person aggrieved by an conditions attached to such a licence may appeal to a Magistrates' Court.

3.1.3 *Driver's Licence*
Town Police Clauses Act 1847 Sections 46 – 50
Local Government (Miscellaneous Provisions) Act 1976 Section 59

No person shall act as the driver of a hackney carriage without first obtaining a licence from the local authority. If the proprietor of a hackney carriage employs a person as a driver, the proprietor shall retain possession of the driver's licence until that person leaves his employment.

A council shall not grant a licence unless:
   i)   satisfied that the applicant is a fit and proper person to hold a driving licence;
   ii) that he has held an ordinary driving licence (not being a provisional licence) for at least 12 months.

For the purpose of satisfying themselves as to whether an applicant is a fit and proper person, the council may send a copy of the application to the chief officer of police for the area, requesting his observations. The police must respond to such a request.

The council may attach such conditions to the grant of a licence as they consider reasonably necessary.

Appeal: Appeal against a refusal to issue a driver's licence, or against any condition imposed on one which is granted, lies to magistrates' court.

The council may revoke a driver's licence upon a second conviction, of the driver or the proprietor, for an offence relating to hackney carriages.

3.2 **Offences**

3.2.1 *Offences by Driver or Proprietor*
Offences which may be committed in relation to the use of a hackney carriage include:
   i)   Use, drive, allow to stand or ply for hire, without a licence, or while not displaying a licence number (Town Police Clauses Act 1847, Section 45).
   ii) The driver on a hackney carriage stand, who refuses or neglects without reasonable excuse to drive to any place within the prescribed distance. (Town Police Clauses Act 1847, Section 53).
   iii) Act as a driver without a licence, or during the time a licence is suspended. Lend or part with his licence (except to a proprietor) (Town Police Clauses Act 1847, Section 47).
   iv) A proprietor commits an offence if he employs a person as a driver who has not obtained a licence, or during the time his licence is suspended (Town Police Clauses Act 1847, Section 53).
   v)   A proprietor commits an offence who permits a hackney carriage to be used without the number of persons to be carried being clearly marked on the vehicle. The driver will commit an offence if he refuses to carry up to this number when required to do so by the hirer (Town Police Clauses Act 1847, Section 52).
   vi) The proprietor and the driver will commit an offence by taking as a fare a greater sum than is allowed under by-laws (Town Police Clauses Act 1847, Section 58).

3.2.2 *Hackney Carriage Stands*
Local Government (Miscellaneous Provisions) Act 1976 Section 64

A person commits an offence who:
- without reasonable excuse
- causes or permits any vehicle other than a hackney carriage
- to wait on a hackney carriage stand
- during the period for which the stand is appointed.

3.2.3 *Exception*
The driver of a public service vehicle will have a defence if she shows that she parked there to avoid obstruction to traffic or for other compelling reason, but only for so long as was reasonably necessary to put down or pick up passengers.

3.2.4 *Explanation*
Hackney carriage stand: A district council may provide hackney carriage stands in the area, after consulting the police and public, and taking account of bus stops and other factors, so as to avoid obstruction being caused. A stand will be clearly marked as such, with prescribed traffic signs.

Period: A hackney carriage stand may be designated as such for a particular period of the day, not necessarily for the whole 24 hours. This information will be displayed.

PRIVATE HIRE VEHICLES

4.1 Licensing

4.1.1 *Licensing of Operators, Drivers and Vehicles*
Local Government (Miscellaneous Provisions) Act 1976 Section 46

(1) Except as authorised by this part of this Act:
    a) no person being the proprietor of any vehicle, not being a hackney carriage or London cab in respect of which a vehicle licence is in force, shall use or permit the same to be used in a controlled district as a private hire vehicle without having for such a vehicle a current licence under Section 48 of this Act.
    b) no person shall in a controlled district act as a driver of any private hire vehicle without having a current licence under Section 51 of this Act.
    c) no person being the proprietor of a private hire vehicle licensed under the Part of this Act shall employ as a driver thereof for the purpose of any hiring any person who does not have a current licence under Section 51 of this Act.
    d) no person shall in a controlled district operate any vehicle as a private hire vehicle without having a current licence under Section 55 of this Act.
    e) no person licensed under the said Section 55 shall in a controlled district operate any vehicle as a private hire vehicle:
        i) if for the vehicle a current licence under the said Section 48 is not in force; or,
        ii) if the driver does not have a current licence under the said Section 51.

(2) If any person knowingly contravenes the provisions of this Section, he shall be guilty of an offence.

4.1.2 *Conditions in Relation to Vehicle Licensing*
Local Government (Miscellaneous Provisions) Act 1976 Section 48

Provided that a district council shall not grant a licence unless they are satisfied that:
- a) the vehicle is:
  - i) suitable in type, size and design for use as a private hire vehicle;
  - ii) not of such a design and appearance as to lead any person to believe that the vehicle is a hackney carriage;
  - iii) in a suitable mechanical condition;
  - iv) safe; and
  - v) comfortable.
- b) that there is in force in relation to the use of the vehicle a policy of insurance or such security as complies with the requirements of Part VI of the Road Traffic Act 1988,

and shall not refuse such a licence for the purpose of limiting the number of vehicles in respect of which such licences are granted by the council.

4.1.3 *Conditions Relating to Driver Licensing*
Local Government (Miscellaneous Provisions) Act 1976 Section 51

A district council shall consider applications for licences to drive private hire vehicles. A council shall not grant a licence unless:
- i) satisfied that the applicant is a fit and proper person to hold a driving licence;
- ii) that he has held an ordinary driving licence (not being a provisional licence) for at least 12 months.

For the purpose of satisfying themselves as to whether an applicant is a fit and proper person, the council may send a copy of the application to the chief officer of police for the area, requesting his observations. The police must respond to such a request.

The council may attach such conditions to the grant of a licence as they consider reasonably necessary. The council must keep a register of the holders of private hire vehicle drivers' licences, which shall be available for public inspection during office hours.

Appeal: Appeal against a refusal to issue a driver's licence, or against any condition imposed on one which is granted, lies to magistrates' court (Section 52).

4.1.4 *Explanation*
Operator/proprietor: A person must be licensed to act as an operator. The operator of private hire vehicles is the person who runs a business, takes orders from customers and engages drivers to fulfil those orders. An operator must use only licensed vehicles and licensed drivers. A proprietor does not have to be licensed as such, but may not use or permit use of a vehicle which is not licensed, nor shall she employ an unlicensed driver.

An operator may or may not also be the proprietor of vehicles. Some operators however, do not own vehicles themselves, but engage owner/drivers to work for them.

Vehicle: The council has powers to impose conditions on the type and size of vehicles which they will licence. In particular, they may reject a vehicle which looks like a hackney carriage. A council has no power to limit the number of licensed vehicles in its area.

One area only: An operator may only make use of vehicles and drivers licensed by the council of the district in which she operates (*Dittah v Birmingham City Council* (1993) – also cited as *Dittah v DPP* (1993)).

4.2 **Operator Records**
Local Government (Miscellaneous Provisions) Act 1976 Section 56

(1) For the purposes of this part of this Act every contract of hire of a private hire vehicle licensed under this Part of this Act shall be deemed to have been made with the operator who accepted the booking for that vehicle whether or not he provided the vehicle.

(2) Every person to whom an operator's licence has been granted by a district council shall keep a record in such form as the council may, by condition attach to the grant of the licence prescribe, and shall enter therein, before the commencement of the journey, such particulars of every booking for a private hire vehicle invited or accepted by him, whether by accepting the same from the hirer or by undertaking it at the request of another operator, as the district council may by condition prescribe and shall produce such record on request to any authorised officer of the council or to any constable.

(3) Every person to whom an operator's licence has been granted by a district council shall keep such records as the council may, by conditions attached to the grant of the licence, prescribe of the particulars of any private hire vehicle operated by him and shall produce the same on request to any authorised officer of the council or to any constable for inspection.

(4) A person to whom an operator's licence has been granted by a district council shall produce the licence on request to any authorised officer of the council or any constable for inspection.

(5) If a person without reasonable excuse contravenes the provisions of this Section he shall be guilty of an offence.

4.2.1 *Explanation*

Booking: To avoid any doubt, the operator who accepts a booking is responsible for keeping a record of that booking, irrespective of who provides the vehicle. An operator may use his own vehicle, one belonging to an owner-driver who works for him, or even farm the business out to another operator.

Records: The operator is required to keep records of every booking which he accepts. He must also keep such other records as the council may require, as a condition attached to his operator's licence.

An authorised officer of the council, or any constable, may require production of these records.

INSPECTION OF VEHICLES

5.1 Power to Stop and Inspect Vehicles
Local Government (Miscellaneous Provisions) Act 1976 Section 68

Any authorised officer of the council in question, or any constable shall have power at all reasonable times to inspect and test, for the purpose of ascertaining its fitness, any hackney carriage or private hire vehicle, and if he is not satisfied as to the fitness of the hackney carriage or private hire vehicle, or as to the accuracy of its taximeter he may by notice in writing require the proprietor of the hackney carriage or private hire vehicle to make it or its taximeter available for further inspection and testing at such reasonable time and place as may be specified in the notice, and suspend the vehicle licence until such time as such authorised officer or constable is so satisfied;

Provided that, if the authorised officer or constable is not satisfied before the expiration of a period of two months, the said licence shall, by virtue of this Section, be deemed to have been revoked.

5.1.1 *Explanation*
Inspect and test: A council official or a constable, has power to test and inspect the vehicle. However, the council official does not have the power to stop a vehicle.

Suspend/revoke: If the initial inspection gives cause to doubt the vehicle's fitness to be used as a hackney carriage or private hire vehicle, as the case may be, or doubt as to the accuracy of its taximeter, the licence may be suspended until the operator submits it for a more detailed test. If the vehicle has not been passed as fit for use within two months, the licence is considered to be revoked.

5.2 Accidents
Local Government (Miscellaneous Provisions) Act 1976 Section 50

If a hackney carriage or private hire vehicle is involved in an accident:
  - which causes damage materially affecting the safety, performance or appearance of the vehicle, or the comfort or convenience of persons carried in it
  - the proprietor shall report to the council which has licensed the vehicle
  - as soon as practicable and in any case within 72 hours.

(This does not affect any liability to report the accident to the police, under the provisions of the Road Traffic Act 1988.)

5.3 Obstructing Officers
Local Government (Miscellaneous Provisions) Act 1976 Section 73

(1) Any person who:
  a) wilfully obstructs an authorised officer or constable acting in pursuance of this part of this Act or the 1847 Act; or
  b) without reasonable excuse fails to comply with any requirements properly made to him by such officer or constable under this part of this Act; or
  c) without reasonable cause fails to give such an officer or constable so acting any other assistance or information which he may reasonably require of such person for

the purpose of the performance of his function under this Part of this Act or the Act of 1847;

shall be guilty of an offence.

(2) If any person, in giving any such information as is mentioned in the preceding subsection, makes any statement which he knows to be false, he shall be guilty of an offence.

VEHICLE DOCUMENTS

6.1 Production of Documents

6.1.1 *Driver's licence*
Local Government (Miscellaneous Provisions) Act 1976 Section 53

A driver of a hackney carriage or private hire vehicle licensed by a council, shall produce her licence for inspection upon the request of an authorised officer of the council or of a constable. The licence shall be produced forthwith, or within 5 days either at the council offices (if the request is made by a council officer), or at a police station within the council area, nominated by the driver (if the request is made by a constable).

Offence: Failure without reasonable excuse to produce the licence when requested.

6.1.2 *Vehicle Licence and Insurance*
Local Government (Miscellaneous Provisions) Act 1976 Section 50

The proprietor of a hackney carriage or private hire vehicle licensed by a council shall , on the request of an authorised officer of the council, produce for inspection the vehicle licence and the certificate of insurance or security.

Offence: The proprietor commits an offence if he fails without reasonable excuse to produce a document when requested to do so.

6.2 Suspension or Revocation of Licences

6.2.1 *Vehicle Licence*
Local Government (Miscellaneous Provisions) Act 1976 Section 60

Notwithstanding any provisions of the 1847 Act, a council may suspend, revoke or refuse to renew a hackney carriage or private hire vehicle licence on any of the following grounds:
a) the vehicle is unfit for use as such;
b) any offence or non-compliance with the relevant provisions of this Act or the 1847 Act, by the operator or driver;
c) any other reasonable cause.

6.2.2 *Driver's Licence*
Local Government (Miscellaneous Provisions) Act 1976 Section 61

Notwithstanding any provisions of the 1847 Act, a council may suspend, revoke or refuse to renew a hackney carriage or private hire driver's licence on any of the following grounds:
a) since the licence was granted, the driver
   – has been convicted of any offence involving dishonesty, indecency or violence; or

- has been convicted of an offence under the relevant parts of this Act or the 1847, or has failed to comply with a provision thereof;
b) any other reasonable cause.

6.2.3 *Private Hire Operator's licence*
Local Government (Miscellaneous Provisions) Act 1976 Section 62

A council may suspend, revoke or refuse to renew a private hire operator's licence on any of the following grounds:
a) any offence under, or non-compliance with, the provisions of this part of the Act;
b) any conduct on the part of the operator which appears to the council to render him unfit to hold the licence;
c) any material change since the licence was granted in any of the circumstances of the operator on the basis of which the licence was granted;
d) any other reasonable cause.

6.2.4 *Appeal*
Appeal against a council's decision to revoke, suspend or refuse to renew a licence, lies to magistrates' court.

Chapter 60: Miscellaneous Traffic Matters

NOTICE OF INTENDED PROSECUTION (NIP)

1.1 Requirement for NIP
Road Traffic Offenders Act 1988 Section 1

(1) Subject of Section 2 of this Act, a person shall not be convicted of an offence to which this Section applies unless:

    a) he was warned at the time the offence was committed that the question of prosecuting him for some one or other of the offences to which this Section applies would be taken into consideration, or

    b) within fourteen days of the commission of the offence a summons for the offence was served on him, or

    c) within fourteen days of the commission of the offence a notice of the intended prosecution specifying the nature of the alleged offence and the time and place where it is alleged to have been committed, was:

        i) in the case of an offence under Section 28 or 29 of the Road Traffic Act 1988 (cycling offences) served on him

        ii) in the case of any other offence, served on him or on the person, if any, registered as the keeper of the vehicle at the time of the commission of the offence.

(1A) A notice may be served on a person:

    a) by delivering it to him;

    b) by addressing it to him and leaving it at his last known address;

    c) by sending it by registered post, recorded delivery service or first class post addressed to him at his last known address.

(2) A notice shall be deemed for the purposes of subsection (1)(c) above to have been served on a person if it was sent by registered post or recorded delivery service addressed to him at his last known address, notwithstanding that the notice was returned as undelivered or was for some other reason not received by him.

(3) The requirement of subsection (1) above shall in every case be deemed to have been complied with unless the contrary is proved.

(4) Schedule 1 of this Act shows the offences to which this Section applies.

1.2 When NIP is Not Required
Road Traffic Offenders Act 1988 Section 2

(1) The requirements of Section 1(1) of this Act does not apply in relation to an offence, if at the time of the offence or immediately after it, an accident occurs owing to the presence on a road of the vehicle in respect of which the offence was committed.

(2) The requirements of Section 1(1) of this Act do not apply in relation to an offence in respect of which:

    a) a fixed penalty notice (within the meaning of Part III of this Act) has been given or fixed under any provision of that Part, or

b) a notice has been given under Section 54(4) of this Act (provisional endorsable fixed penalty notice – see Chapter 55).

(3) Failure to comply with the requirement of Section 1(1) of this Act is not a bar to the conviction of the accused in the case where the court is satisfied:
   a) that neither the name and address of the accused, nor the name and address of the registered keeper, if any, could with reasonable diligence have been ascertained in time for a summons to be served or for a notice to be served or sent in compliance with the requirement, or
   b) that the accused by his own conduct contributed to the failure.

1.3 Explanation

Warning at the time: The purpose of the NIP procedure is to make a person aware, while events should still be fresh in her memory, that there is a likelihood of her being prosecuted for one of the specified offences. If she is not made aware of this until some time has elapsed, she may be less able to recall the circumstances and to mount an effective defence against the prosecution evidence.

Written notice: If the person is not warned at the time of the offence that she may be prosecuted, a summons within 14 days, or a written notice within 14 days, will do instead. In the case of a motor vehicle, service of the written notice may be on the alleged offender or on the registered keeper of the vehicle.

Service by post: A written notice will be considered served if it is sent by recorded delivery, registered post or first class post to the person's last known address. When it is sent by registered post or recorded delivery, whether it is actually delivered matters not.

Accident: If the purpose of the NIP procedure is to remind a driver about events, it seems reasonable that a warning notice is not required when, immediately before or at the time the offence in question is committed, an accident occurs involving the offender's vehicle. The accident should serve as a reminder. If a driver fails to conform to a red traffic light and two seconds later is involved in a collision, no notice of intended prosecution will be needed.

The fact that a driver was seriously injured in the accident does not negate that he would be aware that he had been involved in an accident (*DPP v Pidhajeckyj* (1991)).

Fixed penalty notice: If an offender has been issued with a fixed penalty notice, or with a provisional one in the case of a driver unable to produce her licence at the time, there is no need for a NIP.

Unable to trace: The lack of a warning notice will not be a bar to prosecution where:
   i) neither the offender's name and address, nor that of the registered keeper, could be ascertained, despite reasonable diligence having been applied in seeking to do so; **or**
   ii) the accused's own conduct contributed to failure to serve a summons or NIP in time.

In many cases, both these elements will be involved, as where a person has bought a second-hand car and failed to register that ownership, the previous owner having notified DVLC that he has sold it.

1.4 **Offences Subject to NIP Procedure**
Road Traffic Offender Act 1988 (as amended) Schedule 1

Section	Offence
2 Road Traffic Act 1988 (hereafter RTA)	Dangerous driving
3 RTA	Careless and Inconsiderate driving
22 RTA	Leaving vehicle in dangerous position
28 RTA	Dangerous cycling
29 RTA	Careless inconsiderate cycling
35 RTA	Fail to comply with traffic directions
36 RTA	Fail comply with traffic signs
16 Road Traffic Regulation Act 1984 (hereafter RTRA)	Speeding (contravention of temporary restriction)
17 RTRA	Speeding (traffic regulation on special roads)
88(7) and 89(1) RTRA	Speeding generally

Note: The need for a NIP applies also to an offence of aiding and abetting any of the listed offences.

DANGER TO OTHER ROAD USERS

2.1 **Leaving a Vehicle in a Dangerous Position**
Road Traffic Act 1988 Section 22

2.1.1 *Offence*
A person commits an offence if:
- being the person in charge of a vehicle
- he causes or permits the vehicle or a trailer drawn by it to remain at rest on a road
- in such a position or in such condition or in such circumstances as to involve danger of injury to other persons using the road.

2.1.2 *Explanation*
Causes or permits: These terms are explained in Chapter 52.

Vehicle: The offence is not restricted to mechanically propelled vehicles; it could be committed by a person in charge of a horse and cart.

Position, condition, circumstances: It is somewhat misleading to refer to this offence as 'dangerous position.' The condition of the vehicle itself, or other attendant circumstances, could give rise to danger of injury. There is however, another offence, of using a vehicle in a dangerous condition (See Chapter 52).

2.2 Causing Danger to Other Road Users
Road Traffic Act 1988 Section 22A

(1) A person is guilty of an offence if he intentionally and without lawful authority or reasonable cause:
   a) causes anything to be on or over the road, or
   b) interferes with a motor vehicle, trailer or cycle, or
   c) interferes (directly or indirectly) with traffic equipment,
   in such circumstances that it would be obvious to a reasonable person that to do so would be dangerous.

2.2.2 Meaning of Terms

(2) In subsection (1) above 'dangerous' refers to danger either of injury to any person while on or near a road, or of serious damage to property on or near a road; and in determining for the purposes of that subsection what would be obvious to a reasonable person in a particular case, regard shall be had not only to the circumstances of which he could be expected to be aware, but also to the circumstances shown to have been within the knowledge of the accused.

(3) In subsection (1) above 'traffic equipment' means:
   a) anything lawfully placed on or near a road by a highway authority;
   b) a traffic sign lawfully placed on or near a road by a person other than the highway authority;
   c) any fence, barrier or light lawfully placed on or near a road:
      i) for guarding, lighting and signing in streets where works are undertaken or
      ii) by a constable or a person acting under the instructions (whether general or specific) of a chief officer of police.

(4) For the purposes of subsection (3) above anything placed on or near a road shall unless the contrary is proved be deemed to have been lawfully placed there.

(5) In this Section road does not include footpath or bridleway.

2.2.3 Explanation

Intentionally/lawful authority, etc: The lorry driver who loses a crate from his load on a motorway may be prosecuted for insecure load, but will not be liable for this offence because he did not intentionally cause the crate to be on the road. Police officers who deploy a device across the road to deflate the tyres of a vehicle which is being pursued, will be acting with lawful authority or reasonable cause.

Danger: This includes danger of serious damage, as well as of injury to a person. Demonstrators who throw nails on the road in an effort to stop lorries, as part of a protest, may not be endangering the safety of the drivers, but will be liable because they are causing danger of serious damage to the vehicles.

Signs: The term includes all signs lawfully placed, whether a permanent sign erected by the highway authority, a temporary police sign or even a warning triangle placed on the road to warn of a broken down vehicle. Barriers, lamps and the like at road works are included, and these frequently feature in such offences, where the mindless miscreant thinks it fun to throw warning lamps and barriers into the trench, leading to the risk of someone falling into it.

Reasonable person: It is will not amount to a defence for the accused to claim that it never occurred to him that what he did was dangerous. The test is whether a reasonable person would have realised that such conduct was dangerous.

2.2.4 *Arrest and Punishment*
The offence is triable either way, and carries a maximum sentence of seven years on indictment. It is therefore an arrestable offence. This reflects the wide range of possible seriousness of the offence, from the youth who picks up a warning lamp from roadworks and throws it over the hedge, to a situation where persons may be killed or seriously injured, e.g. by interfering with a vehicle carrying hazardous chemicals.

TAMPERING WITH OR TAKING HOLD OF MOTOR VEHICLES
3.1 Tampering
Road Traffic Act 1988 Section 25

If, while a motor vehicle is on a road or on a parking place provided by a local authority, a person:
   a) gets on to the vehicle, or
   b) tampers with the brake or other parts of its mechanism,
   without lawful authority or reasonable cause he is guilty of an offence.

3.1.1 *Explanation*
Road or council car park: The offence will not be committed by tampering with a vehicle on private premises. Many public car parks, not run by the local authority, e.g. at supermarkets, cinemas, etc, will, however, fall within the meaning of 'road' (See Chapter 50).

Mechanism: There is no guidance in the Act as to what is meant by 'mechanism' but it will, presumably, include the engine, transmission, and ancillary motors, etc.

Get on: The offence may be committed without any tampering, merely by getting on to the vehicle.

Lawful authority or reasonable cause: Lawful authority derives from some lawful power, as when a constable authorises the removal of a vehicle which is causing obstruction. Whether a cause is reasonable will be a matter of fact for the court to decide in any particular case. If youths are playing football in a car park and the ball lands on top of a parked lorry, does a youth have 'reasonable cause' for climbing on to the lorry, to fetch the ball?

3.2 Holding or Getting on to a Vehicle
Road Traffic Act 1988 Section 26

A person commits an offence if:
   (1) For the purpose of being carried:
      – without lawful authority or reasonable cause
      – he takes or retains hold of, or gets on to a motor vehicle or trailer
      – while it is in motion on a road.

   (2) For the purpose of being drawn:
      – he takes or retains hold of a motor vehicle or trailer
      – while it is in motion on a road.

3.2.1 *Explanation*

Lawful authority ... excuse: Getting on to a moving vehicle in order to hitch a lift will not amount to an offence if the offender comes up with a reasonable excuse for doing so. However, taking hold in order to be drawn along will be an offence no matter what the excuse.

Purpose: There is a difference between this offence and that of tampering, when a person gets on to a vehicle. For this offence to be committed, the purpose must be to be carried, and the vehicle must be in motion.

In motion: The offence of getting on to be carried will not be committed by a person who jumps on to a vehicle, e.g. when it is stopped at traffic lights. The aim of the legislation is to prohibit dangerous practices, not to prevent people 'trespassing' on vehicles.

Retains: The offence will be committed by someone who takes hold of a motor vehicle or trailer while it is stopped, but then continues to retain hold once the vehicle starts moving.

Drawn: This offence may be committed by a cyclist, for example, who holds on to a vehicle in order to be towed.

DRIVING OTHER THAN ON A ROAD

4.1 **Offence**
Road Traffic Act 1988 Section 34

(1) Subject to the provisions of this Section, if without lawful authority a person drives a motor vehicle:
   a) on to or upon any common land, moorland or land of any other description, not being land forming part of a road, or
   b) on any road being a footpath, or bridleway,
   he is guilty of an offence.

(2) It is not an offence under this Section to drive a motor vehicle on any land within fifteen yards of a road, being a road on which a motor vehicle may lawfully be driven, for the purposes only of parking the vehicle on that land.

(3) A person shall not be convicted of an offence under this Section with respect to a vehicle if he proves to the satisfaction of the court that it was driven in contravention of this Section for the purposes of saving life or extinguishing fire or meeting any other like emergency.

(4) It is hereby declared that nothing in this Section prejudices the operation of:
   a) right of the public over commons and waste lands, or
   b) any bylaws applying to any land
   or affects the law of trespass to such land or any rights or remedy to which a person may by law be entitled in respect of any such trespass or in particular confers a right to park a vehicle on any land.

4.1.1 *Explanation*

Lawful authority: The park ranger or volunteer worker, for example, taking materials across land to repair a section of footpath, will have lawful authority.

Motor vehicle: The offence applies only to a motor vehicle (one intended or adapted for use on roads), so if the vehicle in question is intended only for use off-road, the offence does not arise.

Footpath, bridleway: A footpath is a highway restricted to persons on foot, not driving or riding animals. The term 'footpath' refers to a way which is a highway in its own right; the term does not include a pavement or footway which runs along the side of a road. A bridleway is a highway over which persons may ride or lead a horse, and there may be a right in a particular case to drive other animals also. On neither of these is it permitted to travel with a vehicle, although cycling may be permitted on some bridleways.

15 yards: The motorist who fancies having a picnic in a shady dell on the moor, should ensure that she drives no more than 15 yards away from the road, when parking her vehicle.

REMOVAL OF VEHICLES

5.1 Police Powers

5.1.1 *To Require Vehicle to be Moved*
Removal and Disposal of Vehicles Regulations 1986 Regulation 3

(1) This regulation shall apply to a vehicle which:
   a) has broken down, or been permitted to remain at rest, on a road in such position or in such condition or in such circumstances as to cause obstruction to persons using the road or as to be likely to cause danger to such persons, or
   b) has been permitted to remain at rest or has broken down and remained at rest on a road in contravention of a prohibition or restriction.

(2) A constable may require the owner, driver or other person in control or in charge of any vehicle to which this regulation applies to move or cause to be moved the vehicle and any such requirement may include a requirement that the vehicle shall be moved from that road to a place which is not on that or any other road, or that the vehicle shall not be moved to any such road or to any such position on the road as may be specified.

5.1.2 *To Move Vehicle*
Removal and Disposal of Vehicles Regulations 1986 Regulation 4

Where a vehicle:
   a) is a vehicle to which regulation 3 of these regulations applies, or
   b) having broken down on a road or on any land in the open air, appears to a constable to have been abandoned without lawful authority, or
   c) has been permitted to remain at rest on a road or on any land in the open air in such a position or in such condition or in such circumstance as to appear to a constable to have been abandoned without lawful authority;
then subject to the provisions of Section 99 and 100 of the Road Traffic Regulation Act 1984 a constable may remove or arrange for the removal of the vehicle, and, in the case of a vehicle which is on a road he may remove it or arrange for its removal from that road, or may move it or arrange for its removal to another position on that or another road.

5.1.3 *Explanation*
Broken ... at rest: The powers, to require that a vehicle be moved, applies equally to a situation where the vehicle has broken down, as it does to a vehicle which has been deliberately brought to a halt or parked. Clearly, if a driver is seeking to get his broken down van moved as quickly as possible,

there is little point in a police officer intervening. In a situation where the driver is waiting for a friend to come and give him a tow, or is seeking to repair the vehicle rather than to move it, the application of these provisions may lead to a speedier resolution of a traffic flow problem.

Obstruction, danger, restriction: A lorry stopped on a narrow stretch of road during rush hour may be moved because it is causing an obstruction. However, a vehicle will equally be liable to be removed if it is parked on double yellow lines.

Abandoned on land: Police have powers to remove vehicles on land other than a road, which appear to have been abandoned without lawful authority. However, a local authority has similar powers (see below).

Sections 99 and 100: These relate to procedures for impounding vehicles and charging for their release.

Same road, different road: When a constable exercises these powers, she may require that the vehicle be moved (or may move the vehicle):
- to a place which is not on that road, or on any other road; or
- to a particular road; or
- to a specified place on that road.

Examples would include 'move it from this stretch of road', 'take it at least 50 yards past the road works', 'take it into one of the side streets', etc.

5.2 **Local Authority Powers**
Refuse Disposal (Amenity) Act 1978 Section 3

Where it appears to a local authority that a motor vehicle in their area is abandoned without lawful authority on any land in the open air or on any other land forming part of a highway, it shall be the duty of the authority subject to the provisions of this Section, to remove the vehicle.

5.2.1 *Explanation*
Motor vehicle: The term extends beyond what is usually meant by the term – any mechanically propelled vehicle intended or adapted for use on roads – to include:
- any such vehicle whether or not in a fit state for such use
- any trailer intended or adapted for attaching to such vehicle
- any chassis or body of such vehicle or trailer, with or without wheels
- anything attached to such vehicle or trailer.

DOCUMENTS AND DETAILS

6.1 **Police Powers – Driving Licences**
Road Traffic Act 1988 Section 164

(1) Any of the following persons:
    a) a person driving a motor vehicle on a road,
    b) a person whom a constable has reasonable cause to believe has been the driver of a motor vehicle at the time when an accident occurred owing to its presence on a road,
    c) a person whom a constable or vehicle examiner has reasonable cause to believe

has committed an offence in relation to the use of the vehicle on a road, or

d) a person:

   i) who supervises the holder of a provisional licence while the holder is driving a motor vehicle on a road, or,

   ii) whom a constable or vehicle examiner has reasonable cause to believe was supervising the holder of a provisional licence while driving, at the time when an accident occurred owing to the presence of the vehicle on a road or at a time when an offence is suspected of having been committed by the holder of the provisional licence in relation to the use of the vehicle on a road,

   must, on being so required by a constable, or vehicle examiner, produce his licence and its counterpart for examination, so as to enable the constable or vehicle examiner to ascertain the name and address of the holder of the licence, the date of issue, and the authority by which it was issued.

(2) A person required by a constable under subsection (1) above to produce his licence must in prescribed circumstances, on being so required by the constable, state his date of birth.

(3) If:

   a) the Secretary of State has:

      i) revoked a licence, or

      ii) revoked or suspended a large goods vehicle drivers licence or a passenger carrying vehicles drivers licence, and

   b) the holder of the licence fails to deliver it and its counterpart to the Secretary of State or the traffic commissioner as the case may be, a constable or vehicle examiner may require him to produce the licence and its counterpart, and upon being produced seize them and deliver them to the Secretary of State.

(4) Where a constable has reasonable cause to believe that the holder of a licence, or any other person, has knowingly made a false statement for the purpose of obtaining the grant of the licence, the constable may require the holder to produce it and its counterpart to him.

(4A) Where a constable to whom a provisional licence has been produced by a person driving a motor bicycle has reasonable cause to believe that the holder was not driving it as part of the training being provided on a training course for motor cyclists, the constable may require him to produce the prescribed certificate of completion of a training course for motor cyclists.

(5) Where a person has been required to produce a licence and its counterpart to the court and fails to do so, a constable may require him to produce them and, upon their being produced may seize them and deliver them to the court.

(6) If a person required under the preceding provisions of this Section to produce a licence and its counterpart or state his date of birth or to produce his certificate of completion of a training course for motorcyclists fails to do so he is, subject to subsection (7) to (8A) below guilty of an offence.

(7) Subsection (6) above does not apply where a person is required on any occasion under the preceding provisions of this Section to produce a licence and its counterpart:

   a) produces on that occasion a current receipt for the licence and its counterpart and, if required to do so produces that licence and its counterpart in person immediately on their return at a police station that was specified on that occasion, or

b) within seven days after that occasion produces such a receipt at a police station that was specified by him on that occasion and, if required to do so, produces the licence and its counterpart in person immediately on their return at that police station.

(8) In proceedings against any person for the offence of failing to produce a licence and its counterpart it shall be a defence for him to show that:

a) within seven days after production of his licence and its counterpart was required he produced them in person at a police station that was specified by him at the time their production was required, or

b) he produced them in person there as soon as was reasonably practicable, or

c) it was not reasonably practicable for him to produce them there before the day on which proceedings commenced,

and for the purposes of this subsection the laying of the information shall be treated as the commencement of the proceedings.

(8A) Subsection (8) above shall apply in relation to a certificate of completion of a training course for motor cyclists as it applies in relation to a licence.

6.1.1 *Explanation*

Is or was driving: A person who actually is driving may be required to produce his driving licence and counterpart, for no other reason than he is driving. A person who is not driving may be required to produce his licence and counterpart if the constable has reason to believe that he has committed an offence arising from using a motor vehicle on a road, or has been involved in an accident as a driver. In addition, when the driver is a provisional licence holder, the person who is, or who is suspected was, supervising him at the time, may also be required to produce his driving licence.

Motor bicycle: If the vehicle concerned is a motor bicycle and the rider produces a provisional licence, he may also be required to produce the certificate issued upon successfully completing the basic training course for motor bicycle riders (unless, of course, on the occasion in question, he was riding the bike on a road as part of that training). Failure to produce the certificate amounts to an offence.

Receipt: A person who has surrendered his driving licence to the police upon being issued with an endorsable fixed penalty notice, should have a receipt for his licence and may produce this instead. He may then be required to produce his licence and counterpart as soon as they are returned to him.

Date of birth: A constable may demand a person asked for his licence, to give his date of birth, in order that it may be checked against the date encoded in the driver number on the licence. The grounds on which a date of birth may be required are:

(1) The person fails to produce his licence forthwith; **or**

(2) He produces it forthwith; **and**
    i)   the driver number has been altered, removed or defaced; or
    ii) the person is the supervisor for a provisional licence holder and the constable has reason to suspect that he is under 21; or
    iii) the constable has reason to suspect that the licence:

- was not granted to that person, or
- was granted to him in error, or
- contains an alteration made with intent to deceive.

Motor Vehicles (Driving Licences) Regulations 1996 Regulation 77

Delayed production: A person prosecuted for failure to produce his licence (and counterpart) when required will have a defence if it is produced within 7 days at a police station of his choice. Production must be in person, not by sending someone else along with them. If the licence (and counterpart) are not produced within 7 days, the defence will remain valid if:
- they are produced as soon thereafter as is reasonably practicable; or
- if he proves that it was not reasonably practicable to produce them before the commencement of proceedings for the offence.

If a driver is stopped on her way to the airport, from where she intends to fly off for a fortnight in the sun, producing her licence as soon as she returns will probably be considered reasonable.

Other grounds for requiring licence: A constable may demand a licence from a person suspected of having obtained it by means of false statement, when he is required by a court to produce it, or where the licence has been revoked.

6.2 **Police Powers – Name and Address, Insurance and Other Documents**
Road Traffic Act 1988 Section 165

(1) Any of the following persons:
   a) a person driving a motor vehicle (other than an invalid carriage) on a road, or
   b) a person whom a constable or a vehicle examiner has reasonable cause to believe have been the driver of a motor vehicle (other than an invalid carriage) at the time when an accident occurred owing to its presence on a road, or
   c) a person whom a constable or vehicle examiner has reasonable cause to believe to have committed an offence in relation to the use on a road of a motor vehicle (other than an invalid carriage),
   must, on being so required by a constable or vehicle examiner, give his name and address and the name and address of the owner of the vehicle and produce the following documents for examination.

(2) Those documents are:
   a) the relevant certificate of insurance or certificate of security, or such other evidence that the vehicle is not or was not being driven in contravention of Section 143 of this Act as may be prescribed by regulations made by the Secretary of State.
   b) in relation to a vehicle to which Section 47 of this Act applies, a test certificate issued in respect of the vehicle as mentioned in subsection (1) of that Section, and
   c) in relation to a goods vehicle, a plating certificate or goods vehicle test certificate.

(3) Subject to subsection (4) below, a person who fails to comply with a requirement under subsection (1) above is guilty of an offence.

(4) A person shall not be convicted of an offence under subsection (3) above by reason of only failure to produce any certificate or other evidence in proceedings against him for the offence where he shows that:

a) within seven days after the date on which the production of the certificate or other evidence was required it was produced at a police station that was specified by him at the time when its production was required, or

b) it was produced there as soon as reasonably practicable, or

c) it was not reasonably practicable for it to be produced there before the date on which the proceedings were commenced, and for the purposes of this subsection the laying of information shall be treated as the commencement of the proceedings.

(5) A person:

a) who supervises the holder of a provisional licence while the holder of such a licence is driving on a road a motor vehicle (other than an invalid carriage), or

b) whom a constable or vehicle examiner has reasonable cause to believe was supervising the holder of such a licence while driving, at a time when an accident occurred owing to the presence of the vehicle on a road, or at a time when an offence was suspected of having been committed by the holder of a provisional licence in relation to the use of the vehicle on a road, must on being so required by a constable, give his name and address and the name and address of the owner of the vehicle.

(6) A person who fails to comply with a requirement under subsection (5) above is guilty of an offence.

6.2.1 *Explanation*

Driver: Those persons who may be required to give details and produce documents are the same as those who may be required to produce driving licences, i.e. driving, suspected offence, suspected accident.

Documents: The documents which may be required to be produced are a certificate of insurance or other evidence that the vehicle is being used lawfully in respect of requirements for insurance (Section 143), a test certificate if the vehicle requires one (Section 47), and a goods vehicle test certificate, if applicable.

Note: There are various other documents which a constable, or other authorised person such as a vehicle examiner, may require, in relation to goods vehicles. These are not dealt with in this book.

Delayed production: The same provisions apply as pertain to driving licences (see paragraph 6.1.1 above).

Supervisor: When the driver concerned is the holder of a provisional licence, any person who is or was supervising him at the time in question, may be required to give her own name and address, and that of the owner of the vehicle.

6.3 **Identity of Driver**
Road Traffic Act 1988 Section 172

(1) This Section applies:

a) to any offence under the preceding provisions of this Act except:
   i) an offence under Part V, or
   ii) an offence under Section 13,16,51(2),61(4),67(9),68(4)96 or 120

b) to any offence under Section 25,26 or 27 of the Road Traffic Offenders Act 1988

c) to any offence against any other enactment relating to the use of vehicles on a roads, and

d) to manslaughter, by the driver of a motor vehicle.

(2) Where the driver of a vehicle is alleged to be guilty of an offence to which this Section applies:

a) the person keeping the vehicle shall give such information as to the identity of the driver as may be required to give by or on behalf of the chief officer of police, and

b) any other person shall if required as stated above give any information which it is in his power to give and may lead to he identification of the driver.

(3) Subject to the following provisions, a person who fails to comply with the requirement under subsection (2) above shall be guilty of an offence.

(4) A person shall not be guilty of an offence by virtue of paragraph (a) of subsection (2) above if he shows that he did not know and could not with reasonable diligence have ascertained who the driver of the vehicle was.

(5) Where a body corporate is guilty of an offence under this Section and the offence is proved to have been committed with the consent or connivance of, or to be attributable to neglect on the part of, a director, manager, secretary or similar officer of the body corporate, a person who was purporting to act in any such capacity, he, as well as the body corporate, is guilty of an offence and liable to be proceeded against and punished accordingly.

(7) A requirement under subsection (2) may be made by written notice served by post, and where it is so made:

a) it shall have effect as a requirement to give the information within the period of 28 days beginning with the day on which the notice is served, and

b) the person on whom the notice is served shall not be guilty of an offence under this Section if he shows either that he gave the information as soon as reasonably practicable after the end of that period or that it has not been reasonably practicable for him to give it.

(8) Where the person on whom the notice under subsection (7) above is to be served is a body corporate, the notice is duly served on the secretary or clerk.

(9) The proper address of any person in relation to the service on him of a notice under subsection (7) above is:

a) in the case of the secretary or clerk of a body corporate, that of the registered or principle office of that body or (if the body corporate is the registered keeper of the vehicle concerned) the registered address, and

b) in any other case, his last known address at the time of service.

6.3.1 *Explanation*

Offences: If the driver of a vehicle is alleged to be guilty of an offence, then the police may require the registered owner of that vehicle, or any other person who may have information, to give information, to assist in identifying the offender. These provisions apply to most of the offences created by the Road Traffic Act 1988, to offences under the Road Traffic Offenders, Sections 25, 26 27 (failing to give date of birth to a court upon conviction, failing to surrender a driving licence to a court, failing to produce a driving licence to a court) and to most offences under other Acts relating to the use of vehicles on roads. Some of the exclusions are offences relating to:

– driving instruction (Part V)
– motor cycle helmets (Section 16)
– goods vehicle plating and testing (Section 51(2))
– driving with uncorrected defective eyesight (Section 96)
Similar provision is made in legislation relating to registration and licensing of vehicles.

Vehicle: These provisions are not confined to drivers of motor vehicles. The rider of a pedal cycle is a 'driver' for the purposes of these provisions, and offences such as careless and dangerous cycling are offences to which the Section applies.

Keeper of the vehicle: The registered keeper of the vehicle must give such information as he may be required to give.. by the police, concerning the identity of the driver. The fact that the registered keeper does not know who the driver was is not sufficient excuse. The keeper will have a defence only if he proves, not only that he did not know the driver's identity, but also that he could not with reasonable diligence have ascertained who the driver was. An employer who does not have a system of recording who was driving a particular company vehicle at a particular time, may have difficulty convincing a court that 'reasonable diligence' had been exercised.

Other person: Any person other than the registered keeper of a vehicle may be required to give information which it is within his power to give. A defence of reasonable diligence does not apply; if the person does not have the information, then he will not be liable for failing to give it. A requirement may be made of any person, e.g. a witness to an accident, a driver (not being the registered keeper) who has lent the vehicle to someone else, etc.

By or on behalf of: Information must be required by or on behalf of the chief officer of police. A chief officer may authorise some or all of the members of a police force to require information on her behalf. One hardly expects a chief constable or commissioner to go round in person seeking the identities of offending drivers.

Requirement: A requirement may be made verbally or in writing. If a written requirement is sent by post, the reply must be forthcoming within 28 days, or an offence is committed, subject to the person concerned showing that he gave the required information as soon as he reasonably could, or that he could not reasonably give the information.

Otherwise than for a written requirement by post, there is no time limit, but the information should be given in a reasonable time (*Lowe v Lester* (1987)).

Company liability: If the registered keeper of a vehicle is a company, rather than an individual, the provisions apply, and the company may be prosecuted for failure to supply information. In addition, a director or manager may be held personally responsible, if it shown that he consented or connived in the company's failure to disclose information.

6.3.2 *Punishment*

A person convicted of an offence of failing to provide information when required, shall be liable to a fine. Except where the defendant is a company, conviction also carries obligatory endorsement and discretionary disqualification, if the alleged offences relate to a motor vehicle. Thus, a person who fails to assist in identifying the offending driver, puts his own driving licence at risk.

6.4 **Forgery of Vehicle Documents**
Road Traffic Act 1988 Section 173

(1) A person who, with intent to deceive:
- a) forges, alters or uses a document or other thing to which this Section applies, or
- b) lends to, or allows to be used by, any other person a document or other thing to which this Section applies, or
- c) makes or has in his possession any document or other thing so closely resembling a document or other thing to which this Section applies as to be calculated to deceive,

is guilty of an offence.

(2) This Section applies to the following documents and other things:
- a) any licence under any Part of this Act or, in the case of a licence to drive, any counterpart of such a licence
- b) any test certificate, goods vehicle test certificate, plating certificate, certificate of conformity or Ministers approval certificate (within the meaning of Part II of this Act)
- c) any certificate required as a condition of any exception prescribed under Section 14 of this Act, (exempt from wearing seat belt)
- cc) any seal required by regulations made with respect to speed limiters
- d) any plate containing particulars required to be marked on a vehicle by regulations or containing other particulars required to be marked on a goods vehicle
- e) any records required to be kept by virtue of Section 74 of this Act, (operator required to keep maintenance records)
- f) any document which is issued as evidence of the result of a test of competence to drive
- ff) any certificate provided for by regulations, relating to the completion of a training course for motorcyclists
- g) any badge or certificate prescribed by regulations relating to driving instructors
- h) any certificate of insurance or certificate of security
- j) any document produced as evidence of insurance
- k) any document which may be produced in lieu of a certificate of insurance or a certificate of security
- l) any international road haulage permit, and
- m) a certificate issued upon completeion of a course for disqualified drivers.

(3) In the application of this Section to England and Wales 'forges' means makes a false document or other thing in order that it may be used as genuine.

6.4.1 *Explanation*

Intent to deceive: Police officers searched a house in connection with a matter not related to driving. They found a driving licence, but left it there. Later they returned and asked to see the licence. When the defendant produced it, the police found that it had been obtained by submitting false details. He was convicted but won his appeal, when the court held that to produce a false driving licence to the police for a purpose which has nothing to do with driving, does not amount to this offence (*R v Howe* (1982)).

Forge: A person will 'forge' if he makes a false document or other thing in order that it may be used as genuine. A document is false if it tells a lie about itself (for further explanation, see Chapter 28).

Use, lend, allow to be used: There is no need to alter details on a driving licence or other document, in order to be guilty of an offence under this Section; using another person's licence, whether it be stolen or borrowed, will amount to an offence. If the licence is borrowed, the person whose licence it is may be liable for lending it, or for allowing it to be used. In each case, for the offence to be complete, the offender must have an intention to deceive.

Document: Virtually any document relating to a vehicle or a driver, is covered by these provisions, even down to the seal on a speed limiter.

6.5 **False Statements to Obtain Documents**
Road Traffic Act 1988 Section 174

(1) A person who knowingly makes a false statement for the purpose:
   a) of obtaining the grant of a licence under any Part of this Act to himself or any other person, or,
   b) of preventing the grant of any such licence, or,
   c) of procuring the imposition of a condition or limitation in relation to any such licence, or,
   d) of securing the entry or retention of the name of any person in the register of approved instructors maintained under Part V of this Act, or,
   e) of obtaining the grant of an international road haulage permit to himself or any other persons,
   is guilty of an offence.

(3) A person who, in supplying information or producing documents for the purposes of goods vehicle test certificates, type approval or conformity certificates, or goods vehicle weights:
   a) makes a statement which he knows to be false in a material particular or recklessly makes a statement which is false in a material particular, or
   b) produces, provides, sends or otherwise makes use of a document which he knows to be false in a material particular or recklessly produces, provides, sends or otherwise makes use of a document which is false in a material particular,
   is guilty of an offence.

(4) A person who:
   a) wilfully makes a false entry in any record required to be made or kept by regulations retaining to goods vehicle maintenance records, or
   b) with intent to deceive, makes use of any such entry which he knows to be false, is guilty of an offence.

(5) A person who makes a false statement or withholds any material information for the purpose of obtaining the issue:
   a) of a certificate of insurance or certificate of security under Part VI of this Act, or,
   b) of any document which may be produced in lieu of a certificate of insurance or a certificate of security,
   is guilty of an offence.

6.5.1 *Explanation*
Document: These provisions apply to licences, driving instructor registration, insurance documents and certain road haulage permits.

False statement: For the most part, the offender must know that his statement is false in a material particular, although in relation to certain offences relating to goods vehicle documentation, a statement made recklessly which turns out to be false, will suffice.

6.6 Issue of False Documents
Road Traffic Act 1988 Section 175

If a person issues:
   a) any document relating to insurance, or
   b) a test certificate or certificate of conformity (within the meaning of Part II of this Act),
   and the document or certificate so issued is to his knowledge false in any material particular, he is guilty of an offence.

6.6.1 *Explanation*
Document: The documents to which this provision applies are insurance documents and test certificates.

Knowledge: The person issuing the document must know that it is false, if he is to be liable for the offence.

6.7 Police Powers to Seize Documents
Road Traffic Act 1988 Section 176

   (1) If a constable has reasonable cause to believe that a document produced to him:
      a) in pursuance of Section 137 of this Act (driving instructors certificate), or
      b) in pursuance of any of the preceding provisions of the Part of this Act,
      is a document in relation to which an offence has been committed under Sections 173, 174 or 175 of this Act or under Section 115 of the Road Traffic Regulation Act 1984 (parking meter tickets, etc) he may seize the document.

   (1A) Where a licence to drive or its counterpart of a licence may be seized by a constable under subsection (1) above, he may also seize the counterpart or the licence, as the case may be, produced with it.

   (2) When a document is seized under subsection (1) above, the person from whom it was taken shall, unless:
      a) the document has been previously returned to him, or
      b) he has been previously charged with an offence under any of those Sections,
      be summoned before a magistrates' court to account for his possession of the document.

   (4) If a constable, or vehicle examiner has reasonable cause to believe that a document or plate carried on a motor vehicle or by the driver of the vehicle is a document or plate to which this subsection applies, he may seize it. (For the purposes of this subsection the power to seize includes the power to detach from a vehicle).

   (5) Subsection (4) above applies to a document or plate in relation to which an offence has been committed under Sections 173, 174 or 175 of this Act in so far as they apply:
      a) to documents evidencing the appointment of examiners, or
      b) to goods vehicle test certificates, plating certificates, certificates of conformity or Minister's approval certificates (within the meaning of Part II of this Act), or

c) to plates containing plated particulars (within the meaning of that part) or containing other particulars required to be marked on goods vehicles, or

d) to records required to be kept by virtue of Section 74 of this Act, or

e) to international road haulage permits.

(6) When a document or plate is seized under subsection (4) above, either the driver or owner of the vehicle shall, if the document or plate is still detained and neither of them has previously been charged with an offence in relation to the document or plate under Section 173, 174 or 175 of this Act, be summoned before a magistrates' court to account for his possession of, or the presence on the vehicle of, the document or plate.

(7) The court must make such an order respecting the disposal of the document or plate and award such costs as the justice of the case may require.

(8) In this Section 'counterpart' in relation to a licence to drive under Part III of this Act, has the same meaning as in that Part.

6.7.1 *Explanation*

Constable: The power to seize a forged or altered driving licence, for example, may be exercised by a constable, but not by a civilian enquiry office clerk employed by the police.

Document: The power extends to any document or other thing suspected of being:
- forged, altered used, lent, etc with intent to deceive (Section 173)
- obtained by a false statement (Section 174)
- issued by a person who knew it was false (Section 175).

TESTING OF VEHICLES

7.1 Powers to Test Vehicles on Premises
Road Vehicles (Construction and Use) Regulations 1986 Regulation 76

(1) Subject to the conditions specified in paragraph (2), the following persons are hereby empowered to test and inspect the brakes, silencers, steering gear and tyres of any vehicle on any premises where that vehicle is located:
- a constable in uniform;
- certain other authorised examiners in relation to hackney carriages, goods vehicles and public service vehicles.

(2) Those conditions are:
a) any person empowered as there mentioned shall produce his authorisation if required to do so

b) no such person shall enter any premises unless the consent of the owner of those premises has first been obtained

c) no such person shall test or inspect any vehicle on any premises unless:
   i) the owner of the vehicle consents thereto, or
   ii) notice has been given to that owner personally or left at his address not less than 48 hours before the time of the proposed test or inspection, or has been sent to him at least 72 hours before that time by recorded delivery service to his address last known to the person giving notice; or

iii) the test or inspection is made within 48 hours of an accident to which Section 170 of the Road Traffic Act applies and in which the vehicle was involved.

(3) For the purposes of this regulation, the owner of the vehicle shall be deemed to be in the case of a vehicle:
   a) which it is for the time being registered, and is not being used under a trade licence, the registered owner
   b) used under a trade licence, the holder of that licence; or
   c) exempt from excise duty, the person resident outside the United Kingdom who has brought the vehicle into Great Britain
   and in cases (a) and (b) the address of the owner as shown on the said register or, as the case may be on the licence, may be treated as his address.

7.1.1 *Explanation*

Scope of test: The powers apply only in respect of those parts mentioned.

Lights: Corresponding provisions in the Road Vehicles Lighting Regulations 1989, regulation 28, allow for the testing of vehicle lighting.

Consent of owner of premises: This is an over-riding requirement, not subject to any exceptions.

Consent of owner of vehicle: A test may be carried out if the owner of the vehicle consents, or has been notified. In the case of an accident, no consent or notification is required so long as the test is carried out within 48 hours of the accident.

7.2 **Testing on Roads**
Road Traffic Act 1988 Section 67

(1) An authorised examiner may test a motor vehicle on a road for the purposes of:
   a) ascertaining whether the following requirements, namely:
      i) the construction and use requirements, and
      ii) the requirement that the condition of the vehicle is not such that its use on a road would involve a danger of injury to any person
      are complied with as respects the vehicle;
   b) bringing to the notice of the driver any failure to comply with those requirements.

(2) For the purpose of testing a vehicle under this Section the examiner:
   a) may require the driver to comply with his reasonable instructions, and
   b) may drive the vehicle.

(3) A vehicle shall not be required to stop for a test except by a constable in uniform.

(4) The following persons may act as authorised examiners for the purposes of this Section:
   a) a constable authorised so to act by or on behalf of the chief officer of police;
   b) a person appointed by the police authority for a police area, to act under the directions of the chief officer of police;
   c) other authorised examiners, in respect of hackney carriages, goods vehicles, or appointed by the Secretary of State.

(5) A person authorised as an examiner, with the exception of a police constable, must produce his authority to act, if required to do so.

(6) On the examiner proceeding to test a vehicle under this Section, the driver may, unless the test is required under subsection (7) or (8) below to be carried out forthwith, elect that the test be deferred to a time, and carried out at a place, fixed in accordance with Schedule 2 to this Act, and the provisions of the Schedule shall apply accordingly.

(7) Where it appears to a constable that, by reason of an accident having occurred owing to the presence of the vehicle on a road, it is requisite that a test should be carried out forthwith, he may require it to be carried out and, if he is not to carry it out himself, may require that the vehicle shall not be taken away until the test has been carried out.

(8) Where in the opinion of the constable the vehicle is apparently so defective that it ought not to be allowed to proceed without a test being carried out, he may require the test to be carried out forthwith.

(9) If a person obstructs an authorised examiner acting under this Section, or fails to comply with the requirements of this Section, he is guilty of an offence.

(10) In this Section and in Schedule 2 to this Act:
   a) 'test' includes 'inspect' or 'inspection', as the case may require, and
   b) references to a vehicle include reference to a trailer drawn by it.

7.2.1 *Explanation*

Scope of test: A test under these provisions, is not limited to specified components such as brakes, etc, as is the case in relation to tests on premises.

Drive: An examiner may drive a vehicle for the purpose of a test; otherwise the driver must comply with reasonable requests from the examiner to enable the test to be carried out.

Stop: An authorised examiner has no power to stop a vehicle; the services of a constable in uniform will be required for this purpose.

Authorised constable: Any constable in uniform is empowered to test a vehicle on premises, but in this case, only those who are specially trained, and have written authority, may do so.

However, in a case where a constable who was not authorised to examine vehicles, obtained evidence of a defective handbrake by the simple method of applying the brake fully, then pushing the vehicle to show that the handbrake had no effect, it was held that this evidence was admissible. In this case, the driver co-operated, but if he had refused consent, the constable, not being an authorised examiner, would not have had any power to require that the test take place (*Stoneley v Richardson* (1973). Thus, if there is a defect which does not require the skills of a vehicle examiner, such as defective lamp or bald tyre, there is no reason why the evidence of a constable who is not an authorised examiner, should not be given to prove an offence.

Deferred test: A driver may elect to defer a roadside test, in accordance with provisions set out in Schedule 2 to the Act.

However, a constable – but not any of the other authorised examiners – and the constable concerned need not herself be authorised – may require that a test be carried out forthwith if, because the vehicle has been in an accident, or because of its poor state, the constable believes that it should stay where it is until it is examined.

CARRIAGE OF DANGEROUS GOODS BY ROAD
Carriage of Dangerous Goods by Road Regulations 1996

8.1 Scope of Regulations

8.1.1 *Dangerous Substance*
The provisions of the regulations cover the carriage by road of substances such as – chemicals with hazardous affects, gasses or other substances which are highly flammable or which may explode, infectious materials, etc.

8.1.2 *Warning Signs*
A motor vehicle or trailer being used for the carriage of dangerous materials must be fitted with danger signs, hazard warning panels and orange coloured panels, in accordance with the requirements of the regulations. Included in the warning panels will be codes which identify substances so that emergency services may take appropriate action in the event of a leakage, spillage, fire or other emergency. The type and position of panels to be displayed vary according to the category of the dangerous goods carried.

8.1.3 *Transportation Documentation*
The operator of a vehicle being used for the carriage of dangerous goods must ensure that the driver is in possession of Transportation Documentation before commencing a journey. This documentation must comprise details of the goods being carried, including designation and classification of the goods, amounts, and emergency information. The **emergency information** should include – dangers inherent in the goods – measures to be taken in event of accident or other emergency – details of treatment to be given to any person coming in contact with the goods – details of fire-fighting equipment which must **not** be used – measures to be taken to deal with any leakage or spillage.

8.2 Requirements

8.2.1 *Offence*
A breach of the requirements of the regulations will amount to an offence under Section 15 of the Health and Safety at Work Act 1974. The enforcement of most of these will be a matter for specialists, but non-specialist police officers may discover breaches of some of the regulations, a selection of which appears below.

8.2.2 *Documentation*

(1) A vehicle operator must not supply false or misleading information to the driver relating to the dangerous goods to be carried.

ii) The driver shall ensure that the Transport Documentation is kept readily available on the vehicle at all times when dangerous goods are being carried. If a trailer is detached from the motor vehicle, the driver must give the occupier of the premises where the trailer is kept, a copy of the Transport Documentation, and the occupier must then keep it readily available. In addition, the driver must affix a copy of the Transport Documentation to the trailer itself, in a readily visible position.

iii) The driver must ensure that any documentation relating to dangerous goods which are not being carried at that time is either – removed from the vehicle – or placed in a securely closed container, clearly marked to show that it does not relate to any dangerous goods then being carried.

8.2.3 *Information and Warning Panels*

i) The operator must ensure that information is displayed on the vehicle as required by the regulations.

ii) No person shall cause or permit such information to be displayed on a vehicle which is not being used for the carriage of dangerous goods. Any warning panel or danger sign which does not relate to the dangerous goods being carried, must be removed or covered.

iii) No person shall cause or permit other information to be displayed on a vehicle which, when read in conjunction with the information required by the regulations, would be likely to confuse the emergency services.

iv) The operator and the driver must ensure that all danger signs, hazard warning panels, etc, required by the regulations, are kept clean and free from obstruction.

v) No person shall remove any danger sign, hazard warning panel etc, or falsify the information thereon.

8.2.4 *Supervision and Parking*

i) The operator and the driver shall ensure that when a vehicle being used for the carriage of dangerous goods is parked, the parking brake is applied and it is:
   a) supervised at all times by a competent person who is aged 18 years or over (or younger than 18 if she is a member of the armed forces); or
   b) it is parked in an isolated position, having been secured, in one of the following places, in descending order of priority:
      1 unsupervised in the open in a secure depot or factory premises;
      2 in a supervised vehicle park;
      3 in a public or private vehicle park where the vehicle is not likely to suffer damage from any other vehicle;
      4 in a suitable open space, separated from the public highway and from dwellings, where the public does not normally pass or assemble.

Exception

The restrictions on where the vehicle may be parked do not apply if the vehicle has been damaged or has broken down on a road and the driver has gone to seek assistance, provided he first takes all reasonable steps to secure the vehicle and its contents.

8.2.5 *Carrying Passengers*

The driver of a vehicle being used for the carriage of dangerous goods shall not cause or permit any person, other than a member of the vehicle crew, to be carried for the sole purpose of transporting that person.

8.3 **Production of Documentation**

The driver of a vehicle being used for the carriage of dangerous goods shall ensure that the

Transportation Documentation is produced upon the request of any police constable or goods vehicle examiner.

8.4 Defence

In any proceedings for an offence arising out of breach of these regulations, the accused shall have a defence if he proves:

a) that the offence arose through the act or default of another person, not being an employee of the accused; and

b) that he took all reasonable precautions and exercised all due diligence to avoid commission of that offence.

To rely on this defence, the accused must first give written notice to the prosecution, at least 7 days before the court hearing, giving such information as he has available, identifying or assisting in identifying the other person.

8.5 Explanation

Documentation and information: The marking of vehicles and tanks containing dangerous goods, and the availability of the Transportation Documentation, is intended to enable fire brigade staff and others to take appropriate action to deal with any emergency which may arise when a vehicle is on a road or is parked elsewhere.

For this reason, warning panels, etc, must not be displayed when a vehicle is not carrying any dangerous goods. Documentation and warning panels should not relate to any dangerous goods not being carried at that time, e.g. which may have been carried on a previous occasion. If such documentation is carried in the cab of a vehicle, it must be locked in a secure container, clearly marked, so as not to lead to confusion should some emergency arise.

Parking: The places where a vehicle may be parked when not attended by the driver or other competent person, are listed in order of priority. If no secure depot or factory premises is readily available, then the vehicle may be left in a supervised vehicle park. If no supervised vehicle park is available, then it may be left in an unsupervised vehicle park. As a last resort, it may be left somewhere else which is not a highway, not near houses, and where the public are not likely to appear. Only in the case of damage or breakdown, may it be left unattended on a road, while the driver goes off to seek assistance.

Passengers: A passenger ,who is not a member of the vehicle crew, must not be carried for the sole purpose of carrying him. Hitchhikers are definitely out, but, e.g. a vehicle examiner exercising his powers, could be carried, or a mechanic who is seeking to repair a defect, so long as the purpose is not merely to move that passenger from one place to another.

Defence: Note that an operator may not use the defence, that the offence arose due to the fault of someone else, if the other person is his employee.

8.6 Driver Training
Carriage of Dangerous Goods by Road (Driver Training) Regulations 1996

Drivers must undergo specified training before being allowed to drive vehicles carrying dangerous goods on roads. A driver is issued with a certificate upon completion of training, to which the following requirements apply:

Reg 6   A driver of a vehicle engaged in carrying dangerous goods must ensure that the relevant training certificate is kept by him so as to be immediately available during the whole of the journey.

Reg 7   The driver shall produce the certificate upon the request of any goods vehicle examiner or police constable (or in the case of radio active goods, upon the request of an appointed inspector).

8.7 Carriage of Explosives by Road
Carriage of Explosives by Road Regulations 1996

These regulations make similar provisions to the carriage of explosives as apply to dangerous goods, albeit the requirements are more stringent in many respects. They include a duty upon a driver to produce the Transport Documentation upon the request of any goods vehicle examiner or constable.

Index

M